ELEVENTH EDITION

EXPLORING
Marketing Research

ELEVENTH EDITION

EXPLORING
Marketing Research

Barry J. Babin
Louisiana Tech University

William G. Zikmund

CENGAGE
Learning®

Australia • Brazil • Japan • Korea • Mexico • Singapore • Spain • United Kingdom • United States

Exploring Marketing Research, 11th Edition
Barry J. Babin, William G. Zikmund

Vice President, General Manager, Social Science & Qualitative Business: Erin Joyner

Product Director: Jason Fremder

Senior Product Manager: Michael Roche

Senior Content Developer: Elizabeth Lowry

Senior Content Developer: John Rich

Product Assistant: Jamie Mack

Marketing Manager: Jeff Tousignant

Marketing Coordinator: Christopher P. Walz

Manufacturing Planner: Ron Montgomery

Art and Cover Direction, Production Management and Composition: Lumina Datamatics, Inc.

Cover Image: © Dimitri Otis/Photographer's Choice RF/Getty Images

Intellectual Property
Analyst: Diane L. Garrity
Project Manager: Betsy Hathaway

Library of Congress Control Number: 2015931012

ISBN: 978-1-305-26380-2

Cengage Learning
20 Channel Center Street
Boston, MA 02210
USA

Cengage Learning is a leading provider of customized learning solutions with employees residing in nearly 40 different countries and sales in more than 125 countries around the world. Find your local representative at **www.cengage.com**

Cengage Learning products are represented in Canada by Nelson Education, Ltd.

To learn more about Cengage Learning Solutions, visit **www.cengage.com**

Purchase any of our products at your local college store or at our preferred online store **www.cengagebrain.com**

Printed in the United States of America
Print Number: 02   Print Year: 2016

First, to my wonderful family and second, to my colleagues and students
who continue to be a source of inspiration.

BRIEF CONTENTS

CONTENTS

PART TWO
Designing Research Studies

PART THREE
Measurement

CHAPTER 10
Measurement and Attitude Scaling, 268

CHAPTER 11
Questionnaire Design, 303

PREFACE

Never before has marketing research been more exciting or offered more and better career opportunities. Today's decision makers are under more pressure than ever to act, and to act fast. To take effective actions, they need intelligence, and intelligence begins with information. That's where research steps in. Research provides insight that leads to better decision-making. Researchers have access to more data than ever before to help provide that insight. Tracking consumers is easy today as virtually every move we make leaves some type of data trail. Also, never before has communicating with consumers been easier in a world where so many consumers are connected all the time. Now, finding gems of insight amidst the colossal amounts of intelligence seems a lot like searching for a needle amidst a mountain of hay. Complicating the search further is the fact that markets change more quickly than ever, meaning that in the search for the needle, the hay keeps shifting around. Thus, "search" cannot be removed from "research."

Decision-making in so many industries, both for-profit and not-for-profit, depends on input from research. The research process described in this text helps provide that input. The process enables a company to identify its customers and design products that maximize the value they receive from a purchase. In return, the company receives value as the customers spend their hard-earned money. The result: customers win and businesses win! All are better off.

A lot has changed since the first edition of this text. One thing that has not changed though is that businesses succeed by coming together with customers to create value that addresses real consumer needs. Although addressing needs remains the *raison d'être* for business, the way consumer needs get addressed is ever changing. Value creation today involves all sorts of technologies. Today, value creation involves much more than computers and the Internet. Smartphones mean billions of consumers can access your business at their fingertips, GPS systems point consumers to market offerings, drones help provide information and may even make deliveries, tap and pay systems involving iPay or Google Wallet make transactions faster and easier than ever. For the market researcher, the key advantage is that all of these systems leave behind a trail of information ready to mine for insight. That's where this text comes in: *Exploring Marketing Research* equips students with the knowledge and skills involved in this basic research process. By mastering this process, students will know how to frame questions to get valuable answers, where to look for those answers, and know how to use tools that help convert raw data into intelligence.

Chapter 3 introduces this process, which includes six stages. Researchers must first work together with decision makers to decide why they are looking for that metaphorical needle in the haystack. The next two stages plot out the way to go about finding the needle. Next are two stages that focus on the actual search for the needle. The process concludes when the market researcher communicates the benefits of finding "pointed" information that can help mend problems or create something really new and special to the decision maker. Success in this process usually merits the researcher a reward that is a bit more valuable than that needle!

New to *Exploring Marketing Research*

To ensure that students are able to conduct market research with an understanding of all the latest theories and techniques available to them, the eleventh edition is substantially revised and updated. The last few editions maintained a consistent chapter structure from edition to edition. However, given the dynamic nature of marketing research, this edition places a greater division between the "soft" and "hard" sides of marketing research. The earlier parts place emphasis more on describing research designs and different sources of data and data processes. The latter part focuses more specifically on modern tools that help form a basis for marketing analytics. You'll notice in the latter chapters, we shift terminology a little and talk more about the work of the analyst. Often, the researcher and the analyst may be one in the same. But, in larger firms and on larger projects, the function of the analyst is specifically focused on data analysis, often using inferential statistical tools.

The revisions in the text also better reflect data collection approaches suitable to the information age. Technological and social developments of the last few decades are revolutionizing information systems, sources of and ways of gathering secondary data, survey processes, sampling, questionnaire design, qualitative analysis including focus group interviews, and communication of results. Practically every chapter includes significant coverage of technology-related topics. Most chapters also include review questions and activities that get students involved with the latest research technologies in a hands-on way. For example, "The Survey This!" feature provides firsthand experience with the advantages and disadvantages of using online questionnaires and then analyzing the data that this approach provides.

Key features of the eleventh edition include:

- Project Outline—Chapter 16 includes an outline (downloadable in the student resources) suitable for use as a student project. The outline functions as a guide for the steps necessary to conduct a marketing research project like one suitable to serve as a term-long project in a marketing research course. The outline is geared to fit almost any type of comprehensive research project. By selecting only parts of the outline, a smaller project could be designed.
- Survey This!—Students respond to an online questionnaire using Qualtrics software. The questionnaire involves students' opinions, activities, and interests regarding numerous everyday behaviors ranging from involvement with social networking media to study habits. In the early chapters, this feature is useful for critiquing the way questionnaires are constructed and how research hypotheses are addressed in a survey. In later chapters, students can use data from the ongoing survey to get experience with marketing analytics tools. Students also get access to Qualtrics to design their own questionnaires as described below.
- Increased coverage of marketing analytics. The final five chapters contain mostly new coverage of more advanced analytical tools including data mining approaches using decision trees, multivariate data analysis approaches and even a primer on structural equations modeling, a tool suitable for testing theory. In this revision, the division between data analysis and research design parts is more clear.
- Tips of the Trade—Each chapter contains a useful list of important tips that correspond to the particular stage of the research process discussed in the chapter. The tips provide information addressing practical questions such as interview length, question wording, interviewer involvement, sample size requirements, and guides for data reliability and validity, as well as useful tips for testing hypotheses using inferential statistics.
- Chapter Vignettes—The first sixteen chapters open with a story relevant to the material featured in that particular chapter. Some of these vignettes involve famous brands and companies,

so the reader may well be familiar with some of the topics. Other vignettes involve "slice of life" stories describing a businessperson's struggle to make smart decisions and demonstrate how research is intertwined with this struggle.

- More emphasis on "how to"—The boxed material, chapter objectives, and end-of-chapter materials seek to emphasize research in action or steps used to perform different approaches illustrated in the text. Boxed materials take the form of Research Snapshots that cover ethical angles of research, provide illustrations of research in practice, and offer relevant tips or detailed "how-to" examples. The chapter learning objectives provide coherence and structure to the chapters, each culminating with objective-directed end-of-chapter materials. In later chapters, the Research Snapshots provide step-by-step guides describing how to perform many of the marketing analytics approaches.

- Software Friendly—*Exploring* recognizes that different students and instructors interact with multiple software platforms. Here, the illustrations do not focus on a single software platform. Rather, the how-to guides illustrate how to perform different analysis routines in multiple platforms. Most advanced analytical/statistical tools are illustrated in SPSS, SAS, and JMP (a fast growing analytical tool). The more basic tools also include illustrations for EXCEL.

- Substantial Coverage on International Business Issues—The examples and illustrations make much greater use of international business. Readers of this book may end up working or dealing with issues anywhere in the world, so the increased international examples will increase awareness of research issues beyond North America and open up domestic students to global market dynamics. This is a particularly important emphasis because cultural and language barriers often present challenges for the researcher.

- Substantial Attention to Qualitative Research—Big data also creates a big demand for qualitative research tools. In response, several chapters provide insight into how to gather and use data not expressed in the form of quantities. Chapter 5 focuses exclusively on qualitative research. Phenomenology, grounded theory, ethnography, and case study approaches are all covered. Qualitative research is dramatically being changed by the Internet as consumers leave more and more artifactual data behind on social networking websites, company chat rooms, blogs, social networks, micro-blogs (such as tweets left on Twitter), and more. Just think about the potential gold mine of data available in all of the online consumer feedback, ratings, and recommendations.

Organization of the Book

The eleventh edition of *Exploring Marketing Research* follows the logic of the marketing research process itself. The book is organized into seven parts, and each part presents the basic research concepts for one of the stages in the research process; each part also discusses how these concepts relate to decisions about conducting specific projects.

Part 1: Introduction emphasizes the interplay between research and business and how the importance and scope of research varies with the type of business orientation that characterizes a company. Included in this discussion is an overview of computerized data management and information systems, an overview of the entire marketing research process, and an explanation of how all of this is changing due to the Internet.

Without high ethical standards, no business is good. Thus, the introductory materials also include an emphasis on business ethics and the special ethical problems associated with marketing research.

Part 2: Designing Research Studies covers the essentials involved in starting to study business problems. This part emphasizes decision-making, problem definition, and the process of how researchers translate business problems into research questions and perhaps even research hypotheses. The part includes coverage of research proposals in some detail, and the reader is encouraged to see these as the written agreement that helps put the decision maker and the researcher on the same page.

Chapter 5 emphasizes qualitative research applications. One role played by qualitative research is helping to separate business problem symptoms from true issues that researchers can attack with marketing research. However, qualitative research extends far beyond problem definition; it allows greater potential for discovery as well as deeper and potentially more meaningful explanations in marketing research.

Other chapters in this part include other ways of obtaining data. This includes a detailed discussion of secondary data and emphasizes its increasing importance in an increasingly data-rich world. Other chapters include descriptions of survey designs (how to conduct, administer, and design survey instruments) observational studies (data on actual consumer behaviors) and causal designs involving marketing experiments.

Part 3: Measurement gives readers working knowledge of building blocks absolutely critical to effective marketing research. This part describes the basics of measurement theory. Key topics include descriptions of the different levels of scale measurement and how this affects the interpretation of results. Basic ways to measure human attitudes and practical matters dealing with questionnaire design are also discussed. An increased emphasis is placed on the use of new technologies for conducting interviews. For instance, how does asking a question in an electronic format change options for respondents and the researcher? Students can again get firsthand experience with state-of-the-art questionnaire design and surveying tools with the Qualtrics assignments.

Part 4: Sampling and Sample Statistics explains the difference between a population and a sample. Two chapters cover important issues that provide a basis for statistical inference. One important topic describes reasons why sampling is needed and why samples can be used to confidently allow predictions about larger numbers of people (i.e., populations). Another chapter provides useful guides for determining how large a sample is needed to make inferences with desired levels of confidence. Basic issues related to sampling distributions also are covered.

Part 5: Basic Data Analytics (and Reporting) covers basic processes necessary in translating raw data into market intelligence. The part presents some of the most commonly used methods for analyzing data. For instance, basic descriptive statistics related to central tendency and dispersion are discussed in detail as a basis for understanding approaches that follow.

The chapters also cover inferential statistics including often-used univariate and bivariate approaches such as the chi-square test and t-tests. Elementary ANOVA applications are discussed in the context of analyzing experiments. Data mining approaches using sequential cross-classification are covered. Both simple and multiple regression also get covered as an introduction to general linear modeling procedures. Last, but certainly not least, the part concludes with a chapter on presenting research results. The chapter includes the outline useful in creating a student (individual or group) marketing research project. Also, basic guidelines for constructing research reports and presentations that are delivered orally or presented online are discussed.

Part 6: Beyond the Basics of Marketing Analytics provides more detail on linear modeling approaches and commonly used multivariate statistical approaches. More detailed coverage of topics such as statistical moderation and mediation are covered, including step-by-step approaches for testing hypotheses involving moderation or mediation. Big data analytics applications involving multivariate tools like cluster analysis also are discussed. This edition includes much more thorough coverage of logistical regression, factorial designs, and factor analysis and concludes with a primer on structural equations modeling (SEM) sufficient to allow users to test basic theoretical models and to provide a basis for more extensive study of SEM and other multivariate data analysis approaches.

Part 7: Comprehensive Cases with Computerized Databases makes up the last section of the book. These cases provide materials that challenge students to apply and integrate the concepts they have learned throughout the text. Instructors will find that these cases provide some flexibility either to expand or simplify the assignment to suit the demands of varying course assignments.

The cases provide more variety and include some that involve analysis of internal marketing problems as well as an opportunity to use qualitative research. When quantitative data are included, they can be easily analyzed with basic statistical tools like SPSS or JMP. Excel files are also included with the same data. These files can be read directly by statistical programs like SAS, SPSS, JMP, or other programs. The eleventh edition includes a new comprehensive case suitable for application of multivariate data analysis tools.

Superior Pedagogy

More than other marketing research textbooks, the eleventh edition of *Exploring Marketing Research* addresses students' need to comprehend all aspects of the marketing research process. The following features facilitate learning throughout the book:

- **Learning Objectives.** Each chapter begins with a concise list of learning objectives that emphasize the major areas of competency the student should achieve before proceeding to the next chapter. The key is to avoid labeling everything a major learning objective and to provide the instructors with flexibility for emphasizing additional material from each chapter as they see fit.

- **Major Headings Keyed to Learning Objectives.** All first-level headings, with the exception of those labeled "Introduction," are keyed to learning objectives. This should be an aid in developing assessment rubrics and makes the book more user friendly in terms of identifying key material. Example assessment rubrics are available in the instructional resources.

- **Research Snapshots.** All of the box materials share a common title, Research Snapshots. Each chapter contains three Research Snapshots. The boxes explore marketing research processes in a variety of modern businesses situations, ranging from international considerations to research ethics. In later chapters in particular, boxes illustrate research techniques and step-by-step instructions for producing statistical results across multiple platforms.

- **Writing Style.** An accessible, interesting writing style continues as a hallmark of this book. With a careful balance between theory and practice and a sprinkling of interesting examples and anecdotes, the writing style clarifies and simplifies the market research process. In addition, the text offers a comprehensive treatment of important and current topics.

- **Statistical Approach.** Given the increased emphasis in industry on marketing analytics, the eleventh edition provides greater coverage of analytical tools. That said, the emphasis remains one that takes a simple approach to give full coverage to basic tools like those used to test hypotheses involving differences between means or relationships among variables. Cross-tabulation, *t*-tests, ANOVA, and regression are covered in sufficient depth to allow a student to master these techniques. More complex analytical tools are covered in sufficient detail to also allow students to perform basic applications (factor analysis, cluster analysis, SEM). The text includes screen shots to get students started running statistics using EXCEL, SAS, JMP, or SPSS, (check for software availability with this text).

  In addition, easy-to-follow, click-through sequences can walk a student through a few of the most basic approaches to producing statistical results.

- **Key Terms.** Learning the vocabulary of marketing research is essential to understanding the topic, and *Exploring Marketing Research* facilitates this with key terms. First, key concepts are boldfaced and completely defined when they first appear in the textbook. Second, all key terms and concepts are listed at the end of each chapter, and many terms are highlighted in a marginal glossary. Third, a glossary summarizing all key terms and definitions appears at the end of the book for handy reference. A glossary of frequently used symbols is also included.

- **Research Activities.** The end-of-chapter materials include a few real-world research activities intended to provide actual research experience for the student. Most provide an opportunity for the student to gain experience with multiple content areas. Some involve ethical aspects of research, and some involve Internet usage.

- **Cases.** Extensive cases taken from real-life situations illustrate marketing research concepts and build knowledge and research skills. These cases offer students the opportunity to participate actively in the decision-making process, one of the most effective forms of learning. Video cases are also available via the instructor section of the book's website (www.cengagebrain.com).

Resources for Students

To promote learning and competency, it is also important to provide students with well-crafted resources. In addition to covering the latest information technology, the eleventh edition includes the following student resources:

- To access additional course materials and companion resources, please visit **www.cengagebrain.com.** At the Cengage Brain home page, search for ISBN 9781305263529 using the search box at the top of the page. This will take you to the product page where free companion resources can be found.
- The Dedicated Website **www.cengagebrain.com,** developed especially for the new edition, includes chapter quizzes that allows you to test and retest your knowledge of chapter concepts. Each chapter has a quiz to encourage retesting. In addition, the website features downloadable flashcards of key terms, the very best online marketing research resources available, and much more.

Survey and analytical skills are essential to effective marketing research. Survey skills include an ability to translate research questions into survey items that respondents, usually consumers, answer. These answers produce data and analytics turns that data into market intelligence! *Exploring* provides students with real experience in both state of the art survey and analytical technologies. Students gain access to commercial quality survey creation and data analysis software with student versions of two market-leading products: The Qualtrics Research Suite for building surveys and *JMP* point and click statistical software from the SAS Institute. One access card (see the front of the book) provides a code and instructions for downloading *JMP* statistical software while another access card provides access to the Qualtrics Research Suite, the premier survey software tool in the industry, is bound inside the back cover of the book. Note that e-book versions of this title will not have access to these products. As well, some instructors might want to expose and assign the SPSS Statistical Software as part of their course. An optional packaging option providing students with access to SPSS is available with *Exploring Marketing Research*. Contact your Cengage Learning consultant for procedures for adding SPSS to your bookstore order. Following are descriptions of all of these products:

- *JMP* is a statistics software package for Windows and Macintosh computers from SAS, the market leader in analytics software and services. Unlike the traditional SAS interface, *JMP* provides point-and-click accessibility and integrates easily with Excel spreadsheets. *JMP* student edition is a streamlined, easy-to-use version that provides extensive marketing analytics capabilities and easily produces graphical output. The textbook provides many *JMP* illustrations. Once data is imported, students will find that most procedures require just two or three mouse clicks. *JMP* provides an interface to explore data visually and interactively, which enhances students' engagement with the data and enables them to tackle difficult statistical problems with ease. *JMP* can import data from a variety of formats, including Excel and other statistical packages, and you can easily import or copy and paste graphs and output into documents and presentations. *JMP* functions in the same way on both Windows and Mac platforms and instructions contained with this book apply to both platforms.
- The Qualtrics Research Suite was built for marketing researchers by marketing researchers. Enclosed with each new copy of *Exploring Marketing Research* is an access code that gives you access to a tool that makes survey creation easy enough for a beginner while at the same time sophisticated enough for the most demanding academic or corporate researcher. Qualtrics allows you to create and deploy surveys, and provides data for analysis. A survey included in the book in the Survey This! box on page 4 invites users to respond to a sample survey. Then the sample survey data collected from students who have used *Exploring Marketing Research* around the globe are made available for learning exercises throughout learning experience. Exercises and questions stemming from the survey engage students in critically evaluating survey items and questionnaire construction in the early chapters and in the later chapters, actual data provide a resource for hands-on analytics revealing insights into actual students' attitudes and behaviors. Qualtrics access requires the code provided in the access card available with each new copy of the book.

■ SPSS Statistics Student Version provides real-world software for students to do data analysis with one of the world's leading statistical software packages. This student-friendly version is virtually identical to the professional version in function and appearance. Marketing faculty around the world have relied on SPSS for decades. SPSS Student Version promotes better decision-making and productivity through faster performance, accurate results, increased productivity and effectiveness using a range of specialized techniques. SPSS Student Version integrates with other technologies and tools, making it easy to access common data types, external programming languages, and file types. Access is available only when bundled with text. IBM SPSS Statistics Student Version for Windows (ISBN-10: 1285838033 | ISBN-13: 9781285838038)

ACKNOWLEDGMENTS

Certainly, no list of acknowledgments will be complete. So many people have assisted in this project. Chief among these would be to the late Bill Zikmund for carrying the weight of this project for each of the first eight editions. I enjoy carrying the project along into hopefully many more editions as the premier marketing research text. Also, thanks go to some of my team. My current and former graduate assistants including Christian Bushardt, Nina Krey, David Locander, Lauren Brewer, Kevin James, David Shows, Melanie Gardner, and Christina Chung have helped share some of the workload on other endeavors freeing up time for me to spend on this project. David was particularly helpful in getting the Survey This! feature underway. I would be remiss not to also mention the support and patience of my family. Thanks especially to Laurie (Dr. Laurie Babin) for carefully proofreading all the chapters in this book and providing suggested corrections. Also, thanks go to all the great faculty who mentored me during my days in the Ph.D. program at LSU. Most notable among these are Joseph F. Hair, Jr. and the late William R. Darden.

Special thanks go to all the good people at Cengage Learning who helped make this project possible. Thanks to my publishers, John Rich and Mike Roche, for motivating the whole team to stay on schedule. Also, a special thanks to Elizabeth Lowry and the rest of the production team. They provided tremendous support through the writing and production process, including assistance with proofing, permissions, photos, and exhibits.

Many colleagues contributed ideas for this book. They made many suggestions that greatly enhanced this book. For their insightful reviews of the manuscript for this or previous editions of *Exploring Marketing Research*, I would like to thank the following:

Karen Goncalves
Nichols College

Carol Bienstock
Radford University

Steven V. Cates
Averett University

Stephanie Noble
The University of Mississippi

Bob Lauman
Webster University

Natalie Wood
St. Joseph's University

Robert Jaross
Florida International University

Terry Paul
The Ohio State University

Mike Parent
Utah State University

Stephen Batory
Bloomsburg University

Michael R. Hyman
New Mexico State University

Rick Saucier
St. John's University

Xin Zhao
University of Utah

Gerald Albaum
University of New Mexico

William Bearden
University of South Carolina

Joseph A. Bellizzi
Arizona State University–West, Emeritus

James A. Brunner
University of Toledo

F. Anthony Bushman
San Francisco State University

Thomas Buzas
Eastern Michigan University

Roy F. Cabaniss
Huston-Tillotson College

Michael d'Amico
University of Akron

Ron Eggers
Barton College

H. Harry Friedman
City University of New York–Brooklyn

Ron Goldsmith
Florida State University

Larry Goldstein
Iona College

David Gourley
Arizona State University

Jim Grimm
Illinois State University

Christopher Groening
University of Missouri

Al Gross
Robert Morris College

Don Heinz
University of Wisconsin

Craig Hollingshead
Texas A&M University–Kingsville

Victor Howe
University of Kentucky

Roy Howell
Texas Tech University

Rhea Ingram
Columbus State University–Georgia

P. K. Kannan
University of Maryland

Susan Kleine
Arizona State University

David B. Klenosky
Purdue University

C. S. Kohli
California State University–Fullerton

Jerome L. Langer
Assumption College

James H. Leigh
Texas A&M University

Larry Lowe
Bryant College

Karl Mann
Tennessee Technological University

Charles R. Martin
Wichita State University

Marlys Mason
Oklahoma State University

Tom K. Massey
University of Missouri–Kansas City

Sanjay Mishra
University of Kansas

G. M. Naidu
University of Wisconsin–Whitewater

Charles Prohaska
Central Connecticut State University

Alan Sawyer
University of Florida

Robert Schaffer
California State University–Pomona

Leon G. Schiffman
City University of New York–Baruch

David Shows
Appalachian State University

K. Sivakumar
Lehigh University

Mark Speece
Central Washington University

Harlan Spotts
Western New England College

Wilbur W. Stanton
Old Dominion University

Bruce L. Stern
Portland State University

James L. Taylor
University of Alabama

Gail Tom
California State University–Sacramento

Deborah Utter
Boston College

David Wheeler
Suffolk University

Richard Wilcox
Carthage College

Margaret Wright
University of Colorado

Clifford E. Young
University of Colorado–Denver

William Lee Ziegler
Bethune-Cookman College

Thanks also to all of the students who have inspired me and reinforced the fact that I made a great career decision over two decades ago. Thanks also to my close colleagues Mitch Griffin, Dave Ortinau, and Jim Boles for their continued support and insight.

Barry J. Babin
Max P. Watson, Jr. Professor of Business Research and Chair
Department of Marketing & Analytics
Louisiana Tech University
January 2015

IN REMEMBRANCE

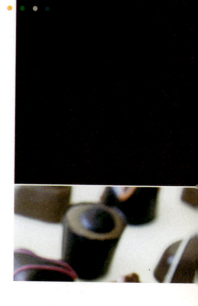

William G. Zikmund (1943–2002)

A native of the Chicago area, William G. Zikmund was a professor of marketing at Oklahoma State University and died shortly after completing the eighth edition. He received a Ph.D. in business administration with a concentration in marketing from the University of Colorado.

Before beginning his academic career, Professor Zikmund worked in marketing research for Conway/Millikin Company (a marketing research supplier) and Remington Arms Company (an extensive user of marketing research). Professor Zikmund also served as a marketing research consultant to several business and nonprofit organizations. During his academic career, Professor Zikmund published dozens of articles and papers in a diverse group of scholarly journals, ranging from the *Journal of Marketing* to the *Accounting Review* to the *Journal of Applied Psychology*. In addition to *Exploring Marketing Research*, Professor Zikmund authored *Essentials of Marketing Research*, *Business Research Methods*, *Marketing*, *Effective Marketing*, and a work of fiction, *A Corporate Bestiary*.

Professor Zikmund was a member of several professional organizations, including the American Marketing Association, the Academy of Marketing Science, the Association for Consumer Research, the Society for Marketing Advances, the Marketing Educators' Association, and the Association of Collegiate Marketing Educators. He served on the editorial review boards of the *Journal of Marketing Education*, *Marketing Education Review*, *Journal of the Academy of Marketing Science*, and *Journal of Business Research*.

ELEVENTH EDITION

EXPLORING
Marketing Research

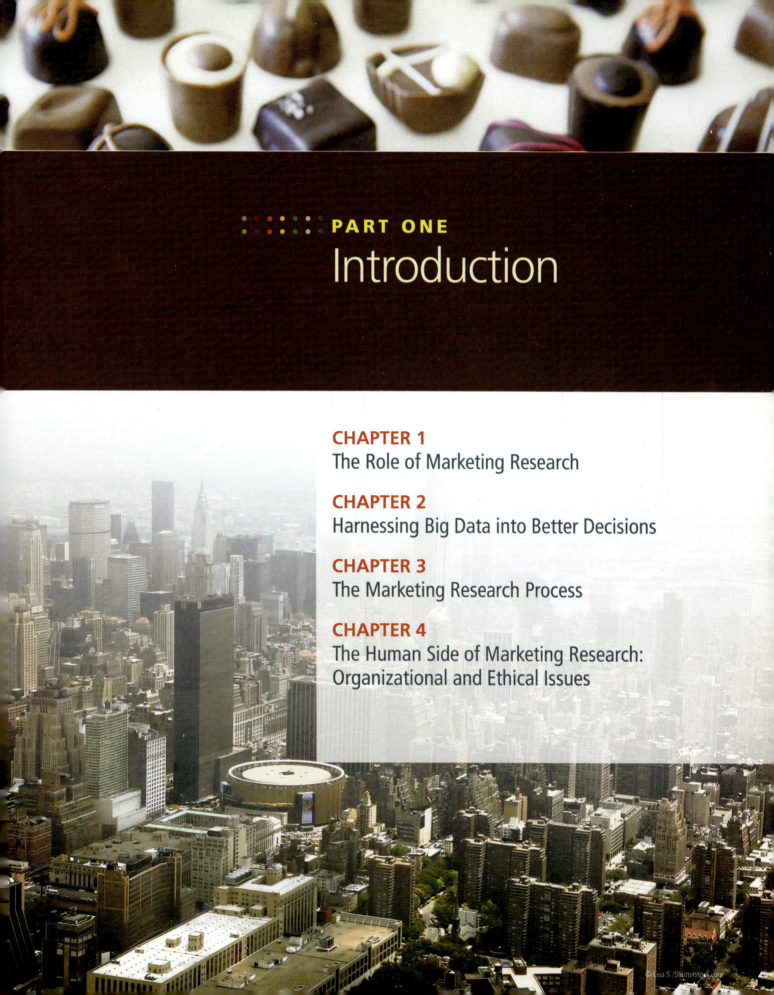

The Role of Marketing Research

LEARNING OUTCOMES

After studying this chapter, you should be able to:

1. Know what marketing research is and what it does for business
2. Understand the difference between basic and applied marketing research
3. Understand how the role of marketing research changes with the orientation of the firm
4. Be able to integrate marketing research results into the strategic planning process
5. Know when marketing research should and should not be conducted
6. Appreciate the way that technology and internationalization are changing marketing research

Chapter Vignette:

Samapple!

Consumers today love their technological devices. Most of us are seldom far from our smartphones, tablets, notebooks—we are hooked on electronics. Apple represented the king of technology brands for many years. The company took advantage of a hip and smug image to portray competitors like Microsoft as out-of-date and old-fashioned. Apple's late founder, Steve Jobs, once bragged about how Apple did not need consumer research signaling the attitude that they knew what to make without needed input from the market.

In the technology world, even months can make a difference and today, Apple is no longer America's favorite technology brand. In fact, a consumer survey shows Apple is America's fifth favorite "technology" brand trailing Amazon, Samsung, Sony, and even the old fuddy-duddy, Microsoft. Samsung's Galaxy brand is particularly hip and their advertising campaign effectively portrayed it as hip and cool whereas Apple customers stand in line "waiting for the next best thing" that is already here—in their Galaxy smartphone! Samsung uses a great deal of consumer research as input into its designs even going so far as to create a "band-aid" feel in the product design in response to consumer input that the previous models did not feel sturdy

or comfortable. In China, consumers are increasingly keen on brands like Coolpad over Apple.

The fact is, as product markets become increasingly competitive, knowledge of consumers becomes the primary tool in gaining competitive advantage through effective design and positioning. Marketing research offers companies a tool to integrate market data into effective decision-making.[1]

Introduction

When one considers all the complexities involved in getting a product to the market successfully, things like packaging may easily seem like minor details. However, when managers make decisions without adequate information, they can quickly realize that some details are not so minor after all. From high-tech electronics companies to snack food companies, companies require information as input to decision making. Marketing research can provide that information. Without the input that marketing research provides, key business decisions including those shaping product and package design, pricing, distribution, market potential, and promotion design become guesswork.

We open with two examples illustrating how business decisions require intelligence and how research can provide that intelligence. The following illustrations focus specifically on how marketing research encourages innovation in the form of new products or improvements in existing value propositions and the marketing of those offerings. Imagine yourself in the role of a brand manager as you read these examples and think about the information needs you may have in trying to build a successful brand.

Viral marketing is a focus of attention for many firms these days. Is viral marketing a fad or is it something that really pays off for firms? Coca-Cola launched a 70-second video called "Unlock the 007 in You" in conjunction with the 50th anniversary of the James Bond motion picture series. The video depicts a train station scene where a Coke Zero vending machine customer reads a message on the machine to get to a platform across the station in 70 seconds to win tickets to the latest Bond premier. Along the way, the customer has to dodge fruit vendors, delivery men, a pack of small dogs, and lots of other obstacles all while bystanders hum or play the familiar Bond theme. In the end, the consumer arrives just in time and receives orders to "sing" the Bond song to win the tickets. Can you hear it now?

That particular video has been viewed over 11,000,000 times. However, Coke is not concerned with the views. This particular promotional effort intended to motivate viewers to share the link with others. It worked! This was the most shared video YouTube ad of 2012. Unruly Media Inc. provides services to companies aimed at getting videos not only to turn viral but also to get them shared. Unruly acknowledges that a very small percentage of video exposures lead to sharing. In fact, a share rate of 1 percent would be very high. However, when an ad does get shared, Unruly research suggests that consumers who view a shared video end up liking the video 15 percent more than if they discovered the video on their own.[1] That's important because liking of the video leads to almost twice the purchase likelihood for the advertised product.

● ● ● ● ● ●

Unruly researches the impact of viral videos. (source is unrulymedia.com)

The coffee industry, after years of the "daily grind," has proved quite dynamic over the past few years. After a steady decline, research on consumers' beverage purchases shows that coffee sales began rebounding around 1995. By 2007, research indicates that although practically all coffee drinkers visit gourmet coffee shops, younger coffee consumers, particularly those under the age of 30, drink most of their coffee the *gourmet* way.[2] But, how much is too much to pay for coffee? Even at a Starbucks store, you might guess that a consumer would be unhappy to pay about $60 for a pound of ground coffee. However, research shows that these younger, relatively affluent coffee drinkers are paying this price routinely, and they are doing it to make their coffee at home.

Source: unruly.com

The widespread adoption of single-serve pod-based roasted coffee brewers, one cup at a time, has stimulated sales of coffee pods. The unit cost of coffee in the pod approaches $60 a pound, six times more than the price of bagged coffee. Research shows that in the upper middle income, 18- to 34-year-old demographic, a consumer uses a single-serve coffee pod for 65 percent of their coffee. In other demographics, that number is about 50 percent or less. Because of the high margin associated with this consumption, many companies are looking at opportunities to sell other products to this lucrative demographic. Green Mountain is considering products including soup pods and other

Source: www.qualtrics.com

This book introduces the reader to the world of marketing research. Marketing research represents the eyes and the ears of the competitive business firm. The researcher's job is to determine what information is needed so that data can be analyzed and become intelligence. Consumers play a crucial role in this process. They often are research participants and, with or without their knowledge, they provide the information needed. One way that consumers (and sometimes employees or managers) take part is by participating in surveys. Most readers have probably participated in surveys previously. Here is another chance to do so, only this time, you will first play the role of a research participant. Later, you will fill the role of a research analyst and even a key marketing decision-maker as you try to make sense of data provided by the many users of this textbook.

Your first interaction with the "Survey This!" feature is simply to play the role of respondent and respond to the entire survey as honestly and completely as possible. Go to the URL provided in the preface and by your instructor, and simply participate. Your answers will be anonymously stored in the database along with all the other students using this book around the country and, in some cases, the world. Once you've completed the survey, you can visit the course website and get a copy of the questions contained in the questionnaire and data from a sample of previous users.

beverages including Coke pods! Coke liked this idea so much, they bought a 10 percent share in Green Mountain coffee, a leader in coffee pods.[3]

These examples illustrate the need for information in making informed business decisions. Unruly uses research to advise advertisers on ways to make videos go viral, get shared and eventually drive sales. The fact that coffee pods provide such convenience to a specific but substantial demographic demonstrates that the market is very willing to pay high prices for convenient alternatives. As a result, companies are trying to find other ways to leverage the pod concept into profits. One can easily see how research can be used to examine new concepts and product changes in progressively more complex stages, setting the stage for more successful product introductions. New product research represents only the tip of the iceberg when it comes to the types of marketing research conducted and used every day. This chapter introduces basic concepts of marketing research and describes how research can play a crucial role in successful marketing and business success in general.

What Is Marketing Research?

Part of business involves studying the different things that come together to create a business environment. Marketing research would not exist if business didn't exist. Thus, understanding marketing research requires at least a cursory understanding of business.

Business and Marketing Research

In its essence, business is very simple. Successful companies offer things to consumers that they are willing to buy. That means that consumers view the propositions offered by companies as providing varying degrees of value. In other words, products are ultimately a bundle of value-producing benefits. Many factors affect consumer perceptions of value and successful companies are those that keenly understand the value equation. With this in mind, several key questions help provide understanding:

1. *What do we sell?* This includes not only the benefits that are easily seen, but also the more emotional benefits such as the comfort and relaxation of enjoying a cup of gourmet coffee in a pleasant atmosphere or the esteem that comes from having the latest electronic gadget. Companies offer value propositions that provide the potential for value beyond merely tangible product features.

2. *How do consumers view our company?* Companies likewise often define themselves too narrowly based only on the physical *product* they sell. They should think about just whom their customers would choose if they chose another alternative. For instance, how is Starbucks viewed relative to its competitors? Who are the competitors? Does Starbucks compete more directly with Maxwell House, Keurig, McDonald's, or something completely unassociated with coffee like a local lounge? If Starbucks provides value through relaxation and social interaction, a lounge may sometimes be an alternative. Ultimately, companies ask themselves "Are we viewed more or less favorably relative to alternatives?"

3. *What does our company/product mean?* What knowledge do people have of the company and its products? Do they know how to use them? Do they know all the different needs the company can address? What does our packaging and promotion communicate to consumers? Does our total value proposition signal the quality that we offer?

4. *What do consumers desire?* How can the company make the lives of its customers better, and how can it do this in a way that is not easily duplicated by another firm? Part of this lies in uncovering the things that customers truly desire, but which they can often not put into words.

Answering these questions requires information. Marketing research's function is to supply information that helps provide these answers, thereby leading to more informed and more successful decision-making. Managers who use this information reduce the risk associated with decision-making.

All business problems require information for effective decision-making. Can researchers deliver the right information in a useful form and on time? Research seeks to deliver accurate and precise information that can make marketing strategy and management more effective.[4] Marketing research attempts to supply accurate information that reduces the uncertainty in decision-making. Very often, managers make decisions with little information for various reasons, including insufficient time to conduct research or management's belief that they already know enough. Relying on seat-of-the-pants decision-making—decision making without research—is like betting on a long shot at the racetrack because the horse's name is appealing. Occasionally the long shot pays off. More often, long-run uninformed decision-making is unwise. Marketing research helps decision-makers shift from intuitive guesswork to a more systematic, objective, and effective approach.

Marketing Research Defined

Marketing research is the application of the scientific method in searching for the truth about market and marketing phenomena. Research applications include defining marketing opportunities and problems, generating and evaluating marketing ideas, monitoring performance, and generally understanding the marketing process and the way consumers extract value from consumption. Marketing research includes idea generation and theory development, problem definition, information gathering, analyzing data, and communicating the findings including potential implications. Although marketing researchers ask a lot of questions, research clearly involves a lot more than just surveys and questionnaires.

This definition suggests that the marketing research process is neither accidental nor haphazard. Literally, research (*re*-search) means "to search again." The term connotes patient study and scientific investigation wherein the researcher takes another, more careful look to try and successively know more. Ultimately, all findings tie back to some theory.

The definition also emphasizes, through reference to the scientific method, that any information generated should be accurate and objective. The researcher should be personally detached and free of bias attempting to find truth. Research isn't performed to support preconceived ideas but to test them. If bias enters into the research process, the value of the research is considerably reduced. We will discuss this further in a subsequent chapter.

Marketing research

The application of the scientific method in searching for the truth about marketing phenomena. These activities include defining marketing opportunities and problems, generating and evaluating marketing ideas, monitoring performance, and understanding the marketing process.

Care for Some Horns and Halos?

Horns and Halos are not a new breakfast cereal! Both for profit and not-for-profit institutions benefit from research describing how consumers make decisions related to nutrition. The federal government issues rules and regulations describing what types of information must be provided to consumers. Today, American consumers will find nutrition labels on practically all packaged food, on fast-food restaurant menus and even on fresh foods. The government specifically requires nutrition labels on fresh chicken and beef. Although the intention is to create more informed decisions, research suggests the result is not always so clear.

Researchers have adopted strange sounding terms to describe how consumers sometimes make misguided decisions. A halo effect refers to a consumer, sometimes mistakenly, believing that certain food categories are healthy. For instance, anything called a salad might have a halo. A horn on the other hand refers to the fact that some categories are always perceived to be unhealthy, like steak. Experimental research shows that the use of nutrition labels alone have little effect on consumer judgments of food healthiness. However, the use of nutrition labels may interact with halos and horns in a way that may create more accurate perceptions of inaccurate horns. In

other words, some steaks are relatively healthy (like a sirloin) and the labels may help identify that fact. Other research shows the difficulty in deciding what causes healthy or unhealthy diets. Although some research attributes the availability of fast food with increased obesity for instance, other research likewise attributes the federal school lunch program with obesity. Marketing research sometimes presents surprising results.

Sources: Burton, S., L. A. Cook, E. Howlett and C. L. Newman (2014), "Broken Halos and Shattered Horns: Overcoming the Biasing Effects of Prior Expectations through Objective Information Disclosure," *Journal of the Academy of Marketing Science,* in press. C. L. Newman, E. Howlett and S. Burton (2014), "Implications of Fast Food Restaurant Concentration for Preschool-Aged Childhood Obesity," *Journal of Business Research,* in press.

Clearly, marketing research is relevant to all aspects of the marketing mix. Research can facilitate managerial decision making about each of the four Ps: product, pricing, promotion, and place (distribution). By providing valuable input for marketing mix decisions, marketing research decreases the risk of making bad decisions in each area.

Finally, this definition of marketing research is limited by one's definition of *marketing*. Although one could hardly argue that research aimed at designing better products for a for-profit corporation like Coca-Cola is clearly marketing research, marketing research also includes efforts that assist nonprofit organizations such as the American Heart Association, the university alumni association, or a parochial elementary school. Every organization exists to satisfy social needs, and each requires marketing skills to produce and distribute their products and services. Governments also can use research in much the same way as managers at Samsung or Coke. For instance, the Food and Drug Administration (FDA) is an important user of marketing research, employing it to address the way people view and use various food and drugs. One such research study funded by the FDA addressed the question of how point of sale materials might influence consumers' perceptions, or better misperceptions, of the healthiness of fresh food offerings.[5] The Research Snapshot describes a typical nutrition-related marketing research project. This book explores marketing research as it applies to all organizations and institutions engaging in marketing activities.

Applied and Basic Marketing Research

One useful way to describe research is based on the specificity of its purpose. Is the research intended to address a very specific problem or is it meant to describe some overall marketing phenomenon?

Applied Marketing Research

Applied marketing research is conducted to address a specific marketing decision for a specific firm or organization. If Green Mountain Coffee is trying to decide what other beverages could be profitably sold through its pod systems, applied marketing research can help provide answers. Similarly, the research that identifies the best segments to approach with its new products is applied research. Applied research is relatively specific and claims to help a particular organization make better decisions regarding that issue.

Applied marketing research

Research conducted to address a specific marketing decision for a specific firm or organization.

Basic Marketing Research

Basic marketing research doesn't address the needs of a specific organization and doesn't typically address a specific business decision. Instead, basic research expands marketing knowledge in general and not at solving a particular business's problem. Basic research can test the validity of a general marketing theory (one that applies to all of marketing) or to learn more about some market phenomenon like social networking. A great deal of basic marketing research addresses the ways in which retail atmosphere influences consumers' emotions and behavior.[6] From such research, we can learn how much the physical place creates value for consumers above and beyond any items purchased. This basic research does not examine the problem from any single retail or service provider's perspective. However, Starbucks' management may become aware of such research and apply the results in deciding how to design its stores. Thus, these two types of research are not completely independent.

Researchers sometimes use different terms to represent the same distinction. Some reserve the term *marketing research* to refer to basic research. Then, the term *market research* is used to capture applied research addressing the needs of a firm within a particular market. Although the distinction is very useful in describing research, very few aspects of research apply only to basic or only to applied research. Here, we will use the term *marketing research* more generally to refer to either type of research.

Basic marketing research

Research conducted without a specific decision in mind that usually does not address the needs of a specific organization. It attempts to expand the limits of marketing knowledge in general and is not aimed at solving a particular pragmatic problem.

The Scientific Method

All marketing research, whether basic or applied, involves the scientific method. The **scientific method** is the way researchers go about using knowledge and evidence to reach objective conclusions about the real world. The scientific method is the same in social sciences such as marketing as in physical sciences such as physics. Marketing researchers apply the scientific method as their way to understand marketing phenomena.

Exhibit 1.1 briefly illustrates the scientific method. Researchers usually begin with some understanding of theory in the problem area. Consumer researchers usually are familiar with

Scientific method

The way researchers go about using knowledge and evidence to reach objective conclusions about the real world.

© 2016 Cengage Learning®

EXHIBIT 1.1
The Scientific Method

Product oriented

Describes a firm that prioritizes decision making in a way that emphasizes technical superiority in the product.

Production oriented

Describes a firm that prioritizes efficiency and effectiveness of the production processes in making decisions.

Marketing concept

A central idea in modern marketing thinking that focuses on how the firm provides value to customers more than on the physical product or production process.

Marketing orientation

The corporate culture existing for firms adopting the marketing concept. It emphasizes customer orientation, long-term profitability over short-term profits, and a cross-functional perspective.

Customer oriented

Describes a firm in which all decisions are made with a conscious awareness of their effect on the consumer.

Stakeholder orientation

Recognizing that multiple parties are affected by firm decisions.

consumer behavior theory and by elaborating on this theory and/or combining theoretical knowledge with pure discovery, research questions emerge. Discovery can involve any means of idea generation, including exploratory techniques that we will discover later or even eureka types of experiences like when the apple fell on Newton's head! The early stages of the research process in particular work better when creative thinking is applied. A host of creative thinking tools exist that managers and researchers can and should apply. The researcher then develops formal research hypotheses that play a key role through the remainder of the process. The next step involves testing hypotheses against empirical evidence (facts from observation or experimentation). Results either support a particular hypothesis or do not support that hypothesis. From the results, new knowledge is acquired that may lead to a new theory or modification of an existing theory.

Use of the scientific method in applied research ensures objectivity in gathering facts and testing creative ideas for alternative marketing strategies. In basic research, scientific research contributes to conclusions that over time contribute to the development of general laws about phenomena like price and value. The scientific method is the philosophy and way of doing *scientific* research, the results of which are the basis for knowledge growth and better decision making. Much of this book deals with scientific methodology.

Marketing Research and Strategic Management Orientation

Organizations over time adopt a certain way of going about their business. These ways represent strategic management orientations and they provide a common theme for decision-making. A firm can be **product oriented**. A product-oriented firm prioritizes decision making in a way that emphasizes technical superiority of their offerings. Thus, input from technicians and experts are very important in making critical decisions. The goal is to make what the firm sees as the best products possible. A firm can be **production oriented**. Production orientation means that the firm prioritizes efficiency and effectiveness of the production processes in making decisions. Here, input from engineers and accountants becomes important as the firm seeks to drive costs down. Production-oriented firms are usually very large firms manufacturing products in very large quantities resulting in good economies of scale. Marketing research may take a backseat with these orientations.

In contrast, marketing research is a primary tool enabling implementation of a marketing orientation.[7] The **marketing concept** is a central idea in modern marketing thinking that focuses more on how the firm provides value to customers than on the physical product or production process. The orientation has evolved over time as product- and production-oriented firms respond to changes in the competitive and economic environments. When a firm adapts the marketing concept, it develops a **marketing orientation.** A marketing-oriented firm must:

1. Be **customer oriented**—means that all firm decisions are made with a conscious awareness of their effect on the consumer
2. Emphasize long-run profitability rather than short-term profits or sales volume
3. Adopt a cross-functional perspective, meaning that marketing is integrated across other business functions

Going further, a **stakeholder orientation** recognizes that multiple parties are affected by firm decisions. When a company makes a decision to change a product line based on marketing research, that decision affects customers, employees, and their families; the owners of the company (shareholders in a public company); and even society in general. Good decision-making considers how all are affected when making decisions. Exhibit 1.2 provides an overview of business orientations.

Customer Orientation

According to the marketing concept, the consumer should be the primary focus of attention, the pivot point about which the business moves to achieve the balanced best interests of all other stakeholders in the long run. According to this philosophy, the firm creates offers with consumers' needs in mind. The creation of value for consumers, after all, is the reason that a firm exists. Therefore, unlike the other two orientations, marketing research addressing consumer desires, beliefs, and attitudes becomes essential.

How could a good piece of luggage be designed without consumer research? Those who travel frequently, particularly by air, are very fussy about the bag they carry. When all is considered, research shows that price is hardly the most important criterion for the frequent traveler. These consumers are willing to plunk down hundreds and sometimes even over $1,000 for the right bag. Well-known

Marketing research provides input that can make a traveler happy about the bag they tote through an airport

companies like Samsonite and lesser well-known companies, at least to the general public, like Mandarina Duck, use consumer input to design *perfect* bags. What factors do consumers consider more important than price and essential in a good bag? First, rollers. Not just any rollers, smooth and sturdy rollers and increasingly, four instead of two wheels. That enables the bag to stand up and provide an easy place to rest a computer or purse. Second, size. It has to hold at least a few days' attire but has to fit in the overhead bin of an airplane. Third, separate storage for items like shoes and toiletries and preferably, a garment compartment for more dressy attire. Fourth, sturdiness. The bag should stand abuse and last years, not months! Fifth, unique and fun appearance. When you travel a lot, the bag should have personality that says something about the consumer. Thus, a bag that is a special khaki orange color with grey accents not only is fun, but unique enough to stand out in a crowd and much easier to pick out on a carousel should you have to check it. Mandarina Duck is a leader in style but does not take a backseat in function.[8] Consumer research plays a big role in this research.

Although technology firms are traditionally thought of as prototypically product oriented, that view is changing. In a work at home, smartphone at the ready environment, consumers realize they have a lot of choices. In the past, companies often issued phones and computers from brands like Gateway and Blackberry. Today, employees often want to use their own favorite technologies to help do their jobs. One result is that even IT guys in companies have had to become consumer oriented! They are now charged with helping employees leverage their own technologies into greater productivity.[9]

Product Orientation	Production Orientation	Marketing Orientation	Stakeholder Orientation
Internal focus	Internal focus	External focus	External focus
Emphasize product superiority	Emphasize efficiency and low costs	Emphasize customer tastes and desires	Emphasize a balance in satisfying all parties touched by organization
Product research is critical	Process research is important	Customer research is essential	Consumer research important
Narrow or even niche markets served	Mass markets often required for success	Identifiable market segments matched with unique product	Select segments served balanced with great concern for public persona

EXHIBIT **1.2**

Types of Business Orientations

© 2016 Cengage Learning®

Long-Run Profitability

Customer orientation does not mean slavery to consumers' every fleeting whim. Implicit in the marketing concept is the assumption of the continuity of the firm. Thus, the firm must eventually experience profitability to survive although its orientation may be more toward building strong relationships with customers.

Lego works hard to build relationships with customers. Not only do they do research to try to predict how today's children would like to interact with the Lego brand, but they also study the market to integrate carefully their marketing efforts. Lego monitors social networks and general Internet communication constantly searching for positive and negative mentions of the brand. They refer to this as their **online sentiment analysis**.[10] Lego.com provides visitors with an interactive Lego experience from which Lego harvests more information about their customers and potential customers. This aggressive research approach allows them to build and maintain strong relationships with its customers.

The second aspect of the marketing concept argues against profitless volume or sales volume for the sake of volume alone. Sometimes, the best decision for a customer and the best decision in the end for the firm is the sale that is not made. For instance, a parts supplier might be able to mislead a customer about the relative quality of the parts he or she sells and make an immediate sale. However, when the parts begin to fail sooner than expected, the customer will almost certainly not do business with this firm again. If instead the salesperson had been honest and suggested another supplier, he or she may be able to find another opportunity to do business with that firm.

Online sentiment analysis
Using data indicating the total positive or negative mentions of a brand on the Internet to assess and understand the strength of the brand.

A Cross-Functional Effort

The marketing concept requires the firm to provide marketing information to be provided to and used by all the functional areas of a business. Information must be integrated into decisions for all areas. Production needs accurate forecasts to know how much should be produced; the design team needs input on consumer tastes, strategic management personnel need to understand the meaning of the brand, and so on. Problems are almost certain to arise from lack of an integrated, company-wide effort. The marketing concept stresses a cross-functional perspective to achieve consumer orientation and long-term profitability. The first panel of Exhibit 1.3 illustrates a firm in which every department works independently. The walls between the areas of the firm illustrate a lack of cross-functionality and, consequently, a lack of market orientation. The second panel illustrates a firm without barriers between the functions where marketing personnel work cross-functionally with other areas to achieve long-term profitability.

When a firm lacks organizational procedures for communicating marketing information and coordinating marketing efforts, the effectiveness of its marketing programs will suffer. Marketing research findings produce some of the most crucial marketing information; thus, such research is management's key tool for finding out what customers want and how best to satisfy their needs. In a competitive marketplace, managers recognize the critical need for conducting marketing research. When conducted competently, the firm bases decisions on valid and reliable facts communicated effectively to decision makers.

In a marketing-oriented firm, marketing researchers serve more than the external customers who buy the firm's offerings. Marketing research also serves internal customers with information. The internal customers include employees all along the value production chain from frontline service and sales employees, to production managers to the CEO. In fact, in a market-oriented organization, all employees are marketers in that they serve internal and external customers. An accountant who prepares a report for a sales manager should view the manager as a customer who uses the information to make decisions benefiting external customers. All employees share the common focus of providing value to customers; in such organizations, the focus on customers becomes tacit knowledge.[11] Stakeholder-oriented companies also place a keen focus on processes that serve customers as well as others impacted by firm decisions.

a) Isolated Functions

b) Cross-Functionality

© 2016 Cengage Learning®

Keeping Customers and Building Relationships

Marketers often talk about getting customers, but keeping customers is equally important. Effective marketers work to build long-term relationships with their customers. The term **relationship marketing** communicates the idea that a major goal of marketing is to build long-term relationships with the customers contributing to their success. Once an exchange is made, effective marketing stresses managing the relationships that will bring about additional exchanges. Effective marketers view making a sale not as the end of a process but as the start of the organization's relationship with a customer. Satisfied customers will return to a company that has treated them well if they need to purchase the same product in the future. If they need a related item, satisfied customers know the first place to look. Harley-Davidson is a company that over time has developed a familial-type bond with its loyal customers. The research snapshot describes some of the ways Harley seeks for and uses information to serve better its markets at home and abroad.

In a company that practices total quality management, manufacturing's orientation toward lowest-cost productivity should harmonize with marketing's commitment to quality products at acceptable prices. For example, when Ford Motor Company advertises that "Quality Is Job One," the production department must make sure that every automobile that comes off the assembly line meets consumers' quality specifications. The notion that quality improvement is every employee's job must be integrated throughout the organization so that marketing and production will be in harmony. If this notion conflicts with manufacturing's desire to allow for variations from quality standards, the firm must implement statistical quality controls and other improvements in the manufacturing operation to improve its systems and increase productivity.

Chapters 8 discusses the measurement of quality, customer satisfaction, and value in detail. Throughout this book, however, we will explain how marketing research can help a company achieve the goal of creating valuable experiences for customers.

Marketing Research: A Means for Implementing the Marketing Concept

The real estate business has its ups and downs. Part of the reasons for these is that the things that appeal to consumers change over time. Companies like Camden Properties and Riverstone Residential manage apartment complexes all over the United States. In some markets, the apartment business is extremely competitive. These companies have learned several things about the

EXHIBIT 1.3
Isolation versus Cross-Functionality of Marketing in a Firm

Relationship marketing

Communicates the idea that a major goal of marketing is to build long-term relationships with the customers contributing to their success.

Hog Means Family

Relationships are built around value. To provide value, a firm needs to know what a product means to its customers. Harley-Davidson Inc., whose motorbikes often are affectionately known as Hogs, relies on research to understand what it means. More than anything else, Harleys these days mean family and families do not keep secrets from each other. Harley practices a wide variety of research and one recent tool involves mining social media sites. For instance, Harley-Davidson discovered a link between Kirchart skateboards and the Hog. Searching for the brand's name on social network sites like Facebook, they discovered a link to a YouTube video in which professional skateboarders for Heath Kirchart rode Harley-Davidson motorcycles across the country on their summer tour. Because of this information, Harley leveraged this information by becoming an official sponsor of Kirchart's tours.

Does this iconic American brand translate into foreign markets? That's a question for research. Harley opened its first dealerships in India just a few years ago. Indian consumers were more accustomed to scooters than Hogs, but the rising middle class and a new demand for luxury products creates opportunity. Survey research among Indian consumers showed a favorable opinion toward the brand. However, high duties imposed by the Indian government and difficult emission

© Andrey Armyagov/Shutterstock.com

regulations proved too much of a barrier for Harley for several years. Successful lobbying of the Indian government eased some of the restrictions and Harley now offers 12 models ranging from a smallish 883 cc model to the 1800 cc model more fitting of the title Hog. In this way, Harley can address the needs of the luxury market and those desiring a more practical bike that still makes a statement. The result, some new additions to a now international family.

Sources: Fournier, S. and J. Avery (2011), "The Uninvited Brand," *Business Horizons* (in press). Lee, B. (2013), "The Power of Peer Influence," *ABA Bank Marketing*, 45, 24–27.

---

modern apartment shopper. One big trend in their favor is that younger Americans tend to favor apartment complex living over stand-alone housing. Buying and owning a home is not as important a goal to younger generations as it was in the past. A second big trend is understanding how apartments ultimately are selected. It turns out that one of the biggest factors in judging the quality of a complex is its landscaping. Therefore, a lot of large apartment complexes invest heavily in sod, shrubs and even trees. Even a new complex can seem to be secluded in greenery. The landscaping gives the complex tremendous curb appeal that ultimately helps build sales. In addition, the landscaping may well keep the tenants happy longer, decreasing problems with turnover.

Research promotes firm success in other ways as well. For instance, during the introduction of a new product, accurate forecasting of the product's potential sales volume is an essential basis for estimating its profitability. A firm considering the introduction of a cat snack that contains hairball medicine might rely on a test market experiment to determine the optimal price for this new concept. Extensive testing should be done to ensure that the marketing program is fine-tuned to maximize the firm's profitability while satisfying consumers.

Analysis of data may also be a form of marketing research that can increase efficiency. Online shoppers can see some evidence of this in their routine browsing at places like Amazon or Barnes and Noble. Look at what happens toward the bottom of the screen when browsing a product. Notice how often the page will show what other products you may have an interest in. These suggestions are built from data showing what things consumers tend to buy together.

Marketing Research and Strategic Marketing Management

Effective marketing management requires research. Think about the role that celebrity endorsers play for many companies. Given their importance, numerous firms monitor the favorability of different celebrities and firms seek this research information in making endorsement decisions.

The Davie-Brown Index represents an independent research source providing such data on celebrities from all corners of the entertainment world. Among football quarterbacks, Peyton Manning is seen as more appealing and trendsetting than others like Tom Brady, Tony Romo, or Drew Breeze, and he represents a good candidate to send positive signals about a brand. On the other hand, newcomers like Johnny Manziel create a lot of attention and can drive sales of licensed products, but he may not send as positive an image as does Peyton.

Opendorse rates all celebrities based on how many dollars a single social network follower brings in sales. Interestingly, although the National Football League (NFL) is viewed as the top sports institution in the United States, no NFL player cracks the top 10. Tiger Woods, Roger Federer and Phil Mickelson make up the top 3. Peyton Manning is the top NFL player but he is not even in the top 10 endorsers based on dollars per follower![12] Data like these help firms know whether to invest in celebrity endorsers. The prime managerial value of marketing research comes from the reduced uncertainty that results from information and facilitates decision making about marketing strategies and tactics to achieve an organization's strategic goals.

Developing and implementing a marketing strategy involves four stages:

1. Identifying and evaluating market opportunities.
2. Analyzing market segments and selecting target markets.
3. Planning and implementing a marketing mix that will provide value to customers and meet organizational objectives.
4. Analyzing firm performance.

Exhibit 1.4 illustrates the integration of research and marketing strategy and the way they come together to create value in the marketplace.

Marketing Research

Identify and Evaluate Market Opportunities

Analyze Market Segments and Select Target Markets

Plan and Implement Marketing Mix

Value

Firm Performance

© 2016 Cengage Learning®

EXHIBIT 1.4

Marketing Research Cuts Decision Risk with Input That Leads to Value

Identifying and Evaluating Market Opportunities

One job that marketing research performs is monitoring the environment for signals indicating a business opportunity. A mere description of a social or economic activity, such as trends in consumer purchasing behavior, may help managers recognize problems and identify opportunities for enriching marketing efforts. In some cases, this research can motivate a firm to take action to address consumer desires in a way that is beneficial to both the customers and to the firm.

At times, evaluating opportunities may involve something as mundane as tracking weather trends. Consumers have a physical need to maintain some degree of physical comfort. Thus, changes in temperature patterns may create business opportunities for utility companies, appliance companies, and even beverage companies as more consumers will select a hot beverage like hot chocolate when the weather is cold and dreary. Companies can also adjust their logistic distribution patterns based on the weather. When Hurricane Katrina hit the Gulf Coast of the United States, several chainsaw companies (such as Poulan) and companies that manufacture generators (such as Honda) began directing inventory toward those areas even before the hurricane actually struck. As a result, many home supply stores like Home Depot and Lowe's were able to maintain inventories of these vital products despite an increase in demand of over 1,000 percent! Thus, the misfortune of a hurricane created a business opportunity that also provided real value to consumers. In this case, the businesses and the consumers all benefited from the fact that firms scan the opportunity for trends.

Malls sometimes have research firms housed within them because the firm can interact with a steady stream of consumers. Some shopping centers in Texas near the United States–Mexican border spotted an opportunity when they realized that a significant number of the shoppers in their mall indicated their residency in Mexico. A survey project was launched to profile these consumers. The results revealed that these consumers were typically from somewhere near Monterey, Mexico, typically households with children and typically relatively high in household income.[13] The results to that study can be used to market to other consumers living near Monterey who match this profile and encourage them to take a day trip across the border to do some shopping.

Market opportunities may be evaluated using many performance criteria. Estimates of market sales potential allow managers to evaluate the profitability of various opportunities. Accurate sales forecasts are among the most useful pieces of planning information a marketing manager can have. Complete accuracy in forecasting the future is not possible because change is one of the few constants in marketing. Nevertheless, objective forecasts of demand or of changes in the environment can provide a strong foundation for a sound marketing strategy.

Fun in the snow depends on weather trends, equipment, and clothing—all subjects for a market researcher.

age fotostock / SuperStock

Analyzing and Selecting Target Markets

The second stage in developing a marketing strategy involves analyzing market segments and selecting target markets. Marketing research is a major source of information for determining which characteristics of market segments distinguish them from the overall market. Such research can help "locate" or describe a market segment in terms of demographic characteristics. Geo-demographics can be important to study and track in this effort. **Geo-demographics** refers to information describing the demographic profile of consumers in a particular geographic region. The company may learn that consumers in a particular postal code within a region tend to be middle-aged, have multiple children over the age of twelve, and have college degrees and white-collar jobs. Once the company knows the geo-demographics of a market segment, the consumers within that segment can be reached by choosing media appealing to that particular profile. For example, *Architectural Digest* is a magazine that is read predominantly by consumers with very high social status in the most exclusive ZIP codes in the United States.

Geo-demographics
Refers to information describing the demographic profile of consumers in a particular geographic region.

Planning and Implementing a Marketing Mix

Using the information obtained in the two previous stages, marketing managers plan and execute a marketing-mix strategy. Marketing research may be needed to support specific decisions about any aspect of the marketing mix. For instance, the research can evaluate an alternative course of action. For example, advertising research might investigate whether an actress like Julia Roberts or a singer like Katy Perry would make a better spokesperson for a specific brand of hair coloring. Research might be conducted involving test ads with each celebrity examining questions such as whether or not attitudes toward the brand are higher for Julia or for Katy. Perhaps not as obviously, research also would address how much credibility is associated with each celebrity based on how much a consumer would believe that the celebrity would actually use that particular product.

An overall research plan involves all marketing strategy elements. Once research identifies a target market and media that can be used in promotion, the benefits required to create value for the customers must be known and communicated, the appropriate price to capture that value must be determined and not overlooked, and the best channel of distribution to reach the targeted consumers must be determined. The integration of all of this research leads to effective brand management.[14] The following examples describe marketing research for each element of the marketing mix.

Product Research

Product research takes many forms and includes studies designed to evaluate and develop new products and to learn how to adapt existing product lines. Concept testing exposes potential customers to a new product idea to judge the acceptance and feasibility of the concept. Product testing reveals a product prototype's strengths and weaknesses or determines whether a finished product performs better than competing brands or according to expectations. Brand-name evaluation studies investigate whether a name is appropriate for a product. Package testing assesses size, color, shape, ease of use, and other attributes of a package. Product research encompasses all applications of marketing research that seek to develop product attributes that will add value for consumers.

Product testing research provides valuable input to companies, customers, and policy makers.

The idea of a smokeless cigarette has been around for decades. Products like Reynolds's Premier, perhaps the most famous (or infamous) smokeless cigarette, typically failed because the experience was too different from traditional smoking. After all, one can hardly smoke if there is no smoke! The latest concept is an E-cigarette. E-cigarettes contain a battery-powered tube that heats liquid containing varying degrees of nicotine. When a user puffs on the device, it produces smoke, or more precisely, a steam-like (but smokeless) water vapor. Research suggested the importance of something that looks like smoke in simulating an authentic smoking experience. Proponents, such as the National Vapers Club, argue that the product is a safer alternative to regular cigarettes. However, further product testing is underway to provide input to policy makers like the U.S. FDA to determine both the actual safety and the perceptions that the various brands of E-cigarettes send to consumers.[15]

Pricing Research

Pricing

Involves finding the amount of monetary sacrifice that best represents the value customers perceive in a product after considering various market constraints.

In many ways, pricing research represents typical marketing research. Many test markets address the question of how consumers will respond to a product offering two different prices. **Pricing** strategy involves finding the amount of monetary sacrifice that best represents the value customers perceive in a product after considering various market constraints. Most organizations conduct pricing research. Starbucks may seem expensive now, but if the price doubled, would Starbucks lose half of its customers? How much extra are Toyota customers willing to pay for each extra mpg? How much is one willing to pay to place a bid in an online auction? Pricing research also investigates the way people respond to pricing tactics. How do consumers respond to price reductions? How much are people willing to pay for some critical product attribute? Do consumers view prices and/or quantity discounts as fair in a given category?[16] Do price gaps among national brands, regional brands, and private labels exist? Most importantly, research also addresses the way consumers determine perceived value.

Pricing research by its nature also involves consumer quality perceptions. Do groceries priced at 99 cents really sell a lot more than groceries priced at $1? A great deal of research explores the effects of "odd-ending" prices. For the most part, overall effects due to odd-ending prices seem subtle and overall to have very little effect. However, when other variables are considered, the results become clearer. Research suggests that for premium brands, odd-ended pricing can lower sales whereas for discount brands, a 99-cent ending price can enhance sales.[17] Like other aspects of research, the story often is not as straightforward as some may think.

Marketing channel

A network of interdependent institutions that performs the logistics necessary for consumption to occur.

Supply chain

Another term for a channel of distribution, meaning the link between suppliers and customers.

Distribution Research

Distribution involves the marketing channels that will physically "distribute" products from a producer to a consumer. A **marketing channel** is a network of interdependent institutions that perform the logistics necessary for consumption to occur. Some channels are very short and involve only a producer and a consumer, and some are very long involving many transportation, wholesale, and retail firms. It may be somewhat obvious why the term **supply chain** is sometimes used to refer to a channel of distribution. Distribution is necessary to remove the separations between buyers and sellers.

● ● ● ● ● ● ●

What types of marketing research would be useful to Redbox?

Distribution research is typified by studies aimed at selecting retail sites or warehouse locations. A survey of retailers or wholesalers may be conducted because the actions of one channel member can greatly affect the performance of other channel members. Distribution research often is needed to gain knowledge about retailers' and wholesalers' operations and to learn their reactions to a manufacturer's marketing policies. It may also be used to examine the effect of just-in-time ordering systems or exclusive distribution on product quality. Research focused on developing and improving the efficiency of marketing channels is extremely important.

Consider today how the distribution channel for the entertainment industry is changing. Just a couple of decades ago, most Americans relied on the big three networks (CBS, NBC, ABC) for entertainment and even news. The customer typically watched programs on one of the networks when the network showed the program. Advertisers paid the networks to host shows. Today, the major three networks are just fractions of what they once were and consumers watch many network programs online from the network websites or from YouTube. Netflix and iTunes give other examples of new channel options for consumers looking for a little electronic entertainment. Although these are high tech options, Redbox created another novel channel option by making movies available in vending machines. So, when consumers visit Walgreens, they can also get a movie. Locations become critically important for Redbox. Location studies are indeed important for retailers and other members of the distribution channel.

Promotion Research

Promotion is the communication function of the firm responsible for informing and persuading buyers. **Promotion research** investigates the effectiveness of advertising, premiums, coupons, sampling, discounts, public relations, and other sales promotions. However, among all of these, firms spend more time, money, and effort on advertising research.

The marketing research findings of Zales, a large jewelry retailer, helped in the creation of advertising with large, one-word headlines that simply asked, "Confused?" "Nervous?" or "Lost?" The advertisements overtly acknowledged the considerable emotional and financial risks that consumers face in jewelry purchases. Research had shown that typical consumers felt unable to determine the relative quality of various jewelry items, believed jewelry purchases were expensive and needed reassurance about their purchases, especially because they often purchased jewelry for someone else. This promotion helped communicate an effective message of empathy with the consumer.

Similarly, a business in transition must effectively communicate its meaning. Take Dunkin' Donuts (DD), for example. The first DD opened in 1950 and although it grew into the largest doughnut store in the world with thousands of units, the brand became stale, pardon the pun. The firm launched an aggressive market research effort aimed at freshening up DD.[18] What did the research reveal? Among other things consumers saw the brand as:

- Strongly associated with donuts
- Unhealthy
- Morning
- Uninviting interiors
- Down to earth

Using this research, the company began to emphasize the aspects that signaled DD products as part of a routine. DD customers are on the go and have things to do and a quick place to get a bite for breakfast and a cup of coffee fits into the routine. The company is spending money livening up its stores and changing the menu offering, taking advantage of new contact points such as Instagram. More than 1 million DD Twitter and Instagram mobile coupons are redeemed via tablets and smartphones each year with many tying into the company's DD Perks loyalty program. The loyalty program helps feed the notion that DD is strongly linked to morning and coffee rituals. Dunkin' Donuts' brand transformation into DD is not happening overnight, but market research is providing the key input needed to freshen up the brand.

The Integrated Marketing Mix

Marketing today focuses increasingly on the fact that different promotional decisions should not be made in isolation. Instead, the concept of **integrated marketing communication** is adopted, meaning that all promotional efforts (advertising, public relations, personal selling, event marketing, social networking, and so forth) should be coordinated to communicate a consistent image. Likewise, more generally, marketing firms realize that the elements of the marketing mix itself must work together. For instance, a change in price can affect the quality of the product, which may also influence decisions about distribution. From a research standpoint, the **integrated marketing mix** means that research studies often investigate effects of various combinations of marketing mix elements on important outcomes like sales and image. Research suggests that consumer-oriented firms are particularly oriented toward integrating all aspects of their marketing into a single message.[19]

Integration means sending a consistent message. Part of DD's transformation from a donut shop into a morning ritual experience involves replacing the visual image of donuts with coffee. Everywhere the consumer encounters the brand they see coffee and coffee beverages featured

Promotion

The communication function of the firm responsible for informing and persuading buyers.

Promotion research

Investigates the effectiveness of advertising, premiums, coupons, sampling, discounts, public relations, and other sales promotions.

Integrated marketing communication

Means that all promotional efforts (advertising, public relations, personal selling, event marketing, and so forth) should be coordinated to communicate a consistent image.

Integrated marketing mix

The effects of various combinations of marketing-mix elements on important outcomes.

David Zanzinger / Alamy

● ● ● ● ● ●

Best Buy has reinvented the traditional Geek image and made it work for them.

Total value management

Trying to manage and monitor the entire process by which consumers receive benefits from a company.

Performance-monitoring research

Refers to research that regularly, sometimes routinely, provides feedback for evaluation and control of marketing activity.

Marketing metrics

Quantitative ways of monitoring and measuring marketing performance.

much more prominently than donuts. Similarly, other brands like Best Buy leverage their Geek Squad (computer nerds who portray the idea of computer services) into a consistent message. Even more identifiable, Aflac's duck gives the brand strong presence (a disability insurance company). In fact, the duck is probably better known than the firm's product!

Analyzing Marketing Performance

After a marketing strategy has been implemented, marketing research may serve to inform managers whether planned activities were properly executed and are accomplishing what they were expected to achieve. In other words, marketing research may be conducted to obtain feedback for evaluation and control of marketing programs. This aspect of marketing research is especially important for successful **total value management**, which attempts to manage the entire process by which a consumer receives benefits from a company.

Performance-monitoring research refers to research that regularly, sometimes routinely, provides feedback for evaluation and control of marketing activity. For example, most firms continuously monitor wholesale and retail activity to ensure early detection of sales declines and other anomalies. In the grocery and drug industries, sales research may use Universal Product Codes (UPCs) on packages read by electronic cash registers and computerized checkout counts to provide valuable market-share information to store and brand managers interested in the retail sales volumes of their products. Market-share analysis and sales analysis are the most common forms of performance-monitoring research. Almost every organization compares its current sales with previous sales and with competitors' sales. However, analyzing marketing performance is not limited to the investigation of sales figures.

Marketing metrics refer to quantitative ways of monitoring and measuring marketing performance. Research derives marketing metrics that allow a firm to know whether the resources invested in marketing activities have met their quantitative business goals. Marketing metrics allow the firm to assess the return on investment (ROI) associated with marketing activities. Recent research suggests that the more firms emphasize value creation in their marketing, the higher are these key performance metrics.[20] Thus, value appears to pay.

When Is Marketing Research Needed?

The need to make intelligent, informed decisions ultimately motivates marketing research. Not every decision requires marketing research. Thus, when confronting a key decision, a marketing manager must initially decide whether to conduct marketing research. The determination of the need for marketing research centers on (1) time constraints, (2) the availability of data, (3) the nature of the decision to be made, and (4) the value of the research information in relation to costs.

Time Constraints

Systematic research takes time. In many instances management believes that a decision must be made immediately, allowing no time for research. Managers often make decisions without adequate information or thorough understanding of market situations. Although making decisions without researching a situation is not ideal, sometimes the urgency of a situation precludes the use of research. The urgency with which managers often want to make decisions often conflicts with the marketing researchers' desire for rigor in following the scientific method.

Availability of Data

Often managers already possess enough information to make sound decisions without additional marketing research. When they lack adequate information, however, research must be considered. This means that data need to be collected from an appropriate source. If a potential source of data exists, managers will want to know how much it will cost to get the data.

If the data cannot be obtained or obtained in a timely fashion, this particular research project should not be conducted. For example, many nations do not have reliable population census data due to underdevelopment, corruption, ongoing conflicts, transient migration, etc. Organizations engaged in international business often find that data about business activity or population characteristics that are readily available in the United States are nonexistent or sparse in developing countries. Imagine the problems facing marketing researchers who wish to investigate market potential in places like Uzbekistan, Yugoslavian Macedonia, and Rwanda.

Nature of the Decision

The value of marketing research depends on the nature of the managerial decision to be made. A routine tactical decision that does not require a substantial investment may not seem to warrant a substantial expenditure for marketing research. For example, a computer company must update its operator's instruction manual when it makes minor product modifications. The research cost of determining the proper wording to use in the updated manual is likely too high for such a minor decision. The nature of the decision is not totally independent of the next issue to be considered: the benefits versus the costs of the research. In general, however, the more strategically or tactically important the decision, the more likely it is that research will be conducted.

Benefits versus Costs

Marketing research can be costly but it can also be of great benefit. Earlier we discussed some of the managerial benefits of marketing research. In any decision-making situation, managers must identify alternative courses of action and then weigh the value of each alternative against its cost. Marketing research can be thought of as an investment alternative. When deciding whether to make a decision without research or to postpone the decision in order to conduct research, managers should ask three questions:

1. Will the payoff be worth the investment?
2. Will the information gained by marketing research improve the quality of the marketing decision enough to warrant the expenditure?
3. Is the proposed research expenditure the best use of the available funds?

Consider a food company considering a change in packaging such as a move from Styrofoam to paper cups for coffee or from plastic to styrene for snacks. Firms often may make such decisions with little or no research input. Management may not appreciate the value of research into this issue because they believe the research costs exceed the potential benefits. Perhaps managers view a change in packaging as so inconsequential that extensive testing is unnecessary to make a quality decision. However, managers often end up regretting the decision not to do research. SunChips changed their packaging material to compostable paper and saw a tremendous drop in sales as customers ridiculed the packages publicly including on YouTube videos. One problem the brand overlooked was how incredibly noisy the new packages would be. In hindsight, perhaps more research was merited although a comparison of the loss in sales revenue with the costs of conducting further market tests would be needed to better address this question. Exhibit 1.5 outlines the criteria for determining when to conduct marketing research.

EXHIBIT **1.5**
Should We Conduct
Marketing Research?

Factor	Conduct Market Research	Do Not Conduct Market Research
Time	Sufficient time is available before decision will be made.	Time pressure requires a decision before adequate research can be completed.
Data Availability	Firm does not have access to data but data can be obtained.	Firm already has relevant data or data cannot be obtained.
Nature of Decision	Decision is of considerable strategic or tactical importance.	Decision is NOT of considerable strategic or tactical importance.
Benefits versus Costs	Potential value of research exceeds costs of conducting research.	Costs of research exceed potential value of project.
	GO!	STOP!

Marketing Research in the Twenty-First Century

Marketing research, like all business activity, continues to change. Changes in communication technologies and the trend toward an ever more global marketplace have played a large role in many of these changes.

Communication Technologies

Virtually everyone is "connected" today. Increasingly, many people are "connected" nearly all the time. The typical college student spends hours a day on YouTube, Facebook or other social networking sites that connect him or her to the Internet. Each move provides access to information but also leaves a record of data that tells a great deal about that particular consumer. Thus, we have more data than ever and we have better ways to store the data. Today, the amount of information formally contained in an entire library can rest easily in a single personal computer. Storage capacity overall is virtually unlimited.

The speed with which people exchange information continues to increase. During the 1970s, exchanging information overnight from anywhere in the continental United States was heralded as a near miracle of modern technology. Today, we can exchange information from nearly anywhere in the world to nearly anywhere else in the world almost instantly. A researcher can get on Skype and interview decision makers anywhere in the world as long as an Internet connection is present. Our mobile phones and handheld data devices enable us to converse, but they also serve as a means of communication that can even involve marketing research data. Marketing researchers arm trained interviewers with iPads and similar devices that can display graphic images to respondents and provide a structured guide to the interview. Thus, the expressions "time is collapsing" and "distance is disappearing" capture the tremendous revolution in the speed and reach of our communication technologies.

As recently as the 1970s, most computer applications required expensive mainframe computers found only in very large corporations, major universities, and large governmental/military institutions. Researchers could expect to wait hours or even longer to get results from a statistical program involving 200 respondents. Today, even the most basic laptop computers can solve complicated statistical problems involving thousands of data points in practically a nanosecond. Soon, small, inexpensive appliances like a smartphone will access software and data existing on the cloud (large servers that supply information and software to large numbers of Internet users), eliminating the need for specialized software and a conventional laptop computer.

Global Marketing Research

Marketing research has become increasingly global as more and more firms take advantage of markets that have few, if any, geographic boundaries. Some companies have extensive international

© Iurii Osadchi/Shutterstock.com

Who's Watching What?
(a shot of winter Olympics??)

For decades, Nielsen's name is synonymous with television ratings. Back in the day of three major U.S. networks when every home had a landline phone and families gathered in front of the television each night, that job was much easier. Today, consumers are viewing programs on demand and live streaming during broadcasts. That means consumers are *watching* their tablets, phones, computers, and even smartwatches, in addition to televisions.

Nielsen is facing competition from a number of firms including ComScore who believe they can better account for nontraditional viewing. This criticism was fueled by NBC after Nielsen reported disappointing ratings numbers for the 2014 Winter Olympics held in Sochi, Russia. Some say the low ratings are indicative of American's actual interest, particularly when the Olympics were absent of U.S. stars such as Lindsay Vonn who was sidelined with an injury that took her out of the Olympics. Nielsen acknowledges the changing trends and is involved in developing better mechanisms to track viewers'

engagement with television shows. Nielsen acquired Arbitron in 2014 in part to secure their "people meter" technology, which is a small device a person keeps on them that detects computer codes signaling viewing and listening behaviors across multiple media devices including computers and smartphones. Networks are beginning to stream their broadcasts live and companies that buy advertising need accurate viewing numbers to know how much an ad on a given show is worth.

Sources: Sharma, A. and C. S. Stewart (2014), "Nielsen Feels Digital Heat from Rivals," *Wall Street Journal*, (2/12), B1-B7. Gregory, S. (2014), "America Is Short on Star Power with Lindsey Vonn Out," *Time*, (1/8), 1.

marketing research operations. Upjohn conducts marketing research in 160 different countries. Nielsen Holdings NV, founded in New York in 1923 and still based in the Big Apple, but now incorporated in the Netherlands, is the world's largest marketing research company. Less than half of its business comes from the United States these days. Nielsen researches all manner of topics internationally. It is probably best known as the television ratings company (see Research Snapshot). However, their consumer watch business is heavily involved in research for clients in consumer goods markets. A recent Nielsen report described research demonstrating consumer receptivity to retail private labels across over a dozen countries.[21] U.S. consumers report a 39 percent willingness to switch from a name brand to a lower priced store private label. That's about in the middle of the pack and similar to consumers in Spain and the Netherlands. Chinese consumers express the lowest willingness to switch to private labels at only about 15 percent willingness to switch, whereas Greek consumers are most favorable toward private labels registering a near 70 percent willingness to switch to the cheaper private labels. A client operating retail stores in all of these countries would find this data extremely helpful in shaping their promotional strategy for each country's stores.

Companies that conduct business globally must understand the nature of those particular markets and judge whether they require customized marketing strategies. For example, although the fifteen nations of the European Union (EU) share a single formal market, marketing research shows that Europeans do not share identical tastes for many consumer products. Marketing researchers have found no such thing as a typical European consumer; language, religion, climate, and centuries of tradition divide the EU nations. Scantel Research, a British firm that advises companies on color preferences, found inexplicable differences in Europeans' preferences in medicines. The French prefer to pop purple pills, but the English and Dutch favor white ones. Consumers in all the three countries dislike bright red capsules, which are big sellers in the United States. This example illustrates that companies that do business in Europe must research throughout Europe to adapt to local customs and buying habits.[22]

Even companies that produce iconic brands in their own country are now doing research internationally. Brown-Forman, the parent company of Jack Daniels (the classic American "Sour Mash" or Bourbon Whiskey), is now interviewing consumers in the far corners of the world. Jack

Culturally cross-validate

To verify that the empirical findings from one culture also exist and behave similarly in another culture.

Daniels is a global brand that one can find practically any where they go. However, consumers in different cultures do not all consume Jack Daniels similarly. The internationalization of research places greater demands on marketing researchers and heightens the need for research tools that allow us to **culturally cross-validate** research results, meaning that the empirical findings from one culture also exist and behave similarly in another culture. The development and application of these international research tools are an important topic in basic marketing research.

TIPS OF THE TRADE

- Throughout this text, a Tips of the Trade section provides helpful hints for using and doing marketing research. The first tip is to pay attention to these sections as helpful references.
- Customers and employees are valuable sources for input that leads to innovation in the marketplace and in the workplace.
- Business problems ultimately boil down to information problems because with the right information, the business can take effective action.
- Research plays a role before, during, and after key marketing decisions.

  - Research helps design marketing strategies and tactics before action is taken.
  - Once a plan is implemented, research monitors performance with key metrics providing valuable feedback.
  - After a plan is implemented, research assesses performance against benchmarks and seeks explanations for the failure or success of the action.

- Research that costs more than the right decision could return should not be conducted.
- Marketing researchers must stay in touch with changes in media technology and the way consumers contact companies with those devices.

∷ SUMMARY

This chapter had six learning outcomes. After reading the chapter, the student should be competent in each area described by a learning outcome.

1. Know what marketing research is and what it does for business. Marketing research is the application of the scientific method in searching for the truth about market and marketing phenomena. Research applications include defining marketing opportunities and problems, generating and evaluating marketing ideas, monitoring performance, and generally understanding the marketing process and the way consumers extract value from consumption. Thus, it is the intelligence-gathering function in business. This intelligence assists in decisions ranging from long-range planning to near-term tactical decisions. Although many business decisions are made "by the seat of the pants" or based on a manager's intuition, this type of decision making carries with it a large amount of risk. By first researching an issue and gathering intelligence on customers, competitors, and the market, a company can make a more informed decision. The result is less risky decision making.

2. Understand the difference between basic and applied marketing research. Applied marketing research seeks to facilitate managerial decision-making. Basic or pure research seeks to increase knowledge of theories and concepts. Both are important. Applied research examples are emphasized in this text although practically all of the tools and techniques that are discussed are appropriate to either type of research. Some use the term *market research* to refer to applied research and *marketing research* to refer to basic research.

3. Understand how the role of marketing research changes with the orientation of the firm. Every company has a particular operating orientation. Production-oriented companies emphasize producing outputs as efficiently as possible. Generally, this leads to an emphasis on low-cost production and low-cost positioning in the marketplace. Product-oriented companies emphasize producing a sophisticated product that is also technologically advanced. Firms that are oriented around the marketing concept become very consumer oriented. Market-oriented firms view all employees as customers who need marketing intelligence to make good decisions. Stakeholder oriented companies try to balance concerns of all internal and external constituencies, including consumers. Marketing-oriented and stakeholder oriented companies tend to do more marketing research and emphasize marketing research more than do other firms.

4. Be able to integrate marketing research results into the strategic planning process. Marketing research is a means of implementing the marketing concept, the most central idea in marketing. The marketing concept says that a firm must be oriented both toward consumer satisfaction and toward long-run profitability (rather than toward short-run sales volume). Marketing research can help implement the marketing concept by identifying consumers' problems and needs, improving efficiency, and evaluating the effectiveness of marketing strategies and tactics. The development and implementation of a marketing strategy consist of four stages: (1) identifying and evaluating opportunities, (2) analyzing market segments and selecting target markets, (3) planning and implementing a marketing mix that will provide value to customers and meet the objectives of the organization, and (4) analyzing firm performance. Marketing research helps in each stage by providing information for strategic decision-making. In particular, marketing research aimed at the marketing mix seeks information useful in making better decisions about product design, promotion, distribution, and pricing.

5. Know when marketing research should and should not be conducted. Marketing managers determine whether marketing research should be conducted based on (1) time constraints, (2) availability of data, (3) the nature of the decision to be made, and (4) the benefit of the research information versus its cost. Research should only be conducted when time is available, relevant data can be found and does not already exist, the decision can be shaped by information, and the benefits outweigh the cost of doing the research.

6. Appreciate the way that technology and internationalization are changing marketing research. Technology has changed almost every aspect of marketing research. Modern computing and media technologies including smart devices (phones, watches, tablets, etc.) and social networking make data collection, study design, data analysis, data reporting, and practically all other aspects of research easier and better in many respects. Researchers do have to be aware of the multiple ways that companies interact with consumers. Furthermore, as more companies do business outside their own borders, companies are doing research in an international marketplace. This places a greater emphasis on research that can assess the degree to which research tools can be applied and interpreted the same way in difference cultures. Thus, research techniques often must culturally cross-validate results.

∴ KEY TERMS AND CONCEPTS

applied marketing research, *7*

basic marketing research, *7*

culturally cross-validate, *22*

customer oriented, *8*

geo-demographics, *15*

pricing, *16*

integrated marketing communication, *17*

integrated marketing mix, *17*

marketing channel, *16*

marketing concept, *8*

marketing metrics, *18*

marketing orientation, *8*

marketing research, *5*

online sentiment analysis, *10*

performance-monitoring research, *18*

product oriented, *8*

production oriented, *8*

promotion, *17*

promotion research, *17*

relationship marketing, *11*

scientific method, *7*

stakeholder orientation, *8*

supply chain, *16*

total value management, *18*

:: QUESTIONS FOR REVIEW AND CRITICAL THINKING

1. What advantages does research offer to the decision maker over seat-of-the-pants decision-making?
2. Define a marketing orientation and a product orientation. Under what strategic orientation(s) is there a greater need for marketing research?
3. What are the four key questions helpful in understanding the value equation for a given firm?
4. Define *marketing research* and describe its task. How is it different from research in the physical sciences?
5. In what stage of the scientific method is creativity and creative thinking most important? Briefly explain.
6. Which of the following organizations are likely to use marketing research? Why? How?
   a. Manufacturer of breakfast cereals
   b. An online auction Internet site like Quibids
   c. Manufacturer of nuts, bolts, and other fasteners
   d. The Federal Trade Commission
   e. A hospital
   f. A company that publishes marketing textbooks
   g. Google
7. An automobile manufacturer is conducting research in an attempt to predict the type of car design consumers will desire in the year 2022. Is this basic or applied research? Explain.
8. Define online sentiment analysis. How can it be helpful in brand management?
9. What is the definition of an *integrated marketing mix*? How might this affect the research a firm conducts?
10. Comment on the following statements:
    a. Marketing managers are paid to take chances with decisions. Marketing researchers are paid to reduce the risk of making those decisions.
    b. A marketing strategy can be no better than the information on which it is formulated.
    c. The purpose of research is to solve marketing problems.
11. List the conditions that help a researcher decide when marketing research should or should not be conducted.
12. How have technology and internationalization affected marketing research?
13. What types of tools does the marketing researcher use more given the ever-increasing internationalization of marketing?
14. Apple, Facebook, Coca-Cola, Microsoft, Walmart, Pfizer, Google. Given the introduction to marketing research presented here, rank the companies based on how important you believe marketing research is to each's success. What do you think is each firm's operating orientation?

:: RESEARCH ACTIVITIES

1. Suppose you owned a jewelry store in Denton, Texas. You are considering opening a second store just like your current store. You are undecided on whether to locate the new store in another location in Denton, Texas, or in Birmingham, Alabama. Why would you decide to have some marketing research done before making the decision? Should the research be conducted? What demographic data about Birmingham or Denton might be useful in making the decision?
2. Find examples of news articles from the most recent week involving the use of marketing research in making decisions about each element of the marketing mix. The *Wall Street Journal* is a good source for such stories.
3. Find a list of the ten most popular smartphone apps at the current time. Is there anything in common among the apps? Do they indicate any trends about consumers in general or a particular segment of consumers? What is that trend? Which companies may benefit from such a trend?

Harnessing Big Data into Better Decisions

LEARNING OUTCOMES

After studying this chapter, you should be able to:

1. Know why concepts like data, big data, information, and intelligence represent value

2. Understand the four characteristics that describe data

3. Know what a decision support system is and the technology tools that help make it work

4. Recognize some of the major databases and how they are accessed

5. Understand the basic concept of marketing analytics and its potential to enhance decision-making

6. Be sensitive to the potential ethical issues of tracking consumers' behavior electronically

Dimitri Otis/Getty Images

Chapter Vignette:

Marketing Research Is Good for You!

Todd lives in Toronto and works a 40-hour week. When not at work, Todd likes being a couch potato. He spends a lot of time watching the Maple Leafs, Blue Jays, and other sports events. He subscribes to a premium television service to make sure he has access to what he wants to see when he wants to see it. He uses apps to order pizza regularly and often swipes his loyalty card at nearby fast-food restaurants. Todd doesn't like to cook! He receives a personalized invitation to participate in a clinical trial of a new obesity drug.

Across town, Jane stops for Asian food in a restaurant and is handed an electronic tablet for a menu. The home page says, "Hungry after your workout?"

Unbeknownst to Todd, all of this behavior is known to Blue-Chip Marketing, a company that combines consumer data with health facts to assist marketing efforts for companies, many in health-related fields. From his Internet behavior, social networking, the fact that his phone is often near the couch, and he subscribes to the premium television service, Todd becomes very interesting to Blue-Chip. A statistical model used by Blue-Chip puts these things together to predict that Todd is obese. With these models, they can more carefully identify candidates for trials without even having to ask any questions.

Also unbeknownst to Jane, the fact that she checked in at her gym 90 minutes before going through the turnstile at the restaurant is already known and the restaurant informed. An electronic turnstile system detects her presence (or at least her phone's presence) and the message is pushed to the restaurant. The hostess can then quickly choose the best opening page for the tablet before giving it to the customer.

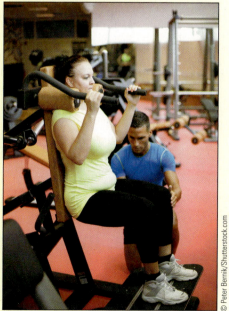

© Peter Bernik/Shutterstock.com

This is marketing today. Decisions that used to require considerable time and judgment can now be nearly or completely automated and they can be applied at the individual customer level. The heart of this process is data, big data we might say. This chapter provides an overview of how marketing research today uses data, including big data, to help feed into decision systems that hopefully improve marketing performance.[1]

Introduction

Data have always been the fuel that marketing research uses to create knowledge. As long as research itself has been conducted, data provide the answer to research questions, allow exploration of ideas, and provide the testing mechanism for hypotheses. In its basic form **data** are recorded facts or measures of certain phenomena. The phenomena could include objects or events. Objects might include the amount of sales attributed to a specific product in a specific country, the color of a package, or the price of a product. Data about events may include survey responses indicating how consumers feel during a service experience, the amount a consumer purchases during a sale, or the amount of time a consumer spends on an online game.

Data

Recorded facts or measures of certain phenomena (things).

Today, a typical notebook computer has a memory capacity of over 100 GB (gigabytes). 1 GB = 1,024 MB (megabytes and 1 MB = about 1 million characters). Marketing research grew rapidly in the 1950s and 1960s. Part of the growth was fueled by the growth in computing power, which made analytical analysis using computationally complex statistics possible. In 1956, the most powerful IBM mainframe computer contained 50 disks (hard drives) that enabled a storage capacity of almost 5 MB. Not until 1980 did a mainframe computer have a 1 MB memory capacity.[2] Even a simple computer today has more than 1,000 times the capacity of the most powerful computer of three decades ago.

The ability to store and record data continues to grow. So today many of our everyday activities leave data traces behind. When we use our smartphone, browse the Web, use Facebook, make a purchase at a retail outlet, or drive a car with our GPS navigation system, we are leaving behind data. Through these simple types of activities, we leave behind 2.5 quintillion bytes of data each day.[3] Thus, everything about data has become bigger except the devices that enable us to record and store that data. The tremendous growth in data has led many to use the term "big data." While there is considerable disagreement about just what comprises **big data**,[4] we can think of it as large quantities of data taken from multiple, varied sources that were not intended to be used together, that are available to be analytically applied to provide input to organizational decision-making.

Big data

Large quantities of data taken from multiple, varied sources that were not intended to be used together, that are available to be analytically applied to provide input to organizational decision-making.

Like the growth of marketing research that occurred in the early days of sophisticated computational devices, the advances in big data technology are leading to another surge in the growth of the marketing research industry. As a result, marketing researchers with strong analytical skills are in high demand. That growth is expected to create nearly 2,000,000 "big data" jobs by 2015.[5] Thus, a career in marketing research is a real possibility for many readers of this book.

This chapter discusses big data, data systems, and the role decision support systems and predictive analytics play in helping firms make informed marketing decisions. The decision support systems can be complicated and extensive, extending beyond the internal organizational walls. Marketing research plays an important role in making sense out of the glut of data now available. Today, data technology allows businesses to more easily integrate research findings into marketing strategy and operations.

Data, Information, and Intelligence Equal Value

In everyday language, terms like *information* and *data* are often used interchangeably. Researchers use these terms in specific ways that emphasize how useful each can be. Marketing managers may not be as intimately involved in finding and analyzing data; however, the decisions that they

Review the questionnaire that you responded to in the last chapter. Later, you'll be asked to analyze data with the hope of predicting and explaining some important outcomes with marketing implications. At this point, think about how any given section of the questionnaire might be used as input to decision making by an educational institution or a communications firm. To start understanding the data better, print the questionnaire and use the downloaded data to write the variable names beside each question. Save the questionnaire for later use in helping identify items on the questionnaire.

Source: www.qualtrics.co

make based on the input received from research will make or break the firm. In this way, data, information, and intelligence all have the potential to create value to the firm through better decision-making.

Data by themselves do not provide valuable input to decision-making. For instance, raw data showing the amount of Wi-Fi usage in Starbucks stores means very little. That data has to be put into a usable form. **Information** is data formatted (structured) to support decision making or define the relationship between two or more data points. **Market intelligence** is the subset of information that actually has some explanatory power enabling effective decisions to be made. So, there is more data than information, and more information than intelligence. Most data are irrelevant to any specific decision-making situation and therefore not always valuable. When data become information, their relevance is examined more closely through some analytical procedure. Conclusions are drawn from the structured data (i.e., information) to actually shape marketing decisions. The result is market intelligence derived from data analysis, and this should enable better decision-making, better value provided to customers in that their desires are more closely met and thereby more value for the firm in the form of improved organizational performance.[6]

Think again about the millions of facts recorded by Amazon each day. Each time a product is sold, facts about that transaction are recorded and become data. The data include the selling price of purchased items, the amount of time a shopper spent on a given Web page, the number of consumers visiting a page without making a purchase, comments left by consumers, and much more. One way that Amazon tries to use big data is in improving customer service.[7] Each time a consumer interacts with Amazon.com, data are recorded. So, Amazon systems know a lot about the consumer, including things like phone numbers, address, credit card or other payment information, purchase history, and data on previous chats, e-mails, or phone calls. When a customer initiates a complaint online, all of this information is available to provide better service. Sometimes in under a minute, the consumer receives a call from an Amazon call center. The representative already knows the person's name and number and has pulled up information on common complaints about the recent purchase. As a result, the consumer's problem can often be addressed in less than 2 minutes.

Information

Data formatted (structured) to support decision making or define the relationship between two or more data points.

Market intelligence

The subset of information that actually has some explanatory power enabling effective decisions to be made.

The Characteristics of Valuable Information

Four important characteristics do much to determine the value of information. Exhibit 2.1 provides an overview of the characteristics discussed on the next page.

EXHIBIT **2.1**
Characteristics of
Valuable Data

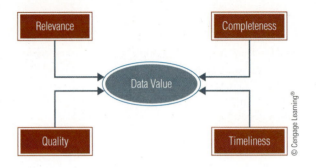

© Cengage Learning®

Relevance

Relevance

The characteristic of data reflecting how pertinent these particular facts are to the situation at hand. When data are relevant, a change in that fact is associated with a change in an important outcome.

Relevance is the characteristic of data reflecting how pertinent these particular facts are to the situation at hand. Put another way, the facts are logically connected to the situation. Unfortunately, irrelevant data and information often creep into decision making. One particularly useful way to distinguish relevance from irrelevance is to think about how things change. Relevant data are facts about things that will materially alter the situation if they change. So, this simple question becomes important:

Will a change in the data coincide with a change in some important outcome?

American consumers' dietary trends are relevant to the restaurant industry. For instance, if Americans become more health-conscious, sales of doughnuts are likely to change. This may lead a restaurant like Dunkin' Donuts to rethink its product offering. However, information on the height of Mount Washington is irrelevant because it isn't going to change any time soon and even if it did, it would not affect U.S. doughnut preferences.

Completeness

Information completeness

Having the right amount of information.

Information completeness refers to having the right amount of information. Marketing managers must have sufficient relevant information to develop explanations and predictions useful in decision-making. For example, managers trying to make a key decision about launching a technological innovation to their current software commission a quick research study in which consumers are asked to rate the perceived usefulness of the technological improvement. Based on the high usefulness scores, the managers launch the innovation only to find decreased sales and increased customer complaints. The complaints send a loud signal that the innovation made the product too complex. In their haste to act, the managers acted without input on this critical variable.

A follow-up study demonstrated that perceived complexity was equally as important in predicting adoption of new technologies and that as consumers see innovations as more complex, they find less value in the product. Theory can play a big role in helping to make information more complete and in this case a theory known as the technology acceptance model describes some key pieces of information in predicting the success of technological innovations.[8]

Quality

Data quality

How accurately the data actually match reality.

Data quality reflects how accurately the gathered data actually match reality. High-quality data are valid and reliable—both concepts we'll turn to in detail later. In this chapter, we emphasize the vast quantity of data now available not in small part due to new technologies.

Not all data are equal in quality. Professional sales managers equip their salespeople with a plethora of technology to record information about sales calls. The data have numerous uses, not the least of which is allowing data systems to compute an expected value of the customer. In this way, the salesperson can know how much effort to put into winning each particular prospect. However, salespeople often are pinched for time and wait until the end of the day or even the end of the week to enter the required information. A pharmaceutical salesperson may wonder, "Did I spend 5 minutes or 12 minutes answering questions?" "Did the doctor make me wait 10 minutes or more?" "Did the doctor ask for samples or did I just leave them?" Each inaccurate answer lowers data quality and means the decision system's statistical models are less reliable. Managers can take advantage of technology by placing a GPS tracking device on the sales manager's smartphone or tablet. The tracking devices record the time spent in each location automatically. However, sales managers might weigh the increased accuracy against the reality of management spying on its salespeople. Researchers offer this advice as a guide to enhanced data quality:[9]

1. Automate data collection and entry when feasible.
2. Inspect the data and cleanse for obvious errors.
3. Be mindful of the costs and benefits of efforts at improving data quality.

Timeliness

Timeliness means the data are not so old that they are irrelevant. Generally, timeliness requires highly current data. Imagine car companies currently trying to predict the types of cars that would interest consumers. Think of all the changes in the operating environment that have taken place since 2008. The economy went from boom to bust and consumer confidence dropped consequently. Fuel prices have fluctuated wildly ranging anywhere from a U.S. average for regular gas of $1.60 per gallon in late 2008 to nearly $4.10 per gallon in July of that same year only to briefly fall to nearly $1.60 by the first of 2009. Car preference will change with these environmental factors, so data collected in one time period may not be entirely accurate. Similarly, imagine how the dramatic pace of technological change in the electronics industry hinders predicting consumer acceptance of mobile phones. The term **market dynamism** represents the rate of change in environmental and competitive factors.[10] Highly dynamic markets mean greater risk in relying on data, particularly on untimely data.

Global Marketplace

By now, marketers around the world realize the potential marketplace is the entire world. A start-up company in Topeka, Kansas, only needs a website and the company's business isn't just in Kansas anymore. Large companies use a plethora of technology ranging from handheld tablets to satellites to gather and exchange data in an effort to keep track of business details globally.

Consider a simple example. At any moment, United Parcel Service (UPS) can track the status of any shipment around the world. UPS drivers use handheld electronic clipboards called delivery information acquisition devices (DIADs) to record appropriate data about each pickup or delivery. The data are then entered into the company's main computer for record-keeping and analysis. A satellite telecommunications system allows UPS to track any shipment for a customer. Consumers also can get near real-time information on the status of a delivery as information from the DIADs is available through www.ups.com.

Decision Support Systems

Marketing research serves four possible business functions. These functions align with purposes of marketing research:

1. Foundational—answers basic questions such as, "What consumers or consumer segments should the company serve and with what types of products?"
2. Testing—addresses things like new product concepts, product innovations, pricing, or promotional ideas. "How effective will they be?"
3. Issues—examine how specific, broad issues impact the firm. "How will a new competitor, a change in organizational structure, or increased investments in advertising influence the company?"
4. Performance—this type of research monitors specific metrics, including financial statistics like profitability and delivery times with questions such as, "How is variation in product lead-time affecting performance metrics?"

Timeliness
Means the data are not so old that they are irrelevant.

Market dynamism
Represents the rate of change in environmental and competitive factors.

To the Point
"*Facts are stubborn things.*"
—RONALD REAGAN

Bringing Home the Bacon!

Marketers employ big data because it helps them bring home the bacon. A McKinsey study found that companies that orient their marketing and sales decision making around results from the analysis of big data see a 15 to 20 percent improvement in return on investment (ROI). That's an attractive marginal return that likely will send more firms looking for marketing researchers who can make sense of big data.

Sometimes, bringing home the bacon becomes quite literal. A research project using data mining approaches analyzed consumer ratings of nearly 1,000,000 new menu items in an effort to reveal what ingredients most make food taste better. The results are clear. Nothing improves the flavor of food items like sandwiches more than bacon. Fast-food restaurants can use this data in their new product designs to help, well, bring home more bacon! Bacon has its limits, though. The project results showed that consumers did not

© Joe Gough/Shutterstock.com

tend to rate dessert items that contained added bacon any better than the same items without the bacon. Is this the power of big data or big bacon?

Sources: McKinsey and Company (2013), "Big Data, Analytics and the Future of Marketing and Sales," *Forbes*, (7/22), http://www.forbes.com/sites/mckinsey/2013/07/22/big-data-analytics-and-the-future-of-marketing-sales/, accessed March 19, 2014. Thusco, A. (2014), "How Big Data Is Revolutionizing the Food Industry," Wired.com, (February), http://www.wired.com/insights/2014/02/big-data-revolutionizing-food-industry/, accessed March 19, 2014.

The performance category is most relevant in decision support systems. Monitored metrics feed into automated decision-making systems and/or trigger reports for specific managers. These form the basis of a decision support system and best typify the way marketing research assists managers with day-to-day operational decisions.

A marketing **decision support system (DSS)** is a system that helps decision-makers confront problems through direct interaction with computerized databases and systems. A DSS stores and transforms data into organized information that is easily accessible to marketing managers and other specific internal customers of information. DSSs save managers countless hours by making decisions in minutes or even seconds that might otherwise take days or weeks.

Modern decision support systems greatly facilitate **customer relationship management (CRM)**. A CRM system is the part of the DSS that characterizes the interactions between firm and customer. It brings together information about customers, including sales data, market trends, marketing promotions, and the way consumers respond to them based on customer preferences. A CRM system describes customer relationships in sufficient detail so that managers, salespeople, customer service representatives, and perhaps the customers themselves can access information directly, match customer needs with satisfying product offerings, remind customers of service requirements, and know what other products a customer has purchased or might be interested in purchasing. CRM systems can compute the overall lifetime value of each customer. This data point often proves a key metric for triggering decisions.

The CRM systems are specifically responsible for promotions customized to individual customers. Casinos use loyalty or "player's" cards that the customer swipes with each activity. All this information gets stored and eventually the casino knows how to manage the customer by directing offers that the customer's previous behavior suggests a liking-for. Auto service centers can use information about a consumer's car to schedule routine maintenance and help diagnose problems before they occur.

Exhibit 2.2 illustrates how data systems work with a decision support system. Raw, unsummarized data are input to the DSS. Data collected in marketing research projects are a major source of this input, but the data may be purchased or collected by accountants, sales managers, production managers, or company employees other than marketing researchers. Effective marketers spend a great deal of time and effort collecting information for input into the decision support system. Useful information is the output of a DSS. A decision support system requires both

Decision support system (DSS)

A computer-based system that helps decision-makers confront problems through direct interaction with databases and systems.

Customer relationship management (CRM)

Part of the DSS that characterizes interactions between firm and customer.

© 2016 Cengage Learning®

EXHIBIT 2.2
Decision Support Systems Create Intelligence

databases and software. For firms operating across national borders, the DSS becomes part of its global information system.

Databases and Data Warehousing

A **database** is a collection of raw data arranged logically and organized in a form that can be stored and processed by a computer. A customer mailing list is one type of database. Population characteristics may be recorded by state, county, and city in another database.

Data warehousing is the process allowing important day-to-day operational data to be stored and organized for simplified access. More specifically, a **data warehouse** is the multitiered computer storehouse of current and historical data. Data warehouse management requires that the detailed data from operational systems be extracted, transformed, placed into logical partitions (for example, daily data, weekly data, etc.), and stored in a consistent and secure manner. Organizations with data warehouses may integrate databases from both inside and outside the company. Data warehousing allows for sophisticated analysis, such as data mining, discussed later in the book.

More and more, data storage exists in **cloud storage**, meaning data are stored on devices that make the files directly available via the Internet. This means that any authorized user from any computer, smartphone, or tablet with Internet accessibility. Salesforce.com is one of the largest providers of CRM systems.[11] They make the data gathered about customers easy to access by subscribers anywhere by utilizing cloud storage.

Input Management

How does data end up in a data warehouse? In other words, how is the input managed? Input includes all the numerical, text, voice, behavioral, and image data that enter the DSS. Systematic accumulation of pertinent, timely, and accurate data is essential to the success of a decision support system.

DSS managers, systems analysts, and programmers are responsible for the decision support system as a whole, but many functions within an organization provide input data. Marketing researchers, accountants, corporate librarians, sales personnel, production managers, and many others within the organization help collect data and provide input for the DSS. Input data can also come from external sources.

Exhibit 2.3 shows six major sources of data input: internal records, proprietary marketing research, salesperson input, behavioral tracking, Web tracking, and outside vendors and external distributors of data. Each source can provide valuable input.

Database

A collection of raw data arranged logically and organized in a form that can be stored and processed by a computer.

Data warehousing

The process allowing important day-to-day operational data to be stored and organized for simplified access.

Data warehouse

The multitiered computer storehouse of current and historical data.

Cloud storage

Data files stored on devices that make them directly accessible via the Internet

EXHIBIT **2.3**
Six Major Sources of
Marketing Input for Decision
Support Systems

Source:

Internal Records	Customer profiles, previous orders, inventory, product sales histories
Proprietary Marketing Research	Survey findings, test market results, new product forecasts
Salesperson Input	Customer complaints and comments, changes in competitors' goods and services
Behavioral Tracking	Scanner data, click-through sequences, Global Positioning Satellite (GPS) System records, automated customer counts
Web Tracking	Social networking sites, Internet blogs, chat
Outside Vendors and External Distributors	Industry sales trends, competitors' market shares, demographics

© 2016 Cengage Learning®

Internal Records

Internal records, such as accounting reports of sales and inventory figures, provide considerable data that may become useful information for marketing managers. An effective data collection system establishes orderly procedures to ensure that data about costs, shipments, inventory, sales, and other aspects of regular operations are routinely collected and entered into the computer.

Proprietary Marketing Research

Proprietary marketing research

The gathering of new data to investigate specific problems.

Research projects conducted to study specific company problems generate data; this is **proprietary marketing research**. Providing managers with nonroutine data that otherwise would not be available is a major function of proprietary marketing research. Earlier, we discussed four categories of research. Proprietary marketing research may involve either or both of the "testing" and "issues" types of research.

Salesperson Input

Salespeople work in firms' external environments, so they commonly provide essential marketing data. Sales representatives' reports frequently alert managers to changes in competitors' prices and new product offerings. Salespeople also hear customer complaints. As complaint trends become evident, this data may become marketing intelligence that leads to a change in service delivery.

Behavioral Tracking

Modern technology provides new ways of tracking human behavior. Global positioning satellite (GPS) systems allow management to track the whereabouts of delivery personnel at all times. This is the same system that provides directions through an automobile's navigation system. For example, if your delivery person takes a quick break for nine holes of golf or decides to stop at Neil's Bar for a couple of beers mid-afternoon, management can spot these as deviations from the appropriate delivery route. Smartphones generally have GPS capabilities that potentially allow systems to track customer whereabouts and maybe even driving patterns.

Retailers also track purchase behavior at the point of sale. **Scanner data** refers to the accumulated records resulting from in-store point-of-sale data recordings. The **Universal product code**, or UPC, is the bar code on a product containing information on the category of goods, the manufacturer, and product identification based on size, flavor, color, and so on. This is what the optical scanner actually reads. Each time a reader scans a bar code, the information can be stored. Bar code readers are used in many places where data needs to be recorded and used, including in package delivery and on the bag check tickets at the airport.

Scanner data
The accumulated records resulting from in-store point-of-sale data recordings.

Universal product code
UPC is the bar-coded information that contains product information that can be read by optical scanners.

● ● ● ● ● ● ●

GPS devices, like those used in automobile navigation systems, allow management to track delivery personnel or even actual customer behavior.

Web Tracking

The Internet greatly facilitates customer behavior tracking. For instance, Google tracks the "click-through" sequence of customers. Therefore, if a customer is searching for information on refrigerators and then goes to BestBuy.com, Google tracks this behavior and uses the information to calculate the value that a click-through provides as an advertising offer to Best Buy. For instance, if one out of every 500 users that go from a Google search buys a refrigerator at Best Buy, Google can tell them what the referral is worth. The tracking data also allows Google and other search engines to know how much to charge advertisers for premium listings in search results. Search for "used cars" and the results indicated by background shading (usually) are listings that Google sells as advertising. Companies listed on top a list of search results pay more than do companies listed near the bottom of the list.

ACnonoc / Alamy

Search-engine optimizer

Mines Internet data to provide consulting to firms who wish to move up the listing of hits for terms related to their product category.

Some marketing companies serve as search-engine optimizers. A **search-engine optimizer** mines Internet data to provide consulting to firms who wish to move up the listing of hits for terms related to their product category. Given that so many purchases involve an Internet search early in the process, firms see it as critical that they appear somewhere near the top of the search results, and they are willing to pay to get to the top, one way or another.

Marketing researchers also monitor postings and create vehicles such as contests that invite consumers to leave ideas and feedback about the brand. Other sources for information include Internet blogs and chat rooms, where consumers share information about their own experiences, including complaints that serve as a type of warning to other consumers. BlueKai, part of Oracle, and eXelate are companies that specialize in Web tracking.[12] BlueKai trades data on over 200 million U.S. consumers.

Some companies also supply real-time data on Web traffic. Do more consumers visit Amazon.com or Ebay.com? Alexa (alexa.com) provides access to this data. A visit to this website reveals the answer to that question and also provides a demographic breakdown of the visitors to each website. Are women more frequent visitors to Amazon relative to men? This information may be useful when choosing a possible Internet retail channel for goods.

Networks and Electronic Data Interchange

Electronic data interchange (EDI)

Type of exchange that occurs when one company's computer system is integrated with another company's system.

Electronic data interchange (EDI) systems integrate one company's computer system directly with another company's system. Much of the input to a company's decision support system may come through networks from other companies' computers. Companies such as Computer Technology Corporation and Microelectronics market data services allow corporations to exchange business information with suppliers or customers. For example, every evening Walmart transmits millions of characters of data about the day's sales to its apparel suppliers. Wrangler, a supplier of blue jeans, receives the data and applies a model that sends orders to replenish Walmart stock. This DSS lets Wrangler's managers know when to send specific quantities of specific sizes and colors of jeans to specific stores from specific warehouses.

Open source information

Structured data openly shared between companies.

Many firms share information in an effort to encourage more innovation. **Open source information** is a term that captures structured data openly shared between companies. Boeing builds innovative aircraft including the Dreamliner 787 passenger jet and the Phantom Ray unmanned airborne system with sophisticated stealth technology designed for military applications. Hundreds of suppliers manufacture components for these aircraft. Boeing came to a realization around the turn of the century that their core competency is more in systems integration than in manufacturing.[13] As a result, Boeing designs the electronic systems for nearly all of these components but to do so, the suppliers need open access to Boeing data. Without this access, Boeing's pace of innovation would be slower.

Database Sources and Vendors

Some organizations specialize in recording certain marketing and consumer information. In some cases, these companies make that data available either for free or for a fee. Computer technology has changed the way many of these organizations supply data, favoring the development of computerized databases. Many organizations specialize in the collection and publication of high-quality information. One outside vendor for data is Nielsen. As mentioned earlier, Nielsen provides television program ratings, audience counts, and information about the demographic composition of television viewer groups.

Media sources like *Advertising Age*, the *Wall Street Journal*, *Sales and Marketing Management*, and other trade- and business-oriented publications are important sources of information. These publications keep managers up-to-date about the economy, competitors' activities, and other aspects of the marketing environment. In addition, they provide demographic and lifestyle statistics about their particular readers that can be very useful in advertisers' media planning.

Data Archives

Many government agencies around the world are important sources of data. The *Statistical Abstract of the United States* is a typical example of a data archive. The *Abstract* provides a comprehensive statistical summary of U.S. social, political, and economic organization. Users can access the *Abstract* as well as detailed data from the U.S. Census with projections through the current year via the Internet at http://www.census.gov.

Numerous computerized search and retrieval systems and electronic databases are available as subscription services or in libraries. Today, businesspeople access online information search and retrieval services, such as Dow Jones News Retrieval and Bloomberg Financial Markets, without leaving their offices. In fact, some information services can be accessed from remote locations via digital wireless devices.

Data wholesalers put together consortia of data sources into packages offered to municipal, corporate, and university libraries for a fee. Information consumers then access the data through these libraries. Some of the better-known *databases* include Wilson Business Center, Hoovers, ProQuest, INFOTRAC, LexisNexis, and Dow Jones News Retrieval Services. These databases provide all types of information, including recent news stories and data tables charting statistical trends. These companies sometimes become **data retailers** by selling data access directly to the end consumer. For instance, Hoovers data can either be purchased in a single transaction, through a

Data wholesalers
Companies that put together consortia of data sources into packages that are offered to municipal, corporate, and university libraries for a fee.

Data retailers
Companies that provide access to data directly to the end consumer for a fee.

● ● ● ● ● ●

Example data available at alexa.com. This data compares Facebook, Twitter, YouTube, and Pinterest Internet Traffic Rankings.

Historical Traffic Trends ⓘ

Global Rank History   Pro Metrics

twitter.com   facebook.com   youtube.com   pinterest.com

Traffic Metrics ⓘ

Site ⇕	Global Rank ⇕
twitter.com	10 ▲ -1
facebook.com	2
youtube.com	3
pinterest.com	29 ▼ +2

Source: www.alexa.com

● ● ● ● ● ●

Hoovers offers retail access to data in three ways.

Access Hoover's Full Business Database in 3 Ways
Get started – select the tasks below that best describe your need:

Targeted Lead Lists
- Build a custom list of prospects today
- Target your best prospects with 50 search filters
- Phone, email & addresses available

Subscription Access
- On Demand reports and List Building anytime
- Research competitors, financials, history etc.
- Leverage exclusive Customer Analytics and List Cleaning Tools

Integrate Data Quality
- Cloud and API solutions integrate Hoover's data with your Sales applications or CRM
- Leverage over 100 proprietary data elements

Source: www.alexa.com

Big Data Gives and Takes Away

The plethora of data means that managers potentially have more and more intelligence available to make decisions. While sifting through the data is like searching for a needle in a haystack, the likelihood of finding some buried treasure keeps managers motivated to use big data and apply more and more marketing analytics. Another idea of how this might work is with systems that can use sales data tied with GPS tracking to push promotional offers for coffee shops to specific consumers nearby that the data analytics suggest are in the mood for coffee. In these ways, big data brings customers. Big data is also being used in ways not so closely tied to sales. Researchers say that the data that casinos gather can be put together with other information on those same consumers to predict which are most likely to become compulsive gamblers. Although one might first think casinos would like to have gambling addicts as customers given the revenue they could generate, even aside from any moral concerns, the negative publicity that casinos face due to problems with gambling

© Marie C Fields/Shutterstock.com

would make them shy away from using this as a sales tool. Instead, the information may potentially be useful in getting help for casino customers before their gambling problems become severe.

Sources: Berzon, A. and M. Maremont (2013), "Researchers Bet Casino Data Can Identify Gambling Addicts," *Wall Street Journal*, (August 3–4), A1-A10. *Entrepreneur* (2013), "Discovering Buried Treasure," (May), 40.

subscription service, or by integrating the data access through cloud storage. A company may want to research the market potential for a new location in a certain area. For instance, a company that produces and sells devices for dental braces may wish to generate a database concerning all the orthodontists in a given metropolitan area. Data retailers can help with these kinds of data needs.

The DIALOG catalog is a useful source for finding databases. The DIALOG catalog can be searched through ProQuest, which is available through many university libraries. It identifies hundreds of databases in areas including business, science, the law, and humanities. A typical database may have a million or more records, each consisting of a one- or two-paragraph abstract summarizing the major points available in a given source.

Several types of databases from outside vendors and external distributors are so fundamental to decision support systems that they deserve further explanation. The following sections discuss statistical databases, financial databases, and video databases in slightly more detail.

Statistical Databases

Statistical databases contain numerical data for market analysis and forecasting. Often, demographic, sales, and other relevant marketing variables are recorded by geographical area. Geographic information systems use these *geographical databases* and powerful software to prepare computer maps of relevant variables. Nielsen acquired a market segmentation system known as PRIZM and makes a host of statistical data, including segment profiles, available for free online. If a company needs more specific information on a segment, it can engage Nielsen for a fee. A host of other statistical sources are available, including government sources such as the U.S. Census, the FCC, and even the CIA, which maintains a database of country profiles known as the *CIA Factbook*. Other statistical databases include Datastream, part of Thomason-Reuters, and Wharton Research Data Services (WRDS).

Financial Databases

Some statistical databases specialize in financial data. CompuStat publishes an extensive financial database on thousands of companies, broken down by industry and other criteria. To illustrate the depth of this pool of information, CompuStat's Global Advantage offers extensive data on about 100,000 securities in dozens of countries in Europe, the Pacific Rim, and North America. The database also contains statistics on hundreds of banking institutions in the United States.

Video Databases

Video databases and streaming media are having a major impact on the marketing of many goods and services. For example, movie studios provide clips of upcoming films, and advertising

● ● ● ● ● ● ●

Example of statistical data available from Nielsen's PRIZM data.

(Source: http://www.claritas.com/MyBestSegments/Default.jsp?ID=20&pageName=ZIP%2BCode%2BLookup& menuOption=ziplookup#)

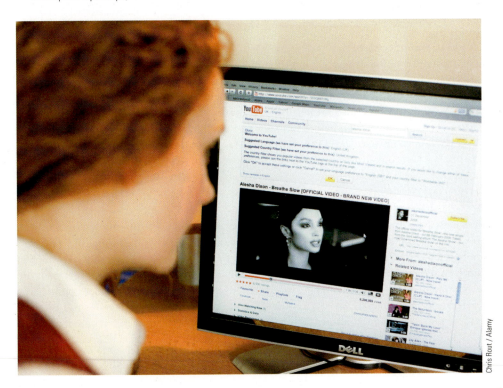

● ● ● ● ● ● ●

YouTube provides a digital archive that can be mined for data or used as a vehicle to test ideas and concepts.

EXHIBIT **2.4** Some Database Sources That Are Widely Available

Database	Description	Availability
Proquest	A collection of databases that include published works such as academic articles, trade periodicals, newspapers, and some statistical databases.	Widely available through university libraries. The libraries pay for the services and grant access to patrons.
LexisNexis	A wide degree of business and media-related content, including business publications, newspapers, and other media sources from 1970. Also maintain a large consumer database (half a billion consumers) including business contacts.	Publication data often available through libraries via library subscription. Consumer data and big data services available for a fee.
U.S. Census	Tremendous amounts of historic and current data about the U.S. population and trends but also a lot of information about various U.S. industries and trends.	Access at www.census.gov. Access to data tables and site is free.
CIA Factbook	Contains statistical data on the countries of the world including demographic data, lifestyle data including religious affiliations, and basic data on commerce and the economy in the country.	Access at: https://www.cia.gov/library/publications/the-world-factbook/. Access is free.
Market Share Reporter	The most comprehensive source for data on the relative market share for publicly traded companies across many industries.	Published by Gale and available on a subscription fee basis. Available at some libraries.
Nielsen	Provides data on consumer media usage, including ratings for television programming and networks. Data from PRIZM segmentation also available among others.	Media data available on a fee for service or subscription basis. Basic PRIZM data on U.S. communities provided free with more detailed data available for a fee.
YouTube	Largest collection of videos in the world. The collection includes advertising, some of which is produced exclusively for YouTube.	YouTube.com (I think you know it). Free.
Alexa	Provides Web usage statistics for public websites. The data include visit information, United States and global rank, demographics of visitors, and more.	Alexa.com. Basic data available for free. More elaborate data and services available for a fee.

agencies put television commercials on the Internet (see http://ispot.tv or *Ad Age*'s http://www.creativity-online.com, for example). YouTube.com is the world's largest video database, and companies routinely produce video commercials for release on YouTube. Each advertisement on YouTube will display how many times the ad has been "viewed" through that particular link. Such data serve as an indicator of the ad's reach and effectiveness. These days, most Super Bowl advertisements can be seen online even before the big game airs. Superbowl-commericals.org operates a site dedicated just to making Super Bowl ads and news about them available online.

The Internet and Research

The Internet in general provides tremendous access to data and information sources. About 2,500,000,000 (2.5 billion) people use the Internet and about 45 percent of those live in Asia.[14] Even though fewer than half of all Asians have access to the Internet, as opposed to nearly three of four North Americans, the sheer size of the population means that most of the Internet users are in Asia. In contrast to the past, a computer is not required as increasingly consumers, particularly in lesser developed parts of the world, access the Internet through a smartphone or similar device. In fact, more people have smartphones than have access to a flush toilet! Web tracking means that there are billions, if not trillions, of traces of data left behind. These means that consumers are doing lots of surfing and leaving behind data with every site they visit.

Can They Read My Mind?

How powerful are today's data tools? Some may say they are too powerful! What if a firm could accurately predict what you were going to buy before you actually placed an order? Would that be a good thing? To get an idea of how that might work, consider how often a consumer receives suggestions from a Web retail site shows what other customers "like you" purchased when they purchased the item being viewed. Data systems like these use previous consumer data to suggest what gets purchased together. Amazon combines data like this with personal information entered into their system, such as from an Amazon Prime account, as well as one's browsing history to build models of what a particular consumer is going to buy. Amazon believes they are so accurate with these predictions that they would like to ship things

to consumers before they even buy them. Currently, the idea is to ship something to a distribution center near a consumer's home to reduce the delivery time once an order is actually placed. However, the technology exists to actually have Amazon make the "purchase" without the consumer even making a selection. Technology like this, although convenient, is controversial. Amazon also has the capability of delivering those products with a fleet of GPS-directed drones that could take the item that was not purchased and drop it off right to your front lawn. What do you think about that?

Sources: Bensinger, G. (2014), "Amazon Wants to Ship Your Package before You Buy It," *Wall Street Journal*, (1/21), B1. CBS News (2014), "Amazon Files Patent for "Anticipatory" Shipping," cbsnews.com/news/amazon-files-patent-for-anticipatory-shipping/, accessed 1/21/14. Manjoo, F. (2013), "Why Bezos's Drone Is More than a Joke," *Wall Street Journal*, (12/5), B1–B7.

Source: www.amazon.com

Navigating the Internet

Parties that furnish information on the World Wide Web are called **content providers**. Content providers maintain websites that contain information about the entity as well as links to other sites. Increasingly, users are able to add content to websites as well. In these cases, such as Wikipedia, the users manage the content. Most Web browsers also allow the user to enter a **Uniform Resource Locator (URL)** into the program. The URL is really just a website address that Web browsers recognize. Twenty years ago, a consumer often needed to know the URL of a site to find it on the Net. Today, modern search engines work so well that one or two key words will generally pull up the intended site or, if not the intended site, one very similar to it!

Most **keyword search** are formed by simply entering a name or phrase. A student doing a term paper on Winston Churchill might simply put "Churchill" in the search window. A Boolean search is a search that combines relevant key words in very specific ways. The operators include words like *and*, *or*, and *not*. So, a search of Churchill will bring up thousands of hits, including Churchill Downs, the home of the Kentucky Derby, as well as a cigar store or two. However, enter "war" and "Churchill" and the search becomes quickly limited to sites that contain both words; enter "war and Churchill" and the search looks for content with that exact expression.

Modern data mining approaches can actually automate Web searches using Boolean operators. Researchers often are charged with monitoring negative information about a brand.[15] When researchers either manually or through an automated system detect negative information near the top of search results for a brand, the firm can take actions to counter the negative information by placing other content online that results in the negative information not appearing so close to

To the Point

"The Net is 10.5 on the Richter scale of economic change."

—NICHOLAS NEGROPONTE

Content providers
Parties that furnish information on the World Wide Web.

Uniform Resource Locator (URL)
A website address that Web browsers recognize.

Keyword search
Takes place as the search engine searches through millions of Web pages for documents containing the keywords.

the top of the results. In fact, the suppression of negative online associations, which many times includes false information about individuals or brands, has spawned an industry of its own as companies specialize in taking such counter measures.

Environmental Scanning

Environmental scanning

Entails all information gathering designed to detect changes in the external operating environment of the firm.

The Internet is an especially useful source for scanning many types of environmental changes. **Environmental scanning** entails all information gathering designed to detect changes in the external operating environment of the firm. Even things beyond the control of the firm can have a significant impact on firm performance.

Information Technology

Smart agent software

Software capable of learning an Internet user's preferences and automatically searching out information in selected websites and then distributing it.

The ability to use behavioral data that consumers generate when interacting with the Internet through any type of device has revolutionized the way some marketing functions are implemented. Today's information technology uses "smart agents" or "intelligent agents" to deliver customized content to a viewer's desktop. **Smart agent software** is capable of learning an Internet user's preferences and automatically searching out information and distributing the information to a user's computer. Numerous vendors offer smart agent software for sale or lease. Companies that purchase software hope to leverage the information consumers leave behind into more customized and therefore more effective sales appeals.

Pull technology

Consumers request information from a Web page and the browser then determines a response; the consumer is essentially asking for the data.

Push or Pull?

Push technology

Sends data to a user's computer without a request being made; software is used to guess what information might be interesting to consumers based on the pattern of previous responses.

Data and information are delivered to consumers or other end users via either **pull technology** or **push technology**. Conventionally, consumers request information from a Web page and the browser then determines a response. Thus, the consumer is essentially asking for information through an e-mail, interactive chat, or automated response. In this case, it is said to be pulled through the channel. The opposite of pull is push. Push technology sends data to a user's device without a request being made. In other words, data analytics and systems that identify the consumer are used to guess what information might entice a consumer into engaging with the company. The goal is to turn a consumer into a customer!

Retailers like Michael Kors make good advantage of push technology.

Source: www.michaelkors.com

Considering that there are more "smart" devices today than there are humans on Earth, the number of opportunities to push content to consumers is almost unlimited. Push technology delivers personalized information to consumers without any intentional effort on the consumers' part. Even if by happenstance you browse at a retail site like Michael Kors, for the next few days you may see banner ads for an item that was on a page you browsed previously. That is an example of push technology. However, that's the tip of the iceberg. One doesn't have to be browsing to receive push messages. Apple's iBeacon system allows an iPhone's location to be detected to a matter of inches. Retailers can place iBeacons in their store to detect other iPhones or other systems running Apple software.[16] If something in your browsing history indicates an interest in a product in the store, a text message or e-mail can be pushed to the phone once a consumer gets within its proximity. In essence, the iBeacon or similar technologies for other brands of smart agents function as a Near Field Communication Device.

Near Field Communication (NFC) Devices

RFID stands for radio frequency identification. A tiny chip, which can be woven onto a fabric, placed in packaging, attached to a card, including credit cards, or otherwise affixed to virtually any product, sends a radio signal that identifies that particular entity uniquely. When the tag comes into proximity of a reader, the reader records the programmed information allowing products and/or consumers to be tracked virtually anywhere. The U.S. military pioneered RFID technology as a logistical tool and Walmart was a leading proponent of the technology based on the improved ability to track goods and feed information into its global information system.[17] Wholesalers take advantage of data created through an RFID system that helps them rotate stock to make sure that the oldest stock goes out first.[18] Pharmaceutical companies also use RFID tags to track the whereabouts of medicines. RFID provides a major source of big data input.[19]

Retailers use RFID technology both to offer customers uniquely tailored promotions and to keep track of customers' shopping behavior. La Croissanterie, a fresh but fast-food chain based in Paris, replaced its traditional cardboard loyalty card with a plastic wallet-sized card that includes an RFID chip.[20] Once a customer enters the store, he or she can tap a smart poster that contains

RFID
Abbreviation for radio-frequency-identification tags that use a small microchip to communicate with data systems.

Loyalty cards like this one from France-based La Croissanterie contain RFID chips enabling the recording of data about individual customers. (From lacroissanterie.fr)

Source: www.lacroissanterie.fr

NFC

Abbreviation for near-field-communication or Wi-Fi-like systems communicating with specific devices within a defined space like inside of a retail unit or near a poster billboard.

NFC (near field communication) technology. **NFC** works like a Wi-Fi system communicating with specific devices within a defined space like inside of a retail unit. The NFC essentially talks to the RFID chip. The smart poster identifies the customer's loyalty status, offers them a promotion based on this status, records all purchases, and updates the customer's status automatically (no hole punchers or stamps used here) but, most importantly from a research standpoint, records all the customer data no matter which of about 200 La Croissanterie units the customer visits. Some market researchers believe that soon, information from RFID chips will be integrated so that when a consumer enters a shopping list into a smartphone, lights may be able to direct the in-store consumer to product options based on what is entered onto the list.[21]

As with the previous example, NFC push marketing no longer requires an RFID device as smartphones can function in much the same way. Smartphone technologies also allow consumers to download applications that allow their phones to be their loyalty card. Market researchers can use NFC data to track shoppers' movement through a store as well. By doing so, they can reveal how products can be placed in stores to increase the length of the path that a consumer takes through the store and, as a result, increase unplanned sales from that customer.[22] Once the consumer accepts such an app, data systems go to work recording information aimed at finding out just what makes customers like him/her receptive to offers.

Increasingly, marketing efforts involve combinations of push and pull efforts. A pop-up generated by a smart agent may entice a consumer to click-through or begin a chat seeking further information. In addition, the more consumers come to accept mobile marketing efforts, the more marketers are likely to even further increase their efforts at employing information technology to enhance value.[23] Currently, in the United States, marketing efforts that actually function through the telephone such as calls or SMS require that consumers opt-in. This is not the case throughout the world, and thus the tools for marketing with push technology vary from place to place. In the end though, all of these tools leave data behind and that data feeds into research.

Cookies

Cookies

Small data files that a content provider can save onto the computer of someone who visits its website.

Cookies, in computer terminology, are small data files that record a user's Web usage history. If a person looks up a weather report by keying in a zip code into a personalized Web page, the fact that the user visited the website and his/her zip code are recorded in the cookie. This is a clue that tells where the person lives (or maybe where he or she may be planning to visit). Websites can then direct information to that consumer based on information in the cookie. So, someone in College Station, Texas, may receive pop-up ads for restaurants in College Station. If that person visits graduate program sites, he or she may receive an advertisement from University of Phoenix or one of its competitors.

Intranets

Intranet

A company's private data network that uses Internet standards and technology.

An **Intranet** is a company's private data network that uses Internet standards and technology. The information on an Intranet—data, graphics, video, and voice—is available only inside the organization or to those individuals whom the organization deems as appropriate participants. Thus, a key difference between the Internet and an Intranet is that security software programs, or "firewalls," are installed to limit access to only those employees authorized to enter the system. Intranets then serve as secure knowledge portals that contain substantial amounts of organizational memory and can integrate it with information from outside sources. The challenge in designing an Intranet is making sure that it is capable of delivering relevant data to decision-makers while still maintaining security.

The Intranet can be extended to include key customers or suppliers as sources of valuable research. Their participation in the Intranet can lead to better new product development efforts. An Intranet lets authorized users, possibly including key customers, look at product drawings, employee newsletters, sales figures, and other kinds of company information. The Mayo Clinic is widely recognized as having an effective Intranet.[24] A big part of the success is deciding how to draw the boundaries that define who can access what. For a medical organization, that can be particularly complicated as the clinic itself interacts with physicians, insurers, pharmaceutical developers, and so forth. On top of this, the Mayo Clinic has to make sure the system complies with the Health Insurance Portability and Accountability Act (HIPAA). **HIPAA** is the U.S. government's

HIPAA

Health Insurance Portability and Accountability Act.

effort to nationalize the privacy of health-related information while trying to still allow the transfer of information as it might better promote improved health.

Marketing Analytics

The terms *marketing analytics* and *predictive analytics* did not exist prior to the birth of the big data era. Both are extensions of traditional data analysis and we return to this in more detail later in the book. For now though, it's important to understand that marketing analytics is a part of marketing research that aids business decision-making. **Marketing analytics** is a general term that refers to efforts to measure relevant data and apply analytical tools in an effort to better understand how a firm can enhance marketing performance. Delta Airlines applies data from ticket sales and follow-up surveys to understand how sensitive its customers are to timing and service issues. Are customers willing to pay more for an 11 a.m. flight than a 5 a.m. flight and are they more satisfied if the flight includes breakfast? Statistical tools are heavily involved in marketing analytics and they can help explain the way the company should respond to consumer information.

Predictive analytics shares much in common with marketing analytics. Broadly speaking, **predictive analytics** refers to linking computerized data mined from multiple sources to statistical tools that can search for predictive relationships and trends. Here, the emphasis is very much on being able to create a pathway to a sale or improved profitability by guessing (with some success) what a consumer is going to do. As the term implies, predictive analytics is more about prediction than about explanation. Software companies like SPSS and SAS offer products that both look for data and then use statistical tools to reveal key predictive relationships. We'll learn more about SPSS and specific statistical tools later in the book.

Information taken from consumers' actual archived behavior along with preference data provided by direct input from the consumer is used to model sales levels that can be achieved with various amounts of discounts. Financial companies like Merrill Lynch use predictive analytics to find service innovations needed to enhance specific customers' satisfaction. In addition, financial firms also apply predictive analytics in fraud detection.[25] Previously, fraud detection was like finding a needle in a haystack. In the big picture, predictive analytics allows companies to better allocate resources (see the Research Snapshot on page 39 for an illustration). Beats finding a needle in a haystack!

Traditional marketing analytics was never meant to handle the enormous amount of data available in today's big data world.[26] Thus, researchers are working on ways to automate analytics as a way of making them more useful. By providing a ready way of converting data into intelligence, almost instantaneously, marketing analytics holds obvious potential to change, and hopefully enhance, the way many marketing decisions are made.

Marketing analytics

A general term that refers to efforts to measure relevant data and apply analytical tools in an effort to better understand how a firm can enhance marketing performance.

Predictive analytics

A system linking computerized data mined from multiple sources to statistical tools that can search for predictive relationships and trends.

Data Technology and Ethics

By this point in the chapter, one may feel a little like *big brother* could be watching. The news today is filled with stories about concerns for data privacy at the individual, national, and international levels. Advances in data technology have in a way made privacy seem like a thing of the past. The rapid advancement has outpaced society's ability to understand the ethical and moral implications of the high volumes of electronic communication, so much of which leaves an enduring and at least semipublic record. After all, text messages, device cameras, Web browsing, social media posts, not to mention e-mail, GPS systems, and mobile phone calls, all leave behind some type of record. Background checks now routinely involve mining records from social media sites. Some of these records can be used in market research and consumers experience some benefits from the intelligence produced.

Several companies today specialize in providing data through knowledge of consumers' whereabouts. **Geolocation technologies** allow your whereabouts and/or movement to be known through digital identification of some type, some of which we mentioned earlier when discussing near field communication. Location information is connected with other information on

Geolocation technologies

Allow whereabouts and/or movement of a consumer or object to be known through digital identification of some kind.

the individual to let users know potentially valuable information about the consumer. Several companies like Turnstyle Analytics and Viasense specialize in constructing a dossier on individual consumers based on where they go and spend time and putting this together with other information, including information from Facebook.[27] Now, without asking a consumer if they are a golfer, the system knows the answer based on how often a person visits a golf course. With that knowledge, when the consumer enters a shopping center parking lot, they may receive an offer from the center's golf store. In some cases, a subscribing retailer may even be alerted that a good customer is in the area.

When consumers use Foursquare (www.foursquare.com) or some other apps to check into bars, restaurants, stores, or theaters, it may be more than their friends who know his/her whereabouts. The behavioral tracking possible with this technology could be used by marketing research firms to feed data systems to push promotional offers to "friends," but the data could be used more strategically to understand the paths consumers take when they are out and about.

The marketing research industry and government agencies are interested in better understanding the ethical implications that come with improved technologies for "snooping." The convenience that a consumer gets from the technologies needs to be weighed against concerns for privacy. True anonymity becomes nearly impossible when data are extracted digitally. Data from social networks identify the user by name. Even if a device does not identify a consumer by name, the IP address of the devices being used allows an identifiable record. Thus, the wide availability of data put together with predictive analytics means that companies and agencies really have the capability to know us quite intimately. At this point, congressional hearings have produced little in the way of legislation on the matter. Many industry leaders believe that self-regulation is called for as an alternative to strict government intervention.[28]

Here are four factors relevant for considering the ethics of data gathered through digital means.

1. Has the consumer implicitly or explicitly consented to being traced? When a consumer places information on Facebook, for instance, that consumer is making the information publicly available and therefore consenting to others seeing and using the information. However, phone conversations are generally considered to be private communications between two individuals. Thus, researchers tracking Facebook or Foursquare information are acting fairly by essentially only joining in on information users have agreed to make public to some extent. Conversely, researchers who might think about eavesdropping on conversations between two individuals are violating their privacy and acting in an unjust manner.

2. Does the tracking behavior violate any explicit or implicit contracts or agreements? As the legal issues involving electronic privacy develop, agreements for use of various technologies will increasingly include statements regarding the limits to which behavior can be traced. Researchers should be mindful of staying within these limits. For instance, if analytical devices predict one's medical condition, conveying that information could violate acts like HIPAA.

3. Can researchers enable users to know what information is available to data miners? Some companies, including a marketing data provider known as Turn, participate in an **open data partnership**. This partnership seeks to allow consumers access to the information collected from their digital interactions and even provides consumers an opportunity to edit the information.[29] The open data partnership potentially represents a fair way of handling data mining activities as at least consumers come to know what information researchers gather and can act to be more secretive if some of that information represents things they would rather keep private.

4. Do the benefits to consumers from tracking their behavior balance out any potential invasion of their privacy? Ethically, any imposition of consumers should be smaller than the benefit consumers obtain from the research activity. Greater convenience for consumers and being able to better communicate to them about desirable products are benefits enhanced from electronic data mining activities. If a company can predict what you would buy before you do, should it be able to complete the transaction without an actual transaction taking place?

Concerned consumers can enhance security when using the Internet by using security settings that place limits on access to sites that collect data or prohibit the storage of cookies once the browser is closed. These settings can also delete one's browsing history at the same time. The consumer pays a price in convenience as the browser will no longer be able to fill in

Open data partnership

Researchers agree to make the information they collect from activities like Web tracking available to the consumers from whom they gather the information.

URLs, names and passwords, and so on automatically. Once again, however, technology creates workarounds to these security precautions. **History sniffing** is a term for activities that covertly discover and record the websites that a consumer visits without using cookies. Perhaps not totally surprisingly, the Internet porn industry advanced the use of this technology—realizing that some of its customers would try to prevent their cookies from being traced. One history sniffing technique relies on the fact that hyperlinks change color from blue to purple when a user clicks through.[30] A browser code uses this technology to build profiles of users based on the sites they visit.

Going further, a consumer concerned that some institutions may know too much based on big data technologies may forgo owning a smartphone or other device that reveals their location. He or she may also stay away from social network sites where personal information may be revealed or even give up e-mail or Internet browsing. However, these steps seem drastic and few are willing to sacrifice these benefits out of concern for privacy. The advancement of technology has moved faster than our ability to understand when knowing too much really is too much.

History sniffing

Activities that covertly discover and record the websites that a consumer visits.

TIPS OF THE TRADE

- Researchers should focus on relevance as the key characteristic of useful data.
- Do so by asking, "Will knowledge of some fact change some important outcome?"
- Automate data collection when possible to enhance data quality.
- Weigh the costs of technology investments against the benefits they will bring.
- Be mindful of ethical concerns when using today's sophisticated data mining techniques.

:: SUMMARY

1. Know why concepts like data, big data, information, and intelligence represent value. From a research perspective, there is a difference between data, information, and intelligence. Data are simply facts or recorded measures of certain phenomena (things); information is data formatted (structured) to support decision making or define the relationship between two facts. Market intelligence is the subset of data and information that actually has some explanatory power enabling effective decisions to be made. Advancing communication technologies mean that consumers are constantly leaving behind data. Thus, researchers today use big data, taken from multiple sources not intended to be used together, to model what consumers are going to do. This data can be supplemented with data found or purchased from data providers. Marketing analytics are employed to try to make sense out of all of this and feed intelligence into the organization's decision systems. When used properly, and with good ethical practices in mind, employing data to make strategic and tactical decisions means greater value for the firm and its customers.

2. Understand the four characteristics that describe data. The usefulness of data to management can be described based on four characteristics: relevance, completeness, quality, and timeliness. Relevant data have the characteristic of pertinence to the situation at hand and when relevant facts change, the decision is affected. Completeness means having the right amount of information for decision making. Missing information can lead to erroneous conclusions. The quality of information is the degree to which data represent the true situation. High-quality data represent reality faithfully and present a good picture of reality. Timely means the data are not so old that they are irrelevant. Generally, timeliness requires highly current data.

3. Know what a decision support system is and the technology tools that help make it work. A marketing decision support system (DSS) is a system that helps decision-makers confront problems through direct interaction with computerized databases and systems. Decision systems systematically integrate marketing data. Marketing data come from six major sources: internal records, proprietary marketing research, salesperson input, behavioral tracking, web tracking, and outside vendors/external distributors. Data warehousing is the process allowing important day-to-day operational data to be stored and organized for simplified access. Data warehouse management requires that detailed data from operational systems be extracted, transformed, and stored (warehoused) so that the various database tables from both inside and outside the company are consistent. The DSS also is greatly aided by CRM systems and tools such as behavioral and Web tracking, among others.

4. Recognize some of the major databases and how they are accessed. A database is a collection of raw data arranged logically and organized in a useful form. Aside from internal databases, marketing researchers can access many publicly available databases, some of which are free and others which come with some sort of fee-based access. The U.S. Census Bureau contains a plethora of information about household demographics, population by region, and overall population trends; however, one can also access data about many industries through census.gov. The *CIA Factbook* provides a wealth of information about international markets. Nielsen provides data on media usage and even on lifestyles and demographics across the United States at the zip code level through PRIZM.

5. Understand the basic concept of marketing analytics and its potential to enhance decision making. *Marketing analytics* is a general term that refers to efforts to measure relevant data and apply analytical tools in an effort to better understand how a firm can enhance marketing performance. Predictive analytics involves mining computerized data sources with statistical tools that can search for predictive relationships and trends. Thus, it combines automated data mining with multivariate and other statistical tools to enhance prediction. The marketing researcher's job in predictive analytics is twofold. First, identify the key sources of information that may create predictive intelligence and second, use analytic tools to build predictive models.

6. Be sensitive to the potential ethical issues of tracking consumers' behavior electronically. Privacy is becoming a rare commodity as consumers enter a myriad of information into websites and pass information through their smart phones. The tracking of consumers can be made more ethical when (a) consumers have implicitly or explicitly consented to being tracked, (b) tracking activities do not violate any agreements with the consumer, (c) systems exist allowing consumers to know what information is gathered, and (d) the benefits to consumers in general outweigh any imposition from the data gathering process. Consumers can take steps to protect their own privacy, but they come at the price of the convenience that smart technologies give us.

:: KEY TERMS AND CONCEPTS

big data, *26*

cloud storage, *31*

content providers, *39*

cookies, *42*

customer relationship management (CRM), *30*

data quality, *28*

data retailers, *35*

data warehouse, *31*

data warehousing, *31*

data wholesalers, *35*

data, *26*

database, *31*

decision support system (DSS), *30*

electronic data interchange (EDI), *34*

environmental scanning, *40*

geolocation technologies, *43*

HIPAA, *42*

history sniffing, *45*

information, *27*

information completeness, *28*

intranet, *42*

keyword search, *39*

market dynamism, *29*

market intelligence, *27*

marketing analytics, *43*

NFC, *42*

open data partnership, *44*

open source information, *34*

predictive analytics, *43*

proprietary marketing research, *32*

pull technology, *40*

push technology, *40*

relevance, *28*

RFID, *41*

scanner data, *33*

search-engine optimizer, *34*

smart agent software, *40*

timeliness, *29*

Uniform Resource Locator (URL), *39*

universal product code, *33*

:: QUESTIONS FOR REVIEW AND CRITICAL THINKING

1. Define big data. How has big data created greater demand for people with research skills?
2. What is the difference between data, information, and intelligence?
3. What are the characteristics of useful information?
4. What is the key question distinguishing relevant data from irrelevant data?
5. How is CRM used as input to a DSS?
6. Define RFID. How can it provide input to a DSS?
7. What types of internal databases might one find in the following organizations?
   a. Hilton Hotels
   b. A major university athletic department
   c. AB Inbev
   d. QuiBids (online auction website)
   e. iTunes
   f. Facebook
8. What type of operational questions could a delivery firm like UPS expect to automate with the company's decision support system?
9. What makes a decision support system successful?
10. What is data warehousing?
11. What is Web tracking? Visit http://www.kbb.com. While there, choose two cars that you might consider buying and compare them. Which do you like the best? What would you do now? What are at least three pieces of data that should be stored in a data warehouse somewhere based on your interaction with *Kelly Blue Book*?
12. Give three examples of computerized databases that are available through your college or university library.
13. Describe what smart agent software is and how it may affect you as a typical consumer.
14. Describe the role of marketing analytics in assisting business decision-making.
15. What is predictive analytics? Think about your behavior in the last 48 hours. List at least 10 things that you've done which may have produced data that could be used as input into a predictive analytics system.
16. Suppose a retail firm is interested in studying the effect of lighting on customer purchase behavior. Which of the following pieces of information is the least relevant and why?
   a. Amount of natural light in the store
   b. The compensation system for store salespeople
   c. The color of the walls in the store
   d. The type of lighting: fluorescent or incandescent
17. How could New Balance, a maker of athletic shoes, use an NFC device like iBeacon (described in chapter)?
18. What are four questions researchers can ask in deciding whether their electronic data gathering systems violate good ethical principles?

:: RESEARCH ACTIVITIES

1. Search the Internet and try to find the earliest use of the phrase "big data." Describe why the term has come to be used.
2. Use the Internet to see if you can find information to answer the following questions:
   a. What is the exchange rate between the U.S. dollar ($) and the Euro (€)?
   b. What are four restaurants in the French Quarter in New Orleans?
   c. What is the most popular novel among teenage girls aged 14–16?
   d. Do more people visit the foxnews.com or cnn.com websites?
3. Casually interview two consumers at least 20 years different in age. Describe to them a use of big data such as the restaurant consumer whose server knew she had worked out before coming to the restaurant just by data produced by her smartphone. How do they react? Is either concerned about the potential breech in privacy? Comment on your results.

Harvard Cooperative Society

Case 2.1

From his office window overlooking the main floor of the Harvard Cooperative Society, CEO Jerry Murphy can glance down and see customers shopping. They make their way through the narrow aisles of the crowded department store, picking up a sweatshirt here, trying on a baseball cap there, checking out the endless array of merchandise that bears the Harvard University insignia.

PHOTODISC GREEN/GETTY IMAGES

Watching Murphy, you can well imagine the Coop's founders, who started the store in 1882, peering through the tiny window-panes to keep an eye on the shop floor. Was the Harvard Square store attracting steady traffic? Were the college students buying enough books and supplies for the Co-op to make a profit? Back then, it was tough to answer those questions precisely. The owners had to watch and wait, relying only on their gut feelings to know how things were going from minute to minute.

Now, more than a hundred years later, Murphy can tell you, down to the last stock-keeping unit, how he's doing at any given moment. His window on the business is the notebook computer that sits on his desk. All day long it delivers up-to-the-minute, easy-to-read electronic reports on what's selling and what's not, which items are running low in inventory, and which have fallen short of forecast. In a matter of seconds, the computer can report gross margins for any product or supplier, and Murphy can decide whether the margins are fat enough to justify keeping the supplier or product on board. "We were in the 1800s, and we had to move ahead," he says of the $55 million business. Now, he considers investing in iBeacon and/or other NFC technology as a way of directing customers toward purchases as they browse through the store.

Questions

1. What is a decision support system? What advantages does a decision support system have for a business like the Harvard Cooperative Society?
2. How would the decision support system of a business like the Harvard Cooperative Society differ from that of a major corporation?
3. Briefly outline the components of the Harvard Cooperative Society's decision support system.
4. How might the Harvard Cooperative Society use the iBeacon technology?

The Marketing Research Process

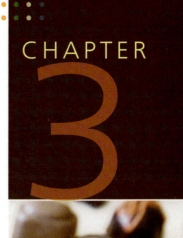

CHAPTER

3

LEARNING OUTCOMES

After studying this chapter, you should be able to:

1. Apply marketing research in making better marketing decisions
2. Classify marketing research as either exploratory research, descriptive research, or causal research
3. List the major stages of the marketing research process and the steps within each
4. Understand the concepts of theory and hypothesis and the critical role they play in research
5. Know the difference between a research project and a research program

Dimitri Otis/Getty Images

Chapter Vignette:

Changing for Wired Students

What are the largest higher education institutions in the United States? What schools come to mind? Is your institution one of the largest? Read on to find out.

Some might say that college students always have been at least a little wired. In this high-tech world though, students don't even need a wire.[1] Changing educational technologies mean today's students enjoy many more choices than did their parents or even their older siblings. Universities offer new degree programs in varied and specific fields including areas like sports marketing and gaming management, and degrees can be obtained without ever physically stepping foot on an actual university campus.

Thinking about an MBA? Although the degree still provides an attractive line on the résumé, some are concerned that the increasingly large number of MBA graduates is decreasing the value

of the degree in terms of the salaries for MBA grads.[2] Over a quarter of a million U.S. students alone attend MBA classes of one form or another at any given time. For universities, the market for the MBA degree is particularly competitive and the fact is that those universities that offer a market-oriented program are most attractive to students. More and more

Source: www.ashford.edu

49

universities see profit potential from online students who don't take up classroom space, require fewer student services, and are sometimes taught by adjunct or part-time faculty who are cheaper than tenure track faculty.[3] Thus, universities are aggressively marketing online MBA programs. Marketing research helps answer important questions that feed into this marketing.

- How much does convenience drive consumer choice relative to quality or price perceptions?
- How much of a price premium is a student willing to pay for online convenience?
- How are nontraditional vis-à-vis traditional MBA programs viewed in terms of value, quality, and prestige?
- What is the demand? Are there enough potential students to make a particular program financially feasible? Where might the students come from?
- Do online MBA offerings cannibalize in-class MBA offerings?
- What kinds of consumer support should the MBA program create to increase the satisfaction of online MBA students?

- What is the impact of promoting online programs on the image of the school's MBA and the image of the college and university overall?
- Can a business school better accomplish the mission of the university with an online MBA program?

The competitive MBA market typifies the landscape of many marketing firms. Clearly, universities could benefit from marketing research addressing some of these key questions. Each university maintains its own academic standards while still trying to attract enough students to make its MBA program feasible. Potential opportunities and potential problems fill this competitive landscape. Decisions made by university faculty and administrators will determine how successfully each school deals with the changing marketplace.

The five largest institutions of higher learning in the United States are University of Phoenix, Kaplan University, Arizona State University, Ashford University, and Miami Dade Community College. Surprised? All five of these have aggressively marketed to nontraditional student segments.

Introduction

This chapter focuses on the marketing research process. This process informs business decisions aiding in solving problems and seizing on opportunities. Quality decision-making drives business success. Marketing researchers contribute to decision making in several key ways. These include

1. Helping to better define the organization's current situation
2. Identifying useful decision statements and related research questions
3. Defining the firm's meaning—how consumers, competitors, and employees view the firm
4. Providing ideas for product improvements or possible new product development
5. Testing ideas that will assist in implementing marketing strategy including innovations
6. Examining how well a marketing theory describes marketing reality

The chapter introduces the types of research that allow researchers to provide input to key marketing decisions. The chapter first discusses stages in the marketing research process and concludes by demonstrating the role that theory plays in better decision-making.

Decision Making and Marketing Research

A college student makes many decisions that affect the future. These include important strategic decisions like whether to go to college or not. If the answer is yes, then a decision is faced about where to attend. Furthermore, the student must decide what subject to major in, what electives to take, which instructors to sign up for, whether to belong to a fraternity or sorority, how much to work outside of school, and so forth. The student may seek out data provided by other students, parents, or various media sources. These data may be critical in reaching decisions. Indeed, the answers to each of these questions shape a student's future, ultimately determine how successful he or she will be, and shape the way he or she is viewed by others.

Likewise, businesses face decisions that shape the future of the organization, its employees, and its customers. In each case, the decisions are brought about as the firm either seeks to capitalize on some opportunity or to lessen any potential negative impacts related to some market problem. Formally defined, **decision making** is the process of developing and deciding among alternative ways of resolving

Decision making

the process of developing and deciding among alternative ways of resolving a problem or choosing from among alternative opportunities

The survey you took as part of this course covers a wide degree of topics. One question in particular deals with a respondent's study habits. How much time do you spend studying for this course? After you've read this chapter, think about how you might design a study investigating the issue of study time for this class. What type of study design would you be using to implement your study? What other parts of the survey might be relevant to your study?

Source: Qualtrics.com

a problem or choosing from among alternative opportunities. A decision-maker must recognize the nature of the problem or opportunity, identify how much information is currently available and how reliable it is, and determine what information is needed to better deal with the situation.

Every decision-making situation can be classified based on whether it best represents a problem or an opportunity, and on whether it represents a situation characterized by complete certainty or absolute ambiguity. A **market opportunity** is a situation that makes some potential competitive advantage possible. Thus, the discovery of some underserved market segment presents such an opportunity. For example, Zynga capitalized on the trend toward free online gaming, particularly via Facebook networks, by offering virtual products, such as virtual (not real) fertilizer, for sale for real money. Zynga discovered that many consumers will willingly buy their way into better game performance.

A **market problem** is a business situation that makes some significant negative consequence more likely. The situation is because of some force acting in or on the firm's market. As more and more consumers turned to mobile devices for gaming instead of accessing games via Facebook, consumers turned away from Zynga offerings to more mobile-friendly games. With consumer data suggesting more and more movement toward more and new mobile devices, Zynga management eventually decided to purchase NaturalMotion, a company specializing in mobile gaming technologies, in an effort to make its games mobile friendly and create more opportunities for customers to interact with its brands.[5] This may look like an example of "if you can't beat them, join them." But, it illustrates how marketing research described consumer trends that motivated a major change in business strategy.

Problems are usually not as obvious as they may seem. In fact, they usually are not easily observable. Instead, problems are inferred from **symptoms**, which are observable cues that serve as a signal of a problem because they are caused by that problem. A drop in market share is generally only a symptom of a market problem and not the problem itself. Research plays a role in identifying the causes of problems so decisions can shape cures and not just treat symptoms in a superficial way. Decision situations are also characterized by how much certainty or ambiguity exists.

Market opportunity

A situation that makes some potential competitive advantage possible.

Market problem

A business situation that makes some significant negative consequence more likely.

Symptoms

Observable cues that serve as a signal of a problem.

Certainty

Complete certainty means that the decision-maker has all information needed to make an optimal decision. This includes the exact nature of the marketing problem or opportunity. For example, an advertising agency may need to know the demographic characteristics of subscribers to magazines in which it may place a client's advertisements. The agency knows exactly what information it needs and where to find the information. If a manager is completely certain about both the problem or opportunity and future outcomes, then research may not be needed at all. However, perfect certainty, especially about the future, is rare.

Uncertainty means that the manager grasps the general nature of desired objectives, but the information about alternatives is incomplete. Predictions about forces that shape future events are educated guesses. Under conditions of uncertainty, effective managers recognize that spending additional time to gather data that clarify the nature of a decision is needed. For instance, a university may understand that there is an objective of increasing the number of MBA students, but it may not know whether an online, weekend, or off-site MBA program is the best way to accomplish the objective. Marketing decisions generally involve uncertainty, particularly when a company is seeking different opportunities.

What symptoms might signal a problem for a new product extension like this?

Ambiguity

Ambiguity means that the nature of the problem itself is unclear. Objectives are vague and decision alternatives are difficult to define. This is by far the most difficult decision situation, but perhaps the most common.

Marketing managers face a variety of problems and decisions. Complete certainty and predictable future outcomes may make marketing research a waste of time. However, under conditions of uncertainty or ambiguity, marketing research becomes more attractive to decision-makers. Decisions also vary in terms of importance, meaning that some may have great impact on the welfare of the firm and others may have negligible impact. The more important, ambiguous, or uncertain a situation, the more likely it is that additional time must be spent on marketing research.

Classifying Decision Situations

Exhibit 3.1 depicts decision situations characterized by the nature of the decision and the degree of ambiguity. Under problem-focused decision making and conditions of high ambiguity, symptoms may not clearly point to some problem. Indeed, they may be quite vague or subtle, indicating only small deviations from normal conditions. For instance, a fast-food restaurant may be experiencing small changes in the sales of its individual products, but no change in overall sales. Such a symptom may not easily point to a problem such as a change in consumer tastes. As ambiguity is lessened, the symptoms are clearer and are better indicators of a problem. A large and sudden drop in overall sales may suggest the problem that the restaurant's menu does not fare well compared to competitors' menus. Thus, a menu change may be in order to deal with the menu problem.

Similarly, in opportunity-oriented research, ambiguity is characterized by marketplace and environmental trends that do not suggest a clear direction. As the trends become larger and clearer, they are more diagnostic, meaning they point more clearly to a single opportunity. Trends showing how consumers may use social networking were not always so evident. Online gaming technologies have had to adapt quickly though as trends to games online at Facebook have shifted more toward smartphone friendly alternatives. A problem for one industry often presents an opportunity for another.

Types of Marketing Research

Effective marketing research reduces uncertainty and helps focus marketing decision-making. Sometimes marketing researchers know exactly what their marketing problems are and can design careful studies to test specific hypotheses. Universities, even not-for-profit universities, face

© Cengage Learning®

EXHIBIT 3.1
Describing Decision-Making Situations

marketing problems. For instance, input from employers, students, and alumni might suggest that a school's curricula are outdated. The problem could even be contributing to low enrollment motivating university administration to address the problem. Thus, marketing researchers working for the university may devise a careful test exploring which of three new, alternative curricula would most improve the public's perception that the curriculum is of high quality. This type of research is problem oriented and seems relatively unambiguous. The marketing research may culminate with researchers preparing a report suggesting the relative effect of each alternative curriculum on enrollment. The decision should follow relatively directly from the research.

In more ambiguous circumstances, marketing managers may be totally unaware of a marketing problem. Alternatively, the company may be scanning the environment for opportunities. For example, a small, private undergraduate university in a mid-sized Texas town may consider adding an online MBA program. University administrators may have little idea as to how this would affect the image of their school among current students, employers, alumni, or faculty. They also may not know exactly what programs would be most desired by its current or potential customer bases. Some preliminary research may be necessary to gain insights into the nature of such a situation. Without it, the situation may remain too ambiguous to make more than a seat-of-the-pants decision. The decision-makers almost certainly need input from marketing research.

The technique or purpose underlying marketing research provides a basis for classification. Experiments, surveys, and observational studies are just a few common research techniques. Classifying research by its purpose shows how the nature of a decision situation influences the research methodology. The following section introduces the three basic research designs, each representing a different type of research, that help researchers create intelligence that leads to better decision-making:

1. Exploratory
2. Descriptive
3. Causal

Matching the particular decision situation with the right type of research is important in obtaining useful research results.

Exploratory Research Design

Exploratory research

Conducted to clarify ambiguous situations or discover ideas that may be potential business opportunities.

Exploratory research aims to clarify ambiguous situations or discover ideas that may amount to true business opportunities. Exploratory research does not provide conclusive evidence from which to determine a particular course of action. In this sense, exploratory research is not an end unto itself. Researchers usually undertake exploratory research with the full expectation that managers will need more research to supply more conclusive evidence. Using exploratory research can sometimes also make the difference in determining the relevance of follow-up research. Rushing into detailed research before knowing exactly what the key decisions should be will likely produce irrelevant data and thereby waste time, money, and effort.

Innovation and Exploratory Research

Exploratory research is particularly useful in new product development.[6] Sometimes, it may reveal insight into radical products like a vacuum tube that could transport people through a line at speeds approaching that of a jet aircraft. Not all ideas are so extreme. Consumer products companies depend on a steady stream of new brand ideas or profitable brand extensions.

A brand like Kraft constantly explores consumer data for clues that might signal a successful product introduction. Kraft combined data taken from scanners with unstructured customer interviews to identify *superconsumers*.[7] The superconsumer epitomizes the Pareto Principle otherwise known as the 80/20 rule (i.e., 80 percent of sales come from 20 percent of customers). In fact, in the case of Kraft Velveeta, scanner purchase data suggested that 10 percent of all customers accounted for half of all brand profits. Exploratory interviews with some of these superconsumers suggested that they were always looking for new opportunities to use Velveeta. As a result, Kraft responded with new product extensions for Velveeta that included individual slices suitable for burgers or sandwiches and shredded Velveeta convenient for salads and tacos. Simple product extensions like these led to over $100 million in sales. Exploratory research can be very profitable.

The data explosion discussed previously also aids exploratory research. The Research Snapshot illustrates how companies are using technological innovations to gather exploratory research. Input gathered through these techniques helps fuel better decision-making.

Exploratory Research and Problem Solving

Exploratory research can be useful in helping to better define a marketing problem or identify a market opportunity. An exploratory design may be implemented to try to reveal not just the symptoms observed in some situation, but potential underlying problems that are causing those symptoms. Usually, this process is not clear and yields numerous potential causes that require further research to pin down probable causes. Patients don't usually go to the doctor and point out their problem (like an ulcer). Instead, they point out symptoms (upset stomach). Similarly, decision-makers usually hear about symptoms and often need help from research to identify and attack problems. Whether facing an opportunity or a problem, businesses need quality information to deal effectively with these situations. The amount of certainty or ambiguity also characterizes all decision situations.

Descriptive Research

Descriptive research

Describes characteristics of objects, people, groups, organizations, or environments; tries to "paint a picture" of a given situation.

Descriptive research, as the name implies, describes characteristics of objects, people, groups, organizations, or environments. Put more simply, descriptive research tries to "paint a picture" of a given situation. Marketing managers frequently need to determine who purchases a product, portray the size of the market, identify competitors' actions, and so on. Descriptive research addresses who, what, when, where, why, and how questions.

Descriptive research often helps describe market segments. What does the organic food market look like? Marketing researchers used simple descriptive surveys to describe consumers who are

Heard It through the Grapevine

The word exploratory itself brings about the idea of newness. The newness is sometimes radical and sometimes incremental. In either case, firms employ exploratory research in an attempt to develop successful innovations. General Electric is discovering innovative ways to use social networking to enhance the GE brand. GE uses the Vine app (Vine.co) to preview short (6 seconds), looping videos via Twitter. They place a video out and then monitor the number of hits and reactions the video generates. One simple video showed how colors move through liquids. The colorful six-second loop quickly generated over 200,000 views. When a video fails to generate hits or gets negative feedback, GE quickly takes it down. Every time someone views a video, the GE brand gets more attention. The tweets also prove useful in exploring ideas for totally new product ideas or for incremental improvements to products or the brand message. GE's use of Vine illustrates how new media technologies can serve as productive exploratory research tools.

Sources: Wells, G. (2014), "Real-Time Marketing in a Real-Time World," *Wall Street Journal*, (March 24), R3. *Advertising Age* (2013), "General Electric Hosts a 6-Second Science Fair on Vine," http://adage.com/article/creativity-pick-of-the-day/general-electric-hosts-a-6secondscience-fair-vine/243552/, accessed April 1, 2014.

heavy consumers (buy a lot) of organic food products. One report shows that annual global organic food sales are just over $80 billion.[8] Fruits and vegetables (i.e., fresh produce) account for nearly 40 percent of those sales although organic meat, poultry, and fish sales are increasing rapidly. The organic beverage market is also growing with organic coffee and tea accounting for just over 35 percent of the global organic beverage market. These data provide a snapshot of the organic grocery market.

Competition for the organic segment is considerable. Over half of Whole Foods's food products are organic and as a result, they appeal to the organic food segment in the United States. Whole Foods's sales have grown continuously except for 2009, reaching over $13 billion in its 367 stores in 2013. In terms of profitability, a Whole Foods store produces average sales of $972 per square foot compared to about $600 for a typical grocery store. Whole Foods's future seems bright but several facts give a reason for some caution. The rate of growth in sales since 2009 has not returned to the levels seen in the early 2000s. Research shows that other grocery outlets have increased the amount of space dedicated to organic goods, some consumers also have been conditioned by years of economic malaise to deprioritize organic and quality relative to price, and Whole Foods's growth in the number of stores has often been in the same metropolitan areas.[9] Boston has nearly thirty Whole Foods stores and as the number of stores increase, sales per store decrease somewhat as the new stores cannibalize customers from the preexisting stores. All of this data represents results from descriptive studies.

Similarly, the university considering the addition of an online MBA program might benefit from descriptive research profiling the market and the potential customers. Online students are not identical to the traditional MBA students. They tend to be older, averaging about 30 years of age. Another key statistic is that the dropout rate for online students is significantly higher than for traditional MBA students. Nearly 14 percent of online students drop before completing a course, compared to 7.2 percent for traditional in-class students.

Accuracy is critically important in descriptive research. If a descriptive study misestimates a university's demand for its MBA offering by even a few students, it can mean the difference between the program sustaining itself or being a drain on already scarce resources. For instance, if a research predicts that twenty students will enroll in a cohort, but only fifteen students actually sign up, the program will likely not generate enough revenue to sustain itself. Therefore, descriptive research forecasting sales revenue and costs or describing consumer attitudes, satisfaction, and commitment must be accurate or decision-making quality will suffer.

adventtr/iStockphoto.co

Feel the Power…

In the end, businesses succeed or fail based on how consumers interact with the brand. If consumers stop buying, the business's days are numbered. With all the talk about big data today, one can form the opinion that research is all about quantities of data. However, some research firms specialize in getting deeply involved with consumers to describe better the motivations behind consumer behavior. The firms refer to such data as thick data. For instance, what does a television mean today? In a study for Samsung, researchers interviewed hundreds of consumers about the way they use their televisions and collected consumer videos of their interactions with TVs. One trend that emerged is that consumers often did not like the way their televisions looked when they were not on. The data described consumer desires to hide their TVs. Because of these descriptive studies, Samsung focused on redesigning TVs into a more sleek and elegant piece of furniture. The data also revealed increasing frustration as the greater choice in channels comes at the price of making it more difficult to find specific programming. Samsung responded to these findings by making their televisions smarter by using patterns in program choices to aid users' ability to find the shows that they would most enjoy. Research provided the key to a more meaningful TV experience.

Sources: Madsbjerg, C. and M. B. Rasmussen (2014), "The Power of Thick Data," *Wall Street Journal* (March 22–23), C3. http://www.samsung.com/us/news/20414, accessed April 2, 2014.

Unlike exploratory research, researchers usually conduct descriptive studies with a considerable understanding of the marketing situation. This understanding, perhaps developed in part from exploratory research, directs the study toward specific issues. Later, we will discuss the role of research questions and hypotheses. These statements help greatly in designing and implementing a descriptive study.

Survey research typifies a descriptive study. Many surveys try to answer questions such as "Why are store A's sales lower than store B's sales?" In other words, a **diagnostic analysis** seeks to detect reasons for market outcomes and focuses specifically on the beliefs, feelings, and reactions consumers have about and toward competing products. A research study trying to diagnose slumping French wine sales among casual consumers might ask a sample of consumers from this segment about the taste of French, Australian, and American wines. The results might indicate a deficiency in taste, suggesting that a reason why this segment is not buying as much

Diagnostic analysis

Seeks to detect reasons for market outcomes and focuses specifically on the beliefs, feelings, and reactions consumers have about and toward competing products.

Jim West / Alamy

French wine is that they do not believe French wines taste as fruity as do wines from Australia. Descriptive research can sometimes provide an explanation by diagnosing differences among competitors, but descriptive research does not provide direct evidence of causality.

Causal Research

If a decision maker knows what *causes* important outcomes like sales and employee satisfaction, then he or she can shape firm decisions in a positive way. Causal inferences are very powerful because they lead to greater control. **Causal research** allows decision-makers to make causal inferences. What brought some event about? That is, causal research seeks to identify cause-and-effect relationships to show that one event actually makes another happen. Heat causes ice to melt. Heat is the cause and melted ice (water) is the effect.

Exploratory and/or descriptive research usually precedes causal research. In causal studies, researchers typically have a substantial understanding of the decision-making situation. As a result, the researcher can make an educated prediction about cause-and-effect relationships that the research will test. The tests are usually quite focused, which is a good thing, but the trade-offs must be considered. Causal research designs can take a long time to implement. In addition, they often involve intricate designs that can be very expensive. Thus, even though managers may often want the assurance that causal inferences can bring, they are not always willing to spend that much time and money.

Causal research
Allows causal inferences to be made—they identify cause-and-effect (x brought about y) relationships.

Causality

Ideally, managers want to know how a change in one event (say, using a new product logo) will change another event of interest, like sales. Causal research attempts to establish that when we do one thing, another thing will follow. A **causal inference** is just such a conclusion. Although we use the term *cause* all the time in everyday language, scientifically establishing something as a cause is not so easy and even researchers sometimes confuse causality with correlation. A researcher requires very specific evidence to draw a causal inference. Three critical pieces of causal evidence are

Causal inference
A conclusion that when one thing happens, another specific thing will follow.

1. Temporal Sequence
2. Concomitant Variance
3. Nonspurious Association

Temporal Sequence
Temporal sequence deals with the time order of events. In other words, having an appropriate causal order, or temporal sequence, is a necessary criterion for causality. The cause must occur before the effect. How could a restaurant manager blame a decrease in sales on a new chef if the drop in sales occurred before the new chef arrived? If advertising causes sales, the advertising must appear before the change in sales.

Temporal sequence
One of three criteria for causality; deals with the time order of events—the cause must occur before the effect.

Concomitant Variation
Concomitant variation occurs when two events "covary," meaning they vary systematically. In causal terms, concomitant variation means that when a change in the cause occurs, a change in the outcome also is observed. We often use the term correlation, discussed in a later chapter, to represent what concomitant variation means. Causality cannot possibly exist when there is no systematic variation between the variables. For example, if a retail store's competition has not changed, then the competitors cannot possibly be responsible for changes in store sales. There is no *correlation* between the two events. On the other hand, if two events vary together, one event may be causing the other. If a university increases its number of online MBA course offerings and experiences a decrease in enrollment in its traditional in-class MBA offerings, the online course offerings may be *causing* the decrease.

Concomitant variation
One of three criteria for causality; occurs when two events "covary," meaning they vary systematically.

One challenge in acting on results discovered by computer mining of big data is sorting out what is actionable. The data may identify patterns that suggest systematic variation, but at times the patterns don't seem practically actionable. More follow-ups on such patterns may be needed before taking action because systematic variation alone doesn't guarantee causality.

EXHIBIT 3.2
Ice Cream Is a Spurious
Cause of Drowning

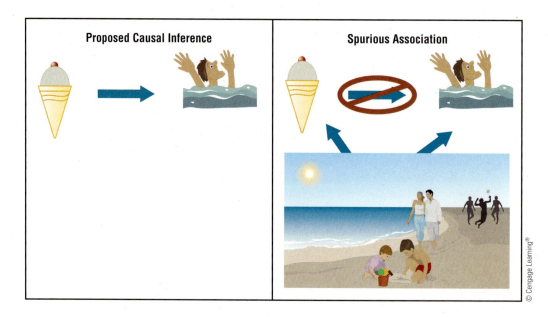

Nonspurious Association

Nonspurious association

One of three criteria for causality; means any covariation between a cause and an effect is true and not simply because of some other variable.

Nonspurious association means any covariation between a cause and an effect is indeed because of the cause and not simply owing to some other variable. A spurious association is one that is not true. Often, a causal inference cannot be made even though the other two conditions exist because both the cause and effect have some common cause; that is, both may be influenced by a third variable. For instance, a city worker notices an alarming trend. On days when a large number of ice cream cones are sold at Virginia Beach, more people drown. So, when ice cream sales go up, so does drowning. Should the city decide to ban ice cream? This would be silly because the concomitant variation observed between ice cream consumption and drowning is spurious. On days when the beach is particularly crowded, more ice cream is sold *and* more people drown. So, the number of people at the beach, being associated with both outcomes, may cause both. Exhibit 3.2 illustrates the concept of spurious association.

Establishing evidence of nonspuriousness can be difficult. If a researcher finds a third variable that covaries with both the cause and effect, causing a significant drop in the correlation between the cause and effect, then a causal inference becomes difficult to support. Although the researcher would like to rule out the possibility of any alternative causes, it is impossible to observe the effect of all variables on the correlation between the cause and effect. Therefore, the researcher must use theory to identify the most likely "third" variables that would relate significantly to both the cause and effect. The research must control for these variables in some way, as we will see in a later chapter devoted to experimental methods. In addition, the researcher should use theory to make sure that the cause-and-effect relationship truly makes sense.

In summary, causal research should do all of the following:

1. Establish the appropriate causal order or sequence of events
2. Measure the concomitant variation (relationship) between the presumed cause and the presumed effect
3. Examine the possibility of spuriousness by considering the presence of alternative plausible causal factors

Degrees of Causality

In everyday language, we often use the word "cause" in an absolute sense. For example, a warning label used on cigarette packages claims "smoking causes cancer." Is this true in an absolute sense?

Absolute causality

The cause is necessary and sufficient to bring about the effect.

Absolute causality means the cause is necessary and sufficient to bring about the effect. Thus, if we find only one smoker who does not eventually get cancer, the claim is false. Although this is a very strong inference, it is impractical to think that we can establish absolute causality in the behavioral sciences.

Why do we continue to do causal research then? Well, although managers may like to be able to draw absolute conclusions, they can often make very good decisions based on less powerful inferences. **Conditional causality** means that a cause is necessary but not sufficient to bring about an effect. This is a weaker causal inference. One way to think about conditional causality is that the cause can bring about the effect, but it cannot do so alone. If other conditions are right, the cause can bring about the effect. We know there are other medical factors that contribute to cancer. For instance, lifestyle and diet are also both plausible causes of cancer. Thus, if one smokes and has a diet and lifestyle that promote cancer, smoking could be a considered a conditional cause of cancer. However, if we can find someone who has contracted cancer and never smoked, the causal inference would be proven wrong.

Contributory causality may be the weakest form of causality, but it is still a useful concept. A cause need be neither necessary nor sufficient to bring about an effect. However, the three types of evidence shown on the previous page can establish causal evidence. For any outcome, there may be multiple causes. So, an event can be a contributory cause of something so long as the introduction of the other possible causes does not eliminate the correlation between it and the effect. This will become clearer when we discuss ways to test relationships later in the text. Smoking then can be a contributory cause of cancer so long as the introduction of other possible causes does not cause both smoking and cancer.

Conditional causality

Means that a cause is necessary but not sufficient to bring about the effect.

Contributory causality

A cause need be neither necessary nor sufficient to bring about an effect; the weakest form of causality.

Experiments

Marketing experiments hold the greatest potential for establishing cause-and-effect relationships. An **experiment** is a carefully controlled study in which the researcher manipulates a proposed cause and observes any corresponding change in the proposed effect. An **experimental variable** represents the proposed cause and the researcher controls this variable by manipulating its value. **Manipulation** means that the researcher alters the level of the variable in specific increments. So, managers often want to make decisions about the price and distribution of a new product. Both price and the type of retail outlet in which a product is placed are considered potential causes of sales. A causal research design would manipulate both the price and distribution and assess the consequences on key outcome variables.

Suppose a company produces a new tablet computer called the Meboard. The company needs research to implement the best marketing mix for the product. The company may manipulate price in an experiment by offering it for $200 among some consumers and $500 among others. Likewise, they manipulate retail distribution by selling the Meboard at discount stores in some consumer markets and at specialty electronic stores in others. The retailer can examine whether price and distribution cause sales by comparing the sales results in each of the four conditions created. Exhibit 3.3 illustrates this study.

A marketing research experiment examined the effect of adding a higher-priced alternative to the set of products sold by a retailer. The researchers manipulated price by creating a scenario that either added a higher or lower priced alternative to a set of products reviewed by a consumer. The results show that for frequently purchased products, adding a higher-priced alternative causes consumers to believe that prices in general were lower.[10] We will say much more about manipulations and experimental designs later.

Experiment

A carefully controlled study in which the researcher manipulates a proposed cause and observes any corresponding change in the proposed effect.

Experimental variable

Represents the proposed cause that the researcher controls by manipulating its value.

Manipulation

Means that the researcher alters the level of the variable in specific increments.

Meboard Sales by Condition		
	Low Price	**High Price**
Specialty Distribution	Peoria, IL Retail Price: $200 Retail Store: Best Buy	Des Moines, IA Retail Price: $500 Retail Store : Best Buy
General Distribution	St. Louis, MO Retail Price: $200 Retail Store: Big Cheap-Mart	Kansas City, MO Retail Price: $500 Retail Store: Big Cheap-Mart

EXHIBIT 3.3

Testing for Causes with Experimental Manipulations

© 2016 Cengage Learning®

Uncertainty Influences the Type of Research

The amount of uncertainty surrounding a marketing situation does much to determine the most appropriate type and amount of research needed. Exhibit 3.4 contrasts the types of research, illustrates this idea, and shows how researchers conduct exploratory research during the early stages of decision-making. At this point, the decision situation is usually highly ambiguous and management is very uncertain about what actions to take. When management is aware of the problem but lacks some key knowledge, researchers conduct descriptive research. Causal research requires tightly defined problems.

Each type of research produces a different type of result. In many ways, exploratory research is the most productive because it produces many ideas. Exploratory research is discovery oriented and relatively unstructured. Too much structure in this type of research may lead to more narrowly focused types of responses that could stifle creativity. At times, managers do take managerial action based only on exploratory research results because management may not be able to or may not care to invest the time and resources needed to conduct further research. Decisions made based only on exploratory research can be more risky because exploratory research does not test ideas.[11] For instance, a business school professor may ask a class of current MBA students for ideas about an online program. Although the students may provide many ideas that sound very good, that particular research design does not test any idea scientifically. An exploratory design is adequate for discovering ideas, but not for testing ideas.

The discovery process often culminates with research questions. These research questions can guide descriptive research designs. Research questions focus the research on specific variables, allowing for a more structured approach capable of producing managerially actionable results. For example, descriptive research might profile a market segment both demographically and psychographically. Results like this can greatly assist firms in taking action by deciding when and where to offer their service for sale.

Researchers who employ causal designs focus very specifically on a small number of research hypotheses. Experimental methods require tight control of research procedures. Thus, causal research is highly structured to produce specific results. Causal research results are often managerially actionable because they suggest that if management changes the value of a "cause," some desirable effect will come about. So, by changing a package's color (i.e., the cause, from orange to blue), higher sales occur. The increased control associated with experiments reduces uncertainty in testing hypotheses.

EXHIBIT **3.4** Characteristics of Different Types of Marketing Research

	Exploratory Research	Descriptive Research	Causal Research
Amount of Uncertainty Characterizing Decision Situation	Highly ambiguous	Partially defined	Clearly defined
Key Research Statement	Research question	Research question	Research hypothesis
When Conducted?	Early stage of decision making	Later stages of decision making	Later stages of decision making
Usual Research Approach	Unstructured	Structured	Highly structured
Examples	"Our sales are declining for no apparent reason" "What kinds of new products are fast-food customers interested in?"	"What kind of people patronize our stores compared to our primary competitor?" "What product features are most important to our customers?"	"Will consumers buy more products in a blue package?" "Which of two advertising campaigns will be more effective?"
Nature of Results	Discovery oriented, productive, but still speculative. Often in need of further research.	Can be confirmatory although more research is sometimes still needed. Results can be managerially actionable.	Confirmatory oriented. Fairly conclusive with managerially actionable results often obtained.

Stages in the Research Process

Marketing research, like other forms of scientific inquiry, involves a sequence of highly interrelated activities. The stages of the research process overlap and not every research project follows exactly through each stage. These particular stages are relevant when the researcher realizes that data collection of some type is necessary. In those instances, marketing research generally follows a pattern represented by these stages:

1. Defining research objectives
2. Planning a research design
3. Planning a sample
4. Collecting data
5. Analyzing data
6. Formulating conclusions and preparing a report

Exhibit 3.5 portrays these six stages as a cyclical or circular-flow process. The circular-flow concept illustrates how one research project can generate new ideas and knowledge that lead to further investigation. Thus, the conclusions and reporting stage connects with the defining the research objectives stage with a dotted line. Notice also, that management is in the center of the process. The researcher cannot properly define research objectives without managerial input. After all, management must ultimately make a decision. Management also may ask for additional research once a report is given. This same general research process applies in basic marketing research and applied market research, whether for profit or nonprofit organizations.[12]

Alternatives in the Research Process

The researcher must choose among a number of alternatives during each stage of the research process. Like choosing a route on a map, no single path fits all journeys. The map analogy is useful because the marketing researcher faces multiple alternatives at each stage. When there are severe time constraints, these constraints override validity, resulting in choosing the fastest alternative. When money and human resources are more plentiful, the appropriate path differs and likely emphasizes validity over speed. Exhibit 3.6 shows the decisions that researchers must make in each stage.

Libraries contain a wealth of information. Studies forming a literature review can be found in the library.

© Andrey_Popov/Shutterstock.com

EXHIBIT **3.5**
Stages of the Research
Process

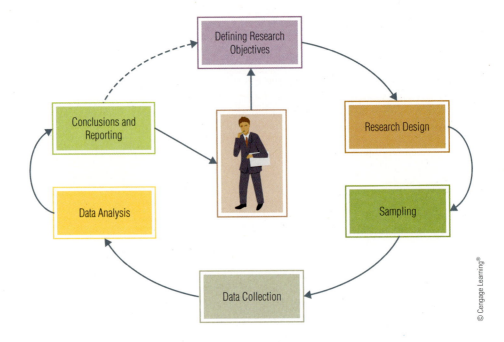

© Cengage Learning®

Defining the Research Objectives

Research objectives

The goals to be achieved by conducting research.

Deliverables

The term used often in consulting to describe research objectives to a research client.

Exhibit 3.6 shows how the research process begins with defining research objectives. **Research objectives** are the goals that researchers intend to achieve through this particular effort. In consulting, researchers use the term **deliverables** to describe the objectives to a research client. The genesis of the research objectives lies in the type of decision situation faced. The objectives may involve exploring a new market's reaction to a new product offering. Alternatively, they may involve testing the effect of a policy change like self-service checkout on perceived service quality. A deliverable may be to quantify any change in service quality in the latter instance. Different types of objectives lead to different types of research designs.

In applied or market research, the researcher cannot list objectives until there is an understanding of the decision situation. The lead researcher and the chief decision-maker must share this understanding for effective research. We often describe this understanding as a *problem statement*. In general usage, the word *problem* suggests that something has gone wrong. This isn't always the case. Actually, the research objective may be to simply clarify a situation, define an opportunity, or monitor and evaluate current operations. Research objectives cannot be developed until managers and researchers have agreed on the actual business "problem" that will be addressed by the research. Thus, they set out to "discover" this problem through a series of interviews and through a document called a *research proposal*.

Managers and researchers alike may not have a clear-cut understanding of the situation at the outset of the research process. Managers may only be able to list symptoms that could indicate a problem. Sales may be declining, but management may not know the exact nature of the problem. Thus, the researcher in this case may only be able to state a research objective in general terms:

"Identify factors contributing to reduced sales."

The researcher needs this preliminary research to discover things that he/she should research more specifically.

Defining the Managerial Decision Situation

In marketing research, the adage "a problem well defined is a problem half solved" is worth remembering. This adage emphasizes that an orderly definition of the research problem lends a sense of direction to the investigation. Careful attention to problem definition allows the researcher to set the proper research objectives. If the purpose of the research is clear, the chances of collecting necessary and relevant information and not collecting surplus information will be much greater.

Albert Einstein noted that "the formulation of a problem is often more essential than its solution."[13] This is good advice for marketing managers but it is difficult to put into practice.

EXHIBIT **3.6** Flowchart of the Marketing Research Process

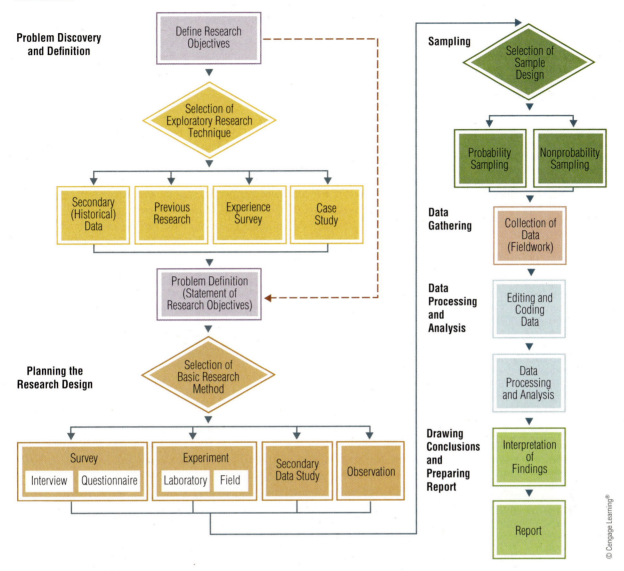

Managers naturally concentrate on finding the right answer instead of asking the right question. They also want one solution quickly rather than having to spend time considering many possible solutions. Further, properly defining a problem often proves more difficult than solving a problem. As a result of the natural tendency to be done with issues, researchers sometimes end up collecting data before carefully thinking out the nature of the marketing problem. When this occurs, the data often do not lead to relevant results.

Marketing research must have clear objectives and definite designs. Unfortunately, little or no planning goes into the formulation of many research problems. Consider the slumping sales of Coca-Cola recently. If Coke sales are down, it's easy to conclude that some problem with the product must exist. Just as in the 1980s, Coke management may consider asking researchers to study the taste of the beverage in an effort to gain competitive positioning against Pepsi, its biggest rival. Right? Is Pepsi Coca-Cola's biggest rival and therefore a source of its problems? Well, Coca-Cola management, as happens so often, may make some false assumptions that would lead them to ignore relevant issues. A scan of consumer trends and perhaps a little exploratory research may lead Coke to some other possible reasons for slumping sales. For instance, consumers are drinking fewer traditional soft drinks overall in favor of alternative drinks like Monster energy drinks or flavored teas. In addition, Coke's preliminary research identified cold weather as an uncontrollable "problem" contributing to consumers desiring Coke less than in the past.[14] Focusing on trying to improve relative to Pepsi is likely inappropriate on closer inspection.

The summary of the managerial decision situation, the research objectives and/or deliverables, and a basic description of the research process represent key elements of a research proposal. Put simply, a **research proposal** is a written statement of the research design emphasizing what the research will accomplish. A research proposal helps get management and the research team on the same page before a major research project begins.

Exploratory Research

Researchers use exploratory research to help discover and define the decisions themselves. Exploratory research progressively narrows the scope of research and helps transform ambiguous problem situations into a more focused project with specific research objectives. Exploration could involve interviews with experts, observation of consumers actually engaged with the product, or analysis of online content describing the product. Exploratory efforts help refine the decision statements and research questions and focus the overall project more toward relevant issues. Exhibit 3.5 indicates that researchers must decide whether to use one or more exploratory research techniques or bypass this stage altogether.

The marketing researcher can employ techniques from four basic categories to obtain insights and gain a clearer idea of the problem: previous research, pilot studies, case studies, and experience surveys. This section will briefly discuss previous research and pilot studies interviews, the most popular type of pilot study.

Previous Research

As a rule, researchers should first investigate previous research to see whether others may have addressed the same research problems previously. Researchers should search previous research reports within the company's archives. In addition, some firms specialize in providing various types of research reports, such as economic forecasts. The Survey of Current Business provides an example of previous research conducted by an outside source.[15]

Literature Review

Previous research may also exist in the public domain. A **literature review** is a directed search of published works, including periodicals, books, as well as publicly available government, industry, or company reports. The reports may discuss theory and/or present empirical results relevant to the research objectives. A literature survey is common in applied market research studies but it is a fundamental requirement of a basic (i.e., marketing) research report. Online searches using common library search tools or Internet search engines often yield many reports on a given subject. A major challenge for the researcher is to sort out the most relevant from among these. Search engines generally sort hits by either relevance or date. Relevance in this case is a function of keyword matches and can be misleading. A perusal of the abstracts of each article may prove more useful in spotting relevance.

Suppose a real estate developer is interested in developing a piece of commercial property. In particular, she has identified this property as a location for a lifestyle center containing places for people to shop, be entertained, dine, work and live—all in one location. Success will depend on attracting people to this place and creating the right feel. The decision to move forward with the project involves many dimensions, including the location, tenant mix, and the physical design or atmosphere of the place, which is affected by things like color, scents, and architecture. Obviously, prudence calls for more than a cursory study of the feasibility of this project and the implications for different types of designs. Before launching an exhaustive study, the researcher can first look through research journals and find hundreds of studies that address the different decision dimensions.[16] The review may give some idea on what type of architecture will work best to create the right atmosphere and enable the research to focus on a smaller set of possibilities.

Pilot Studies

Almost all consumers take a test drive before buying a car. A **pilot study** serves a similar purpose for the researcher. A pilot study is a small-scale research project that collects data from respondents like they are planned in the full study as sort of a dry run. Pilot studies are critical in refining measures and reducing the risk that the full study design contains a fatal flaw that will render its results useless. This is particularly true for experimental research, which depends critically on valid manipulations of experimental variables.[17] Pilot studies also often are useful in fine-tuning research objectives. Researchers sometimes refer to a pilot study as a *pretest*. A **pretest** is a very descriptive

Research proposal
A written statement of the research design emphasizing what the research will accomplish.

Literature review
A directed search of published works, including periodicals and books that discusses theory and presents empirical results that are relevant to the topic at hand.

Pilot study
A small-scale research project that collects data from respondents similar to those to be used in the full study.

Pretest
A small-scale study in which the results are only preliminary and intended only to assist in design of a subsequent study.

© Konstantin L/Shutterstock.com

Previous research results, published literature and pilot studies all may come together to help form a theory of what design would be most successful.

term indicating a small–scale study in which the results are only preliminary and intended only to assist in design of a subsequent study.

A pilot study sometimes includes a focus group interview. A **focus group** interview brings together six to twelve people in a loosely structured format. The technique assumes that individuals are more willing to talk about things when they are able to do so within a group discussion format. Focus group respondents sometimes feed on each other's comments to develop ideas that would be difficult to express in a different interview format. We discuss focus groups in much more detail in Chapter 5.

Imagine how important a pilot test is for a toy company. A pilot study likely would involve children actually interacting with new toy concepts in an effort to understand issues related to product longevity, durability, and safety, among other things. A separate pilot study may involve parents and explore how they select toys for their children and what price points might be appropriate for the toy. In some cases, toy designers end up being very surprised how children actually play with toys during pilot tests.

Exploratory research need not always follow a structured design. Because the purpose of exploratory research is to gain insights and discover new ideas, researchers may use considerable creativity and flexibility. Some companies perform exploratory research routinely as part of environmental scanning. If the conclusions made during this stage suggest marketing opportunities, the researcher is in a position to begin planning a formal, quantitative research project.

Focus group

A small group discussion about some research topic led by a moderator who guides discussion among the participants.

Stating Research Objectives

After identifying and clarifying the problem, with or without exploratory research, the researcher must formally state the research objectives. This statement delineates the type of research needed and what intelligence may result that would allow the decision-maker to make choices that are more informed. The statement of research objectives culminates the process of clarifying the managerial decision into something actionable.

A written decision statement expresses the business situation to the researcher. The research objectives try to address directly the decision statement or statements. As such, the research objectives represent a contract of sorts that commits the researcher to producing the needed research. This is why market researchers express these as deliverables in applied market research. Research objectives drive the rest of the research process. Indeed, before proceeding, the researcher and managers must agree that the objectives are appropriate and will produce relevant information.

What Is a Theory?

Ultimately, theory plays a role in determining the appropriate research objectives. A **theory** is a formal, logical explanation of some event(s) that includes descriptions of how things relate to one

Theory

A formal, logical explanation of some event(s) that includes predictions of how things relate to one another.

another. Researchers build theory through a process of reviewing previous findings of similar studies, simple logical deduction, and knowledge of applicable theoretical areas. For example, if a Web designer is trying to decide what color the background of the page should be, the researcher may first consult previous studies examining the effects of color on things like package design and retail store design. He or she may also find theories that deal with the wavelength of different colors or theories that explain retail atmospherics. This may lead to specific predictions that predict blue as a good background color.[18]

Although some may see theory as only relevant to academic or basic marketing research, theory plays a role in understanding practical market research as well. Before setting research objectives, the researcher must be able to describe the business situation in some coherent way. Without this type of explanation, the researcher would have little idea of where to start. Ultimately, the logical explanation helps the researcher know what variables need to be included in the study and how they may relate to one another. Businesspeople in all sorts of industries rely on theories for clues in how to deal with changes in business situations. The tourism industry relies on theories from many areas including consumer behavior, economics, marketing, and geography.[19] The "Winning Theory" Research Snapshot illustrates how theory and practice come together for improved marketing decisions.

What Is a Hypothesis?

Hypothesis

A formal statement, derived from theory, explaining some specific outcome.

A **hypothesis** is a formal statement explaining some specific outcome. The researcher derives hypotheses (pl.) from theory to point out what things the research will test. In other words, when one states a hypothesis, one makes a proposition. In its simplest form, a hypothesis is a scientific guess. Using our opening vignette as an example, the researcher may use theoretical reasoning to develop the following hypothesis:

> *H1: The more hours per week a prospective MBA student works, the more favorable his/her attitude toward online MBA class offerings.*

Empirical testing

Means that some prediction has been examined against reality using data.

We often apply statistics to data to test hypotheses empirically. **Empirical testing** involves comparing a hypothetical proposition, such as a hypothesis, against reality using data. When the data are consistent with a hypothesis, we say, "The hypothesis is *supported*." When the data are inconsistent with a hypothesis, we say, "The hypothesis is *not supported*." We are often tempted to say that we prove a hypothesis when the data conform to the prediction; this isn't really true. Statistical results cannot prove anything because there is always the possibility that our conclusion is wrong. Now, at times we can be very, very confident in our conclusion, but from an absolute perspective, statistics cannot prove a hypothesis is true. Research reduces but does not eliminate uncertainty.

Exhibit 3.7 illustrates the connections between decision statements, research objectives, and research hypotheses. Although the first two objectives each have one hypothesis, notice that the third has two. In reality, most research projects will involve more than one research objective, and

---

EXHIBIT 3.7 Examples of Decision Statements, Research Objectives, and Research Hypotheses

Decision Statement	Relevant Theory	Research Objective	Hypothesis
Should we allocate more resources toward social networking or television advertising?	Source credibility	Identify relative attitude change associated with message communicated through each medium.	A respondent's attitude will become more positive when exposed to a brand communication through a social network posting than through a television advertisement.
In what ways can we improve our service quality?	Atmospherics (stimulus – organism – response)	Determine how much the physical environment influences consumer perceptions of service quality.	The positive emotions that consumers report in response to the environment are related positively to service quality perceptions.
How much price promotion should be used in marketing brand X?	Brand equity/consumer naïve theories	Determine the effects of price reductions on sales and brand image.	The more a respondent is exposed to price promotions for brand X, the lower the perceived quality of brand X products.

A Winning Theory?

Once customers stop repeating behavior, managers are going to want to know why. This thinking will likely involve some theories. The gaming industry in the United States was a growing industry for many years, particularly since several states loosened laws limiting the ways people can gamble. One of the most basic theories that applies to consumption involves the generalization that as things become less scarce, they become less desirable. Not so long ago, legalized gaming scarcely existed in the United States outside of Nevada. In the 1990s, a small number of states loosened up laws and became tourist destinations for American gamblers. Mississippi became the biggest gambling destination outside of Las Vegas and Atlantic City. As economies worsened, more and more states are relaxing laws on gaming hoping to make up for tax revenues formerly generated by other types of commerce. Today more than forty states are home to casinos in one form or another.

With gaming in so many places, individual casinos struggle. Gaming companies have closed huge casinos in destinations known for gaming including Atlantic City, New Jersey, and Tunica, Mississippi (MS). Mississippi gaming revenue is about half of what it was in the mid-2000s. Not only that, casino patrons are letting go of the slot machines. Someone doesn't even have to leave home to play slots as online gaming can be done from any online device. Based on the idea that scarcity does lower desirability, casinos are launching research to find ways to provide entertainment alternatives that are not so easily copied. For instance, research suggests a growing trend toward table games and away from slot machines. Research likewise suggests that casino customers express a greater willingness to spend money on unique shows and fine dining. Casinos with unique experiences build an immunity to the proliferation of typical gaming houses filled with video machines. Research is playing a role in building a winning theory!

Sources: *Bloomberg Businessweek* (2014), "Casinos Know When to Fold' Em," (April 7–13), 25–26.
Stutz, H. (2014), "Analysts Shrug Off Decline in January Gaming Revenue," (February 28), *Las Vegas Review Journal*, http://www.reviewjournal.com/business/analysts-shrug-decline-january-gaming-revenue, accessed April 5, 2014.

each of these may often involve more than one hypothesis. Think about how you might go about trying to test the hypotheses listed in Exhibit 3.7.

Planning the Research Design

After the researcher has formulated the research problem, he or she must choose the research design. A **research design** is like a recipe that specifies the methods and procedures for collecting and analyzing the needed information. Each design type, exploratory, descriptive, and causal, provides a unique set of options in implementing the design. A research design provides a framework or plan of action for the research. The researcher also must determine the sources of information, the design technique (survey or experiment, for example), the sampling methodology, and the schedule and cost of the research.

Research design

The methods and procedures for collecting and analyzing the needed information for a given type of research.

Selection of the Basic Research Method

Here again, the researcher must make a decision. Exhibit 3.6 shows four approaches for implementing descriptive or causal research: surveys, experiments, secondary data, and observation. The objectives of the study, the available data sources, the urgency of the decision, and the cost of obtaining the data influence technique selection. Later, we describe how experiments typically are exclusive to causal designs.

The most common method of generating primary data is the survey. Most people have seen the results of political surveys by Gallup or Harris Online, and some have been respondents (members of a sample who supply answers) to marketing research questionnaires. A **survey** is a research technique involving interviews of sample units in some form or recorded observations of some behavior. The term *surveyor* is most often reserved for civil engineers who describe a piece of property using a transit. Similarly, marketing researchers describe some market segment using a questionnaire. The task of writing a list of questions and designing the format of the printed or written questionnaire is an essential aspect of the development of a survey research design.

Research investigators may choose to contact respondents by phone (home or mobile), mail (snail or e), via website invitations, social network pages, sometimes text messages, or even in person. An advertiser spending $4 million or more for 30 seconds of commercial time during the Super Bowl reaches out through multiple media vehicles for feedback on its efforts. Some agencies even release Super Bowl ads on the Internet prior to the big game to monitor the number of views and comments the ads might generate. In 2014, Anheuser Busch released its "Puppy Love" ad, with its theme of familial attachment between a puppy and the famous Clydesdales, and went viral before Super Bowl Sunday. In addition, the ad agency will do telephone, text and Internet surveys beginning immediately after the game. Each of these survey methods has advantages and disadvantages. A researcher's task is to find the most appropriate way to collect the needed information.

The objective of many research projects, particularly descriptive research, is to record things that can be observed—for example, the number of automobiles that pass by a proposed site for a gas station, the amount of time somebody spends viewing a web page, or the way people walk through a store. The main advantage of observational techniques is recording data about consumer behavior without relying on self-reports. Researchers collect observations unobtrusively and passively, meaning without a respondent's direct participation.

Automatic devices are often best to *observe* this type of data. For instance, Nielsen Company created the "People Meter," which they attached to television sets to record the programs watched by each household member. Today, Nielsen automatically collects not only real-time viewing but also shows viewed at another time based on DVR recording activity. Automatic observation eliminates the possible bias of respondents stating that they watched the president's State of the Union address rather than *Duck Dynasty*. Today, Nielsen and competitors are developing ways to automatically observe viewing from Netflix and other nontraditional entertainment channels of distribution.

Observation is more complex than mere "nose counting," and the task is more difficult than the inexperienced researcher would imagine. Observation cannot capture all kinds of data. Researchers are often interested in things such as attitudes, opinions, motivations, and other intangible states of mind that they cannot directly observe. Survey data often can help provide additional information and complement intelligence derived from observation. Nielsen, for instance, uses the observational data from the People Meter together with survey data about viewing behavior to determine the ratings that networks use to decide which shows get canceled.

Research companies also hire people to record "observations" of behavior. Research personnel known as **mystery shoppers** act like customers while observing and recording data. Companies pay mystery shoppers to gather data about the way employees treat consumers, the cleanliness of the environment, price points, and other important marketing information. This data addresses questions like: How often are store policies followed? How often are customers treated courteously? Are employees prone to do unethical things? Mystery shoppers sometimes intentionally try to do something that would otherwise be unethical to see how an employee might respond. Even not-for-profit organizations use the mystery shopper approach as a way of trying to find out what is really happening during business hours.

The "Best" Research Approach

No single best research design fits all situations. Researchers often have several alternatives that can achieve a stated research objective. Consider a researcher who must forecast product sales for the upcoming year. Some commonly used forecasting methods are surveying executive opinion, collecting sales force composite opinions, surveying user expectations, projecting trends, and analyzing market factors. Any one of these may yield a reliable forecast.

The ability to select the most appropriate way to implement a research project develops with experience. Inexperienced researchers often jump to the conclusion that a survey methodology is usually the best design because they are most comfortable with this method. Chicago's Museum of Science and Industry wanted to determine the relative popularity of each exhibit. Museum considered a survey approach. Instead, a creative researcher suggested a far less expensive alternative: an unobtrusive observation technique. The researcher suggested that the museum merely keep track of the frequency with which the floor tiles in front of the various exhibits needed replacing, indicating where the heaviest traffic occurred. The tile observation method showed that the chick-hatching exhibit was the most popular. This method provided the same results as a survey and at a much lower cost.

Planning a Sample

If you take your first bite of a steak and conclude that the entire steak is cooked to the desired degree of wellness (rare, medium rare, etc.), you have just conducted a sample. **Sampling** involves any procedure that draws conclusions based on measurements of a portion of the entire population. In other words, a sample is a subset from a larger population. In the steak analogy, the first bite is the sample and the entire steak is the population. If certain statistical procedures are followed, a researcher need not select every item in a population because the results of a good sample should have the same characteristics as the population as a whole. Of course, when samples are erroneous, they do not give reliable estimates of the population. So, should the first bite come from the edge or the center of a steak?

A famous example of error due to sampling is the 1936 *Literary Digest* fiasco. The magazine conducted a survey and predicted that Alf Landon would win over Franklin D. Roosevelt by a landslide in that year's presidential election. This prediction was wrong and Roosevelt won the election. Poor sample selection led to this error. The postmortems showed that *Literary Digest* had sampled its readers as well as telephone subscribers. As has happened since 1936, the sample did not predict the outcome of the election because these people did not represent well the population of actual voters.

Sampling begins with the question, "Who is to be sampled?" The answer to this primary question requires the identification of a target population. Defining this population and determining the sampling units may not be so easy. If, for example, pinterest.com surveys Pinterest users to determine its brand image, the answer may be in error because potential Pinterest users are not included in the sample. Specifying the target population is a crucial aspect of the sampling plan.

The next sampling issue concerns sample size. How big should the sample be? Although management may wish to examine every potential buyer of a product or service, doing so may be unnecessary as well as unrealistic. Typically, larger samples are more precise than smaller ones, but proper probability sampling can allow a small proportion of the total population to give a reliable measure of the whole. A later discussion will explain how large a sample must be to be truly representative of the universe or population.

The final sampling decision is how to select the sampling units. Simple random sampling may be the best-known type. In simple random sampling, every unit in the population has an equal and known chance of selection. However, this is only one type of sampling. For example, a cluster-sampling procedure may reduce costs and make data-gathering procedures more efficient. If members of the population are found in close geographical clusters, a sampling procedure that selects area clusters rather than individual units in the population will reduce costs. Rather than selecting 1,000 individuals throughout the United States, it may be more economical to first select twenty five counties and then sample within those counties. This will substantially reduce travel, hiring, and training costs. In determining the appropriate sampling plan, the researcher will have to select the most appropriate sampling procedure for meeting the established study objectives.

Collecting Data

The data-collection stage begins once the researcher has formalized the sampling plan. Data gathering is the process of gathering or collecting information. Human observers or interviewers may gather data, or machines like scanners or online stat counters may record data automatically.

Obviously, the many research techniques involve many methods of gathering data. Surveys require direct participation by research respondents. This may involve filling out a questionnaire or interacting with an interviewer. In this sense, they are obtrusive. **Unobtrusive methods** of data gathering are those in which the subjects do not have to be disturbed for data to be collected. They may even be unaware that research is going on at all. For instance, a simple count of motorists driving past a proposed franchising location is one kind of data gathering method. No matter how data are collected, it is important to minimize errors in the process. For example, the data gathering should be consistent in all geographical areas. If an interviewer phrases questions incorrectly or records a respondent's statements inaccurately (not verbatim), major data collection errors will result.

Editing and Coding

After a research team completes the fieldwork, someone must convert the data into a format that will answer the marketing manager's questions. This is part of the data processing and analysis stage. Here, the information content is mined from the raw data. Data processing generally begins with editing and coding the data. Editing involves checking the data collection forms for omissions, legibility, and consistency in classification. The editing process corrects problems such as interviewer errors (an answer recorded on the wrong portion of a questionnaire, for example) before the data are analyzed.

Data have to be coded to become useful. Computer-assisted data collection tools provide data downloads in multiple formats such as Excel and Statistical Package for Social Sciences (SPSS), among others. Thus, much of the coding is automatic. When a respondent enters his/her age as 44 years when asked to enter his/her age, that 44 is entered directly into the file with practically the only possibility of error being something caused by the respondent (such as hitting the wrong keys or a dishonest response). However, researchers usually need to perform some additional coding. For instance, items requiring simple open-ended responses require coding in some type of categorical or numeric form.

Analyzing Data

Data analysis

The application of computation, summarizing, and reasoning to understand the gathered information.

Data analysis is the application of computation, summarizing, and reasoning to understand the gathered information. In its simplest form, analysis may involve determining consistent patterns and summarizing the relevant details revealed in the investigation. The nature of the data, the research design, and management's requirements help determine what type of data analysis is most appropriate. Statistical analyses may range from portraying a simple frequency distribution to more complex multivariate analyses approaches. Later chapters will discuss three general categories of statistical analysis: univariate analysis, bivariate analysis, and multivariate analysis.

Drawing Conclusions

The research ends by drawing conclusions from the data analysis. These conclusions speak directly to the research questions developed in the early phases of the project and should fulfill the deliverables promised in the research proposal. Conclusions are what managers and other users of the research are interested in. As a result, the researcher highlights the main conclusions in both a written report and in any oral or electronic presentations resulting from the project.

Researchers prepare a formal report describing these conclusions and the research that leads to them. All too often, research reports are written without due consideration to the sophistication of the client. The researcher should write reports in as simple a manner as possible while still conveying the research adequately. Decision-makers end up ignoring overly complex sounding research reports. We return to this topic in detail Chapter 16 because the importance of effective communication cannot be overstated.

The Research Program Strategy

Research project

A single study addressing one or a small number of research objectives.

Our discussion of the marketing research process began with the assumption that the researcher wished to collect data to achieve a specific marketing objective. When the researcher has only one or a small number of research objectives that can be addressed in a single study, that study is referred to as a **research project**. We emphasize the researcher's need to select specific techniques for solving one-dimensional problems, such as identifying market segments, selecting the best packaging design, or test-marketing a new product.

However, if you think about a firm's marketing mix activity in a given period of time (such as a year), you'll realize that marketing research is not a one-shot activity—it is a continuous process. An exploratory research study may require follow-up in the form of a survey, or a researcher may conduct a specific research project for each aspect of the marketing mix. If a new product is being developed, the different types of research might include market potential studies to identify the size and characteristics of the market; product usage testing to record consumers' reactions to prototype products; brand name and packaging research to determine the product's symbolic connotations; and test-marketing the new product. Thus, when numerous related studies come together to address issues about a single company or phenomenon captured by multiple related research questions, we refer to this as a **research program**. Because research is a continuous process, management should view marketing research at a strategic planning level. The program strategy refers to a firm's overall plan to use marketing research. It is a planning activity that places a series of marketing research projects in the context of the company's marketing plan.

Now that we have outlined the research process, note that the order of topics in this book follows the flowchart of the research process presented in Exhibit 3.4. Keep this flowchart in mind while reading later chapters.

Research program

Numerous research studies that come together to address multiple, related research questions.

TIPS OF THE TRADE

- Diagnostic analysis can help distinguish symptoms from problems.
- Use exploratory research tools in the interviews with managers to help establish research objectives.
- Ambiguous decision-making situations, particularly in opportunity seeking, usually call for exploratory research. With more certainty, very specific research questions will often call for a causal design. For example:
  - In what ways can Digitex leverage its brand name into new industries? Because this is a broad and relatively vague question, discovery-oriented exploratory research addressing the way consumers view Digitex is probably needed.
  - The use of an animated character in a pop-up help window will lead consumers to be more satisfied with the information they receive from the www. edmunds.com website than will the use of a video-taped person. This hypothesis is very specific and suggests a causal research design.
- Don't overlook the first stage of the research process—defining research objectives.
- The deliverables can be the most important part of a research proposal.
  - Good deliverable: Provide a measure of consumer shopping value perceptions for Anthropologie consumers (both store and online shoppers) and a major competitor, Michael Kors.
  - Poor deliverable: Increase profitability at Anthropologie by luring customers from Michael Kors.

:: SUMMARY

1. Apply marketing research in making better marketing decisions. Decision-making means that businesses choose between numerous alternative courses of action. Each course of action likely leads to a different outcome. Marketing research can help identify symptoms from problems, help identify reasonable objectives, and by providing an idea of what outcome will follow from different alternative courses of action, help managers make better decisions in response to both opportunities and problems.

2. Classify marketing research as either exploratory research, descriptive research, or causal research. Marketing research can be described as exploratory, descriptive or causal. Each type of research leads to a different research design. The clarity with which the team defines a decision situation determines whether exploratory, descriptive, or causal research is most appropriate. When the decision is very ambiguous, or the interest is on discovering ideas, exploratory research is most appropriate. Descriptive research attempts to paint a picture of the given situation by describing characteristics of objects, people, or organizations. Causal research identifies cause-and-effect relationships. Three types of evidence are needed to establish causality:

a) Temporal Sequentiality
b) Concomitant Variation
c) Nonspurious Association

3. List the major stages of the marketing research process and the steps within each. The six major stages of the research process are (1) defining research objectives, (2) planning the research design, (3) planning a sample, (4) collecting data, (5) analyzing data, and (6) drawing conclusions. Each stage involves a subsequent set of steps.

4. Understand the concepts of theory and hypothesis and the critical role they play in research. Theory offers a potential logical explanation for events in a given decision situation. Theory requires testing to know how true the explanations might be. Hypotheses are formal statements explaining some specific outcome in a way that is amenable to testing. Theory and hypotheses not only provide an idea of what might be expected in a given situation, but they guide the implementation of research by suggesting what things need to be measured.

5. Know the difference between a research project and a research program. A *research project* addresses one of a small number of research objectives that can be included in a single study. In contrast, a *research program* represents a series of studies addressing multiple research objectives. Many marketing activities require an ongoing research task of some type.

:: KEY TERMS AND CONCEPTS

absolute causality, *58*
causal inference, *57*
causal research, *57*
concomitant variation, *57*
conditional causality, *59*
contributory causality, *59*
data analysis, *70*
decision making, *50*
deliverables, *62*
descriptive research, *54*
diagnostic analysis, *56*
empirical testing, *66*

experiment, *59*
experimental variable, *59*
exploratory research, *54*
focus group, *65*
hypothesis, *66*
literature review, *64*
market opportunity, *51*
market problem, *51*
manipulation, *59*
mystery shoppers, *68*
nonspurious association, *58*
pilot study, *64*

pretest, *64*
research design, *67*
research objectives, *62*
research program, *71*
research project, *70*
research proposal, *64*
sampling, *69*
survey, *68*
symptoms, *51*
temporal sequence, *57*
theory, *65*
unobtrusive methods, *69*

:: QUESTIONS FOR REVIEW AND CRITICAL THINKING

1. List five ways that marketing research can contribute to effective business decision making.
2. Define *market opportunities, market problems,* and *market symptoms.* Give an example of each as it applies to a social networking company.

3. Consider the following list, and indicate and explain whether each best fits the definition of a problem, opportunity, or symptom:
   a. A 12.5 percent decrease in store traffic for a children's shoe store in a medium-sized city mall.

b. The number of recent graduates joining the business school alumni club has dropped 50 percent from 8 years ago.

c. A furniture manufacturer and retailer in North Carolina reads a research report indicating consumer trends toward Australian Jara and Kari wood. The export of these products is very limited and very expensive.

d. The number of cigarette smokers in sub-Saharan Africa is expected to increase dramatically over the next decade.

e. A local fine-dining establishment cannot find enough applicants with sufficient skills to learn how to deliver the quality of service its customers expect.

f. Next winter is expected to bring record-setting cold to most of the United States.

4. What are the three types of marketing research? Indicate which type each item in the list below illustrates. Explain your answers.

a. Establishing the relationship between advertising and sales in the beer industry

b. Identifying target market demographics for a shopping center located in Omaha, Nebraska

c. Estimating the 5-year sales potential for MRI machines in the Ark-La-Tex (Arkansas, Louisiana, and Texas) region of the United States

d. Testing the effect of the inside temperature of a clothing store on sales of outerwear

e. Explain how making grocery orders available for online ordering and drive-through pickup would enhance business performance for Publix supermarkets

5. What is a diagnostic analysis?

6. Describe the type of research evidence that allows one to infer causality.

7. What is an experimental manipulation?

8. Describe how a literature search is useful in marketing research.

9. Do the stages in the research process seem to follow the scientific method?

10. Why is the "define research objectives" of the research process probably the most important stage?

11. Suppose Auchan (http://www.auchan.fr), a hypermarket chain based out of France, was considering opening three hypermarkets in the midwestern United States. What role would theory play in designing a research study to track how the shopping habits of consumers from the United States differ from those in France and from those in Japan? What kind of hypothesis might be examined in a study of this topic?

12. Referring to the question immediately above, what type of research design do you believe would be most useful to provide useful input to the Auchan decision-makers? What deliverable might go along with the research?

13. Describe ways that observation is used to create data for marketing research.

14. What type of research design would you recommend in the situations below? For each applied market research project, what might be an example of a "deliverable"? Which do you think would involve actually testing a research hypothesis?

a. The manufacturer and marketer of flight simulators and other pilot training equipment wishes to forecast sales volume for the next five years.

b. A local chapter of the American Lung Association wishes to identify the demographic characteristics of individuals who donate more than $500 per year.

c. A major music producer wonders how buzz initiated through Facebook might affect the online revenue for new artists.

d. A food company researcher wishes to know what types of food are carried in brown-bag lunches to learn if the company can capitalize on this phenomenon.

e. A researcher wishes to explore the feasibility of a casino in a community where gaming had previously been banned.

f. A political campaign wants to know what resources would be required to make unflattering videos of political opponents go viral on the web.

15. What is the difference between a research project and a research program? Talk to a graduate student or faculty member about a thesis or dissertation involving business research. Describe whether it best represents a research project or research program.

:: RESEARCH ACTIVITIES

1. Look up information about the online MBA programs at the University of Phoenix (http://business.phoenix.edu/business/graduate.aspx). Compare it to the traditional MBA program at your university. Suppose each was looking to expand the numbers of students in their programs. How might the research design differ for each?

2. Visit the Gallup Organization's home page (http://www.gallup.com). The Gallup home page changes regularly. However, it should provide an opportunity to read the results of a recent poll. For example, one poll showed Americans' level of concern or lack of concern with global warming. Summarize your opinion of the poll. Do you believe it is accurate? What companies or organizations might benefit from this data? Gallup provides a basic description of the way it conducts polls on the web site. Take a look at the information available. List the various stages of the research process and how they were (or were not) followed in Gallup's project.

3. Any significant business decision requires input from a research project. Write a brief essay (about 450 words) either defending this statement or refuting it.

4. What is a People Meter? Describe how it works and what data it provides. Suppose you were asked by a supervisor to prepare a blog entry describing your opinion of its validity. What would be your position and how would you defend it?

A New "Joe" on the Block

Case 3.1

Joe Brown is ready to start a new career. After spending 30 years as a market researcher and inspired by the success of Starbucks, he is ready to enter the coffee shop business. However, before opening his first shop, he realizes that a great deal of research is needed. He has some key questions in mind.

- What markets in the United States hold the most promise for a new coffee shop?
- What type of location is best for a coffee shop?
- What is it that makes a coffee shop popular?
- What coffee do Americans prefer?
- How would consumers respond to coffee delivery?

A Google search reveals more previous research on coffee, markets, and related materials than he ever expected. Many studies address taste. For example, he finds several studies that in one way or another compare the taste of different coffee shop coffees. Most commonly, they compare the taste of coffee from Starbucks against coffee from McDonald's, Dunkin' Donuts, Burger King, and sometimes a local competitor. However, it becomes difficult to draw a conclusion as the results seem to be inconsistent.

- One study had a headline that poked fun at Starbucks' high-priced coffee. The author of this study personally purchased coffee at four places, took them to his office, tasted them, made notes, and then drew conclusions. All the coffee was tasted black with no sugar. Just cups of Joe. He reached the conclusion that McDonald's Premium Coffee (at about $1.50 a cup) did not taste quite as good as Starbucks House Blend (at about $1.90 a cup), both of which were much better than either Dunkin' Donuts (at about $1.20) or Burger King (less than $1). This study argued that McDonald's was best, all things considered.
- Another study was written up by a good critic who was simply interested in identifying the best-tasting coffee. Again, he tasted them all black with nothing added. Each cup of coffee was consumed in the urban location near the inner city center where he lived. He reached the conclusion that Starbucks' coffee had the best flavor although it showed room for improvement. McDonald's premium coffee was not as good, but better than the other two. Dunkin' Donuts coffee had reasonably unobjectionable taste but was very weak and watery. The Burger King coffee was simply not very good.
- Yet another study talked about Starbucks becoming a huge company and how it has lost touch with the common coffee shop coffee customer. The researchers stood outside a small organic specialty shop and interviewed 100 consumers as they exited the shop. They asked, "Which coffee do you prefer?" The results showed a preference for a local coffee, tea, and incense shop, and otherwise put Starbucks last behind McDonald's, Burger King, Panera Bread, and Dunkin' Donuts.

PHOTODISC GREEN/GETTY IMAGES

- Still another study compared the coffee-drinking experience. A sample of 50 consumers in St. Louis, Missouri, were interviewed and asked to list the coffee shop they frequented most. Starbucks was listed by more consumers than any other place. A small percentage listed Dunkin' Donuts but none listed McDonald's, despite their efforts at creating a premium coffee experience. The study did not ask consumers to compare the tastes of the coffee across the different places.
- Still another study about Dunkin' Donuts claims that more "hard-working" Americans prefer Dunkin' Donuts coffee to Starbucks.

Joe also wants to find data showing coffee consumption patterns and the number of coffee shops around the United States, so he spends time looking for data on the Internet. His searches don't reveal anything satisfying.

As Joe ponders how to go about starting "A Cup of Joe," he wonders about the relevance of this previous research. Is it useful at all? He even questions whether he is capable of doing any primary research himself and considers hiring someone to do a feasibility study for him. Maybe doing research is easier than using research.

Questions

1. What are the top three key decisions faced by Joe?
2. What are the key deliverables that an outside researcher should produce to help Joe with the key decisions?
3. How relevant are the coffee taste studies cited above? Explain.
4. What flaws in the coffee taste studies should Joe consider in trying to weigh the merits of their results?
5. Try to do a quick search to explore the question: "Are American consumer preferences the same all across the United States?"
6. If a consultant comes in to do the job, what are three key deliverables that would likely be important to Joe in making a decision to launch the Cup of Joe coffee shop?
7. Do you believe there is a way GPS technology such as the iBeacon described in a previous chapter could be an opportunity to sell more Joe? How might that be explored?

Sources: Shiver, J., "Taste Test: The Little Joes Take on Starbucks," *USA Today*, (March 26, 2008), http://www.usatoday.com/money/industries/food/2006-03-26-coffee_x.htm, accessed July 20, 2008; Associated Press, "McDonald's Coffee Beats Starbucks, Says Consumer Reports," *The Seattle Times*, (February 2, 2007), Squidoo (2014), "Starbucks versus Dunkin Donuts Debate: The Coffee Wars," http://jaguarjulie.squidoo.com/starbucksvsdunkindonuts, accessed April 6, 2014.

The Human Side of Marketing Research: Organizational and Ethical Issues

Dimitri Otis/Getty Images

LEARNING OUTCOMES

After studying this chapter, you should be able to:

1. Know when research should be conducted externally and when it should be done internally

2. Understand the career opportunities and career paths available within the marketing research industry

3. Become sensitive to the often conflicting relationship between marketing management and researchers

4. Understand marketing ethics and ways that researchers can face ethical dilemmas

5. Appreciate the rights and obligations of (a) research respondents—particularly children, (b) research clients or sponsors, (c) marketing researchers, and (d) society

6. Avoid situations involving a conflict of interest in performing marketing research

Chapter Vignette:

If It Feels Green Then It Is Green?

Consumers today are concerned about environmental sensitivities and as a result, companies are becoming *greener*. Marketing efforts communicate a company's environmental sensitivity through product packaging, labeling, advertising, and public relations. These efforts are complicated by the fact that knowing what truly is best for the environment is itself a complicated exercise. Do electric cars powered by high-powered batteries containing toxic chemicals really do less harm than would high-efficiency diesel-powered cars with matching power? Consider also that consumers may recharge the electric cars with electricity taken from an oil-burning or coal-burning power plant. These questions are difficult enough for scientists to answer much less for the average consumer. Research suggests that even environmentally "aware consumers" cannot discern the most green product alternative even half of the time and that consumers high in environmental involvement are susceptible to potential green washing.

Put yourself in the place of a young researcher asked to conduct research for a company that markets products from family-owned farms, including one that grows grapes. The family grows grapes the same way they have for almost 200 years. The practices were organic before anybody knew

© nito/Shutterstock.com

what that meant. They ship grapes all over North America and to South Africa. Management asks the researcher for information useful in developing snack packaging that might help tap into consumers' green sensitivities. Management believes that sales will increase by placing the grapes in a green wrapper and putting the word sustainable on the packaging. In fact, management believes this so strongly that they have already invested in equipment and materials to produce the packaging. The researcher plans experiments comparing consumer beliefs about environmental friendliness, attitudes toward the brand, purchase intentions, and perceived tastiness using the green packaging versus using the traditional packaging (no plastic at all with crated grapes selected by the consumer stem by stem). In particular, the researcher examines whether or not consumers perceive this national brand as better than other national brands and the locally grown grapes that it competes with regionally. One thing seems clear, buying green makes consumers feel better and this means another reason why packaging decisions are meaningful to the company.[1]

Introduction

The vignette describes a situation emphasizing marketing research's human side. A company is looking for research to help sell a product, in this case produce. The researcher faces a number of dilemmas. Some of these introduce business ethics into the arena of marketing research. This chapter focuses on marketing research's human side by discussing the people who do, use, and participate in research.

Who Should Do the Research?

The vignette opening this chapter involves a situation in which a company is hiring an outside researcher to conduct a study critical to its marketing strategy. Although this is very typical, many companies have their own employees perform research projects and research programs. Thus, companies sometimes perform in-house research, meaning that employees of the company affected by the research project perform the research. In other cases, companies use an **outside agency** to perform the research, meaning that the company hires an independent, outside firm to perform a research project. In other words, the research is outsourced. Although it would seem that **in-house research** would usually be of higher quality because of the increased knowledge of the researchers conducting the studies, several reasons why employees of the firm may not always be the best people to do the job exist.

Outside agency

An independent research firm contracted by the company that actually will benefit from the research.

In-house research

Research performed by employees of the company that will benefit from the research.

Do It Yourself or Let Your Fingers Do the Walking?

When the firm facing a decision encounters one of the following situations, they should consider having the research performed by an outside agency.

- An outside agency often can provide a fresh perspective. Too much knowledge potentially hinders creativity. When a firm desires new ideas, like those that come from discovery-oriented research, an outsider is not constrained by the groupthink that often affects a company employee. In other words, employees who spend so much time together in their day-to-day work activities begin to act and think alike to a large degree. History reveals many stories of products that remained unsuccessful commercially for years until someone from outside the company discovered a useful application. Most people think of the microwave oven as a marvel of the late twentieth century. A company called Raytheon invented the technology for a microwaves in the 1940s. Raytheon worked on radar systems for the Allied military in World War II. Not until Raytheon acquired an electronics company called Amana in 1965 did anybody realize that microwave technology could be a huge commercial success as a kitchen appliance. Today, a kitchen would be incomplete without a microwave oven.

To the Point

"*To manage a business is to manage its future; and to manage the future is to manage information.*"

—MARION HARPER

By now, you are becoming familiar with the student questionnaire that accompanies this book. Examine the items in the questionnaire and the questionnaire overall for the following issues.

1. Were you required to identify yourself by name in completing the survey?

Please read each of the following statements. After reading each, click on the the circle that best describes how much you agree with each statement.	Strongly Agree	Agree	Neutral	Disagree	Strongly Disagree
I make time to study every day.	○	○	○	○	○
I know the material better after I study.	○	○	○	○	○
I can't study when it's quiet.	○	○	○	○	○
I prefer to not be around others when I study.	○	○	○	○	○
I can study the night before and be ready for a test.	○	○	○	○	○
I like to study with others.	○	○	○	○	○
I arrange time to study with others.	○	○	○	○	○

Source: www.qualtrics.com

2. Can the results (you can access the results through your instructor) be linked to respondents by name?
3. Do any items need to be tied to a name to be useful to the researcher?
4. Are the survey results anonymous? Should they be?

- An outside agency often can be more objective. When a firm is facing a particularly sensitive situation that may even affect a large number of jobs within the company, researchers may have difficulty being objective. Alternatively, if a particular chief executive within the firm is in love with some new idea, researchers may feel a great deal of pressure to present results that are supportive of the concept. In these cases, outside researchers may be a good choice. Outsiders don't have to work for the company and interact with the players involved in the decision on a daily basis. Therefore, they are less concerned about presenting results that may not be truly welcome.

- An outside agency may have special expertise. When a firm needs research requiring a particular expertise that some outside agency specializes in, it may be a good idea to use that firm to conduct the research. For example, if a company is searching for new ideas about how to use its Facebook site, an online focus group interview may be a good idea. Conducting online focus groups may not be a prevalent skill among company employees. However, multiple research firms specialize in this particular type of research. Thus, an outside agency may have greater competency in this specific area.

- An outside agency often has local expertise allowing it to specialize in research from its home area. When a company needs consumer research from a particular country or even from a particular part of a country, the outside agency becomes advantageous because of its knowledge of customs and values. The company probably also knows acceptable ways to get information from consumers in that particular area. For example, a research agency based here in the United States would probably not strongly consider a door-to-door survey for consumer research. However, in other parts of the world, particularly with a less developed communication infrastructure, door-to-door interviews may be a viable option.

Likewise, certain conditions make in-house research more attractive, as described below:

- If a research project needs completing very quickly, chances are that in-house researchers can get started more quickly and get quicker access to internal resources that can help get the project done in short order.

- If the research project requires close collaboration of many other employees from diverse areas of the organization, then in-house research may be preferable. The in-house research firms can usually gain cooperation and can more quickly ascertain just whom they need to interview and where to find those people.

- A third reason for doing a project in-house has to do with economy. Researchers nearly always save money by doing the research in-house relative to hiring an outside agency.

- If secrecy is a major concern, the company should conduct the research in-house. Even though an outside firm might be trusted, that same company may take slightly less care in disguising the research efforts. Thus, other companies may pick up signals in the marketplace that suggest the area of research for a firm.

Exhibit 4.1 summarizes the advantages of doing research internally (in-house) or outsourcing externally (out-house).

EXHIBIT **4.1**
Advantages of In or
Outhouse Research.

- Advantages of In-House
  Research:
  – Quick Turn-Around
  – Better Collaboration
    among Employees
  – Cheaper
  – Greater Secrecy

- Advantages of Out-House
  Research:
  – Fresh Perspective
  – Greater Objectivity
  – Special Expertise
  – Special Market
    Knowledge

© 2016 Cengage Learning®

Working in the Marketing Research Field

Perhaps never before have there been more opportunities to work in the marketing research field.[2] The explosion in data resulting from consumers' near constant use of interactive electronic media and the ability to more conveniently interact with research respondents through the Internet enables businesses to act with more data-driven intelligence than ever before. Marketing research jobs routinely appear as among the top career fields for recent college graduates. This section provides an overview of the types of marketing research organizations that exist and the types of jobs that exist within those organizations.

About three-fourths of all U.S. organizations have a department or individual responsible for marketing research. Consumer product companies, manufacturers, service firms, health-care organizations, social media companies, hotels, and retailers are most likely to have an in-house marketing research department. Marketing research clearly has a presence and this is particularly true for larger firms. Technology provides new ways to gather intelligence and researchers help develop those methods as well as apply analytical routines to the data to extract meaning.

The insurance industry relies significantly on marketing research. Dozens or even hundreds of people are involved with a major company's marketing research. MetLife has been singled out as a role model for exemplary performance and integration of its marketing research team into strategic decision making. The marketing research team has helped MetLife:[3]

- Build stronger relationships with customers
- Integrate customer and competitor information into decision processes
- Have better working relationships with vendors
- Become more market-oriented and entrepreneurial by targeting tailor-made financial advice to generational segments
- Develop informative content that drives consumers to its website

The placement of marketing research within a firm's organizational structure and the structure of the research department itself vary substantially, depending on the firm's degree of market orientation and research sophistication. A marketing research department can easily become isolated with poor organizational placement. Researchers may lack a voice in executive committees when they have no continuous relationship with marketing management. Firms that place the research department at an inappropriately low level end up suffering this mishap. Given the critically important nature of the intelligence coming out of a research department, the organizational structure should place research high enough to ensure that senior management is well informed. Research departments also need to interact with a broad spectrum of other units within the organization. Thus, the position they occupy in the organizational hierarchy should allow them to provide credible information both upstream and downstream. MetLife's marketing research informs senior levels of the organization and seeks input from all levels of the organization.

Research departments that perform a staff function must wait for management to request assistance. Often the term "client" is used by the research department to refer to line management; the entity for whom services are being performed. The research department responds to clients' requests and is responsible for the design and execution of all research.

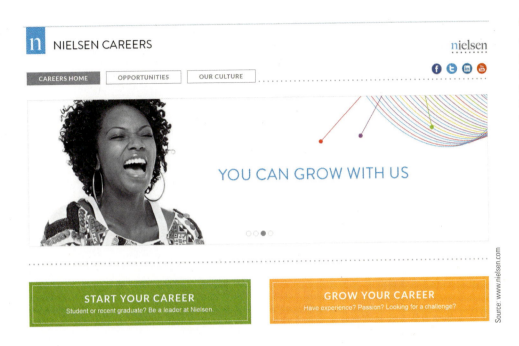

Thousands of people work for large global research firms like Nielsen. Marketing research truly presents a world of career opportunities. [http://sites.nielsen.com/careers/]

Research Suppliers and Contractors

As mentioned in the beginning of the chapter, sometimes obtaining marketing research from an outside organization makes good sense. In these cases, marketing managers must interact with **research suppliers**, who are commercial providers of marketing research services. Market research services are provided by organizations variously classified as marketing research consulting companies, such as Burke or Millward Brown, a division of Kantar; advertising agencies, such as Ipsos MediaCT, a division of Ipsos SA; suppliers of syndicated research services, such as Nielsen Holdings, N.V.; as well as thousands of smaller regional firms, business/management schools, and government agencies. The Nielsen Company alone employs over 34,000 people in more than 100 countries. [4] Research suppliers provide varied services that can be classified into several types.

Research suppliers
Commercial providers of marketing research services.

Syndicated Service

No matter how large a firm's marketing research department is, some projects are too expensive to perform in-house. A **syndicated service** is a marketing research supplier that provides standardized information for many clients in return for a fee. They are a sort of supermarket for standardized research results. For example, J.D. Power and Associates (see Research Snapshot on page 80) sells research about customers' experiences with products they purchase and their reasons for satisfaction or dissatisfaction with those products. Consumers are perhaps most familiar with J.D. Power for their automobile ratings. For instance, J.D. Power traditionally lists Lexus, Toyota, and Honda as the most dependable automobiles. In 2014 however, the Cadillac Escalade ranks as the top scoring premium SUV category based on ownership reports of problems and options in the first 90 days of ownership. [5] Most automobile manufacturers and their advertising agencies subscribe to this syndicated service because the company provides important industry-wide information gathered from a national sample of thousands of consumers. By specializing in this type of customer research, J.D. Power gains economies of scale in being able to apply the same research techniques to a wide array of product categories.

Syndicated service
A marketing research supplier that provides standardized information for many clients in return for a fee.

Syndicated services provide information economically because the information is not specific to one client but interests many. In a way, the costs for producing the results spread among all subscribers. The cost would be prohibitive if a single firm had to conduct this research for its own use. Syndicated service companies offer standardized information measuring media audiences, wholesale and retail distribution data, social media usage, Internet statistics, customer satisfaction, and other forms of data.

The True Power of Research

The customer's voice is powerful in many ways. Many companies turn to J.D. Power to understand the power that comes from the customer's voice. J.D. Power rates competing companies' products and services in many industries based on feedback from thousands of customers. For instance, want to know what tires consumers believe are the best? This might be an important question for retail dealers considering product lines and for auto manufacturers looking to enhance the value of their new cars by using quality OEM component parts. A sample of 29,000 consumers ranks Michelin the best passenger car tire, giving it 5 power star ratings on all dimensions (ride, traction, appearance, wear, and overall). Michelin is tops in all car categories with the exception of performance sports car owners who rate Pirelli tires the best. J.D. Power delivers ratings on things not related to autos as well. Nearly 9,000 customers rated house paint and it turns out the best paint depends on the innie or outie question. For painting inside, Benjamin Moore is best, followed by Sherwin Williams

Juanmonino/iStockphoto.co

and BEHR. For painting outside, Sherwin Williams places first, followed by BEHR and Benjamin Moore. In the marketplace, these performance circles are full of *power*.

Sources: PR, N. (2014, April 16). J.D. Power Reports: Leading Paint Brands Continue to Achieve High Levels of Customer Satisfaction; Application Is the Most Important Factor Across Product Lines. *PR Newswire US.* http://ratings.jdpower.com/automotive/index.htm, accessed April 19, 2014.

Standardized research service

Companies that develop a unique methodology for investigating a specific business specialty area.

• • • • • •

Doing research in a foreign country is often better done by an outside agency with resources in those places.

Rhoda Sidney/PhotoEdit

Standardized Research Services

Standardized research service providers develop a unique methodology for investigating a business specialty area. Several research firms, such as Symphony Health Solutions, specialize in market research for the health-care industry. Standardized research suppliers conduct studies for multiple individual clients using the same methods.

Even when a firm could perform the research task in-house, research suppliers may be able to conduct the project at a lower cost, faster, and relatively more objectively. A company evaluating a new advertising strategy may find an ad agency's research department better able to provide technical expertise on copy development research than could be done within the company itself. Researchers also may wisely seek outside help with research when conducting research in a foreign country in which the necessary human resources and knowledge to collect data effectively are lacking.

Limited Research Service Companies and Custom Research

Limited-service research suppliers specialize in particular research activities, such as field interviewing, data warehousing, or data processing. Full-service research suppliers sometimes contract these companies for ad hoc marketing research projects. The client usually controls these marketing research agencies or management consulting firms, but the research supplier handles most of the operating details of **custom research** projects. These are projects tailored specifically to a client's unique needs.

Exhibit 4.2[6] lists the top twenty suppliers of global research based on 2013 research revenues. Over 100,000 research professionals work for just these fifteen firms that account for almost $18 billion. Most provide multiple

EXHIBIT **4.2** The World's Largest Research Firms

Rank	Organization	Headquarters	Home Country	Web Site	Research Employees (Full-Time)	Number of Countries	Approximate Revenue ($ millions)
1	Nielsen Holdings NV	New York	USA	Nielsen.com	34,000	100	5,429
2	Kantar	London	UK	kantar.com	22,000	80	3,339
3	Ipsos SA	Paris	France	ipsos.com	15,927	85	2,301
4	GfK	Nuremberg	Germany	gfk.com	12,678	68	1,948
5	IMS Health Inc.	Parsippany, NJ	USA	imshealth.com	2,580	74	775
6	Information Resources Inc.	Chicago, IL	USA	IRIworlwide.com	4,035	8	764
7	INTAGE, Inc.	Tokyo	Japan	intage.co.jp	2,465	7	500
8	Westat Inc.	Rockville, MD	USA	wesstat.com	2,019	8	496
9	Arbitron Inc.[a]	Columbia, VA	USA	arbitron.com	1,292	3	450
10	NPD Group Inc.	Port Washington, NY	USA	npd.com	1,230	13	272
11	comScore Inc.	Reston, VA	USA	comScore.com	1,139	22	255
12	Video Research Ltd.	Tokyo	Japan	videor.co.jp	389	2	250
13	IBOPE Group	Sao Paulo	Brazil	IBOPE.com.br	3,024	14	247
14	ICF International Inc	Fairfax, VA	USA	ICFI.com	1,250	6	240
15	JD Power	Westlake Village, CA	USA	jdpower.com	738	8	234
	[a]Acquired by Nielsen at end of 2013				104,766		17,500

Source: Data taken from Honomichl, J. (2013), "Global Top 25: 2010 Honomichl Report," *Marketing News*, (August 30), 20–55.

services ranging from designing activities to fieldwork. Clearly, the exhibit reveals that marketing research is a massive, global industry. Just a few decades ago, the list would comprise solely firms based in the United States. Large research firms now base their operations in places around the globe including Paris, Tokyo, and Sao Paulo, Brazil. The explosion in global data availability will only add to the growth in the industry. Therefore, attractive career opportunities are numerous for those with the right skills and desires.

Custom research

Research projects that are tailored specifically to a client's unique needs.

Size of the Marketing Research Firm

Marketing research organizations themselves consist of layers of employees. Each employee has certain specific functions to perform based on his or her area of expertise and experience. A look at these jobs describes the potential structure of a research organization and gives insight into the types of careers available in marketing research.

Small Firms

The boundary between small firms, mid-sized firms, and large firms, generally speaking, is not precise. Government statistics usually consider firms with fewer than 100 employees to be small. In small firms, the vice president of marketing may be in charge of all significant marketing research. This officer generally has a sales manager to collect and analyze sales histories, trade association statistics, and other internal data. Small marketing companies usually have few resources and special competencies to conduct large-scale, sophisticated research projects.

Director of marketing research

This person provides leadership in research efforts and integrates all staff-level research activities into one effort. The director plans, executes, and controls the firm's marketing research function.

Research analyst

A person responsible for client contact, project design, preparation of proposals, selection of research suppliers, and supervision of data collection, analysis, and reporting activities.

Research assistants

Research employees who provide technical assistance with questionnaire design, data analyses, and similar activities.

● ● ● ● ● ● ●

When market research departments grow, they begin to specialize by product or business unit. More and more firms now have departments devoted to electronic media and/or electronic social networks.

Small research firms often have fewer than five employees regularly involved in marketing research and often operate regionally. Small firms often operate as sole proprietorships and it is not unusual for that to be literally true with a single research professional working alone without additional employees.

Small marketing research firms often have no major corporate clients. Instead, most business for small research firms comes from other small firms, especially start-up firms or even individuals wishing to do a feasibility study. In addition to feasibility studies, small marketing research firms typically conduct consumer attitude assessments and studies assessing the relationship between customer satisfaction and customer loyalty. A small firm can be a good place to start a career or to start your own business. Researchers working for a small firm generally perform all stages of research.

Mid-Sized Firms

Mid-sized firms are those with between 100 and 500 employees. In a mid-sized firm, someone usually holds the position of **director of marketing research**. This person provides leadership in research efforts and integrates all staff-level research activities.

A **research analyst** is responsible for client contact, project design, preparation of proposals, selection of research suppliers, and supervision of data collection, analysis, and reporting activities. Normally, the research analyst is responsible for several projects simultaneously covering a wide spectrum of the firm's organizational activities. He or she works with product or division management and makes recommendations based on analysis of collected data.

Research assistants (or associates) provide technical assistance with questionnaire design, data analyses, and so forth. Another common name for this position is *junior analyst*. The **manager of decision support systems** supervises the collection and analysis of sales, inventory, and other periodic customer relationship management (CRM) data. Research assistants develop sales forecasts for product lines using analytical and quantitative techniques. They provide sales information to decision-makers to satisfy planning, analysis, and control needs. A **forecast analyst** who provides technical assistance, such as running computer programs and manipulating data to forecast sales, may assist the manager of decision support systems.

Personnel within a planning department may perform the marketing research function in a mid-sized firm. At times, they may outsource some research functions. The planner may design research studies and then contract with outside firms that supply research services such as interviewing or data processing. They can combine the input from these outside agencies with their own work to write research reports.

Large Firms

As marketing research departments grow, they tend to specialize by product or strategic business unit. Major firms are those with over 500 employees. Marriott Corporation, for instance, has a director of marketing research for lodging (e.g., Marriott Hotels and Resorts, Courtyard by Marriott, and Fairfield Inn) and a director of marketing research for contract services (e.g., Senior Living Services). Each business unit's research director reports to the vice president of corporate marketing services. Many large organizations have managers of customer quality research who specialize in conducting surveys to measure consumers' satisfaction with product quality.

Exhibit 4.3 illustrates the organization of a major firm's marketing research department. Within this organization, the centralized marketing research department conducts research for all the division's product groups. This is typical of a large research department that conducts much of its own research, including fieldwork. The director of marketing research reports to the vice president of marketing.

Andrew Holt/Alamy

EXHIBIT 4.3 Example Large Market Research Firm's Organizational Chart

The Director of Marketing Research as a Manager

A director of marketing research plans, executes, and controls the firm's marketing research function. This person typically serves on company executive committees that identify competitive opportunities and formulate marketing strategies. The various directors from each functional area generally make up this committee (such as finance, sales, production, and so forth). The director of marketing research provides the research perspective during meetings. For instance, he or she can let the committee know what types of market intelligence might be obtained feasibly given the decision being discussed. Marketing research directors typically face on-the-job issues such as these:

- Skilled research professionals prefer doing research to managing people. However, a director spends more time in meetings and directing others than actually conducting his/her own research.
- Market research's role often is not recognized formally on par with financial management. The director must be an advocate for the function and its capabilities. In doing so, the director is an advocate for the market itself.
- Outstanding research professionals resist giving up responsibility for key decisions about significant research projects. As a result, they delegate only elementary or tedious tasks to subordinates who sometimes end up feeling underutilized and unhappy with their work.

Perhaps never before has the field of marketing research offered so much career potential. The growing demand for people with research skills means many job opportunities in the coming years. Additionally, the salary for many of these jobs is quite attractive. Being a global industry, opportunities exist on every continent and in practically every country. The Research Snapshot gives a rough idea of what marketing research salaries are like internationally.

Manager of decision support systems

Employee who supervises the collection and analysis of sales, inventory, and other periodic customer relationship management (CRM) data.

Forecast analyst

Employee who provides technical assistance such as running computer programs and manipulating data to generate a sales forecast.

Cross-Functional Teams

In a truly market-oriented organization, all employees are involved in the intelligence-gathering and dissemination process. Because of their involvement, employees from different areas of the organization are more likely to communicate and act on marketing information in market-oriented firms.

Cross-functional teams are composed of individuals from various functional areas such as engineering, production, finance, and marketing who share a common purpose. Cross-functional teams help organizations focus on a core business process, such as customer service or new-product development. Working in teams reduces the tendency for employees to focus single-mindedly on an isolated functional activity. In market-oriented firms, cross-functional teams help employees increase customer value since communication about the customer and their specific desires and opinions spreads throughout the firm more naturally and fully.

Cross-functional Teams

Employee teams composed of individuals from various functional areas such as engineering, production, finance, and marketing who share a common purpose.

Learning Marketing Research Can Pay!

Clive Rose/Getty Images

Search career sites and you are likely to find jobs related to marketing research among the fastest growing and most attractive careers around today. Strategic thinking and business always has been interested in intelligence that could lead to better decision making. Today, that interest is as keen as ever, but the growth in data collection, data storage, and data analysis tools make the Big Data Era a big opportunity era for students entering the marketing research field. Thus, marketing research jobs are likely to remain well placed among the top ten career opportunities with U.S. News, ranking it the number one "best business job" of 2014.

The U.S. Bureau of Labor Statistics lists marketing research as a field growing much faster than average. The market research analyst position alone accounts for nearly half a million jobs in the United States. Those individuals working as analysts with only a bachelor's degree average earning over $60,000 per year. Analysts with experience or a master's degree can earn a six-figure salary. The job is always interesting and requires someone who can understand consumer emotion while also having good quantitative skills. An analyst who gets promoted to marketing research director can expect an average salary of over $125,000 per year. Marketing research requires people with other skills too. Data specialists also are needed to manage databases and identify sources of data to supply to analysts. Data administration jobs also are growing faster than average and the salaries can be comparable to the research analyst.

Job opportunities in marketing research exist outside the United States as well. The salaries also can be very lucrative overseas. Salaries in Japan, for example, are considerably higher than in the United States. With the demand high and the salaries good, perhaps marketing research is worth getting into!

Sources: http://www.bls.gov/home.htm, accessed April 20, 2014. http://www.careers-in-marketing.com/mrfacts.htm, accessed April 20, 2014. http://money.usnews.com/careers/best-jobs/market-research-analyst, accessed April 20, 2014.

New-product development often involves a cross-functional team of engineers, finance executives, production personnel, sales managers, and marketing researchers who take an integrated approach to leverage opportunities into success. In the old days, sales and marketing research seldom contributed to new product development until long after the company made key decisions regarding design, product specifications, and manufacturing. Now marketing researchers' input is part of an integrated team effort. Researchers act both as business consultants and as providers of technical services.

Conflict between Marketing Management and Marketing Research

In principle, the functions of marketing research should merge harmoniously with the objectives of marketing management for the benefit of both parties. In practice, the relationship between the marketing research department and the users of marketing research too often involves misunderstanding and conflict.

Top management seldom acknowledges marketing research as a factor when decisions are successful. At times, it's as if acknowledging intelligence developed by research demonstrates weakness by having to rely on marketing input like customer data. The late Steve Jobs epitomized this attitude by often boasting that Apple did no market research in developing their key product line offerings like the iPhone and iPad. However, the truth is that Apple was doing a substantial amount of survey research including descriptive studies providing insight into how people used their phones.[7] Apple reluctantly admitted this in court during its patent infringement case with Samsung while also acknowledging that market research at Apple remains top secret.

Research That Implies Criticism

A product manager who requests a survey of dealer loyalty will not be happy if the survey finds that the dealers are extremely critical. Similarly, a sales manager who informally projects a 5 percent increase in sales will not like hearing from the research department that the market potential indicates sales volume should be up by 20 percent. In each of these situations, marketing research presents information that implies criticism of a line executive's decision. In personal life, a sure way to lose a friend is to be openly critical of him or her. Things are no different in business.

Money

Research budgets are a source of conflict between management and researchers. Financial managers often see research as a cost rather than as an investment or a way of lowering risk. Thus, as is often true in many areas of business, managers often want to spend as little as possible on research. In contrast, researchers often vigorously resist cutting corners in conducting research. For instance, they may feel the need for a large random sample to address a research question using descriptive research. This approach can be very expensive and sometimes time consuming. Inevitably, management's desire to save money and the researcher's desire to conduct rigorous research conflict. Successful research projects often involve compromise between researchers and managers. This may involve working within a budget that will produce meaningful results and sacrifice precision and rigor minimally.

Time

Researchers say, "Good research takes time!" Managers say, "Time is money!" Like oil and water, these two views do not go together easily. A look back at the research process in the last chapter makes it clear that it can take some time to complete a research project. Simply planning one can involve days, if not weeks, of study and preparation. For instance, conducting a literature review or a review of previous studies can take weeks. Without them, the researcher may not be able to develop specific research hypotheses that would direct the project very specifically toward the current issue. Other times, the researcher may wish to interview more people than time can allow or take the time to use a more sophisticated data analysis approach.

A quickly done research project almost certainly means cutting corners. This doesn't mean it can't provide valuable information. But, a study put together quickly and conducted quickly is not as certain to provide valuable answers as would a more deliberately planned project. When studies are rushed, the following sources of error become more prominent than they would be otherwise:

- Conducting a study that is not needed. Taking more time to perform a literature search, including through company and industry reports, may have provided the needed intelligence without a new study.
- Addressing the wrong issue. Taking more time could help make sure the decision statement is well defined and that the research questions that follow will truly address relevant issues, lessening the chance that the research goes in the wrong direction.
- Sampling difficulties. Correctly defining, identifying, and contacting a truly representative sample is a difficult and time-consuming task. However, in some types of research, the quality of results depends directly on the quality of the sample.
- Inadequate data analysis. The researcher may analyze the data quickly and without the rigor that would otherwise be taken. Therefore, certain assumptions may not be considered, and important information within the data is simply not discovered.

Sometimes a marketing researcher will have to submit to the time pressure and do a quick-and-dirty study. A sudden event can make it necessary to acquire data quickly—but rush jobs can sometimes be avoided with proper planning of the research program. Researchers sometimes get backed into a corner where a study simply must be conducted under severe time limitations. When this happens, the researcher is obligated to disclose this limitation to management. The research report and presentation should include all the study limitations, including those that resulted from a shortage of time or money.

Intuitive Decision Making

Managers are decision-makers. They are action-oriented, and they often rely on gut reaction and intuition. Many times their intuition serves them well, so it isn't surprising that they sometimes do not believe a research project will help improve their decision making. Managers sometimes resist research because results may prove counter to managerial intuition or desires. Managers particularly dislike waiting for a research report. Sometimes, decision-makers learn the hard way that informed decisions are usually better.

When managers do use marketing research, they often want simple projects yielding concrete and certain results. Researchers tend to see problems as complex questions answerable only within probability ranges. One aspect of this conflict is the fact that a research report provides findings, but cannot make decisions. Decision-oriented executives may unrealistically expect research to make decisions for them or provide some type of guarantee that the action they take will be correct. Although research provides information for decision making, it does not remove all the uncertainties involved in complex decisions. Certain alternatives may be eliminated, but the research may reveal new aspects of a problem. Although research is a valuable decision-making tool, the executive is not freed from the decision-making task altogether but is simply able to perform the task in a more informed manner.

Presentation of the right facts can be extremely useful. However, decision-makers often believe that researchers collect the wrong facts. Many researchers view themselves as technicians who generate numbers using sophisticated mathematical and statistical techniques; they may spend more time on technical details than on satisfying managerial needs. Each person who has a narrow perspective of another's job is a partial cause of the problem of generating limited or useless information.

Intuition is not a replacement for informed market intelligence.[8] The business news routinely reports stories of preventable product, brand, and advertising blunders. Firms that rely heavily on social media to get their message out have to act fast. The urge to act fast often means ideas are not well tested. Esurance launched a Super Bowl Sunday promotion contest offering $1.5 million to a lucky tweeter. Consumers entered the contest by tweeting any message with the hashtag #EsuranceSave30. All sounds good, right? If Esurance had done even a little preliminary research, it most likely would've revealed the huge problem with this campaign. Large number of tweets contained the hashtag but also contained obscenities, profanities, and ridiculously false statements associated the company with undesirable characters and events.[9] Thus, the unintended result was creating electronic traces associated the brand with dubious words and names.

Future Decisions Based on Past Evidence

Managers wish to predict the future, but researchers measure only current or past events. Back in 1957, Ford introduced the Edsel, one of the classic business failures of all time. One reason for the Edsel's failure was that the marketing research conducted several years before the car's introduction indicated a strong demand for a medium-priced car for the "man on his way up." Production facility and management delays followed and by the time the car hit the market, consumer preference had shifted favoring traditional cars or small imports for suburban wives. Not all research information is so dated, but all research describes what people have done in the past. In this sense, researchers use the past to predict the future.

Likewise, firms easily can get lulled into complacency about consumer behavior. Zynga, an online game company, made important capital decisions based on the idea that consumers would continue to use Facebook as an online gaming platform. Just after making these decisions, consumers abandoned Facebook in large numbers opting instead to use phone and tablet apps for online gaming.

Reducing Conflict between Management and Researchers

Given the conflicting goals of management and research, it is probably impossible to completely eliminate the conflict. However, when researchers and decision-makers work more closely together, there will be less conflict. The more closely they work together, the better the communication between decision-makers and researchers. In this way, business decision-makers will better understand the information needs and work requirements of researchers. It will allow for better planning of research projects and a greater appreciation for the role that research plays in minimizing the riskiness of business decision making. Exhibit 4.4 lists some common areas of avoidable conflict between research and management.

With closer cooperation, managers and researchers become more involved with projects from the beginning. Without cooperation, each party can have unclear role expectations. Research proposals and research job descriptions help make expectations clear. Management shouldn't ask for and researchers shouldn't state unrealistic objectives. Better planning and an annual statement of the research program for the upcoming year also help minimize emergency assignments, which usually waste resources and demoralize personnel.

Marketing researchers likewise will come to understand management's perspective better. Researchers enhance company profits by encouraging better decisions. The closer together managers and researchers work, the more researchers realize that managers sometimes need information urgently. Thus, they should try to develop cost-saving research alternatives and realize that sometimes a quick-and-dirty study is necessary, even though it may not be as scientifically rigorous as might be desired. Sometimes, quick-and-dirty studies still provide usable and timely information. In other words, they should focus practically on results.

Perhaps most important is more effective communication of the research findings and research designs. The researchers must understand the interests and needs of the users of the research. If the researchers are sensitive to the decision-making orientation of management and can translate research results into practical management language, conflict will diminish.

EXHIBIT 4.4 Improving Two-Way Communication to Reduce Conflict

Conflict Area	Top Management	Marketing Research
➢ Role Expectations ➢ Professional Consideration ➢ Resources	➢ Define Research Responsibilities Clearly ➢ Allow for Research in Planning ➢ Budget Responsibly	➢ DO NOT OVERSTATE RESEARCH OBJECTIVES ➢ Sympathize with Management View ➢ Be Decision-Oriented Not Technique-Oriented
➢ Idea Generation ➢ Timeliness ➢ Problem Definition	➢ Be Objective (Open-Minded) ➢ Avoid Quick and Dirty Studies ➢ Emphasize High-Yield Projects	➢ Recognize Time Constraints ➢ Apply Rigor Appropriately
➢ Research Reporting ➢ Consideration of Work	➢ Acknowledge Research Limitations ➢ Minimize Management Filters	➢ Communicate Results Thoroughly but as Simply as Possible ➢ Presume Client (Management) Will Act on Research

© 2016 Cengage Learning®

Ethical Issues in Marketing Research

As in all human interactions, ethical issues exist in marketing research and in science in general. This book considers various ethical issues related to specific aspects of research throughout the text. The remainder of this chapter describes the makeup of ethical issues in research with an emphasis on societal and managerial concerns.

Ethical Questions Are Philosophical Questions

Ethical questions are philosophical questions. Several philosophical theories address how an individual develops a moral philosophy and how the resulting morals affect behavior. The theories include those addressing cognitive moral development, the bases for ethical behavioral intentions, and opposing moral values.[10] Although ethics remains a somewhat elusive concept, what is clear is that not everyone involved in business, or in fact involved in any human behavior, comes to the table with the same ethical standards or orientations.[11]

Marketing ethics

The application of morals to behavior related to the exchange environment.

Marketing ethics is the application of morals to business behavior related to the exchange environment. Generally, good ethics conforms to the notion of "right," and a lack of ethics conforms to the notion of "wrong." Highly ethical behaviors are those that are fair, just, and do not cause one to feel shame.[12] Ethical values can be highly influenced by one's moral standards. **Moral standards** are principles reflecting one's beliefs about what is ethical and what is unethical. More simply, moral standards are rules distinguishing right from wrong. The Golden Rule, "Do unto others as you would have them do unto you," is one such ethical principle.

Moral standards

Principles that reflect beliefs about what is ethical and what is unethical.

An **ethical dilemma** refers to a situation in which one chooses from alternative courses of actions, each with different ethical implications. Each individual develops a philosophy or way of thinking that guides decisions when facing moral dilemmas. Many people use moral standards to guide their actions when confronted with an ethical dilemma. Other people adapt an ethical orientation that rejects absolute principles. These individuals determine ethics based more on the social or cultural acceptability of behavior. To them, an act conforming to social or cultural norms is an ethical act. The sections below contrast these two ethical orientations.

Ethical dilemma

Refers to a situation in which one chooses from alternative courses of actions, each with different ethical implications.

Relativism

Relativism

A term that reflects the degree to which one rejects moral standards in favor of the acceptability of some action. This way of thinking rejects absolute principles in favor of situation-based evaluations.

Relativism is a term that reflects the degree to which one rejects moral standards in favor of the acceptability of some action. This way of thinking rejects absolute principles in favor of situation-based evaluations. Thus, an action is judged as ethical in one situation and unethical in another.

Idealism

Idealism

A term that reflects the degree to which one bases one's morality on moral standards.

In contrast, **idealism** is a term that reflects the degree to which one bases one's morality on moral standards. Someone who is an ethical idealist will try to apply ethical principles like the Golden Rule in all ethical dilemmas.

For example, a student may face an ethical dilemma when taking a test. Another student may arrange to exchange multiple-choice responses to a test via electronic text messages. This represents an ethical dilemma because there are alternative courses of action each with differing moral implications. An ethical idealist may apply a rule that cheating is always wrong and therefore would not likely participate in the behavior. An ethical relativist may instead argue that the behavior is acceptable because many other students are doing the same thing. In other words, the consensus is that this sort of cheating is acceptable, so this student would be likely to go ahead and participate in the behavior. Marketing researchers, marketing managers, and even consumers face ethical dilemmas practically every day.

General Rights and Obligations of Concerned Parties

Everyone involved in marketing research can face an ethical dilemma. Like other areas of marketing, marketing research involves multiple stakeholder groups.[13] For this discussion, we consider four groups of stakeholders:

1. The "doers" of research, or those actually involved in planning and implementing research.
2. The "users" of research, meaning research clients, management, or others who may access research products or reports.
3. The research participants, meaning those people who actually provide the data by being observed or responding in some way.
4. Society at large, including the populations that are affected by research and the governmental institutions that regulate research.

Each party has certain rights and obligations toward the other parties. Exhibit 4.5 shows these relationships. The research process works correctly and benefits stakeholders when all parties respect their respective rights and obligations. Like the rest of business, research works best when all parties act ethically.

Rights and Obligations of the Research Participant

In the past, most data collection took place with the research participant's active consent. Increasingly, marketing researchers use data gathered through participants' passive participation. Both active and passive participation present some potential vulnerability. Thus, marketing researchers need to examine the question, "What ethical duties and obligations are exchanged between the researcher and the research participant?"

Participant's Right to Privacy

Traditional survey research requires that a respondent voluntarily answer questions in one way or another. This may involve answering questions on a website, using a phone (voice or text), through an e-mail request, face to face, or even sending a completed questionnaire by

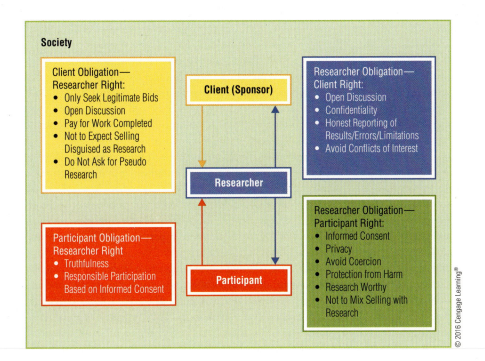

© 2016 Cengage Learning®

EXHIBIT **4.5**

The Rights and Obligations of Marketing Research

Informed consent

When an individual understands what the researcher wants him or her to do and agrees to the research study.

snail mail. In these cases, **informed consent** means that the individual understands what the researcher wants him or her to do and agrees to be a participant in the research study. Before asking questions, the interviewer provides an opportunity for the participant to decline the invitation. In other cases, research participants may not be aware that someone is monitoring them in some way. Today's technology blurs the line between active and passive research, as behavioral and sometimes personal information routinely becomes data via smartphones and other devices. The ethical responsibilities vary depending on whether participation is active or passive.

Active Research

Americans traditionally relished their privacy. The right to privacy is an important issue in marketing research. If a research participant believes the researcher is being too nosy, he or she has the right to refuse participation. However, critics argue that the very old, very young, the poorly educated, and other underprivileged individuals are sometimes unaware of their right to provide informed consent or refuse. Although the researcher should provide a clear indication of the nature of the questions, some surveys initially ask questions that are relatively innocuous and then move to questions of a highly personal nature. Respondents should know their right to refuse includes breaking off an interview at any time.

The privacy issue goes further into other ways that a research project could invade a person's privacy. Do any questions below illustrate any privacy concerns for active research participants?

- "Is a telephone call that interrupts family dinner an invasion of privacy?"
- "Is an e-mail requesting response to a 30-minute survey an invasion of privacy?"
- "Is capturing market information one posts on social network sites an invasion of privacy?"
- "Is a follow up contact to a previous response an invasion of privacy?"

As a practical matter, respondents may feel more relaxed about privacy and feel better informed about the consent decision if they know who is conducting the survey. In a face-to-face interview, interviewers should wear official name tags and provide identification giving their name and the name of their company. Cover letters and e-mail requests likewise should identify the reason for the research, the name of the institution conducting the research and in most cases, the name of the research sponsor.

Generally, research firms deploying interactive interviews practice common courtesy by trying not to do interviews at inconvenient times. Research companies should adhere to the principles of the "do-not-call" policy and should respect consumers' "Internet privacy" even if the company might be technically exempt from the legislation.[14] **Do-not-call legislation** restricts any telemarketing effort from calling consumers either who register with a national or statewide no-call list or who ask the firm directly not to call. U.S. legislators aimed these laws at sales-related calls but legislation in several states, including California, Louisiana, and Rhode Island, extends the laws to apply to "those that seek marketing information." Thus, the legislation effectively protects consumers' privacy from researchers as well as salespeople.[15] Research firms, particularly in these states, should consider subscribing to the do-not-call registry to avoid breeching the law or ethical practice.

Consumers often are confused about the difference between telemarketing efforts and true marketing research. Part of this is because unscrupulous telemarketing firms sometimes disguise their sales efforts by opening conversations with "we are doing research." The resulting confusion contributes to both increased refusal rates and lower trust from the public. In the 1980s, about half of people would respond to questions via an unexpected telephone interview. Today, response rates have dropped to under ten percent.[16] Part of the drop in participation is because consumers cannot easily distinguish telemarketing from legitimate research.

Companies using the Internet to do marketing research also face legislative changes. Much of this legislation aims at properly notifying respondents about the collection of data and informing them of to whom the results will be provided. Researchers should make sure to provide consumers a clear and easy way either to consent to participation in active research on the Internet or to opt out easily. Research companies should be careful to protect research results from being used to contact respondents in sales attempts. Also, the researcher needs to clearly state the degree to which the information that they provide is private.

Do-not-call legislation

Restricts any telemarketing effort from calling consumers who either register with a no-call list or who request not to be called.

Passive Research

Passive research involves different types of privacy issues. Generally, researchers do not view unobtrusive observation of public behavior in places such as stores, airports, sidewalks and museums as an invasion of a person's privacy. Researchers justify this type of observation on the fact that the participants are willfully performing the actions publicly and they are indeed anonymous so long as they are not identified by name or there is not any attempt made to identify them. They are "faces in the crowd." As long as the behavior observed is typical of behavior commonly conducted in public, then there is no invasion of privacy; the public behaviors are tantamount to **implicit consent**. In contrast, recording behavior not typically conducted in public would be a violation of privacy. For example, recording people (without consent) taking showers at a health club using hidden cameras is inappropriate, even if the research addresses ways of improving the health-related aspects of the shower experience.

Implicit consent
Behaviors that are openly performed in public implies that one is willing to have others observe them.

The line between public and private behavior is not always that clear. Technology pushes the limits of implied consent. Typically, we consider phone calls to be private. However, technology exists that allows our phone calls to be stored in massive databases. As discussed in Chapter 2, our smartphones allow our locations to be tracked and recorded. Companies employ GPS tracking, including the capabilities of employees' own smartphones to "spy" on their whereabouts. One company ended up firing one employee based on the GPS evidence that revealed he was having an affair during work hours.[17] The evidence came in the form of his phone ending up at the same address too often and for too long! Other companies place near-field communication devices in employee name badges to track their whereabouts inside the workplace. Interestingly, the research reveals low productivity both from those who spend too much and too little time at their desk.

One can make a better case for companies having the right to monitor employees than they can for consumers to be monitored without their consent, either explicit or implicit. For instance, does implied consent cover web traffic and web activity in general? When someone visits a real casino their behavior can be monitored by the sophisticated video system in the casino. Marketing researchers can use this data to help improve the casino design and casino experience in general. However, when one visits an online gaming site, does implicit consent exist for firms to use the data left behind or even to sell the data to other firms? Virtually all of our interactions online leave data behind and reveal quite a bit about our preferences for *virtually* everything.

Although people shown in a video walking through a casino or in an airport are considered anonymous, electronic tracking confuses the concept of anonymity. A guarantee of **anonymity** assures respondents that they cannot be identified or linked to their response in any way. When a respondent completes a survey using Qualtrics, the user can see a map that shows the location of the person that responded. How is this possible? All the devices that connect to the Internet have Internet Protocol (IP) addresses. The IP address identifies the device and its location. Thus, to the extent that the owner is the user, true anonymity does not exist in the collection of this raw data. Already, consumers can even be pushed personalized appeals based on their Internet activity while they are inside a store.

Anonymity
Assures respondents that they cannot be identified or linked to their response in any way.

The do-not-call legislation protects consumers from unwanted telemarketing. However, regulations and practices designed to sort out the limits of implied consent for electronic media are not yet developed largely. The U.S. Congress as well as governments in other countries is now debating such actions. More importantly, the marketing research industry is considering self-regulation that would provide ethical guidelines concerning how to treat such data.[18] Our lives are improved by the data. Legislation needs to balance the improvements against the loss of privacy that comes from the plethora of real-world tracking.

The Obligation to Be Truthful

When someone willingly consents to participate actively, the researcher assumes he or she will provide truthful answers. Honest cooperation is the primary obligation of the research participant. In return for being truthful, the subject has the right to expect confidentiality. **Confidentiality** means that researchers will not share any individual's information with others. Individuals who truly believe that the researcher maintains confidentiality are more likely to respond truthfully, even about potentially sensitive topics. Likewise, the researcher and research sponsor also may expect the respondent to maintain confidentiality. For instance, if the research involves a new food

Confidentiality
The information involved in a research will not be shared with others.

©Jeanette Dietl/Shutterstock.com

When Nobody Is Looking?

An old adage says that one's character is not defined by doing the right thing when people are looking, but by the actions one takes when nobody is looking. Sometimes, researchers, clients, and participants face subtle, or perhaps even invisible, ways to influence the research process in potentially unethical ways. The client, for example, can simply withhold information. In some instances, the decision to proceed with a project may have already been made behind the scenes but not disclosed to the researcher. Client firms also have "donated" coupons for new products to schools while a test market for that product was underway. The decision-makers were motivated to show that their new product ideas would be successful. The results biased the research.

Researchers can also subtly cross the boundary between good and questionable ethical practices. One way that this takes place is in the tactics used to try to get research respondents to agree to participate. Consider these attempts at social persuasion:

- Tell an electronic survey respondent that results are anonymous when some type of identification gets recorded automatically.
- Tell the potential respondent that the interview will take only a few minutes when the average time to complete is more like 15–18 minutes.
- Tell the potential respondent that the interview contains only five questions and will take only 2 minutes. However, after responding to the fifth question, the respondent is informed that another set of questions has just been added to the survey.
- Telling the potential respondent that "only a few select individuals" qualify to give their opinion when the survey sample is really broad-based.

Field interviewers sometimes practice these techniques even when instructed not to do so. Thus, researchers need to be extremely cautious about the amount of pressure put on research assistants to get participants. Too much pressure may cause the assistants to cross the line and perform actions that question the character of the research firm and the industry overall.

Sources: Bednall, H. B. D., S. Adam, and K. Polcinski (2010), "Using Compliance Techniques to Boost Telephone Response Rates," *International Journal of Market Research,* 52 (2), 155–168. Slsmadi, S. (2010), "Marketing Research and Social Responsibility: Ethical Obligations toward the Society," *Journal of Accounting— Business & Management,* 17 (1), 42–47.

product from Nabisco, then they may not want the respondent to discuss the idea for fear that the idea may fall into the competition's hands. Thus, confidentiality helps ensure truthful responses and protects sensitive information.

Kid's Stuff Is Complicated

Researchers have a special obligation to ensure the safety of children. Children are involved in at least half of all spending in the United States. Thus, researchers need input from children to help create high-value products for children. Legislators rightly have special concern for privacy when business interacts with children in some way. The Children's Online Privacy Protection Act (COPPA), defines a child as anyone under the age of 13. Anyone engaging in contact with a child through the Internet is obligated to obtain parental consent before a child can provide any personal information or identification. Therefore, a researcher collecting a child's name, phone number, or e-mail address without parental consent is violating the law.

In 2013, legislators modified COPPA to make clear that personal information included online activity records, GPS location data, audio recordings made by a child, or videos posted that include the child.[19] In addition, changes in COPPA implement procedures that help verify that parental consent really comes from a parent. Thus, some mechanism such as an official electronic signature is needed to provide consent. Officials also approved the kidSAFE seal program.[20] Companies that comply with COPPA and kidSAFE core safety rules such as making sure a website has only age appropriate content and has specific and clear procedures for handling any parental safety constraints, can earn the seal. The seal intends to provide parents with some degree of comfort in allowing their children to use a website.

Policy makers consider children vulnerable because they may not be able to reasonably reach decisions that keep them safe in all cases. Should researchers allow a child to consent to participating in research without parental consent? Even something as innocuous as offering a child a cupcake for participating in research might not meet all parents' approval. Clearly, researchers should interview children under a certain age only in the presence of a parent. However, will the child respond the same way when a parent is present as when alone? Imagine asking a 14-year-old if he or she enjoys smoking cigarettes or consuming alcohol. How might a parent's presence change the response?[21] The age of consent for marketing research isn't clear even when research is within the guidelines of COPPA. To be safe, researchers should conduct most standard research with children under the age of 16 only with parental consent. When the research involves matters that are for "mature audiences," such as human sexuality or alcohol consumption, then the researchers should seek parental consent for anyone under the age of 18.

Firms that follow COPPA and take other safety precautions can earn this seal of approval – comes from http://www .kidsafeseal.com/aboutourseals .html

Doing research with children can yield extremely useful information. However, it is also more risky than doing research with adults. When in doubt, researchers should consider how they would like to see their own child treated and then go even further to make sure that there are no ethical problems with the use of children in research.

Deception and the Right to Be Informed

Experimental Designs

Experimental manipulations often involve some degree of deception. In fact, without some deception, a researcher would never know if a research subject was responding to the actual manipulation or to their perception of the experimental variable. This is why researchers sometimes use a placebo.

A **placebo** is a false experimental effect used to create the perception of a true effect. Imagine two consumers, each participating in a study of the effect of a new herbal supplement on hypertension. One consumer receives a packet containing the citrus-flavored supplement, which is meant to be mixed in water and drunk with breakfast. The other also receives a packet, but in this case, the packet contains a mixture that will simply color the water and provide a citrus flavor. The second consumer also believes he or she is drinking the actual supplement. In this way, the psychological effect is the same on both consumers, and any actual difference in hypertension must be due to the actual herbs contained in the supplement. Interestingly, experimental subjects often display some placebo effect in which the mere belief that some treatment has been applied causes some effect.

Placebo

A false experimental effect used to create the perception that some effect has been administered.

This type of deception can be considered ethical. Primarily, researchers conducting an experiment must generally (1) gain the willful cooperation of the research subject and (2) fully explain the actual experimental variables applied following the experiment's completion. Every experiment should include a **debriefing** session. The debriefing session is the researcher's opportunity to fully inform subjects about the experiment's purpose and provide a chance for them to ask any questions that they may have about the experiment.

Debriefing

Research subjects are fully informed and provided with a chance to ask any questions they may have about the experiment.

Protection from Harm

Researchers should do everything they can to make sure that participation in research does not endanger participants' safety in any respect. Most marketing research does not expose participants to any harm. However, the researcher should consider every possibility. For example, if the research involves tasting food or drink, the possibility exists that a research participant could have a severe allergic reaction. Similarly, researchers studying retail and workplace atmospherics often manipulate odors by injecting certain scents into the air.[22] The researcher is sometimes in a difficult situation. He or she has to find out somehow what things the subject is allergic to, without revealing the actual experimental conditions. One way a researcher can do this is by asking subjects to provide a list of potential allergies ostensibly as part of a separate research project.

Other times, research may involve some potential psychological harm. This may come in the form of stress or in the form of some experimental treatment, which questions some strongly held conviction. For instance, a researcher studying helping behavior may lead a subject to believe that another person is being harmed in some way. In this way, the researcher can see how much a subject can withstand before doing something to help another person. In reality, the other person is usually a research confederate simply pretending to be in pain. Three key questions that can determine whether the experimental procedures treat a research participant unethically are:

1. Has the research subject provided consent to participate in an experiment?
2. Is the research subject subjected to substantial physical or psychological trauma?
3. Can the research subject be easily returned to his or her initial state?

The issue of consent is tricky in experiments because the researcher cannot reveal exactly what the research is about ahead of time without threatening the validity of the experiment. In addition, the researcher generally provides experimental research subjects with some incentive to participate. We will have more on this later in the book, but ethically speaking, the incentives should always be noncoercive. In other words, a faculty member seeking volunteers should not withhold a student's grade if he or she does not participate in an experiment. Thus, the volunteer should provide consent without fear of harm for saying no and with some idea about any potential risk involved.

If the answer to the second question is yes, then the researcher should not go forward with the research design. If the answer to the second question is no and consent is obtained, then the manipulation does not present an ethical problem, and the researcher can proceed.

The third question is really helpful in understanding how far one can go in applying manipulations to a research subject. If the answer to the third question is no, then the research should not be conducted. Researchers sometimes show interest in reasons why and the implications of consumers wearing tattoos.[23] Consider an experiment that would investigate the effect of an altered mental state on tattoo selection. The research question is, "How does intoxication affect tattoo selection?" Subsequently, the experimental research design presents two potential risks for harm. First, the subject becomes intoxicated. Second, the subject may end up actually obtaining a visible tattoo. If the subject has a hangover, he or she will likely recover. However, tattoos are permanent barring drastic medical attention. Thus, the design is unethical because it presents the possibility of changing the subject in a way that would make returning him or her to normal practically impossible.

Many research companies and practically all universities and business schools maintain a **human subjects review committee**. This committee carefully reviews a proposed research design to try to make sure that no harm can come to any research participant. A side benefit of this committee is that it can also review the procedures to make sure that the research design does not create any legal problems. Sometimes, an organization may use the name **Institutional Review Board** (IRB) to refer to this committee. The harm can potentially even go beyond humans. Any research that involves animals, such as dogs trying food, deserves scrutiny from an IRB.

Human subjects review committee

Carefully reviews proposed research designs to try to make sure that no harm can come to any research participant. Otherwise known as an Institutional Review Board or IRB.

Institutional Review Board

Another name for a human subjects review committee.

Rights and Obligations of the Client Sponsor (User)

Ethical Behavior between Buyer and Seller

The general business ethic expected between a purchasing agent and a sales representative should hold in a marketing research situation. For example, if a purchasing agent has already decided to purchase a product from a friend, the agent would be acting unethically by soliciting bids from others because those bids have no chance of being accepted. Similarly, a client seeking research should only seek bids from firms that have a legitimate chance of actually doing the work. In addition, any section on the ethical obligation of a research client would be remiss not to mention that the user is obligated to pay the provider the agreed-upon wage within the agreed-upon time.

An Open Relationship with Research Suppliers

The client/sponsor has an obligation to encourage the researcher to seek out the truth objectively. Managers and researchers must openly and honestly discuss the key issues and come to a consensus about what decision-statement(s), and thus what research question(s), best describes the need for the research. The more a decision-maker refuses to answer the researcher's questions, the less likely are the parties to come to a useful consensus about the research. Therefore, the researcher is better off not taking this particular job.

Once agreed upon, the research sponsor should support the research team in their effort to obtain information and perform analyses that will provide answers to the research questions. This means that the client needs to be open to actually using the research results. All too often, decision-makers want the research results only if they will support some preconceived answer— in other words the decision is already made and the research is needed for political cover. This is unethical. Time is simply too valuable to ask a researcher to perform a project when the sponsoring agent knows ahead of time that the results will not be used. Unfortunately, as a firm's performance suffers and as top management fails to show ethical leadership, that company tends to practice less ethical research practices as well.[24]

An Open Relationship with Interested Parties

Conclusions should be based on data—not conjecture. Users should not knowingly disseminate conclusions from a research project in a manner that twists them into some desirable interpretation. Twisting the results in a self-serving manner, or to support some political position, poses serious ethical questions. Such actions are morally inappropriate and the client-researcher relationship should be open enough to avoid encouraging anything but honest results.

Advocacy research—research undertaken to support a specific claim in a legal action or to represent some advocacy group—puts a client in a unique situation. Researchers often conduct advocacy research in their role as an expert witness. For instance, a law firm may ask a researcher to present evidence addressing how much a "knock-off" brand diminishes the value of a better-known name brand. In conventional research, the researcher weighs research attributes such as sample size, profiles of people actually interviewed, and number of questions asked, against cost. Trade-offs become appropriate if the research is too costly to conduct relative to the benefit. However, a court's opinion on whether research results are reliable might rely exclusively on any one specific research aspect. Thus, an opposing attorney may magnify the slightest variation from technically correct procedures attempting to demonstrate to the judge or jury that the project is flawed.

Advocacy research presents a number of serious issues that can lead to an ethical dilemma:

- Lawyers' first responsibility is to represent their clients. Therefore, they might be more interested in evidence that supports their client's position than anything else— including truthful results. Presenting accurate research results may harm the client.
- A researcher should be objective. However, he or she runs the risk of conducting research that does not support the desired position. In this case, an unethical lawyer may ask the researcher to present the results in a manner that obfuscates the truth.
- Should the lawyer (in this case a user of research) ask the researcher to take the stand and present an inaccurate picture of the results?

Ethically, the attorney should certainly not put the researcher on the stand and encourage an act of perjury. The attorney may hope to ask specific questions that are so limited that taken alone, they may appear to support the client. However, this is risky because the opposing attorney likely also has an expert witness that can suggest questions for cross-examination. Returning to our branding example, if the research does not support an infringement of the known brand's name, then the brand name's attorney should probably not ask the researcher to take the stand.

The question of advocacy research is one of objectivity: Can the researcher seek out the truth when the sponsoring client wishes to support its position at a trial? The ethical question stems from a conflict between legal ethics and research ethics. Although the courts have set judicial standards for marketing research methodology, perhaps only the client and individual researcher can resolve this question.

To the Point

"We are what we repeatedly do. Excellence then is not act but a habit."

ARISTOTLE

Advocacy research

Research undertaken to support a specific claim in a legal action or represent some advocacy group.

Research Not Advocate

This chapter illustrates that both the customers of research and the producers of research have an ethical responsibility to act in ways that will promote truthful results and the truthful interpretation of results. Client or societal forces create demands for research only if it seems consistent with a conventional viewpoint. Researchers sometimes succumb to pressures and end up violating this principle.

Even academic researchers feel such pressures. A well-known social psychologist illustrates the point. After a long career and accusations levied by research colleagues, he admitted to having materially fabricated data and manipulated results. His research results generally dealt with socially sensitive issues and the fabrications resulted in research papers that tended to support politically correct conclusions. For instance, in studying morality and dietary behavior, the researcher fabricated results suggesting that vegetarians are less selfish than individuals who are not vegetarians. Similarly, a group of climate scientists recently have publicly pointed out the difficulties associated with presenting any study results that run counter to conventional global warming theories. This is against a backdrop of evidence suggesting that researchers who published key pieces leading to the conclusion

of global warming likewise fabricated and manipulated data in ways that supported and exaggerated temperature trends and the implications of those trends. The truth to these issues is difficult to know, but when researchers become advocates, the truth may become even more obscure.

Sources: *Science* (2011), "Around the World," 333 (September 16), 1556. Sterling, T. (2011), "Committee: Dutch Professor Faked Data for Years," http://www.boston.com/news/science/articles/2011/11/03/dutch_psychologist_built_career_on_faked_data/, accessed February 5, 2012. Allegre, C. et al. (2012), "No Need to Panic about Global Warming," *Wall Street Journal,* (January 27), A15. Hubbard, S. (2011), "NASA Study: Global Warming Alarmists Wrong," *Newmax* (July 28), http://www.newsmax.com/Newsfront/NASA-Global-Warming-Alarmists/2011/07/28/id/405200, accessed February 5, 2012.

Privacy

Research participants deserve privacy, as discussed above, and this right means the researcher and sponsor are obliged to respect that right. Suppose a database marketing company is offering an e-mail list compiled by screening millions of households to obtain brand usage information. The list would be extremely valuable to your firm, but you suspect the interviewers misled the individuals who filled out the information forms by telling them they were participating in an anonymous survey. Would it be ethical to purchase the mailing list? If respondents were deceived into providing their names, the practice is certainly unethical. The client and the research supplier have the obligation to maintain respondents' privacy, so selling it or buying it breeches good ethics.

Consider another example. Sales managers know that a marketing research survey of their business-to-business customers' buying intentions includes a means to attach a customer's name to each questionnaire. This confidential information could be of benefit to a sales representative calling on a specific customer. A client wishing to be ethical must resist the temptation to identify those accounts (i.e., those respondents) that are the hottest prospects.

Rights and Obligations of the Researcher

Marketing research firms and marketing research departments should practice good business ethics. Researchers are often the focus of discussions of business ethics because of the necessity that they interact with the public. Several professional organizations offer codes of ethics for marketing researchers, including the American Marketing Association, the European Society for Opinion and Market Research, and the Marketing Research Society.[25] Many of these codes are lengthy and

the full contents are available at the associations' websites. Key code components generally reflect the content of this chapter and prohibit:

- Representing a sales pitch as marketing research
- Providing the name of respondents who were promised anonymity for some purpose other than the research
- Breaching the confidentiality of the research client or research participant
- Doing research for multiple firms competing in the same market
- Disseminating false or misleading results
- Plagiarizing the work of other researchers
- Violating the integrity of data gathered in the field

Unfortunately, researchers often succumb to pressures and violate the principles of ethical research. This even extends to academic researchers who feel pressure to publish research or who become zealous in supporting a social cause as the Research Snapshot illustrates. A well-regarded social psychologist published papers suggesting that people who eat meat are associated with selfishness. However, the pressure to publish and support this position proved too much and the researcher eventually admitted to fabricating data.[26] The discovery of the fabrication led to his resignation.

In addition, the researchers have rights. In particular, once a research consulting firm is hired to conduct some research, they have the right to cooperation from the sponsoring client. Also, the researchers have the right to be paid for the work they do as long as it is done professionally. Sometimes, the client may not like the results. But not liking the results is no basis for not paying. The client should pay the researcher for competent work in full and in a timely manner.

The Purpose of Research Is Research

Mixing Sales and Research

Consumers sometimes agree to participate in an interview that is purported to be pure research, but it eventually becomes obvious that the interview is really a sales pitch in disguise. This is unprofessional at best and fraudulent at worst. The Federal Trade Commission (FTC) has indicated that it is illegal to use any plan, scheme, or ruse that misrepresents the true status of a person seeking admission to a prospect's home, office, or other establishment. No research firm or basic marketing researcher should engage in any sales attempts. Applied market researchers working for the sponsoring company should also avoid overtly mixing research and sales. However, the line is becoming less clear with increasing technology.

Research That Isn't Research

Consider the following typical exchange between a product manager and a marketing researcher. The manager wants to hire the firm to do a test-market for a new product:

Researcher:	*What if the test results are favorable?*
Product manager:	*We'll launch the product nationally.*
Researcher:	*And if the results are unfavorable?*
Product manager:	*They won't be. I'm sure of that.*
Researcher:	*But just suppose they are.*
Product manager:	*I don't think we should throw out a good product just because of one little market test.*
Researcher:	*Then why test?*
Product manager:	*Listen, this is a major product introduction. It's got to have some research behind it!*

The product manager really wants research that will justify a decision he or she has already made. If the test-market's results contradict the decision, the product manager will almost certainly disregard the research. This type of study falls into the category of **pseudo-research** because the purpose is not to gather information for marketing decisions but to bolster a point of view and satisfy other needs.

In this situation, a researcher should walk away from the project if it appears that management strongly desires the research to support a predetermined opinion only. Although it is a fairly easy matter for an outside researcher to walk away from such a job, it is another matter for an in-house researcher to refuse such a job. Thus, avoiding pseudo-research is a right of the researcher but an obligation for the manager.

Pseudo-research

Conducted not to gather information for marketing decisions but to bolster a point of view or satisfy other needs.

Occasionally, managers request marketing research simply to pass blame for failure to another area. A product manager may deliberately request a research study with no intention of paying attention to the findings and recommendations. The manager knows that the particular project is in trouble but plays the standard game to cover up for his or her mismanagement. If the project fails, marketing research will become the scapegoat. The ruse may involve a statement something like this: "well, research should have identified the problem earlier!"

Push Polls

Politicians concocted and specialize in a particular type of pseudo-research A **push poll** is telemarketing under the guise of research intended to "sell" a particular political position or point of view. The purpose of the poll is to push consumers into a predetermined response. For instance, a polling organization calls thousands of potential voters inviting each to participate in a survey. The interviewer then may ask loaded questions that put a certain spin on a candidate. "Do you think that candidate X, who is involved with people known to be linked to scandal and crime, can be trusted with the responsibility of office?" This is a push poll. An honest question may simply ask how much candidate X can be trusted.

Push polling doesn't always involve political candidates, but they usually involve political issues in some way. Residents do not always welcome new Wal-Mart locations based on factors including the increase in traffic and congestion that the store can bring to an area. Chicago area residents received a polling call that went something like this:

The Mayor says that the proposed Walmart would bring over 400 jobs to this area and allow neighborhood residents access to fresh food. Do you support the new Walmart store's construction?

The results indicated that over 70 percent of residents supported the new store.[27] However, the framing of the question by referencing the mayor and the mention of jobs without mentioning potential problems almost certainly swayed the results. Push polls may include only a single question like this whereas legitimate research almost always will ask more questions as researchers search for clues to understand a person's position on an issue.

Service Monitoring

Occasionally, the line between research and customer service is not completely clear. For instance, Toyota may survey all of its new car owners after the first year of ownership. Although the survey appears to be research, it may also provide information that could be used to correct some issue with the customer. For example, if the research shows that a customer is dissatisfied with the way the car handles, Toyota could follow up with the specific customer. The follow-up could result in changing the tires of the car, resulting in a smoother and quieter ride, as well as a more satisfied

Push polling can be used to create a false impression of public opinion on controversial issues.

customer. Should a pattern develop showing other customers with the same opinion, Toyota may need to switch the original equipment tires used on this particular car.

Both research and customer service are involved and because the car is under warranty, no selling attempt exists. Researchers often design satisfaction surveys that include a means of opening a dialog between the company and the customer. Such practice is acceptable as long as the researcher makes the follow-up contact optional. The contact may provide a means of avoiding an experience that diminishes the value of a product.

Misrepresentation of Research

Obviously, one sees that an ethical researcher does not misrepresent study results. This means, for instance, that the researcher states the statistical accuracy of a test precisely and does not overstate or understate the meaning of the findings. Both the researcher and client share this obligation. Consider a researcher reporting a positive relationship between advertising spending and sales. The researcher may also discover that this relationship disappears when the primary competitor's prices are taken into account. In other words, the competitor's prices account for at least part of the observed fluctuation in sales. Thus, it would be questionable, to say the least, to report a finding suggesting that sales could be increased by increasing ad spending without also mentioning the role that competitors' prices play in explaining sales.

Honesty in Presenting Results

Misrepresentation can also occur in the way a researcher presents results. For instance, charts can be created that make a very small difference appear very big. Likewise, they can be altered to make a meaningful difference seem small. Exhibit 4.6 illustrates this effect. Each chart presents exactly the same data. The data represent consumer responses to service quality ratings and satisfaction ratings. Both quality and satisfaction are collected on a 5-point strongly-disagree-to-strongly-agree scale. In frame A, the chart appears to show meaningful differences between men and women, particularly for the service-quality rating. However, notice that the scale range is shown as 4 to 5. In frame B, the researcher presents the same data but shows the full scale range (1 to 5). Now, the differences are reported as trivial.

All charts and figures should reflect fully the relevant range of values reported by respondents. If the scale range is from 1 to 5, then the chart should reflect a 1 to 5 range unless there is some value that is simply not used by respondents. If no or only a very few respondents had reported a 1 for their service quality or satisfaction rating, then it may be appropriate to show the range as 2 to 5. However, if there is any doubt, the researcher should show the full scale range.

The American Marketing Association's marketing Code of Ethic states that "a user of research shall not knowingly disseminate conclusions from a given research project or service that are inconsistent with or not warranted by the data." A dramatic example of a violation of this principle occurred in an advertisement of a cigarette smoker study. The advertisement compared two brands and stated that "of those expressing a preference, over 65 percent preferred" the advertised brand to a competing brand. The misleading portion of this reported result was that most of the respondents did *not* express a preference; they indicated that both brands tasted about the same. Thus, only a very small percentage of those studied actually revealed a preference, and the results were somewhat misleading. Such shading of results violates the obligation to report accurate findings.

Honesty in Reporting Errors and Limitations

Likewise, researchers should not keep any major error occurring during the course of the study a secret. Hiding errors or variations from the proper procedures can distort or shade the results. Similarly, every research design presents some limitations. For instance, the sample size may be smaller than ideal. The researcher should point out the key limitations in the research report and presentation. In this way, the users can understand any factors that qualify the findings. The decision-maker needs this information before deciding on any risky course of action.

Confidentiality

Confidentiality comes into play in several ways. The researcher must abide by any confidentiality agreement with research participants. For instance, a researcher conducting a descriptive research survey may have identified each participant's e-mail address in the course of conducting the

How Results Can Be
Misrepresented in a Report
or Presentation

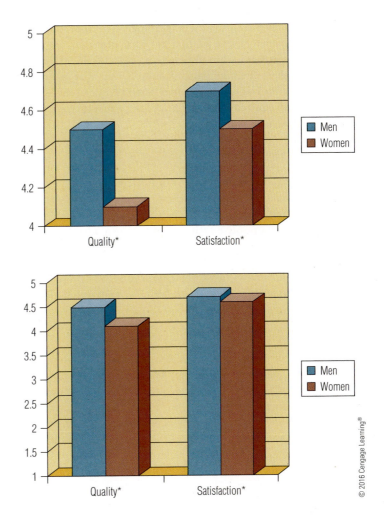

research. After seeing the results, the client may ask for the e-mail addresses as a logical prospect list. However, as long as the researcher assured each participant's confidentiality, he or she cannot provide the e-mail addresses to the firm. Indeed, a commitment of confidentiality also helps build trust among survey respondents.[28]

The marketing researcher often is obligated to protect the confidentiality of the research sponsor. In fact, business clients value marketing researchers' confidentiality more than any other attribute of a research firm.[29] Researchers must honor all implied and expressed promises of confidentiality, whether made to a research participant or research client.

The Role of Society at Large

Societies create and condone governments that oversee and regulate business and consumer activities. The do-not-call legislation provides an example of a way that governments restrict marketing research behavior. The Stop Online Piracy Act (SOPA) deals more with restrictions on consumers and Internet providers like Google with the intention of protecting the owners of intellectual and creative property. Society has an obligation to be fair and enact restrictions only when the benefits are justified in light of the difficulties those restrictions create. Furthermore, one point summarizes all the ethical obligations of marketing research in general. Marketing research offers benefits for individual members of and for society at large. However, research often involves some inconvenience in the form of intrusions like surveys. The potential benefits of the research should always outweigh the burdens placed on members of society. When this is true, the research is justified.

The role of society at large as a stakeholder also makes clear that ethics is not only for business. Business, society, and individuals all have ethical responsibilities. Marketing research value is diminished when any party breeches a responsibility.

The Researcher and Conflicts of Interest

Imagine a researcher conducting a test market for an Apple iPad that includes enhanced interactive video among its benefits. Just after conducting the research, Motorola coincidentally contacts the same researcher. Motorola, who has yet to develop similar interactive video capability, wants research that addresses whether or not an interactive video feature enhances the tablet market. The researcher is now in a difficult position. Certainly, an ethical dilemma exists presenting multiple choices to the researcher, including the following.

- Agreeing to do the research for Motorola and using some results from the Apple study to prepare a report and recommendation for Motorola
- Agreeing to sell the new concept to Motorola without doing any additional research. In other words, provide Apple's company secrets to Motorola
- Conducting an entirely new project for Motorola without revealing any of the results or ideas from the Apple study
- Turning down the chance to do the study without revealing any information about Apple to Motorola

Which is the best choice? Obviously, both of the first two options violate the principle of maintaining client confidentiality. Thus, both are unethical. The third choice, conducting an entirely new study, may be an option. However, it may prove nearly impossible to do the entire project as if the Apple study had never been done. Even with the best of intentions, the researcher may inadvertently violate confidentiality with Apple. The last choice is the best option from a moral standpoint. It avoids any potential **conflict of interest**. In other words, actions that would best serve one client, Motorola, would be detrimental to another client, Apple. Generally, it is best to avoid working for two direct competitors.

This would be a good time to revisit the opening chapter vignette. Does the situation present the researcher with any potential conflicts of interest? How can they be addressed?

Conflict of interest

Occurs when one researcher works for two competing companies.

TIPS OF THE TRADE

- A good way to get started in the marketing research industry is to target either a large marketing research firm or a local research firm with offers to serve as an intern. An internship will provide insight and experience that can provide a leg up on others in getting the job.
- When a company faces a very emotional decision, it is usually better to have the research needed to address the related research questions done by an outside firm.
- Those involved in research should consider the position of others involved in the process. When considering conducting or using research in some manner, one way to help ensure fair treatment of others involved in research is to consider whether you would like to be treated in this manner or whether you would like someone to treat a close member of your family in such a manner.

- Research with particularly vulnerable segments such as children involves special care. When doing research with children under the age of 16, the researcher nearly always needs parental consent.
- Even the appearance of a conflict of interest can taint the research and the researcher. So, wise researchers stay away from such appearances.

© Maridav/Shutterstock.com

∴ SUMMARY

1. Know when research should be conducted externally and when it should be done internally. The company that needs the research is not always the best company to perform the research. Sometimes, an outside supplier is more effective. An outside agency is better when the company desires a fresh perspective, when it would be difficult for inside researchers to be objective, and when the outside firm has some special expertise. In contrast, research in-house is better when the company needs it done very quickly, when the project requires close collaboration of many employees within the company, when the budget for the project is limited, and when secrecy is a major concern. The decision to go outside or stay inside for research depends on these particular issues.

2. Understand the career opportunities and career paths available within the marketing research industry. A marketing research career has never been more attractive. The demand for people with research skills continues to grow as the ability to record data unobtrusively expands with technology. Entry-level jobs may involve simple tasks such as data entry or performing survey research. A research analyst may be the next step on the career path. An experienced analyst typically earns a six-figure salary. Whereas there are several intermediate positions that differ depending on whether one works for a small or large firm, the director of marketing research is the chief information officer in charge of marketing information systems and research projects. The director plans, executes, and controls the marketing research function.

3. Become sensitive to the often conflicting relationship between marketing management and researchers. Researchers and managers often pursue conflicting goals. Some key sources of conflict include money, time, intuition, and experience. Managers want to spend the least amount of money on research as possible, have it done in the shortest time period conceivable, and believe that intuition and experience are good substitutes for research. Researchers will exchange greater expense for more precision in the research, would like to take more time to be more certain of results, and are hesitant to rely on intuition and experience. Better communication is a key to reducing this conflict. One tool that can be useful is the implementation of cross-functional teams.

4. Understand marketing ethics and ways that researchers can face ethical dilemmas. Marketing ethics is the application of morals to behavior related to the exchange environment. Generally, good ethic conforms to the notion of "right" and a lack of ethic conforms to the notion of "wrong." Those involved in marketing research face numerous ethical dilemmas. Researchers serve clients or, put another way, the doers of research serve the users. A doer may find himself or herself tempted to compromise professional standards in an effort to please the user. After all, the user pays the bills. Given the large number of ethical dilemmas involved in research, ethics is highly applicable to marketing research.

5. Appreciate the rights and obligations of (a) research respondents—particularly children, (b) research clients or sponsors, (c) marketing researchers, and (d) society. Each party involved in research has certain rights and obligations. These are generally interdependent in the sense that one party's right often leads to an obligation for another party. Although the rights and obligations of all parties are important, the obligation of the researcher to protect research participants is particularly important. Experimental manipulations can sometimes expose subjects to some form of harm or involve them in a ruse. The researcher must offer subjects the chance to be informed fully of the true purpose of the research during a debriefing. The researcher must also avoid subjecting participants to undue physical or psychological trauma. In the end, the total value of research should exceed the cost to society.

6. Avoid situations involving a conflict of interest in performing marketing research. A marketing research conflict of interest occurs when a researcher faces doing something to benefit one client at the expense of another client. One situation where this occurs is when a researcher could use results obtained in a study done for Brand A to prepare a report for its primary competitor Brand B. The researcher might consider recollecting the data anew for Brand B, but even this opens up the researcher to the appearance of a conflict of interest. The best way to avoid a conflict of interest is to avoid getting involved with multiple projects involving competing firms within some market.

:: KEY TERMS AND CONCEPTS

advocacy research, *95*

anonymity *91*

confidentiality, *91*

conflict of interest, *101*

cross-functional teams, *83*

custom research, *81*

debriefing, *93*

director of marketing research, *82*

do-not-call legislation, *90*

ethical dilemma, *88*

forecast analyst, *83*

human subjects review committee, *94*

idealism, *88*

informed consent, *90*

implied consent *91*

in-house research, *76*

Institutional Review Board, *94*

manager of decision support systems, *83*

marketing ethics, *88*

moral standards, *88*

outside agency, *76*

placebo, *93*

pseudo-research, *97*

push poll, *98*

relativism, *88*

research analyst, *82*

research assistants, *82*

research suppliers, *79*

standardized research service, *80*

syndicated service, *79*

:: QUESTIONS FOR REVIEW AND CRITICAL THINKING

1. What are the conditions that make in-house research preferable? What are the conditions that make outside research preferable? Would the company in the opening vignette have been better off to do the marketing research desired in-house rather than out-house?

2. Read a recent news article from *The Wall Street Journal* or other key source that deals with a new-product introduction or new product idea. Would you think it would be better for that firm to do research in-house or to use an outside agency? Explain.

3. Why is marketing research such an attractive career today?

4. What might the organizational structure of the research department be like for the following organizations?
   a. A large conglomerate like Google
   b. An advertising agency like Wieden and Kennedy
   c. A founder-owned company that operates a 20-unit restaurant chain
   d. A not-for-profit health-care organization like St. Jude Children's Hospital
   e. Your university

5. What problems do marketing research directors face in their roles as managers?

6. What are the managerial motivations that prove a source of conflict with marketing research?

7. What researcher motivations prove a source of conflict with management?

8. Search Internet job sites. Try to gather three to five want ads that are for marketing research positions of some type. Comment on the salary ranges and expected qualifications listed in these ads.

9. What is a cross-functional team? How is it relevant to marketing research?

10. What is the difference between research and pseudo-research? Cite several examples of each.

11. What is the definition of marketing ethics? How are marketing ethics relevant to research?

12. What is the difference between ethical relativism and ethical idealism? How might a person with an idealist ethical philosophy and a person with a relativist ethical philosophy differ with respect to including a sales pitch at the end of a research survey?

13. What is the difference between anonymity and confidentiality? What obligations does a researcher have with respect to confidentiality?

14. How should a marketing researcher help top management better understand the functions and limitations of research?

15. List at least one research obligation for research participants (respondents), marketing researchers, and research clients (sponsors).

16. What is a conflict of interest in a research context? How can such conflicts of interest be avoided?

17. What key questions help resolve the question of whether or not research participants serving as subjects in an experiment are treated ethically?

18. Identify a research supplier in your area and determine what syndicated services and other functions are available to clients.

19. How do societal forces play a role in shaping research ethics?

20. Comment on the ethics of the following situations.
    a. A warehouse club advertises "savings up to 30 percent" after a researcher presented management with survey results suggesting store prices ranged from 5 percent above the competition to 30 percent below the average competitor prices.
    b. A researcher requests the names of guests attending a professional conference, the titles of any movies (in-room) they purchased, a list of products consumed from the mini-bar, and a list of room service purchases.
    c. A researcher tells a potential respondent that an interview will last 10 minutes rather than the 30 minutes he or she actually anticipates.
    d. A respondent tells an interviewer that she wishes to cooperate with the survey, but her time is valuable and, therefore, she expects to be paid for her responses.
    e. An academic researcher performs basic research based on Facebook comments from guys talking about female acquaintances using salacious terms.
    f. A manager for a data service firm asks a researcher for the IP addresses of research respondents to a short consumer survey investigating factors leading to the likelihood of changing service providers.
    g. An online dating company stores the GPS locations of users, tracks their whereabouts, and sells an app that offers users an alert when a lot of "daters" are within a 10-minute radius.

21. Go back and review the example of a researcher wishing to conduct research about consumers and tattoos discussed in the chapter. (a) What ethical concepts does the example illustrate? (b) Describe a way in which the research could be designed to avoid any ethical issues.

∴ RESEARCH ACTIVITIES

1. Find the mission statement of three of the top research firms described earlier in the chapter (see Exhibit 4.2). What career opportunities exist at these firms? Would you consider each firm a small, mid-sized, or large firm? How might a job with one of these firms differ from starting your own research business?

2. Imagine a study being conducted by a senior manager at Apple who is interested in driving more business through iTunes.

The manager's ideas require a huge capital investment and are predicated on Apple operating systems dominating the smartphone (and tablet) market. Do some research on the Internet to find statistics for the market shares of various operating systems. Prepare a chart that displays the relative market shares as if you were presenting to the manager. As a researcher, is there potential for conflict or even ethical consequences based on the results?

Global Eating

Case 4.1

Barton Boomer, director of marketing research for a large research firm, has a bachelor's degree in marketing from Kansas State University. He joined the firm nine years ago after a one-year stint as a marketing research trainee at the corporate headquarters of a western packing corporation. Barton has a wife and two children. He earns $70,000 a year and owns a home in the suburbs. He is typical of a marketing junior research analyst. He is asked to interview an executive with a local restaurant chain, Eats-R-Wee. Eats-R-Wee is expanding internationally. The logical two choices for expansion are either to expand first to other nations that have values similar to those in the market area of Eats-R-Wee or to expand to the nearest geographical neighbor. During the initial interviews, Mr. Big, Vice President of Operations for Eats-R-Wee, makes several points to Barton.

• "Barton, we are all set to move across the border to Ontario and begin our international expansion with our neighbor to the north, Canada. Can you provide some research that will support this position?"

• "Barton, we are in a hurry. We can't sit on our hands for weeks waiting to make this decision. We need a comprehensive research project completed by the end of the month."

• "We are interested in how our competitors will react. Have you ever done research for them?"

• "Don't worry about the fee; we'll pay you top money for a 'good' report."

Marla Madam, Barton's Director of Marketing Research, encourages Barton to get back in touch with Mr. Big and tell him that the project will get underway right away.

Question
Critique this situation with respect to Barton's job. What recommendations would you have for him? Should the company get involved with the research? Explain your answers.

Big Brother Is Watching?

Case 4.2

Technology is making our behavior more and more difficult to keep secret. Right at this very moment, there is probably some way that your location can be tracked in a way that researchers could use the information. Do you have a smartphone with you? Is there an RFID tag in your shirt, your backpack, credit card or some other personal item? Are you in your car, and does it have a GPS device? All of these are ways that your location and movements might be tracked.

For instance, rental cars can be tracked using GPS. Suppose a research firm contracts with an insurance firm to study the way people drive when using a rental car. A customer's every movement is then tracked. So, if the customer stops at a fast-food restaurant, the researcher knows. If the customer goes to the movie when he or she should be on a sales call, the researcher knows. If the customer is speeding, the researcher knows.

Clearly, modern technology is making confidentiality more and more difficult to maintain. Although legitimate uses of this type of technology may assist in easing traffic patterns and providing better locations for service stations, shopping developments, and other retailers, at what point does the collection of such information become a concern? When would you become concerned about having your whereabouts constantly tracked?

Question

Suppose a Geographic Information Systems (GIS) research firm is approached by the state legislature and asked to provide data about vehicle movement within the state for all cars with a satellite tracking mechanism. Based on the movement of the cars over a certain time, the police can decide when a car was speeding. They intend on using this data to send speeding tickets to those who moved too far, too fast. If you are the research firm, would you supply the data? Discuss the ethical implications of the decision.

Photodisc Green/Getty Images

PART TWO

Designing Research Studies

Dimitri Otis/Getty Images

·:::· Qualitative Research Tools

After studying this chapter, you should be able to:

1. Contrast qualitative research with quantitative research
2. Know the role of qualitative research in exploratory research designs
3. Describe the basic orientations of qualitative research
4. Recognize common qualitative research tools and know the advantages and limitations of their use
5. Prepare a focus group interview outline
6. Recognize ways social networking and the *blogosphere* provide opportunities for qualitative research
7. Appreciate the role of exploratory qualitative research in scientific decision-making

Chapter Vignette:

Courtesy, Vans Classic Slip-On

The VF Corporation often doesn't register high top-of-mind awareness. However, consumers are very familiar with some of the many brands within its portfolio. While all the VF brands share a meaning related to an active lifestyle, brands like North Face, Timberland, Wrangler, and Vans each express this meaning in a slightly different way. Even in the recent difficult market times, VF continues to grow. A great deal of the growth comes from the brands that best match specific customer segments with lifestyle products capable of allowing consumers within those segments to express themselves meaningfully. VF is counting on Vans as a leader in their continued growth. To do this, Vans has to continue to understand exactly how the brand can create value and identify more customer segments eager for the same experience.

Qualitative research provides the focus of this chapter and provides tools that allow Vans to understand its value proposition. The Vans brand is long associated with shoes for skateboarding, although many of its shoes never see a skateboard these days. Vans' growth followed input from market research exploring the skateboard culture and the activities, interests, and opinions that appeal to this segment. So, what is in the mind and heart of a *boarder*? Researchers addressed the research question using an ethnographic approach and discovered that a carefree and detached attitude, a free spirit, and a rejection of conventional society were characteristics defining the culture.

Unlike mere shoes, Vans have to help the customer realize these feelings. Thus, Vans can't get by on comfort alone. Growth depends on creating hedonic value more than utilitarian value.

The research led to the adoption of an "off the wall" attitude, literally, as the slogan spun off product ideas, images, an Internet television series, and products that tapped into popular unpop culture! A line of Vans decorated in various Star Wars motifs that attempt to capture the spirit of "off the *wall*" and "out of this *world*" skateboard moves. VF's research is now pointing them toward Europe, where they believe youth markets are eager to experience the "off the wall" lifestyle. Realizing Vans is very much an experience brand, VF is spearheading this effort with the first and only ***House of Vans***. Vans fans can

© Shane White/Shutterstock.com

experience the retail theater in London, England, where tourists from all around Europe can go off the wall. In contrast, VF sees growth for Timberland, with research suggesting a very different meaning, to grow mainly through direct sales. A deep understanding of the brand becomes essential to market growth and success.[1]

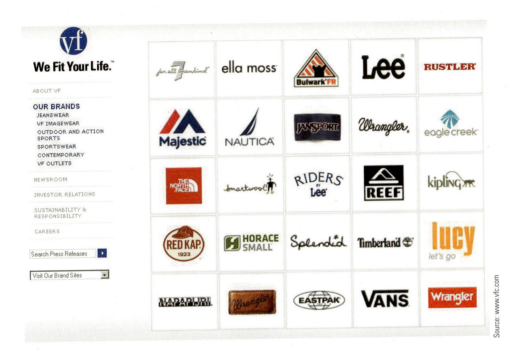

VF Corp, like other diversified marketers, must manage a portfolio of brands each offering a varied interpretation of the overall brand (from vfc.com).

Source: www.vfc.com

Introduction: What Is Qualitative Research?

Chemists sometimes use the term *qualitative analysis* to refer to research that determines the makeup of some compound. In other words, the focus is on the inner meaning of specific chemicals—their *qualities*. As the word implies, qualitative research is interested more in *qualities* than quantities. Therefore, qualitative marketing research is unique in not applying specific numbers to measure marketing variables or using statistical procedures to specify a relationship's strength numerically.

Describing Qualitative Research

Qualitative marketing research is research that addresses marketing objectives through techniques allowing the researcher to provide elaborate interpretations of market phenomena without depending on numerical measurement. The focus is on discovering new insights and true inner meanings. It is very widely applied in practice and many research firms specialize in qualitative research.

Qualitative research designs employ less structure than most quantitative approaches. Participants in qualitative research do not choose numerical (or multiple choice) responses to a specific question. Instead, qualitative approaches are more **researcher-dependent** in that the researcher must extract meaning from open-ended responses, such as text from a recorded interview or a posting on a social networking website like Facebook, or from a collage representing the meaning of some experience, such as skateboarding. The researcher interprets the data to extract its meaning and converts it to information.

Uses of Qualitative Research

Mechanics can't use a hammer to fix everything that is broken. Instead, a mechanic chooses the tool from a toolbox that he/she believes matches best to a given problem. Marketing research is the same. The researcher has many tools available and the research design should try to match the

Qualitative marketing research

Research that addresses marketing objectives through techniques that allow the researcher to provide elaborate interpretations of market phenomena without depending on numerical measurement; its focus is on discovering new insights and true inner meanings.

Researcher-dependent

Research in which the researcher must extract meaning from unstructured responses such as text from a recorded interview or a collage representing the meaning of some experience.

Although we most often think of surveys as ways of collecting quantitative data, we can also use them to collect qualitative data. Take a look at the question that was part of the in-class survey at left in the screenshot.

Find at least three responses in the data that you believe represent qualitative data and try to interpret the results. What approach best fits your attempt to interpret this data? What do you think (what theory) can be learned from the responses to this question? Compare your interpretation to those of other students. How much do you agree with other students and what do you think is the source of disagreement, if any?

best tool to the research objective. Also, just as a mechanic is probably not an expert with every tool, each researcher usually has special expertise with a small number of tools. Not every researcher has expertise with tools that would comprise qualitative research.

Generally, the less specific the research objective, the more likely that qualitative research tools will be appropriate. Also, when the emphasis is on a deeper understanding of motivations or on discovering novel concepts, qualitative research is very appropriate. The following list represents common situations that often call for qualitative research.[2]

1. When a researcher faces difficulty developing specific and actionable decision statements or research objectives. For instance, if, after several interviews with a research client, a researcher still cannot determine what things he/she needs to measure, qualitative research approaches may help with problem definition and, as a result, identify research questions indicating what to measure.
2. When the research objective involves developing a very detailed and in-depth understanding of some phenomena. Qualitative research tools help reveal the primary themes indicating human motivations and the documentation of activities is usually very complete.
3. When the research objective is to learn how consumers use a product in its natural setting or to learn how to express some concept in colloquial terms. A survey can probably ask many useful questions, but watching how someone actually experiences a product will usually be more insightful. Qualitative research produces many product improvement ideas.
4. When some behavior the researcher is studying is particularly context-dependent—meaning the reasons something is liked or some behavior is performed depends very much on the particular situation surrounding the event. The skating environment frames the situation in which researchers understand the Vans brand best.
5. When the researcher needs a fresh approach. This is particularly the case when quantitative research results on some issue have been less than satisfying. Qualitative tools can yield unique insights, many of which may lead to new product ideas.

Each situation also describes a situation that may require an exploratory orientation. In Chapter 3, we indicated that researchers sometimes need exploratory research just to reach the appropriate decision statement and research objectives. Although equating qualitative research with exploratory research is an oversimplification, the application of qualitative tools can help clear up ambiguity and provide innovative ideas.

Qualitative "versus" Quantitative Research

In social science, one can find many debates about the superiority of qualitative research over quantitative research or vice versa.[3] We'll begin by saying that this is largely a superfluous argument in either direction. The truth is that qualitative research can accomplish research objectives that quantitative research cannot. Similarly truthful, but no more so, quantitative research can accomplish objectives that qualitative research cannot. The key to successfully using either is to match the right approach to the right research context.

Many good research projects combine both qualitative and quantitative research.[4] For instance, developing valid survey measures requires first a deep understanding of the concept measured and second a description of the way people express these perceptions in everyday language. Both of these are tasks best suited for qualitative research. However, validating the measure formally to make sure it can reliably capture the intended concept will likely require quantitative research.[5] Also, qualitative research may be needed to separate symptoms from problems and then quantitative research may follow to test relationships among relevant variables.

Quantitative marketing research addresses research objectives through empirical assessments that involve numerical measurement and analytical approaches. Quantitative research is more apt to stand on its own in the sense that it entails less interpretation. It is quite appropriate when a research objective involves a managerial action standard. For example, a salad dressing company considered changing its recipe.[6] Researchers tested the new recipe using a sample of consumers who rated the product using 100-point numeric scales. Management established a rule requiring 90 percent confidence that a majority of consumers would rate the new product higher than the old product before replacing a recipe. The results require little interpretation beyond the computations. A project like this uses both quantitative measurement in the form of numeric rating scales and quantitative analysis in the form of applied statistical procedures.

Quantitative marketing research

Addresses research objectives through empirical assessments that involve numerical measurement and statistical and/or computational analysis.

Contrasting Qualitative with Quantitative Methods

Exhibit 5.1 illustrates some differences between qualitative and quantitative research. Certainly, these are generalities and exceptions apply but it covers some of the key distinctions.

Quantitative researchers direct a considerable amount of activity toward measuring concepts with scales that directly or indirectly provide numeric values. The user inputs the resulting numeric

EXHIBIT 5.1
Comparing Qualitative and Quantitative Research

Qualitative Research	Research Aspect	Quantitative Research
Discover Ideas, Used in Exploratory Research with General Research Objects	Common Purpose	Test Hypotheses or Specific Research Questions
Observe and Interpret	Approach	Measure and Test
Unstructured, Free-Form	Data Collection Approach	Structured Response Categories Provided
Researcher Is Intimately Involved. Results Are Subjective.	Researcher Independence	Researcher Uninvolved Observer. Results Are Objective.
Small Samples—Often in Natural Settings	Samples	Large Samples to Produce Generalizable Results (Results That Apply to Other Situations)
Exploratory Research Designs	Most Often Used	Descriptive and Causal Research Designs

Source: William Zikmund and Barry Babin, *Essentials of Marketing Research*, 5th ed, Cengage Learning, 2012.

The Other Side of the Coin

We usually think about consumer researchers interviewing potential customers about what they like. However, researchers monitor online chatter for both good and bad news about the brand. One doesn't have to search hard for posts about "why I hate ____ (fill in the brand)" or "____ sucks!" Even brands like Apple generate a lot of negative commentary on Tumblr, Facebook, and the Internet in general. Qualitative researchers often find the comments that consumers leave behind useful. These posts or even pictures can provide qualitative data that may lead to insights concerning product problems or the types of consumers who will hate the brand.

The Internet clearly has a nefarious side. Sometimes, negative information is not left by actual customers of the products. Instead, individuals intentionally create negative information, even if it is not true, in the hope that others may see it or that it will get associated with the brand in search engine algorithms. Firms also exist to gerrymander Search-Engine-Optimizer (SEO) results. Qualitative researchers may be able to depict clues that sort out the negative comments left by actual customers from those left behind maliciously. In many ways, qualitative approaches can be useful in detecting marketing problems.

values into statistical computations and hypothesis testing. As will be described in detail later, this process involves comparing numbers in some way. In contrast, qualitative researchers are more interested in observing, listening, and interpreting. The qualitative researcher intimately involves him/herself in the research process and in constructing the results. For these reasons, qualitative research results are researcher-dependent, or **subjective**, meaning that different researchers may reach different conclusions based on the same data. In contrast, when a survey respondent provides a satisfaction score on a quantitative scale, the score is more objective because the number will be the same no matter what researcher is involved in the analysis.

Subjective
Researcher-dependent results with the consequence that different researchers may reach different conclusions (meanings) based on the same interview.

Qualitative research usually involves smaller samples than the typical quantitative study. Instead of sampling hundreds of consumers, a handful of them are usually sufficient as a source of qualitative data. Small samples are perfectly acceptable in discovery-oriented research. All ideas discovered still need testing before companies put them into practice. Does a smaller sample mean that qualitative research is cheaper than quantitative? Perhaps not. Although researchers observe fewer respondents, the greater researcher involvement in both the data collection and analysis can drive up the costs of qualitative research.

Small samples, interpretive procedures that require subjective judgments and an unstructured interview format all make traditional hypotheses testing complicated with qualitative research. Thus, these procedures are not the best for drawing definitive conclusions. A causal design is better suited for testing. These disadvantages for drawing inferences, however, become advantages when the goal is to draw out potential explanations. The researcher spends more time with each respondent and is therefore able to explore much more ground due to the flexibility of the procedures.

Qualitative Research and Exploratory Research Designs

When researchers have limited experience or knowledge about an issue, exploratory research is useful. Exploratory research can be an essential first step to a more rigorous, conclusive, confirmatory study by reducing the chance of beginning with an inadequate, incorrect, or misleading set of research objectives.

Philosophically, we can classify research as either exploratory or confirmatory. Confirmatory research tests hypotheses. The test results help decision-making by suggesting a specific course of action. Exploratory research, on the other hand, is different and plays a key role in developing ideas that lead to research hypotheses in the first place.

Most exploratory research designs produce **qualitative data**. Qualitative data are not characterized by numeric values and instead involve textual, visual, or oral information. The focus of qualitative research is not on numbers but on stories, visual portrayals, meaningful characterizations, interpretations, and other expressive descriptions. Exploratory designs do not usually produce **quantitative data**, which represent phenomena by assigning numeric values in an ordered and meaningful way.

For example, a quantitative researcher may search for numbers that indicate economic trends. This may lead to hypothesis tests concerning how much the economy influences movie consumption. An exploratory researcher is more likely to adopt a qualitative approach that might involve interviews trying to develop a deeper understanding of how changing economic times influence families and why people suffering economically spend scarce resources on movie consumption. Data from the interview may help develop a hypothesis, but it would not test one.

Researchers can sometimes conduct a qualitative study very quickly. Others take a very long time. For example, Coca-Cola researchers can arrange, conduct, and interpret a single focus group analysis involving the company's sales force in a matter of days. This would provide faster results than most descriptive or causal designs. However, other types of qualitative research, such as a participant-observer study aimed at understanding skateboarding, could take months to complete. A qualitative approach can, but does not necessarily, save time.

Idea Generation

Exploratory research plays a big role in new product development, including developing and screening new product ideas. It is particularly useful in idea generation and screening by producing multiple ideas and then narrowing the choices down to a small number of alternatives. In this process, exploratory research may indicate that some new product ideas are unworkable.

Qualitative research can generate ideas for new products, advertising copy, promotional ideas, and product improvements in numerous ways. Researchers using qualitative approaches can ask consumers to describe their product experiences in great detail. This data can reveal the consumer needs that a product can truly address. For example, a consumer may describe their dog food experiences. When asked what he/she wants in a dog food, the reply likely will be, "Something that is good for the dog." Once the consumer is encouraged to continue, however, we may learn that the dog food "smells bad in the refrigerator" and "is messy to clean up." Thus, the interview reveals that needs related to dog food are not entirely centered on the dog.

Idea generation proves difficult for students and for managers alike. Thus, researchers must keep an open mind when conducting qualitative research and interpreting data. No doubt, managers dismiss many good ideas because they sound crazy. But, just think of how many crazy products we use—at least products that would've seemed crazy at some point in time. Here is a quick and simple checklist to help create a creative mindset when looking for new ideas.

1. Quantity Leads to Quality—A breakthrough idea is more likely to exist in a list of 100 than in a list of 3 ideas.
2. Wilder Is Better—In an exploratory mode, encourage respondents to think of wild ideas. Stretch beyond realistic boundaries to see what might be.
3. Do Not Judge—People are naturally judgmental. Premature judgment kills many great ideas. Idea generation is exploratory work and there is no room for judgment here.
4. Question Assumptions—When interpreting a respondent's comments, do not impose assumptions that may not exist. Follow up to examine important assumptions. The phrase "think outside of the box" is all about trying to break through false assumptions.

Qualitative data

Data that are not characterized by numeric values and instead are textual, visual, or oral; focus is on stories, visual portrayals, meaningful characterizations, interpretations, and other expressive descriptions.

Quantitative data

Represent phenomena by assigning numeric values in an ordered and meaningful way.

To the Point

"*Innovation … endows resources with a new capacity to create wealth.*"

—PETER DRUCKER

Probing

Probing is an interview technique that tries to draw deeper and more elaborate explanations from a respondent. Oftentimes, researchers may conduct interviews with key decision-makers in trying to separate symptoms from the relevant issues that should be the focus of the research. Probing techniques often are applied in such interviews. In addition, researchers apply probing techniques in interviews trying to reveal consumer values and motivations that drive specific consumer behaviors. For instance, why do some consumers avoid personal contact and try to communicate with companies only via web communication? Researchers will find probing useful for any of the following reasons:

1. Clarification—ask respondent to explain exactly what certain phrases or terms mean.
2. Free-form thinking—ask for top-of-mind associations by saying, "What does _____ make you think of?"
3. Pause—the researcher may simply wait in silence briefly. The silence can encourage the respondent to explain more deeply as a way of coping with the awkwardness that the silence brings.
4. Contrast—ask respondent to contrast events as similar or different from other events.
5. Meaning—ask respondent to "tell me something" or "tell me more" about some interesting point.
6. Change—ask respondent, "What has changed?" This is particularly useful in separating symptoms from issues when interviewing key decision-makers.

Concept Testing

Concept testing

A frequently performed type of exploratory research representing many similar research procedures all having the same purpose: to screen new, revised, or repositioned ideas.

Research's main role in idea screening is concept testing. **Concept testing** is a frequently performed type of exploratory research representing many similar research procedures all having the same purpose: to screen new, revised, or repositioned ideas. Despite the term *testing*, concept testing approaches are largely qualitative. Typically, respondents read a written statement, view a pictorial representation, or examine a model or sample, and then provide comments. The questions almost always include whether the idea is likable, whether it would be useful, and whether it seems new. Respondents then elaborate on the idea orally, in writing, or through some visual communication. Concept testing allows an initial evaluation prior to the commitment of any additional research and development, manufacturing, or other company resources. Perhaps just as importantly, the researcher interprets respondent comments qualitatively searching for themes to potentially improve the product.

Concept testing processes work best when they not only identify ideas with the most potential but also lead to important refinements. Rite Aid drug stores first successfully concept-tested a new store layout. Dubbed the Wellness Store, the new design features lower shelves, wider aisles, and a more focused merchandise assortment emphasizing personal well-being. Now that the Wellness Store concept seems viable, Rite Aid is further testing a store-within-the-store concept known as Beauty Vision. The Beauty Vision store offers stylish merchandising of beauty-related products such as cosmetics and skincare.[7] The brands include Senna Cosmetics and Alison Raffaele, an upgrade over the old selection. Qualitative insight from consumers was instrumental in developing both concepts. Then, in-store testing provided data supporting and refining the ideas for rollout.

Likewise, if Vans introduces snowboarding and biking products as a way of increasing sales revenues, those products will have to undergo concept screening. Will consumers respond favorably to the ideas of a Vans Cushioned Snowboard or Vans Napoleon Dynamite line? Clearly, concept testing including probing interview techniques will be helpful in this effort.

Exhibit 5.2 shows excellent concept statements for two new alternative chain restaurant concepts. A national franchise operating various chain restaurants that compete with the likes of Hooters and Outback Steakhouse is interested in this concept. The statements portraying the intangibles (brand image, product appearance, name, and price) and a description of the product simulate reality. A researcher conveys the product idea clearly to the research participant, who then responds in some way. Their comments become the key information gleaned from the study.

EXHIBIT **5.2**
Testing New Product
Concepts

Component	Concept	
	Havana's	Bekkah
Brand Image	Family oriented, Cuban themed, with generous portions of modestly priced food	Upscale hangout for on–the-go individuals looking for a change of pace
Atmosphere	Bright colors, Cuban music all day and every day with every restaurant built around a bar featuring genuine '57 Chevys	Muted colors and stone walls giving the appearance of an oasis in an arid climate
Product Assortment	Traditional Cuban slow-cooked meats with generous sides like black beans and fried plantains. Cuban sangria and a wide assortment of beer are featured.	Lebanese meats sliced very thin with traditional Middle Eastern seasonings, a variety of pita breads, feta cheese, and yogurt relishes. Lebanese wines are featured and supplement an otherwise domestic collection.
Price Points	Average ticket per customer is projected to be around $14.	Average ticket per customer is projected to be around $26.
Location	Suburban location around the top 10 largest metropolitan areas in the United States and Canada	Major SMSAs (standard metropolitan statistical areas) across the southern United States from San Diego, CA to Jacksonville, FL

Source: William Zikmund and Barry Babin, *Essentials of Marketing Research*, 5th ed, Cengage Learning, 2012.

Qualitative Research Orientations

Researchers perform qualitative research in many ways using many techniques. Each research-er's orientation toward qualitative research is influenced by the different fields of study. These orientations are each associated with a category of qualitative research. The major categories of qualitative research include:

1. Phenomenology—originating in philosophy and psychology
2. Ethnography—originating in anthropology
3. Grounded theory—originating in sociology
4. Case studies—originating in psychology and in business research

Precise lines between these approaches are difficult to draw, and a particular qualitative research study may involve elements of two or more approaches. However, each category does reflect a somewhat unique approach to human inquiry and approaches to discovering knowledge. Each will be described briefly, followed by a description of some of the more common qualitative techniques used to generate qualitative data.

Phenomenology

What Is a Phenomenological Approach to Research?

Phenomenology represents a philosophical approach to studying human experiences based on the idea that human experience itself is inherently subjective and determined by the contexts in which people live.[8] The phenomenological researcher focuses on how relationships between a person and the physical environment, objects, people, or situations shape a person's behavior. Phenomenological inquiry seeks to describe, reflect upon, and interpret experiences.

Researchers with a phenomenological orientation rely largely on conversational interview tools. The phenomenological interviewer is careful to avoid asking direct questions when at all possible. Instead, the interviewer asks respondents to tell a story about some experience. In

Phenomenology

A philosophical approach to studying human experiences based on the idea that human experience itself is inherently subjective and determined by the context in which people live.

addition, the researcher must do everything possible to make sure a respondent is comfortable telling his/her story. One way to accomplish this is to become a member of the group (e.g., becoming a skateboarder to understand skateboarding culture). Another way may be to avoid having the person use his/her real name. This might be particularly necessary in studying potentially sensitive topics, including smoking, shoplifting, or employee theft.

A phenomenological approach to studying the Vans brand may require considerable time. The researcher may first spend weeks or months fitting in with the person or group of interest to establish a comfort level. The researcher makes careful notes of conversations. If the interviewer seeks an actual interview, he/she would likely not begin by asking a skateboarder to describe his/her shoes. Rather, asking for favorite skateboard incidents or talking about what makes a skateboarder unique may generate productive conversation. Generally, the approach is very unstructured as a way of avoiding leading questions and to provide every opportunity for new insights.

What Is Hermeneutics?

Hermeneutics

An approach to understanding phenomenology that relies on analysis of texts through which a person tells a story about him/herself.

The term *hermeneutics* is important in phenomenology. **Hermeneutics** is an approach to understanding phenomenology that relies on analysis of texts in which a person tells a story about him/herself.[9] The interpretive research extracts meaning by connecting text passages to one another or to themes expressed outside the story. The connections provide a way of coding the key meanings expressed in a story. Although a full understanding of hermeneutics is beyond the scope of this text, qualitative tools often employ some of the key terminology. For instance, a

Hermeneutic unit

Refers to a text passage from a respondent's story that is linked with a key theme from within this story or a theme provided by the researcher.

hermeneutic unit refers to a text passage from a respondent's story that is linked with a key theme from within this story or a theme provided by the researcher.[10] The qualitative researcher uses these passages to interpret the data.

Listening is a necessary skill for phenomenological researchers. A researcher with keen listening skills picks up on the meaningful themes. Furthermore, listening isn't always oral. The Coca-Cola Company invites consumers to tell stories about themselves and Coke products on their social networking websites. After all, this is where a large portion of consumer conversation takes place in these virtual communities these days.[11] Here, hermeneutic units from conversations taking place in an environment where consumers are comfortable and candid reveal key themes about the ways products are used and can spur ideas for product improvement, advertising, or new products.

Computerized software exists to assist in listening by making coding texts and images easy. ATLAS.ti is one such software package that adopts the term *hermeneutic unit* in referring to groups of phrases that are linked with meaning. One useful component of computerized approaches is a word counter. The word counter will return counts of how many times words appear in a story or recorded interview. Frequently reoccurring words or phrases indicate potential key themes. The following Research Snapshot demonstrates the use of hermeneutics in interpreting a story about a consumer shopping for a car.

Word Clouds

Word cloud

A graphical depiction of the frequency with which words occur; words occurring more frequently are shown in correspondingly large type face. Others may use the term *tag cloud* to refer to the same thing.

Numerous software programs, including Atlas Ti, will generate a word cloud from text input. A **word cloud** is a graphical depiction of the frequency with which words occur. The more often a word or phrase occurs, the larger that word is depicted in the graphic. Others may use the term *tag cloud* to refer to the same thing. Word clouds will depict the word or terms that occur most frequently with large, bold typeface. Words or terms that are infrequently occurring are small and light. Word clouds are an easy way to portray the frequency with which terms occur in a given interview, story, or other text data unit. Clients easily understand the graphic. However, the researcher should acknowledge that the frequency of occurrence does not necessarily mean importance. Sometimes, infrequently occurring themes can be very meaningful. Consider the potential consequences of overlooking a pharmaceutical product's side effect like memory loss because consumers seldom mention it in open-ended interviews. Also, in most software, the researcher has to use judgment about terms that are synonyms. For instance, if a story talks about a consumer being embarrassed, guilty, and ashamed when buying personal items at the drug store, should those

"When Will I Ever Learn?"

A hermeneutic approach can be used to provide insight into car shopping experiences. The approach involves a small number of consumers providing relatively lengthy stories about recent car shopping experiences. The goal is trying to discover particular reasons why they eliminate certain car models from consideration. The consumer tells a story of comparing a Ford and a General Motors (GM) minivan. She describes the two vehicles in great detail and ultimately concludes, "We might have gone with the Ford instead because it was real close between the Ford and the GM." The Ford was cheaper, but the way the door opened suggested difficulties in dealing with kids and groceries and the like, and so she purchased the GM model. The researcher in this story goes on to interpret the plotline of the story as having to do with her responsibility for poor consumption outcomes. Consider the following passage.

"It has got GM defects and that is really frustrating. I mean the transmission had to be rebuilt after about 150 miles … and it had this horrible vibration problem. We took a long vacation where you couldn't go over sixty miles an hour because the thing started shaking so bad… . I told everybody, 'Don't buy one of these things.' We should have known because our Buick—the Buick that is in the shop right now—its transmission lasted about 3,000 miles. My husband's parents are GM people and they had one go bad. I keep thinking, When I am

AP Images/Lenny Ignelzi

going to learn? I think this one has done it. I don't think I will ever go back to GM after this."

The research concludes that a hermeneutic link exists between the phrase "When I am going to learn?" and the plot of self-responsibility. The resulting behavior including no longer considering GM products and the negative word-of-mouth behavior are ways of restoring esteem given the events.

Sources: *Journal of Marketing Research* by Winer, Russ. Copyright 1997 by Am Marketing Assn (AMA) (CHIC). Reproduced with permission of Am Marketing Assn (AMA) (CHIC) in the format Textbook via Copyright Clearance Center. Thompson, Craig J., "Interpreting Consumers: A Hermeneutical Framework for Deriving Marketing Insights from the Tests of Consumers' Consumption Stories," *Journal of Marketing Research*, 34 (November 1997), 438–455 (see pp. 443–444 for quotation).

EXHIBIT 5.3

An Example Word Cloud

be treated as a single phrase or as separate terms? As long as the researcher and user understand that a word cloud is for exploratory use, the tool can be quite helpful.

Exhibit 5.3 depicts a word cloud derived from online reviews of a New York City hotel. The exhibit illustrates a way qualitative researchers can try to interpret text left behind by consumers online. In this case, the researcher would likely ignore the words that would be obvious in a hotel review, like *room*, *hotel*, and *booking*, and instead focus on adjectives that may indicate the true impression of the hotel. In this case, the word "smelled" and "smell" likely contain the same meaning and could be indicative of a problem with the hotel. Word clouds provide simple but useful descriptions. One should not jump to conclusions based on the word cloud alone. For instance, we can be quite confident that the hotel smelled, but the word cloud itself does not indicate whether the smell was good or bad. Clearly though, the result suggests potentially relevant themes associated with consumption.

Ethnography

What Is Ethnography?

Ethnography

Represents ways of studying cultures through methods that involve becoming highly active within that culture.

Participant-observation

Ethnographic research approach where the researcher becomes immersed within the culture that he/she is studying and draws data from his/her observations.

Netnography

The application of ethnographic research procedures to online phenomena.

Ethnography represents ways of studying cultures through methods that involve becoming highly active within that culture. **Participant-observation** typifies an ethnographic research approach. Participant-observation means the researcher immerses him/herself within the culture that he/she is studying and draws data from the resulting observations. A *culture* can be either a broad culture, like American culture, or a narrow culture, like urban gangs or skateboarding enthusiasts.[12] Increasingly, ethnographic approaches address the meaning of belonging to and participation in online communities. Often, the researcher participates as a member of the community in employing ethnographic procedures. The term **netnography** sometimes is used to refer to the application of ethnography to online phenomena.[13] A researcher may get involved in an online Vans social community to better understand the brand and the skateboarding lifestyle.

Organizational culture also is relevant for ethnographic study.[14] At times, researchers actually become employees of an organization for an extended period of time. In doing so, they become part of the culture and over time other employees come to act quite naturally around the researcher. The researcher may observe behaviors that the employee would never reveal otherwise. For instance, a researcher investigating the ethical behavior of salespeople may have difficulty getting a car salesperson to reveal any potentially deceptive sales tactics in a traditional interview. However, ethnographic techniques may result in the salesperson letting down his/her guard, resulting in more valid discoveries about the car-selling culture.

Ethnographic (participant-observation) approaches may be useful in understanding how children obtain value from their experiences with toys.

Alyson Aliano/The Image Bank/Getty Images

Observation in Ethnography

Observation plays a key role in ethnography. Researchers today sometimes ask households for permission to place video cameras in their home. In doing so, the ethnographer can study the consumer in a "natural habitat" and use the observations to test new products, develop new product ideas, and develop marketing strategies in general. Companies like Qualvu gather data from small cameras that consumers wear around their neck, something like a necklace.[15] While the consumer shops, the camera is capturing the experience as the consumer sees it.

Ethnographic study can be particularly useful when a certain culture is composed of individuals who cannot or will not verbalize their thoughts and feelings. For instance, ethnography has advantages for discovering insights among children because it does not rely largely on their answers to questions. Instead, the researcher can simply become part of the environment, allow the children to do what they do naturally, and record their behavior.[16]

The opening vignette describes a situation in which ethnographic research may be appropriate. A researcher might blend into a skateboard group. The artifacts shared by the group, including photos posted on the group's wall, may provide meaning. Also, researchers who act as customers can perform ethnography by becoming a natural part of the environment. Researchers posing as restaurant customers developed lists of the most critical service failures in restaurants and interpreted meanings for things such as slow service, inappropriate server behavior, and food waste.[17]

To the Point

"You can tell a lot about a person by the way he eats his jellybeans."

—RONALD REAGAN

Grounded Theory

What Is Grounded Theory?

Grounded theory represents an inductive investigation in which the researcher poses questions about information provided by respondents or taken from historical records. The researcher asks the questions to him/herself and repeatedly questions the responses to derive deeper explanations. Grounded theory is particularly applicable in highly dynamic situations involving rapid and significant change. Two key questions asked by the grounded theory researcher are "What is happening here?" and "How is it different?"[18] The distinguishing characteristic of grounded theory is that it does not begin with a theory but instead extracts one from whatever emerges from an area of inquiry.

Grounded theory
Represents an inductive investigation in which the researcher poses questions about information provided by respondents or taken from historical records; the researcher asks the questions to him/herself and repeatedly questions the responses to derive deeper explanations.

How Is Grounded Theory Used?

Consider a company that approaches a researcher to study whether or not the company sales force is losing its effectiveness. The researcher can use grounded theory to discover a potential explanation. A theory emerges based on text analysis of dozens of sales meeting transcripts recorded over the previous five years. By posing questions about events discussed in the sales meetings and scrutinizing differences in the situations that may have led to the discussion, the researcher develops a theory. The theory suggests that with an increasing reliance on e-mail and other technological devices for communication, the salespeople do not communicate with each other informally as much as they did previously. As a result, the salespeople had failed to bond into a close-knit "community."[19]

Computerized software also can be useful in developing grounded theory.[20] Researchers input text from consumer interviews into a program called NVivo to develop a theory of things that interfere with consumers acting out ethical consumption intentions. The results suggested that consumers who lack deep motivation are unwilling to sacrifice other aspects of product quality only for the sake of appearing to act more responsibly as a consumer.

Case Studies

What Are Case Studies?

Case studies refer to the documented history of a particular person, group, organization, or event. A case study may describe consumers' acceptance or rejection of a particular product or brand. Clinical interviews of individual consumers represent this type of case study.

Case studies
The documented history of a particular person, group, organization, or event.

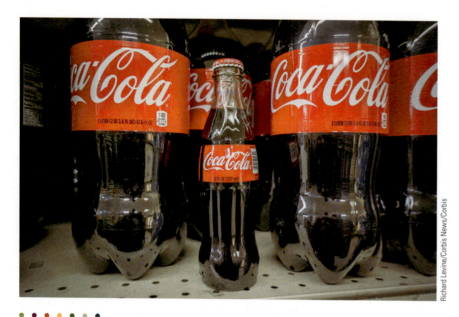

Richard Levine/Corbis News/Corbis

Alternatively, case studies may describe the events of a specific company introducing a new product. Sometimes, case studies document the way some company dealt with a crisis of some type. Case studies, for instance, proved useful in trying to explore ways firms dealt with the financial crisis occurring a few years ago.[21] Textbook cases typify this kind of case study.

Themes are identified by the frequency with which the same term (or a synonym) arises in the narrative case description. The themes may be useful in discovering variables that are relevant to potential explanations. Thematic interpretation is a tool useful across all types of qualitative inquiry, not just in case studies.

Qualitative research reveals that products that are perceived as "authentic" offer more value for consumers.

Themes

Identified by the frequency with which the same term (or a synonym) arises in the narrative description.

How Are Case Studies Used?

Case studies are commonly applied in business. For instance, case studies of brands that sell "luxury" products helped provide insight into what makes up a prestigious brand. A marketing researcher carefully conducted case studies of higher-end wine labels (such as Penfolds Grange), including the methods of production and marketing. This analysis suggested that a key ingredient to a prestige brand may well be authenticity. When consumers know something is authentic, they attach more esteem to that product or brand.[22]

Case studies provide a primary advantage in that a researcher can study an entire organization or entity in depth with meticulous attention to detail. With this highly focused attention, the researcher is able to study the order of events carefully or to concentrate on identifying the relationships among functions, individuals, or entities. Conducting a case study often requires the cooperation of the party studied. This freedom to search for whatever data an investigator deems important makes the success of any case study highly dependent on the alertness, creativity, intelligence, and motivation of the individual performing the case analysis.

Common Techniques Used in Qualitative Research

Qualitative researchers apply a nearly endless number of techniques. These techniques overlap more than one of the categories previously discussed, although each category may display a preference for certain techniques. Exhibit 5.4 lists characteristics of some common qualitative research techniques. Each is then described.

Focus group interview

An unstructured, free-flowing interview with a small group of around six to ten people. Focus groups are led by a trained moderator who follows a flexible format encouraging dialogue among respondents.

Focus Group Interview

The focus group interview is so widely used that many advertising and research agencies do nothing but focus group interviews. A **focus group interview** is an unstructured, free-flowing interview with a small group of people, usually between six and ten. Focus groups are led by a trained moderator who follows a flexible format encouraging dialogue among respondents. Common focus group topics include employee programs, brand meanings, problems with products, advertising themes, or new-product concepts. Unfortunately, all people too

EXHIBIT **5.4** Common Qualitative Research Tools

Tool	Description	Type of Approach (Category)	Key Advantages	Key Disadvantages
Focus Group Interviews	Small group discussions led by a trained moderator	Ethnography, case studies	• Can be done quickly • Gain multiple perspectives • Flexibility	• Results do not generalize to larger population • Difficult to use for sensitive topics • Expensive
Depth Interviews	One-on-one, probing interview between a trained researcher and a respondent	Ethnography, grounded theory, case studies	• Gain considerable insight from each individual • Good for understanding unusual behaviors	• Results not meant to generalize • Very expensive per each interview
Conversations	Unstructured dialogue recorded by a researcher	Phenomenology, grounded theory	• Gain unique insights from enthusiasts • Can cover sensitive topics • Less expensive than depth interviews or focus groups	• Easy to get off course • Interpretations are very researcher dependent
Semi-Structured Interviews	Open-ended questions, often in writing, that ask for short essay-type answers from respondents	Grounded theory, ethnography	• Can address more specific issues • Results can be easily interpreted • Cost advantages over focus groups and depth interviews	• Lack the flexibility that is likely to produce truly creative or novel explanations
Word Association/ Sentence Completion	Records the first thoughts that come to a consumer in response to some stimulus	Grounded theory, case studies	• Economical • Can be done quickly	• Lack the flexibility that is likely to produce truly creative or novel explanations
Observation	Recorded notes describing observed events	Ethnography, grounded theory, case studies	• Can be inobtrusive • Can yield actual behavior patterns	• Can be very expensive with participant observer series
Collages	Respondent assembles pictures that represent their thoughts/feelings	Phenomenology, grounded theory	• Flexible enough to allow novel insights	• Highly dependent on the researcher's interpretation of the collage
Thematic Apperception/ Cartoon Tests	Researcher provides an ambiguous picture and respondent tells about the story	Phenomenology, grounded theory	• Projective, allows to get at sensitive issues • Flexible	• Highly dependent on the researcher's interpretation

Source: William Zikmund and Barry Babin, *Essentials of Marketing Research*, 5th ed, Cengage Learning, 2012.

often use the term loosely to refer to any discussion among a small group of people. Without the appropriate structure and trained leader, a group discussion probably lacks the appropriate focus.

Focus group participants may range from consumers talking about hair coloring, petroleum engineers talking about problems in the "oil patch," children talking about toys, or employees talking about their jobs. A moderator begins by providing an opening statement intended to steer discussion in the intended direction. Ideally, discussion topics emerge at the group's initiative more than that of the moderator's. Consistent with phenomenological approaches, moderators should avoid direct questioning unless absolutely necessary.

Advantages of Focus Group Interviews

Focus groups allow people to discuss their true feelings, anxieties, and frustrations, as well as the depth of their convictions, in their own words. Although other approaches may also do much the same, focus groups offer several advantages:

1. Relatively fast
2. Easy to execute
3. Allow respondents to piggyback off each other's ideas
4. Provide multiple perspectives
5. Give flexibility to allow more detailed descriptions
6. Provide a high degree of scrutiny

Speed and Ease

In an emergency situation, a research company can conduct, analyze, and report on three or four group sessions within about a week. The large number of research firms that conduct focus group interviews makes it easy to find someone to conduct the research. Practically every state in the United States contains multiple research firms that have their own focus group facilities. Companies with large research departments likely have at least one qualified focus group moderator so that they need not outsource the focus group.

Piggybacking and Multiple Perspectives

Piggyback

A procedure in which one respondent stimulates thought among the others; as this process continues, increasingly creative insights are possible.

Furthermore, the group approach may produce thoughts that would not be produced otherwise. The interplay between respondents allows them to **piggyback** off of each other's ideas. In other words, one respondent stimulates thought among the others and, as this process continues, increasingly creative insights are possible. A comment by one individual often triggers a chain of responses from the other participants. The social nature of the focus group also helps bring out multiple views as each person shares a particular perspective.

Flexibility

The flexibility of focus group interviews is advantageous, especially when compared with the more structured and rigid survey format. Numerous topics can be discussed and many insights can be gained, particularly with regard to the variations in consumer behavior in different situations. Responses that would be unlikely to emerge in a survey often come out in group interviews: "*If the day is hot and I have to serve all the kids in the neighborhood, I make Kool-Aid; otherwise, I give them Dr Pepper or Coke.*"

● ● ● ● ● ●

Traditional focus group facilities typically include a comfortable room for respondents, recording equipment, and a viewing room via a two-way mirror.

Marmaduke St. John / Alamy

If a researcher is investigating a target group to determine who consumes a particular beverage or why a consumer purchases a certain brand, situational factors must be included in any interpretations of respondent comments. For instance, in the situation above, the focus group moderator would note the preference for a particular beverage. However, it would be inappropriate to say that Kool-Aid is preferred in general. The proper interpretation is situation-specific. On a hot day, the kids get Kool-Aid. When the weather isn't hot, the kids may get nothing, or if only a few kids are around, they may get lucky and get a Dr. Pepper. A possible interpretation may be: Kool-Aid is appropriate for satisfying large numbers of hot kids, but Dr. Pepper is a treat for a select few friends that is even easier to provide.

Scrutiny

A focus group interview allows closer scrutiny in several ways. First, multiple people can observe the interview live because they are usually conducted in a room containing a two-way mirror. The respondents and moderator are on one side; an invited audience that may include both researchers and decision-makers is on the other. If the decision-makers are located in another city or country, they may watch through an Internet connection (perhaps using Skype or similar technology) or through some other video media. No matter how agents from the decision-maker observe, the fact that they can look in provides a check on the eventual interpretations offered in the report. Second, the focus group organizers generally videotape the session. If video is not feasible, then they will produce an audio recording. Later, detailed examination of the recorded session can offer additional insight and help clear up disagreements about what happened.

Focus Group Illustration

Researchers often use focus group interviews for concept screening and concept refinement. Product development involves a continuous process of examining potential modifications, refinements, and idea generation. This process applies to existing and new products. Philip Morris and Lorillard are developing smokeless, electronic cigarette (e-cigarette) products for the U.K. market, where vaping is catching on. Focus groups with consumers in the United States, where vaping (smoking e-cigarettes) has a longer history, help them understand how U.K. consumers will react to the product and how it might be improved.[23] Voluntary focus group respondents used samples of the product and then discussed it among themselves. The interview results suggest that consumers like the key product features related to tidiness such as the fact that it produces no ashes, no side smoke, and very little odor. Focus group respondents show little concern about how the cigarette actually functions but hope that they will be able to use the product around nonsmokers without irritating them. Some respondents see

Focus groups provide insight to companies by getting consumer reactions to novel new products.

e-cigarettes as a way of ending tobacco habits. This example illustrates how focus groups help develop and refine products and provide ideas for effectively marketing products once released.

Focus Group Respondents

What is a research supplier's responsibility when recruiting individuals to participate in a focus group? Practically every focus group interview requires that respondents be screened based on some relevant characteristic. For example, if the topic involves improving parochial school education, the group should probably not include non-parents or parents with no plans of having children. The respondents in this case should be parents who are likely to put or are currently putting a child through school.

Even after careful screening, some consumers that fit the desired profile make poor focus group participants. Respondents are inappropriate if they are either unwilling to express their views or they are overbearing. The group dynamics suffer when one or more respondents are too quiet or are a loudmouth. When a researcher finds good focus group participants, he/she may be tempted to use them over and over again. Is this appropriate? This is a dilemma a focus group planner may well face. Consider a research client viewing videotapes of a series of six focus groups conducted about new kitchen appliance designs. The client realizes that four respondents appear in more than one of the six focus group interviews and that ten respondents appear in focus group videos conducted by the same researcher on another topic six months previous. Whenever diversity of opinion is needed, relying on what essentially become professional focus group respondents is not likely appropriate. The researcher should take the extra effort to find new respondents rather than relying on conveniently available and appropriately talkative respondents.

Group Composition

A traditional focus group's ideal size is six to ten people. A very small group has less potential for good ideas and each person is very susceptible to influence from the others. In a very large group, some participants may have difficulty getting their ideas across.

Homogeneous groups allow researchers to concentrate on consumers with similar lifestyles, experiences, and communication skills. When every participant is more or less similar to the others, the discussion carries forward with less likelihood of becoming overly confrontational. Additionally, marketing campaigns generally communicate with specific market segments consisting of relatively homogenous consumers. Ethnographers like to deal with unique cultures. If an ethnographic researcher is looking to do a focus group about Vans, he/she may recruit participants from a local skate park or from members of an online social community.

Imagine how the opinions of the electronic cigarette would vary among a group of smokers and nonsmokers. Management would probably be nearsighted not to consider the input from nonsmokers because they ultimately will influence the acceptable places where these devices can be used. Although any one focus group consisting of both smokers and nonsmokers might be lively, it is very likely to be confrontational. If the researcher involves multiple interviews, the researcher may consider doing one with a mixed group, but researchers generally prefer separate interviews for disparate groups. The researcher obtains diversity in the sample by using different groups even though each group is homogeneous. For instance, in discussing smokeless cigarettes, four groups might be used:

1.   Single current smokers
2.   Married smokers whose spouses do not smoke
3.   Former smokers
4.   Nonsmokers

Although each group is homogenous, researchers obtain opinions from diverse respondents. Many research firms apply a rule of thumb that four different focus group sessions, each in a different city, can satisfy exploratory research needs dealing with common consumer product issues.

Environmental Conditions

A focus group session may typically take place at the research agency in a room specifically designed for this purpose. These agencies' facilities include the studio-like rooms where the focus groups are conducted, viewed, and recorded. Participants receive refreshments prior to the interview to help create a more relaxed atmosphere conducive to a free exchange of ideas. A relaxed atmosphere helps create a more open and intimate discussion of personal experiences and sentiments.

The Focus Group Moderator

During a focus group interview, a **moderator** ensures that everyone gets a chance to speak as he/she facilitates the discussion.

Several qualities characterize a good focus group moderator:

1. A moderator must develop rapport with the group and make all participants feel comfortable. Good moderators show genuine interest in people, establish rapport, gain participants' confidence, and make them feel eager to talk.
2. A moderator must be a good listener. Careful listening allows the researcher to separate productive discussion directed toward accomplishing the stated research objective from discussions that will take the group in an irrelevant direction. Without good listening skills, the interview may fail to address the issues that motivated the effort.
3. A good moderator does not interject his/her personal opinion. Good moderators usually say less rather than more. They can stimulate productive discussion with generalized follow-ups such as, "Tell us more about that incident," or "How are your experiences similar or different from the one you just heard?" The moderator must be particularly careful not to ask leading questions such as "You do like Red Bull, don't you?"
4. A moderator directs verbal traffic capably without turning off productive participants. The discussion needs to remain focused around the research objective. A moderator does not give the group total control of the discussion because it may well quickly lose focus. He/she normally has prepared questions on topics that aim to draw out ideas related to the research objective and therefore managerial issues. Normally, he/she starts out by encouraging a general discussion (i.e., "tell me what comes to mind when you think of a skate park") but usually *focuses* in on specific topics as the session progresses. Ideally, the group covers topics with little to no prompting.

Moderator

A person who leads a focus group interview and ensures that everyone gets a chance to speak and facilitates the discussion.

Focus Groups as Diagnostic Tools

Focus groups typify exploratory research but they also can be helpful in later stages of a research project. Sometimes, the findings from surveys or other quantitative techniques raise more questions than they answer. Managers who are puzzled about survey research results may use focus groups as a way of better understanding what consumer surveys are actually saying. In such a situation, the focus group supplies diagnostic help as a follow up to other research.

Focus groups are also excellent diagnostic tools for spotting problems with ideas as an idea screening technique. The moderator presents a marketing concept to the group and then seeks elaborate comments on the idea. This usually leads to lengthy lists of potential product problems and some ideas for overcoming them. People are naturally inclined to offer reasons why things won't work so this approach can be effective. Mature products can also be "focused-grouped" for improvements in this manner.

Depth Interviews

An alternative to a focus group is a depth interview. A **depth interview** is a one-on-one interview between a professional researcher and a research respondent. Depth interviews are much the same as a psychological, clinical interview, but with a different purpose. The researcher asks many questions and follows up each answer with probes for additional elaboration. Exhibit 5.5 provides an excerpt from a depth interview. The interviews allow the researchers to develop a theory of the way children react to product advertisements. In each case, the child was elaborating on their reactions to or memories of advertisements.

Like focus group moderators, the interviewer's role is critical in a depth interview. He/she must be a highly skilled individual who can encourage the respondent to talk freely without

Depth interview

A one-on-one interview between a professional researcher and a research respondent conducted about some relevant business or social topic.

EXHIBIT **5.5** Example Results from a Depth Interview

Respondent Comments	Interpreted Meaning
"I like to watch [Barbie ads] because I like to see how pretty the Barbies are and if there is going to be, like, a new kind of Barbie. There is one Barbie … that comes with some little lipstick-type thing on a towel. You dip it in water and put the lipstick on the Barbie. The Barbie's lipstick turns darker."	Children look forward to seeing some advertisements and take value from viewing them.
"It's like a fairy tale on the commercial, I mean people can't really be thin. And they can't just pop out of it like that. That's not real."	Children are not detached from reality when viewing the ads.
"The Honey Comb commercial has never left my head because it's got all those details in it. It's got bright colors, and music and kids with interesting things in it. That's what makes it stay in my head. I don't like that kind of cereal or the new kinds. I don't like sweet cereal. I just like the commercials though."	Children appreciate the hedonic value aspects of viewing advertisements.
"I don't like that one (Chip's Ahoy ad) because it made me too hungry. Cookies are my favorite. And we're not allowed to have snacks."	Signifies the role of parents in facilitating the consumption of children.

Source: Taken from Moore, E.S. and R.J. Lutz (2000), "Children, Advertising, and Product Experiences: A Multimethod Inquiry," *Journal of Consumer Research*, 27 (June), 31–48.

influencing the direction of the conversation. Probing questions are critical. Interviews often employ the "what has changed approach" in depth interviews with managerial employees.

Laddering

Laddering

A particular approach to probing asking respondents to compare differences between brands at different levels that produces distinctions at the attribute level, the benefit level, and the value or motivation level. Laddering is based on the classical repertory grid approach.

Laddering is a term used for a particular approach to probing, asking respondents to compare differences between brands at different levels. A repertory grid interview is an approach developed in the mid–twentieth century to conduct interviews that drew out the way people distinguished concepts. Laddering evolved from the repertory grid interview and is very useful in identifying the potential meaning of brand names. What usually results with laddering is that respondents first distinguish things using attribute-level distinctions, second are benefit-level distinctions, and third are distinctions at the value or motivation level. Laddering, for example, can then distinguish two brands of skateboarding shoes based on (a) the materials they are made of, (b) the comfort they provide, and (c) the excitement they create.

Depth Interview Procedure

Each depth interview may last more than an hour. Not only does the researcher conduct the interview, with each interview producing about the same amount of text as does a focus group interview, but the resulting data must be analyzed and interpreted. Thus, depth interviews are time consuming. The interviewer also must be keenly aware of what is happening and record both surface reactions and subconscious motivations of the respondent. Analysis and interpretation of such data are highly subjective, and it is difficult to settle on a true interpretation.

Depth interviews provide more insight into a particular individual than do focus groups. In addition, since the setting isn't really social, respondents are more likely to discuss sensitive topics than are those in a focus group. Buick took depth interviews into respondents' homes. Here, respondents discussed their ideas about cars and car brands in great detail, sometimes going on for 2 hours or more.[24] The comfortable surroundings no doubt aided the discussion. Following the interviews, Buick researchers felt as though Buick customers desire premium items and special features but they aren't inclined to pay a premium price for a car. Also, they picked up on perceptions that consumers viewed Buick as a brand for older people.

Depth interviews are particularly advantageous when the focus is on some unique or unusual behavior. For instance, depth interviews revealed characteristics of consumer misbehavior, ranging from things like not honoring reservations, changing price tags, service belligerence, and even shoplifting.[25] Depth interviews are similar to focus groups in many ways. Focus groups and depth interviews cost about the same as long as only one or two respondents are interviewed in depth. However, if a dozen or more depth interviews are included in a report, the costs are higher than focus group interviews because of the increased interviewing and analysis time.

Conversations

Holding **conversations** in qualitative research is an informal data-gathering approach in which the researcher engages a respondent in a discussion of the relevant subject matter. This approach is almost completely unstructured and the researcher enters the conversation with few expectations. The goal is to have the respondent produce a dialogue about his/her lived experiences.

A conversational approach to qualitative research is particularly appropriate in phenomenological research and for developing grounded theory. In our Vans experience, the researcher may simply tape-record a conversation about becoming a "skater." The resulting dialogue can then be analyzed for themes and plots. The result may be some interesting and novel insight into the consumption patterns of skaters, for example, if the respondent said,

> *"I knew I was a real skater when I just had to have Vans, not just for boarding, but for wearing."*

This theme may connect to a rite-of-passage plot and show how Vans play a role in this process.

A conversational approach is advantageous because conducting a single interview is usually inexpensive. Unlike depth interviews or focus groups, the researcher doesn't have to pay respondents because they are enthusiasts freely discussing their behavior. Often, the conversation takes place spontaneously, with little set up or with little need for any formal setting such as a focus group studio. They are relatively effective at getting at sensitive issues once the researcher establishes a rapport with them. Conversational approaches, however, are prone to produce a small portion of relevant information because they are not steered in the same way as a depth interview or focus group. Additionally, the data analysis is very much researcher-dependent.

Conversations

An informal qualitative data-gathering approach in which the researcher engages a respondent in a discussion of the relevant subject matter.

Semi-Structured Interviews

Semi-structured interviews usually come in written form and ask respondents for short essay responses to specific open-ended questions. Respondents are free to write as much or as little as they want. The interview design separates questions into sections typically and within each section, probing questions follow the opening question. In face-to-face semi-structured, oral interviews, structured follow-ups are more difficult than with the written approach.

Advantages to semi-structured interviews include an ability to address very specific issues and the fact that responses are usually easier to interpret than with other qualitative approaches. In written form, the researcher prepares all questions ahead of time and thus the presence of an interviewer is not necessary. For this reason, among others, semi-structured interviews are relatively cost-effective.

Some researchers interested in studying car salesperson stereotypes used qualitative semi-structured interviews to map consumers' cognitions (memory). The semi-structured interview began with a free-association task:

> *List the first five things that come into your mind when you think of a "car salesman."*

A probing question followed:

> *Describe the way a typical "car salesman" looks.*

Questions about how the car salesperson acts and how the respondent feels in the presence of a car salesperson followed this probe. The results led to research showing how the information that consumers process differs in the presence of a typical car salesperson as opposed to a less typical car salesperson.[26] One suggestion that followed addressed the way car salespeople dress. Perhaps something other than the prototypical attire would help create a less negative reaction.

Free-Association and Sentence-Completion Methods

**Free-association
techniques**

Record respondents' first
(top-of-mind) cognitive
reactions to some stimulus.

Free-association techniques simply record a respondent's first cognitive reactions (top-of-mind) to some stimulus. The Rorschach or inkblot test typifies the free-association method. Respondents view an ambiguous figure and say the first thing that comes to their mind. Free-association techniques allow researchers to map a respondent's thoughts or memory.

The sentence-completion method is based on free-association principles. Respondents simply are required to complete a few partial sentences with the first word or phrase that comes to mind. For example:

People who drink beer are _____.
A man who drinks a dark beer is _____.
Light beer is most liked by _____.

Answers to sentence-completion questions tend to be more extensive than responses to word-association tests. Although the responses lack the ability to probe for meaning as in other qualitative techniques, they are very effective in finding out what is on a respondent's mind. They can also do so in a quick and very cost-effective manner. Researchers often employ free-association and sentence-completion tasks in conjunction with other approaches. For instance, they provide effective icebreakers in focus group interviews.

Observation

Field notes

The researcher's descriptions of
what he/she actually observes
in the field; these notes then
become the text from which
meaning is extracted.

Throughout this chapter, we describe how observation is an important qualitative tool. The participant-observer approach typifies how researchers use observation to explore various issues. The researcher's field notes play a large role in this process. **Field notes** are the researcher's descriptions of what he/she actually observes in the field. These notes then become the text from which he/she extracts meaning.

Observation may also take place in visual form. Researchers may observe consumers in their home, as mentioned earlier, or try to gain knowledge from photos observed there or pinned on an Internet site like pinterest.com. Observation can either be very inexpensive, such as when a research associate sits at Starbucks and simply observes customer behavior, or it can be very expensive as is the case in most participant-observer studies. Observational research is keenly advantageous for gaining insight into things that respondents cannot or will not verbalize.

This Pinterest user has a deeply
felt relationship with Harley-
Davidson (photo found on
pinterest.com).

Collages

Marketing researchers sometimes have respondents prepare a collage to represent their experience with some good, service, or brand. Harley-Davidson commissioned research comparing collages depicting feelings about Harley-Davidson created by Harley owners with those of collages created by owners of a competing brand. The collages of "Hog" owners revealed themes of artwork and the freedom of the great outdoors. These themes did not emerge in the non-Hog groups. Confirmatory research followed which helped Harley continue its growth by appealing more specifically to sensitivities of its market segments.[27] Today, pinterest.com provides a good way to do qualitative research about brands. Multiple pages exist that depict in pictures the way people feel and use Harley-Davidson products and many, many other brands. Each page is a virtual collage providing data for interpretation.

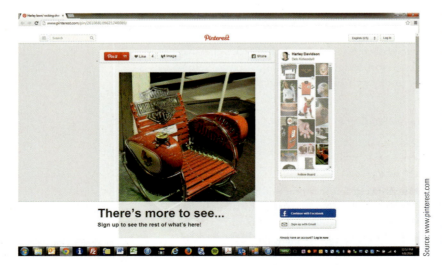

Source: www.pinterest.com

Thematic Apperception Test (TAT)

A **thematic apperception test (TAT)** presents subjects with an ambiguous picture(s) in which consumers and products are the center of attention. The investigator asks the subject to tell what is happening in the picture(s) now and what might happen next. Hence, the approach elicits themes (*thematic*) based on the perceptual-interpretive (*apperception*) use of the pictures. The researcher then analyzes the contents of the stories provided by respondents.

The picture or cartoon stimulus must be sufficiently interesting to encourage discussion but ambiguous enough not to disclose the nature of the research project. Clues should not be given to the character's positive or negative predisposition. Researchers contrasting the meaning of coffee brands may depict an ambiguous figure preparing coffee from a package of Folgers coffee to some subjects and to others, the same figures substituting Illy coffee (an Italian gourmet brand). The respondents could then be asked to describe the user. Surely, the Folgers and Illy users would be described differently. The differences might reveal ideas about the marketing of the two brands based on the meanings interpreted from the TAT. In much the same way, a TAT may be used to get a description of someone wearing Vans shoes.

A **picture frustration** version of the TAT uses a cartoon drawing in which the respondent suggests a dialogue in which the characters might engage. Exhibit 5.6 is a purposely ambiguous illustration of an everyday occurrence. The picture depicts two office workers and the respondent describes what the woman might be saying. This approach could be used for discussions about products, packaging, the display of merchandise, store personnel, and so on.

Projective Research Techniques

A TAT represents a projective research technique. A **projective technique** is an indirect means of questioning enabling respondents to project beliefs and feelings onto a third party, an inanimate object, or a task situation. Projective techniques usually encourage respondents to describe a situation in their own words with little prompting by the interviewer. The typical assumption is that

Thematic apperception test (TAT)

A test that presents subjects with an ambiguous picture(s) in which consumers and products are the center of attention; the investigator asks the subject to tell what is happening in the picture(s) now and what might happen next.

Picture frustration

A version of the TAT using a cartoon drawing in which the respondent suggests a dialogue in which the characters might engage.

Projective technique

An indirect means of questioning enabling respondents to project beliefs and feelings onto a third party, an inanimate object, or a task situation.

EXHIBIT **5.6**

Picture Frustration Version of TAT

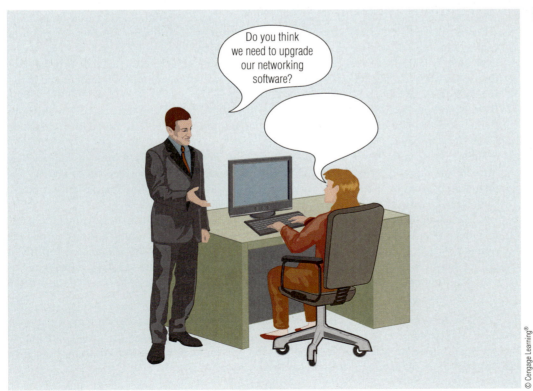

© Cengage Learning®

respondents interpret the situation within the context of their own experiences, attitudes, and personalities. This allows respondents to express opinions and emotions otherwise hidden from others and possibly even themselves. All projective techniques are particularly useful in studying sensitive issues.

Researchers interested in motivations for buying a hybrid automobile may ask a question like, "What would a person like you do to decide whether or not to trade their current automobile for a hybrid car such as a Prius?"[28] This question may elicit far different answers than the obvious one of concern for the environment. They deal more with questions of status or image portrayed by the car. Although some question whether or not respondents really do project the reporting of others' behavior on themselves, the results from projective interviews can be useful in exploratory research. Also, when studying very sensitive topics involving things like abuse of other people, embarrassing behavior, or treating customers or coworkers inappropriately, projective approaches can yield better results than asking people directly to self-report immoral behavior.

Preparing a Focus Group Outline

Discussion guide

A focus group outline that includes written introductory comments informing the group about the focus group purpose and rules and then outlines topics or questions to be addressed in the group session.

Focus group researchers use a discussion guide to help control the interview and guide the discussion into product areas. A **discussion guide** includes written introductory comments informing the group about the focus group purpose and rules and then outlines topics or questions to be asked in the group session. Thus, the discussion guide serves as the focus group outline. Some discussion guides will have only a few phrases in the entire document. Others may be more detailed. The amount of content depends on the nature and experience of the researcher and the complexity of the topic.

A marketing researcher conducting a focus group interview for a cancer center had the following objectives in mind when preparing the guide for the interview and conducting the interview:

- The first question was very general, asking that respondents describe their feelings about being out in the sun as an icebreaker. This opening question aimed to elicit the full range of views within in the group. Some individuals might view being out in the sun as a healthful practice, whereas others view the sun as deadly. The hope is that by exposing the full range of opinions, respondents would be motivated to explain fully their own position. This was the only question asked specifically of every respondent. Each respondent had to give an answer before free discussion began. In this way, individuals experience a nonthreatening environment encouraging their free and full opinion.
- The second question asks whether participants could think of any reason one should warn them about sunlight exposure. This question intends only to introduce the idea of a warning label.
- Subsequent questions became increasingly specific. They first asked about possible warning formats that might be effective. The moderator allows focus group participants to react to any formats suggested by another respondent. After this discussion, the moderator will introduce some specific formats the cancer center personnel have in mind.
- Finally, the moderator presents the "bottom-line" question: "What format would be most likely to induce people to take protective measures?" There would be probing follow-ups of each opinion so that a respondent couldn't simply say something like "the second one." All focus groups finish up with a catchall question asking for any comments, including any thoughts they wanted passed along to the sponsor (which was only then revealed as the Houston-based cancer center).

Researchers who planned the outline established certain objectives for each part of the focus group. The initial effort was to break the ice and establish rapport within the group. The logical flow of the group session then moved from general discussion about sunbathing to more focused discussion of types of warnings about danger from sun exposure.

In general, the following steps allow for an effective focus group discussion guide:

1. Welcome and introductions should take place first. Respondents begin to feel more comfortable after introducing themselves.
2. Begin the interview with a broad icebreaker that does not reveal too many specifics about the interview. Sometimes, this may even involve respondents providing some written story or their reaction to some stimulus like a photograph, film, product, or advertisement.
3. Questions become increasingly more specific as the interview proceeds. However, the moderator will notice that a good interview will cover the specific question topics before they are asked. This is preferable as respondents do not feel forced to react to the specific issue; it just emerges naturally.
4. If there is a very specific question to ask, such as explaining why a respondent would either buy or not buy a product, the moderator should save that question for last.
5. A debriefing statement should provide respondents with the actual focus group objectives and answer any questions they may have. This is also a final shot to gain some insight from the group.

Disadvantages of Focus Groups

Focus groups offer many advantages. Like practically every other research technique, the focus group has some limitations and disadvantages, too. Problems with focus groups include those discussed as follows.

First, focus groups require objective, sensitive, and effective moderators. Moderators may often find it difficult to remain completely objective. In large research firms, a lead researcher may provide the focus group moderator only enough information to conduct the interview effectively. The focus group moderator's opinion shouldn't influence the interview or its results. Although many people, even some with little or no background to do so, conduct focus groups, good moderators become effective through a combination of objectivity, good people skills (which cannot be taught), training (in qualitative research), and experience. Without them, the exercise could provide misleading results.

Second, researchers do not select focus group participants randomly and thus a focus group is not a representative, random sample. Participants do not represent the entire target market in any statistical sense. Consequently, focus group results are not useful in making inferences about a larger population.

Third, although not so much an issue with online formats where respondents can remain anonymous, traditional face-to-face focus groups may not be useful for discussing sensitive topics. A focus group is a social setting and usually involves people with little to no familiarity with each other. Therefore, issues that people normally do not like to discuss in public may also prove difficult to discuss in a focus group.

Fourth, focus groups cost a considerable amount of money, particularly when not conducted by someone employed by the company desiring the focus group. Focus group prices vary regionally, but the following figures provide a rough guideline.

Renting Facilities and Equipment	$ 1,200
Paying Respondents ($100/person)	$ 1,000
Researcher Costs	
• Preparation	$ 800
• Moderating	$1,000
• Analysis and Report Preparation	$1,500
Miscellaneous Expenses	$ 500

Thus, a client can expect a professional focus group to cost around $6,000. However, most marketing topics will call for multiple focus groups. A series of interviews does not increase the costs proportionately, however, because the only element repeated is the interview itself. Thus, a research firm's price for doing two or three interviews increases about $2,000 to $3,000 per interview.

Modern Technology and Qualitative Research

The chapter to this point mentions several ways that the Internet provides ways of conducting qualitative research. Technological advances have greatly improved researchers' ability to perform all aspects of marketing research, but perhaps they are changing qualitative marketing research more than any other area. This section focuses on ways that technology enables and facilitates modern qualitative research.

Facilitating Interviewing

Videoconferencing Technologies

The videoconferencing industry has grown dramatically in recent years. Most managers routinely conduct meetings using some Internet-based interface such as Skype, Adobe Connect, G+ Hangout, or Megameeting, just to name a few. Researchers can use these tools to conference with managers scattered in offices all around the world. However, researchers also apply the tools to conduct focus group interviews.

FocusVision Network of New York is a marketing research company that provides specialized videoconferencing equipment and services and numerous technological platforms with which to conduct focus group interviews. In addition to doing in-person focus groups, FocusVision can conduct them via webcams. A focus group via webcam allows advantages such as being able to push out images and information via the computer screen during the interview. Online focus groups also can involve a video game in some way.[29] Although these are not customized for focus groups, they provide a less expensive alternative to services specialized for online focus groups.

Interactive Media and Online Focus Groups

Online focus group

A qualitative research effort in which a group of individuals provides unstructured comments through some online medium.

Internet applications of qualitative exploratory research are growing rapidly and involve both formal and informal applications. Formally, the term **online focus group** refers to a qualitative research effort in which a group of individuals provides unstructured comments through some online medium. This could involve videoconferencing but commonly participants examine an Internet display and then use their keypad to make remarks either during a chat-room session or in the form of a blog. Because respondents enter their comments into the computer, transcripts of verbatim responses are available immediately after the group session. Online groups can be quick and cost-efficient. However, because there is less interaction between participants, group synergy and snowballing of ideas may be diminished.

Companies like this one leverage technology to provide alternative means of conducting Focus Group Interviews.

Online focus groups allow access to groups that might be hard to tap otherwise. Sermo (sermo.com) is an online community of physicians that provides data to advertising agencies working for pharmaceutical firms and other institutions with a focus on health-care administration. At Sermo, on-demand focus groups comprised of physicians provide fast and efficient feedback on numerous issues related to product effectiveness, usage, and brand messaging.[30] Compared to the price of an in-person physician focus group, the $10,000–$16,000 price per interview is a bargain.

Several companies have established a form of informal, "continuous" focus group by establishing an Internet blog for that purpose.[31] We might call this technique a **focus blog** when the intention is to mine the site for business research purposes. General Motors, P&G, American Express, Fandango, and Lego all use ideas harvested from their focus blogs. Although real-life, in-person focus group respondents are paid to participate for 90 minutes, bloggers usually participate for absolutely no fee at all! Thus, technology provides potential cost advantages over traditional focus group approaches.[32]

Online versus Face-To-Face Focus Group Techniques

A research company can facilitate a formal online focus group by setting up a private, electronic chat room for that purpose. Participants in formal and informal online focus groups feel that their anonymity is very secure. Often respondents will say things in this environment that they would never say otherwise. For example, a lingerie company was able to get insights into how it could design sexy products for larger women. Online, these women freely discussed what it would take "to feel better about being naked."[33] One can hardly imagine how difficult such a discussion might be face to face. Increased anonymity can be a major advantage for a company investigating sensitive or embarrassing issues.

Because participants do not have to be together in the same room at a research facility, the number of participants in online focus groups can be larger than in traditional focus groups. Twenty-five participants or more is not uncommon for the simultaneous chat-room format, where entries are typed and not spoken. Participants can be at widely separated locations, even in different time zones, because the Internet does not have geographical restrictions. Of course, a major disadvantage is that often the researcher does not exercise as much control in precisely who participates. In other words, a person could very easily not match the desired profile or even answer screening questions in a misleading way simply to participate.

A major drawback with online focus groups is that moderators cannot see body language and facial expressions (bewilderment, excitement, interest, etc.). Thus, they cannot fully interpret how people are reacting. Also, moderators' ability to probe and ask additional questions on the spot is reduced in online focus groups. Research that requires focus group members to actually touch something (such as a new easy-opening packaging design) or taste something is not generally suitable for an online format.

Social Networking

Social networking is one of the most impactful trends in recent times. For many consumers, particularly younger generations, social networking sites like Facebook, Tumblr, Ning, Baidu, and Twitter are primary tools for communicating with friends both far and near, known and unknown. Social networking takes the place of large volumes of e-mail, phone calls, and even face-to-face communications. While the impact that social networking will eventually have on society is an interesting question, what is most relevant to marketing research is the large portion of this information that discusses marketing and consumer-related information.

Companies can assign research assistants to search these sites for information related to their particular brands. A Twitter search, for instance, shows quickly who is talking about the product. Companies can get a sense for what these customers are thinking through their tweets.[34] The research analyst codes the information as either positive or negative. When too much negative information appears, the company can take steps to try and protect the brand. In addition, many companies like Proctor & Gamble (P&G) and Ford maintain their own social networking sites for the purpose of gathering research data. In a way, these social networking sites are a way that companies can eavesdrop on consumer conversations and discover key information about their products.

Focus blog

A type of informal, "continuous" focus group established as an Internet blog for the purpose of collecting qualitative data from participant comments.

To the Point

"Necessity, mother of invention."

—WILLIAM WYCHERLEY

Research Knows Almost No Boundaries!

Qualitative research knows *almost* no boundaries! Well, at least not for Ford. Large companies like Ford are increasingly using qualitative research including phenomenology, ethnography, and grounded theory. Ford now relies on qualitative input to help with ideas for product design, marketing campaign design, concept testing, and even relationships with suppliers. The advances in technologies have helped make automakers more willing to base decisions on consumer input. Some feel that, for perhaps the first time, companies like Ford may now place consumer input above cost cutting in making key decisions.

Ford used information posted online, in-home ethnography, and traditional focus groups to refine a global marketing campaign centered around the Ford Mustang. Marketing researchers interpreted all of this input in a way that placed great emphasis on the feelings associated with driving a Mustang. As a result, Ford developed a slogan and campaign built around "No boundaries!" However, early concept testing showed that this slogan did not create a positive impression in some Asian cultures. Thus, after a few adjustments and further testing, they settled on "Make Every Day Exciting!" Additionally, grounded theory approaches are helping companies better see into the future by building predictive theories about what characteristics might create value for consumers into the future. Qualitative research points toward the Mazda 3 as a potential success rivaling the Ford Focus.

Sources: Flint, D. and B. Woodruff, "The Initiators of Changes in Customers' Desired Values: Results from a Theory Building Study," *Industrial Marketing Management*, 30 (2008), 321–330. http://www.thecarconnection.com/compare/mazda_mazda3_2014_choices, accessed May 11, 2014.

© Transtock/Jupiter Images

Field Approaches for Interpreting Online Text

Interpretative researchers apply specialized approaches to making sense of consumers' online postings. Some researchers look at the posting as a drama consisting of an act, agency, scene, and purpose.[35] For instance, the wall of a Facebook group, like "I bet I can find 1,000,000 people who hate Heneken," provides a scene in which an act takes place. The act consists of the various posts consumers leave on the site. Classifying the posts into categories found in a dramatic play help bring sense to the texts consumers openly leave behind.

Other interpretative researchers use the term netnography to describe the application of ethnography to comments made in online communities. The researcher blends in as part of a virtual community and in doing so, he/she gains access to the myriad of comments consumers leave behind about all manner of businesses.[36] Like other uses of social networking in marketing research, the reduced costs relative to traditional ethnography are an important motivator of netnography.

Ethics

Netnography also illustrates ethical dilemmas that qualitative researchers face when dealing with online data. For instance, should the online researcher identify him/herself to the community as a researcher? If so, the community may not respond the same way. Alternatively, the researcher is extracting data without the informed consent of the participants otherwise. If a researcher takes the latter approach, he/she has a special duty to protect the identity of participants and to protect the brand community itself from harm. If this is the case, the netnography approach is similar to anonymously observing consumers moving about in a public environment.

Software Development

Interpretive Software

Computerized qualitative analysis is now commonly used. Two commonly used programs are ATLAS.ti (discussed earlier) and NVivo. These can save a lot of time by helping to identify themes and connections within text. In fact, today's programs can even assist in interpreting videotapes and photographs for meaning.

Computerized analysis of depth interviews with service providers and their customers revealed interesting key themes dealing with the friendship or bond that forms between them. Some of the themes that emerged included the feeling that meetings were more like get-togethers with a friend, the feeling that the service provider wants to give something back to a client, and the belief that one can share one's true thoughts and feelings with a client. On the not-so-positive side, a theme that also emerged was that sometimes the friendships are not mutual. Comments like "I thought she would never leave" or "Won't he give me a break?" would be consistent with that theme.[37]

Some interpretative software is available as freeware. An SWR is available from the U.S. Centers for Disease Control and Prevention (http://www.cdc.gov/hiv/software/answr.htm) as is EZ-Text (http://www.cdc.gov/hiv/software/ez-text.htm). Transana will read video- and audiotape data and is available from the Wisconsin Center for Education Research (http://www.transana.org).

Text Mining

Generally, when managers think of data mining capabilities, they think of statistical analyses of large volumes of quantitative data. However, modern predictive analytic software enables text data to be mined from various sources including social networking sites, recorded conversations from call centers, e-mail contacts, and many more sources. Large companies, including Sikorsky Aircraft, one of the largest helicopter companies in the world, and Cablecom, a Swiss telecommunications firm, employ text mining as a way of reducing customer churn. Leading statistical analysis companies such as SAS and SPSS offer advanced text mining capabilities. Although these programs can be expensive, they offer companies the ability to extract meaning from the tremendous amounts of verbal information generated by their customers, partners, and competitors.

The word cloud described earlier in the chapter is a useful tool to combine with text mining. Online reviews provide useful input for text mining. However, the researcher needs to keep in mind that a large percentage of online posts may not be authentic. Anyone can post an comment and sometimes anyone is somebody with an ax to grind (such as a disgruntled employee) or somebody paid to post information. Estimates suggest that one-fourth or more of online posts are fake. Some researchers provide online interpretive tools that look for signs that an online review is fake and provide the user with some idea of how likely a review is to be legitimate.[38]

Exploratory Research in Science and in Practice

Any research tool, qualitative or quantitative, can be misapplied. Some people believe that a good statistician can support practically any argument. Well, this may be part of urban legend but certainly statistics can be misleading. Qualitative research is no exception and researchers can apply these tools improperly and produce misleading results. Hopefully, the researcher has simply erred when this occurs. Intentionally misleading others with research results is blatantly unprofessional. A researcher needs to know what research tool to apply, how to apply it, and when to apply it to practice the craft professionally.

Misuses of Exploratory Qualitative Research

Exploratory research cannot take the place of conclusive, confirmatory research, and confirmatory research cannot take the place of discovery-oriented, exploratory tools. Qualitative tools generally offer the researcher a great deal of flexibility to cover a wide range of topics. As such, they are well suited to explore marketing issues. Subjectivity is a drawback of interpretive approaches, but that weakness predominantly limits testing—particularly hypothesis testing. The term *interpretive* research sometimes is nearly synonymous with qualitative research. When only one researcher interprets the meaning of what a single person said in a depth interview, one should be very cautious before making major marketing decisions on these results. Is the result **replicable**? Replicable means the same conclusion is intersubjectively certifiable—another researcher's interpretation

Replicable

Something is intersubjectively certifiable meaning the same conclusion would be reached based on another researcher's interpretation of the research or by independently duplicating the research procedures.

would match (or they would get the same result by conducting the same research procedures). The temptation is to act on one interpretation because having other researchers interpret things like depth interviews takes resources that are not always readily available.

Indeed, many researchers frowned on qualitative methodologies for years based on a few early and public misapplications during the so-called motivational research era. Although many of the ideas produced during this time had some merit, as can sometimes be the case, too few researchers did too much interpretation of too few respondents. Compounding this, marketers were quick to act on the results, believing that the results peaked inside one's subliminal consciousness and therefore held some type of extra power. Thus, often the research was flawed based on poor interpretation, as was the decision process when the deciders acted prematurely. Psychologists applied projective techniques and depth interviews to consumers frequently in the late 1950s and early 1960s, producing some interesting and occasionally bizarre reasons for consumers' purchasing behavior:

■   A woman is very serious when she bakes a cake because unconsciously she is going through the symbolic act of giving birth.
■   A man buys a convertible as a substitute mistress and a safer (and potentially cheaper) way of committing adultery.
■   Men who wear suspenders are reacting to an unresolved castration complex.[39]

Decades later, researchers for McCann-Erickson and other advertising agencies interviewed women about roaches. Among other qualitative techniques, a form of TAT involving story completion about an encounter with an insect was applied in understanding the meanings of insects in consumers' lives. Research like this revealed themes including:

■   The joy of victory over roaches (watching them die or seeing them dead).
■   Using the roach as a metaphor through which women can take out their hostility toward men (women generally referred to roaches as "he" instead of "she" in their stories).
■   A pervasive fear and hatred of roaches. When Orkin tested ads depicting roaches running on the television screen, viewers actually threw things at the screen before even thinking about whether the bugs were real. Although viewers felt real fear during the ads, Orkin decided to run the ads and even started a contest for people who could tell stories about damaging a television during the ad.[40]

Even today, we have the Pillsbury Doughboy as evidence that useful ideas originated from motivational research. However, many companies became frustrated when decisions based on motivational research approaches proved poor. Thus, marketing researchers moved away from qualitative tools during the late 1960s and 1970s. Today, however, qualitative tools have won acceptance once again as researchers realize they have greater power in discovering insights that would be difficult to capture in typical survey research (which is limited as an exploratory tool).

Scientific Decision Processes

Objectivity and replicability are two characteristics of scientific inquiry. Are focus groups objective and replicable? Would three different researchers all interpret focus group data identically? How should a facial expression or nod of the head be interpreted? Have subjects fully grasped the idea or concept behind a nonexistent product? Have respondents overstated their interest because they tend to like all new products? Many of these questions reduce to a matter of opinion that may vary from researcher to researcher and from one respondent group to another. Medical labs such as Bayer find that results from the academic literature are often difficult to replicate in their own labs.[41] Although many reasons for this may exist, replicating exploratory conclusions is particularly problematic because they are not meant to be conclusive. Therefore, a focus group, or a depth interview, or TAT alone does not best represent a complete scientific inquiry.

However, if thoughts discovered through these techniques survive preliminary evaluations and are developed into conceptually sound research hypotheses, they can be further tested. These tests may involve survey research or an experiment testing an idea very specifically. Thus, exploratory research approaches using qualitative research tools are very much a *part* of *scientific* inquiry.

An exploratory research design is the most productive design, meaning the tools used produce more discoveries than do other research designs. A company cannot determine the most important product benefits until all benefits obtained from consuming the product are known.

Before making a *scientific* decision, a research project should include a confirmatory study using objective tools and an adequate sample in terms of both size and how well it represents a population. But, is a *scientific* decision approach always used or needed?

In practice, many marketing managers make decisions based solely on the results of focus group interviews or some other exploratory result. Given that some decisions involve relatively small risk, a scientific decision process is not always justified. However, as risk increases, the confidence that comes along with a rigorous research and decision process becomes well worth the investment. The primary barriers to scientific decisions are (1) time, (2) money, and (3) emotion.

Time

Sometimes, researchers simply lack sufficient time to follow up on exploratory research results. Marketing companies feel an increasingly urgent need to get new products to the market faster. Thus, a seemingly good idea generated in a focus group (like Diet Vanilla or Ginger Dr Pepper) is never tested. Managers may see the risk of delaying a decision as greater than the risk of proceeding without completing the scientific process. Thus, although the researcher may wish to protest, there may be logical reasons for deciding now. The decision-makers should be aware, though, that the conclusions drawn from exploratory research designs are just that—exploratory. Thus, there is less likelihood of good results from the decision than if the research process had involved further testing.

Money

Similarly, researchers sometimes do not follow up on exploratory research results because the cost is too high. The research team may already have spent thousands of dollars on qualitative research. Managers who are unfamiliar with research will be very tempted to wonder, "Why do I need yet another study?" and "What did I spend all that money for?" Thus, they choose to proceed based only on exploratory results. Again, the researcher has fulfilled the professional obligation as long as he/she makes the tentative nature of any ideas derived from exploratory research clear in the research report.

Again, this isn't always a bad approach. If a decision does not involve a great deal of risk or can be reversed easily, the best course of action may be to proceed to implementation without spending more time and money on confirmatory research. Remember, research should never cost more than the benefits that can come from an effective decision.

Emotion

Time, money, and emotion are all related. Decision-makers sometimes become so anxious to have something resolved, or they get so excited about some novel discovery resulting from a focus group interview, they may act rashly. Perhaps some of the ideas produced during the motivational research era sounded so enticing that decision-makers got caught up in the emotion of the moment and proceeded without the proper amount of testing. Thus, as in life, when we fall in love with something, we are prone to act irrationally. The chances of emotion interfering in this way can be lessened by making sure multiple decision-makers are involved in the decision process.

TIPS OF THE TRADE

- Qualitative research tools are most helpful when
  - The decision-makers don't know exactly what issues to take action on
  - Some specific behavior needs to be studied in depth
  - When the value of a product changes dramatically from situation to situation or consumer to consumer
  - When exploring a research area with the intent of studying it further
  - Concept testing

- Focus group questions should start with more general questions and work to the more specific.

- Don't be afraid to use props such as advertisements, photos, or actual products to get respondents talking.

- Apply qualitative tools to data already existing on the Internet such as social networking sites, corporate feedback listings, and blogs.

- The overall value of a research tool is not determined by whether it is quantitative or qualitative but by the value that it produces.

:: SUMMARY

1. Contrast qualitative research with quantitative research. The chapter emphasizes that any argument about the overall superiority of qualitative versus quantitative research is misplaced. Rather, each approach has advantages and disadvantages that make it appropriate in certain situations. The most noticeable difference is the relative absence of numbers in qualitative research. Qualitative research relies more on researchers' subjective interpretations of text or other visual material. In contrast, the numbers produced in quantitative research are objective in the sense that they don't change simply because someone else computed them. Qualitative research involves small samples. Quantitative research usually uses large samples. Qualitative procedures are generally more flexible and produce deeper and more elaborate explanations than quantitative research.

2. Know the role of qualitative research in exploratory research designs. The high degree of flexibility that goes along with most qualitative techniques makes it very useful in exploratory research designs. Therefore, exploratory research designs most often involve some qualitative research technique. Many of the things that some criticize qualitative research for, such as lack of structure, actually are advantageous in an exploratory design.

3. Describe the basic orientations of qualitative research. Phenomenology is a philosophical approach to studying human experiences based on the idea that human experience itself is inherently subjective and determined by the context within which a person experiences something. It lends itself well to conversational research. Ethnography represents ways of studying cultures through methods that include high involvement with that culture. Participant-observation is a common ethnographic approach. Grounded theory represents inductive qualitative investigation in which the researcher continually poses questions about a respondent's discourse in an effort to derive a deep explanation of their behavior. Case studies are documented histories of a particular person, group, organization, or event.

4. Recognize common qualitative research tools and know the advantages and limitations of their use. Two of the most common qualitative research tools include the focus group interview and the depth interview. The focus group has some cost advantage per respondent because it would take ten times as long to conduct the interview portion(s) of a series of depth interviews compared to one focus group. However, the depth interview is more appropriate for discussing sensitive topics. Researchers today though have a wide variety of tools at their disposal aside from the focus group and depth interview.

5. Prepare a focus group interview outline. A focus group outline should begin with introductory comments followed by a very general opening question that does not lead the respondent. More specific questions should be listed until a blunt question directly pertaining to the study objective is included. It should conclude with debriefing comments and a chance for question-and-answers with respondents.

6. Recognize ways social networking and the *blogosphere* provide opportunities for qualitative research. Social network postings are replete with postings about brands, products, and consumer experiences. These natural conversations are fertile data for interpretative researchers. Some companies have even established a focus blog that is a source for continuous commentary on a company. Consumer reviews on sites like tripadvisor.com provide another source of data online. A key strength of these approaches is cost effectiveness, although virtually no control can be exercised over the respondents. Internet-based communication tools also greatly facilitate focus groups involving participants who need not travel to a focus group facility. This can be particularly useful when groups consist of professionals who would be unlikely to take the time to participate otherwise.

7. Appreciate the role of exploratory qualitative research in scientific decision-making. Qualitative research has a rightful place in scientific discovery, and the idea that qualitative research is somehow lacking in rigor because it is not quantitative is simply misplaced. Risks do come with using exploratory research procedures in general to make scientific decisions. Although not all decisions require a scientific decision process, companies sometimes do make major decisions using only exploratory research. A lack of time, money, and strong emotions to move on all represent barriers to a scientific decision process. Ultimately, the researcher's job is to make sure that decision makers understand the increased risk that comes along with basing a decision only on exploratory research results.

:: KEY TERMS AND CONCEPTS

:: QUESTIONS FOR REVIEW AND CRITICAL THINKING

1. Define *qualitative* and *quantitative* research. Compare and contrast the two approaches.
2. Describe the term *interpretive research*.
3. What types of situations call for qualitative research?
4. Consider the chapter vignette. Illustrate how researchers could apply at least four different qualitative tools to the business situation described in the opening vignette.
5. Define probing. Describe an illustration of the way probing might reveal ideas for a new product or a product improvement in the grocery or fast-food industry.
6. What are the basic categories (orientations) of qualitative research?
7. Of the four basic categories of qualitative research, which do you think is most appropriate for a qualitative approach designed to better define a marketing situation prior to conducting confirmatory research?
8. How might ethnography be used in concept testing?
9. What type of qualitative research would you suggest in the following situations?
   a. A product manager suggests development of a non-tobacco cigarette blended from wheat, cocoa, and citrus.
   b. A research project has the purpose of evaluating potential brand names for a new insecticide.
   c. A manager must determine the best site for a drive-in convenience store in an urban area.
   d. An advertiser wishes to identify the symbolism associated with posting selfies online.
   e. Searching for ideas for new smartphone or tablet applications.
   f. Determining what might make a consumer willing to pay to play an online video game.
10. What are the key differences between a focus group interview and a depth interview?
11. Visit some social network sites for large companies like Honda, Qantas Airlines, Target, Auchan, and Marriott. Is there any evidence that they are using their Internet sites in some way to conduct a continuous online focus blog or intermittent online focus groups?
12. What is *laddering*? How might it be used in trying to understand which fast-food restaurant different segments of customers prefer?
13. How is a focus group outline used by a focus group moderator?
14. List at least four ways that recent technological advances have advanced the use of qualitative research. Explain your choices. Do you know any even newer ways that technological advancements could provide data in the form of text or picture messages? Can you think of a way that SMS text messages or MMS messages might provide qualitative input?
15. Comment on the following remark by a marketing consultant: "Qualitative exploration is a tool of marketing research and a stimulant to thinking. In and by itself, however, it does not constitute market research."
16. A researcher tells a manager of a wine company that he has some "cool ethnography results from Facebook postings" suggesting that young consumers like the idea of a plastic individual serving size bottles that could be vended or offered at the cash register. Even before the decision-maker sees the report, the manager begins purchasing small plastic bottles and the new bottling equipment. Comment on this situation.
17. Under what circumstances might it be unethical to use consumer postings on a brand community Facebook site as data in qualitative research?
18. A packaged goods manufacturer receives many thousands of customer e-mails every year. Some are complaints, some are compliments. They cover a broad range of topics. Are these e-mails a possible source for interpretative research? Why or why not?

:: RESEARCH ACTIVITIES

1. How might the following industries use an Internet social networking site for exploratory research? Search several well-known brand names on Facebook. Do you see any evidence that the brands in these industries are using the site to collect data useful in qualitative research?
   a. Energy drinks
   b. Vacation resorts
   c. Online game designers
   d. Insurance companies
2. Go back to the opening vignette. What if Vans approached you to do a focus group interview that explored the idea of offering casual attire (off-board) aimed at their primary segment (skateboarders) and offering casual attire for male retirees? How would you recommend the focus group(s) proceed? Prepare a focus group outline(s) to accomplish this task.
3. Interview two people about their exercise behavior. In one interview, try to use a semi-structured approach by preparing questions ahead of time and trying to have the respondent complete answers for these questions. With the other, try a conversational approach. What are the main themes that emerge in each? Which approach do you think was more insightful? Do you think there were any "sensitive" topics that a respondent was not completely forthcoming about?
4. Search the Internet for some online posts from consumers describing Walmart shopping experiences. An experience that amounts to a complaint qualifies as relevant. Make sure the descriptions contain at least 200 words. Create a word cloud using freeware or other software and interpret it in an effort to explore ways to improve the Walmart experience.

Disaster and Consumer Value

After September 11, 2001, U.S. consumers showed a desire to tone down their consumer activities. They ordered simpler foods in restaurants and spent more time at home. Therefore, a lot of marketing campaigns began emphasizing down-home themes.

At some point after a disaster, it is time to get back to business. But, major catastrophic events are likely to leave permanent changes on consumers and employees in those areas. Suppose you are approached by the owner of several delicatessens and full-service wine stores in a Gulf Coast area recently devastated by a hurricane. All of the owners' units suffered damaged and have been closed for months. Now, the owner is considering reopening all of the units. The business decisions the company faces include whether to reopen all of the units (or only those in areas suffering minimal devastation) and whether they should maintain the same brand positioning they had previous to the hurricane. They would like to have a report from you within eighty days.

1. How could each classification of qualitative research be used here?
2. What qualitative research tool(s) would you recommend be used and why?
3. Where would you conduct any interviews and with whom would you conduct them?
4. Are there ethical issues that you should be sensitive to in this process? Explain.
5. What issues would arise in conducting a focus group interview in this situation?
6. Prepare a focus group outline.

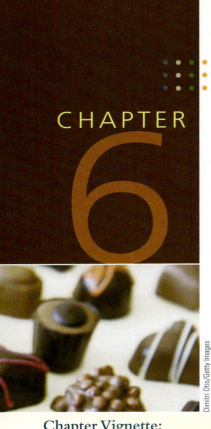

Dimitri Otis/Getty Images

Secondary Data Research in a Digital Age

After studying this chapter, you should be able to:

1. Discuss the advantages and disadvantages of using secondary data
2. Understand common objectives addressed by secondary data
3. Identify various internal and proprietary sources of secondary data
4. Give examples of various external sources of secondary data
5. Describe the impact of single-source data and globalization in the big data era

Chapter Vignette:

You Bet Your Life!

Suppose you or a loved one had to go into the hospital for heart surgery. Clearly, this is serious business! Research suggests that the majority of health-care customers do research before receiving critical services. In fact, nine of ten consumers say they would believe information about hospitals posted in social networks. Well, today consumers have abundant sources of data about doctors and hospitals at their fingertips. Numerous organizations including insurance companies and government agencies publish health-care statistics online. Medicare.gov, for instance, puts hospital satisfaction data at a consumer's fingertips. Is the food good in the hospital? You can look up the satisfaction data on this and many other criteria. One controversial statistic available online is the hospital's mortality rate. If you are going in for heart surgery, perhaps you'd like to know what the odds of survival might be? These statistics are available. Further, if these data are available for consumers, it's also available to health-care marketing organizations and other agencies that may search for intelligence by putting such statistics available with other data.

However, are these data all useful? How reliable are Facebook posts about a hospital? How reliable are the mortality rates posted on websites? Some argue that one must be very cautious about using this data. For example, some hospitals will not take certain high-risk patients. Those that do may

report higher mortality rates but those rates are not because of a lack of skill of the doctors as much as it is the fact that the typical patient is more severely ill. Also, fraud in online posts also is a reality of the Internet and makes postings online less than 100 percent reliable. The fact that the data are easily available, meaning it just needs to be found, represents a huge advantage of secondary data. But, convenient data are not always good data. Unlike other data, the researcher had no control over the data collection. However, the data's validity still needs careful scrutiny just as if the researcher collected it him/herself.[1]

© spotmatik/Shutterstock.com

Introduction

Market researchers are always working under budget constraints. As a result, they are wise to ask if the data needed to examine the research questions already exist. If so, the analysis can proceed quickly and efficiently. If not, a much more laborious process lies ahead. This chapter focuses on instances where the data may indeed already exist in some usable format. Given the big data explosion described in an earlier chapter, the chances are better than ever that some data relevant to a given marketing problem already exists.

Using Secondary Data in Marketing Research

Researchers often look for secondary data at some point in the research process. **Secondary data** are facts and information collected and recorded by someone else prior to and for purposes other than the current project. Secondary data usually are historical and already assembled. They require no additional access to the entities that originally provided the data observations in some way. For hospitals, the secondary data originates from sources including patient satisfaction surveys, observed waiting times, insurance company reports, and routine reporting required of hospitals.

Secondary data

Data that have been previously collected for some purpose other than the one at hand.

Advantages

The primary advantage of secondary data that they are readily available. Obtaining secondary data generally is faster and less expensive than acquiring primary data. This is particularly true given that most secondary data is digitally stored and accessible electronically. In many situations, researchers can access secondary data nearly instantaneously.

Consider the money and time saved by researchers who obtain updated population estimates for U.S. towns from an external source. Instead of doing expensive fieldwork themselves, researchers can acquire population estimates online from the U.S. Census Bureau. The use of secondary data eliminates many of the activities normally associated with primary data collection, such as sampling, fieldwork, and data entry.

Access provides another secondary data advantage. Sometimes, companies cannot get the needed data using primary data collection procedures. For example, a manufacturer of farm implements could not duplicate the information in the *Census of Agriculture* because much of the information (e.g., amount of taxes paid) might not be accessible to a private firm. Banks like to know life-event data about customers such as when are children born, when are children moving out of the house, when is retirement, and so forth.[2] Collecting this data from customers proves difficult or impossible due to regulations limiting what a bank can ask customers. Health-care agencies face similar regulatory restrictions. In this case, researchers can apply analytical tools to secondary data showing the demographic profiles by neighborhood and data similarly profiling lifestyle information about those same neighborhoods. When the researcher takes secondary data from multiple sources and applies data analysis to guess when someone might be having a baby or retiring, big data is helping supply intelligence.

To the Point

"If I have seen farther than others, it is because I have stood on the shoulders of giants."

—ISAAC NEWTON

Disadvantages

The researchers using secondary data in most cases did not collect the data. As a result, the individuals who originally gathered the data did so for an entirely different reason. Secondary data then do not fit the particular research question perfectly. The question is, do they fit well enough to be useful? Researchers should consider the following in deciding whether to use the data:

- Do the data apply to the population of interest?
- Do the data apply to the time period of interest or are they too old to be relevant?
- Do the secondary data appear in the correct units of measurement?
- Do the data offer facts relevant to the research question?
- Do the data include enough variables to describe the phenomena of interest in adequate detail?

- Are the data reliable and valid?
- Can the data be analyzed in conjunction with other secondary and/or primary data?

Researchers have to take care not to assume that secondary information is relevant, useful, and reliable simply because it is available. Consider the following typical situations:

- A researcher interested in forklift trucks finds 12-year-old secondary data on forklift trucks grouped together in a broader category also counting industrial trucks and tractors.
- An investigator who wishes to study consumers earning more than $300,000 per year finds secondary data in which household income is reported in levels with the highest indicating the number of households at $200,000 per year or more.
- A brewery that wishes to compare its per-barrel advertising expenditures with those of competitors finds that some companies' data report the cost of point-of-purchase promotional expenditures with advertising and others do not.
- Data from a previous warranty registration database show where consumers like to buy certain products such as garden supplies and pet food.

Secondary data often do not adequately satisfy research needs because:

1. the data are too old,
2. of variation in definitions of terms,
3. the use of different units of measurement, and
4. inadequate information to verify the data's validity or to allow any potential explanation for behavior.

In primary data collection, the researcher determines when data are collected and defines variables included in research question(s). Contrast this to a researcher investigating market potential for a new product within the Hispanic market in Chicago using secondary data reported as "percent white," "percent nonwhite," and "other." Researchers frequently encounter secondary data that report on a population of interest that is similar, but not directly comparable, to their population of interest.

Units of Measurement

Units of measurement may cause problems if they do not conform exactly to a researcher's needs. For example, consider a researcher comparing college students' grades across transcripts from different countries. In the United States, grades are typically on a 0 to 4 scale (F, D, C, B, or A). In France, records indicate grades using a 20-point scale. Places like Turkey, China, and Indonesia use other scales. Can the researcher directly compare students' grades to assist university administrators in making graduate school admission decisions? In contrast, standardized tests like the GMAT or GRE use the same scale no matter where a student takes the test. Thus, administrators may find it easier to compare students based on standardized test scores. Interestingly, though, the GMAT and GRE each use a different scale making comparisons across the two tests difficult.

Sometimes, data using different scales is amenable to rescaling. **Data transformation** is the process of changing the original form of data to a format more suitable for achieving a stated research objective. Researchers may find it easy to compare sales over the years by transforming all sales figures mathematically to some base year by using the inflation rate. For instance, $1 in 1980 = $2.29 in 2000, $2.86 in 2010, and $3.21 in 2014. Looked at from the other direction, $1 in 2014 represents only $0.31 of buying power in 1980. Some data, such as U.S. Gross Domestic Product (GDP) estimates, are provided in constant (i.e., transformed) dollars. Similarly, one can easily convert dollar values to euros or any other major currency using the exchange rate for that particular day. A quick Internet search will yield numerous websites that assist in this calculation, allowing for easy transformation of currency values. However, standardized tests assign points differently, so transforming a GRE score to a GMAT score, for instance, is problematic. Thus, valid transformations are not always possible.

Reliability and Validity

Researchers today might easily be more tempted than ever to use secondary data given the tremendous explosion of secondary data sources arising from increases in consumer tracking and data storage technologies. However, the usefulness of the results still depends on data quality. In some ways, having more data complicates the process of sorting out high from low quality data.

This brings us to another potential disadvantage of secondary data. That is, the user has no control over the data's reliability and validity—topics we will discuss in more detail later. But for now, think of these as representing data accuracy or trustworthiness. Although timely and pertinent secondary data may fit the researcher's requirements, the data could be inaccurate. The research methods used to collect the data may have somehow introduced bias to the data. For example, media often publish data from surveys to identify the characteristics of their subscribers or viewers. These data will sometimes exclude derogatory data from their reports. Some data releases are notorious for being "revised" later. Economic growth rates, the number of jobs created per quarter, and even the weather fall into this category. Initial weather data reported a May average temperature in Arkansas of 95.2 °F, the hottest on record. Weeks later, the corrected report lowered that *slightly* to 85 °F, just about normal.[3] Good researchers are suspicious of and avoid data with a high likelihood of bias or that have a history of substantial revision.

Many sites make Internet traffic data available. However, raw reports of Internet traffic are very dubious. Over one-third of Internet traffic is fraudulent.[4] The increasing value of Internet advertising has spawned a host of unscrupulous efforts at boosting traffic counts including the introduction of computer viruses that spawn fake visits to websites. Advertisers pay for Web advertising based on traffic counts, and various intermediaries between the advertisers and the media selling advertising often participate in these unethical activities. The inaccurate traffic means marketers are paying unfair prices for online ads.

Thus, the researcher must work diligently to assess the reputation of the organization that gathers and reports data. Also, they must critically assess the original research design. Unfortunately, such evaluation may be impossible because he/she cannot find or obtain full information explaining the original research's procedures in detail. At other times, such as in assessing Web traffic, determining a true hit on a page from a fraudulent hit based on automatic recording of data falls into the virtually impossible category.

Researchers should verify data whenever possible. **Cross-checks** from multiple sources—that is, comparison of the data from one source with data from another—should be made to determine the similarity of independent projects. When the data are not consistent, researchers should attempt to identify reasons for the differences or to determine which data are most likely to be correct. When the researcher cannot verify the reliability and validity of the data, he/she must determine whether using the data is worth the risk. Exhibit 6.1 illustrates issues that useful in deciding whether to rely on secondary data. At times, situations may dictate that a researcher move forward even when the researcher is uncertain about one of these issues. The researcher has a duty at that point to inform the decision-maker of the risks involved in relying on questionable secondary data.

Data transformation

The process of changing the original form of the data to a format suitable to achieve the research objective; also called data transformation.

Cross-checks

The comparison of data from one source with data from another source to determine the similarity of independent projects.

EXHIBIT 6.1
To Use or Not to Use
Secondary Data?

Typical Objectives for Secondary-Data Research Designs

We could never list all possible purposes of secondary data in marketing research. However, secondary data plays a role in many commonly occurring marketing research questions. Exhibit 6.2 shows three general categories of research objectives: fact-finding, model building, and database marketing.

Fact-Finding

The simplest objective of secondary-data research is fact-finding. A restaurant serving breakfast might be interested in knowing what new products are likely to entice consumers. Secondary data available from National Eating Trends, a service of the NPD Group, show that the most potential may be in menu items customers can eat on the go.[5] According to data from the survey of eating trends, the increased prevalence of nutrition and calorie counts on menus has not significantly affected consumer choices. In addition, although overall restaurant sales dropped during the economic downturn of 2009–2014, Chili's, a casual restaurant, has seen their sales go up. Another research firm, Market Facts, says almost half of consumers say they would pay extra for cheese on menu items. These simple facts would interest a researcher who was investigating today's dining market.

Identification of Consumer Behavior for a Product Category

Another typical objective for a secondary research study might be to uncover all available information about consumption patterns for a particular product category or to identify demographic trends that affect an industry. For example, a company called Servigistics offers software that scans a company's own parts inventory data and compares it with marketing objectives and competitors' prices to suggest potential price adjustments. Kia Motors tried using this service in

Broad Objective	Specific Research Example
Fact-Finding	Identifying Web traffic, consumption patterns, tracking trends
Model Building	Forecasting market potential, sales in a time-period, selecting locations, determining relationships with sales
Database Marketing	Developing prospect lists, predicting future customer behavior, data mining

EXHIBIT 6.2
Common Objectives of
Secondary Data Studies

© 2016 Cengage Learning®

place of the usual method of marking up cost by a set fraction. By considering secondary data including internal inventory data and external data about competitors' prices, it was able to make service parts a more profitable segment of its business.[6] This example illustrates the wealth of factual information about consumption and behavior patterns available by carefully considering and analyzing secondary data.

Trend Analysis

Marketers watch for trends in the marketplace and the environment. **Market tracking** is the observation and analysis of trends in industry volume and brand share over time. Scanner research services and Internet analytics firms, as well as other organizations, provide facts about sales volume to support this work.

Almost every large consumer goods company routinely investigates brand and product category sales volume using secondary data. This type of analysis typically involves comparisons with competitors' sales or with the company's own sales in comparable time periods. It also involves industry comparisons among different geographic areas.

Market tracking

The observation and analysis of trends in industry volume and brand share over time.

Environmental Scanning

In many instances, the fact-finding process simply seeks to identify trends. Environmental scanning entails information gathering and fact-finding designed to detect early indications of environmental changes. As mentioned in Chapter 2, the Internet and social media provide an easy tool facilitating environmental scanning. However, other means of environmental scanning include periodic reviews of contemporary publications and reports. Marketers today understand the importance of emerging markets. With golf growth slowing in the United States, companies like Callaway, Ping, and Titleist, as well as other companies involved in the resort business, may benefit from news reports showing that golf is booming in China. Mission Hills, in Shenzhen, boasts twenty-two golf courses and claims to be the world's largest golf resort. The reports also describe a noticeable number of young children on the practice grounds.[7] These trends may provide opportunities for many golf-related businesses.

VICTOR FRAILE / Alamy

Does It Matter?

Secondary data, by its name, may seem to lack power compared to primary data. However, with secondary data, researchers can test research questions that would be difficult to examine any other way. For example, what matters when it comes to firm performance? Does customer satisfaction ultimately lead to superior firm performance? Given that firm performance is a property of the company and not of its customers or employees, the researcher cannot directly capture this with surveys. Therefore, researchers turn to secondary data to try to isolate controllable variables that drive firm performance.

Basic marketing research addresses this issue by tapping into secondary data sources such as the Nielsen database, Compustat, and the American Consumer Satisfaction Index (ACSI). What should companies emphasize? Advertising, services, value or satisfaction? Statistical models using secondary data suggest that advertising, satisfaction, and services all play a role. But, as an industry is more competitive, services and value come to the top in shaping a firm's stock value.

So, what matters? It seems like firms should allocate scarce resources toward increasing services and greater value. Service and value are never secondary!

Sources: Grewal, P., M. Chandrashkaran, and A. V. Citrin (2010), "Customer Satisfaction Heterogeneity and Shareholder Value," *Journal of Marketing Research*, 47 (August), 612–626. Fang, E., R. W. Palmatier, and J. B. Steencamp (2008), "Effect of Service Transition Strategies on Firm Value," *Journal of Marketing*, 72 (September), 1–14. Luo, X. and C. Homburg (2007), "Neglected Outcomes of Consumer Satisfaction," *Journal of Marketing*, 71 (April), 133–149. Horowitz, B. (2014), "McDonald's: Last in Satisfaction—Again," *Wall Street Journal*, (June 20), B6.

Many media outlets today offer push technology targeted to specific customer types. Push technology uses "electronic smart agents," custom software that filters, sorts, prioritizes, and stores information for later viewing.[8] The true value of push technology is that the researcher who is scanning the environment can specify the kinds of news and information he/she wants, have it delivered to his/her device quickly, and view it at leisure. However, early push technologies proved bothersome because they provided too much irrelevant information. Today's technologies work together with search engine histories to direct users toward more relevant information faster. Smart agents and apps like Instapaper and Little Printers put the user more in control,[9] creating a combination of push and pull, and hopefully allowing the user to avoid information overload.

Model Building

Model building

A mathematical representation of the relationship between two or more variables; shows how one thing responds to changes in another.

Model building, the second general objective for secondary research, is more complicated than simple fact-finding. **Model building** involves specifying relationships between two or more variables, perhaps extending to the development of descriptive, explanatory or predictive analytics. The models try to specify how one thing changes in coordination with another. Models need not include complicated mathematics, though. In fact, decision-makers often prefer simple models that everyone can readily understand to complex models that are difficult to comprehend. In particular, models should allow for a visual representation of how some important outcome, like market share or sales, can be changed. Mathematical model builders often use secondary data. A great deal of big data analysis involves scouring internal and external data sources for variables that help model sales or market share.

Estimating Market Potential for Geographic Areas

Marketers often estimate market potential using secondary data. In many cases, a trade association or another source publishes exact sales figures. However, when the desired information is unavailable, the researcher may estimate market potential by transforming secondary data from two or more sources. For example, managers may find secondary data about market potential for a country or other large geographic area, but this information may not be broken down into smaller geographical areas, such as by metropolitan area, or in terms unique to the company, such as sales territory. In this type of situation, researchers often need to make projections for the geographic area of interest.

Suppose a Belgian Abbey Ale (beer) company is looking for opportunities to expand sales by exporting or investing in other countries. Managers decide to begin by estimating market potential for several potential target markets. Secondary research uncovered data for per capita beer consumption in numerous sources, such as Data Monitor, a company that catalogs commercial statistics by country. Population estimates are available in several places, including the Census Bureau and through the CIA (see www.cia.gov to access the *World Factbook*). Exhibit 6.3 illustrates the main findings compiled.

The trade area market potential for the Czech Republic in 2015 is found by multiplying the country's population estimate[10] by the per capita beer consumption:

$$10,500,000 \text{ people} \times 182 \text{ liters/person} = 1,911,000,000 \text{ liters}$$

That's over a bottle a day per person. To get a sense of the expected sales volume, the marketer would have to multiply this amount by the price per liter at which beer typically sells. Although the Czech Republic may be an attractive market, greater overall volume might be offered by other markets with larger overall populations. As Exhibit 6.3 reveals, China, although with the lowest per capita consumption of the countries shown in the exhibit, offers the largest opportunity in terms of the total potential market for beer sales. Brazil and the United States also display relatively high total beer consumption. Although China, Brazil, and the United States aren't known so much for beer consumption, as is Germany, the sheer size of the markets makes them attractive targets for the brewery.

Decision-makers should consider the calculated market potential for each country a rough estimate. Also, the marketer should consider whether each country is experiencing growth or decline in demand. For example, beer consumption is barely growing in Europe and Japan, but it is expanding in Latin America (at about 4 percent a year) and growing even faster in China (by at least 6 percent a year). Additionally, the researcher can probably find information on competitive intensity (how many competing beer companies) in each area and adjust projections for the competition.

Forecasting Sales

Sales forecasting is the process of predicting sales totals over a specific period. Accurate sales forecasts, especially for products in mature, stable markets, frequently come from secondary-data research that identifies trends and extrapolates past performance into the future. Marketing researchers often use internal company sales records to project sales. A rudimentary model would multiply past sales volume by an expected growth rate. A researcher might investigate a secondary source and find that industry sales normally grow about 10 percent per year; multiplying company sales volume by 10 percent would give a basic sales forecast.

Exhibit 6.4 illustrates trend projection using a moving average projection of growth rates. Average ticket prices for a Major League Baseball game are secondary data from Team Marketing Report (**http://www.teammarketing.com**). The moving average is the sum of growth rates for the past three years divided by three (number of years). The resulting number is a forecast of the percentage increase in ticket price for the coming year. Using the three-year average growth rate

Country	2015 Population (thousands)	Annual Volume Consumed (thousand liters)	Annual per Capita Beer Consumption (liters)	Share of World Market
Czech Republic	10,500	1,911	182	0.01
Germany	81,000	8,650	107	0.05
Australia	22,750	1,830	80	0.01
United States	320,000	24,250	75	0.13
Brazil	203,000	12,800	63	0.07
China	1,400,000	44,201	32	0.24

EXHIBIT 6.3
Market Potential for Select Geographic Areas by Country

© 2016 Cengage Learning®

of 1.2 percent for the 2012, 2013, and 2014 sales periods, we can forecast the average ticket price for 2015 as follows:

$$\$27.93 + (\$27.93 \times .012) = \$28.27$$

A Major League Baseball team is probably more interested in financial metrics like revenue. Using the ticket price for any season, one can compute average home ticket sales revenue for any upcoming season by multiplying the average Major League attendance projection times the number of home games (81) times the average ticket price. For the year 2015, the estimated attendance using the three-year moving average is 30,665. Thus, the estimated revenue for a typical team is:

$$30{,}665 \text{ tickets/game} \times 81 \text{ games} \times \$28.27 \text{ per ticket} = \$70{,}218{,}864$$

The moving average forecasting is best suited to a static competitive environment. More dynamic situations make other sales forecasting techniques more appropriate. We'll discuss other forecasting methods later in the book, but simple moving averages like the three-year moving average are often applied in practice.

Analysis of Trade Areas and Sites

Site analysis techniques

Techniques that use secondary data to select the best location for retail or wholesale operations.

Marketing managers examine trade areas using **site analysis techniques** that help management select the best locations for retail or wholesale operations. Secondary-data research helps managers make these site selection decisions. Some organizations, especially franchisers, have developed special computer software based on analytical models to select sites for retail outlets. The researcher must obtain the appropriate secondary data for analysis with the computer software.

EXHIBIT **6.4**
Secondary Data for Major League Baseball Ticket Prices with Moving Average

Year	Average Ticket Price ($)	Percentage Change from Previous Year	Three-Year Moving Average
1996	11.20	5.2%	3.5%
1997	12.36	10.4%	5.8%
1998	13.59	10.0%	8.5%
1999	14.91	9.7%	10.0%
2000	16.67	11.8%	10.5%
2001	18.99	13.9%	11.8%
2002	18.30	−3.6%	7.4%
2003	19.01	3.9%	4.7%
2004	19.82	4.3%	1.5%
2005	21.17	6.8%	5.0%
2006	22.21	4.9%	5.3%
2007	22.70	2.2%	4.6%
2008	25.43	12.0%	6.4%
2009	26.64	4.5%	6.3%
2010	26.74	0.4%	5.6%
2011	26.92	0.7%	1.9%
2012	26.98	0.2%	0.4%
2013	27.73	2.7%	1.2%
2014	27.93	0.7%	1.2%

© 2016 Cengage Learning®

The **index of retail saturation** offers one way to investigate retail sites and to describe the relationship between retail demand and supply.[11] The calculation gives an idea of how much revenue a market generates per a specific amount of retail space:

$$\text{Index of retail saturation} = \frac{\text{Local market potential (demand)}}{\text{Local market retailing space}}$$

For example, Exhibit 6.5 shows the relevant secondary data for shoe store sales in a five-mile radius surrounding a Florida shopping center. Data like these are available from numerous vendors of market information such as Mapping Analytics. First, to estimate local market potential (demand), we multiply population by annual per capita shoe sales in the trade area. Then, we sum the selling floor size over all shoe stores in the trade area. These two figures make the numerator and denominator of the calculation, respectively:

$$\text{Index of retail saturation} = \frac{\$14,249,000}{94,000\,\text{sq.ft.}} = \$152/\text{sq.ft.}$$

Although the index is called saturation, a higher number actually indicates a less saturated area. An index value above 200 is considered to indicate exceptional opportunities. Trade area maps represent market potential using colors that indicate varying degrees of market potential. The result is a geographic information system (GIS) that pull secondary data together from multiple sources to provide useful information for better decision making.

Advertising Response

A great deal of modeling in marketing research focuses on how advertising influences consumers and business performance including the way advertising intensity affects the rate at which a service is adopted or disadopted (meaning a consumer ends the service agreement). Particularly in public services such as cable television, historic records on diffusion and firm advertising are readily available. The models include a relationship between the firm's own advertising and the primary competitor's advertising.[12] Additionally, other models show that although banner ad click through rates are very low, they do contribute to increased sales. With social media and the

Index of retail saturation

A calculation that describes the relationship between retail demand and supply as a ratio of sales potential per unit area of retail sales space.

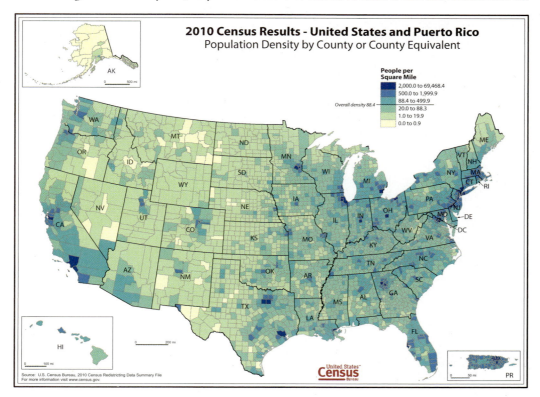

Data Mining Tools May Analyze Population Densities or Traffic Patterns to Help with Location Decisions

Internet, advertising effectiveness often is tied to quantities of exposures driven by websites with high traffic counts.

Some models are more focused on classification than response. They may try to show overlap between groups of people or communication. For instance, they may mine social networking data to identify common networks of people whose communication overlaps across Facebook, Twitter, and Myspace.[13] Advertisers can use this knowledge to send a carefully targeted message to a consumer in one social network that will then expand to others by virtue of the overlap.

Data Mining

Large corporations' decision support systems often contain millions or even hundreds of millions of records of data. In Chapter 2, we introduced the term *data mining* in discussing what happens after huge volumes of data become stored electronically and are accessible by a firm's research analysts. Data mining helps clarify the underlying meaning of the data.

Data mining

The use of powerful computer analytical routines to dig automatically through huge volumes of data searching for useful patterns of relationships.

The term **data mining** refers specifically to the use of powerful computer analytical routines to dig automatically through huge volumes of data searching for useful patterns of relationships. The analytics can take many forms from simple correlational routines to routines that involve artificial intelligence. For example, **neural networks** are a form of artificial intelligence in which a computer mimics the way human brains process information and make decisions. This type of data mining can help predict fast-food preference.[14] Neural networks simulate consumer decision making and work like human memory by relying on rules that have more often been shown to be true. For example, lemonade and Chick-fil-A become associated. If a consumer likes lemonade, he/she will more often go to Chick-fil-A. The program would use lemonade preference as one of a host of predictive criteria.

Neural networks

A form of artificial intelligence in which a computer is programmed to mimic the way human brains process information.

Market-basket analysis is a form of data mining that analyzes anonymous point–of–sale transaction databases to identify coinciding purchases or relationships between products purchased and other retail shopping information.[15] Auchan, a large French hypermart firm, identified an interesting pattern among the scanner data gathered as customers pay for the things they buy. They noticed that a higher than expected number of customers who bought baby diapers also bought beer (they end up in the market basket together). A quick follow-up suggested further that most of the diaper and beer buyers were men. As a result, management decided to move some beer displays closer to the diapers and as a result, they raised the proportion of beer and customer buyers even higher.

Market-basket analysis

A form of data mining that analyzes anonymous point-of-sale transaction databases to identify coinciding purchases or relationships between products purchased and other retail shopping information.

Customer discovery is a data–mining application that similarly involves mining data to look for patterns that can increase the value of customers. For example, Macy's commissioned data-mining techniques looking for patterns of relationships among the huge volumes of previous sales records. Macy's sent out millions of catalogs, but not every customer got the same catalog; in fact, tens of thousands versions of the catalog were carefully tailored to specific customers.[16] Female customers thirty years of age saw more handbags, accessories, shoes, and women's clothing than did middle-aged males. Further, if her individual records show purchases of baby clothing, she will probably see many things for toddlers. The result is that the customer sees more purchase possibilities that have a high probability of addressing some current need or desire.

Customer discovery

Involves mining data to look for patterns identifying who is likely to be a valuable customer.

Most retailers today maintain electronic records of every purchase made by a consumer. By using data mining to combine these records with data from other customers, the companies can generate suggested sales attempts in real time. More and more, marketers can mine text data for meaning. Data-mining routines mine Internet chatter and interpret words and phrases in ways that allow the development of models of customer satisfaction in specific industries.[17] The research snapshot describes a similar process by which management stays in touch with online buzz to model brand equity.

Database Marketing and Customer Relationship Management

Database marketing

The use of customer databases to promote one-to-one relationships with customers and create precisely targeted promotions.

A customer relationship management (CRM) system maintains customer databases containing customers' names, addresses, phone numbers, past purchases, responses to past promotional offers, and other relevant data such as demographic and financial data. **Database marketing** is the practice of using CRM databases to develop one-to-one relationships and precisely targeted promotional efforts with individual customers. Banks use database marketing to model not only a customer's

What's That Buzzing Sound?

Bees aren't the only creatures that buzz. Consumers do, too, and more and more they create that buzz online. Just think about it, the Internet is filled with billions of consumer conversations. Obviously, these billions of data points contain a lot of useful information. But, a lot of it is useless, too. How can a firm make sense of this? One solution: data-mining software designed for the blogosphere.

Buzzmetrics, a part of Nielsen online, serves firms by monitoring electronic conversations, letting firms know whether conversation about their brand is up or down on any given time period. Want to know if a Super Bowl ad had any impact? The buzz an ad creates from the time it becomes public is a good indicator. No buzz, probably not much sizzle in terms of market effectiveness. Is *Dancing with Stars* still popular? If people aren't talking about it online then that show may be losing its sizzle. Today, there is an app for just about everything. Conventions put their events schedule in apps and provide easy ways for conventioneers to use a

Twitter feed or leave comments on Facebook or other sites. Smart agents mine this content for buzz to help know what makes a convention successful.

Sources: Alahnah, M. and D. Khazanchi (2010), "The Importance of Buzz," *Marketing Research*, 22 (Summer), 20–25. Lee, S. S. and C. H. Lee (2014), "An Exploratory Study of Convention Specific Social Media Usage by Attendees: Motivations and Effect of Generations on Choice of Convention Information Source and Intention to Use Mobile Application," *Journal of Convention & Event Tourism*, 15, 135–149.

lifetime value, but his/her lifetime potential value.[18] This allows managers to steer customers toward processes that enhance their value.

Effective database marketing requires vast amounts of secondary data to be integrated into a CRM system. Transaction records, which often list items purchased, prices, and customers' names and addresses, are the building blocks for many databases. Analysts supplement these records with data customers provide directly, such as data on a warranty card, surveys, or even other secondary data purchased from third parties. For example, credit services may sell databases about applications for loans, credit card payment history, and other financial data. Several companies, such as Donnelley Marketing and Nielsen (with PRIZM), collect primary data and then sell demographic data that can be related to small geographic areas, such as those with a certain zip code. (Remember that when the vendor collects the data, they are primary data, but when the database marketer incorporates the data into his/her database, they are secondary data.)

Sources of Internal Secondary Data

More and more, the exact distinction between internal and external secondary data becomes blurry with modern information technology. Some accounting documents are indisputably internal records of the organization. Researchers in another organization cannot have access to them. Clearly, a book published by Cengage and located in a university library is external to the company. However, in today's world of electronic data interchange, data gathered by an industry organization may appear in a catalog and may be purchased. For example, international beverage consumption statistics broken down by category are available for purchase from an online information vendor and then made available to company analysts for instantaneous access within the DSS. The formerly external data is now available internally.

Internal data are data that originate in the organization and represent events recorded by or generated by the organization. **Proprietary data** is perhaps a more descriptive term and emphasizes the fact that company owns and controls the data.

Internal data

Data that originate in the organization and represent events recorded by or generated by the organization.

Proprietary data

Secondary data owned and controlled by the organization.

Internal and Proprietary Data

Most organizations routinely gather, record, and store internal data to help them solve future problems. An organization's accounting system can usually provide a wealth of information. Routine documents such as sales invoices allow external financial reporting, which in turn can be a source of data for further analysis. If company employees properly code the data into a company database, the researcher may be able to conduct more detailed analysis using the decision support system. Companies organize sales information in several different ways including by account, by product, or by sales territory. The coding allows retrieval of information about orders delivered, back orders, and unfilled orders. Other useful sources of internal data include salespeoples' call reports, customer complaints, service records, warranty card returns, product returns, archived focus group recordings, and other records. As you can see, the data provide opportunities to forecast and potentially explain important outcomes to the firm including sales and return rates.

Researchers frequently aggregate or disaggregate internal data. A wine store compared its sales records to names registered on its e-mail mailing list. As a result, the store owner realized that the old 80/20 rule was no exaggeration. In fact, about 15 percent of customers accounted for 80 percent of all sales. As a result, the store concentrated on extra incentives for the best customers to visit the store more often.

Internet technology is making it easier to research internal and proprietary data. Often, companies set up secure, internal networks allowing employees to store and share proprietary data within the organization. An **enterprise search**, which is like an Internet search but focuses on data within the enterprise's internal network, considers not only how many views a particular data page records, but also users' historical search patterns in determining what data might be useful. In addition, other companies have purchased specialized enterprise search software, such as Autonomy, which searches internal sources plus such external sources as news and government websites.[19]

Some firms like Boeing, Apple, and Honda use open-source software in an effort to develop innovations. The result is an **open-source innovation** effort that involves allowing other firms real-time access to otherwise proprietary data within the enterprise. The GENIVI Alliance represents a cooperative effort where firms from multiple automobile manufacturers share access to data with software and communications companies in an effort to create better automotive audio, communication, and entertainment systems.[20]

Enterprise search
A search driven by an Internet type search engine that focuses on data within an organization's internal network.

Open-source innovation
Effort that involves allowing other firms real-time access to otherwise proprietary data within the enterprise in an effort to expand the solution space developing innovations.

External Secondary Data Sources

External data
Facts observed, recorded, and stored by an entity outside of the researcher's organization.

External data are facts observed, recorded, and stored by an entity outside of the researcher's organization. The government, universities, newspapers and journals, trade associations, and other organizations perform these services either to serve industry or to offer for sale. Today, computerized access is the rule of the day making external data nearly as accessible as internal data. The Research Snapshot on the next page illustrates a company that specializes in data archives.

Information as a Product and Its Distribution Channels

Secondary data offers value, and thus, companies buy and sell data access regularly. Just as bottles of perfume or plumbers' wrenches go from production to consumer in different ways, secondary data also flow through various channels of distribution. Many users, such as Fortune 500 corporations, purchase documents and computerized lifestyle and population data from companies like Nielsen. However, smaller companies lacking the budget necessary to buy data from these companies can get a wealth of data free from sources like the U.S. Census Bureau (www.census.gov).

Libraries

Traditionally, libraries' vast storehouses of information have served as a bridge between users and producers of secondary data. The library staff deals directly with the creators of information, such

Uncle Sam Finds You!

In a nation with an all-volunteer military, finding recruits is an ongoing need. The project is especially challenging in wartime, when more service members are necessary but the costs of serving are too daunting for many citizens. One way that the Department of Defense meets this challenge is by reviewing data that exist in a variety of sources. Its Joint Advertising, Market Research & Studies (JAMRS) project operates over a dozen research initiatives that make data available to military recruiters in all branches of the U.S. armed services. Some involve data collection, but many apply already-existing data (secondary data) to the task of recruitment.

JAMRS is partly a data warehouse storing all information gathered as potential recruits visit or contact recruiting stations. JAMRS also pays for data from third-party research firms. For example, it uses the PRIZM market segmentation data gathered and sold by Nielsen (who acquired Claritas who originally developed PRIZM), a marketing research firm. The PRIZM data describe the purchasing and media behavior of many market segments. Recruiters can use the data to identify the activities of potential recruits that live in their region—for example, to identify the magazines they read.

The U.S. Marines are learning more about applying secondary data in predicting individuals with a high probability

The military is very interested in marketing research

of enlisting. Given privacy restrictions, Marine recruiters, and those for other branches, are limited in what information they can keep about prospects. For example, Marine recruiters cannot use information from the cookies of someone who visits a recruiting website. So instead, they put together information about interests from secondary sources and try to match those to profiles of successful recruits.

Sources: "Market Research and Studies," *Joint Advertising, Market Research & Studies,* JAMRS website, http://jamrs.defense.gov/, accessed June 18, 2014. *Ad Age* (2013), "How the Marine Corps Enlists Big Data for Recruitment Efforts," http://adage.com/article/datadriven-marketing/marine-corps-enlists-big-data-recruitment/291009/, accessed June 18, 2014.

---

as the federal government, and intermediate distributors of information, such as abstracting and indexing services. More and more, libraries access content through large consortiums that work with publishers to put together collections and make them available through search engines such as Ebscohost. The user need only locate the appropriate secondary data on the library *shelves* (physical or virtual). Large corporations also maintain libraries as do public institutions like the United Nations and the Library of Congress. As a result of the convenience of Internet access, university students don't actually visit the school library as much as in the past. Libraries are innovating to provide other reasons for people to actually visit the library.

The Internet

Today, vast amounts of secondary data are conveniently available over the Internet. Library Spot, at **http://www.libraryspot.com**, provides links to online libraries, including law, medical, academic, and government libraries. The virtual reference desk features links to calendars, dictionaries, encyclopedias, maps, and other sources typically found at a traditional library's reference desk. Remember, though, not all sources are equal as some are more credible than are others. Exhibit 6.6 lists some popular Internet addresses where one can find potentially useful data.

The opening vignette illustrates how companies find secondary data via the Internet. Consumers also use information posted here as a form of secondary data to aid in their own purchases. J.D. Power (jdpower.com) provides consumer ratings of many, many products. For instance, a consumer can look there and find what airlines customers score the highest and lowest. For 2014, Alaska Airlines and Delta Airlines top the list, whereas United and U.S. Air score the

EXHIBIT **6.6**
Selected Internet Sources for
Secondary Data

Source	Description	URL
U.S. Census Bureau	Demographic information about the United States overall and by state and county. Information about U.S. business and the economy.	www.census.gov
CIA *Factbook*	Profiles of over 250 countries providing descriptive statistics of population, commerce, geography, religion, history, and much more.	www.cia.gov
FedStats	A portal containing links to reports and data compiled by most federal agencies ranging from agriculture to education.	fedstats.sites.usa.gov
Datamonitor	Offers a very large collection of current business reports on industries, countries, markets, consumption statistics as well as tracking data for new product launches. Subscription required.	www.datamonitor.com
Advertising Age	Media source for advertising industry news and access to hundreds of research reports on specific issues within and affecting the industry (for a fee).	www.adage.com
YouTube	Online access to over 10 billion videos. User videos can reveal insights into product improvements. Huge source for television and video advertising.	www.youtube.com
Kantar Media	Source focusing on the integrated global media industry. Excellent source for statistics and reports on viewership, Internet usage, and basic consumer profiles such as the British teen market.	www.kantarmedia.com
European Union Commission	Comprehensive collection of statistics on Europe overall and the individual nations within the European Union. Statistics include detailed economic performance data, immigration, demographic data, and much more.	ec.europa.eu/eurostat
The Wall Street Journal Online	Provides a real-time view of business news and financial statistics including stock values, exchange rates, and more. Some content is free.	www.wsj.com
Harvard Business School	Not a database per se but like at most libraries, links to dozens of sources for data both public and private can be found here.	http://www.library.hbs.edu/all_databases.html
The ACSI	Customer satisfaction ratings for hundreds of large firms doing business in the U.S. Data are available by industry and free of charge.	http://theacsi.org/
Quandl.com	A venture launched by a Canadian technology company that aims to become a repository for quantitative data of all types, with a particular emphasis on economic data and data on international markets.	http://Quandl.com
Chinability	A convenient collection of reports and links to data reports and other sources related to the Chinese economy and business climate.	www.chinability.com

lowest.[21] Consumers also leave behind comments and ratings and ask questions and get answers from other consumers who they may not even know. Consumers place more value on information provided by consumers who respond quickly to Internet queries for information, whose previous responses are positively evaluated by other consumers, and who seem to show knowledge in their responses.[22] Marketing researchers similarly weigh information posted by consumers based on some assessment of credibility.

Vendors

The information age offers many channels besides libraries through which to access data. Many external producers make secondary data available directly or through intermediaries, which are often called *vendors*. Vendors such as Factiva (www.factiva.com) now allow managers to participate in a community and access thousands of external databases. Hoovers (http://www.hoovers.com), for instance, specializes in providing information about thousands of companies' financial situations and operations.

Producers

Classifying external secondary data by the nature of the producer of information yields six basic sources: publishers of books and periodicals, government sources, media sources, trade association sources, commercial sources, and consumer sources. The following section discusses some secondary data sources briefly.

Periodicals

Professional journals such as the *Journal of the Academy of Marketing Science, Journal of Marketing, Journal of Marketing Research, The Journal of Business Research, Journal of Advertising Research, American Demographics,* and *The Public Opinion Quarterly,* as well as commercial business periodicals such as the *Wall Street Journal, Fortune,* and *Bloomberg Businessweek,* contain much useful material. *Sales and Marketing Management's Survey of Buying Power* is a particularly useful source of information about markets. To locate data in periodicals, indexing services such as the *ABI/INFORM and Business Periodicals Index* and the *Wall Street Journal Index* are very useful. Guides to data sources also are helpful. Most university libraries provide access to at least some of these databases.

Government Sources

Government agencies produce data prolifically. Most of the data published by the federal government can be counted on for accuracy and quality of investigation. Most students are familiar with the U.S. *Census of Population,* which provides a wealth of data.

The *Census of Population* is only one of many resources that the government provides. Banks and savings and loan companies rely heavily on the *Federal Reserve Bulletin* and the *Economic Report of the President* for volumes of data related to things like consumer credit and industrial productivity. Builders and contractors use the information in the *Current Housing Report and Annual Housing Survey* for their research. The ProQuest® *Statistical Abstract of the United States* is an extremely valuable source of information about the social, political, and economic organizations of the United States.

The federal government is a leader in making secondary data available on the Internet. Visit FedStats (**http://fedstats.sites.usa.gov/**) for a central access point with links to many useful statistics. FedStats provides links to the sources mentioned above. Additionally, the following list provides illustrations of the types of facts easily found by exploring this portal:

- Energy production statistics by state and for the country overall. The top four energy-producing states in the United States are West Virginia, Texas, Wyoming, and Louisiana.
- Economic data series, current and historical, such as gross domestic product, retail sales data, and personal income by state. A map of personal income shows that states in the south tended to experience economic growth, whereas other areas, particularly in the west, showed economic declines during the end of the last decade.
- Over a dozen reports documenting and providing statistics about what people eat across the United States broken down by state, in-home versus out-of-home, food category, and how much people pay.

State, county, and local government agencies can also be useful sources of information. Many state governments publish state economic models and forecasts, and many cities have metropolitan planning agencies that provide data about the population, economy and transportation systems in their town. Fortunately, many state and community statistics can be accessed from fedstats.gov, but each state's economic development agency website is a good place to look for more on a particular state.

To the Point

"*The man who does not read good books has no advantage over the man who cannot read them.*"

—MARK TWAIN

Fedstats (fedstats.sites.usa .gov) is a convenient portal to secondary data sources such as the Bureau of Labor Statistics (www.bls.gov).

This chart comes from bls.gov. The darker shaded blue states showed the highest income personal growth and states shaded violet had personal income declines for the 2012–2013 time period

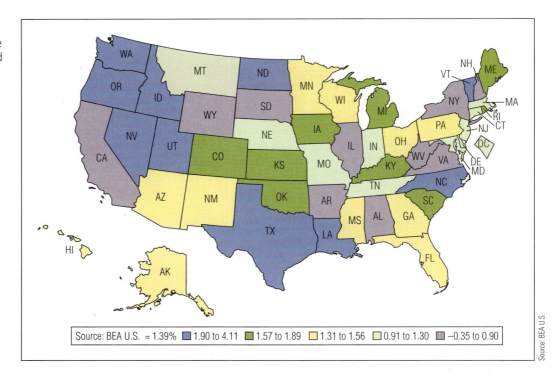

Media Sources

Information on a broad range of subjects is available from broadcast, Internet, and print media. The *Wall Street Journal* (wsj.com), the *Financial Times* (ft.com), and *Bloomberg Businessweek* (businessweek.com) are valuable sources for information on the economy and many markets. The latest stock values for publicly traded companies are available and may prove useful as a measuring stick to assess effectiveness of these companies' major strategic initiatives. Wsj.com is an excellent source for video updates on the latest business trends and news stories.

Trade Association Sources

Trade associations, such as the Food Marketing Institute or the American Petroleum Institute, serve the information needs of a particular industry. The trade association collects data on a number of topics of specific interest to firms, especially data on market size and market trends. Association members have a source of information that is particularly germane to their industry questions. For example, the Recording Industry Association of America (RIAA) provides reports tracking trends in the music industry that are useful to the artists, management companies, and the media in general. As one area of focus, the RIAA compiles a great deal of information related to protecting intellectual and creative property rights.

Commercial Sources

Numerous firms specialize in selling and/or publishing information. For example, the Polk Company specializes in information relevant to automobile marketing, such as the percentage of car buyers relying on the Internet in the search process and the relative health of dealerships by area. Datamonitor offers subscribers an impressive collection of reports, many of which are inter-active, and they allow tracking of industry leaders globally, basic descriptions of markets, and statis-tics on new product introductions. *Fortune* rates the most admired companies annually in addition to providing the Fortune 500 list of the largest U.S. companies. Walmart tops that list with revenue approaching $½ trillion.[23] Exxon-Mobile comes in second with revenues topping $430 billion/year. Here are a few sources of specialized data not mentioned earlier or in Exhibit 6.6.

Market-Share Data. A number of syndicated services supply either wholesale or retail sales vol-ume data based on product movement. Information Resources, Inc. collects market-share data using Universal Product Codes (UPC) and optical scanning at retail store checkouts. Symphonies' InfoScan is a syndicated retail tracking service that collects scanner data from more than 90,000 retailers, including supermarkets, drug stores, and mass merchandisers. This data allows an estimate of market share for just about any consumer goods brand. InfoScan now tracks sales in other coun-tries, including France, Germany, Italy, and the United Kingdom. The *World Market Share Reporter* also is available through the reference desk in many university libraries and available online to sub-scribers. Gale Research publishes and markets the *Reporter* in a domestic and global version each year. The *Reporter* provides market share reports based on aggregated sales data.

Walmart operates its own in-store scanner system called Retail Link. Walmart suppliers get free online access to data.[24] The data contains information on sales allowing vendors to know things like the percentage of stores that have their merchandise on the shelf as well as total sales data across all of Walmart. Given Walmart's dominant role in the U.S. marketplace, share estimates from Retail Link are good proxies for overall market share.

Consumer Attitude and Public Opinion Research. Many research firms offer specialized syndicated services that report findings from attitude research and opinion polls. For example, the Futures Company provides custom research, tailored for specific projects, and several syndicated services. Future's public opinion research studies, such as the voter and public attitude surveys that appear in *Time* and other news magazines, are a source of secondary data. One of the firm's services is the *Yankelovich MONITOR,* a syndicated annual census of changing social values and an analysis of how they can affect consumer marketing. The *MONITOR* charts the growth and spread of new social values, characterizes the types of customers who support the new values and those who continue to support traditional values, and outlines the ways in which people's values affect purchasing behavior.

Harris Interactive is another public opinion research firm that provides syndicated and custom research for business. One of its services is the Harris survey. This survey, released three times per week, monitors the pulse of the American public on topics such as inflation, unemployment, energy, consumer products, politics, and so on. A recent poll gauges Americans' opinions about driving and smartphone use. Based on a poll of over 2,000 adult Americans, over 90 percent of Americans believe that sending or reading texts while driving is dangerous or very dangerous.[25] Nearly 70 percent believe talking on a handheld phone is dangerous or very dangerous. None-theless, nearly three in four report talking on a handheld phone while driving and just under half report texting while driving, with 14 percent admitting to frequently texting and driving. Millennials report the highest incidence of texting and driving (24 percent frequently texting while driving).

Consumption and Purchase Behavior Data. NPD's National Eating Trends (NET) is the most detailed database available on consumption patterns and trends for more than 4,000 food and bev-erage products. This is a syndicated source of data about the types of meals people eat and when and how they eat them. The data, called *diary panel data,* are based on records of meals and diaries kept by a group of households that have agreed to record their consumption behavior over an extended period of time.

National Family Opinion (NFO), Marketing Research Corporation of America (MRCA), and many other syndicated sources sell diary panel data about consumption and purchase behavior. Since the advent of scanner data, diary panels are more commonly used to record purchases of apparel, hardware, home furnishings, jewelry, and other durable goods, rather than purchases of non-durable consumer packaged goods. More recently, services have been tracking consumer behavior online, collecting data about sites visited and purchases made over the Internet.

Advertising Research. Advertisers can purchase readership and audience data from a number of firms. W. R. Simmons and Associates measures magazine audiences; Arbitron measures radio audiences; Nielsen Media Measurement estimates television audience ratings. By specializing in collecting and selling audience information on a continuing basis, these commercial sources provide a valuable service to their subscribers.

Assistance in measuring advertising effectiveness is another syndicated service. For example, Roper Starch Worldwide measures the impact of advertising in magazines. Roper provides readership information for the client's or its competitors' ads.

Consumer Data

Consumer data includes all information left behind online intentionally or unintentionally. This includes social network posts, consumer feedback on sites like TripAdvisor or Urbanspoon, GIS data recording a person's whereabouts through the smartphone, YouTube videos, everything deposited in cookies, and much more. As is clear by this point in the chapter, firms make ample use of this as a big data source that feeds into discovery and marketing analytics. Forty-three percent of managers feel big data reflecting consumer habits gives their firm competitive advantage.[26]

Single-Source and Global Research in the Big Data Era

As business has become more global, so has the secondary data industry. Any business with a website is a global company with potential to reach consumers anywhere in the world. As a result, many companies, large and small, need data on markets near and far. Single-source data firms help companies in that effort and provide ready access to data about global markets. This data has the potential to be productive input into marketing analytics routines.

Many private companies exist solely to provide secondary data and many marketing research firms provide this canned data as a big part of their business. Additionally, many government entities provide secondary information based on statistics that they must collect in administering programs in their own country. It's hard to think of a topic for which no secondary data would exist.

Single-Source Data-Integrated Information

Nielsen Company offers data from both its television meters and scanner operations. The integration of these two types of data helps marketers investigate the impact of television advertising on retail sales. In other ways as well, users of data find that merging two or more diverse types of data into a single database offers many advantages.

PRIZM by Claritas Corporation (a Nielsen entity), GfK Mediamark Research & Intelligence, and many other syndicated databases report product purchase behavior, media usage, demographic characteristics, lifestyle variables, and business activity by geographic area such as zip code. Although such data are often called *geodemographic,* they cover such a broad range of phenomena that no one name is a good description. These data use small geographic areas as the unit of analysis.

Single-source data

Diverse types of data offered by a single company; usually integrated on the basis of a common variable such as geographic area or store.

The marketing research industry uses the term **single-source data** for diverse types of data offered by a single company. Ideally, a firm could go to a single source and get any type of secondary data they may need. Quandl.com seeks to be a clearinghouse for all manner of quantitative statistical data, particularly economic and market data.

Government Agencies

Many countries include an office or have ties to a professional organization that is responsible for storing and making data about key market elements available. The Japan Management Association provides secondary research data to government and industry. One ongoing survey tracks Japanese executives' opinions on pressing business matters. The Institute's goal is to allow global firms access to its enormous store of data about Japan to develop and plan business in Japan.

Secondary data compiled outside the United States have the same limitations as domestic secondary data. However, international researchers should watch for certain pitfalls that frequently are associated with foreign data and cross-cultural research. First, data may simply be unavailable in certain countries. Second, researchers may question the accuracy of some data. This is especially likely with official statistics that may be adjusted for the political purposes of foreign governments. Finally, although economic terminology may be standardized, various countries use different definitions and accounting and recording practices for many economic concepts. For example, different countries may measure disposable personal income in radically different ways. International researchers should take extra care to investigate the comparability of data among countries. Exhibit 6.7 lists some potential sources for marketing information about various parts of the world.

The U.S. government and other organizations compile databases that may aid international marketers. The CIA's *World Factbook* and the National Trade Data Bank (NTDB) are especially useful for exploring potential markets overseas. The NTDB, the U.S. government's most comprehensive source of world trade data, illustrates what is available. The NTDB was established by the Omnibus Trade and Competitiveness Act. Its purpose was to provide "reasonable public access, including electronic access" to an expert promotion data system that was centralized, inexpensive, and easy to use. The CIA's *World Factbook* contains a tremendous amount of data useful in a preliminary assessment of foreign market potential.

The U.S. Department of Commerce has the responsibility for operating and maintaining the NTDB and works with federal agencies that collect and distribute trade information to keep the NTDB up to date. Over 1,000 public and university libraries offer access to the NTDB through the Federal Depository Library system. By using the NTDB, small- and medium-sized companies get immediate access to information that until now only Fortune 500 companies could afford.

Topics in the NTDB include export opportunities by industry, country, and product; foreign companies or importers looking for specific products; how-to market guides; demographic, political, and socioeconomic conditions in hundreds of countries; and much more. NTDB offers one-stop shopping for trade information from more than twenty federal sources. You do not need to know which federal agency produces the information: All you need to do is consult NTDB.

• United States fedstats.sites.usa.gov/	• South America http://www.internetworldstats.com/south.htm
• South Africa http://www.statssa.gov.za	• Norway http://www.ssb.no
• Australia http://www.nla.gov.au/oz/stats.html	• United Nations http://www.un.org/esa
• Japan http://www.stat.go.jp/	• Global Information from the *CIA Factbook* http://www.cia.gov
• United Kingdom http://www.statistics.gov.uk	
• France http://www.insee.fr	

EXHIBIT 6.7

Some Example Sources of Global Marketing Information

© lynx_v / Shutterstock

© 2016 Cengage Learning®

TIPS OF THE TRADE

■ Always consider the possibility that secondary data may exist which can address the research question at hand adequately.

■ Check on the reliability and validity of secondary data. Most reputable sources provide details describing details of the research methods that allow the data quality to be assessed. Try to use multiple sources to corroborate data.

■ Secondary data are particularly useful for trend analysis, environmental scanning, and estimating market potential for geographic areas. Secondary data are useful in a big data context.

■ Government sites such as the Census Bureau (**www.census .gov**), the CIA *World Factbook* (**www.cia .gov**), and FedStats (www.fedstats.gov) are great sources for data about industries, businesses, and consumers, not only in the United States, but also around the world.

© paffy/Shutterstock.com

∴ SUMMARY

1. Discuss the advantages and disadvantages of using secondary data. Someone other than the researcher typically gathers secondary data for some purpose other than the researcher's research question. The chief advantage of secondary data is availability, meaning they are almost always less expensive to obtain and faster to obtain than primary data. Often, researchers use secondary data when relevant primary data are impossible or impractical to obtain. The biggest disadvantage stems from the fact that secondary data were not collected with the researcher's needs in mind. In addition, the researcher may not know the quality of the data in terms of reliability and validity. One way to do this is to cross-check the data using a different source; of course, that isn't always possible.

2. Understand the typical objectives addressed by secondary data. Secondary research designs address many common marketing problems. Three general categories of research objectives often addressed with secondary data are fact-finding, model building, and database marketing. A typical fact-finding study might seek to uncover all available information about consumption patterns for a particular product category or to identify business trends that affect an industry. Model building is more complicated and involves specifying relationships between two or more variables to understand retail locations and advertising responses. Data mining allows marketers to find hidden gems in the volumes of secondary data. More and more, consumers leave their purchase records and conversations about products and brands behind online and provide a great deal of valuable secondary data useful in data mining and even in database marketing efforts.

3. **Identify various internal and proprietary sources of secondary data.** Managers often get data from internal proprietary sources such as accounting records. Data mining is the use of powerful computers to dig through volumes of data to discover patterns about an organization's customers and products. It is a broad term that applies to many different forms of analysis.

4. **Give examples of various external sources of secondary data.** External data are generated or recorded by another entity. Governments, trade organizations, media outlets, and syndicated data sources all record information and make it available for use by others. Sometimes, the data are available free, but other times a fee or subscription must be paid to use the data. The chapter provides an exhibit with some key sources of secondary data. Fedstats.gov is nearly a one-stop source for any statistical information compiled by the U.S. federal government. Private sources like Datamonitor and Kantar Media are comprehensive sources of secondary data collected from various other sources and deal more specifically with marketing new products and monitoring brand perceptions.

5. **Describe the impact of single-source data and globalization on secondary data research in the big data era.** Single-source data firms help companies in that effort and provide ready access to data about global markets. Government resources also offer substantial amounts of data about international markets. As business has become more global, so has the secondary-data industry. International researchers should watch for pitfalls that can be associated with foreign data and cross-cultural research, such as problems with the availability and reliability of data. However, secondary data from single-source outlets and government portals can be synthesized and even combined with data from other sources to perform model building and, in doing so, typify the big data research era.

:: KEY TERMS AND CONCEPTS

cross-checks, *145*
customer discovery, *152*
data transformation *145*
data mining, *152*
database marketing, *152*
enterprise search, *154*

external data, *154*
index of retail saturation, *151*
internal data, *153*
market-basket analysis, *152*
market tracking, *147*
model building, *148*

neural networks, *152*
open source innovation, *154*
proprietary data, *153*
secondary data, *143*
single-source data, *160*
site analysis techniques, *150*

:: QUESTIONS FOR REVIEW AND CRITICAL THINKING

1. Define secondary data. What is the primary advantage of using secondary data to a marketing researcher?
2. Thinking of secondary data as advantageous, how might a bank or health-care organization use a big data approach using secondary data to predict peak periods for loans or emergency care?
3. What questions should a researcher ask about secondary data in deciding whether or not the data are useful?
4. What factors might discourage a researcher from using a particular secondary data source?
5. In what ways might a researcher determine if a specific secondary data source is sufficiently reliable and valid to address a research question presuming the source does not describe the study methodology in detail?
6. Identify some typical research objectives for secondary-data studies.
7. What is model building? How does it use secondary data? What are some examples of different applications of model building in marketing research?
8. What would be a source for the following data?

a. Population, average income, and employment rates for Oregon
b. European trends in automobile ownership
c. Divorce trends in the United States
d. Use of Facebook and Twitter by age and region
e. Annual sales of the top ten U.S. fast-food companies
f. Top ten websites ranked by number of unique visitors
g. Attendance at professional sports events held in Canada and China

9. Suppose you are a marketing research consultant and a client comes to your office and says, "I must have the latest information on the supply of and demand for Idaho potatoes within the next 24 hours." What would you do?
10. What type of data source does the CIA *World Factbook* represent? What kind of data can one find there?
11. Report the following data:
a. U.S. gross domestic product for the first quarter of 1965.
b. U.S. exports of goods and services for the calendar year 2014

    c. U.K. imports of goods and services for the calendar year 2012

    d. U.S. gross domestic product for the first quarter of 2014

    e. Number of fast-food restaurants currently operating in North Dakota

    f. For any of a–e, are the data unavailable?

    g. For any of a–e, would you be uncomfortable relying on the number provided? Explain why or why not.

12. Suppose Walmart is planning on locating a new neighborhood store in downtown Richmond. Suppose the city has hired you to report on the net economic and cultural impact of allowing this Walmart in the middle of downtown. Online, you come across many cities reporting traffic statistics in downtowns with a Walmart location. In every large city with a Walmart, traffic statistics indicate considerable congestion. Should you use that data in your analysis? What are the risks in doing so? Could the data be used to skew opinions one way or the other?

13. Do you believe it is ethical for an employer to mine social networking sites for personal information about employees? Does it matter if the information refers to behavior solely away from work or that is somehow tied to things done while at work? Address the same issue for a marketing research firm that distributes entertainment to mobile devices (movies, music, games). Is it ethical for them to search for relationships and market segments using information people post about themselves on the Internet?

:·: RESEARCH ACTIVITIES

1. Use secondary data to learn the size of the current U.S. golf market and to profile the typical golfer. Can secondary data address research questions related to changes and trends in the U.S. golf market?

2. Where could a researcher working for the U.S. Marine Corps (**http://www.marines.com**) find information that would identify the most productive areas of the United States in which to recruit? What would you recommend?

3. Compare population data from the CIA *World Factbook* for Uruguay, the United States, South Africa, Japan, and Italy with population data for those countries found through some other source (perhaps one originating in each country). Do the different data sources agree? Comment.

4. Try to find the U.S. market share for the following companies within 30 minutes:

    a. Home Depot

    b. Burger King

    c. Marlboro

    d. Google

    e. Was this a difficult task? If so, why do you think it is this difficult?

5. Use the Internet to learn what you can about Indonesia.

    a. Check the corruption index for Indonesia at **http://www. transparency.org**.

    b. What additional kinds of information are available from the following sources?

        1. Go to http://freetheworld.com/member.html and view information for Indonesia.

        2. Visit the CIA's *World Factbook* (http://www.cia.gov/ library/publications/the-world-factbook/).

        3. Go to Google, Yahoo! or another search engine, and use "Indonesia" as a search word. Does it reveal any other convenient data source?

    c. Based on what you find, would you recommend that either Canes or Quick (both fast-food chains) should expand operations in Indonesia?

6. Go to Statistics Norway at **http://www.ssb.no**. What data, if any, can you obtain in English? What languages can be used to search this website? What databases might be of interest to the business researcher?

7. Suppose you were working for a company that wanted to start a business selling handmade acoustic guitars that are reproductions of classic vintage guitars. Pricing is a big part of the decision. Secondary information is available via the Internet. Use eBay (**http://ebay.com**) to identify four key brands of acoustic guitars by studying the vintage acoustic guitars listed for sale. Since the company wishes to charge premium prices, they will model after the most expensive brand. What brand seems to be associated with the highest prices?

8. Visit a social networking site (assuming you can log into a site). Search for information about Starbucks. Is there anything useful that turns up in your search that could be used by Starbucks to improve their sales and overall business operations? Explain.

Demand for Gas Guzzlers

Case 6.1

In fall 2005, Hurricanes Katrina and Rita churning in the Gulf of Mexico damaged oil rigs and refineries, contributing to a spike in oil prices. Many observers expressed confidence that those events were the long-expected trigger that would kill off demand for SUVs and other gas-guzzling vehicles.[18] They were only partly right.

In the months leading up to the hurricanes, sales of SUVs had already been falling, according to data from *Automotive News*. Automakers had been shifting ad dollars away from these products. CNW Market Research said that in August 2005, consumers had for the first time placed fuel economy ahead of performance when ranking factors for choosing a new vehicle. When gas prices approached three dollars a gallon in September 2005, marketers felt sure that fuel economy would remain a top concern. Advertisers began creating more ads featuring vehicles' gas mileage.

But by the end of the year, attitudes were shifting again. The National Automobile Dealers Association surveyed consumers visiting its website for information about car purchases, and it learned they ranked price as most important, followed by make and model, then performance. Fuel economy ranked last, with 3 percent considering it most important and 11 percent considering it least important. What's a carmaker to do? General Motors gathers data from the shoppers who visit websites such as **www.kbb.com** to look up information, and it is analyzing the data to identify the price of fuel at which car buyers adjust their priorities.

Questions

1. From the standpoint of an automobile company, what sources of information in this chapter offer relevant secondary data?
2. Suggest two or three other sources of data that might be of interest to auto companies interested in forecasting demand.
3. Online or at your library, look for information about recent trends in SUV purchases. Report what you learned and forecast whether SUV sales are likely to recover or continue their decline. What role do gas prices play in your forecast?

PHOTODISC GREEN/Getty Images

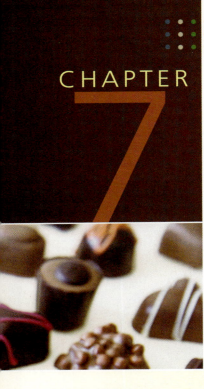

Dimitri Otis/Getty Images

:::: Survey Research

After studying this chapter, you should be able to:

1. Define surveys and describe the type of information that may be gathered in a survey
2. Identify sources of error in survey research
3. Summarize the ways researchers gather information through personal interviews
4. Know the advantages and disadvantages of conducting surveys using self-administered questionnaires
5. Appreciate the importance of pretesting questionnaires
6. Describe ethical issues that arise in survey research

Chapter Vignette:

Mobile Surveys Catching On, and Catching Respondents "On the Go!"

esearchers today are taking advantage of smartphone technologies that provide several ways to capture consumer opinions. While phone calls to conduct surveys via voice communication are possible in some instances, researchers know they do not have to talk to consumers to be able to communicate with them via a smartphone, tablet, or phablet. Consumers of all ages use text messaging as a way of communicating efficiently. The implications for this new skill shared by so many have not been lost on survey companies. Mobile surveying technologies integrate short message service (SMS) survey capability into their products. Recipients of a mobile survey can receive an SMS text message, where they can answer single or multiple-choice questions, or even provide open-ended responses to questions anytime or anywhere. The use of these types of "instant feedback" survey responses can have many different business applications.

For example, marketing researchers may wish to capture consumer reactions to products over time, or may wish to get an instant "first impression" as they use a product initially. Perhaps a firm wishes to capture instant feedback from a training exercise or may wish to capture or understand respondent attitudes to a particular part of a meeting or event. In fact,

current researchers interested in experiential surveying use mobile surveys to capture people's feelings at that particular instant, and thus can create a longitudinal understanding of people's attitudes and emotional states over time. During a hotel stay, a customer might get several opportunities to rate the service instantly via an opt-in text survey.

Mobile surveying is an exciting new way to capture data on respondents, no matter where they are. Texting is routine now—perhaps the next time you see someone furiously texting on their cell phone, they are responding to a mobile survey "on the go!"

© Jack Frog/Shutterstock.com

Introduction

Marketing research focuses on human behavior. So, the marketing researcher needs input from or about people, and perhaps asking people questions is the simplest way to obtain that input. We use the term **respondents** for the people who answer the questions during a survey. Researchers conduct interviews via e-mail, through the Internet, text messaging, or even through an actual face-to-face question-and-answer discussion. A survey represents a way of describing public opinion by collecting primary data through communicating directly with individual sampling units. Surveys provide a snapshot at a given point in time. More precisely, this is a **sample survey** because respondents' opinions presumably represent a sample of the larger target population's opinion. For consumer-oriented firms, sample surveys represent a primary tool for staying in touch with the population of consumers.

Credit: B. O'Kane / Alamy

Respondents

People who answer an interviewer's questions verbally or provide answers to written questions through any media delivery (paper or electronic).

Sample survey

A more formal term for a survey emphasizing that respondents' opinions presumably represent a sample of the larger target population's opinion.

Surveys indicate that 40 percent of consumers select an electronics product brand only after deciding in which store to shop. As a result, Sony felt the need to redesign its brand image in a way that attracted more attention and made more of an emotional connection with consumers.[1] Sony followed up this key finding with a variety of research projects, both qualitative and quantitative, which helped them identify changes to their logo and packaging that not only enabled them to be more prominent in stores, but also helped sell the brand and not just the product. Not to be outdone, Samsung and Apple both offer store within a store concepts at Best Buy as a way of getting their brands to stand out above the rest.

The Types of Information Gathered Using Surveys

Information gathered in a survey varies considerably, depending on the objectives. Surveys often address multiple research questions relevant to the marketing mix. Typically, surveys describe what is happening, what people believe, what they are like, or reveal reasons for a

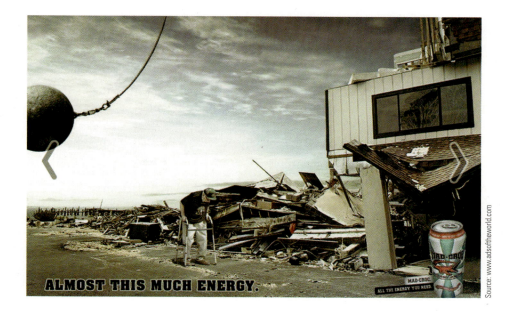

ALMOST THIS MUCH ENERGY.

Source: www.adsoftheworld.com

● ● ● ● ● ● ●

A survey can provide input that would help advertisers know how consumers interpret an ad like this before going public.

Source: http://adsoftheworld. com/media/print/madcroc_old_ man?size=_original, 4/12/2011, the company website is madcroc.com

Using the face scale, please adjust the face until it matches the way you feel about your university experience.

Courtesy of Qualtrics.com

particular marketing activity. Marketers can make decisions about what products to sell, what the prices should be, where to sell them, how to generate buzz and other things. Questions about product use, desirable features, and Web habits help with product development and advertising messages.

More specifically, surveys gather information to assess consumer knowledge and awareness of products, brands, or issues and to measure consumer attitudes, feelings, and behaviors. Additionally, surveys describe consumer characteristics, including purchasing patterns, brand usage, and descriptive characteristics including demographics and lifestyle. Thus, psychographic research involves surveys. Surveys are good tools for gathering demographic information and information on media exposure helpful in planning a market segmentation strategy.

A survey commissioned by eBay learned that almost 60 percent of people receive unwanted gifts, and 15 percent have sold an unwanted gift online. In addition, the survey indicated that selling unwanted gifts online was twice as common among the 25- to 34-year-old demographic. The survey potentially suggests a possible source of demand for eBay's services.[2] Other surveys indicate that consumers who receive gifts believe the giver will be more upset about regifting than do the actual givers. Further, givers voice a preference for regifting a gift than to have someone to whom they gave a gift throw it away.[3] Although consumer surveys are a common form of marketing research, not all survey research involves consumer opinion. Frequently, studies focus on other populations like wholesalers, retailers, or industrial buyers.

The term *survey* is most often associated with quantitative research. Most surveys seek to quantify certain factual information. However, aspects of surveys may also be qualitative. In new-product development, a survey often has a qualitative objective of refining product concepts. Surveys can reveal stylistic, aesthetic, or functional changes based on respondents' open-ended suggestions. Evaluating the qualitative nature of advertising may also be an objective of survey research.[4] An energy drink company created a viral ad depicting an elderly man moving along with the aid of a walker while trying to dodge a wrecking ball. The energy drink provides a boost to his step, enabling him to navigate the sidewalk without being smashed. Before going mainstream with the ad, the company applied a short survey following YouTube views, asking viewers what they thought of the ad. Based on the responses, the ad agency tried to judge whether the ad communicated product benefits and good feelings or whether the image offended respondents.

Advantages and Disadvantages of Survey Research

Survey research presents numerous advantages. Surveys provide a quick, often inexpensive, efficient, and accurate means of assessing information about a population. Researchers also can apply fairly straightforward statistical tools in analyzing sample survey results. Surveys are quite flexible and, when conducted properly, the results are extremely valuable to the manager.

Show Us Some Love

Lots of marketers like to survey past customers to assess their service quality and customer satisfaction. Did you ever have a service employee tell you that you might be invited to participate in a survey, and if you were to receive such an invitation, "Can you give us all 5s (a perfect score)?" The employee adds, "We aim always to exceed customer expectations!" Sure enough, a few days later the invitation to participate in the survey arrives via e-mail. The questionnaire contains several questions for which the respondent is to indicate whether or not the service quality was "much less than expected," "less than expected," "exactly what you expected," "slightly better than expected," or "exceeded expectations." The scores range from 1 to 5, respectively. The customer thinks about the service. Being very familiar with the company's service, she fully expected the service to be outstanding and the service was outstanding. She knows that the employee wants

her to mark 5. But, honestly, answer 3, exactly as expected, is exactly correct. She puts 3. When a manager looks at the data, her response is flagged to represent a unhappy customer. If the goal of the company is truly to represent their customers' perceptions, have they introduced any sources of error illustrated in Exhibit 7.1 into the process?

One of the key disadvantages is that survey results are no better than the quality of the sample and answers obtained. A survey opens the door to errors in general and those errors contribute to misleading results. In addition to these general disadvantages, each individual survey tool introduces unique disadvantages. By understanding the nature of these errors, researchers can reduce the likelihood of producing misleading results by better matching a survey approach to a given situation.

Sources of Error in Surveys

A manager who is evaluating the quality of a survey must estimate its accuracy. The manager must consider all the possible sources of mistakes. Exhibit 7.1 outlines the various forms of survey errors.[5] From one perspective, total survey error contains two major sources, sampling error and systematic error due to some issue with the respondent or the survey administration.

In this chapter, we focus on errors that most directly distract from the representativeness of the survey results. In other words, a good survey should provide a snapshot of some larger population, such as all consumers in California or all consumers in the United States. Survey results from a sample should generalize to a larger population. Unfortunately, many factors can inhibit a survey's representativeness and a good researcher strives to understand the *total error* that can creep into survey results.[6] Later in the book, we'll focus more on topics related to scaling and measurement error.

Random versus Systematic Sampling Error

Successful surveys portray a representative cross-section of a particular population. Even with technically proper random probability samples, however, statistical errors occur because of chance variation in the elements selected for the sample. These statistical problems are unavoidable but become smaller as a sample grows in size. **Sampling error** refers to inadequacies of the actual respondents to represent the population of interest. Part of sampling error arises because of random fluctuation but part occurs because of a sampling frame's inappropriateness.

Sampling error

Error arising because of inadequacies of the actual respondents to represent the population of interest.

169

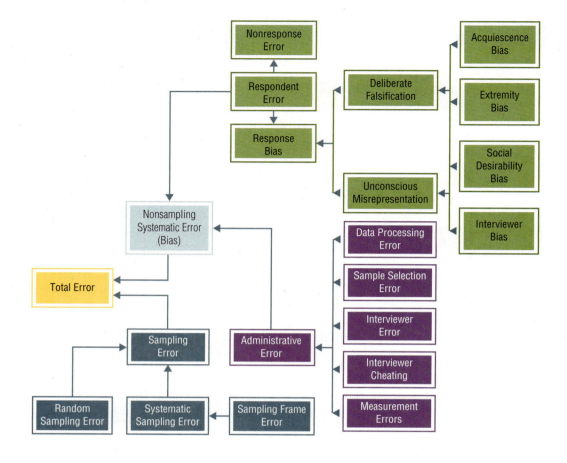

Systematic error

Error resulting from some
imperfect aspect of the
research design that causes
respondent error or from a
mistake in the execution of the
research.

Population parameter

Refers to some true value
of a phenomenon within a
population.

Sample bias

A persistent tendency for the
results of a sample to deviate
in one direction from the
true value of the population
parameter.

Respondent error

A category of sample bias
resulting from some respondent
action such as lying or inaction
such as not responding.

Conversely, **systematic error** results from some imperfect aspect of the research design or from a mistake in the execution of the research. Systematic errors include all sources of error other than those introduced directly by the sampling procedure. Therefore, systematic errors are *nonsampling errors*. Respondent and research administrator mistakes are primary sources for systematic errors.

The term **population parameter** refers to some true value of a phenomenon within a population. For instance, the number of Red Bulls consumed in 2015 by first-year university students in Indiana truly exists. Determining this number without error presents a formidable challenge. Given the difficulty in identifying the population parameter directly, researchers choose instead to estimate the number using a sample of these students. A **sample bias** exists when results of a particular sample deviate in one direction from the true value of the population parameter. For instance, if the researcher selects respondents during May of 2015, the Red Bull parameter estimate may be biased upward because the sample members were facing final exams. Systematic errors arise from two general categories: respondent error and administrative error.

Respondent Error

Surveys ask people for answers and hopefully people give truthful answers. Error exists otherwise and respondent error results. Response bias and nonresponse error bias are the two major categories of **respondent error**.

Nonresponse Error

Surveys rarely obtain 100 percent response rates, but a researcher employing a text message questionnaire about energy drink consumption may face a serious problem. The researcher must believe that sample members who respond to a text message questionnaire are not any different from sample members who did not respond. Sample members who refuse or cannot respond are **nonrespondents**. **Nonresponse error** is the statistical difference between a parameter value obtained using only actual survey respondents compared to the value obtained from a survey (hypothetical) including input also from those who did not respond (i.e., the nonrespondents). In other words, what would the value be if all potential sample members had responded? Of course, knowing precisely how big this error truly is becomes practically impossible because nonrespondents, by definition, did not provide information!

In a phone survey, nonresponse occurs when a call goes unanswered. The number of **no contacts** in survey research has been increasing for a host of reasons, including restrictions in who can be contacted and changes in technology. Increasingly, households do not have a home telephone. A traditional phone survey cannot reach these members of the sampling frame. Most people today screen out unwanted communications or at the least just do not answer unrecognized numbers. An e-mail request sent to a potential respondent via an old unused e-mail address likewise creates nonresponse through no contact.

Refusals occur when people are unwilling to participate in the research. A research team reviewed fifty mail surveys of pediatricians conducted by the American Academy of Pediatrics (AAP) and found that response rates declined through the first decade of the twenty-first century. In the early years of the study period, an average 70 percent of pediatricians returned completed surveys; the response rate fell to an average 63 percent in the second half of the period.[7] No contacts and refusals can seriously bias survey data. In the case of the pediatricians, the researchers found little difference in the response rates attributable to differences in such easy-to-measure variables as age, sex, and type of membership in the AAP, leaving them to wonder whether the cause of refusals was some unknown but important difference among these doctors.

Researchers often investigate the causes of nonresponse. For example, a study analyzed a large database collected by AT&T and found that the effort required to participate in an ongoing study contributes to the problem.[8] People tend not to respond to questions that are difficult to answer. If a project requires that the same respondents answer multiple surveys, expect higher participation to the first the series of surveys and participation to fall off as the series progresses.

How can a researcher assess nonresponse error? Comparing the sample demographics with the demographics of the target population provides one means of checking for potential response bias. For instance, if we know that 54 percent of freshmen university students in Indiana are female (based on state census counts), and our resulting sample in the Red Bull consumption survey turns out to be 75 percent male, we know females are underrepresented. Thus, the Red Bull consumption estimate would exhibit bias (error) to the extent that men and women do not drink as much Red Bull.

Researchers know that those who are most enthusiastic about an issue are more likely to respond. **Self-selection bias** is a problem that frequently plagues self-administered questionnaires. Consumers decide where to shop, eat, and get their cars serviced and whether to answer a questionnaire. Thus, a researcher conducting a survey about consumer attitudes toward Abercrombie and Fitch (A&F) should expect more favorable responses than normal if he/she conducts the survey within an A&F store or if he/she uses a customer database for the sampling frame. In either case, the potential respondent has made a conscious selection to patronize A&F. Self-selection bias distorts survey results because favorable respondents are overrepresented. Oftentimes, self-selection bias can reflect more extreme attitudes than those that truly exist in a wider population.

Response Bias

A **response bias** occurs when respondents answer questions in a way that slants meanings away from true population values. As a result, willfully or not, the respondent contributes to misleading results. If a distortion of measurement occurs because respondents' answers are false or misrepresented, the resulting sample bias will be a response bias. When researchers identify response bias, they should include a corrective measure.

Deliberate Falsification. Occasionally people deliberately give false answers. A response bias occurs when people misrepresent answers. Consider a survey about grocery store prices. Rather than appear ignorant or unconcerned about prices, a respondent may provide their best estimate and not tell the truth—namely, that they cannot remember. Sometimes respondents become bored

Nonrespondents

Sample members who are mistakenly not contacted or who refuse to provide input in the research.

Nonresponse error

The statistical differences between a survey that includes only those who responded and a perfect survey that would also include those who failed to respond.

No contacts

Potential respondents in the sense that they are members of the sampling frame but who do not receive the request to participate in the research.

Refusals

People who are unwilling to participate in a research project.

Self-selection bias

A bias that occurs because people who feel strongly about a subject are more likely to respond to survey questions than people who feel indifferent about it.

Response bias

A bias that occurs when respondents either consciously or unconsciously answer questions with a certain slant that misrepresents the truth.

with the interview and provide answers just to finish the survey. Other times, respondents try to look smart by giving answers they think are expected. Similarly, respondents sometimes give answers simply to please the interviewer or to qualify as a respondent to obtain some incentive. Falsification comes in several forms.

Unconscious Misrepresentation. Even when a respondent is consciously trying to be truthful and cooperative, response bias can arise from the question format, the question content, or some other stimulus. For example, the administration technique can bias results. The results of two in-flight surveys concerning aircraft preference illustrate this point. Passengers flying on Boeing 747s preferred that plane over an Airbus A-380 (74 percent versus 19 percent), whereas passengers flying on an Airbus A-380 preferred it to the 747 (56 percent versus 38 percent). Obviously, presence in one company's aircraft biased the results.[9] Respondents could hardly make a fair comparison of planes when the awareness of one alternative was so much greater.

Respondents may not be able to give precise answers in some cases. Consider the following question:

When was the last time you went 36 hours without checking Facebook? _____days

Respondents may have to guess because they do not know the exact answer. In other cases, consumers cannot adequately express their feelings in words. The cause may be questions that are vague, ambiguous, or not specific enough. Researchers may ask someone to describe his or her frustration when using a computer. If the researcher has a specific interest in software usage, he or she will likely be disappointed with the answers. Language differences also may be a source of misunderstanding. A French researcher used an instrument developed in France to assess lunch habits. However, the French word for lunch, *dejeuner*, means "breakfast" in Quebec.

Many respondents will answer questions even though they have given them little thought. For example, in most investigations of consumers' buying intentions, the predictability of the intention scales depends on how close the subject is to making a purchase. The intentions of subjects who have little knowledge of the brand or the store alternatives or who have not yet made any purchase plans are relatively unlikely to predict purchase behavior accurately. Additionally, as more time passes since a purchase or a shopping event, the more people tend to underreport information about that event. Time lapse influences people's ability to communicate specific factors precisely.

Unconscious misrepresentation bias may also occur because consumers unconsciously avoid facing the realities of a future buying situation. Housing surveys record that Americans overwhelmingly continue to aspire to own detached, single-family dwellings (preferably single-level, ranch-type structures that require two to five times the amount of land per unit required for attached homes). However, builders know that *attached* housing purchases by first buyers are more common than respondents expect.

Types of Response Bias

Response bias falls into four specific categories: acquiescence bias, extremity bias, interviewer bias, and social desirability bias. These categories overlap and are not mutually exclusive. A single biased answer may be distorted for many complex reasons, some distortions being deliberate and some being unintentional misrepresentations.

Acquiescence Bias.   A tendency for a respondent to maintain a consistent response style often tending to try to go along and agree with the viewpoint of a survey is known as **acquiescence bias**. One good way to think about acquiescence bias is in the context of new-product research. Questions about a new-product idea generally elicit some acquiescence bias because respondents give positive connotations to most new ideas. For example, consumers responded favorably to survey questions about pump baseball gloves (the pump inserts air into the pocket of the glove, providing more cushioning). However, when these expensive gloves hit the market, they sat on shelves. When conducting new-product research, researchers should recognize the high likelihood of acquiescence bias.

A less common form of acquiescence comes in the form of respondents tending to disagree with all questions. A survey administered by a group protesting a new Walmart location in a residential area may show abnormally high disagreement with supporting the development. Other times, a respondent may be trying to respond with desirable responses because he believes the researcher will withhold a promised incentive for participation if the answers do not support the research purpose.

Acquiescence bias

Tendency of a respondent to maintain a consistent response style often tending to try to go along and agree with the viewpoint of a survey.

Other times, a respondent is just not putting much effort into responses, resulting in consistent responses. Thus, acquiescence bias occurs whenever a respondent displays:

1. a tendency to concur with a particular position,
2. a tendency to please the researcher or answer consistent with the perceived research purpose by providing consistent responses,
3. lazily gives consistent answers that result in deviations from true responses.

Extremity Bias. Some individuals tend to use extremes when responding to questions. In other words, they will tend to use the furthest left or right ends of a scale. Response styles vary from person to person, and extreme responses may cause an **extremity bias** in the data.[10] Extremity bias is common in consumer satisfaction scales. The trick for the researcher in deciding if the data are valid is to sort out extremity bias from true responses like the kind that may result from self-selection (mentioned above).

Interviewer Bias. Response bias may arise from the interplay between interviewer and respondent. If the interviewer's presence influences respondents to give untrue or modified answers, **interviewer bias** results. Sometimes respondents may give answers they believe will please the interviewer rather than the truthful responses. Respondents may wish to appear intelligent and wealthy—of course they read *Architectural Digest* rather than the *National Enquirer*.

Interviewer characteristics, including age, sex, style of dress, tone of voice, facial expressions, or other nonverbal characteristics, may influence a respondent's answers. In a research study on sexual harassment against saleswomen, male interviewers might not obtain as candid responses from saleswomen as female interviewers would. Thus, interviewer techniques in which the interviewer remains unseen have an advantage of preventing this particular type of interviewer bias.

Many interviewers, contrary to instructions, shorten or rephrase questions to suit their needs. A researcher doing survey research for major U.S. newspapers asked a question about the Nazi holocaust in the following fashion:

"Do you believe it seems possible or does it seem impossible to you that the Nazi Extermination of the Jews never happened?"[11]

Obviously, this question is confusing and yielded a result that should be meaningless. Instead, an unscrupulous blogger may use the results to state that 1 in 4 respondents believe the holocaust never occurred, or conversely that only 1 in 4 believe it did occur, when the survey results have no clear meaning.

This potential influence on responses can be avoided to some extent if interviewers receive training and supervision that emphasize the necessity of appearing neutral. Also, researchers with strong opinions may be steered toward other projects or be made aware that misleading results are unethical and likely do not further their cause in the long run.

Social Desirability Bias. **Social desirability bias** occurs because a respondent wishes to create a favorable impression or somehow save face during an interview. Respondents may inflate income, overstate education, or report heightened sensitivity to environmental issues. If the source for the research is known, imagine how it may bias answers to sensitive questions such as "Did you vote for the President in the last election?" "How often do you see a roach in your home?" "Do you color your hair?" or "How often do you go to church?"

The social desirability bias is especially significant in the case of research that addresses sensitive or personal topics, including respondents' sexual behavior. A researcher surveyed teens, asking the following question:

■ Have you ever *received* any nude pictures of a friend or peer via text message, Instagram, or Facebook?

Fifteen percent of teens reported "yes" to this question. The researcher also asked the following:

■ Have you ever *sent* nude pictures to your friends or posted them on Facebook or Instagram?

Only 4 percent indicated "yes" to this question.[12] Do you believe that the large difference in percentage is due to socially desirable responding? Do teens feel pressure to say they receive nude photos? Are teens unwilling to admit to sending or posting nude photos? An alternative explanation is that a few individuals send large numbers of photos of themselves or others in the nude to large numbers of teens. The social desirability makes it difficult to attribute any definitive meaning to this survey result.

Extremity bias

A category of response bias that results because some individuals tend to use extremes when responding to questions.

Interviewer bias

A response bias that occurs because the presence of the interviewer influences respondents' answers.

Social desirability bias

Bias in responses caused by respondents' desire, either conscious or unconscious, to gain prestige or appear in a different social role.

Administrative Error

When a research employee improperly administers or executes his/her task, he/she creates **administrative error**. Administrative errors result from carelessness, confusion, neglect, omission, or some other blunder. Four terms describe the different types of administrative error:

- **Data processing error** results when data are improperly edited, coded, or entered into a computer. The accuracy of data processed by a computer depends on correct data entry and programming. Data processing error is reduced by establishing careful procedures for verifying each step in the data processing stage.

- **Sample selection error** results in an unrepresentative sample due to error in either sample design or execution of the sampling procedure. Executing a sampling plan free of procedural error is difficult. A firm that wants to represent a city's adult population and selects a sample from a telephone directory introduces systematic error in several ways, including:
  - many households have unlisted numbers and do not appear in the directory,
  - many households do not have a home (landline) phone,
  - cell phones are not listed in conventional directories.

Web responders also may be dishonest in some way as a means of being included as a respondent. For example, a respondent trying to earn a $1 incentive to answer a survey intended only for people living in Texas, Louisiana, or Mississippi answered the "in which state do you live?" with 25 different states before trying Texas. Obviously, this respondent cannot live in all of those places and further investigation suggested this respondent did not even live in the United States. Including this person would create sample selection bias.

- **Interviewer error** occurs when interviewers record answers incorrectly, such as checking the wrong response or not writing fast enough to record respondents' statements verbatim. Also, selective perception may cause interviewers to misrepresent subtlety contrary opinions.
- **Interviewer cheating** occurs when an interviewer falsifies entire questionnaires or fills in answers to questions that respondents skipped. Some interviewers cheat to finish an interview as quickly as possible or to avoid questions about sensitive topics. The term *curb-stoning* refers to interviewers filling in responses for respondents that do not really exist. Research firms can reduce interviewer cheating by recontacting a small number of respondents to verify previously recorded responses. In this way, curb-stoners might get revealed and face the consequences associated with this unethical behavior.

Administrative error

An error caused by the improper administration or execution of the research task.

Data processing error

A category of administrative error that occurs because of incorrect data entry, incorrect computer programming, or other procedural errors during data analysis.

Sample selection error

An administrative error caused by improper sample design or sampling procedure execution.

Interviewer error

Mistakes made by interviewers failing to record survey responses correctly.

Interviewer cheating

The practice of filling in fake answers or falsifying questionnaires while working as an interviewer.

● ● ● ● ● ● ●

When is the researcher ever certain about who is really providing survey answers?

© Twin Design/Shutterstock.com

What Can Be Done to Reduce Survey Error?

Knowing the many sources of error in surveys, you may have lost some of your optimism about survey research. Don't be discouraged! The discussion above emphasizes negativity because it is important for marketing managers to realize that surveys are not a panacea. Once one knows about the problems, steps can be applied to reduce survey errors. We'll discuss some ways to reduce error through effective questionnaire and sampling design in upcoming chapters. The good news lies ahead!

Ways Marketing Researchers Conduct Survey Interviews

When most people think of interviewing, they envision two people engaged in a face-to-face dialogue or in a phone conversation. However, people don't always communicate in a two-way fashion. Sometimes, communication is one-way with little chance for spontaneous interaction. For example, traditional print advertisements employ one-way communication because they are noninteractive. The ad provides no mechanism in which the consumer talks back to the company. Likewise, we can summarize marketing communications with survey respondents into interactive and noninteractive media.

Interactive Survey Approaches

Interactive survey approaches allow spontaneous two-way interaction between an interviewer and an respondent. Even when the communication is electronic, interactive approaches try to capture the dynamic exchange made possible through face-to-face interviews. Survey respondents, thus, need not be passive audience members. Today's interactive approaches allow respondents to be involved in two-way communication using electronic media such as smartphones or live Web interfaces. More detail on various electronic survey tools follows later in this chapter.

Noninteractive Media

Noninteractive survey approaches do not facilitate two-way communications and are largely a vehicle by which respondents give answers to static questions. The traditional questionnaire received by mail, completed by a respondent, and mailed back to the researcher does not allow a real-time, dynamic exchange of information and is therefore noninteractive. Noninteractive questionnaires do have merit, but this type of survey is less flexible than surveys using interactive communication media. In fact, noninteractive media can be the best approach in some situations. Simple opinion polls, awareness studies, and even surveys assessing consumer attitudes can generally be collected adequately via one-way communication.

Conducting Personal Interviews

A **personal interview** is a form of direct, interactive communication in which an interviewer asks respondents questions face-to-face. This versatile and flexible method is a two-way conversation between interviewer and respondent. Personal interviews are truly interactive. Traditionally,

Electronic dating services have become a popular, successful example of electronic interactive media.

Interactive survey approaches
Communication that allows spontaneous two-way interaction between the interviewer and the respondent.

Noninteractive survey approaches
Communication approach by which respondents give answers to static questions that does not allow a two-way or dynamic dialog.

Personal interview
Interactive face-to-face communication in which an interviewer asks a respondent to answer questions.

Getting Sleepy, Sleepy, Sleepy

Many people suffer from insomnia, or trouble sleeping. What do people do when they can't sleep? Well, many of them turn to their smartphone, tablet, or computer to surf the Internet, check out what's happening on Pinterest, Facebook, or Instagram, or check their e-mail. All of these options increase the likelihood that the insomniac will respond to a survey request from a marketing researcher. While insomniacs may seem to be somewhat of a captive audience for surveys, they don't respond in the same way as other respondents. In fact, insomniacs produce greater response error, particularly in the form of unconscious misrepresentation due to a difficulty in paying attention when one is so sleepy. This can lead to acquiescence bias of the type associated with low involvement. While it's clear that insomniacs increase error overall, they do seem to give fewer deliberate falsifications such as those that lead to social desirability bias. In other words, they are more likely to give their actual occupation compared to well-rested respondents who display a tendency to make their jobs seem more important and prestigious than they really are when answering a survey.

© wavebreakmedia/Shutterstock.com

Sources: Barber, L. K., Barnes, C. M., & Carlson, K. D. (2013). "Random and Systematic Error Effects of Insomnia on Survey Behavior." *Organizational Research Methods, 16*(4), 616–649. Fisher, J. D., & Houseworth, C. A. (2013). "Occupation Inflation in the Current Population Survey." *Journal of Economic & Social Measurement, 38*(3), 243–261.

researchers have recorded interview results using paper and pencil, by reading questions and recording answers. Today, computers are increasingly supporting survey research by automatically recording responses. In this section, we examine the general characteristics of face-to-face personal interviews, then compare and contrast door-to-door personal interviews with personal interviews conducted in shopping malls and those conducted on the phone.

Gathering information through face-to-face contact with individuals goes back many years. Military inscription and tax rates were set based on periodic censuses in ancient Egypt and Rome. During the Middle Ages, the merchant families of Fugger and Rothschild prospered in part because their far-flung organizations enabled them to get information before their competitors could.[13] Today, survey researchers present themselves in airports, shopping centers, and train stations and announce, "Good afternoon, my name is ___. I am with ___ Research Company, and we are conducting a survey on ___."

Advantages of Personal Interviews

Marketing researchers find that personal interviews offer many unique advantages.

Opportunity for Feedback

Personal interviews provide the opportunity for feedback and clarification. For example, if a consumer is reluctant to provide sensitive information, the interviewer may offer reassurance that his or her answers will be strictly confidential. Personal interviews offer the lowest chance that respondents will misinterpret questions, because an interviewer who senses confusion can clarify the instruction or questions. Circumstances may dictate that at the conclusion of the interview, the respondent be given additional information concerning the purpose of the study. This clarification is easily accomplished with a personal interview. If the feedback indicates that some question or set of questions is particularly confusing, the researcher can make changes that make the questionnaire easier to understand.

Probing Complex Answers

Another important characteristic of personal interviews is the opportunity to follow up by probing. If a respondent's answer is too brief or unclear, the researcher may request a more comprehensive or clearer explanation. The interviewer probes for clarification with standardized questions such as "Can you tell me more about what you had in mind?" (See Chapter 5 for an expanded discussion of probing.) Depending on the research purpose, personal interviews vary in the degree to which questions are structured and in the amount of probing required. The personal interview is especially useful for obtaining unstructured information. Skilled interviewers can handle complex questions that cannot easily be asked in telephone or mail surveys.

Length of Interview

If the research objective requires an extremely lengthy questionnaire, personal interviews may be the only option. A general rule of thumb on mail and e-mail surveys is that they should not take more than 12 minutes to complete and telephone interviews typically should take less than 10 minutes. In contrast, a personal interview can be much longer, perhaps an hour or even more. However, the longer the interview, no matter what the form, the more the respondent should be compensated for their time and participation. Researchers should also be clear about how long participation should take in the opening dialogue requesting participation.

Completeness of Questionnaire

The social interaction between a well-trained interviewer and a respondent in a personal interview increases the likelihood that the respondent will answer all the items on the questionnaire. The respondent who grows bored with a telephone interview may terminate the interview at his or her discretion simply by hanging up. Self-administered mail questionnaires require more effort from respondents and as such, they may just skip questions that require lengthy written answers. **Item nonresponse**—failure to provide an answer to a question—occurs less often when an experienced interviewer asks questions directly.

Item nonresponse
Failure of a respondent to provide an answer to a survey question.

Props and Visual Aids

Interviewing respondents face-to-face allows the investigator to show them new product samples, sketches of proposed advertising, or other visual aids. When Lego Group wanted to introduce new train model sets for its famous building bricks, the company targeted adults who build complex models with its product. The company invited adults who were swapping ideas at the Lego website to visit the New York office, where they viewed ideas and provided their opinions. The respondents wound up rejecting all the company's ideas, but they suggested something different: the Santa Fe Super Chief set, which sold out within two weeks of introduction due only to enthusiastic word of mouth.[14] Telephone interviews could not have yielded such rich results.

Marketing research that uses visual aids has become increasingly popular with researchers who investigate film concepts, advertising problems, and moviegoers' awareness of performers. Research for movies often begins by showing respondents videotapes of the prospective cast. Respondents see video clips and evaluate a movie's appeal based on the clips. This helps researchers know which scenes to use in trailers.

High Participation Rate

Although some people are reluctant to participate in a survey, the presence of an interviewer generally increases the percentage of people willing to complete the interview. People are often more hesitant to tell a person "no" face-to-face than they are over the phone, in a mail request, or through another impersonal contact. Respondents typically are required to do no reading or writing—all they have to do is talk. A personable interviewer can also do much to improve response rates. Many people enjoy sharing information and insights with friendly and sympathetic interviewers.

What a Disaster

When disaster strikes, consumers probably don't feel like responding to a survey. However, marketing research among disaster victims can be extremely helpful in informing companies and public institutions like FEMA to know what things need to be done to assist disaster victims. If the population that you wish to represent is disaster victims, the sampling frame will also make up disaster victims. This changes the way the research is approached. After a disaster, the researcher cannot expect that the victim will have access to the Internet, smartphone, or landline telephone. In these cases, a personal interview sometimes is the only choice. After the massive earthquake that hit Japan, researchers performed personal interviews with Tokyo residents asking them about what information is proving most helpful. The research suggested that sources of information offered great value, while sources simply trying to pick up one's spirits offered little value. Similarly, after a hurricane, tornado, or bushfire strikes, the victims become very valuable in providing information that may help greatly assist future victims. However, when one thinks about it, the less effected victims are likely to be those that most easily have access to a phone or Internet. If a problem solver is trying to identify steps that can best provide aid to disaster victims, ignoring the personal interview could be a disaster.

Sources: Hong, C., Hiroyasu, S., & Keiko, Y. (2013). "Disaster Mitigation and Ad Likeability: Japanese Public's Attitudes Toward Post-March 11 PSAS." *American Academy of Advertising Conference Proceedings*, 182. Hickson, H., & Lehmann, J. (2014). "Exploring Social Workers' Experiences of Working with Bushfire-Affected Families." *Australian Social Work*, 67(2), 256–273.

Disadvantages of Personal Interviews

Personal interviews also have disadvantages. Respondents are not anonymous and as a result may be reluctant to provide confidential information to another person. Suppose a survey asked top executives, "Do you see any major internal instabilities or threats to the achievement of your marketing objectives?" Many managers may be reluctant to tell the interviewer his/her thoughts about this sensitive question because complete anonymity is impossible.

Interviewer Influence

Imagine telling others about the past weekend. Would you have the same conversation with your mother as with your grandfather? Or, what about a roommate? In the same way, respondents act differently with different interviewers. One study's results suggest that male interviewers produced larger amounts of variance compared to female interviewers when 85 percent of respondents are female. Older interviewers who interviewed older respondents produced more variance than other age combinations, whereas younger interviewers who interviewed younger respondents produced the least variance.

Differential interviewer techniques may be a source of bias. The rephrasing of a question, the interviewer's tone of voice, and the interviewer's appearance may influence respondents' answers. Consider the interviewer who has conducted 100 personal interviews. During the next one, he or she may lose concentration and either selectively perceive or anticipate the respondent's answer. The interpretation of the response may differ somewhat from what the respondent intended. Typically, the public thinks of a person who does marketing research as a dedicated scientist. Unfortunately, some interviewers do not fit that ideal. Considerable interviewer variability exists. Cheating is possible; interviewers cut corners to save time and energy or fake parts of their reports by dummying up part or all of a questionnaire. Control over interviewers is important to ensure that difficult, embarrassing, or time-consuming questions are handled properly.

Lack of Anonymity of Respondent

Because a respondent in a personal interview is not anonymous, he or she may be reluctant to provide confidential information to the interviewer. Researchers take care to phrase sensitive questions to avoid social desirability bias. For example, the interviewer may show the respondent a card that lists possible answers and ask the respondent to read a category number rather than be required to verbalize sensitive answers.

Cost

Personal interviews are expensive, generally substantially more costly than mail, e-mail, Internet, or phone surveys. The geographic proximity of respondents, the length and complexity of the questionnaire, and the number of people who are nonrespondents because they could not be contacted (not-at-homes) all influence the cost of personal interviews.

Mall Intercepts

Interviewers conduct personal interviews in respondents' homes or offices or in many other places including shopping centers and airports. The phrase **mall-intercept interview** applies to a technique involving random approaches to respondents asking for participation in a survey. Interviewers intercept potential respondents in a public area and then complete the interview in a convenient place. Sometimes interviewees are asked to taste new food items or to view advertisements. The locale for the interview generally influences the participation rate, and thus the degree to which the sample represents the general population.

When the researchers need a sample representative of the U.S. consumer population, he/she needs to keep in mind that each shopping center has its own market characteristics. Larger bias follows to the extent that a particular shopping center likely has a unique demographic or psychographic profile. However, personal interviews in shopping centers are appropriate when the target group is a special market segment, such as households with school-aged children. A mall intercept approach may be particularly appropriate during the back to school sales period. The mall-intercept interview allows the researcher not only to interview, but to have respondents interact with physical objects, including backpacks, tablets, bicycles, and so on. Mall intercepts are great when demonstration is part of the research design. For example, electronics manufacturers often do not want to test new appliances in consumers' homes because of difficulty in moving and setting up appliances. Thus, bringing respondents to the appliances is a better option. The mall intercept approach also reduces response biases, including the types of acquiescence bias that come from low-response involvement and deliberative falsifications particularly in reporting observable demographic characteristics.

Mall-intercept interview
Personal interviews conducted in a shopping center or similar public area.

Door-to-Door Interviews

The presence of an interviewer at the door generally increases the likelihood that a person will be willing to complete an interview, presuming someone answers the door. Because **door-to-door interviews** increase the participation rate and are conducted at a person's residence, they provide a more representative sample of the general population than other survey approaches such as e-mail. People who do not have telephones, who have unlisted telephone numbers, or who are otherwise difficult to contact may be reached using door-to-door interviews. However, door-to-door interviews may under-represent some groups and over-represent others based on the geographic areas covered.

Door-to-door interviews may exclude individuals who live in multiple-dwelling units with security systems, such as high-rise apartment dwellers, or executives who are too busy to grant personal interviews during business hours. Other people, for security reasons, simply will not open the door when a stranger knocks. Telephoning an individual in one of these subgroups to make an appointment ahead of time or advertising the fact that interviewers will be canvassing a neighborhood may increase the likelihood that someone answers the door. However, obtaining

Door-to-door interviews
Personal interviews conducted at respondents' doorsteps in an effort to increase the participation rate in the survey.

a representative sample of security-conscious consumers may prove difficult. For these reasons, door-to-door interviews are becoming a thing of the past as a widely employed survey approach.

Callbacks

Callbacks

Attempts to try and contact those sample members missed in the initial attempt.

When an interviewer's first attempt to contact a potential respondent fails, a systematic procedure calling for more attempts should be in place. **Callbacks**, or attempts to try and contact those sample members missed in the initial attempt, can substantially reduce nonresponse error. Callbacks in door-to-door interviews are important because not-at-home individuals (e.g., working parents) may systematically vary from those who *are* at home (nonworking parents, retired people, and the like). Callbacks, although useful, can be very expensive because interviewers must return to areas already canvased for responses, meaning travel time between sampling units can be great. Callbacks are not possible with mall intercept interviews. In nonpersonal modes, like e-mail surveys, callbacks can be automated. In computer-assisted telephone interviews (sometimes referred to by the acronym **CATI**), the computer automatically schedules initial calls and autodials a callback when a call to a specific number is unanswered. Many public opinion researchers believe CATI remains a good alternative for representativeness compared to other survey types.[15]

CATI

Acronym for computer-assisted telephone interviews where a computer routine automatically selects numbers from a sampling frame and schedules calls and callbacks.

Global Considerations

Marketing researchers recognize that the manner of conducting and the receptiveness to personal interview varies dramatically around the world. For example, in some Arab nations, a female mall-intercept interviewer may not be able to interview a male respondent. In many countries, the idea of discussing grooming behavior and personal-care products with a stranger would be highly offensive. Personal interviews on such topics would be a bad idea. Thus, cultural norms play a role in selecting a survey approach.

Researchers face both cultural and social norms when doing research that requires business-people to participate. For example, conducting business-to-business interviews in Japan during business hours is difficult because managers, strongly loyal to their firm, believe that they have an absolute responsibility to stick to the job! Managers also understandably feel uncomfortable answering too many questions about their decision-making asked by a company researcher. In these instances, an outside research company might get better responses.

To the Point

"*People have really odd opinions. They tell me I'm skinny as if that's supposed to make me happy.*"

ANGELINA JOLIE

● ● ● ● ● ● ●

Phone surveys were less complicated back when phones were phones.

Source: www.telephonearchive.com

Telephone Interviews

Remember when a telephone was a just telephone? Probably not. Phones come in many forms these days. The interviewer these days typically sits at a computer that lists the questions and provides a survey form on which the interviewer records the respondent's answers (another example of how CATI takes place). Researchers using phone interviews these days need to ponder this question: Are all types of phones equally prone to error?

Landline Phones

Landline telephone interviews have been a mainstay of commercial survey research since the 1940s. Traditionally, researchers consider data gathered in a phone interview comparable to that collected in a face-to-face interview. Phone interviews even possess advantages over face-to-face interviews as respondents are sometimes more forthcoming with information on a variety of personal topics while tucked away comfortably at home out of the sight of the interviewer.

Pollsters and many market researchers still consider an in-home phone interview survey capable of providing samples relatively representative of household populations in the United States and other developed nations. For instance, researchers used telephone interviews with over 1,600 households in Israel to assess the impact of regular drinking on social well-being among people who live daily with the realities of war and terrorism. The results point to the benefits of social drinking where people gather with family and friends as a tool in coping with trauma.[16] Several recent events including legislation making calls more difficult and decreasing landline phone ownership are challenging the assumption that phone interviews provide good representativeness.

No-Call Legislation

"No-call" legislation dates back to the mid-2000s. Marketers cannot call phone numbers listed on the do-not-call registry. The legislation exists at the federal and state levels and is not unique to the United States. The legislation originally targeted telemarketers, and although marketing research efforts do not always fall under the legislation, many commercial marketing research firms honor the do-not-call registry. Consumers who opt-in to the system are unlikely to welcome survey research calls.

Information about do-not-call lists for each state can be found at the Direct Marketing Association's Web site at http://www.the-dma.org/government/donotcalllists.shtml.

What You Should Know About the National Do Not Call Registry

The National Do Not Call Registry gives you a choice about whether to receive telemarketing calls at home. Most telemarketers should not call your number once it has been on the registry for 31 days. If they do, you can file a complaint at this Website. You can register your home or mobile phone for free.

Scammers have been making phone calls claiming to represent the National Do Not Call Registry. The calls claim to provide an opportunity to sign up for the Registry. These calls are not coming from the Registry or the Federal Trade Commission, and you should not respond to these calls.

Attention sellers and telemarketers: Go to https://telemarketing.donotcall.gov to access the National Do Not Call Registry.

Source: Direct Marketing Association

Marketers and marketing researchers can obtain the do-not-call lists of phone numbers from the FTC for $59 per area code. A subscriber can purchase the entire registry for just over $16,000. Although this may seem expensive, the FTC levies fines on the order of $10,000 per violation (per call), so obtaining the registry is a wise investment for those wishing to contact consumers via the telephone. The FTC's do-not-call website (http://donotcall.gov) provides access to detailed information for consumers and organizations.

Robocalls

A phone call conducted by an autodialer and using a recorded voice message system.

The feds do take violations very seriously. One company found this out the hard way.[17] Versatile Marketing Solutions (VMS) purchased consumer phone numbers from companies who provide sales leads services without checking the do-not-call lists. In fact, the sales leads had been created when unsuspecting households responded to **robocalls** with a brief "survey" from "Tom with Home Protection" about home security. A robocall is an autodialed phone call conducted by a recorded voice message system. VMS allegedly placed millions of calls to households who responded to the fake survey from Tom. Although VMS argued that the robocall respondents had opted in for calls about security, their arguments were not persuasive and in the end VMS agreed to a $3.4 million fine for the illegal calls. Using a survey to disguise selling is unethical.

The Canadian government instituted a nearly identical do-not-call program. The Canadian Radio-Television and Telecommunications Commission imposes steep fines for calls made to people on the Canadian do-not-call list. Other countries in Europe and elsewhere are also considering similar or even more aggressive legislation.

Ownership

We used to think that every household had a phone. Think again. Landline phone penetration is about 60 percent in the United States and slightly less in Europe.[18] That means that marketing researchers interested in representative samples in either place are starting out with a large piece of the population excluded from the list when landline phones are used. The percentage of cell-phone-only households varies with demographics. Younger consumers are more likely to shun a landline phone as are consumers in the southern and western United States.[19] As a result, a sampling frame consisting of landline phone numbers creates the risk of increased error in the form of coverage bias. **Coverage bias** refers to misrepresentation of a population by survey results that disproportionately represent one group over another.

Coverage bias

Misrepresentation of a population by survey results that disproportionately represent one group over another.

Even if the sampling frame is adequate to represent the population, the fact that different types of people are more or less likely to respond contributes to sample selection error as well. One in six households with landline phones reports not taking any incoming calls with their landline phone. Many other calls fail because of caller ID or due to hang-ups. To the extent that any of these issues are associated systematically with respondent characteristics, systematic error in the form of coverage bias becomes a strong possibility. Does one's personality relate to not answering, hanging up, or getting on a do-not-call list? Obviously, the chance of administrative error in the form of sample selection bias seems highly plausible. Thus, landline phone interviews are still widely used, but researchers no longer automatically think of them as producing pristine data.

Researchers today supplement landline sampling frames with some other survey mode, potentially including a cell phone list as a way of reducing coverage error. Pollsters who correctly guess how much landline calls need to be supplemented with cell phone calls end up showing more accuracy in predicting election winners. More and more, though, even other modes are mixed into the sampling frame in an effort to gain adequate coverage of a population.

Mobile Phones

Mobile-phone interviews differ from landline phones most obviously because they reach individuals rather than households. However, there are other less obvious distinctions.

■ In the United States, telemarketing toward mobile phone numbers is prohibited unless the user opts in.

■ The recipient of a mobile phone call is more likely to be distracted than are other respondents. The respondent may be driving a car, on the metro, or walking down a noisy street. Factors such as these are not conducive to a high-quality interview.

- The area codes for mobile phones are not necessarily geographic. For instance, a person who moves from Georgia to Washington can choose to keep the old phone number. As a result, a researcher conducting a voice call survey may be unable to determine whether a respondent fits into the desired geographic sampling population.
- The phones have varying abilities for automated responses and differing keypads. Some requests, such as "hit pound sign," may be more difficult to do on some keypads than on others.

Mobile phones are ubiquitous in most developed and even in some not so developed countries. Mobile phone penetration exceeds 100 percent in most developed nations. In some countries, such as the UAE, Bahrain, and Qatar, mobile phone ownership exceeds two phones for every person![20] Even in underdeveloped countries, consumers have quickly adopted mobile phones. In fact, out of 7 billion people worldwide, over 6 billion have access to a mobile phone, compared to 4.5 billion who have access to a flush toilet![21] Thus, mobile phones allow access to the masses. The consumer movement toward solely mobile phones may have less effect on research in Europe and other nations where researchers include mobile phone numbers alongside landline phone numbers in a sample frame listing. However, each sampling unit's chance of being contacted is multiplied by the number of phones he or she owns. Ideally, a sampling frame could be drawn that includes both a phone number and a name to identify a potential respondent. However, methods like random number dialing cannot identify people.

Phone Interview Characteristics

Phone interviews have several distinctive characteristics that set them apart from other survey techniques. These characteristics present significant advantages and disadvantages for the researcher.

Random Digit Dialing

Marketing researchers used to be tempted to use a telephone directory as a sampling frame. However, the typical telephone directory presents problems. Foremost, not every resident chooses to list their home phone number in the directory. Because people with unlisted phone numbers typically differ demographically and psychologically from those who list their numbers, unlisted phone numbers can introduce coverage bias. Researchers try to resolve the problem of unlisted phone numbers with random digit dialing. **Random digit dialing** in its simplest form takes telephone exchanges (area code + the first three numbers) for a geographic area and using computer-generated random numbers, adds the last four digits to obtain a phone number to call. The process excludes mobile phone numbers and if the firm complies, numbers on the do-not-call list. Random digit dialing also helps overcome the problem due to unlisted numbers, new listings, and recent changes in phone numbers. In the vast majority of random digit dialing, the computer actually selects the number from the list of potential respondents and places the call. Unfortunately, the refusal rate in commercial random digit dialing studies is higher than the refusal rate for telephone surveys that use only listed telephone numbers.

Random digit dialing
Use of telephone exchanges and random numbers to develop a sample of respondents in a landline phone survey.

Landline versus Mobile Phone Results

Exhibit 7.2 provides a summary of potential differences in surveying by landline or mobile phones. Researchers should not be surprised to observe differences in the characteristics of heavy mobile phone users versus consumers who rely mostly on landline phone communications. For instance, compared to mobile phone users:[22]

- Mobile phones are less likely to be shared than a landline phone.
- Calls to mobile phone numbers are more likely than landline numbers to result in someone answering the phone—particularly during weekday working hours. About one in three calls to mobile phones are answered as opposed to about one in four calls to landline numbers.
- Calls to mobile phone numbers are less likely to result in someone answering the phone on weekends than are landline numbers. Respondents answer less than one in three calls to mobile phones on the weekends as opposed to nearly four in ten calls to landline numbers.

EXHIBIT **7.2**
Comparing and Contrasting
Landline and Mobile Phones

	Landline Phone	Mobile Phone
Sampling units	Better for sampling household populations	Better for sampling populations of individual consumers/employees
Reaching respondents	Low probability of contact during working hours	Higher probability of getting an answer except on weekends
Cooperation	Once someone answers, slightly more willing to cooperate	Once someone answers, they often are preoccupied and less willing to talk particularly at any length
Restrictions	Do not call legislation restrictions may apply	Mobile phone numbers cannot be autodialed or conducted with computer voice-assistance unless respondent gives written consent
Cost to respondent	Generally none	Charges may apply and respondent should receive compensation
Geography	Area codes and exchanges indicate location of household	Phone numbers are not good indicators of individuals' locations
Population	Tends to be older than median, married, own fewer electronic durable goods per person	Tend to be younger (not eligible to participate), single, college-educated, likely to own more electronic durable goods per person
Technology	Relatively static	Changing rapidly with greater likelihood for visual presentation and text input
Ownership	About 60 percent in the United States and decreasing here and abroad	Over 90 percent in the United States with nearly 60 percent being smartphones
Expense	Relatively economical	Relatively expensive due to added requirements of use

- Refusals are higher for calls to mobile phone numbers than for calls to landline numbers.
- Mobile phone users should be duly compensated for their responses given the potential costs involved and the calls should be kept to a short duration given that a mobile phone user is more likely in a situation involving attention to some other activity.
- Mobile phone users are different demographically than landline users. Mobile phone respondents tend to be younger, more likely college educated, and more affluent.
- Mobile phone users own different things than landline users. A survey suggests that mobile phone users are more likely to own durable goods like tablets, computers, and even music players.[23]

These factors all affect the equivalence of data and samples obtained from landline and mobile-phone sampling. Researchers should consider these factors before making a quick decision that any type of phone interviewing will satisfy the data needs at hand. In the end, a thorough understanding of the population of interest is essential in judging which type of interview is most appropriate.

Speed

One advantage of telephone interviewing is the relative speed of data collection. Data collection with mail or personal interviews can take weeks. In contrast, interviewers can conduct hundreds of telephone interviews within a few hours. When an interviewer enters a respondent's answers directly into a computerized system, data processing speeds up even more relative to any other approach involving manual data coding and entry.

Cost

As the cost of personal interviews continues to increase, landline phone interviews appear relatively inexpensive. Estimates indicate that landline telephone interviews cost 25 percent of a comparable door-to-door personal interview. Mobile surveys are considerably more expensive than landline survey approaches because research personnel must dial and conduct them.

Absence of Face-to-Face Contact

Telephone interviews are more impersonal than face-to-face interviews. Respondents may answer embarrassing or confidential questions more willingly in a telephone interview than in a personal interview. However, mail and Internet surveys, although not perfect, are better media for gathering extremely sensitive information because they seem more anonymous. Some evidence suggests that people provide information on income and other financial matters only reluctantly, even in telephone interviews. Such questions may be personally threatening for a variety of reasons, and high refusal rates for this type of question occur with each form of survey research.

The inability of the interviewer to see respondents can cause problems. If a respondent pauses to think about an answer, the interviewer may simply interpret the pause as "no response" and go on to the next question. Hence, there is a greater tendency for interviewers to record no answers and incomplete answers in telephone interviews than in personal interviews.

Cooperation

One trend is very clear. In the last few decades, telephone response rates have fallen. Analysis of response rates for the long-running Survey of Consumer Attitudes conducted by the University of Michigan found that response rates fell from a high of 72 percent to 67 percent during the period from 1979 to 1996 and then even faster after 1996.[24] Lenny Murphy of the data collection firm Dialtek says survey response rates fell to below 20 percent by the mid-2000s.[25] Now, just over half of all calls get answered and less than 10 percent of calls actually result in a survey response.[26]

Famous research companies like Pew or Nielsen usually identify themselves by name when calling as evidence suggests that respondents may be slightly more likely to answer if they recognize the firm to be a research firm and not a telemarketer or political call.[27] Once someone answers the phone, over half of respondents do not agree to the interview. Respondents who answer the call but do not provide data are not particularly helpful in the research process. When companies put extra resources into reaching sample units, such as doing repeated callbacks and paying financial incentives for a response, the response rate can approach 20 percent. A general rule is that across all survey modes greater representation requires greater financial and human resources from the interview firm.

Refusal to cooperate with interviews is directly related to interview length. Survey research finds that interviews of 5 minutes or less have refusal rates of about half of that of surveys that take between 6 and 12 minutes. A good rule of thumb is to keep telephone interviews under 10 minutes. In general, 30 minutes is the most time a researcher can expect a respondent to take when answering a survey unless he/she is highly interested in the survey subject, or highly paid to respond.

Another way to encourage participation is to send households an invitation to participate in a survey. The invitation can describe the purpose and importance of the survey and the likely duration of the survey. The invitation can also encourage subjects to be available and reassure them that the caller will not try to sell anything. In a study comparing response rates, the rates were highest among households that received an advance letter, somewhat lower when the notice came on a postcard, and lowest with no notice.[28]

Incentives to Respond

Respondents should receive some incentive to respond. Research addresses different types of incentives. For telephone interviews, tests of different types of survey introductions suggest that not all introductions are equally effective. A financial incentive or some significant chance to win a desirable prize will produce a higher telephone response rate than a simple assurance that the research is not a sales pitch, a more detailed description of the survey, or an assurance of confidentiality.[29]

Lack of Visual Medium

Visual aids cannot be used in traditional telephone interviews, meaning that they are not ideal for packaging/design research, copy testing of television and print advertising, and concept tests that require visual materials. Likewise, certain attitude scales and measuring instruments require the respondent to see a graphic scale, so they are difficult to use over the phone. Facetime or Skype video calls via a smartphone, tablet, or computer offer the possibility of presenting still or video images to respondents to accompany verbal dialog. Researchers may take greater advantage of this technology in the coming years. However, the phone is still inappropriate as a survey medium when respondents need to physically interact with a product.

Central Location Interviewing

Research agencies or interviewing services typically conduct all telephone interviews from a central location. Such **central location interviewing** allows firms to hire a staff of professional interviewers and to supervise and control the quality of interviewing more effectively. When telephone interviews are centralized and computerized, an agency or business can benefit from additional cost economies. Research firms gain even better cost economies by outsourcing interviews to offshore call centers where labor costs are very low. However, a respondent will quickly become impatient with an interviewer who is difficult to understand. The cost savings that come from using interviewers who have difficulty communicating are soon outweighed by subsequent problems.

Central location interviewing

Telephone interviews conducted from a central location, allowing firms to hire a staff of professional interviewers and to supervise and control the quality of interviewing more effectively.

Global Considerations

Different cultures often have different norms about proper telephone behavior. For example, business-to-business researchers have learned that Latin American businesspeople will not open up to strangers on the telephone. So, researchers in Latin America usually find personal interviews more suitable than telephone surveys. In Japan, respondents consider it ill-mannered if telephone interviews last more than 20 minutes. Laws governing researchers' ability to call via landline or mobile phones also vary based on factors such as do-not-call laws and the legality of calling mobile phone numbers. The U.S. Telephone Consumer Protection Act (TCPA) states:

"The TCPA forbids calling a cell phone using any automated telephone dialing system (autodial [*sic* CATI]) without prior express [written] consent. This rule applies to all uses of autodialers and predictive dialers, including survey and opinion research. This applies to intra-state calls, inter-state calls and calls from outside the United States and accidental calls are not exempt."[30]

Researchers need to follow very specific procedures for calling cell phone numbers in the United States, including the added expense of manual dialing and the use of a live interviewer (rather than a recorded computer device). This may not be the case in other countries, including much of Europe. Thus, mobile phone calls may provide a more convenient research tool outside the United States.

Surveys Using Self-Administered Questionnaires

Marketing researchers distribute questionnaires to consumers in many ways (see Exhibit 7.3). They insert invitations to participate via pop-ups in websites and Facebook posts (or other social networking sites). They insert questionnaires in packages and magazines. They may place questionnaires at points of purchase, in high-traffic locations in stores or malls, or on tabletops in restaurants. Traditionally, survey researchers sent printed questionnaires via snail mail.

EXHIBIT **7.3**
Options for Self-Administered
Questionnaires

Researchers can administer surveys like these without the added expense of interview personnel. No matter how the **self-administered questionnaires** are distributed, they are different from interviews because the respondent takes responsibility for reading and answering the questions him/herself.

In mall intercepts, a research assistant usually stands by to answer any questions and/or provide basic instructions. The assistant does not typically read questions to respondents. More and more, the assistant hands the person an electronic tablet or takes them to a kiosk where each respondent completes the task electronically or on paper. In settings away from a research assistant completely, response quality becomes totally dependent on the questionnaire's ability to communicate the respondent task clearly and unambiguously. Below, we elaborate on a few of the more widely used survey techniques for self-administered questionnaires.

Self-administered questionnaires

Surveys in which the respondent takes the responsibility for reading and answering the questions without having them stated orally by an interviewer.

Mail Questionnaires

A traditional **mail survey** is a self-administered questionnaire sent to respondents through a postal service. Most often, the general postal service, or snail mail, provides delivery. However, when fears of a low response rate, as typically occurs when the sample consists of professional workers like physicians or consultants, an express courier service like FedEx is a better but more expensive option. When researchers are concerned that the questionnaire actually gets delivered to the designated recipient, the courier (or postal agent) will obtain a certified return receipt.

Mail questionnaires have several advantages and disadvantages.

Mail survey

A self-administered questionnaire sent to respondents through the mail.

Geographic Flexibility

Mail questionnaires can reach a geographically dispersed sample simultaneously because interviewers are not required. Researchers can reach respondents who are located in isolated areas or those who are otherwise difficult to reach. For example, a pharmaceutical firm may find that doctors are not available for personal or telephone interviews. However, a mail or courier survey can reach both rural and urban doctors who practice in widely dispersed geographic areas.

Cost

Mail questionnaires are relatively inexpensive compared with personal interviews, though they are not cheap. Most include follow-up mailings, which require additional postage and printing costs. And it usually isn't cost-effective to try to cut costs on printing—questionnaires photocopied on low-grade paper have a greater likelihood of being thrown in the wastebasket than those prepared with more expensive, high-quality printing.

Low response rates contribute to high cost as researchers mail multiple questionnaires for every one that respondents send back. Each questionnaire goes out with a return postage paid reply envelope, otherwise researchers should not expect respondents to return completed questionnaires. Very often, a second wave of questionnaires follows the first in an effort to increase responses. So, printing and postage costs add up quickly, not to mention the costs of any incentive provided to increase response rate.

Exhibit 7.4 illustrates the cost of mail questionnaires per response. Typically, researchers mail out 1,000 or more questionnaires. Nonrespondents represent the highest cost item. Response rates are substantially higher when a questionnaire is sent by Fedex or other courier company. This exhibit assumes a 50 percent response rate for a courier versus 20 percent for snail mail, along with realistic assumptions for other cost items (cost of labor excluded). As that ratio increases, the cost of using a courier approaches that of snail mail. In fact, if the snail mail response rate were to fall to 12 percent, the respondent cost for snail mail would approach $40 with nonresponse accounting for almost $35 of that cost. When a high response rate becomes critical, a courier can present a viable option for delivery.[31]

Respondent Convenience

Respondents complete mail surveys at their convenience so they are more likely to take time to think about their replies. Mail questionnaires allow the respondent to check records before responding. A manager replying to a survey about the number of workers hired in the last six months could easily check the records to get a more accurate answer than memory would provide. The added convenience helps minimize the annoyance factor of survey research.

EXHIBIT 7.4
Costs of Snail Mail versus Courier Surveys

Standard Snail Mail

Overnight Courier

- Printing
- Postage
- Return postage
- Envelopes
- Incentive
- Nonrespondent cost

Standard Snail versus Overnight

Item	Standard Snail Mail Per Response	Standard Snail Mail Total	Overnight Courier Per Response	Overnight Courier Total
Printing	0.75	$1,500	0.75	$600
Postage	1.00	$2,000	15.00	$12,000
Return postage	0.80	$1,600	0.80	$640
Envelopes	0.20	$400	0.20	$160
Incentive	2.00	$4,000	2.00	$1,600
Nonrespondent cost	19.00	$7,600	18.80	$7,500
Respondent Cost	**$23.75**	**$9,500**	**$37.50**	**$15,000**

Respondent Anonymity

In the cover letter that accompanies a mail or self-administered questionnaire, marketing researchers almost always state that the respondents' answers will be confidential. With this promise, the researcher cannot share information about any particular respondent by name. Respondents are even more likely to provide sensitive or embarrassing information when the researcher provides for anonymity, meaning responses cannot be traced to any individual. Researchers can guarantee confidentiality in practically any research. Electronic surveys, telephone responses, and personal interviews all make anonymity easier to promise than to actually deliver. Mail surveys provide an alternative where the researcher can implement respondent anonymity with little difficulty.

A market researcher asked the following question through two approaches, "Have you borrowed money at a regular bank?" Researchers noted a 17 percent response rate for personal interviews and a 32 percent response rate for the mail survey. Although random sampling error may have accounted for part of this difference, the results suggest that for research on personal and sensitive financial issues, mail surveys provide a greater sense of confidentiality—the likely explanation being greater perceived anonymity.

Absence of Interviewer

Although the absence of an interviewer can induce respondents to reveal sensitive or socially undesirable information, this lack of personal contact can also be a disadvantage. The respondent does not have the opportunity to question the interviewer. Problems that might be clarified in a personal or telephone interview can remain misunderstandings in a mail survey.

Standardized Questions

Mail questionnaires typically are highly standardized, and the questions are quite structured. Questions and instructions must be complete but straightforward. Any ambiguity likely leads to response error. With a mail survey, once the company mails the questionnaires, it is difficult to change the format or the questions.

Time Is Money

If time is a factor in management's interest in the research results, or if attitudes are rapidly changing, mail surveys may not be a good communication medium. A minimum of two or three weeks is necessary for receiving the majority of the responses. Follow-up mailings require an additional two or three weeks. The time between the first mailing and the cut-off date (when questionnaires will no longer be accepted) normally is six to eight weeks. Even personal interviews are faster in many cases.

Length of Mail Questionnaire

Mail questionnaires vary considerably in length, ranging from extremely short postcard questionnaires to multipage booklets that require respondents to fill in thousands of answers. A general rule of thumb is that a paper questionnaire should not exceed six pages in length. Time wise, any questionnaire taking more than 10 minutes is considered lengthy and response rates will be low. When a questionnaire requires a respondent to expend significant effort, an incentive is generally required to induce the respondent to return the questionnaire. The following sections discuss several ways to pursue higher response rates even when questionnaires are relatively long.

Response Rates

Fewer than 5 percent of respondents return poorly designed mail questionnaires. The basic calculation for obtaining a **response rate** is to the number of legitimately completed questionnaires returned divided by the total number of sample members provided a chance to participate. Typically, the number in the denominator is adjusted for faulty addresses and similar problems that reduce the number of eligible participants.

Response rate

The number of questionnaires returned and completed divided by the number of sample members provided a chance to participate in the survey.

Response rates represent a major issue of mail questionnaires. When response rates are extremely low, one wonders whether people who responded are unusual, meaning somehow not representative of the population. Nonresponse error might be high if so. If response rates are very high, respondents could be complying due to undue incentives that amount to coercion. The incentive may be more responsible for answers than honest cooperation. In any event, rarely will a mail survey exceed a 50 percent response rate, and those types of response rates usually require tremendous effort and expense.

Mail survey respondents are usually better educated and more likely to be a homeowner than nonrespondents. If they return the questionnaire at all, poorly educated respondents who cannot read and write well may skip open-ended questions to which they are required to write out their answers. Thus, systematic differences may correspond to differences between groups.

A researcher also has no assurance that the intended subject is the person who fills out the questionnaire. The wrong person answering the questions may be a problem when surveying corporate executives, physicians, and other professionals. Busy professionals may pass questionnaires on to subordinates to complete. This problem is not unique to mail surveys because electronic and telephone surveying also provide no guarantee that the actual response comes from a legitimate respondent.

Increasing Response Rates for Mail Surveys

Who responds to mail surveys? Individuals who are interested in the general subject of the survey are more likely to respond than those with little interest. Wine enthusiasts are more likely than the average supermarket consumer to answer a survey addressing wine purchases. If the survey aims at measuring the typical supermarket attitudes and behaviors toward wine buying, the heavy responses by enthusiasts could represent error. People who hold extreme positions on an issue are more likely to respond than individuals who are largely indifferent to the topic. To minimize this bias, researchers have developed a number of techniques to increase the response rate to mail surveys. Designing and formatting attractive questionnaires and wording questions so that they are easily understood also help ensure a good response rate. However, special efforts beyond reply postage and follow-ups may be required even with a sound questionnaire.

Cover Letter

Cover letter

Letter that accompanies a questionnaire to induce the reader to complete and return the questionnaire.

A **cover letter** that accompanies a questionnaire is an important means of inducing a reader to complete and return the questionnaire. Exhibit 7.5 illustrates a cover letter and some of the points considered by a marketing research professional to be important in gaining respondents' attention and cooperation. The first paragraph of the letter explains why the study is important. The basic appeal alludes to the social usefulness of responding. Two other frequently used appeals are asking for help ("Will you do us a favor?") and the egotistical appeal ("Your opinions are important!"). Most cover letters promise confidentiality, invite the recipient to use an enclosed postage-paid reply envelope, describe any incentive or reward for participation, explain that answering the questionnaire will not be difficult and will take only a short time, and describe how the person was scientifically selected for participation.

A personalized letter addressed to a specific individual shows the respondent that he or she is important. Including an individually typed cover letter on letterhead rather than a printed form is an important element in increasing the response rate in mail surveys.[23]

Incentives Help

Researchers can increase a respondent's motivation for returning a questionnaire by offering monetary incentives or premiums. Although pens, lottery tickets, and a variety of premiums have been used, monetary incentives appear to be the most effective and least biasing incentive. Money attracts attention and creates a sense of obligation. Often, cover letters try to boost response rates with messages such as "We know that the attached dollar cannot compensate you for your time, but please accept it as a token of our appreciation." Response rates increase dramatically when a monetary incentive goes to a charity of the respondent's choice rather than directly to the respondent.

EXHIBIT 7.5
A Cover Letter Requesting
Participation in a Survey

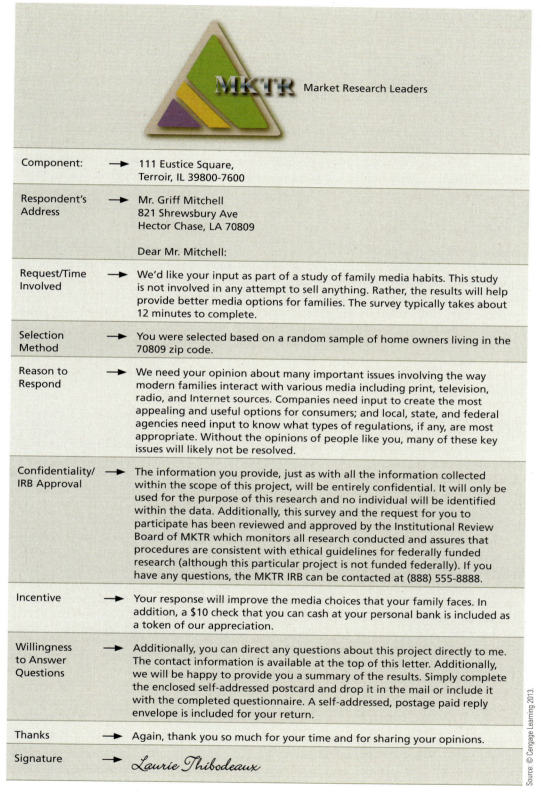

MKTR   Market Research Leaders

Component:	→	111 Eustice Square, Terroir, IL 39800-7600
Respondent's Address	→	Mr. Griff Mitchell 821 Shrewsbury Ave Hector Chase, LA 70809 Dear Mr. Mitchell:
Request/Time Involved	→	We'd like your input as part of a study of family media habits. This study is not involved in any attempt to sell anything. Rather, the results will help provide better media options for families. The survey typically takes about 12 minutes to complete.
Selection Method	→	You were selected based on a random sample of home owners living in the 70809 zip code.
Reason to Respond	→	We need your opinion about many important issues involving the way modern families interact with various media including print, television, radio, and Internet sources. Companies need input to create the most appealing and useful options for consumers; and local, state, and federal agencies need input to know what types of regulations, if any, are most appropriate. Without the opinions of people like you, many of these key issues will likely not be resolved.
Confidentiality/ IRB Approval	→	The information you provide, just as with all the information collected within the scope of this project, will be entirely confidential. It will only be used for the purpose of this research and no individual will be identified within the data. Additionally, this survey and the request for you to participate has been reviewed and approved by the Institutional Review Board of MKTR which monitors all research conducted and assures that procedures are consistent with ethical guidelines for federally funded research (although this particular project is not funded federally). If you have any questions, the MKTR IRB can be contacted at (888) 555-8888.
Incentive	→	Your response will improve the media choices that your family faces. In addition, a $10 check that you can cash at your personal bank is included as a token of our appreciation.
Willingness to Answer Questions	→	Additionally, you can direct any questions about this project directly to me. The contact information is available at the top of this letter. Additionally, we will be happy to provide you a summary of the results. Simply complete the enclosed self-addressed postcard and drop it in the mail or include it with the completed questionnaire. A self-addressed, postage paid reply envelope is included for your return.
Thanks	→	Again, thank you so much for your time and for sharing your opinions.
Signature	→	*Laurie Thibodeaux*

Source: © Cengage Learning 2013.

Advance Notification

Advance notification that a questionnaire will be arriving can increase response rates in some situations. Nielsen has used this technique to ensure a high cooperation rate in filling out diaries of television watching. Advance notices that go out closer to the questionnaire mailing time produce better results than those sent too far in advance. The optimal lead-time for advance notification is about three days before the mail survey is to arrive. Advanced notification can come in the form of a postcard, a phone call, or even an e-mail. A recent survey about respondent eating behavior employed a postcard prenotification for half of the sample and no reminder for the other half (control group).[32] The prenotification group obtained a response rate of 24 percent compared to 20 percent in the control group. This may not seem too impressive, but the authors conclude that the added costs of using the reminder were more than compensated for by the enhanced response rate.

Survey Sponsorship

Sometimes response quality is enhanced when the survey sponsor remains anonymous. Respondents who know who the research is for may, perhaps unintentionally, provide biased results. One business-to-business marketer wished to conduct a survey of its wholesalers to learn their stocking policies and their attitudes concerning competing manufacturers. A mail questionnaire sent on corporate letterhead very likely will yield a much lower response rate than a questionnaire using a commercial marketing research firm's letterhead.

Sponsorship by well-known and prestigious organizations such as universities or government agencies sometimes improves response rates. A mail survey sent to members of a consumer panel will receive an exceptionally high response rate because panel members have already agreed to cooperate as part of membership.

Keying Mail Questionnaires with Codes

A marketing researcher planning a follow-up letter, postcard, or e-mail would prefer not to disturb respondents who already have completed and returned a completed questionnaire. However, if the survey process is completely anonymous, the researcher has no way of knowing who has responded and who has not. Thus, the researcher has no choice but to send any second waves to everyone in the sample. One alternative is to clandestinely code questionnaires in a way that allows the researcher to know who has responded and remove them from the sample list. In this way, individual codes key questionnaires to individual members of the sampling frame. This code can appear on the questionnaire itself or on the envelope. For instance, blind keying might involve using a room number in the reply address as the code. Each envelope would contain a different room number and the sample list would include that number beside each person's name. The code might also appear somewhere on the questionnaire itself and in some cases a statement might indicate the number's purpose in identifying individual responses and not individual people. The researcher has to be cautious, as it would be unethical to promise anonymity if some type of identification coding is used.

Self-Administered Questionnaires Using Other Forms of Distribution

Drop-off method

A survey method that requires the interviewer to travel to the respondent's location to drop off questionnaires that will be picked up later.

Other forms of self-administered printed questionnaires share many characteristics with mail questionnaires. When the research involves a long questionnaire, the drop-off method may be helpful. The **drop-off method** means that a research assistant physically drops the questionnaire off at a potential respondent's office or home. The assistant may arrange a time to come back and get the completed questionnaire. Clearly, this is an expensive method of distributing questionnaires but the response rate is generally improved. In the United States, researchers employ drop-offs when the sample involves businesspeople who are best reached at their place of work. Marketing researchers who study service provider behavior also may find this an effective means of administration. In this case, responding employees may deposit completed questionnaires into a collection box for later pickup. At times, the questionnaire may contain a postage paid envelope for return via snail mail.

E-Mail Surveys

E-mail surveys involve making the questionnaire available to a potential respondent via e-mail. Today, respondents receive requests to participate in surveys more by e-mail than any other distribution method. E-mail surveys can put a respondent together with a questionnaire in one of three ways.

E-mail surveys

Survey requests distributed through electronic mail.

Using E-Mail

Three ways to contact respondents via email include the following:

- A questionnaire can be included in the body of an e-mail. In this case, the questionnaire should be very short (no more than ten questions). These are likely to receive a relatively high response rate.
- Questionnaires can be included as attachments. To complete the questionnaire, a respondent must open the questionnaire, respond via radio boxes and areas to write short answers, save the questionnaire, and then reattach it to a reply e-mail. Researchers can use common software such as Microsoft Word or Adobe Acrobat to create these files. Alternatively, the respondent may have the option of marking the questionnaire with a pen or pencil and returning via fax or mail. As might be expected, response rates are low with this approach given all the effort and inconvenience of dealing with the attachment and, as a result, professional researchers typically avoid this approach.
- A third option is to include a hyperlink within the body of an e-mail that will direct the respondent to a Web-based questionnaire. The respondent then completes the response directly on that website. This approach is the most common way of soliciting responses via e-mail. In essence, the e-mail survey becomes a Web-based Internet survey.

Sampling and E-mail

Like phone surveys, most, but not all, people in developed countries have access to e-mail. E-mail easily reaches businesspeople, middle-aged, and young adults. Researchers now consider e-mail a viable alternative for contacting research respondents and perhaps as representative as the landline for contacting wide cross-sections of the population.

Advantages and Disadvantages of E-mail

The benefits of incorporating a questionnaire in an e-mail include the speed of distribution, lower distribution and processing costs, faster turnaround time, more flexibility, and less manual processing of paper questionnaires. The speed of e-mail distribution and the quick response time are major advantages when dealing with time-sensitive issues.

Some researchers also believe that respondents are more candid in e-mail than in person or on the telephone. One caveat would exist when dealing with research directed at employers using company e-mail addresses. Employees often believe that their e-mails are not secure and "eavesdropping" by a supervisor could possibly occur. The belief that a response is not secure is particularly strong when the questionnaire is contained in the e-mail itself and a reply e-mail is needed to return a completed questionnaire. When the questionnaire deals with confidential subject matter, the respondent should enter responses via a questionnaire accessed through a hyperlink-accessible Web questionnaire. In this way, the ability to get candid responses remains an advantage.

In general, the guidelines for printed mail surveys apply to e-mail surveys. For example, delivering the material in the cover letter remains important despite the fact that people do not like e-mails that are more than two or three lines. For e-mail surveys, the researcher may include only personal information (if respondents are referred to by name), the request/time involved, and the selection method in the e-mail. The remaining sections can be included as the first page of the questionnaire providing an option for the recipient to opt in or out at the bottom.

Also, if the e-mail lists more than one address in the "to" or "CC" field, all recipients will see the entire list of names. This lack of anonymity has the potential to cause response bias and nonresponse error. E-mail requests should be addressed to a single person. Alternatively, the blind carbon copy, or BCC, field can be used if the same message must be sent to an entire sample. A drawback to this approach is that some spam filters will identify any message addressed to a large number of respondents as junk e-mail. Bulk-mailing programs exist that attempt to work around this problem by e-mailing potential respondents a few at a time. As can be seen, the problems associated with successful delivery to respondents remain a disadvantage of e-mail surveys.

Internet Surveys

Internet survey

A self-administered survey administered using a Web-based questionnaire.

An **Internet survey** is a self-administered questionnaire posted on a website. Typically, respondents know the questionnaire exists either by simply coming across it while browsing, through a pop-up notification, or via an e-mail containing a hyperlink, as described above. A consumer may randomly encounter the request while browsing a retailer's website. Many travel-related pages routinely provide survey invitations on their sites. Facebook pages also commonly include survey invitations. Today, a consumer might participate in an Internet survey as a way of earning some benefit. Pandora.com hosts short Internet surveys that allow consumers to listen for four hours uninterrupted after participating. The only distinction between an Internet survey and an e-mail survey hosted on a Web platform like Qualtrics is the way the researcher invites respondent participation.

Speed and Cost-Effectiveness

Internet surveys allow marketers to reach a large audience (possibly a global one), personalize individual messages, and secure confidential answers quickly and cost-effectively. The computer-based survey eliminates the costs of printing, postage, and data entry, as well as other administrative costs. Once the researcher develops the questionnaire and obtains a mailing list (e-mails of potential respondents in this case), the incremental cost of reaching additional respondents is minimal. The low incremental cost means that large samples are possible relative to other interview techniques. Speed isn't greatly affected either, as even surveys using large samples can be conducted in a week or less.

An invitation from a website allows respondents to earn benefits by participating in surveys like this one from Pandora

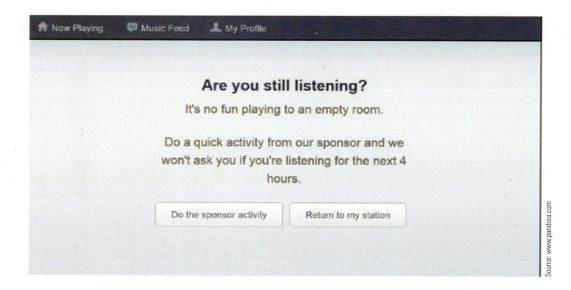

Source: www.pandora.com

Visual Appeal and Interactivity

Internet survey designs allow more interactivity than paper-based surveys. For instance, questions can change based on the specific responses provided. A respondent might initially write in the name of the last retailer in which he or she spent more than $100: Walmart. Subsequent questions asking the respondent to rate the shopping experience can "pipe in," or fill in, the name Walmart into questions. The Internet also is an excellent medium for the presentation of visual materials, such as photographs or drawings of product prototypes, advertisements, videos, or movie trailers.

Respondent Participation and Cooperation

Internet survey respondents who intentionally click through a link they stumble across while browsing display high category involvement. For example, Ticketmaster quickly obtained more than 10,000 responses based on a survey invitation placed on their home page. The responses helped Ticketmaster better understand its customer purchase patterns and evaluate visitor satisfaction with the site. A response like this is possible only when consumers are involved and believe their cooperation will help make the experience better. Survey respondents can be crowdsourced using social networking and relevant web pages. The idea behind **crowdsourcing** is that if many, many people are exposed to requests for participation, even a small percentage of completers can generate a large sample. Caution is needed in such cases, though, as the sample is not likely to represent the population very well.

> **Crowdsourcing**
> Inviting many, many people to participate in a project via the Internet and/or social networks so that even a small percentage of completers can generate a large sample.

Academic researchers sometimes crowdsource responses from Internet workers. For example, Amazon's Mechanical Turk allows workers with an account to opt-in to survey requests in return for small financial payments, often less than $1 per survey. These types of responses can be useful in some specific research instances, particularly in pretesting portions of surveys. Results, however, should not be considered generalizable, and the researcher needs to be particularly wary of acquiescence bias as Internet workers learn through experience how to end up getting paid as a top priority (a requester can refuse to pay a worker if he/she is unhappy with the response). Thus, Internet workers are particularly eager to "please" the researcher. A more complete discussion of the pros and cons of using Internet workers in marketing research is beyond the scope of this chapter. However, researchers should remain skeptical about these responses, particularly when the research involves an experimental design or the true demographic profile (sex, age, occupation, etc.) is important.[33] The Research Snapshot illustrates some of the considerations concerning this type of crowdsourcing.

Today, many e-mail surveys employ members of consumer panels who have previously indicated a willingness to cooperate by completing questionnaires. Panel members click-through a hyperlink to a survey hosted on a server like the one maintained by Qualtrics. Different security settings can provide some confidence that the respondent who received the e-mail request is the one who actually responds. Panel members receive small incentives to respond. When professionally managed, panels give the researcher a good chance at deriving a sample that can adequately represent many populations such as consumers in Florida, consumers in the United States and Canada, salespeople in Germany, and so forth. The drawback to using panels is price. While prices vary considerably, a researcher can expect legitimate panel access prices to range from about $5 per complete response to over $25 per complete response. As a population becomes more difficult to access (such as CAT scan salespeople with less than 5 years' experience), or as quality of the response becomes more important, panel access becomes increasingly expensive.

Accurate Real-Time Data Capture

Internet surveys in effect allow respondents to record their own answers directly into a data file. Survey software also can prohibit improper data entry. For example, on a paper questionnaire a respondent might incorrectly check two responses even though the instructions call for a single answer. Online survey tools can make this type of mistake impossible by barring a second response and/or activating a warning message. Thus, the data capture is more accurate than when humans do the data entry. The researcher can watch the surveys come in and give input into when to stop the survey process.

Moving Around

A marketing researcher was pretesting marketing materials for application in a later survey targeting consumers in specific U.S. states. As a good measure, rather than asking are you from the state of Texas, for example, the researcher includes an initial screening question that asks, "In what state do you reside?" One frustrated worker left a message for the researcher (written exactly as the worker composed it): "i m from texas and I try to work on your task but it showing that you are not qualify to work on task and i put all the states (AL, FL, GA, LA, MS, NC, SC, TN, TX) it showing same for all states … notify me so I can work…. I don't have much time now … its near to expire." In other words, the worker first tried an ineligible state as a state of residence, then another state, then another, then another, all in a matter of minutes (actually the worker said 30 hours). However, once the worker tried

one state, his/her device's IP address was recorded and entry into the survey was blocked no matter what state was selected. IP addresses in fact can help identify one's location, although a savvy worker can employ software to mask actual location.

Callbacks

E-mail survey samples drawn from consumer panels allow for easy callbacks via e-mail. Computer software sends e-mail reminders automatically and like other survey forms, they can marginally increase responses.[34] Computer software can sometimes identify nonrespondents or respondents who started but did not complete a questionnaire and send those people customized messages. Sometimes follow up e-mails offer additional incentives to those individuals who previously quit with only a few additional questions left to answer. When researchers assure respondents of complete anonymity, no individual computer tracking should take place, leaving the only callback option a reminder sent to the entire sample qualified by an "excuse me" message for those who may have already responded.

Personalized and Flexible Questioning

Survey software allows questioning to branch off into two or more different lines depending on a respondent's answer to a filtered question. In other words, the computer program asks questions in a sequence determined by the respondent's previous answers. This ability to sequence questions based on previous responses is a major advantage of computer-assisted surveys. The computer can be programmed to skip from question 6 to question 9 if the answer to question 6 is "no." Information can be piped in based on previous responses making questions less ambiguous and more relevant. Fewer, less ambiguous, and more relevant questions mean a survey that is easier to answer and thus increases response rates and response quality.

A related advantage of using a Web survey is that it can prompt respondents when they skip over a question. In a test comparing telephone and Internet versions of the same survey, the rate of item nonresponse was less for the Internet version, which issued a prompt for each unanswered item.[35] This was likely not a simple matter of motivation, because the rate of respondents who actually took the Web version was less than for the telephone version, even though the researchers offered a larger incentive to those asked to go online. Online survey software can force a respondent to answer questions by blocking them from moving further if they've left a forced response question blank. Research suggests that forced responding does not increase survey nonresponse nor does it present evidence of biased answers.[36] However, researchers may not always be comfortable with this choice as we will see below.

Respondent Anonymity

Respondents are more likely to provide sensitive or embarrassing information when they remain anonymous. In fact, Internet survey respondents may get the sense of anonymity that may come from the vastness of the Internet. However, a researcher using typical Internet survey approaches cannot guarantee anonymity. As mentioned in Chapter 2, the IP addresses for computers, smartphones, and tablets provide unique identifiers that reveal where the device was (by identifying the communication portal like a Wi-Fi device) when the response was recorded and includes, in essence, a signature for that particular device. Thus, researchers typically can go as far as promising confidentiality but without taking specific precautions to block the identification of the IP address (for instance, if combined with an intercept method many respondents are using the same device), complete anonymity does not come with Internet surveys.

Improving Response Rates

Methods for improving response rates for an Internet survey are similar to those for other kinds of survey research. A request delivered through Facebook may improve response likelihood. The subject line should refer to a topic likely of interest to the audience, and legal as well as ethical standards dictate that it may not be deceptive. Thus, the line might be worded in a way similar to the following: "Please give your opinion on [subject matter of interest]." Researchers should avoid gimmicks like dollar signs and the word *free,* either of which is likely to alert the spam filters installed on most computers.

Research suggests that the manner of invitation can enhance participation.[37] Invitations containing phrases like "shorter than the typical survey" or "participate and earn a chance to win cash prizes" increase participation. In contrast, "participate and earn frequent flyer miles" or "introducing a new credit card" lowers participation.

Unlike mail surveys, Internet surveys do not offer the opportunity to send a physical incentive, such as a dollar bill, to the respondent. Incentives to respond to a survey must be in the form of a coupon or a promise of a future reward. A coupon can be included that contains a discount code which can be applied at a retail website or even in a store. For example, a respondent might receive a $10 coupon good at **www.target.com** or in any Target store as a thanks for participating. Otherwise, a promise can be offered: "As a token of appreciation for completing this survey, the sponsor of the survey will make a sizable contribution to a national charity. You can vote for your preferred charity at the end of the survey." Generally, promises are less effective than an incentive in hand.

Researchers also can use prenotification for Web surveys. The research firm can send e-mail notices, phone messages, postcards, and/or letters informing potential respondents that an e-mail will be arriving containing a survey invitation. Researchers studying why students enroll in the universities that they attend might involve contacting recent college applicants. The applicants might first receive a letter indicating that a survey invitation will arrive via e-mail. With a study like this, one might expect about 20 percent of potential respondents to click through to the questionnaire, and all but a small percentage of these would respond, for an overall response rate of just under 20 percent and a **click-through response rate** of about 90 percent. Recall that highly engaged respondents are more likely to respond. Alternatively, they may receive only the e-mail invitation.

Mail notification has several potential advantages. Spammers do not send notifications via mail, so the survey may end up having a little more legitimacy. Additionally, the prenotification establishes the potential for a relationship and can even include a request to put the sender on the recipient's safe sender list. However, research provides no evidence of substantial response rate gains by using snail mail prenotification and any gains need to be weighed against the extra costs involved with physically mailing notices.[38] Telephone call prenotifications are slightly more effective but also add costs. Thus, nonautomatic prenotifications are used only when there are great concerns about responses.

Internet surveys, even those not associated with a panel, are often directed toward a finite population. For example, all members of the Atlanta area Sales and Marketing Executives

Click-through response rate

The portion of potential respondents exposed to a hyperlink to a survey who actually click-through to view the questionnaire.

Association might comprise a population of interest for researchers studying attitudes toward customer relationship management programs. Research shows that a combination of pop-up notification on a software user forum's home page plus a single e-mail notification (to all members of the forum) yields an overall response rate of about 14 percent.[39] Thus, respondent characteristics that indicate a stake in the issues studied are most responsible for increasing response rates.

With Internet surveys, we can track both click rate, which assesses the portion of potential respondents who actually take a look at the questionnaire, and, if an e-mail request is sent, overall response rates based on the number of invitations. Generally, except for very long questionnaires, many respondents who click through to view a questionnaire also respond to it. Some researchers argue that the true response rate for an Internet survey initiated by an e-mail invitation should be the ratio of completed questionnaires to the number of click-throughs. This opinion argues that logically, the only respondents with a chance to respond are those that clicked through and many surveys close once a quota of completes is obtained. With this rationale, Internet survey response rates equal or exceed telephone and snail mail surveys. Like every other type of survey, Internet surveys have both advantages and disadvantages.

After reviewing hundreds of studies dealing with the use of incentives in increasing participation in surveys of all types, researchers reached the following conclusions:[40]

1. Incentives increase response rates across all survey modes.
2. Prepaid monetary incentives increase response rates better than promised incentives or lotteries.
3. The response rates increase with the size of incentive although published research does not consider large incentives (over $20).
4. The use of incentives can systematically influence what type of person responds to a survey across all modes.
5. Maximizing response rate does not guarantee sample representativeness. The use of incentives should be monitored for possibilities of increasing error while also increasing response rates.

Response Quality

Internet surveys are still in their infancy in many ways. However, the prospects for a bright future are good. Surveys asking potential respondents questions that can be compared with known population demographics can be used to compare the response quality of different survey media. For instance, basic demographic information for each U.S. ZIP code is available through http://www.census.gov. Random samples taken from ZIP codes asking respondents to report these basic statistics should produce results that match the census data with allowance for a small amount of error.[41] If the results show that certain demographics are under represented and others are over-represented, nonresponse bias exists. At this point, Web-based survey approaches produce data that is as good as traditional landline phone surveys.

Text-Message Surveys

Text-message surveys have all the advantages of mobile-phone surveys, including increased reach, but share the disadvantages in terms of reaching only respondents who have opted in with expressed consent. However, text-message surveys are catching on in other countries and are ideal for surveys involving only a few very short questions. Additionally, MMS messages can include graphic displays or even short videos.

Choosing an Appropriate Survey Approach

Each survey administration technique has advantages and disadvantages. A researcher who must ask highly confidential questions may use an anonymous mail survey, thus sacrificing follow-up possibilities to avoid interviewer bias. If a researcher must have considerable control over question phrasing (and potentially rephrasing), centralized location telephone interviewing may provide both control and a user-friendly format.

To determine the appropriate technique, the researcher must ask several questions:

- Is the assistance of an interviewer necessary?
- Are respondents interested in the issues being investigated?
- Will cooperation be easily attained?
- How quickly is the information needed?
- Will the study require a long and complex questionnaire?
- How large is the budget?

The criteria—cost, speed, anonymity, and so forth—may differ for each project.

Exhibit 7.6 summarizes some major advantages and disadvantages of different survey approaches. It emphasizes typical types of surveys. For example, a creative researcher might be able to design highly versatile and flexible mail questionnaires, but most researchers use standardized questions. An elaborate mail survey may be more expensive than a short personal interview, but generally this is not the case. One research team investigating consumer medical issues tested several different modes for generating results when the ability to generalize to a population was important.[42] In the end, once cost per valid response was considered, a generic snail mail survey proved most cost-effective based on a combination at $23 per response with a 7.5 percent response rate (compared to $25 for a personalized snail mail questionnaire with a 10.5 percent response rate—both proving cheaper than telephone and directed Internet surveys where response rates were less than 5 percent).

More and more, though, survey researchers employ **mixed-mode survey** approaches that employ more than one approach in a given survey. This means the sampling frame must be accessible from more than one survey mode. Polling organizations traditionally relied heavily on landline telephone surveys. However, the accuracy in representing populations of interest (such as voters or consumers) declined due to coverage error associated with declining incidence and the resulting nonresponse bias. Thus, polling organizations today supplement landline calling with cell phone calling and even some Internet surveys. Accurate polls come from sampling approaches that best match modes to subgroups within a population.

Mixed-mode survey

Term used to refer to a survey approach that uses more than one survey medium to reach potential respondents.

Pretesting Survey Instruments

A researcher spending $300,000 to survey a few thousand consumers does not want to find out after data collection that most respondents misunderstood some questions, all gave the same answer to a key variable, or misinterpreted the response instructions for an entire set of items. Researchers can minimize these possibilities by employing various screening procedures during *pretesting*. **Pretesting** involves trial runs using the survey instrument with a group of colleagues or actual respondents to iron out fundamental problems in instructions, items, or design of a questionnaire. Researchers benefit by spotting problems in the pretest and rightly inferring that a problem with this very small sample will likely be a problem in the full sample once data collection actually begins.

Broadly speaking, survey researchers choose from three basic ways of pretesting. The first two involve screening the questionnaire with other research colleagues, and the third—the one most often called pretesting—is a trial or pilot test with an actual group of respondents. First, when screening the questionnaire with other research professionals, the investigator asks them to look for such problems as difficulties with question wording, leading questions, and bias due to question order. An alternative type of screening might involve a client or the research manager who ordered the research. Often, managers ask researchers to collect information, but when they see the questionnaire, they feel that it does not really address their decision statements. The researchers then need either to explain things better to the client and/or make changes. Secondly, other research experts may sometimes be asked to judge the content of survey items as a way of trying

Pretesting

Screening procedure that involves a trial run with a group of respondents to iron out fundamental problems in the survey design.

To the Point

"Practice is the best of all instructors."

— PUBLILIUS SYRUS

CIRCA 42 BC

EXHIBIT **7.6**   Advantages and Disadvantages of Typical Survey Methods

Characteristic:	Door-to-Door Personal Interview	Mall Intercept Personal Interview	Telephone Interview	Snail Mail Survey	E-mail / Internet Survey
Speed of data collection	Moderate	Fast	Very fast	Slow	Fastest
Geographic flexibility	Limited to moderate	Confined mostly to urban and suburban areas	High	High	High (worldwide)
Respondent cooperation	Moderate in getting an answer. Excellent once respondent agrees to participate	Good in agreement to respond. Moderate cooperation thereafter	Difficult to get an answer. Good cooperation thereafter. Varies landline versus cell	Moderate all the way around	Low from general population but high when hot button issue presented or sample is a computer panel
Versatility of questioning	Quite versatile	Extremely versatile	Limited versatility, particularly for cell calls	Not versatile; requires highly standardized format	Good versatility for logical branching and respondent assignment
Questionnaire length	Long	Moderate	Moderate for landline and short for cell	Moderate but varies depending on incentive	Moderate but varies depending on incentive
Item non response rate	Low	Medium	Medium	High	Software can assure none
Possibility for respondent misunderstanding	Low	Low	Average	High	High
Degree of researcher or interviewer influence on responses	High	High	Moderate	Lowest	Low with exceptions depending on data source
Supervision of interviewers	Moderate	Moderate to high	High, especially with central location interviewing	Not applicable	Not applicable
Anonymity of respondent	Lowest	Moderate	Low	Highest	Moderate
Ease of callback or follow- up	Difficult	Most difficult	Easy	Easy, but takes time	Difficult if respondents are unknown. Easy if sample drawn from e-mail list
Cost	Highest	Moderate to high	Low to moderate	Low	Low to moderate depending on potential cost of access to sample
Special features	Visual materials may be shown or demonstrated; extended probing possible	Taste tests, product trials, viewing of marketing materials possible. Ideal for representing population of mall/shopping center shoppers	Fieldwork and supervision of data collection are simplified. Distinction must be made between landline and mobile/cell phone calls	Respondent may answer questions at own convenience; has time to reflect on answers	Streaming media software allows use of graphics and animation as well as random assignment to experimental conditions

to verify that the items are measuring what the researcher intended. Later, we return to this idea under the heading of validity.

The third form is basically a trial run of the entire research project. Once the researcher has decided on the final questionnaire, data are collected with a small number of respondents (perhaps as many as 100 but sometimes as few as three dozen) to determine whether the questionnaire needs refinement. The researcher is keen to spot problem items and analyzes these data for suspicious patterns indicating potential problems. For example, a researcher might find that all respondents indicate the same answer to a specific question. Such a result is highly unlikely when more than a handful of respondents are included. Thus, a response like this probably indicates a problem with item wording.

Unfortunately, although the value of a pretest is readily apparent, researchers often press forward without it due to time and budget concerns. The risk of collecting some items that end up not being very helpful increases without a pretest. Needless to say, pretests are highly recommended in almost all types of primary data collection efforts.

Ethical Issues in Survey Research

Chapter 4 mentioned that codes of ethics express researchers' obligation to protect the public from misrepresentation and exploitation under the guise of marketing research. Thou shall not disguise selling as research! Many ethical issues apply to survey research, such as respondents' right to privacy, the use of deception, respondents' right to be informed about the purpose of the research, the need for confidentiality, the need for honesty in collecting data, and the need for objectivity in reporting data.

At this time, a few points are worth emphasizing. Researchers should not ask for information in a misleading way. Also, researchers must be careful to guard the resulting data carefully. For instance, a researcher may end up with data that identifies children's responses to several different new products. The data may also contain demographics and other material. Once that data becomes stored on a laptop or server, it is vulnerable to theft or misplacement. The researcher should follow good security procedures in protecting the data stored on various storage mediums.

Additionally, technology brings new issues to the forefront. Although e-mail is an extremely useful tool, researchers should avoid needlessly contributing to spam volume by sending unsolicited e-mails seeking survey respondents. At times, this may be the only way to reach a population, but whenever possible, e-mail requests for responses are better directed toward individuals who in some way may have indicated that the e-mail isn't so unwanted. For example, members of consumer response panels opt in and thus give their explicit approval to receive such e-mails. Additionally, consumers who query about certain information may end up being good research respondents. Consider someone who has sought information about hybrid cars from a website like Kelley Blue Book **(www.kbb.com)**. A website like this may even include a place where a consumer can register and indicate whether they are open to further contact. If they appear open to responding to research that may be tied to new automobiles or environmentally sensitive products, sending a survey about attitudes toward new car features may not be an imposition. On the other hand, phoning someone during dinner or filling up a busy executive's inbox with requests to participate in irrelevant surveys pushes the boundaries of good ethics.

Technology brings other ethics challenges. Survey software can require someone to answer a question but this too could be seen as unethical by some—including some IRBs. A way around this and to maintain high ethical integrity is to include a "don't know" or "prefer not to answer" option. Certainly, as technology continues to evolve, even more ethics challenges may face survey researchers. Also, the researcher needs to be mindful about technology and the lack of complete anonymity that comes with many forms of electronic responses.

TIPS OF THE TRADE

■ Even a perfectly written survey will produce erroneous results when the sample is incapable of adequately representing a population due to survey error

■ The longer the questionnaire, the lower the response rate. Anything longer than 10 minutes will get very low response rates unless special steps are taken, such as:
  • Look for respondents who are essentially a captive audience; like students in a class or people waiting for a plane
  • Use a survey research panel
  • Try to target the survey toward individuals who are highly involved in the topic
  • Offer a nontrivial incentive to respond

■ Telephone surveys can still produce high-quality results. However, consider supplementing with a mixed-mode approach that involves a combination of landline calls, cell calls, and Internet surveys
  • In the United States, cell calls cannot be automated unless a potential respondent has opted in
■ E-mail surveys and Internet surveys are good approaches for most types of surveys given an adequate sampling frame like those that come from professionally managed panels
■ Any pretest is better than no pretest

∴ SUMMARY

1. Define surveys and describe the type of information that may be gathered in a survey.
A survey represents a way of describing public opinion by collecting primary data through communicating directly with individual sampling units. Surveys provide a snapshot at a given point in time. More precisely, this is a sample survey because the respondents' opinions presumably represent a sample of the larger target population's opinion. Members of the sample are known as respondents. Surveys gather information to assess consumer knowledge and awareness of products, brands, or issues and to measure consumer attitudes, feelings, and behaviors. Additionally, surveys describe consumer characteristics, including purchasing patterns, brand usage, and descriptive characteristics including demographics and lifestyle. Surveys provide a quick, efficient, and accurate means of assessing information about a population.

2. Identify sources of error in survey research. Two major forms of error are common in survey research. The first, sampling error is inadequacy of respondents to represent a population of interest even if other survey aspects are valid. Sampling error results from random sampling error, chance variation given that a sample is some fraction of the entire population, and systematic sampling error that results from a flawed sampling frame. The second major category of error, systematic error, takes several forms. Nonresponse error is caused by sampling units that fail to respond to a survey. This type of error can be detected by comparing the demographics of the sample population with those of the target population and making a special effort to contact underrepresented groups. In addition, response bias occurs when a response to a questionnaire is falsified or misrepresented, either intentionally or inadvertently. Administrative error also contributes to nonsampling, systematic error. Administrative error represents a flaw in the execution of the survey or sample plan. Exhibit 7.1 summarizes the sources of error.

3. Summarize the ways researchers gather information through personal interviews. An interactive survey approach facilitates two-way communication where the respondent and the interviewer truly have a personal dialogue. A face-to-face personal interview typifies this approach, but other media, including mobile phones and landline phones, allow two-way communication. Face-to-face interviews can be conducted door-to-door, although this mode is used less and less these days. Mall intercepts provide another alternative for personal interviews. They give the advantage of allowing respondents to interact with actual products or marketing stimuli. Landline telephone interviews are still widely used when a representative sample becomes a priority. Mobile phone surveys have potential, but legal restrictions like the Telephone Consumer Protection Act (TCPA) make using them more difficult and expensive than landline surveys.

4. Know the advantages and disadvantages of conducting surveys using self-administered questionnaires. Self-administered questionnaires provide less interactivity than personal interviews but provide increased efficiency. Self-administered surveys can be administered through snail mail-delivered paper questionnaires or e-mail and Internet-based survey approaches. They typically are less expensive than personal interviews although gathering representative data generally is expensive through any means. Self-administered questionnaires also can provide for faster data collection. The structured response though provides little flexibility to stray beyond the questions written on the survey.

5. Appreciate the importance of pretesting questionnaires. Pretesting a questionnaire is a useful way to discover problems while they can still be corrected. Pretests may involve screening the questionnaire with other research professionals and/or conducting a trial run with a relatively small set of respondents. Despite their obvious value, researchers too often move forward without adequately pretesting survey instruments and sampling frames.

6. Describe ethical issues that arise in survey research. Researchers must protect the public from misrepresentation and exploitation. This obligation includes honesty about the purpose of a research project and protection of subjects' right to refuse to participate or to answer particular questions. Researchers also should protect the confidentiality of participants and record responses honestly. If a survey cannot be administered in a way that prohibits any unique identification of respondents, researchers should not promise anonymity. Lastly, as technology evolves, researchers should be mindful of ways that good ethics can be breeched in sometimes subtle ways, including adding volumes of spam and breeches of confidentiality.

:: KEY TERMS AND CONCEPTS

acquiescence bias, *172*
administrative error, *174*
callbacks, *180*
central location interviewing, *186*
click-through response rate, *197*
computer-assisted telephone interviewing (CATI), *180*
cover letter, *190*
coverage bias, *182*
crowd-sourcing, *195*
data processing error, *174*
door-to-door interviews, *179*
drop-off method, *192*
e-mail surveys, *193*
extremity bias, *173*
interactive survey approaches, *175*

Internet survey, *194*
interviewer bias, *173*
interviewer cheating, *174*
interviewer error, *174*
item nonresponse, *177*
mail survey, *187*
mall-intercept interviews, *179*
mixed-mode survey, *199*
no contacts, *171*
noninteractive survey approaches, *175*
nonrespondents, *171*
nonresponse error, *171*
personal interview, *175*
population parameter, *170*
pretesting, *199*
random digit dialing, *183*

refusals, *171*
respondent error, *170*
respondents, *167*
response bias, *171*
response rate, *189*
robocalls, *182*
sample bias, *170*
sample selection error, *174*
sample survey, *167*
sampling error, *169*
self-administered questionnaires, *187*
self-selection bias, *171*
social desirability bias, *173*
systematic error, *170*

:: QUESTIONS FOR REVIEW AND CRITICAL THINKING

1. What is a survey? Give an example of one that you've recently participated in. Find an example of survey results reported in the *Wall Street Journal*.
2. What is *self-selection bias*? Describe it as a source of total survey error.
3. Do surveys tend to gather qualitative or quantitative data? What types of information are commonly measured with surveys?
4. What potential sources of error listed in Exhibit 7.1 might be associated with the following situations?
   a. In an Internet survey of frequent fliers aged 50 and older, researchers conclude that price does not play a significant role in airline travel because only 25 percent of the respondents check off price as the most important consideration in determining where and how they travel, whereas 35 percent rate price as being unimportant. Management decides prices can be increased with little loss in business.
   b. A telephone survey of big city voters finds that most respondents do not like negative political ads—that is, advertising by one political candidate that criticizes or exposes secrets about the opponent's "dirty laundry." Researchers conclude that negative advertising should not be used.
   c. A survey accessed through Instagram produces results ranking Apple Macbooks as far superior to other PCs for business applications. A retailer decides to reduce inventory of PCs other than Macbooks.
   d. Researchers who must conduct a 45-minute personal interview offer $175 to each respondent because they believe that people who will sell their opinions are more typical than someone who will talk to a stranger for free for 45 minutes. Management uses the results to adjust their services offering.
   e. A company's sales representatives are asked what percentage of the time they spend traveling, talking on the telephone, participating in meetings, working on the computer, in training, and filling out reports for management. The survey is conducted via the company's e-mail network. Management concludes that sales reps are not spending enough time performing selling in the field.
   f. A health insurance company obtains a 75 percent response rate from a sample of college students contacted by mobile phone in a study of attitudes toward life insurance. Survey respondents received a code for a free meal from Canes Chicken Fingers Restaurant. The company is concerned that consumers are less interested in life insurance these days.
5. A sample of 14-year-old schoolchildren is asked if they have ever smoked a cigarette. The students are asked to respond orally in the presence of other students. What types of error might enter into this process?
6. Why is response rate a concern for survey researchers? Are there other issues that should be of greater concern?
7. A researcher sends out 2,000 questionnaires via e-mail and promises respondents anonymity. Fifty surveys are returned because the e-mail addresses are inaccurate. Of the 1,950 delivered questionnaires, 100 are completed and e-mailed back. However, 40 of these respondents wrote that they did not want to participate in the survey. The researcher indicates the response rate was 5.0 percent. Is this the right thing to do? What concerns might you have about this approach?
8. Define interactive and noninteractive survey approaches. Why might a researcher choose an interactive survey approach over a noninteractive survey approach?
9. Suppose a firm wanted to conduct an interactive survey to predict whether to push marketing efforts aimed at families expecting their first child through Pinterest, Instagram, or Facebook efforts. The researcher is considering using a single-mode approach consisting of a telephone survey. Critique this decision and offer suggestions for improvement.
10. A publisher offers teenage boys (aged 14–17 years) one of four best-selling famous rock posters as an incentive for filling out a ten-page mail questionnaire about what makes a good guitar. What are the pros and cons of offering this incentive? Yes or no, should the incentive be offered (explain)?
11. What do you think should be the maximum length of a self-administered e-mail questionnaire using no financial incentive?
12. A survey researcher reports that "205 usable questionnaires out of 942 questionnaires delivered in our mail survey converts to a 21.7 percent response rate." What are the subtle implications of this statement?
13. What is do-not-call legislation? What effect has it had on survey research?
14. Agree or disagree with this statement: Landline and mobile-phone surveys are essentially the same and can be used in the same situations with the same results.
15. What are the advantages and disadvantages of e-mail surveys? What are the situations when they may not be appropriate?
16. What is a click-through rate? How is it relevant to e-mail surveys?
17. What is the difference between an e-mail and an Internet survey?
18. Evaluate the following survey designs:
   a. A text-message survey asking the potential respondent to indicate with yes or no responses whether they are driving or not, whether they are alone, whether they believe the roads in their area can adequately handle traffic, whether more money should be devoted to better roadways, whether or not traffic is adequately policed, and whether or not automatic cameras should be used to issue speeding tickets. The sample is drawn from people who have agreed to be contacted via mobile phone regarding their new Subaru purchase.
   b. A shopping mall that wishes to evaluate its image places packets including a questionnaire, cover letter, and stamped return envelope in the mall where customers can pick them up if they wish.
   c. An e-mail message is sent asking respondents to complete a questionnaire on a website. Respondents answer the questions and then have the opportunity to play a slot-machine game on the website. Each respondent is guaranteed a monetary incentive but has the option to increase it by repeatedly playing the slot-machine game.

d. A mall-intercept interviewing service is located in a regional shopping center. The facility contains a small room for television and movie presentations. Shoppers are used as sampling units to evaluate television commercials. However, mall-intercept interviewers recruit additional subjects for television commercial experiments by offering them several complimentary tickets for special sneak previews of movies. Individuals contacted at the mall are allowed to bring up to five guests. In some cases, respondents try to sell their complimentary tickets through Facebook and Craig's List posts.

e. *Time* magazine opts to conduct a mobile-phone survey rather than mail survey for a study to determine the demographic characteristics and purchasing behavior of its subscribers in the United Kingdom, France, and the United States.

19. Under what conditions might someone conducting a mail survey use an overnight courier to send questionnaires to sampling units?

20. What type of survey approach is most likely to yield the highest response rate? What approach(es) will yield the lowest response rate? What can be done to improve response rates in e-mail and Internet surveys?

21. Comment on the ethics of the following situations:

a. A researcher plans to use invisible ink to code questionnaires to identify respondents in a mail survey designed to get honest opinions from people who have filed to run for political office. The code will allow their identities to be known by the researcher.

b. A political action committee conducts a survey about its particular cause. At the end of the questionnaire, it includes a request for a donation.

c. A telephone interviewer calls at 1 P.M. on Sunday and asks the person who answers the phone to take part in an interview.

d. An industrial marketer wishes to survey its own distributors. It invents the name "Mountain States Marketing Research" and sends out an e-mail questionnaire under this name.

22. How might the marketing research industry take action to ensure that the public believes that landline phone surveys and door-to-door interviews are legitimate activities and that firms that misrepresent and deceive the public using marketing research as a sales ploy are not true marketing researchers?

23. Go to the Pew Internet and American Life page at **http://www.pewinternet.org**. Several reports based on survey research will be listed. Select one of the reports. What were the research objectives? What were the first three questions on the survey?

::RESEARCH ACTIVITY

1. Ask a small sample of students at your local university to report their GPA. Then, try to find the average GPA of students at your school. If you have to, ask several professors to give their opinion. Does it seem that the student data are subject to error? Explain.

2. Look for opportunities to participate in surveys online. Is the sponsor identified and if so, how might it influence responses? Comment on the surveys with respect to their ability to deliver error-free data to the sponsor.

Case 7.1

SAT and ACT Writing Tests

The SAT and ACT college entrance exams once were completely multiple-choice, but both tests recently began including an essay portion (which is optional for the ACT). Some researchers have investigated how the essay tests are used by one group they serve: the admissions offices of the colleges that look at test results during the selection process.[37]

Early survey research suggests that some admission officers harbor doubts about the essay tests. ACT, Inc., reported that among the schools it surveyed, only about one-fifth are requiring that applicants take the writing portion of the exam. Another one-fifth merely recommend (but don't require) the essay.

Kaplan, Inc., which markets test preparation services, conducted surveys as well. Kaplan asked 374 colleges whether they would be using the SAT writing test in screening candidates. Almost half (47 percent) said they would not use the essay at all. Another

22 percent said they would use it but give it less weight than the math and verbal SAT scores.

Kaplan also surveys students who take the exams for which it provides training. On its website, the company says, "More than 25 percent of students ran out of time on the essay!"

Questions

1. What survey objectives would ACT have in asking colleges how they use its essay test? What objectives would Kaplan have for its survey research?

2. If you were a marketer for the College Board (the SAT's company) or ACT, Inc., what further information would you want to gather after receiving the results described here?

3. What sources of error or response bias might be present in the surveys described here?

National Do-Not-Call Registry

Case 7.2

Citizens' annoyance with phone calls from salespeople prompted Congress to pass a law setting up a National Do-Not-Call Registry. The registry was soon flooded with requests to have phone numbers removed from telemarketers' lists. By law, salespeople may not call numbers listed on this registry. The law makes exceptions for charities and researchers. However, a recent poll suggests that even though phone calls from researchers may be legal, they are not always well received.

In late 2005, Harris Interactive conducted an Internet survey in which almost 2,000 adults answered questions about the National Do-Not-Call Registry. About three-quarters of the respondents said they had signed up for the registry, and a majority (61 percent) said they had since received "far less" contact from telemarketers. In addition, 70 percent said that since registering, they had been contacted by someone "who was doing a poll or survey" and wanted them to participate. But apparently respondents weren't sure whether this practice was acceptable. Only one-fourth (24 percent) of respondents said they knew that researchers "are allowed to call," and over half (63 percent) weren't sure about researchers' rights under the law.

Questions

1. Was an online survey the best medium for a poll on this subject? What were some pros and cons of conducting this poll online?
2. How might the results have differed if this poll had been conducted by telephone?
3. As a researcher, how would you address people's doubts about whether pollsters may contact households listed on the Do-Not-Call Registry?

Observation

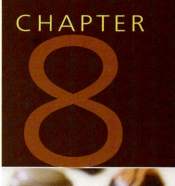

LEARNING OUTCOMES

After studying this chapter, you should be able to:

1. Discuss the role of observational technologies as marketing research tools
2. Know the difference between direct and contrived observation
3. Identify ethical issues particular to research using observation
4. Explain the observation of physical objects and message content
5. Describe major types of mechanical observation
6. Summarize techniques for measuring physiological reactions

Dimitri Otis/Getty Images

Chapter Vignette:

Goople Peeking!

Earlier, we discussed the ways that big data analysis can help companies predict consumer behavior. Well, huge companies like Google and Apple take data collection to the extreme by tracking individuals' every waking hour and more. Your iPhone is observing more than your mug shot on Facetime. Your iPhone sends data back to Apple that indicates your every movement. Android systems have similar capabilities. We can refer to the combination of Apple and Google in observing your behavior through electronic means "Goople" peeking. Even things that you may have forgotten, Goople knows. Did you go to Starbucks before work or during work? How long did you stay there? Did you use your phone to pay? Did you search any terms on your smartphone's browser? Did you like anything on Facebook? Did you respond to a survey or visit a blog? Did you spend time looking at the new merchandise display? Did you get from point A to point B faster than the speed limit allows? Google depends on advertising revenue and the more they know, the more they can carefully target content toward your behaviors. Apple considers how they may become a tool for conducting the bulk of consumer transactions by expanding iTunes technology to draw money right from your bank account. Once consumers find out about all of this peeking at their behavior, they are typically alarmed at the loss of privacy. A consumer can take a few steps to prevent an Android device from tracking geographic locations and an Apple user can do the same although it is a bit more complicated. However, even with Wi-Fi and GPS turned off, cell signals continue to track locations. Thus, when asked, few consumers say they are willing to give up the convenience that comes with a smartphone in return for a measure of privacy. Perhaps the entire meaning of privacy is changing with technology. How does it feel to know Goople is peeking at you right this minute?[1]

Source: www.ibtimes.com

Introduction

Scientists rely heavily on observation. This was true yesterday, is true today, and certainly will be true tomorrow. Simple observation has played a key role in scientific discoveries for as long as people have pursued knowledge. Bernoulli developed the laws of buoyancy and fluid dynamics by *observing* what happened to his bathwater when he entered the tub; it went up in proportion to his mass. What a simple observation! According to legend, Newton developed the laws of gravitation by *observing* (and feeling) the way an apple fell onto his head while he rested under the tree. Observations play a key role in discovering ideas and developing theories. Inductive learning begins with collections of observations. Researchers also deductively develop logical theories that in turn test these ideas through the use of observation of the specific phenomena of interest. This chapter is all about observing marketing behavior directly.

Technology and Observation in Marketing Research

Observation

The systematic process of recording the behavioral patterns of people, objects, and occurrences as they take place.

In marketing research, **observation** is a systematic process of recording actual behavioral patterns of people, objects, and events as they take place. No questioning or communicating with people is needed. Researchers who use observation method data collection either witness and record information while watching events take place or take advantage of a tracking system such as checkout scanners, information in cookies, or GPS tracking. These tracking systems can observe and provide data such as whether a specific consumer purchased more products on discount or at regular price, or how much time a consumer spent viewing a particular Web page before either exiting or clicking through to the next page. Advances in technology have given a bigger role for observational research tools in marketing research.

Observation can be a useful part of either qualitative or quantitative research. Additionally, actual observations of behavioral patterns can be part of an exploratory, descriptive, or even a causal design. For instance, researchers studying compliance with a diet program might manipulate different features of the program and then observe actual eating and exercise habits. These observations would play a key role as a dependent variable in a causal design. More often, however, observation is associated with qualitative research and with exploratory research designs. Observation is nearly synonymous with ethnographic research as researchers often try to blend into the environment and simply scrutinize the germane behavior. Callaway Golf may plant ethnographic researchers as caddies (who carry clubs for golfers) on nice golf courses to observe the actual behavior of golfers on the golf course. The caddies blend into the environment in a manner traditional to ethnographic research. Scientific observation is scarcely distinguished from simple observation. However, scientific observation addresses a research question aimed at discovering or testing market knowledge, whereas simple observation has no such motivation.

Technological Advances and Observation

We've covered numerous ways Internet, cellular, social networking and near-field technologies have fueled big data analytics. Because most of this data gathering involves no two-way communication (no survey or interview), these types of data qualify as behavioral observational. They leave behind a systematic recording of what people actually did and in that sense do not suffer from problems such as memory inaccuracy that may from time to time plague survey data. Plus, these technologies enable data collection to be automated.

The chapter vignette stresses observation of individual consumers using computers and telecommunication technologies, but observation goes further than just peeking at individuals. Now, Apple can see how it feels to have their behavior tracked. Google's acquisition of Skybox satellite services gives Google the capability to track Apple's supply chain activity and predict company secrets in advance. For example, by tracking images around Apple production facilities, Google may be

Observational data predicting what other companies are doing could be useful to competitors' marketing decisions.

able to know in advance when Apple is about to release a new iPhone or iPad version. Data analytics could signal when the inflow of deliveries and outflow of materials, observed from a satellite, are abnormal and consistent with the patterns observed during previous new product introductions. The data may get combined with other unstructured data to suggest steps that Google could take to capitalize on the information. Google may, for instance, send sales executives to visit Samsung and Motorola and discuss how their advertisements on Google should change to prepare for the introduction. The companies may speed up their own new product introductions or modifications. How will Apple feel about getting Goopled? Evolving communication technologies clearly have changed the role of observation in marketing research.

What Can Be Observed?

Exhibit 8.1 summarizes primary types of phenomena that can end up recorded in observational research. These phenomena range from the pathway that one takes walking from store to store to the number of visits to political websites. Some observed behaviors are rather obvious, like the time it takes to get checked out at Wendy's. Others, though, can be much more inconspicuous. For instances, photos posted online contain codes that often reveal when and where the photo was taken. Facebook then stores this data, which can be useful in predicting user behavior.

The exhibit provides the impression that observational methods can cover a wide range of phenomena. Researchers use data to study phenomena related to these behaviors for numerous reasons. Not the least of the advantages of observational data is the fact that it is behavior. Observational data itself typically records behavior with little error because observational techniques are often simple and more and more occur automatically. Observational data collected automatically avoids expenses required with more labor-intensive processes. A Skybox satellite may seem expensive to a small company, but for Google, it's a few million dollars that provides technology to take high-resolution images of the Earth twice daily. Consequently, the price for any particular observation is miniscule. If the observational data are already stored, they also have all the advantages of secondary data.

However, observational research is not perfect. While often one's behavior is observed easily, the reason for the behavior cannot be observed. Valuable explanations as to why someone behaves as they do may lie in phenomena that researchers cannot observe directly. Thus, the inability to tap into these latent variables represents a limitation to observational research tools.[2] This issue leads to another disadvantage of observational research. Analytical models using this data often provide better predictive power than they do explanatory power. Pharmaceutical companies use huge databases of medical observations to predict things like the potential side effects of their products.

Perhaps you recall answering these questions about opinions and preferences for technological products. Take a look at the results from this section of the survey. In what ways does the survey try to employ behavioral observation, if at all? How might this information be useful to companies that sell small electronic appliances? Are there other places in the survey where behavioral observation has been or could be combined with this traditional survey approach?

www.qualtrics.com

EXHIBIT 8.1 Different Types of Observable Behaviors Tracked by Marketing Research

Observable Phenomenon	Illustration	Technologies Used to Observe
Physical Movements	The ways shoppers move through shopping centers and stores	Video, GPS and NFC
Verbal Behavior	Statements recorded at the Walmart complaint line, posted on blogs, social networks, or sites like TripAdvisor	Voice recordings and Internet archives
Expressive Behavior and Physiological Reactions	Facial expressions of consumers in a restaurant, the body language of consumers waiting for service, or the amount of sweat produced under stress	Human observations, video or tools like GSR
Spatial Tensions and Locations	How close shoppers stand to a service provider while getting advice about what clothes look good	Human observations or video
Temporal Patterns	How long patients in a doctor's office will wait before going to the counter to complain	Human observations or timing devices
Physical Objects	What brands of shoes, clothing, and skateboards teens at a skate park own and use	Human observation
Verbal and Pictorial Records	Photographs or videos of early childhood Christmas experiences including photos posted on Instagram, Facebook, or other social network sites	Data archiving techniques, human observation
Neurological Activities	Brain activity in response to a consumer experiencing joy or disgust while reading advertising copy	Facial recognition or devices like fMRI
Internet Activities	Websites viewed, time spent viewing, social networking habits—what do consumers *like*? Search engine histories—what are consumers looking for?	Cookies and other tags that identify devices
Geographical Information	Where is someone physically located at any given time?	GPS tools, IP addresses, cell tower IDs
Physical Distribution	Movement of raw materials and finished products across the globe	NFC, satellite observation

While these studies are economical, the companies often are disappointed with the conclusions derived from them as they often end up conflicting with explanations derived from studies using other research designs.[3] Initial observational research associated one osteoporosis drug with increased risk of cancer of the esophagus. However, clinical data accumulated over time failed to display such an effect. Another limitation is that the observation period often is short. Observing behavior patterns that occur over a period of several days or weeks generally is too costly or even impossible. Big data technologies may change this, however, as various aspects of a person's everyday behavior can be captured through their phone.

The Research Snapshot illustrates a way that consumers are tracked with observations.

All That Jazz!

It's amazing how much the things we like to consume say about ourselves. For instance, how much do we know about somebody if we know what they like to drink or what music they like to listen to? Probably a lot!!

Researchers gather observational data on our Web behavior based on the assumption that we browse the things we like. For instance, consider two consumers, one who "likes" Smoking Loon and 2-Buck Chuck on Facebook and the other who "likes" Robert Mondavi and Sterling wines. The first two being edgy wine brands while the last two represent traditional California wine. Going further, the research can match these to political preferences evidence through online behavior in an effort to know how people vote. The study shows that the first wine lover leans heavily left in his or her politics while the latter leans heavily right.

Like music? In much the same way, Pandora is leveraging observational data suggesting a relationship between music preference and politics to sell advertising to political campaigns. Consider two consumers, one who creates a Bob Marley station with a touch of Daft Punk on Pandora and the other who creates a Yanni station with a touch of Frank Sinatra. How will these consumers vote? Probably no surprise but the Marley listener is going to vote democratic while the Yanni listener leans right. Knowing a consumer's preferences provides powerful information because knowing a few preferences allows one to predict many others.

Sources: Wilson, R. (2013), "What Your Favorite Drink Says about Your Politics, in One Chart," *Washington Post*, (12/31), http://www.washingtonpost.com/blogs/govbeat/wp/2013/12/31/what-your-favorite-drinksays-about-your-politics-in-one-chart/, accessed February 22. Dwoskin, E. (2014), "Pandora Ads Tie Music to Politics," *Wall Street Journal*, February 14, B1–B2.

Keith Beaty/Getty Images

The Nature of Observation Studies

Marketing researchers can observe people, objects, events, or other phenomena using either human observers or machines designed for specific observation tasks. Human observation best suits a situation or behavior that is not easily predictable in advance of the research. In this sense, observational research fits best with a discovering orientation. Researchers employ a wide range of mechanical and electronic tools to capture consumer behavior. Mechanical observation, as performed by supermarket scanners or traffic counters, can very accurately record situations or types of behavior that are routine, repetitive, or programmatic. Cookies stored on computers record online browsing histories. Sophisticated machines that assess biological reactions such as a lie detector or neurological activities also make mechanical observations.

Human or mechanical observation is often **unobtrusive**, meaning no communication with a respondent takes place. For example, rather than asking customers how much time they spend shopping in the store, a supermarket manager might observe and record the time when a shopper enters and leaves the store. The unobtrusive nature of observational data collection often generates data without a subject's knowledge. A situation in which an observer's presence, or the mechanical device doing the recording, is easily known to the subject involves **visible observation**. A situation in which a subject is unaware that any observation is taking place is **hidden observation**. Hidden, unobtrusive observation minimizes respondent error. When respondents are unobtrusively recorded in a public area, an agreement to participate in research is not generally required. In such a situation, the respondent is in a public space and each person's identify is almost always unknown. On the other hand, a consumer who agrees to wash his or her hair in front of a video camera is visibly observed and should have provided formal consent to be involved in the research.

The data are recorded when and as the actual event takes place. Thus, they are free from nuisances like social desirability bias or memory problems.

Unobtrusive

No communication with the person being observed is necessary so that he or she is unaware that he or she is an object of research.

Visible observation

Observation in which the observer's presence or mechanical measurement device is obviously known to the subject.

Hidden observation

Observation in which the subject is unaware that observation is taking place.

Observation of Human Behavior

Whereas surveys emphasize verbal responses, observation studies emphasize and allow for the systematic recording of nonverbal behavior. Toy manufacturers such as Fisher Price use the observation technique because children often cannot express their reactions to products. By observing children at play with a proposed toy, doll, or game, marketing researchers may be able to identify the elements of a potentially successful product. Toy marketing researchers might observe play to answer the following questions:

■ How long does the child's attention stay with the product?
■ Does the child put the toy down after 2 minutes or 20 minutes?
■ Are the child's peers equally interested in the toy?

Behavioral scientists have recognized that nonverbal behavior can be a communication process by which individuals exchange meanings. Head nods, smiles, raised eyebrows, winks, and other facial expressions or body movements serve as communication symbols. Observation of nonverbal communication may hold considerable promise for the marketing researcher. For example, a hypothesis about customer-salesperson interactions is that the salesperson would signal status based on the importance of each transaction. In low-importance transactions, in which potential customers are plentiful and easily replaced (say, a shoe store), the salesperson may show definite nonverbal signs of higher status than the customer. When customers are scarce, as in big-ticket purchase situations (real estate sales), the opposite should be true, with the salesperson showing many nonverbal indicators of deference. One way to test this hypothesis would be with an observation study using the nonverbal communication measures shown in Exhibit 8.2. Each row in the table indicates an aspect of nonverbal communication that one might observe in a common market situation.

Of course, researchers would not ignore verbal behavior. In fact, in certain observation studies, verbal expression is very important.

EXHIBIT **8.2** Observing and Interpreting Nonverbal Communication

Behavior		Description	Example
Facial Expressions		Expressions of emotion such as surprise (eyes wide open, mouth rounded and slightly open, brow furrowed)	A consumer reacts to the price quoted by a salesperson.
Body Language		Posture, placement of arms and legs	A consumer crosses arms as salesperson speaks, possibly indicating a lack of trust.
Eye Activity		Eye contact, staring, looking away, dilated pupils. In U.S. culture, not making eye contact is indicative of a deteriorating relationship. Dilated pupils can indicate emotion or degree of honesty.	A consumer avoids making eye contact with a salesperson knowing that he or she will not make a purchase.
Personal Space		Physical distance between individuals; in the United States, people like to be about eight feet apart to have a discussion.	A consumer may back away from a salesperson who is viewed to be violating one's personal space.
Gestures		Responses to certain events with specific body reactions or gestures	A consumer who wins something (maybe at the casino or a sports contest) lifts arms, stands tall, and sticks out chest.
Manners		Accepted protocol for given situations	A salesperson may shake a customer's hand, but should not touch a customer otherwise.

Direct and Contrived Observation

Researchers need always to take care of how much they interject themselves into a data collection situation. In a phenomenological approach, the researcher is often very much within the research situation. Consider the case where researchers ask restaurant employees to talk about working in a restaurant and how much emphasis restaurant management places on hygiene and customer safety. The researcher has to ask questions and may even provide some prop or stimulus to help get the respondent started. On the other hand, hidden cameras placed within the restaurants could record behavior and provide data without the need for a researcher's presence. Alternatively, an ethnographer may actually take a job in the restaurant and perform certain acts to see how other employees react. This brings us to the difference between direct and contrived observation.

Direct Observation

Direct observation can produce detailed records of what people actually do during an event. The observer plays a passive role, making no attempt to control or manipulate a situation, instead merely recording what occurs. He or she must make every effort not to interject him- or herself into the situation. For example, recording traffic counts and traffic flows within a supermarket can help managers design store layouts that maximize a typical customer's exposure to the merchandise offered while also facilitating search efforts. This data gathered through observation often are more accurate than what one would get by asking consumers about their movement through a store. A manufacturer can then better determine shelf locations, sales displays, the arrangement of departments and merchandise within those departments, the location of checkout facilities, and other characteristics that improve the shopping value consumers obtain from visiting a store.

For instance, if directly questioned in a survey, most shoppers would inaccurately portray the time they spent in each department. Likewise, many respondents would likely overstate the amount of effort they put into washing hands when directly questioned by a researcher. With the direct observation method, the data consist of records of events made as they occur. An observation form often helps keep researchers' observations consistent and ensures that they record all relevant information. A respondent is not required to recall—perhaps inaccurately—an event after it has occurred; instead, the observation is instantaneous. Direct observation such as described in the Research Snapshot dealing with hygiene may greatly reduce problems with perceptual distortion that lead to response error.

Direct observation

A straightforward attempt to observe and record what naturally occurs; the investigator does not create an artificial situation.

Why Use Direct Observation?

In many cases, direct observation is the most straightforward form of data collection—or the only form possible. A produce manager for Auchan (a France-based hypermart firm) may periodically gather competitive price information from Carrefour (also a France-based hypermart firm) stores within competing areas. Both Carrefour and Auchan can monitor each other's promotions by observing advertisements posted on the competitor's website (see **http://www.auchan.fr** and **http://www.carrefour.fr**), for example. In other situations, observation is the most economical technique. In a common type of observation study, a shopping center manager may observe the license plate (tag) numbers on cars in its parking lot. These data, along with automobile registration information, provide an inexpensive means of determining where customers live.

Researchers sometimes can obtain certain data more quickly or easily using direct observation than by other methods. If a research question involves what demographic characteristics are associated with spending time in a food court, a researcher can simply observe the gender, race, and other visible respondent characteristics rather than employing a survey. Researchers investigating a diet product may use observation when selecting respondents in a shopping mall. Overweight people may be prescreened by observing pedestrians, thus eliminating a number of screening interviews. Direct observation's advantages often make it the simplest, quickest, and most accurate way to gather data. On the other hand, direct observation has limited flexibility because not all phenomena are observable.

Errors Associated with Direct Observation

Although direct observation involves no interaction with the subject, the method is not error-free. When human observers record behaviors, the observer may record events subjectively. The same visual cues that may influence the interplay between interviewer and respondent (e.g., the subject's age or sex) may come into play in some direct observation settings, such as when the observer subjectively attributes a particular economic status or educational background to someone. A middle-aged person in a business suit will prime someone of high social class and the observer will frame expectations around that stereotype. We refer to a distortion of measurement resulting from the cognitive behavior or actions of the witnessing observer as **observer bias**. In a research project using observers to evaluate whether a retailer's salesclerks are rude or courteous, field-workers rely on their own interpretations of people or situations during the observation process. In these instances, nuisance situational factors such as the observer's own mood may bias their interpretations of others.

Also, accuracy may suffer if the observer does not record every detail that describes the persons, objects, and events in a given situation. Generally, the observer should record as much detail as possible. However, the pace of events, the observer's memory, the observer's writing speed, and other factors will limit the amount of detail that can be recorded.

Interpretation of observation data is another potential source of error. Facial expressions and other nonverbal communication may have several meanings. Does a smile always mean happiness? Does the fact that someone is standing or seated next to the president of a company necessarily indicate the person's status? Error creeps in the more pure observation moves into subjective judgment.

Observer bias

A distortion of measurement resulting from the cognitive behavior or actions of a witnessing observer.

To the Point

"What we see depends mainly on what we look for."

—SIR JOHN LUBBOCK

Contrived Observation

Most observation takes place in a natural setting, but sometimes the investigator intervenes to create an artificial environment to test a hypothesis. This approach is called **contrived observation**. Contrived observation can increase the frequency of occurrence of certain behavior patterns, such as employee responses to complaints. An airline passenger complaining about a meal or service from the flight attendant may actually be a researcher recording the attendant's reactions. If situations were not contrived, the research time spent waiting and observing would expand considerably. A number of retailers use observers called *mystery shoppers* to visit a store and pretend to be interested in a particular product or service. After leaving the store, the "shopper" evaluates the salesperson's performance.

The Research Snapshot on the next page discusses direct observation of hand washing in public restrooms. Similarly, a study compared results from self-reported questionnaire data, focus group data, and observational data concerning hygiene among restaurant employees. The questionnaire responses suggested that 95 percent of employees washed their hands thoroughly after handling raw chicken, but that number averaged about 82 percent in the face-to-face interview condition, and when observation provides the data, 75 percent of the restaurant employees did not wash their hands adequately after handling raw chicken.[4] This direct observation could be turned into a contrived situation if a participant observer, pretending to be a new employee, asked another employee to assist by in some way handling raw chicken, and then observed the other employee's behavior. In the latter case, the researcher has interjected him- or herself into a situation, but perhaps for a very good reason. This may allow a hypothesis stating that interruptions will be associated with less hand washing compared to a no interruption condition.

Contrived observation

Observation in which the investigator creates an artificial environment in order to test a hypothesis.

What We Say and What We Do

Michael Haegele / Bridge / Corbis

Most people know that hand washing is a fundamental way to stay healthy, not to mention simple good manners. So, when you ask them, most people say they faithfully wash their hands. But according to observational research, what people say about this behavior is not what they necessarily do.

Survey results based on a broad sample of American adults indicate that 96 percent of respondents say that "they always wash" their hands after using a public restroom. Do you think survey results on this topic may be subject to any response error? Many other studies examine hand washing using observational research designs. Typically, these studies employ research assistants who observe others' behavior in public restrooms while pretending to be just another public restroom user. Across dozens of studies of this type, results suggest that only 19 percent of people worldwide properly wash their hands with soap and water after using the bathroom. Researchers employed this observational research approach in a large-scale study of public restroom usage in a U.S. college town. Results from that study show that 78 percent of female users washed their hands with soap and water following use of the toilet while only 50 percent of male users did the same. Several factors influenced these percentages, including the presence of a sign stating the importance of hand washing in disease prevention. The sign increased hand washing among females but not males. Time of day also influences results with hand-washing frequency falling as the day wears on. People who use their cell phone while in the toilet become less likely to wash hands. What do you make of the difference between survey and observational results? Realize too that with this method, no user was ever alone in the restroom. Might this influence results?

In the United States alone, nearly 50,000,000 people seek health care at clinics or emergency rooms each year because of food-borne illnesses. Estimates suggest that this number could be nearly cut in half if people just washed their hands after using the bathroom or otherwise coming into tactile contact with fecal matter, urine, mucus or other germ and bacterial carrier. Thus, hand washing is a legitimate cause of hand wringing among decision-makers in food and health-related industries.

Source: Freeman, M. C., Stocks, M. E., Cumming, O., Jeandron, A., Higgins, J. T., Wolf, J., & Curtis, V. (2014), "Systematic Review: Hygiene and Health: Systematic Review of Hand Washing Practices Worldwide and Update of Health Effects," *Tropical Medicine & International Health*, 19(8), 906–916. Borchgrevink, C. P., JaeMin, C., & SeungHyun, K. (2013). Hand Washing Practices in a College Town Environment. *Journal of Environmental Health*, 75(8), 18–24.

Complementary Evidence

Observational study results may amplify the results of other forms of research by providing *complementary evidence* concerning individuals' "true" feelings. Researchers typically conduct focus group interviews behind two-way mirrors from which marketing executives observe as well as listen to what is occurring. This additional data source allows for interpretation of nonverbal behavior such as facial expressions or head nods to supplement information from interviews.

For example, in one focus group session concerning how women use hand lotion, researchers observed that all the women's hands were above the table while they were casually waiting for the session to begin. Seconds after the women were told that the topic was to be hand lotion, all their hands were placed out of sight. This observation, along with the group discussion, revealed the women's anger, guilt, and shame about the condition of their hands. Although they felt that people expected them to have soft, pretty hands, their household tasks include washing dishes, cleaning floors, and doing other chores, are hard on the hands.

Other research studies combine visible observation with personal interviews. During or after in-depth observations, researchers ask individuals to explain their actions.[5] Direct observation of women applying hand and body lotion identified two kinds of users. Some women slapped on the lotion, rubbing it briskly into their skin. Others caressed their skin as they applied the lotion. When the interviewer asked about their behavior, the researchers were able to interpret this finding.

Women who slapped the lotion on were using the lotion as a remedy for dry skin. Those who caressed their skin were more interested in making their skin smell nice and feel soft.

Researchers also may follow up observations of customers in a shopping center with survey research. For example, if customers are observed looking into the window of a store for more than 30 seconds but then moving on without going in, researchers may intercept them with a few questions potentially revealing reasons for this behavior.

Recording the decision time necessary to make a choice is a relatively simple, unobtrusive task easily accomplished through direct observation; it is also an example of complementary evidence. Survey responses combined with information on how long the respondent took to make a choice reveal more than either type of data alone. Recorded choice time is a measure of **response latency**. This measure is based on the hypothesis that the longer a decision-maker takes, the more difficult that decision was and the more thought the respondent put into the choice. A quick decision presumably indicates an easy or obvious choice. Computer-administered surveys can incorporate an automatic measure of response latency. The ability to combine behavioral observations with survey responses is a big advantage of Web-based surveys over paper-and-pencil approaches. Imagine how cumbersome a survey would become if respondents had to manually time themselves and enter the number of seconds it took to make responses.

Response latency

The amount of time it takes to make a choice between two alternatives; used as a measure of the strength of preference.

Ethical Issues in the Observation of Humans

Observational researchers' tools are sometimes akin to snooping or spying.[6] Observation methods introduce a number of ethical issues, many raising the issue of the respondent's right to privacy. Suppose a research firm approaches a company interested in acquiring information about how women put on their bras by observing behavior in a spa dressing area. The researcher considers approaching spas in several key cities about placing small cameras inconspicuously to observe women getting dressed. Obviously, such a situation raises an ethical question. Even if the dressing room is an area where women often do dress where others can observe them, women do not expect to have their dressing behavior recorded and viewed. Therefore, unless the researcher can find a way to have women consent to such observation, this observational approach is unethical.

If the researcher obtains permission to observe someone, the subject may not act naturally. So, at times there is a strong temptation to observe without obtaining consent or gaining input from an Institutional Review Board (IRB). Many times, such as monitoring people walking through and waiting in an airport, obtaining consent from individual respondents is impractical if not impossible. Further, asking for consent just before the actual observation will likely change the behavior.

Source: © Cengage Learning 2013.

EXHIBIT **8.3**

Is the Observation Ethical?

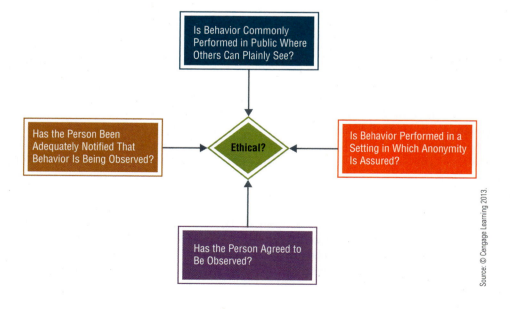

New technologies afford opportunities to observe behaviors of interest to marketing managers. Deep-packet inspection refers to the ability of an Internet service provider to read data transmitted by users. The observation of this data might clue researchers in on how consumers search for marketing information. Observers may also snoop on Facebook and other social networking sites and both observe and provoke online comments all motivated by the need to discover information about consumers.

So, when should researchers feel comfortable collecting observational data? Although exceptions exist to every rule, here are four questions that can help address this question (depicted in Exhibit 8.3):

1. Is the behavior being observed commonly performed in public where it is expected that others can observe the behavior?
2. Is the behavior performed in a setting in which the anonymity of the person being observed is assured (meaning there is no practical way to identify individuals)?
3. Has the person agreed to be observed?
4. Has the person been adequately notified that their behavior (including data transfers) is being observed?

If the answer to the first two questions is "yes," then there is not likely a violation of privacy in collecting observational research data. If the answer to the third and/or fourth question is "yes," then gathering the data also is likely ethical. Otherwise, the researcher should carefully consider input from an IRB or other authority before proceeding with the research.

Also, some might see contrived observation as unethical based on the notion of entrapment. To *entrap* means to deceive or trick into difficulty, which clearly is an abusive action. For instance, in the hand-washing example given, when the experimenter interrupts the real employee, he/she may entrap the employee into a lower probability of washing hands thoroughly. In this instance, if the employee was harmed or caused harm to others (by getting in trouble with a superior or making someone ill) then clearly the intrusion is unethical. However, if no possibility of harm exists, then the researcher can likely proceed although this particular instance should be done under the auspices of an IRB.

Given that the Internet is not just a source that provides information but also a source of recorded information, many have concerns that any information (whether true or not) has potential to harm someone's reputation. A prank photo of a graduate student for example could surface in a background check and harm the student's chance at getting a job. These concerns underlie "Right to Be Forgotten" movements that include legislative efforts.[7] The initiatives are growing quickly in Europe following an EU court ruling supporting "a right to be forgotten." The ruling requires search providers like Google to respond to individuals' requests to remove information from search results. As a result, Google is hiring a staff to review individually the thousands and thousands of requests. However, Google thus far is reticent to remove information appearing in published sources. Given the complexity of dealing with Google on these matters, an industry of companies who assist individuals in these efforts has spawned with France's Reputation VIP leading the way.

● ● ● ● ● ● ●

Even if fashion companies could learn a lot about the types of problems consumers typically have when purchasing and wearing clothes, would observation through two-way mirrors (a mirror that reflects on one side but can be seen through from the other) be appropriate?

© iStockphoto.com/pkline

Observation of Physical Objects

Physical phenomena may be the subject of observation study. Physical-trace evidence is a visible mark of some past event or occurrence. For example, the wear on library books indirectly indicates how many people actually handle and/or check out books and, therefore, wear represents a proxy for popularity based on the assumption that more wear means more readers. A classic

Artifacts

The things that people made and consumed within a culture that signal something meaningful about the behavior taking place at the time of consumption.

example of physical-trace evidence in a nonprofit setting was erosion on the floor tiles around the hatching-chick exhibit at Chicago's Museum of Science and Industry. These tiles were replaced every six weeks; tiles in other parts of the museum did not need to be replaced for years. The selective erosion of tiles, indexed by the replacement rate, was a measure of the relative popularity of exhibits.

Artifacts

Clearly, a creative marketing researcher has many options for determining the solution to a problem. The story about Charles Coolidge Parlin, generally recognized as one of the founders of commercial marketing research, examining garbage cans at the turn of the twentieth century illustrates another study of physical traces. Physical traces often involve artifacts. **Artifacts** are things that people made and consumed within a culture that signal something meaningful about the behavior taking place at the time of consumption. Ethnographers are particularly interested in examining artifacts, and Parlin's garbage can escapades illustrate how a marketing researcher can apply an ethnographic approach involving observation of artifacts.

Parlin designed an observation study to persuade Campbell's Soup Company to advertise in the *Saturday Evening Post*. Campbell's was reluctant to advertise because it believed that the *Post* was read primarily by working people who would prefer to make soup from scratch, peeling the potatoes and scraping the carrots, rather than paying ten cents for a can of soup. To demonstrate that rich people weren't the target market, Parlin selected a sample of Philadelphia garbage routes. Garbage from each specific area of the city that was selected was dumped on the floor of a local National Guard Armory. Parlin had the number of Campbell's soup cans in each pile counted. The results indicated that the garbage from the rich people's homes didn't contain many cans of Campbell's soup. Although they may not have made soup from scratch themselves, their housekeepers may have. The garbage piles from the blue-collar area showed a larger number of Campbell's soup cans. This observation study was enough evidence for Campbell's. They advertised in the *Saturday Evening Post*.[8]

A scientific project conducted at the University of Arizona adopted this research approach in which aspiring archaeologists sifted through garbage for over thirty years. They examine soggy cigarette butts, empty milk cartons, and half-eaten Big Macs in an effort to understand modern life. Like other research involving observation, we can compare the observed garbage data with the results of surveys about food consumption. Garbage does not lie. This type of observation can correct for potential overreporting of healthful item consumption and underreporting consumption of, say, cigarettes or fast food.

Picking through the garbage on the side of the road can reveal behaviors of fast-food customers.

FRANK PERRY/AFP/Getty Images

Inventories

Another application of observing physical objects is to count and record physical inventories through retail or wholesale audits. This method allows researchers to investigate brand sales on regional and national levels, market shares, seasonal purchasing patterns, and so on. Marketing research suppliers offer audit data at both the retail and the wholesale levels.

An observer can record physical-trace data to discover information a respondent could not recall accurately. For example, measuring the number of ounces of liquid bleach used during a test provides precise physical-trace evidence without relying on the respondent's memory. The accuracy of respondents' memories is not a problem for the firm that conducts a pantry audit. The pantry audit requires an inventory of the brands, quantities, and package sizes in a consumer's home rather than responses from individuals. The problem of untruthfulness or some other form of response bias is avoided. For example, the pantry audit prevents the possible problem of respondents erroneously claiming to have purchased prestige brands. However, gaining permission to physically check consumers' pantries is not easy, and the fieldwork is expensive. In addition, the brand in the pantry may not reflect the brand purchased most often if consumers substituted it because they had a coupon, the usual brand was out of stock, or another reason.

Researchers studying hand washing employed an interesting observational approach involving inventories. They decided to measure hand washing by electronically monitoring the soap remaining in the restroom dispenser following each use.[9] In other words, the soap use unobtrusively assessed whether a user washed his or hands or not if one presumes that soap-use equates to hand washing (as hygiene experts presume). The study also explored the use of signs by displaying either a disgusting message or an informational message near the soap dispenser. Results show that:

1. just over 30 percent of men and 65 percent of women washed their hands,
2. that men were more likely to wash after exposure to a disgusting message,
3. while women were more likely to wash when exposed to the informational message.

Thus, the soap inventory served as an observational measurement tool.

Content Analysis

Besides observing people and physical objects, researchers sometimes use **content analysis**, which obtains data by observing and analyzing the contents or messages of advertisements, newspaper articles, television programs, letters, Web pages, blogs, Facebook photos, tweets, and the like. This method involves systematic analysis as well as observation to identify the specific information content and other characteristics of the messages. Content analysis studies the message itself and involves the design of a systematic observation and recording procedure for quantitative description of the manifest content of communication. This technique measures the extent of emphasis or omission of a given analytical category. For example, content analysis of advertisements might evaluate their use of words, themes, characters, or space and time relationships. Content analysis often counts the frequency of themes or occurrences within a given hermeneutic unit. For instance, the frequency with which women, African Americans, Hispanics, or Asians appear in advertising displayed on a television program represents a topic amenable to content analysis.

Content analysis might be used to investigate questions such as whether some marketers use certain themes, appeals, claims, or even deceptive practices more than others or whether recent consumer-oriented actions by the Federal Trade Commission have influenced the contents of advertising. For instance, content analysis of tweets from large companies aimed at consumers described the way companies seem to be using Twitter. The findings suggest that companies use tweets to share hyperlinks to other sites and hashtags more than they do to share photo or video content.[10] Content analysis also can explore the information content of television commercials directed at children, the company images portrayed in ads, and numerous other aspects of advertising.

Study of the content of communications sometimes involves more than simply counting the items. Researchers sometimes perform content analysis of YouTube content in an effort in understanding what types of videos might influence consumer behavior. For instance, a content analysis

Content analysis

The systematic observation and quantitative description of the manifest content of communication.

employed judges who watched sample retail advertisements placed on YouTube by companies and then judged the ads based on whether they were more emotional or informational in nature. Ideally, multiple judges (at least two or three coders) perform the coding task, allowing for an assessment of rater reliability or how replicable are the results. In this study, the retail ads that were deemed more effective tended to be judged as informational more than emotional.[11]

Mechanical Observation

In many situations, the primary—and sometimes the only—means of observation is mechanical rather than human. Video cameras, traffic counters, and other machines help observe and record behavior. Some unusual observation studies have used motion-picture cameras and time-lapse photography. An early application of this observation technique photographed train passengers and determined their levels of comfort by observing how they sat and moved in their seats. Another time-lapse study filmed traffic flows in an urban square and resulted in a redesign of the streets. Similar techniques may help managers design store layouts and resolve problems in moving people or objects through spaces over time. The soap inventory study of hand washing also illustrates a mechanical observation application.

Television, Radio, and Digital Monitoring

Television monitoring

Computerized mechanical observation used to obtain television ratings. Nielsen's People Meter technology best illustrates television (or more broadly, media) monitoring.

Portable People Meter 360 (PPM 360)

Device that looks and functions much like a small cell phone but automatically detects broadcast signals, satellite radio and tv transmissions, and most other digital signals.

Perhaps the best-known marketing research project involving mechanical observation and computerized data collection is Nielsen's **television monitoring** system for estimating national television audiences. Nielsen Media Research uses a consumer panel and a monitoring device called a People Meter to obtain ratings for television programs nationwide.[12] We introduced this device in Chapter 3 to illustrate observation-based research. A company called Arbitron pioneered the technology and Nielsen acquired Arbitron in 2014. The Nielsen People Meter gathers data on what program is on a television and who is watching it at the time. The electronic devices capture information on program choices and the length of viewing time. This observational data is supplemented with consumer diaries that together provide valuable input on ratings, which helps price advertising time by program and lets advertisers know what programs reach the targeted audience.

Critics of the People Meter argue that subjects in Nielsen's panel grow bored over time and don't always record when they begin or stop watching television. More recently, innovations answer this objection with a new measuring system called the **Portable People Meter 360 (PPM 360).**[13]

● ● ● ● ● ●

Traffic cameras that monitor speeding on major highways are becoming commonplace in Europe, Australia, and even in some parts of the United States. Would car companies learn anything from the observed behavior?

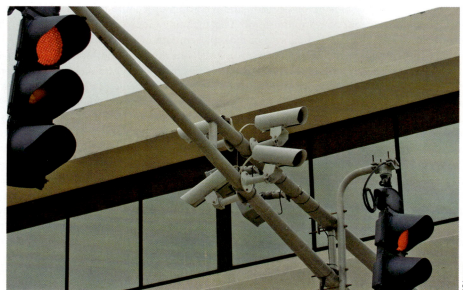

AP Images

PPM 360 is a device that looks and functions much like a small cell phone. The panel participant carries this with them and it automatically detects broadcast signals, satellite radio and television transmissions, and most other types of digital signals. Thus, the ratings are not based only on panel members interacting with traditional media like home-based television sets or AM/FM radios. Participants receive points that lead to modest compensation amounts whenever they turn the PPM360 on. Arbitron's meter simplifies the participants' role and collects data on exposure to radio and television programming outside the home.

Other devices monitor advertising on all types of digital media. For instance, Pretesting Group's PeopleReader™ unobtrusively measures the time a user spends on viewing printed advertising pages or pages displayed on a computer or other smart device such as a tablet. The company argues that they can assess consumer stopping power with the device or the degree to which an advertisement engages consumers and shifts their attention to the ad and away from the focal media.

Monitoring Web Traffic

Computer technology makes gathering detailed data about online behavior easy and inexpensive. The greater challenges are to identify which measures are meaningful and to interpret the data correctly. For instance, most organizations record the level of activity at their websites. They may count the number of *hits*—mouse clicks on a single page of a website. If the visitor clicks on many links, that page receives multiple hits. Similarly, they can track *page views,* or single, discrete clicks to load individual pages of a website. Page views more conservatively indicate how many users visit each individual page on the website and may also be used to track the path or sequence of pages that each visitor follows. Web traffic monitoring also allows a company to know how a potential customer came to their site and where they went afterward. Did someone make a reservation at Sofitel.com after visiting bing.com? This question can be answered. We also can monitor what type of device a consumer viewed a Web page on and where that device was located at the time of the viewing. Additionally, companies can track comments about their brands left on blogs and social networking sites. Thus, all the billions of clicks made on the Internet each day leave behind a trail that indicates our behavior.

Web Traffic and Buzz

Marketers need to know if advertising is effective. For most advertising, that means it must be viewed. For companies placing ads online and on social media sites, knowing how many people even may have seen the ad becomes an important statistic. A **click-through rate (CTR)** for these ads can be computed in the same way as in assessing survey response rates to obtain the percentage of people exposed to a Web-based advertisement who actually click on the corresponding hyperlink which takes them to the company's website. If 10,000 people view a page and 100 click on the ad, the click through rate is 1 percent.

Click-through rate (CTR)
Proportion of people who are exposed to a hyperlinked Internet ad who actually click on its hyperlink to enter the website.

Counting hits or page views can suggest the amount of interest or attention a website is receiving, but these measures are flawed. First, hits do not differentiate between a lot of activity by a few visitors and a little activity by many visitors. In addition, the researcher lacks information about the meaning behind the numbers. If a user clicks on a site many times, is the person finding a lot of useful or enjoyable material, or is the user trying unsuccessfully to find something by looking in several places? Additionally, some hits are likely made by mistake. The consumers may have had no intention of clicking through the ad or may not have known what they were doing when they clicked on the ad.

A more specific count is the number of *unique visitors* to a website. This measurement counts the initial access to the site but not multiple hits on the site by the same visitor during the same day or week. Operators of websites can collect the data by attaching small files, called *cookies*, to the computers of visitors to their sites and then tracking those cookies to see whether the same visitors return. Google, Facebook, and Apple rely heavily on research specialists who use analytical tools to gather data from consumers' cookies and other computer residuals to help forecast who may buy what and when. Two such companies, DataLogix and Acxiom, are pioneers in using smartphone and computer information from individual users to predict not only Web sales but also in-store sales.[14] Google and Facebook dominate online advertising and hope to grow this revenue stream even more by linking ad spends with them to consumer spending in the store. Facebook claims that retail store Bud Light sales increased 3.3 percent solely in response to Anheuser-Busch's Facebook advertising.

While the technology behind such tracking is complex and proprietary, you can get a sense for how this works each time you visit a website surrounded by banner ads for a retail site and even for a specific product that you recently viewed online. The technology allows consumers' personal data (including e-mail addresses, names) and data extracted from cookies and smart devices to be linked with in-store purchase histories. Personal identities are replaced with a numbering system in a process called hashing that purports to protect individuals' personal identities.

Research companies provide their clients with assessments of more than website effectiveness as the resulting data includes assessments of advertising effectiveness and social media buzz. Imagine how a company like Paramount might be interested in whether or not news about new products stirs up any activity online. **Conversation volume** represents a measure of the amount of Internet postings that involve a specific name or term. That name or term could be a brand name, a destination name, or the name of an event. Motion picture producers rely heavily on conversation volume to assess the success of motion pictures. The Oscar nominated movie "Gravity" saw heavy conversation volume before release that analysts coded mostly negative.[15] However, after release, the conversation volume increased in quantity and in tone. The buzz turned from mostly negative to mostly positive. Similarly, analysts monitor Twitter for positive or negative tweets. Researchers consider this observational data because they do not perform an interview of any type for its acquisition.

Extrapolating product success purely based on Web traffic or even online conversation volume can produce inaccurate projections. Mere counts of brand-name usage do not reveal whether the usages are in a positive or negative light. In addition, many brand names can be confounded by other meanings.[16] Just imagine all the reasons why someone may search or use the word "kiss." Further, consumers employ differing levels of computer security systems limiting researchers' access to information. Difficulties such as these strongly point toward the need for observational data from the Internet to be professionally analyzed before relying on it for important decisions.

Numerous websites provide basic Web traffic statistics. Some sites provide services for free and others for a fee. Alexa.com allows users to compare traffic among competing websites and get basic demographic information about the consumers who frequent those sites. Exhibit 8.4 illustrates how one can use these sites to better understand Web traffic. Other Web traffic statistics providers include statcounter.com, click.com, and Google Analytics, among others.

Conversation volume

A measure of the amount of Internet postings that involve a specific name or term.

Kiss has many meanings.

Kristoffer Tripplaar / Alamy

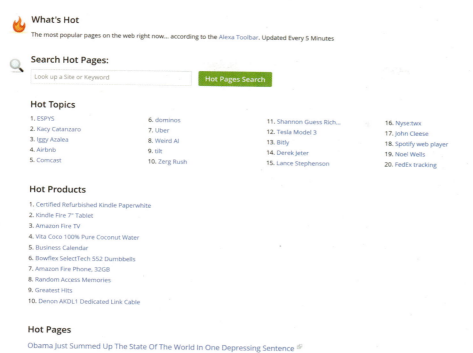

Source: www.alexa.com

Alexa.com makes information about the most popular web sites and product interest available based on actual web traffic.

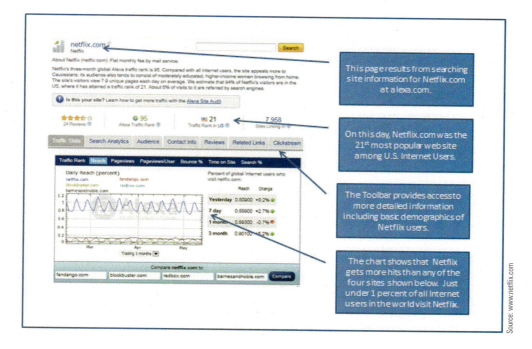

Source: www.netflix.com

EXHIBIT **8.4**
Using Web Stat Providers

CTR and Online Advertising

As online advertising has become more widespread, marketing research has refined methods for measuring the effectiveness of the advertisements. Applying the CTR to the amount spent on the advertisement gives the advertiser a *cost per click*. This presents a practical way to evaluate advertising effectiveness. However, marketers rarely see getting consumers to click on an ad as its primary objective. Companies more often expect advertising to help them meet sales goals.

Google has benefited from CTR research indicating that the highest CTRs tend to occur on pages displaying search results. Not surprisingly, someone who searches for the term *kayaks* is more likely to be interested in an advertisement offering a good deal on kayaks. The company showed Vanguard, for example, that banner ads cost the financial firm less than fifty cents per click and generated a 14 percent CTR. That CTR is far above typical response rates for direct-mail advertising, but it does not indicate whether online clicks are as valuable in terms of sales.[17] If the company makes more than fifty cents per customer clicking through, the ads are an effective sales tool.

Scanner-Based Research

Lasers performing optical character recognition and bar code technology like the universal product code (UPC) and RFID tags have accelerated the use of mechanical observation in marketing research. A number of syndicated services offer secondary data about product category movement generated from retail stores using scanner technology.

This technology allows researchers to investigate questions that are demographically or promotionally specific. Scanner research has investigated the different ways consumers respond to price promotions and the effects of those differences on a promotion's profitability. One of the primary means of implementing this type of research is through the establishment of a **scanner-based consumer panel** to replace consumer purchase diaries. In a typical scanner panel, each household carries a shopper card, which members present at checkout. A scan of the card allows recording of a household's purchase information as data.

Scanner-based consumer panel

A type of consumer panel in which participants' purchasing habits are recorded with a laser scanner rather than a purchase diary.

Aggregate data, such as actual store sales as measured by scanners, are available to clients and industry groups. For instance, data from Information Resources Inc. (IRI) have indicated a downward trend in sales of hair-coloring products. Demographic data suggest that an important reason is the aging of the population; many consumers who dye their hair reach an age at which they no longer wish to cover their gray hair. A smaller segment of the population is at an age where consumers typically begin using hair coloring.[18]

Data from scanner research parallel data provided by a standard mail diary panel, with some important improvements:

1. The data measure observed (actual) purchase behavior rather than reported behavior (recorded later in a diary).
2. Substituting mechanical for human record-keeping improves accuracy.
3. Measures are unobtrusive, eliminating interviewing and the possibility of social desirability or other bias on the part of respondents.
4. More extensive purchase data can be collected, because all UPC categories are measured. In a mail diary, respondents could not possibly reliably record all items they purchased.
5. The data collected from computerized checkout scanners can be combined with data about advertising, price changes, displays, and special sales promotions. Researchers can scrutinize them with powerful analytical software provided by the scanner data providers.

Scanner data is a mechanical observation form that requires no input from customers. From time to time, media express concerns about the accuracy of scanner pricing data. In an exhaustive study of scanner data from a single western state, researchers determined that overall scanner error is less than 5 percent, that undercharges were more common than overcharges, and that those errors often resulted from temporary price changes associated with short-term price promotions.[19] The key to this type of research was the sales data recorded by scanners.

Camera Surveillance

Modern society increasingly relies on cameras to keep tabs on all sorts of behaviors Camera surveillance is practically everywhere in New York city including almost every private apartment building.[20] Cameras watch the entry doors and hallways as well as all other public spaces.

Apartment managers say that the decrease in dealing with criminal incidences and lower insurance rates more than makes up for the modest cost of camera surveillance systems. In particular, they note the decrease in illicit drug sales that used to occur commonly just out the front door of many apartment buildings.

Likewise, cameras planted inconspicuously in shopping centers, stores, and downtown streets can be useful in marketing research. Shopping center security video can help identify problems with merchandising and the types of things that attract consumers to come into and remain in an environment. This is only the tip of the iceberg as cameras have many more applications than these.

Researchers sometimes ask and get permission to place cameras inconspicuously in consumers' homes, offices, or even cars.[21] Microsoft commissioned research involving the observation of 50 homes via inconspicuous, in-home cameras. The research addressed problems encountered by consumers when using Windows products in their homes. Microsoft was able to study the consumer behavior involved and try to find a way to reduce the problems identified. Other companies, including Kimberly-Clark, Sony, and Old Spice, have also successfully applied observational research using cameras. The Old Spice research involved videos of guys taking showers in their homes (with permission and swimsuits), and the Kimberly-Clark research involved young parents wearing small hat cams while changing a baby's diaper. This type of observation allows close inspection of activities in places and at times when having an actual observer present would not work.

Marketing researchers are also using something dubbed a Mindcam to understand various aspects of consumer activity, such as shopping.[22] A small camera and microphone combination records all the sights and sounds experienced by the shopper. Typically, an interview follows up where the consumer tries to explain his or her behavior and any purchases made. Small cameras and other recording devices make these types of developments possible.

Smartphones

Modern people are increasingly dependent upon their smartphones and other devices such as tablet computers. Most people don't realize how much information is recorded through their everyday use of the phone. All text messages, browsing, and phone calls leave behind some kind of record. In this way, phones serve as a type of mechanical behavior recorder. As referenced earlier, smartphones also contain GPS devices capable of recording the phone's, and thus most likely the user's, whereabouts anytime the phone is connected. Observations from smartphones might reveal:[23]

- when people are happy based on their message content,
- their political opinions,
- when the customer may be unhappy with their smartphone service provider,
- where a person likes to party on the weekend,
- what types of websites a person likes.

Like other areas, technology may outpace the ethics of using this type of data. The benefits of allowing researchers access to the data are being weighed against privacy concerns as policy makers ponder legal limits on what can be recorded and shared.

Measuring Physiological Reactions

Marketing researchers have used a number of other mechanical devices to evaluate consumers' physical and physiological reactions to advertising copy, packaging, and other stimuli. Five major categories of mechanical devices are used to measure physiological reactions: (1) eye-tracking monitors, (2) pupilometers, (3) psychogalvanometers, (4) voice-pitch analyzers, and (5) neurological activity.

● ● ● ● ● ● ●

Physiological responses to advertising can be recorded with a device like this one.

AP Images/The Leavenworth Times, John Richmeier

Eye-Tracking Monitor

Eye-tracking monitor

A mechanical device used to observe eye movements; some eye monitors use infrared light beams to measure unconscious eye movements.

A magazine or newspaper advertiser may wish to grab readers' attention with a visual scene and then direct it to a package or coupon. Or a television advertiser may wish to identify which selling points to emphasize. Eye-tracking equipment records how the subject reads a print ad or views a television commercial and how much time a respondent spends looking at various parts of a stimulus. In physiological terms, the gaze movement of a viewer's eye is measured with an **eye-tracking monitor**, which measures unconscious eye movements. Originally developed to measure astronauts' eye fatigue, modern eye-tracking systems need not keep a viewer's head in a stationary position. The devices track eye movements with invisible infrared light beams that lock onto a subject's eyes. The light reflects off the eye, and eye-movement data are recorded while another tiny video camera monitors which magazine page is being perused. The data are analyzed by computer to determine which components in an ad (or other stimuli) were seen and which were overlooked. Eye-tracking monitors have recently been used to measure the way subjects view e-mail and Web marketing messages. OgilvyOne has used this technology to learn that people often skip over more than half of the words in e-mail advertising, especially words on the right side of the message. Interestingly, consumers generally ignore the word *free*.[24]

Other physiological observation techniques are based on a common principle: that adrenaline is released when the body is aroused. This hormone causes the heart to enlarge and to beat harder and faster. These changes increase the flow of blood to the fingers and toes. The blood vessels dilate, and perspiration increases, affecting the skin's electrical conductivity. Other physical changes following the release of adrenaline include dilation of the pupils, more frequent brain wave activity, higher skin temperature, and faster breathing. Methods that measure these and other changes associated with arousal can apply to a variety of marketing questions, such as subjects' reactions to advertising messages or product concepts.

Pupilometer

A mechanical device used to observe and record changes in the diameter of a subject's pupils.

Pupilometer

A **pupilometer** observes and records changes in the diameter of a subject's pupils. A subject is instructed to look at a screen on which an advertisement or other stimulus is projected. When the brightness and distance of the stimulus from the subject's eyes are held constant, changes in pupil size may be interpreted as changes in cognitive activity that result from the stimulus, rather than from eye dilation and constriction in response to light intensity, distance from the object, or other physiological reactions to the conditions of observation. This method of research is based on the assumption that increased pupil size reflects positive attitudes toward and interest in advertisements.

Psychogalvanometer

A **psychogalvanometer** measures galvanic skin response (GSR), a measure of involuntary changes in the electrical resistance of the skin. This device is based on the assumption that physiological changes, such as increased perspiration, accompany emotional reactions to advertisements, packages, and slogans. Excitement increases the body's perspiration rate, which increases the electrical resistance of the skin. The test is an indicator of emotional arousal or tension and can be used to help detect dishonest responses as a lie detector.

Psychogalvanometer

A device that measures galvanic skin response, a measure of involuntary changes in the electrical resistance of the skin.

Voice-Pitch Analysis

Voice-pitch analysis is a relatively new physiological measurement technique that gauges emotional reactions as reflected in physiological changes in a person's voice. Abnormal frequencies in the voice caused by changes in the autonomic nervous system are measured with sophisticated, audio-adapted computer equipment. Computerized analysis compares the respondent's voice pitch during warm-up conversations (normal range) with verbal responses to questions about his or her evaluative reaction to television commercials or other stimuli. This technique, unlike other physiological devices, does not require the researcher to surround subjects with mazes of wires or equipment.

Voice-pitch analysis

A physiological measurement technique that records abnormal frequencies in the voice that are supposed to reflect emotional reactions to various stimuli.

Neurological Devices

What happens inside a consumer's brain during everyday activities like browsing advertisements online. More and more, we are able to observe what goes on in the consumer's mind.

Companies like Visiontrack specialize in research that tracks how the eye moves during an activity. Think about how useful this might be to companies considering product placements within video games or in designing more efficient instrument panels for airplanes.

Source: www.tobii.com

Magnetic resonance imaging (MRI)

A machine that allows one to measure what portions of the brain are active at a given time.

Neurological activity can reveal how much thought takes place and what types of feelings a person is probably experiencing. Similar processes involve things such as **magnetic resonance imaging (MRI)** or transcranial magnetic simulation.[25] If these things sound complicated, it's because they are. These tools allow actual direct observation of what is going on in the mind of a respondent by assessing and identifying where electromagnetic activity is taking place within the brain. Thus, these techniques may revolutionize research on information processing.

Marketing researchers employ the technology by having paid respondents view advertisements in an MRI machine.[26] The results help identify the patterns of cognitive and emotional reactions the ads may generate, at least when ads are viewed in an MRI machine. For instance, the brain activation patterns of consumers exposed to cigarette advertising versus anti-smoking ads are contrasted using MRI recordings. These tests are accomplished via the volunteer participation of consumers who must lie completely still inside the device for periods exceeding 30 minutes. Thus, the tools remain obtrusive and expensive, both factors limiting their application in practice. However, advancing technology provides smaller and more portable neurological measuring devices more amenable to studying consumer behavior somewhat more realistically. Researchers also should be concerned about the ethical implications of looking into someone's mind. As barriers such as these are overcome, observations of brain activity may become a mainstay of observational marketing research.

Physiological measures have disadvantages and advantages. All of these devices assume that physiological reactions are associated with persuasiveness or predict a cognitive response. However, no strong theoretical evidence demonstrates exactly how physiological changes drive future sales. Another major problem with physiological research is the *calibration,* or sensitivity, of measuring devices. Identifying arousal is one thing, but precisely measuring *levels* of arousal is another. In addition, most of these devices are expensive and require an artificial setting for their use. However, as a prominent researcher points out, physiological measurement is coincidental: "Physiological measurement isn't an exit interview. It's not dependent on what was remembered later on. It's a live blood, sweat, and tears, moment-by-moment response, synchronous with the stimulus."[27]

TIPS OF THE TRADE

- Once someone knows that others are watching, the researcher cannot be sure how much that knowledge changes behavior.

- Researchers should strongly consider using measures of response latency when studying information processing. Computer-aided survey technology makes observing response latency easy and accurate.

- Complementary evidence combining observational and nonobservational approaches provide more complete explanations.

- The anonymity of people whose behavior is captured using observational data collection should be protected at all times unless consent has been obtained to identify the person.

:: SUMMARY

1. Discuss the role of observation technologies as marketing research tools. Scientific observation is the systematic process of recording the behavioral patterns of people, objects, and occurrences as they take place. Researchers use observation to record: (1) physical actions; (2) verbal behavior, such as sales conversations; (3) expressive behavior; (4) spatial relations and locations; (5) temporal patterns; (6) physical objects; (7) verbal and pictorial records; (8) neurological activity; (9) Internet activity; (10) geographic information; and (11) physical distribution in supply chains. Observational data is very advantageous in capturing behavior as it actually happens. Technology provides new ways of recording behavior automatically, and as a result, reliance on observation is increasing.

2. Know the difference between direct and contrived observation. The most advantageous observational data techniques are unobtrusive, meaning the observation takes place without the knowledge of the observed person. Direct observation involves watching and recording what naturally occurs, without creating an artificial situation. For some data, observation is the most direct or the only method of collection. For example, researchers can measure response latency, the time it takes individuals to decide such as in choosing among alternatives. Contrived observation creates situations that prompt some reaction to be measured such as the case with mystery shoppers who pose as customers and complain about bad service (even if it isn't bad).

3. Identify ethical issues particular to research using observation. Contrived observation, hidden observation, and other observation research tools, including the use of electronic tracking via Web browsing or cell phone use, have the potential to involve deception or violate one's privacy. For this reason, these methods often raise ethical concerns about subjects' right to privacy and right to be informed. The chapter includes a short checklist that can be useful in determining the morality of an observational data gathering approach. An overriding concern when consent cannot or is not obtained is whether the person freely performs the observed behavior in public. Technological advances also create concern over individuals' "right to be forgotten."

4. Explain the observation of physical objects and message content. Physical-trace evidence serves as a visible record of past events. Researchers may examine whatever evidence provides such a record, including inventory levels, the contents of garbage cans, or the items in a consumer's pantry. Researchers can take advantage of artifacts that are left behind to try and explain the behavior associated with that particular object. Content analysis obtains data by observing and analyzing the contents of the messages in written or spoken communications.

5. Describe major types of mechanical observation. Mechanical observation uses a variety of devices to record behavior directly. It may be an efficient and accurate choice when the situation or behavior to be recorded is routine, repetitive, or programmatic. National television audience ratings are based on mechanical observation (e.g., People Meters) and computerized data collection. Website traffic and content are monitored easily through residuals left on computers. Bar-code scanners automatically record purchase data and RFID tags can also track the movement of goods. Smartphones record many aspects of behavior including geographic location and movement.

6. Summarize techniques for measuring physiological reactions. Physiological reactions, such as arousal or eye movement patterns, may be observed using a number of mechanical devices. Eye-tracking monitors identify the direction of a person's gaze, and a pupilometer observes and records changes in the diameter of the pupils of subjects' eyes, based on the assumption that a larger pupil signifies a positive attitude. A psychogalvanometer measures galvanic skin response as a signal of a person's emotional reactions. Voice-pitch analysis measures changes in a person's voice and associates the changes with emotional response. MRIs and similar devices allow recording of neurological (i.e., brain) activity.

:: KEY TERMS AND CONCEPTS

artifacts, *218*

click-through rate (CTR), *221*

content analysis, *219*

contrived observation, *214*

conversation volume, *222*

direct observation, *213*

eye-tracking monitor, *226*

hidden observation, *211*

observation, *208*

observer bias, *214*

magnetic resonance imagery (MRI), *228*

psychogalvanometer, *227*

Portable People Meter 360 (PPM 360) *220*

pupilometer, *226*

response latency, *216*

scanner-based consumer panel, *224*

television monitoring, *220*

unobtrusive observation, *211*

visible observation, *211*

voice-pitch analysis, *227*

:: QUESTIONS FOR REVIEW AND CRITICAL THINKING

1. Yogi Berra, the late baseball player and coach who was famous for mind-boggling sayings, said, "You can observe a lot just by watching." How does this fit in with the definition of scientific observation?
2. What are the major advantages of unobtrusive observation over other types of data collection?
3. What are the major limitations of observational data collection techniques?
4. What is the difference between direct and contrived observation?
5. What is conversation volume? What sources provide this type of data?
6. The chapter showed a photograph of a traffic monitoring camera. Do you think the use of these cameras to issue speeding tickets is ethical? What types of behavior might cameras like these capture that would help automobile designers produce products that better match our needs as drivers?
7. What is "the right to be forgotten" movement?
8. A multinational fast-food corporation plans to locate a restaurant in La Paz, Bolivia. Secondary data for this city are sketchy and outdated. How might you determine the best location using observational data collection? How might satellite imagery be useful?
9. What does it mean to use complementary evidence? Describe how observational data taken from users' smartphone browser history could be supplemented with complementary evidence to answer questions about some aspect of consumer behavior.
10. Click-through rates for advertisements placed in websites typically are usually very, very low (1 percent or less). What types of error might exist in using click-through rate data as a measure of an advertisement's success?
11. Outline a research design using observation for each of the following situations:
    a. A bank wishes to collect data on the number of customer services and the frequency of customer use of these services.
    b. A state government wishes to determine the driving public's use of seat belts.
    c. A fast-food franchise wishes to determine how long a customer entering a store has to wait for his or her order.
    d. University food services wonder if a smartphone app with which students can order food ahead of time will cut down on wait times and food waste.
    e. An overnight package delivery service wishes to observe delivery workers beginning at the moment when they stop the truck, continuing through the delivery of the package, and ending when they return to the truck.
    f. A political consulting agency would like to study consumers' reactions as they view national candidates' political commercials airing on cable and broadcast television.
12. What is an artifact to a marketing researcher? How might one use artifacts to study the types of things that fans at major sporting events might be willing to purchase when attending an event? Can artifacts also be used to study ergonomics in the office? If so, how?
13. What is a scanner-based consumer panel?
14. What are the major types of mechanical observation? What types of observations might Twitter potentially have access to that would be of interest to basic marketing researchers?
15. How can a marketing researcher determine if an observational data collection involving hidden cameras is ethical?
16. Comment on the ethics of the following situations:
    a. During the course of telephone calls to investors, a stockbroker records respondents' voices when they are answering sensitive investment questions and then conducts a voice-pitch analysis. The respondents do not know that their voices are being recorded.
    b. A researcher plans to invite consumers to be test users in a simulated kitchen located in a shopping mall and then to videotape their reactions to a new microwave dinner from behind a two-way mirror (one that an observer behind the mirror can see through but the person looking into the mirror sees only the reflection).
    c. A marketing researcher arranges to purchase the trash from the headquarters of a major competitor. The purpose is to sift through discarded documents to determine the company's strategic plans.
    d. A political research firm considers technology that activates a consumer's tablet microphone to "observe dinner time conversations" in an effort to produce better political ads.
17. What is a psychogalvanometer?
18. Look back to the chapter on qualitative research and find the definition for ethnography. Why is observation such a big part of this important qualitative research approach?
19. What is an MRI device and how can it be used in research studying advertising effectiveness?

:: RESEARCH ACTIVITIES

1. William Rathje, a researcher at the University of Arizona, Department of Anthropology, has become well known for the "Garbage Project." The project involves observational research. Use **http://www.ask.com** to find information about the garbage project at the University of Arizona. What is the name of the book that describes some of the key findings of the Garbage Project? How do you think it involves observational research?
2. The Internet is filled with webcams. For example, Pebble Beach Golf Club has several webcams (**http://www.pebblebeach.com**). How could a researcher use webcams like these to collect behavioral data? In your short time viewing these webcams, are there any research questions that you think might be addressed based on behaviors that can be observed in these views? If so, what might one or two be?
3. Review the evidence presented regarding hand washing behaviors (or the lack thereof). Report results based on the way the data were obtained. What accounts for the differences in survey, observational, and mechanical-based studies? Do a little research of your own on hand washing and compare to the results reported here. Can you think of other ethical ways to "observe" this behavior that are not stated in this chapter?

Mazda and Syzygy

Case 8.1

When Mazda Motor Europe set out to improve its website, the company wanted details about how consumers were using the site and whether finding information was easy. Mazda hired a research firm called Syzygy to answer those questions with observational research.[28] Syzygy's methods include the use of an eye-tracking device that uses infrared light rays to record what areas of a computer screen a user is viewing. For instance, the device measured the process computer users followed in order to look for a local dealer or arrange a test drive. Whenever a process seemed confusing or difficult, the company looked for ways to make the website easier to navigate.

To conduct this observational study, Syzygy arranged for sixteen subjects in Germany and the United Kingdom to be observed as they used the website. The subjects in Germany were observed with the eye-tracking equipment. As the equipment measured each subject's gaze, software recorded the location on the screen and graphed the data. Syzygy's results included three-dimensional contour maps highlighting the "peak" areas where most of the computer users' attention was directed.

Questions

1. What could Mazda learn from eye-tracking software that would be difficult to learn from other observational methods?
2. What are the shortcomings of this method?
3. Along with the eye-tracking research, what other research methods could help Mazda assess the usability of its website? Summarize your advice for how Mazda could use complementary methods to obtain a complete understanding of its website usability.

Twitter Metrics

Case 8.2

Media companies rely greatly on observational data in an effort to convince advertisers to purchase advertising on their platform.[29] The media giants of Google, Facebook, Twitter, and so on report their observational research results often to send signals that advertising on that platform pays off. A standard measure is the number of monthly active users. Active users are defined as people who have an account and log-in during the month. That number can be divided into the number of unique active users and the number of total active users; the latter number counting each log-in and the former counting only the number of individuals who logged in at least one time during the month. These data are recorded automatically as users interact with the site. Thus, they are the result of observational data measurement. However, in 2014 Twitter's active user metrics stopped growing and actually showed some periods of declining usage. Growth dropped from near 20 percent in 2012 to nearly 0 at the beginning of 2014. As a result, Twitter considered whether these metrics really were the best to demonstrate how much consumers actually interact with Twitter, and as consequence, how good of an advertising platform Twitter actually is.

Twitter management examined observational data about how people ended up at its website (where did they link to Twitter) and how long they spent on the site. Based on the research, Twitter marketing managers argue that the old metrics do not accurately portray Twitter's value as an advertising tool. Many people actually interact with Twitter without logging in. For instance, if a Twitter feed is referenced in a news story, people often click through without logging in. In addition, other media often pick up images of Twitter artifacts (tweets and feeds) and place them in their own stories. Thus, indirect exposure results even if people do not actually visit Twitter. Management decided that one of the metrics used by researchers in the report, monthly unique visitors, as opposed to active users, is a better indicator of Twitter's value as an advertising medium. Through 2014, monthly active users averaged about 50,000,000. However, the monthly unique visitors number averaged about 120,000,000. Over two times as many visitors as users. Thus, Twitter began to feed this number to potential advertisers in sales efforts.

Questions

1. Comment on the validity of the observational data used to form Twitter's metrics.
2. Do you agree that the number of unique visitors is a more accurate measure than the number of unique active users with respect to the value of Twitter as an advertising tool?
3. How might complementary evidence be added to this to improve Twitter's sales pitches to advertisers?
4. How does Twitter traffic compare to that of Facebook and YouTube?

Tulsa's Central Business District

Case 8.3

The metropolitan Tulsa Chamber of Commerce recognized that there was a critical gap between the availability of timely information about the central business district (CBD) and the need for this information for investment decision making, commercial marketing efforts, and the continued pursuit of the goal of downtown revitalization. The Chamber of Commerce undertook four separate research projects to gather information about the CBD. One project was a physical inventory of the existing downtown commercial base. The objectives of the study were to determine what types of establishments were operating in the CBD and the number of vacancies there and to generally profile the commercial geography of the CBD. The researchers found that the central business district was based on the U.S. Bureau of the Census classification scheme. The CBD was identified as the area encompassed by the inner dispersal loop (a system of expressways), which corresponded identically with census tract 25 (see Case Exhibit 8.3–1).

A team of ten pedestrian fieldworkers covered each block in the inner dispersal loop. The fieldworkers used the observation form in Case Exhibit 8.2–2 to record the company name, address, primary business activity, estimated frontage, and other relevant information about each building site or office. Fieldworkers recorded Standard Industrial Classification (SIC) codes for retailers. SIC codes for all other establishments were recorded by research assistants after the data were collected. All the data were identified by census block.

Questions

1. Evaluate this research design.
2. What changes, if any, would you make in the observation form?
3. What problems would you expect in the data collection stage?
4. What techniques would you use to analyze the data?

Conducting Marketing Experiments

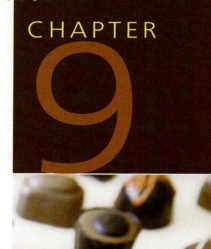

LEARNING OUTCOMES

After studying this chapter, you should be able to:

1. Know the basic characteristics of research experiments
2. Design an experiment using the basic issues of experimental design
3. Know tools for maximizing the validity of experiments with an emphasis on minimizing demand characteristics
4. Weigh the trade-off between internal and external validity
5. Recognize the appropriate uses of test-marketing
6. Avoid unethical experimental practices

Dimitri Otis/Getty Images

Chapter Vignette:

Warning! This Product May Cause . . .

"**W**hat cigarette do you smoke, Doctor?" This was the question posed in a 1949 ad for Camel cigarettes. Not surprisingly, the result stated in the ad was that more doctors smoked Camels than any other cigarette. The intended inference here is obvious—if doctors choose Camels, then they must not cause as many harmful effects as those of other cigarettes! The whole question of smoking has advanced a great deal since that time. Inevitably, debates about smoking involve questions of cause.

- Does smoking cause cancer?
- Does smoking cause death?
- Does advertising cause people to smoke?
- Does smoking cause popularity?

Warning labels say things like "Smoking causes lung cancer, heart disease, and emphysema." In U.S. courts, plaintiffs' attorneys and in some cases state governments have successfully argued that cigarette companies are responsible for the health problems and even deaths associated with long-term smoking.[1] As a result, tobacco companies have paid huge settlements. However, a U.K.-based tobacco company, Imperial Tobacco, faced with a £500,000 lawsuit filed on behalf of a cancer patient who had smoked Player Cigarettes for 40 years, is basing a legal defense on the notion that a lack of certainty remains over whether or not cigarettes cause cancer. They claim that the only evidence for this is statistical association and that many other factors are also statistically associated with the occurrence of cancer including a patient's socioeconomic status, childhood experiences (orientation toward healthy behaviors like exercise and diet), ethnicity, personality, and diet.

© Squareplum/Shutterstock.com

Imperial Tobacco's claim that no experimental evidence isolates the extent to which smoking truly causes cancer provided the basis for their legal defense.[2] Further, they argued that advertising could not have caused the plaintiff to begin smoking. The Imperial defense was successful as the court ruled in their favor stating that the causal evidence was insufficient to hold the company responsible.

Nonetheless, many lawsuits in U.S. courts name the brand that a smoker first started smoking even if the person smoked many brands of cigarettes in the years and decades that followed. This tactic is based on the assumption that the branding and advertising efforts initially caused a person to smoke. The research evidence on this point is mixed, but researchers now are turning their attention toward experiments testing hypotheses related to the effectiveness of anti-smoking advertisements—particularly those aimed at adolescents. Typically, these experiments involve multiple groups of individuals, each subjected to a different set of conditions, and then each measured on variables related to their actual smoking behavior or favorableness toward smoking.[3] For instance, the procedures call for assignment to magazines with different types of ads to each of four groups:

- Group 1 views a magazine with several actual ads for cigarettes.
- Group 2 views a magazine with several anti-smoking ads that emphasize negative effects on health.
- Group 3 views a magazine with several anti-smoking ads that emphasize negative effects on one's social life.
- Group 4 views a magazine with no cigarette or anti-smoking ads.

The researchers analyze the differences across groups to examine the effectiveness of the ads. In this case, groups 2 and 3 should be less favorably inclined toward smoking than either group 1 or group 4 if anti-smoking ads are effective. Then, we can compare results from groups 2 and 3 to each other to see whether teens react with more fear at the thought of becoming ill or becoming less popular! The extent to which the researchers can truly establish causal evidence eventually will boil down to control.

Introduction

Most students are familiar with scientific experiments from studying physical sciences like physics and chemistry. The term *experiment* typically conjures up an image of a chemist surrounded by bubbling test tubes and Bunsen burners. Behavioral and physical scientists have used experimentation far longer than have marketing researchers. Nevertheless, both social scientists and physical scientists use experiments for much the same purpose.

Experiments are widely used in causal research designs. Experimental research allows a researcher to control the research situation to evaluate the potential for *causal* relationships among variables. The marketing experimenter manipulates one or more independent variables and holds constant all other possible independent variables while observing effects on dependent variables. A researcher can control variables in an experiment to a degree not possible in a survey.

A simple example would be thinking about how changes in drink prices might cause changes in drink sales. Price would be an independent variable and sales would be a dependent variable. The marketing researcher can experimentally control drink price by setting it at different levels and then study this problem by examining consumer reactions to each level in the form of drink sales.

A marketing experiment investigated the influence of price on consumer feelings and efficacy (ability on a task). The experimenter gave each subject in the experiment an energy drink. After consuming the energy drink, subjects took a cognitive test. In half the cases, the researcher told subjects that the energy drink cost $2. In the other half of the cases, the researcher told subjects that the energy drink cost $4. Each subject went through exactly the same process with the exception of the stated price of the energy drink. Does price cause performance? The results showed that the subjects in the $4 condition outperform those in the $2 condition. That is, they did better on the cognitive test. The explanation is that they felt more confident and that carried over into better performance.

The Characteristics of Experiments

Examples are probably the best way to illustrate marketing experiments. Here, we illustrate the characteristics of experiments by describing a study aimed at testing hypotheses inferring the potential causal effects of color. We will refer back to this example throughout this chapter and begin by describing the key characteristics of experiments in this section of the chapter.

By now, perhaps you have had an opportunity to explore the editing features of the Qualtrics survey platform. As the name implies, the tool edits a "survey." Typically, we think of surveys in association with descriptive research designs. Consider the following points in trying to understand the role such tools may play in causal designs.

1. What types of variables can be measured using survey items created with Qualtrics?
2. Would it be possible to implement an experimental manipulation within or in conjunction with a Qualtrics survey application?
3. Is it possible to create a manipulation check with a Qualtrics survey item?
4. How might computer technology assist in randomly assigning subjects to experimental conditions?

© George Doyle & Ciaran Griffin

Subjects

Let's take a look at an experiment investigating how color and lights might influence shoppers. This particular research is highly relevant for those involved in retail management and design. The key decisions facing managers is how to alter color and lighting to produce favorable consumer reactions. A corresponding research question is, "What is the effect of color and lighting on shopper patronage (patronage means how much someone would shop and buy in a store)?"[4]

Over two hundred female consumers participated in the experiment. Researchers refer to participants in experimental research as **subjects** rather than respondents—the term typically used for participants in survey research. This is because the researcher subjects research participants to some experimental treatment. In addressing the color and lighting research question, the experimental task involved asking subjects to provide responses to a "new fashion store" concept. The hypothetical new store would sell women's clothing and accessories to the fashion-minded professional woman.

Subjects

The sampling units for an experiment, usually human participants in research who are subjected to some experimental manipulation.

Experimental Conditions

Perhaps the characteristic that most differentiates experimental research from survey research is the manner in which independent variables are created rather than simply measured. The illustration experiment involves two relevant independent variables. Researchers created fictitious store environments for the experiment. Four different hypothetical store environments were created corresponding to different combinations of the independent variable values. Thus, the only thing differing among the four is the particular combination of the predominant store color and the type of lighting.

The experimenter created the color independent variable by variously designing the new store as either predominantly blue or predominantly orange. Similarly, the experimenter created the lighting independent variable by designing the hypothetical store as either having bright or soft lights. Exhibit 9.1 illustrates the four different experimental conditions created by combining the two possible values for each independent variable. An **experimental condition** refers to one of the possible levels of an experimental variable manipulation.

The procedures assigned subjects randomly to one of these four conditions. As a result, each subject group experienced a store with one of the four color and lighting combinations as shown in the Exhibit. Thus, all participants within a group received the same description. Subjects in different groups received different descriptions. By analyzing differences among the groups, the researcher can see what effects occur due to the two experimentally controlled independent variables.

Experimental condition

One of the possible levels of an experimental variable manipulation.

Background color can be used as an experimental variable in this way.

EXHIBIT 9.1
Experimental Conditions in Color and Lighting Experiment

		Color	
		Blue	**Orange**
Lighting:	Soft	¼ of Participants	¼ of Participants
	Bright	¼ of Participants	¼ of Participants

Blocking variables

Categorical variables included in the statistical analysis of experimental data as a way of statistically controlling or accounting for variance due to that variable.

Covariate

A continuous variable included in the statistical analysis as a way of statistically controlling for variance due to that variable.

Independent variables that are not experimental conditions can also be included as a means of statistical control in the analysis of experiments. Researchers refer to these as either blocking variables or covariates. **Blocking variables** are categorical variables like a subject's gender or ethnicity. For example, researchers may group results based on whether respondents are male or female. On the other hand, we refer to a continuous variable expected to show a statistical relationship with a dependent variables as a **covariate**. Once statistical analysis begins, researchers treat blocking variables in a similar way as experimental variables and covariates like a regression variable. We'll cover the statistical analysis of experiments later in the text.

Effects

The key outcome, or dependent variable, in this example is a subject's perception of how much he or she would patronize the store. In this case, a rating scale asking how much each participant thought he/she would actually visit and buy things at the hypothetical store. The possible scores ranged from 0 (would not shop) to 300 (definitely would shop). A higher score means higher patronage. Effects are the characteristics of experiments that allow hypotheses to be tested. We can classify effects in several ways. Here, we will focus on the difference between main effects and interaction effects.

Main Effects

Main effect

The experimental difference in dependent variable means between the different levels of any single experimental variable.

A **main effect** refers to the experimental difference in means between the different levels of any single experimental variable. In this case, there are two potential main effects, one for color and one for lighting.

Exhibit 9.2 shows the average patronage score for each experimental condition. The results show that among experimental subjects who rated a blue store, an average patronage score of 153.8 was reported, which is considerably higher than the average of 131.8 reported by subjects who rated an orange store. The lighting experimental variable, however, doesn't seem to make as much difference. Subjects in the soft lighting condition reported an average of 144.7 and subjects in the bright lighting condition reported only a slightly lower average of 140.4.

EXHIBIT **9.2**
Consumer Average Patronage
Scores in Each Condition

		Color		
		Blue	**Orange**	
Lighting:	Soft	148.5	140.1	144.7
	Bright	159.1	122.6	140.4
		153.8	131.8	

Source: © Cengage Learning 2013.

Thus, the conclusion at this point seems to be that changing a store's color can change consumer patronage. A blue store is better than an orange store! On the other hand, lighting doesn't seem to make much difference. Or does it?

Interactions

An **interaction effect** is a change in a dependent variable due to a specific combination of independent variables. In this case, it's possible that the combination of color and lighting creates effects that are not clearly represented in the two main effects.

Interaction effect

Differences in a dependent variable due to a specific combination of independent variables.

Researchers often depict experimental results with a line graph as shown in Exhibit 9.3. The lines drawn at different heights corresponding to the means for blue and orange depict a color main effect. If the lines were at the same height, no main effect due to color exists. However, the blue line is higher than the orange line. The midpoints of the lines correspond to the means of 153.8 and 131.8 for the blue and orange conditions, respectively. A lighting main effect is less obvious because the difference between the midpoint between the two soft points (144.7) is not too different than the corresponding height of the midpoint between the two bright points (140.4). When the lines have very different slopes, an interaction is likely present. In this case, the combination of lights and color is presenting an interaction leading to the following interpretation.

The best possible reaction occurs when the store has a blue color with bright lights and the worst combination occurs when the store is orange with bright lights. In contrast, the means are essentially the same for either color when the lights are soft. So, lights may indeed matter. When the lights are soft, there is little difference in patronage between a blue and orange store. But, when the lights are bright, there is quite a difference between blue and orange.

One can contrast the pattern of results depicted in Exhibit 9.3 with those from another experiment shown in Exhibit 9.4 on the next page. Here, researchers conducted an experiment to see how different promotions offered by a nightclub might affect the amount of drinks a college student would have during the promotion.[5] The researchers were also interested in potential differences between men and women—a blocking variable. Notice that the line for men is higher than the line for women, suggesting a main effect of sex; men have more drinks than women. Also, the mean number of drinks is higher for the 50-cent drink promotion than for either of the other

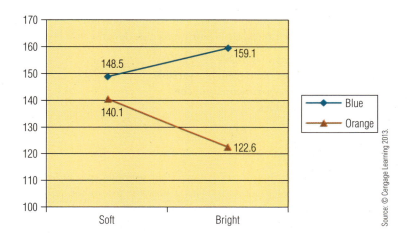

EXHIBIT **9.3**
Experimental Graph Showing
Results within Each Condition

Source: © Cengage Learning 2013.

EXHIBIT 9.4
Results from Nightclub
Promotion Experiment

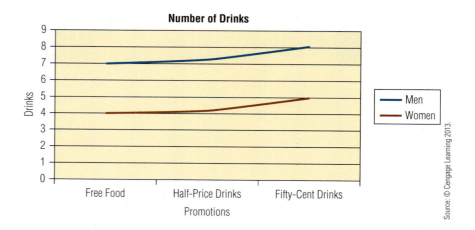

Source: © Cengage Learning 2013.

two. But, in contrast to our illustration given, the lines are parallel to each other, suggesting that no interaction effect has occurred. In other words, men and women respond to the promotions in the same way.

Summary of Experimental Characteristics

Experiments differ from ordinary survey research. The differences can be understood by identifying special characteristics of experiments. These characteristics include the following:

■ Experiments use subjects instead of respondents. The experimental implementation exposes subjects to some treatment by manipulating an experimental variable. Survey respondents do not react to any experimental treatment or manipulation.

■ Experimental variables become the key independent variables. The researcher creates the experimental variables rather than simply measuring them. Measured independent variables are called blocking variables or covariates in experiments.

■ Experimental effects exist to the extent that treatment groups exhibit differences between means. Main effects are differences in the means based on a single experimental variable (treatment). Interaction effects are differences in means based on combinations of two or more variables.

Basic Issues in Experimental Design

Experimental design is a major research topic and entire courses and books are devoted only to designing experiments. Here, we provide an introduction into experimental design. The terminology introduced in describing experimental characteristics will be helpful in learning how to implement a simple experimental design. Fortunately, most experimental designs in marketing are relatively simple and this introduction should provide a sufficient basis for implementing such designs.

Experimental designs involve no less than four important design elements:

1. Manipulation of the independent variable.
2. Selection and measurement of the dependent variable.
3. Selection and assignment of experimental subjects.
4. Control over extraneous variables.

Manipulation of the Independent Variable

Recall from Chapter 3, the thing that makes independent variables special in experimentation is that the researcher can actually create its values. This is how the researcher manipulates, and therefore controls, independent variables. In our color experiment, the researcher manipulated the values of the color independent variable by assigning it a value of either blue or orange. Experimental

Thomas Michael Corcoran / PhotoEdit

independent variables represent hypothesized causal influences. Therefore, experiments are very appropriate in causal designs.

An **experimental treatment** is the term referring to the way an experimental variable is manipulated. For example, the illustration manipulates the store color experimental treatment by assigning subjects randomly to evaluate either a blue or orange store environment. Thus, there were two levels (or values) of the color variable. A medical researcher may manipulate an experimental variable by treating some subjects with one drug and the other subjects with a separate drug. Experimental variables often involve treatments with more than two levels. For instance, prices of $99, $149, and $219 might represent treatments in a pricing experiment examining how price causes sales for a new Samsung tablet computer. Treatments function experimentally as independent or predictor variables through manipulations.

Experimental variables like these cannot only be described as independent variables, but they also can be described as a *categorical variable* because they take on a value to represent some classifiable or qualitative aspect. Color, for example, is either orange or blue. Advertising copy style is another example of a categorical or classificatory variable that a researcher could manipulate in an experiment. In other situations, an independent variable may truly exist as a *continuous variable*. When this is the case, the researcher must select appropriate levels of that variable as experimental treatments. For example, lighting can vary from dark to any level of brightness. Price can take on any value but the researcher will only include levels representing relevant distinctions in price in an experiment. Before conducting the experiment, the researcher decides on levels that would be relevant to study. The levels should be noticeably different and realistic.

Experimental and Control Groups

In perhaps the simplest experiment, the researcher manipulates an independent variable over two treatment levels resulting in two groups, an experimental group and a control group. An **experimental group** is one in which an experimental treatment is administered. A **control group** is one in which no experimental treatment is administered. For example, consider an experiment studying how advertising affects sales. In the experimental group, the advertising budget may be set at $200,000 more than the normal level. In the control condition, advertising remains unchanged at the normal level. All other conditions are controlled and thus are the same across the groups. The control group serves as a baseline for comparison. At the end of the experiment, the researcher compares sales (the dependent variable) in the two treatment groups to determine whether the level of advertising (the independent variable) had any effect. Note that this simple experiment can only produce a main effect. Multiple independent variables are necessary for an interaction to occur.

Experimental treatment

The term referring to the way an experimental variable is manipulated.

Experimental group

A group of subjects to whom an experimental treatment is administered.

Control group

A group of subjects to whom no experimental treatment is administered which serves as a baseline for comparison.

Cell

Refers to a specific treatment combination associated with an experimental group.

Several Experimental Treatment Levels

The advertising/sales experiment with one experimental and one control group may not tell the advertiser everything he or she wishes to know. If the advertiser wished to understand the functional nature of the relationship between sales and advertising at several treatment levels, he/she might include additional experimental groups with advertising expenditure increases of $250,000, $500,000, and $1 million. This experiment may still involve a control variable. By analyzing more groups, each with a different treatment level, the researcher can achieve a more precise result than in the simple experimental group–control group experiment described above. This design also can produce only a main effect; in this case, a main effect of advertising expenditure.

More Than One Independent Variable

An experiment can also be made more complicated by including the effect of another experimental variable. Our extended example involving retail atmosphere would typify a still relatively simple two-variable experiment. Since there are two variables, each with two different levels, the experimental design creates four experimental groups. Often, the term **cell** refers to a treatment combination within an experiment. The formula described below shows how to compute the number of cells involved in any experiment:

$$K = (T_1)(T_2)..(T_m)$$

where $K =$ the number of cells, $T_1 =$ the number of treatment levels for experimental group number one, $T_2 =$ the number of treatment levels for experimental group number two, and so forth through the m th experimental group (T_m). In the illustration experiment, there are two experimental variables each with two levels so the computation is quite simple:

$$K = 2 \text{ (color levels)} \times 2 \text{ (lighting levels)} = 4 \text{ } cells$$

Including multiple variables allows a comparison of experimental treatments on the dependent variable. Since there are multiple experimental variables, this design involves both main effects and interactions.

Selection and Measurement of the Dependent Variable

Selecting dependent variables is crucial in experimental design. Unless the dependent variables are relevant and truly represent an outcome of interest, the experiment will not be useful. Sometimes, the logical dependent variable is fairly obvious. If researchers introduce a new cinnamon, pink grapefruit tea mix in a test-market, sales volume is most likely to be a key dependent variable. However, if researchers are experimenting with different forms of advertising copy appeals, defining the dependent variable may be more difficult. For example, measures of advertising awareness, recall, changes in brand preference, or sales might be possible dependent variables. In the retail atmosphere example, retail patronage was the key dependent variable. However, other potential dependent variables might include perceived product quality, excitement, or price perceptions.

Choosing the right dependent variable is part of the problem definition process. Like the problem definition process in general, researchers sometimes rush through this and don't devote the careful attention to the selection that is needed. The experimenter's choice of a dependent variable determines what type of answer a researcher can provide to assist managers in decision making.

The introduction of a product known as Crystal Pepsi, a clear cola, illustrates the need to think beyond consumers' initial reactions. When PepsiCo introduced Crystal Pepsi the initial trial rate was high, but only a small percentage of customers made repeat purchases. The brand never achieved high repeat sales within a sufficiently large market segment. Brand awareness, trial purchase, and repeat purchase are all possible dependent variables in an experiment. The dependent variable therefore should be considered carefully and more than one can be included in an experiment. Thorough problem definition will help the researcher select the most important dependent variable(s).

Goldfishing or Bluefishing?

Food marketers are often claiming that their brand tastes better than the competitors. When a claim like this is made, it has to be supported somehow or else the company making the claim is liable and risks being sued for making a false or unsubstantiated claim. Thus, research is often needed to produce evidence supporting such claims. Marketers need to be very careful, however, that this type of research is conducted in a rigorous fashion.

Sea Snapper brand gourmet frozen fish products claimed in advertising that their fish sticks are preferred more than two to one over the most popular brand, Captain John's.[6] The advertisements all included a definitive statement indicating that research existed that substantiated this claim. Captain John's sued Sea Snapper over the claim and based the suit on the fact that the research was faulty. Sea Snapper managers conducted taste tests involving four hundred consumers who indicated that they regularly ate frozen food products. Two hundred tasted Sea Snapper premium fish sticks and the other two hundred tasted Captain John's premium fish sticks. Results showed a main effect with an average preference score for

Sea Snapper of 78.2 compared to 39.0 for Captain John's. Case closed? Not hardly. Captain John's attorney hired a marketing research firm to assist in the lawsuit.

The research firm was unable to duplicate the result. After intense questioning of subjects involved in the original research, it turned out that Sea Snapper fish sticks were always presented to consumers on a blue plate while Captain John's were always presented to consumers on a goldfish-colored (an orangish gold) plate. Therefore, the Sea Snapper results could be attributable to a variable other than taste and Captain John's came out as the winner of this legal action—with the help of marketing research.

Jo van den Berg/Getty Images

© George Doyle & Ciaran Griffin

Selection and Assignment of Test Units

Test units are the subjects or entities whose responses to the experimental treatment are measured. Individual consumers, employees, organizational units, sales territories, market segments, brands, stores, websites, or other entities may be the test units. People are the most common test units in most marketing and consumer behavior experiments. In our retail atmospherics example, individual consumers are the test units.

Test units

The subjects or other entities whose responses to the experimental treatment are measured or observed.

Sample Selection and Random Sampling Errors

As in other forms of marketing research, random sampling errors and sample selection errors may occur in experimentation. For example, experiments sometimes go awry based on the geographic area chosen for a particular investigation. A case in point is an experiment testing a new lubricant for outboard boat motors by Dow Chemical Company. The research team tested the lubricant in Florida. They thought the hot, muggy climate would provide the most demanding test. In Florida the lubricant was a success. However, the story was quite different when consumers in Michigan bought and used the product. Although the lubricant sold well and worked well during the summer, the following spring Dow discovered the oil had congealed, allowing the outboard engines, idle all winter, to rust. The rusting problem never came to light in Florida, where the engines were in year-round use. Thus, sample selection error occurs because of flaws in procedures used to assign experimental test units. Testing units in Florida created error because the goal was understanding how the product worked in places other than Florida— like Michigan.

Systematic or nonsampling error may occur if the sampling units in an experimental cell are somehow different than the units in another cell, and this difference affects the dependent variable. For example, suppose some professors are interested in testing the effect of providing snacks during exams on students' scores. The experimental variable is snacks, manipulated over three levels: (1) fruit, (2) cookies, and (3) chocolate. The test units in this case are individual students.

Systematic or nonsampling error

Occurs if the sampling units in an experimental cell are somehow different than the units in another cell, and this difference affects the dependent variable.

241

Although experiments are often administered in groups, if all groups are not the same, then systematic error is introduced.

When the professors conduct the experiment, for convenience, they decide to give all of the 8 a.m. classes chocolate for a snack, all of the 1 p.m. classes get fruit, and all of the 7 p.m. classes get cookies. While this type of procedure is often followed, if our tastes and digestive systems react differently to different foods at different times of the day, systematic error is introduced into the experiment. Furthermore, because the night classes contain students who are older on average, the professors may reach the conclusion that students perform better when they eat cookies, when it may really be due to the fact that students who are older perform better no matter what they are fed.

Randomization

Randomization

The random assignment of subject and treatments to groups; it is one device for equally distributing the effects of extraneous variables to all conditions.

Randomization—the random assignment of subject and treatments to groups—is one device for equally distributing the effects of extraneous variables to all conditions. Randomizing assignments does not eliminate nuisance variables but controls for them because they likely exist to the same degree in every experimental cell. All cells should yield similar average scores on the dependent variables if it were not for the experimental treatments administered in a particular cell. In other words, the researcher would like to set up a situation where everything in every cell is the same except for the experimental treatment. Random assignment of subjects allows the researcher to make this assumption, thereby reducing the chance of systematic error. With proper randomization, the characteristics of each experimental group tend to be the same as the population characteristics.

Matching

Matching subjects on the basis of pertinent background information is another technique for controlling systematic error. Matching involves assigning subjects in a way that a particular characteristic is the same in each group. If a subject's sex is expected to influence dependent variable responses, as it may in a taste test, then the researcher may make sure that there are equal numbers of men and women in each experimental cell. In general, if a researcher believes that certain extraneous variables may affect the dependent variable, he or she can make sure that the subjects in each group are the same on these characteristics.

For example, in a taste test experiment for a dog food, it might be important to match the dogs in various experimental groups on the basis of age or breed. That way, the same number of

Basset Hounds and Dobermans will test formulas A, B, and C. Although matching can be a useful approach, the researcher can never be sure that sampling units are matched on all characteristics. Here, for example, even though breeds can be matched, it is difficult to know if all dogs live in the same type of environment (indoors, outdoors, spacious, cramped, with table scraps or without, etc.).

Repeated Measures

Experiments that expose an individual subject to more than one level of an experimental treatment involve a **repeated measures** design. Although this approach has advantages, including being more economical since the same subject provides data on multiple conditions, the design has drawbacks that limit its usefulness. We will discuss these in more detail later.

Repeated measures
Experiments in which an individual subject is exposed to more than one level of an experimental treatment.

Extraneous Variables

The fourth decision about the basic elements of an experiment concerns control over variables that may systematically influence the dependent variable(s). Earlier we classified total survey error into two basic categories: random sampling error and systematic error. The same dichotomy applies to all research designs, but the terms *random (sampling) error* and *systematic error* are used frequently when discussing experiments.

Experimental Confounds

We already discussed how systematic error can occur when extraneous variables, or the conditions of administering the experiment, influence the dependent variables. When this occurs, the results will be confounded because the design fails to control for or eliminate all extraneous variables. A **confound** in an experiment means that an alternative explanation exists beyond the experimental variables for any observed differences in the dependent variable. Once a potential confound is identified, the validity of the experiment is severely questioned.

Recall from the Research Snapshot on page 241 that the experimental procedures involved a taste test. The Research Snapshot illustrates how a confound can ruin an experiment. Sea Snapper fish sticks were always presented on a blue plate and Captain John's fish sticks were always presented on a goldfish-colored plate. The plate's color is confounding the explanation that the difference in brands is responsible for the difference in liking. Is the difference in liking due to the color or the product quality?

In a simple experimental group–control group experiment aimed at employee task efficiency, if subjects in the experimental group are always administered a treatment (an energy drink) in the morning and then have their efficiency measured also in the morning, and the control group always has their efficiency measured in the afternoon, a constant error has been introduced. In other words, the results will show a difference not only due to the treatment, but also due to the added efficiency that naturally occurs in the morning. In such a situation, time of day represents a confound. On the other hand, other types of error are random and not constant. For example, the natural fluctuations in efficiency that occur from day to day. Random errors are less of a problem for experiments than are constant errors because they do not cause systematic changes in outcomes.

Confound
An experimental confound means that there is an alternative explanation beyond the experimental variables for any observed differences in the dependent variable.

Identifying Extraneous Variables

Most students of marketing realize that the marketing mix variables—price, product, promotion, and distribution—interact with uncontrollable forces in the market, such as competitors' activities and consumer trends. Thus, marketing experiments are subject to the effect of extraneous variables. Because extraneous variables can produce confounded results, researchers must make every attempt to identify them before the experiment.

The chapter vignette illustrates how important isolating causes can be in developing theoretical explanations. Does cigarette advertising cause young people to smoke? One of the primary reasons for the inconclusiveness of this debate is the failure for most of the research to control for extraneous variables.[7] For instance, consider a study in which two groups of U.S. high school students are studied over the course of a year. One is exposed to a greater percentage of foreign video media in which American cigarettes are more often shown in a flattering and glamorous light. In fact, the video programming includes cigarette commercials. The other group is a control group in which their exposure to media is not controlled. Subjects are left free to view whatever they may choose. At the end of the year, the experimental group reports a greater frequency and incidence of cigarette smoking. Did the increased media exposure involving cigarettes cause smoking behavior?

Although the result seems plausible at first, the careful researcher may ask the following questions:

■ Was the demographic makeup of the two groups the same? While it is clear that the ages of the two groups are likely the same, different ethnic groups have different smoking rates. Approximately 10 percent of high school students report smoking (smoking cigarettes every day), but the rate is higher among some demographic groups.[8] White teens, for instance, had a higher smoking rate in 2013 than did Hispanic teens. Therefore, if one group contained disproportionately more white teens than Hispanic teens, we might expect the study to report different smoking rates than if the sample were proportionately representative of the white to Hispanic population.

■ How did the control group fill the time consumed by the experimental group in being exposed to the experimental treatment? Could it be that it somehow dissuaded them from smoking? Perhaps they were exposed to media with more anti-smoking messages?

■ Were the two groups of the same general achievement profiles? Those who are high in the need for achievement may be less prone to smoke than are other students.

■ Although it is a difficult task to list all possible extraneous factors, some that even sound unusual can sometimes have an effect. For example, did the students have equally dispersed birthdays? Researchers have even shown that smoking rates correspond to one's birthday, meaning that different astrological groups have different smoking rates.[9]

Because an experimenter does not want extraneous variables to affect the results, he or she must control or eliminate such variables. It is always better to spend time thinking about how to control for possible extraneous variables before the experiment since often there is nothing that can be done to salvage results after a confounding effect is identified.

Demand Characteristics and Experimental Validity

Demand characteristic

Experimental design element or procedure that unintentionally provides subjects with hints about the research hypothesis.

Most experiments involve some directed task performed by experimental subjects. Tasks like these are typically linked to the experimental hypotheses. The term **demand characteristic** refers to an experimental design element that unintentionally provides subjects with hints about the research hypothesis. Researchers cannot reveal the research hypotheses to subjects before the experiment or else they can create a confounding effect. Think about the retail atmospherics experiment. If the subjects were told before they participated that they were going to be involved in an experiment to see if they liked stores that were predominantly orange or predominantly blue, the researcher would never be sure if their responses to the dependent variable were really due to the differences in the experimental stimuli or due to the fact that the subjects were trying to provide a "correct" response, knowing that the experiment is about color. Once subjects believe they know the hypotheses, there is little hope that they will respond naturally.

Demand effect

Occurs when demand characteristics actually affect the dependent variable.

So, knowledge of the experimental hypothesis creates a confound. This particular type of confound is known as a **demand effect**. Demand characteristics make demand effects very likely.

Experimenter Bias and Demand Effects

Demand characteristics are aspects of an experiment that *demand* (encourage) that the subjects respond in a particular way. Hence, they are a source of systematic error. If participants recognize the experimenter's expectation or demand, they are likely to act in a manner consistent with the experimental treatment. Even slight nonverbal cues may influence their reactions.

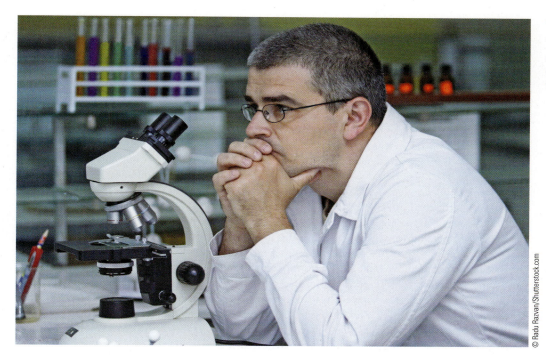

● ● ● ● ● ● ●

The experimenter unintentionally can create a demand effect by smiling, nodding, or frowning at the wrong time.

© Radu Razvan/Shutterstock.com

The person administering experimental procedures often creates prominent demand characteristics. If an experimenter's presence, actions, or comments influence the subjects' behavior or sway the subjects to slant their answers to cooperate with the experimenter, the experiment has introduced *experimenter bias*. When subjects slant their answers to cooperate with the experimenter, they are exhibiting behaviors that might not represent their behavior in the marketplace. For example, if subjects in an advertising experiment understand that the experimenter is interested in whether they changed their attitudes in accord with a given advertisement, they may answer in the desired direction. When researchers pay subjects to participate in experiments, the subjects become particularly eager to please and are more likely to try to respond as they believe the researcher wants them to respond rather than answering questions in a natural way. Acting in a manner oriented toward pleasing the researcher reflects a demand effect rather than a true experimental treatment effect.

Reducing Demand Characteristics

Although it is practically impossible to eliminate demand characteristics completely from experiments, researchers can take several steps aimed at reducing them. Many of these steps make it difficult for subjects to know what the researcher is trying to find out. Some or all of these may be appropriate in a given experiment:

1. Use an experimental disguise.
2. Isolate experimental subjects.
3. Use a "blind" experimental administrator.
4. Administer only one experimental treatment level to each subject.
5. Avoid using subjects who are paid based on performance in the task.

Experimental Disguise

The experimental administrator can tell subjects that the purpose of the experiment is somewhat different from the actual purpose. Most often, administrators simply tell less than the complete "truth" about what is going to happen. For instance, in the retail atmosphere study, the instructions informed subjects that the study sought their reaction to a new retail store concept. This really is true, but the instructions included nothing about color, lighting, or any other potential experimental effect.

In other cases, more deceit may be needed. Psychologists studying how much pain one person may be willing to inflict on another might use a ruse telling the subject that they are actually interested in the effect of pain on human performance. The researcher tells the actual subject to administer a series of questions to another person (who is actually a research assistant) and to provide the person with an increasingly strong electric shock each time an incorrect answer is given. In reality, the real dependent variable has something to do with how long the actual subject will continue to administer shocks before stopping.

Placebo

A false experimental treatment disguising the fact that no real treatment is administered.

A **placebo** is an experimental deception involving a false treatment. A **placebo effect** refers to the corresponding effect in a dependent variable that is due to the psychological impact that goes along with knowledge that a treatment has been administered. A placebo is particularly important when the experimental variable involves physical consumption of some product. The placebo should not be different in any manner that is actually noticeable by the research subject. If someone is told that a special food additive will suppress appetite, and they are supposed to sprinkle it on their dinner before eating as part of an experiment, another group should receive a placebo that looks exactly like the actual food additive but actually is some type of inert compound. Both groups are likely to show some difference in consumption compared to someone undergoing no effect. The difference in the actual experimental group and the placebo group would represent the true effect of the additive.

Placebo effect

The effect in a dependent variable associated with the psychological impact that goes along with knowledge of some treatment being administered.

Placebo effects exist in marketing research. For example, when subjects are told that an energy drink is sold at a discount price, they believe it is significantly less effective than when it is sold at the regular, non-discounted price.[10] Later, we will return to the ethical issues involved in experimental deception.

Isolate Experimental Subjects

Researchers should minimize the extent to which subjects are able to talk about the experimental procedures with each other. Although it may be unintentional, discussion among subjects may lead them to guess the experimental hypotheses. For instance, it could be that different subjects receive different treatments. The experimental integrity will be higher when each only knows enough to participate him/herself and the procedures prevent one subject from being concerned about other subjects.

Unfortunately, with social networking, experiments that take an extended time to complete allow subjects who ordinarily would have no way of contacting each other to communicate online. Pharmaceutical researchers worry that this social chatter online can damage the validity of their drug experiments.[11] For instance, social chatter in one experiment spread tips to subjects about when an inoculation would contain the placebo instead of the intended effect. If the subject knows the treatment is a placebo, it is no longer a placebo! Given the difficulty in completely isolating people in such a case, the researchers may seek pledges of confidentiality from the subjects promising not to discuss the experiment online.

Use a "Blind" Experimental Administrator

When possible, the research assistants actually administering the experiment do not know the experimental hypotheses. Ignorance can be bliss in this case as the big advantage is that if the administrator does not know what exactly is being studied, he/she will not likely give off clues that result in demand effects. Like the subjects, administrators often do their job best when they know only enough to guide subjects through the task.

Administer Only One Experimental Condition Per Subject

When subjects observe more than one experimental treatment condition, they are much more likely to guess the experimental hypothesis. Despite the cost advantages, most researchers should avoid administering multiple treatments to an individual subject. In the retail atmospherics example, if subjects responded first to a blue retail store concept, and then saw the same store that was exactly the same except the walls had become orange, then they are very likely to know that the researcher is interested in color.

Paying for Performance

Researchers often pay an incentive for respondents' cooperation. However, when the incentive depends on the researcher approving the cooperation of individual respondents, and the subjects are aware of this condition, acquiescence bias creeps in as the subjects become increasingly interested in pleasing the researcher as the incentive grows larger. In other words, the subjects believe there is a way they are supposed to respond and think about that instead of or in addition to responding to the experimental stimuli. A pay for performance incentive creates a demand characteristic as subjects are more attentive to the reason for the experiment than they may be otherwise.

Establishing Control

The major difference between experimental research and descriptive research is an experimenter's ability to control variables by either holding conditions constant or manipulating the experimental variable. If the color of beer causes preference, a brewery experimenting with a new clear beer must determine the possible extraneous variables other than color that may affect an experiment's results and attempt to eliminate or control those variables. Marketing theory tells us that brand image and packaging design are important factors in beer drinkers' reactions. Therefore, the researcher may wish to control the influence of these variables. He or she may eliminate these two extraneous variables by packaging the test beers in plain brown packages without any brand identification.

When extraneous variables cannot be eliminated, experimenters may strive for **constancy of conditions**. This means that subjects in all experimental groups participate in identical conditions except for the differing experimental treatments. The principle of matching discussed earlier helps make sure that constancy is achieved.

A supermarket experiment involving four test products shows the care that must be taken to hold all factors constant. The experiment required that all factors other than shelf space remain constant throughout the testing period. In all stores the shelf level (i.e., height) that had existed before the tests was to stay the same throughout the test period. Only the *amount* of shelf space (the treatment) was supposed to change. One problem involved store personnel accidentally changing shelf level when stocking the test products creating an alternative explanation for any change in sales. Thus, the researcher sought to minimize this problem by auditing each store four times a week. In this way, a change in shelf height could be detected in a minimum amount of time. The experimenter personally stocked as many of the products as possible, and the cooperation of stock clerks also helped reduce treatment deviations.

If an experimental method requires that the same subjects be exposed to two or more experimental treatments, an error may occur due to the *order of presentation*. For instance, if researchers are examining the effects of different levels of graphical interface on video game enjoyment and subjects are asked to view each of four different levels, the order in which they are presented may influence enjoyment. Subjects might enjoy one level simply because it follows a very poor level. **Counterbalancing** attempts to eliminate the confounding effects of order of presentation by requiring that one fourth of the subjects be exposed to treatment A first, one fourth to treatment B first, one fourth to treatment C first, and finally one fourth to treatment D first. Likewise, the other levels are counterbalanced so that the order of presentation is rotated among subjects.

Constancy of conditions
Means that subjects in all experimental groups are exposed to identical conditions except for the differing experimental treatments.

Counterbalancing
Attempts to eliminate the confounding effects of order of presentation by requiring that one fourth of the subjects be exposed to treatment A first, one fourth to treatment B first, one fourth to treatment C first, and finally one fourth to treatment D first.

Basic versus Factorial Experimental Designs

In *basic experimental designs* a single independent variable is manipulated to observe its effect on a single dependent variable. However, we know multiple factors influence complex marketing dependent variables such as recommendations, sales, product usage, and preference. The simultaneous change in independent variables such as price and advertising may have a greater influence on sales than if either variable is changed alone. *Factorial experimental designs* are more sophisticated than basic experimental designs and allow for an investigation of the interaction of two or more independent variables.

Laboratory Experiments

A marketing experiment can be conducted in a natural setting (a field experiment) or in an artificial or laboratory setting. In social sciences, the actual laboratory may be a behavioral lab, which is somewhat like a focus group facility. However, the experimental procedures may turn a classroom or an area in a shopping center into an experimental lab.

Laboratory experiment

The researcher has more complete control over the research setting and extraneous variables.

In a **laboratory experiment** the researcher maximizes control over the research setting and extraneous variables. For example, some advertising researchers recruit subjects and bring them to the agency's office or perhaps a mobile unit designed for research purposes. Researchers then expose subjects to a television commercial within the context of a program that includes competitors' ads among the commercials shown. While viewing the ads, a lie detector type device measures the subjects' physiological arousal. The researcher measures trial purchase intentions for the focal product as well. In a short time span, the marketer is able to collect information on emotional responses and consumer decision making. Our retail atmospheric experiment also illustrates a laboratory experiment.

Tachistoscope

Device that controls the amount of time a subject is exposed to a visual image.

Other laboratory experiments may be more controlled or artificial. For example, a **tachistoscope** allows a researcher to experiment with the visual impact of advertising, packaging, and so on by controlling the amount of time a subject sees a visual image. Each stimulus (for example, package design) is projected from a slide to the tachistoscope at varying exposure lengths (1/10 of a second, 2/10, 3/10, etc.). The tachistoscope simulates the split-second duration of a customer's attention to a package in a mass display.

Field Experiments

Field experiments

Research projects involving experimental manipulations that are implemented in a natural environment.

Field experiments are research projects involving experimental manipulations implemented in a natural environment. They can be useful in fine-tuning marketing strategies and determining sales forecasts for different marketing mix designs.

Facebook routinely implements field experiments by subjecting subscribers to various manipulations. The experiments attracted considerable attention given that Facebook conducts these tests without the knowledge of the subjects.[12] One experiment involved almost 700,000 users who became subjects as Facebook manipulated newsfeeds to provide the users with relatively high amounts of either positive or negative news. The research questions that were being examined dealt with whether or not the nature of the news (positive or negative) influences social networking behavior. Thus, Facebook measured how many positive or negative posts followed exposure to this experimental treatment. In fact, they discovered that they could manipulate users as those with more bad news posted more critical posts and those exposed to good news posted more positive posts. The results have implications for decisions related to how they sell advertising.

Experiments vary in their degree of artificiality and control. Exhibit 9.5 shows that as experiments increase in naturalism, they begin to approach a pure field experiment. As they become more artificial, they approach a pure laboratory experiment.

Generally, subjects know when they are participating in a laboratory experiment. Performance of certain tasks, responses to questions, or some other form of active involvement is characteristic of laboratory experiments. In field experiments, as in test-markets, subjects do not even know they have taken part in an experiment. Ethically, researchers should gain consent before having someone participate in an experiment. However, with field experiments consent is implied because subjects are not asked to do anything departing from their normal behavior nor do they typically know they are subjects in an experiment. The researchers should nonetheless maintain all precautions with respect to safety and confidentiality.

Facilities like this one can break down the food that companies sell and tell them exactly what it should taste like. Is this a good way to test the taste of new products?

Source: Analytical food laboratories

Mike McQueen/Terra/Corbis

● ● ● ● ● ● ●
The naturally occurring noise that exists in the field can interfere with experimental manipulations.

Advantages of Between-Subjects Designs

A basic question faced by the researchers involves how many treatments a subject should receive. For economic reasons, the researcher may wish to apply multiple treatments to the same subject. For instance, in the retail atmosphere experiment, each subject could rate each combination of colors and lighting. Thus, four observations on the dependent variable can be obtained from a single subject. Such a design is called a **within-subjects design**. Within-subjects designs involve repeated measures because with each treatment the same subject is measured.

In contrast, the researcher could decide that each person will receive only one treatment combination. This is referred to as a **between-subjects design**. Each dependent variable is measured only once for every subject.

Between–subjects designs are usually advantageous although they are usually more costly. The validity of between–subjects designs is higher because by applying only one treatment combination to one subject, the researcher reduces demand characteristics greatly. When a subject sees multiple conditions, he or she is more likely to be able to guess what the study's purpose might be. In addition, as we will see later, statistical analyses of between–subjects designs are simpler than within–subjects designs. This also means the results are easier to report and explain to management.

Within-subjects design
Involves repeated measures because with each treatment the same subject is measured.

Between-subjects design
Each subject receives only one treatment combination.

Laboratory experiments ← Artificial environmental setting   Natural environmental setting → Field experiments

EXHIBIT 9.5
The Artificiality of Laboratory Versus Field Experiments

Internal versus External Validity

As mentioned earlier, researchers always face trade-offs. Experiments are no exception and many of the design decisions affect an experiment's validity—but not all validity is created equal.

Internal Validity

Internal validity

Exists to the extent that an experimental variable is truly responsible for any variance in the dependent variable.

Internal validity exists to the extent that an experimental variable is truly responsible for any variance in the dependent variable. In other words, does the experimental manipulation truly cause changes in the specific outcome of interest? If the observed results were influenced or confounded by extraneous factors, the researcher will have problems making valid conclusions about the relationship between the experimental treatment and the dependent variable.

Thus, a lab experiment enhances internal validity because it maximizes control of outside forces. If we wish to know whether a certain odor causes increased productivity among service workers, we may set up a task in a room with a tightly controlled airflow so we can be sure that the specific odor exists in the air in the amount and intensity desired. We can also control temperature, lighting, density, sounds, and many other factors that would be difficult or impossible to control outside of a lab environment. If the only thing that varies from subject to subject is the odor, then we can safely say that any differences in performance must be attributable to human reactions to the scent.

Manipulation Checks

Internal validity depends in large part on successful manipulations. Manipulations should be carried out in such a way that it varies the experimental variable over meaningfully different levels. If the levels are too close together, the experiment may lack the power necessary to observe differences in the dependent variable. In a pricing experiment, it may be that manipulating the price of an automobile over two levels, \$25,800 and \$26,950, would not be successful in creating two truly different price categories.

Manipulation check

A validity test of an experimental manipulation to make sure that the manipulation does produce differences in the independent variable.

The validity of manipulations is examined with a **manipulation check**. If a researcher administers a drug in different dosages that should affect blood sugar levels, the researcher could actually measure blood sugar level after administering the drug to make sure that the dosages were different enough to produce a change in blood sugar. In marketing, the manipulation check often consists of a survey question or two. In the pricing example, subjects may answer a question about how low they believe the price of the car to be. A valid manipulation would produce substantially different average responses to that question in a "high" and "low" price group. Manipulation checks should always be administered after dependent variables in self-response format experiments. This keeps the manipulation check item from becoming a troublesome demand characteristic.

Extraneous variables can jeopardize internal validity. The six major ones are *history, maturation, testing, instrumentation, selection,* and *mortality.*

History

History effect

Occurs when some change other than the experimental treatment occurs during the course of an experiment that affects the dependent variable.

A **history effect** occurs when some change other than the experimental treatment occurs during the course of an experiment that affects the dependent variable. A common history effect occurs when competitors change their marketing strategies during a test-marketing experiment. History effects are particularly prevalent in repeated measures experiments that take place over an extended time. If we wanted to assess how much a change in recipe improves individual subjects' consumption of a food product, we would first measure their consumption and then compare it with consumption after the change. Since several weeks may pass between the first and second measurement, there are many things that could occur that would also influence subjects' diets.

Although it may sound extreme, examining the effect of some dietary supplement on various health-related outcomes may require that a subject be confined during the experiment's course. This may take several weeks. Without confining the subject in something like a hospital setting, there would be little way of controlling food and drink consumption, exercise activities, and other factors that may also affect the dependent variables.

A special case of the history effect is the **cohort effect**, which refers to a change in the dependent variable that occurs because members of one experimental group experienced different historical situations than members of other experimental groups. For example, two groups of managers used as subjects may be in different cohorts because one group encountered different experiences over the course of an experiment. If the experimental manipulation involves different levels of financial incentives and performance is the dependent variable, one group may be affected by an informative article appearing in a trade magazine during the experiment. Since the other group participated prior to this group, members of that group could not benefit from the article. Therefore, the possibility exists that the article rather than the change in incentive is truly causing differences in performance.

Cohort effect
Refers to a change in the dependent variable that occurs because members of one experimental group experienced different historical situations than members of other experimental groups.

Maturation

A **maturation effect** is a function of time and the naturally occurring events that coincide with growth and experience. Experiments taking place over longer time spans may see lower internal validity as subjects simply grow older or more experienced. Suppose an experiment were designed to test the impact of a new compensation program on sales productivity. If this program were tested over a year's time, some of the salespeople probably would mature as a result of more selling experience or perhaps gain increased knowledge. Their sales productivity might improve because of their knowledge and experience rather than the compensation program.

Maturation effect
A function of time and the naturally occurring events that coincide with growth and experience.

Testing

Testing effects are also called *pretesting effects* because the initial measurement or test alerts or primes subjects in a way that affects their response to the experimental treatments. Testing effects only occur in a before-and-after study. A before-and-after study is one requiring an initial baseline measure to be taken before an experimental treatment is administered. So, before-and-after experiments are a special case of a repeated measures design. For example, students taking standardized achievement and intelligence tests for the second time usually do better than those taking the tests for the first time. The effect of testing may increase awareness of socially approved answers, increase attention to experimental conditions (that is, the subject may watch more closely), or make the subject more conscious than usual of the dimensions of a problem.

Testing effects
A nuisance effect occurring when the initial measurement or test alerts or primes subjects in a way that affects their response to the experimental treatments.

Instrumentation

A change in the wording of questions, a change in interviewers, or a change in other procedures used to measure the dependent variable causes an **instrumentation effect**, which may jeopardize internal validity. If the experiment involves a personal interview with different interviewers asking questions after than before exposure to a treatment, the varying mannerisms of the interviewer may influence subject responses. If the same interviewers ask questions for both before and after a subject is exposed to an experimental manipulation, some problems may still arise. With practice, interviewers may acquire increased skill in interviewing, or they may become bored and decide to reword the questionnaire in their own terms. To avoid this problem, new interviewers are hired, but different individuals are also a source of extraneous variation due to instrumentation variation. There are numerous other sources of instrument decay or variation. Again, instrumentation effects are problematic with any type of repeated measures design.

Instrumentation effect
A nuisance that occurs when a change in the wording of questions, a change in interviewers, or a change in other procedures causes a change in the dependent variable.

Selection

The selection effect is a sample bias that results from differential selection of respondents for the comparison groups, or sample selection error, discussed earlier.

Mortality

If an experiment takes place over a period of a few weeks or more, some sample bias may occur due to the **mortality effect (sample attrition)**. Sample attrition occurs when some subjects withdraw from the experiment before it is completed. Mortality effects may occur if subjects drop

Mortality effect (sample attrition)
Occurs when some subjects withdraw from the experiment before it is completed.

from one experimental treatment group disproportionately from other groups. Consider a sales training experiment investigating the effects of close supervision of salespeople (high pressure) versus low supervision (low pressure). The high-pressure condition may misleadingly appear superior if those subjects who completed the experiment did very well. If, however, the high-pressure condition caused more subjects to drop out than the other conditions, this apparent superiority may be due to the fact that only very determined and/or talented salespeople stuck with the program.

External Validity

External validity

Is the accuracy with which experimental results can be generalized beyond the experimental subjects.

External validity is the accuracy with which experimental results are generalizable beyond the experimental subjects. External validity increases as subjects comprising a sample truly represent some defined population meaning that the results extend to market segments or groups of people. The higher the external validity, the more researchers and managers can count on the fact that any results observed in an experiment will also be seen in the "real world" (marketplace, workplace, sales floor, etc.).

SUV safety continues to improve, but car companies including GM, Jeep, Toyota and Suzuki still face liability lawsuits based on claims that a design contributed to a high propensity of roll-over.[13] The companies experiment with various types of suspensions and test the equipment in labs. Once the companies' design minimizes rollover problems in the lab, they move outside to a test track and see how a real vehicle handles. However, even this test leaves room for lawyers to argue that the tests lack external validity. After all, a track is not a highway and the test drivers are not typical SUV owners. Lab experiments are associated with low external validity because experimental procedures exact demanding control but do not adequately represent real-world intricacies. In other words, the experimental conditions may be too artificial. When a study lacks external validity, the researcher will have difficulty repeating the experiment with any change in subjects, settings, or time.

Convenient Subjects

Behavioral experiments conducted by basic marketing researchers such as academics often involve the use of convenient subjects rather than individuals randomly selected from some representative sampling frame (as we will discuss in Chapter 12). College students and crowdsourcing via social networks or Internet sites provide common approaches to finding convenient subjects, which results in a convenience sample. Convenience, time, money, and a host of other practical considerations often lead to using subjects from these easily accessible sources.

The issue of external validity represents a key concern in predicting how representative an experiment's results may be. Students are easily accessible, but they often are not representative of the total population. This is not always the case, however, and sometimes researchers focus on behaviors for which students have some particular expertise. Research directed at understanding how young adults react to Facebook promotions or how different studying techniques affect test performance can have a great deal of internal and external validity using students. This is because students fit within the population of interest. However, researchers wishing to conduct an experiment addressing a research question aimed at understanding how renovating church facilities affects clergy members' job satisfaction would probably not benefit much from using typical undergraduate business students as subjects. Why would anyone expect these students to behave like clergy?

Basic researchers often use college students as experimental subjects. This practice is widespread in academic studies. Some evidence shows that students are quite similar to household consumers, but other evidence indicates that they do not provide sufficient external validity to represent most populations. This is particularly true when students substitute or play the role of business-people. However, research results also display wide variance across different groups of students even for straightforward and seemingly predictable relationships.[14] For instance, the study showed that the relationship between attitude toward capitalism and perceptions of ethics in business ranged from −.15 to +.55 across a few dozen samples of undergraduate business students. The instability in results raises caution when using students in general, not just in terms of external validity.

As an alternative to students without sacrificing convenience, basic researchers turn to samples crowd-sourced via Amazon's Mechanical Turk or other sources that serve as a conduit to Internet workers. Here, one can entice individual workers to serve as experimental subjects in return for small cash payments. The relatively low costs and speed with which researchers can obtain data in this manner are very enticing and often serve as justification for using "mechanical" subjects (see the Research Snapshot on the next page).

However, the researcher needs to use particular caution in deciding whether these subjects are suitable for their purpose. Many of these "workers" spend hours a day performing tasks online. As such, they participate in many online experiments. Although some may see this experience as a good thing, the expertise actually creates a form of expertise bias as the subjects become particularly sensitive to any demand characteristic. Because Internet workers also believe their pay is contingent upon the way they respond, acquiescence bias also becomes a real possibility as the workers are eager to please and thus may not , or may not be able to, respond naturally.

In addition, screening questions are sometimes ineffective. Workers want to get paid. Thus, they often may answer screening questions in a manner that will get them included in the sample whether or not they actually fit the criteria. If a study is only about middle-aged males, workers of other types can still claim to fit this criterion to participate in the study. Also, social networking sites exist where workers converse with one another. Topics include which worker requests are worth doing and advice on how a worker *should* respond. As we saw earlier in the chapter when discussing social network postings' effects on drug experiments, this chatter enhances the possibility that the results are confounded by knowledge and amount to demand artifacts rather than true effects.

Researchers are not likely to stop using this source because it is so convenient, but great caution needs to be taken. Workers with the greatest amount of experience should be avoided as candidates for experiments. Screening needs to be done in a manner that subjects cannot easily detect. This may include allowing subjects that don't match the desired profile to participate in some way so they can get paid and feel like they completed the task. The experimenter should conduct the experiment over a very short timeframe (a couple of hours) to minimize the effect of chatter. With respect to internal validity, Internet workers crowd-sourced for pay perhaps provide better respondents to surveys that do not involve experimental manipulations where researchers are just seeking opinions.

Not all convenience subjects are the same. For instance, the research snapshot suggests that the time of the semester can affect what students participate in university research. Thus, an effect that exists at the end of the term may look a little different than the effect that might exist at the beginning of a term. Technology provides some alternatives to student subjects and more researchers are taking advantage of these opportunities.

In both surveys and experiments, researchers should consider using **attention filters**. Attention filters are items that have known and obvious answers included just to see if participants are playing along. A common attention filter item might be:

Have you ever had a fatal heart attack while watching television?

If someone answers yes, they would have to be in the afterlife to be telling the truth. Thus, their answers would be suspect. Research suggests that both students and Internet workers sometimes fail attention filters like this. In fact, a researcher using a convenience sample from these sources may expect 30 percent of subjects to be paying so little attention that they fail simple checks like these.[15]

Attention filters

Items that have known and obvious answers included just to see if participants are playing along.

Trade-Offs between Internal and External Validity

Naturalistic field experiments tend to have greater external validity than artificial laboratory experiments. Marketing researchers often must trade internal validity for external validity. Retail researchers sometimes conduct field experiments concerning merchandising, traffic flow, and a host of other issues. Retailers invest a lot of resources into their store designs. One important decision involves when to remodel a store. A research team implemented a field experiment examining changes in customer perceptions of the atmosphere, service quality, and store sales due to a remodel.[16] They measured the key dependent variables before and at two points in time after the remodel. In particular, they were interested in how the remodel affects new and old customers. The researchers conclude that a remodel leads to significant increases in spending and improved perceptions following the remodel. This finding is particularly strong among new store customers

RESEARCH SNAPSHOT

Mechanical Students

"Who needs extra credit?" Ever get asked that question in class? Well then, you know the answer. The bulk of experimental psychological research relies on student subjects and counts on them performing their duty to execute faithfully and honestly the instructions provided. However, are students equally able and motivated to do that? It turns out that male students are more likely to participate late in a term compared to female students. Also, the more conscientious students are, the more likely they are to participate early in the term. As a consequence, students with better grades participate early and those who are desperate for extra credit late in the term jump on the opportunity. If these factors also influence response quality then researchers may find different results for an experiment conducted in week 2 as opposed to week 13!

Students may become mechanical and simply move through the procedures motivated only by getting through and receiving credit. Enter Mechanical Turk. Amazon provides opportunities for browsers to become "workers" and participate in "human intelligence tasks (HIT)" for small amounts of pay. If a browser is bored, perhaps they'll take place in a short experiment on price policies for 40 cents. These "workers" opt into the experiment by clicking through an invitation link placed on the site. These workers are not all the same. More workers come from India than any other place. Most "workers" from India report being male (almost 2 of 3), college-educated (8 of 10), and report little concern about privacy. U.S. "workers" tend slightly toward reporting being male (6 of 10), younger than the general population, and college-educated (4 of 10). They also tend to be more socially and politically liberal than the population in general and, unlike their Indian coworkers, express greater concern about privacy.

Thus, mechanical subjects may replace mechanical students.

Sources: Chandler, J., Mueller, P., & Paolacci, G. (2014). "Nonnaïveté Among Amazon Mechanical Turk Workers: Consequences and Solutions for Behavioral Researchers." *Behavior Research Methods,* 46, 112–130. Kang, R., Brown, S., Dabbish, L., & Kiesler, S. (2014, July). Privacy Attitudes of Mechanical Turk Workers and the US Public. In Symposium on Usable Privacy and Security (SOUPS). Witt, E.A.,Donnelon, M.B., & Orlando, M.J. (2011), "Timing and Selection Effects within a Psychology Subjects Pool: Personality and Sex Matter," *Personality and Individual Differences,* 50 (February), 355–359.

who increase spending 16 percent after the remodel, with the increase falling only slightly to 14 percent after 12 months. Thus, a remodel seems to *cause* an increase in sales and improved perceptions of service quality and the store atmosphere.

Laboratory experiments with many controlled factors usually are high in internal validity, while field experiments like the remodel study generally have less internal validity, but greater external validity. While the store remodel study takes place in a real setting, giving some confidence that other remodels may produce similar outcomes, did the remodel really cause the change? Perhaps some road construction occurred simultaneously with the remodel and redirected traffic. Perhaps a competing store closed during the time of the remodel. The remodel may have coincided with a change in product assortment. Any of these factors may also drive a change in sales. Ideally, researchers could balance internal and external validity by using both experimental approaches. Results from lab experiments would be followed up with some type of field test.

Test-Marketing

The most common type of field marketing experiment is the test–market. Test-marketing has three broad primary uses in marketing research. Each use can be broken down more specifically to look at some issue in close detail. The three broad uses are as follows:

1. Forecasting the success of a newly developed product.
2. Testing hypotheses about different options for marketing mix elements.
3. Identifying weaknesses in product designs or marketing strategies.

254

Forecasting New Product Success

Test-markets frequently provide pilot tests for new products. The basic idea for a prototypical test-market is simple. A product is marketed on a small-scale under actual market conditions and the results allow a prediction of success or failure once the product is introduced on a large scale. Do people really want skinny beers? Heineken used a test-market to forecast the success of Heineken Premium Light (HPL) beer, which led Miller to test its own skinny beer (MGD 64) version, and now these beers have substantial market share.[17] Heineken also experiments with the type of can. Its light beer now comes in a skinny 8.5 ounce can as a result of positive tests.[18]

Companies using test-markets should realize that a new product concept also involves issues like advertising, pricing, supply chains, and retail placement. These issues may also be manipulated within a test-market. Estimates can then be made about the optimal advertising level, the need for product sampling, retail channel fit, or perhaps even advertising and retail channel selection interaction. Test-marketing permits evaluation of the entire new product concept, not just the physical good itself.

A researcher conducting a test-market may evaluate not only new products' sales as a dependent variable, but also existing products' sales as relevant dependent variables. This was a major concern in the introduction of HPL and MGD 64. Test-marketing allows a firm to determine whether a new offering will cannibalize sales from existing products, meaning that consumers are choosing the new offering as a replacement for another product offered by the same company. If Miller's MGD 64 sales in a test-market are impressive but sales of their other beers drop proportionately, then Miller would be less inclined to go through all the effort and expense of a full-scale new product launch.

Testing the Marketing Mix

Test-markets are equally useful as a field experiment manipulating different marketing plans for existing products. A manager can study any element of the marketing mix with a test-market.

Advertising researchers also can test the effectiveness of different media. Proctor and Gamble (P&G) owns many brands. Are they better off trying to engage customers and potential customers on Facebook, Instagram, or Twitter? The company can test the relative effectiveness of each with one or two brands with the hope of generalizing results to many brands. One test compared

Test-marketing can be used to determine the impact of different promotional approaches on sales and brand image.

Susan Van Etten

the engagement levels of the same brand video posted on the three social network media.[19] The conclusions were drawn by comparing engagement rates among brand followers across the three media. In the end, Facebook produced a miniscule engagement rate of 0.07 percent (that's 7 hundredths (1/100) of a percent) compared to an even lower rate 0.03 percent on Twitter. In contrast, Instagram produced an engagement rate of 4.2 percent. Thus, when engaging with videos, Instagram clearly produces the highest engagement.

Identifying Product Weaknesses

Test-market experimentation also allows identification of previously undetected product or marketing plan weaknesses. The company can deal with the weaknesses before committing to the actual sales launch. Although often this use of test-markets is accidental, in the sense that it isn't the reason for conducting the test-markets, companies save huge sums of resources by spotting problems before the full-scale marketing effort begins. Often, this use of test-marketing occurs when a product underperforms in at least one location. Researchers can then follow up with other research approaches to try and reveal the reason for the lack of performance. Once identified, product modifications address these faults specifically.

McDonald's test-marketed pizza periodically for years. The first test-market provided lower than expected sales results. The reasons for the underperformance included a failure to consider competitors' reactions and problems associated with the small, single portion pizza, which was the only way McPizza was sold. Additionally, McPizza didn't seem to bring any new customers to McDonald's. In the next round of test-marketing, the marketing strategy repositioned the pizza, shifting to a 14-inch pizza that was only sold from about 4 p.m. until closing. With still underwhelming results, McDonald's test-marketed "Pizza Shoppes" within the test McDonald's where employees could be seen assembling ingredients on ready-made pizza dough. As a result of the tests, McDonald's has shied away from pizza for the U.S. adult market. Pizza-like products, however, exist and succeed at many McDonald's locations in other nations.

When a product fails its market test, the test-market does not fail! In most cases, this represents an important *research success*. Encountering problems in a test-market either properly leads the company to introduce the new product or to make the planned change in marketing strategy. Thus, decision-makers avoid a huge mistake. In addition, test-market results may lead management to make adjustments that will turn the poor test-market results into a market success. The managerial experience gained in test-marketing can be extremely valuable, even when the performance results are disappointing.

Projecting Test-Market Results

Test-marketing is all about generalizing results. In other words, researchers do a trial test on a small-scale with the hope that the small-scale results will match those achieved in a full-scale product introduction. Therefore, external validity is a key consideration in designing a test-market. Test-markets are not appropriate for research questions that require very rigorous control of internal validity. However, the fundamental reason that test-markets are conducted is the hope that results can be accurately projected from the sample to the entire market or population of customers. Researchers take several steps to try to make these projections as accurate as they possibly can.

Most researchers support sales data with consumer survey data during test-markets. These help monitor consumer awareness and attitudes toward the test-marketed product as well as the repeat-purchase likelihood. Frequently this information is acquired via consumer panels.

Estimating Sales Volume: Some Problems

Test-marketing is all about estimating how well the product involved will do in the marketplace. Researchers project sales based on how well the product performs in the test-market. Numerous methodological factors cause problems in estimating national sales results based on regional tests. Often, these problems result from mistakes in the design or execution of the test-market itself.

Overattention

If managers give too much attention to a new product launch within a test-market, the product may be more successful than it would under more normal marketing conditions. In the test-market, the firm's advertising agency may make sure that the test-markets have excellent television coverage (which may or may not be representative of the national television coverage). If sales-people are aware of the test-market, they may spend unusual amounts of time making sure the new product is available or displayed better. This also means that managers should avoid any added incentives that would encourage extra sales efforts to sell the test-marketed product.

Unrealistic Store Conditions

The test-market should offer the product under the same conditions that would likely exist under real conditions. If greater effort leads to a relatively advantageous but unrealistic merchandising advantage, the results will not be valid. For example, extra shelf facings, eye-level stocking, and other conditions resulting from unrealistic distribution efforts would probably distort the test-market.

This situation may result from research design problems or overattention, as previously described. For example, if retailers know that someone is paying more attention to their efforts with a given product, they may give it artificially high distribution and extra retail support.

Reading the Competitive Environment Incorrectly

Another common mistake is to assume that the competitive environment will be the same nationally as in the test-market. If competitors are unaware of a test-market, the results will not measure competitors' reactions to company strategy. Competitors' responses after a national introduction may differ substantially from the way they reacted in the test-market. On the other hand, competitors may react to a test-market by attempting to undermine it. If they know that a firm is testing, they may attempt to disrupt test-market results with increased promotions and lower prices for their own products, among other potential acts of **test-market sabotage**.

Test-market sabotage
Intentional attempts to disrupt the results of a test-market being conducted by another firm.

Time Lapse

One relatively uncontrolled problem results from the time lapse between the test-market experiment and the national introduction of the product. Often, the period between the test-market and national introduction is a year or more. Given the time needed to build production capacity, develop channels of distribution, and gain initial sales acceptance, this may be unavoidable. However, the longer the time between the test-market and the actual selling market, the less accurate one should expect the results to be.

Advantages of Test-Marketing

This discussion of test-marketing should make it clear that test-markets are advantageous in ways that are very difficult to match with other research approaches. The key advantage of test-marketing is the real-world setting in which the experiment is performed. Although focus groups and surveys also can be useful in describing what people may like in a new product, the actual behavior of consumers in a real test-market location is far more likely to lead to accurate projections.

A second advantage of test-marketing is that researchers can easily communicate results to management. Although the experiment itself can be difficult to implement for a host of reasons, most related to small-scale or temporary marketing, the data analysis is usually very simple. Very often, the same procedures used in any simple experiment provide a way of producing test-market results. As we will see, this relies heavily on comparing means in some way. Researchers find marketing managers much more receptive to these types of results than they may be to results drawn from complicated mathematical models or qualitative approaches relying on deep subjective interpretation. Many consumer industries depend heavily on test-market results for help in decision making. The Research Snapshot on page 254 illustrates a typical test-market application and some problems that can occur.

Disadvantages of Test-Marketing

Test-markets also have disadvantages. Although the power of test-markets in providing accurate predictions are apparently such that companies would use test-markets for all major marketing changes, this is hardly the case. The disadvantages are such that test-markets are used less frequently than one might think.

Cost

Test-marketing is very expensive. Consider that for most new products, companies have to actually create production facilities on a small-scale, develop distribution within selected test-market cities, arrange media coverage specific to those locations, and then have systems and people in place to carefully monitor market results. All of this leads to high cost overall and very high unit costs. Heineken faced all these issues in test-marketing HPL. As a result, each six-pack could cost several times over the actual selling price. However, when HPL was introduced throughout the United States, the economies of scale that come with full-scale marketing left unit costs below the selling price.

Test-marketing a packaged-goods product typically costs millions. As with other forms of marketing research, decision-makers must weigh the value of the information against the research costs. The expense of test-marketing certainly is a primary reason why marketing managers refuse to use the approach. Although they do reduce error in decision making, they are not perfect and certainly some risk remains in basing decisions on test-market results. If they were risk-free, managers would use them far more frequently. Because they are not risk-free and are very expensive, managers may decide to make go or no-go decisions based on less expensive techniques that are often less accurate.

Time

Test-markets cost more than just money. Test-markets cannot be put together overnight. Simply planning a test-market usually takes months. Actually implementing one takes much longer. On top of the time for planning and implementation, researchers also must decide how long is long enough. In other words, when is the amount of data collected sufficient to have confidence in drawing valid conclusions?

The appropriate time period for a test-market varies depending on the research objectives. Sometimes, as in Procter & Gamble's testing of its unique new products Febreze, Dryel, and Fit Fruit & Vegetable Wash, the research takes several years. In other situations, as in P&G's testing of Encaprin pain reliever (a product that ultimately failed in national distribution), the time period may be shorter. HPL's test-markets lasted less than a year, relatively short by most standards.

Thus, even a quickly planned and implemented test-market can cost the firm a year or more in time. During this time, competitors are also trying to gain competitive advantage. The fear that competitors may make a big move first puts added pressure on marketing managers to move quickly. For this reason, the time costs associated with test-markets are a primary reason for forgoing them.

How long should a test-market be? Test-markets should be long enough for consumers to become aware of the product, have a chance to purchase it, consume it, and repurchase it at least one more time. Thus, it must be longer than the average purchase cycle for that particular product. A test-market that is too short may overestimate sales, because typically the early adopters are heavy users of the product. Thus, projections are based on consumers who are far from average.

Loss of Secrecy

As pointed out in the Research Snapshot on next page, one drawback to actual field experimentation is that the marketplace is a public forum. Therefore, secrets no longer exist. In the case of a new product, not only does the competition know about the new product, but a competitor can sometimes benefit from the test-market by monitoring the same dependent variables as is the

The Hidden in Hidden Valley Ranch

A few years ago, Hidden Valley Ranch (HVR) conducted a field market experiment to examine how effective three new flavors of salad dressings would be in the marketplace. Thus, there were three levels of the experimental variable, each representing a different flavor. HVR had to produce small batches of each flavor, get them bottled, and ship them to their sales representatives, who then had to stock the dressings in the participating retail stores. All of this was very expensive and the costs to produce each bottle used in a test-market were almost $20.

So, the first day of the test was consumed with sales reps placing the products in the salad dressing sections of retail stores. The second day, each rep went back to each store to record the number of sales for each flavor. By the third day, all of the bottles of all flavors had sold!! Amazing! Was every flavor a huge success?? Actually, one of HVR's competitors had sent their sales reps around beginning on the second day of the test to buy every bottle of the new HVR dressings in every store it had been placed in. Thus, HVR was unable to produce any sales

ZUMA Press/Newscom

data (the dependent variable) and the competitor was able to break down the dressing in their labs and determine the recipe.

This illustrates one risk that comes along with field tests. Once a product is available for sale, there are no secrets. Also, you risk espionage of this type that can render the experiment invalid.

© George Doyle & Ciaran Griffin

sponsoring firm. This may cause them to launch a competing product. In some cases, the competitor can even beat the originating company to the national marketplace.

Selecting test-markets is, for the most part, a sampling problem. The researcher seeks a sample of test-market cities that is representative of the population comprised of all consumers in the relevant market area. If a new product is being launched throughout Australia, for example, the researcher must choose cities that are typical of all Australians.

Thus, test-market cities should represent the entire competitive marketplace. For companies wishing to market a product through the United States, there is no single ideal test-market city. Nevertheless, the researcher must usually avoid cities that are not representative of the nation. Regional or urban differences, atypical climates, unusual ethnic compositions, or different lifestyles may dramatically affect a marketing program. Sometimes, although the researchers may wish to sell a product throughout the entire region of the United States, they may have a certain benefit segment in mind. Food companies may consider introducing a product for segments that enjoy spicy food, for example. In this case, they may choose cities known to favor spicier, more flavor-filled foods, such as New Orleans and San Antonio. In this case, those test-market city populations fit the benefit segment and in this way represent the relevant population better than more typical cities.

Certain cities are used repeatedly for test-market operations because researchers see them as typical of U.S. consumers overall. Whereas some larger cities like Tampa, Peoria, and San Antonio provide potential test-markets, test-markets often take place in smaller cities. Exhibit 9.6 lists several popular U.S. test-markets. Their popularity lies in how close they come to duplicating the average U.S. demographic profile.

A look at the table suggests Grand Junction as an apparently representative location. However, marketers may sometimes adjust the test-market to match the marketing strategy for a product. If a product is geared toward a certain consumer segment, for example, the Hispanic market, then Midland, Texas, may make more sense.

EXHIBIT **9.6**
Test-Market Areas and How
They Compare to Nation

Metropolitan Area	Population	Median Age	Percent of Family HHS	Hispanic Population
Cedar Rapids, IA	262,421	35.2	58.0%	3.5%
Eau Claire, WI	164,570	33.2	59.6%	1.9%
Grand Junction, CO	147,554	37.3	58.5%	13.9%
Columbus, OH	1,967,066	31.5	53.0%	5.4%
Wichita Falls, TX	151,201	32.5	62.3%	18.9%
Birmingham (Hoover), AL	1,140,300	35.5	55.0%	3.2%
Midland, TX	156,780	33.3	71.0%	38.0%
Entire U.S.A.	316,128,839	37.6	55.0%	16.0%

Source: © Cengage Learning 2013.

Americans and Canadians are similar in many respects. However, one shouldn't assume that a product that is successful in the United States will be successful in Canada. Thus, even after a successful American launch, a company may wish to conduct a test-market in Canada. In addition, even if Canadians like a new product, a unique marketing approach may be in order. Generally, Calgary, Alberta represents a prime test-market location for the Canadian market. When Italy's Podere Castorani Winery wished to expand to Canada, Calgary provided the test-market location. Likewise, when Shell introduced a fast-pay charge system, Calgary again proved a suitable test-market. Edmonton also is frequently used to test-market products. Imperial Tobacco selected Edmonton for a test-market of SNUS, a smokeless, spitless tobacco product, positioned as a safe alternative relative to smoking cigarettes.[20]

Like the United States, Canada is comprised of many different ethnic segments. Companies should also be aware that French Canada is quite different from the rest of the country. Edmonton may represent Canadians well enough but not French Canadians. Thus, companies may consider a test-market in Quebec City, Quebec, to see how French Canadian consumers will react.

Test-marketing in Europe can be particularly difficult. Although companies can test their products country by country, the sheer costs involved with test-marketing motivate firms to look for cities more representative of large parts of Europe. Copenhagen, Denmark, is one such city. While the population is somewhat homogenous demographically, the Danes tend to be multilingual and open to product innovation. Copenhagen is particularly representative of northern Europe. Other cities to be considered include Frankfurt, Germany, Birmingham, England, and Madrid, Spain.

Ethical Issues in Experimentation

Ethical issues with experimentation were discussed in Chapter 4 so we touch on them lightly here. The question of deception is a key ethical dilemma in experimentation. Although deception is necessary in most experiments, when debriefing procedures return subjects to their prior condition, then the experiment is probably consistent with good moral standards. When subjects have been injured significantly or truly psychologically harmed, debriefing will not return them to their formal condition and the experiment should not proceed. Therefore, we offer additional commentary on debriefing.

Researchers should debrief experimental subjects following an experimental procedure. In fact, many academic researchers, such as those conducting basic marketing research, are required to debrief subjects by their university IRB procedures. Debriefing experimental subjects by communicating the purpose of the experiment and the researcher's hypotheses about the nature of consumer behavior is expected to counteract negative effects of deception, relieve stress, and provide an educational experience for the subject.

Proper debriefing allows the subject to save face by uncovering the truth for himself. The experimenter should begin by asking the subject if he has any questions or if he found any part of the experiment odd, confusing, or disturbing. This question provides a check on the subject's suspiciousness and effectiveness of manipulations. The experimenter continues to provide the subject cues to the deception until the subject states that he believes there was more to the experiment than met the eye. At this time, the purpose and procedure of the experiment [are] revealed.[21]

Debriefing therefore is critical because it allows us to return subjects to normal. If this cannot be done through a simple procedure like debriefing, the experiment is likely to be unethical. If an experimenter, for example, took 100 nonsmokers, divided them into 4 groups of 25, and had them smoke 20 or 50 cigarettes a day for 5 years (manipulation 1) that were either called Nicky's or BeFrees (manipulation 2), no debriefing could restore them to normal and therefore, this experiment should never be conducted.

In addition to the Facebook experiments feeding disproportionately negative news as part of an experimental treatment embedded in newsfeeds, Facebook conducted experiments involving a treatment that locked users out of their Facebook accounts for potentially fraudulent behavior.[22] The manipulation involved creating the impression among users in the experimental condition that they are suspect of creating a false identity. Facebook gathered the data as an effort to better understand their own anti-fraud measures. However, some subjects became alarmed about the e-mails and compounding the matter, they were never debriefed. After facing public scrutiny, Facebook now claims to have implemented review procedures that amount to an IRB to approve research.

Additionally, there is the issue of test-markets and efforts extended toward interfering with a competitor's test-market. When a company puts a product out for public consumption, they should be aware that competitors may also now freely consume the product. If a competitor buys a lot of the product, the test-market results will be misleading. Further, any design secret is probably no longer secret as competitors dissect the new product. When a company actively attempts to sabotage or invalidate another company's test-market or they aim to infringe on some patent/copyright protection, those acts are ethically questionable. Finally, all of the cautions listed in Chapter 4 concerning the integrity of the data including the avoidance of any steps that tend to "massage" the data to be consistent with hypotheses apply stringently.

Peoria is considered more representative of the general U.S. population than is Miami.

TIPS OF THE TRADE

- Experiments test for causal evidence and thus represent the primary tool for causal research designs.
- Experimental manipulations in marketing research should possess the following characteristics:
  - Comprise distinct categories or magnitudes.
  - Two, three or, at the most, four treatment levels per experimental variable— particularly when multiple experimental variables are used in a single study.
  - Administered randomly across subjects.
- Experimental graphs are useful in displaying results, particularly when interactions are involved.
- Laboratory experiments provide greater internal validity at the cost of lower external validity.

- That's a primary way that basic researchers justify student subjects as legitimate.
- Great care needs to be taken in using Internet crowdsourcing to find subjects for research.
- Response error is often very high in the form of maturation, acquiescence, and dishonesty.
- Field experiments, including test-markets, increase external validity at the cost of internal validity.
  - Traditional test-markets remain expensive and technology offers some virtual alternatives. Test-markets also take a lot of time and involve a loss of secrecy.
  - When a product can easily be duplicated by competitors who obtain an actual product, then a test-market may not be wise.

∷ SUMMARY

1. Know the basic characteristics of research experiments. Independent variables are created through manipulation in experiments rather than through measurement. The researcher creates unique experimental conditions, each representing a unique level of an independent variable. Researchers refer to human sampling units as subjects in an experiment rather than respondents. This is because researchers subject them to experimental manipulations. Experimental manipulations are examined for the extent to which they affect outcomes. Main effects are due to differences in observed outcomes based on any single experimental variable. Interaction effects are due to combinations of independent variables.

2. Design an experiment using the basic issues of experimental design. Systematic experimental error occurs because sampling units (research subjects) in one experimental cell are different from those in another cell in a way that affects the dependent variable. In an experiment involving how people respond to color, the researcher would not want to have all males in one color group and all females in another. Randomization is an important way of minimizing systematic experimental error. If research subjects are randomly assigned to different treatment combinations, then the differences among people that exist naturally within a population should also exist within each experimental cell. Additionally, the researcher must try to control for all possible extraneous variables. Extraneous variables can render any causal inference as spurious. Control is necessary to reduce the possibility of confounding explanations.

3. Know tools for maximizing the validity of experiments with an emphasis on minimizing demand characteristics. Demand characteristics are experimental procedures that somehow inform the subject about the actual research purpose. Demand effects can result from demand characteristics. When this happens, the results are confounded. Demand characteristics can be minimized by following these simple rules: using an experimental disguise, isolating experimental subjects, using a "blind" experimental administrator, administering only one experimental treatment combination to each subject, and avoid using subjects who believe they are paid based on their performance. The more experiments someone participates in, the more likely they are to succumb to demand characteristics. A between-subjects design means that every subject receives only one experimental treatment combination. The main advantages of between-subjects designs are the reduced likelihood of demand effects and simpler analysis and presentation, all of which can improve validity.

4. Weigh the trade-off between internal and external validity.   Lab experiments offer higher internal validity because they maximize control of extraneous variables. High internal validity is a good thing because we can be more certain that the experimental variable is truly the cause of any variance in the dependent variable. Field experiments maximize external validity because they take place in a more natural setting, meaning that the results are more likely to generalize to the actual business situation. The increased external validity comes typically at the expense of internal validity and vice-versa.

5. Recognize the appropriate uses of test-marketing.   Major uses of test-marketing include forecasting the success of a newly developed product, testing hypotheses about different options for marketing mix elements, and identifying weaknesses in product designs or marketing strategies. The two major advantages of test-markets discussed in the chapter are the real-world setting and the ease in interpretation and communication of results. These advantages have to be weighed against several key disadvantages. These include the great amount of money that it costs to conduct a test-market, the length of time it takes to design, implement, and analyze a test-market, and the loss of secrecy that comes when the product is marketed publicly.

6. Avoid unethical experimental practices.   Experiments involve deception. Additionally, research procedures sometimes expose subjects to stressful or possibly dangerous manipulations. Every precaution should be made to ensure that subjects are not harmed. Debriefing subjects about the true purpose of a lab experiment following its conclusion is important for the ethical treatment of subjects. If debriefing can restore subjects to their pre-experimental condition, the experimental procedures are likely consistent with ethical practice. If the procedures change subjects in some way that makes it difficult to return them to their prior condition or subjects them to undue distress, then the experimental procedures probably go beyond what ethical researchers consider appropriate.

:: KEY TERMS AND CONCEPTS

attention filters, *253*
between-subjects design, *249*
blocking variables, *236*
cell, *240*
cohort effect, *251*
confound, *243*
constancy of conditions, *247*
control group, *239*
counterbalancing, *247*
covariate, *236*
demand characteristic, *244*
demand effect, *244*
experimental condition, *235*

experimental group, *239*
experimental treatment, *239*
external validity, *252*
field experiments, *248*
history effect, *250*
instrumentation effect, *251*
interaction effect, *237*
internal validity, *250*
laboratory experiment, *248*
main effect, *236*
manipulation check, *250*
maturation effect, *251*
mortality effect (sample attrition), *251*

placebo, *246*
placebo effect, *246*
randomization, *242*
repeated measures, *243*
subjects, *235*
systematic or nonsampling error, *241*
tachistoscope, *248*
test-market sabotage, *257*
test units, *241*
testing effects, *251*
within-subjects design, *249*

:: QUESTIONS FOR REVIEW AND CRITICAL THINKING

1. Define *experimental condition, experimental treatment,* and *experimental group.* How are these related to the implementation of a valid manipulation?

2. A tissue manufacturer that has the fourth-largest market share plans to experiment with a 50¢ off coupon during November and a buy one, get one free coupon during December. The experiment will take place at Target stores in St. Louis and Kansas City. In addition, coupons will be issued either through the Internet or in the local newspaper. Sales will be recorded by

scanners from which mean tissue sales for each store for each month can be computed and interpreted.

a. What are the experimental variable and the dependent variable?

b. Prepare a mock experimental graph that shows hypothetical results (simply guess at what the mean values for each experimental condition would be).

c. What types of people would make good subjects for this experiment?

3. What is the difference between a *main effect* and an *interaction* in an experiment? In question 2, what will create a main effect? Is an interaction possible?

4. How can experimental graphs be used to show main effects and interactions?

5. What purpose does the random assignment of subjects serve?

6. Why is an experimental confound so damaging to the conclusions drawn from an experiment?

7. What are demand characteristics? How can they be minimized?

8. Suppose researchers were experimenting with how much more satisfied consumers are with a "new and improved" version of some existing product. How might the researchers design a placebo within an experiment testing this research question? Is using such a placebo ethical or not?

9. If a company wanted to know whether to implement a new management training program based on how much it would improve return on investment in its southwest division, would you recommend a field or lab experiment?

10. Suppose you wanted to test the effect of three different e-mail requests inviting people to participate in a survey posted on the Internet. One simply contained a hyperlink with no explanation, the other said if someone participated $10 would be donated to charity, and the other said if someone participated he or she would have a chance to win $1,000. How would this experiment be conducted differently based on whether it was a between-subjects or within-subjects design? What are the advantages of a between-subjects design?

11. What is a manipulation check? How does it relate to internal validity?

12. When conducting an experiment, should a researcher seek participants to serve as subjects who participate in experiments an average of 4 hours a day or more? Take a yes or no stance and justify your answer.

13. Define internal validity and external validity. It's been said that external validity decreases when internal validity is high. Do you believe that is so? Explain your answer.

14. The idea of nonspurious association was introduced in Chapter 3. How does a confounding variable affect whether an association is spurious or nonspurious?

15. Why is a test-market usually considered an experiment?

16. When is test-marketing likely to be conducted? When is it not as appropriate? Which type of validity is most relevant to test-marketing?

17. What are the advantages and disadvantages of test-marketing?

18. What role does debriefing play in ensuring that experimental procedures are consistent with good ethical practice?

19. A university researcher asks students to participate in an experiment that takes 4 hours to complete in the last week of a semester. Each student receives 5 points extra credit. Another researcher conducts the same experiment using Internet crowd-sourced subjects paid $0.50 to participate. The subjects know they will be paid after the researcher checks the quality of each subject's response. Contrast these two approaches including a discussion of any ethical issues that might be involved.

:: RESEARCH ACTIVITIES

1. Consider the situation of a researcher approached by Captain John's in the Research Snapshot on page 241.
   a. Provide a critique of the procedures used to support the claim that Sea Snapper's product is superior. Prepare it in a way that it could be presented as evidence in court.
   b. Design an experiment that would provide a more valid test of the research question, "Do consumers prefer Sea Snapper fish sticks compared to Captain John's fish sticks?"

2. Conduct a taste test involving some soft drinks with a group of friends. Pour them several ounces of three popular soft drinks and simply label the cups A, B, and C. Make sure they are blind to the actual brands. Then, let them drink as much as they want and record how much of each they drink. You may also ask them some questions about the drinks. Then, allow other subjects to participate in the same test, but this time, let them know what the three brands are. Record the same data and draw conclusions. Does brand knowledge affect behavior and attitudes about soft drinks?

3. Consider the information in the chapter describing Facebook's experiments with their own users. Do you see any evidence of such experiments going on today at Facebook, Instagram, or Twitter? Would you consider Facebook's experimentation lab or field experiments? Given the backlash Facebook experienced from conducting the experiments, what advice would you have for them to improve the way they go about conducting experiments through their platform?

Examining Product Failure at No-Charge Electronics

Case 9.1

No-Charge Electronics owner Buzz Auphf needs to know how much product failure affects customer loyalty. Buzz contacts David Handy, a local market researcher, and they ultimately decide on examining a research question asking, "How do current customers react to different levels of product failure?" David designs the following experiment to examine the causal effect of product failure on customer purchase intentions, satisfaction, and loyalty.

The experiment is implemented via e-mail using a sample of current and prospective customers. Three free Netflix movies are provided as an incentive to participate. Subjects are asked to click through to an Internet site to download a product that will enhance their computer's graphics capability. In the low-failure condition, after the subjects click to the site, there is no change

in the graphics of their computers. In the high-failure condition, once they click through to the site, the subjects' computers go into an infinite loop of obscene graphical images until a message arrives indicating that a severe virus has infected their computer and some files may be permanently damaged. This goes on for 45 minutes with no remedy. At that time, a debriefing message pops up telling subjects that it was all part of an experiment and that their computer should now function properly. Prepare a position statement either agreeing or disagreeing that the experiment is consistent with good ethical practice.

Tooheys

Case 9.2

Sixty-six willing Australian drinkers helped a Federal Court judge decide that Tooheys didn't engage in misleading or deceptive advertising for its 2.2 beer. The beer contains 2.2 percent alcohol, compared to 6 percent for other beers, leading to a claim that could be interpreted as implying it was non-alcoholic.

Volunteers were invited to a marathon drinking session after the Aboriginal Legal Service claimed Tooheys' advertising implied beer drinkers could imbibe as much 2.2 beer as they wanted without becoming legally intoxicated. Drunken driving laws prohibit anyone with a blood-alcohol level above 0.05 from getting behind the wheel in Australia.

So, an experiment was conducted to see what happens when a lot of 2.2 is consumed. But the task wasn't easy or that much fun. Some subjects couldn't manage to drink the required 10 "middies," an Aussie term for a beer glass of 10 fluid ounces, over the course of an hour.

Thirty-six participants could manage only nine glasses. Four threw up and were excluded. Two more couldn't manage the "minimum" nine glasses and had to be replaced.

Justice J. Beaumont observed that consuming enough 2.2 in an hour to reach the 0.05 level was "uncomfortable and therefore an unlikely process." Because none of the ads mentioned such extreme quantities, he ruled they couldn't be found misleading or deceptive.[23]

Questions

1. Would a lab experiment or a field experiment be more "valid" in determining whether Tooheys could cause a normal beer consumer to become intoxicated? Explain.
2. Describe an alternate research design that would have higher validity.
3. Is the experiment described in this story consistent with good ethical practice?
4. Is validity or ethics more important?

::::::: **PART THREE**

Measurement

Hill Street Studios/Getty Images

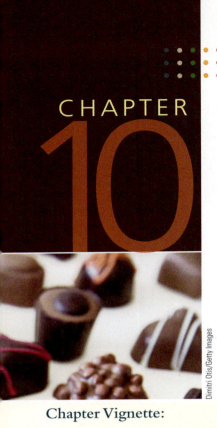

Dimitri Otis/Getty Images

Measurement and Attitude Scaling

Chapter Vignette:

Do You Know How to Score?

*I*n sports, one can always know who won a match by looking at the final score. Although sports statisticians keep track of countless statistics, in the end, the final score is all that is needed to judge the outcome. In business, one can't always tell how a team is doing. Certainly, marketing managers would like to know how well they were doing with a single score. For a long time, marketers gauged performance by their customer satisfaction score. Over time though, the relationship between satisfaction and overall performance proved weaker than first thought. Some analysts believe they now know what that single score might be. Indeed, the net promoter score (NPS) proposes to be the single indicator that tells how well a business has performed. Researchers can easily apply the NPS by asking them a single survey item scored on a 0 to 10 scale, as such:

On the 0 to 10 point scale shown below, how likely is it that you would recommend Spirit Airlines to a friend or colleague?										
0	1	2	3	4	5	6	7	8	9	10

Consumers' responses equal their scores. A score of 6 or below is associated with a label of detractor, a score of 7 or 8 is labeled passively satisfied, and a score of 9 or 10 signifies a promoter. Companies with a high proportion of promoters tend to outperform competitors significantly. A primary reason is that these loyal, promoter customers help perform the sales and promotion functions for the firm.

Robert Llewellyn/Photolibrary/Getty Images

Obviously, the simplicity of this approach is attractive to many businesses. However, the method is not without controversy. Questions about the usefulness and the validity of the NPS approach have surfaced. Some question exactly what the NPS item measures. The NPS best represents intent to spread positive word of mouth. Some researchers question the one-size-fits-all approach or suggest that although the item may predict, the prediction accuracy is far from perfect and leaves room for other concepts to explain variance in performance. Models that predict do not always offer useful explanations. Some researchers claim that without controlling for other factors, any correlation between the NPS and things like profitability could be misleading. Factors such as the length of the relationship between a firm and a customer and the type of industry may change the nature of the relationship between the NPS and performance. However, despite the NPS shortcomings, it is doubtful that competitive firms would trade even a single promoter for dozens of detractors or even a handful of passively satisfied customers. So, this single item certainly helps managers know the score![1]

Introduction

Anyone who has ever followed a recipe knows the importance of good measurement. Following a recipe may seem easy, but understanding the quantities represented and the units of measure can be critical. Confuse salt with sugar or tablespoons for teaspoons and the dish is ruined. Just as in the culinary arts, researchers can measure business and marketing in more than one way. Also, researchers often may have to use imperfect measurement devices. Measure a concept poorly and the "recipe" is a likely disaster. Only in this case, the "recipe" is usually an important business decision poorly made instead of a ruined dish.

What Needs to Be Measured?

Managers can't know if their strategies are creating value and the firm is performing well without valid measurement. However, decision-makers often express problems in terms of things that are complex and abstract. Managers want to "out-perform" their competitors but knowing exactly what good performance means is not so simple. A measure cannot be any better than the concepts' definitions. Measurement then, begins with a definition.

Measurement is the process of describing some property of a phenomenon, usually by assigning numbers some systematic way. Good measurement results when the assignment produces both reliable and valid measures. The decision statement, corresponding research questions, and any subsequent research hypotheses determine what concepts researchers need to measure. The numbers convey information about the phenomenon. When numbers are used, the researcher must have a rule for assigning a number to an observation in a way that provides an accurate description.

We can illustrate measurement by thinking about the way instructors assign students' grades. Instructors try systematically to represent students' varying levels of performance; how well a student has mastered the course material. A grade represents student performance. Students with higher performance should receive a different grade than do students with lower performance. Even the concept of student performance defies a universally applied measurement approach. Consider the following options:

1. A student can be assigned a letter corresponding to his/her performance as is typical of U.S.-based grading systems.

   a. A—Represents excellent performance
   b. B—Represents good performance
   c. C—Represents average performance
   d. D—Represents poor performance
   e. F—Represents failing performance

2. A student can be assigned a number from 1 to 20, which is the system more typically used in France.

   a. 20—Represents outstanding performance
   b. 11–20—Represent differing degrees of passing performance
   c. Below 11—Represent failing performance

Measurement

The process of describing some property of a phenomenon of interest, usually by assigning numbers in a systematic way that aims to be reliable and valid.

Take a look at the section of the student survey shown in the screen-shot. Suppose someone thought the items made a composite scale and you are asked to analyze its quality. An-swer the following questions:

1. Is the level of measurement nominal, ordinal, interval, or ratio?
2. Assuming the scale items repre-sent studying concentration, do you think any of the items need to be reverse-coded before a summated scale could be formed? If so, which ones?

3. Using the data for these items, compute the coefficient α and draw some conclusion about the scale's reliability.
4. At this point, how much can be said about the scale's validity? Are there any items that do not belong on the scale?

© George Doyle & Ciaran Griffin

Please read each of the following statements. After reading each, click on the the circle that best describes how much you agree with each statement.

	Strongly Disagree	Disagree	Neutral	Agree	Strongly Agree
I make time to study every day.	○	○	○	○	○
I know the material better after I study.	○	○	○	○	○
I can't study when it's quiet.	○	○	○	○	○
I prefer to not be around others when I study.	○	○	○	○	○
I can study the night before and be ready for a test.	○	○	○	○	○
I like to study with others.	○	○	○	○	○
I arrange time to study with others.	○	○	○	○	○

www.qualtrics.com

3. A student can be assigned a number corresponding to a percentage performance scale.

   a. 100 percent—Represents a perfect score indicating the best performance.
   b. 60–99 percent—Represents differing degrees of passing performance, each number representing the proportion of correct work.
   c. 0–59 percent—Represents failing performance but still captures proportion of correct work.

4. A student can be assigned one of two letters corresponding to performance.

   a. P—Represents a passing mark
   b. F—Represents a failing mark

Each measurement scale has the potential of producing error or some lack of validity. Exhibit 10.1 illustrates a common student performance measurement application.

Often, instructors may use a percentage scale all semester long and then at the end, have to assign a letter grade for a student's overall performance. Does this produce any potential measurement

EXHIBIT **10.1**

Are There Any Validity Issues with This Measurement?

Student	Percentage Grade	Difference from Next Highest Grade	Letter Grade
1	79.4%	0.5%	C
2	70.0%	9.4%	C
3	69.0%	1.0%	D
4	79.9%	NA	B

problems? Consider two students who have percentage scores of 79.4 and 70.0, respectively. The most likely outcome when these scores are translated using a conventional ten-point spread into "letter grades" is that each receives a C (70–80 percent range for a C). Consider a third student who finishes with a 69.0 percent average and a fourth student who finishes with a 79.9 percent average.

Which students are happiest with this arrangement? The first two students receive the same grade, even though their scores are over 9 percentage points apart. The third student gets a grade lower (D) performance than the second student does, even though their percentage scores are only 1.0 percentage point different. The fourth student, who has a score only 0.5 percentage points higher than the first student, would receive a B. Thus, the measuring system (final grade) suggests that the fourth student outperformed the first (assuming that 79.9 is rounded up to 80) student (B versus C), but the first student did not outperform the second (each gets a C), even though the first and second students have the greatest difference in percentage scores.

One can make a case that error exists in this measurement system. In fact, all measurement systems present the potential for error. Researchers, if we are to represent concepts truthfully, must make sure that the measures used are accurate enough to yield useful conclusions. Making use of measures requires that the researcher at least somewhat understands the flaws in the particular measurement tools used. When this is the case, researchers can sometimes account for the error statistically. Ultimately, scientific research would be impossible without measurement.

Concepts

A researcher has to know what to measure before knowing how to measure something. The research questions should emphasize the relevant concepts involved in the decision facing the firm. A **concept** can be thought of as a generalized idea that represents something of identifiable and distinct meaning. Demographic concepts such as *age*, *sex*, and *number of children* are relatively concrete concepts having relatively unambiguous meanings. They present few problems in either definition or measurement. Other concepts are more abstract. Concepts such as *loyalty*, *personality*, *performance*, *channel power*, *trust*, *corporate culture*, *guilt*, *customer satisfaction*, *value*, and so on are more difficult to both define and measure. Consumer involvement may seem like a simple idea until the researcher tries to unambiguously define it and measure it. Recently, marketing managers use the term engagement to represent how much a consumer is interested in and interacts with a brand. Engagement and involvement seem very similar. If, however, engagement and involvement are different concepts, marketing researchers must develop distinct scales for each concept.[2]

Concept

A generalized idea that represents something of identifiable and distinct meaning.

Operational Definitions

Researchers measure concepts through a process known as **operationalization**. This process involves identifying scales that correspond to properties of the concept. **Scales**, just as a scale you may use to check your weight, are measurement devices that provide a range of values that correspond to different characteristics or amounts of a characteristic in a concept. In other words, scales provide **correspondence rules**, which indicate that a certain value on a scale corresponds to some true value of a concept. Hopefully, they do this in a truthful way. A student receiving an A should be among the best performers in a class.

Here is an example of a correspondence rule: "Assign numerals 1 through 7 according to how much individual customers trust a sales representative. If a customer judges a sales representative as completely trustworthy, assign a 7. If the sales rep is perceived as completely untrustworthy, assign the numeral 1. Numbers between 1 and 7 represent varying degrees of trust." The opening vignette describes the concept of NPS and its correspondence rules.

Operationalization

The process of identifying scale devices that correspond to properties of a concept involved in a research process.

Scales

A device providing a range of values that correspond to different characteristics or amounts of a characteristic exhibited in observing a concept.

Correspondence rules

Indicate the way that a certain value on a scale corresponds to some true value of a concept.

Variables

Researchers use the variance in concepts to make meaningful diagnoses. Therefore, when we defined *variables*, we really were suggesting that variables capture different values of a concept. Scales capture a concept's variance and, as such, the scales provide the researcher's variables. Consider the following hypothesis:

H1: Salesperson experience is related positively *to salesperson job performance.*

The hypothesis implies a relationship between two variables, experience and job performance. The variables capture variance in the experience and performance concepts. One employee may have fifteen years of experience and be a top performer. A second may have ten years' experience and be a good performer. The scale used to measure experience is quite simple in this case and would involve providing the number of years an employee has been with the company. Job performance, not quite so simple a concept, might involve a correspondence rule with which a supervisor places an employee into one of several performance categories.

Constructs

Sometimes, a single variable cannot capture a concept alone. Using multiple variables to measure one concept often provides a more complete account of some concept than could any single variable. Even in the physical sciences, scientists apply multiple measurements to obtain representations that are more accurate. As concepts become more abstract, multiple items become necessary for good measurement.

A **construct** is a term used for latent concepts measured using multiple variables. By latent, we mean the concept is not directly observable and instead we infer a value by using multiple indicators such as individual scale items. For instance, a salesperson's customer orientation is inferred by using responses to scale items like these (each captured on a 1–5 scale of some type):[3]

Construct

A term used to refer to latent concepts measured with multiple variables.

1. I offer the product that is best suited to a customer's problem.
2. A good employee has to have the customer's best interests in mind.
3. I try only to sell my customers things that will provide him/her value.
4. I put my customer's best interests before the profitability of my company.
5. I try to find out what kind of products will be most helpful to a customer.

Marketing researchers deal with many latent constructs that represent concepts such as personality, lifestyle, consumer traits like price consciousness, representations of experiences including consumer emotions, and consumption outcomes such as value perceptions.

Operational definitions translate conceptual definitions into measurement scales. An operational definition is like a manual of instructions or a recipe. Even the truth of a statement like "Gaston makes good seafood gumbo" depends on the definition of gumbo and the ingredients used in the gumbo. If salesperson customer orientation is defined as a salesperson placing relatively high priority on the customer's best interests, then applying the five items stated previously provides an operational definition.

Levels of Scale Measurement

Nominal scales

Represent the most elementary level of measurement in which values are assigned to an object for identification or classification purposes only.

Marketing researchers use many scales. Not all scales capture the same richness in a measure and not all concepts require a rich measure. But, a researcher can classify all measures based on the way they represent distinctions between observations of a variable. The four levels or types of scale measurement are *nominal, ordinal, interval,* and *ratio level scales.* Traditionally, the level of scale measurement is important because it determines the mathematical comparisons that are allowable. Each of the four scale levels offers the researcher progressively more power in testing the validity of a scale and analyzing the way it corresponds to other concepts. The largest line of demarcation in this respect lies between the ordinal and interval levels. We begin though by taking a look at the most basic type of measurement system.

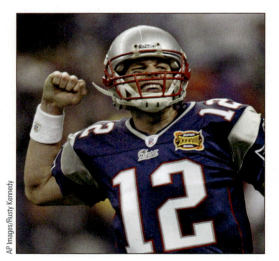

Athletes wear nominal numbers on their jerseys.

Nominal Scale

Nominal scales represent the most elementary level of measurement. A nominal scale assigns a value to an object for identification or classification purposes. The value can be a number, but does not have to be a number, because nominal scales do not represent quantities. In this sense, a nominal scale is truly a qualitative scale. Nominal scales are extremely useful even though some may consider them elementary.

Marketing researchers use nominal scales quite often. For instance, suppose Barq's Root Beer experimented with three different types of sweeteners (cane sugar, corn syrup, or fruit extract) in an effort to decide which created the best tasting soft drink. Basically, Barq's researchers designed a taste test experiment. Experimental subjects taste one of the three recipes and then rate how much they like it and how likely they would be to buy that particular drink. The researchers would like the experiment to be blind so that he/she does not bias subjects' perceptions. Thus, when subjects actually taste one of the three root beers, the cups containing the drinks say X, Y, or Z, not cane sugar, corn syrup, or fruit extract. The X, Y and Z become the measuring system that represents the variance in sweeteners.

Nominal scaling is arbitrary in the sense that each label can be assigned to any of the categories without introducing error; for instance, in the root beer example, the researcher can assign the letter Z to any of the three options without damaging scale validity. Cane sugar could just as properly be labeled Z as X, or Y, or even A, or B. The researcher might use numbers instead of letters without any change in the validity of the measuring system. If so, cane sugar, corn syrup, and fruit extract might be identified with the numbers 1, 2, and 3, respectively, or even 543, −26, and 8080, respectively. Either set of numbers is equally valid since the numbers are not representing different quantities. They are simply identifying the type of sweetener.

We encounter nominal numbering systems all the time. Uniform numbers are nominal numbers. Tom Brady is identified on the football field by his jersey number. What is his number? Airport terminals are identified with a nominal numbering system. In the Atlanta airport, a departing traveler can go through terminals T, A, B, C, D, and E before reaching a departure gate at terminal F. School bus numbers are nominal in that they simply identify a bus. Elementary school buses sometimes use both a number and an animal designation to help small children get on the right bus. So, bus number "8" may also be the "tiger" bus.

The first drawing in Exhibit 10.2 depicts the number 7 on a horse's colors. This is merely a label to allow bettors and racing enthusiasts to identify the horse. The assignment of a 7 to this horse does not mean that it is the seventh fastest horse or that it is the seventh biggest or anything else meaningful. But, the 7 does let you know when you have won or lost your bet!

EXHIBIT 10.2

Nominal, Ordinal, Interval, and Ratio Scales Provide Different Information

Source: © Cengage Learning 2013.

EXHIBIT 10.3

Facts about the Four Levels of Scales

Level	Examples	Numerical Operations	
Nominal	Yes – No Female – Male Buy – Did Not Buy Postal Code: _____	Counting	• Frequencies • Mode
Ordinal	Rankings Choose from the Following: • Dissatisfied • Satisfied • Very Satisfied • Delighted Indicate Your Level of Education: • HS Diploma • Some College • Bachelor's Degree • Graduate Degree	Counting and Ordering	• Frequencies • Mode • Median • Range
Interval	100-Point Job Performance Ratings Assigned by Supervisors: 0% = Worst Performers 100% = Best Performers Temperature-Type Attitude Scales: Low Temperature = Bad Attitude High Temperature = Good Attitude	Common Arithmetic Operations	• Mean • Median • Variance • Standard Deviation
Ratio	Amount Purchased Salesperson Sales Volume Likelihood of performing some act: • 0% = No Likelihood to • 100% = Certainty Number of stores visited Time spent viewing a particular web page Number of web pages viewed	All Arithmetic Operations	• Mean • Median • Variance • Standard Deviation

Exhibit 10.3 lists some nominal scales commonly used by marketing researchers. Nominal scale properties mean the numbering system simply identifies things.

Ordinal Scale

Ordinal scales

Ranking scales allowing things to be arranged based on how much of some concept they possess.

Ordinal scales have nominal properties, but they also allow for categorization based on how much a characteristic exists relative to others. In other words, an ordinal scale is a ranking scale. When a professor assigns an A, B, C, D, or F to a student at the end of the semester, he or she is using an ordinal scale. An A represents relatively greater performance than B, which is relatively greater performance than C, and so forth.

Surveys often ask research participants to *rank order* things based on preference. So, preference is the concept, and the ordinal scale lists the options from most to least preferred, or vice versa. Five objects can be ranked from 1–5 (least preferred to most preferred) or 1–5 (most preferred to least preferred) with no loss of meaning. In this sense, ordinal scales are somewhat arbitrary, but not nearly as arbitrary as a nominal scale.

When marketing professors take some time off, they sometimes like to place a wager. They may place a wager on a horse race online or even go to the racetrack itself. The race results are described with an ordinal scale consisting of three categories: win, place and show. A horse finishing in the "show" position has finished after the "win" and "place" horses (see the second drawing in Exhibit 10.2). This ordinal scale captures the order of finish accurately, to which one can apply an ordered number rule:

■ Assign 1 to the "win" position
■ Assign 2 to the "place" position
■ Assign 3 to the "show" position

Shooting at Los Angeles International Airport

Friday's attack at LAX took place in Terminal 3 at about 9:20 a.m. local time.

Sources: Los Angeles International Airport; Reuters
Staff, 01/11/2013

Without nominal scales, how would you know which terminal to go to at this airport?

Sometimes, the winning horse defeats the place horse by only a fraction (wins by a "nose"). The place horse defeats the show horse by 20 seconds or more. Yet, they still finish 1, 2, and 3. An ordinal scale does not tell by how much a horse won. But, the scale is good enough to separate winning bets from losing bets. Typical ordinal scales in marketing research ask respondents to rate brands, companies, and the like as excellent, good, fair, or poor. Researchers know excellent is higher than good, but they do not know by how much.

Interval Scale

Interval scales have both nominal and ordinal properties, but they also capture information about differences in quantities of a concept. So, not only would a sales manager know that a particular salesperson outperformed a colleague, but the manager would know by how much. If a professor assigns grades to term papers using a numbering system ranging from 1.0–20.0 points, not only does the scale represent the fact that a student with a 16.0 outperformed a student with a 12.0, but the scale would show by how much (4.0 points).

The third drawing in Exhibit 10.2 depicts a horse race in which the win horse is one second ahead of the place horse, which is 20 seconds ahead of the show horse. Not only are the horses identified by the order of finish, but the difference between each horse's performance is known. So, using an interval scale we know horse number 7 and horse number 6 performed similarly, but horse number 5 performed not nearly as well.

A classic example of an interval scale is a Fahrenheit temperature scale. Consider the following weather:

- June 6 was 80° F
- December 7 was 40° F

The interval Fahrenheit scale lets us know that December 7 was 40° F colder than June 6. But, we cannot conclude that December 7 was twice as cold as June 6. Although the actual numeral 80 is indeed twice as great as 40, remember that this is a scaling system. In this case, the scale is not iconic, meaning that it does not exactly represent some phenomenon. In fact, these temperatures can be converted to the more common Celsius scale. Then, the following would result:

- June 6 was 26.7° C
- December 7 was 4.4° C

Interval scales

Scales that have both nominal and ordinal properties, but that also capture information about differences in quantities of a concept from one observation to the next.

Obviously, now we can see that December 7 was not twice as cold as June 6. December 7 was 40° F or 22.3° C cooler, depending upon your thermometer. Interval scales are very useful because they capture relative quantities in the form of distances between observations. No matter what thermometer is used, December 7 was colder than June 6.

Ratio Scale

Ratio scales that they have all the properties of interval scales with the additional attribute of representing absolute quantities. Interval scales represent only relative meaning whereas ratio scales represent absolute meaning. In other words, ratio scales provide iconic measurement. Zero, therefore, has meaning in that it represents an absence of some concept.

An absolute zero is a defining characteristic in determining between ratio and interval scales. For example, money is a way to measure economic value. Consider the following items offered for sale in an online auction:

- Antique railroad pocket watch circa 1910—sold for $50
- Authentic Black Forest cuckoo clock—sold for $75
- Antique gold-filled Elgin wristwatch circa 1950—sold for $100
- "Antique" 1970s digital watch—did not sell and there were no takers for free

We can make the ordinal conclusions that the cuckoo clock was worth more than the pocket watch and that the wristwatch was worth more than the cuckoo clock, all of which were worth more than the 1970s digital watch. We can make interval conclusions such as that the cuckoo was worth $25 more than the pocket watch. We can also conclude that the wristwatch was worth twice as much as the pocket watch and that the 1970s watch was worthless (selling price = $0.00). The latter two conclusions are possible because money price represents a ratio scale.

Temperature can also be captured by a ratio scale. The Kelvin scale begins at 0 K, corresponding to −273.2° on the Celsius scale (an interval scale). This temperature is known as absolute zero. Zero K is the point at which the kinetic energy of atoms in a water molecule approaches 0, meaning that they are moving as slowly as possible. This is as cold as water can get since there is no way of slowing the molecules further (they never completely stop). Thus, 0 K indeed has absolute meaning.

Mathematical and Statistical Analysis of Scales

Although it is true that one can perform mathematical operations with numbers from nominal scales, the result may not have a great deal of meaning. For instance, a school district may perform mathematical operations on school bus numbers. With this, they may find that the average school bus number is 77.7 with a standard deviation of 20.5. Will this help them use the buses more efficiently or better assign bus routes? Probably not. Thus, although you can put nominal numbers into formulas and perform calculations with almost any numbers, the researcher has to know the meaning behind the numbers before drawing useful conclusions.[4]

Discrete Measures

Discrete measures are those that take on only one of a finite number of values. A discrete scale is most often used to represent a classificatory variable. Therefore, discrete scales, possessing nominal properties, do not represent intensity of measures, they represent only membership. Common discrete scales include any yes-or-no response, matching, color choices, or practically any scale that involves selecting from among a small number of categories. Thus, when someone selects from the following responses

- Disagree
- Neutral
- Agree

the result is a discrete value that can be coded 1, 2, or 3, respectively. When discrete scales represent an ordered arrangement of agreement, as in this case, they can possess ordinal properties and nominal properties.

Certain statistics are most appropriate for discrete measures. Exhibit 10.3 shows statistics for each scale level. The central tendency of a discrete measure, whether nominal or ordinal, is best captured by the mode. When a student wants to know what the most likely grade is for MKTG 4311, the mode will be very useful. Observe the results below from the previous semester:

A	5 Students	D	6 Students
B	20 Students	F	6 Students
C	12 Students		

The mode is a "B" since more students obtained that value than any other value. Therefore, the "average" student would expect a B in MKTG 4311.

Continuous Measures

Statistical terminology sometimes draws the distinction between statistics used for *discrete* versus *continuous* measures. **Continuous measures** are those assigning values anywhere along some scale range in a place that corresponds to the intensity of some concept. Ratio measures are continuous measures. Thus, when we measure sales for each salesperson using the dollar amount sold, we are assigning continuous measures. We could construct a number line ranging from the least to the most amount sold and a spot on the line would correspond exactly to a salesperson's performance.

Strictly speaking, interval scales are not necessarily continuous. Consider the following common type of survey question:

Continuous measures
Measures that reflect the intensity of a concept by assigning values that can take on any value along some scale range. Continuous measures require at least interval level measurement.

	Strongly Disagree	Disagree	Neutral	Agree	Strongly Agree
I enjoy participating in online auctions	1	2	3	4	5

This is a discrete scale because only the values 1, 2, 3, 4, or 5 can be assigned. Furthermore, it is an ordinal scale because it only orders based on agreement. We really have no way of knowing that the difference in agreement somebody marking a 5 and somebody marking a 4 is the same as the difference in agreement between somebody marking a 2 and somebody marking 1. The scale difference is 1 in either case, but is the difference in true agreement the same? There is no way to know. Therefore, the mean is not an appropriate way of stating central tendency, and we really shouldn't use many common statistics on these responses.

However, as a scaled response of this type takes on more values, the error introduced by assuming that the differences between the discrete points are equal becomes smaller. Imagine a *Likert scale* with a thousand levels of agreement rather than three or four. The differences between the different levels become so small with a thousand levels that only tiny errors are possible by assuming each interval is the same. Therefore, marketing researchers generally treat interval scales containing five or more categories of response as interval. When fewer than five categories are used, this assumption is inappropriate. Consequently, marketing researchers treat interval scales as continuous when five or more categories are used.

The researcher should keep in mind, however, the distinction between ratio and interval measures. Errors in judgment are possible when one treats interval measures as ratio. For example, the concept of attitude is usually measured with an interval scale. An attitude of zero means nothing—literally. In fact, attitude only has meaning in a relative sense. Therefore, attitude takes on meaning when a researcher compares one person's response to another person's response. Zero on an interval scale is arbitrary.

Means and standard deviations provide acceptable statistics for continuous data. Using the actual quantities for arithmetic operations is permissible with ratio scales. Thus, the ratios of scale values are meaningful. A ratio scale has all the properties of nominal, ordinal, and interval scales. However, the same cannot be said in reverse. An ordinal scale, for example, has nominal properties, but it does not have interval or ratio properties.

Reliable and Valid Measures

Earlier, we distinguished constructs as concepts that require multiple variables to measure them adequately. Looking back to the chapter vignette, could it be that multiple items will be required to adequately represent the concept of customer promotion? Likewise, a consumer's commitment toward some brand or store is usually represented by multiple items.

Attribute

A single characteristic or fundamental feature of an object, person, situation, or issue.

An **attribute** is a single characteristic or fundamental feature of an object, person, situation, or issue. Attribute assessment is common in marketing research. The measures of attributes are often combined to represent some less concrete concept.

Indexes and Composites

Index measure

Assigns a value based on a mathematical formula separating low scores from high scores. Index formulas often put several variables together.

Multi-item instruments for measuring a construct are either called *index measures* or *composite measures*. An **index measure** assigns a value based on a mathematical formula separating low scores from high scores. Index formulas often put several variables together. For example, researchers often form a social class index using three weighted variables: income, occupation, and education. Sociologists see occupation as the single best indicator and it gets the highest weight. A person with a highly prestigious occupation and a graduate degree but lacking a very high income would be more characteristic of high social class than one with a very high income but lacking formal education and a prestigious occupation.

Indexes do not require that the different attribute measures used in the formula strongly correlated with each other. A person's income does not always relate strongly to their education. The American Consumer Satisfaction Index (ACSI) provides a level of American consumers' general satisfaction with businesses based on scores across diverse and unrelated industries and competitors within those industries. Users can compare scores across brands and across industries.[5] In 2014, Samsung phone owners report slightly higher satisfaction than iPhone users. Overall, American consumers report higher satisfaction with soft drinks than they do with wireless service providers.

Composite scales

Assign a value to an observation based on a mathematical derivation of multiple variables to create an operational measure of a construct.

Composite scales also assign a value based on a mathematical derivation of multiple variables but do so to represent a latent construct. For example, a restaurant satisfaction scale might result from combining respondent scores from the following questions assessed with 10-point scales:

■ How satisfied are you with your restaurant experience today?
■ How pleased are you with your visit to our restaurant today?
■ How content are you with the overall restaurant experience today?
■ How satisfied are you with the overall service quality provided today?

For most practical applications, one computes composite measures and indexes in the same way.[6] However, researchers distinguish composite representations of constructs from index measures in that a composite representation of a construct is valid only when its indicators relate to each other both theoretically and statistically. In the customer satisfaction items listed above, one can hardly imagine that respondents would say they were highly satisfied and then provide a low score for how pleased they felt. That would seem very unusual. The item responses therefore should display positive correlations.

Computing Scale Values

Summated scale

A scale created by simply summing (adding together) the response to each item making up the composite measure. The scores can be but do not have to be averaged by the number of items making up the composite scale.

Exhibit 10.4 demonstrates how a researcher creates a composite measure from individual rating scales. This particular scale assesses how much a consumer trusts a website.[7] This particular composite represents a **summated scale**. One creates a summated scale by summing the response to each item making up the composite measure. In this case, the consumer would have a trust score of 13 based on responses to five items. A researcher may sometimes choose to average the scores rather than summing them. The advantage to this is that the composite measure is expressed on the same scale as are the items that make it up. So, instead of a 13, the consumer would have a score of 2.6. The information content is the same.

RESEARCH SNAPSHOT

Recoding Made Easy

Most survey-related software makes scale recoding easy. The screenshot shown here is from SPSS, perhaps the most widely used statistical software in survey-related marketing research. All that needs to be done to reverse-code a scale is to go through this click-through sequence:

1. Click on transform.
2. Click on recode.
3. Choose to recode into the same variable.
4. Select the variable(s) to be recoded.
5. Click on old and new values.
6. Use the menu that appears to enter the old values and the matching new values. Click add after entering each pair.
7. Click continue.

Courtesy of spss statistics 17.0.

This would successfully recode variable X13 in this case. Other software, including Qualtrics, provide easy procedures like these for recoding variables. A recoding routine can be employed in Excel as well by employing the appropriate formula in a new column.

Item	Strongly Disagree (SD) → Strongly Agree (SA)				
This site appears to be more trustworthy than other sites I have visited.	SD	(D)	N	A	SA
My overall trust in this site is very high.	SD	D	(N)	A	SA
My overall impression of the believability of the information on this site is very high.	SD	(D)	N	A	SA
My overall confidence in the recommendations on this site is very high.	SD	(D)	N	A	SA
The company represented in this site delivers on its promises.	SD	D	N	(A)	SA
Computation: Scale Values: SD=1, D=2, N=3, A=4, SA=5					
Thus, the Trust score for this consumer is $2 + 3 + 2 + 2 + 4 = 13$					

EXHIBIT 10.4
Computing a Composite Scale

Source: © Cengage Learning 2013.

Sometimes, a response may need to be reverse-coded before computing a summated or averaged scale value. **Reverse coding** is a specific type of recoding in which the value assigned for a response takes on a value opposite to that normally assigned to the scale labels. If a sixth item was included on the trust scale that said, "I do not trust this website," reverse coding would be necessary to make sure a composite made sense. The content of this item is the reverse of trust (distrust), so the item score is reversed for consistency yielding a trust scale and not a distrust scale. Thus, on a 5-point scale, the values are:

Reverse coding

Means that the value assigned for a response is treated oppositely from the other items.

- 5 becomes 1
- 4 becomes 2
- 3 stays 3
- 2 becomes 4
- 1 becomes 5

The Research Snapshot above shows how a recode can be carried out using SPSS. SAS JMP contains a very similar recode option. Sometimes, one can come up with a simple mathematical

279

Courtesy of spss statistics 17.0

Reverse coding in SPSS is straightforward.

expression to recode a measure. For instance, if the variable above was named T1, the following mathematical expression would perform the recoding:

$$T1 = 6 - T1$$

Survey software also accommodates automatic recoding. Qualtrics, for example, provides an option to automatically recode variables. After choosing the recode option, a window opens that allows the user to assign values manually to each response category.

Reliability

Reliability

An indicator of a measure's internal consistency.

Reliability is an indicator of a measure's internal consistency. Consistency is the key to understanding reliability. A measure is consistent when multiple attempts at measuring something converge on a common result. If a professor's marketing research tests are reliable, a student should tend toward consistent scores on all tests. In other words, a student that makes an 80 on the first test should make scores close to 80 on all subsequent tests. If it is difficult to predict what students would make on a test by examining their previous test scores, the tests probably lack reliability.

Internal Consistency

Internal consistency

Represents a measure's homogeneity or the extent to which each indicator of a construct converges on some common meaning.

Internal consistency is a term used by researchers to represent a composite measure's homogeneity. An attempt to measure trust may require asking several similar but not identical questions. An overall measure often comprises a *battery* of scale items. *Internal consistency* of a multiple-item composite measure can be assessed by correlating scores on subsets of items making up a scale. Internal consistency is not a concern for index measures that do not represent latent constructs.

Split-half method

A method for assessing internal consistency by checking the results of one-half of a set of scaled items against the results from the other half.

The **split-half method** of checking reliability takes half the items from a scale (for example, odd-numbered items) and checks them against the results from the other half (even-numbered items). The two scale *halves* should correlate highly (approaching an absolute value of 1.0). They should also produce similar scores. Multiple techniques exist for estimating scale reliability, all based on this basic principle of correspondence.

Coefficient alpha (α)

The most commonly applied estimate of a multiple item scale's reliability. It represents the average of all possible split-half reliabilities for a construct.

Coefficient alpha (α) is the most commonly applied estimate of a composite scale's reliability.[8] Coefficient α estimates internal consistency by computing the average of all possible split-half reliabilities for a multiple-item scale. The coefficient demonstrates whether the different items converge on some single point. Many researchers use coefficient α as the sole indicator of a scale's quality largely because statistical programs like SPSS and SAS's JMP readily provide the result. Coefficient α can only take on values ranging from 0, meaning no consistency among items (they are all statistically independent), to 1, meaning complete consistency (all items correlate perfectly with each other).

Generally speaking, researchers consider scales exhibiting a coefficient α between 0.80 and 0.96 as possessing very good reliability. Scales with a coefficient α between 0.70 and 0.80 are considered to have good reliability, and an α value between 0.60 and 0.70 indicates fair reliability. When the coefficient α is below 0.60, the scale has poor reliability.[9] Researchers generally report coefficient α for each composite measure involved in a study. A full accounting of measurement quality, though, should also include other indicators aimed at a more thorough assessment of validity as shown below.

Test-Retest Reliability

The **test-retest method** of determining reliability involves administering the same scale or measure to the same respondents at two separate times to test for stability. If the measure is stable over time, the test, administered under the same conditions each time, should obtain similar results. Test-retest reliability represents a measure's repeatability.

Suppose a researcher at one time attempts to measure buying intentions and finds that 12 percent of a population is willing to purchase a product. A few weeks later under similar conditions, the researcher assesses intentions in the population again and finds the result to be 12 percent. The measure, thus, appears reliable. High stability correlation or consistency between two measures at time 1 and time 2 indicates high reliability.

Assume that a person does not change his or her mind about dark beer with time. A scale item like the one shown below:

I prefer dark beer to all other types of beer

should produce the same score in November 2015 as it would in April 2013 or December 2016. When a measuring instrument produces unpredictable results from one testing to the next, the results lack consistency and suggest an unreliable measure. Research based on unreliable measures is itself unreliable because of measurement error.

Reliability is a necessary but insufficient condition for validity. A scale can display high reliability but still lack validity. For example, a composite scale assessing purchase intention may consistently indicate that respondents are 40 percent likely to purchase a new product. The measure is valid to the extent that 40 percent of the population actually does purchase the product. In reality, ten percent of consumers end up purchasing the product. Thus, the scale would be consistent but not valid. A reliable but invalid instrument will yield consistently inaccurate results. Perhaps you've come across results from polls or other research in the media that appear reliable but inaccurate in this manner?

Validity

Good measures should be both precise and accurate. Reliability represents how precise a measure is in that the different attempts at measuring the same thing converge on the same point. Accuracy deals more with how a measure assesses the intended concept. **Validity** is the accuracy of a measure or the extent to which a score truthfully represents a concept.

Reliability
Scale: Positive Feelings

Case Processing Summary

		N	%
Cases	Valid	457	100.0
	Excluded[a]	0	.0
	Total	457	100.0

[a]Listwise deletion based on all variables in the procedure.

Reliability Statistics

Cronbach's Alpha	N of Items
.960	5

Item-Total Statistics

	Scale Mean if Item Deleted	Scale Variance if Item Deleted	Corrected Item-Total Correlation	Cronbach's Alpha if Item Deleted
Excited	14.58	51.459	.859	.955
Happy	14.16	51.611	.886	.950
Interested	14.04	50.138	.891	.949
Pleased	14.29	51.352	.910	.946
Satisfied	14.30	51.603	.886	.950

Here are some results from using a software package to estimate coefficient alpha for a 5-item scale measuring the positive feelings shoppers had during a shopping trip. The results show a value of 0.96 for the scale. Also, the item-total statistics indicate that all the items correlate highly with the scale. Overall, these are positive results.

Test-retest method
Administering the same scale or measure to the same respondents at two separate points in time to test for stability.

Validity
The accuracy of a measure or the extent to which a score truthfully represents a concept.

A golfer may hit reliable but not valid putts and thus tend to miss them in some repeated fashion. This golfer's putts tend to converge to the left of—rather than in—the hole!

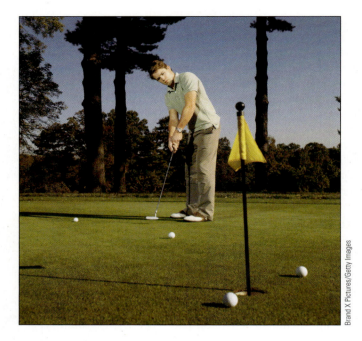

Brand X Pictures/Getty Images

Achieving validity is not a simple matter. Researchers who study job performance often resort to asking employees to self-rate their own performance. A multiple item self-rated performance scale is usually reliable, but does one's opinion reflect his/her actual job performance? Perhaps some bias creeps in causing the scale to represent something besides true job performance.

Researchers need to know if their measures are valid. The question of validity expresses the researcher's concern with accurate measurement. Validity addresses the problem of whether a measure indeed measures what it is supposed to measure. When a measure lacks validity, any conclusions based on that measure are also likely to be faulty.

Students should be able to empathize with the following validity problem. Consider the controversy about highway patrol officers using radar guns to clock speeders. An officer clocks a driver at 75 mph in a 55 mph zone. However, the same radar gun registered 28 mph when aimed at a house. The error occurred because the radar gun had picked up impulses from the electrical system of the squad car's idling engine. The house was probably not speeding—and the radar gun was probably not completely valid.

Establishing Validity

Researchers attempt to assess validity in many ways. The following questions represent some of these approaches:

- Is there a consensus among experts that the scale items actually correspond to the definition of the concept being measured?
- Does the latent construct (factor) fully capture all systematic variation among a scale's items?
- Does any particular measure of the concept correlate with other measures of the same concept?
- Can the behavior associated with the concept be accurately predicted using the specific measurement scale?

Face (content) validity

Extent to which individual measures' content match the intended concept's definition.

Criterion validity

The ability of a measure to correlate with other standard measures of similar constructs or established criteria.

The three basic aspects of validity are *face* or *content validity*, *criterion validity*, and *construct validity*.

Face (content) validity refers to the extent to which individual measures' content match the intended concept's definition. One way to check this involves using a few experts to judge how well each item in a scale represents the concept definition. This test provides evidence of face validity when the judges tend to agree that the items' content matches the concept. If expert judges cannot be used, the researcher him/herself must carefully inspect each item's content.

Criterion validity addresses the question, "Does my measure correlate with measures of similar concepts or known quantities?" Criterion validity may be classified as either *concurrent validity* or *predictive validity* depending on the time sequence in which the new measurement scale and the criterion measure are correlated. If the researcher applies the new measure at the same time as the criterion measure, then concurrent validity is relevant. Predictive validity is established when a new measure predicts a future event. The two measures differ only on the basis of a time dimension.

A practical example of predictive validity is illustrated by a commercial research firm's test of the relationship between a rough commercial's effectiveness (as determined, for example, by recall scores) and a finished commercial's effectiveness (also by recall scores). Ad agencies test animatic, photomatic, or live-action rough commercials before developing actual finished commercials. One marketing research consulting firm suggests that this testing has high predictive validity. Rough commercial recall scores provide correct estimates of the final finished commercial recall scores more than 80 percent of the time.[10]

Construct Validity

Construct validity exists when each measure involved in a project reliably and truthfully represents a unique concept. Construct validity is multifaceted and exists to the extent that a scale exhibits the following characteristics:

1. Face validity
2. Criterion validity
3. Convergent validity
4. Discriminant validity
5. Fit validity

Criterion validity and face validity were discussed in the preceding paragraphs. **Convergent validity** depends on internal consistency meaning that multiple measures converge on a consistent meaning. Highly reliable scales contain convergent validity. One indicator of convergent validity is that each scale item should display high correlation with the actual construct (or latent factor) being measured. **Discriminant validity** represents how unique or distinct is a measure. A scale should not correlate too highly with a measure of a different construct. For example, a customer satisfaction measure should not correlate too highly with a cognitive dissonance scale if the two concepts are truly different. As a rough rule of thumb, when two scales are correlated above 0.75, discriminant validity may be an issue. In addition, each individual scale item should correlate more highly with the construct.

Fit validity is a little more complex to understand but can be thought of as the extent to which a researcher's proposed measurement approach (how all the constructs in a study will be measured) fully explains the covariation (the way each item corresponds with all other items measured) among all the items involved in the research. High fit validity suggests the absence of influence of unmeasured concepts on the scale items employed. Multivariate statistical procedures like confirmatory factor analysis can be useful in establishing construct validity. We return to this topic in the marketing analytics chapters.

Construct validity

Exists when a measure reliably measures and truthfully represents a unique concept; consists of several components including face validity, convergent validity, criterion validity, discriminant validity and fit validity.

Convergent validity

Depends on internal consistency so that multiple measures converge on a consistent meaning.

Discriminant validity

Represents how unique or distinct is a measure; a scale should not correlate too highly with a measure of a different construct.

Fit validity

Represents the extent to which a researcher's proposed measurement approach it represents than with other constructs.

Reliability versus Validity

The differences between reliability and validity can be illustrated by picturing target shooting as illustrated in Exhibit 10.5. Suppose someone fires an equal number of rounds with a century-old rifle and a modern rifle.[11] The shots from the older gun end up considerably scattered, but those from the newer gun cluster closely together. The inconsistency of the old rifle compared with that of the new one indicates lower reliability.

The target on the right of the Exhibit shows results from a new, low priced air gun. All the shots cluster tightly but on the edge of the target. The shots fired with the new gun indicate a reliable tool because they are consistent with each other. The shots are reliable, but not valid because they miss the target by a substantial margin. If you've tried to target shoot at a carnival, you may have used a gun like this.

EXHIBIT 10.5
Reliability and Validity on Target

Old Rifle
Low Reliability
(Target A)

New Rifle
High Reliability
(Target B)

New Rifle—Bad Shot
Reliable but not Valid
(Target C)

What Is an Attitude?

Attitude

An enduring predisposition to consistently respond in a given manner to various aspects of the world; composed of affective, cognitive, and behavioral components.

What does one mean when they accuse someone of having a "bad attitude"? The idea is that one's disposition about the relevant matter is not positive and the result is less than productive behavior. Formally, an **attitude** is a social-psychological concept defined as a relatively enduring predisposition to respond consistently to various things including people, activities, events, and objects. Attitudes are predispositions toward behavior and as such represent rules that inform a person of the appropriate reaction in a given situation. If someone has a negative attitude toward broccoli, then that person is likely to avoid eating, smelling, or even approaching any dish with the obvious presence of broccoli. If a fan "loves the Bulldogs," he or she is more likely to buy tickets and attend their games. Additionally, attitudes are latent constructs, and because of this, they are not directly observable.

Social psychologists believe that attitudes have three identifiable components:

1. An affective component that expresses how much affinity someone has toward the relevant matter. More simply, this is the feeling of liking or not liking something. For example, a consumer might say "I love Chick-fil-A." This expresses strong affinity.
2. A cognitive component that represents a person's awareness and knowledge of the relevant matter. In other words, what a person believes about the subject matter. When someone says, "Chick-fil-A has a wide selection," they are expressing a belief about this particular consumer alternative. Together with other relevant beliefs about Chick-fil-A, the beliefs comprise knowledge—which need not be correct to shape attitude.
3. A behavioral component representing the action undertaken as a result of the affective and cognitive components. If the attitude is positive, the person will display approach responses. If the attitude is negative, the person will display avoidance reactions. "I'll never eat at Chick-fil-A again" expresses a behavioral component of a negative attitude. Researchers often capture the behavioral component using intentions toward future behavior.

Sometimes researchers need to study overall attitude. Other times, they may focus on one of these components more than others. Whenever overall attitude or any of these components are measured through survey research, the researcher is conducting attitudinal research.

Research results generally show that attitudes do predict behavior with at least some accuracy. Consequently, marketing managers place a great deal of importance on attitudes. If a marketing approach changes consumers' aggregate attitude about some product, sales volume changes consequently. If employees' aggregate attitude about their job improves, their work output is likely to increase proportionately. Further, if knowledge about a product can be changed, the product can be repositioned to capture some new market.

For example, research results show consumers on average have a more positive attitude toward Starbucks than Dunkin' Donuts. When Dunkin' Donuts' (DD) marketing management drilled down into the results, they discovered that consumers who like to relax with a snack and beverage did not find the typical DD inviting. Thus, DD launched large-scale remodels of their units into themed interiors. DD introduced four different themes: original blend, dark roast, cappuccino, and jazz brew.[12] Each included better seating, lighting, and wide-screen TVs. As a result, attitudes improved among the segment of consumers looking for a place to relax and snack past breakfast time. The change in décor helped spur an increase in sales in the remodeled units.

● ● ● ● ● ● ●

Marketing Researchers measure attitudes and behavioral intentions about all manner of things, including eating "mor chikin" at Chick-fil-A.

Attitude Measures and Scaling

Researchers face a wide variety of choices in measuring attitudinal concepts. One reason for the variety is that no complete consensus exists over just what constitutes an attitude or an attitudinal variable. Researchers generally agree however that the affective, cognitive, and behavioral components of an attitude can each be measured effectively. However, attitudes may also be interpreted using qualitative techniques like those discussed in Chapter 5. Even if no agreement exists over the precise boundaries delineating attitudinal variables from others, researchers widely apply approaches used to measure attitude components in measuring many attitude-like variables.

Physiological Measures

Research may assess the affective (emotional) components of attitudes through physiological measures like galvanic skin response (GSR), blood pressure, magnetic resonance imaging (MRI), and pupil dilation. These measures provide a means of assessing affect without verbally questioning the respondent. In general, they can provide a gross measure of likes or dislikes, but they are not extremely sensitive to the different gradients of an attitude. Researchers studying attitudes toward music used a physiological approach in studying what types of music tend to become popular.[13] MRI recordings for instance, showing brain activity consistent with increased liking, correlate positively with purchases of music.

Self-Report Scales

In contrast to physiological measures, an entire class of psychological measures involve gaining a respondent's structured response to some specific query or stimulus. Researchers can ask respondents to rank, rate, sort, or choose one of multiple responses as a way of indicating a response. A **ranking task** requires the respondent to rank order a small number of stores, brands, feelings, or objects based on overall preference or of some characteristic of the stimulus. Rankings provide ordinal measurement. **Rating** requires the respondent to estimate the magnitude or the extent to which some characteristic exists or some choice is preferred. Researchers typically treat most rating scales as yielding better than ordinal measurement.

The rating task involves marking a response indicating one's position using one or more attitudinal or cognitive scales. A **sorting** task might present the respondent with several product concepts on cards and require the respondent to classify the concepts by placing the cards into stacks, each representing a different meaning. Another type of attitude measurement requires

Ranking task
A measurement task that requires respondents to rank order a small number of stores, brands, or objects on the basis of overall preference or some characteristic of the stimulus.

Rating
A measurement task that requires respondents to estimate the magnitude of a characteristic or quality that a brand, store, or object possesses.

Sorting
A measurement task that presents a respondent with several objects or product concepts and requires the respondent to arrange the objects into piles or classify the product concepts.

Choice

A measurement task that identifies preferences by requiring respondents to choose between two or more alternatives.

respondents to make a **choice** between two or more alternatives. If a respondent chooses one object over another, the researcher assumes that the respondent prefers the chosen object, at least in this setting.

Marketing researchers commonly use rating scales to measure attitudes. This section discusses many rating scales designed to enable respondents to report the intensity of their attitudes. In its most basic form, attitude scaling requires that an individual agree or disagree with a statement or indicate how much some term describes his or her feeling. For example, respondents in a political poll may be asked whether they either agree or disagree with a statement like, "Politicians are likable." Or, an individual might indicate whether he or she likes or dislikes jalapeño bean dip. This type of self-rating scale merely classifies respondents into one of two categories, thus having only the properties of a nominal scale, and the types of mathematical analysis that may be used with this basic scale are limited.

Simple attitude scaling can be a practical way of implementing a survey when questionnaires are extremely long, when respondents have little education, or for other specific reasons. In fact, a number of simplified scales are merely checklists where a respondent indicates past experience, preference, or likes and dislikes simply by checking an item. Common checklist questions may ask respondents to tick off the following from a list of brands:

■ Which yogurt brands are you familiar with?
■ Which yogurt brand among those that you are familiar has the highest quality?
■ Which yogurt brand offers the most value?
■ Which yogurt brand do you use the most often?

Simple approaches like these produce results that are easy to convey to management.[14] In addition, they sometimes overcome problems common to rating scale approaches that we will touch on later. Marketers might even consider a Facebook "like" as an indicator of a favorable attitude. The value of like as an indicator of marketing success however remains uncertain.[15]

Scales with better than ordinal measurement quality are needed to discern small differences between attitudes or to scale different brands along a continuum. The following sections describe some popular techniques for measuring attitudes quantitatively.

Measuring the Affect Component

Not all rating approaches are the same. Exhibit 10.6 displays an interesting approach to get respondents to rate their affect toward some object. Respondents are asked to choose a "manikin" from each row to show not only their general affective state (like or dislike), but the degree to which they get emotionally aroused (the middle row), and how much the thing being rated makes them feel small (unimportant) or important. This approach is useful in all manner of measures involving emotion.

EXHIBIT **10.6**

Novel Approach to Rating Affect

Sources: Morris, J. D. (1995), "Observations: SAM: The Self-Assessment Manikin: An Efficient Cross-Cultural Measurement of Emotional Response," *Journal of Advertising Research*, 35, 63–68. Morris, J. D., C. Woo and A. J. Singh (2005), "Elaboration Likelihood Model: A Missing Intrinsic Emotional Implication," *Journal of Targeting, Measurement and Analysis for Marketing*, 14 (October), 79–98.

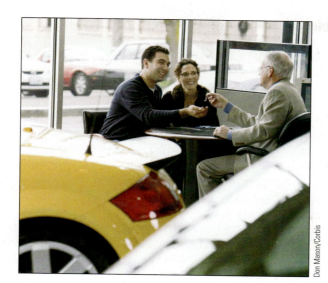

Don Mason/Corbis

Generally, consumers act in a way consistent with their attitudes. Therefore, attitudes are a popular marketing research topic.

Category Scales

I like the idea of attending Cool State University.

☐   *Yes*   ☐   *No*

Expanding the response categories provides the respondent with more flexibility in the rating task. Even more information is provided if the categories are ordered according to a particular descriptive or evaluative dimension. Consider the following question:

How often do you think favorably about attending Cool State University?

☐   *Never*   ☐   *Rarely*   ☐   *Sometimes*   ☐   *Often*   ☐   *Very often*

This **category scale** measures attitude with greater sensitivity than a two-point response scale. By having more choices, the potential exists to provide more information. However, a researcher will create measurement error if he/she uses a category scale for something that is truly bipolar (yes/no, female/male, member/non-member, and so on).

Response category wording is an extremely important factor. Exhibit 10.7 shows some common wordings used in category scales measuring common marketing research variables. As you can see, the more categories, the more difficulty a researcher has in coming up with precise and readily understandable category labels.

Category scale

A rating scale that consists of several response categories, often providing respondents with alternatives to indicate positions on a continuum.

The Likert Scale

The Likert scale may well be the most commonly applied scale format in marketing research. Likert scales are simple to administer and understand. Likert scales were developed by and named after Rensis Likert, a 20th century social scientist. With a **Likert scale**, respondents indicate their attitudes by checking how strongly they disagree or agree with carefully constructed statements. The scale results reveal the respondent's attitude ranging from very positive to very negative. Individuals generally choose from multiple response alternatives such as strongly agree, agree, neutral, disagree, and strongly disagree. Researchers commonly employ five choices, although they also often use six, seven or even more response points. In the following example, from a study of food-shopping behavior, there are five alternatives:

Likert scale

A measure of attitudes designed to allow respondents to rate how strongly they disagree or agree with carefully constructed statements, ranging from very positive to very negative attitudes toward some object.

I like to go to Walmart when buying food for my family.				
Strongly Disagree	Disagree	Neutral	Agree	Strongly Agree
☐	☐	☐	☐	☐
(1)	(2)	(3)	(4)	(5)

EXHIBIT 10.7 Commonly Applied Category Scale Descriptions

Quality				
Excellent	Good	Fair	Poor	
Very good	Fairly good	Neither good nor bad	Not very good	Not good at all
Well above average	Above average	Average	Below average	Well below average
Importance				
Very important	Fairly important	Neutral	Not so important	Not at all important
Interest				
Very interested		Somewhat interested		Not very interested
Satisfaction				
Completely satisfied	Somewhat satisfied	Neither satisfied nor dissatisfied	Somewhat dissatisfied	Completely dissatisfied
Very satisfied	Quite satisfied	Somewhat satisfied	Not at all satisfied	
Frequency				
All of the time	Very often	Often	Sometimes	Hardly ever
Very often	Often	Sometimes	Rarely	Never
All of the time	Most of the time	Some of the time	Just now and then	
Truth				
Very true	Somewhat true	Not very true	Not at all true	
Definitely yes	Probably yes	Probably no	Definitely no	
Uniqueness				
Very different	Somewhat different	Slightly different	Not at all different	
Extremely unique	Very unique	Somewhat unique	Slightly unique	Not at all unique

Source: © Cengage Learning 2013.

The researcher (or survey software) assigns scores to each possible response. In this example, numerical scores of 1, 2, 3, 4, and 5 are assigned to each level of agreement, respectively. Here, strong agreement indicates the most favorable attitude on the statement and receives a score of 5.

Realize that if the statement were worded in a way that indicated dislike for shopping for food at Walmart, a 5 would mean a less favorable attitude about this activity. For example, responses to the item above could even be combined with those from an item like this:

Walmart is a bad place to shop for fresh foods.				
Strongly Disagree	Disagree	Neutral	Agree	Strongly Agree
☐	☐	☐	☐	☐
(1)	(2)	(3)	(4)	(5)

Before one could form a composite scale with these items, the responses to this last item would have to be reverse coded as shown previously.

Remember too, an attitude score is arbitrary and has little cardinal meaning—in other words, attitude scores are at best interval and clearly not ratio. They could also just as easily be scored so that a higher score indicated less favorable attitudes. However, the convention is to score attitude scales so that a higher score means a more favorable attitude. In this way, researchers can compare consumer attitudes for competing brands with higher scores indicating relatively more favorable predispositions.

Selecting Items for a Likert Scale

Typically, a researcher will use multiple items to represent a single attitudinal concept. The researcher may generate a large number of statements before putting together the final questionnaire. A pretest may be conducted using these items allowing for an *item analysis* to be performed. The item analysis helps select items that evoke a wide response (meaning all respondents are not selecting the same response point such as all strongly agree), allowing the item to discriminate among those with positive and negative attitudes. Items are also analyzed for clarity or unusual response patterns. Thus, the final Likert items should be clearly understood and elicit an accurate range of responses corresponding to respondents' true attitudes.

Semantic Differential

A **semantic differential** is a scale type on which respondents describe their attitude using a series of bipolar rating scales. Bipolar rating scales involve respondents choosing between opposing adjectives—such as "good" and "bad," "modern" and "old-fashioned," or "clean" and "dirty." One adjective anchors the beginning and the other the end (or poles) of the scale. The subject makes repeated judgments about the concept under investigation on each of the scales. Exhibit 10.8 shows an example semantic differential approach for assessing consumer attitudes toward a branded video displayed on Instagram.

Semantic differential
A measure of attitudes that consists of a series of bipolar rating scales with opposite terms on either end.

EXHIBIT 10.8
An Example of a Semantic Differential Scale

What's your favorite flavor of Cheerios cereal?

We have more than a dozen delicious varieties.

ORIGINAL CHEERIOS

A family favorite for years. Its wholesome goodness is good for heart health, too.

HONEY NUT CHEERIOS

An irresistible taste of golden honey that also provides 12 essential vitamins and minerals.

MULTI GRAIN CHEERIOS

A delicious way to help manage your weight with 20 grams of whole grain per serving.

Source: www.Cheerios.com

How does the Cheerios ad make you feel? Use the scales below to indicate your feelings.

Sad	○ ○ ○ ○ ○ ○ ○	Happy
Pleased	○ ○ ○ ○ ○ ○ ○	Displeased
Depressed	○ ○ ○ ○ ○ ○ ○	Cheerful
Good	○ ○ ○ ○ ○ ○ ○	Bad

The scoring of the semantic differential can be illustrated using the scale bounded by the anchors "complex" and "simple." Respondents are instructed to check the place that indicates the nearest appropriate adjective. From left to right, the scale intervals represent the belief that the stimulus is somewhere between extremely simple and extremely complex. One advantage provided by using scale labels over each category is the ability to influence the distribution of responses.

How complex is the new Internet TV control to work?

Extremely Simple	Very Simple	Simple	Neither Simple nor Complex	Complex	Very Complex	Extremely Complex
☐	☐	☐	☐	☐	☐	☐
(–3)	(–2)	(–1)	(0)	(1)	(2)	(3)

Semantic Differentials And Meaning

The semantic differential technique originally was developed as a method for measuring the meanings of objects or the "semantic space" of interpersonal experience.[16] Researchers see the semantic differential as versatile and useful in a wide variety of business situations.

When opposites are available, the semantic differential is a good scale choice. In typical attitude or image studies, simple anchors such as very unfavorable and very favorable work well. However, the validity of the semantic differential depends on finding scale anchors that are semantic opposites and this can sometimes prove difficult. For example, consider the following scale in which the respondent is asked to place a check on the space closest to the way they feel about the phrase:

Shopping at the GAP makes me:
Sad __ __ __ __ __ __ __ Happy

Few would question that sad is the opposite of happy. However, what if this were to be combined with an item capturing how angry shopping at the GAP makes a respondent feel? Then, what would the opposite of angry be? Clearly, using happy as the opposite of angry would present a problem because the items above suggests happy is the opposite of sad. Thus, a semantic differential may not be best for capturing anger unless some distinctive and unambiguous opposite exists.

Scoring Semantic Differentials

Like Likert scales, a numerical score can be assigned to each position on a semantic differential scale. For a seven-point semantic differential the scores could be 1, 2, 3, 4, 5, 6, 7 or −3, −2, −1, 0, +1, +2, +3. Marketing researchers generally assume that the semantic differential provides interval data. This assumption does have critics who argue that the data have only ordinal properties because the numerical scores are arbitrary and there is no way of knowing that the differences between choices are equal. Practically, the vast majority of social science researchers treat semantic differential scales as metric (at least interval). This is justified because the amount of error introduced by assuming the intervals between choices are equal (even though this is uncertain at best) is fairly small.

Constant-sum scale
A measure of attitudes in which respondents are asked to divide a constant sum to indicate the relative importance of attributes; respondents often sort cards, but the task may also be a rating task.

Constant-Sum Scale

A **constant-sum scale** demands that respondents divide points among several attributes to indicate their relative importance. Suppose Samsung wishes to determine the importance of smartphone attributes such as reliability, battery life, video/audio quality, camera quality, voice (call) quality, and an economical service plan. Respondents might divide a constant sum of 100 points to indicate the relative importance of those attributes as such:

Divide 100 points among the following characteristics of a smart phone indicating how important each characteristic is when determining which phone will deliver the best overall experience.	
Reliability	20
Battery Life (length of time between charges)	20
Video Quality	5
Audio Quality	10
Camera Quality	10
Voice (Call) Quality	20
Economical Service	15
Total	100

The constant-sum scale requires respondents to understand that their responses should total to the total number of points. In the case above, that number is 100. As the number of stimuli increases, this technique becomes increasingly complex. Fortunately, electronic questionnaires eliminate math errors by having the software trigger an error notice whenever responses do not match the total. The respondent could adjust the responses until the sums do indeed match the total. If respondents follow the instructions correctly, the results will approximate interval measures.

This technique may be used for measuring brand preference. The approach, which is similar to the paired-comparison method, is as follows:

Divide 100 points among the following brands based on your degree of preference for each:	
Coca-Cola	30
Pepsi-Cola	25
Dr Pepper	45
Total	100

Although the constant sum scale is widely used, strictly speaking, the scale is flawed because the last response is completely determined by the way the respondent has scored the other choices. Although this is probably somewhat complex to understand, the fact is that practical reasons often outweigh this concern.

Graphic Rating Scales

A **graphic rating scale** presents respondents with a graphic continuum. The respondents are allowed to choose any point on the continuum to indicate their attitude. Exhibit 10.9 shows a traditional graphic scale, ranging from one extreme position to the opposite position. Typically a respondent's score is determined by measuring the length (in millimeters) from one end of the graphic continuum to the point marked by the respondent. Many researchers believe that scoring in this manner strengthens the assumption that graphic rating scales of this type are interval scales. Alternatively, the researcher may divide the line into predetermined scoring categories (lengths) and record respondents' marks accordingly. In other words, the graphic rating scale has the advantage of allowing the researcher to choose any interval desired for scoring purposes. Electronic questionnaires allow the use of a slider scale. The sliders function much the same as a graphics rating scale as shown in Exhibit 10.9.

Research to investigate children's attitudes has used happy-sad face scales. Exhibit 10.10 illustrates one such approach. Here, the respondent chooses an attitude by sliding the scale up and

Graphic rating scale
A measure of attitude that allows respondents to rate an object by choosing any point along a graphic continuum. Electronic slider scales work much the same way.

EXHIBIT 10.9
Graphic Rating Scale

Please evaluate each attribute in terms of how important it is to you by placing an X at the position on the horizontal line that most reflects your feelings.

Seating comfort	Not important _____ Very important
In-flight meals	Not important _____ Very important
Airfare	Not important _____ Very important

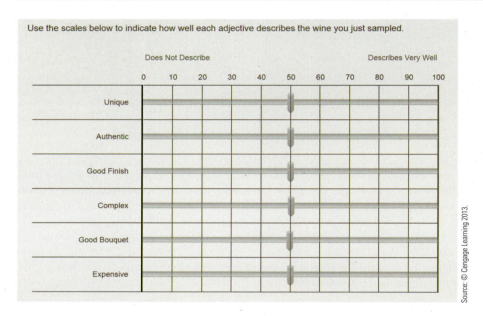

Source: © Cengage Learning 2013.

down using the tab to the right of the face. As the respondent moves the left or right, the face smiles or frowns, correspondingly. The first respondent is fairly pleased with the idea of hot break-fast items at McDonalds. However, the second respondent has a very negative attitude toward the idea. Notice the position of the tab corresponding to each face.

Among the attitude rating approaches discussed in this chapter, Likert scales and semantic differentials account for the majority of applications. The Research Snapshot below suggests that attitudes can help make a story complete.

EXHIBIT 10.10
Using Face Scales to Assess Attitudes

Respondent 1

Respondent 2

Someone Tell Me

Attitude measurement remains a mainstay of marketing research. What factors influence consumer attitudes? Given the large amount of time that people spend online, today a wide range of sources influences consumer attitudes. Personal sources have always been a big part of attitude change, as reflected in the concept of subjective norms, which is the desire to conform to what you think people you like would like you to do. Now, however, many unfamiliar sources online may sway attitudes. Over 60 percent of consumers say that social networks can influence their attitudes about products. Among social network sites such as Facebook, Pinterest, Twitter, YouTube, and Instagram, Facebook remains the most influential according to consumer surveys. Other sites, such as Tripadvisor and Urbanspoon, provide a portal for online reviews.

Whether this will remain the same is yet to be seen. As the number of fraudulent or questionable online reviews grows, perhaps online "likes" and recommendations will begin to lose some influence. Consumer opinion surveys suggest a belief that companies should not encourage their employees, for example, to leave likes on Facebook or write positive reviews online. Other companies actually pay Internet workers to leave behind reviews as if the workers were customers. Even when consumers have doubts about the credibility of a recommendation, the information left online still may have impact. The ease with which such information can be accessed may well trump concerns about its veracity.

Sources: Gallivan, R. (2014), "Amide Fake Reviews, Consumers Are Skeptical of Social Media Advertising," Digits, http://blogs.wsj.com/digits/2014/06/03/amid-fake-reviews-consumers-skeptical-of-social-media-marketing/, accessed July 4, 2014. The Digital Letter (2014), "62% of Consumer Prefer Facebook over Pinterest and Twitter As Their Social Commerce Channel," http://blog.thelettertwo.com/2014/08/12/62-of-consumers-prefer-facebook-over-pinterest-twitter-as-their-social-commerce-channel/, accessed August 16, 2014.

Ranking

A ranking is different than a rating scale in that respondents simply order alternatives on some characteristic. Consumers often *rank order* their preferences so, in this sense, ranking scales have considerable validity. An ordinal scale may be developed by asking respondents to rank order (from most preferred to least preferred) a set of objects or attributes. Respondents easily understand the task of rank ordering product attributes or arranging a set of brand names according to preference. Like the constant-sum scale, however, the ranking scale suffers from inflexibility in that if we know how someone ranked five out of six alternatives, we know the answer to the sixth. Thus, a respondent does not rate each category independently as in a typical ratings scale. Additionally, ordinal scaling only allows us to know that one option is preferred over another—not how much one option is preferred over another.

Paired Comparisons

Consider a situation in which a chain saw manufacturer learned that a competitor had introduced a new lightweight (6-pound) chain saw. The manufacturer's lightest chain saw weighed 9 pounds. Executives wondered if they needed to introduce a 6-pound chain saw into the product line. The research design employed a **paired comparison** approach. The company built a prototype of a 6-pound chain saw. Then, they painted both the 9- and 6-pound saws from their competitor the same color as their own 9- and 6-pound chain saws so color differences would not be responsible for any preferences. Respondents then saw two chain saws at a time and picked the one they preferred. Three pairs of comparisons allowed the researchers to determine the saw each respondent liked best.

To the Point

"My tastes are very simple. I only want the best."

—OSCAR WILDE

Paired comparison

A measurement technique that involves presenting the respondent with two objects and asking the respondent to pick the preferred object; more than two objects may be presented, but comparisons are made in pairs.

The following question illustrates the typical format for asking about paired comparisons.

I would like to know your overall opinion of two brands of adhesive bandages. They are Curad and Band-Aid. Overall, which of these two brands—Curad or Band-Aid—do you think is the better one? Or are both the same?

Curad is better.   ____
Band-Aid is better.   ____
They are the same.   ____

If researchers wish to compare four brands of pens on the basis of attractiveness or writing quality, six comparisons $[(n)(n-1)/2]$ will be necessary. Paired comparisons sometimes require respondents to assess similarity instead of preference by asking which of the two choices is more similar to some third choice. With either similarity or preference, if the number of comparisons is too large, respondents become fatigued and do not carefully discriminate the choices.

Direct Assessment of Consumer Attitudes

Attitudes, as hypothetical constructs, cannot be observed directly. We can, however, infer one's attitude by the way he or she responds to multiple attitude indicators. The researcher can then sum the scores on the multiple indicators of attitude. Consider the following three semantic differential items capturing a consumer's attitude toward Microsoft Word:

very bad ___ ___ ___ ___ ___ ___ ___ *very good*

very unfavorable ___ ___ ___ ___ ___ ___ ___ *very favorable*

very negative ___ ___ ___ ___ ___ ___ ___ *very positive*

A summed score over these three items would represent a latent (unobservable) attitude construct. How do you feel about Microsoft Word? Use the scale to find your score.

The decision whether to use ranking, sorting, rating, or a choice technique is determined largely by the problem definition and especially by the type of statistical analysis desired. For example, ranking provides only ordinal data, limiting the statistical techniques that may be used.

How Many Scale Categories or Response Positions?

Should a category scale have four, five, or seven response positions or categories? Or should the researcher use a graphic scale with an infinite number of positions? The original developmental research on the semantic differential indicated that five to eight points is optimal. However, the researcher must determine the number of meaningful positions that is best for the specific project. This issue of identifying how many meaningful distinctions respondents can practically make is basically a matter of sensitivity. For example, how sensitively can students discriminate the difficulty of college courses? The answer to the question may help determine the number of response categories.

The number of response categories can influence research conclusions. Think about a service employee asked to respond to an item asking about job satisfaction using a two-point response scale of either "no" or "yes." Can the two-point scale adequately capture the range of responses that employees might actually feel? Would we really expect that all people who respond "yes" have the same amount of satisfaction? Typically, a yes or no satisfaction question will yield about 80 percent yes responses. In other words, the data are typically skewed with a small number of scale points. If the scale is expanded to the typical five-point Likert format, the "yes" responses are likely to be spread across multiple categories. Similarly, a scale with too few points may suppress variance that truly exists. Thus, a scale should be adequately sensitive to capture a respondent's opinion or feelings.

What happens if the same question is asked with scales of varying numbers of response categories? Some research suggests that skewness is reduced by including more scale points, particularly for attitudinal and satisfaction type items. Additionally, including more scale points produces less extreme patterns of results with typical responses closer to the midpoint of the scale. Thus, as long as adding category responses does not become taxing to respondents, more categories are better than fewer. However, scales with five to ten scale points typically display results suggesting they are appropriate for use in statistical procedures like regression.[17]

Others offer a few caveats to these findings. Research finds that less capable respondents sometimes provide more valid responses with fewer rather than more scale points.[18] In addition, the inclusion of labels over all scale points tends to produce slightly more acquiescence bias than a scale with labels only on the end point. As a result, the use of labels over all choices is preferable when scores will be compared directly across respondents. Scores with only the ends labeled are somewhat preferable for use with statistics like regression analysis.

Balanced or Unbalanced Rating Scale?

The fixed-alternative format may be balanced or unbalanced. For example, the following question, which asks about parent-child decisions relating to television program watching, is a **balanced rating scale**:

Who decides which movies your family will see?

Child decides all of the time.	*Child decides most of the time.*	*Child and parent decide together.*	*Parent decides most of the time.*	*Parent decides all of the time.*
＿＿＿	＿＿＿	＿＿＿	＿＿＿	＿＿＿

Balanced rating scale
A fixed-alternative rating scale with an equal number of positive and negative categories; a neutral point or point of indifference is at the center of the scale.

This scale is balanced because a neutral point, or point of indifference, is at the center of the scale. **Unbalanced rating scales** may be used when responses are expected to be distributed at one end of the scale, producing a skewed distribution. The skewed distribution may indicate error and can also interfere with the ability to draw meaningful statistical inferences. Marketing researchers often face situations where "end-piling" will occur. One reason for this is that researchers often ask questions for which respondents are fully expected to give more positive than negative responses. For instance, satisfaction scales (job or customer) generally show this pattern. After all, if an employee has stayed in one job for some years or a customer has already selected a place to do business, we should expect that they would provide a positive response. Unbalanced scales, such as the following one, may mitigate this type of "end piling":

Unbalanced rating scales
A fixed-alternative rating scale that has more response categories at one end than the other, resulting in an unequal number of positive and negative categories.

Completely Dissatisfied	Dissatisfied	Somewhat Satisfied	Satisfied	Completely Satisfied
☐	☐	☐	☐	☐

The scale contains three "satisfied" responses and only two "dissatisfied" responses above. Researchers choose between a balanced or unbalanced scale depending on the nature of the concept or knowledge about attitudes toward what is measured. When researchers expect respondents are predisposed toward one end of a concept or the other, unbalanced scales are appropriate. Satisfaction and importance scores usually skew toward positive responses, so unbalanced scales may better capture any true variance that exists.

Forced-Choice Scales?

In many situations, a respondent does not have a strong attitude or opinion toward an issue. A **forced-choice rating scale** compels the respondent to answer using some design or technical aspect. Design-wise, the scale can eliminate a neutral response. A balanced scale with an even number of scale choices accomplishes this task. Consider the Likert item shown below:

Forced-choice rating scale
A fixed-alternative rating scale that requires respondents to choose one of the fixed alternatives.

	Strongly Disagree	Disagree	Slightly Disagree	Slightly Agree	Agree	Strongly Agree
The U.S. Federal Tax Code is fair to all American taxpayers	1	2	3	4	5	6

Technically, software can require a respondent to fill in an answer before finishing the survey. Unanswered items are flagged with some indicator.

Some IRBs suggest that forcing a response by using survey technology borders on unethical. One way around this problem is to use a **non-forced-choice scale** including either a "no opinion" or "don't know" category, as in the following example:

> *How does your attitude toward Community Bank compare with your attitude toward First National Bank?*

> ☐ *Community Bank is much better than First National Bank.*
> ☐ *Community Bank is better than First National Bank.*
> ☐ *Community Bank is worse than First National Bank.*
> ☐ *Community Bank is much worse than First National Bank.*
> ☐ *Don't know.*

Non-forced-choice scale

A fixed-alternative rating scale that provides a "don't know" or "no opinion" category or allowing respondents to indicate that they cannot say which alternative is their choice.

Asking this type of question allows the investigator to separate respondents who cannot make an honest comparison. The argument for forced choice is that people really do have attitudes, even if they are only somewhat knowledgeable about alternatives and should be able to answer the question. Respondents are not provided with an easy out by simply selecting "neutral." The use of forced-choice questions is associated with higher incidences of "no answer." Perhaps when respondents really can't make up their mind, they will leave an item blank if they are given that choice.

Opponents of the forced choice approach argue that error results when respondents are required to answer questions for which they lack a firm position, and they argue that response rates will be lower because respondents will quit when forced to answer questions. However, research indicates that forced choice items do not tend to produce greater error, supporting the argument that people do have some opinion on practically all issues.[19] Further, the total survey response rate and item response rate (leaving items blank or choosing "don't know") is not affected by forced choice approaches. Thus, researchers can apply forced choice responses without significant risk of harming the survey process.

Single or Multiple Items?

Whether to use a single item or a measure made up from responses to several items depends on several characteristics of the phenomenon.

- The complexity of the phenomenon measured
- The number of dimensions of the phenomenon
- The level of abstraction of the phenomenon

Hopefully, the definition of the concept studied makes answers to these questions simple. A single item can assess some very simple or concrete concepts.

> *"Did you watch Big Brother last night?"*
> _____ yes _____ no
> *"Do you like pistachio ice cream?"*
> Don't Like at All _____ _____ _____ _____ _____ Like a Lot

Other indices such as social class require multiple items to form an index. Latent constructs like the personality trait of extraversion generally require multiple item scales for valid measures. Multiple item scales provide the researcher more flexibility and power in assessing validity.

Attitudes and Intentions

Multi-attribute model

A model that constructs an attitude score based on the multiplicative sum of beliefs about an option times the evaluation of those belief characteristics

Behavioral researchers often model behavior as a function of intention, which in turn, is considered a function of attitudes. Attitudes are considered a function of a person's beliefs about some activity weighted by their evaluations of those characteristics. This type of research is sometimes referred to as a **multi-attribute model** or reasoned action approach. For example, a consumer's attitude to opt in to SMS advertising can be modeled by their intention to do so, which in turn, is a function of their attitude.[20] Likewise, a researcher may first measure attitude as a way of knowing how likely a consumer would be to respond to a survey request posted on Facebook.

Multi-attribute Attitude Score

Attitudes are modeled with a multi-attribute approach by taking belief scores assessed with some type of rating scale like those described and multiplying each belief score by an evaluation also supplied using some type of rating scale, and then summing each resulting product. For instance, a series of Likert statements might assess a respondent's beliefs about the reliability, price, service, and styling of a Honda Fit.

	Strongly Disagree	Disagree	Neutral	Agree	Strongly Agree
The Honda Fit is the most reliable car in its class.	SD	D	N	A	SA
The Honda Fit has a low price for a car of its type.	SD	D	N	A	SA
I know that my Honda dealer will provide great service if I buy a Honda Fit.	SD	D	N	A	SA
The Honda Fit is one of the most stylish cars you can buy.	SD	D	N	A	SA

Then, respondents may use a simple rating scale to assess how good or bad is each characteristic. For example, the scale may appear something like this with instructions for the respondent to indicate the relative evaluation of each characteristic.

All things considered ...						
Buying a car that is reliable is						
Very bad ☐	☐	☐	☐	☐	☐	Very good
Buying a car with a low price is						
Very bad ☐	☐	☐	☐	☐	☐	Very good
Buying a car from a dealer with excellent service is						
Very bad ☐	☐	☐	☐	☐	☐	Very good
Buying a car with the latest styling is						
Very bad ☐	☐	☐	☐	☐	☐	Very good

The respondent's attitude toward buying a Honda Fit would be found by multiplying beliefs by evaluations. If a respondent provided the following belief scores using Likert scales for each belief item

Honda Fit reliability	*5*
Honda Fit pricing	*3*
Honda Fit dealer service	*2*
Honda Fit styling	*1*

and the following evaluation scores using the rating scale shown in the preceding

Reliability	*6*
Low pricing	*3*
Dealer service	*4*
Styling	*2*

then her attitude score could be computed as

Beliefs	×	Evaluations	=	(B)(E)
5		6		30
3		3		9
2		4		8
1		2		2
	Total			49

The multi–attribute attitude score for this consumer would be 49. A researcher may also ask respondents to rate a competitor's product. In this case, the product might be a Chevy Sonic. Using the same four characteristics, a score for the competitor can be obtained. The scores can then be compared to see which brand has a competitive advantage in terms of consumer attitudes.

Marketing researchers employ this approach frequently. The key advantages lie in how diagnostic the results can be. Not only can a researcher provide management with feedback on the relative attitude scores, but he or she can also identify characteristics that are most in need of being improved. In particular, poor belief scores on characteristics that respondents rate very favorably (or as highly important) indicate the characteristics that managers should change to improve competitive positioning. In this case, the Fit does well on reliability, and the strong belief score on this characteristic is largely responsible for shaping this consumer's attitude. If the Chevy Sonic scored only a 2 on reliability, the result would diagnose a problem that managers should address. The Sonic has a relatively low score on a very meaningful characteristic.

Behavioral Intention

According to reasoned action theory, people form intentions consistent with the multi–attribute attitude score. Intentions represent the behavioral expectations of an individual toward an attitudinal object. Typically, the component of interest to marketers is a buying intention, a tendency to seek additional information, or plans to visit a showroom. Category scales for measuring the behavioral component of an attitude ask about a respondent's likelihood of purchase or intention to perform some future action, using questions such as the following:

How likely is it that you will purchase a Honda Fit within the next 6 months?

○ Very Unlikely

○ Unlikely

○ Somewhat Unlikely

○ Undecided

○ Somewhat Likely

○ Likely

○ Very Likely

TIPS OF THE TRADE

- Research questions and hypotheses reveal the concepts to measure during the research.
- When planning to use parametric statistical analysis, scales with at least 5 response points provide the greatest flexibility.
- Coefficient α provides an estimate of scale reliability. It is only applicable to multiple item scales with three or more items to be formed into a composite. The following guide can be used in judging the results from estimating coefficient α.
  – Above 0.8, very good reliability
    • Scale can be used as is from a reliability standpoint.
  – From 0.7 to 0.79, good reliability
    • Scale can be used as is from a reliability standpoint.
  – From 0.6 to 0.69, fair reliability
    • Scale can be used as is with caution.
  – Below 0.6, further refinement or modifications to the scale should be made before using.
- Whenever there is a question about the number of scale points to use, it is better to use more rather than fewer scale points.
- Forced choice questions have their place in marketing research.
  – Researchers should strongly consider providing a "don't know" response option when using forced choice mechanisms.
- Attitude scores have no absolute meaning, so results for more than one brand are needed to provide diagnostic recommendations.

© George Doyle & Ciaran Griffin

∷ SUMMARY

1. Determine what things need to be measured to address a research question. Researchers can always know what key concepts he or she must measure by examining the research questions. The research questions are interrogative statements about changes, patterns, or relationships among the concepts relevant to the decision problem. Thus, the researcher must measure these concepts to address the research questions. Hypotheses, which are derived from research questions, often state that one concept is related to another or that differences in some outcome concept will be observed across different levels of some categorical variable. Therefore, the concepts listed in hypotheses must have operational measures to perform the research. Every concept measured requires a conceptual and operational definition. Operational definitions tell how individual variables come together to represent a concept.

2. Distinguish levels of scale measurement. Four levels of scale measurement can be identified. Each level is associated with increasingly more complex properties. Nominal scales assign numbers or letters to objects for identification or classification. Ordinal scales arrange objects based on relative magnitude of a concept. Thus, ordinal scales represent rankings. Interval scales also represent an ordering based on relative amounts of a concept, but they also capture the differences between scale values. Thus, interval scales allow stimuli to be compared to each other based on the difference in their scale scores. Ratio scales are absolute scales, starting with absolute zeros at which there is a total absence of the attribute. Nominal and ordinal scales are discrete. The mode is the best way to represent central tendency for discrete measures. Ratio measures are continuous, and interval scales are generally treated as continuous. For continuous measures, the mean represents a valid representation of central tendency.

3. Create an index or composite measure. Indexes and composite measures are formed by combining scores mathematically from multiple items. For instance, a composite score can be formed by adding a respondent's scores to multiple scale items, each intended to represent the same concept. The end result of the addition is a summed scale. Index scores and composite measures scores are generally obtained in much the same way. However, they differ theoretically from composite measures of latent constructs in that index scores do not have to relate theoretically or statistically to one another.

4. Assess scale reliability and validity. Reliability, validity, and sensitivity are characteristics associated with good measurement. Internal consistency is necessary for good reliability and is assessed most often using coefficient α. Coefficient α should be at least above 0.6 for a scale to be considered as acceptably reliable. Validity is assessed in components. A construct measure that exhibits adequate construct validity is one that is likely well measured. Construct validity consists of face or content validity, convergent validity (internal consistency), discriminant validity, criterion validity, and fit validity. Multivariate statistical procedures like factor analysis can be helpful in providing evidence of construct validity.

5. Understand why the concept of attitude is so important in marketing research. Attitudes are a relatively enduring predisposition to respond consistently to various things including people, activities, events, and objects. Attitudes are predispositions toward behavior and, as such, represent rules that inform a person as to the appropriate reaction in a given situation. Attitudes consist of three components: (a) the affective, or the emotions or feelings involved; (b) the cognitive, or awareness or knowledge; and (c) and the behavioral, or the predisposition to action. Attitudes are so important to business because they tend to predict behavior. If we know one's attitude toward a brand, we can predict with some accuracy whether he or she may purchase and use that brand's products.

6. Design a scale that measures an attitudinal concept. Numerous scaling approaches exist for assessing an attitude. With a Likert scale, respondents indicate their attitudes by checking how strongly they agree or disagree with carefully constructed statements. An attitude can be represented with a series of Likert scale items. Typically, Likert scales contain between five and seven response points. A five-item Likert scale states a phrase with which a respondent expresses agreement. The response points would be "strongly disagree," "disagree," "neutral," "agree," and "strongly agree." A semantic differential uses a series of attitude scales anchored by bipolar adjectives and can be used to create a simple scale that directly measures one's attitude toward some object or activity. Constant-sum scales require the respondent to divide a constant sum into parts, indicating the weights to be given to various attributes of the item being studied. A forced-choice question uses an even number of response points and eliminates a neutral middle from the choice set.

7. Implement a multi-attribute model. A multi-attribute model represents a respondent's attitude about some activity, object, event, or idea by taking belief scores assessed with some type of rating scale and multiplying each belief score by an evaluation of the matching characteristic, also supplied using some type of rating scale, and then summing those products together. These attitude scores are expected to predict behavioral intentions with some degree of confidence. Multi-attribute models provide highly diagnostic information to competitive businesses and thus, they are widely applied.

∴ KEY TERMS AND CONCEPTS

attribute, 278
attitude, 284
balanced rating scale, 295
category scale, 287
choice, 286
coefficient alpha (α), 280
composite measures, 278
concept, 271
constant-sum scale, 290
construct, 272
construct validity, 283
continuous measures, 277
convergent validity, 283
correspondence rules, 271
criterion validity, 282

discrete measures, 276
discriminant validity, 283
face (content) validity, 282
fit validity, 283
forced-choice rating scale, 295
graphic rating scale, 291
index measure, 278
internal consistency, 280
interval scales, 275
Likert scale, 287
measurement, 269
multi-attribute model, 296
non-forced-choice scale, 296
nominal scales, 272
operationalization, 271

ordinal scales, 274
paired comparison, 293
ranking task, 285
rating, 285
reliability, 280
reverse coding, 279
ratio scales, 276
scale, 271
semantic differential, 289
sorting, 285
split-half method, 280
summated scale, 278
test-retest method, 281
unbalanced rating scale, 295
validity, 281

:: QUESTIONS FOR REVIEW AND CRITICAL THINKING

1. Define *measurement*. How is your performance in a marketing research class being measured?
2. What is the difference between a *concept* and a *construct?* In what ways is the definition of the term *variable* similar or different?
3. Consider the following research questions or hypotheses. What variables need to be measured in each?
   a. Do consumers who spend more time and are more committed to Facebook spend more money at Amazon.com?
   b. What are the demographic characteristics of consumers who belong to the PowerUp Rewards program (loyalty program) of GameStop (video games and accessories) stores?
   c. The temperature inside the supermarket will determine how much time shoppers spend in the store such that when the store is cold they will spend less time shopping than when the store is warm.
   d. Product price is related positively to product quality.
   e. Consumer perceptions of value from a service provider are related negatively to the likelihood of switching service providers.
4. An official in the financial office is considering an applicant for financial aid. The officer uses the following process. If the student has a GPA in the 90th percentile among the admission group, 5 points are added. If the student has an ACT or SAT score in the 90th percentile among the admission group, 5 points are added. If the student comes from a family whose cumulative household income was less than $60,000/year for the last 3 years, 8 points are added. If the student is from out of state, 5 points are added. What variables are being used to determine eligibility for this financial aid? What would your approximate score be on this scale? Is it best described as an index or a composite scale? Explain your response.
5. What role does an operational concept definition play in planning a research project?
6. Describe the concept of measurement level and the four different levels of scale measurement.
7. Consider the different grading measuring scales described at the beginning of the chapter. Describe what level of measurement is represented by each. Which method do you think contains the least opportunity for error?
8. Look at the responses to the following survey items that describe how stressful consumers believed a Christmas shopping trip was using a ten-point scale ranging from 1 (no stress at all) to 10 (extremely stressful):
   a. How stressful was finding a place to park? 9
   b. How stressful was the checkout procedure? 5
   c. How stressful was trying to find exactly the right product? 4
   d. How stressful was finding a store employee? 6
   i. What would be the stress score for this respondent based on a summated scale score?
   ii. What would be the stress score for this respondent based on an average composite scale score?
   iii. Do any items need to be reverse-coded? Why or why not?
   iv. How could the concept of split-half reliability be applied using a sample of 100 respondents who gave answers to these four questions?

9. How is it that marketing researchers can justify treating a seven-point Likert scale as interval?
10. What are the components of construct validity? Describe each.
11. Why might a researcher wish to use more than one question to measure attitude toward obtaining an Amazon Prime account?
12. How can a researcher assess the reliability and validity of a multi-item composite scale?
13. Indicate whether the following measures use a nominal, ordinal, interval, or ratio scale:
    a. Prices on the stock market
    b. Marital status, classified as "married" or "not married"
    c. Whether a respondent has ever been unemployed
    d. Professorial rank: assistant professor, associate professor, or professor
    e. Course grades: A, B, C, D, or F
    f. Blood-alcohol content
    g. Number of Facebook friends
    h. The color of one's eyes
    i. The size of one's pupils
    j. Time spent per day using a smartphone or tablet?
14. What is an *attitude?* Why do businesses place so much emphasis on measuring attitudinal concepts?
15. Attitudes are sometimes called tri-partite, meaning they have three components. What are the three components of an attitude?
16. Distinguish between *rating* and *ranking.* Which is a better attitude measurement technique? Why?
17. Construct a Likert scale that would measure student attitudes toward constructing a new business building on campus using a forced choice approach.
18. What are key differences between a five-item and a six-item Likert scale?
19. Describe the way a semantic differential scale could be constructed to measure the behavioral component of attitudes.
20. What is a fundamental weakness of a constant sum or ranking scale?
21. In each of the following, identify the type of scale and evaluate it:
    a. A U.S. representative's questionnaire sent to constituents:

    Do you favor or oppose the Fair Tax proposal?

In Favor	Opposed	No Opinion
☐	☐	☐

    b. How favorable are you toward the Fair Tax proposal?

    Very unfavorable ☐ ☐ ☐ ☐ ☐ ☐ *Very favorable*
    c. A psychographic statement asking the respondent to circle the appropriate response:

    I shop a lot for specials.

Strongly Disagree	Disagree	Neutral	Agree	Strongly Agree
1	2	3	4	5

22. What is a multi-attribute model of consumer attitudes?
23. Look at the table. The b columns represent belief scores for two competing products. The e column represents the evaluations of

those characteristics. Compute the attitude score for each competitor and comment on the competitive positioning of each.

Characteristic	$b_{\text{Brand A}}$	$b_{\text{Brand B}}$	e
Price	5	3	6
Quality	6	2	3
Convenience	1	2	4
Ease of use	3	5	1
Looks	1	7	5

24. If a Likert summated scale has 10 scale items, do all 10 items have to be phrased as either positive or negative statements, or can the scale contain a mix of positive and negative statements? Explain.
25. What are the advantages of using a slider scale?
26. A researcher thinks many respondents will answer "don't know" or "can't say" if these options are printed on an attitude scale along with categories indicating level of agreement. The researcher does not print either "don't know" or "can't say" on the questionnaire because the resulting data would be more complicated to analyze and report. Is this proper?

:: RESEARCH ACTIVITIES

1. Define each of the following concepts, and then operationally define each one by providing correspondence rules between the definition and the scale:
   a. A good bowler
   b. Purchasing intention for a hair salon
   c. Consumer involvement with cars
   d. A workaholic
   e. Fast-food restaurant
   f. Online social networking addict
   g. Attitude toward leaving advice (reviews) on Tripadvisor.com
2. Use the ACSI scores found at **http://www.theacsi.org** to respond to this question. Using the most recent two years of data, test the following two hypotheses:

   a. American consumers are more satisfied with breweries than they are with wireless telephone services.
   b. American consumers are more satisfied with discount and department stores than they are with automobile companies.
   c. American consumers are most satisfied with Southwest Airlines relative to other airlines.
3. Go to **http://www.queendom.com/tests.** Click on the lists of personality tests. Take the hostility test. Do you think this is a reliable and valid measure of how prone someone is to generally act in a hostile manner? Would it be ethical to assign prospective employees a hostility score to be used in a hiring index based on results from this or a similar test?

Satisfaction with Mass Marketing

Case 10.1

A retail consultant studies local Walmart stores to try to assess customer satisfaction with the shopping experience. She begins by examining the ACSI scores for retailers. In the late 2000s, Walmart instituted a policy of increasing the width of the aisles and decreasing the amount of floor space containing huge product displays. Management believes that this was a bad move because when consumers see less, they buy less. Managers argue that the best operating policy is "piling high and selling cheap!" Put as much product on the sales floor as possible and price them as low as possible. This policy is supported by keeping distribution costs low. In addition, management believes that labor costs must be kept low to maintain profitability. The local Walmart is worried about losing business to smaller local supermarkets and dollar stores.

Questions
1. What type of attitude scale is used by the ACSI, if any?
2. What type of attitude study might you design if you were the consultant?
3. Design a survey that would measure beliefs and attitudes toward Walmart and a competing dollar store.
4. How would you use results from this approach to diagnose potential problems for Walmart?

PHOTODISC GREEN/Getty Images

Questionnaire Design

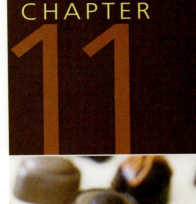

CHAPTER 11

LEARNING OUTCOMES

After studying this chapter, you should be able to:

1. Know the key decisions in questionnaire design
2. Choose between open-ended and fixed-alternative questions
3. Avoid common mistakes in writing questionnaire items
4. Minimize problems with order bias
5. Understand principles of survey flow
6. Use latest survey technology to reduce respondent error
7. Appreciate the importance of pretesting survey instruments

Chapter Vignette:

Ask a Sensitive Question, Get a Sensitive Answer

Survey researchers believe that the responses people give to questionnaire items provide a valid representation of the interests, opinions, or behaviors studied. Researchers should always pay careful attention to how a question is asked, but particularly so when the subjects are sensitive and reveal potentially self-incriminating or embarrassing facts about a person. Consider how a typical respondent might react to the following questions:

- Are your Facebook friends annoying?
- How much time do you spend viewing pornographic websites or videos?
- When you are behind the wheel of a car, are you always a responsible driver?
- Are you very satisfied with your home life?
- Are you satisfied when you think about whether you have exceeded your career aspirations?

A large percentage of respondents would agree with the first question. In fact, growth in Facebook users in the United States has ceased and younger consumers, in particular, are turning to other platforms such as Tumblr, Vine, and Instagram as more convenient outlets for social networking. Despite the lack in growth, Facebook has more than 1,000,000,000 users. So, do Facebook users put up with annoying friends? Also,

if the question was asked in a survey initiated on a friend's Facebook site, would the answer be the same?

Nearly nine in ten respondents would say they would never visit a pornographic website or watch a pornographic video. Yet, pornographic websites are highly visited. Some estimates suggest that 30 percent of all bandwidth on the Internet is consumed by people viewing pornographic content. Pornographic sites have more viewers than Netflix, Amazon, and Twitter combined. A study also asked respondents anonymously whether or not their driving contributed to a recent automobile accident (the survey gave both parties in a recent accident a chance to respond). Maybe it's not so surprising, but the vast majority of people who have recently been in a car accident, when surveyed, say that the other driver was to blame for the incident. Thus, questions that involve self-incrimination may not yield truthful results.

Marketing researchers must take care in asking *relevant* questions in ways that produce the most *truthful* results. The question order can be important. Imagine how responses to the last two questions listed above might change if the order is reversed. The way a researcher words a question also can influence how much a respondent believes that the answer is truly anonymous and can't be linked to him or her personally. Thus, truthful results result from not only asking the right question, but from asking it the right way.[1]

Introduction

Survey researchers use a questionnaire like a carpenter uses a hammer. The questionnaire is the primary tool for building responses to research questions. Many people may believe asking a question is very simple. However, the quality of response cannot be good when the question is bad.

Questionnaire design is one of the most critical stages in the survey research process. Businesspeople and managers who are inexperienced at marketing research frequently believe that constructing a questionnaire is a simple task that they can do without the assistance of a professional researcher. Amateur researchers like these think they can write an effective questionnaire in minutes. Unfortunately, newcomers who naively believe asking questions is easy generally end up with useless results. Ask a bad question and you get bad results!

Basic Considerations in Questionnaire Design

People don't understand questions just because the wording is grammatically correct. Respondents may not know what the researcher is talking about. For instance, a question may ask about a product that the respondent doesn't know. Alternatively, a question may not mean the same thing to everyone interviewed. Finally, people may refuse to answer personally sensitive questions. A skilled survey researcher composes the questionnaire in a way that minimizes error due to potential issues like these.

Even though we discuss questionnaire items as questions, often they are not questions at all but simply words, statements, phrases, or images used to evoke a response. We saw examples of different approaches to question/item design in the previous chapter. The chapter uses the terms *question* and *item* interchangeably.

For a questionnaire to fulfill a researcher's purposes, the questions must meet the basic criteria of *relevance* and *accuracy*. To achieve these ends, a researcher who is systematically planning a questionnaire's design must make several decisions—typically, but not always, the decisions take place in the following sequence:

To the Point

"Before I refuse to take your questions, I have an opening statement."

—RONALD REAGAN

1. What should be asked?
2. How should questions be phrased?
3. In what sequence should the questions be arranged?
4. What questionnaire layout will best serve the research objectives?
5. How can the questionnaire encourage complete responses?
6. How should the questionnaire be pretested and then revised?

What Should Be Asked?

Certain decisions made during the early stages of the research process will influence the questionnaire design. The preceding chapters stressed good problem definition and clear research questions. This leads to specific research hypotheses that, in turn, clearly indicate what the researcher must measure. Different types of questions may be better at measuring certain things than are others. In addition, the communication medium used for data collection—that is, telephone interview, personal interview, snail mail, or Web-based questionnaire—must be determined. This decision is another forward linkage that influences the structure and content of the questionnaire. The specific questions asked will be a function of the previous decisions.

The latter stages of the research process will have an important impact on questionnaire wording. Researchers should consider the data analysis tools that he/she will use when designing questionnaires. Certain question types do not yield data appropriate for certain statistical tools.

Questionnaire Relevancy

A questionnaire is *relevant* to the extent that all information collected addresses a research question and helps a decision-maker address a current marketing problem. Asking a wrong question or an irrelevant question is a common pitfall. If the marketing task is to pinpoint store image problems, questions asking for political opinions may be irrelevant. The researcher should be specific about data needs and have a rationale for each questionnaire item. Irrelevant questions are more than a nuisance because they make the survey needlessly long. In a study where two samples representing the same types of businesspeople received either a one- or three-page printed questionnaire, the response rate was nearly twice as high for the one-page survey.[2]

Conversely, many researchers, after conducting surveys, find that they omitted some important questions. Therefore, when planning the questionnaire design, researchers must think about possible omissions. Is information on the relevant demographic and psychographic variables being collected? Would certain questions help clarify the answers to other questions? Will the results of the study provide the answer to the marketing manager's problem?

Questionnaire Accuracy

Once a researcher decides what to ask, accuracy becomes the primary concern. *Accuracy* means that the information is valid, meaning it faithfully represents reality. Although experienced researchers generally believe that questionnaires should use simple, understandable, unbiased, unambiguous, and nonirritating words, they cannot produce a systematic procedure for ensuring effective question writing across all types of projects. Obtaining accurate answers from respondents depends strongly on the researcher's ability to design a questionnaire that facilitates recall and motivates respondents to cooperate. Respondents tend to be more cooperative when the subject of the research interests them. In addition, when questions are not lengthy, difficult to answer, or ego threatening, respondents are more likely to respond and provide unbiased answers.

Question wording and sequence also substantially influence accuracy, which can be particularly challenging when designing a survey for diverse audiences. Wine industry executives rely on questionnaires to assess what U.S. markets know about wine. Expert wine drinkers might recognize what a researcher means by common wine terms such as *Champagne* and *Burgundy*. They understand the terminology and see items using such terms as *accurately worded*. However, respondents with less expertise may interpret the same questions differently. These respondents may inaccurately associate all sparkling wine with "champagne" and may think of a California "burgundy" when answering the question (Champagne and Burgundy are both names that refer specifically to wines from regions in France).[3] Thus, even relatively simple questions can produce inaccurate answers.

Question Phrasing: Open- or Closed-Ended Statements?

Questions can be phrased in many ways. The researcher may choose from many standard question formats developed over time in previous research studies. This section presents a classification of question types and provides some helpful guidelines for writing questions.

Open-Ended Response versus Fixed-Alternative Questions

We can separate questionnaire items into two basic types based on the amount of freedom respondents have in providing a response. The following sections define open-ended or closed question formats.

Open-ended response | **Open-ended response questions** pose a problem or topic and ask respondents to answer in

questions

Questions that pose a problem and ask respondents to answer in their own words.

their own words. If the interviewer asks a question in a personal interview, the interviewer may probe for more information, as in the following examples:

- *What search engines can you think of other than Google.com?*
- *How do you feel about the political and economic situation today?*
- *What things do you like most about your iPad?*
- *Why do you avoid buying clothes at Walmart?*
- *How much extra are you willing to pay for an electric car?*

Fixed-alternative

questions

Questions in which respondents are given specific, limited-alternative responses and asked to choose the one closest to their own viewpoint.

Open-ended response questions are free-answer questions. **Fixed-alternative questions**—sometimes called *closed-ended questions*—give respondents a limited number of specific alternative responses from which to choose. For example:

Do you blog/have your own Myspace/Facebook-type (or other social networking) page?	
Yes ☐	No ☐

How much time daily do you spend working on your blog/Myspace/Facebook-type page?			
I don't blog ☐	less than 30 minutes a day ☐	30 minutes to 1 hour a day ☐	more than one hour/day ☐

How much time do you spend studying Marketing Research weekly?			
Less than an hour ☐	Between 1 and 2 hours ☐	Between 2 and 3 hours ☐	Greater than 3 hours ☐

Courtesy of Qualtrics.com

Using Open-Ended Response Questions

Open-ended response questions offer several advantages. They are particularly beneficial when the researcher implements an exploratory research design. At this point, researchers may not even know the relevant range of responses to some question. Consider an open-ended question concerning willingness to pay for an electric car. Are consumers willing to pay anything extra? What is the most that people might be willing to pay? Early on, the researcher may have no good idea of what to expect. The initial responses may be helpful in assessing ranges of responses that might be useful in developing structured responses used in a descriptive design. However, researchers can employ numeric open-ended responses with some confidence based on evidence suggesting that open-ended willingness to pay measures accurately forecast demand.[4]

Open-ended questions also identify which words and phrases people spontaneously give to the free-response question. Respondents are free to answer with whatever is at the top of their minds. By obtaining free and uninhibited responses, the researcher may find some unanticipated reaction toward the product. Such responses will reflect the flavor of the language that people use in talking about goods or services and thus may provide a source of new ideas for advertising copywriting or ways to word structured scale items.

Open-ended response questions also are valuable at the beginning of an interview. They are good first questions because they allow respondents to warm up to the questioning process and can stimulate memory for past events. The following question illustrates an open-ended question as an opener:

This question may be followed up with structured questions about how the sense of nostalgia influences feelings about brands or retailers. Further, the open-ended response provides the potential for interpretive research approaches that potentially provide deep insights into the experience.

Open-ended responses also offer some disadvantages. The cost of administering open-ended response questions is on average higher than that of administering fixed-alternative questions. As each respondent's written answer offers a somewhat unique perspective, someone must manually summarize, categorize, or interpret the responses. Once a classification scheme is developed, a data editor can code responses within each data record.

Another potential disadvantage of open-ended responses is an increased possibility of interviewer bias. In an oral interview, interviewer instructions state that answers are to be recorded verbatim. Rarely does even the best interviewer record every word spoken by the respondent. Interviewers have a tendency to take shortcuts. When this occurs, the interviewer may well introduce error because the final answer may reflect a combination of the respondent's and interviewer's ideas.

Also, articulate individuals tend to give longer answers to open-ended response questions. Such respondents often are better educated and from higher-income groups, and therefore, they may not be representative of the entire population. Yet, these better-educated, wealthier respondents may give a disproportionately large share of the responses.

Fixed-Alternative Questions

In contrast, fixed-alternative questions require less interviewer skill, take less time, and are easier for the respondent to answer. This is because answers to closed questions are classified into standardized groupings prior to data collection. Standardizing alternative responses to a question provides comparability of answers, which facilitates coding, tabulating, and ultimately interpreting the data.

However, when a researcher is unaware of the potential responses to a question, he/she should not use fixed-alternative questions. If the researcher assumes what the responses will be but is in fact wrong, he or she will have no way of knowing the extent to which the assumption was incorrect. Sometimes, the researcher only becomes aware of this type of error after launching the survey. Consider, for instance, the fixed-alternative question about willingness to pay for an electric car. What if the researcher chose those particular price categories without careful consideration of the potential range of responses, and then, more than half of respondents select "more than $3,000"? Then, the question format has likely suppressed variation and should probably have included categories above $3,000.

Unanticipated alternatives emerge when respondents believe that closed answers do not adequately reflect their feelings. They may make comments to the interviewer or write additional answers on the questionnaire indicating that the exploratory research did not yield a complete array of responses. After the fact, researchers can't do very much to correct a closed question that does not provide a valid set of alternatives. Therefore, a researcher may find exploratory research with open-ended responses valuable before writing a descriptive questionnaire. The researcher should strive to ensure that there are sufficient response choices to include the relevant range of responses as well as an "other" choice for respondents who do not see their answer among the choice set.

How much more are you willing to pay for an electric car as opposed to a diesel car with the same horsepower?

- ○ $0
- ○ $1 - $249
- ○ $250 - $749
- ○ $750 - $1,499
- ○ $1,500 - $2,999
- ○ More than $3,000
- ○ Other _____

Also, a fixed–alternative question may tempt respondents to check an answer that is more prestigious or socially acceptable than the true answer. Rather than stating that they do not know why they chose a given product, they may select an alternative among those presented, or as a matter of convenience, they may select a given alternative rather than think of the most correct response.

Most questionnaires mix open-ended and closed questions. As we have discussed, each form has unique benefits. In addition, a change of pace can eliminate respondent boredom and fatigue.

Types of Fixed-Alternative Questions

This section identifies and classifies different types of fixed-alternative questions.

The **simple-dichotomy (dichotomous-alternative) question** requires the respondent to choose one of two alternatives. The answer can be a simple "yes" or "no" or a choice between "this" and "that." For example:

Did you make any calls with a home (landline) phone during the last 7 days?

☐ *Yes* ☐ *No*

Several types of questions provide the respondent with *multiple-choice alternatives*. The **multiple-choice question** requires the respondent to choose one—and only one—response from among several possible alternatives. For example:

The **frequency-determination question** is a multiple-choice question that asks for an answer about the general frequency of occurrence. For example:

Attitude rating scales, such as the Likert scale, semantic differential, slider scale, and so on, are fixed-alternative questions, too. Chapter 10 discussed these scale types.

The **checklist question** allows the respondent to provide multiple answers to a single question. The respondent indicates past experience, preference, and the like merely by checking off

Simple-dichotomy (dichotomous-alternative) question
A fixed-alternative question that requires the respondent to choose one of two alternatives.

Multiple-choice question
A fixed-alternative question that requires the respondent to choose one response from among multiple alternatives.

Frequency-determination question
A fixed-alternative question that asks for an answer about general frequency of occurrence.

Checklist question
A fixed-alternative question that allows the respondent to provide multiple answers to a single question by checking off items.

items. In many cases the choices are adjectives that describe a particular object. A typical checklist question might ask the following:

Please check which source below you use most to obtain the latest financial news.

- ○ Wall Street Journal
- ○ Bloomberg Businessweek
- ○ USA Today
- ○ Financial Times
- ○ Facebook
- ○ Twitter
- ○ Local Newspaper
- ○ Fox Businessnews
- ○ CNBC
- ○ Other

Courtesy of Qualtrics.com

A major problem in developing dichotomous or multiple-choice alternatives is the framing of response alternatives. There should be no overlap among categories. Alternatives should be *mutually exclusive*, meaning only one dimension of an issue should be related to each alternative. The following listing of self-report, personal income groups illustrates a common error:

- ■ Under $20,000
- ■ $20,000–$40,000
- ■ $40,000–$60,000
- ■ $60,000–$80,000
- ■ $80,000–$100,000
- ■ $100,000 or more

How many respondents with incomes of $40,000 will be in the second group and how many will be in the third group? A respondent who actually had a $40,000 income could equally as likely choose either. Researchers have no way of knowing how a true $40,000-per-year respondent responded. Grouping alternatives without forethought about analysis is likely to diminish accuracy.

Also, few people relish being in the lowest category and some may not wish to report belonging to the highest income group either. To negate the potential bias caused by respondents' tendency to avoid an extreme category, researchers often include a category lower than the lowest expected answer and a category higher than the highest expected answer.

Phrasing Questions for Self-Administered, Telephone, and Personal Interview Surveys

The means of data collection—telephone interview, personal interview, self-administered Web-based questionnaire—will influence what is the best question format and phrasing. In general, questions for mail, Internet, and telephone surveys must be less complex than those used in personal interviews. Questionnaires for telephone and personal interviews should be written in a conversational style. Exhibit 11.1 illustrates how a question may be revised for a different medium.

In a telephone survey about attitudes toward police services, the questionnaire not only asks about general attitudes such as how much respondents trust their local police officers and whether the police are "approachable," "dedicated," and so on, but it also provides basic scenarios to help respondents put their expectations into words. For example, the interviewer tells respondents to imagine that someone had broken into their home and stolen items and that the respondent

EXHIBIT **11.1**
Best Question Formats Vary by the Interview Medium

Format for Internet or snail-mail self-administered survey:

How satisfied are you with your mobile phone service provider?

○ Very Dissatisfied

○ Quite dissatisfied

○ Somewhat dissatisfied

○ Slightly dissatisfied

○ Neither satisfied nor dissatisfied

○ Slightly satisfied

○ Somewhat satisfied

○ Quite satisfied

○ Very satisfied

Format for telephone or personal interview:

How satisfied are you with your mobile phone service provider? Would you say that you are very dissatisfied, dissatisfied, neither dissatisfied or satisfied, satisfied, or very satisfied?
_____ very dissatisfied
_____ dissatisfied
_____ neither
_____ satisfied
_____ very satisfied

© Cengage Learning®

called the police to report the crime. The interviewer then asks how quickly or slowly the respondent expects the police to arrive.[5]

When a question is read aloud, remembering the alternative choices can be difficult. Consider the following question from a personal interview:

There has been a lot of discussion about the potential health risks to nonsmokers from secondhand tobacco smoke. How serious a health threat to you personally is the inhaling of this secondhand smoke, often called passive smoking: Is it a very serious health threat, somewhat serious, not too serious, or not serious at all?

1. Very serious
2. Somewhat serious
3. Not too serious
4. Not serious at all
5. (Don't know)

The last portion of the question was a listing of the four alternatives that serve as answers. The interviewer uses the listing at the end to remind respondents of the alternatives. The fifth alternative, "Don't know," is in parentheses because, although the interviewer knows it is an acceptable answer, it is not read. The researcher only uses this response when the respondent truly cannot provide an answer.

Avoiding Mistakes

No one size fits all rules determine how to develop a questionnaire. Fortunately, research experience has yielded some guidelines that help prevent the most common mistakes.

Simpler Is Better

Words used in questionnaires should be readily understandable to all respondents. The researcher usually has the difficult task of adopting the conversational language of people at lower education levels without talking down to better-educated respondents. Remember, not all people have the vocabulary of a college graduate. Many consumers, for instance, have never gone beyond a high school education.

To the Point

"*I don't know the rules of grammar. . . . If you're trying to persuade people to do something, or buy something, it seems to me you should use their language, the language they use every day, the language in which they think. We try to write in the vernacular.*"

—DAVID OGILVY

Respondents can probably tell an interviewer whether they are married, single, divorced, separated, or widowed, but providing their *marital status* may present a problem. Researchers should avoid technical jargon commonly used by top corporate executives when surveying retail workers, industrial users, or consumers. "Brand image," "positioning," "marginal analysis," and other corporate language may not have the same meaning for or even be understood by a store owner-operator in a retail survey. The vocabulary used in the following question from an attitude survey on social problems probably would confuse many respondents:

> *When effluents from a paper mill can be drunk and exhaust from factory smokestacks can be breathed, then humankind will have done a good job in saving the environment. . . . Don't you agree that what we want is zero toxicity, meaning no effluents?*

Besides being too long, complex, and confusing, this question is leading.

Avoid Leading and Loaded Questions

Leading question

A question that suggests or implies certain answers.

Leading and loaded questions are a major source of bias. A **leading question** suggests or implies certain answers. A media study of environmental consciousness asked consumers this question:

Many concerned individuals are washing their clothes less often because of concerns for the environment. How has concern for the environment affected your washing behavior?

- ○ Wash rarely
- ○ Wash less often
- ○ Wash about the same
- ○ Wash more often
- ○ Was much more

Courtesy of Qualtrics.com

The potential "bandwagon effect" implied in this question threatens the study's validity. *Partial mention of alternatives* is a variation of this phenomenon:

What do you usually drink first thing in the morning?

- ○ Coke
- ○ Coffee
- ○ Milk

Courtesy of Qualtrics.com

This item may produce an artificially high percentage of Coke, coffee, and milk drinkers because other categories, such as water, tea, or juice, do not appear.

Loaded question

A question that suggests a socially desirable answer or is emotionally charged.

A **loaded question** suggests a socially desirable answer or is emotionally charged. Consider the following question:

What most influences your opinion on controversial political issues?

- ○ Analysis based on knowledge
- ○ Media officials
- ○ Late night comedians
- ○ Coworker opinion

Courtesy of Qualtrics.com

CHAPTER 11 Questionnaire Design ● 313

Most respondents will choose the first response. Why? Even though the question is not that emotionally charged, the first response builds self-esteem more so than the other choices by making the choice seem logical and well thought out.

Certain answers to questions are more socially desirable than others. For example, a truthful answer to the following classification question might be painful:

Where did your rank academically in your high school graduation class?

- ○ 1st (top) quarter
- ○ 2nd quarter
- ○ 3rd quarter
- ○ 4th (bottom) quarter

Courtesy of Qualtrics.com

When taking personality or psychographic tests, respondents frequently can interpret which answers are most socially acceptable even if those answers do not portray their true feelings. For example, what are the socially desirable answers to the following questions on a self-confidence scale?

	Strongly Disagree	Disagree	Neither Agree nor Disagree	Agree	Strongly Agree
I am capable of handling myself in most social situations	○	○	○	○	○
I seldom fear that my actions will cause others to have low opinions of me	○	○	○	○	○

Courtesy of Qualtrics.com

An experiment conducted in the early days of polling illustrates the unpopularity of change.[6] Comparable samples of respondents were simultaneously asked two questions about the presidential succession. One sample was asked,

"Would you favor or oppose adding a law to the Constitution preventing a president from succeeding him/herself more than once?"

The other sample was asked,

"Would you favor or oppose changing the Constitution in order to prevent a president from succeeding him/herself more than once?"

Fifty percent of respondents answered negatively to the first question. For the second question, 65 percent of respondents answered negatively. Thus, the public would rather add to than change the Constitution even though an addition is a change.

Asking respondents "how often" they use a product or visit a store leads them to generalize about their habits, because there usually is some variance in their behavior. In generalizing, a person is likely to portray an *ideal* behavior rather than an *average* behavior. For instance, brushing your teeth after each meal may be ideal, but busy people may skip brushing occasionally. An introductory **counterbiasing statement** or preamble to a question that reassures respondents that their "embarrassing" behavior is not abnormal may yield truthful responses:

Some people have the time to brush three times daily but others do not. How often did you brush your teeth yesterday?

If a question embarrasses the respondent, it may elicit no answer or a biased response. This is particularly true with respect to personal or classification data such as income or education. The problem may be mitigated by introducing the section of the questionnaire with a statement such as this:

To help classify your answers, we'd like to ask you a few questions. Again, your answers will be kept in strict confidence.

Counterbiasing statement
An introductory statement or preamble to a potentially embarrassing question that reduces a respondent's reluctance to answer by suggesting that certain behavior is not unusual.

Split-ballot technique

Using two alternative phrasings of the same question for respective halves of a sample to elicit a more accurate total response than would a single phrasing.

A question statement may be leading because it is phrased to reflect either the negative or the positive aspects of an issue. To control for this bias, the wording of attitudinal questions may be reversed for 50 percent of the sample. This **split-ballot technique** is used with the expectation that two alternative phrasings of the same question will yield a more accurate total response than will a single phrasing. For example, in a study on economy car buying behavior, one-half of a sample of imported-car purchasers received a questionnaire in which they were asked to agree or disagree with the statement:

"*Small domestic cars are cheaper to operate than small imported cars.*"

The other half of the import-car owners received a questionnaire in which the statement read:

"*Small imported cars are cheaper to operate than small domestic cars.*"

The results to the two questions were averaged to get an opinion score for perceived economy of imports versus domestics.

Avoid Ambiguity: Be as Specific as Possible

Items on questionnaires often are ambiguous because they are too general. Consider such indefinite words as *often, occasionally, regularly, frequently, many, good,* and *poor.* Each of these words has many different meanings. For one consumer *frequent* reading of *Fortune* magazine may be reading six or seven issues a year. Another consumer may think reading two issues a year is frequent.

Questions such as the following one, used in a study measuring the reactions of consumers to a television boycott, should be interpreted with care:

> Please indicate the statement that best describes your family's television viewing during the boycott of the Exploration Network.
>
> ○ We did not watch the Exploration Network
> ○ We watched hardly any programs on the Exploration Network
> ○ We occasionally watched programs on the Exploration Netowrk
> ○ We watched a lot of programs on the Exploration Network

Courtesy of Qualtrics.com

Some marketing scholars suggest that the rate of diffusion of an innovation depends on the perception of product attributes such as *divisibility,* which refers to the extent to which the consumer may try an innovation on a limited scale.[7] An empirical attempt to test this theory using semantic differentials was a disaster. Pretesting found that the bipolar adjectives *divisible–not divisible* were impossible for consumers to understand because they did not have the theory in mind as a frame of reference. A revision of the scale used these bipolar adjectives to assess the extent to which a respondent felt he/she could try out a new product:

Testable ___ ___ ___ ___ ___ ___ ___ *Not testable*
(sample use possible)　　　　　　*(sample use not possible)*

However, the question remained ambiguous because the meaning was still unclear sending the researchers back for more pretesting using more concrete wording such as "can you try before you buy?"

A brewing industry study on point-of-purchase advertising (store displays) asked:

> What degree of durability do you prefer in your point-of-purchase advertising?
>
> ○ Permanent (lasting more than 6 months)
> ○ Semipermanent (lasting 1 to 6 months)
> ○ Temporary (lasting less than 1 month)

Courtesy of Qualtrics.com

Here the researchers clarified the terms *permanent, semipermanent,* and *temporary* by defining them for the respondent. However, the question remained somewhat ambiguous. Beer marketers often use a variety of point-of-purchase devices to serve different purposes—in this case, what is the purpose? In addition, analysis was difficult because respondents were merely asked to indicate a preference rather than a *degree* of preference. Thus, the meaning of a question may not be clear because the frame of reference is inadequate for interpreting the context of the question. A student research group asked this question:

What media do you rely on most?

☐ *Television*

☐ *Radio*

☐ *Web sources*

☐ *Social networks*

☐ *Newspapers*

This question is ambiguous because it does not ask about the content of the media. "Rely on most" for what—news, sports, finance, entertainment?

Avoid Double-Barreled Items

A question covering several issues at once is referred to as a **double-barreled question** and should always be avoided. Making the mistake of asking two questions rather than one is easy—for example,

Double-barreled question

A question that may induce bias because it covers two or more issues at once.

> *Please indicate how much you agree with the following statement:*
> *Labor unions and management are most responsible for the current economic crisis.*

When a respondent agrees, so they mean both unions and management, unions or management are responsible? One cannot tell.

When multiple questions are asked in one question, the results may be exceedingly difficult to interpret. Consider the following question from a magazine survey titled "How Do You Feel about Being a Woman?"

Between you and your husband, who does the housework (cleaning, cooking, dishwashing, laundry) over and above that done by any hired help?

○ I do all of it
○ I do almost all of it
○ I do over half
○ We split the work fifty-fifty
○ My hustand does over half

Courtesy of Qualtrics.com

The answers to this question do not tell us if the wife cooks and the husband washes the dishes. The next Research Snapshot provides additional insight into this question.

A survey by a consumer-oriented librarian asked a sample of visitors,

Are you satisfied with the present system of searching for materials using a smart device or computer?

☐ *Yes*   ☐ *No*

A respondent may feel torn between a "yes" to one part of the question and "no" to the other part. The answer to this question does not tell the researcher the source of any problem should someone answer "no". Further, a Likert statement from a study dealing with student perceptions of managerial ethics:

Top international sales managers sometimes buy liquor and prostitutes for important customers.

Strongly Disagree	Disagree	Neither Agree or Disagree	Agree	Strongly Agree
○	○	○	○	○

Courtesy of Qualtrics.com

The item intends to discover students' attitudes about selling as a career.[8] However, perhaps this would be better as two separate questions rather than one to learn respondents' specific beliefs. Then no ambiguity would exist about beliefs concerning what sales managers might buy for customers. A sales manager who takes a customer out for dinner may buy drinks but might never think of buying prostitutes. So, as is, what would a strongly agree or strongly disagree response really mean?

Avoid Making Assumptions

Consider the following question:

Should Macy's continue its excellent gift wrapping program?

○ yes

○ No

This question has a built-in assumption: that people believe the gift-wrapping program is excellent. By answering "yes," the respondent implies that the program is, in fact, excellent and that things are fine just as they are. When a respondent answers "no," the opinion is to discontinue the program implying that it isn't excellent. But, perhaps the respondent thinks Macy's should wrap gifts but doesn't buy the built-in excellence assumption. What answer would that respondent mark?

Another frequent mistake is assuming that the respondent had previously thought about an issue. For example, the following question appeared in a survey concerning Jack-in-the-Box:

"Do you think Jack-in-the-Box restaurants should consider changing their name?"

Respondents have not likely thought about this question beforehand. Most respondents answered the question even though they had no prior opinion concerning the name change. Researchers that desire an informed opinion will end up with responses based on too low a level of involvement in a case like this.

Avoid Taxing Respondents' Memory

A simple fact is that sometimes, we can't remember everything. Researchers writing questions about past behavior or events should recognize that certain questions may make serious demands on the respondent's memory. Writing questions about prior events requires a conscientious attempt to minimize the problems associated with forgetting.

In many situations, respondents cannot recall details without some type of assistance. For example, a telephone survey conducted during the 24-hour period following the airing of the Super Bowl might establish whether the respondent watched the Super Bowl and then asked:

Do you recall any commercials on that program?

Who Really Does Housework?

Who does housework? What seems like a simple question becomes not so simple when one needs a precise answer. One recent survey suggests that, on average, women spent approximately 42 hours a week doing housework compared to approximately 23 hours a week for men. According to these results, women do almost twice as much housework as men. On closer inspection, however, these results suggests that the average married couple spends 65 hours a week doing housework. Really? Do couples really put in nearly 10 hours a day on housework?

That result doesn't seem plausible on first glance, but a number of factors related to survey design may influence the result. First, what is housework? Does housework include driving the kids to school, driving to the grocery store, or driving to work? Does it include time going out to get the newspaper or time spent perusing food catalogs for recipe ideas? A broader definition of housework will yield higher numbers. Second, respondents who do very little housework are not that likely to report to such a survey. Thus, response bias may occur based on the type of person who does respond. Third, the question is prone to socially desirable responding. The socially desirable response for both men and women is to admit to doing a significant amount of housework.

Perhaps an interesting side note is that the more couples report doing housework, the higher the frequency of intimacy

Cardinal / Corbis

they report. On top of this, men report an average of 34 hours a week of work outside the home and women about 20. This doesn't seem to leave a lot of time for other activities. Perhaps one factor behind the apparent relationship is that respondents who report a lot of housework exhibit a response pattern using the upper ends of scales more than the lower parts. If researchers want accurate answers to such questions, they should insure confidentiality, have a very good definition of the phenomena being studied, and be able to convey that definition in a survey instrument. Sometimes, behavioral evidence can validate (or invalidate) survey results. People who do more housework do not have more children than other couples. Does this behavioral result say anything about potential bias in the survey results?

Sources: Craig, L. and P. Simminski (2011), "If Men Do More Housework, Do Their Wives Have More Babies?" *Social Indicators Research,* 101 (2), 255–58. Shellenbarger, S. (2009), "Housework Pays Off Between the Sheets," *Wall Street Journal,* (October 21), D1–D3.

If the answer is positive, the interviewer might ask, "What brands were advertised?" These two questions measure **unaided recall**, because they give the respondent no clue as to the brand of interest.

If the researcher suspects that the respondent may have forgotten the answer to a question, he or she may rewrite the question in an **aided-recall** format—that is, in a format that provides a clue to help jog the respondent's memory. For instance, the question about an advertised beer in an aided-recall format might be "Do you recall whether there was a brand of beer advertised on that program?" or "I am going to read you a list of beer brand names. Can you pick out the name of the beer that was advertised on the program?" Aided recall is less taxing to the respondent's memory.

Telescoping and squishing are two additional consequences of respondents' forgetting the exact details of their behavior. *Telescoping* occurs when respondents believe that past events happened more recently than they actually did. The opposite effect, *squishing,* occurs when respondents think that recent events took place longer ago than they really did. A potential solution to this problem may be to refer to a specific event that is memorable—for example, "How often have you gone to a sporting event since the World Series?" Because forgetting tends to increase over time, the question may concern a recent period: "How often did you watch any Netflix programming last week?" In situations in which "I don't know" or "I can't recall" is a meaningful answer, simply including a "don't know" response category may solve the question writer's problem. Exhibit 11.2 summarizes some key wording mistakes and tips on minimizing them.

Unaided recall

Asking respondents to remember something without providing any clue.

Aided-recall

Asking the respondent to remember something and giving them a clue to help.

EXHIBIT **11.2**
Avoiding Common Wording
Mistakes in Questionnaire
Design

Order Bias

Question Sequence

The order of questions, or the question sequence, may serve several functions for the researcher. If the opening questions are interesting, simple to comprehend, and easy to answer, respondents' cooperation and involvement can be maintained throughout the questionnaire. Asking easy-to-answer questions teaches respondents their role and builds their confidence.

A mail survey among department store buyers drew an extremely poor return rate. A substantial improvement in response rate occurred, however, when researchers added some introductory questions seeking opinions on pending legislation of great importance to these buyers. Respondents completed all the questions, not only those in the opening section.

In their attempt to "warm up" respondents toward the questionnaire, student researchers frequently ask demographic or classificatory questions at the beginning. This generally is not advisable, because asking for personal information such as income level or education may embarrass or threaten respondents. Asking potentially embarrassing questions or personal questions at the end of the questionnaire usually is better. At that point, the respondent may be comfortable with the questioning in general, but also, if the respondent breaks off at that point, the researcher still has a nearly complete questionnaire to work with.

Order bias

Results when a particular sequencing of questions affects the way a person responds or when the choices provided as answers favors one response over another.

Order bias results when a particular sequencing of questions affects the way a person responds or when the choices provided as answers favors one response over another. In political elections involving candidates lacking high visibility, such as elections for county commissioners and judges, the first name listed on a ballot often receives the most votes. For this reason, election boards should consider ballots that list candidate's names in different positions across voters as a way of equaling out any votes that just go to the first person on the list.

Asking specific questions before asking about broader issues is a common cause of order bias. For example, bias may arise if questions about happiness with life in general are asked before asking about happiness with specific aspects of one's life. Consider the following three questions (each rated out of 100 points):

1. Tell us how happy you are with your life in general? _____
2. Tell us how happy you are with your marriage? _____
3. Tell us how happy you are with your career achievements? _____

Responses to question 1 are on average higher when asked in this order. Asking questions 2 and/or 3 first significantly lowers average reported happiness with life. Respondents may overlook specific aspects when answering the general question but then overweight these aspects relative to other nonmentioned aspects.[9] Specific questions may thus influence the more general ones more than general questions will influence specific ones.

Because of this bias, ask general questions before specific questions to obtain the best idea of the true overall impression. This procedure, known as the **funnel technique**, allows the researcher to understand the respondent's overall frame of reference before asking questions that are more specific. The funnel technique reduces bias from one or two specific items.

Funnel technique

Asking general questions before specific questions in order to obtain unbiased responses.

Randomized Presentations

Consider how later answers might be biased by previous questions in this questionnaire on environmental pollution:

Mark the response that best matches your feelings about the severity of each environmental issue.

	Not Severe	Somewhat Severe	Severe	Very Severe	Extremely Severe
Air pollution from automobiles	○	○	○	○	○
Air pollution from open fires	○	○	○	○	○
Air pollution from industrial smoke	○	○	○	○	○
Air pollution from foul odors	○	○	○	○	○
Noise pollution from airplanes	○	○	○	○	○
Noise pollution from cars, trucks, scooters, motorcycles	○	○	○	○	○
Noise pollution from industry	○	○	○	○	○
Noise pollution from loud music	○	○	○	○	○

Courtesy of Qualtrics.com

Not surprisingly, researchers found that the responses to the air pollution questions were highly correlated—in fact, almost identical. With attitude scales, an *anchoring effect* also may exist. The first concept measured tends to become a comparison point from which one makes subsequent evaluations. One way to avoid order bias is to randomize question order. Each respondent receives the questions in a different order depending upon the randomization routine. For instance, a set of twenty questions can be assigned positions using random numbers to assign the order. Internet surveys make randomizing question order convenient and easy. Randomization of items on a questionnaire susceptible to the anchoring effect reduces bias.[10] Even the different response categories can be randomized. These options practically eliminate order bias.

A related problem is bias caused by the order of alternatives on closed questions. To avoid this problem, researchers can employ electronic questionnaires making randomization of the choices easy. This makes sense for multiple-choice responses that do not have a logical order. For instance, a question asking respondents to choose their favorite brand of potato chip could randomize the alternatives to avoid the one on top getting more responses just out of convenience. Alternatively, the standard Likert scale format is logically ordered from 1 representing the strongest disagreement (lowest agreement) to 5, in the case of a 5-point scale, representing the highest agreement. Randomizing the response order in such a case could be confusing to the respondent. With complete randomization, question order is random and respondents see response alternatives in different random positions.

Not surprisingly, marketing researchers rarely print alternative questionnaires with either randomized questions or responses. If printed questionnaires are used, randomization would make data coding very difficult and create a high opportunity for coding error. Thus, printed survey instruments are disadvantageous when randomization is needed.

Randomized Response Techniques

Randomized response techniques

Involve randomly assigning respondents to answer either the question of interest (embarrassing) or a mundane and unembarrassing question.

Researchers who need to ask embarrassing or incriminating questions sometimes employ randomized response approaches that try to demonstrate to the respondent that even the researcher would not be able to know how the respondent answered the question. **Randomized response techniques** involve randomly assigning respondents to answer either the question of interest (embarrassing) or a mundane question free from the possibility of embarrassment. Researchers use an approach like this when studying sensitive issues including sexually transmitted diseases, sexual behaviors, pornography consumption, cigarette consumption, abortion, and voting behaviors, among other things.[11] The following illustration gives an idea of how this works.

Suppose a marketing researcher was studying relationships between manufacturing firms' sales personnel and a retail firms' buying agents. The researcher wants the answer to this question:

H) Have you ever lied about a product's shipping date in order to close a deal?

Rather than asking this question alone. The survey offers respondents an alternate question:

T) Choose a card from the deck provided. Is the card red?

Alternate questions H and T are followed by a single "yes" or "no" response scale. The instructions then tell respondents to flip a coin. If the flip turns out heads, respondents should answer question H. If the flip turns out tails, respondents should answer question T. In this way, respondents get the idea (which is true) that the researcher can't tell what question the respondent answered.

However, in any group of respondents, the researcher can compute the percentage of people who lied based on the observed numbers of "yes" responses and the known statistical probability of a coin flip. In other words, any difference from 50 percent "yes" can be attributed to the presumably honest answers of respondents.[12] Thus, researchers can address hypotheses involving whether or not automobile industry personnel lie about delivery dates more often than computer industry personnel or whether one culture or sex differs from another. The use of randomized response techniques remains controversial based in part on the willingness and ability of respondents to follow procedures. For now, researchers should consider using the approach when studying relatively capable respondents.

Survey Flow

Survey flow

The ordering of questions through a survey.

Survey flow refers to the ordering of questions through a survey. Previously, we discussed order bias as one aspect of survey flow. Other aspects of survey flow can affect response quality. This section discusses issues that facilitate good flow and thereby valid responses.

Oftentimes certain sections of a questionnaire are irrelevant to a particular respondent. Asking a question that does not apply to the respondent or that the respondent is not qualified to answer may be irritating or cause a biased response or even a survey breakoff. A **breakoff** means the respondent stops answering questions resulting in an incomplete survey. We'll have more on breakoffs later in the chapter.

Breakoff

Term referring to a respondent who stops answering questions before reaching the end of the survey.

A **filter question** can serve as a **branching** mechanism directing respondents to an appropriate part of the questionnaire using skip logic. Asking:

"Where do you generally have check-cashing problems in Springfield?"

Filter question

A question that screens out respondents who are not qualified to answer a second question.

may elicit a response even though the respondent has had no check-cashing problems. He or she may wish to please the interviewer with an answer. The respondent could first encounter a filter question such as:

"Do you ever have a problem cashing a check in Springfield? _____ Yes _____ No"

Branching

Directing respondents to alternative portions of the questionnaire based on their response to a filter question.

The responses provided would branch respondents who say "yes" to questions about the places where checks cannot be cashed while respondents who say "no" skip to the next block of questions.

Exhibit 11.3 gives an example of a flowchart plan for a survey addressing a rental car company's sponsorship of a top racer in the Tour de France bicycle race. In this case, the company (Europcar) is evaluating the sponsorship's effectiveness across different markets and potential

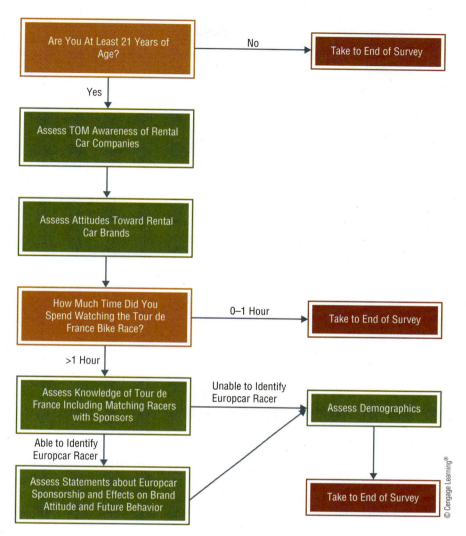

EXHIBIT 11.3

Survey Flow for Tour de France Sponsorship

markets. The first question serves as a filter and qualifies respondents based on whether or not they are old enough to rent a car. Next, respondents provide unaided top of mind awareness and then rate attitudes toward rental car companies, including Europcar. Respondents then reveal whether they spent any significant time viewing the Tour de France. If the respondent viewed for more than one hour, questions assessing the respondent's awareness of sponsorships are provided and so forth. The survey allows research questions involving how much the awareness of Europcar is affected by the sponsorship and how attitudes toward the company might be changed relative to the sponsorship.

Good survey flow, sometimes called *layout*, and physical attractiveness are crucial in mail, Internet, and other self-administered questionnaires. For different reasons, a good layout in questionnaires designed for face-to-face and telephone interviewers is also important.

Traditional Questionnaires

A good layout is neat and attractive, and the instructions for the interviewer should be easy to follow. The responses "It Depends," "Refused," and "Don't Know" enclosed in a box to the side indicate that these answers are acceptable but responses from the 5-point scale are preferred.

Survey researchers can increase response rates by investing in an attractive and well-designed questionnaire. Self-response printed questionnaires should never be overcrowded. Margins should be of decent size, white space should be used to separate blocks of print, and the unavoidable columns of multiple boxes should be kept to a minimum. A question should not begin on one page and end on another page. Splitting questions may cause a respondent to read only part of a question, to pay less attention to answers on one of the pages, or to become confused. For Web-based surveys, again do not crowd a page and try to minimize the amount of scrolling a respondent has to do to see all the items.

Researchers should strive to keep questionnaires as short as possible. A booklet form of questionnaire is preferable to stapling a large number of pages together. Also, do not try to put too many questions on a page—paper or electronic. In situations in which it is necessary to conserve space on the questionnaire or to facilitate data entry or tabulation of the data, a multiple-grid layout may be used. The **multiple-grid (matrix table) question** presents several similar questions and corresponding response alternatives arranged in a grid format. For example:

Multiple-grid (matrix table) question

Several similar questions of the same format all arranged in a grid format.

By using several forms, special instructions, and other tricks of the trade, the researcher can design the questionnaire to facilitate the interviewer's job of following interconnected questions. Exhibit 11.4 illustrates portions of an interview form used by a telephone interviewer. Note how the layout and easy-to-follow instructions for interviewers in Questions 1, 2, and 3 help the interviewer follow the question sequence.

Instructions often appear in capitalized or bold letters to alert the interviewer that it may be necessary to proceed in a certain way. For example, if a particular answer is given, the instructions say to skip certain questions or go to a special sequence of questions. To facilitate coding, fixed alternative responses can be precoded when possible, as in Exhibit 11.4. Skip logic can easily be built into electronic questionnaires to perform this routing automatically.

Layout is extremely important when questionnaires are long or require the respondent to fill in a large amount of information. In many circumstances, using headings or subtitles to indicate groups of questions will help the respondent grasp the scope or nature of the questions to be asked. Thus, at a glance, the respondent can follow the logic of the questionnaire.

Survey Technology

Many guidelines for laying out paper questionnaires apply to Internet questionnaires too. Given the increasing reliance on Internet or Web-based surveys, we discuss many survey flow issues in this important context. Survey software programs like Qualtrics allow several special features that facilitate design and allow important data to be collected that may be difficult otherwise. Smartphones and tablet computers also provide another medium for administering surveys. These same software programs often provide formats amenable to these media as well. Earlier, we learned

1. Did you take the car you had checked to the Standard Auto Repair Center for repairs?

   −1 Yes   (SKIP TO Q. 3)   −2 No

2. (IF NO, ASK:) Did you have the repair work done?

   −1 Yes   −2 No

   ↓   ↓

1. Where was the repair work done?_____   1. Why didn't you have the car repaired?

   _____   _____

                                                        _____

                                                        _____

2. Why didn't you have the repair work done
    at the Standard Auto Repair Center?_____

   _____

   _____

   _____

3. (IF YES TO Q. 1, ASK:) How satisfied were you with the repair work? Were you . . .

   −1 Very satisfied

   −2 Somewhat satisfied

   −3 Somewhat dissatisfied

   −4 Very dissatisfied

   (IF SOMEWHAT OR VERY DISSATISFIED:) In what way were you dissatisfied?

   _____

   _____

   _____

4. (ASK EVERYONE:) Do you ever buy gas at the 95th Street Standard Center?

   −1 Yes   −2 No   (SKIP TO Q. 6)

5. (IF YES, ASK:) How often do you buy gas there?

   −1 Always

   −2 Almost always

   −3 Most of the time

   −4 Part of the time

   −5 Hardly ever

6. Have you ever had your car washed there?

   −1 Yes   −2 No

7. Have you ever had an oil change or lubrication done there?

   −1 Yes   −2 No

EXHIBIT 11.4

Illustrates Portions of an Interview Form Used by a Telephone Interviewer

how electronic questionnaire designs facilitate randomization. Here, we learn about a few other features of self-administered Internet surveys.

Response Quality

Once a respondent agrees to participate, he or she has an ethical obligation to complete the task in a responsible fashion. However, this is not always the case. For instance, the researcher can build in questions that test whether or not the respondent is paying attention. Consider the following item:

Choose "disagree" to this item for administrative purposes.

- ○ Strongly Disagree
- ○ Disagree
- ○ Neutral
- ○ Agree
- ○ Strongly Agree

Courtesy of Qualtrics.com

Suppose a respondent chooses "strongly agree." Obviously, he or she is not responding responsibly. At this point, the researcher can build in branching or skip logic that breaks the survey off if a respondent selects anything other than "disagree." An alternative is to build in a popup that reminds the respondent to pay attention.

Timing

Survey software provides easy mechanisms for timing respondents as they move through a survey. The software routinely records the total time that someone spends responding to a survey. However, the survey also can record time spent on individual pages or even individual questions. The timers produce potentially useful behavioral data and also help identify types of respondent error such as speeding. The presumption is that **speeders**, those who move through a survey much faster than the average respondent, he/she cannot be providing reliable responses.

Speeders

Respondents who take relatively little time to move through a survey—so little that the veracity of their responses is questionable.

Typically, "timing questions" record the amount of time a respondent took before clicking somewhere on a page, the amount of time until they made the last click on a page, and the total amount of time they spent on a page. The time a respondent spent on a page can be an important outcome in studies involving attitude change or information processing. For example, ad features may be built in precisely to encourage consumers to spend more time viewing the ad. Timing also can provide another check on response quality. For instance, if respondents spend less time on a page than it takes to read a question, then they are not likely paying very close attention and, as a result, the response quality is called into question.

Similarly, if the total time spent responding is too fast, indicating a speeder, then the respondent may be marking responses randomly or without paying attention.[13] Respondents who take one and one-half standard deviations less time than usual appear likely to be offering "satisficing" responses leading to substantially high response error. Thus, those taking a standard deviation and half less than the median response are flagged as speeders. In some instances though, particularly with short questionnaires, even less deviation may indicate speeding. Research suggests that m-Turk workers are on average speeders relative to other types of respondents.[14]

Randomized Assignment

At times, the researcher needs to assign a certain set of items to specific respondents. In implementing experimental designs, the researcher assigns a certain set of conditions to each respondent. For instance, in a 2 X 2 between-subjects experiment examining the effect of price level (below or above market price) and quality (an extended warranty that lasts 2 years versus a basic warranty that last 60 days), the researcher needs to assign each subject to one of the four experimental conditions. Electronic survey software facilitates this assignment. One way to accomplish this is to place each of the four stimuli in a separate survey block and then to set up a survey flow that randomly assign subjects to one of those four blocks. Typically, the software will allow even assignment to help make sure that approximately the same number of subjects respond to each of the four conditions.

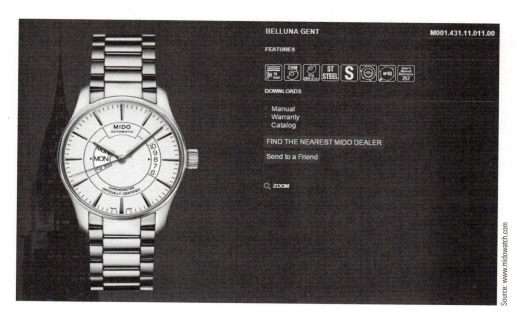

EXHIBIT 11.5

Tracking Points of Interest Using a Heat Map. Heat Maps Identify What Spots in a Graphic Attract a Respondent's Attention.

Physical Features

Several physical features of questionnaires can influence responses.

Tracking Interest

Electronic questionnaires sometimes allow us to come close to tracking behavior beyond timing using special question types such as a heat map. Exhibit 11.5 displays a **heat map question** tracking the way a respondent views an advertisement for a watch. The dashed lines that form a grid would not be visible to the respondent. However, any cursor activity in each grid would be recorded, allowing the researcher to know what parts of the ad captured the respondent's attention the most. This type of question mimics behavioral pupil tracking and provides an indication of what parts of an advertisement or image capture the most attention.

Heat map question

A graphical question that tracks the parts of an image or advertisement that most capture a respondent's attention.

Status Bar

With a paper questionnaire, a respondent can flip through a questionnaire and know about how many questions are in a survey. Multiple page Web-based surveys do not provide this opportunity. However, the researcher may provide a **status bar** as a visual indicator of questionnaire length. The status bar usually resembles a thermometer and the more the bar is filled the closer the respondent is to the finish. Exhibit 11.6 shows an online survey page including a status bar at the bottom of the page. In this case, the respondent appears to be nearly finished.

Status bars are a matter of courtesy to the respondent. However, when a survey involves multiple branches, the status bar can sometimes be misleading. The survey in the exhibit initially asked a filter question, "Do you drive an automobile?" Respondents who indicated "no" were taken immediately to the end of the survey. Thus, the more branching a survey involves, the less useful the status bar becomes.

Status bar

In an Internet questionnaire, a visual indicator that tells the respondent what portion of the survey he or she has completed.

Prompting

Web-based surveys allow limited interactivity. One useful piece of feedback comes in the form of a prompt message. Prompting, in this form, informs the respondent that he/she has skipped an item or provided implausible information. In Exhibit 11.6, the message tells the respondent that the question describing the car must be answered before moving forward with the survey. In this case, the researcher has set this question to be a forced response. In other instances, a prompt may indicate that implausible answers have been provided such as when a constant scale sum does not add up to the proper total.

Prompting of this type reduces item nonresponse (fewer items are skipped) at the expense of increasing breakoffs.[15] Respondents may get frustrated with the demands to provide answers and

EXHIBIT 11.6
Illustration of Status Bar
and Prompts

Sorry, you cannot continue until you correct the following:

• Issue 1
   • *Please answer this question.*

Please answer this question.
Please select the car your drive most often from the alternatives shown below.

Make   ▢
Model ▢
Year   ▢

When do you believe you would be in the market to purchase a new car or truck?

○ 0-6 months
○ 7 months to 12 months
◉ 1 - 2 years
○ 3 - 5 years
○ Not in forseeable future

Survey Completion
0% ▭ 100%

simply quit answering all questions. This is particularly true if the prompt asks a respondent to fill in open-ended items or items a respondent views as sensitive or personal. Overall, prompts should be used for critical questions because blank answers to these are practically equivalent to a survey nonresponse anyway.

Piping

Piping software

Software that allows question answers to be inserted into later questions.

Survey software can systematically or randomly manipulate the questions a respondent sees. **Piping software** allows responses to a previous question to be inserted into later questions. For instance, a researcher studying vacation destinations conducts an online survey about consumer perceptions of their most recent vacation spot. After initial screening to make sure the person has taken a vacation in the past year, the respondent encounters this question:

In what place (resort area, city, or geographic region) did you spend the largest part of your most recent vacation?

Whatever the respondent writes in this box will be inserted into future questions about the destination. If the respondent put Disney World, the future question would appear as:

How many nights did you stay at Disneyworld?

Piping makes question wording much simpler because the respondent's answer replaces repetitive use of phrases such as "your most recent vacation destination."

Pretesting and Revising Questionnaires

Many novelists write, rewrite, revise, and rewrite again certain chapters, paragraphs, or even sentences. The researcher works in a similar world. Rarely does he or she write only a first draft of a questionnaire. Usually the questionnaire is tried out on a group, selected on a convenience basis, that is similar in makeup to the one that ultimately will be sampled. Although the researcher should not select a group too divergent from the target market—for example, selecting business students as surrogates for businesspeople—pretesting does not require a statistical sample. The pretesting process allows the researcher to determine whether respondents have any difficulty understanding the questionnaire and whether there are any ambiguous or biased questions. This process is exceedingly beneficial and may also involve not just the content of the questions but the method of asking as shown in the Research Snapshot on the next page. Making a mistake with twenty-five or fifty subjects can avoid the potential disaster of administering an invalid questionnaire to several hundred individuals.

For a questionnaire investigating teaching students' experience with Web-based instruction, the researcher had the questionnaire reviewed first by university faculty members to ensure the questions were valid, and then asked twenty teaching students to try answering the questions and indicate any ambiguities they noticed. Their feedback prompted changes in the format and wording. Pretesting was especially helpful because the English-language questionnaire was used in a school in the United Arab Emirates, where English is spoken but is not the primary language.[14]

Tabulating the results of a pretest helps determine whether the questionnaire will meet the objectives of the research. A **preliminary tabulation** often illustrates that, although respondents can easily comprehend and answer a given question, that question is inappropriate because it does not provide relevant information to help solve the marketing problem. Consider the following example from a survey among distributors of high-tech medical equipment such as MRI machines:

Preliminary tabulation

A tabulation of the results of a pretest to help determine whether the questionnaire will meet the objectives of the research.

Please indicate the percentage of new client contacts that you have made in the last two years that originated from the following sources:	
Email	0
Phone Call	0
Linked-In Message	0
Facebook Message	0
In-person Cold Call	0
Professional Meeting Attendance	0
Other	0
Other	0
Total	0

Courtesy of Qualtrics.com

Although this may seem like a simple question, pretesting may uncover potential problems. For instance, can respondents add up scores to total 100? If using an online format, the survey software can use a routine to prompt respondents should the scores not total to 100. But, if the task is too difficult, the researcher should revise the question. Also, is some other category frequent enough in occurrence to be listed as one of the options? If an open-ended "other" box reveals some category showing up a lot, the item should include it as an explicit choice. If, on the other hand, very few pretest respondents choose any response for "other," only one "other" response should be used to avoid confusion that may come from including two.

What administrative procedures should be implemented to maximize the value of a pretest? Administering a questionnaire exactly as planned in the actual study often is not possible. For example, mailing out a questionnaire might require several weeks that simply cannot be spared. Pretesting a questionnaire in this manner would provide important information on response rate

I Give Up!

The questionnaire design not only aims to get valid data—but design features also assist in getting data at all. No matter what the interview mode, a large portion of respondents give up before finishing and abandon the survey. With snail-mail questionnaires, the number is impossible to determine. However, phone interviews and online surveys allow an assessment of not only how many breakoffs occur but also when they occur. When designing online surveys, keep the following guidelines in mind when attempting to minimize nonresponse problems due to breakoffs:

- Make sure the questionnaire is visually appealing and easy to read. Clutter causes respondents to give up.
- Don't put too many questions on a single page or the task looks burdensome and leads respondents to give up.
- Sensitive questions lead respondents to give up.
- Respondents give up in the face of long questions.
- Open-ended questions in a majority closed-ended survey lead respondents to give up.
- The more sophisticated the sample, the more items capturing greater variance (like sliders and high response rates)

and those not containing labels on all response categories can be used effectively.

- One important element in a pretest is estimating how many people give up without finishing.
- Follow these rules and you won't have to give up on Web-based surveys.

Sources: Peychev, A. (2009), "Survey Breakoff," *Public Opinion Quarterly*, 71 (Spring), 74–97. Weijters, B., E. Cabooter, and N. Schillewaert (2010), "The Effect of Rating Scale Format on Response Styles: The Number of Response Categories and Response Category Labels," *International Journal of Research in Marketing*, 27, 236–47.

but may not point out why questions were skipped or what questions are ambiguous or confusing. Personal interviewers can record requests for additional explanation or comments that indicate respondents' difficulty with question sequence or other factors. This is the primary reason why researchers employ interviewers often in pretest work. Self-administered questionnaires are not reworded as personal interviews, but interviewers are instructed to observe respondents and ask for their comments after they complete the questionnaire. When pretesting personal or telephone interviews, interviewers may test alternative wordings and question sequences to determine which format best suits the intended respondents.

No matter how the pretest is conducted, the researcher should remember that its purpose is to uncover any problems that the questionnaire may cause. Thus, pretests typically are conducted to answer questions about the questionnaire such as the following:

- Can the questionnaire format be followed by the interviewer [respondent for self-response]?
- Does the questionnaire flow naturally and conversationally?
- Are the questions clear and easy to understand?
- Can respondents answer the questions easily?
- Which alternative forms of questions work best?
- What overall and item response rates can be expected?

Pretests also provide means for testing the sampling procedure—to determine, for example, whether interviewers are following the sampling instructions properly and whether the procedure is efficient. Pretests also provide estimates of the response rates for mail surveys and the completion rates for telephone surveys.

Usually a questionnaire goes through several revisions. The exact number of revisions depends on the researcher's and client's judgment. The revision process usually ends when both agree that the desired information is being collected in an unbiased manner.

Designing Questionnaires for Global Markets

Marketing research is now a global enterprise. Researchers must take cultural factors into account when designing questionnaires. The most common problem involves translating a questionnaire into other languages. A questionnaire developed in one country may be difficult to translate because equivalent language concepts do not exist or because of differences in phrasing and vernacular. Although Spanish is spoken in both Mexico and Venezuela, one researcher found out that the Spanish translation of the English term *retail outlet* works in Mexico but not in Venezuela. Venezuelans interpreted the translation to refer to an electrical outlet.

Counting on an international audience to speak a common language such as English does not necessarily bridge these gaps, even when the respondents actually do speak more than one language. Cultural differences incorporate many shades of meaning that may not be captured by a survey delivered in a language used primarily for, say, business transactions. In a test of this idea, undergraduate students in twenty-four countries completed questionnaires about attitudes toward school and career. Half received the questionnaire in English, and half in their native language. The results varied, with country-to-country differences smaller when students completed the questionnaire in English.[16]

Some survey software tools like Qualtrics provide a free translation service that will allow one to write a survey in one language and have it administered in another. This may be useful for very exploratory surveys and as a first effort in translation. Marketing researchers usually apply more rigor in making sure the meanings match across languages.

International marketing researchers often have questionnaires back translated. **Back translation** is the process of taking a questionnaire that has previously been translated from one language to another and having it translated back again by a second, independent translator. The back translator is often a person whose native tongue is the language that will be used for the questionnaire. This process can reveal inconsistencies between the English version and the translation. For example, when a soft-drink company translated its slogan "Baby, it's cold inside" into Cantonese for research in Hong Kong, the result read "Small Mosquito, on the inside, it is very cold." In Hong Kong, *small mosquito* is a colloquial expression for a small child. Obviously the intended meaning of the advertising message had been lost in the translated questionnaire.[17]

Back translation

Taking a questionnaire that has previously been translated into another language and having a second, independent translator translate it back to the original language.

TIPS OF THE TRADE

- Keep questionnaire wording simple
  - Use shorter words that have concrete meaning
  - Use shorter statements—one line is best—never more than two lines
  - When questioning about frequency, try to use numbers instead of vague terms like *rarely*.
- Design questionnaire for the least capable respondent in the sampling frame.
- In general, funnel respondents from general to specific questions.
- Randomize question order when possible to avoid order bias.

- Once a questionnaire exceeds a dozen questions, build in automated response quality checks.
- Keep appearance of questionnaire neat and clean to avoid breakoffs.
- Pretests are invaluable in spotting things such as mistake-prone questions, projected overall response rates, and item response rates based on breakoffs.
  - A revised questionnaire is better than an initial questionnaire.
- Use random assignment to balance out presentation of experimental conditions.
- Be aware that speeding can kill response quality.

:: SUMMARY

1. Know the key decisions in questionnaire design. The data gathered via a questionnaire must be both relevant and accurate to be of value. A researcher systematically planning a survey faces several decisions that will shape the value of the questionnaire. What should be asked? How should questions be phrased? In what sequence should the questions be arranged? What questionnaire layout will best serve the research objectives? How can the questionnaire encourage complete responses? How should the questionnaire be pretested and revised if needed?

2. Choose between open-ended and fixed-alternative questions. Open-ended response questions pose some question and ask a respondent to answer in his or her own words. They provide the respondent with flexibility and may allow for meaningful, interpretive conclusions. Open-ended response questions are especially useful in exploratory research or at the beginning of a questionnaire. However, they make a questionnaire more expensive to analyze and interpret because an interviewer must review each response. As a result, interviewer bias can influence the responses to such questions. Alternatively, fixed-alternative questions require less interviewer skill, take less time, are easier to answer, and encourage breakoffs less. In fixed-alternative questions, the researcher provides respondents with specific limited alternative responses and asks them to choose the one closest to their own viewpoint. Care must be taken to formulate the responses so that they do not overlap and to make sure all plausible response categories are provided.

3. Avoid common mistakes in writing questionnaire items. Survey language should be simple to allow for variations in vocabulary and knowledge. Researchers with strong opinions should seek assistance in making sure a questionnaire is free of leading or loaded questions, which subtly encourage one response over another. Two other common problems are item ambiguity and double-barreled questions, which asks two or more questions at the same time. By keeping each question short and stated with simple, concrete terminology, these problems can be reduced. Researchers who ask respondents about past specific behaviors should consider giving some sort of assistance to prime memory or employ aided-recall questions.

4. Minimize problems with order bias. A person's response to a question can vary based on where in the sequence of items that question appears. Researchers often employ the funnel technique of survey design. This technique involves asking the most general questions about some subject first and the most specific questions about a subject last. Once all subjects have been covered, any remaining sensitive or demographic items are included. Randomization also plays a role in reducing order bias. Survey software makes the randomization of questions and the randomization of responses simple—both approaches reduce order bias. The randomized response technique also offers a way to make respondents comfortable answering even very embarrassing questions.

5. Understand principles of survey flow. Survey flow refers to the ordering of questions through a survey. Some surveys involve branching that takes respondents to different parts of the questionnaire based on a response to a specific question. Branching is implemented by having respondents who do not qualify based on a filter question skip questions that a qualified respondent answers.

6. Use latest survey technology to reduce respondent error. Internet surveys allow researchers effective tools to monitor respondents as they move through a survey. Response quality checks and timing questions monitor whether a respondent is paying attention. Respondents who are not fulfilling their responsibility can be branched out of the survey or given a prompt to notify them of a problem. Internet questionnaires also can include special questions that track behavior including timing and heat-map questions.

7. Appreciate the importance of pretesting survey instruments. Pretesting helps reveal errors while they can still be corrected easily. A preliminary tabulation may show that, even if respondents understand questions, the responses are not relevant to the marketing problem. Often, the most efficient way to conduct a pretest is with interviewers to generate quick feedback. International marketing researchers must take cultural factors into account when designing questionnaires. The most widespread problem involves translation into another language. International questionnaires are often back translated.

:: KEY TERMS AND CONCEPTS

aided-recall, *317*
back translation, *329*
branching, *320*
breakoff, *320*
checklist question, *309*
counterbiasing statement, *313*
double-barreled question, *315*
filter question *320*
fixed-alternative questions, *306*
frequency-determination question, *309*

funnel technique, *319*
heat map question, *325*
leading question, *312*
loaded question, *312*
multiple-choice question, *309*
multiple-grid (matrix table) question, *322*
open-ended response questions, *306*
order bias, *318*
piping software, *326*
preliminary tabulation, *327*

randomized response
   techniques, *320*
simple-dichotomy (dichotomous-
   alternative) question, *309*
speeders, *324*
split-ballot technique, *314*
status bar, *325*
survey flow, *320*
unaided recall, *317*

:: QUESTIONS FOR REVIEW AND CRITICAL THINKING

1. What are six critical questions for a researcher in designing a questionnaire?

2. Evaluate and comment on the following questions taken from several questionnaires:

   a. A university computer center survey on the university health center:

      Check the response that best reflects how often you use the university health center.

      _____ *Infrequently*
      _____ *Occasionally*
      _____ *Frequently*
      _____ *Never*

   b. A survey of advertising agencies:

      Do you understand and like the Federal Trade Commission's new corrective advertising policy?

      _____ *Yes*   _____ *No*

   c. A survey on a new, small electric car:

      Assuming 90 percent of your driving is in town, would you buy this type of car?

      _____ *Yes*   _____ *No*

      If this type of electric car had the same initial cost as a current General Motors full-size, fully equipped car, went from 0 to 60 mph in 16 seconds, and could go 175 miles between recharging, would you buy one?

      _____ *Yes*   _____ *No*

   d. A *student survey:*

      Since the beginning of this semester, approximately what percentage of the time do you get to campus using each of the forms of transportation available to you per week?

      *Walk*_____
      *Bicycle*_____
      *Public transportation*_____
      *Drive*_____

   e. A survey of DH motorcycle company's retail dealers:

      Should the DH company continue its generous cooperative advertising program?

   f. A survey of media use by residents of a retirement community in Florida:

Courtesy of Qualtrics.com

   g. A government survey of consumers who have sold a car during the year:

      > When you sold your car recently, which of the following reflects your opinion of the deal?
      >
      > ○ I feel like it was a big financial loss to me
      > ○ I feel like it was a big financial gain to me
      > ○ The sale really added to my income for the year
      > ○ I think I was paid about as much as the car was worth

      Courtesy of Qualtrics.com

   h. A pro-modern art society's face-to-face survey of the general public:

      Modern art adds greatly to the quality of life in our community. Do you believe that more tax dollars should go to support modern art?
      _____ *Yes*   _____ *No*

   i. A telephone survey of the U.S. general public:

      In the next year, after accounting for inflation, do you think your real personal income will go up or down?
      ___ *Go up more than 15%*
      ___ *Go up more than 5%*
      ___ *Go up*
      ___ *Stay the same*
      ___ *Go down*
      ___ *Go down 5%*
      ___ *Go down more than 5%*
      ___ *(Don't know)*

j. A paper-and-pencil survey of the students registering to use the placement center:

Many of the firms that interview screen applicants based on GPA. What is your GPA?

GPA = ___   Comment:

k. A telephone survey of voters:

Since agriculture is vital to our state's economy, how do you feel about the administration's farm policies?

A) *Strongly favor*

B) *Somewhat favor*

C) *Somewhat oppose*

D) *Strongly oppose*

E) *Unsure*

3. The following question was asked of a sample of television viewers using a snail-mail survey approach:

What type of fan do you consider yourself to be for different sports and sports programs?

- *Diehard Fan: Watch games, follow up on scores and sports news multiple times a day*
- *Avid Fan: Watch games, follow up on scores and sports news once a day*
- *Casual Fan: Watch games, follow up on scores and sports news occasionally*
- *Championship Fan: Watch games, follow up on scores and sports news only during championships or playoffs*
- *Non-Fan: Never watch games or follow up on scores*
- *Anti-Fan: Dislike, oppose, or object to a certain sport*

Does this question do a good job of avoiding ambiguity? If this is exactly how it looked, what improvements would you suggest?

4. What is the difference between a *leading question* and a *loaded question*?

5. Design one or more open-ended response questions to measure reactions to public smartphone usage by others. What advantages and disadvantages does the open-ended format provide?

6. What are some general guidelines for avoiding common mistakes in writing questionnaire items?

7. Do you think the order of the questions below might affect responses? Explain.

8. When might a researcher wish to randomize both question order and the order of responses? Provide an example.

9. Define randomized response technique. Provide an example company that might benefit from using the technique in its marketing research?

10. Design a short telephone survey interview form that measures what types of programs residents of Peoria would like to see available through Netflix.

11. What advantages do Internet surveys offer in terms of order bias and survey flow?

12. Define the term *survey "breakoff."*

13. List at least three factors that increase nonresponse through breakoffs.

14. Provide an example where a filter-item is needed to implement branching in a survey.

15. What is a status bar? When might a status bar be inappropriate?

16. The Apple Assistance Center exists to solve problems for users of MacBook, iPhone, and iPad products. Design a text-message questionnaire that assesses users' satisfaction with the Apple Assistance Center.

17. Respondents have a duty to follow the survey instructions once they agree to participate. Are Internet or personal surveys better for making sure respondents maintain integrity in responding?

18. Visit pollseverywhere.com. What types of surveys may benefit from questions administered via pollseverywhere.com?

19. Define pretesting. Pretests costs time and money. How should a researcher decide if further pretesting is needed?

20. What is back translation?

:: RESEARCH ACTIVITY

1. Search the Internet to find out a little about Nando's Chicken Restaurant. Design a Web-based survey with a five-item questionnaire assessing how consumers in your town would react to a Nando's location.

2. Using Qualtrics, design an eight-question Internet survey that assesses how effective the introductory Marketing course at your school has been. Include a filter question that first asks respondents whether they have completed the course and branch those that have not completed it out of the survey.

3. Try to find two friends that know the same foreign language. Write ten Likert questions that measure how exciting a retail store environment is to shop in. Have one of your friends interpret the question into the foreign language. Have the other take the translation and state each question in English. How similar is the translated English to the original English? Comment.

4. Use the survey flow feature in Qualtrics to set up an assignment of subjects to questions that ask each about their attitude toward either Instagram, Tumblr, Pinterest or Snapchat, which includes randomization so that only each subject answers about only one of the social media outlets.

Frontier Golf Simulators

Case 11.1

It's "Virtually" the Same Game?!

The business of sports is growing tremendously and it is fueled in part by athletes that take on celebrity status. None typifies this better than Tiger Woods. Tiger is a brand representing a multimillion dollar entity unto itself. Traditionally, golf had a stigma of being for wealthy, stodgy, old businessmen who hardly knew how to have a good time. That image is common in many countries outside of the United States to this day. Companies like Nike and Callaway have invested large sums of money and effort to draw a different and more diverse demographic to the game of golf.

With the changing demographic of the actual players comes a marketing challenge of just how to best meet the needs of these segments that are quite new to the game. For instance, indoor golf simulators have started to increase in popularity and offer a chance to play some golf even in an urban setting. These simulators have the distinct advantage of being able to accurately show the player's ball flight and ball spin, as well as the actual yardage the ball travels. A further advantage is that with these simulators, a foursome can finish an entire round of golf in just under an hour instead of four hours or more! Additionally, this round of golf can be played at St. Andrews or Pebble Beach without the expense and hassle of traveling to these mystical sites.

Brian Scheler is the director of marketing for Frontier Golf Simulators, a San Antonio, Texas-based company which operates five state-of-the-art golf simulators. The pricing structure is either $30 per hour for "walk-ins" or a player can take a membership much like he or she might at a real golf club. In addition to the simulators, the facility has a restaurant and bar so that patrons can eat and drink while they tee it up. Brian has the unique challenge of marketing and ultimately selling time on these simulators. Unfortunately, Mr. Scheler is unsure how to best spend his very limited marketing budget. Mr. Scheler understands that the traditional golfer has different wants and needs than does the entertainment-seeking golfer. Does virtual golf offer value in the same way as real golf? If not, the simulators may not appeal to real or traditional golfers at all.

Faced with not knowing exactly what people like most about the simulators, Brian decides to create a survey to determine what people like most about their simulator experience and how to most effectively market his product to maximize the customer's experience and ultimately create returning customers.

1. What are some of the issues Brian should consider when designing the survey?
2. What types of issues can be addressed with open-ended questions and what type of issues can be addressed with fixed-alternative questions?
3. How would the structure of the survey change if Brian decides to administer the survey via the telephone versus face-to-face mall-intercept interviews?
4. Develop a survey that will address Brian's need to better understand his customers.

Source: Prepared by Kevin James, University of Texas-Tyler

A Lengthy Affair

Case 11.2

Sandy Sultan has just received a job for one of the top accounting firms in her town. The firm is expanding into business consulting and she has been hired as the firm's marketing researcher. A drug store client has hired the firm to help deal with its competitive situation. One of the partners comes in and tells Sandy that the project calls for developing a questionnaire that evaluates the importance of forty drug store characteristics, have respondents rate the drug store on each of the forty characteristics, and then have respondents rate each of the ten competing drug stores in town on these same characteristics. After the meeting Sandy goes back to her office feeling depressed.

Sandy believes that this questionnaire will induce respondent fatigue because it will be far too long. Can she really go through with this project?

1. Should Sandy do exactly what the partner suggests or risk losing the business for the firm and perhaps her job by suggesting a different approach?
2. What might be an alternative approach?
3. How many questionnaire items would be needed if Sandy moved forward as suggested?
4. What type of branching might be useful in survey of this type?

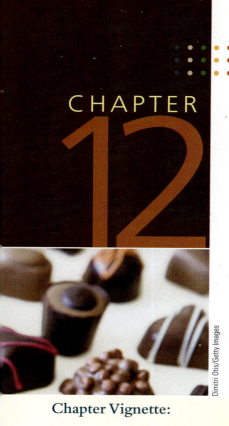

Dimitri Otis/Getty Images

Sampling Designs and Sampling Procedures

LEARNING OUTCOMES

After studying this chapter, you should be able to:

1. Explain reasons for taking a sample rather than a complete census
2. Describe the process of identifying a target population and selecting a sampling frame
3. Compare random sampling and systematic (nonsampling) errors with an emphasis on how the Internet is intertwined with this issue
4. Identify the types of nonprobability sampling, including their advantages and disadvantages
5. Summarize various types of probability samples
6. Discuss how to choose an appropriate sample design

Chapter Vignette:

Harvest Time at Domaine Chandon

Napa Valley's Domaine Chandon is the United State's largest producer of sparkling wine. The company, whose parent is the French company Moët & Chandon, among the largest Champagne producers in France and owners of the prestigious Dom Pérignon brand, produces millions of bottles of Napa Valley sparkling wine annually. More recently, Domaine Chandon also emphasizes still wines (non-sparkling) produced from the better vineyard parcels including noteworthy bottlings of Pinot Noir and Pinot Meunier.

Harvest time arrives in the Napa Valley every fall. October typically marks harvest, but depending on the weather, the best time to harvest grapes for wine production can vary from early September until about Thanksgiving. Pick grapes too early, and the wine becomes too acidic and "green." Pick grapes too late, and the wine becomes too alcoholic and "fat." Choosing the best time to harvest is crucial to making good wine and therefore to business success.

Sampling is an extremely relevant topic to the wine industry and takes place in many, many forms. Perhaps no sample is more critical, though, than the sample used to determine if the grapes are ready for harvest. Think of looking out over the thousands of acres of vineyard, each with thousands of vines, and each one of those with thousands of grapes. The winemaking team cannot possibly test every grape or even

© Gyuszko-Photo/Shutterstock.com

every vine. Think of the different ways one might try to gather a sample of grapes and use those to judge the quality of all the other fruit. The winemaking team could:

1. Stop conveniently along the long drive onto their property toward their 5-star restaurant and taste a few dozen grapes while also taking brix readings (sugar level measure) with a mechanical device.
2. Send workers out to select a bunch of grapes from each vineyard and have them sent to the lab for tasting and analysis (including brix readings).

3. Go out to the highest point on the property and the lowest point on the property and gather fruit for tasting and analysis.
4. Have workers go out and taste one grape from every vine and record the results on a tablet computer.
5. Take a tractor and drive through the vineyards in a large circle to gather bunches of fruit for analysis back in the lab.
6. Use a computer routine to randomly select 200 GPS coordinates throughout the property and have a bunch of fruit selected from each of those coordinates for tasting and brix analysis.

Every day that harvest doesn't take place brings the possibility of disaster due to disease or bad weather. A prolonged rain during this time will likely dilute the flavor of the fruit and bring on rot. Thus, management is very interested in getting the harvest done. In much the same way, researchers sample populations of people to try to know when they are ready to make a purchase or to just know their feelings and opinions. Just as with Domaine Chandon, if the researcher makes a bad sampling decision, the result is likely to produce bad wine—or management whining!

Introduction

Sampling is a critical part of the marketing research process. However, sampling also is a part of everyday life. Most websites that sell books provide a way for potential customers to sample their products. Typically, they'll allow a customer to see the first chapter or the first few pages. A customer in a bookstore, on the other hand, picks up a book, looks at the cover, skims a few pages throughout the book, and gets a sense of the writing style and content before deciding whether the book is worth buying. Which sampling process provides a better indication of the entire book? This chapter tries to provide insight that allows an answer to questions like this one.

Like a bookstore consumer, marketing researchers use sampling because usually contacting the entire population is impossible, inconvenient, or far too expensive. For researchers, the process of sampling can be quite complex. Sampling is a central aspect of marketing research, requiring in-depth examination. In the end, sampling does much to determine how realistic marketing results will be and to what extent they can predict outcomes of marketing decisions. However, like in everyday life, researchers often face resource limitations that encourage them to use less than the most rigorous sampling approach.

The sampling process involves drawing conclusions about an entire population by taking measurements from only a portion of all population elements. A **sample** is a subset of some larger population that researchers observe or measure in some way in an effort to estimate what the entire population is like. In statistical terms, sample observation allows the researcher to estimate population parameters.

Sampling is defined in terms of the population being studied. A **population (universe)** is any complete group—for example, of people, sales territories, stores, products, or college students—whose members share some common set of characteristics. Each individual member is referred to as a **population element**. A relevant population for many durable goods might be all U.S. homeowners. They share the fact that they own a home in the United States. The researcher then faces many choices about how to sample this important consumer population.

Researchers might like to study every element of a population to draw some conclusion with the most certainty. A **census** is an investigation involving measurement of all the individual elements that make up the population—a total enumeration rather than a sample. Thus, if we wished to know whether more Texans drive pickup trucks than sedans or SUVs, we could contact every Texan driver and find out whether they drive a pickup truck, a sedan, or an SUV. We would then know the answer to this question definitively.

Sample
A subset of some larger population that is measured or observed in some way to infer what the entire population is like.

Population (universe)
Any complete group of entities that share some common set of characteristics.

Population element
An individual member of a population.

Census
An investigation involving measurement of all the individual elements that make up a population.

Why Sample?

When a customer visits a tasting room in Napa Valley, he or she *samples* the producer's wine. The customer samples wine by having a small taste from multiple bottles of wine, each containing a different type of wine. From this, the consumer decides if he or she likes a particular wine. If each guest consumed the entire bottle before making a decision, he or she would be far too inebriated to have any idea about the other bottles. In addition, if the goal is to decide whether or not the wines taste good, giving each person a bottle of wine would soon get very expensive. Thus, the customer is left to make judgments based on a very small sample. Similarly, and for some of the same reasons (costs), scientific studies try to draw conclusions about populations by measuring a small sample rather than taking a census.

Pragmatic Reasons

Marketing research projects almost always have budget and time constraints. If Ford Motor Corporation wished to take a census of past purchasers' reactions to the company's recalls of defective models, the researchers would have to contact millions of automobile buyers. Some of them would be inaccessible (e.g., out of the country). In fact, Ford would find it impossible to contact all these people. Constraints usually prevent researchers concerned with large populations from using data derived from a census.

On the other hand, a researcher who wants to investigate a population with an extremely small number of population elements may elect to conduct a census rather than a sample because the cost, labor, and time drawbacks would be relatively insignificant. For a company that wants to assess salespersons' satisfaction with its computer networking system, circulating a questionnaire to all twenty-five of its employees is practical. In that case, no inferential statistics (we will cover these in a later chapter) are necessary, as any observed difference is a true difference. In most situations, however, many practical reasons favor sampling. Sampling cuts costs, reduces labor requirements, and gathers vital information quickly. These advantages may be sufficient in themselves for using a sample rather than a census, but there are other reasons. The Research Snapshot on page 342 describing the origins of the Gallup poll describe its very practical origins. Ultimately, sampling is a practical matter.

Accurate and Reliable Results

Another major reason for sampling is that most properly selected samples give results that are reasonably accurate. If the elements of a population are quite similar, only a small sample is necessary to accurately portray the characteristic of interest. Thus, a population consisting of 10,000 eleventh-grade students in all-boys Catholic high schools will require a smaller sample than a broader population consisting of 10,000 high school students from coeducational, public, secondary schools.

A visual example of how different-sized samples allow one to draw conclusions is provided in Exhibit 12.1. A sample is similar to a jigsaw puzzle that isn't solved yet. Even without looking at the box cover, the puzzler probably doesn't have to wait until every piece is in place to draw a conclusion of what the picture will be. However, as more pieces are put in place, which is analogous to more units being sampled, conclusions can be made with greater confidence. Thus, larger samples allow conclusions to be drawn with more confidence that they truly represent the population.

A sample may even on occasion be more accurate than a census. Interviewer mistakes, tabulation errors, and other nonsampling errors may increase during a census as workers suffer from burnout, fatigue, incompetence, or dishonesty. In a sample, increased accuracy may sometimes be possible because the fieldwork and tabulation of data can be more closely supervised. In a field survey, a small, well-trained, closely supervised group may do a more careful and accurate job of collecting information than a large group of nonprofessional interviewers who try to contact everyone. The U.S. Census Bureau conducts surveys on samples of populations as a way of checking the accuracy of the actual census of those populations. If the conclusions drawn from the sample disagree with the census results, the census is deemed inaccurate and becomes a candidate to be redone because an accurate census is required by law every ten years.

EXHIBIT 12.1
A Puzzle Is a Sample Until It Is Done! The Sample Allows One to Guess at the Picture.

POLKADOT IMAGES/JUPITER IMAGES

Destruction of Test Units

Many research projects, especially those in quality-control testing, require the destruction of the items being tested. Even if it was possible to test every grape prior to the harvest, this would mean there would be nothing left to make wine with! This is the exact situation in many marketing strategy experiments. For example, if an experimental sales presentation were presented to every potential customer, no prospects would remain to be contacted after the experiment. In these examples, the test units have been destroyed or ruined for the purpose of the research project. Obviously, the destruction of test units presents a major argument not to do research using a census rather than a sample.

Identifying a Relevant Population and Sampling Frame

Before taking a sample, researchers must make several decisions. Exhibit 12.2 presents these decisions as a series of sequential stages, but the order of the decisions does not always follow this sequence. These decisions are highly interrelated. The steps listed in this exhibit are discussed here and in the next two chapters.

Defining the Target Population

The first question in sampling is, "What population are we trying to project?" In other words, what larger group is intended to be represented by using a sample? This question is rarely as easy as it may seem and often the matter isn't given much thought. However, researchers should always address the question of generalization in any research report or article.

EXHIBIT 12.2

Stages in the Selection of a Sample

Define the Target Population

▼

Select a Sampling Frame

▼

Determine if a Probability or Nonprobability Sampling Method Will Be Chosen

▼

Plan Procedure for Selecting Sampling Units

▼

Determine Sample Size

▼

Select Actual Sampling Units

▼

Conduct Fieldwork

© Cengage Learning 2013.

Polling agencies conduct research to predict election results. What is the relevant population? *Registered voters* seem to be a reasonable choice and fortunately, a list of registered voters is generally available in public records. However, the actual election results will be determined by who actually votes, not who is registered to vote. If a study is supposed to represent those who actually will vote, registered voters no longer form the most relevant population. Identifying a sample that represents likely voters is much more difficult because no such list exists.

The population must be defined accurately for the research to produce good results. One survey concerning organizational buyer behavior had purchasing agents whom sales representatives regularly contacted rate preferred product characteristics. After the research proved less than helpful, investigators discovered that industrial engineers were actually making the purchasing decisions. For consumer research, the appropriate population element frequently is the household rather than an individual member of the household. This presents some problems if household lists are not available or if input cannot be obtained from the entire household.

Consider how difficult identifying a relevant population is for a company like Anthropologie or Michael Kors. What is the population of "fashion consumers"? However, the entire population of fashion consumers is likely not relevant for either of these companies. Clearly, no precise list of population members exists in this case. Even if they are directing a study at "loyal customers," questions such as defining a loyal or a disloyal consumer remain. Companies that use loyalty programs can maintain a list, but the presumption is that only these consumers are truly loyal. In other words, no consumers that do not have a card are loyal. This assumption may be reasonable but is clearly not perfect. Thus, a sample drawn from this list is more precisely described as representing the population of customers who have a loyalty card than as representing truly loyal customers.

One approach for defining the target population is to ask and answer questions about crucial population characteristics. This list illustrates the process:

- Is a list available that matches our population? If so, can we use it? Is valid contact information available and can they be reached with an appropriate communication method?
  - A mobile phone service provider like Verizon or AT&T would have a list of all of its customers. But, they would not have a list of potential customers.
- Who are we not interested in?
  - Researchers studying the behavior of retail buyers (who make decisions for retailers about what will be sold in the store) are not interested in undergraduate college students.
- What are the relevant market segment characteristics?
  - Companies generally appeal only to specific market segments. For example, consider Abercrombie and Fitch's (A&F) brand image. Certainly, A&F shoppers belong to a specific market segment with specific characteristics.
- Are we only interested in a regional population? If so, how do we determine the borders?
  - For example, does the "U.K. market" include England, Scotland, and Wales (Great Britain)? Or does it include only England, or does it also include Northern Ireland, or maybe even the Republic of Ireland, which is not actually part of the United Kingdom?
  - What states comprise the southern United States or the western United States? Does either include Hawaii?
- Should the study include multiple populations?
  - When launching a new product in multiple countries, each country may constitute a distinct population rather than the entire population. Each population may need to be contacted through a different medium with a different approach.

Answers to these questions help researchers and decision makers focus on the right populations of potential respondents. The sample is implemented using the tangible, identifiable characteristics that also define the population. A baby food manufacturer might define the population as women of childbearing age. However, a more specific *operational definition* would be women between the ages of 18 and 50. Although this definition by age may exclude a few women who are capable of childbearing and include some who are not, it is still more explicit and provides a manageable basis for the sample design. Perhaps there are other reasons why this isn't a perfect population description. One important thing to remember is that if the population members cannot be reached by an appropriate communication method, they cannot be part of a sample.

George Gallup's Nation of Numbers

Civil engineers conduct surveys using a transit that takes measures at specific points, and from that information, he or she generates a description of a piece of land. In somewhat the same way, George Gallup pioneered sampling theories that allow a sample survey to determine public opinion. You didn't have to talk to everybody, he said, as long as you randomly selected interviews according to a sampling plan.

Most of Gallup's work was based on the idea of random sampling. Today, truly random sampling has become increasingly difficult based on changes in the methods of communication. Door-to-door sampling is almost unheard of and even random-digit dialing will likely lead to systematic variation from the characteristics of most populations. Although most polling agencies stick to telephone interviews to predict things like election outcomes, with varying success, major companies have turned to the Web to generate samples. The results are not perfect, but companies like Proctor & Gamble, General Mills, and McDonald's are discovering ways that the shortcomings of online samples can be corrected using many of the same techniques that phone interviewers have used for years. The ease and convenience of online surveying offers a tremendous advantage, just as Gallup found that sampling offered an advantage over canvassing an entire population. Thus, online surveys, just like sampling, are here to stay.

Sources: Excerpted from "George Gallup's Nation of Numbers," *Esquire* (December 1983), pp. 91–92; Helm, B., "Online Polls: How Good Are They?" *Businessweek* 4088 (June 16, 2008), 86.

Bettmann/Corbis

Obviously, A&F caters to a specific market segment with specific demographic and lifestyle characteristics. A researcher studying A&F customers would err by studying the "clothing market."

Source: www.abercrombie.com

The Sampling Frame

Sampling frame

A list of elements from which a sample may be drawn; also called working population.

In practice, the sample will be drawn from a list of population elements that often differ somewhat from the defined target population. A list of elements from which the sample may be drawn is called a **sampling frame**. The sampling frame is also called the *working population* because these units will eventually provide units involved in analysis. A simple example of a sampling frame would be a list of all members of the American Medical Association. Similarly, companies that maintain consumer panels can provide a list of individuals that comprise a sampling frame.

A **sampling frame error** occurs when certain sample elements are excluded or when the entire population is not accurately represented in the sampling frame. An election poll relying on a telephone directory as a sampling frame uses households with listed phone numbers, not households who are likely to vote. Phone directories are very limited as discussed earlier because of multiple reasons including the fact that they typically do not include cell phones. The Research Snapshot describes this issue in more detail.

In practice, almost every list excludes some members of the population. For example, would a university e-mail directory provide an accurate sampling frame for a given university's student population? Perhaps the sampling frame excludes students who registered late and includes students who have resigned from the university. The e-mail directory also will likely list only the student's official university e-mail address. However, many students may not ever use this address, opting to use a private e-mail account instead. Thus, the university e-mail directory could not be expected to perfectly represent the student population. However, a perfect representation isn't always possible or needed.

Sampling Services

Some firms, called *sampling services* or *list brokers,* specialize in providing lists or databases that include the names, addresses, phone numbers, and e-mail addresses of specific populations. Lists offered by companies such as this are compiled from subscriptions to professional journals, credit card applications, warranty card registrations, and a variety of other sources. One sampling service obtained its listing of households with children from an ice cream retailer who gave away free ice cream cones on children's birthdays. The children filled out cards with their names, addresses, and birthdays, which the retailer then sold to the mailing list company.

A valuable source of names is Equifax's series of city directories. Equifax City Directory provides complete, comprehensive, and accurate business and residential information. The city directory records the name of each resident over eighteen years of age and lists pertinent information about each household. The reverse directory pages offer a unique benefit. A **reverse directory** provides, in a different format, the same information contained in a telephone directory. Listings may be by city and street address or by phone number, rather than alphabetical by last name. Such a directory is particularly useful when a retailer wishes to survey only a certain geographical area of a city or when census tracts are to be selected on the basis of income or another demographic criterion. Many such directories are easily accessible via the Internet.

Online Panels

Online survey services routinely provide access to **online panels** for a modest fee. Researchers contract with the panel provider to get access to a relevant sampling frame. The typical panel comprises a list of e-mail addresses with each address identifying an individual who has agreed to participate in research surveys. Qualtrics, the company that hosts the survey involved in the Survey This! features provides access to such panel services. Online panels contain millions of potential respondents. As a result, panel managers can easily stratify the entire sampling frame on many characteristics of interest and provide a narrower sampling frame representing a specific occupation, users of particular online services, or recent purchasers of some durable goods. The more specific the profile requested, the more expensive the panel. Panel members typically receive some small incentive in return for their membership. The incentive could be a small cash payment, coupons, or contributions to nonprofits. Later, we discuss the advantages and disadvantages of using an online panel as a sampling frame.

Sampling Frames for International Marketing Research

The availability of sampling frames varies dramatically around the world. Not every country's government conducts a census of population. In some countries telephone directories are incomplete, no voter registration lists exist, and accurate maps of urban areas are unobtainable. However, in Taiwan, Japan, and other Asian countries, a researcher can build a sampling frame relatively easily because those governments release some census information. If a family changes households, updated census information must be reported to a centralized government agency

Sampling frame error

An error that occurs when certain sample elements are not listed or are not accurately represented in a sampling frame.

Reverse directory

A directory similar to a telephone directory except that listings are by city and street address, or by phone number rather than alphabetical by last name.

Online panels

Lists of respondents who have agreed to participate in marketing research along with the e-mail and contact information of these individuals.

before communal services (water, gas, electricity, education, and so on) are made available.[1] This information is then easily accessible in the local *Inhabitants' Register.* Fortunately, many of the online panels include members from nations around the world. The panels can be stratified by country or by region within a country just as they can in the United States. For example, if a company wishes to survey part-time fast-food employees in Canada and Japan, a panel can probably provide potential respondents.

Sampling Units

Sampling unit

A single element or group of elements subject to selection in the sample.

The elements of a population must be selected according to a specified procedure when sampling. The **sampling unit** is a single element or group of elements that is eligible for selection via the sampling process. For example, an airline may sample passengers by taking every twenty-fifth name on a complete list of passengers flying on a specified day. In this case the sampling unit would be the same as the element. Alternatively, the airline could first select certain flights as the sampling unit and then select certain passengers on each flight. In this case the sampling unit would contain many elements.

Primary sampling unit (PSU)

A term used to designate a unit selected in the first stage of sampling.

If the target population has first been divided into units, such as airline flights, additional terminology must be used. A unit selected in the first stage of sampling is called a **primary sampling unit (PSU)**. A unit selected in a successive stage of sampling is called a **secondary sampling unit** or (if three stages are necessary) **tertiary sampling unit**. When there is no list of population elements, the sampling unit generally is something other than the population element. In a random-digit dialing study, the sampling unit will be telephone numbers.

Secondary sampling unit

A term used to designate a unit selected in the second stage of sampling.

Tertiary sampling unit

A term used to designate a unit selected in the third stage of sampling.

Random Sampling and Nonsampling Errors

An advertising agency sampled a small number of shoppers in grocery stores that used Shopper's Video, an in-store advertising network. The agency hoped to measure brand awareness and purchase intentions. Investigators expected this sample to be representative of the grocery-shopping population. However, if a difference exists between the value of a sample statistic of interest (for example, the sample group's average willingness to buy the advertised brand) and the value of the corresponding population parameter (the population's average willingness to buy), a *statistical error* has occurred. Earlier, we introduced two basic causes of differences between statistics and parameters:

1. random sampling errors
2. systematic (nonsampling) error

Random sampling error

The difference between the sample result and the result of a census conducted using identical procedures.

An estimation made from a sample is not the same as a census count. **Random sampling error** is the difference between the sample result and the result of an accurate census. Of course, the result of a census is unknown unless someone actually takes one. Random sampling error occurs because of chance variation in the selection of sampling units. The sampling units, even if properly selected according to sampling theory, may not perfectly represent the population because of chance variation.

Picture fifty students in a typical undergraduate research class. If the class is the population and the instructor uses a random sample of ten students to estimate the average height of a student in the class, a random selection process should make sure that the ten tallest students are not selected for the sample. Although this is theoretically possible, the odds that this would occur are astronomical. The difference between the average of the ten students and the actual average of the population (fifty students) represent random sampling error.

Random Sampling Error

Random sampling error will come back into play later when the issue of hypothesis testing surfaces. At this point, recognize that *random sampling error* is a technical term that refers *only* to statistical fluctuations that occur because of chance variations in the elements selected for the sample. Random sampling error is a function of sample size. As sample size increases, random sampling error decreases.

Let's return to the classroom of fifty students. If the researcher is very lazy, a sample of 1 can be used to estimate student height. The chance of randomly selecting the tallest student is 1 in 50, the same as the odds of selecting the student that matched the median. Either way, the confidence that the sample is matching the true population value should not be very high. A strong likelihood exists that by doubling the sample size to two observations, the estimated value could change a great deal. Conversely, if the researcher is very cautious, a sample of forty-nine might be taken. Now, even if the tallest person in the class is in the sample, there are forty-eight other observations that are also considered. The estimate of the average height now is much more confident. Also, the value should not change very much when one more observation is added to the calculation. When someone releases poll results and describes them with a margin of error of 3, 5, or 10 percent, that margin of error is determined by the sample size.

Systematic Sampling Error

Systematic (nonsampling) errors result from nonsampling factors, primarily the nature of a study's design and the correctness of execution. These errors are systematic in some way and *not* due to chance fluctuations. For example, in our classroom example, if a researcher chose a sampling frame consisting of all students sitting in the first two rows, a strong likelihood exists that systematic error would be introduced because shorter students tend to sit up front in an effort to see what is going on instead of the back of another student's head. Sample biases such as these account for a large portion of errors in marketing research. Errors due to sample selection problems are nonsampling errors and should not be classified as random sampling errors.

Systematic But Not Obvious Sampling Error

We touched on some of these topics in earlier chapters. For example, telephone samples cannot represent the entire U.S. population because people without a landline phone usually share something in common with each other. For instance, they tend to be younger than average. Likewise, a random sample of U.S. homeowners would not represent all U.S. consumers because homeowners tend to be relatively older and more likely to have children than apartment dwellers. If a researcher cannot obtain a random, representative sample, he or she should aim to gather a sample that matches the population demographically.

Facebook surveys allow researchers to reach a large sample rapidly—both an advantage and a disadvantage. Sample size requirements can be met overnight or in some cases almost instantaneously. A researcher can, for instance, release a survey during the morning in the Eastern Standard Time zone and have all sample size requirements met before anyone on the West Coast wakes up. If rapid response rates are expected, and a national sample is desired, steps must be taken to distribute the questionnaire evenly across all time zones. In addition, a survey released during the middle of the day, just like a phone sample conducted in the middle of the day, is likely to exclude people with full-time jobs in a systematic way because they are at work. Thus, the survey should probably remain active for a minimum of 12 hours or so.

The ease and low cost of an Internet survey also contributes to the flood of online questionnaires. As a result, frequent Internet users may be more selective about which surveys they bother answering. Researchers investigating college students' attitudes toward environmental issues found that those who responded to an e-mail request sent to all students at a school scored higher on environmental concern than students contacted individually through systematic sampling.[2] The researchers concluded that students who cared about the issues were more likely to respond to the online survey.

Website Visitors

Many Internet surveys use volunteer respondents who happen to visit an organization's website intentionally or by happenstance. These *unrestricted samples* are clearly not random samples. They may not even represent people with an interest in that particular website because of the haphazard manner by which many respondents arrived at a particular site.

A better technique for sampling website visitors is to select sampling units randomly. Survey software can be used to trigger a pop-up survey to each one-hundredth (or whatever number) visitor. Or, the software can even adjust the triggering of the survey based on information gathered on the respondent's Web behavior. For example, the opportunity to become a respondent might be timed so that at least 30 seconds have to be spent on the home page before the respondent becomes part of the sampling frame. This may prevent random page visitors from becoming a large part of the sample. Respondents who are selected to participate are first prompted to see if they would like to participate. If the person clicks "Yes," the site presents the questionnaire as a pop-up or as a new browser window.

Randomly selecting website visitors can cause a problem by overrepresenting frequent visitors. Several programming techniques and technologies (using cookies, registration data, or prescreening) are available to help accomplish more representative sampling based on site traffic. Cookies contain information that reveals the frequency of visits.

Panel Samples

Consumer panels provide a practical sampling frame in many situations. A good panel provider knows basic characteristics of each member. Panels become particularly useful in screening out sampling units who do not fit the characteristics of a relevant population. If the relevant population is men, the e-mail addresses belonging to female respondents are omitted from the frame. However, panels are not perfect.

Panel sampling frames may contain a high proportion of respondents who simply like to fill out questionnaires or give their opinion. Either case presents the opportunity for sample bias. Fortunately, research suggests that personality variables do not relate strongly to panel membership.[3] However, attempts to validate survey results using different panels or different communication methods often show variance.[4] Thus, as the concern for representativeness increases, the more steps the researcher must take to ensure that the sampling units do indeed represent the population.

Consider Harris Interactive Inc., an Internet survey research organization, which maintains a panel of more than 6 million individuals internationally. A database this large allows the company to draw simple random samples, stratified samples, and quota samples from its panel members.[5] Harris Interactive oversamples, meaning it sends disproportionately more invitations to demographic groups known to under-respond such as males 18 to 24 years old. Practically all groups can be reached through panel surveys with the possible exception of the elderly (over 75 years of age) and the impoverished.

To ensure that survey results are representative, Harris Interactive uses a *propensity-weighting* scheme. The research company does parallel studies—by phone as well as over the Internet—to test the accuracy of its Internet data-gathering capabilities. Researchers look at the results of the telephone surveys and match those against the Internet-only survey results. Next, they use propensity weighting to adjust the results, taking into account the motivational and behavioral differences between the online and offline populations. (How propensity weighting adjusts for the difference between the Internet population and the general population is beyond the scope of this discussion.)

In addition to these steps, panel members may be asked screening questions to make sure that the screening characteristics are accurately working. For example, a researcher interested in coffee shop drinkers in the Midwest may want respondents to compare other shops to Starbucks. Thus, the population may be limited to consumers who frequent Starbucks. Although the online panel may be screened to include only communities where Starbucks has coffee shops, the researcher would be well advised to include screening questions that check on the familiarity of respondents with Starbucks.

Opting In

In many cases, researchers place survey links on websites or social network pages. Anyone who visits the page can potentially become part of the sample that responds to the particular survey. In this case, if a visitor clicks through and responds to the survey, he or she has not been selected from a sampling frame. Instead, the term **opt in** refers to this behavior as the respondent decided on his/her own accord to respond and provide data for the researcher. In other cases, the opt in may be more general and represent an agreement to participate in research in general. Such is the case when a panel solicits members.

Opting in
The term referring to the fact that a respondent decides to participate in a research project on his/her own accord.

By whatever technique the sampling frame is compiled, it is important *not* to send unauthorized e-mail to respondents. If individuals do not *opt in* to receive e-mail from a particular organization, they may consider unsolicited survey requests to be spam. A researcher cannot expect high response rates from individuals who have not agreed to be surveyed. Spamming is not tolerated by experienced Internet users and can easily backfire, creating a host of problems—the most extreme being complaints to the Internet service provider (ISP), which may shut down the survey site.

Low response rates also can be a problem for survey results. This can occur when after someone opts in, they opt out by not finishing the task. Presuming the goal is to generalize to some population, if the low response rates do not occur systematically, the researcher should conclude that some characteristic correlates with responding. If that's the case, then the sample's ability to generalize is damaged. Also, low response rates can increase expense as additional sampling units or even samples may be required. Survey completion rates can be enhanced by embedding highly interesting questions at key points in the survey at which point respondents may otherwise sense fatigue.[6] However, care needs to be taken to make sure the questions don't cause certain types of people to respond more than other types of people.

Sites like Amazon's Mechanical Turk provide another opportunity for respondents to opt in to surveys. However, these respondents do not participate as members of any panel but rather as an unscreened, paid respondent. Therefore, respondents who participate after coincidentally or intentionally finding a survey on a website of this type are not random and cannot be considered representative of the general consumer population.

Less Than Perfectly Representative Samples

Random sampling errors and systematic errors associated with the sampling process may combine to yield a sample that is less than perfectly representative of the population. Exhibit 12.3 illustrates two nonsampling errors (sampling frame error and nonresponse error) related to sample design. The total population is represented by the area of the largest rectangle. Sampling frame errors eliminate some potential respondents. Random sampling error (due exclusively to random, chance fluctuation) may cause an imbalance in the representativeness of the group. Additional errors will occur if individuals refuse to be interviewed or cannot be contacted. Such nonresponse error may also cause the sample to be less than perfectly representative. Notice that if the top half of the total population comes from one part of town and the bottom half comes from another part of town, by the time the planned sample is reached, the portion from the lower part of the exhibit is overrepresented and this continues to the actual sample where 25 percent more of the sample (represented by four people as opposed to three) comes from the lower portion of town. The actual sample overrepresents this portion of town.

EXHIBIT 12.3 Errors Associated with Sampling

Total Population

Sampling Frame

Planned Sample

Respondents (Actual Sample)

Sampling Frame Error

Random Sampling Error

Nonresponse Error

Probability versus Nonprobability Sampling

Probability sampling

A sampling technique in which every member of the population has a known, nonzero probability of selection.

Nonprobability sampling

A sampling technique in which units of the sample are selected on the basis of personal judgment or convenience; the probability of any particular member of the population being chosen is unknown.

Several alternative ways to take a sample are available. The main alternative sampling plans may be grouped into two categories: probability techniques and nonprobability techniques.

In **probability sampling**, every element in the population has a *known, nonzero probability* of selection. The simple random sample, in which each member of the population has an equal probability of being selected, is the best-known probability sample.

In **nonprobability sampling**, the probability of any particular member of the population being chosen is unknown. The selection of sampling units in nonprobability sampling is quite arbitrary, as researchers rely heavily on personal judgment. Technically, no appropriate statistical techniques exist for measuring random sampling error from a nonprobability sample. Therefore, projecting the data beyond the sample is, technically speaking, statistically inappropriate. Nevertheless, researchers sometimes find nonprobability samples best suited for a specific research purpose. As a result, nonprobability samples are pragmatic and are used in market research.

Data taken from Internet samples can be divided into probability and nonprobability samples. With probability samples, the likelihood of any panel member being selected as a potential respondent is fixed, nonzero, and known. Likewise, any relevant stratified portion of a panel being selected is fixed, nonzero, and known. Well-managed panels represent probability samples as the panel management procedures control invitations to participate in any survey. Thus, results derived from samples whose members are selected randomly from such panels can generalize to the sampling frame and perhaps even to broader populations like U.S consumer households presuming panel membership is maintained to provide such representation. On the other hand, crowdsourced data from any Web source, including Mechanical Turk, clearly represents nonprobability sampling. The researcher has no control over who clicks through to respond or who sees the work request.

Although probability sampling is preferred, nonprobability sampling becomes a reality when expedience or thriftiness overrides precision. A nonprobability sample always presents a limitation in terms of generalizability. The following sections provide some terminology relevant to the use of various sampling approaches.

Convenience Sampling

Convenience sampling

The sampling procedure of obtaining those people or units that are most conveniently available.

To the Point

"A straw vote only shows which way the hot air blows."

— O. HENRY

As the name suggests, **convenience sampling** refers to sampling by obtaining people or units that are conveniently available. A research team may determine that the most convenient and economical method is to set up an interviewing booth from which to intercept consumers at a shopping center. News media often present person-on-the-street interviews that ask passersby to answer questions or offer opinion on matters of the day. The interviews offer a *survey* of opinion. Given the prevalence of media headquarters in New York City, the interviews often take place on the streets near Times Square. Often, the results are comical. Many passersby cannot answer questions like who is the vice president of the United States, where Israel is on a map, or what the names of two U.S. Supreme Court justices are. Do you think these survey results, although convenient to the national news bureaus located in New York, provide an accurate portray of typical Americans? Although it may not seem scientific, marketing researchers also sometimes choose respondents because they are convenient.

Researchers generally use convenience samples to obtain results quickly and economically. At times, a sample through other means may be impractical or impossible to obtain. For example, many Internet surveys are conducted with volunteer respondents who, either intentionally or by happenstance, come across a survey invitation on Facebook, Twitter, or some other website. Although this method produces a large number of responses quickly and at low cost, visitors to a website comprise a convenience sample. Respondents, thus, may not be representative because of the haphazard manner by which many of them arrived at the website or because of self-selection bias.

Similarly, research looking at cross-cultural differences in organizational or consumer behavior typically uses convenience samples. Rather than selecting cultures with characteristics relevant to the hypothesis being tested, the researchers conducting these studies often choose cultures to which they have access (for example, because they speak the language or have contacts in that culture's organizations). Further adding to the convenience, cross-cultural research often defines "culture" in terms of nations, which are easier to identify and obtain statistics about. But, complications exist with this approach, including the fact that many nations include several cultures and some people in a given nation may be more involved with the international business or academic community than with a particular ethnic culture.[7] Here again, the use of convenience sampling limits how well the research represents the intended population.

The user of research based on a convenience sample should remember that projecting the results beyond the specific sample is inappropriate. Convenience samples are best used for exploratory research when additional research will subsequently be conducted with a probability sample. University professors conducting marketing research will frequently use a student sample out of convenience. This can be appropriate if the emphasis in the research design lies in internal validity. In other words, to see if the effect put forth in a hypothesis holds under circumstances allowing maximum control of outside effects, such as in a lab experiment. The use of student sampling is inappropriate when the researcher intends the results to generalize to a larger population.

Researchers studying employees often will study those from one company or even one unit of a company. These studies are convenience samples unless the sole intent is to generalize no further than the particular company or unit. Data derived from paid crowdsourcing like M-Turk requests also clearly represent convenience samples with similar precautions about generalization.

Judgment Sampling

Judgment (purposive) sampling is a nonprobability sampling technique in which an experienced individual selects the sample based on his or her judgment about some appropriate characteristics required of the sample member. Researchers select samples that satisfy their specific purposes, even if they are not fully representative. The consumer price index (CPI) is based on a judgment sample of market-basket items, housing costs, and other selected goods and services expected to reflect a representative sample of items consumed by most Americans. Test-market cities often are selected because they are viewed as typical cities whose demographic profiles closely match the national profile. A fashion manufacturer regularly selects a sample of key accounts that it believes are capable of providing information needed to predict what may sell in the fall. Thus, the sample is selected to achieve this specific objective.

Judgment (purposive) sampling

A nonprobability sampling technique in which an experienced individual selects the sample based on personal judgment about some appropriate characteristics of the sample member.

Quota Sampling

Suppose your university administration wants to investigate the experiences of the undergraduate student body. Although 95 percent of the students are full-time, the administration may wish to ensure that both full-time and part-time students are included in the sample. In this case, the researcher may decide to have the sample of 200 students consist of 150 full-time and 50 part-time students. This quota would ensure that the part-time students are well represented, whereas strict probability sampling procedures might not include a sufficient number of those students (10).

The purpose of **quota sampling** is to ensure that the various subgroups in a population are represented on pertinent sample characteristics to the exact extent that the investigators desire. Stratified sampling, a probability sampling procedure described in the next section, also has this objective, but it should not be confused with quota sampling. In quota sampling, the interviewer has a quota to achieve. For example, the interviewer may be assigned 100 interviews, 75 with full-time students, and 25 with part-time students. The interviewer is responsible for finding enough people to meet the quota. Aggregating the various interview quotas yields a sample that represents the desired proportion of each subgroup.

Quota sampling

A nonprobability sampling procedure that ensures that various subgroups of a population will be represented on pertinent characteristics to the exact extent that the investigator desires.

Possible Sources of Bias

The logic of classifying the population by pertinent subgroups is essentially sound. However, because respondents are selected according to a convenience sampling procedure rather than on a probability basis (as in stratified sampling), the haphazard selection of subjects may introduce bias. For example, a college professor hired some of his students to conduct a quota sample based on age. When analyzing the data, the professor discovered that almost all the people in the "under 25 years" category were college-educated. Interviewers, being human, tend to prefer to interview people who are similar to themselves.

Quota samples tend to include people who are easily found, willing to be interviewed, and middle class. Fieldworkers exercise considerable leeway in the selection of actual respondents. Interviewers often concentrate their interviewing in areas with heavy pedestrian traffic such as downtowns, shopping malls, and college campuses. Those who interview door-to-door learn quickly that quota requirements are difficult to meet by interviewing whoever happens to appear at the door. People who are more likely to stay at home generally share a less active lifestyle and are less likely to be meaningfully employed. One interviewer related a story of working in an upper-middle-class neighborhood. After a few blocks, he arrived in a neighborhood of mansions. Feeling that most of the would-be respondents were above his station, the interviewer skipped these houses because he felt uncomfortable knocking on doors that would be answered by these people or their hired help.

Advantages of Quota Sampling

The major advantages of quota sampling over probability sampling are speed of data collection, lower costs, and convenience. Although quota sampling has many problems, carefully supervised data collection may provide a representative sample of the various subgroups within a population. Quota sampling may be appropriate when the researcher knows that a certain demographic group is more likely to refuse to cooperate with a survey. For instance, if older men are more likely to refuse, a higher quota can be set for this group so that the proportion of each demographic category will be similar to the proportions in the population. A number of laboratory experiments also rely on quota sampling because it is difficult to find a sample of the general population willing to visit a laboratory to participate in an experiment.

Snowball Sampling

Snowball sampling

A sampling procedure in which initial respondents are selected by probability methods and additional respondents are obtained from information provided by those initial respondents.

Snowball sampling involves using some process for selecting a few initial respondents and then uses those respondents to seek out additional respondents. The researcher may use a probability sampling approach to contact the initial respondents. However, a nonprobability approach also is used such as when students are asked to snowball initial respondents or when Facebook friends are asked to invite their own Facebook friends. The approach can be useful when the relevant market segment is narrow and potentially difficult to reach otherwise. Suppose a manufacturer of sports equipment is considering marketing a mahogany croquet set for serious adult players. This market is certainly small. An extremely large sample would be necessary to find 100 serious adult croquet players. It would be much more economical to survey, say, 300 people, find 15 serious croquet players, and ask them for the names of other croquet players.

Reduced sample sizes and costs are clear-cut advantages of snowball sampling. However, bias is likely to enter into the study because a person suggested by someone also in the sample has a higher probability of being similar to the first person. If there are major differences between those who are widely known by others and those who are not, this technique may present some serious problems. However, snowball sampling can locate and recruit heavy users, such as consumers who buy more than twenty-five houseplants each year. The approach may identify potential focus group participants, and because generalizability is not a concern, the focus group organizer can use snowball sampling.

Probability Sampling

All probability sampling techniques employ chance selection procedures. The random probability process eliminates bias inherent in nonprobability sampling procedures. Note that the term *random* refers to the procedure for selecting the sample members and not the data in the sample. *Randomness* characterizes a procedure whose outcome cannot be predicted because it depends on chance. Randomness should not be thought of as unplanned or unscientific—it is the basis of all probability sampling techniques. This section will examine the various probability sampling methods.

Simple Random Sampling

Simple random sampling is a sampling procedure ensuring that each element in a population has an equal chance of being included in a sample. Examples include drawing names from a hat and selecting the winning raffle ticket from a large drum. If the names or raffle tickets are thoroughly stirred, each person or ticket should have an equal chance of being selected. In contrast to other, more complex types of probability sampling, this process is simple in that only one stage of sample selection is required.

Although drawing names or numbers out of a fishbowl, rolling dice, or turning a roulette wheel may be an appropriate way to draw a sample from a small population, when populations consist of large numbers of elements, sample selection can be based on tabled random numbers or computer-generated random numbers (see **http://www.samurajdata.se/~cj/rnd.html** or **http://random.org** for simple random number generators).

Suppose a researcher is interested in selecting a simple random sample of all Honda auto dealers in California, New Mexico, Arizona, and Nevada. Presume that 105 Honda dealers exist in these states and the researcher would like a sample of 25 dealerships. Each dealer's name is assigned a number from 1 to 105. The researcher can then use a random number generator, like those available online or in Excel, to find 25 random numbers between 1 and 105. He or she can then contact the 25 dealerships corresponding to the 25 random numbers drawn. For example, if 60 is the random number generated, then the dealer assigned that number earlier is selected for the sample.

Random number generators greatly facilitate random sample selection. A number is first assigned to each element of the population (i.e., alphabetical, chronological, digits from a student number, etc.). Assuming the population is 99,999 or fewer, five-digit numbers may be selected from the table of random numbers merely by reading the numbers in any column or row, moving up, down, left, or right. A random starting point should be selected at the outset. For convenience, we will assume that we have randomly selected as our starting point the first five digits in columns 1 through 5, row 1, of the table generated by random.org, mentioned previously. The first number in our sample would be 73265; moving down, the next numbers would be 34663, 62549, and so on.

The random-digit dialing technique of sample selection requires that a telephone interviewer identify the exchange or exchanges of interest (the first three numbers in a phone number after the area code) and then use a table of numbers to select the next four numbers. In practice, however, the exchanges are not always selected randomly. Researchers who wanted to find out whether black Americans with African ancestry prefer being called "black" or "African-American" narrowed their sampling frame by selecting exchanges associated with geographic areas where the proportion of this population was at least 30 percent. The reasoning was that this made the survey procedure far more efficient, considering that the researchers were trying to contact a group representing less than 15 percent of U.S. households. This initial judgment sampling raises the same issues we discussed regarding nonprobability sampling. In this study, the researchers found that respondents were most likely to prefer the term *black* if they had attended schools that were about half black and half white.[8] If such experiences influence the answers to the question of interest to the researchers, the fact that blacks who live in predominantly white communities are underrepresented may introduce bias into the results. The result reduces the generalizability of the results.

Systematic Sampling

Suppose a researcher wants to take a sample of 1,000 from a population of 2,000,000 names. With **systematic sampling**, he or she would draw every 2,000th name from a list of population members. This simple process illustrates how to find the interval between selected observations:

$$\text{Interval} = \frac{\text{Population Size}}{\text{Sample Size}} = \frac{2,000,000}{1,000} = 2,000$$

A starting point is selected randomly; then every *n*th number on the list is selected. In this case, the researcher selects every 2,000th name. Because the starting point may well not be at the beginning, this may actually yield only 999 names. A random number can be used to select one more if the sample needs to be exactly 1,000.

Simple random sampling

A sampling procedure that assures each element in the population of an equal chance of being included in the sample.

To the Point

"Make everything as simple as possible, but not simpler."

—ALBERT EINSTEIN

Systematic sampling

A sampling procedure in which a starting point is selected by a random process and then every *n*th number on the list is selected.

Exhibit 12.4 illustrates this process. Here, suppose someone wished to take a sample of the average monthly temperature in Colombia over a 100-month period. Thus, the exhibit shows the first in what will be a total of 104 total observations. If a sample of twenty is to be obtained, every fifth observation is taken. A die is rolled to find what the first observation will be. Thus, the sequence of selected observations is shown in the rows indicated by "select" in the random starting point column.

EXHIBIT **12.4**

Systematically Sampling from a List

	Observation	Month	Year	Average Temperature (C°)
Random Starting Point	1	January	2010	4
	2	February	2010	6
	3	March	2010	10
	4	April	2010	15
	5	May	2010	16
	6	June	2010	22
Select	7	July	2010	26
	8	August	2010	22
	9	September	2010	27
	10	October	2010	19
	11	November	2010	10
Select	12	December	2010	6
	13	January	2011	22
	14	February	2011	9
	15	March	2011	9
	16	April	2011	12
Select	17	May	2011	18
	18	June	2011	26
	19	July	2011	30
	20	August	2011	31
	21	September	2011	24
Select	22	October	2011	14
	23	November	2011	12
	24	December	2011	7
	25	January	2012	5
	26	February	2012	4
Select	27	March	2012	9
	28	April	2012	14
	29	May	2012	18
	30	June	2012	24
	31	July	2012	24
Select	32	August	2012	25

Although systematic sampling is not actually a random selection procedure, it does yield random results if the arrangement of the items is not in some sequence corresponding to the interval in some way. The problem of *periodicity* can occur otherwise. Returning to Exhibit 12.4, what would happen if the average temperature in this time period were compared with a historical average of 17 degrees and a sample was formed with a sampling interval of 12 and a random starting point of August? Obviously, the comparison would be biased because all of the readings would be summertime readings. This could hardly be considered random.

Stratified Sampling

The usefulness of dividing the population into subgroups, or *strata*, whose members are more or less equal with respect to a characteristic, was illustrated in our discussion of quota sampling. The first step is the same for both stratified and quota sampling: choosing strata on the basis of existing information—for example, classifying retail outlets based on annual sales volume. However, the process of selecting sampling units within the strata differs substantially. In **stratified sampling**, a subsample is drawn using simple random sampling within each stratum. This is not true of quota sampling.

The reason for taking a stratified sample is to obtain a more efficient sample than would be possible with simple random sampling. Suppose, for example, that urban and rural groups have widely different attitudes toward energy conservation, but members within each group hold very similar attitudes. Random sampling error will be reduced with the use of stratified sampling because each group is internally homogeneous, but there are comparative differences between groups. More technically, a smaller standard error may result from this stratified sampling because the groups will be adequately represented when strata are combined.

Another reason for selecting a stratified sample is to ensure that the sample will accurately reflect the population on the basis of the criterion or criteria used for stratification. This is a concern because occasionally simple random sampling yields a disproportionate number of one group or another, and consequently, the sample ends up being less representative than it could be.

A researcher can select a stratified sample as follows. First, a variable (sometimes several variables) is identified as an efficient basis for stratification. A stratification variable must be a characteristic of the population elements known to be related to the dependent variable or other variables of interest. The variable chosen should increase homogeneity within each stratum and increase heterogeneity between strata. The stratification variable usually is a categorical variable or one easily converted into categories (i.e., subgroups). For example, a pharmaceutical company interested in measuring how often physicians prescribe a certain drug might choose physicians' training area as a basis for stratification. In this example the mutually exclusive strata are medical doctors (MDs) and osteopathic doctors (ODs).

Next, for each separate subgroup or stratum, a list of population elements must be obtained. (If such lists are not available, they can be costly to prepare, and if a complete listing is not available, a true stratified probability sample cannot be selected.) Using a table of random numbers or some other device, a *separate* simple random sample is then taken within each stratum. Of course, the researcher must determine how large a sample to draw for each stratum. This issue is discussed in the following section.

Proportional versus Disproportional Sampling

If the number of sampling units drawn from each stratum is in proportion to the relative population size of the stratum, the sample is a **proportional stratified sample**. Sometimes, however, a researcher selects a disproportional stratified sample to try to obtain an adequate number of sampling units in each stratum. Sampling more heavily in a given stratum than its relative population size warrants is not a problem if the primary purpose of the research is to estimate some characteristic separately for each stratum and if researchers are concerned about assessing the differences among strata.

Suppose a research question concerned what was the average total bill of retail customers in Missouri based on the average total reported by retail stores. The percentage breakdown of

Stratified sampling
A probability sampling procedure in which simple random subsamples that are more or less equal on some characteristic are drawn from within each stratum of the population.

Proportional stratified sample
A stratified sample in which the number of sampling units drawn from each stratum is in proportion to the population size of that stratum.

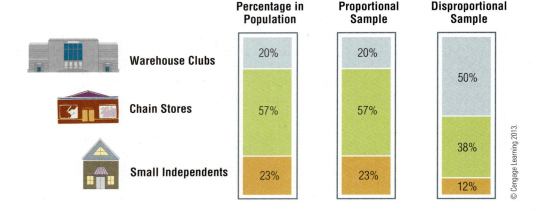

EXHIBIT 12.5
Disproportional
Sampling: Hypothetical
Example

Missouri retail outlets is presented in Exhibit 12.5. A proportional sample of retail stores would use the same percentages as in the population. However, the small percentage of warehouse club stores underrepresents the relative amount of money consumers spend in these large stores. To avoid underrepresenting the large warehouse clubs in the sample, the researcher can take a disproportional sample.

Disproportional stratified sample

A stratified sample in which the sample size for each stratum is allocated according to analytical considerations.

In a **disproportional stratified sample**, the sample size for each stratum is not allocated in proportion to the population size but is dictated by analytical considerations, such as variability in store sales volume. The logic behind this procedure relates to the general argument for sample size: As variability increases, sample size must increase to provide accurate estimates. Thus, the strata that exhibit the greatest variability are sampled more heavily to increase sample efficiency—that is, produce smaller random sampling error. Complex formulas (beyond the scope of an introductory course in marketing research) have been developed to determine sample size for each stratum. A simplified rule of thumb for understanding the concept of optimal allocation is that the stratum sample size increases for strata of larger sizes with the greatest relative variability. Other complexities arise in determining population estimates. For example, when disproportional stratified sampling is used, the estimated mean for each stratum has to be weighed according to the number of elements in each stratum in order to calculate the total population mean.

Cluster Sampling

Cluster sampling is an economical sampling approach that retains the characteristics of a probability sample. Consider a researcher who must conduct 500 personal interviews with physicians scattered throughout the United States. Travel costs are likely to be enormous because the amount of time spent traveling will be substantially greater than the time spent in the interviewing process. If a pharmaceutical marketer can assume the product will be equally successful in Phoenix and Baltimore, cluster sampling provides an alternative. The assumption is that respondents in a cluster that is sampled are the same as respondents in an unsampled cluster.

Cluster sampling

An economically efficient sampling technique in which the primary sampling unit is not the individual element in the population but a large cluster of elements; clusters are selected randomly.

In **cluster sampling**, the primary sampling unit is no longer the individual element in the population (e.g., grocery stores) but a larger cluster of elements located in proximity to one another (e.g., cities). The *area sample* is the most popular type of cluster sample. A grocery store researcher, for example, may randomly choose several geographic areas as primary sampling units and then interview at a sample of grocery stores within the geographic clusters. Interviews are confined to these clusters only. No interviews occur in other clusters. Cluster sampling is classified as a probability sampling technique because of either the random selection of clusters or the random selection of elements within each cluster. Some examples of clusters appear in Exhibit 12.6.

Cluster samples become attractive when lists of a sample population are not available. For example, when researchers investigating employees and self-employed workers for a downtown revitalization project found that a comprehensive list of these people was not available, they decided to take a cluster sample, selecting organizations (business and government) involved in the project as the clusters. A sample of firms within the central business district was developed using stratified

RESEARCH SNAPSHOT

Had Too Much?

When has a customer had too much to drink? Health and government agencies are interested in marketing research on consumers' reported consumption of alcoholic beverages. However, marketing research on the topic is complicated by multiple issues. Some respondents may view the topic as personally sensitive and be hesitant to respond or respond truthfully. Not only will this lead to respondent error but systematic sampling error may increase as these respondents opt out.

Moreover, if the intent is to represent the U.S. adult population, and the questions involve self-reported numbers of drinks and intoxication, what should the sampling frame be? Should the sampling frame take into account factors beyond demographics such as the height and weight of consumers? Should it account for situational factors and the types of service environments in which consumers drink? Research suggests large variations in the amount of drinks necessary for someone to become intoxicated based on these factors and other things, such as the amount and types of foods consumed while drinking. As in a lot of marketing research, what

seems at first like a simple matter of asking a few questions, quickly becomes complex. In this case, trying to get a sampling frame and sampling scheme that adequately represents the relevant population is itself a question requiring a great deal of study.

Sources: Beck, M. (2011), "Testing the Limits of Tipsy," *Wall Street Journal* (August 2), D. Reynolds, K. and L. Harris (2009), "Dysfunctional Customer Behavior Severity: An Empirical Examination," *Journal of Retailing*, 85 (3), 321–35.

Population Element	Possible Clusters in the United States
U.S. adult population	States Counties Metropolitan Statistical Areas Census Tracts Blocks Households
College seniors	Colleges
Manufacturing firms	Counties Metropolitan Statistical Areas Localities Plants
Airline travelers	Airports Planes
Sports fans	Football Stadiums Basketball Arenas Baseball Parks

EXHIBIT **12.6**
Examples of Clusters

© Cengage Learning 2013.

probability sampling to identify clusters. Next, individual workers within the firms (clusters) were randomly selected and interviewed concerning the revitalization project.

Ideally a cluster should be as heterogeneous as the population itself—a mirror image of the population. A problem may arise with cluster sampling if the characteristics and attitudes of the elements within the cluster are too similar. For example, geographic neighborhoods tend to have residents of the same socioeconomic status. Students at a university tend to share similar beliefs. This problem may be mitigated by constructing clusters composed of diverse elements and by selecting a large number of sampled clusters.

Multistage Area Sampling

Multistage area sampling

Sampling that involves using a combination of two or more probability sampling techniques.

Multistage area sampling is a cluster sampling approach involving multiple steps that combine some of the probability techniques already described. Typically, geographic areas are randomly selected in progressively smaller (lower-population) units. For example, a political pollster investigating an election in Texas might first choose counties within the state to ensure that different areas are represented in the sample. In the second step, precincts within the selected counties may be chosen. As a final step, the pollster may select blocks (or households) within the precincts, then interview all the blocks (or households) within the geographic area. Researchers may take as many steps as necessary to achieve a representative sample.

The U.S. Census Bureau provides maps, population information, demographic characteristics for population statistics, and so on, by several small geographical areas; these may be useful in sampling. Census classifications of small geographic areas vary, depending on the extent of urbanization within Metropolitan Statistical Areas (MSAs) or counties.

What Is the Appropriate Sample Design?

A researcher who must decide on the most appropriate sample design for a specific project will identify a number of sampling criteria and evaluate the relative importance of each criterion before selecting a sampling design. This section outlines and briefly discusses the most common criteria. The Research Snapshot on the previous page illustrates how important the sampling design would be to any survey about U.S. drinking habits.

Degree of Accuracy

Selecting a representative sample can be crucial for a researcher desiring to make accurate predictions or forecasts. However, the degree of accuracy required or the researcher's tolerance for sampling and nonsampling error may vary from project to project, especially when cost savings or another benefit may be a trade-off for a reduction in accuracy.

For example, when the sample is part of an exploratory research project, accuracy may not be the highest priority. For other, more conclusive projects, the sample result must precisely represent a population's characteristics, and the researcher must be willing to spend the time and money needed to achieve that accuracy. When researchers use a convenience sample, they may sometimes even think backward and only describe what population the results might extend to based on the sample that can be obtained. Typically, a market research report will qualify results based on sampling characteristics.

Resources

The cost associated with the different sampling techniques varies tremendously. If the researcher's financial and human resources are restricted, certain options will have to be eliminated. For a typical graduate student working on a thesis or dissertation, conducting a representative, national survey is often out of the question because of limited resources. Managers concerned with the cost of the research versus the value of the information often will opt to save money by using a nonprobability sampling design rather than make the decision to conduct no research at all.

Time

A researcher who needs to meet a deadline or complete a project quickly will be more likely to select a simple, less time-consuming sample design. A researcher may have questions about an online panel and how well it represents the relevant population of consumers in the United States. However, he or she can obtain the online panel very quickly and may be willing to trade-off speed for any increased accuracy that would come from drawing his or her own sampling frame.

Advance Knowledge of the Population

Advance knowledge of population characteristics, such as the availability of lists of population members, is an important criterion. In many cases, however, no list of population elements exists. This is especially true when the population element is defined by ownership of a particular prod-uct or brand, by experience in performing a specific job task, or on a qualitative dimension. A lack of adequate lists may automatically rule out systematic sampling, stratified sampling, or other sampling designs, or it may dictate that a preliminary study, such as a short telephone survey us-ing random digit dialing, be conducted to generate information to build a sampling frame for the primary study. Social media can be used to reach out to brand fans. Proctor & Gamble could reach Tide fans by going to the detergent's Facebook page. However, because they would not find a list of all Tide users by doing so, nor could one be generated from this page, the resulting sample would be a convenience sample.

National versus Local Project

Geographic proximity of population elements will influence sample design. When population elements are unequally distributed geographically, a cluster sample may become much more attractive. A sample that represents all households in the United States and Canada becomes the goal for the few household products that show no regional, demographic, or lifestyle bias. Few products exhibit this characteristic. For instance, market researchers investigating opinions of North American consumers about the Fiat Mini should sample from large urban areas rather than rural areas based on the knowledge that rural residents do not often purchase a Fiat.

TIPS OF THE TRADE

- Online panels are a practical reality in marketing research. A sample can be obtained quickly and gen-erally comes close to matching general population parameters if the results come from a well-managed panel. Well-managed panels can provide a probability sample. Like many things though, the better run pan-els are more expensive than more haphazardly man-aged panels.
- Crowdsourced panels (such as M-Turk) involve consumers who opt in and provide little ability for generalization in the vast majority of marketing and consumer research settings.
- Convenience samples do have appropriate uses in marketing research. Convenience samples (including student samples) are particularly appropriate when:
  - Exploratory research is conducted.
  - The researcher is primarily interested in internal validity (testing a hypothesis under any condition) rather than external validity (understanding how much the sample results project to a target population).
- When cost and time constraints only allow a convenience sample:
  - Researchers can try to think backward and project on the population for whom the results apply based on the nature of the convenience sample. Of course, this depends on reliable data describing the demographic and other rel-evant population characteristics of individual respondents.
- The research report should address the adequacy of the sample. The report should qualify the generalizability of the results based on sample limitations.

∴ SUMMARY

1. Explain reasons for taking a sample rather than a complete census. Sampling involves drawing conclusions about an entire population by taking measurements from only a portion of that population. The practical nature of research is clearly illustrated in sampling. Sampling is used because of the practical impossibility of measuring every population member. Seldom would a researcher have the time or budget to do so. Also, a researcher would rarely need to measure every unit, as a well-designed and executed sampling plan can yield results that may even be more accurate than an actual census. Samples also are needed in cases where measurement involves destruction of the measured unit.

2. Describe the process of identifying a target population and selecting a sampling frame. The first problem in sampling is to define the target population. Incorrect or vague definition of this population is likely to produce misleading results. The chapter contains an example list of questions that illustrate considerations needed in making a decision about the relevant population. A sampling frame is a list of elements, or individual members, of the overall population from which the sample is drawn. A sampling unit is a single element or group of elements subject to selection in the sample. Sometimes, a list of actual population members exists and can serve as a sampling frame. More often, the researcher will need the assistance of a directory, panel, or mailing list in forming the sampling frame.

3. Compare random sampling and systematic (nonsampling) errors with an emphasis on how the Internet is intertwined with this issue. Two sources of discrepancy between the sample results and the population parameters exist. One, random sampling error, arises from chance variations of the sample from the population. Random sampling error is a function of sample size and may be estimated using the central-limit theorem (discussed in a later chapter). Systematic, or nonsampling, error comes from sources such as sampling frame error, mistakes in recording responses, or nonresponses from persons who are not contacted or who refuse to participate. When researchers do not have an accurate list of population members, some type of systematic error becomes very likely. Internet surveys and consumer panels are very convenient but make truly random selection difficult. Thus, when these methods are chosen, extra care needs to be taken to make sure that the sample has characteristics that indeed allow it to represent the target population.

4. Identify the types of nonprobability sampling, including their advantages and disadvantages. The two major classes of sampling methods are probability and nonprobability techniques. Nonprobability techniques include convenience sampling, judgment sampling, quota sampling, and snowball sampling. They are convenient to use but more subject to systematic sampling error. Sorting out the systematic sampling error from the random sampling error also proves problematic.

5. Summarize various types of probability samples. Probability samples are based on chance selection procedures. These include simple random sampling, systematic sampling, stratified sampling, and cluster sampling. With these techniques, random sampling error can be accurately predicted. The process for selecting sample units from a population is described in the chapter. A true probability sample can be costly both in terms of money and time.

6. Discuss how to choose an appropriate sample design. A researcher who must determine the most appropriate sampling design for a specific project will identify a number of sampling criteria and evaluate the relative importance of each criterion before selecting a design. The most common criteria concern accuracy requirements, available resources, time constraints, knowledge availability, and analytical requirements. Internet sampling presents some unique issues. Convenience samples drawn from website visitors or social networks are problematic with respect to generalizability. Drawing a probability sample from an established consumer panel whose members opt in can be effective.

∴ KEY TERMS AND CONCEPTS

census, *337*
cluster sampling, *354*
convenience sampling, *348*
disproportional stratified sample, *354*
judgment (purposive) sampling, *349*
multistage area sampling, *356*
nonprobability sampling, *348*
online panels, *343*
opt in, *346*

population (universe), *337*
population element, *337*
primary sampling unit (PSU), *344*
probability sampling, *348*
proportional stratified sample, *353*
quota sampling, *349*
random sampling error, *344*
reverse directory, *343*
sample, *337*

sampling frame, *342*
sampling frame error, *343*
sampling unit, *344*
secondary sampling unit, *344*
simple random sampling, *351*
snowball sampling, *350*
stratified sampling, *353*
systematic sampling, *351*
tertiary sampling unit, *344*

:: QUESTIONS FOR REVIEW AND CRITICAL THINKING

1. If you decide whether you want to see an entire movie based on a 90 second YouTube clip, are you using a sampling technique? Could this be described as a scientific sampling technique? Explain your answer.

2. What is the difference between a population and a sample? What are the reasons why a sampling process is so often used in place of a census? Why is it that a population can sometimes be as accurate as, or more accurate than, a census?

3. Define sample, sampling unit, sampling frame, and population.

4. How might the target population differ for a researcher doing separate projects for two retailing companies—one for A&F and one for Nordstrom?

5. Name some possible sampling frames for research questions involving the following:
   a. Online travel agencies
   b. Frequent Instagram users
   c. Golf course greenskeepers (responsible for the condition of the golf course)
   d. Dog owners
   e. Harley-Davidson owners
   f. Tattoo wearers
   g. Minority-owned businesses
   h. Women over six feet tall
   i. High school students who will consider architecture as a career
   j. Fast-food consumers in California

6. Describe the difference between a random and systematic sampling error.

7. What is a nonprobability sample? Give some examples.

8. Is a convenience sample ever appropriate? Explain.

9. When would a researcher use a judgment, or purposive, sample?

10. What are pros and cons of using M-Turk crowdsourcing to provide a sample for a marketing research study? Would you advise someone trying to predict which type of appeals for energy efficient technology for new automobiles will be effective on U.S. consumers to use a sample taken from M-Turk?

11. A telephone interviewer asks, "I would like to ask you about race. Are you Native American, Hispanic, African-American, Asian, or white?" After the respondent replies, the interviewer says, "We have conducted a large number of surveys with people of your background, and we do not need to question you further. Thank you for your cooperation." What type of sampling is likely being used?

12. What role can screening questions play in trying to understand and control systematic variance from sources such as Internet surveys, online panels, or other types of directories?

13. What are the benefits of stratified sampling?

14. What geographic units within a metropolitan area are useful for sampling?

15. Outline the step-by-step procedure you would use to select the following:
   a. A random sample of 275 students from your university
   b. A quota sample of fifty light users and fifty heavy users of beer in a shopping mall intercept study
   c. A sample of regular Twitter users to explore social network links
   d. A stratified sample of fifty mechanical engineers, forty electrical engineers, and forty civil engineers from the subscriber list of an engineering journal

16. Selection for jury duty is supposed to be a totally random process. Comment on the following computer selection procedures, and determine if they are indeed random:
   a. A program instructs the computer to scan the list of names and pick names that were next to those from the last scan.
   b. Three-digit numbers are randomly generated to select jurors from a list of licensed drivers. If the weight information listed on the license matches the random number, the person is selected.
   c. The juror source list is obtained by merging a list of registered voters with a list of licensed drivers.

17. Provide an example of marketing research in which a sample that is truly representative of all of North America is needed. If you cannot provide an actual example, try to contrive a situation that would require such a sample. How often would such a target population be needed?

18. To ensure a good session, a company selects focus group members from a list of articulate participants instead of conducting random sampling. The client did not inquire about sample selection when it accepted the proposal. Is this ethical?

19. Go to **http://www.reversephonedirectory.com** and put in a few phone numbers that you know. Make sure that you put an equal number of cell and home phone numbers. Given the results that you obtain, do you believe this directory is useful to generate a list of names and numbers for a telephone survey? Do you think such an approach could be useful if a company was willing to pay for a list?

20. Go to the U.S. Census Bureau's home page at **http://www.census.gov,** click on quick facts. You can find profiles of every state from this website. Suppose a representative sample of the state of Louisiana is used to represent the current U.S. population. How well does Louisiana represent the United States overall? How well does Louisiana represent California or Maine? Use the profiles of the states and of the country to form your opinion. If a researcher is resource limited and uses only a single state to help predict success of a new product to be launched nationally, how should he or she go about discussing generalizability of the research results?

:: RESEARCH ACTIVITY

1. Develop a sampling plan to study the lunch habits of undergraduate and graduate students of your university. Research questions involve who has the most market share and what the preferred food types and price points are for this particular school. Explain your choices.

Who's Fishing?

Case 12.1

Washington Times columnist Gene Mueller writes about fishing and other outdoor sporting activities.

Mueller commented that although interest groups express concerns about the impact of saltwater fishers on the fish population, no one really knows how many people fish for recreation or how many fish they catch. This situation would challenge marketers interested in the population of anglers.

How could a marketer get an accurate sample? One idea would be to contact residents of coastal counties using random-digit dialing. This sampling frame would include many, if not all, of the people who fish in the ocean, but it would also include many people who do not fish—or who fish for business rather than recreation. A regional agency seeking to gather statistics on anglers, the Atlantic Coastal Cooperative Statistics Program, prefers to develop a sampling frame more related to people who fish.

Another idea would be to use state fishing license records. Privacy would be a drawback, however. Some people might not want their records shared, and they might withhold phone numbers. Further complicating this issue for Atlantic fishing is that most states in the Northeast do not require a license for saltwater fishing. Also exempt in some states are people who fish from the shore and from piers.

A political action group called the Recreational Fishing Alliance suggests that charter fishing businesses collect data.

Questions

1. Imagine that an agency or business has asked for help in gathering data about the number of sports anglers who fish off the coast of Georgia. What advice would you give about sampling? What method or combination of methods would generate the best results?
2. What other criteria besides accuracy would you expect to consider? What sampling methods could help you meet those criteria?

Big Data Basics: Describing Samples and Populations

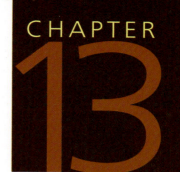

LEARNING OUTCOMES

After studying this chapter, you should be able to:

1. Use basic descriptive statistics to analyze data and make basic inferences about population metrics
2. Distinguish among the concepts of population, sample, and sampling distributions
3. Explain the central-limit theorem
4. Use confidence intervals to express inferences about population characteristics
5. Understand major issues in specifying sample size
6. Know how to assess the potential for nonresponse bias

Dimitri Otis/Getty Images

Chapter Vignette:
It's a Numbers Game

Business students often associate numbers more with a discipline like accounting than with marketing. However, when one gets involved in marketing research, he or she quickly sees that this conclusion is inaccurate. Marketing depends a great deal on numbers and on mathematics—particularly statistics. Never has this been truer than in the big data era where companies find shortages of marketing researchers capable of analyzing all the numbers that are stored about customers and their choices. The key to using all of these numbers, that comprise data, is to summarize them in a way that is both meaningful and easily understood by management.

Although marketing analysts sometimes employ very complicated statistics, more often than not, very basic summary statistics contain key insights that indicate firm performance. Perhaps no industry gathers more data on their customers and perspective customers than the automobile industry. Several websites such as Kelly Blue Book (kbb.com) or Edmunds (edmunds.com) summarize some of this data.

Simple summary measures include mean satisfaction and quality scores, consumer star ratings, top box scores, bottom box scores, and the net promoter score (NPS) discussed earlier. These metrics provide summary measures of how owners feel and what they think about owning a certain car. Top box scores give frequency counts of how many respondents rate the car with the highest score possible (for instance score the car 10 on a 0 to 10 point scale). Bottom box scores do the opposite; that is, they provide a frequency count indicating how many respondents give the car the lowest score possible (for instance score the car 0 out of 10). The NPS reveals the frequency of consumers who will recommend the car to others, or more specifically, the frequency of promoters and detractors.

All of these measures represent elementary statistics. Although all of these measures for a given car correlate with one another, each measure contains some unique information.[1] For instance, the top box score is most associated with loyalty. The bottom box score is most associated with consumers who are actively spreading negative word of mouth or WOM. Means scores may be useful in comparing satisfaction or other metrics like gas mileage among alternatives. The bottom line is that a marketer can't run from numbers forever. Eventually, the numbers catch up to us all. Thankfully, for many who fear complicated mathematics, all of these metrics truly are elementary. This is particularly a good thing when researchers have to communicate results to managers who may be quantitatively challenged themselves!

Introduction

This chapter provides an entrée into the world of marketing analytics. As suggested in the vignette, although big data analysis sounds like a very complicated thing to do, we can learn a lot from summarizing the data with elementary, basic statistics. This chapter gives an overview of some of the most commonly used of these basic statistics. All of these statistics are univariate in the sense that only one variable is involved. This overview also provides good background for understanding equations related to sample size requirements. These equations complement the material in the previous chapter, providing us with a better understanding of the usefulness of a particular sample.

Descriptive Statistics and Basic Inferences

The boom in demand for marketing research analysts exists because raw data alone are seldom useful. Raw data are just numbers and words with little meaning. Analysts must somehow identify diagnostic data, meaning data useful in decision-making, and then summarize the information. Otherwise, the decision-makers will be lost amidst the vast quantities of data available to even small businesses today. The most basic statistical tools for summarizing information from data include frequency distributions, proportions, and measures of central tendency and dispersion. Statistics like these often provide a summary number that allows analysts to compare the characteristics of a sample with some population benchmark, characteristics of another sample, or some other critical value. Analysts and decision-makers refer to such numbers as **metrics**. After providing summary metrics, the researcher then adds to that information about the sample validity. The combination of summary metrics from basic statistics *and* a valid sample proves vital in making effective marketing and business decisions.

Databases like those available through census.gov and the CIA *Factbook* provide a glimpse into the way analysts can represent volumes of data with summary statistics. At these sites, we can find table after table of figures associated with numbers of births, number of workers by industry, populations, and other data that represent *statistics*. Specifically, these tables provide descriptive statistics. Another type of statistics, **inferential statistics**, allows inferences about a whole population from a sample. For example, a firm test-markets a new product in Sacramento and Birmingham because it wishes to make an inference from these sample markets to predict what will happen throughout the United States. Therefore, two applications of statistics exist:

1. to describe characteristics of the population or sample and
2. to generalize from a sample to a population.

Metrics

A summary number that allows analysts to compare the characteristics of a sample with some population benchmark, characteristics of another sample, or some other critical value.

Inferential statistics

A summary representation of data from a sample that allows us to understand (i.e., infer from sample to population) an entire population.

What Are Sample Statistics and Population Parameters?

Inferential statistics allow us to make a judgment about a population using data from a sample. Recall, a sample is a subset, usually a very small portion of the total number of elements in a given population. Data from a sample are always uncertain. Certainty in judging the population comes only from a census, meaning all population elements are measured.

Sample statistics are summary measures computed only from the sample data. **Population parameters** are summary characteristics of information describing a specific population. Sample statistics become inferential when we use them to make inferences (guesses) about population parameters.[2] In our notation, we will generally represent population parameters with Greek lowercase letters—for example, μ or α—and sample statistics with English letters, such as X or S. We use parameter estimates derived from a sample (English letters) to guess what the population characteristics (Greek letters) might be.

Sample statistics

Summary measures about variables computed using only data taken from a sample.

Population parameters

Summary characteristics of information describing the properties of a population.

Using data from the Survey This! feature, try to come up with answers to these questions:

1. Suppose a marketing manager was trying to determine how many students had only one e-mail account that they used regularly. The manager's intention is to market additional Internet services to students who have only one or no e-mail account.

   a. What is the proportion of students in the sample that have more than one e-mail account?
   b. If the student population is 5 million students, what sample size is needed to estimate the actual proportion of students with more than one active e-mail account within ±1 percent?
   c. What sample size is needed to estimate the actual proportion of students with more than one active e-mail account within ±5 percent?
   d. If the decision to launch this marketing activity involves an investment of approximately $75,000 for this company (with median annual revenues of $3 million), what level of precision would you recommend?

Do you have more than one email address that you use regularly?

Yes   No

How often do you check your email?

1-3 times a week   4-6 times a week   1-2 times a day   3-4 times a day   >4 times a day

Do you Instant Message?

Yes   No

Source: www.qualtrics.com

Frequency Distributions

One of the most common ways to summarize sample data is to construct a *frequency table,* or **frequency distribution**. Frequency distributions can be depicted with a table or a chart and indicate the number of times (i.e., the frequency) a particular value of a variable occurs. If your instructor took a sample of student grade observations at the end of the term, the table would indicate how many students made A, and how many made B, C, D, and F. Exhibit 13.1 illustrates a frequency distribution of sample of credit union customers' responses to a question that asked:

- How much money do you currently have (i.e., what is your current balance) in the local university credit union checking account?

Frequency distributions are particularly useful in summarizing nominal or ordinal variables. The table provides a quick summary of balances reported by these respondents.

A frequency calculation also typically includes the distribution of relative frequency, or a **percentage distribution**. To develop a frequency distribution of percentages, divide the frequency

Frequency distribution

A table or chart summarizing the number of times a particular value of a variable occurs.

Percentage distribution

A frequency distribution organized into a table (or graph) that summarizes percentage values associated with particular values of a variable.

EXHIBIT **13.1**

Frequency Distribution of Deposits

Amount	Frequency (Number of People Who Hold Deposits in Each Range)
Under $3,000	499
$3,000–$4,999	530
$5,000–$9,999	562
$10,000–$14,999	718
$15,000 or more	811
	3,120

Source: © Cengage Learning®

Percentage Distribution
of Deposits

Amount	Percent (Percentage of People Who Hold Deposits in Each Range)
Under $3,000	16
$3,000–$4,999	17
$5,000–$9,999	18
$10,000–$14,999	23
$15,000 or more	26
	100

Source: © Cengage Learning®

of each value by the total number of observations, and multiply the result by 100. Based on the data in Exhibit 13.1, Exhibit 13.2 shows the percentage distribution of account balances; that is, the percentage of people holding deposits within each range of values.

Probability

The long-run relative frequency with which an event will occur.

Probability is the long-run relative frequency with which an event will occur. Inferential statistics uses the concept of a probability distribution, which is conceptually the same as a percentage distribution, except that the data represent probabilities. Exhibit 13.3 shows the probability distribution of the credit union balances. In other words, the table shows how likely a sample respondent is to have a balance within each range listed.

Proportions

Proportion

The percentage of elements that meet some criterion for membership in a category.

When a frequency distribution portrays only a single characteristic in terms of a percentage of the total, it defines the **proportion** of occurrence. A proportion, such as the proportion of freshman at a university, indicates the percentage of population elements that successfully meet a criterion for membership in a category. A proportion may be expressed as a percentage, a fraction, or a decimal value. In the example used here and illustrated in Exhibit 13.3, the probabilities are equal to the proportion of consumers in each deposit category. For example, 23 percent have a bank balance between $10,000 and $14,999.

Top-Box/Bottom-Box Scores

Top-box score

The portion of respondents who choose the most positive choice in a multiple-choice question usually dealing with customer opinion.

Managers are often very interested in the proportion of consumers choosing extreme responses. A **top-box score** generally refers to the portion of respondents who choose the most favorable response toward an option usually related to customer opinion. The top-box metric can show, for instance, the portion of consumers who would most likely recommend a business to a friend or be most likely to make a purchase. The logic is that respondents who choose the extreme response are really unique compared to the others. Managers often ask about the top-box metric.[3]

Probability Distribution
of Deposits

Amount	Probability
Under $3,000	.16
$3,000–$4,999	.17
$5,000–$9,999	.18
$10,000–$14,999	.23
$15,000 or more	.26
	1.00

Source: © Cengage Learning®

Sometimes, however, the opposite perspective is more diagnostic. Thus, managers are well-served also to examine the **bottom-box score**, the portion of respondents who choose the least favorable response to some question about customer opinion. The bottom-box metric is more diagnostic of customer problems and often signals a need for some managerial reaction. Analysts often apply measures to consumers who already are brand customers. Thus, the top-box often contains the largest group of responses. In cases like these in particular, the bottom-box score is very useful.

Bottom-box score

The portion of respondents who choose the least favorable response to some question about customer opinion.

Central Tendency Metrics

On a typical day, a sales manager counts the number of sales calls each sales representative makes. He or she wishes to inspect the data to find the center, or middle area, of the frequency distribution. Put another way, what is the most typical number of sales calls? The analyst can represent central tendency with basic descriptive statistics like the mean, median, or mode. Each is determined in a slightly different way.

The Mean

We all use the notion of an average on a regular basis. The **mean** is just the mathematical average of a set of numbers and represents the most common representation of central tendency. As such, it is a widely used metric. To express the mean mathematically, we use the summation symbol, the capital Greek letter *sigma* (Σ). A typical use might look like this:

Mean

A basic statistic that quantifies central tendency computed as the arithmetic average.

$$\sum_{i=1}^{n} X_i$$

which is a shorthand way to write the sum of

$$X_1 + X_2 + X_3 + X_4 + X_5 + \cdots + X_n$$

Below the Σ is the initial value of an index, i in this case, and above it is the final value of i, which also equals n, the total number of observations.

Suppose a sales manager supervises the eight salespeople listed in Exhibit 13.4. To express the sum of the salespeople's calls in Σ notation, we just number the salespeople (this number becomes the index number) and associate subscripted variables with their numbers of calls:

We then write an appropriate Σ formula and evaluate it:

$$\sum_{i=1}^{8} X_i = X_1 + X_2 + X_3 + X_4 + X_5 + X_6 + X_7 + X_8$$

$$= 4 + 3 + 2 + 5 + 3 + 3 + 1 + 5$$

$$= 26$$

Index		Salesperson	Variable		Number of Calls
1	=	Mike	X_1	=	4
2	=	Patty	X_2	=	3
3	=	Billie	X_3	=	2
4	=	Bob	X_4	=	5
5	=	John	X_5	=	3
6	=	Frank	X_6	=	3
7	=	Chuck	X_7	=	1
8	=	Samantha	X_8	=	5
		Total		=	26

EXHIBIT 13.4
Number of Sales Calls per Day by Salesperson

Source: © Cengage Learning®

This notation is the numerator in the formula for the arithmetic mean:

$$\text{Mean} = \frac{\sum\limits_{i=1}^{n} X_i}{n} = \frac{26}{8} = 3.25$$

The notation $\sum\limits_{i=1}^{n} X_i$ means add together all the Xs whose subscripts are between 1 and n inclusive, where n equals 8 in this case. The formula shows that the mean number of sales calls in this example is 3.25.

Researchers generally wish to know the population mean, μ (lowercase Greek letter *mu*), which is calculated as follows:

$$\mu = \frac{\sum\limits_{i=1}^{N} X_i}{N}$$

where

N = number of members in the population

In the case of the sales manager, the total population of salespeople under his or her supervision is 8. N would be 8. Often, though, we will not have complete data needed to calculate a population mean, μ, so we will calculate a sample mean, $\overline{X}$ (read "X bar"), with the following formula:

$$\overline{X} = \frac{\sum\limits_{i=1}^{n} X_i}{n}$$

where

n = number of observations made in the sample

More likely than not, you already know how to calculate a mean. However, knowing how to distinguish among the symbols $\sum$, μ, and X is helpful to understand statistics.

In this introductory discussion of the summation sign ($\sum$), we have used detailed notation that includes the subscript for the initial index value (i) and the final index value (n). However, from this point on in the chapter, we'll omit the details for simplicity and the symbol $\sum$ will mean summed overall observations in the sample.

The mean is the most widely applied measure of central tendency. However, the mean can sometimes be misleading, particularly when extreme values or outliers are present. Thus, researchers sometimes rely on other central tendency indicators.

The Median

Median

A measure of central tendency that is the midpoint; the value below which half the values in a distribution fall.

The next measure of central tendency, the **median**, is the midpoint of the distribution, or the 50th percentile. In other words, the median is the value below which half the values in the sample fall. In the sales manager example, 3 is the median because half the observations are greater than 3 and half are less than 3. In cases like this, with an even number of observations, the median equals the average of the two middle observations, in this case both are 3.

The median is a better metric for central tendency in the presence of extreme values or outliers. For instance, a professor gives a marketing research test and one student makes a 99, another makes a 98, the next highest grade is 51, and the remaining 17 grades range from 30 to 50. If the professor curves the grades so that everyone who scores "above average" will pass, the result could be only 5 or 6 students passing as the mean would be on the order of 46. Perhaps the students would prefer the professor curve based around the median, which would mean that half of the students would pass by definition.

The Mode

Mode

A measure of central tendency; the value that occurs most often.

In fashion merchandising, *mode* refers to the most popular fashion. In statistics the **mode** is the measure of central tendency that identifies the value that occurs most often. In our example of sales calls, Patty, John, and Frank each made three sales calls. The value 3 occurs most often, so 3 is the mode. The mode is determined by listing each possible value and noting the number of times each value occurs. The mode is the best measure of central tendency for data that is less than interval and for data approaching a unimodal distribution with one large peak (many observations have the same response with relatively few other responses).

Dispersion Metrics

The mean, median, and mode summarize the central tendency of frequency distributions. Accurate analysis of data also requires knowing the tendency of observations to depart from the central tendency. Thus, another way to summarize the data is to calculate the dispersion of the data, or how the observations vary from the mean. Consider, for instance, the twelve-month sales patterns of the two products shown in Exhibit 13.5. Both have a mean monthly sales volume of 200 units, but the dispersion of observations for product B is much greater than that for product A. There are several measures of dispersion.

The Range

The simplest representation of dispersion is the range, the distance between the smallest and the largest values of a frequency distribution. In Exhibit 13.5, the range for product A is between 196 units and 202 units (6 units), whereas for product B the range is between 150 units and 261 units (111 units). The range does not take into account all the observations; it merely tells us about the extreme values of the distribution.

Just as people may be fat or skinny, distributions may be fat or skinny. Although we do not expect all observations to be exactly like the mean, in a skinny distribution they will lie a short distance from the mean. Product A is an example; the observations are close together and reasonably close to the mean. In a fat distribution, such as the one for product B, they will be spread out. Exhibit 13.6 illustrates this concept graphically with two frequency distributions that have identical modes, medians, and means but different degrees of dispersion.

	Units Product A	Units Product B
January	196	150
February	198	160
March	199	176
April	200	181
May	200	192
June	200	200
July	200	201
August	201	202
September	201	213
October	201	224
November	202	240
December	202	261
Average	**200**	**200**

EXHIBIT **13.5**
Sales Levels for Two Products with Identical Average Sales

Source: © Cengage Learning®

EXHIBIT 13-6
Low Dispersion versus High Dispersion

The interquartile range is the range that encompasses the middle 50 percent of the observations—in other words, the range between the bottom quartile (lowest 25 percent) and the top quartile (highest 25 percent).

Deviation Scores

A method of calculating how far any observation is from the mean is to calculate individual deviation scores. To calculate a deviation from the mean, use the following formula:

$$d_{i_i} = X_i - \overline{X}$$

For the value of 150 units for product B for the month of January, the deviation score is -50; that is, $150 - 200 = -50$. If the deviation scores are large, we will have a fat distribution because the distribution exhibits a broad spread.

Why Use the Standard Deviation?

Statisticians have derived several quantitative indexes to reflect a distribution's spread, or variability. The *standard deviation* is perhaps the most valuable indicator of spread, or dispersion. Students often have difficulty understanding it. Learning about the standard deviation will be easier if we first look at several other potential metrics indicating dispersion. Each of these has certain limitations that the standard deviation does not.

First is the average deviation. We compute the average deviation by calculating the deviation score of each observation value (i.e., its difference from the mean), summing these scores, and then dividing by the sample size (n):

$$\text{Average deviation} = \frac{\Sigma(X_i - \overline{X})}{n}$$

Although this measure of spread seems interesting, it is never used. Positive deviation scores are canceled out by negative scores with this formula, leaving an average deviation value of zero no matter how wide the spread may be. Hence, the average deviation is a useless spread measure.

One might correct for the disadvantage of the average deviation by computing the absolute values of the deviations. In other words, we ignore all the positive and negative signs and use only the absolute value of each deviation. The formula for the mean absolute deviation is

$$\text{Mean absolute deviation} = \frac{\Sigma|X_i - \overline{X}|}{n}$$

Because this procedure eliminates the problem of always having a zero score for the deviation measure, it becomes even more useful to express deviations in terms of variance.

Variance

Another means of eliminating the sign problem caused by the negative deviations canceling out the positive deviations is to square the deviation scores. The following formula gives the mean squared deviation:

$$\text{Mean squared deviation} = \frac{\Sigma(X_i - \overline{X})^2}{n}$$

This result is useful for describing the overall variability. However, we typically wish to make an inference about a population from a sample, and so the divisor $n - 1$ is used rather than n in most practical marketing research problems.[4] The divisor changes from n to $n - 1$ to provide an unbiased estimator. This equation for spread, called sample **variance**, has the following formulation:

$$\text{Variance} = S^2 = \frac{\Sigma(X_i - \bar{X})^2}{n - 1}$$

Variance

A metric of variability or dispersion. Its square root is the standard deviation.

Variance Sample variance is a very good index of dispersion. The variance, S^2, will equal zero if and only if each and every observation in the distribution is the same as the mean. The variance will grow larger as the observations tend to differ increasingly from one another and from the mean.

Standard Deviation

Variance is an extremely important and useful analytical concept. That said, it has one drawback as a summary metric showing dispersion. The variance reflects a squared unit of measurement. For instance, if measures of sales in a territory are made in dollars, the mean number will be reflected in dollars, but the variance will be in squared dollars. Because of this, statisticians often take the square root of the variance. Using the square root of the variance for a distribution, called the **standard deviation**, eliminates the drawback of having the measure of dispersion in squared units rather than in the original measurement units. The formula for the standard deviation is

$$S = \sqrt{S^2} = \sqrt{\frac{\Sigma(X_i - \bar{X})^2}{n - 1}}$$

Standard deviation

A quantitative index of a distribution's spread, or variability; the square root of the variance for a distribution.

Exhibit 13.7 illustrates that the calculation of a sample standard deviation requires the researcher to first calculate the sample mean. In the example with eight salespeople's sales calls (Exhibit 13.4), we calculated the sample mean as 3.25. Exhibit 13.7 illustrates how to calculate the standard deviation for these data.

Let's return to thinking about the original purpose for measures of dispersion. We want to summarize the data from survey research and other forms of marketing research. Indexes of central tendency, such as the mean, help us interpret the data. In addition, we wish to calculate a measure of variability that will give us a quantitative index of the dispersion of the distribution. We have looked at several measures of dispersion to arrive at two very adequate means of measuring dispersion: the variance and the standard deviation. The term given is for the sample standard deviation, S. The variance gives us a summary indicator of the reasonable ranges of variable observations. If we are assessing the utilitarian value someone finds from their Amazon Prime membership, the mean would provide the central tendency and the standard deviation the

X	$(X - \bar{X})^1$	$(X - \bar{X})^2$
4	$(4 - 3.25) = $ .75	.5625
3	$(3 - 3.25) = $ −.25	.0625
2	$(2 - 3.25) = -1.25$	1.5625
5	$(5 - 3.25) = $ 1.75	3.0625
3	$(3 - 3.25) = $ −.25	.0625
3	$(3 - 3.25) = $ −.25	.0625
1	$(1 - 3.25) = -2.25$	5.0625
5	$(5 - 3.25) = $ 1.75	3.0625
Σ[a]	0[a]	13.5000

$$n = 8 \qquad \bar{X} = 3.25$$

$$S = \sqrt{\frac{\Sigma(X - \bar{X})^2}{n - 1}} = \sqrt{\frac{13.5}{8 - 1}} = \sqrt{\frac{13.5}{7}} = \sqrt{1.9286} = 1.3887$$

[a]The summation of this column is not used in the calculation of the standard deviation.

EXHIBIT 13-7

Calculating a Standard Deviation: Number of Sales Calls per Day for Eight Salespeople

Source: © Cengage Learning®

dispersion. A small standard deviation (in the extreme 0) would mean that all respondents report about the same value. A large standard deviation reveals a lack of consensus about the value derived from Amazon prime. In addition, predictive statistical techniques require variance to work. Statistically, practically all meaning comes from some aspect of variance or covariance.

The term for the population standard deviation, σ, which is conceptually very similar, has not been given (the divider would be n rather n–1). Nevertheless, you should understand that σ measures the dispersion in the population and S measures the dispersion in the sample. These concepts are crucial to understanding statistics.

Distinguish between Population, Sample, and Sample Distribution

Roulette is a common casino game and a casino may contain many roulette wheels. If someone wanted to know whether the roulette wheels were fair, they may make many observations of which number the ball lands on as the result of a spin. The results would follow some pattern. It might not be possible to record the results of all spins of the roulette wheel, but someone could probably record results over a several-hour period on one or more wheels. This basic image provides the idea behind statistical distributions.

The Normal Distribution

Normal distribution

A symmetrical, bell-shaped distribution that describes the expected probability distribution of many chance occurrences.

One of the most common probability distributions in statistics is the **normal distribution**, commonly represented by the *normal curve*. This mathematical and theoretical distribution describes the expected distribution of sample means and many other chance occurrences. Think of it as a tally of observed values. The normal curve is bell shaped, and almost all (99.7 percent) of its values are within ±3 standard deviations from its mean. An example of a normal curve, the distribution of IQ scores, appears in Exhibit 13.8. The IQ score is normed to 100 meaning that 100 is an average IQ score. In this example, 1 standard deviation for IQ equals 15. Someone with an IQ score of 70 is 2 standard deviations below average and scores better than 2.14 percent of others. A person scoring 145 is 3 standard deviations above average and better than 99.8 percent of others. As another example, if you plot your blood pressure every day for 100 days and tallied the results (as if on a number line), they would likely produce a normal distribution.

● ● ● ● ● ●

By recording the results of spins of the roulette wheel, one could find the distribution of the results. If the wheel is fair, what should the distribution look like?

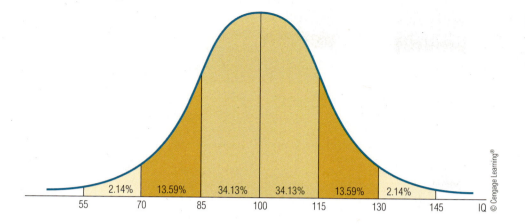

EXHIBIT **13-8**
Normal Distribution: Distribution of Intelligence Quotient (IQ) Scores

The **standardized normal distribution** is a specific normal curve that has several characteristics:

1.   It is symmetrical about its mean.
2.   The mean identifies the normal curve's highest point (the mode) and the vertical line about which this normal curve is symmetrical.
3.   The normal curve has an infinite number of cases (it is a continuous distribution), and the area under the curve has a probability density equal to 1.
4.   The standardized normal distribution has a mean of 0 and a standard deviation of 1.

Exhibit 13.9 illustrates these properties. Exhibit 13.10 is a summary version of the typical standardized normal table found at the end of most statistics textbooks. A more complex table of areas under the standardized normal distribution can be found on the Internet at **http://www .mathsisfun.com/data/standard-normal-distribution-table.html** or in the statistical appendix on the www.cengagebrain.com.

The standardized normal distribution is a purely theoretical probability distribution, but it is a most useful distribution in inferential statistics. Statisticians have spent a great deal of time and effort making it convenient for researchers to find the probability of any portion of the area under the standardized normal distribution. All we have to do is transform, or convert, the data from other observed normal distributions to the standardized normal curve. In other words, the standardized normal distribution is extremely valuable because we can translate, or transform, any normal variable, X, into the standardized value, Z. Exhibit 13.11 illustrates how either a skinny distribution or a fat distribution can be converted into the standardized normal distribution. This ability to transform normal variables has many pragmatic implications for the marketing researcher.

Standardized normal distribution

A purely theoretical probability distribution that reflects a specific normal curve for the standardized value, Z.

To the Point

"*To study the abnormal is the best way of understanding the normal.*"

—WILLIAM JAMES

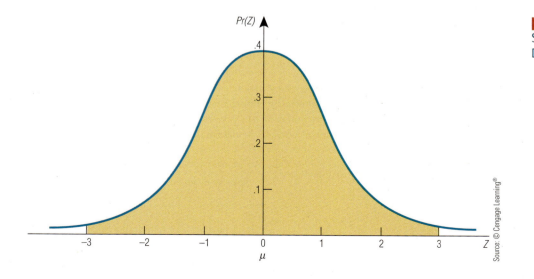

EXHIBIT **13-9**
Standardized Normal Distribution

EXHIBIT **13-10** Standardized Normal Table: Area under Half of the Normal Curve[a]

Z Standard Deviations from the Mean (Units)	Z Standard Deviations from the Mean (Tenths of Units)[a]									
	.0	.1	.2	.3	.4	.5	.6	.7	.8	.9
0.0	.000	.040	.080	.118	.155	.192	.226	.258	.288	.315
1.0	.341	.364	.385	.403	.419	.433	.445	.455	.464	.471
2.0	.477	.482	.486	.489	.492	.494	.495	.496	.497	.498
3.0	.499	.499	.499	.499	.499	.499	.499	.499	.499	.499

[a] Area under the segment of the normal curve extending (in one direction) from the mean to the point indicated by each row-column combination. For example, about 68 percent of normally distributed events can be expected to fall within 1.0 standard deviation on either side of the mean (0.341 × 2). An interval of almost 2.0 standard deviations around the mean will include 95 percent of all cases (.477 + .477).

EXHIBIT **13-11**

Standardized Values Can Be Computed from Flat or Peaked Distributions Resulting in a Standardized Normal Curve

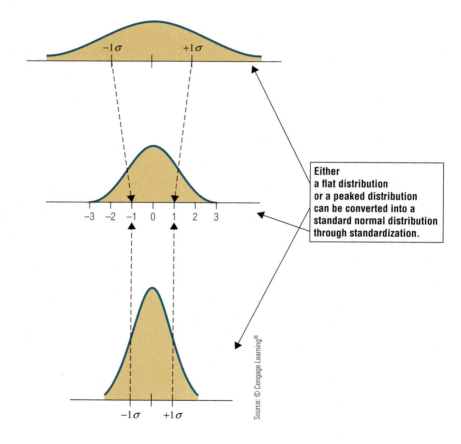

Either a flat distribution or a peaked distribution can be converted into a standard normal distribution through standardization.

Computing the standardized value, Z, of any measurement expressed in original units is simple: Subtract the mean from the value to be transformed, and divide by the standard deviation (all expressed in original units). The formula for this procedure and its verbal statement follow. In the formula, note that σ, the population standard deviation, is used for calculation.[5]

$$\text{Standardized value} = \frac{\text{Value to be transformed } - \text{ Mean}}{\text{Standard deviation}}$$

$$Z = \frac{X - \mu}{\sigma}$$

where

μ = hypothesized or expected value of the mean

Estimation of Parameters and Confidence Intervals

Apple, Samsung, and other marketers who introduce new products with much fanfare could rely on sampling and statistical estimation to prepare for the new product launch. Using past data, they can form expectations about when sales should peak. For instance, a new phone's sales may peak 30 days after its release. They know from data that by the end of the first month, X percent of all sales of this new product are realized. With this information, the company can tell within 5 percent how many units of this new product will be sold in total. Making a proper inference about population parameters is highly practical for a marketer that must have the inventory appropriate for a short selling season.

Suppose you are a product manager for Con-Agra Foods and you recently invited Facebook friends of Swiss Miss to test a reformulated Swiss Miss Healthy Green Cocoa Mix. As a result, 800 households participated in the Green Cocoa trial. After the trial, 80 percent of sample respondents said they would buy the product when available on retailer shelves. Among that 80 percent, 76 percent reported that they never previously tried a diet or low-calorie cocoa mix while 84 percent reported that they had previously tried such a product. How can you be sure there were no statistical errors in this estimate? How confident can you be that these figures approximate the actual population of cocoa mix consumers?

Point Estimates

Our goal in using statistics is to make an estimate about population parameters. A population mean, μ, and standard deviation, σ, are constant and typically unknown. Such is the case if we are evaluating advertising options and would like to know how much time married men aged 21–29 years spend using Twitter each week. The real population values are unknown so we need to guess them using a sample. As we have discussed, $\overline{X}$ and S are random variables that will vary from sample to sample with a certain probability (sampling) distribution. The Research Snapshot on the next page illustrates making estimates of what is normal.

Consider a practical example of a 24-hour fitness company considering the addition of racquetball to their facilities. The company needs an estimate of the average number of days customers participate in this sport each week. When statistical inference is needed, the population mean, μ, is a constant but unknown parameter. To estimate the average number of playing days, we could take a sample of 300 racquetball players throughout the area where our entrepreneur is thinking of building club facilities. If the sample mean, $\overline{X}$, equals 2.6 days per week, we might use this figure as a **point estimate**. This single value, 2.6, would be the best estimate of the population mean. However, we would be extremely lucky if the sample estimate were exactly the same as the population value. A less risky alternative would be to calculate a confidence interval.

Point estimate
An estimate of the population mean in the form of a single value, usually the sample mean.

Confidence Intervals

If we specify a range of numbers, or interval, within which the population mean should lie, we can be more confident that our inference is correct. A **confidence interval estimate** is based on the knowledge that $\mu = \overline{X} \pm$ an amount that matches sampling error. After calculating an interval estimate, we can determine how probable it is that the population mean will fall within this range of statistical values. In the racquetball project, the researcher, after setting up a confidence interval, would be able to make a statement such as, "With 95 percent confidence, I think that the average number of days played per week is between 2.3 and 2.9." This information can be used to estimate market demand because the researcher has a certain confidence that the interval contains the value of the true population mean.

The crux of the problem for a researcher is to determine how much random sampling error to tolerate. In other words, what should the confidence interval be? How much of a gamble

Confidence interval estimate
A specified range of numbers within which a population mean is expected to lie; an estimate of the population mean based on the knowledge that it will be equal to the sample mean plus or minus a small sampling error.

Are You Facebook Normal?

Are you normal? A quiz at www.blogthings.com will give you an answer to that question (a site that offers many quizzes where one can compare themselves with others and find things out about themselves—like what is your number? Or color?) It consists of twenty questions covering things like whether or not you change towels every day, whether you have closer to $40 or $100 on hand, whether you are comfortable using the bathroom with another person in the room, and so forth. Once the user finishes the quiz, the site provides him or her with a normal score by comparing the responses to the overall distribution of responses. Similarly, Facebook users can test how "normal" they are and compare their normalness to their Facebook friends. This Facebook app asks questions about how much you like your body, how you really feel about the people you know, and whether you think you are

mentally ill. Millions have responded to these questions and one's normalness is determined against that distribution. The author of this book scored 55 percent normal on blogthings but only 19 percent normal according to Facebook. I suppose that brings us back to test reliability!

Confidence level

A percentage or decimal value that tells how confident a researcher can be about being correct; it states the long-run percentage of confidence intervals that will include the true population mean.

should be taken that μ will be included in the range? Do we need to be 80 percent, 90 percent, or 99 percent sure? The **confidence level** is a percentage or decimal value that indicates the probability that the results will be correct. Traditionally, scientific researchers use a 95 percent confidence level. Although there is nothing magical about a 95 percent confidence level, we select this confidence level in our examples based on convention.

As mentioned, the point estimate gives no information about the possible magnitude of random sampling error. The confidence interval gives the estimated value of the population parameter, plus or minus an estimate of the error. We can express the idea of the confidence interval as follows:

$$\mu = \overline{X} \pm \text{a small sampling error}$$

More formally, assuming that the researchers select a large sample (more than thirty observations), the small sampling error is given by

$$\text{Small sampling error} = Z_{c.l.}\, S_{\overline{X}}$$

where

$Z_{c.l.}$ = value of Z, or standardized normal variable, at a specified confidence level (*c.l.*)

$S_{\overline{X}}$ = standard error of the mean

The precision of our estimate is indicated by the value of $Z_{c.l.}S_{\overline{X}}$. Let's start by finding the range of possible error, E, as follows:

$$E = Z_{c.l.}\, S_{\overline{X}}$$

Thus,

$$\mu = \overline{X} \pm E$$

where

$\overline{X}$ = sample mean (commonly pronounced X-bar)

E = range of sampling error

or

$$\mu = \overline{X} \pm Z_{c.l.}\, S_{\overline{X}}$$

The expression of "confidence" using $\pm E$ is stated as one-half of the total confidence interval. One-half of the interval is less than the mean and the other half is greater than the mean.

The following step-by-step procedure can be used to calculate confidence intervals:

1. Calculate $\overline{X}$ from the sample.
2. Assuming σ is unknown as is generally the case, estimate the population standard deviation by finding S, the sample standard deviation.
3. Estimate the standard error of the mean, using the following formula:

$$S_{\overline{X}} = \frac{S}{\sqrt{n}}$$

4. Determine the Z-value associated with the desired confidence level. Divide the confidence level by 2 to determine what percentage of the area under the curve to include on each side of the mean.
5. Calculate the confidence interval.

The following example shows how calculation of a confidence interval can be used in preparing a demographic profile, a useful tool for market segmentation. Suppose a client plans to open a sporting goods store in downtown Houston to cater to working women who play golf. In a survey of 100 women who work in downtown Houston, the research analyst hired by the client finds that the mean age $(\overline{X})$ in the sample is 37.5 years, with a standard deviation (S) of 12.0 years. Even though 37.5 years is the "expected value" and the best guess for the true mean age in the population (μ), the likelihood is that the mean is not exactly 37.5. Thus, a confidence interval around the sample mean provides useful intelligence to the client:

1. $\overline{X} = 37.5$ years
2. $S = 12.0$ years
3. Then, $S_{\overline{X}} = \dfrac{12.0}{\sqrt{100}} = 1.2$

4. Suppose you wish to be 95 percent confident—that is, assured that 95 times out of 100, the estimates from a sample of 100 would include the population parameter. Including 95 percent of the area requires that 47.5 percent (one-half of 95 percent) of the distribution on each side be included. From a Z-table (see Exhibit 13.10 or the full table available on the companion website), you find that 0.475 corresponds to the Z-value 1.96.
5. Substitute the values for $Z_{c.l.}$ and $S_{\overline{X}}$ into the confidence interval formula:

$$\mu = 37.5 \pm (1.96)(1.2)$$

$$= 37.5 \pm 2.35$$

You, the analyst, report back to the client that the μ is between the range from 35.2 to 39.9 years. Intervals constructed in this manner will contain the true value of μ 95 percent of the time.

Step 3 can be eliminated by entering S and n directly in the confidence interval formula:

$$\mu = \overline{X} \pm Z_{c.l.}\frac{S}{\sqrt{n}}$$

Remember that $S/\sqrt{n}$ represents the standard error of the mean, $S_{\overline{X}}$. Its use is based on the central-limit theorem.

If you wanted to increase the probability that the population mean will lie within the confidence interval, you could use the 99 percent confidence level, with a Z-value of 2.57. You may want to calculate the 99 percent confidence interval for the preceding example; you can expect that μ will be in the range between 34.4 and 40.6 years.

We have now examined the basic concepts of inferential statistics. You should understand that sample statistics such as the sample means, $\overline{X}$s, can provide good estimates of population parameters such as μ. You should also realize that there is a certain probability of being in error when you estimate a population parameter from sample statistics. In other words, there will be a random sampling error, which is the difference between the survey results and the results of surveying the entire population. If you have a firm understanding of these basic terms and ideas, which are the essence of statistics, the remaining statistics concepts will be relatively simple for you. The Research Snapshot shows how simple descriptive statistics can be used to contrast Walmart and Target shoppers.

Sample Size

When asked to evaluate a marketing research project, most people, even those with little marketing research training, begin by asking, "How big was the sample?" Intuitively we know that the larger the sample, the more accurate the research.

Random Error and Sample Size

Random sampling error varies with sample size. In statistical terms, increasing the sample size decreases the width of the confidence interval at a given confidence level. Our estimates become more precise. Following from above, we compute a confidence interval from sample statistics as

$$\text{Confidence interval} = \overline{X} \pm Z\frac{S}{\sqrt{n}}$$

One can easily see that the equation includes the sample size in the denominator that determines the error range (E):

$$E = Z\frac{S}{\sqrt{n}}$$

Thus, if n increases, E decreases.

Students familiar with the law of diminishing returns in economics will easily grasp the concept that increases in sample size reduce sampling error at a *decreasing rate*. For example, doubling a sample of 1,000 will reduce random sampling error by 1 percentage point, but doubling the sample from 2,000 to 4,000 will reduce random sampling error by only another half percentage point. More technically, random sampling error is inversely proportional to the square root of n. Thus, at some pointing, analysts find it inefficient to increase the sample further. Given the budget and the relative degree of imprecision that the decision-maker will tolerate, the marketing research analyst makes an informed decision on how big a sample will be used.

Factors in Determining Sample Size for Questions Involving Means

Three factors are required to specify sample size: (1) the variance, or heterogeneity, of the population; (2) the magnitude of acceptable error; and (3) the confidence level. Suppose a researcher wishes to find out whether nine-year-old boys are taller than seven-year-old boys. Intuitively we know that even with a very small sample size, we can obtain the correct information. This is based on the fact that the determination of sample size depends on the research question and the variability within the sample.

The *variance*, or *heterogeneity*, of the population is the first necessary bit of information. As introduced earlier in the chapter, we often use the *standard deviation* of the population to represent response heterogeneity. Only a small sample is required if the population is homogeneous. For example, predicting the average age of graduate business students requires a smaller sample than predicting the average age of people who visit the zoo. As *heterogeneity* increases, so must sample size. A pharmaceutical company testing the effectiveness of an acne medicine, for instance, should require a sample large enough to account for the varying range of skin types.

The *magnitude of error*, or the confidence interval, is the second necessary bit of information. Defined in statistical terms as E, the magnitude of error indicates how precise the estimate must be, or in other words, the *precision level*. From a managerial perspective, the importance of the decision

Target and Walmart Shoppers Really Are Different

Scarborough Research conducts ongoing consumer research about American consumer habits. The result is a sample including over 220,000 adults in eighty-one designated market areas used to estimate characteristics of the U.S. population. One motivation behind the research was the question: "How different are regular Walmart shoppers from regular Target shoppers?"

When survey respondents identified the stores in which they shop, 40 percent named both Target and Walmart. However, 31 percent shopped at Walmart but not Target and 12 percent shopped at Target but not Walmart. Target shoppers who shunned Walmart were more likely to shop at more upscale stores, including Macy's and Nordstrom. To a Target-only shopper, value is defined by style, selection, quality, and a pleasant experience. Walmart shoppers who stay away from Target were more likely to shop at discounters such as Dollar General and Kmart. Walmart shoppers define value in a utilitarian way by emphasizing price and one-stop shopping convenience. Digging a little deeper,

research suggests that not all Walmart shoppers are alike. Walmart recently tried adding more upscale brands hoping consumers would morph the image into something closer to Target. However, they soon cut back on this new strategy based on reduced sales from the core segment.

How accurately do you think the Scarborough sample captures these two stores segments?

Sources: Merrilees, B., and D. Miller (2010), "Brand Morphing Across Segments," *Journal of Business Research*, 63 (November), 1129–34 and Troy, M. (2011), "Loyalty on the Line as Wal-Mart Ads Tempt Target Shoppers," Retailtoday.com (April), accessed August 14, 2014.

to the well-being of the firm will probably influence the analyst's specifications of this range. If, for example, the acne medication tests favorably both in terms of user results and sales within a test-market sample, the firm may launch capital investments necessary to begin production of the medicine on a global scale. Given the resources involved should the firm commit to production, the tolerance in precision is likely very small and, as a result, so will the acceptable range of error. In other cases, the estimate need not be extremely precise. For example, knowing the household incomes of the acne medication users may not be so important a question particularly because the medication is available by prescription and will be covered by most insurance plans. Thus, the analysts may be happy with an error in estimated income of ±\$5,000 in total household income instead of $E = \pm\$500$. Seldom would a marketing researcher need more precision than ±\$1,000 in estimating a market segment's mean household income.

The third factor of concern is the *confidence level*. In our examples, we will typically use the 95 percent confidence level. This, however, is an arbitrary decision based on convention; there is nothing sacred about the 0.05 chance level (i.e., the probability of 0.05 of the true population parameter being incorrectly estimated). Exhibit 13.16 summarizes the information required to determine sample size. In fact, while basic researchers use 0.05 most often, applied marketing researchers more commonly are content with less precision.

Variable	Symbol	Typical Source of Information
Standard deviation	S	Pilot study or rule of thumb
Magnitude of error	E	Managerial judgment or calculation ($ZS_{\bar{x}}$)
Confidence level	$Z_{c.l.}$	Managerial judgment

Source: © Cengage Learning®

EXHIBIT 13-16
Statistical Information Needed to Determine Sample Size for Questions Involving Means

Estimating Sample Size for Questions Involving Means

Once the preceding concepts are understood, determining the actual size for a simple random sample is quite easy. The researcher must follow three steps:

1. Estimate the standard deviation of the population.
2. Make a judgment about the allowable magnitude of error.
3. Determine a confidence level.

The only problem is estimating the standard deviation of the population. Ideally, similar studies conducted in the past will give a basis for judging the standard deviation. In practice, researchers who lack prior information conduct a pilot study to estimate the population parameters so that another, larger sample of the appropriate sample size may be drawn. This procedure is called **sequential sampling** because researchers take an initial look at the pilot study results before deciding on a larger sample to provide more definitive results.

The first step involves estimating the standard deviation. A rule of thumb for estimating the value of the standard deviation is to expect it to be one-sixth of the range. If researchers conducting a study on tablet purchases expect the price paid to range from $100 to $700, a rule-of-thumb estimate for the standard deviation would be $100 ($600 × 1/6).

For the moment, assume that the standard deviation has been estimated in some preliminary work. If our concern is to estimate the mean of a particular population, the formula for sample size is

$$n = \left(\frac{ZS}{E}\right)^2$$

where

Z = standardized value that corresponds to the confidence level

S = sample standard deviation or estimate of the population standard deviation

E = acceptable error amount, plus or minus error factor (recall the range is one-half of the total confidence interval)[8]

Suppose a survey researcher studying annual expenditures on lipstick wishes to have a 95 percent confidence level ($Z = 1.96$) and a range of error (E) of less than $2. If the estimate of the standard deviation is $29 based on a pilot study, the required sample size is calculated as follows:

$$n = \left(\frac{ZS}{E}\right)^2 = \left(\frac{(1.96)(29)}{2}\right)^2 = \left(\frac{56.84}{2}\right)^2 = 28.42^2 = 808$$

On the other hand, if a range of error (E) of $4 is acceptable, the required sample size becomes much smaller:

$$n = \left(\frac{ZS}{E}\right)^2 = \left(\frac{(1.96)(29)}{4}\right)^2 = \left(\frac{56.84}{4}\right)^2 = 14.21^2 = 202$$

Thus, doubling the range of acceptable error reduces sample size requirements dramatically. Stated conversely in a general sense, doubling sample size will reduce error by only approximately one-quarter. Thus, the added precision from a larger sample may often not be worth the added costs.

Population Size and Required Sample Size

The Nielsen Company estimates television ratings. Throughout the years, is it possible to rate 100 million plus viewers with a sample of approximately 5,000 households? The answer to that question is that in most cases the size of the population does not have a major effect on the sample size. Even though the population is very large, a sample that comprises only a small portion of the population can be accurate. As suggested earlier, the variance of the population has a greater effect on sample size requirements than does the population size.

Sometimes, the population size may be small, such as Boeing or Airbus trying to make inferences about firms that might purchase a new airliner. When the population is relatively small, a finite correction factor is applied to adjust sample size requirements. Typically, an analyst applies this correction when the sample will represent more than 5 percent of a finite population. If the sample is large relative to the population, the foregoing procedures may overestimate the required sample size. The finite correction factor for small samples is

$$\sqrt{\frac{(N - n)}{(N - 1)}}$$

where

N = population size

n = sample size

Determining Sample Size for Proportions

Researchers frequently are concerned with determining sample size for problems that involve estimating population proportions or percentages. When the question involves the estimation of a proportion, the researcher requires some knowledge of the logic for determining a confidence interval around a sample proportion estimation (p) of the population proportion (π). For a confidence interval to be constructed around the sample proportion (p), an estimate of the standard error of the proportion (S_p) must be calculated and a confidence level specified.

The precision of the estimate is indicated by the value $Z_{c.l.} S_p$. Thus, the plus-or-minus estimate of the population proportion is

$$\text{Confidence interval} = p \pm Z_{c.l.} S_p$$

If the researcher selects a 95 percent probability for the confidence interval, $Z_{c.l.}$ will equal 1.96 (from Z-table). The formula for S_p is

$$S_p = \sqrt{\frac{pq}{n}} \text{ or } S_p = \sqrt{\frac{p(1 - p)}{n}}$$

where

S_p = estimate of the standard error of the proportion

p = proportion of successes

$q = 1 - p$, or proportion of failures

Suppose that 20 percent of a sample of 1,200 television viewers recall seeing an advertisement. The proportion of successes (p) equals 0.2, and the proportion of failures (q) equals 0.8. We estimate the 95 percent confidence interval as follows:

$$\text{Confidence Interval} = p \pm Z_{c.l.} S_p$$

$$= 0.2 \pm 1.96 S_p$$

$$= 0.2 \pm 1.96 \sqrt{\frac{p(1 - p)}{n}}$$

$$= 0.2 \pm 1.96 \sqrt{\frac{0.2(1 - 0.2)}{1.200}}$$

$$= 0.2 \pm 1.96 \sqrt{\frac{0.16}{1.200}}$$

$$= 0.2 \pm 1.96(0.0115)$$

$$= 0.2 \pm 0.023$$

Thus, the population proportion who see an advertisement is estimated to be included in the interval between 0.177 (0.2 − 0.023) and 0.223 (0.2 + 0.023), or roughly between 18 and 22 percent, with 95 percent confidence (95 out of 100 times).

Sample size for a proportion requires the researcher to make a judgment about confidence level and the maximum allowance for random sampling error. Furthermore, the size of the proportion influences random sampling error, so an estimate of the expected proportion of successes must be made, based on intuition or prior information. The formula is

$$n = \frac{Z_{c.l.}^2 \, pq}{E^2}$$

where

n = number of items in sample

$Z_{c.l.}^2$ = square of the confidence level in standard error units

p = estimated proportion of successes

$q = 1 - p$, or estimated proportion of failures

E^2 = square of the maximum allowance for error between the true proportion and the sample proportion, or $Z_{c.l.} \, S_p$ squared

Suppose a researcher believes that a simple random sample will show that 60 percent of the population (p) recognizes the name of an automobile dealership. The researcher wishes to estimate with 95 percent confidence ($Z_{c.l.}$ = 1.96) that the allowance for sampling error is not greater than 3.5 percentage points (E). Substituting these values into the formula gives

$$n = \frac{(1.96)^2 (0.6)(0.4)}{0.035^2}$$

$$= \frac{(3.8416)(0.24)}{0.001225}$$

$$= \frac{0.922}{0.001225}$$

$$= 753$$

Determining Sample Size on the Basis of Judgment

Just as sample units may be selected to suit the convenience or judgment of the researcher, sample size may also be determined on the basis of managerial judgments. Using a sample size similar to those used in previous studies provides the inexperienced researcher with a comparison with other researchers' judgments.

Another judgmental factor that affects the determination of sample size is the selection of the appropriate item, question, or characteristic to be used for the sample size calculations. Several different characteristics affect most studies, and the desired degree of precision may vary for these items. The researcher must exercise some judgment to determine which item will be used. Often the item that will produce the largest sample size will be used to determine the ultimate sample size. However, the cost of data collection becomes a major consideration, and judgment must be exercised regarding the importance of such information.

Another consideration stems from most researchers' need to analyze various subgroups within the sample. For example, suppose an analyst wishes to look at differences in retailers' attitudes by geographic region. The analyst will want to make sure to sample an adequate number of retailers in the New England, mid-Atlantic, and South Atlantic regions to ensure that subgroup comparisons are reliable. There is a judgmental rule of thumb for selecting minimum subgroup sample size.

Each subgroup to be separately analyzed should have a minimum of 100 units in each category of the major breakdowns. The total sample size is computed by totaling the sample sizes necessary for these subgroups.

Assess the Potential for Nonresponse Bias

Researchers must provide an assessment of generalizability in their reports. How much can we count on metrics derived analytically to truly represent the relevant population? As we see above, sample size and heterogeneity influence the generalizability assessment, as do the concepts of probability and nonprobability sampling from the previous chapter. Earlier, we introduced the notion of nonresponse bias. Nonresponse bias, in particular the bias caused when sample units provide no response, can significantly damage generalizability.

The reason that nonresponders must be considered routinely a threat to external validity is that there could be some systematic reason that members selected for inclusion from a sampling frame did not respond. People with very busy lives are less likely to respond to a survey request than people with a lot of time on their hands. People with very busy lives likely share other things in common. They likely work more hours, are more likely to be involved in family activities (be married and have children in the home), share commonalities in age and lifestyle, and so forth. Any systematic connection between sample unit characteristics and their likelihood to respond is a potential source for bias.

The concern for potential bias brings us back to the notion of response rates. Researchers worry particularly for the potential of bias when survey response rates are low. Given that response rates from randomly drawn probability samples are commonly less than 10 percent, the concern for bias exists practically all the time. In fact, though, a high response rate does not free the sample from nonresponse bias. Consider the case when a financial incentive encourages people to respond. In those cases, the respondents who most need or who are most sensitive to the incentive are more likely to respond. Again, a systematic influence creates the potential for bias.

A detailed treatment of the topic goes beyond the scope of this chapter. However, some basic procedures can be followed in an effort to increase confidence in the generalizability of the sample.[9] These pieces of advice complement the discussion of probability and nonprobability sampling from the previous chapter.

1. A well-managed sampling frame that contains accurate information on individual respondents provides the greatest potential for generalizability. A Nielsen panel provides an example of such a sampling frame.

2. **Auxiliary variables** provide a useful means of detecting potential systematic reasons for nonresponse (or conversely response). Auxiliary variables are those that the researcher should build into a survey that allow a comparison between sample units that do respond and those that do not respond. Auxiliary variables do not have to be involved in the research questions. For instance, a consumer panel manager should know basic demographic information and other factoids about every member of the panel. The best auxiliary variables are those known to correlate with survey participation or those that might influence dependent variables. For any project using a sample derived from the panel, the researcher can measure these same variables and then compare the known sampling frame values with the values of those who do respond as a way of indicating potential problems with generalizability. For instance, the following hypothetical values on auxiliary variables illustrate their use:

Auxiliary variables

Auxiliary variables are those that the researcher should build into a survey that allow a comparison between sample units that do respond and those that do not respond.

Auxiliary Variable	Known Value in Sampling Frame	Values Observed among Respondents
Percent female	50.5%	60.1%
Average time online daily	3.9 hours	4.2 hours
Political identification	31% Democrat/27% Republican/40% independent	38% Democrat/30% Republican/25% independent
Percent owning home	64%	52%

In this case, the data are not supporting generalizability. The values observed among sample respondents differ significantly on all but one auxiliary variable (average time online daily is about the same). Thus, the researcher would have to caution management against making strong inferences about the population from this sample. However, even when the sample response rate is low, if a number of auxiliary variables show correspondence, the researcher can express confidence in generalizability as the chance of something systematic causing non-response is not evident. The use of auxiliary variables further illustrates the advantage of using a probability sample taken from a well-managed sampling frame with known characteristics.

3.   A high response rate in and of itself does not guarantee freedom from bias.

4.   Post hoc sampling procedures can be employed, which adjust the contact of individuals in a way that tries to over–contact types of people that were not likely to respond to the initial sampling plan.

Although researchers often avoid the question of generalizability, particularly when the research employs convenience samples, it remains a critical question because the answer determines how well a sample represents a population.

TIPS OF THE TRADE

- Measures of central tendency provide overall summaries of the level to which some phenomenon exists on average. The appropriate central tendency statistic varies with the nature of the data.
  - The mean is the most commonly used measure of central tendency.
  - The median is more appropriate than the mean as a measure of central tendency when the data display extreme values or outliers.
  - The mode is appropriate when the data are less than interval.
- Sample size estimates often require some estimate of the standard deviation that will exist in the sample.
  - Larger samples allow predictions with greater precision that can be expressed over a smaller range.
  - Increases in precision usually require disproportionately large increases in sample size and bring about inefficiencies.

- The amount of risk involved in a decision determines how much precision is needed.
  - Greater precision means more resources are required.
  - The balance between precision and resources generally answers the sample size question.
  - Only the riskiest of decisions require very large samples (i.e., 1,000 or more).
  - Samples of 300 to 500 respondents can provide adequate results for most marketing decisions.
- Low response rates (under 10 percent) are common in marketing research.
  - Researchers should employ auxiliary variables to compare sample characteristics with the values known to exist in the relevant population.
  - A well-managed sampling frame provides the best tool to accomplish the check for nonresponse bias.

:: SUMMARY

1. Use basic descriptive statistics to analyze data and make basic inferences about population metrics. Calculating a mean and a standard deviation to "describe" or profile a sample is a commonly applied descriptive statistical approach. The term *metrics* is used almost interchangeably with the noun, statistics, but emphasizes the fact that values will be compared. Inferential statistics investigate samples to draw conclusions about entire populations. A frequency distribution shows how frequently each response or classification occurs. A simple tally count illustrates a frequency distribution. A proportion indicates the percentage of group members that have a particular characteristic. Three commonly applied measures of central tendency are the mean, median, and mode. For most samples, the mean, median, and mode produce different values. Measures of dispersion further describe a distribution. The range is the difference between the largest and smallest values observed. The most useful measures of dispersion are the variance and standard deviation.

2. Distinguish among the concepts of population, sample, and sampling distributions. The techniques of statistical inference are based on the relationship among the population distribution, the sample distribution, and the sampling distribution. The population distribution is a frequency distribution of the elements of a population. The sample distribution is a frequency distribution of a sample. A sampling distribution is a theoretical probability distribution of sample means for all possible samples of a certain size drawn from a particular population. The sampling distribution's mean is the expected value of the mean, which equals the population's mean. The standard deviation of the sampling distribution is the standard error of the mean, approximately equal to the standard deviation of the population, divided by the square root of the sample size.

3. Explain the central-limit theorem. The central-limit theorem states that as the sample size increases, the distribution of sample means of size *n*, randomly selected, approaches a normal distribution. This means that even if a distribution has a nonnormal distribution, the distribution of averages taken from samples of these numbers is normally distributed. This allows inferential statistics to be used. This theoretical knowledge can be used to estimate parameters and determine sample size.

4. Use confidence intervals to express inferences about population characteristics. Estimating a population mean with a single value gives a point estimate. The confidence interval estimate is a range of numbers within which the researcher is confident that the population mean will lie. The confidence level is a percentage that indicates the long-run probability that the confidence interval estimate will be correct. Many research problems involve the estimation of proportions. Statistical techniques may be used to determine a confidence interval around a sample proportion.

5. Understand the major issues in specifying sample size. The statistical determination of sample size requires knowledge of (1) the variance of the population, (2) the magnitude of acceptable error, and (3) the confidence level. Several computational formulas are available for determining sample size. Furthermore, a number of easy-to-use tables have been compiled to help researchers calculate sample size. The main reason a large sample size is desirable is that sample size is related to random sampling error. A smaller sample makes a larger error in estimates more likely.

6. Know how to assess the potential for nonresponse bias. Nonresponse bias causes problems because it means that the sampling units that participated are different from those that did not participate. Auxiliary variables are an important tool in assessing the potential for such bias. A well-managed sampling frame, which provides a probability sample, is a primary tool in dealing with nonresponse bias. The end goal is assessing the generalizability of the metrics observed in the sample.

:: KEY TERMS AND CONCEPTS

auxiliary variables, *385*
bottom-box score, *365*
central-limit theorem, *375*
confidence interval estimate, *377*
confidence level, *378*
frequency distribution, *363*
inferential statistics, *362*
mean, *365*
median, *366*

metrics, *362*
mode, *366*
normal distribution, *370*
percentage distribution, *363*
point estimate, *377*
population distribution, *373*
population parameters, *362*
probability, *364*
proportion, *364*

sample distribution, *373*
sample statistics, *362*
sampling distribution, *374*
sequential sampling, *382*
standard deviation, *366*
standard error of the mean, *374*
standardized normal distribution, *371*
top-box score, *364*
variance, *369*

:: QUESTIONS FOR REVIEW AND CRITICAL THINKING

1. What is the difference between descriptive and inferential statistics?
2. Define the analytical notion of metrics.
3. Suppose the speed limits in thirteen countries in miles per hour are as follows:

Country	Highway Miles per Hour
1. Italy	87
2. France	82
3. Hungary	75
4. Belgium	75
5. Portugal	75
6. Great Britain	70
7. Spain	62
8. Denmark	62
9. Netherlands	62
10. Greece	62
11. Japan	62
12. Norway	56
13. Turkey	56

What is the mean, median, and mode for these data? Feel free to use your computer (statistical software or spreadsheet) to get the answer. Which is the best measure of central tendency for this data?

4. Prepare a frequency distribution for the data in question 3.
5. Why is the standard deviation rather than the average deviation typically used?
6. Calculate the standard deviation for the data in question 3.
7. Draw three distributions that have the same mean value but different standard deviation values. Draw three distributions that have the same standard deviation value but different mean values.
8. A smartphone manufacturer surveyed 100 retail phone outlets in each of the firm's sales regions. An analyst noticed that in the South Atlantic region the average retail price was $165 (mean) and the standard deviation was $30. However, in the Mid-Atlantic region the mean price was $170, with a standard deviation of $15. What do these statistics tell us about these two sales regions?

9. A marketing analytics professional stated that "all information in data comes from variability." Do you agree? Why or why not?
10. What is the sampling distribution? How does it differ from the sample distribution?
11. What would happen to the sampling distribution of the mean if we increased the sample size from 5 to 25?
12. Suppose a fast-food restaurant wishes to estimate average sales volume for a new menu item. The restaurant has analyzed the sales of the item at a similar outlet and observed the following results:
    $\overline{X} = 500$ (mean daily sales)
    $S = 100$ (standard deviation of sample)
    $n = 25$ (sample size)
    The restaurant manager wants to know into what range the mean daily sales should fall 95 percent of the time. Perform this calculation.
13. In the example on page 382 of research on lipstick, where $E = \$2$ and $S = \$29$, what sample size would we require if we desired a 99 percent confidence level?
14. Suppose you are planning to sample cat owners to determine the average number of cans of cat food they purchase monthly. The following standards have been set: a confidence level of 99 percent and an error of less than 5 units. Past research has indicated that the standard deviation should be 6 units. What is the required sample size?
15. What is a standardized normal curve?
16. Using the formula in this chapter, a researcher determines that at the 95 percent confidence level, a sample of 2,500 is required to satisfy a client's requirements. The researcher actually uses a sample of 1,200, however, because the client has specified a budget cap for the survey. What are the ethical considerations in this situation?
17. Draw the distribution that should result from an honest roulette wheel. Draw the distribution from a dishonest roulette wheel.

Assuming samples of 500 spins were taken from each wheel, what would the distribution of sample means of 10 look like for each wheel?

18. A random number generator and other statistical information can be found at **http://www.random.org.** Flip some virtual coins. Perform twenty flips with an Aurelian coin. Perform twenty flips with a Constantius coin. Perform frequency tables for each result. What conclusion might you draw? Would the result change if you flipped the coins 200 times or 2,000 times?

19. What role do auxiliary variables play in inferential marketing statistics?

:: RESEARCH ACTIVITIES

1. Look up at least five academic journal articles (such as the *Journal of Business Research, Journal of the Academy of Marketing Science, Journal of Marketing, Journal of Personal Selling and Sales Management, Journal of Consumer Research*) in an area of interest to you that involve survey research. Do they all discuss the sample and sample size? From any description about the sample provided, can the reader make a judgment about what population the statistics generalize to (presuming inferential statistics are involved)?

2. Use an online library service to find basic business research studies that report a "response rate" or number of respondents compared to number of contacts. You may wish to consult journals, such as the *Journal of Business Research*, the *Journal of Marketing*, the *Journal of the Academy of Marketing Science*, or the *Journal of Personal Selling and Sales Management*. Find at least ten such studies. What is the average response rate across all of these studies? Do the resulting sample sizes seem adequate? Do the researchers mention whether or not the results generalize to some population? Write a brief report on your findings.

3. This activity would make a good in-class assignment. Assign each student a random number. Then, randomly select eight students and ask each a small number of survey questions such as (feel free to add a few of your own):
   a. What is your political affiliation?
   b. What is your religious affiliation?
   c. Do you park a car on campus?
   d. What is your major?
   e. How old are you in years?
   Now, assuming your instructor compiles results for the entire class, compare your results from your sample of eight to the class results. How well does your sample generalize to the entire class? Compare your results and then that of the entire class to data available from your university website on these questions (some of this should be available from institutional research at your school). How well do your sample eight and the sample that is your entire class generalize to the entire university? This illustrates the use of auxiliary variables.

Coastal Star Sales Corporation

Download the data sets for this case from **www .cengagebrain.com.** *or request them from your instructor.*

Coastal Star Sales Corporation is a West Coast wholesaler that markets leisure products from several manufacturers. Coastal Star has an eighty-person sales force that sells to wholesalers in a six-state area, which is divided into two sales regions. Case Exhibit 13.1–1 shows the names of a sample of eleven salespeople, some descriptive information about each person, and sales performance for each of the last two years.

Questions

1. Calculate a mean and a standard deviation for each variable.
2. Set a 95 percent confidence interval around the mean for each variable.
3. Calculate the median, mode, and range for each variable.
4. Organize the data for current sales into a frequency distribution with three classes: (a) under $500,000, (b) $500,000 to $999,999, and (c) $1,000,000 and over.
5. Organize the data for years of selling experience into a frequency distribution with two classes: (a) less than five years and (b) five or more years.
6. Convert the frequency distributions from question 5 to percentage distributions.

CASE EXHIBIT 13.1-1 Salesperson Data: Coastal Star Sales Corporation

Region	Salesperson	Age	Years of Experience	Sales Previous Year	Sales Current Year
Northern	Jackson	40	7	$ 412,744	$ 411,007
Northern	Gentry	60	12	1,491,024	1,726,630
Northern	La Forge	26	2	301,421	700,112
Northern	Miller	39	1	401,241	471,001
Northern	Mowen	64	5	448,160	449,261
Southern	Young	51	2	518,897	519,412
Southern	Fisk	34	1	846,222	713,333
Southern	Kincaid	62	10	1,527,124	2,009,041
Southern	Krieger	42	3	921,174	1,030,000
Southern	Manzer	64	5	463,399	422,798
Southern	Weiner	27	2	548,011	422,001

Source: © Cengage Learning®

Source: © Cengage Learning®

::::::: **PART FIVE**

Basic Data Analytics

© Nonstock/Jupiter Images

Dimitri Otis/Getty Images

⠿ Basic Data Analysis

LEARNING OUTCOMES

After studying this chapter, you should be able to:

1. Prepare qualitative data for interpretation or data analysis
2. Know what descriptive statistics are and why they are used
3. Create and interpret tabulation and cross-tabulation tables
4. Perform basic data transformations
5. Understand the basics of testing hypotheses using inferential statistics
6. Be able to use a p-value to make statistical inferences
7. Conduct a univariate *t*-test.

Chapter Vignette:

Don't Tell Me!

Most people think that the last thing businesses like to hear is a consumer complaint. However, a bigger problem may occur when consumers don't complain. Complaints can provide key data that allow businesses to improve the way they deal with customers. By improving service, the businesses keep more customers and become more profitable. Thus, when consumers truly have a problem, management should welcome complaints. From another perspective, a relatively large number of complaints indicates a potential problem with management. Thus, many businesses set specific targets for minimizing complaints. Realizing that some consumers are chronic complainers, most of these targets don't strive for perfection but settle on some reasonable number. For instance, a business may set a target of fewer than twenty-five complaints per week. Research is needed to help set the target and then assess firm performance against that standard.

Who complains the most? A recent study examined the demographics of the "complainer." Among 162 complainers in the sample (out of 237 consumers in total with 75 reporting no bad experiences in the last twelve months), the results reveal how many people in each group make up the "complainer":

Age	< 25	26–39	40–53	54 or more
Percentage	43.6	35.3	66.7	65.9

IS_ImageSource /iStockphoto.com

Does this mean that older people are more likely to complain? Does this mean that older consumers are better sources of marketing information or just chronic complainers that the firm may be better off without? Perhaps part of the answer lies in drawing meaning from basic statistics like these.[1]

Introduction

We now turn to research tools that allow researchers to make inferences beyond central tendency and dispersion. As researchers, we infer whether some condition exists in a population based on what we observe in a sample. Alternatively, the research could be more exploratory and the researcher could be using statistics simply to search for some pattern within the data. Basic marketing analytics like those discussed in this chapter, though elementary, can provide powerful insight into marketing decision-making.

Coding Qualitative Responses

Researchers often summarize and bring meaning to qualitative data by developing some type of logical coding scheme. The researcher sometimes uses interpretive software to assist in coding observations into categories. A researcher will even combine an interpretive approach with basic quantitative analyses to address a research question. Either way, some coding is necessary. Any mistakes in coding can dramatically change the conclusions. **Coding** represents the way a specific meaning is assigned to a response within previously edited data. Codes represent the meaning in data by assigning some measurement symbol to different categories of responses. This may be a number, letter, or word. The proper form of coding relates back to the level of scale measurement. Researchers code nominal data by using a word, letter, or any identifying mark. On the other hand, numbers typically are most appropriate for ordinal, interval, and ratio measures.

Thus, **codes** often, but not always, are numerical symbols. However, codes, more broadly speaking, are rules for interpreting, classifying, and recording data. In qualitative research, the codes are usually words or phrases that represent themes. In purely interpretive research, numbers are seldom used for codes. For example, a qualitative researcher may apply a code to a hermeneutic unit describing in detail a respondent's reactions to several different glasses of wine. After reading through the text several times, and applying a word-counting routine, the researcher realizes that appearance, the nose (aroma), and guessing (trying to guess what the wine will be like or what type of wine is in the glass) are important themes. A code is assigned to these categories. After considerable thought and questioning of the experience, the researcher builds a network, or grounded theory, that suggests how a wine may come to be associated with feelings of romance.

Coding
The process of assigning a numerical score or other character symbol to previously edited data.

Codes
Rules for interpreting, classifying, and recording data in the coding process; also, the actual numerical or other character symbols assigned to raw data.

Structured Qualitative Responses and Dummy Variables

Qualitative responses to structured questions, such as "yes" or "no," can be stored in a data file literally ("yes" or "no") or with letters such as "Y" or "N." Alternatively, they can be represented with numbers, one each to represent the respective category. Since this represents a nominal numbering system, the actual numbers used are arbitrary.

Even though the codes are numeric, the variable is classificatory. Any numbers assigned serve only to separate affirmative from negative responses. For statistical purposes the research may consider adopting **dummy coding** for dichotomous responses like "yes" or "no." Dummy coding assigns a 0 to one category and a 1 to the other. So, for yes/no responses, a 0 could be "no" and a 1 would be "yes." Similarly, a "1" could represent a female respondent and a "0" would be a male respondent. Dummy coding provides the researcher with more flexibility in how structured, qualitative responses are analyzed statistically. Dummy coding can be used when more than two categories exist, but because a dummy variable can only represent two categories, multiple dummy variables are needed to represent a single qualitative response that can take on more than two categories. In fact, the rule is that if k is the number of categories for a qualitative variable, $k - 1$ dummy variables are needed to represent the variable.

An alternative to dummy coding is **effects coding**. Effects coding is performed by assigning a $+1$ to one value of a dichotomous variable and a -1 to the other. Dummy coding is more widely used in general, although effects coding has some advantages in the way experimental results are presented. Either way is an acceptable technique for coding structured qualitative data. Both

Dummy coding
Numeric "1" or "0" coding where each number represents an alternate response such as "female" or "male."

Effects coding
An alternative to dummy coding using the values of -1 and $+1$ to represent two categories of responses.

Source: www.qualtrics.com

dummy and effects coding represent qualitative phenomena in a way that facilitates basic data analysis.

Class coding is another approach that can be used if the data are not going to be directly used to perform computations. **Class coding** assigns numbers to categories in an arbitrary way merely as a means of identifying some characteristic. If packages come in three colors, the class codes may be 1 for blue, 2 for red, and 3 for green. This coding works for representing treatment conditions in experimental variables.

Class coding

Coding that assigns numbers to categories in an arbitrary way merely as a means of identifying some characteristic.

The Nature of Descriptive Analysis

Descriptive analysis

The elementary transformation of raw data in a way that describes the basic characteristics such as central tendency, distribution, and variability.

Perhaps the most basic statistical analysis is descriptive analysis. **Descriptive analysis** is the elementary transformation of data in a way that describes the basic characteristics such as central tendency, distribution, and variability. A researcher takes responses from 1,000 American consumers and tabulates their favorite soft drink brand and the price they expect to pay for a six-pack of that product. The mode for favorite soft drink and the average price across all 1,000 consumers would be descriptive statistics that describe central tendency in two different ways. Averages, medians, modes, variance, range, and standard deviation typify widely applied descriptive statistics.

Descriptive statistics can summarize responses from large numbers of respondents in a few simple statistics. When a sample is used, the sample descriptive statistics are used to make inferences about characteristics of the entire population of interest. The researcher examining descriptive statistics for any one particular variable is using univariate statistics. Because they are so simple, descriptive statistics are used very widely.

In Chapter 10, we learned that the level of scale measurement can help the researcher choose the most appropriate statistical tool. Exhibit 14.1 shows the specific descriptive statistic appropriate for each level of measurement. Also, remember that all statistics appropriate for lower-order scales (nominal is the lowest) are suitable for higher-order scales (ratio is the highest). So, a frequency table could also be used for interval or ratio data. Frequencies can be represented graphically as shown and are a good way of visually depicting typical survey results.

Consider the following data. Sample consumers were asked where they most often purchased beer. The result is a nominal variable that can be described with a frequency distribution (see the bar chart in Exhibit 14.1). Ten percent indicated they most often purchased beer in a drug store, 45 percent indicated a convenience store, 35 percent indicated a grocery store, and 7 percent indicated a specialty store. Three percent listed "other" (not shown in the bar chart). The mode is convenience store since more respondents chose this than any other category. A similar distribution may have been obtained if the chart plotted the number of respondents ranking each store as their favorite type of place to purchase beer.

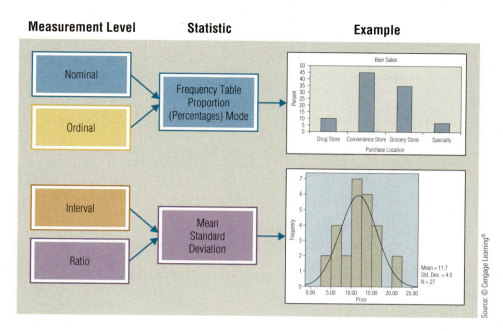

Source: © Cengage Learning®

EXHIBIT 14.1
Levels of Scale Measurement and Suggested Descriptive Statistics

The bottom part of Exhibit 14.1 displays example descriptive statistics for interval and ratio variables. In this case, the chart displays results of a question asking respondents how much they typically spend on a bottle of wine purchased in a store. The mean and standard deviation are displayed beside the chart as 11.7 and 4.5, respectively. Additionally, the frequency distribution is shown with a histogram. A **histogram** is a graphical way of showing the frequency distribution in which the height of a bar corresponds to the frequency of a category. Histograms are useful for any type of data, but with continuous variables (interval or ratio) the histogram is useful for providing a quick assessment of the distribution of the data. A normal distribution line is superimposed over the histogram providing an easy comparison to see if the data are skewed or multimodal.

Histogram

A graphical way of showing a frequency distribution in which the height of a bar corresponds to the observed frequency of the category.

Creating and Interpreting Tabulation

Tabulation refers to the orderly arrangement of data in a table or other summary format. When this tabulation process is done by hand the term *tallying* is used. Counting the different ways respondents answered a question and arranging them in a simple tabular form yields a **frequency table**. The actual number of responses to each category is a variable's frequency distribution. A simple tabulation of this type is sometimes called a *marginal tabulation*.

Tabulation tells the researcher how frequently each response occurs. This starting point for analysis requires the researcher to count responses or observations for each category or code assigned to a variable. A frequency table showing where consumers generally purchase beer can be computed easily. The tabular results that correspond to the chart would appear as follows:

Tabulation

The orderly arrangement of data in a table or other summary format showing the number of responses to each response category; tallying.

Frequency table

A table showing the different ways respondents answered a question.

Response	Frequency	Percent	Cumulative Percentage
Drug store	50	10	10
Convenience store	225	45	55
Grocery store	175	35	90
Specialty	35	7	97
Other	15	3	100

The frequency column shows the tally result or the number of respondents listing each store, respectively. The percent column shows the total percentage in each category. The cumulative percentage shows the percentage indicating either a particular category or any preceding category as their preferred place to purchase beer. From this chart, the mode indicates that the typical consumer buys beer at the convenience store since more people indicate convenience store as the place where they usually buy beer than any other category.

Similarly, Americans' responses to the simple question of "Who is your favorite movie star?" were recently tabulated. Overall, Tom Hanks, Denzel Washington, Jennifer Lawrence, Julia Roberts, and Sandra Bullock were the top five based on frequency of being mentioned as the favorite among 2,300 respondents.[2] However, the response varied by generation. For respondents aged 18−36 (Echo Boomers), Jennifer Lawrence was the favorite. For respondents aged 37−48 (Gen X), Tom Hanks ranked first as was also the case for Boomers (49−67), while John Wayne led the pack among the Matures (68+). The idea that generation may influence choice of favorite movie star brings us to cross-tabulation.

Who is your favorite movie star? Does your choice agree with others of your generation?

Cross-Tabulation

Cross-tabulation

The appropriate technique for addressing research questions involving relationships among multiple less-than interval variables; results in a combined frequency table displaying one variable in rows and another in columns.

A frequency distribution or tabulation can address many research questions. As long as a question deals with only one categorical variable, tabulation is the best approach to communicate the result. Although frequency counts, percentage distributions, and averages summarize considerable information, simple tabulation may not yield the full value of the research when multiple variables are involved. **Cross-tabulation** is generally a more appropriate technique for addressing research questions involving relationships among multiple less-than interval variables. A cross-tabulation is a combined frequency table. Cross-tabulation allows the inspection and comparison of differences among groups based on nominal or ordinal categories. One key to interpreting a cross-tabulation table is comparing the observed table values with hypothetical values that would result from pure chance.

Exhibit 14.2 summarizes cross-tabulations from consumers' responses to different ways of obtaining music in the United States.[3] The study contrasts a questionable method of obtaining music online (downloading from an illegal file sharing site) by a basic demographic variable—generation. A sample of 214 consumers of varying ages provides the data. When given a choice between obtaining a music file via the Internet, 166 of the 214 would choose to purchase it legally from a site like iTunes while 48 would obtain it free even if the download were illegal. The cross-tabulation comes by looking at how generation membership (a less-than interval variable) influences choice of methods to obtain the music. Exhibit 14.2 breaks down the results and suggests that the echo boomer generation displays a preference toward obtaining the music illegally (35 of 53) while older generations tend toward purchasing the music rather than downloading illicitly.

Contingency table

A data matrix that displays the frequency of some combination of possible responses to multiple variables; cross-tabulation results.

Contingency Tables

Exhibit 14.3 shows an example of cross-tabulation results using contingency tables. A **contingency table** is a data matrix that displays the frequency of some combination of possible responses to

EXHIBIT 14.2
Cross-Tabulation from Consumer Ethics Survey

Generation	Purchase	Download	Total
Echo Boomer	18	35	53
Gen X	41	12	53
Boomer	54	1	55
Mature	53	0	53
	166	48	214

Source: © Cengage Learning®

(A) Cross-Tabulation of Question "Do you shop at Target?" by Sex of Respondent

	Yes	No	Total
Men	150	75	225
Women	180	45	225
Total	330	120	450

(B) Percentage Cross-Tabulation of Question "Do you shop at Target?" by Sex of Respondent, Row Percentage

	Yes	No	Total (Base)
Men	66.7%	33.3%	100% (225)
Women	80.0%	20.0%	100% (225)

(C) Percentage Cross-Tabulation of Question "Do you shop at Target?" by Sex of Respondent, Column Percentage

	Yes	No
Men	45.5%	62.5%
Women	54.5%	37.5%
Total	100%	100%
(Base)	(330)	(120)

Source: © Cengage Learning®

EXHIBIT **14.3**

Different Ways of Depicting the Cross-Tabulation of Biological Sex and Target Patronage

multiple variables. Two-way contingency tables, meaning they involve two less–than interval variables, are used most often. A three-way contingency table involves three less–than interval variables. Beyond three variables, contingency tables become difficult to analyze and explain easily.

Two variables are depicted in the contingency table shown in panel A:

■ Row Variable: Biological Sex ___Male ___Female
■ Column Variable: "Do you shop at Target? YES or NO"

Several conclusions can be drawn initially by examining the row and column totals:

1. 225 men and 225 women responded as can be seen in the Total column. This means that altogether 450 consumers responded.
2. Out of this 450 total consumers, 330 consumers indicated that "yes" they do shop at Target and 120 indicated "no," they do not shop at Target. This can be observed in the column totals at the bottom of the table. These row and column totals often are called **marginals** because they appear in the table's margins.

Researchers usually are more interested in the inner cells of a contingency table. The inner cells display conditional frequencies (combinations). Using these values, we can draw some more specific conclusions:

3. Out of 330 consumers who shop at Target, 150 are male and 180 are female.
4. Alternatively, out of the 120 respondents not shopping at Target, 75 are male and 45 are female.

This finding helps us know whether the two variables are related. If men and women equally patronize Target, we would expect that hypothetically, 165 of the 330 shoppers would be male and 165 would be female. Clearly, these hypothetical expectations (165 male/165 female) are not

Marginals

Row and column totals in a contingency table, which are shown in its margins.

observed. What is the implication? A relationship exists between respondent sex and shopping choice. Specifically, Target shoppers are more likely to be female than male. Notice that the same meaning could be drawn by analyzing non-Target shoppers.

A two-way contingency table like the one shown in part A is referred to as a *2 × 2 table* because it has two rows (Men and Women) and two columns (Yes and No). Each variable has two levels. A two-way contingency table displaying two variables, one (the row variable) with three levels and the other with four levels, would be referred to as a *3 × 4 table*. Any cross-tabulation table may be classified according to the number of rows by the number of columns (*R* by *C*).

Percentage Cross-Tabulations

Statistical base

The number of respondents or observations (in a row or column) used as a basis for computing percentages.

When data from a survey are cross-tabulated, percentages help the researcher understand the nature of the relationship by making relative comparisons simpler. The total number of respondents or observations may be used as a **statistical base** for computing the percentage in each cell. When the objective of the research is to identify a relationship between answers to two questions (or two variables), one of the questions is commonly chosen to be the source of the base for determining percentages. For example, look at the data in parts A, B, and C of Exhibit 14.3. Compare part B with part C. Selecting either the row percentages or the column percentages will emphasize a particular comparison or distribution. The nature of the problem the researcher wishes to answer will determine which marginal total will serve as a base for computing percentages.

Elaboration and Refinement

The *Oxford Universal Dictionary* defines *analysis* as "the resolution of anything complex into its simplest elements." Once a researcher has examined the basic relationship between two variables, he or she may wish to investigate this relationship under a variety of different conditions. Typically, a third variable is introduced into the analysis to elaborate and refine the researcher's understanding by specifying the conditions under which the relationship between the first two variables is strongest and weakest. In other words, a more elaborate analysis asks, "Will interpretation of the relationship be modified if other variables are simultaneously considered?"

Elaboration analysis

An analysis of the basic cross-tabulation for each level of a variable not previously considered, such as subgroups of the sample.

Elaboration analysis involves the basic cross-tabulation within various subgroups of the sample. The researcher breaks down the analysis for each level of another variable. If the researcher has cross-tabulated shopping preference by sex (see Exhibit 14.3) and wishes to investigate another variable (say, marital status), a more elaborate analysis may be conducted. Exhibit 14.4 breaks down the responses to the question "Do you shop at Target?" by sex and marital status. The data show women display the same preference whether married or single. However, married men are much more likely to shop at Target than are single men. The analysis suggests that the original conclusion about the relationship between sex and shopping behavior for women be retained. However, a relationship that was not discernible in the two-variable case is evident. Married men more frequently shop at Target than do single men.

The finding is consistent with an interaction effect. The combination of the two variables, sex and marital status, is associated with differences in the dependent variable. Interactions between variables examine moderating variables. A **moderator variable** is a third variable that changes the nature of a relationship between the original independent and dependent variables. Marital status is a moderator variable in this case. The interaction effect suggests that marriage changes the relationship between sex and shopping preference.

Moderator variable

A third variable that changes the nature of a relationship between the original independent and dependent variables.

EXHIBIT 14.4

Cross-Tabulation of Marital Status, Sex, and Responses to the Question "Do You Shop at Target?"

	Single		Married	
	Men	Women	Men	Women
"Do you shop at Target?"				
Yes	55%	80%	86%	80%
No	45%	20%	14%	20%

Source: © Cengage Learning®

In other situations, the addition of a third variable to the analysis may lead us to reject the original conclusion about the relationship. When this occurs, the elaboration analysis suggests the relationship between the original variables is spurious.

How Many Cross-Tabulations?

Surveys may ask dozens of questions and hundreds of categorical variables can be stored in a data warehouse. Computer-assisted marketing researchers can "fish" for relationships by cross-tabulating every categorical variable with every other categorical variable. Thus, every possible response becomes a possible explanatory variable. A researcher addressing an exploratory research question may find some benefit in such a fishing expedition. Marketing analytics software exists that automatically searches through volumes of cross-tabulations looking for relationships. These results may provide some insight into the market segment structure for some product. Alternatively, the program may flag the cross-tabulations suggesting the strongest relationship. CHAID (chi-square automatic interaction detection) software exemplifies software that makes searches through large numbers of variables possible. Data-mining can be conducted with CHAID or similar techniques and may suggest useful relationships. A recent application paired promotion types against the type of product and suggests that coupons work best in getting consumers to come to your restaurant but television advertising works best in selling automobiles.[4] Although marketing analytics that mines data for information that may predict sales sounds complicated, cross-tabulation provides a basis for many of the search routines.

Outside of exploratory research, researchers should conduct cross-tabulations that address specific research questions or hypotheses. When hypotheses involve relationships among two categorical variables, cross-tabulations are the right tool for the job. However, as the number of categorical variables becomes greater, depicting the results in a table shown in a report or presentation becomes difficult and complicated to interpret. Therefore, as the number of variables moves beyond three, analysts may not depict them in a report.

Data Transformation

Simple Transformations

Data transformation (also called **data conversion**) is the process of changing the data format from the original form into a format more amenable to analytics appropriate for achieving the given research objectives. Researchers often recode the raw responses into modified or new variables. For example, many researchers believe that less response bias will result if interviewers ask respondents for their year of birth rather than their age. This presents no problem for the research analyst because a simple data transformation is possible. The raw data coded as birth year can easily be transformed to age by subtracting the birth year from the current year. In fact, some software automatically records dates in formats such as the amount of time since the arrival of January 1, 1900, or the arrival of January 1, 1980, considered the birth date of the PC age. The analyst may find it helpful to transform these into more user friendly formats.

In earlier chapters, we discussed recoding and creating summated scales. Reverse coding and the creation of composite scales represent common data transformations.

Collapsing or combining adjacent categories of a variable is a common form of data transformation used to reduce the number of categories. A Likert scale may sometimes be collapsed into a smaller number of categories. For instance, consider the following Likert item administered to a sample of state university seniors:

Data transformation

Process of changing the data from their original form to a format suitable for performing a data analysis addressing research objectives.

To the Point

"*All that we do is done with an eye to something else.*"

—ARISTOTLE

	Strongly Disagree	Disagree	Neutral	Agree	Strongly Agree
I am satisfied with my college experience at this university	☐	☐	☐	☐	☐

The following frequency table describes results for this survey item:

Strongly Disagree	Disagree	Neutral	Agree	Strongly Agree
110	30	15	35	210

The distribution is bimodal because two peaks exist in the distribution, one at either end of the scale. Since the vast majority of respondents (80 percent = (110 + 210)/400) indicate either strongly disagree or strongly agree, the variable responses act a lot like a categorical variable. Customers either strongly disagreed or strongly agreed with the statement. So, the researcher may wish to collapse the responses into two categories. While multiple ways exist to accomplish this, the researcher may assign the value 0 to all respondents who either strongly disagreed or disagreed and the value 1 to all respondents who either agreed or strongly agreed. Respondents marking neutral would be excluded from analysis.

Perhaps the 110 dissatisfied students differ in some important way from the 210. Perhaps their exam scores are also bimodal. Exhibit 14.5 shows an example of a bimodal distribution. Here, 125 students scored 45 and 125 scored 95. Only 100 students made some score between these values. Thus, the mean or mode would be a misleading indicator of expected values with a true bimodal distribution.

Problems with Data Transformations

Median split

Dividing a data set into two categories by placing respondents below the median in one category and respondents above the median in another.

Researchers often perform a median split to collapse a scale with multiple response points into two categories. The **median split** means respondents below the observed median go into one category and respondents above the median go into another. Although this is common, the approach is best applied only when the data do indeed exhibit bimodal characteristics. When the data are unimodal, such as would be the case with normally distributed data, a median split will lead to error.

Exhibit 14.6 illustrates this problem. Clearly, most respondents either slightly agree or slightly disagree with this statement. The central tendency could be represented by the median of 3.5, a mean of 3.5, or the mode of 3.5 (3 and 4 each have the same number of responses so the mode is set between the two). The "outliers," if any, appear to be those not indicating something other

EXHIBIT **14.5**
Bimodal Distributions Are Consistent with Transformations into Categorical Values

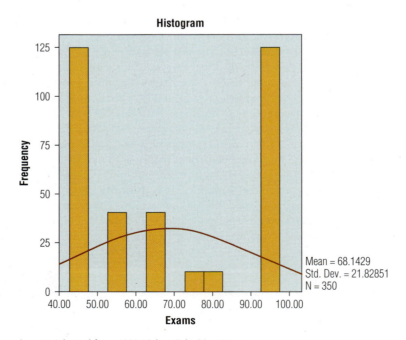

Source: Adapted from 1987 Nielsen Television Report.

EXHIBIT **14.6**
The Problem with Median Splits with Unimodal Data

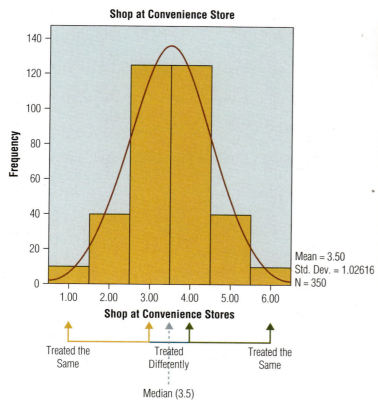

Shop at Convenience Store

Mean = 3.50
Std. Dev. = 1.02616
N = 350

Frequency Distribution: X1 = I Do Most of My Shopping at Convenience stores.		
Response Category (Code)	Counts	Cumulative Percentage
Strongly Disagree (1)	10	2.86%
Disagree (2)	40	14.29%
Slightly Disagree (3)	125	50.00%
Slightly Agree (4)	125	85.71%
Agree (5)	40	97.14%
Strongly Agree (6)	10	100.00%

Median = 3.5

Recode to Complete Data Transformation:

Old Values	1	2	3	4	5	6
New Values	1	1	1	2	2	2

Source: © Cengage Learning®

than slight agreement or slight disagreement. In all likelihood, the respondents indicating slight disagreement are more similar to those indicating slight agreement than they are to those respondents indicating strong disagreement. Yet, the recode places values 1 and 3 in the same new category, but places values 3 and 4 in a different category (see the recoding scheme in Exhibit 14.6). The distribution does not support a median split into two categories and so a transformation collapsing these values into agreement and disagreement is inappropriate.

When a sufficient number of responses exist and a variable is ratio, the researcher may choose to delete one-fourth to one-third of the responses around the median to effectively ensure a bimodal distribution. This helps to mitigate the logical inconsistency illustrated in Exhibit 14.6. Median splits should always be performed only with great care and with adequate justification, though, as the inappropriate collapsing of continuous variables into categorical variables ignores the information contained within the untransformed values. Justification for a median split commonly is found in the ability to apply a more parsimonious statistical approach than would be possible using the raw data values.

Index Numbers

The consumer price index and wholesale price index are secondary data sources that are frequently used by marketing researchers. Price indexes, like other **index numbers**, represent simple data transformations that allow researchers to track a variable's value over time and compare a variable(s) with other variables. Recalibration allows scores or observations to be related to a certain base period or base number.

For instance, if the data are time-related, a base year is chosen. The index numbers are then computed by dividing each year's activity by the base-year activity and multiplying by 100. Index

Index numbers

Scores or observations recalibrated to indicate how they relate to a base number.

RESEARCH SNAPSHOT

Wine Index Can Help Retailers

Indexes can be very useful, and researchers are sometimes asked to create index values from secondary data.

How much wine do consumers in different countries consume? Some standard of comparison would be helpful in assessing this question. Using 1968 U.S. wine consumption as a standard (just over 4 liters/person), the current wine consumption index for the following countries is as shown here:

Country	Index
Israel	0.25
South Africa	1.78
U.S.A.	2.59
U.K.	5.01
France	11.26
Luxembourg	12.12
Vatican City	15.36

Consumers in the United States, according to these statistics, drink just over 2½ times as much wine per capita as they did in 1968. That's a lot more than the typical Israeli consumer who on average drinks only a quarter as much today as the typical American consumer did in 1968 (1.0 liter/year). In contrast, Vatican City has the highest per capita wine consumption at 62.2 liters/year per capita for an index of 15.4. Although many may think of French consumers as drinking the most wine, they trail several countries, including Vatican City and Luxembourg, with an index of 11.3.

Consumption statistics are helpful in making decisions about the amount of space and attention given to wine across retail space in different countries. Although these statistics may point to a country like Luxembourg or France as a more attractive market for wine than the United States, if one considers the consumption data in the form of gross consumption per year rather than per capita consumption per year, this view may seem incorrect. The United States overall is the world's largest consumer market for wine at a total consumption of 2.9 billion liters per year compared to France, coming in at second place at 2.8 billion liters per year, and Vatican City at 52,000 liters per year. Clearly, you can see the form in which the analysts present the data can lead to different conclusions.

Sources: Per capita consumption figures derived from The Wine Institute, http://www.wineinstitute.org/, accessed September 3, 2014.

numbers require ratio measurement scales. Marketing managers may often chart consumption in some category over time. Grocers may wish to chart the U.S. wine consumption index. Using 1968 as a base year (4.05 liters per year), the 2014 U.S. wine consumption index is about 2.6, meaning that the typical American consumer drinks 10.5 liters of wine per year (see the Research Snapshot).[5]

Tabular and Graphic Methods of Displaying Data

Tables, graphs, and charts may simplify and clarify data. Graphical representations of data may take a number of forms, ranging from a computer printout to an elaborate pictograph. Tables, graphs, and charts, however, all facilitate summarization and communication. For example, see how the simple frequency table and histogram shown in Exhibit 14.6 provide a summary that quickly and easily communicates meaning that would be more difficult to see if all 350 responses were viewed separately.

Today's researcher has many convenient tools to quickly produce charts, graphs, or tables. Even basic word processing programs include chart functions that can construct the chart within the text document. Bar charts (histograms), pie charts, curve/line diagrams, and scatter plots are among the most widely used tools. Some choices match well with certain types of data and analyses.

To the Point

"The thing to do is to supply light."

—WOODROW WILSON

Hypothesis Testing Using Basic Statistics

Descriptive research and causal research designs often climax with hypotheses tests. Generally, hypotheses should be stated in concrete fashion so that the method of empirical testing seems almost obvious.

Empirical testing typically involves inferential statistics. This means that an inference can be made about some population based on observations of a sample representing that population. Statistical analysis can be divided into several groups based on how many variables are involved:

- **Univariate statistical analysis** tests hypotheses involving only one variable.
- **Bivariate statistical analysis** tests hypotheses involving two variables.
- **Multivariate statistical analysis** tests hypotheses and models involving multiple (three or more) variables or sets of variables and potentially involving multiple equations.

For now, the focus is on univariate statistics. Thus, we examine statistical tests appropriate for drawing inferences about a single variable.

Hypothesis Testing Procedure

Hypotheses are tested by comparing an educated guess with empirical reality. The process can be described as follows:

- First, the hypothesis is derived from the research objectives. The hypothesis should be stated as specifically as possible and should be theoretically sound.
- Next, a sample is obtained and the relevant variables are measured. In univariate tests, only one variable is of interest.
- The measured value obtained in the sample is compared to the value either stated explicitly or implied in the hypothesis. If the value is consistent with the hypothesis, the hypothesis is supported. If the value is not consistent with the hypothesis, the hypothesis is not supported.

An example univariate hypothesis is illustrated here:

H1: The average number of children per family in zip code 70360 is greater than 1.5.

If a sample is drawn from this zip code and the average number of children per family is 0.075, the hypothesis is not supported. If the average number of children is 3.3, the result supports the hypothesis. As the mean becomes smaller than 3.3 and approaches the theoretical expected value of 1.5, the chance becomes smaller that the data support the stated hypothesis. The exact point where the hypothesis changes from not being supported to being supported depends on how much risk the researcher is willing to accept and on the variability of the measure.

Typical univariate hypotheses set up a comparison of some observed sample mean against a benchmark value. The test addresses the question, "Is the sample mean truly different from the benchmark?" But, how different is really different? If the observed sample mean is 1.55 and the benchmark is 1.50, would the hypothesis still be supported? Probably not! When the observed mean is so close to the benchmark, we do not have sufficient confidence that a second set of data using a new sample taken from the same population might not produce a finding conflicting with the benchmark. In contrast, when the mean turns out well above 1.50, perhaps 3.3, then we could more easily trust that another sample would not produce a mean equal to or less than 1.50.

While the terminology of null and alternative hypotheses is common in statistical theory, it is also commonly confusing. Therefore, we'll avoid using the term *null hypothesis* when at all possible. Students usually understand hypothesis testing more easily by focusing on what the findings should look like if the proposed hypothesis is true. If the hypothesis mentioned earlier is true, an observed sample's mean should be noticeably greater than 1.50. We test to see if this idea can be supported by the empirical evidence. A statistical test's significance level or p-value becomes a key indicator of whether or not a hypothesis can be supported.

Univariate statistical analysis

Tests of hypotheses involving only one variable.

Bivariate statistical analysis

Tests of hypotheses involving two variables.

Multivariate statistical analysis

Statistical analysis involving three or more variables or sets of variables or even multiple equations.

Significance Levels and p-values

Significance level

A critical probability associated with a statistical hypothesis test that indicates how likely an inference supporting a difference between an observed value and some statistical expectation is true. The acceptable level of Type I error.

A **significance level** is a critical probability associated with a statistical hypothesis test that indicates how likely it is that an inference supporting a difference between an observed value and some statistical expectation is true. The term **p-value** stands for probability value and is essentially another name for an *observed* or *computed* significance level. Exhibit 14.7 discusses interpretations of p-values for different kinds of statistical tests. The probability in a p-value is that the statistical expectation (null) for a given test is true. So, low p-values mean there is little likelihood that the statistical expectation is true. This means the researcher's hypothesis positing (suggesting) a difference between an observed mean and a population mean, or between an observed frequency and a population frequency, or for a relationship between two variables, is likely supported.

p-value

Probability value, or the observed or computed significance level; p-values are compared to significance levels to test hypotheses.

Traditionally, researchers have specified an acceptable significance level for a test prior to the analysis. Later, we will discuss this as an acceptable amount of Type I error. Most typically, researchers set the acceptable amount of error, and therefore the acceptable significance level, at 0.1, 0.05, or 0.01. If the p-value resulting from a statistical test is less than the prespecified significance level, the results support a hypothesis implying differences. To illustrate, if an analyst is comparing sales in two districts and sets the acceptable Type I error at 0.1 and the p-value resulting from the test is 0.03, then the results support a hypothesis suggesting differences in sales in the two districts.

Type I and Type II Errors

Hypothesis testing using sample observations is based on probability theory. We make an observation of a sample and use it to infer the probability that some observation is true within the population the sample represents. Because we cannot make any statement about a sample with complete certainty, there is always a chance that an error will be made. When a researcher makes the observation using a census, meaning that every unit (person or object) in a population is measured, then conclusions are certain. Researchers very rarely use a census, though, and thus, they are susceptible to two types of inferential errors (see Research Snapshot on page 405).

EXHIBIT 14.7
p-Values and Statistical Tests

Test Description	Test Statistic	
Compare an Observed Mean with Some Predetermined Value	Z or t-test—Low p-Values Indicate the Observed Mean Is Different Than Some Predetermined Value (Often 0)	$\alpha = .025$ $\alpha = .025$ $m = 3.0$ $\overline{X}$
Compare an Observed Frequency with a Predetermined Value	X^2—Low p-Values Indicate That Observed Frequency Is Different Than Predetermined Value	$df = 1$ 1
Compare an Observed Proportion with Some Predetermined Value	Z or t-test for Proportions—Low p-Values Indicate That the Observed Proportion Is Different Than the Predetermined Value	50%
Bivariate Tests:		
Compare Whether Two Observed Means Are Different from One Another	Z or t-test—Low p-Values Indicate the Means Are Different	$\mu = 0$
Compare Whether Two Less-Than Interval Variables Are Related Using Cross-Tabs	X^2—Low p-Values Indicate the Variables Are Related to One Another	$df = 3$ 3
Compare Whether Two Interval or Ratio Variables Are Correlated to One Another	t-test for Correlation—Low p-Values Indicate the Variables Are Related to One Another	$r = 0$

Source: © Cengage Learning®

Type I Error

Suppose the observed sample mean described earlier leads to the conclusion that the mean is greater than 1.5 when in fact the true population mean is equal to 1.5. A Type I error has occurred. A **Type I error** occurs when a condition that is true in the population is rejected based on statistical observations. When a researcher sets an acceptable significance level a priori (α), he or she is determining how much tolerance he or she has for a Type I error. Simply put, a Type I error occurs when the researcher concludes that there is a statistical difference based on a sample result when in reality one does not exist in the population. When testing for relationships, a Type I error occurs when the researcher concludes a relationship exists when in fact one does not exist.

Type I error

Occurs when a condition that is true in the population is rejected based on statistical observations in a sample

Type II Error

Conversely, if our null hypothesis is indeed false, but we conclude that we should not reject the null hypothesis, we make what is called a Type II error. In this example, our null hypothesis that the mean is equal to 1.5 is not true in the population. However, our sample data indicates the mean does not differ from 1.5. So, a Type II error is the probability of failing to reject a false hypothesis. This incorrect decision is called beta (β). In practical terms, a Type II error means that our sample does not show a difference between an observed mean and a benchmark when in fact the difference does exist in the population. Alternatively, for correlation type relationships, a **Type II error** is created when the sample data suggests that a relationship does not exist when in fact a relationship does exist. Such an occurrence is related to statistical power. A sample size is sometimes too small to provide the power needed to find a relationship.

Unfortunately, without increasing sample size, the researcher cannot simultaneously reduce Type I and Type II errors. They are inversely related. Thus, reducing the probability of a Type II error increases the probability of a Type I error. In marketing problems, Type I errors generally are considered more serious than Type II errors. Thus, more emphasis is placed on determining the significance level, α, than in determining β.[6]

Type II error

Occurs when the sample data suggests that a relationship does not exist when in fact a relationship does exist

Univariate Tests of Means

At times, a researcher may wish to compare some observation against a preset standard. A univariate t-test is appropriate for testing hypotheses involving some observed mean against some specified value such as a sales target. The t-distribution, like the standardized normal curve, is a symmetrical, bell-shaped distribution with a mean of 0 and a standard deviation of 1.0. When sample size (n) is larger than 30, the t-distribution and Z-distribution are almost identical. Therefore, while the t-test is strictly appropriate for tests involving small sample sizes with unknown standard deviations, researchers commonly apply the t-test for comparisons involving the mean of an interval or ratio measure. The precise height and shape of the t-distribution vary with sample size.

More specifically, the shape of the *t*-distribution is influenced by its degrees of freedom (*df*). The degrees of freedom are determined by the number of distinct calculations that are possible given a set of information. In the case of a univariate *t*-test, the degrees of freedom are equal to the sample size (*n*) minus one. If a sample size is 46 (*n*=46) then the degrees of freedom for a univariate *t*-test is 45 (*df*=46−1=45).

Exhibit 14.8 illustrates *t*-distributions for 1, 2, 5, and an infinite number of degrees of freedom. Notice that the *t*-distribution approaches a normal distribution rapidly with increasing sample size. This is why, in practice, marketing researchers usually apply a *t*-test even with large samples. The practical effect is that the conclusion will be the same since the distributions are so similar with large samples and the correspondingly larger numbers of degrees of freedom.

Another way to look at degrees of freedom is to think of adding four numbers together when you know their sum—for example,

4

2

1

+X

12

The value of the fourth number has to be 5. The values of the first three digits could change to any value (freely vary), but the fourth value would have to be determined for the sum to still be

equal to 12. In this example there are three degrees of freedom. Degrees of freedom can be a difficult concept to understand fully. For most basic statistical analyses, the user only needs to remember the rule for determining the number of degrees of freedom for a given test. Today, with computerized software packages, the number of degrees of freedom is provided automatically for most tests.

Ultra-luxury car makers may set a sales goal that involves selling more than 1,000 cars per year worldwide as a means of deciding whether to put that car into production. The research question of "Will sales exceed 1,000 cars?" involves a univariate analysis. More specifically, a univariate *t*-test may result from survey data of prospective customers.

To calculate a *t* statistic, one uses this formula:

$$t = \frac{\overline{X} - \mu}{S_{\overline{X}}}$$

with *n* − 1 degrees of freedom. Suppose a researcher for a luxury car manager believes that the average number of cars sold would be twenty per week. The manager records the number

EXHIBIT 14.8

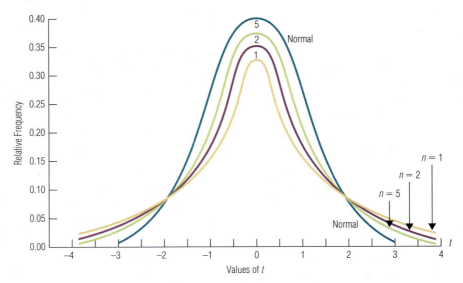

of sales for the first twenty–five weeks of a new prototype production run. Are the sales different from twenty per week? The substantive hypothesis is

$H_1: \mu \neq 20$

1. The researcher calculates a sample mean and standard deviation. In this case, suppose $\overline{X} = 22$ and S (sample standard deviation) $= 5$.
2. The standard error is computed $(S_{\overline{X}})$:

$$S_{\overline{X}} = \frac{S}{\sqrt{n}}$$
$$= \frac{5}{\sqrt{25}}$$
$$= 1$$

3. The researcher then finds the t–value associated with the desired confidence level or statistical significance. If a 95 percent confidence level is desired, the significance level is 0.05.
4. The critical values for the t–test are found by locating the upper and lower limits of the confidence interval. The result defines the regions of rejection. This requires determining the critical value of t. For 24 degrees of freedom ($n = 25$, $df = n - 1$), the critical t–value is 2.064.
5. The formula provides this result:

$$t_{abs} = \frac{\overline{X} - \mu}{S_{\overline{X}}}$$

$$t_{abs} = \frac{22 - 20}{1} = \frac{2}{1} = 2$$

The observed mean of 22 is inserted for the sample mean $(\overline{X})$ and the hypothesized value of 20 is inserted for the population mean (μ). We can see that the observed t–value of 2.00 is less than the critical t–value of 2.064 at the 0.05 level when there are $25 - 1 = 24$ degrees of freedom. As a result, the p-value is greater than 0.05 and the hypothesis is not supported. We cannot conclude with 95 percent confidence that the mean is not 20.

The Z-distribution and the t-distribution are very similar, and thus the Z-test and t-test will provide much the same result in most situations. However, when the population standard deviation (σ) is known, the Z-test is most appropriate. When σ is unknown (the situation in most business research studies), and the sample size greater than 30, the Z-test can also be used. When σ is unknown and the sample size is small, the t-test is most appropriate.

TIPS OF THE TRADE

- A frequency table can be a very useful way to depict basic tabulations.
- Cross-tabulation and contingency tables are a simple and effective way to examine relationships among less-than interval variables.
  - When a distinction can be made between independent and dependent variables (that are nominal or ordinal), the convention is that rows are independent variables and columns are dependent variables.
- A continuous variable that displays a bimodal distribution is appropriate for a median split.
  - Median splits should be performed on variables that display a normal distribution only with caution.
  - Importantly, median splits on continuous variables should be performed only after deleting one-fourth to one-third of the responses around the median to help prevent logically inconsistent classifications.

∴ SUMMARY

1. Prepare qualitative data for interpretation or data analysis. Qualitative data interpretation benefits from coding. Coding can help identify key themes. Coding involves assigning some representative value to units of data having similar meaning. One of the most basic forms of coding is dummy coding. Dummy coding involves representing dichotomies with values of 0 and 1.

2. Know what descriptive statistics are and why they are used. Descriptive analyses provide descriptive statistics. These include measures of central tendency and variation. Statistics such as the mean, mode, median, range, variance, and standard deviation are all descriptive statistics. These statistics provide a basic summary describing the basic properties of a variable.

3. Create and interpret tabulation and cross-tabulation tables. Statistical tabulation is another way of saying that we count the number of observations in each possible response category. In other words, tabulation is the same as tallying. Tabulation is an appropriate descriptive analysis for less-than interval variables. Frequency tables and histograms are used to display tabulation results. Cross-tabulation is the appropriate technique for assessing relationships among multiple less-than interval variables. The key to interpreting a cross-tabulation result is to compare actual observed values with hypothetical values that would result from pure chance. When observed results vary from these values, a relationship is indicated.

4. Perform basic data transformations. Data transformations are often needed to assist in data analysis and involve changing the mathematical form of data in some systematic way. Basic data transformations include reverse coding, summating scales, creating index numbers, and collapsing a variable based on a median split.

5. Understand the basics of testing hypotheses using inferential statistics. Hypothesis testing can involve univariate, bivariate, or multivariate statistics. Hypotheses are derived from research questions and should be stated in specific and testable terms. A sample is drawn. The sample represents a relevant population and then an inference about the population is made based on the descriptive statistics developed from the sample.

6. Be able to use a p-value to make statistical inferences. A p-value is the probability value associated with a statistical test. The probability in a p-value is the probability that the expected value for some test distribution is true. In other words, for a t-test, the expected value of the t-distribution is 0. If a researcher is testing whether or not a variable is significantly different from 0, then the p-value that results from the corresponding computed t-value represents the probability that the true population mean is actually 0. For most marketing research hypotheses, a low p-value supports the hypothesis. If a p-value is lower than the researcher's acceptable significance level (i.e., 0.05), then the hypothesis is usually supported.

7. Conduct a univariate t-test. A univariate t-test allows a researcher to test inferences comparing some sample observation against a predetermined standard. Often, the predetermined standard represents some benchmark such as a sales target or scrap rate. The t-test results allow an inference about a relevant population based on the mean derived from a sample.

∴ KEY TERMS AND CONCEPTS

bivariate statistical analysis, *403*
class coding, *394*
coding, *393*
codes, *393*
contingency table, *396*
cross-tabulation, *396*
data transformation, *399*
descriptive analysis, *394*
dummy coding, *393*

effects coding, *393*
elaboration analysis, *398*
frequency table, *395*
histogram, *395*
index numbers, *401*
marginals, *397*
median split, *400*
moderator variable, *398*
multivariate statistical analysis, *403*

p-value, *404*
significance level, *404*
statistical base, *398*
tabulation, *395*
Type I error, *405*
Type II error, *405*
univariate statistical analysis, *403*

:: QUESTIONS FOR REVIEW AND CRITICAL THINKING

1. How does coding allow qualitative data to become useful to a researcher?
2. What are five descriptive statistics used to describe the basic properties of variables?
3. What is a *histogram*? What is the advantage of overlaying a normal distribution over a histogram?
4. A survey asks respondents to respond to the statement "My work is interesting." Interpret the frequency distribution shown here (taken from an SPSS output):

Category Label	Code	Abs. Freq.	Rel. Freq. (Pct.)	Adj. Freq. (Pct.)	Cum. Freq. (Pct.)
Very true	1	650	23.9	62.4	62.4
Somewhat true	2	303	11.2	29.1	91.5
Not very true	3	61	2.2	5.9	97.3
Not at all true	4	28	1.0	2.7	100.0
	•	1,673	61.6	Missing	
	Total	2,715	100.0	100.0	
Valid cases	1,042		Missing cases	1,673	

5. Use the data in the following table to
   a. prepare a frequency distribution of the respondents' ages;
   b. cross-tabulate the respondents' genders with cola preference; and
   c. identify any outliers.

Individual	Gender	Age	Cola Preference	Weekly Unit Purchases
John	M	19	Coke	2
Al	M	17	Pepsi	5
Bill	M	20	Pepsi	7
Mary	F	20	Coke	2
Jim	M	18	Coke	4
Karen	F	16	Coke	4
Tom	M	17	Pepsi	12
Sassi	F	22	Pepsi	6
Amie	F	20	Pepsi	2
Dawn	F	19	Pepsi	3

6. Data on the average size of a soda (in ounces) at all thirty major league baseball parks are as follows: 14, 18, 20, 16, 16, 12, 14, 16, 14, 16, 16, 16, 14, 32, 16, 20, 12, 16, 20, 12, 16, 16, 24, 16, 16, 14, 14, 12, 14, 20. Compute descriptive statistics for this variable. Comment on the results. Presuming the first fifteen are drink sizes in the American League and the last fifteen are drink sizes in the National League, test the hypotheses: Soft drink sizes are larger at American League Ball Parks than at National League Ball Parks. Do the data represent a sample or a census?

7. The following computer output shows a cross-tabulation of frequencies and provides frequency number (N) and row (R) percentages.
   a. Interpret this output including an impression about whether or not the row and column variables are related.
   b. Critique the way the analysis is presented.

Have You Read a Book in Past three months	Have High School Diploma?		
	Yes	No	Total
Yes	489	174	663
	73.8	26.2	
No	473	378	851
	55.6	44.4	
	. . . . . .	. . . . . .	. . . . . .
Total	962	552	1514

8. List and describe at least three basic data transformations.
9. What conditions suggest that a ratio variable should be transformed into a dichotomous (two group) variable represented with dummy coding?
10. A data processing analyst for a research supplier finds that preliminary computer runs of survey results show that consumers love a client's new product. The employee buys a large block of the client's stock. Is this ethical?

11. Use a website such as **http://www.styledrops.com** to find some prices for four Prada handbags, four Gucci handbags, four Yves Saint Laurent handbags, four Burberry handbags, and four Ferragamo handbags. Enter these into a spreadsheet. Using the lowest priced Prada handbag as a base, compute an index displaying the price of all other handbags. Which brand offers the best value in your opinion? Compute the appropriate statistic for central tendency using the spreadsheet or some other software. Use the chart feature to depict the prices as a frequency distribution.
12. Describe the basic hypothesis testing procedure.
13. What is a p-value and how is it used?
14. A researcher is asked to determine whether a productivity objective (in dollars) of better than $75,000 per employee is possible. A productivity test is done involving twenty employees. What conclusion would you reach? The sales results are as follows:

28,000	105,000	58,000	93,000	96,000
67,000	82,500	75,000	81,000	59,000
101,000	60,500	77,000	72,500	48,000
99,000	78,000	71,000	80,500	78,000

:: RESEARCH ACTIVITIES

1. Go the website for the Chicago Cubs baseball team (**http://chicago.cubs.mlb.com**). Use either the schedule listing or the statistical information to find their record in the most recently completed season. Create a data file with a variable indicating whether each game was won or lost and a variable indicating whether the game was played at home in Wrigley Field or away from home. Using a computer and software such as Excel, SPSS, JMP, or SAS,

a. Compute a frequency table and histogram for each variable.
b. Use cross-tabulations to examine whether a relationship exists between where the game is played (home or away) and winning.
c. Extra Analysis: Repeat the analyses for the Houston Astros baseball team (**http://www.astros.com**). What does this suggest for the relationship between playing at home and winning?

Body on Tap

Case 14.1

A few years ago Vidal Sassoon, Inc., took legal action against Bristol-Myers over a series of TV commercials and print ads for a shampoo that had been named Body on Tap because of its beer content.[7] The prototype commercial featured a well-known high fashion model saying, "In shampoo tests with over 900 women like me, Body on Tap got higher ratings than Prell for body. Higher than Flex for conditioning. Higher than Sassoon for strong, healthy-looking hair."

The evidence showed that several groups of approximately 200 women each tested just one shampoo. They rated it on a six-step qualitative scale, from "outstanding" to "poor," for twenty-seven separate attributes, such as body and conditioning. It became clear that 900 women did not, after trying both shampoos, make product-to-product comparisons between Body on Tap and Sassoon or between Body on Tap and any of the other brands mentioned. In fact, no woman in the tests tried more than one shampoo.

The claim that the women preferred Body on Tap to Sassoon for "strong, healthy-looking hair" was based on combining the data for the "outstanding" and "excellent" ratings and discarding the lower four ratings on the scale. The figures then were 36 percent for Body on Tap and 24 percent (of a separate group of women) for Sassoon.

When the "very good" and "good" ratings were combined with the "outstanding" and "excellent" ratings, however, there was only a difference of 1 percent between the two products in the category of "strong, healthy-looking hair."

The research was conducted for Bristol-Myers by Marketing Information Systems, Inc. (MISI), using a technique known as blind monadic testing. The president of MISI testified that this method is typically employed when what is wanted is an absolute response to a product "without reference to another specific product." Although he testified that blind monadic testing was used in connection with comparative advertising, that was not the purpose for which Bristol-Myers retained MISI. Rather, Bristol-Myers wished to determine consumer reaction to the introduction of Body on Tap. And Sassoon in-house research expert stated flatly that blind monadic testing can not support comparative advertising claims.

Question

Comment on the professionalism of the procedures used to make the advertising claim. Why do you believe the researchers performed the data transformations described?

Premier Motorcars

Case prepared by Mitch Griffin, Bradley University. Premier Motorcars is the new Fiat dealer in Delavan, Illinois. Premier Motorcars has been regularly advertising in its local market area that the new Fiat 500 averages 30 miles to a gallon of gas and mentions that this figure may vary with driving conditions. A local consumer group wishes to verify the advertising claim. To do so, it selects a sample of recent purchasers of the Fiat 500. It asks them to drive their cars until at least two tanks of gasoline have been used up and then calculate the mileage in miles per gallon. The researcher can then calculate descriptive statistics indicating what the actual mileage of the Fiat 500 is based on the observations from the sample. The data in Case Exhibit 14.2−1 portray the results of the tests.

Questions

1. Formulate a statistical hypothesis appropriate for the consumer group's purpose.
2. Calculate the mean average miles per gallon. Compute the sample variance and sample standard deviation.
3. Construct the appropriate statistical test for your hypothesis, using a 0.05 significance level.
4. Use at least two different software packages to conduct the statistical test. For instance, use Excel and a statistics package like SPSS or JMP. Are the results the same? Comment.

CASE EXHIBIT 14.2–1   Miles per Gallon Information

Purchaser	Miles Per Gallon	Purchaser	Miles Per Gallon
1	30.9	13	27.0
2	24.5	14	26.7
3	31.2	15	31.0
4	28.7	16	23.5
5	35.1	17	29.4
6	29.0	18	26.3
7	28.8	19	27.5
8	23.1	20	28.2
9	31.0	21	28.4
10	30.2	22	29.1
11	28.4	23	21.9
12	29.3	24	30.9

Source: Case prepared by Mitch Griffin, Bradley University.

© MaxyM/Shutterstock.com

Dimitri Otis/Getty Images

CHAPTER 15

Testing for Differences between Groups and for Predictive Relationships

LEARNING OUTCOMES

After studying this chapter, you should be able to:

1. Choose an appropriate statistic based on data characteristics
2. Compute a χ^2 statistic for cross-tab results
3. Use a *t*-test to compare a difference between two means
4. Conduct a one-way analysis of variance test (ANOVA)
5. Appreciate the practicality of modern statistical software packages
6. Understand how the General Linear Model (GLM) can predict a key dependent variable

Chapter Vignette:
Doubling Down

How many times have you heard somebody try to blame something on "big business." Well, people make up businesses. Interestingly, though, many people have double standards when laying moral blame for the same actions.

John is about to trade in his car and knows that some repair is needed that is not obvious but needs to be fixed to avoid permanent damage to the car. John takes the car to Carmax where an agent named Patrice greets him. Should John tell Patrice about the problem? Is that the morally correct thing to do?

By now, you've probably made some judgment of John's action should he not disclose the problem. Put the shoe on the other foot now. What if Patrice, the Carmax sales agent, were selling a car with the same problem to John? Should she disclose the problem to John? Does your moral judgment of this

act differ from the one mentioned earlier? If you would judge John's act as less morally incorrect than Patrice's, then you, like a large number of people, are displaying a double standard. A dubious act performed by a consumer is judged as more ethical than the very same act performed by someone associated with a business.

Researchers build hypotheses around this double standard and test them using simple tests of differences between ethical judgments. The research puts various dubious scenarios before experimental subjects and asks them to rate how ethical the person's behavior was using a scale ranging from 1 = totally unethical to 7 = totally ethical. These scenarios were split across 127 subjects so that half read a scenario involving a consumer engaging in the act while the other half read the same scenario with the exception that a businessperson performs the same act. Across the four scenarios, the results show:

Act Performed by:	Scenario:			
	Deceive in Negotiation	Hide Product Defect	Overstate Third Party Offer	Apply Time Pressure
Consumer	5.4	3.7	5.3	6.0
Business	3.6	1.7	3.4	5.0

Source: © Cengage Learning 2013.

The differences between the means support the double standard hypothesis. When a consumer performs the act, subjects judge the act more ethically. However, given that the results come from a sample and not a census, a statistical test is needed to judge how confident one can be about a conclusion that the means are different between the two conditions. In this case, an independent samples *t*-test confirms that the means are significantly different with 95 percent confidence.

One reason for the difference may be neutralization, or more simply, the extent to which excuses are available for an otherwise unethical act. For instance, if subjects excuse the consumer based on the thought that his or her action "won't really hurt anybody," then the act is judged as more ethical. Correlational studies shed light on this issue. This chapter sheds light on statistical tools researchers use to reach such conclusions.[1]

Introduction

The vignette describes some ethical judgment comparisons across two experimental groups. If we look at the customer (business) condition as a categorical variable and ethical judgments as an interval variable, these comparisons really involve drawing inferences about how one experimental variable influences another, ethical judgments. A surprising number of inferences involve two variables. The automated search for relationships between two variables provides the backbone for automated big data searchers. Sometimes, the marketing analytics person reduces a more complex analysis involving multiple variables to a series of two-variable comparisons because presenting the results becomes very simple. This chapter illustrates some common ways to perform bivariate and other elementary statistical tests.

What Is the Appropriate Test Statistic?

Marketing researchers commonly examine differences in behaviors like sales, characteristics, beliefs, opinions, emotions, or attitudes. In the most basic experimental design, the researcher tests differences between subjects assigned to an experimental group and subjects assigned to the control group. A survey researcher may be interested in whether male and female consumers purchase a product in the same amount. A researcher also may test whether or not a firm's business units in Europe are as profitable as its business units located in the United States. Such tests are bivariate **tests of differences** when they involve only two variables. In these tests, one variable often acts like a dependent variable while a classification or grouping variable acts as an independent variable.

> **Tests of differences**
> An investigation of a hypothesis stating that two (or more) groups differ with respect to measures of another variable.

Exhibit 15.1 on page 414 illustrates that the type of measurement, the nature of the comparison, and the number of groups compared influence the statistical choice. Often researchers are interested in testing differences in mean scores between groups or in comparing the distribution showing how two groups' scores vary across response categories. We will focus our attention on these issues.[2] The rest of the chapter focuses on how to choose the right statistic for two-group comparisons and perform the corresponding test. Exhibit 15.1 on page 414 provides a frame of reference for the rest of the chapter by illustrating various possible comparisons involving a few golfers.

More generally, choosing the right statistic boils down to what type and how many variables are involved in a particular research question or hypothesis. Commonly, hypotheses can be expressed either as tests of differences between groups or as relationships between variables. Research questions and hypotheses typically imply that variables are either dependent or independent. Dependent variables are those that respond to independent variables. In a causal research design, independent variables cause dependent variables.

The answers to two questions make finding an appropriate analytical approach easy:

1. How many independent variables (IV) and dependent variables (DV) are involved in the analysis?
2. What is the scale level of the independent and dependent variables involved in the analysis?

EXHIBIT **15.1** Some Bivariate Hypotheses

Information	Golfer			Hypothesis or Research Question	Level of Measurement Involved	Statistic Used	Comment	Result
	Dolly	**Lori**	**Mel**					
Average Driver Distance (meters)	135	150	185	Lori hits her drives further than Dolly	Golfer = Nominal; Drive Distance = Ratio	Independent Samples t-test to compare mean distance	The data for Lori and Dolly are used	Supported ($t = 2.07$, $df = 56$, $p < .05$)
σ	30	25	30					
Average 7-Wood Distance (meters)	140	145	150	Mel hits her driver further than her 7-wood	Club = Nominal (7-wood or driver); 7-Wood Distance = Ratio	Paired-Samples t-test to compare mean distances for Mel	Only the data for Mel are used (std of diff = 30)	Supported ($t = 6.39$, $df = 29$, $p < .05$)
σ	30	30	30					
Sample size (number of balls hit)	28 drives 28 7-woods	30 drives 28 7-woods	29 drives 28 7-woods	A relationship exists between golfers and 7-wood distance	Golfer = Nominal; Distance = Ratio	One-Way ANOVA to compare means for the three groups	All data for 7-wood distance are used (MSE = 30)	Not supported ($F = 0.83$, ns)
Number of Drives in Fairway	4	22	11	Mel drives the ball more accurately than Dolly	Golfer = Nominal; Accuracy = Nominal (Right, Fairway, Left)	Cross-Tabulation with χ^2 Statistic	Resulting cross tabulation table is 2 rows × 3 columns (rows = golfer and columns = accuracy (fairway, right left)	Supported ($\chi^2 = 10.3$, $df = 3$, $p < .05$)
Drives missing right of fairway	16	7	9	A relationship exists between golfers and accuracy	Golfer = Nominal; Accuracy = Nominal (Right, Fairway, Left)	Cross-Tabulation with χ^2 Statistic	Cross-tabulation is now 3 rows × 3 columns	Supported ($\chi^2 = 23.7$, $df = 4$, $p < .05$)
Drives missing left of fairway	8	1	9					

Exhibit 15.2 provides a useful guide in choosing a test. For instance, with one nominal IV and one nominal DV, the analyst employs cross-tabulation with a χ^2 test. When a single IV represents a nominal classification variable and the DV is interval, the analyst employs one-way ANOVA (an independent samples t-test can provide the same result if the classification variable contains only two categories). Notice that in several other cases the appropriate statistic would be a statistic that is beyond the scope of this chapter. Fortunately, the tests described in this chapter represent those commonly used in marketing research and account for a large bulk of analytics and inferential tests. Users may find it useful to refer back to this particular exhibit when trying to decide which statistical tool fits a given research question or hypothesis.

Market research reports very often involve cross-tabulation tables. For instance, consider an analyst asked to examine the following research question addressing the effectiveness of Bridgestone's "Made in the USA" advertising campaign:

When given a choice, would a golfer from the USA be more likely to choose Bridgestone golf balls than Titleist golf balls relative to a golfer from Europe?

The research question involves a categorical (nominal) independent variable, a consumer's country, and a categorical (nominal) dependent variable, brand of golf ball selected when given a choice of the two. Thus, the test would involve a single less-than interval dependent variable and a single less-than interval independent variable. The appropriate analytical tool for a statistical inference is a χ^2 test computed from the corresponding 2 (USA/Europe) × 2 (Bridgestone/Titleist) cross-tabulation table. If the test involved choosing between three brands (Bridgestone, Titleist, and Callaway), the appropriate analytical tool remains cross-tabulation with a χ^2 test.

Are men or women more preoccupied with their smartphones and social networking sites? You may be able to answer this question by looking at the data from the student survey. Test the following hypotheses using data obtained from the survey:

H_1: Women are more likely than men to have a Facebook site.

H_2: Men make more phone calls each day than do women.

H_3: Women receive more e-mail than do men.

H_4: Men spend more time online daily than do women.

H_5: The better a student feels about his or her living arrangements, the more time he or she spends studying.

How many text messages do you send daily?

How many text messages do you receive daily?

How many cell phone calls do you make in a day?

How many cell phone calls do you receive in a day?

Source: www.qualtrics.com

EXHIBIT **15.2**
Choosing the Right Statistic

Independent Variables:	Dependent Variables		
	1 Nominal / Ordinal DV	1 at Least Interval DV	More than 1 DV
1 Nominal/Ordinal IV	Cross-Tabulation with χ^2 Test	t-test or One-Way ANOVA	Multivariate Analysis
2 or More Nominal/ Ordinal IVs	Cross-Tabulation with χ^2 Test	n-Way ANOVA	Multivariate ANOVA
At Least 1 Nominal/ Ordinal IV and at Least 1 Interval or Ratio IV	Multivariate Analyses— (Logistic Regression)	Full-Factorial ANCOVA	Multivariate MANCOVA
1 Interval/Ratio IV	t-test	Simple Regression	Multivariate Regression
1 or More Interval/ Ratio IVs	Multivariate Analyses— (Logistic Regression)	Multiple Regression	Multivariate Analyses such as Path Model

Color Code:

Beyond the Scope of this Text

Dependent Variable Condition

Variations of the GLM illustrated in Chapter

Bivariate test illustrated in Chapter

Independent Variable Condition

Source: © 2016 Cengage Learning®

Cross-Tabulation Tables: The χ^2 Test for Goodness-of-Fit

Cross-tabulation was introduced in the previous chapter as a way of representing relationships between variables. Cross-tabulations are intuitive and easily understood. They also lend themselves well to graphical analysis using tools like bar charts. Cross-tabulation also can be very useful in big data analytics.

Two-variable cross-tabulations communicate analytical results easily and clearly. Thus, analysts use them very much. Cross-tabulations are much like tallying. When two variables exist, each with two categories, four cells result. Each cell contains the count of observations matching a particular combination of characteristics. The χ^2 distribution provides a means for testing the statistical significance of a contingency table. In other words, the bivariate χ^2 test examines the statistical significance of relationships between two less–than interval variables.

The χ^2 test for a contingency table involves comparing the observed frequencies (O_i) with the expected frequencies (E_i) in each cell of the table. The goodness- (or closeness-) of-fit of the observed distribution with the expected distribution is captured by this statistic. Remember that the convention is that the row variable is the independent variable and the column variable is the dependent variable. Although cross-tabulation is appropriate when both variables are nominal or ordinal, interval variables are used in a cross-tabulation if the response range is very small. Such is the case if a variable only takes on values of 1, 2, or 3, for example. Once a variable has more than four categories, a cross-tabulation table loses its advantage of simplicity in communicating the result.

We could use a χ^2 test to examine a research question asking whether or not Papa John's restaurants were more likely to be located in a stand-alone location or in a shopping center. The univariate (one-dimensional) analysis suggests that the majority of the locations (60 percent) are stand-alone units:

Location	One-Way Frequency Table
Stand-alone	60 stores
Shopping Center	40 stores
Total	100 stores

Is there any effect of location on Papa John's restaurants? Suppose the researcher analyzes the situation further by examining the following bivariate hypothesis:

Stand-alone locations are more likely to be profitable than are shopping center locations.

While the researcher is unable to obtain the dollar figures for the profitability of each unit, a press release indicates which Papa John's units were profitable and which were not. Cross-tabulation using a χ^2 test is appropriate because

- the independent variable (location) is less–than interval; and
- the dependent variable (profitable/not profitable) is less–than interval.

The data can be recorded in the following 2×2 contingency table:

Location	Profitable	Not Profitable	Total
Stand-alone	50	10	60
Shopping Center	15	25	40
Totals	65	35	100

Several conclusions appear evident. One, it seems that more stores are profitable than not profitable (65 versus 35, respectively). Secondly, more of the profitable restaurants seem to be in stand-alone locations (50 out of 65). However, is the difference strong enough to be statistically significant?

Is the observed difference between stand-alone and shopping center locations the result of chance variation due to random sampling? Is the discrepancy more than sampling variation? The χ^2 test allows us to conduct tests for significance in the analysis of the $R \times C$ contingency table (where R = row and C = column). The formula for the χ^2 statistic is the same as that for one-way frequency tables:

$$\chi^2 = \sum \frac{(O_i - E_i)^2}{E_i}$$

where

χ^2 = chi-square statistic
O_i = observed frequency in the ith cell
E_i = expected frequency in the ith cell

Again, as in a univariate χ^2 test, a frequency count of data that nominally identify or categorically rank groups is acceptable.

If the researcher's hypothesis is true, the frequencies shown in the contingency table should not resemble a random distribution. In other words, if location has no effect on profitability, the profitable and unprofitable stores would be spread evenly across the two location categories. This is really the logic of the test in that it compares the observed frequencies with the theoretical expected values for each cell.

After obtaining the observations for each cell, the expected values for each cell must be obtained. The expected values for each cell can be computed easily using this formula:

$$E_{ij} = \frac{R_i C_j}{n}$$

where

R_i = total observed frequency count in the ith row
C_j = total observed frequency count in the jth column
n = sample size

Only the total column and total row values are needed for this calculation. Thus, the calculation could be performed before the data are even tabulated. The following values represent the expected values for each cell:

Location	Profitable	Not Profitable	Total
Stand-alone	(60 × 65)/100 = 39	(60 × 35)/100 = 21	60
Shopping Center	(40 × 65)/100 = 26	(40 × 35)/100 = 14	40
Totals	65	35	100

Notice that the row and column totals are the same for both the observed and expected contingency matrices. These values also become useful in providing the substantive interpretation of the relationship. Variance from the expected value indicates a relationship.

The actual bivariate χ^2 test value is calculated in the same manner as for a univariate test. The one difference is that one finds the degrees of freedom by multiplying the number of rows minus one $(R - 1)$ times the number of columns minus one $(C - 1)$ rather than simply the number of cells minus one:

$$\chi^2 = \sum \frac{(O_i - E_i)^2}{E_i}$$

with $(R - 1)(C - 1)$ degrees of freedom. One can plug in the observed and expected values into the formula as follows:

$$\chi^2 = \frac{(50 - 39)^2}{39} + \frac{(10 - 21)^2}{21} + \frac{(15 - 26)^2}{26} + \frac{(25 - 14)^2}{14}$$

$$= 3.102 + 5.762 + 4.654 + 8.643$$

$$= 22.16$$

The number of degrees of freedom equals 1:

$$(R - 1)(C - 1) = (2 - 1)(2 - 1) = 1$$

From an Internet chi-square calculator (such as http://stattrek.com/online-calculator/chi-square.aspx) or the chi-square distribution table on the companion website (**www.cengagebrain.com**), we see that the critical value at the 0.05 probability level with 1 *df* is 3.84. Thus, we are 95 percent confident that the observed values do not equal the expected values when the $\chi^2 = 3.84$ and we have 1 *df* as in a 2×2 contingency table. As the χ^2 becomes greater, we would have more confidence that the row variables are associated with systematic differences in the column variables. Before the analyst concludes support for the hypothesis, he or she must check and see that the deviations from the expected values are in the hypothesized direction. Since the difference between the stand-alone locations' observed profitability and the expected values for that cell are positive, the hypothesis is supported. Location is associated with profitability. Thus, testing the hypothesis involves two key steps:

1. Examine the statistical significance of the χ^2 resulting from the observed contingency table.
2. Examine whether the differences between the observed and expected values are consistent with the hypothesized prediction.

Proper use of the χ^2 test requires that each expected cell frequency (*E*) have a value of at least 5. If this sample size requirement is not met, the researcher should take a larger sample as a way of increasing the frequency.

JMP is a point and click statistics software package from SAS, one of the pioneers in statistical software. JMP makes a trial version available at jmp.com. The JMP screenshot on at the left shows a cross-tabulation result depicting whether the living arrangement of a university student influences the type of transportation the student uses to get to class. The mosaic frame at the top of the output depicts in colors the proportion of students living in each type of place who take each of the three types of transportation listed. The contingency table shows the cross-tabulation results. The top number in each cell shows the observed cell frequency count and the bottom numbers show the percentage of the column and row totals that this cell comprises. The numbers in the bottom of the output show the chi-square statistic result. In this case, the χ^2 of 73.4 with 4 *df* is associated with a very low p-value (<0.0001) meaning there is

A "contingency analysis" or cross-tab result performed in SAS JMP. This one suggests a relationship between where students live and how they get to school. Notice the significant chi-square result at the bottom of the results.

Doing a Cross-tab

Contingency analysis is simplified with statistical software. In this case, SAS JMP and SPSS provide very easy ways to perform the tests. In SAS JMP:

1. Click on Analyze.
2. Choose Fit Y by X.
3. Enter a nominal or ordinal independent variable as an X factor and a nominal or ordinal dependent variable as a Y factor. Click OK.
4. The results will appear in an output box. Contingency analysis can also be accessed through the consumer analysis function.

In SPSS:

1. Click on Analyze.
2. Choose Descriptive Statistics.
3. From the choices, select Cross-Tabs.
4. Enter a nominal or ordinal independent variable as in the Row box and a nominal or ordinal variable in the Column box.

5. Click on Statistics and choose Chi-Square. Then click Continue to close the Statistics box and then OK.
6. The results will appear in the output.

Contingency results from SPSS. The results point to significantly greater switching among AT&T store customers relative to Verizon store customers.

Carrier * Choice Crosstabulation

			Choice		Total
			Switch	Keep	
Carrier	Verizon	Count	24	41	65
		% within Carrier	36.9%	63.1%	100.0%
		% within Choice	28.9%	83.7%	49.2%
		% of Total	18.2%	31.1%	49.2%
	ATT	Count	59	8	67
		% within Carrier	88.1%	11.9%	100.0%
		% within Choice	71.1%	16.3%	50.8%
		% of Total	44.7%	6.1%	50.8%
Total		Count	83	49	132
		% within Carrier	62.9%	37.1%	100.0%
		% within Choice	100.0%	100.0%	100.0%
		% of Total	62.9%	37.1%	100.0%

Chi-Square Tests

	Value	df	Asymp. Sig. (2-sided)	Exact Sig. (2-sided)	Exact Sig. (1-sided)
Pearson Chi-Square	36.962[a]	1	.000		
Continuity Correction[b]	34.803	1	.000		
Likelihood Ratio	39.515	1	.000		
Fisher's Exact Test				.000	.000
Linear-by-Linear Association	36.682	1	.000		
N of Valid Cases	132				

a. 0 cells (0.0%) have expected count less than 5. The minimum expected count is 24.13.

b. Computed only for a 2x2 table

little chance that the observed and expected cell values are equal. Thus, we conclude a relationship exists between living arrangement and type of transportation. Dorm dwellers tend to walk, apartment dwellers take the bus, and students living in houses tend to drive to campus.

A separate graphic (p. 419) displays contingency results generated by the SPSS software. In this case, the results depict a tally of customers who received a promise to be paid $20 for visiting their carrier's phone store to see the newest Samsung phone. The column variable indicates that overall, 83 customers switched and 49 kept their old phones. Among the 83 who switched, 59 visited the AT&T store and 24 visited the Verizon store. In contrast, 41 of 65 customers who visited the Verizon store kept their old phone. The χ^2 of 37.0 with 1 df (p < 0.0001) suggests the relationship between the brand of phone store visited and switching phones is significant.

The *t*-Test for Comparing Two Means

When a researcher needs to compare means for a variable grouped into two categories based on some less-than interval variable, a *t*-test is appropriate. One way to think about this is as testing the way a dichotomous (two-level) independent variable is associated with changes in a continuous dependent variable. Several variations of the *t*-test exist.

Independent Samples *t*-Test

Independent samples *t*-test

A test for hypotheses stating a difference in means of an at-least interval dependent variable divided into two groups formed based on some less-than interval classificatory variable.

Most typically, the research analyst will apply the **independent samples *t*-test** to test for differences between means taken from two independent samples or groups. For example, if we measure the price for some designer jeans at 30 different retail stores, of which 15 are Internet-only stores (pure clicks) and 15 are bricks and mortar stores, we can test whether the prices are different based on store type with an independent samples *t*-test. The *t*-test for difference of means assumes the two samples are drawn from normal distributions and that the variances of the two populations are approximately equal (homoscedasticity). Another way to look at the test is that it uses a nominal or ordinal independent variable (that classifies things into two groups) to predict an interval or ratio dependent variable.

Independent Samples *t*-Test Calculation

The *t*-test actually tests whether the differences between two group means is zero. Not surprisingly, this idea can be expressed as the difference between two population means:

$$\mu_1 = \mu_2, \text{which is equivalent to,} \mu_1 - \mu_2 = 0$$

However, since this is inferential statistics, we test the idea by comparing two sample means:

$$(\overline{X}_1 - \overline{X}_2 = 0)$$

A verbal expression of the formula for *t* is

$$t = \frac{\text{Sample mean 1} - \text{sample mean 2}}{\text{Variability of random means}}$$

Thus, the *t*-value is a ratio with information about the difference between means (provided by the sample) in the numerator and the standard error in the denominator. The question is whether the observed differences have occurred by chance alone. To calculate *t*, we use the following formula:

$$t = \frac{\overline{X}_1 - \overline{X}_2}{S_{\overline{X}_1 - \overline{X}_2}}$$

where

$\overline{X}_1$ = mean for group 1

$\overline{X}_2$ = mean for group 2

$S_{\overline{X}_1 - \overline{X}_2}$ = pooled or combined standard error of difference between means

A **pooled estimate of the standard error** is a better estimate of the standard error than one based on the variance from either sample. The pooled standard error of the difference between means of independent samples can be calculated using the following formula:

$$S_{\overline{X}_1 - \overline{X}_2} = \sqrt{\left(\frac{(n_1 - 1)S_1^2 + (n_2 - 1)S_2^2}{n_1 + n_2 - 2} \right) \left(\frac{1}{n_1} + \frac{1}{n_2} \right)}$$

where

S_1^2 = variance of group1

S_2^2 = variance of group2

n_1 = sample size of group 1

n_2 = sample size of group 2

Are business majors or sociology majors more positive about a career in business? A *t*-test can be used to test the difference between sociology majors and business majors on scores on a scale measuring attitudes toward business. We will assume that the attitude scale is an interval scale. The result of the simple random sample of these two groups of college students is shown next:

Business Students	Sociology Students
$\overline{X}_1$ = 16.5	$\overline{X}_2$ = 12.2
S_1 = 2.1	S_2 = 2.6
n_1 = 21	n_2 = 14

> **Pooled estimate of the standard error**
>
> An estimate of the standard error for a *t*-test of independent means that assumes the variances of both groups are equal.

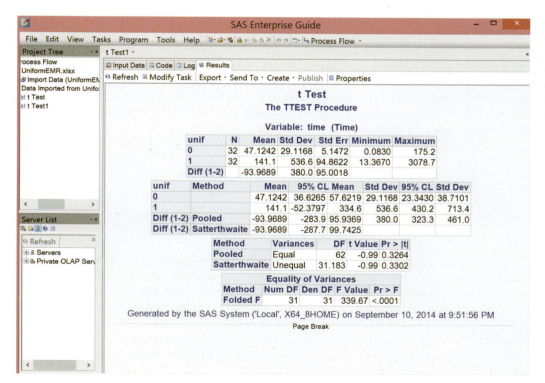

> This graphic shows an independent *t*-test conducted with SAS. Click on Analyze, choose ANOVA, select a classification variable and an analysis variable, and click Run.

SAS Enterprise Guide

t Test1

Input Data Code Log Results

Refresh Modify Task | Export · Send To · Create · Publish Properties

t Test

The TTEST Procedure

Variable: time (Time)

unif	N	Mean	Std Dev	Std Err	Minimum	Maximum
0	32	47.1242	29.1168	5.1472	0.0830	175.2
1	32	141.1	536.6	94.8622	13.3670	3078.7
Diff (1-2)		-93.9689	380.0	95.0018		

unif	Method	Mean	95% CL Mean		Std Dev	95% CL Std Dev	
0		47.1242	36.6265	57.6219	29.1168	23.3430	38.7101
1		141.1	-52.3797	334.6	536.6	430.2	713.4
Diff (1-2)	Pooled	-93.9689	-283.9	95.9369	380.0	323.3	461.0
Diff (1-2)	Satterthwaite	-93.9689	-287.7	99.7425			

Method	Variances	DF	t Value	Pr > |t|
Pooled	Equal	62	-0.99	0.3264
Satterthwaite	Unequal	31.183	-0.99	0.3302

Equality of Variances

Method	Num DF	Den DF	F Value	Pr > F
Folded F	31	31	339.67	<.0001

Generated by the SAS System ('Local', X64_8HOME) on September 10, 2014 at 9:51:56 PM

Page Break

A high score indicates a favorable attitude toward business. This particular *t*-test tests whether the difference in attitudes between sociology and business students is significant. A higher *t*-value is associated with a lower p-value. As the *t* gets higher and the p-value gets lower, the researcher has more confidence that the means are truly different. The relevant data computation is

$$S_{\overline{X}_1 - \overline{X}_2} = \sqrt{\left(\frac{(n_1 - 1)S_1^2 + (n_2 - 1)S_2^2}{n_1 + n_2 - 2}\right)\left(\frac{1}{n_1} + \frac{1}{n_2}\right)}$$

$$= \sqrt{\left(\frac{(20)(2.1)^2 + (13)(2.6)^2}{33}\right)\left(\frac{1}{21} + \frac{1}{14}\right)}$$

$$= 0.797$$

The calculation of the *t*-statistic is

$$t = \frac{\overline{X}_1 - \overline{X}_2}{S_{\overline{X}_1 - \overline{X}_2}}$$

$$t = \frac{16.5 - 12.2}{0.797}$$

$$= \frac{4.3}{0.797}$$

$$= 5.395$$

In a test of means between groups, degrees of freedom are calculated as follows:

$$df = n - k$$

where
$n = n_1 + n_2$
k = number of groups

In our example *df* equals 33 (21+14−2). If the 0.01 level of significance is selected, reference to the tabled values of the *t*-distribution (see www.cengagebrain.com or a web based p-value calculator) yields the critical *t*-value. The critical *t*-value of 2.75 must be surpassed by the observed *t*-value if the hypothesis test is to be statistically significant at the 0.01 level. The calculated value of *t*, 5.39, exceeds the critical value of *t* for statistical significance, so it is significant at $\alpha = 0.01$. The p-value is less than 0.01. In other words, this research shows that business students have significantly more positive attitudes toward business than do sociology students. The Research Snapshot on page 424 provides an overview of situations calling for an independent samples *t*-test.

Practically Speaking

In practice, computer software is used to compute the *t*-test results. Exhibit 15.3 displays a typical *t*-test printout. These particular results examine the following research question:

RQ: Does religion relate to price sensitivity in restaurants?

This question was addressed by asking a sample of 100 consumers to report how much they would be willing to pay per person for a nice dinner at one of the better restaurants in town. A research assistant showed each respondent a menu from the restaurant and then asked the respondent what amount per person he or she would pay (including tip) if dining there. The sample included 57 Catholics and 43 Protestants. Because no direction of the relationship is stated (no hypothesis is offered), a two-tailed test is appropriate. Although instructors still find some value in having students learn to perform the *t*-test calculations, practitioners almost always generate and interpret computer generated results today.

EXHIBIT 15.3 Independent Samples *t*-test Results

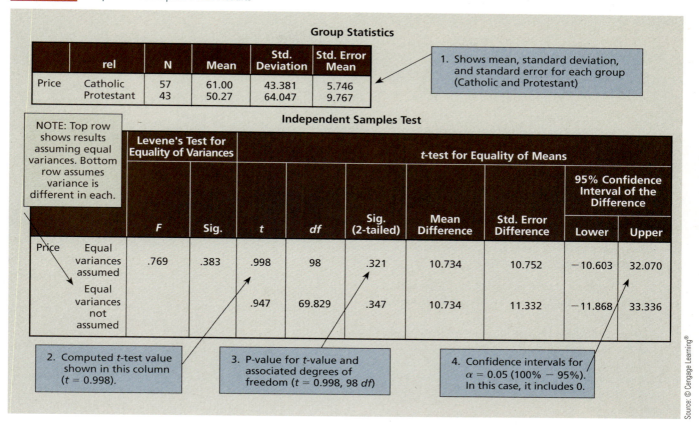

Group Statistics

	rel	N	Mean	Std. Deviation	Std. Error Mean
Price	Catholic	57	61.00	43.381	5.746
	Protestant	43	50.27	64.047	9.767

1. Shows mean, standard deviation, and standard error for each group (Catholic and Protestant)

NOTE: Top row shows results assuming equal variances. Bottom row assumes variance is different in each.

Independent Samples Test

		Levene's Test for Equality of Variances		t-test for Equality of Means						95% Confidence Interval of the Difference	
		F	Sig.	t	df	Sig. (2-tailed)	Mean Difference	Std. Error Difference	Lower	Upper
Price	Equal variances assumed	.769	.383	.998	98	.321	10.734	10.752	−10.603	32.070
	Equal variances not assumed			.947	69.829	.347	10.734	11.332	−11.868	33.336

2. Computed *t*-test value shown in this column (*t* = 0.998).

3. P-value for *t*-value and associated degrees of freedom (*t* = 0.998, 98 *df*)

4. Confidence intervals for $\alpha = 0.05$ (100% − 95%). In this case, it includes 0.

The interpretation of the *t*-test is made simple by focusing on either the p-value or the confidence interval and the group means. Here are the basic steps:

1. Examine the difference in means to find the "direction" of any difference. In this case, Catholics are willing to pay over $10 more than Protestants.
2. Compute or locate the computed *t*-test value. In this case, *t* = 0.998.
3. Find the p-value associated with this *t* and the corresponding degrees of freedom. Here, the p-value (two-tailed significance level) is 0.321. This suggests a 32 percent chance that the means are actually equal given the observed sample means. Assuming a 0.05 acceptable Type I error rate (α), the appropriate conclusion is that the means are not significantly different.
4. The difference can also be examined using the 95 percent confidence interval ($-10.603 < \overline{X}_1 - \overline{X}_2 < 32.070$). Since the confidence interval includes 0, we lack sufficient confidence that the true difference between the population means is not really 0. The result suggests that it may well be 0.

A few points are worth noting about this particular result. First, strictly speaking, the *t*-test assumes that the two population variances are equal. A slightly more complicated formula exists that will compute the *t*-statistic assuming the variances are not equal.[3] The software provides both results when reporting independent samples *t*-test results. The sample variances appear considerably different in this case as evidenced by the standard deviations for each group (43.4, 64.0). Nonetheless, the conclusions are the same using either assumption. In marketing research, we often deal with values that have variances close enough to assume equal variance. This isn't always the case in the physical sciences where variables may take on values of drastically different magnitude. Thus, the rule of thumb in marketing research is to use the equal variance assumption. In the vast majority of cases, the same conclusion will be drawn using either assumption.

Marketing Expert "T-eeze"

When is an independent samples *t*-test appropriate? Once again, we can find out by answering some simple questions:

- Is the dependent variable interval or ratio?
- Can the dependent variable scores be grouped based upon some meaningful categorical variable?
- Does the grouping result in scores drawn from independent samples (hint: this means that one respondent's score on the DV does not influence another respondent's score on the DV)?
- Are two groups involved in the research question?

When the answer to all questions is yes, an independent samples *t*-test is appropriate. To conduct the test in SPSS:

1. Click on Analyze and then choose Compare Means.
2. From the options shown, choose independent samples *t*-test.
3. Move the dependent variable into the Test Variables box.
4. Place the independent variable into the Grouping Variable box.
5. Click on Define Groups and enter the two values of the independent variable to be compared (0 and 1 if dummy coded). Click Continue.
6. Then click OK and the results will appear in the output window.

In JMP:

1. Click on Analyze and then choose Fit Y by X.
2. Place the interval or ratio dependent variable in the Y Response box.

3. Place the less-than interval independent variable in the X Factor box.
4. Click on OK. Results will appear in an output box.
5. Click on the small red upside down triangle next to "Oneway Analysis…"
6. The *t*-test results will appear.

In Excel, *t*-test results can be obtained by going to formulas, then selecting "t.test" from the statistical functions and entering the location of the values for each group, respectively. The variables must be sorted by the values of the independent variable before the function can compute the values. A *t*-test also can be accessed from the Data Analysis add-in for Excel. After clicking on Data Analysis, choose *t*-test: Two Samples Assume Equal (or Unequal as may be appropriate) Variances and enter the data in the same manner.

Second, notice that even though the means appear to be not so close to each other, the statistical conclusion is that they are the same. The substantive conclusion is that Catholics and Protestants would not be expected to be willing to pay different prices. Why is it that the means do not appear to be similar, yet that is the conclusion? The answer lies in the variance. Respondents tended to provide very wide ranges of acceptable prices. Notice how large the standard deviations are compared to the mean for each group. Since the *t*-statistic is a function of the standard error, which is a function of the standard deviation, a lot of variance means a smaller *t*-value for any given observed difference. When this occurs, the researcher may wish to double-check for outliers. A small number of wild price estimates could be inflating the variance for one or both groups. An additional consideration would be to increase the sample size and test again.

Third, a *t*-test is used even though the sample size is greater than 30. Strictly speaking, a *Z*-test can test this difference. Researchers often employ a *t*-test even with large samples. As samples get larger, the *t*-test and *Z*-test tend to yield the same results. Although a *t*-test can be used with large samples, a *Z*-test should not be used with small samples. Also, a *Z*-test can be used in instances where the population variance is known ahead of time.

Paired-Samples *t*-Test

What happens when a researcher needs to compare two means that are not from independent samples? Such might be the case when the same respondent provides two comparable scores; for instance, when a respondent rates both how much he or she likes shopping on retail websites and how much he or she likes shopping in real retail stores. Since the liking scores are both provided by the same person, the assumption that they are independent is not realistic. Additionally, if one compares the prices the same retailers charge in their stores with the prices they charge on their websites, the samples cannot be considered independent because each pair of observations is from the same sampling unit.

A **paired-samples *t*-test** is appropriate in this situation. The idea behind the paired-samples and another *t*-test can be seen in the following computation:

$$t = \frac{\bar{d}}{s_d / \sqrt{n}}$$

where $\bar{d}$ is the average difference between means, s_d is the standard deviation of the observed differences between means, and n is the number of observed differences between means. The test has degrees of freedom equal to one minus the total number of paired differences. Researchers also can compute the paired-samples *t*-test using statistical software. For example, using SPSS, the click-through sequence would be:

>   *Analyze → Compare Means → Paired-Samples t-test*

A dialog box then appears in which the "paired variables" should be entered. When a paired-samples *t*-test is appropriate, the two numbers being compared are usually scored as separate variables.

Exhibit 15.4 displays a paired-samples *t*-test result. A sample of 208 amusement park consumers was asked to rate how satisfied they felt both before and after visiting a new water rapids ride. The research question is, "How does the new water attraction affect customer satisfaction?" Each respondent provided two satisfaction scores much as in a within-subjects experimental design. The bar chart depicts the means for each variable (satisfied1 is the score before and satisfied2 is the

Paired-samples *t*-test

An appropriate test for comparing the scores of two interval variables drawn from related populations.

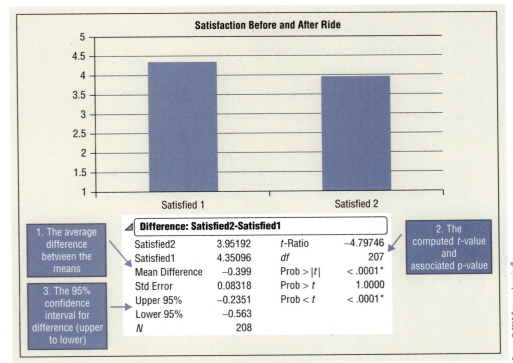

Source: © 2016 Cengage Learning®

EXHIBIT 15.4

Illustration of Paired-Samples *t*-test Results

score after riding the new attraction). The *t*-test results suggest that average difference of -0.40 (rounded to 2 decimals) is associated with a *t*-value of -4.8. As can be seen using either the p-value (p <0.0001) or the confidence interval ($-0.24 < \bar{d} < -0.56$), which does not include 0, the difference is significantly different from 0. Therefore, the results suggest that the new attraction may not have been such a good idea!

Management researchers have used paired–samples *t*-tests to examine the effect of downsizing on employee morale. For instance, job satisfaction for a sample of employees can be measured immediately after the downsizing. Some months later, employee satisfaction can be measured again. The difference between the satisfaction scores can be compared using a paired-samples *t*-test. Results suggest that the employee satisfaction scores increase within a few months of the downsizing as evidenced by statistically significant paired-samples *t*-values.[4]

The Z-Test for Comparing Two Proportions

What type of statistical comparison can be made when the observed statistics are proportions? Suppose a researcher wishes to test the hypothesis that wholesalers in the northern and southern United States differ in the proportion of sales they make to discount retailers. Testing whether the population proportion for group 1 (p_1) equals the population proportion for group 2 (p_2) is conceptually the same as the *t*-test of two means. This section briefly describes **Z-test for differences of proportions**, which requires a sample size greater than 30.

The test is appropriate for a hypothesis of this form:

$$H_0: \pi_1 = \pi_2$$

which may be restated as

$$H_0: \pi_1 - \pi_2 = 0$$

Comparison of the observed sample proportions p_1 and p_2 allows the researcher to ask whether the difference between two *large* random samples occurred due to chance alone. The Z-test statistic can be computed using the following formula:

$$Z = \frac{(p_1 - p_2)(\pi_1 - \pi_2)}{S_{p_1 - p_2}}$$

where

p_1 = sample proportion of successes in group 1

p_2 = sample proportion of successes in group 2

$\pi_1 - \pi_2$ = hypothesized population proportion 1 minus hypothesized population proportion 2

$S_{p_1 - p_2}$ = pooled estimate of the standard error of differences in proportions

To calculate the standard error of the differences in proportions, use the formula

$$S_{p_1 - p_2} = \sqrt{\bar{p}\,\bar{q}\left(\frac{1}{n_1} + \frac{1}{n_2}\right)}$$

where

$\bar{p}$ = pooled estimate of proportion of successes in a sample

$\bar{q} = 1 - \bar{p}$, or pooled estimate of proportion of failures in a sample

n_1 = sample size for group 1

n_2 = sample size for group 2

To calculate the pooled estimator, $\bar{p}$, use the formula

$$\bar{p} = \frac{n_1 p_1 + n_2 p_2}{n_1 + p_2}$$

Z-test for differences of proportions

A technique used to test the hypothesis that proportions are significantly different for two independent samples or groups.

One-Way Analysis of Variance (ANOVA)

When the means of more than two groups or populations are to be compared, one-way **analysis of variance (ANOVA)** is the appropriate statistical tool. ANOVA involving only one grouping variable is often referred to as *one-way* ANOVA because only one independent variable is involved. Another way to define ANOVA is as the appropriate statistical technique to examine the effect of a less-than interval independent variable on an at-least interval dependent variable. Thus, a categorical independent variable and a continuous dependent variable are involved. An independent samples *t*-test can be thought of as a special case of ANOVA in which the independent variable has only two levels. When more levels exist, the *t*-test alone cannot handle the problem.

The statistical null hypothesis for ANOVA is stated as follows:

$$\mu_1 = \mu_2 = \mu_3 = \cdots = \mu_k$$

The symbol k is the number of groups or categories for an independent variable. In other words, all group means are equal. The substantive hypothesis tested in ANOVA is

At least one group mean is not equal to another group mean.

As the term *analysis of variance* suggests, the problem requires comparing variances to make inferences about the means.

Consider how a sample of prices for a notebook computer could be explained by the source of the price. Specifically, the independent variable could be thought of as "source," meaning the advertised price was for a website purchase or for an instore purchase. The dependent variable is price. Since only two groups exist for the independent variable, either an independent samples *t*-test or one-way ANOVA could be used. The results would be identical.

However, assume that source involved three group levels. Prices would now be compared based on whether the retailer was a bricks–and–clicks retailer (multichannel, meaning real and virtual stores), a bricks–only store (only physical stores) or a clicks–only retailer (virtual or Internet stores only). One-way ANOVA would be the choice for this analysis.

Simple Illustration of ANOVA

ANOVA's logic is fairly simple. Look at the following data table describing how much coffee respondents report drinking each day based on which shift they work (GY stands for Graveyard shift, which is typically from about 5:00 p.m. until about 1:00 a.m.).

Day	1
Day	3
Day	4
Day	0
Day	2
GY	7
GY	2
GY	1
GY	6
Night	6
Night	8
Night	3
Night	7
Night	6

The following table displays the means for each group and the overall mean:

Shift	Mean	Std. Deviation	N
Day	2.00	1.58	5
GY	4.00	2.94	4
Night	6.00	1.87	5
Total	4.00	2.63	14

Analysis of variance (ANOVA)

Analysis involving the investigation of the effects of one treatment variable on an interval-scaled dependent variable—a hypothesis-testing technique to determine whether statistically significant differences in means occur between two or more groups.

EXHIBIT **15.5** Illustration of ANOVA Logic

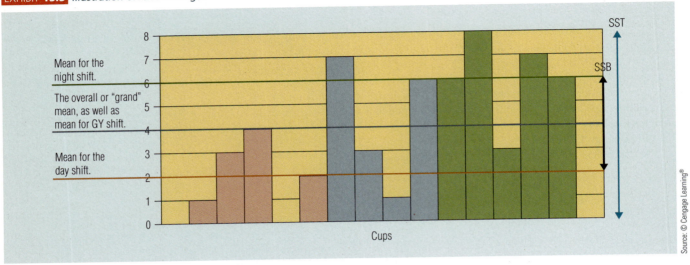

Exhibit 15.5 plots each observation with a bar. The long blue vertical line illustrates the total range of observations. The lowest is 0 cups and the highest is 8 cups of coffee for a range of 8. The overall mean is 4 cups. Each group mean is shown with a different colored line that matches the bars corresponding to the group. The day shift averages 2 cups of coffee a day, the graveyard shift 4 cups, and the night shift 6 cups of coffee per day.

Here is the basic idea of ANOVA. Look at the dark double-headed arrow in Exhibit 15.5. This line represents the range of the differences between group means. In this case, the lowest mean is 2 cups and the highest mean is 6 cups. Thus, the blue vertical line corresponds to the total variation (range) in the data and the thick double-headed black vertical line corresponds to the variance accounted for by the group differences. As the thick black line accounts for more of the total variance, then the ANOVA model suggests that the group means are not all the same, and in particular, not all the same as the overall mean. This also means that the independent variable, in this case work shift, explains the dependent variable. Here, the results suggest that knowing when someone works explains how much coffee they drink. Night-shift workers drink the most coffee.

Partitioning Variance in ANOVA

The responses to any continuous variable contain a certain amount of variance. We have been discussing variable comparisons created by separating observations into groups. ANOVA works by breaking the total variance in a response down into components that are either due to some grouping variable or due to variance within groups.

Total Variability

An implicit question with the use of ANOVA is, "How can the dependent variable best be predicted?" Without any additional information, the error in predicting an observation is minimized by choosing the central tendency, or mean for an interval variable. For the coffee example, if no information was available about the work shift of each respondent, the best guess for coffee drinking consumption would be four cups. The total error (or variability) that would result from using the **grand mean**, meaning the mean over all observations, to predict all values can be thought of as:

Grand mean

The mean of a variable over all observations.

$$SST = \text{Total of (observed value} - \text{grand mean)}^2 = \sum_{t=1}^{n}\left(x_i - \bar{\bar{x}}\right)$$

Although the term *error* is used, this really represents how much total variation exists among the measures.

Using the first observation, the error of observation would be

$$(1 \text{ cup} - 4 \text{ cups})^2 = 9$$

The same squared error could be computed for each observation and these squared errors totaled to give SST.

Between-Groups Variance

ANOVA tests whether "grouping" observations explains variance in the dependent variable. In Exhibit 15.5, the three colors reflect three levels of the independent variable, work shift. Given this additional information about which shift a respondent works, the prediction changes. Now, instead of guessing the grand mean, the group mean would be used. So, once we know that someone works the day shift, the prediction would be that he or she consumes 2 cups of coffee per day. Similarly, the graveyard and night-shift predictions would be 4 and 6 cups, respectively. Thus, the **between-groups variance** can be found by taking the total sum of the weighted difference (weighted by the sample size of each group or n_g) between group means and the overall mean as shown:

$$SSB = \text{Total of } n_{group}(\text{group mean} - \text{grand mean})^2$$

Between-groups variance
The sum of differences between the group means and the grand mean summed over all groups for a given set of observations.

The weighting factor (n_{group}) is the specific group sample size. Let's consider the first observation once again. Since this observation is in the day shift, we predict 2 cups of coffee will be consumed. Looking at the day shift group observations in Exhibit 15.5, the new error in prediction would be

$$(2 \text{ cups} - 4 \text{ cups})^2 = (2)^2 = 4$$

The error in prediction has been reduced from 3 using the grand mean to 2 using the group mean. This squared difference would be weighted by the group sample size of 5, to yield a contribution to SSB of 20.

Next, the same process could be followed for the other groups yielding two more contributions to SSB. Because the graveyard shift group mean is the same as the grand mean, that group's contribution to SSB is 0. Notice that the night-shift group mean is also 2 different than the grand mean, like the day shift, so this group's contribution to SSB is likewise 20. The total SSB then represents the variation explained by the experimental or independent variable. In this case, total SSB is 40. The reader may look at the statistical results shown in Exhibit 15.6 to find this value in the Sums of Squares column.

Within-Group Error

Finally, error within each group would remain. Whereas the group means explain the variation between the total mean and the group mean, the distance from the group mean and each individual observation remains unexplained. This distance is called **within-group error or variance**. The values for each observation can be found by

$$SSE = \text{Total of (Observed Mean} - \text{Group Mean)}^2 = \sum_{i=1}^{n}(x_i - \bar{x}_g)^2$$

Within-group error or variance
The sum of the differences between observed values and the group mean for a given set of observations; also known as total error variance.

Again, looking at the first observation, the SSE component would be

$$SSE = (1 \text{ cup} - 2 \text{ cups})^2 = 1 \text{ cup}$$

This process could be computed for all observations and then totaled. The result would be the total error variance—a name sometimes used to refer to SSE since it is variability not accounted for by the group means. These three components are used in determining how well an ANOVA model explains a dependent variable.

EXHIBIT 15.6 Interpreting ANOVA

Tests of Between-Subjects Effects (Dependent Variable: Coffee)

Source	Type III Sum of Squares	df	Mean Square	F	Sig.
Corrected Model	40.000[a]	2	20.000	4.400	.039
Intercept	221.538	1	221.538	48.738	.000
Shift	40.000	2	20.000	4.400	.039
Error	50.000	11	4.545		
Total	314.000	14			

[a]R Squared = .444 (Adjusted R Squared = .343)

1. This row shows overall *F*-value testing whether all group means are equal. The sums of squares column calculates the SST, SSE, and SSB (shift row).

Shift	Mean	Std. Error	95% Confidence Interval	
			Lower Bound	Upper Bound
Day	2.000	.953	2.099	4.099
GY	4.000	1.066	1.654	6.346
Night	6.000	.953	3.901	8.099

2. This column shows the group means for each level of the independent variable.

Source: © Cengage Learning®

The *F*-Test

F-test

A procedure used to determine whether there is more variability in the scores of one sample than in the scores of another sample.

The **F-test** is the key statistical test for an ANOVA model. The *F*-test determines whether there is more variability in the scores of one sample than in the scores of another sample. The key question is whether the two sample variances are different from each other or whether they are from the same population. Thus, the test breaks down the variance in a total sample and illustrates why ANOVA is *analysis of variance*.

The *F*-statistic (or *F*-ratio) can be obtained by taking the larger sample variance and dividing by the smaller sample variance. Using tabled values of the *F*-distribution (see www.cengagebrain .com) is much like using the tables of the *Z*- and *t*-distributions that we have previously examined. These tables portray the *F*-distribution, which is a probability distribution of the ratios of sample variances. These tables indicate that the distribution of *F* is actually a family of distributions that changes quite drastically with changes in sample sizes. Thus, degrees of freedom must be specified. Inspection of an *F*-table allows the researcher to determine the probability of finding an *F* as large as a calculated *F*.

Using Variance Components to Compute *F*-Ratios

In ANOVA, the basic consideration for the *F*-test is identifying the relative size of variance components. The three forms of variation described briefly earlier are:

1. SSE—variation of scores due to random error or within-group variance due to individual differences from the group mean. This is the error of prediction.
2. SSB—systematic variation of scores between groups due to manipulation of an experimental variable or group classifications of a measured independent variable or between-group variance.
3. SST—the total observed variation across all groups and individual observations.

The Research Snapshot on page 432 provides additional insight into the mechanics of ANOVA. In addition, the Web resources provided with the text provide some illustrations of how to perform an analysis like this using SPSS, JMP, SAS, or EXCEL.

Thus, we can partition total variability into *within-group variance* and *between-group variance*. The F-distribution is a function of the ratio of these two sources of variances:

$$F = f\left(\frac{SSB}{SSE}\right)$$

A larger ratio of variance between groups to variance within groups implies a greater value of F. If the F-value is large, the results are likely to be statistically significant.

A Different but Equivalent Representation

F also can be thought of as a function of the between-group variance and total variance.

$$F = f\left(\frac{SSB}{SST - SSE}\right)$$

In this sense, the ratio of the thick black line to the blue line representing the total range of data presents the basic idea of the F-value.

Source: © Cengage Learning®

EXHIBIT 15.7

How to do One-Way ANOVA using SAS JMP, SPSS, and EXCEL.

JMP: Click Analyze and then fit Y by X. Enter interval or ratio Y response and nominal or ordinal X Factor. Then click OK.

SPSS: Click Analyze and then choose "Compare Means." Select "One-Way ANOVA" from the options and enter data as shown here. Then click OK.

EXCEL: After adding the data analysis pack, select ANOVA and enter data as shown here. Then click OK.

Is the Price Right?

Marketing researchers often find themselves in situations where they would like to test relationships between a combination of nominal and continuous variables with some continuous dependent variable.

Some marketing researchers recently sought to explore combinations of wine label characteristics and the way they influence how much a consumer is willing to pay. The research questions involved whether customers are willing to pay (WTP) a higher price when (a) the label describes the wine with a technical versus casual description (EXP1), (b) the wine is from France or Oregon (EXP2), and (c) when the consumer's wine knowledge varies ($Q5_2$). Consumers tasted a wine (actually in all cases they tasted the same wine) and were shown the bottle. The label contained the two experimental variables: the description of the wine (either technical or casual) and the origin of the wine (France/Oregon). Wine knowledge was assessed based on the results of a 100 point test assessing how knowledgeable each respondent was about wine. The model can be expressed as:

$$WTP = \bar{\bar{Y}}_{WTP} + \Delta EXP1 + \Delta EXP2 + \Delta EXP1 \times \Delta EXP2 + BQ5_2$$

The researchers examine the research question using a GLM approach within SPSS. They agree that a 0.1 Type I error rate is

Univariate Analysis of Variance

Tests of Between-Subjects Effects

Dependent Variable: WTP

Source	Type III Sum of Squares	df	Mean Square	F	Sig.
Corrected Model	2714.807[a]	4	678.702	4.239	.003
Intercept	27818.172	1	27818.172	173.762	.000
Q5₂	558.065	1	558.065	3.486	.065
Exp1	39.563	1	39.563	.247	.620
Exp2	1233.614	1	1233.614	7.706	.007
Exp1 × Exp2	766.289	1	766.289	4.786	.031
Error	16009.383	100	160.094		
Total	96353.000	105			
Corrected Total	18724.190	104			

a. R Squared =.145 (Adjusted R Squared = .111)

Means by Condition

		Description		
		Casual	Technical	Overall
Place of Origin	Oregon	22.04	24.69	23.37
	France	33.59	26.89	30.24
	Overall	27.82	25.8	26.8

acceptable in this analysis. After opening the data file, the researcher chooses Analyze, General Linear Model, then Univariate. After entering the correct variables the program produces the results:

$$WTP = \bar{\bar{Y}}_{WTP} + \Delta EXP1 + \Delta EXP2 + \Delta EXP1 \times \Delta EXP2 + BQ5_2$$

The ANOVA table suggests that the model explains a significant amount of variance in WTP. The wine's origin significantly affects WTP. Subjects are willing to pay an average of $30.50 when the wine is French but only $23.53 when they believe it is from Oregon. In addition, the interaction between origin and the presentation of information is significant as seen by the F of 4.86 for Exp1× Exp 2. The means by condition suggests that presenting a technical description results in a higher price when the wine is from Oregon ($25.74 versus $21.32) but a lower price when the wine is from France ($33.94 versus $27.06). Finally, the parameter estimate (not shown here) for wine knowledge is −0.09 suggesting that for every point higher in wine knowledge, the subjects are willing to pay 9 cents less for the wine. As a decision maker for a wine company, how could you use this information?

Source: See Moulard, J.G., B.J. Babin, M. Griffin (2015), "How Aspects of a Place Affect a Wine's Authenticity and Value Perception: The Role Country of Origin and Technical Terroir," *International Journal of Wine Business Research*, forthcoming.

Practically Speaking

Exhibit 15.6 displays the ANOVA result for the coffee-drinking example. Again, today, an analyst will use software to get answers even for a small problem like this. The days of hand calculations are gone. Even though this example presents a small problem, one-way ANOVA models with more observations or levels are interpreted in the same way.

In interpreting results, the first thing to check is whether the overall model *F* is significant (see Exhibit 15.6). In this case, the computed *F* = 4.40 with 2 and 11 degrees of freedom. The p-value associated with this value is 0.039. Thus, we have high confidence in concluding that the group means are not all the same. Second, the researcher must remember to examine the actual means for each group to properly interpret the result. Doing so, the conclusion reached is that the night-shift people drink the most coffee, followed by the graveyard-shift workers, and then lastly, the day-shift workers.

Statistical Software

Businesses increasingly rely on data driven marketing analytics. The marketing research analyst has access to statistical software that facilitates statistical analysis by quickly and easily providing results for *t*-tests, cross-tabulations, ANOVA, GLM, and more. Some data mining routines even automate some of this analysis. Some of the most common statistical software packages are SPSS, now owned by IBM, SAS, and its new user friendly product called JMP (a free trial is available at jmp.com). Excel includes basic data analysis functions and an add-in data analysis function that contains procedures like ANOVA. Basic JMP components also become available on the Excel toolbar if both packages are installed on a computer. Most universities provide students with access to one or more of these software packages. A host of other packages are available on the Web including freeware like *R* (r-project.org). However, for marketing researchers, packages like SPSS and JMP offer an easy to use interface and a standardized approach to statistics. Thus, they remain widely used.

General Linear Model

Multivariate dependence techniques are variants of the **general linear model (GLM)**. Simply, the GLM is a way of modeling some process based on how different variables cause fluctuations from the average dependent variable. Fluctuations can come in the form of group means that differ from the overall mean as is in ANOVA or in the form of a significant slope coefficient as in regression.

General linear model (GLM)

A way of explaining and predicting a dependent variable based on fluctuations (variation) from its mean. The fluctuations are due to changes in independent variables.

GLM Equation

The basic idea can be thought of as follows:

$$\hat{Y}_i = \overline{\overline{Y}} + \Delta X + \Delta F + \Delta XF$$

Here, $\overline{\overline{Y}}$ represents a constant, which can be thought of as the overall mean of the dependent variable, ΔX and ΔF represent changes due to main effect independent variables (such as experimental variables) and blocking independent variables (such as covariates or grouping variables), respectively, and ΔXF represents the change due to the combination (interaction effect) of those variables. Realize that Y_i in this case could represent multiple dependent variables, just as X and F could represent multiple independent variables. This form is an ANOVA representation. An Analysis of Covariance (ANCOVA) representation would add a continuous covariate (X_c):

$$\hat{Y}_i = \overline{\overline{Y}} + \Delta X + \Delta F + \Delta XF + BXc$$

B is a regression coefficient as described later.

Regression analysis and *n*-way ANOVA represent common forms that the GLM can take. SAS and SPSS both contain programs specifically referred to by GLM. They are particularly useful in analyzing data from experiments but GLM can also be used to produce regression results.

Regression Analysis

Simple regression investigates a *straight-line relationship* of the type

$$Y = \alpha + \beta X$$

where Y is a continuous dependent variable and X is an independent variable that is usually continuous, although a dichotomous nominal or ordinal variable can be included in the form of a dummy variable. Alpha (α) and beta (β) are two parameters that must be estimated so that the equation best represents a given set of data. These two parameters determine the height of the regression line and the angle of the line relative to horizontal. When these parameters change, the line changes. Together, they represent the changes from the overall mean of the dependent variable for a regression form of the GLM. Regression techniques have the job of estimating values for these parameters that make the line *fit* the observations the best.

The result is simply a linear equation, or the equation for a line, just as in basic algebra! Parameter α represents the Y intercept (where the line crosses the y-axis) and β is the slope coefficient. The slope is the change in Y associated with a change of one unit in X. Slope may also be thought of as rise over run. That is, how much Y rises (or falls, if negative) for every one unit change in the x-axis. A mathematical estimation of the line completes the regression progress by providing estimates for the intercept (b_0) and slope coefficient (b_1):

$$Y_i = b_0 + b_1 X_1 + e_i$$

Interpreting Multiple Regression Analysis

Multiple regression analysis is an extension of simple regression analysis allowing a metric dependent variable to be predicted by multiple independent variables. Thus, one dependent variable is explained by more than one independent variable. When trying to explain sales, plausible independent variables include prices, economic factors, advertising intensity, and consumers' incomes in the area. A simple regression equation can be expanded to represent multiple regression analysis:

$$Y_i = b_0 + b_1 X_1 + b_2 X_2 + b_3 X_3 + \cdots + b_n X_n + e_i$$

Parameter Estimate Choices

The estimates for α and β are the key to regression analysis. In most business research, the estimate of β is most important. The explanatory power of regression rests with β because this is where the direction and strength of the relationship between the independent and dependent variable is explained. A Y-intercept term is sometimes referred to as a constant because α represents a fixed point. An estimated slope coefficient is sometimes referred to as a regression weight, regression coefficient, parameter estimate, or sometimes even as a *path* estimate. The term *path* estimate is a descriptive term adapted because of the way hypothesized causal relationships are often represented in diagrams:

$$X \xrightarrow{\beta_1} Y$$

For all practical purposes, these terms are used interchangeably. Parameter estimates can be presented in either raw or standardized form. One potential problem with raw parameter estimates is due to the fact that, like covariance values, they reflect the measurement scale range. So, if a simple regression involved distance measured with miles, very small parameter estimates may indicate a strong relationship. In contrast, if the very same distance is measured with centimeters, a very large parameter estimate would be needed to indicate a strong relationship. Generally, the raw slope coefficient is abbreviated with a small letter **b**.

Researchers often explain regression results by referring to a **standardized regression coefficient (β)**. A standardized regression coefficient, like a correlation coefficient, provides a common metric allowing regression results to be compared to one another no matter what the original scale range may have been. Due to the mathematics involved in standardization, the standardized Y-intercept term is always 0.

Researchers use shorthand to label regression coefficients as either "raw" or "standardized." The most common shorthand is as follows:

- B_0 or b_0—raw (unstandardized) Y-intercept term; an estimate of what was referred to as α earlier.
- B_1 or b_1—raw regression coefficient or estimate.
- β_1—standardized regression coefficients.

The bottom line is that when the actual units of measurement are the focus of analysis, such as might be the case in trying to forecast sales during some period, raw (unstandardized) coefficients are most appropriate. When the goal is explanation of some outcome by examining a series of relationships, standardized regression coefficients are more appropriate because they allow for the size of the relationship for each independent variable to be compared directly. A β of 0.6 is a stronger relationship than a β of 0.2. With unstandardized coefficients, this comparison cannot be directly made.

Steps in Interpreting a Multiple Regression Model

Multiple regression models often are used to test some proposed theoretical model. For instance, a researcher may be asked to develop and test a model explaining business unit performance. Why do some business units outperform others? Multiple regression models can be interpreted using these steps:

1. Examine the model F-test. If the test result is not significant, the model should be dismissed and there is no need to proceed to further steps.
2. Examine the individual statistical tests for each parameter estimate. Independent variables with significant results can be considered a significant explanatory variable.
3. Examine the model R^2. No cutoff values exist that can distinguish an acceptable amount of explained variation across all regression models. However, the absolute value of R^2 is more important when the researcher is more interested in prediction than explanation. In other words, the regression is run for pure forecasting purposes. When the model is more oriented toward explaining which variables are most important in explaining the dependent variable, cutoff values for the model R^2 are inappropriate.
4. A next step would be to diagnose multicollinearity. Simply put, this is the extent to which the independent variables are redundant. A detailed discussion of this topic is beyond the scope of this particular text. However, a simple check for problems can be obtained by taking a look at the Variance Inflation Factors (VIF). Most statistical packages allow these to be computed. VIFs of between 1 and 2 are generally not indicative of problems with multicollinearity. As they become larger, the results become more susceptible to interpretation problems because of overlap in the independent variables.

Exhibit 15.8 illustrates this step-by-step process using regression results from an SPSS output an SPSS. The regression model explains marketing employees' bonuses for a Fortune 500 company. The independent variables are Tools (a dummy variable representing whether the employee uses a new social network mining tool coded 1 if the employee installed the software and 0 if not), Hours (number of hours working in field per week), and Exp (experience in the industry in years). In this case, the researcher is using a maximum acceptable Type I error rate of 0.05. The conclusion reached from this analysis is that hours spent in the field pays off in increased bonus amounts ($\beta = 0.69$, p < 0.05).

EXHIBIT 15.8

Illustration of Steps for Interpreting a Multiple Regression Model

TIPS OF THE TRADE

- Cross-tabulations are widely applied in market research reports and presentations.
  - Cross-tabs can be very useful in big data analysis exploring data for useful relationships.
  - Cross-tabulations are appropriate for research questions involving predictions of categorical dependent variables using categorical independent variables.
  - When more than four categories exist, cross-tabulation tables can become difficult to present clearly.
  - Independent variables are placed in rows and dependent variables are placed in columns.
- A t-test can be used to compare means.

- An independent samples t-test predicts a continuous (interval or ratio) dependent variable with a categorical (nominal or ordinal) independent (grouping) variable.
  - A paired-samples t-test compares means from two different responses from the same sampling unit. Therefore, the sampling is dependent.
- A one-way ANOVA extends the concept of an independent samples t-test to more than two groups.
- Simple hand calculations can be useful in learning what statistical procedures actually do. However, in conducting actual tests, take advantage of computer software whenever permissible.

© GEORGE DOYLE & CIARAN GRIFFIN

::SUMMARY

1. Choose an appropriate statistic based on data characteristics. A skilled researcher can quickly determine the appropriate statistic for a given research question. In this chapter, we learned that if the researcher can distinguish independent from dependent variables, know how many of each are involved in the analysis, and know the level of scale measurement for each, choosing the right statistic becomes easy.

2. Compute a χ^2 statistic for cross-tab results. Bivariate statistical techniques analyze scores on two variables at a time. A cross-tabulation is a useful way of depicting and analyzing the way two categorical variables are related to one another. For instance, a nominal independent variable may be used to predict a nominal dependent variable. Cross-tabulations are very useful and lend themselves well to depicting results in charts. The χ^2 statistic is the test statistic appropriate for testing relationships among variables used in a cross-tabulation table. Higher χ^2 values are generally associated with lower p-values and therefore greater probability of a relationship between the row and column variables. The process of testing a hypothesis using a χ^2 statistic is similar in concept to practically all the hypotheses testing procedures that follow.

3. Use a t-test to compare a difference between two means. When a researcher needs to compare means for a variable grouped into two categories based on some less–than interval variable, a t-test is appropriate. An independent samples t-test examines whether a dependent variable like price differs based on a grouping variable like biological sex. Statistically, the test examines whether the difference between the mean for men and women is different from 0. Larger t-values are associated with smaller p-values and statistical significance. A paired–samples t-test examines whether the means from two variables that are not independent are different. A common situation calling for this test is when the two observations are from the same respondent or sampling unit. A simple before–and–after test calls for a paired-samples t-test so long as the dependent variable is continuous.

4. Conduct a one-way analysis of variance test (ANOVA). ANOVA is the appropriate statistical technique to examine the effect of a less-than interval independent variable on an at-least interval dependent variable. Conceptually, ANOVA partitions the total variability into three types: total variation, between-group variation, and within-group variation. As the explained variance represented by SSB becomes larger relative to SSE or SST, the ANOVA model is more likely to be significant, indicating that at least one group mean is different from another group mean.

5. Appreciate the practicality of modern statistical software packages. Hand calculations using a simple calculator can sometimes be a good way for getting the feel of exactly what some statistic is doing; however, even small applications are usually better performed with the help of some statistical software whether it be Excel, SPSS, SAS, JMP, or some other package. This saves time and helps reduce mathematical errors. Almost all commercial statistical software provide point and click convenience.

6. Understand how the General Linear Model (GLM) can predict a key dependent variable. The General Linear Model is a widely used way of representing statistical effects as systematic deviations from the population mean. ANOVA and Linear Regression are among the most common forms of the GLM. The results should be analyzed based on how well they account for variation in the dependent variable and based on what specific independent variables relate significantly to the dependent variable.

:: KEY TERMS AND CONCEPTS

analysis of variance (ANOVA), *427*
between-groups variance, *429*
F-test, *430*
general linear model (GLM), *433*
grand mean, *428*
independent samples *t*-test, *420*
multiple regression analysis, *434*

paired-samples *t*-test, *425*
pooled estimate of the standard error, *421*
standardized regression coefficient (β), *434*
tests of differences, *413*
within-group error or variance, *429*
Z-test for differences of proportions, *426*

:: QUESTIONS FOR REVIEW AND CRITICAL THINKING

1. What statistical test of differences is appropriate in the following situations?
   a. Comparison of average campaign contributions (in $) of Democrats, Republicans, and Independents.
   b. Advertising managers and brand managers have responded "Yes," "No," or "Not sure" to an attitude question. The advertising and brand managers' responses are to be compared.
   c. One-half of a sample received an incentive in a mail survey while the other half did not. A comparison of response rates is desired.
   d. A researcher believes coupon links pushed through Facebook.com will generate more sales than coupon links pushed through Twitter.com.
   e. A manager wishes to compare the job performance of a salesperson before ethics training with the performance of that same salesperson after ethics training.

2. Perform a χ^2 test on the following data (hint: set up a spreadsheet to perform the calculations as a good way of learning what the test really does):
   a. Do managers and line employees differ in their response to the statement, "Increased regulation is the best way to ensure safe products"?

	Agree	Disagree	No Opinion
Managers	58	66	8
Line Employees	34	24	10
Totals	92	90	18

   b. Test the following hypothesis with the following data: Women are more likely to have a pinterest.com account. Do you have a pinterest.com account?

	Yes	No
Male	25	75
Female	80	20

3. Interpret the following computer cross-tab output including a χ^2 test. Variable EDUCATION is a response to "What is your highest level of educational achievement?" HS means a high school diploma, SC means some college, BS means a bachelor's degree, and MBA means a master of business administration. Variable WIN is how well the respondent did on a set of casino games of chance. A 1 means they would have lost more than $100, a 2 means they approximately broke even, and a 3 means they won more than $100. What is the result of exploring a

research question that education influences performance on casino gambling? Comment on your conclusion and any issues in interpreting the result.

The SAS System
The FREQ Procedure
Table of Education by WIN

Education Frequency Percent Row Pct Col Pct	1	2	3	Total
MBA	3	10	4	17
	1.12	3.72	1.49	6.32
	17.65	58.82	23.53	
	3.19	10.31	5.13	
BS	11	19	12	42
	4.09	7.06	4.46	15.61
	26.19	45.24	28.57	
	11.70	19.59	15.38	
SC	33	30	27	90
	12.27	11.15	10.04	33.45
	35.67	33.33	30.00	
	35.11	30.93	34.62	
HS	47	38	35	120
	17.47	14.13	13.01	44.61
	29.17	31.67	29.17	
	50.00	39.18	44.57	
Total	94	97	78	269
	34.94	36.06	29.00	100.00

Win spans columns 1, 2, 3.

Statistics for Table of Education by WIN

Statistic	df	Value	Prob
Chi-Square	6	7.5275	0.2748

Sample Size = 269

4. A store manager's computer-generated list of all retail sales employees indicates that 70 percent are full-time employees, 20 percent are part-time employees, and 10 percent are furloughed or laid-off employees. A sample of 50 employees from the list indicates that there are 40 full-time employees, 6 part-time employees, and 4 furloughed/laid-off employees. Conduct a statistical test to determine whether the sample is representative of the population.

5. Test the following hypothesis using the data summarized in the following table. Interpret your result:

H1: Internet retailers offer lower prices for tablet computers than do traditional in-store retailers.

Retail Type	Average Tablet Price	Standard Deviation	n
E-tailers	$371.95	$50.00	25
In-store retailers	$360.30	$45.00	25

6. Selected territories in a company's eastern and western regions were rated for sales potential based on the company's evaluation system. A sales manager wishes to conduct a t-test of means to determine whether there is a difference between the two regions. Conduct this test, preferably using a statistical software package, and draw the appropriate conclusion:

Region	Territory	Rating	Region	Territory	Rating
West	1	74	East	8	81
West	2	88	East	9	63
West	3	78	East	10	56
West	4	85	East	11	68
West	5	100	East	12	80
West	6	114	East	13	79
West	7	98	East	14	69

How would this result change if the company only had seven territories in the West and seven in the East?

7. How does an independent samples t-test differ from the following?
   a. one-way ANOVA
   b. paired-samples t-test
   c. a χ^2 test

8. Are t-tests or Z-tests used more often in marketing research? Why?

9. A sales force received some management-by-objectives training. Are the before/after mean scores for salespeople's job performance statistically significant at the 0.05 level? The results from a sample of employees are as follows (use your computer and statistical software to solve this problem):

Salesperson	Before	After	Salesperson	Before	After
Carlos	4.84	5.43	Tommy	4.00	5.00
Sammy	5.24	5.51	Laurie	4.67	4.50
Melanie	5.37	5.42	Ronald	4.95	4.40
Philippe	3.69	4.50	Amanda	4.00	5.95
Cargill	5.95	5.90	Brittany	3.75	3.50
Dwight	4.75	5.25	Mathew	3.85	4.00
Amy	3.90	4.50	Alice	5.00	4.10
Kallua	3.20	3.75	Jake	4.00	5.15

10. Using the "CAR" data that accompanies the text (see website), consider the following problem. The data describe attitudes of car owners from Germany and the United States toward their automobiles. The variable "ATT" is how much respondents like their current car (attitude), "ATTNEW" is their attitude toward a new car called the Cycle. The "COUNTRY" variable is self-explanatory. The "SPEND" variable is how much the respondents spend on average on products to keep their cars clean (in Euros). Using SPSS or other statistical software, test the following hypotheses:

H1: The owners' attitudes toward the Cycle are more favorable than attitudes toward their current cars.
H2: Germans like their cars more than Americans.

11. Interpret the following output examining group differences for purchase intentions. The three groups refer to consumers from three states: Florida, Minnesota, and Hawaii.

Tests of Between-Subjects Effects
Dependent Variable: int2

Source	Type III Sum of Squares	df	Mean Square	F	Sig.
Corrected Model	681.746[a]	2	3340.873	3.227	0.043
Intercept	308897.012	1	308897.012	298.323	0.000
State	6681.746	2	3340.873	3.227	0.043
Error	148068.543	143	1035.444		
Total	459697.250	146			
Corrected Total	154750.289	145			

[a]R Squared = 0.043 (Adjusted R Squared = 0.030)

Law
Dependent Variable: int2

State	Mean	Std. Error	95% Confidence Interval Lower Bound	Upper Bound
F	37.018	4.339	28.441	45.595
M	50.357	4.965	40.542	60.172
H	51.459	4.597	42.373	60.546

12. The following table gives a football team's season–ticket sales, percentage of games won, and number of active alumni for the years 1998–2015.

Year	Season-Ticket Sales	Percentage of Games Won	Number of Active Alumni
1998	4,995	40	NA
1999	8,599	54	3,450
2000	8,479	55	3,801
2001	8,419	58	4,000
2002	10,253	63	4,098
2003	12,457	75	6,315
2004	13,285	36	6,860
2005	14,177	27	8,423
2006	15,730	63	9,000
2007	15,805	70	9,500
2008	15,575	72	9,530
2009	15,900	75	9,550
2010	14,010	80	9,560
2011	12,500	82	9,575
2012	10,900	30	9,540
2013	9,998	25	9,580
2014	12,750	78	9,705
2015	14,050	78	10,000

a. Enter the data into an electronic file.
b. Estimate a regression model for sales = Percentage of games won.
c. Estimate a regression model for sales = Number of active alumni.
d. Estimate a multiple regression model predicting sales using variables of your choice.
e. If *sales* is the dependent variable, which of the two independent variables do you think explains sales better? Explain.

13. Interpret the following GLM results. Following from an example in the chapter, *performance* is the performance rating for a business unit manager. *Sales* is a measure of the average sales for that

```
                        The SAS System
                       The GLM Procedure
                  Dependent Variable: Performance

                                    Sum of
    Source              DF          Squares      Mean Square   F Value   Pr > F
    Model                3      173.6381430      57.8793810     13.87    <.0001
    Error               36      150.2341040       4.1731696
    Corrected Total     39      323.8722470

              R-Square    Coeff Var      Root MSE    Performance Mean
              0.536132    2.514731       2.042834         81.23468

    Source              DF     Type III SS     Mean Square   F Value   Pr > F
    Dummy                1     136.9511200     136.9511200     32.82    <.0001
    Sales                1      22.4950649      22.4950649      5.39    0.0260
    Experience           1       2.2356995       2.2356995      0.54    0.4689
Level of    -------Performance------- ----------Sales---------- ----Experience--------
Dummy   N     Mean      Std Dev       Mean       Std Dev       Mean        Std Dev
0      22  79.4848842  1.78987031  15979.7723  2008.32604  23.8984087   8.27327485
1      18  83.3733171  2.50773844  16432.0080  2015.18863  20.6788050   8.96324112
```

unit. *Experience* is the number of years the manager has been in the industry. The variable *dummy* has been added. This variable is a 0 if the manager has no advanced college degree and a 1 if the manager has an MBA. Do you have any recommendations?

14. Interpret the following regression results. All of the variables are the same as in number 13. These results are produced with a regression program instead of the GLM-univariate ANOVA program.

a. What do you notice when the results are compared to those in number 13? Comment.
b. List the independent variables in order from greatest to least in terms of how strong the relationship is with performance.
c. When might one prefer to use an ANOVA program instead of a multiple regression program?

```
                    The SAS System
                   The REG Procedure
                    Model: MODEL1
            Dependent Variable: performance

            Number of Observations Read 40
            Number of Observations Used 40
```

Analysis of Variance

Source	DF	Sum of Squares	Mean Square	F Value	Pr > F
Model	3	173.63814	57.87938	13.87	<.0001
Error	36	150.23410	4.17317		
Corrected Total	39	323.87225			

Root MSE	2.04283	R-Square	0.5361
Dependent Mean	81.23468	Adj R-Sq	0.4975
Coeff Var	2.51473		

Parameter Estimates

Variable	Label	DF	Parameter Estimate	Standard Error	t-Value	Pr > |t|	Standardized Estimate
Intercept	Intercept	1	72.68459	2.88092	25.23	<.0001	0
Dummy	Dummy	1	3.80621	0.66442	5.73	<.0001	0.66546
Sales	Sales	1	0.00038324	0.00016507	2.32	0.0260	0.26578
Experience	Experience	1	0.02829	0.03866	0.73	0.4689	0.08475

:: RESEARCH ACTIVITIES

1. How ethical is it to do business in different countries around the world? An international organization, Transparency International, keeps track of the perception of ethical practices in different countries. Visit the website and search for the latest corruption indices (**http://cpi.transparency.org/cpi2013/results/**). Using the data found here for 2013, test the following research questions.

   a. Are nations from Europe and North America perceived to be more ethical than nations from Asia, Africa, and South America? Include Australia and New Zealand with Europe.

   b. Are there differences among the corruption indices between 2005 and 2013?

2. Using the retail data available in the resources for this chapter, examine the following research questions: (1) Verizon consumers have a more favorable attitude than do AT&T consumers. (2) Are consumers with a coupon willing to pay the same amount as are consumers without a coupon? (3) Does the combination of store/phone brand and coupon influence willingness to pay (WTP_ACC)? The following table contains a guide to the file.

X1	X2	X3	INT1	INT2	INT3	Traditional	ATT1	ATT2	ATT3	ATT4	Q31	Q32	Q135	AGE	WTP_ACC	TotTime
Retail Phone Store. 0=Verizon, 1=ATT	Where promotion was delivered, 0=BNM (physical store) and 1=Online	Was$s Off Coupon Provided, 0=no, 1=yes	Intention Likert Scale Item 1	Intention Likert Scale Item 2	Intention Likert Scale Item 3	Did respondent view phone as traditional	Attitude Semantic Differential 1	Attitude Semantic Differential 2	Attitude Semantic Differential 3	Attitude Semantic Differential 4	Switch or keep old phone? 0 =switch, 1 =keep	Time of day store visited. 1= day,2= night	Gender, 1=male,2 =female	in years	Willingness topay for phone plus add-ons and accessories	Total times shopping

Old School versus New School Sports Fans

Case 15.1

Download the data sets for this case from **www.cengagebrain.com** *or request them from your instructor.*

Three academic researchers investigated the idea that, in American sports and society, there are segments with conflicting views about the goal of competition in society (i.e., winning versus self-actualization) and the acceptable/desirable way of achieving this goal. Persons who believe in "winning at any cost" in sports can be labeled new school individuals according to the researchers. The new school is founded on notions of the individual before the team, loyalty to the highest bidder, and high-tech production and consumption of professional sports. On the other hand, people may value the traditions and process of sports more highly. They believe that "how you play the game matters." The researchers label these individuals as old school individuals. The old school emerges from old-fashioned American notions of the team before the player, sportsmanship, and competition simply for "love of the game."

The researchers tried to measure New School/Old School orientation by asking agreement with several attitude statements (the survey contained over 15 items in total but only 10 were used here after some initial analyses). The scores on these ten statements

allowed the researchers to form a composite measure representing Old School orientations. Based on their composite scores, respondents were grouped into low, middle, and high Old School groups. A low Old School orientation conversely could be thought of as a high New School orientation. One research question of interest is whether men and women differ in their orientation toward competition in sports. Case Exhibit 15.1–1 shows the computer output of a cross-tabulation to relate the gender of the respondent (GENDER) with the New School/Old School grouping (OLDSKOOL). In the results, the Pearson Chi-Square can be used to interpret statistical significance.

Questions

1. Is this form of analysis appropriate for the research question?
2. Interpret the computer output and critique the analysis.
3. Explore the GLM (General Linear Model) procedure in SAS, SPSS, or JMP (access using "fit model") by testing a model using show_off as the dependent variable and gender as the independent variable.
   a. Interpret the result.
   b. Add age as a covariate and repeat the analysis. Interpret the result.

CASE EXHIBIT 15.1-1 SPSS Output

Contingency Table				
	OLDSKOOL			
Count **Total %** **Col %** **Row %** **Expected**	**Low**	**Middle**	**High**	**Row Totals**
Woman	37	40	8	85
	13.70	14.81	2.96	31.48
	45.68	27.03	19.51	
	43.53	47.06	9.41	
	25.5	46.5926	12.9074	
Men	44	108	33	185
	16.30	40.00	12.22	68.52
	54.32	72.97	80.49	
	23.78	58.38	17.84	
	55.5	101.407	28.0926	
Column Totals	81	148	41	270
	30.00	54.81	15.19	

(Continued)

Tests			
N	DF	-LogLike	RSquare (U)
270	2	5.7424309	0.0218
Test	ChiSquare	Prob>ChiSq	
Likelihood Ratio	11.485	0.0032*	
Pearson	11.654	0.0029*	

Source: © Cengage Learning®

International Operations at CarCare Inc.

Case 15.2

CarCare is considering expanding its operations beyond the United States. The company wants to know whether it should target countries with consumers who tend to have a positive attitude toward their current cars. It has gathered data on U.S. and German car owners. The data are included in the "car" data set that can be viewed on the website at **www.cengagebrain.com** (car.sav or car.xls) or available from your instructor. Using the data, conduct a correlation and simple regression analysis using spending as the dependent variable and attitude toward the current car as the independent variable.

1. Test the hypothesis: Attitude toward one's car is related positively to spending for car-care products.
2. Would you recommend they do more research to identify nations with relatively favorable attitudes toward the cars they own?

PHOTODISC GREEN/GETTY IMAGES

Communicating Research Results

CHAPTER 16

LEARNING OUTCOMES

After studying this chapter, you should be able to:

1. Create an outline for a research project using the basic parts of a final report
2. Explain how to use tables for presenting numerical information
3. Summarize how to select and use the types of research charts
4. Know how to give an effective oral presentation
5. Discuss the importance of Internet reporting and research follow-up

Chapter Vignette:

Effective Research Is a Stone's Throw Away

The Rosetta Stone represents one of the greatest findings in the history of communication. The stone dates back to several centuries before Christ but was discovered near the ancient city of Rosetta, Egypt, at the end of the eighteenth century. What made this discovery so special? The etchings on the stone represented a decree to the peoples of that time, which was written not only in hieroglyphics but also in ancient Greek. French and British researchers worked for decades and eventually produced a translation between the ancient Greek and the hieroglyphic script. They learned that hieroglyphics were not just pictures but that over time, hieroglyphics had developed into a language with symbols that took on phonetic characteristics including sound. This breakthrough meant that scores of ancient etchings could now communicate effectively because of the translation code made possible by the Rosetta Stone.[1]

Fortunately, marketing researchers don't have to write research reports on stones, but effective communication can still be pretty hard! The research report is the tool that translates what most people could not possibly understand into a useful report that communicates important information for business managers, marketing executives, policy makers, or other marketing researchers. Marketing practitioners lack working knowledge of multivariate data analysis, ethnography, phenomenology, or most other technical aspects of marketing research.

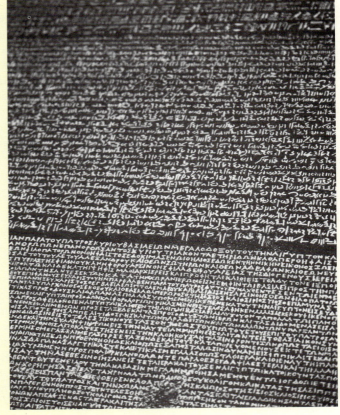

So even if researchers conduct the marketing research properly, the research can still be a complete failure if the researcher is unable to produce a user-friendly, concise, and actionable research report. In fact, science itself is of little use unless one can effectively communicate its meaning.[2]

In fact, employers often view excellent writing skills as a necessary requisite when evaluating marketing research candidates. Unfortunately, these same employers are often disappointed with technical employees' communication skills. These employees are expected not only to write formal research reports but also to make effective oral presentations and, increasingly, to deliver effective and accurate communication via Internet media, including online meetings, blogs, and even tweets. Imagine the chore of translating results of a months-long research project into a 140-character tweet![3] Sounds like a job for another Rosetta Stone!

Introduction

Researchers can easily be tempted into rushing through the research report. By the time the report is written, the researchers may well feel exhausted or burned out and ready to move on to something new. With all the *real* work done, the results jut need to be documented. This feeling can be disastrous, however. If people who need to use the research results have to wade through a disorganized presentation, find themselves confused by technical jargon, or find sloppiness of language or thought, they will probably discount the report and make decisions as if the project never started. So the research report is a crucial means for communicating the whole project's benefits. This chapter explains the communication of research results using written reports, presentations, and follow-up conversations.[4] The Research Snapshot on the next page shows how difficult accurate communication can be.

The Project and the Report

Research report

An oral presentation or written statement of research results, strategic recommendations, and/or other conclusions to a specific audience.

A **research report** is a formal presentation and/or written statement that communicates research results and draws appropriate conclusions following from a research project. The report provides the *answers* and documents procedures to the interested audience. For an applied market research project, the report presents the results accomplishing the proposal's deliverables, including specific managerial recommendations. In fact, deliverables should be a logical conclusion of the report contents. A basic marketing researcher writes a similar report that often takes the form of a white paper or scholarly research paper targeted for publication in a research journal such as the *Journal of Marketing*, the *Journal of the Academy of Marketing Science*, or the *Journal of Business Research*. A written research report often coincides with a formal presentation delivered in person and/or via the Internet.

To the Point

"It is a luxury to be understood."

—RALPH WALDO EMERSON

Report Format

Every significant research project produces a report of some kind. Report contents are specific to each report. The research report documents the entire life of the research project. Market and marketing researchers tend to follow some conventions with respect to the **report format**. This research report format follows consensus about what ordered parts and contents comprise a professional research document. A conventional format makes the document user friendly.

Report format

A standard outline that marketing research reports use as a guide to make sure that the key elements are presented in a logical and usable order.

In fact, although we think of the research report as the culmination of a research project, the report outline that describes the standard format serves as a useful guide for the entire research project. In fact, such an outline serves as a template for a research project. If students are asked to complete a research project for this class, the report outline can also serve as a step-by-step guide in completing the project. Thus, the student resources for the text contain a file with the outline that can be used as a guide. The student needs to complete the relevant parts noted in the research outline to finish the project. Not all parts are included in all reports. However, parts that are common to all reports are noted in the outline.

Now, the end is near. The Survey This! feature has covered quite a bit of ground about marketing research students' preferences and behaviors. The topics include how students interact with technology, what are their preferences for communicating and studying, and how they spend their time, among other things. Additionally, you may be interested in comparing how different groups of respondents are similar or alike. Perhaps you are curious about some of these issues. Develop at least three research questions. Examine these questions using the data from the survey. Prepare a written report and slide show presentation that could be used to brief an interested audience of businesspeople who wish to better serve this particular market. Try to pick issues that you are truly curious about and you'll find yourself anxious to get to the answer!

Source: www.qualtrics.com

© GEORGE DOYLE & CIARAN GRIFFIN

Large research companies also use standard templates that allow the researcher to fill in the custom information derived from the specific research project. These large companies may also employ a technical writing staff to assist in the production of reports. Not every report fits the exact template, and occasionally some reports may omit a section or include other sections that are not part of the basic template. But most research projects will follow an outline that includes the following major elements:

1. Title page
2. Letter of transmittal
3. Letter of authorization
4. Table of contents (and lists of figures and tables)
5. Executive summary
   a. Objectives
   b. Results
   c. Conclusions
   d. Recommendations
6. Body
   a. Introduction
      1. Background
      2. Objectives
   a. Methodology
   b. Results
   c. Limitations
   d. Conclusions and recommendations
7. Appendix
   a. Data collection forms
   b. Detailed calculations
   c. General tables
   d. Bibliography
   e. Other support material

Exhibit 16.1 illustrates this format graphically.

RESEARCH SNAPSHOT

Statistics show 20 percent of report statistics are misleading. Oh Yeah??!!

People may not like math, but when it comes to making judgments, people like numbers. Just consider how many news stories in the paper or news report some poll results, trends, or other statistics. Similarly, many ads make claims backed up by statistics. Consider these *facts* taken from newspaper reports:

"Visa announced that its new credit card will carry an adjustable rate set monthly at four percent above the prime rate, in line with other variable-rate cards."

This is a common mistake: confusing *percentage* and *percentage points*. A rate set so slightly above the prime rate would be an unusually good bargain. For example, at the time of this writing, the U.S. federal prime rate is 3.25 percent; prime plus 4 percent would be just 3.38 percent, far below the rates charged by most credit cards. The writer probably meant Visa would charge prime rate plus four percentage points, which in this example would be 7.25 percent.

"Battling Hunger, a food pantry, said it delivered 110,000 tons of food to Detroit last Thanksgiving. The food was delivered to help residents there overcome the effects of a severe economic slump, particularly in the automobile industry."

Can you spot any problems with such statements? Looking carefully, each of these examples is potentially misleading. Misleading reports may not have to do with the numbers themselves, but with other details such as

the units of measure or standards of comparison. In this case, 110,000 tons equals 220 million pounds of food. Can that be reasonable? Even if the food pantry served a million people—all of Detroit plus some suburbanites—it would have distributed 220 pounds of food to each individual. Not likely. When numbers are this unrealistic, the writer should check the calculations, including the decimal point's location, and the units. Perhaps this writer meant 110,000 pounds or 110 tons.

"More Americans tell pollsters they are currently more often happy than worried."

This seems simple enough. However, what the story does not point out is that the poll results contain only results taken on the weekend. People who are polled on weekdays give the opposite picture—they are more worried than happy. So pay attention to the details before jumping to conclusions.

Sources: Based on Bialik, C. (2009), "In Ads, 1 Out of 5 Stats Is Bogus," *Wall Street Journal*, (March 11), 12. Bialik, C. (2011), "U.S. News—The Numbers Guy: Happy? Statisticians Aren't Buying It," *Wall Street Journal* (March 26), 2.

EXHIBIT 16.1 Report Format

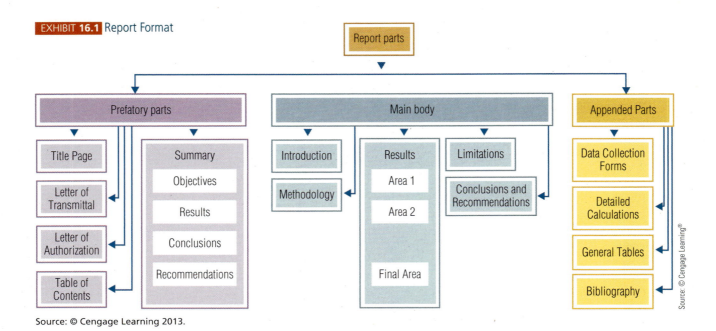

Source: © Cengage Learning 2013.

Tailoring the Format to the Project

The format of a research report may need to be adjusted for two reasons: (1) to obtain the proper level of formality and (2) to decrease the complexity of the report. The format given here is for the most formal type of report, such as one for a large project done within an organization or one done by a research agency for a client company. A formal report typically arrives to the client bound in a permanent cover and may be hundreds of pages long. Electronic versions usually are made available and are typically in a pdf format to maximize compatibility. If the report contains potentially sensitive information, the electronic files are password protected.

In less-formal reports, parts are shorter or sometimes omitted. Just as we choose our clothing to match the formality of an occasion, not every report comes dressed, so to speak, in a tuxedo or long evening gown. A formal report includes all prefatory parts in detail—title page, copies of letters of transmittal and authorization, and table of contents. Like changing into an everyday business suit from a tuxedo, dropping down to the next lower level of formality involves eliminating parts of the prefatory material that are inessential in such a situation and reducing the complexity of the report body as well. In general, as the report moves down through the sport coat and slacks and then blue jeans stages, more prefatory parts are dropped, and the complexity and length of the report body are reduced.

How does the researcher decide on the appropriate level of formality? The general rule is to include all the parts needed for effective communication in the particular circumstances—and no more. This depends on how far up in management the report is expected to go and how routine the matter is. A researcher's immediate supervisor does not need a 100-page, *black-tie* report on a routine project. However, the board of directors does not want a one-page *blue jeans* report on a big project that backs a major expansion program. The researcher may take a formal report presented to top management and strip it of some prefatory parts (and thus reduced in formality) for wider circulation within the company. The condensing of the report in this fashion would take place only with top management approval.

The Parts of the Report

Typically, research reports follow the same general outline. Research reports are a form of technical writing, and as such, readers may well expect the paper to follow this format. Here, the old adage "If it ain't broke, don't fix it" truly applies.

Title Page

The *title page* provides a name for the report, tells for whom the report was prepared (when prepared for a specific entity and not for public consumption), tells who performed the research (lists at least the primary investigators responsible) and wrote the report, and gives the date of release or presentation. The report's title should give a concise indication of the purpose of the research project. Researchers often find it challenging to come up with a title that is both descriptive and brief. Generally, a shorter title is better, and a good rule of thumb is not to extend the title far beyond twelve words. The title page also provides contact information for both the preparer and the recipient. On confidential reports, the title page lists names of individuals to whom the report should be circulated. The research team makes sure to bound formal reports neatly and often covers the entire work with a title fly-page, which lists only the title of the report.

Letter of Transmittal

Relatively formal and very formal reports include a *letter of transmittal*. The transmittal letter's purpose is to announce formally the release of or delivery of the report to the recipient. A transmittal letter gives the research personnel a chance to establish some rapport with the users of the report. Thus, this is typically the only part of a formal report that allows the writer to strike a personal or even slightly informal tone. The transmittal should not dive into the report findings, although providing a broad overview of the research objectives accomplished by the research is permissible.

A transmittal letter's opening paragraph releases the report and briefly identifies the factors of authorization. The letter comments generally on findings and matters of interest regarding the research. The closing section expresses the writer's personal interest in the project just completed

To the Point
"The covers of this book are too far apart."
—AMBROSE BIERCE

and in doing additional, related work. Overall, the letter explains how the report represents a key deliverable and invites further discussion on the matter.

Letter of Authorization

The *letter of authorization* is a letter to the researcher that approves the project, details who has responsibility for it, and describes the resources available to support it. The researcher receives and does not write this letter; however, he or she may include it in the report to signify client approval of the work. In many situations, simply referring to the authorization in the letter of transmittal suffices. If so, the letter of authorization need not be included in the report. In some cases, though, the reader may be unfamiliar with the authorization or may need detailed information about it. In such cases, the report should include this letter, preferably an exact copy of the original.

The Table of Contents

A *table of contents* is essential to any report more than a few pages long. It should list the divisions and subdivisions of the report with page references. The table of contents and the final outline of the report coincide with one another, but the table of contents usually shows only the first-level subheadings and at most only up to the second-level subheadings. For short reports, it is sufficient to include only the first-level headings. If the report includes many figures or tables, a list of these should immediately follow the table of contents. Theses and dissertations, which are often a research report of sorts, nearly always include a list of exhibits.

The Executive Summary

The *summary,* or *executive summary* as it is called more often, briefly explains why the research project was conducted, what aspects of the problem were considered, what the outcome was, and what should be done. The executive summary is a vital part of the report. Studies have indicated that nearly all managers read a report's summary, while only a minority read the body of the report. Thus, the writer's only chance to produce an impact may be in the executive summary.

The researcher should write the executive summary only after writing the rest of the report. The executive summary represents the essence of the report. Executive summaries should be one page long (or, at most, two pages), so the writer must carefully sort out what is important enough to be included in it. Several pages of the full report may have to be condensed into one summarizing sentence. Some parts of the report may be condensed more than others; the number of words in the summary need not be in proportion to the length of the report section being discussed. The summary should be self-sufficient. In fact, the summary is often detached from the report and circulated by itself.

The summary contains four elements. First, it states the objectives of the report, including the most important background information and the specific purposes of the project. Second, it presents the methodology and results, third the conclusions and fourth, any recommendations. These are opinions based on the results and constitute an interpretation of the results. Finally come recommendations, or suggestions for action, based on the conclusions. In many cases, managers prefer not to have recommendations included in the report or summary. Whether or not recommendations are to be included should be clear from the particular context of the report.

The Body

Introduction section

The part of the body of a research report that discusses background information and the specific objectives of the research.

The *body* constitutes the bulk of the report. It begins with an **introduction section** setting out the background factors that made the project necessary as well as the objectives of the report. It continues with discussions of the methodology, results, and limitations of the study and finishes with conclusions and recommendations based on the results.

The introduction explains why the researcher conducted the project and what the research procedures aimed to discover. Introductions should include the basic authorization and submittal data. The relevant background comes next. Enough background should be included to explain why the project was worth doing, but the background need not include unessential historical factors. The question of how much background is enough depends on the needs of the audience. A government report that will be widely circulated requires more background than a company's internal report on customer satisfaction. The last part of the introduction explains exactly what the project tried to discover. It discusses the statement of the problem and research questions as stated in the research proposal. Each purpose presented here should have a corresponding entry in the results section later in the report.

The second part of the body is the **research methodology section**. This part is a challenge to write because it must describe the research process, which often includes potentially complex, technical procedures, and do so in a manner appropriate for the audience. Complex technical details can be included in a technical appendix. Sometimes, the report includes a glossary of technical terms. Four points should be included in the research methodology section:

1. *Research design.* Was the study exploratory, descriptive, or causal? Did the data come from primary or secondary sources? Were results collected by survey, observation, or experiment? A copy of the survey questionnaire or observation form should be included in the appendix. Why was this particular design suited to the study?
2. *Sample design.* What was the target population? What is the sampling frame? What sample units are selected? How were they selected? How large was the sample? What was the response rate? The researcher should save detailed computations to support these explanations for the appendix.
3. *Data collection and fieldwork.* How many and what types of fieldworkers were used? What training and supervision did they receive? Was the work verified? This section is important for establishing the degree of accuracy of the results.
4. *Analysis.* This section should outline the general statistical methods used in the study, but the information presented here should not overlap with what is presented in the results section.

The **results section** should make up the bulk of the report and should present, in some logical order, those findings of the project that bear on the research objectives. The report organizes results as a continuous narrative, designed to be convincing but not to oversell the project. Summary tables and charts aid the interpretation portrayed in the discussion. These tables and charts may serve as points of reference to the data and free the prose from excessive regurgitation of detailed facts. Comprehensive or detailed charts, however, should be included in an appendix.

Because no research is perfect, a professional report includes a discussion of limitations. The researcher should report problems arising with nonresponse error or other sampling procedures. However, the discussion of limitations should avoid overemphasizing the weaknesses; its aim should be to provide a realistic basis for assessing the results.

The last part of the body is the **conclusions and recommendations section**. As mentioned earlier, conclusions are opinions based on the results, and recommendations are suggestions for action. The conclusions and recommendations are presented in this section in more detail than in the summary, and the text should include justification as needed.

The Appendix

The *appendix* presents the "too . . ." material. Any material that is too technical or too detailed to go in the body should appear in the appendix. This includes materials of interest only to some readers or subsidiary materials not directly related to the objectives. Some examples of appendix materials are data collection forms, detailed calculations, discussions of highly technical questions, detailed or comprehensive tables of results, and a bibliography (if appropriate). Much appendix material gets posted securely online for access on an as-needed basis.

Basic Marketing Research Report

The outline described applies especially to applied market research projects. When basic research reports are written, such as might be submitted and potentially published in an academic business journal, the outline changes slightly since some components become irrelevant. A common outline used in basic marketing research proceeds as follows:

1. Abstract
2. Introduction

Research methodology section

The part of the report body that describes the research process, which often includes explanations of potentially complex, technical procedures

Results section

The part of the body of a report that presents the findings of the project. It includes tables, charts, and an organized narrative.

Conclusions and recommendations section

The part of the body of a report that provides opinions based on the results and suggestions for action.

3. Background
   a. Literature review
   b. Hypotheses
4. Research Methods
5. Results
6. Discussion
   a. Implications
   b. Limitations
   c. Future research
7. Conclusions
8. References
9. Appendixes

Using Tables Effectively

Graphic aids

Pictures or diagrams used to clarify complex points or emphasize a message.

Used properly, **graphic aids** can clarify complex points or emphasize a message. Used improperly or sloppily, they can distract or even mislead a reader. Graphic aids work best when they are an integral part of the text. The graphics should always be interpreted in the text. This does not mean that the writer should exhaustively explain an obvious chart or table, but it *does* mean that the text should point out the key elements of any graphic aid and relate them to the discussion in progress.

Several types of graphic aids may be useful in research reports, including tables, charts, maps, and diagrams. The following discussion briefly covers the most common ones, tables and charts. The reader interested in other types of graphic material should consult more specialized sources.

Creating Tables

Tables are most useful for presenting numerical information, especially when several pieces of information have been gathered about each item discussed. For example, consider how hard following the information in Exhibit 16.2 might be with only narrative text and no graphical aids. Using tables allows a writer to point out significant features without getting bogged down in

EXHIBIT **16.2** Basic Data Table Illustration

Number of Graphic | Title | Column Headings

Table 162E. Bottled Water Sales Volume—2001 to 2011
(In millions of $US)

Country	2001	2002	2003	2004	2005	2006	2007	2008	2009	2010	2011
World-wide	55,618	59,543	63,950	66,916	71,092	75,851	81,112	84,866	88,862	93,239	98,058
United States	10,247	11,413	12,253	13,214	14,343	15,610	16,966	17,010	17,107	17,217	17,343
Germany	9,427	9,979	10,577	10,728	11,281	11,958	12,648	13,293	13,931	14,573	15,212
China	1,497	1,752	2,214	2,589	3,246	4,028	4,971	6,108	7,474	9,122	11,104
Italy	5,824	6,135	6,500	6,675	6,972	7,276	7,590	7,910	8,231	8,547	8,862
France	4,191	4,251	4,287	4,323	4,364	4,409	4,520	4,620	4,706	4,782	4,851
Japan	2,445	2,682	2,973	3,236	3,374	3,531	3,702	3,887	4,091	4,319	4,573
Brazil	2,620	2,651	2,713	2,884	3,059	3,224	3,390	3,578	3,780	4,009	4,268

Note: Sales volume based on average retail price per liter by total liters sold by country.
Source: Data Monitor Interactive Consumer Database.

Row Headings | Notes including sources

detail. The body of the report should include only relatively short summary tables, with comprehensive tables reserved for an appendix.

Each table should include the following elements:

- *Number.* The number is indexed to the List of Exhibits/Tables/Figures/Charts provided along with the table of contents. For an electronic report, this list may be hyperlinked to the graphics list for easy navigation. Some authors prefer to use the term *exhibit* to refer to all tables, charts, and figures—all graphics in general. Others prefer to number tables, charts, and figures separately.
- *Title.* The title should indicate the contents of the table and be complete enough to be intelligible without referring to the text.
- *Stubheads and bannerheads.* The stubheads contain the captions for the rows of the table, and the bannerheads (or boxheads) contain those for the columns.
- *Notes.* Any explanations or qualifications for particular table entries or sections should be given in notes placed at the bottom of the table or footnotes appearing at the bottom of the page.
- *Source notes.* If a table is based on material from one or more secondary sources rather than on new data generated by the project, the sources should be acknowledged, usually below the table.

Using Charts Effectively

Charts translate numerical information into visual form to summarize and communicate meaning. Often, the researcher sacrifices numerical precision in return for easy communication in transferring data to graphical form. Each chart should include the following elements:

- *Figure number.* Reports number charts (and other illustrative material) consecutively and usually do so separately from tables. The numbers allow for easy reference from the text. If there are many charts, a list of them should be included after the table of contents.
- *Title.* The title should describe the contents of the chart with just a few words. Numbers sometimes go at the top and sometimes at the bottom of a graphic. However, the placement should remain consistent across all charts in a document.
- *Explanatory legends.* A good graphic includes keys to aid in the explanation and to help the reader interpret the chart without the necessity of reading the report in detail. Explanatory legends of this sort include color codes to match to chart components, labels for axes, scale numbers, and a way to understand any abbreviations.
- *Source and footnotes.* Any secondary sources for the data should be acknowledged. Footnotes may be used to explain items, although they are less common for charts than for tables.

Charts are subject to distortion, whether unintentional or deliberate. Researchers must use special care to represent true scale values faithfully in all graphical aids. In fact, presenters can intentionally alter scale values in an effort to skew the interpretation of the data. Intentionally altering scales for this purpose is clearly unethical and unintentionally doing so is sloppy.

A particularly severe kind of distortion comes from treating unequal intervals as if they were equal. Typically, someone does this when trying to distort the interpretation of some meaning intentionally. Exhibit 16.3 shows this type of distortion. Here, both charts show the rate of change in U.S. gross domestic product over a period from 2011 to 2014. Does one chart appear to show more steady growth than the other does? The top chart shows greater fluctuation including two periods of declining growth. The bottom chart shows only steady growth. On close inspection, however, the two charts are not using the same intervals. The top chart shows every quarter from 2011 to 2014 in addition to annualized data. The bottom omits the first quarter of each year. Perhaps not coincidentally, the periods of lowest growth tended to happen in the first quarter over this period.

Researchers sometimes are tempted to choose the scale values for axes on charts in a way that may make a small finding seem much larger than it really is. Consider Exhibit 16.4. It displays results of an experiment testing the difference between two alternative advertising designs on purchase intention. Subjects recorded their purchase intentions after viewing one of the ads using a 10-point scale scored from 1 (Extremely Unlikely to Buy) to 10 (Very Likely to Buy).

EXHIBIT **16.3**
Two Differing Depictions
of the Same Data

EXHIBIT **16.4**
Axes Values Can Influence
Interpretation

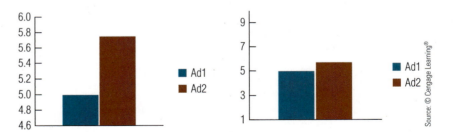

Both frames in the exhibit display exactly the same data. However, would a reader draw the same conclusion from either frame? Frame A makes ad 2 seem much more advantageous relative to ad 1. In contrast, frame B leads to the conclusion that there is very little difference between the two. In this case, frame A is misleading because notice that the y-axis uses a minimum value of 4.6 and a maximum value of 6.0, while frame B uses the actual scale minimum and maximum values of 1 and 10. Researchers sometimes feel the need to exaggerate the size of an effect by choosing a misleading scale range to make some effect seem relatively important. Often, the researcher gets confused about the difference between statistical significance and practical significance and tries to turn one into the other by making the graphic exaggerate an effect.

Distortions can also occur by accident as statistical tools that generate such graphs may automatically insert inappropriate minimum and maximum values. Interaction effects can be particularly prone to distortions. Consider Exhibit 16.5, which shows the very same effect as depicted automatically by two separate software packages. The exhibits depict an interaction effect between

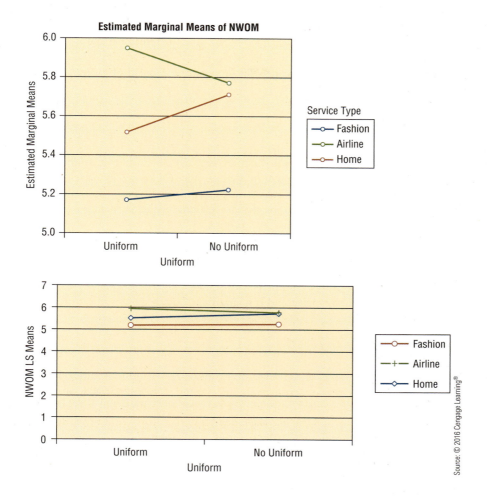

Source: © 2016 Cengage Learning®

EXHIBIT **16.5**
A Small-Scale Range for the
Y-Axis Can Mislead the User

two nominal, experimental variables (service type depicts the type of service a subject is describing, and uniform depicts whether the service employee involved in a situation wore a uniform). The dependent variable is how likely the subject would be to spread negative word of mouth (NWOM). Frame A shows the results in a chart automatically generated by SPSS. Frame B shows the results in a chart automatically generated by JMP. Unless the reader looks closely, frame A points to a conclusion that subjects react quite differently across the three service types. Notice the difference in slopes of the lines that can signify an interaction. Frame B, however, shows that all three lines are similar and leads to the conclusion that the combination of service type and uniform does not make much of a difference. Now, look closely at the y-axes. Frame A compresses the response range of NWOM to 5.2 to 5.9, only 0.7 out of a total scale range of 7 points. Frame B, on the other hand, depicts the full scale range. In this case, frame B gives the more accurate picture. The actual statistical result for the interaction produces an $F_{(df = 2,203)}$ or 0.42, which yields a *p*-value of 0.7 (not statistically significant).

Researchers sometimes get so emotionally involved in doing and presenting research that they may not realize their graphics are misleading. Often, a misleading graphic results from zeal or carelessness rather than intentional deception. Unfortunately, misleading graphics are all too common. Again, however, the researcher should always use great caution in making sure that graphics do nothing to encourage an inappropriate conclusion. Otherwise, the chart may contribute to the old adage "Statistics don't lie, but liars use statistics."

Marketing researchers should always try to present results as faithfully as possible. In this case, using the entire scale range would lead to a more accurate conclusion. In other instances where a larger range of values may be in play, perhaps in plotting the price someone actually paid for their last car, the minimum axes value need not be 0, but it should reflect the minimum plausible price that someone would pay. For example, one may set the scale range in this instance by the actual minimum and maximum prices reported across all respondents. The researcher may need to remove outliers to depict the results accurately. However, the researcher should have eliminated true outliers prior to reaching the point of interpreting the final statistical results and preparing the report graphics. Also, the researcher needs to report the removal of outliers so the user can understand what constituted an abnormal response.

Pie Charts

One of the most useful kinds of charts is the pie chart, which shows the composition of some total quantity at a particular time. As shown in the example in Exhibit 16.6, each angle, or *slice*, is proportional to its percentage of the whole. Companies often use pie charts to show sources of sales revenues or to depict the relative size of market segments. Each slice in a pie chart should contain a label or legend identifying the slice and giving the percentage of the total comprised by that segment. The writer should not try to include too many small slices; about six slices is a typical maximum. In this case, the pie chart shows results from a sample of several hundred tenth graders depicting their favorite means of communicating with friends. A company is interested in how to get students to spread advice on help with school assignments. The pie chart quickly depicts the results and points to Snapchat and Instagram as attractive communication vehicles.

Line Graphs

Line graphs are useful for showing the relationship of one variable to another. The dependent variable generally is shown on the vertical axis and the independent variable on the horizontal axis. The most common independent variable for such charts is time, but it is by no means the only one. Exhibit 16.7 shows a *simple line graph* depicting the proportion of worldwide Internet users over time. The increasing slope visually suggests steady growth.

Bar Charts

A bar chart shows changes in the value of a dependent variable (plotted on the vertical axis) at discrete intervals of the independent variable (on the horizontal axis). A simple bar chart is shown in Exhibit 16.8 on page 455.

The *multiple-bar chart* shows how multiple variables relate to the primary variable. In each of these cases, each bar or segment of the bar needs to be clearly identified with a different color or pattern. The writer should not use too many divisions or dependent variables. Too much detail obscures the essential advantage of charts, which is to make relationships easy to grasp.

EXHIBIT 16.6

A Pie Chart Depicting a Sample of Tenth Graders' Choice to a Question Asking Their Favorite Means of Communication

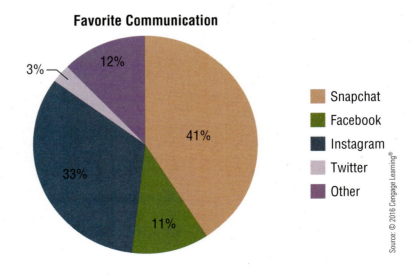

Favorite Communication

- Snapchat
- Facebook
- Instagram
- Twitter
- Other

Source: © 2016 Cengage Learning®

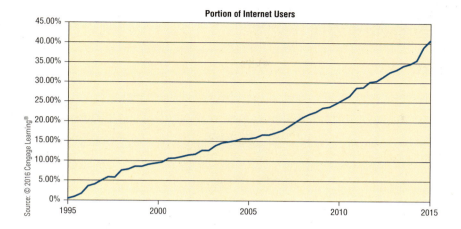

Source: © 2016 Cengage Learning®

EXHIBIT 16.7

A Line Graph Depicting
Percentage of Internet Users
Worldwide by Year

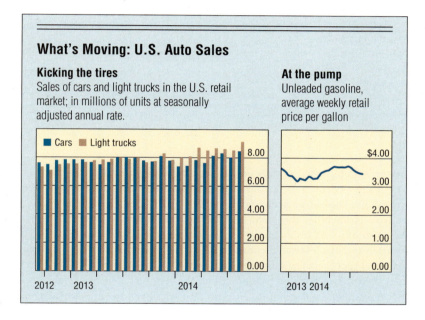

EXHIBIT 16.8

Graphic Combining a
Multiple-Bar Chart and a
Line Chart to Depict Trends in
Car versus Truck Sales in the
United States.

Oral Presentation

The conclusions and recommendations of most research reports are presented orally as well as in writing. The purpose of an **oral presentation** is to highlight the most important findings of a research project and provide clients or line managers with an opportunity to ask questions. The oral presentation may be as simple as a short video conference with a manager at the client organization's location or as formal as a report to the company board of directors. One rule stands above all when preparing a presentation—be as straightforward as possible.

Realize this rule also applies in nontraditional presentation formats. Today's researcher has to be prepared to give personalized presentations to busy executives and to use Internet-based tools to prepare presentations that can be viewed at the user's leisure. The Research Snapshot discusses these trends briefly.

In a traditional oral presentation, preparation is the key to effectiveness. Communication specialists often suggest that a person preparing an oral presentation begin at the end.[5] In other words, while preparing a presentation, a researcher should think about what he or she wants the client to know when it has been completed. The researcher should select the three or four most

Oral presentation

A spoken summary of the major findings, conclusions, and recommendations, given to clients or line managers to provide them with the opportunity to clarify any ambiguous issues by asking questions.

Presentation Today?

In the 1960s, a marketing research presentation probably meant going through some key results using a flip chart and magic marker. In the 1970s and 1980s, the presenter turned to overhead projectors. The LCD projector and the common types of presentation software that we use today became the tool of choice in the late 1990s. The projectors themselves have become increasingly small and portable, enabling presentations to be given just about anywhere where a power source is available.

However, the modern marketing researcher doesn't even need a projector. Increasingly, tablet computers are used to give presentations to small groups. In fact, the researcher doesn't even need to be present for the presentation as Skype-type software programs and communication enable the presentation to be delivered over the Internet. In either case, the researcher needs to be keenly aware how the presentation format will affect communication. A tablet computer offers a small screen so even fewer words per slide is

© Dragon Images/Shutterstock.com

the rule. For remote presentations, the researcher may wish to take advantage of on-screen annotations that allow the user to easily know where in the screen the key information can be found and to include any additional explanations. Similarly, if the presentation is to be completely canned and viewed by the users without the presence of the researcher, these types of visual and voice-over annotations can be extremely useful. These technological tools are real trends in presentations today.

Sources: Brodkin, J. (2011), "The Complicated New Face of Personal Computing," *Network World*, 28 (1/10), 12–16. "iDeal Tool of Sales Trade," *Pharmaceutical Executive* (2011), 31 (May), 84–86.

important findings for emphasis and rely on the written report for a full summary. The researcher also needs to be ready to defend the results of the research. This is not the same as being defensive; instead, the researcher should be prepared to deal in a confident, competent manner with the questions that arise. Remember that even the most reliable and valid research project is worthless if the managers who must act on its results are not convinced of its importance.

As with written reports, researchers need to adapt the presentation to the audience. Delivering an hour-long formal speech when a 10-minute discussion is what management asked for (or vice versa) will reflect poorly on both the presenter and the report. The terminology also needs to be appropriate for the audience. A group of marketing researchers can tolerate more jargon than a group of managers.

Lecturing or reading to the audience is sure to impede communication at any level of formality. The presenter should refrain from reading prepared text word for word. By relying on brief notes, familiarity with the subject, and as much rehearsal as the occasion calls for, the presenter will foster better communication. He or she should avoid research jargon and use short, familiar words. The presenter should maintain eye contact with the audience and repeat the main points. Because the audience cannot go back and replay what the speaker has said, an oral presentation often is organized around a standard format: *Tell them what you are going to tell them, tell them, and tell them what you just told them.*

Graphic and other visual aids can be as useful in an oral presentation as in a written one. Presenters can choose from a variety of media. Slides, overhead-projector acetates, and on-screen computer-generated graphics are useful for larger audiences. For smaller audiences, the researcher may put the visual aids on posters or flip charts. Another possibility is to make copies of the charts for each participant, possibly as a supplement to one of the other forms of presentation. Still another is to use a small personal computer or a tablet computer to flip through a presentation. This latter option is best if the audience is only one person.

Whatever medium is chosen, each visual aid should be designed to convey a simple, attention-getting message that supports a point on which the audience should focus its thinking. As they do in written presentations, presenters should interpret graphics for the audience. The best slides are easy to read and interpret. Large typeface, multiple colors, bullets that highlight, and other artistic devices can enhance the readability of charts.

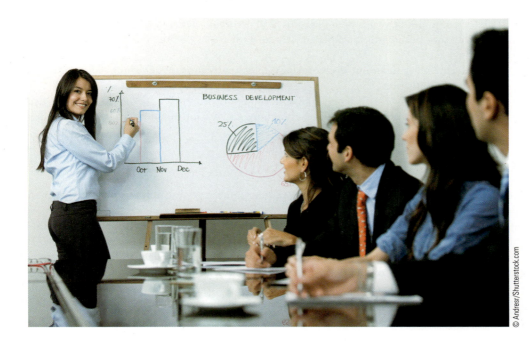

Subtle Gestures Can Improve a Presentation.

Using gestures during presentations can also help convey the message and make presentations more interesting. Also, invite participation from the audience. Here are some tips on actually making the presentation:[6]

■ Generally, introduce yourself while displaying the title of the presentation. Acknowledge any others who materially assisted in the project.
■ Open up your arms to embrace your audience. Keep your arm actions at the height between your waist and shoulders.
■ Drop your arms to your sides when not using them.

Some gestures are used to draw attention to points illustrated by visual aids. For these, gesturing with an open hand can seem more friendly and can even release tension related to nervousness. In contrast, a nervous speaker who uses a laser pointer may distract the audience as the pointer jumps around in the speaker's shaky hand.[7]

Reports on the Internet and Follow-Up

Many clients want numerous employees to have access to research findings. One easy way to share data is to make executive summaries and reports available on a company intranet or in an appropriate place on the Internet. In addition, a company can use information technology on the Internet to design questionnaires, administer surveys, analyze data, and share the results in a presentation-ready format. Real-time data capture allows for beginning-to-end reporting. A number of companies offer fully Web-based research management systems—for example, many companies also provide online research reports on key topics of interest.

Self-Contained Presentations

The researcher should keep some key points in mind when preparing a stand-alone presentation that can be viewed at the convenience of the user:

1. Make sure the title page indicates who did the research and for whom it was done.
2. Keep in mind that viewers may use all sorts of media devices to view the presentation. As a result, simpler is better. Keep any videos, audio, or photos in as small a file as possible and in a file that would work on almost any device.

3. Limit the number of words on a slide just as in an oral presentation.
4. Annotate any potentially complex material with text call–outs or simple audio or video recordings.
5. Use self-advancing slides but always include an easy way for the user to move forward, stop, or repeat the presentation.
6. Include links to any technical appendices that support the work.
7. On the last slide, provide clear and unambiguous contact information for easy follow-up.

Follow-Up Reports

Research follow-up

Recontacting decision-makers and/or clients after they have had a chance to read over a research report in order to determine whether additional information or clarification is necessary.

Research reports and oral presentations should communicate research findings so that managers can make business decisions. In many cases, the manager who receives the research report is unable to interpret the information and draw conclusions relevant to managerial decisions. For this reason, effective researchers do not treat the report as the end of the research process. They conduct a **research follow-up**, in which they recontact decision-makers and/or clients after the latter have had a chance to read over the report. The purpose is to determine whether the researchers need to provide additional information or clarify issues of concern to management. Just as marketing research may help an organization learn about its customers' satisfaction, the research follow-up can help marketing research staffers ensure the satisfaction of their customers, marketing managers.

TIPS OF THE TRADE

- Research reports, like all communications, are interpreted by the receiver. Try to be clear and unambiguous in preparing the research report.
- Research reports should generally follow the principles of good technical writing.
- Whenever possible, have someone else proof the report and slides before submitting them to the client or editor.
- Whenever possible, stick to the standard outline for the paper.
- The executive summary is critically important because on occasion it is the only part read in detail by the client.
  - Keep it short—about 400 words maximum except for the longest reports.
  - Highlight the key findings with bullet points.
  - Write it last—after finishing the rest of the report and presentation.
- Consider the audience in preparing the report and presentation.
- Make the communication understandable.
  - Avoid jargon and put any complex statistical output in a technical appendix.
  - Use charts and tables to illustrate findings.
- Good ethical practices dictate that charts, graphics, and tables be presented in a way that minimizes the likelihood of misinterpreting meaning.
- Presentation slides should be clear and legible.
  - Err toward larger font, not smaller.
  - Err toward fewer words, not more.
  - When slides are posted to be viewed via the Internet, annotate complex issues with pop-ups or balloon inserts.

Source: © Cengage Learning 2013

∵ SUMMARY

1. Create an outline for a research project using the basic parts of a final report. A research report is an oral or written presentation of research findings directed to a specific audience to accomplish a particular purpose. Report preparation is the final stage of the research project. The consensus is that the format for a research report should include certain prefatory parts, the body of the report, and appended parts. The report format should be varied to suit the level of formality of the particular situation. The prefatory parts of a formal report include a title page, letters of transmittal and authorization, a table of contents, and a summary.

2. Explain how to use tables for presenting numerical information. Tables present large amounts of numerical information in a concise manner. They are especially useful for presenting several pieces of information about each item discussed. Short tables are helpful in the body of the report; long tables are better suited for an appendix. Each table should include a number, title, stubheads and bannerheads, footnotes for any explanations or qualifications of entries, and source notes for data from secondary sources.

3. Summarize how to select and use the types of research charts. Charts present numerical data in a way that highlights their relationships. Each chart should include a figure number, title, explanatory legends, and a source note for secondary sources. Pie charts show the composition of a total (the parts that make up a whole). Line graphs show the relationship of a dependent variable (on the vertical axis) to an independent variable (horizontal axis). Most commonly, the independent variable is time. Bar charts show changes in a dependent variable at discrete intervals of the independent variable—for example, comparing one year with another or one subset of the population with another. Researchers need to pay careful attention to avoid distorted interpretations of graphics based on manipulations of the scale values used on axes or some other intentional or careless inaccuracy.

4. Know how to give an effective oral presentation. Most research projects are reported orally as well as in writing, so the researcher needs to prepare an oral presentation. The presentation should defend the results without being defensive. The presentation must be tailored to the situation and the audience. The presenter should practice delivering the presentation in a natural way, without reading to the audience. Graphic aids are useful supplements when they are simple and easy to read. Gestures also add interest and emphasis.

5. Discuss the importance of Internet reporting and research follow-up. Posting a summary of results online gives clients ready access to that information. Some online survey software processes the data and displays results in a presentation-ready format. Keep in mind that users often access online materials using many different types of media devices. Self-contained presentations should stay simple. In the follow-up stage of a research project, the researchers recontact decision-makers after submitting the report. This helps the researchers determine whether they need to provide further information or clarify any issues of concern to management.

∵ KEY TERMS AND CONCEPTS

conclusions and recommendations section, *449*
graphic aids, *450*
introduction section, *448*
oral presentation, *455*
report format, *444*

research follow-up, *458*
research methodology section, *449*
research report, *444*
results section, *449*

∵ QUESTIONS FOR REVIEW AND CRITICAL THINKING

1. What are the parts of a market research report?
2. How does an applied market research report differ from a basic or marketing research report?
3. What types of tables might be used to describe some of the various statistical tests discussed in previous chapters?
4. What is the difference between a *basic marketing research paper* and *an applied market research report?*
5. What is a *pie chart?* What is a *bar chart?* When might one be preferable over the other?

6. Why might a researcher create a graphic that leads a user to over-estimate the size of some effect? Describe with an example.

7. How might a marketing researcher unintentionally distort results of an independent *t*-test examining brand A's customer satisfaction against brand B's customer satisfaction where customer satisfaction is measured on a 0 to 100 point satisfaction scale (0 = no satisfaction to 100 = complete satisfaction)? How might the researcher intentionally distort the interpretation of these results?

8. What are some basic business research journals? Find some published research reports in these journals. How do they meet the standards set forth in this chapter?

9. What rules should be followed when preparing slides for self-contained presentations like those posted online?

10. What ethical concerns arise when you prepare (or read) a report?

11. Prepare an exhibit like Exhibit 16.2 that shows the per capita bottled water consumption for the countries listed. Population stats for each country can be found in the CIA Factbook (https://www.cia.gov/library/publications/the-world-factbook/). Sort the countries from most to least consumption per capita. What exhibit would be more valuable for someone looking for opportunities in the bottled water industry?

∴ RESEARCH ACTIVITY

1. This activity can be used for the term-long project. In the resources that accompany this book, you will find a PowerPoint file that contains a detailed outline for a research project. This file contains a skeleton or template of a final research presentation. The outline also serves as the framework for a research report. Using instructions from your instructor regarding the topic and nature of a research report, fill in the information needed to turn the outline into an actual research report. In some cases, you will need to insert slides to fill in a section. For example, the results will likely take multiple slides to communicate effectively. Your instructor will provide guidance as to other details in terms of turning this into an oral presentation, a formal written report, a slidenet.com presentation or other Internet presentation, and so forth. This activity gives you the opportunity to gain real-world research expertise.

2. Input "Amazon.com" or "Apple" in an Internet search engine along with other key words that may lead you to research reports that describe some aspect of these mammoth companies' marketing efforts. Try limiting results with the word *report* should you be overwhelmed with information. Find one of the articles that actually presents some research reports, such as consumer reactions to innovations. Prepare PowerPoint slides that contain appropriate charts to present the results.

3. Using data from Exhibit 15.6, which described coffee drinking habits by the shift that workers work (shown again here), prepare a pie chart(s) and at least one other type of chart that depicts some meaning from the data. For instance, show the proportion of workers in each shift (a pie chart works well for this) and show the means of coffee drinking by shift. Use a statistical package like SAS JMP or SPSS to create the charts. Also, create the charts using Excel or PowerPoint. What software seems to be the most easy and most flexible in creating charts?

Ex15_6_coffee - JMP

File   Edit   Tables   Rows   Cols   DOE   Analyze   Graph   Tools   View   Window   Help

Ex15_6_coffee

	Shift	Cups
1	Day	1
2	Day	3
3	Day	4
4	Day	0
5	Day	2
6	GY	7
7	GY	2
8	GY	1
9	GY	6
10	Night	6
11	Night	8
12	Night	3
13	Night	7
14	Night	6

Columns (2/1)
- Shift ✳
- Cups ✳

Rows

All rows	14
Selected	0
Excluded	0
Hidden	0
Labelled	0

Consumer Price Knowledge

case 16.1

A recent study investigated one major area of marketing decisions: pricing practices.[8] Specifically, the study addressed consumer knowledge and attitudes about the practice of online retailers adjusting their prices according to customer characteristics, such as how frequently they buy from the retailer. Price discrimination has long been commonplace in many industries, but the Internet provides a way of implementing large-scale price discrimination. Realize that price discrimination isn't always a bad thing for individual consumers as sometimes he or she is the beneficiary of a low price.

For example, a rental car company may offer a consumer a low rate on a rental car if the person's recent Web history has shown a search for hotels. Someone who goes straight to the rental car site may not get such a discount. Another website selling cameras charged different prices for the same model depending on whether

the visitor to the site had previously visited sites that supply price comparisons. In general, price discrimination is legal unless it discriminates by race or sex or involves antitrust or price-fixing laws (such as two competitors agreeing to charge certain prices).

The study consisted of telephone interviews conducted with a sample of 1,500 adults, screened to find persons who had used the Internet in the preceding thirty days. The questionnaire gathered demographic data and data about Internet usage. In addition, the interviewer read seventeen statements about basic laws and practices related to price discrimination and the targeting of consumers according to their shopping behaviors. Respondents were asked whether each of these statements was true or false. Case Exhibits 16.1–1, 16.1–2, 16.1–3, and 16.1–4 summarize some of the results from this study.

Questions

1. The information provided here is not detailed enough for a formal report, but assume that you are making an informal report in a preliminary stage of the reporting process. Which of these findings do you want to emphasize as your main points? Why?
2. Prepare a written summary of the findings, using at least two tables or charts.
3. Prepare two tables or charts that would be suitable to accompany an oral presentation of these results. Are they different from the visual aids you prepared for question 2? Why or why not?

CASE EXHIBIT 16.1–1

Selected Information about the Sample

Sex	
Male	48%
Female	52%
Online Connection at Home	
Dial-up connection only	31%
Cable modem (with/without dial-up)	18%
DSL (with/without dial-up)	25%
Cable or DSL with another method	13%
Don't know	4%
No connection at home	9%
Self-Ranked Expertise Navigating the Internet	
Beginner	14%
Intermediate	40%
Advanced	34%
Expert	12%

Source: Joseph Turow, Lauren Feldman, and Kimberly Meltzer, "Open to Exploitation: American Shoppers Online and Offline," APPC report, June 2005, p. 15, downloaded at http://www.annenbergpublicpolicycenter.org.

CASE EXHIBIT 16.1–2

Responses to Selected Knowledge Questions

Statement	Response*		
	True	**False**	**Don't Know**
Companies today have the ability to follow my activity across many sites on the web.	**80%**	8%	12%
It is legal for an *online* store to charge different people different prices at the same time of day.	**38%**	29%	33%
By law, a site such as Expedia or Orbitz that compares prices on different airlines must include the lowest airline prices.	37%	**32%**	31%
It is legal for an *offline* store to charge different people different prices at the same time of day.	29%	**42%**	29%
When a website has a privacy policy, it means the site will not share my information with other websites or companies.	59%	**25%**	16%

*When the numbers do not add up to 100%, it is because of a rounding error. **Boldface** type indicates the correct answer.

Source: Joseph Turow, Lauren Feldman, and Kimberly Meltzer, "Open to Exploitation: American Shoppers Online and Offline," APPC report, June 2005, p. 20, downloaded at http://www.annenbergpublicpolicycenter.org.

(Continued)

Responses to Selected Attitude Questions

Statement	Response*			
	Agree	Disagree	Neutral	Don't Know
It's okay if a store charges me a price based on what it knows about me.	8%	91%	—	1%
It's okay if an *online* store I use charges different people different prices for the same products during the same hour.	11%	87%	1%	1%
It would bother me to learn that other people pay less than I do for the same products.	76%	22%	1%	1%
It would bother me if websites I shop at keep detailed records of my buying behavior.	57%	41%	2%	1%
It's okay if a store I shop at frequently uses information it has about me to create a picture of me that improves the services it provides for me.	50%	41%	2%	1%

*When the numbers do not add up to 100%, it is because of a rounding error.

Source: Joseph Turow, Lauren Feldman, and Kimberly Meltzer, "Open to Exploitation: American Shoppers Online and Offline," APPC report, June 2005, p. 22, downloaded at http://www.annenbergpublicpolicycenter.org.

Predicting Knowledge Score from Selected Demographics

	Unstandardized Regression Coefficient (B)	Standardized Regression Coefficient (β)
Education	0.630*	0.200
Income	0.383*	0.150
Self-perceived ability to navigate Internet	0.616*	0.149
Constant	2.687	
R^2	0.148	

*Significance <0.001 level.

Source: Joseph Turow, Lauren Feldman, and Kimberly Meltzer, "Open to Exploitation: American Shoppers Online and Offline," APPC report, June 2005, p. 29, downloaded at http://www.annenbergpublicpolicycenter.org.

Source: http://online.wsj.com/mdc/public/page/2_3022-autosales .html#autosalesA, accessed September 21, 2014.

A Final Note on Marketing Research

Hopefully, after reading and studying the material in this book, you can now understand and apply basic processes that help identify key information needs and turn raw data into intelligence. Thus, after sifting through a vast sea of information, this intelligence helps someone make a better decision, which, in turn, helps make someone's life better. The consumer who gets something of greater value is better off and the people who produced and marketed the product also are better off. Marketing research is a very important and useful area of knowledge that can lead to meaningful skills. The set of cases that follows provides the reader with one last chance to gain experience through real-world applications of marketing research. If you are still hungry for more about marketing research, there are many more advanced topics that can increase your skills in one of the specialized areas of research!

© Mila Supinskaya/Shutterstock.com

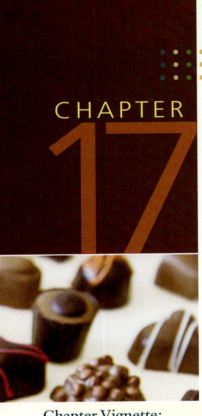

Beyond the Basics in Basic Data Analysis

LEARNING OUTCOMES

After studying this chapter, you should be able to:

1. Compute an F-statistic
2. Know what a factorial design means in an ANOVA context
3. Appreciate the potential complexity of experimental designs
4. Use post-hoc comparisons
5. Know when a specific contrast is appropriate
6. Understand how sequential chi-square analyses are useful in discovering meaning in big data

Chapter Vignette:

Beyond the Basics of Marketing Analysis

The first five parts of the book provide a solid background in the essentials of marketing research. In particular, students now should feel comfortable with the notion of transforming data into intelligence. Likewise, students now should know what types of data are available, know methods of obtaining data, know how to assess the basics of data quality including validity, have an awareness of statistical software useful in interpreting and analyzing data and know how to perform basic marketing analytic procedures.

Having mastered these basics, the following chapters move beyond the basics. Given the increasing demand for marketing analysts, these chapters go deeper in detail and breadth with respect to the marketing analyst's toolbox. In particular, the chapter highlights several approaches used in big data discovery. The first chapter in this part (chapter 17) provides an insight into some more advanced issues in basic data analysis. These topics include details about ANOVA itself, an introduction into more complex experimental designs, and describe specific tests that involve statistical contrasts. In addition, other uses of the chi-square tests are described including a tool used in big data analysis. The second chapter (18) goes beyond the basics of linear regression. It takes a closer look at the notion of correlation, introduces the concept of covariance, distinguishes explanation and prediction, and provides a look at the arithmetic of Ordinary Least Squares (OLS). In the next (Chapter 19), we examine ways to test specific types of hypotheses using tests of mediation and moderation including hierarchical multiple regression analysis. Chapters 20 to 22 provide an introduction to multivariate data analysis. The first two of these chapters are divided among dependence techniques and interdependence techniques, respectively. The final chapter provides a basic overview of structural equations analysis with an emphasis on the notion of theory testing.

SURVEY THIS!

This chapter expands on some of the analysis approaches examined in earlier chapters. Here is a chance to explore data analysis in more detail. The chapter closes by talking about data mining approaches using cross-tabulation. To get an idea of how this works, use the data from the Survey This feature to examine at least five cross-tabulations aimed at some common behavior. Are any of the cross-tabulations statistically significant? Does any pattern emerge that might be useful to a decision-maker?

Do you have more than one email address that you use regularly?

Yes   No

Survey Powered By Qualtrics®

Introduction

Once upon a time, a Blackberry phone was so alluring to its owners that its common nickname was a "Crackberry." Many Blackberry owners probably could never imagine breaking their Crackberry habit. What types of things make customers stay loyal to their smartphone brand? Phone manufacturers do considerable research, both before and after the launch of new products, in an effort to make better decisions about designing phones. For instance, researchers may wish to know how the size, shape, and brand of a phone influence how much customers may become attached to their phone. This question may require some type of analysis beyond those covered in the first parts of the book. In particular, a more complex experimental design provides an alternative approach. The analysis still involves the General Linear Model (GLM). Another approach might be to mine data collected unobtrusively as consumers use their phones. This chapter takes a closer look at issues related to GLM ANOVA models and exploring data using sequential chi-square analyses.

Computing an F-Statistic

F for One-Way ANOVA

Earlier, we described the χ^2 statistic as perhaps the most basic of statistical tests of association. Although manual calculations are almost unheard of these days, understanding the way one would compute a statistic can be very useful in learning. In this case, the basic statistic of ANOVA, and for GLM in general, is the **F-statistic**. The F-statistic, like in regression, involves the ratio of systematic variance to error variance. As you will see, it is very similar to the χ^2 statistic. The data in Exhibit 17.1 are from a hypothetical company's test-market experiment on phone pricing. Three pricing treatments were administered in four separate areas each (12 test locations, A–L, were required). These data will be used to illustrate ANOVA. In the mathematical illustration, we are testing only the effect of the price manipulation on sales. Thus, only one effect is considered.

F-statistic

Basic test statistic of ANOVA and GLM in general involving the ratio of systematic to error variance.

Terminology for the variance estimates is derived from the calculation procedures, so an explanation of the terms used to calculate the F-ratio should clarify the meaning of the analysis of variance technique. The calculation of the F-ratio requires that we partition the total variation into two parts:

$$\begin{array}{ccc} \text{Total sum of squares} & & \text{Within-group} & & \text{Between-group} \\ (SST) & = & \text{sum of squares} & + & \text{sum of squares} \\ & & (SSE) & & (SSB) \end{array}$$

or

$$SST = SSE + SSB$$

EXHIBIT 17.1

Test Market Involving Product Pricing

Test Area and Locations	Price:	Sales in Thousands of Units			
		$99	$89	$119	Row Totals
1 = A, B, C		130	145	153	428
2 = D, E, F		118	143	129	390
3 = G, H, I		87	120	96	303
4 = J, K, L		84	131	99	314
Totals		419	539	477	1435
Column Means		104.75	134.75	119.25	119.58

SST, which equals the total sum of observed values' deviations from the overall or grand mean ($(\overline{\overline{Y}})$), computed by squaring the deviation of each score from the grand mean and summing these values (or squares):

$$SST = \sum_{i=1}^{n} \sum_{j=1}^{c} (Y_{ij} - \overline{\overline{Y}})^2$$

where

Y = individual score—that is, the ith observation or test unit in the jth group

$\overline{\overline{Y}}$ = grand mean

n = number of all observations or test units in a group

c = number of jth groups (or columns)

In our example,

$$
\begin{aligned}
SST = & (130 - 119.58)^2 + (118 - 119.58)^2 + (87 - 119.58)^2 \\
& + (84 - 119.58)^2 + (145 - 119.58)^2 + (143 - 119.58)^2 \\
& + (120 - 119.58)^2 + (131 - 119.58)^2 + (153 - 119.58)^2 \\
& + (129 - 119.58)^2 + (96 - 119.58)^2 + (99 - 119.58)^2 \\
= & \ 5{,}948.9
\end{aligned}
$$

SSE, the variability that we observe within each group, or the error remaining after using the groups to predict observations, is calculated by squaring the deviation of each score from its group mean and summing these scores:

$$SSE = \sum_{i=1}^{n} \sum_{j=1}^{c} (Y_{ij} - \overline{Y}_j)^2$$

where

Y = individual score

$\overline{Y}_j$ = group mean for the jth group

n = number of observations in a group

c = number of jth groups

In our example,

$$
\begin{aligned}
SSE = & (130 - 104.75)^2 + (118 - 104.75)^2 + (87 - 104.75)^2 + (84 - 104.75)^2 \\
& + (145 - 134.75)^2 + (143 - 134.75)^2 + (120 - 134.75)^2 + (131 - 134.75)^2 \\
& + (153 - 119.25)^2 + (129 - 119.25)^2 + (96 - 119.25)^2 + (99 - 119.25)^2 \\
= & \ 4{,}148.25
\end{aligned}
$$

SSB, the variability of the group means about a grand mean, is calculated by squaring the deviation of each group mean from the grand mean, multiplying by the number of items in the group, and summing these scores:

$$SSB = \sum_{j=1}^{c} n_j(\overline{Y}_j - \overline{\overline{Y}})^2$$

where

$\overline{Y}_j$ = mean for the *j*th group (in this case, the mean per price each group)

$\overline{\overline{Y}}$ = grand mean

n_j = number of items in the *j*th group

In our example,

$$SSB = 4(104.75 - 119.58)^2 + 4(134.75 - 119.58)^2$$
$$+ 4(119.25 - 119.58)^2$$
$$= 1,800.68$$

The next calculation requires dividing the various sums of squares by their appropriate degrees of freedom. These divisions produce the variances, or *mean squares*. To obtain the mean square between groups, we divide *SSB* by $c - 1$ degrees of freedom:

$$MSB = \frac{SSB}{c - 1}$$

In our example,

$$MSB = \frac{1,800.68}{3 - 1} = \frac{1,800.68}{2} = 900.34$$

To obtain the mean square within groups, we divide *SSE* by $cn - c$ degrees of freedom:

$$MSE = \frac{SSE}{cn - c}$$

In our example,

$$MSE = \frac{4,148.25}{12 - 3} = \frac{4,148.25}{9} = 460.91$$

Finally, the *F*-ratio is calculated by taking the ratio of the mean square between groups to the mean square within groups. The between-groups mean square is the numerator and the within-groups mean square is the denominator:

$$F = \frac{MSB}{MSE}$$

In our example,

$$F = \frac{900.34}{460.91} = 1.95$$

There will be $c - 1$ degrees of freedom in the numerator and $cn - c$ degrees of freedom in the denominator:

$$\frac{c - 1}{cn - c} = \frac{3 - 1}{3(4) - 3} = \frac{2}{9}$$

The critical value of *F* at the 0.05 level for 2 and 9 degrees of freedom indicates that an *F* of 4.26 would be required to support the idea that *F* is not 1 (equal values for the numerator and denominator). In our example, the mean differences due to the treatment do not account for significant variation in the dependent variable. In this case, it appears that varying the price treatments ends up yielding approximately the same sales volume.

The information produced from an analysis of variance is traditionally summarized in table form. Exhibits 17.2 and 17.3 summarize the formulas and data from our example. Exhibit 17.3 displays a typical way of presenting the data in a table. In addition, Exhibit 17.4 displays the results of this analysis using SAS JMP.

EXHIBIT 17.2
ANOVA Summary Table

Source of Variation	Sum of Squares	Degrees of Freedom	Mean Square	F-Ratio
Between groups	$SSB = \sum_{j=1}^{c} n_j (\overline{Y}_j - \overline{\overline{Y}})^2$	$c - 1$	$MSB = \dfrac{SSB}{c-1}$	—
Within groups	$SSE = \sum_{i=1}^{n} \sum_{j=1}^{c} (Y_{ij} - \overline{Y}_j)^2$	$cn - c$	$MSE = \dfrac{SSE}{cn-c}$	$F = \dfrac{MSB}{MSE}$
Total	$SST = \sum_{i=1}^{n} \sum_{j=1}^{c} (Y_{ij} - \overline{\overline{Y}})^2$	$cn - 1$	—	

where c = number of groups
n = number of observations in a group
cn = total number of observations

Source: © Cengage Learning®

EXHIBIT 17.3
Pricing Experiment ANOVA Table

Source of Variation	Sum of Squares	Degrees of Freedom	Mean Square	F-Ratio
Between groups	1,800.68	2	900.34	—
Within groups	4,148.25	9	460.91	1.953
Total	5,948.93	11	—	—

Source: © Cengage Learning®

EXHIBIT 17.4
GLM F Computation in JMP

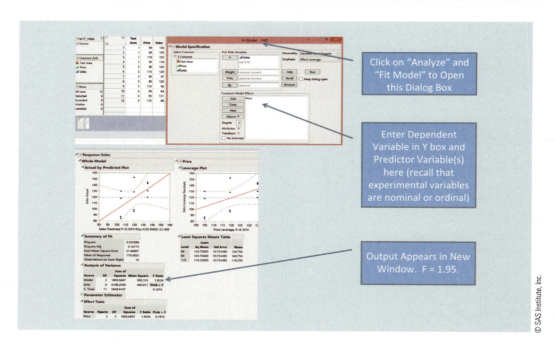

© SAS Institute, Inc.

ANOVA for Complex Experimental Designs

Randomized block design (RBD)

Variation of GLM ANOVA allowing the analyst to control statistically for the impact of a nominal or ordinal control, or blocking variable.

To test for statistical significance in a randomized block design, another version of analysis of variance is utilized. A **randomized block design (RBD)** allows the analyst to control statistically for the impact of a nominal or ordinal control, or blocking variable. The linear model for the RBD for an individual observation is:

$$Y_{ij} = \mu + \alpha_j + \beta_i + \varepsilon_{ij}$$

where

Y_{ij} = individual observation on the dependent variable

μ = grand mean

α_j = jth treatment effect

β_i = ith block effect

ε_{ij} = random error or residual

The statistical objective is to determine whether significant differences exist among treatment means and block means. An F-ratio results for each source of effects.

The same logic that applies in single-factor ANOVA—using variance estimates to test for differences among means—applies in ANOVA for randomized block designs. Thus, to conduct the ANOVA, we partition the total sum of squares (SS_{total}) into nonoverlapping components.

$$SS_{total} = SS_{treatments} + SS_{blocks} + SS_{error}$$

The sources of variance are defined as follows:

Total sum of squares:

$$SS_{total} = \sum_{i=1}^{r} \sum_{j=1}^{c} (Y_{ij} - \overline{\overline{Y}})^2$$

where

Y_{ij} = individual observation

$\overline{\overline{Y}}$ = grand mean

r = number of blocks (rows)

c = number of treatments (columns)

Treatment sum of squares:

$$SS_{treatments} = \sum_{i=1}^{r} \sum_{j=1}^{c} (\overline{Y}_j - \overline{\overline{Y}})^2$$

where

$\overline{Y}_j$ = jth treatment mean

$\overline{\overline{Y}}$ = grand mean

Block sum of squares:

$$SS_{blocks} = \sum_{i=1}^{r} \sum_{j=1}^{c} (\overline{Y}_i - \overline{\overline{Y}})^2$$

where

$\overline{Y}_i$ = ith block mean

$\overline{\overline{Y}}$ = grand mean

Sum of squares error:

$$SS_{error} = \sum_{i=1}^{r} \sum_{j=1}^{c} (Y_{ij} - \overline{Y}_i - \overline{Y}_j - \overline{\overline{Y}})^2$$

The SS_{error} may also be calculated in the following manner:

$$SS_{error} = SS_{total} - SS_{treatments} - SS_{blocks}$$

The degrees of freedom for $SS_{treatments}$ are equal to $c - 1$ because $SS_{treatments}$ reflects the dispersion of treatment means from the grand mean, which is fixed. Degrees of freedom for blocks are $r - 1$ for similar reasons. SS_{error} reflects variations from both treatment and block means. Thus, $df = (r - 1)(c - 1)$.

Mean squares are calculated by dividing the appropriate sum of squares by the corresponding degrees of freedom.

Exhibit 17.5 represents an ANOVA table for the randomized block design. It summarizes what has been discussed and illustrates the calculation of mean squares.

EXHIBIT 17.5
ANOVA Table for Randomized Block Designs

Source of Variation	Sum of Squares	Degrees of Freedom	Mean Square
Between blocks	SS_{blocks}	$r - 1$	$\dfrac{SS_{blocks}}{r - 1}$
Between treatments	$SS_{treatments}$	$c - 1$	$\dfrac{SS_{treatments}}{c - 1}$
Error	SS_{error}	$(r - 1)(c - 1)$	$\dfrac{SS_{error}}{(r - 1)(c - 1)}$
Total	SS_{total}	$rc - 1$	—

Source: © Cengage Learning®

F-ratios for treatment and block effects are calculated as follows:

$$F_{treatment} = \frac{\text{Mean square treatment}}{\text{Mean square error}}$$

$$F_{blocks} = \frac{\text{Mean square blocks}}{\text{Mean square error}}$$

Factorial Designs

Factorial design

An experimental design fully implemented with two or more experimental variables, meaning observations are taken for every level of every experimental variable.

Factorial designs expand on the idea of one-way ANOVA. A **factorial design** produces an experimental design fully implemented with two or more experimental variables, meaning observations are taken for every level of every experimental variable. A factorial design, a one-way analysis of variance, and a multiple regression model share some things in common. The sum of squares for each of the treatment factors (rows and columns) is similar to the between-groups sum of squares in the single-factor ANOVA model. Each treatment sum of squares is calculated by taking the deviation of the treatment means from the grand mean. Determining the sum of squares for the interaction is a new calculation because this source of variance is not attributable to the treatment sum of squares or the error sum of squares.

ANOVA for a Factorial Experiment

In a two-factor experimental design the linear model for an individual observation is

$$Y_{ijk} = \mu + \beta_i + \alpha_j + I_{ij} + \varepsilon_{ijk}$$

where

Y_{ijk} = individual observation on the dependent variable

μ = grand mean

β_i = ith effect of factor B—row treatment

α_j = jth effect of factor A—column treatment

I_{ij} = interaction effect of factors A and B

ε_{ijk} = random error or residual

You'll notice the theoretical representation above matches with the estimated form of the GLM introduced in Chapter 15:

$$\hat{Y}_{ijk} = \overline{\overline{Y}} + \Delta X + \Delta F + \Delta XF$$

This representation of a two-way ANOVA allows prediction of the dependent variable based on changes in the mean due to factor X, factor F, and the combined effect of X and F. This two-way ANOVA can be generalized to k-way ANOVA where k represents the number of factors involved in an experiment.

Partitioning the Sum of Squares for a Two-Way ANOVA

In terms of the details, we can now partition the total sum of squares into distinct and overlapping portions:

Sum of squares total	=	Sum of squares rows (treatment B)	+	Sum of squares columns (treatment A)	+	Sum of squares interaction	+	Sum of squares error

or

$$SS_{total} = SSR_{treatment\ B} + SSC_{treatment\ A} + SS_{interaction} + SS_{error}$$

Sum of squares total:

$$SS_{total} = \sum_{i=1}^{r}\sum_{j=1}^{c}\sum_{k=1}^{n}(Y_{ijk} - \overline{\overline{Y}})^2$$

where

Y_{ijk} = individual observation on the dependent variable

$\overline{\overline{Y}}$ = grand mean

j = level of factor A

i = level of factor B

k = number of an observation in a particular cell

r = total number of levels of factor B (rows)

c = total number of levels of factor A (columns)

n = total number of observations in the sample

Sum of squares rows (treatment B):

$$SSR_{treatment\ B} = \sum_{i=1}^{r}(\overline{Y}_i - \overline{\overline{Y}})^2$$

where

$\overline{Y}_j$ = mean of ith treatment—factor B

Sum of squares columns (treatment A):

$$SSC_{treatment\ A} = \sum_{j=1}^{c}(\overline{Y}_j - \overline{\overline{Y}})^2$$

where

$\overline{Y}_j$ = mean of jth treatment—factor A

Sum of squares interaction:

$$SS_{interaction} = \sum_{i=1}^{r}\sum_{j=1}^{c}\sum_{k=1}^{n}(Y_{ij} - \overline{Y}_i - \overline{Y}_j - \overline{\overline{Y}})^2$$

RESEARCH SNAPSHOT

Illustrating a Factorial Design Analysis

The graphic at the right displays results for the uniform experiment. Here, two experimental variables are involved in a 2 (uniforms or no uniform for service providers) × 3 (service types: fashion store, airline, home store) between-subjects design. The dependent variable in this case is willingness to spread negative word of mouth (NWOM) about the service. In this case, the results suggest that the factorial model F is significant (F = 2.42, with 5 and 203 degrees of freedom, p < .05). Given the model is significant, the individual variables are examined to see which may create significant differences in the dependent variable. In this case, only one fixed factor, service type, is associated with significant differences in NWOM. The table of estimated means suggests that subjects report the lowest NWOM for fashion stores (5.2) and the most for airlines (5.9), which appears similar to the mean NWOM for fashion stores (5.6). Neither the uniform main effect nor interaction creates a significant effect on NWOM in this case.

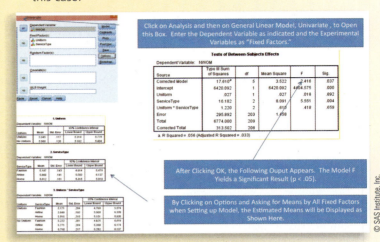

The above is one form of calculation. However, $SS_{\text{interaction}}$ generally is indirectly computed in the following manner:

$$SS_{\text{interaction}} = SS_{\text{total}} - SSR_{\text{treatment B}} - SSC_{\text{treatment A}} - SS_{\text{error}}$$

Sum of squares error:

$$SS_{\text{error}} = \sum_{i=1}^{r}\sum_{j=1}^{c}\sum_{k=1}^{n}(Y_{ijk} - \overline{Y}_{ij})^2$$

where

$\overline{Y}_{ij}$ = mean of the interaction effect

These sums of squares, along with their respective degrees of freedom and mean squares, are summarized in Exhibit 17.6.

The Research Snapshot illustrates how to examine a factorial design using the GLM procedure in SPSS.

EXHIBIT 17.6

ANOVA Table for Two-Factor Design

Source of Variation	Sum of Squares	Degrees of Freedom	Mean Square	F-Ratio
Treatment B	$SSR_{\text{treatments B}}$	$r - 1$	$MSR_{\text{treatment B}} = \dfrac{SSR_{\text{treatment B}}}{r - 1}$	$\dfrac{MSR_{\text{treatment B}}}{MS_{\text{error}}}$
Treatment A	$SSC_{\text{treatments A}}$	$c - 1$	$MSC_{\text{treatment A}} = \dfrac{SSC_{\text{treatment A}}}{C - 1}$	$\dfrac{MSC_{\text{treatment A}}}{MS_{\text{error}}}$
Interaction	$SS_{\text{interaction}}$	$(r - 1)(c - 1)$	$MS_{\text{interaction}} = \dfrac{SSC_{\text{interaction}}}{(r - 1)(c - 1)}$	$\dfrac{MS_{\text{interaction}}}{MS_{\text{error}}}$
Error	SS_{error}	$rc(n - 1)$	$MS_{\text{error}} = \dfrac{SS_{\text{error}}}{rc(n - 1)}$	
Total	SS_{total}	$rcn - 1$		

Source: © Cengage Learning®

In the next three sections we illustrate other ways to partition variance and examine specific research questions either within a GLM ANOVA framework itself or as part of some specific test within the overall experiment. Although we will not present the detailed equations for those tests in the sections below, realize that each is formed by breaking down the sums of squares to isolate a specific effect.

Complex Experimental Designs

Experiments like those presented to this point in the book represent the most commonly employed approaches to causal designs in market and marketing research. However, the researcher sometimes is not presented with an ideal situation. For instance, resource limitations may lead the researcher to use a more complicated experimental design. The analyst then may need to use more complicated analytics to extract meaning from the data.

Within-Subject Designs

In Chapter 9, we introduced the notion that sometimes a subject may see more than one combination of experimental treatments. The researcher may wish to apply multiple treatments to the same subject for various reasons. Not the least of these is to create a design that is cheaper to implement. In other times, the researcher may be interested in the difference created in the same subject based on exposure to more than one treatment. Either way, subjects will be assessed multiple times.

For instance, in a retail atmosphere experiment like the one described in Chapter 9, each subject could rate each combination of colors (blue and orange) and lighting (bright and soft) instead of only one combination. Thus, the design produces four observations on the dependent variable from each subject as opposed to a single observation in a between-subject design. Such a design is called a **within-subjects experimental design**. Within-subjects designs involve repeated measures because with each treatment the same subject is measured. Thus, an elementary one factor, within-subjects design could be analyzed with a paired samples t-test.

Within-subjects experimental design
Experimental subjects are exposed to multiple treatment combinations in the same experiment.

Demand Artifacts

Between-subjects designs are usually advantageous although they are usually more costly. The validity of between-subjects designs often is higher because by applying only one treatment combination to one subject, the researcher reduces demand characteristics greatly. When a subject sees multiple conditions, he or she is more likely to guess the study's purpose. Exhibit 17.7 illustrates the differences between a between-and within-subjects design. Although the same amount of data on dependent variables can be collected using one-fourth as many subjects by implementing a within-subjects design, the internal validity may be threatened by repeated exposure to different treatment levels. After a subject has seen a product in the bright lights and blue condition, and then sees the same product and evaluates it once more in the soft lights and blue condition, and then once more in the bright lights and orange condition, and finally one more time in the bright lights and blue condition, he or she is likely to be clued in that the experiment is about lights and color. Thus, the results could constitute a **demand artifact**. A demand artifact results when the differences between treatment level could be caused by awareness of the treatments rather than a genuine response to the treatments.

Demand artifact
Observed effects are due to awareness of the treatments rather than a genuine response to the treatments.

Data Analysis of Within-Subjects Designs

A within-subjects design calls for a repeated measures analysis. This complicates things a bit in several ways. Not the least is how to enter the data. Is each row in a data set going to constitute an individual observation or is each row going to constitute all observations on each subject? The

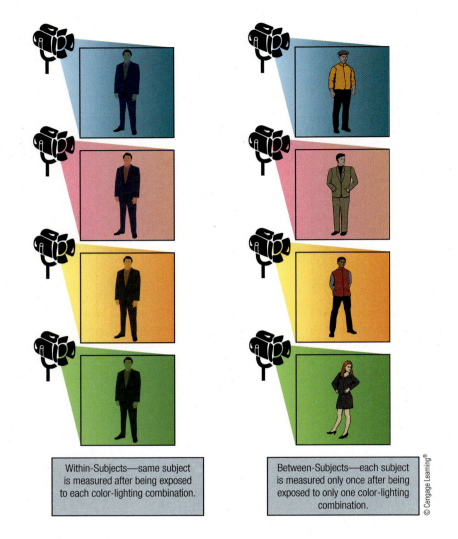

Within-Subjects—same subject is measured after being exposed to each color-lighting combination.

Between-Subjects—each subject is measured only once after being exposed to only one color-lighting combination.

© Cengage Learning®

first approach would involve stacking individual observations on top of one another. If a subject were measured four times, four rows of data are needed to represent that entire response. More typically, data analysts do not stack the responses for repeated measures and instead use one row to represent all measures for a subject. By avoiding stacking, the data are in a more user friendly format for most statistical software including SPSS and JMP.

Exhibit 17.8 illustrates this more common approach for data entry. In this particular data, only the first 12 observations are depicted. In actuality, 133 sandwich shop "locations" were involved in a field experiment that delivered a new promotion about the shop either through Facebook (FB), Pinterest (PIN) or E-mail (EM). The researcher then recorded sales one day prior to the promotion (Sales1), the day of the promotion (Sales2), two days following (Sales3) and three days following the promotion (Sales4). The promotional material displayed a new product and instructions on how to receive a discount to try it. In the promotion, the new product was depicted on either a blue, green, red, or white background.

Suppose the analyst needed to address the research questions of whether sales changed from the day prior until the day after the promotion (sales1, sales2, sales3) and whether the three promotion types are equally effective (FB, EM, PIN). The relevant GLM estimation could be thought of as:

$$\hat{Y}_{it} = \overline{\overline{Y}} + \Delta X + \Delta T + \Delta XT,$$

Location	Promo	Color	Sales1	Sales2	Sales3	Sales4
1	FB	blue	70.6	56.3	71.0	69.9
2	PIN	green	68.4	56.7	60.0	63.6
3	PIN	red	68.3	62.2	58.8	58.6
4	PIN	white	59.2	62.4	62.0	67.6
5	EM	blue	75.0	69.2	65.7	66.6
6	FB	green	66.7	65.0	65.5	62.6
7	PIN	red	61.1	61.2	70.0	58.1
8	FB	white	65.2	62.8	72.0	60.8
9	FB	blue	80.9	56.5	78.2	76.1
10	EM	green	78.3	69.3	76.1	66.8
11	EM	red	64.1	72.0	69.2	65.6
12	FB	white	66.0	63.9	62.5	65.8

EXHIBIT 17.8

Repeated Measures Data in Excel

Source: © 2016 Cengage Learning®

Where $\hat{Y}_{it}$ is the predicted value of sales for location i at time t. $\bar{\bar{Y}}$ is the observed grand mean of sales across all observations, ΔX is the adjustment to the grand mean due to the experimental or between-subjects factor, promotion, ΔT is the adjustment due to the "Time" or which repetition of the measurement is being considered (the within-subjects factor), ΔXT is the potential interaction between promotion and time.

The Research Snapshot illustrates how to use SPSS or SAS JMP to perform this within-subjects ANOVA problem. The results suggest, using a type I error rate (α) of 0.05, that the within-subjects factor is not significant ($F_{2,29} = 0.37$, $p = 0.69$, which exceeds 0.05). Therefore, the sales do not vary significantly over the three time periods. Results also suggest that the between-subjects factor, promotion type, does lead to significant changes in sales ($F_{2,130} = 19.1$, $p < .0001$). Exhibit 17.9 plots the estimated means from this analysis. Finally, the interaction between Promo and Time also is not significant ($F_{4,258} = 1.95$, $p = 0.10$, which is greater than 0.05). Thus, by observing the means in light of this analysis, the researcher can report back that the Pinterest promotions were associated with lower sales than either e-mail or Facebook (significant between-subjects main effect), but that the change in sales over the period did not vary with promotion type (insignificant interaction).

Unbalanced Designs

A factorial design that is well-implemented is considered a **balanced experimental design**; one in which approximately equal numbers of subjects are exposed to each combination of treatment levels. Thus, in a 2×2 between-subjects design implemented in a sample of 80 consumers, 20 subjects would respond to each of the experiment's four cells. Small deviations do not present

Balanced experimental design

One in which approximately equal numbers of subjects are exposed to each combination of treatment levels. An unbalanced design presents unequal cell sizes.

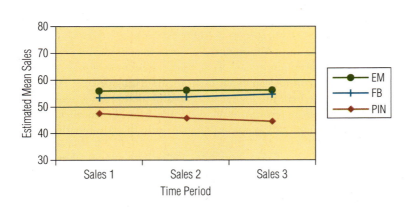

EXHIBIT 17.9

Estimated Means for Promotion Type and Time of Sales (Note: This is from JMP Output.)

Analyzing a Within-Subjects Design

A within-subjects design involves a variation of the GLM procedure. In this case, the procedure is a little more involving than the factorial design described above. Using the data partially shown in Exhibit 17.8 and the research questions described in the chapter, the illustration shown here describes how to get results using SAS JMP.

- JMP can be installed as a toolbar in Excel. Analysis windows can then be opened directly from Excel.
- Click on "Fit Model" and then enter the series of measures of dependent measures in the Y window.
- Choose "Manova" here.
- Enter any between subjects factors in the "corrected model effects" window. Then click "run."
- Initial results will appear in this box. To finish, click on "choose response" and then enter a name for the series of repeated measures (Time is the default), then click "univariate tests also" and then "OK."

© SAS Institute, Inc.

After running this analysis, JMP presents a fairly compact output:

The output shows the results for the between-subjects effect (Promo) and the within-subjects effect, including the interaction between the two. As described in the text, only the between-subjects factor is statistically significant at the 0.05 Type I error rate. Check to see that you can find the numbers for statistical tests described in the text.

In SPSS, here are the steps that would perform the same test:

- Click on Analyze, then drill down to "General Linear Model" and choose "Repeated Measures."
- In this box, enter a name for the within-subject factor, enter then number of levels (how many times a subject has been measured on the dv), then click "define."
- In this box, slide the three within subject measures of interest into this window, enter the between subjects factor below, choose any options, then click "OK." Results will appear in the output window.

© SAS Institute, Inc.

The two programs will produce the same results. In this case, sales do not change much from time to time, but promotion through Pinterest does not seem as effective as the other choices.

---

significant problems for statistical analysis and standard practices can proceed if, for example, the cell sizes would be 18, 22, 19, 21.

Obviously, then, an unbalanced experimental design is one with unequal numbers of subjects per experimental cell. In the extreme, an **incomplete experimental design** results in some empty cells. The incomplete design complicates data analysis in many ways, not the least of which is the inability to analyze all interactions. Although the analysts may prefer to have data on all possible combinations as it presents a straightforward data analysis, sometimes some combinations of treatment levels are implausible (consider an experiment manipulating price, brand prestige, and other factors over multiple levels where the lowest price and highest prestige would present an unrealistic combination). In addition, resource limitations may limit the number of subjects recruited to participate in an experiment and as a consequence, only the combinations most likely to be considered realistic are used.

Incomplete experimental design

An experimental design that results in some empty cells (some combinations of treatments with no observations).

Post-Hoc Contrasts

In all of the GLM results analyzing experimental data the individual experimental variables' effects are estimated and the statistical significance of those tests is provided by an F-statistic. We've seen many examples of these tests of significance previously. When an experimental variable has only two levels, and a single experimental variable is involved, a one-way ANOVA produces this test of statistical significance. However, what if the experimental variable involves more than two levels? Consider the data in Exhibit 17.10. These results are from an experiment in which the researcher is examining the research question:

Are consumers equally willing to pay for movies of any genre (drama, comedy, adventure)?

The researcher designs a movie trailer that experimental subjects access within an online survey framework. The movie description manipulates the genre over these three levels: drama, comedy, and adventure. If the F-statistic for movie genre is statistically significant, the results still do not reveal whether the mean willingness to pay (WTP) for one movie type is statistically different from the others. Thus, the analyst will employ some type of more specific tests to compare every level of the experimental variable against every other level. A **post-hoc comparison** tests the statistical significance of all possible group differences between means. Typically, a post-hoc

Post-hoc comparison

Tests the statistical significance of all possible group differences between means even when no hypothesis about such differences exist.

EXHIBIT **17.10**

Mean WTP by Experimental Condition(s)

Movie Type	Rating	WTP	Sex	Age
Drama	PG	8	1	50
Comedy	PG	12	0	35
Adventure	PG	15	1	25
Drama	PG	9	0	45
Comedy	PG	12	1	40
Adventure	PG	10	0	38
Drama	PG	9	1	70
Comedy	PG	7	0	29
Adventure	PG	9	1	48
Drama	PG	12	0	51
Comedy	PG	7	1	21
Adventure	PG	16	0	35
Drama	PG	13	1	33
Comedy	PG	11	0	39
Adventure	PG	14	1	49
Drama	R	18	0	56
Comedy	R	11	1	27
Adventure	R	14	0	47
Drama	R	7	1	22
Comedy	R	12	0	60
Adventure	R	16	1	55
Drama	R	7	0	25
Comedy	R	8	1	24
Adventure	R	10	0	32
Drama	R	9	1	27
Comedy	R	4	0	23
Adventure	R	12	1	46
Drama	R	9	0	39
Comedy	R	11	1	40
Adventure	R	15	0	65

Source: © 2016 Cengage Learning®

comparison is made in exploring potential specific differences when no specific hypothesis addresses differences between specific groups.

Several variations of post-hoc comparisons exist. Perhaps the most commonly applied is the **Tukey Honestly Significant Difference (HSD)** technique. While we will not present the formula for the test here, it can be thought of as a quantitative examination of the distance between groups formed by each level of the experimental variable and whether that difference is equal to zero. SPSS and JMP make post-hoc comparisons very easy. In SPSS, follow this sequence:

Tukey Honestly Significant Difference (HSD)

The most commonly applied post-hoc comparison technique.

1. Choose GLM–Univariate.
2. Enter WTP as the Dependent Variable and Movie Type as a Fixed Factor.
3. Select Post hoc from the buttons on the left.
4. Place a check in the box by Tukey.
5. Click OK.

In JMP, the following sequence produces the same result for a one-way ANOVA:

1. Chose Fit Y by X.
2. Enter WTP as the Y variable and Movie Type as an X-Factor.
3. Click Run.
4. Click red tab at top of analysis and choose Means/Anova.
5. In the same tab, click Compare Means.

Alternatively, one could use "fit model" and follow a similar process but select "multiple comparisons" to get the t-test instead of "compare means." Fit model is appropriate for factorial designs.

In this case, the ANOVA results suggest that Movie Type does indeed cause differences in WTP. The F-statistic for Movie Type is 4.25 with 2 and 27 degrees of freedom. The p-value is 0.025, which is statistically significant (presuming a 0.05 Type I error rate). The means by experimental condition are:

Adventure	$13.10
Comedy	$ 9.50
Drama	$10.10

From this result, the analyst cannot conclude whether the significant result is due to differences between any one pair of conditions or due to multiple comparison differences. The Tukey HSD in this case yields the results shown in Exhibit 17.11. The first row depicts the difference of 3.60 between the means for the adventure and comedy conditions. The 95 percent confidence interval ranges from 0.32 to 6.89. The p-value for the difference test is 0.029. Thus, the mean WTP for adventure movies is statistically higher than for comedy movies. Neither of the other two comparisons yields a significant difference because the confidence interval includes 0, or alternatively, because the p-value is greater than 0.05. Thus, after conducting the ANOVA and discovering a significant difference in WTP by movie type, the post-hoc comparison then suggests more specifically what the nature of that difference is.

Several drawbacks limit the confidence that one has in post-hoc comparison results. For example, post-hoc comparisons across all combinations can yield many specific tests. For example, in a 3 × 3 between-subjects design, 9 cells exist leading to 15 potential comparisons, 3 for each main effect comparison and 9 for the comparisons of interaction combinations. At some point, just by chance, a result is likely to be significant. Alternatively, each individual comparison produces relatively lower power. Thus, post-hoc comparisons have disadvantages in terms of both type I and type II error. Other types of post-hoc comparisons exist. For

EXHIBIT 17.11

Tukey's HSD Results for WTP by Movie Type

Comparison	Difference	CL	UL	p-value
Adventure-Comedy	3.60	0.32	6.89	0.029
Adventure-Drama	3.00	−0.28	6.28	0.078
Drama-Comedy	0.60	−2.68	3.88	0.893

example, Scheffe's test provides a more conservative test with respect to type I error (taking into account the problems with capitalizing on chance). A full discussion of all of these tests is beyond the scope of this text. However, they all function in the same manner as the Tukey's HSD test.

Planned Comparison

Many times, researchers may believe that any effect observed in an ANOVA is due to some specific comparison of cell means. When the researcher hypothesizes specific differences ahead of time, the appropriate analytical approach is known as a **planned comparison**. A planned (or a priori) comparison represents an alternative approach to examining specific differences between means of different effect combinations in ANOVA. Three key differences between planned contrasts and post-hoc comparisons exist. First, a planned comparison is appropriate when a hypothesis exists ahead of time specifying the specific combination expected to yield a significant difference. Second, the analyst only tests the combinations involved in hypotheses. Third, planned comparisons contain more statistical power. As a consequence, planned comparisons are inappropriate for exploratory analysis. If the researcher is trying to explore or discover the sources for a significant main effect or interaction, post-hoc tests are more appropriate.

The combination of individual or group means representing a planned comparison is known as a **contrast**. Contrasts are created with arithmetic that specifies positive and negative weights to the groups or individual cells that will be compared. The positive and negative weights must sum to 0. For example, consider a main effect with three levels: L1, L2, and L3. Perhaps the three groups could represent different levels of price matching for an electronics store. L1 could represent no price matching; L2 could represent a guarantee to match the prices of competing retailers; and L3 could represent the guarantee to beat the prices of competitors by discounting the price by 5 times the difference in price. In this case, the researcher hypothesizes ahead of time that any significant main effect of price matching will be due to the difference between L3 and the other levels. In other words, the price-beating guarantee (L3) will produce significantly more positive attitudes than either no price matching (L1) or the mere price-matching guarantee (L2). The arithmetic for such a contrast amounts to:

$$C = (0.5)L1 + (0.5)L2 + (-1.0)L3$$

Notice that the sum of the weights is 0.

If the researcher hypothesized that the only significant differences would be between the no price matching (L3) and price matching (L2), a contrast could be represented with the following equation:

$$C = (1.0)L1 + (-1.0)L2 + (0.0)L3$$

Unlike the post-hoc comparisons, every planned comparison is independent of the others. Thus, no adjustment is made to the type I error rate. Each test has a type I error rate of α. As a consequence, the researcher inflates the likelihood of finding a significant result by chance if he or she conducts multiple planned comparisons with the same data. The post-hoc comparison methods like Tukey's HSD adjust the type I error rate based on the knowledge that all possible comparisons are computed.

Consider a researcher analyzing how likely a university student would be to attend a school's home basketball game based on where they live. The variable "type" divides students into those that live in an on-campus dormitory, an off-campus apartment, or in a house. Type then has three levels. The researcher believes that students who live in an apartment are less likely to attend a university sporting event because they are more distracted by the social nature of apartment living. Thus, the researcher hypothesizes a priori that:

Students who live in an apartment will report significantly lower intentions to attend a basketball game than students who live in a dorm or a house.

Planned comparison

A test of differences between specific cells in an experimental design that is based on some specific hypothesized condition corresponding to that contrast.

Contrast

The combination of individual or group means representing a planned comparison.

Conducting a Planned Comparison

Planned comparisons can be conducted within a GLM analysis in both SPSS and JMP. In SPSS, one would follow the following sequence to get the result in the student basketball attendance example:

1. Click Analyze and choose General Linear Model.
2. Enter Q11_2INT as the dependent variable.
3. Enter Type as a fixed factor.
4. Click on Options and put a check in the "contrast coefficient matrix" box.
5. Click Continue and then OK.

SPSS will perform all possible contrasts and the researcher must identify the one corresponding to the prediction and ignore the others. In this case, we find it at the end of the analysis:

Contrast Results (K Matrix)

		Dependent Variable
Type Deviation Contrast[a]		Q11_2INT
Level 2 vs. Mean	Contrast Estimate	−.678
	Hypothesized Value	0
	Difference (Estimate − Hypothesized)	−.678
	Std. Error	.251
	Sig.	.009
	95% Confidence Interval for Difference	
	Lower Bound	−1.180
	Upper Bound	−.176

In JMP, one would follow the following sequence:

1. Click Analyze.
2. Click Fit Model.
3. Enter Q11_2INT as the Y variable.
4. Enter Type as the Model Effect.
5. Click Run and the ANOVA results appear.
6. Click on the red triangle above the "TYPE" graph and choose LS means Contrast.
7. Use the contrast matrix to indicate the specific contrast of interest.

8. Click Done and the results appear.

The researcher conducts the study and gathers 64 responses. An ANOVA conducted using GLM with Q11_2INT (How likely are you to attend the next home basketball game? The scale ranging from 1 = "No Chance of Attending" to 7 = "Certain to Attend") yields the following results:

Model $F_{(df = 2,61)} = 3.66$ p = 0.032

The estimated means for each group are:

Dorm	5.27
Apartment	4.24
House	5.23

Thus, the results suggest a difference in the group means based on the independent variable of living arrangements (TYPE). This result does not test the hypothesis, though. A planned contrast is necessary to perform this test. With Dorm, Apartment, and House as levels 1, 2, and 3 of TYPE, respectively, a contrast can be set up as follows:

$$C = (0.5)L1 + (−1.0)L2 + (0.5)L3$$

The analyst tests this planned contrast to yield the following result:

$$F_{(df = 1,61)} = 7.3, p = 0.009$$

Thus, given the p-value of less than 0.05, an acceptable alpha of 0.05, and the means in the pattern corresponding to the hypothesis (the mean reported intent to attend is lowest for the apartment condition), the analyst can report support for the hypothesis. Apartment students do seem less likely to attend a game than are students with other living arrangements.

The Research Snapshot gives some insight into how to perform these tests with statistical software. Remember when setting up a contrast equation, the sum of all the weights must be 0. The "contrast" condition(s) contain the unique weights. In this case, the unique weight of -1.0 is on L2, the apartment condition. The other conditions share the weight of $+0.05$.

Mining Big Data with Sequential χ^2 Tests

The planned comparison test illustrates the way a researcher would examine a specific theory-based experiment. When it comes to analyzing big data though, market researchers work in very much of an exploratory mode. In a justification mode, researchers avoid fishing expeditions; in an exploratory mode, however, a fishing expedition fits the bill just fine. Thus, data mining is much more about prediction than explanation. The search becomes identifying characteristics that have a statistical relationship with some outcome of interest. In marketing, the outcomes of interest commonly are variables like purchase behavior, visit behavior, and loyalty behavior such as switching, complaining, and WOM. When mining big data, a researcher pays little attention to theoretical explanation in selecting variables to include as potential predictors of key outcomes. In fact, the researcher may turn selection over to some automated process.

Automatic interaction detection refers to a computerized procedure that searches for variables within a data set that relate systematically with a dependent variable. Oftentimes, the output comes in the form of a decision-tree. A **decision-tree** graphically depicts what-if analyses in a tree-like diagram with branches indicating the chances of some event occurring. For instance, if a researcher needs to identify what characteristics of locations are successful for a fast-food restaurant, he or she can create a decision-tree. The tree would split out characteristics of successful and unsuccessful locations. For instance, a basic split may show that locations on corners are twice as likely to succeed as locations not on corners. Further, among those locations on corners, those facing a shopping center are again twice as likely to succeed as those that do not face a shopping center. Thus, the decision-maker can then get an idea of what would happen if a location were (were not) on a corner and then were (were not) facing a shopping center.

A great deal of software exists to create decision-trees based on some form of automatic interaction detection. Perhaps the most basic is something known as **chi-square automatic interaction detection, or CHAID**. CHAID forms the tree by creating branches based on progressive contingency matrices and the corresponding chi-square value. A high chi-square indicates a place for a branch. Once the data are split, CHAID looks for the highest possible chi-square value within that branch. In the end, the resulting decision-tree profiles characteristics most associated with the targeted value of a dependent variable.

CHAID typically is performed on data sets containing thousands of observations such as typifies a retailer's customer data. We can illustrate this using a small data set (the "city location" data available [as SPSS, SAS, JMP, Excel] in the online resources). This data represents information on 35 fast-food locations for a fictional sandwich shop we'll call Out-&-N. Out-&-N wishes to mine this data to identify the types of places attractive for future locations based on likelihood of success. Exhibit 17.12 describes the variables in the data set.

Automatic interaction detection

Refers to a computerized procedure that searches for variables within a data set that relate systematically with a dependent variable.

Decision-tree

Graphically depicts what-if analyses in a tree-like diagram with branches indicating the chances of some event occurring.

Chi-square automatic interaction detection, or CHAID

Refers to a computerized procedure that searches for variables within a data set that relate systematically with a dependent variable.

EXHIBIT **17.12** Variables in "City Location" Data

Var.:	Success	Region	Win	Capital	Univ	N-out	Coast	Temp	POP
Info:	Did Location Succeed?	Part of Country	Has City Won a Sports Championship?	Is City a Capital City?	Does City Have a University?	Does City Have an In-N-Out location?	Is City on Major Body of Water?	Average Summer Temp.	Population
Values	0 = Fail	1 = South 2 = West	0 = No	0 = No	0 = No	0 = No	0 = Inland	°F	1000s
	1 = Success	3 = North	1 = Yes	1 = Yes	1 = Yes	1 = Yes	1 = Coast		

Source: © 2016 Cengage Learning®

Suppose the marketing analyst begins to address the question of what makes a good location by taking the variables region, win, capital, university, and N-out (In-N-Out Burger, who is Out-&-N's major competitor) and performs CHAID. Exhibit 17.13 displays the CHAID decision-tree. The top of the tree shows that 20 of 35 locations, or 57.1 percent, have succeeded while 15, or 42.9 percent, have failed. CHAID first computes all possible contingency matrices and finds the one that produces the highest chi-square. In this case, the chi-square formed by con-trasting region between the south and all other regions (CHAID collapsed the West and North) forms the first split. The chi-square is 5.1 with 1 degree of freedom and the adjusted p-value (adjusted for the fact that multiple chi-squares are being performed in this tree) is 0.071. Given the small sample and the practical nature of the analysis, a type I error rate of 0.15 is used. Follow-ing this branch initially, we see:

1. In the south,
   a. 10 locations have succeeded
   b. 2 locations have failed
2. In the west and north,
   a. 19 locations have failed
   b. 10 locations have succeeded

All CHAID software (this tree was created by SPSS) includes graphical aids. Notice the bar charts at the bottom of each box in the decision-tree. The blue bars represent successes and the green failures. The decision-maker will be looking for a box where the blue bar is highest relative to the green bar. This will indicate a combination of factors (an interaction) leading to the highest probability of success. At the second level, we can see the following:

1. The decision-maker was very interested in region because the choice of new locations can be controlled. Thus, the researcher instructed SPSS to "force the first variable" and listed region as the first independent variable. CHAID splits the "South" branch by the "Univ" variable ($\chi^2 = 2.4$, df = 1, p < 0.15).
   a. Among cities with a university in the South:
      i. 6 locations have succeeded
      ii. 0 location have failed
   b. Among cities without a university in the South:
      i. 4 locations have succeeded
      ii. 2 locations have failed
2. CHAID splits the "West and North" branch by the "Win" variable ($\chi^2 = 3.2$, df = 1, p < 0.15).
   a. Among cities with a sports championship:
      i. 5 locations have succeeded
      ii. 2 locations have failed
   b. Among cities without a sports championship:
      i. 5 locations have succeeded
      ii. 11 locations have failed
3. CHAID then splits the "West and North by No Championship" branch by Capital city ($\chi^2 = 5.7$, df = 1, p < 0.15).
   a. Among cities in the "West and North with no championship" and which are not a capital city:
      i. 5 locations have succeeded
      ii. 4 locations have failed
   b. Among cities in the "West and North with no championship" and which are a capital city:
      i. 0 locations have succeeded
      ii. 7 locations have failed

The market researcher reports clear evidence back to the decision-maker using this decision-tree. From the CHAID results, the company should seek locations in university towns/cities in the south. All locations (100 percent) with this combination of variables have succeeded. Conversely, the company should avoid locations in the west or north with bad sports teams (no champion-ships) that are not capital cities. All locations with this combination of characteristics have failed.

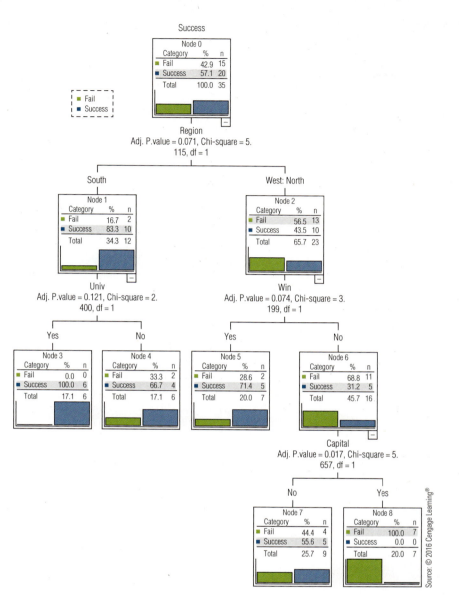

EXHIBIT **17.13**
A Decision-Tree for Retail
Locations

The results of CHAID are actionable based on probabilities. CHAID results predict success. However, CHAID also illustrates the difference between prediction and explanation. While some results may make sense (perhaps the menu fits southern university students' tastes), others often seem to defy a reasonable explanation. For this reason, CHAID is not considered a tool for theoretical research. In addition, when samples are large enough, the analyst will split the sample randomly and then see if results obtained in one half of the data can be validated using the second half of the data.

Beyond the chi-square tests, software routines create decision-trees in many other ways. Often the computer routine will not only search for interactions, but also will search for the best means of portioning the data. Thus, quickly decision-trees can become a bit of black box. All of the procedures work in much the same way as CHAID, and usually produce similar looking decision-trees. For instance, **CART** stands for classification and regression technique. CART uses a combination of cross-classification and simple regression to produce decision-trees based on significant interactions. Overall, automatic interaction detection gives a very good overview into the way big data analysis is automated using basic statistical routines.

CART

Stands for classification and regression technique. An automatic interaction routine combining cross-classification and regression analysis.

Creating a Decision-Tree

While many specialized software programs exist to create decision-trees, SPSS and JMP both are capable of doing these types of analyses. In SPSS, one would follow these steps to create a decision-tree:

1. Click Analyze.
2. Choose "Classify" and from the list of choices choose "Tree."
3. Enter a categorical dependent variable in the Dependent Variable box.
4. Enter the independent variables of interest.
   a. CHAID will classify any continuous variable entered.
   b. If one variable is of special interest, list it first and then check the box beside "Force first variable."
   c. The user can explore options to see a variety of approaches.
5. Click OK.

In JMP, one can follow these steps:

1. Click Analyze.
2. Go to "Modeling" and choose "Partition."
3. Enter a categorical dependent variable in the Y box.
4. Enter independent variables into the X box.
5. Click "OK."
6. Use the red tabs to create "splits."

In addition to the tree, JMP produces a cross-classification graphic like this one:

Each dot represents an observation. In this case the observations represent mushrooms, and the dependent variable is whether it is poisonous or edible (this data set is a JMP sample data set). The different sections of the graphic depict the tree results produced by partitioning. The red dots are poison mushrooms and the green dots are edible. While it's good to know that bruised mushrooms are *often* okay to eat, it's much more important to know that unbruised mushrooms from the woods are probably poisonous!

TIPS OF THE TRADE

- Avoid complex experimental designs if at all possible.
  - Within-subjects designs are economical but yield the highest likelihood of demand artifacts.
- Post-hoc tests are useful in trying to isolate the source of significant ANOVA results, particularly when main effects involve more than two levels.
- Use a planned contrast when testing a hypothesis derived from theory that points to some specific conditions (cells) where a difference is expected. The weights in a contrast equation must sum to zero.
- Data mining techniques like CHAID are only for use in exploratory analysis.

∴ SUMMARY

1. Compute an F-statistic. An F-statistic is the basic inferential test in GLM procedures including ANOVA and regression. The F-statistic involves the ratio of systematic variance to error variance. SSB represents variance around the group means. This is the variability accounted for by experimental variables. SSE represents the variability that is not explained by SSB in standard ANOVA. SST is the sum of SSB and SSE.

2. Know what a factorial design means in an ANOVA context. A factorial design represents an experimental design that is fully implemented. By fully implemented, we mean that observations are taken on every combination of experimental variables. No cells are left empty. A one-way ANOVA contains only as many cells as there are levels of the experimental variable. A two-way ANOVA contains as many cells as the number of levels of each experimental variable multiple by each other. The two-way ANOVA concept can be expanded into k-way ANOVA where k is the number of treatment variables. A factorial design involves interpretation of main effects and interactions.

3. Appreciate the potential complexity of experimental designs. Resource limitations sometime lead the research away from standard, between-subject factorial designs into more complex designs. Complex designs call for more complex data analytics than do between-subject factorial designs. One of the main complications comes from a within-subjects design. Within-subjects designs call for repeated measures analytics. ANOVA then partitions out any between-subjects effects from within-subjects effects.

4. Use post-hoc comparisons. A post-hoc comparison tests the statistical significance of all possible group differences between means. Post-hoc comparisons represent an exploratory approach to predicting group means. While many variations of post-hoc comparisons exist, Tukey's Honestly Significant Difference (HSD) technique is applied widely. One of the drawbacks of post-hoc comparisons is that, cell by cell, the tests have limited statistical power.

5. Know when a specific contrast is appropriate. In stark contrast to post-hoc contrasts, planned comparisons provide a mechanism for testing specific cells or combinations of cells against one another. Planned comparisons are different from post-hoc comparisons in multiple ways. (1) A planned comparison is appropriate when hypotheses exist specifying the specific combination(s) of effects that are associated with the dependent variable. (2) The analyst only tests the combinations specifically referred to in a hypothesis. When a contrast equation is set up, the sum of all the weights must equal zero.

6. Understand how sequential chi-square analyses are useful in discovering meaning in big data. Automatic interaction detection refers to an automated procedure by which a routine searches all possible combinations between the dependent variable and different levels of the independent variable. The most basic form of automatic interaction detection is CHAID. CHAID involves taking every possible chi-square, finding the largest, and then splitting up the data based on that result. Then, within each branch, taking every chi-square and splitting the samples again based on the chi-square results. CHAID represents a basic form of big data mining. The results are depicted in a decision-tree that makes prediction of characteristics that are associated with success in some dependent variable easily understood.

∴ KEY TERMS AND CONCEPTS

:: QUESTIONS FOR REVIEW AND CRITICAL THINKING

1. What are the abbreviations and formulas and their meaning for the "partitioning" of the total variance in a dependent variable? Include the ANOVA abbreviations for total variation.
2. What is the formula for error remaining in an ANOVA after using the group results to predict the dependent variable?
3. What is the formula for the variability around a group mean in an ANOVA?
4. Give the formula for SS_{blocks}. Explain the equation. Which other component of ANOVA is most similar to SS_{blocks} and why?
5. Give the definition of a factorial design.
6. What would the equation be for any particular observation response as a result of some three-factor factorial design?
7. What is SSB, SST, and SSE in the following data representing responses to different types of promotion provided through Facebook?

Type of Promotion	Gender	Purchase Amount
25% Off	M	$75
25% Off	F	$100
25% Off	M	$80
25% Off	F	$95
25% Donated	M	$60
25% Donated	F	$50
25% Donated	M	$75
25% Donated	F	$45

8. Describe an experiment that would likely produce demand artifacts. What alternative design might avoid the occurrence of demand artifacts?
9. Define balanced experimental design and incomplete experimental design. As a market research analyst, which would you prefer to analyze data for and why?
10. Suppose a researcher conducted a 2 × 4 between-subjects design where device type (cell phone versus computer) and type of advertisement (text only, text and graphics, text and photos, no text but a speaking avatar) are the predictors of intentions to "like" the ad. The researcher expects that the device type will be a significant predictor with phone users having lower intentions than computer users. After conducting the test, he is concerned about what level of "advertisement type" is the most unique. What type of tests would be appropriate and why?
11. What is CHAID? How does it produce a decision-tree?

:: RESEARCH ACTIVITIES

1. Conduct a repeated measures analysis using the data shown in Exhibit 17.8. Include Sales4 as an additional within-subjects measure. How do the results compare with those shown in the chapter using only Sales1, Sales2, and Sales3? What recommendations would you make for a decision-maker based on these results?
2. Using the data shown in Exhibit 17.10, run a factorial ANOVA using GLM that includes sex as a blocking variable, age as a covariate, and movie type and rating as experimental variables. All of the variables predict WTP. Explain your results. Create tables, if necessary, to communicate your results.
3. Use the city location data to create a decision-tree using automatic interaction detection in SPSS, SAS, or JMP. In contrast with the results in the chapter, do not force region to be the first variable, include all nominal variables, and include temperature as another dependent variable. What is the best combination of results to attract customers according to this analysis? Explain your results.

Advanced Topics in Linear Analytics

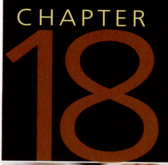

CHAPTER
18

LEARNING OUTCOMES

After studying this chapter, you should be able to:

1. Understand the meaning of covariance and correlation theoretically
2. Compute a covariance and correlation matrix
3. Separate causal relationships from other types of relationships to build explanations
4. Use multiple regression for predictive purposes
5. Appreciate the arithmetic of OLS

Dimitri Otis/Getty Images

Effective marketing results in positive outcomes for an organization's stakeholders. Marketing depends on good performance on variables that take on values based on a variety of company actions, consumer characteristics, and environmental conditions. Thus, these outcomes are truly *dependent* variables. The quantitative benchmarks that indicate firm performance as dependent variables represent **marketing metrics**. Market researchers then apply various statistical approaches in an effort to show how these marketing metrics come to be and what controllable factors might influence them in a positive way.

Key marketing metrics include basic outcomes like traffic counts, sales, margin, repeat behavior, and net promoter score (NPS), and others that are less obvious, including life-time-value to customer acquisition costs (CAC, or customer lifetime value), and the percentage of new customers in a period that were generated by some specific marketing attempt.[1] Outcomes like these, and others, help managers know what marketing tools pay off the most.

Chapter 14 introduced bivariate analyses and briefly touched on the concept of multiple linear regression. In this chapter, and in the two that follow, we go deeper in depth into linear analytics. This chapter provides a foundation for understanding the more complex analytics presented in the final chapters. Linear tools are far from limiting and provide the researcher with considerable flexibility not only in benchmarking performance with marketing analytics but also in understanding what factors actually drive positive and negative analytics.

What determines how many text messages a typical student sends daily? This question can be addressed with correlation or simple regression analysis. The Survey This! data may shed some light on this issue. Use number of text messages sent and three other variables of your choice to explore this issue. Use variables that are better than ordinal. Conduct a correlation analysis from a correlation matrix and build a predictive regression model. Interpret the results and draw an appropriate conclusion.

Understanding Covariance and Correlation

Marketing metrics

Quantitative benchmarks that indicate firm performance and serve as dependent variables for the market researcher.

Measures of association capture how much one variable changes as another variable(s) changes. In other words, measures or statistics of association show how variables move together. When variables change in response to one another, that is they move together, we say they are related to one another.

Measures of association

Capture how much one variable changes as another variable(s) changes (i.e., move together).

Covariance

A simple statistic that indicates how much one variable relates to another is statistical covariation. **Covariance** is the absolute amount of association between two variables determined by how a change in one variable corresponds systematically to a change in another. The formula for sample covariance is:

Covariance

Is the absolute amount of association between two variables determined by how a change in one variable corresponds systematically to a change in another.

$$S_{xy} = \mathbf{Cov}_{(x,y)} = \frac{\sum\limits_{i=1}^{n} (X_i - \overline{X})(Y_{i-}\overline{Y})}{n-1}$$

where X_i and Y_i represent the ith observation of X and Y, respectively, and $\overline{X}$ and $\overline{Y}$ are the sample means of X and Y, respectively. Given that most statistics described in earlier chapters represent sample values rather than populations, we provide the formula for the sample covariance first. The sample covariance comes into play when the analyst needs to perform a statistical inference. The statistical significance of a computed covariance can be tested with a t-test. The resulting t-value is compared to a critical value to determine if the covariance is statistically different than 0.

However, inferences are not always needed. The population covariance (σ_{xy}) would be similarly computed by substituting the population means (μ_x, μ_y) for the respective sample means and changing the denominator to n instead of $n-1$:

$$\sigma_{xy} = \mathbf{Cov}_{(x,y)} = \frac{\sum\limits_{i=1}^{n} (X_i - \mu_x)(Y_i - \mu_y)}{n}$$

As samples become large, the difference between the two results becomes negligible.

Another way to think of covariance is as the average cross-product. Literally, the numerator of the equation is summing the products of deviations from average for X and Y (i.e., cross-multiplying

Obs	Days (Y1)	Sales (Y2)	NPS (X)	(Y-Ȳ)	(X-X̄)	Product
1	55.0	$39	1	39.9	−3.7	−146.18
2	27.0	$133	2	11.9	−2.7	−31.64
3	19.0	$171	3	3.9	−1.7	−6.44
4	18.0	$163	3	2.9	−1.7	−4.78
5	15.0	$396	4	−0.1	−0.7	0.09
6	11.0	$505	5	−4.1	0.3	−1.38
7	12.0	$362	5	−3.1	0.3	−1.04
8	12.0	$334	5	−3.1	0.3	−1.04
9	13.0	$424	5	−2.1	0.3	−0.71
10	14.0	$612	5	−1.1	0.3	−0.38
11	8.0	$512	6	−7.1	1.3	−9.51
12	5.0	$575	6	−10.1	1.3	−13.51
13	3.0	$509	6	−12.1	1.3	−16.18
14	4.0	$575	7	−11.1	2.3	−25.98
15	11.0	$820	7	−4.1	2.3	−9.64
Mean	15.1	408.6	4.7			−17.9
Sample Covariance						−19.2

EXHIBIT 18.1
Calculating Covariance

Source: © 2016 Cengage Learning®

the deviations from mean). As the deviations from mean become larger together, that is, for both X and Y, the covariance value becomes larger, meaning more *co*-variation. Conversely, think of what happens when for one observation (i), either X or Y is exactly equal to its mean. The cross-product for that observation would be 0 because anything multiplied by 0 is 0. The net results for that observation would be no contribution to covariance. If associated values of X_i and Y_i differ from their means in the same direction, their covariance will be positive. If the values of X_i and Y_i tend to deviate in opposite directions (one negative and one positive), their covariance will be negative.

Exhibit 18.1 illustrates how to calculate a covariance. In this case, a spreadsheet has been used to help with the arithmetic. The data for this problem are provided in a file in the student resources (exhibit 18_1data.xls). The data include a sample comprised of 15 observations, each a health services firm's customer. Variables include the number of days since the last contact between the customer and the firm (either in person, online, or by phone), the NPS from the customer, and the average monthly sales to that customer.

For now, sales are not used as interest is on the covariance between the NPS (X) and days since last contact. The $(Y - \bar{Y})$ and $(X - \bar{X})$ columns contain the subtraction of each observation score on Y and X, respectively, from the observed mean. For instance, in the first row, $55.0 - 15.1 = 39.9$ and $1.0 - 4.7 = -3.7$. Those two values are *crossed*, meaning multiplied, to get the product of -146.18. This process of computing cross-products is repeated for each observation. Here, the deviations in days tend to be opposite in sign to the deviations in NPS. By summing the 15 cross-products and dividing by n, the observed covariance of -17.9 is obtained. If the researcher is interested in a sample estimate of the covariance, the sum of the 15 cross-products is divided by $n - 1$ instead of n, or 14 instead of 15, to yield the estimate of sample covariance of -19.2.

What does this tell us? The fact that the sign is negative indicates that the higher the NPS reported, the fewer days between customer contacts. Thus, the two variables are negatively related. In this instance, management is made aware that an increase in NPS is associated with more frequent contact with customers. Covariance statistics can be very powerful. However, researchers sometimes wish to express the relationship between variables on a standardized scale. This brings us to the correlation coefficient.

Correlation

A **correlation coefficient** is a statistical measure of association between two variables expressed on a range of −1 to +1. Statistically speaking, correlation is a standardized representation of

Correlation coefficient

Is a statistical measure of association or covariation between two variables expressed on a scale of −1 to +1. It is standardized covariance and generally represented by the letter r.

covariance. Several different correlation statistics exist based on the measurement level of the variables. Relationships between continuous variables are represented by the Pearson product-moment correlation. A Spearman correlation is more appropriate for ordinal-level data. The researcher should be familiar with these terms as software packages often will provide various options for the actual computation.

Here, we focus on the Pearson product-moment correlation coefficient. Like with covariance, a *t*-test can be used to see if a correlation is significantly different from 0. If the value of *r* equals +1.0, a perfect positive relationship exists. The two variables are really one! If the value of *r* equals −1.0, a perfect negative relationship exists. The implication is that one variable is a mirror image of the other. As one goes up, the other goes down in proportion and vice versa. No correlation is indicated if *r* equals 0. This means as one variable goes up, the other is as likely to go up as it is down or it may even remain unchanged. Knowing the value of one variable says nothing reliable about the value of another. A correlation coefficient indicates both the magnitude of the linear relationship and the direction of that relationship. For example, if we find that $r = -0.85$, we know we have a very strong inverse, or negative, relationship—that is, the greater the value measured by variable X, the lower the value measured by variable Y.

The formula for calculating the correlation coefficient for two variables X and Y can be expressed as follows:

$$r_{xy} = r_{yx} = \frac{\sum_{i=1}^{n}(X_i - \overline{X})(Y_i - \overline{Y})}{\sqrt{\sum_{i=1}^{n}(X_i - \overline{X})^2 \sum_{i=1}^{n}(Y_i - \overline{Y})^2}}$$

An alternative way to express this formula is as follows:

$$r_{xy} = r_{yx} = \frac{\sigma_{xy}}{\sqrt{\sigma_x^2 \sigma_y^2}}$$

where

σ_x^2 = overall variance of X

σ_y^2 = overall variance of Y

σ_{xy} = overall covariance of X and Y

As mentioned earlier in text, a correlation coefficient is a standardized measure of covariance. Covariance coefficients retain information about the absolute scale ranges. Thus, large values tend to produce larger numbers, and in this sense, more information is available. A covariance representing distance in millimeters will be much larger than a covariance representing the same distance in kilometers. In this sense, covariance coefficients are advantageous compared with correlation coefficients. However, this same characteristic means that covariance coefficients can be compared to one another only when all measures use the same numeric scale. Thus, researchers often find the correlation coefficient more useful because they can compare two correlations without regard for the amount of variance exhibited by each variable separately.

Standardized variables

Result from subtracting the mean of a variable from each observation (as in Exhibit 18.1) and dividing by the standard deviation of that variable. Standardized variables are often called Z-scores.

Scatter plot

A simple plot graphically depicting the corresponding values of variables onto one another in a Cartesian plane.

Another way to compute correlation involves standardizing the variables. **Standardized variables** result from subtracting the mean of a variable from each observation (as in Exhibit 18.1) and dividing by the standard deviation of that variable. Standardized variables are often called Z-scores. Standardized variables eliminate information about the actual scale values of a variable and instead express values as standard deviations from the mean. Correlation then becomes the average cross-product of the standardized variables.

Exhibit 18.2 illustrates plots of X and Y, each depicting a different type of relationship. Each frame represents a **scatter plot**, which simply means that X and Y values are plotted on one another in a Cartesian plane. Each diagram shows a second set of axes that reorient the data around the mean of X and the mean of Y. So, each observation is represented not only by its raw values but also by the deviations from each mean. We can easily see from the earlier equations that

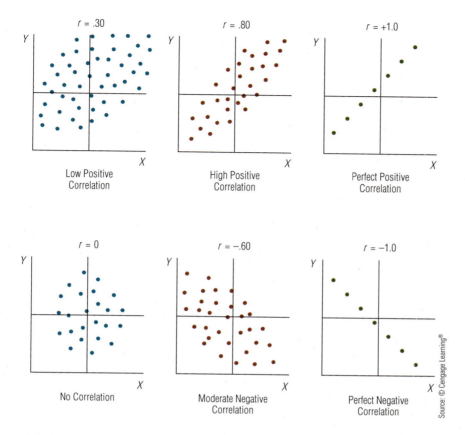

Source: © Cengage Learning®

EXHIBIT 18.2

Scatter Diagram to Illustrate Correlation Patterns

the sum of the products of deviations from the variable means is an important determinant in calculating covariance and correlation:

$$\sum_{i=1}^{n} (X_i - \overline{X})(Y_i - \overline{Y})$$

Notice that in the no-correlation condition, the observations are scattered rather evenly about the space. A correlation of zero happens when positive cross-products of deviations are canceled out by an approximately equal number of negative cross-products of deviations. Sum these deviations up and something around 0 results.

Exhibit 18.3 provides a more detailed illustration. The exhibit depicts an alternative set of axes by drawing a line through the plane at the means of both X and Y. Notice that one data point in each quadrant depicts graphically the distance from the mean and the observed value. The $(X_i - \overline{X})$ distances are depicted with a green dashed line and the $(Y_i - \overline{Y})$ distances are depicted with a red dashed line. For point 1, the product of the two deviations would be positive because each of the deviations is positive. In fact, the same would be true for each point in quadrant 1. For point 3, the product of the deviations also would be positive because each of the deviations is negative (a negative value × a negative value = positive value). In contrast, point 2's cross-product is negative because the X deviation (green line) is positive, but the Y deviation (red line) is negative. For point 4, the Y deviation is positive and the X deviation is negative, again producing a negative cross-product. While we use only these four points to illustrate, the cross-products in each carry the same sign. Thus, when the points are scattered all over the plane, the sum of the cross-products approaches 0 as the negative and positive cross-products cancel each other out. In fact, the correlation between X and Y for these values is almost nothing, 0.01.

In contrast, if the values are less scattered and take a pattern like the second frame in Exhibit 18.2, the positive cross-products would overwhelm the negative cross-products and a positive relationship becomes evident. Thus, as the data tend to move together, the cross-products will add up to something. That something may be negative or positive depending on where the points fall

EXHIBIT **18.3**
Sums of Cross-Products Help
Understand Association

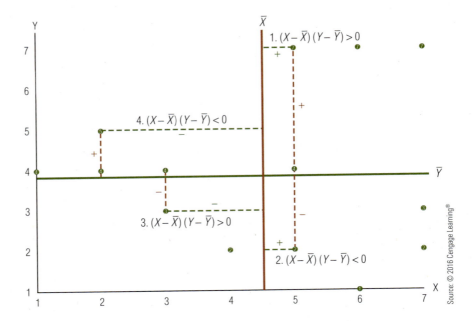

relative to the axes created by the variable mean values. Graphical depictions like those shown in Exhibits 18.2 and 18.3 provide a very good conceptual understanding of covariation, correlation, regression, and measures of association in general.

As an even simpler way of understanding measures of association, one could count the number of observations in each quadrant. If about the same number of points appear in each of the four quadrants, chances are the association between two variables is not very strong. Consequently, the covariance and correlation approach 0.

Correlation Calculation Illustrated

We illustrate correlation coefficient computations with a simple example. Today, researchers do not need to calculate correlation manually. However, the calculation process also helps illustrate exactly what correlation means. Setting up a spreadsheet to do the calculations also provides a good means of learning. Consider an investigation made to determine whether the average number of hours worked in manufacturing industries relates to unemployment. A correlation analysis of the data is carried out in Exhibit 18.4.

Notice that the exhibit breaks down the different components needed to compute variances as well as covariance and correlation. The correlation between the two variables (hours worked and unemployment rate) is -0.635, indicating a **negative (inverse) relationship**. When the number of hours goes up, unemployment comes down. This makes intuitive sense. If factories are increasing output, regular workers will typically work more overtime and new employees will be hired (reducing the unemployment rate). Both variables are probably related to overall economic conditions.

Negative (inverse) relationship

Means that as one variable goes up, the other goes down (the plots would be mostly in quadrants 2 and 4 in Exhibit 18.3).

Coefficient of Determination

Recall earlier that we can represent dispersion with either variance (σ^2) or standard deviation (σ). Variance equals the squared standard deviation for a variable. The coefficient of determination and correlation share the same type of correspondence. While correlation presents a standardized representation of association or correspondence between two variables, one may ask instead how much do the variances of two variables overlap. If we wish to know the proportion of *variance* in Y that overlaps X (or vice versa), we can calculate the **coefficient of determination** (R^2) by squaring the correlation coefficient:

Coefficient of determination

The amount of variance in one variable that overlaps with another. Typically expressed as the R^2 between a dependent variable and an independent variable(s).

$$R^2 = r_{xy}^2 = \left(\frac{\sigma_{xy}}{\sqrt{\sigma_x^2 \sigma_y^2}} \right)^2$$

EXHIBIT **18.4**
Correlation Analysis of Number of Hours Worked in Manufacturing Industries with Unemployment Rate

Unemployment Rate (X_i)	Number of Hours Worked (Y_i)	$X_i - \bar{X}$	$(X_i - \bar{X})^2$	$Y_i - \bar{Y}$	$(Y_i - \bar{Y})^2$	$(X_i - \bar{X})(Y_i - \bar{Y})$
5.5	39.6	.51	.2601	−.71	.5041	−.3621
4.4	40.7	−.59	.3481	.39	.1521	−.2301
4.1	40.4	−.89	.7921	.09	.0081	−.0801
4.3	39.8	−.69	.4761	−.51	.2601	.3519
6.8	39.2	1.81	3.2761	−1.11	1.2321	−2.0091
5.5	40.3	.51	.2601	−.01	.0001	−.0051
5.5	39.7	.51	.2601	−.61	.3721	−.3111
6.7	39.8	1.71	2.9241	−.51	.2601	−.8721
5.5	40.4	.51	.2601	.09	.0081	.0459
5.7	40.5	.71	.5041	.19	.0361	.1349
5.2	40.7	.21	.0441	.39	.1521	.0819
4.5	41.2	−.49	.2401	.89	.7921	−.4361
3.8	41.3	−1.19	1.4161	.99	.9801	−1.1781
3.8	40.6	−1.19	1.4161	.29	.0841	−.3451
3.6	40.7	−1.39	1.9321	.39	.1521	−.5421
3.5	40.6	−1.49	2.2201	.29	.0841	−.4321
4.9	39.8	−.09	.0081	−.51	.2601	.0459
5.9	39.9	.91	.8281	−.41	.1681	−.3731
5.6	40.6	.61	.3721	.29	.0841	.1769

$$\bar{X} = 4.99$$

$$\bar{Y} = 40.31$$

$$\sum(X_i - \bar{X})^2 = 17.8379$$

$$\sum(Y_i - \bar{Y})^2 = 5.5899$$

$$\sum(X_i - \bar{X})(Y_i - \bar{Y}) = -6.3389$$

$$r = \frac{\sum(X_i - \bar{X})(Y_i - \bar{Y})}{\sqrt{\sum(X_i - \bar{X})^2 \sum(Y_i - \bar{Y})^2}} = \frac{-6.3389}{\sqrt{(17.8379)(5.5899)}} = \frac{-6.3389}{\sqrt{99.712}} = -.635$$

The coefficient of determination, R^2, measures that part of the total variance of Y that we can account for by knowing the value of X. In the example about unemployment and hours worked, $r = -0.635$; therefore, $R^2 = 0.403$. About 40 percent of the variance in unemployment overlaps with, or is accounted for by, the variance in hours worked, and vice versa. The coefficient of determination represents a measure of association between a dependent variable and the independent variable(s) employed to predict it. Sometimes, statisticians use the expression that R^2 represents the amount of variance *explained* in a regression equation. Later, we will see that an explanation requires more than just overlapping variance. But one can easily see that *R-squared* really is just r squared!

Covariance and Correlation Matrix

Exhibit 18.3 displays the correlation between two variables. As we move toward *multi* variable analyses, the researcher places interest on more than two variables. When this is the case, a **covariance matrix** summarizes all the information contained in a set of metric variables. A

Covariance matrix

Contains the covariance for every pair of variables among a set of metric variables with the off-diagonal elements displaying covariances and the diagonal elements displaying variance.

What Makes Someone Attractive?

What are the things that make someone attractive? Many people are interested in this question. Among these are companies that hire people to sell fashion. The correlation matrix below was computed with SPSS. The correlations show how different characteristics relate to each other. Variables include a measure of fit, meaning how well the person matches a fashion retail concept, attractiveness, weight (how overweight someone appears), age, manner of dress (how modern), and personality (warm–cold). Thus, a sample of consumers rated a model shown in a photograph on those characteristics. The results reveal the following:

Correlations

		Fit	Attract	Weight	Age	Modern	Cold
Fit	Pearson Correlation	1	0.831**	−0.267*	0.108	−0.447**	−0.583**
	Sig. (2-tailed)		0.000	0.036	0.404	0.000	0.000
	N	62	62	62	62	62	62
Attract	Pearson Correlation	0.831**	1	−0.275*	0.039	−0.428**	−0.610**
	Sig. (2-tailed)	0.000		0.030	0.766	0.001	0.000
	N	62	62	62	62	62	62
Weight	Pearson Correlation	−0.267*	−0.275*	1	0.082	0.262*	0.058
	Sig. (2-tailed)	0.036	0.030		0.528	0.040	0.653
	N	62	62	62	62	62	62
Age	Pearson Correlation	0.108	0.039	0.082	1	−0.019	0.104
	Sig. (2-tailed)	0.404	0.766	0.528		0.882	0.423
	N	62	62	62	62	62	62
Modern	Pearson Correlation	−0.447**	−0.428**	0.262*	−0.019	1	0.603**
	Sig. (2-tailed)	0.000	0.001	0.040	0.882		0.000
	N	62	62	62	62	62	62
Cold	Pearson Correlation	−0.583**	−0.610**	0.058	0.104	0.603**	1
	Sig. (2-tailed)	0.000	0.000	0.653	0.423	0.000	
	N	62	62	62	62	62	62

*Correlation is significant at the 0.05 level (2-tailed).

**Correlation is significant at the 0.01 level (2-tailed).

Thus, if the model seems to "fit" the store concept, she seems attractive. If she is too big, she is seen as less attractive. Age is unrelated to attractiveness or fit. Modern dress style and coldness of personality also are associated with lower attractiveness.

Using these correlations, a retailer can help determine what employees should look like!

Correlations can be found using SPSS by navigating as shown:

Correlations

	Age	Weight	Oxy	Runtime	RunPulse	RstPulse	MaxPulse
Age	1.0000	-0.2405	-0.3118	0.1952	-0.3161	-0.1509	-0.4149
Weight	-0.2405	1.0000	-0.1628	0.1435	0.1815	0.0440	0.2494
Oxy	-0.3118	-0.1628	1.0000	-0.8622	-0.3980	-0.3994	-0.2367
Runtime	0.1952	0.1435	-0.8622	1.0000	0.3136	0.4504	0.2261
RunPulse	-0.3161	0.1815	-0.3980	0.3136	1.0000	0.3525	0.9298
RstPulse	-0.1509	0.0440	-0.3994	0.4504	0.3525	1.0000	0.3051
MaxPulse	-0.4149	0.2494	-0.2367	0.2261	0.9298	0.3051	1.0000

Covariance Matrix

	Age	Weight	Oxy	Runtime	RunPulse	RstPulse	MaxPulse
Age	27.69247	-10.54083	-8.73983	1.42538	-17.05161	-6.04946	-20.00860
Weight	-10.54083	69.36504	-7.22105	1.65825	15.49866	2.79056	19.03372
Oxy	-8.73983	-7.22105	28.37938	-6.37255	-21.73524	-16.21008	-11.55748
Runtime	1.42538	1.65825	-6.37255	1.92492	4.46125	4.76114	2.87476
RunPulse	-17.05161	15.49866	-21.73524	4.46125	105.10323	27.53226	87.35054
RstPulse	-6.04946	2.79056	-16.21008	4.76114	27.53226	58.05591	21.30538
MaxPulse	-20.00860	19.03372	-11.55748	2.87476	87.35054	21.30538	83.98065

A Correlation Matrix and Corresponding Covariance Matrix for Variables Related to Exercise Performance.

covariance matrix contains the covariance for every pair of variables in the off-diagonal elements and contains the variance for each variable on the diagonal. In other words, the covariance matrix, often abbreviated with a bold capital **S**, is a square matrix summarizing all the relationships among variables that retains the absolute scale values. **S** captures both the common scatter (covariance and variance) and the level (higher values result from larger numbers) of the set of variables.

A **correlation matrix** is a standardized covariance matrix. While it retains all the information about relationships in the off-diagonal elements (the actual correlations), the information about the level of variables is removed as all the variances become standardized to 1. Every diagonal element is 1. One way to produce the correlation matrix is to first standardize all variables, yielding Z-scores that express variable values in standard deviations away from the mean, and then compute all possible covariances. Researchers often compute correlation matrices early on as they provide a quick summary of how variables are corresponding with each other. The Research Snapshot on page 493 provides an overview of how to create correlation matrices using SPSS software.

Correlation matrix

A standardized covariance matrix.

Causality and Explanation

In Chapter 3, we discussed the conditions necessary to draw causal conclusions:

1. Temporal sequence
2. Concomitant variance
3. Nonspurious association

In regression analysis, we provide evidence of concomitant variance in the form of significant parameter coefficients. When a parameter estimate shows a significant relationship as evidenced by the coefficient size and the corresponding t-value, the dependent variable varies systematically, or covaries, with that particular independent variable. The issue of temporal sequence must be sorted out logically as regression does not provide a method to determine sequence. In experiments, the effort to isolate the effect of experimental variables through a system of manipulation and control helps establish nonspurious evidence of causation. In traditional descriptive survey research, control through random assignment and manipulation is not possible. However, the analysts still can employ statistical control.

Control Variables

Control variables are those not involved in any causal assertion or hypothesis, but are measured and included in an effort to understand the true effect of hypothesized variables on dependent variables. Another way to think of this is that control variables discount the effect of independent variables to the extent that their influence may also be attributed to a control variable. Exhibit 18.5 illustrates the way control variables allow statistical control to isolate the effect of an independent variable.

Control variables

Those predictor variables not involved in any causal assertion or hypothesis, but measured and included in an effort to understand the true effect of hypothesized variables on dependent variables.

Courtesy of JMP.

EXHIBIT 18.5
Partialling the effect
of X on Y

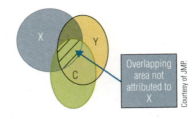

Overlapping
area not
attributed to
X

The ovals shown in Exhibit 18.5 represent the variance of the independent variable X, the dependent variable Y, and a control variable C. The area of overlap between X and Y represents the shared variation between the two variables. Similarly, the overlap between C and Y represents the shared variation between the control variable and the dependent variable. Without considering C, X shares about 30 percent of common variance with Y. Thus, the R^2 between the two variables would be about 0.30. However, the three ovals overlap each other where X, C, and Y come together. This particular area cannot be attributed to X because C may really be the variable driving Y. Thus, this area would be taken away from the effect of X and Y. Thus, the percent of variation attributed to X uniquely drops to about 15 percent. By including the control variable, we are able to partial out the true effect of X on Y.

Multicollinearity

Occurs when multiple predictor variables correlate with each other.

Exhibit 18.5 also illustrates the notion of **multicollinearity**, which occurs when multiple predictor variables included in a regression analysis correlate with each other. The result is that the independent variables are not independent. Multicollinearity can potentially bias regression coefficient estimates to the extent that renders the model incapable of offering results that can *explain* the dependent variable. The good news about multicollinearity is that small to modest levels do not present a major problem in interpreting the effect of independent variables. As multicollinearity becomes large, though, the parameter estimates and the parametric tests of those estimates become unreliable.

Variance inflation factor

Represents an overall estimate of variance overlap among the independent variables.

How much correlation, or shared variance, among independent variables is large? While a rule of thumb would suggest potential issues with multicollinearity when independent variables are related 0.6 or higher, a diagnostic statistic exists to shed some light on the issue. The **variance inflation factor** (VIF) represents an overall estimate of variance overlap among the independent variables. How much overlap is too much? In typical marketing research, a VIF of or 5 of more is a clear indication of problems with multicollinearity. When VIFs are between 2 and 5, the analyst becomes cautious and looks for signs that indicate the results are suspicious, such as implausible standardized regression coefficients ($\beta > |1|$), unusual t-values, or unstable parameter coefficients. A sign of an unstable parameter coefficient is presented when any particular parameter coefficient(s) shows substantial changes in value when one variable is added to a regression model. VIFs near 1.0 indicate little correlation among predictors and no problems with multicollinearity. Chapter 15 displayed results of a regression that included the VIFs in the output, and the Research Snapshot on page 500 on how to get multiple regression results gives a step-by-step guide on how to get these results.

Adjusted R^2

An assessment of amount of variance in the dependent variable that uniquely overlaps with variance in the independent variables. As multicollinearity increases, it becomes lower than unadjusted R^2.

Typical regression results report two R^2 values. In addition to the unadjusted, or overall R^2, the output displays an **adjusted R^2**. The adjusted R^2 tries to take into account the fact that multiple independent variables have some *overlap*, as shown in Exhibit 18.5. Thus, the adjusted R^2 can be only lower or equal to the overall R^2. Only when all independent variables are unrelated to one another will the overall R^2 equal the adjusted R^2. As the independent variables exhibit increasingly high multicollinearity, the adjusted R^2 becomes lower than the overall R^2.

A multiple regression often includes two to five experimental variables of interest, and perhaps at least as many control variables. Analysts hope the control variables will help isolate the effect of any given independent variable and prevent the results from pointing to some accidental generalization as an important effect. Chapter 3 pointed to contributory causality as a suitable goal for marketing research. Analysts hope that including the correct control variables allows the researcher to know how much an independent variable actually affects a dependent variable.

Residuals

In Chapter 15, we introduced the multiple regression equation:

$$Y_i = b_0 + b_1 X_1 + b_2 X_2 + b_3 X_3 + \ldots + b_n X_n + e_i$$

Here, we have not changed the equation but acknowledge that some of the independent variables could be control variables as opposed to independent variables intended to explain some outcome. Although we think of e_i as error in that it represents the portion of the dependent variable not accounted for by the set of predictors, analysts often use the term *residual* instead. A **residual** means the portion left over (*unexplained*) after the predictor variables are included in a model intended to represent *Y*.

A major assumption of any GLM, including linear regression, is that the residual terms are independent. Thus, they should exhibit no systematic pattern. They should not tend to be large for small values of some independent variable and small for large values of that same variable. Most regression programs provide an easy mechanism to plot residuals. If the residual plot suggests the residuals are independent, the analysts can conclude that he/she has omitted no significant predictor of the dependent variable. If residuals are random and no multicollinearity is present, we conclude that the model has explanatory power and evidence of nonspurious association is present.

Residuals should be random in every sense. Residuals should not be related to the predicted values ($\hat{Y}$) or to any independent variable. Thus, plots of residuals against either should reveal no pattern. In other words, when residual plots reveal a random distribution of dots, the researcher can conclude that the error is **white noise**. White noise is the term that refers to a random distribution of error that presents no discernable meaning. The term comes from the noise that an AM radio makes when it is not detecting the signal from any one radio station stronger than any other. Similarly, the sound that a fan makes produces no discernable meaning, only a steady hum.

A clear pattern in residuals indicates a deficiency in the model with respect to its explanatory power. **Underspecification** means a model does not include a complete set of variables that would be necessary to offer a complete explanation of the dependent variable. Control variables provide a useful means of reducing underspecification. Underspecification leads to a pattern in residuals. Thus, the analyst cannot rule out the potential spuriousness of some relationship evident in an underspecified model. Consequently, underspecification reduces the explanatory power of a model. As a consequence, the analyst often finds it useful to plot residuals.

Exhibit 18.6 presents multiple regression results predicting an individual's time in a 50-m race (*Y* in seconds). The independent variables (X_1 and X_2) are age (in years) and weight (in kilograms). Note that the model F of 1.16 is not significant ($p > 0.10$ for a type I error rate of 0.10). Thus, the model does not explain a significant portion of the variance in race time. The bottom of the diagram shows a plot of residuals against row number, or observation number. The residual plot displays a clear pattern. The early observations produce negative residuals while the later observations

Residual

Portion of dependent variable variance left over (*unexplained*) after the predictor variables are included in a model intended to represent *Y*.

White noise

The term that refers to a random distribution of error that presents no discernable meaning.

Underspecification

Means a model does not include a complete set of variables that would be necessary to offer a complete explanation of the dependent variable.

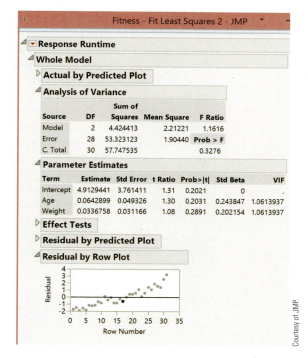

EXHIBIT 18.6

Multiple regression results predicting an individual's time in a 50-meter race (*Y* in seconds)

Courtesy of JMP.

Running Diagnostic Regressions

How do we obtain comprehensive multiple regression results like these? Here's how to get these results in SPSS using data predicting Y with X, X2, X4, X5, and X3R:

1. After opening the data set, click on Analyze.
2. Choose Regression and then select the Linear Regression option.
3. Put Y in the dependent variable window and X1, X2, X4, X5, and X3R in the independent variables window.
4. Click on Statistics and put a check by *collinearity diagnostics* (to obtain VIFs) and click OK.
5. Click on Plot and put ZRESID in the Y window and the desired option as X (in this case we put the Dependent variable).
6. Click Continue and then OK after returning to the Linear Regression window.
7. Interpret the results.

In Excel, with the standard data analysis plugins, you can click on *data* and then *data analysis* and choose *regression* from the pop-up window. Then, enter the corresponding ranges of the dependent and independent variables. Although Excel performs the standard multiple regression analysis in a straightforward manner, Excel is not that convenient for gaining diagnostics. Thus, one of the statistics packages is preferable at this point. In JMP, here is how to get the results:

1. After opening the data, click on Analyze.
2. Click on Fit Model.
3. Enter Y in the Y box.
4. Enter X1, X2, X4, X5, and X3R in the Construct Model Effects box.

5. In the Personality menu, select Standard Least Squares (the default).
6. In the Emphasis menu, select Minimal Output and then click Run.
7. The results will pop up. Right-click within the Parameter Estimates area, chose Column and then put a check by Std Beta and by VIF.
8. In the small red triangle at the top (beside Response Y), choose Row Diagnostics and then select a residual plot such as Plot Residual by Row to obtain results.

Courtesy of the author.

Here, the results suggest that the overall model predicts a significant portion of the variance in Y (F = 38.0, $p < 0.0001$) with an adjusted R^2 of 0.79. Also, X1 is negatively related to Y while X4 and X5 are positively related to Y ($p < 0.05$). However, the VIFs in this case display some values between 2 and 5. These values present the possibility of problems associated with modest multicollinearity, which can make it difficult to rely on individual parameter estimates for explanatory purposes. Also, the plot of residuals shows a slight tendency to increase with larger values of the dependent variable. Both findings lead the analyst to provide caution to users in terms of interpreting the results with great confidence. The absence of both systematic variation among residuals and multicollinearity provide the regression results with explanatory power by giving the analyst confidence in the information provided by a regression's parameter coefficients.

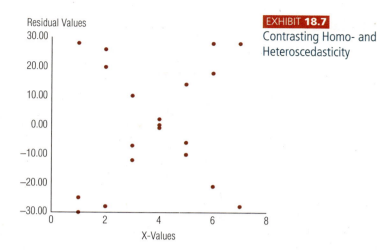

EXHIBIT **18.7**
Contrasting Homo- and Heteroscedasticity

produce positive residuals. If the model was truly *explaining* all the variance in race time possible to be explained, the residuals would display a random pattern centered around 0 on the y-axis. Thus, the analyst concludes from this analysis that some other variable(s) exists that can explain race time.

Exhibit 18.7 contrasts plots of systematic versus random residuals. In the frame on the left, the plot of residuals against the independent variable, X, displays a random pattern with no easily detectable difference in the size of residuals for any value of X. The right frame depicts a different outcome. Here, we see larger values (in absolute value) of residuals for smaller values or larger values of X and smaller values of residuals for X-values close to the scale midpoint of 4. An X-pattern is evident. The left frame of no pattern depicts a state known as **homoscedasticity**, while the right frame displays a condition of **heteroscedasticity** where the residuals change with the values of some variable. In other words, the variance of residuals is not the same across the range of X.

A pattern in residuals suggests an underspecified model. That means some factor is not accounted for, which would remove the observed pattern. In the race time example earlier, the analyst may search for other variables that could be added to the model that may make the residual pattern appear more homoscedastic. Perhaps information about exercise habits or heart efficiency may be helpful. A random pattern of residuals would give the analyst considerably more confidence in concluding that significant regression coefficients do indeed *explain* the dependent variable.

Homoscedasticity

The variability of residuals is constant across the range of values so that no pattern emerges in a residual plot.

Heteroscedasticity

The variability of residuals changes across the range of values so that some pattern emerges in a residual plot against a model variable.

Steps in Regression Aimed at Explanation

Research questions that lead to the need for explanation can be addressed with regression analysis provided the appropriate data are available. The analytical approach in doing so is captured in these steps that are a little more elaborate than those described in Chapter 15:

1. Select the appropriate dependent variable and independent variables based on the research questions or the hypotheses derived from them.
2. Select any relevant control variables available in the data set and include as additional independent variables.
3. Perform multiple regression with appropriate software.
4. Interpret overall Model F and R^2. The Model F should be statistically significant and the R^2 should be of a size to be practically significant to the researcher. While it is impossible to give a cut-off range for R^2 that applies to all situations, values less than 10 percent are often suspected as practically insignificant. If the model is statistically and practically significant, proceed to step 5.
5. Examine VIFs for potential multicollinearity. If no concerns emerge, proceed.
6. Interpret individual parameter estimates. Consider the statistical significance of each variable, the valence of the relationship (positive or negative), and the relative size of the relationship as best captured with the standardized regression coefficients (β).
7. Examine residual plots. If no patterns emerge, and homoscedasticity is evident, the researcher can confidently interpret the resulting parameter coefficients for explanatory meaning.

EXHIBIT 18.8
The Disadvantage
of Unstandardized
Regression Weights

12.5 cm

Estimated Regression Line: $\hat{Y} = 22 + .07X_1$

0.000078 miles

Estimated Regression Line: $\hat{Y} = 0.00014 + .0000004X_1$

Regression for Prediction

Not all regressions are intended to explain some dependent variable. At times, the researcher's concern is merely prediction. In other words, the question involves forecasting what Y might be more than on why Y comes to take on that value. In these cases, the researcher charges the analysts with generating an accurate prediction of Y for any values of $X_1, X_2, \ldots X_k$ as a priority over the explanatory interpretation of β. The predicted values of Y are represented as $\hat{Y}$, which can be computed from the raw (unstandardized) regression coefficients.

Raw regression weights, or slope coefficients (b_i), have the advantage in prediction because they retain the scale metric—which is also their key disadvantage. If the purpose of the regression analysis is forecasting (i.e., generating predicted values), then raw parameter estimates must be used. This is another way of saying when the researcher's primary interest is in prediction.

Thus, when the researcher wants to predict how much product will be sold based on the amount of shelf space, raw regression coefficients must be used. Consider regression results like those shown in Exhibit 18.8. The simple regression results intend to predict what sales for a consumer product are going to be based on how much shelf-space the product gets on a Target plan-o-gram (a schematic showing how shelves should be laid out in a store). Given those results, a forecast for 14 cm of shelf space can be found as follows:

$$\hat{Y} = 22 + 0.07(14) = 23.0$$

Exhibit 18.8 shows the same result can be found by using the equation representing the distance in miles just to illustrate the nature of b relative to β. If the goal is prediction, the researcher can add other variables. Perhaps shelf-height also affects sales. Lighting, distance from the aisle center, average traffic on the aisle, number of competitor products within the section, and other variables may also be available. Eventually, the analyst may gather data on 25 or more independent variables. At this point, multicollinearity is a distinct possibility. However, multicollinearity does not detract from the predictive power of the model. The $\hat{Y}$ values computed from the model are still accurate. Thus, the model with multicollinearity still retains predictive power. However, multicollinearity, as do other data issues with the independent variables, creates problems with the parameter estimates, their standard errors, and the resulting t-values for parameter statistical significance. Consequently, the problems may render the model useless from an explanatory standpoint but still useful from a prediction standpoint.

Visual Estimation of a Simple Regression Model

As mentioned earlier, simple regression involves finding a best-fit line given a set of observations plotted in a two-dimensional space. Many ways exist to estimate where this line should go. Estimation techniques involve terms such as instrumental variables, maximum likelihood, visual estimation, and ordinary least squares (OLS). We focus on the latter two in this text.

Suppose a researcher is interested in forecasting sales for a construction distributor (wholesaler) in Florida. The distributor believes a reasonable association exists between sales and building permits issued by counties. Using bivariate linear regression on the data in Exhibit 18.9, the researcher will be able to explain sales potential (Y) in various counties based on the number of building permits (X).

The data are plotted in a scatter diagram in Exhibit 18.10. In the diagram the vertical axis indicates the value of the dependent variable, Y, and the horizontal axis indicates the value of the

EXHIBIT 18.9
Relationship of Sales
Potential to Building
Permits Issued

Dealer	Y Dealer's Sales Volume (Thousands)	X Building Permits
1	77	86
2	79	93
3	80	95
4	83	104
5	101	139
6	117	180
7	129	165
8	120	147
9	97	119
10	106	132
11	99	126
12	121	156
13	103	129
14	86	96
15	99	108

Source: © Cengage Learning®

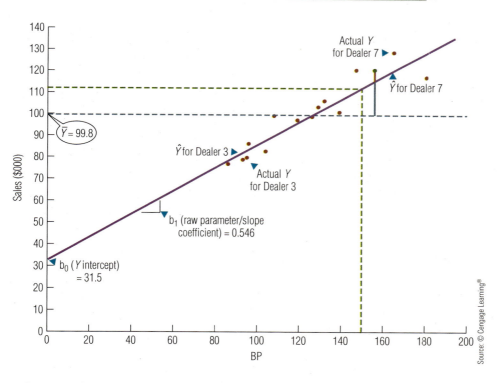

EXHIBIT 18.10
The Best-Fit Line or Knocking
Over the Pins

Source: © Cengage Learning®

independent variable, X. Each single point in the diagram represents an observation of X and Y at a given point in time. The values are simply points in a Cartesian plane.

One way to determine the relationship between X and Y is to simply visually draw the best-fit straight line through the points in the figure. That is, try to draw a line that goes through the center of the plot of points. If the points are thought of as bowling pins, the best-fit line can be thought of as the path that would on average knock over the most bowling pins. For any given value of the independent variable, a prediction can be made by selecting the dependent variable that goes along with that value. For example, if we want to forecast sales if building permits are 150, we simply follow the dotted green lines shown in the exhibit to yield a prediction of about 112. The better one can estimate where the best-fit line should be, the less will be the error in prediction.

Errors in Prediction

Any method of drawing a line can be used to perform regression. However, some methods will obviously have more error than others. Consider our bowling ball line example. One person may be better at guessing where the best-fit line, meaning the one that would knock over the most pins, should go. We would know who was better by determining the total error of prediction.

Let's consider error by first thinking about what value of sales would be the best guess if we had no information about any other variable. In that case, our univariate best guess would be the mean sales of 99.8. If the green spot corresponding to 156 building permits ($X = 156$) were predicted with the mean, the resulting error in prediction would be represented by the distance of the blue-and-red vertical line.

Once information about the independent variable is provided, we can then use the prediction provided by the best-fit line. In this case, our best-fit line is the *bowling ball* line shown in the exhibit. The error in prediction using this line would be indicated by the red vertical line extending from the regression line to the actual observation. Thus, it appears that at least for this observation, our prediction using the regression line has reduced the error in prediction that would result from guessing with the mean. Statistically, this is the goal of regression analysis. We would like an estimation technique that would place our line so that the total sum of all errors over all observations is minimized. In other words, no line fits better. Although with good guess work, visual estimation may prove somewhat accurate.

Time-Series Analysis

Economist and finance researchers focus much more on time-series analyses than do marketing researchers, and entire books can be devoted to this topic alone.[2] Generally, time-series models place an emphasis on prediction over explanation. The goal is to forecast some dependent variable for a future time period. In terms of explanatory power, a problem with time-series analysis is **auto-correlation**. Auto-correlation refers to the fact that observations from different time periods are almost always correlated with each other. Thus, the residuals are unlikely to be independent of each other without corrective measures. One simple corrective measure involves including a variable that accounts for the time period. Thus, the multiple regression formulation becomes

Auto-correlation
The extent to which observations from different time periods are correlated with each other.

$$Y_i = b_0 + b_1 X_1 + b_2 X_2 + b_3 X_3 + \ldots + b_n X_n + b_t t_p + e_i$$

where the addition of t_p represents the time period (from period 1 to period p) and b_t is the regression coefficient corresponding to the time variable.

Ordinary Least-Squares Illustrated

The researcher's task is to find the best means for fitting a straight line to the data. OLS is a relatively straightforward mathematical technique that guarantees that the resulting straight line will produce the least possible total error in using X to predict Y. The logic is based on how much better a regression line can predict values of Y compared to simply using the mean as a prediction (see Exhibit 18.10) for all observations no matter what the value of X may be.

Using Squared Deviations

Unless the dependent and independent variables are perfectly related, no straight line can connect all observations. More technically, the procedure used in the least-squares method generates a straight line that minimizes the sum of squared deviations of the actual values from this predicted regression line. With the symbol e representing the deviations of the observations from the regression line, no other line can produce less error. The deviations are squared so that positive and negative misses do not cancel each other out. The OLS criterion minimizes the total squared error of prediction:

$$\textit{Sum of squared errors} = SSE = \sum_{i=1}^{n} e_i^2$$

where

$e_i = Y_i - \hat{Y}_i$ (the residual = the difference between the actual observed value and the estimated value of the dependent variable for any of i observations)

Y_i = actual observed value of the dependent variable

$\hat{Y}_i$ = estimated or predicted value of the dependent variable (pronounced Y-hat)

n = number of observations

i = number of the particular observation

The general equation for any straight line can be represented as $Y = b_0 + b_1 X$. If we think of this as the true hypothetical line that we try to estimate with sample observations, the regression equation will represent this with a slightly different equation:

$$Y_i = b_0 + b_1 X_1 + e_i$$

The equation means that the predicted value for any value of X (X_i) is determined as a function of the estimated slope coefficient, plus the estimated intercept coefficient, plus some error.

The raw parameter estimates can be found using the following formulas:

$$b_1 = \frac{n(\sum X_i Y_i) - (\sum X_i)(\sum Y_i)}{n(\sum X_i^2) - (\sum X_i)^2}$$

and

$$b_0 = \overline{Y} - b_1 \overline{X}$$

where

Y_i = ith observed value of the dependent variable

X_i = ith observed value of the independent variable

$\overline{Y}$ = mean of the dependent variable

X = independent variable

$\overline{X}$ = mean of the independent variable

n = number of observations

b_0 = intercept estimate

b_1 = slope estimate (regression weight)

The careful reader may notice some similarity between the correlation calculation and the equation for b_1. In fact, the standardized regression coefficient from a simple regression equals the Pearson correlation coefficient for the two variables. Once the estimates are obtained, a predicted value for the dependent variable can be found for any value of X_i with this equation:

$$\hat{Y}_i = b_0 + b_i X_i$$

Statistical Significance of Regression Model

As with ANOVA, the researcher needs a way of testing the statistical significance of the regression model. Also like ANOVA, an F-test provides the answer to this question.

The overall F-test for regression can be illustrated with Exhibit 18.10. Once again examine the multicolored line showing the predicted value for $X = 156$.

1. The total line, including the blue-and-red line, represents the *total deviation* of the observation from the mean:

$$Y_i = \overline{Y}$$

2. The blue portion represents how much of the total deviation is *explained* by the *regression* line:

$$\hat{Y}_i - \overline{Y}$$

3. The red portion represents how much of the total deviation is not explained by the regression line (also equal to e_i):

$$(Y_i - \hat{Y}_i)$$

These three components are mathematically related because the total deviation is a sum of what is explained by the regression line and what is not explained by the regression line. This can be expressed mathematically as

$$(Y_i - \overline{Y}) = (\hat{Y}_i - \overline{Y}) + (Y_i - \hat{Y}_i)$$

	Deviation	Deviation
Total	explained by	unexplained by
deviation =	the regression +	the regression
(SST)	(SSR)	(SSE)

Just as in ANOVA, the total deviation represents the total variation to be explained. Thus, the partitioning of the variation into components allows us to form a ratio of the explained variation versus the unexplained variation. The corresponding abbreviation for this partitioning is

$$SST = SSR + SSE$$

F-test (regression)

A statistical test of the relative magnitude of SSR to SSE. Helps test if the regression model predicts significant amount of variance in Y.

An **F-test (regression)**, or an *analysis of variance,* can be applied to a regression to test the relative magnitudes of the SSR (sums of squares—regression) and SSE (sums of squared errors) with their appropriate degrees of freedom. The equation for the F-test is

$$F_{(k-1)(n-k)} = \frac{SSR/(k-1)}{SSE/(n-k)} = \frac{MSR}{MSE}$$

where

MSR is an abbreviation for mean squared regression

MSE is an abbreviation for mean squared error

k is the number of parameters estimated includes intercept so $k-1=2-1=1$ for simple regression

n is the sample size

Once again, researchers today do not need to and do not calculate this statistic by hand. Regression programs will produce an *ANOVA* table, which will provide the F-value and a p-value (significance level), and will generally show the partitioned variation in some form. For the sales example, the following table is obtained:

ANOVA

	df	SS	MS	F	p-value
Regression (SSR)	1	3398.48911	3398.489	91.29854	0.0000003
Residual (SSE)	13	483.910892	37.22391		
Total	14	3882.4			

Thus, building permits explain a significant portion of the variation in sales as evidenced by the very low p-value.

R^2

The coefficient of determination, R^2, reflects the proportion of variance explained by the regression line. In this example, R^2 can be found with this formula:

$$R^2 = \frac{SSR}{SST} = \frac{3398.5}{3882.4} = 0.875$$

The coefficient of determination may be interpreted to mean that 87.5 percent of the variation in sales is explained by the independent variable building permits.

What is an *acceptable* R^2 value? This question is asked frequently. However, guidelines for R^2 values are neither simple nor straightforward. Indeed, good and bad values for the coefficient of determination depend on so many factors that a single precise guideline is considered inappropriate. The focus should be on the F-test. However, in practice, do not expect to often see a simple regression result with an R^2 anywhere near 0.875. They will normally be considerably lower.

TIPS OF THE TRADE

- Linear statistical techniques are extremely useful in predicting or explaining marketing metrics.
- A covariance matrix summarizes all information about relationships and variability among a set of variables and a correlation matrix summarizes all information about relationships.
- Control variables allow the researcher to build better explanations to the extent that they provide evidence of nonspuriousness between an independent variable of interest and a dependent variable (such as a key marketing metric).
- VIFs provide a signal indicating how much multicollinearity may be a problem. In most typical marketing research,

  - VIFs less than 2 generally rule out multicollinearity as a problem.
  - VIFs greater than 5 indicate a problem with multicollinearity.
  - VIFs between 2 and 5 may suggest a problem, particularly if parameter coefficients show abnormalities or instability.
- The pattern of residuals plotted against the independent variable(s), the dependent variable can help the researcher understand whether a regression model is underspecified.

:: SUMMARY

1. Understand the meaning of covariance and correlation theoretically. Covariance and correlation are very widely used statistical concepts because they summarize the extent to which any two variables are related to each other. Covariance represents relationships in values determined by the actual scale measurements employed to represent them. Correlation represents relationships on a standardized scale ranging from -1.0 to $+1.0$. Positive relationships mean that as one variable goes up, so does the other. Negative relationships mean that as one variable goes up, the other goes down.

2. Compare a covariance and correlation matrix. A covariance matrix arranges all possible covariances into a square table with equal numbers of rows and columns. Each row (column) shows all the covariances for a particular variable. The diagonal element contains the variance for each variable. A correlation matrix is a standardized covariance matrix. Each row (column) contains all the correlations for a particular variable. The diagonal element includes a 1 in each position.

3. Separate causal relationships from other types of relationships to build explanations. Causal findings are very powerful because they allow explanation to take place. A spurious relationship cannot be causal. Thus, the analyst needs to examine the potential that a significant relationship observed through correlation or regression is spurious. Control variables help in determining whether a relationship is spurious. In addition, a model that exhibits a random pattern of residuals is likely free of underspecification. As such, the relationships observed in the model, presuming it is free of multicollinearity, are likely to be nonspurious.

4. Using multiple regression for prediction. An analyst who is focusing on prediction more than explanation need not be as concerned about factors like multicollinearity that interfere with the interpretation of individual regression coefficients and their statistical tests. Instead, the analyst should be concerned that the predicted values of the dependent variable $(\hat{Y})$ are as accurate as possible. As such, the emphasis switches away from interpreting causality or the statistical significance of parameter coefficients to the model's R^2. Data mining routines emphasize prediction and often add variables based solely on their ability to improve predictive power.

5. Appreciate the arithmetic of OLS. OLS estimation mathematically determines the best-fitting regression line for the observed data. The idea of OLS is to find a line that minimizes the squared distance between the regression line comprising all estimated values of Y $(\hat{Y})$ and the actual observed values (Y_i). The line determined by this method may be used to forecast values of the dependent variable, given any value for the independent variable. The regression analysis also involves an ANOVA (analysis of variance) table that contains values used in calculating the coefficient of determination (R^2).

:: QUESTIONS FOR REVIEW AND CRITICAL THINKING

1. Explain the concept of marketing metrics and how measures of association are relevant to the concept.
2. List and define at least three measures of association from this chapter.
3. How is it that covariance can be said to be the average cross-product?
4. Using the information shown in Exhibit 18.1, create a spreadsheet to compute the covariance between *sales* and *NPS*.
5. Using the information shown in Exhibit 18.1, compute the correlation between sales and NPS. Is the correlation statistically significant? Use a statistical package of some type to obtain results of the *t*-test for the significance of the correlation.
6. If variable *Y* and variable *Z* are correlated -0.707, what is the interpretation?
7. What is a scatter plot? Presuming quadrants are formed by creating axes using the means of *X* and *Y*, what quadrants would most points fall into if the two variables show a moderately strong positive correlation?
8. Explain why a covariance matrix can be said to contain more information than a correlation matrix.
9. What role do control variables play in a multiple regression model?
10. Define white noise in a statistical sense.
11. How do the steps in interpreting multiple regression differ if the analyst is charged with building a predictive rather than explanatory model?
12. In terms of the sums of squares (SS), what is the equation for a regression model's *F*-statistic.
13. The following table gives a football team's season-ticket sales, percentage of games won, and number of active alumni for the years 2001–2015.

Year	Season-Ticket Sales	Percentage of Games Won	Number of Active Alumni
2001	4,995	40	NA
2002	8,599	54	3,450
2003	8,479	55	3,801
2004	8,419	58	4,000

Year	Season-Ticket Sales	Percentage of Games Won	Number of Active Alumni
2005	10,253	63	4,098
2006	12,457	75	6,315
2007	13,285	36	6,860
2008	14,177	27	8,423
2009	15,730	63	9,000
2010	15,805	70	9,500
2011	15,501	50	9,502
2012	14,450	67	9,520
2013	13,750	80	10,100
2014	14,750	35	9,890
2015	12,500	70	11,150

   a. Produce a correlation matrix for the variables. Interpret the correlation between each pair of variables. Use some software to help produce the correlation matrix.
   b. Estimate a regression model for sales = Percentage of games won. Interpret the results.
   c. Estimate a regression model for sales = Number of active alumni. Interpret the results.
   d. Conduct a multiple regression to explain ticket sales as a key marketing metric. Interpret the results.
   e. Conduct a multiple regression model to predict ticket sales in 2016 presuming that a simple 3-year moving average is used to forecast winning percentage and number of alumni.
14. In question 13, what role does time play in influencing the interpretation of the model results?
15. Interpret the correlations among the different forms of consumer expenditures shown in the following table? The last column shows household income.

Year	Travel and Gas Expense	Data Services	Visa MC Charges	Car Insurance Expenses	Housing	Total Taxes	HH Income
1	$ 939	$ 61	$ 828	$ 9,400	$ 11,228	$ 14,764	$ 79,428
2	1,119	76	1,312	10,200	12,707	17,211	87,745
3	1,298	110	2,639	10,900	14,947	22,658	98,105
4	1,650	122	3,792	11,500	17,064	28,210	102,064
5	1,804	132	4,490	13,925	20,351	44,219	111,295
6	1,762	164	5,408	14,763	22,097	48,750	127,332
7	1,832	191	6,838	16,395	25,256	59,999	147,437
8	1,823	238	8,281	17,933	28,275	62,888	156,124
9	1,893	273	9,501	18,002	29,669	70,279	164,955
10	1,981	238	11,351	19,052	32,622	75,121	185,489
11	2,074	284	14,262	21,082	37,702	85,200	216,572

:: RESEARCH ACTIVITY

1. Take a look at the data below. *X1* represents an Internet survey respondent's rating of how satisfied they are with their Snapchat app and *Y1* represents the respondent's rating of how likely they would be to recommend the app to a friend.

Obs	Y1	X1
1	5	3
2	7	6
3	2	4
4	5	5
5	3	4
6	2	1
7	6	5
8	1	1
9	5	4
10	6	5
11	7	7
12	3	3

a. Draw a scatter plot of the variables.
b. Using visual estimation, draw the line that appears to best fit the data.
c. What can you say about the relationship between satisfaction with the Snapchat app and the likelihood of recommending?
d. Use a protractor to measure the angle between the *x*-axis and the line you drew. What is it?
e. Find the cosine of the angle.
f. Now, enter the data into the software of your choice and conduct a simple regression predicting likelihood of recommending Snapchat. Interpret the results.
g. Also, using the software, compute the covariance and correlation between the two variables.
h. Compare the values of the correlation, the standardized regression coefficient, the covariance, and the unstandardized regression coefficient.
i. How close is the cosine of the angle to the correlation?
j. If the cosine is close to the correlation and standardized regression coefficient (which should be the same), then you visually estimated the simple regression with accuracy because the cosine of an angle is another way of expressing correlation. Comment on your accuracy.

2. This activity is a project that can be carried out in a team of two students. It provides an exercise in searching for data and building a model using the U.S. Census data (census.gov). Check for the latest data showing the annual number of *New Housing Starts* or *New Residential Construction* (these names reflect the same information). Now, search for data related to retail sales. In particular, try to find data on durable goods sales like furniture and home furnishing retailer sales. Also, find data on motor vehicle sales and grocery store sales. Build a data set that includes all of these variables being careful to match them time-wise (annually, for example, by year). Much of the data can be downloaded into a spreadsheet file or as plain text. Think about these variables. Presuming you are in the retail furniture business, build a regression model that explains the relationship between new residential construction and sales in your industry. How good is the model you developed for explanatory purposes? How good is it for predictive purposes? Prepare a report that summarizes all your findings.

International Operations at CarCare Inc

Case 18.1

CarCare is considering expanding its operations beyond the United States. The company wants to know whether it should target countries with consumers who tend to have a positive attitude toward their current cars. It has gathered data on U.S. and German car owners. The data are included in the "car" data set that can be viewed on the Web site at www.cengagebrain.com (car.sav or car.xls) or available from your instructor. Using the data, conduct a correlation and simple regression analysis using spending as the dependent variable and attitude toward the current car as the independent variable.

1. Test the hypothesis: Attitude toward one's car is related positively to spending for car-care products.
2. Would you recommend they do more research to identify nations with relatively favorable attitudes toward the cars they own?

[Note: This data set was referred to for the first time in Chapter 15.]

:: KEY TERMS AND CONCEPTS

adjusted R^2, *498*
auto-correlation, *504*
coefficient of determination, *494*
control variables, *497*
correlation coefficient, *491*
correlation matrix, *497*
covariance, *490*

covariance matrix, *495*
F-test (regression), *506*
heteroscedasticity, *501*
homoscedasticity, *501*
marketing metrics, *490*
measures of association, *490*
multicollinearity, *498*

negative (inverse) relationship, *494*
residual, *499*
scatter plot, *492*
standardized variables, *492*
underspecification, *499*
variance inflation factor, *499*
white noise, *499*

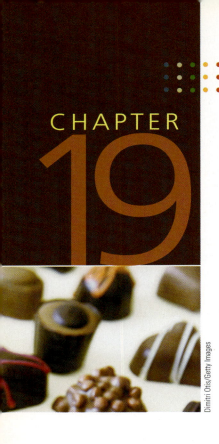

Dimitri Otis/Getty Images

CHAPTER 19

Testing Hypotheses with GLM Procedures

LEARNING OUTCOMES

After studying this chapter, you should be able to:

1. Test hypotheses with regression analysis
2. Understand the basics of interpreting hypotheses of mediation
3. Know that moderation accounts for context effects
4. Conduct and interpret hierarchical linear regression

Introduction

The General Linear Model (GLM) takes on any one of several forms depending on the nature of the data and the type of hypotheses involved in a market research project. In earlier chapters, we introduced several variations of the GLM. In this chapter, we focus on how specific hypotheses involving the GLM are tested and interpreted. In particular, the chapter focuses on interpreting output with respect to specific hypotheses proposing common types of relationships, including tests of mediation and moderation. Both mediation and moderation are commonly offered as theoretical processes by which predictor variables shape outcomes. As a consequence, any marketing analysts should develop a working knowledge of both concepts.

Testing Hypotheses with Regression Analysis

Chapter 3 defined theory and hypothesis. The two terms are not interchangeable. A theory represents a much more comprehensive explanation than does a hypothesis. A hypothesis represents a specific prediction about two variables. Sometimes, the hypothesis may involve more than two variables and propose that, in some way, the dependent variable is a function of two other variables. A theory, however, represents an integration of multiple generalizations and proposes an explanatory process that allows not only prediction but also explanation of the way one set of variables brings about other outcomes. Linear models play a key role in testing hypotheses and, as we will see later, in testing theory as well. Here we focus on the way we use GLM, in the form of multiple regression, to test specific types of hypotheses.

Peruse the Survey This! data looking for an opportunity to run multiple regression. For instance, what if a researcher is interested in factors related to students' attitude toward studying?

Form a summated scale using at least four of the items above. Then, use at least three other variables to run multiple regression. Experiment with a test of moderation using at least one other variable. What do your results say about how students come to have a positive or negative attitude toward studying?

Studying for me is:

Important						Not Important
Not Essential						Essential
Boring						Exciting
Enjoyable						A chore
A burden						Fun
Acceptable						Unacceptable
Exhausting						Invigorating
Intense						Relaxing

Source: www.qualtrics.com

Stating Hypotheses Effectively

As described in Chapter 3, researchers derive hypotheses from research questions, and often, some theory provides a rationale for these research questions. Although the basic idea of a hypothesis may seem simple, writing a hypothesis in good form proves difficult. The hypotheses in the study represent informed guesses about how some outcome reacts to certain inputs. Thus, very often, hypotheses imply causality. A researcher must develop a hypothesis with explanatory logic that separates theoretically meaningful findings from mere accidental generalizations.[1] The following points illustrate considerations that influence how well a hypothesis(es) is written. Good hypotheses:

1. Are shorter, not longer

   a. State any hypothesis in as few words as possible. More words lead to greater likelihood of ambiguity.

2. Are specific, not general

   a. State things in terms of the actual phenomena measured. For instance, if a study measures intentions but not actual behavior, the hypotheses should be stated in terms of behavioral intentions and not actual behavior.

   b. State the specific direction of a proposed relationship.

      i. Is the relationship between X and Y positive or negative? If positive, the greater (lower) the value of X, the greater (lower) the value of Y.

         1. Positive relationships mean as X goes up, so does Y.
         2. Negative relationships mean as X goes up, Y goes down.
         3. Avoid stating equilibrium hypothesis suggesting that X will be equal to Y.

      ii. Greater or less than

         When predictor variables are less than interval, hypotheses often are stated in terms of one value being greater than or less than average.

3. Are meaningful, not trivial

   a. Hypotheses should propose relationships that are of key interest to the decision statement at hand.

4. Are questionable, not certain

   a. Present relationships that are not presumed true based on inspection or presumed true based on a plurality of input from previous studies examining the variables. For example, in a study of coffee consumption, a hypothesis such as the following can be presumed true based on a plethora of previous research:

   Attitudes toward drinking coffee are related positively to intentions to drink coffee.

5. State something, not nothing

   a. A hypothesis should propose that something exists, like a relationship:

   Respondents' price sensitivity relates positively to their satisfaction with discount stores.

   b. As opposed to stating that something does not exist, as in:

   Respondents' price sensitivity does not influence their satisfaction with discount stores.

   Tautology

   Circular reasoning; stating that one variable results from something that is exactly or practically the very same variable.

   c. Do not state a **tautology** (a circular explanation), such as:

   The more a subject likes a brand, the more favorable his/her attitude toward that brand will be.

      i. In this case, the distinction between liking and attitude is not very meaningful. Liking is a virtual synonym for a positive attitude. Thus, the statistic is virtually equivalent to saying that as a subject likes a brand, he/she will like the brand. Not very satisfying as an explanation!

6. Should invite a comparison with data

   a. A hypothesis should imply the way the test should take place. In terms of hypotheses tested by regression results, the hypotheses should be stated in terms of relationships:

   Respondents' price sensitivity relates positively to their satisfaction with discount stores.

   b. This hypothesis clearly indicates what needs to be measured: price sensitivity and satisfaction with discount stores.

   c. The hypothesis states the nature of the relationship. In this case, the hypothesis test outcome would be determined by the regression coefficient relating these two variables. A positive regression coefficient would support the hypothesis. An insignificant relationship or a relationship that is negative would fail to support the hypothesis.

Exhibit 19.1 summarizes the characteristics of a hypothesis well-stated.

EXHIBIT 19.1
Characteristics of a
Hypothesis Well Stated

1. Are shorter not longer
2. Are specific not general
   a. State things in terms of the actual phenomena measured
   b. Gives the direction of the finding
3. Are meaningful not trivial
4. Are questionable not certain
5. State something not nothing
6. Invite a comparison with data

Courtesy of JMP

Testing Basic Hypotheses with Multiple Regression

In the remainder of the chapter, we use a data set that includes variables related to a sample of golfers and their satisfaction with their golf game. In this research, each golfer played 25 rounds of golf using the same brand of driver and the same golf ball. A GPS app allowed the respondent to easily record the distance of each drive hit during the course of the 25 rounds. The variables involved in the data set include the following:

- *Club brand.* A nominal variable coded as brand A, B, or C.
- *Brand of golf ball.* A nominal variable coded as brand A, B, or C.
- *Distance.* The average distance of a drive during the 25 rounds.
- *Price paid.* The price of the golf balls used in the rounds of golf (each participant received the balls for free but was told what the price of the ball is in retail shops).
- *Durability.* The average number of shots before a ball was worn out.
- *Handicap.* The golfer's average handicap during the time of the test. A handicap represents the potential skill of a golfer. The higher the handicap, the lower the potential skill of the golfer.
- *Satisfaction.* The golfers' satisfaction ratings indicating how satisfied they are with their golfing experience scored on a 7-point scale ranging from 1 (felt no satisfaction at all) to 7 (felt completely satisfied).

We begin by examining some direct hypotheses. A great deal of golf promotion emphasizes enhancing a golfer's ability to hit the ball a long way. Thus, given all the marketing effort addressed at the topic, golf equipment companies must believe that customer satisfaction is determined by the distance a customer can drive a golf ball. In addition, a host of evidence in consumer behavior supports a price–quality relationship. In other domains, such as energy drinks, experimental subjects receiving a more expensive stimulant actually perform better than those who receive the same stimulant but are told it cost lest. Furthermore, because they are not paying for the golf balls, they are likely to be happier about getting expensive balls. Thus, the researcher works with the following two hypotheses:

> H1: The distance that respondents hit the golf ball is related positively to their satisfaction with the golf experience.
>
> H2: The price of the golf balls is related positively to respondents' satisfaction with the golf experience.

We now turn to testing these hypotheses using multiple regression.

Testing Direct Effect Hypotheses

The most basic type of hypothesis in descriptive or causal research designs is the direct effect. If the independent variable is an experimental variable, the term *main effect* would apply as well. In descriptive research, such as in typical survey research, the direct effect is often between two interval or better variables. A **direct effect** assesses the relationship between an independent variable and a dependent variable where the hypothesis suggests a relationship that depends on no other variable.

In a regression context, the analyst assesses a direct effect through a straightforward examination of the parameter coefficient between the independent and the dependent variable. A direct effect may be tested along with the presence of control variables. The control variables

Direct effect

The relationship between an independent variable and a dependent variable where the hypothesis suggests a relationship that depends on no other variable.

make the test of direct effects more conservative as the relationship between the independent and dependent variables is maximized when no other variables relate to the independent variable and dependent variable. To the extent that the independent variable and control variables relate to one another, the regression coefficient observed without the presence of control variables (covariates) will be greater than the parameter coefficient observed in the presence of control variables.[2]

In the golfer data, a direct effect hypothesis offered by the researcher is:

> H1: The average distance of respondents' drives relates positively to satisfaction with the golf experience.

The researcher develops this hypothesis through a logical foundation and marketing theory that suggests that as people experience signs of improvement they will be more satisfied with the experience. The researcher briefs the analyst suggesting control for golf skill is in order. Thus, the analyst includes handicap as a control variable in the regression (in reality, other variables would likely be used as control, but for purposes of illustration here, we include only handicap as a control). Exhibit 19.2 provides the parameter estimates resulting from the regression analysis.

The overall model F statistic is 15.2 with 2 and 60 degrees of freedom. The corresponding p-value is less than 0.0001. At an acceptable type I error rate of 0.05, this model predicts a significant portion of the variance in golfer satisfaction. The overall model R^2 is 0.336 and the adjusted R^2 is 0.314. Thus, the overall model is significant suggesting that the analyst can move on to interpret the regression coefficients. As seen in Exhibit 19.2, the effect of the independent variable, distance, is significant ($t = 4.66$, with a p-value <0.0001) with a raw parameter (slope) coefficient of $b = 0.05$ and a standardized regression coefficient, β, of 0.54. Every yard increase in average driving distance increases satisfaction by 0.05 points. The control variable, handicap, yields a b of -0.03 and a β of -0.09, which is not significant ($t = 0.41$, $p > 0.05$). Thus, the results *support* a positive relationship between the distance of drives and satisfaction with the golf experience. The word *support* is appropriate. We do not prove the result with inferential statistics. Results either support or do not support a prediction. In this case, the results support H1.

EXHIBIT 19.2

Regression Results for Direct Effect of Distance

Independent Variable	b	β	t-value	p-value
Distance	0.05	0.54	4.66	0.0001
Handicap	−0.03	−0.09	0.41	0.4133

Source: © 2016 Cengage Learning®

How to Run Regression in SAS, JMP, EXCEL, and SPSS

Although many software programs are now point and click, some analysts still use programs like SAS that require some elementary coding. Running a regression model like the one discussed in this chapter is simple in SAS. The lines below could be entered into the SAS data window:

Data Golfer;

    Input Club $ Brand $ Distance Durable Price Handicap Satis;
    Cards;

A	B	188	200	18	18	1
A	B	205.8	218	40	10	3
A	A	245	227	52	28	1
A	A	245.1	235	52	20	1
A	A	248	279	45	15	3
A	A	248	238	45	17	3
A	A	251.1	306	60	7	5
A	A	251.1	268	60	10	5
A	A	251.2	288	50	9	3
A	A	251.2	310	50	14	3
A	B	256.4	220	45	12	3
A	B	262.9	219	45	10	3
A	B	263.2	261	40	10	3
A	C	263.2	289	33	12	5
A	C	264.7	279	33	14	5
A	B	265	267	40	9	4
A	B	265	263	40	10	4
A	C	268.8	245	30	14	5
A	C	269.7	233	30	9	5
A	C	277.5	301	28	2	7
A	C	282.5	288	28	0	7
B	B	210	288	44	9	4
B	B	237.2	197	38	17	5
B	A	240.2	257	57	15	4
B	A	244.4	284	43	21	6
B	A	250	284	44	22	6
B	A	253.9	259	55	16	4
B	B	254.5	245	40	16	4
B	B	254.5	247	40	18	4
B	B	257	197	34	18	5
B	B	262.8	207	45	12	4
B	B	264	199	50	11	4
B	B	264.3	288	44	9	4
B	A	265.5	237	48	14	6
B	C	265.5	222	24	14	7
B	C	265.5	208	24	15	7
B	C	267.4	264	38	10	5
B	C	267.4	243	38	11	5
B	C	270.5	273	24	3	5
B	A	270.9	269	48	13	6
B	C	275.2	247	21	7	5
B	A	290	278	49	11	7
C	A	244.4	264	41	12	1
C	A	244.4	220	45	18	2
C	A	244.6	273	40	13	1
C	B	245.1	217	39	11	3
C	B	245.5	217	27	14	4
C	C	245.6	240	34	14	4
C	A	248.8	301	45	25	5
C	A	250.1	290	44	20	5
C	A	254.6	219	48	16	2
C	B	255.9	228	44	12	3
C	C	257	270	38	16	5
C	B	260.6	244	36	9	4
C	B	264.4	221	30	15	4
C	B	266.6	240	35	17	4
C	C	270.7	245	30	7	5
C	C	272.1	248	30	4	5
C	C	272.9	271	20	11	5
C	C	275.6	298	39	8	6
C	C	276	278	36	15	5
C	C	280.1	288	40	9	6
C	C	300	274	22	10	5;

run;

proc, reg;
model satis = Distance Handicap /stb;

run;
This would produce the following output:

RESEARCH SNAPSHOT

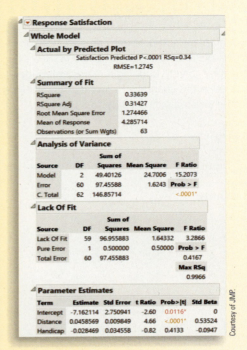

chapter 19

The REG Procedure
Model: MODEL1
Dependent Variable: Satis

Number of Observations Read	63
Number of Observations Used	63

Analysis of Variance					
Source	DF	Sum of Squares	Mean Square	F Value	Pr > F
Model	2	49.40126	24.70063	15.21	<.0001
Error	60	97.45588	1.62426		
Corrected Total	62	146.85714			

Root MSE	1.27447	R-Square	0.3364
Dependent Mean	4.28571	Adj R-Sq	0.3143
Coeff Var	29.73755		

Parameter Estimates						
Variable	DF	Parameter Estimate	Standard Error	t Value	Pr > |t|	Standardized Estimate
Intercept	1	-7.16211	2.75094	-2.60	0.0116	0
Distance	1	0.04586	0.00985	4.66	<.0001	0.53524
Handicap	1	-0.02847	0.03456	-0.82	0.4133	-0.09470

In JMP, the analyst would open the data file or click on JMP from within Excel, choose *Fit Model*, enter Satisfaction as the Y variable, Distance and Handicap as the *Construct Model Effects*, and then click *Run* with all the defaults used.

In Excel, if JMP is not installed, one could click on *data* and then choose the *data analysis* plug-in from the tool bar. Enter the column storing Satisfaction as the *Input Y Range*, remembering to tick off *Labels* when highlighting the first row, which contains the variable names. Then, after making sure that distance and handicap are in columns right next to each other, highlight and enter that range as the *Input X Range*. Then, click OK and the results will appear in a new sheet. Note that the results do not include standardized coefficients.

In SPSS, click *Analyze*, and then choose *Regression* and select Linear from that list of options. Then, enter Satisfaction as the dependent variable and Distance and Handicap as independent(s), as shown:

No matter which software is used, you will get the same results!

The Basics of Testing Mediation

Sometimes, the researcher may speculate that some process exists by which one variable works through another to help bring about the effect captured by a dependent variable. A **mediator variable** fits between an independent variable and a dependent variable and serves to facilitate a relationship between an independent variable and a dependent variable. In other words, a mediator goes between X and Y. Physically, we can think about the kitchen faucet. Water is always in the pipe that runs through the wall to the faucet. But water will flow into the sink only when the facet handle is turned to open. The more the handle is turned, the more the water flows. Likewise, marketing researchers often think of price effects as involving mediation in some way. For instance, price promotions can increase sales. However, price promotions may increase sales only when the promotion creates a perception of increased value.[3] Thus, perceived value mediates the effects of price promotions on sales.

In addition, the presence of a mediator is associated with indirect effects. An **indirect effect** is a relationship consisting of two parts. The first part is the relationship between an independent variable and a mediator variable. The second part is the relationship between the mediator and the ultimate dependent variable. Price promotions affect purchase behavior indirectly through their impact on value perceptions. If price promotions affect value perceptions only a little, then the indirect effect through value perceptions will be small.

Mediator variable

Fits between an independent variable and a dependent variable and serves to facilitate a relationship between an independent variable and a dependent variable.

Indirect effect

A relationship consisting of two parts. The first part is the relationship between an independent variable and a mediator variable.

EXHIBIT 19.3
Breaking Down Mediation

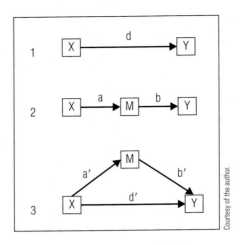

Courtesy of the author.

Conditions of Mediation

Exhibit 19.3 depicts a way to go about examining mediation. The exhibit helps make these points:

1. The first stage depicts the notion that X is related to (causes) Y. However, it says nothing about how that relationship may come to be. As a necessary condition for mediation, d, the relationship between X and Y, must be practically and statistically significant. The relationship can be established using simple regression or with a correlation coefficient.
2. The second frame depicts the notion that the relationship between X and Y is indirect and works through an intervening, or mediating, variable, M. As a necessary condition for mediation, a, the relationship between X and M, must be practically and statistically significant. As above, a nontrivial, significant parameter coefficient from a simple regression or correlation provides a test of this effect. Similarly, b, the effect of M on Y must be practically and statistically significant and can be examined in the same way. The indirect effect of X on Y can be found by multiplying a and b:

    a. $IE_{xy} = a \times b$

3. The third stage depicts the comparative effects of direct and indirect effects of X on Y. If M mediates the relationship of X on Y, then the effect must work entirely or largely through M. A multiple regression model with Y as the dependent variable and M and X as independent variables (and possibly some control variables) provides the needed evidence. Presuming evidence of a relationship between X and Y is established by estimating d in step 1, and that an indirect effect exists as described in step 2, and d' is estimated in this step, the comparison of d and d' provides crucial evidence.

    a. If $|d'| \geq |d|$, no evidence of mediation exists.
    b. If $|d'| < |d|$, but d' remains statistically significant, **partial mediation** exists.
    c. If $|d'|$ is not significantly different than 0, **complete mediation** exists.

Partial mediation

Condition created when the direct relationship between X and Y remains significant but is reduced in the presence of a mediator.

Complete mediation

Condition created when the direct relationship between X and Y is insignificant in the presence of a mediator; the relationship of X on Y is entirely indirect.

Mediation Illustrated

Using the golfer satisfaction example, we illustrate a test for mediation. Here, the researcher hypothesizes that price (X) affects satisfaction (Y) but that the relationship works through distance (M) as a mediator. Following the standard protocol discussed earlier in text using a type I error rate of 0.10 because of a relatively small sample:

1. A simple regression predicting satisfaction with golf ball price suggests that price does significantly relate negatively to satisfaction:

    a. $\beta_x = -0.27, t = -2.24, p < 0.10$

2. Separate simple regression models provide evidence suggesting that price paid affects distance and that distance affects satisfaction.

    a. $\beta_{XM} = -0.22, t = -1.8, p < 0.10$

    b. $\beta_{MY} = 0.57, t = 5.47, p < 0.10$

3. A multiple regression produces results suggesting that the direct effect of X on Y shown in part 1 becomes insignificant (not different than 0) when distance (M) is included as an additional predictor.

    a. $\beta_{XY} = -0.16, t = -1.47, p > 0.10$ (ns − not significant)

    b. $\beta_{MY} = 0.54, t = 5.06, p < 0.10$

    c. $IE_{xy} = \beta_{XM} \times \beta_{MY} = -0.22 \times 0.54 = -0.12$

In this example, we could conclude that distance fully mediates the effect of price on golf experience satisfaction. The direct effect of price on satisfaction shown in step 1a becomes insignificant in step 3a. A t-test for the significance of the indirect effect can be computed by combining the standard errors of prediction of the different equations. In this case, the indirect effect is significant.

Details of Mediation

In recent years, academic researchers have raised issues about potential biases that can occur in calculating the statistical significance of mediation effects. While a complete discussion is beyond the scope of this book, the issue has to do with model specification.[4] One assumption of the parametric tests of linear regression techniques is that the independent variables are independent of each other and that residual terms are independent (of the predicted values, independent variables, and each other). However, to the extent that any unaccounted-for variable exists that relates to both M and Y, the residuals for a regression predicting M with X, and Y with M and X, will not be independent. Consequently, the t-tests and parameter coefficients are biased to the extent that such variables exist.

   The analyst faces several questions when considering how to deal with the potential bias.

1. Can the bias be ignored?

    a. When the analyst is interested only in an assessment of the potential mediation of the relationship between X and Y, he or she may choose to ignore the bias. Such an approach is inconsistent with the conservative nature of theoretical statistical approaches.

    b. The analyst can ignore the bias if an examination of the residuals for predicted values of Y in the step 3 multiple regression suggests no obvious patterns (white noise) or if an additional analysis of the residuals for M (from step 2) and Y (from step 3) suggests no residual correlation. Realize that control variables used in the tests of mediation also can be helpful in trying to rule out potential alternative causes of M and Y. Thus, control variables should be considered as a routine part of hypothesis testing using regression techniques.

2. What are the implications of the potential bias for the regression results?

    a. Like with multicollinearity and heteroscedasticity, the t-tests of the parameter coefficients become unreliable as the bias becomes substantial. Consequently, the researcher may not be able to rely on traditional parametric tests within regression analysis to examine the statistical significance of the mediated effects.

3. Are alternative approaches available to assess the statistical significance of a mediated effect?

    a. One alternative for dealing with the potential for correlated residuals involves more complicated linear modeling approaches. In the final chapter of this book, we cover a full information approach that can correct for the potential residual correlation.

Bootstrapping

Involves taking the available data and using sampling with replacement to generate many samples (typically 500, 1,000, or 2,000) and using average values of parameters in those samples to draw inferences.

b. Another work-around for the bias problem with mediation involves obtaining a test of the indirect effect via statistical bootstrapping. **Bootstrapping** involves taking the available data and using sampling with replacement, generating many, many samples (typically 500, 1,000, or 2,000) and estimating the parameters in each of those samples. Then, rather than examining any of the individual *t*-tests in those regressions, the analyst relies on a test of whether or not the mean of all of the regression estimates for the indirect effect that forms mediation is significantly different than 0. Fortunately, several statistical macros exist to perform this analysis and the researcher need not do this manually. We illustrate their use in the section that follows.

Using a Mediation Macro

Researchers' desire to offer explanations rather than only predictions creates concern over the mechanism of observed covariation. Mediation, being one of the commonly proposed explanations for causal effects, provides a focus for much discussion among researchers.[5] The availability of aids to assist in estimating mediation is one consequence of all this discussion. For instance, the website http://www.afhayes.com/ provides a host of macros for download. One versatile macro known as PROCESS is available as an add-in for both SPSS and SAS. PROCESS can be used for various types of mediation and moderation tests.[6]

We take a break from the golfer satisfaction data to illustrate mediation test using this macro. Exhibit 19.4 illustrates a basic application of PROCESS (for use in SPSS) using a data set that involves consumer perceptions of a service environment. The example involves data collected by a high-end retail firm concerned about the impact of service on consumers. For simplicity of illustration, only three variables are involved in the analysis:

■ X = DumL: A dummy variable capturing the appearance of service personnel as either matching the appearance in a new age advertising campaign (coded 1) or matching the traditional appearance of the retailer (coded 0). The appearance is manipulated in the store as part of a field experiment.

■ M = CongA: A 7-point scale indicating the extent to which a subject believes the service employee who served them fits the brand image (1 = does not fit to 7 = fits very well). Notice in the exhibit that the *Model Number* is set to *4*. PROCESS can perform many other tests, but 4 is the model representing basic mediation.[7]

■ Y = Careabout: A 7-point scale indicating how much a subject believes the service employee cares about each customer as a person (1 = does not care to 7 = cares very much).

EXHIBIT 19.4
Using the PROCESS Macro

Courtesy of SPSS statistics 17.0.

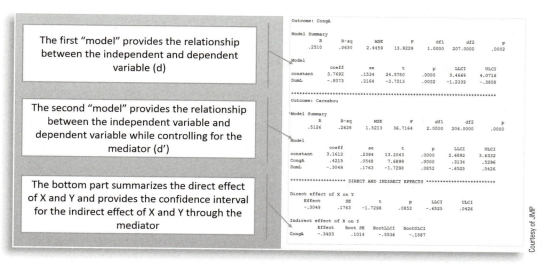

The first "model" provides the relationship between the independent and dependent variable (d)

The second "model" provides the relationship between the independent variable and dependent variable while controlling for the mediator (d')

The bottom part summarizes the direct effect of X and Y and provides the confidence interval for the indirect effect of X and Y through the mediator

EXHIBIT 19.5
Mediation Analysis Macro Output

Exhibit 19.5 shows the results obtained. A simple regression predicting Careabout (Y) with CongA (X) suggests a significant relationship (d). The parameter estimate is -0.65 with a t-value of -3.34 ($p < 0.001$). The first frame of the results suggests that the independent variable of DumL (X) significantly relates to CongA (M) with a parameter coefficient of -0.81 and a t-value of -3.73 ($p < 0.001$).

Next, the results show a multiple regression predicting Y with both X and M. Here, the results suggest that CongA (M) significantly affects Careabout (Y). The resulting parameter estimate is 0.42 ($t = 7.69, p < 0.001$), suggesting that as subjects view the employee as fitting the brand image, they report a higher degree of caring. In addition, the results show that the effect of DumL (X) become insignificant when controlling for M (d') ($b = -0.31, t = -1.73, p > 0.05$). Finally, the results show the bootstrap results for testing the effect of the indirect effect ($a' \times b'$). The confidence interval of the estimate (-0.34) ranges from -0.55 to -0.15. The fact that 0 is not included in the confidence interval supports the statistical significance of the mediator. In this case, the results support complete mediation of the relationship between DumL and Careabout by CongA.

Mediation Terminology

Mediation results can be described in a number of ways. Presuming that the simple direct effect (d) and the indirect effect of X on Y are statistically significant, complete (sometimes called full) mediation results when the effect of X on Y become insignificant in the presence of M. For instance, in the example results shown in Exhibit 19.5, the fact that d' becomes insignificant in the presence of M makes the case for complete mediation. Partial mediation results when the effect of X on Y when controlling for M remains significant but is reduced in size compared to the simple relationship. In other words, d' remains significant but is less than d.

Moderation Means Context Effects

Sometimes, researchers propose research questions that involve combinations or variables affecting some marketing outcome. The combination effects were described earlier (see Chapter 15) as interactions. In a regression context, an interaction effect can be shown as follows:

$$\hat{Y} = b_0 + b_1X_1 + b_2X_2 + b_3X_1X_2$$

where b_3 represents the effect of the interaction of X_1 and X_2 on the dependent variable.

An interaction plays a big role in examining statistical **moderation**, which represents the fact that some third variable affects the relationship between an independent and a dependent variable. Very often, the moderator accounts for some context. For example, researchers provide evidence that the difference in price between a national brand and a store brand affects sales of the store brand.[8] As the store brand is priced less, it gains more market share. However, the effect is not the same across all situations.

Moderation
The process by which some third variable affects the relationship between an independent and a dependent variable.

If the stores are in Europe, relative to the United States, the effect of the price difference is smaller. In this instance, the region (Europe versus the United States) moderates the effect of price differential on sales.

In an experiment, both the independent variable and the moderator variable often are categorical (nominal or ordinal). When this is the case, GLM procedures can assess the interaction by testing a full-factorial design, and a plot of the means by experimental conditions will reveal the nature of an interaction. In addition, if the interaction is between two experimental variables randomly assigned across all experimental subjects, the interaction term ends up being independent of the two experimental variables. Thus, it presents no problems with multicollinearity and the analyst can follow standard procedures. If the interaction term in an ANOVA turns out to be significant, evidence of moderation exists and the effect size can be interpreted directly.

In survey research, though, both the independent variable and the moderator variable are generally at least interval. As such, the regression model includes the moderation effect as a continuous variable interaction between an independent variable and a moderator. In the model (as shown earlier in text), the moderator variable is created by multiplying the two independent variables by each other (moderator $= X_1 \times X_2$). Unlike in an experiment, the interaction term ends up being related to both independent variables because it is a mathematical function of them (i.e., the product of the independent variables). Thus, the analyst must take some additional steps to assess the extent to which moderation exists, if at all.

In either ANOVA or regression, moderators often account for context in some way. For instance, a relationship may vary based on culture. Consider how a price discount may be received across two cultures, one in which consumers do not expect to bargain for routine purchases and the other where bargaining is part of practically anything a consumer buys. The relationship between an advertised price discount and the likelihood of purchase may well be stronger in a country where consumers do not expect to bargain. In other countries, a discount is always expected whether advertised or not. Thus, the relationship between price promotion and intentions to purchase would be greater in those countries where bargaining is not routine.

In this way, culture represents a **context variable**, or one that captures factors unique to time, space, conditions, or person traits that may affect some hypothesized relationship. Time pressure, time of day, region, and demographic variables provide common context variables.

Context variable

Accounts for factors unique to time or space that may affect some hypothesized relationship.

Hierarchical Regression Analysis

Examining context effects with moderators in regression involves a test of interactions in one way or another. Thus, problems with a lack of independence of independent variables occurs with continuous variable interactions. One step to mitigate the potential effects of multicollinearity when employing interactions in multiple regression analysis is to mean-center or standardize the variables. Mean-centering is accomplished by subtracting the overall mean of each variable from each observation. Standardization involves taking Z-scores for the variables, as described earlier (see Chapter 18). These steps reduce, but do not eliminate, the potential problems due to related predictors. Rather than testing the effect of all predictors, including the interaction, in a single multiple regression analysis, the analyst often employs hierarchical regression analysis when using continuous variable interactions.

Hierarchical regression

adding sets of predictor variables sequentially in multiple stages of a regression analysis and examining the change in the models' predictive power at each step.

Hierarchical regression involves adding sets of predictor variables sequentially in multiple stages of a regression analysis and examining the change in the models' predictive power at each step. The focus shifts to a difference in the model F statistics and R^2 at each subsequent stage. The following steps illustrate the hierarchical regression process:

1. Enter all control variables and use them to predict Y. Interpret the model results.

2. Add all the independent variables to the regression model and predict Y. Interpret the model results with an emphasis on the change in model results.

   a. Any independent variables involved in forming an interaction should be mean-centered or standardized.

b. If the change in R^2 represents a significant increase in predictive power, then the independent variables are deemed to significantly predict the dependent variable.

3. Add the interaction term(s) to the regression model and predict Y. Interpret the model results with an emphasis on the change in model results.

a. If the change in R^2 represents a significant increase in predictive power, then the moderator variables are deemed to significantly predict the dependent variable.

b. Realize that the regression coefficients could be unreliable in the presence of the multicollinearity that routinely affects regression models with continuous variable interactions. Thus, the primary test of significance comes from the change in model F rather than the t-test for parameter coefficients. The change in model F is found by applying the following equation:

i. $$\Delta F_{(df = k_2 - k_1,\ n - k_{total} - 1)} = \frac{\dfrac{R_2^2 - R_1^2}{k_2 - k_1}}{\dfrac{1 - R_2^2}{n - k_2 - 1}}$$

where R_2^2 represents the coefficient of determination for the second model (including the additional predictors), R_1^2 represents the coefficient of determination for the base model (with fewer independent variables), k_2 is the number of predictor variables in second (next level) model, k_1 is the number of predictor variables in the base model, and n is the sample size.

4. Use the predicted values of Y at two values of the independent variable (such as $+/-1$ standard deviation away from the mean) to plot the moderation results as routinely done for an interaction in ANOVA.

ANOVA[a]						
Model		Sum of Squares	df	Mean Square	F	Sig.
1	Regression	14.190	1	14.190	6.525	.013[b]
	Residual	132.667	61	2.175		
	Total	146.857	62			
2	Regression	52.190	3	17.397	10.842	.000[c]
	Residual	94.667	59	1.605		
	Total	146.857	62			
3	Regression	52.193	4	13.048	7.994	.000[d]
	Residual	94.664	58	1.632		
	Total	146.857	62			

EXHIBIT **19.6**
Hierarchical Regression Results

Model Summary									
					Change Statistics				
Model	R	R Square	Adjusted R Square	Std. Error of the Estimate	R Square Change	F Change	df1	df2	Sig. F Change
1	.311[a]	.097	.082	1.475	.097	6.525	1	61	.013
2	.596[b]	.355	.323	1.267	.259	11.841	2	59	.000
3	.596[c]	.355	.311	1.278	.000	.001	1	58	.969

a. Predictors: (Constant), Handicap
b. Predictors: (Constant), Handicap, Zscore: Ball Price, Zscore(Distance)
c. Predictors: (Constant), Handicap, Zscore: Ball Price, Zscore(Distance), ModDisPri

		Coefficients[a]							
		Unstandardized Coefficients		Standardized Coefficients				Collinearity Statistics	
Model		B	Std. Error	Beta	t	Sig.		Tolerance	VIF
1	(Constant)	5.484	.505		10.868	.000			
	Handicap	−.093	.037	−.311	−2.554	.013		1.000	1.000
2	(Constant)	4.526	.478		9.470	.000			
	Handicap	−.019	.035	−.062	−.534	.596		.800	1.250
	Zscore(Distance)	.795	.177	.516	4.483	.000		.824	1.214
	Zscore: Ball Price	−.222	.169	−.145	−1.318	.192		.909	1.100
3	(Constant)	4.529	.486		9.321	.000			
	Handicap	−.019	.036	−.063	−.531	.598		.797	1.255
	Zscore(Distance)	.798	.202	.519	3.945	.000		.643	1.555
	Zscore: Ball Price	−.221	.173	−.144	−1.277	.207		.877	1.140
	ModDisPri	.005	.140	.005	.039	.969		.735	1.361

a. Dependent Variable: Satisfaction

Hierarchical Regression Illustration

Exhibit 19.6 illustrates results from hierarchical regression using the golfer data from the beginning of the chapter. The hierarchical regression involves three stages:

1. Handicap is entered as the control variable in Model 1. Results (model results shown in the top frame) suggest that the control variable significantly predicts golfer satisfaction and yields an R^2 of 0.082 ($F = 6.525, p < 0.05$). The regression coefficient ($b = −0.09, \beta = −0.31, t = −2.55, p < 0.05$, coefficients rounded to two decimals) suggests the effect is negative, meaning as handicap gets higher, satisfaction with the golf experience is lower.
2. In Model 2, the routine adds the standardized direct effects of distance and ball to the regression equation from step 1. The addition of the two direct effects significantly improves the predictive power over the model containing only the control variable as seen in the test of significance for the change in F. In this case, the change in F is 11.8 ($p < 0.001$). The change in R^2 is 0.259. The parameter coefficients for the model suggest a positive relationship; as distance increases, so does satisfaction ($b = 0.80, \beta = 0.52, t = 4.48, p < 0.0001$). In contrast, the parameter coefficient for ball price suggests a negative relationship, but the relationship is not significant ($b = −0.22, \beta = −0.14, t = −1.32, p > 0.10$).
3. In Model 3, the interaction represents the moderator (ModDisPri) formed by multiplying the standardized distance variable by the standardized ball price variable. The addition of the interaction in this case does not contribute significantly to the predictive power of the model. The change in R^2 is 0 (Model 2 and Model 3 have $R^2 = 0.355$) and the change in F is 0.001, which is not significant ($p = 0.97$). Because of the insignificance of the change in F at this stage, the results do not support the case for moderation.
4. Given that the interaction is not significant, the researcher need not likely plot the interaction means. The analyst would draw the conclusion that distance drives satisfaction positively as a direct effect, but no interaction, and therefore no moderation, is suggested by these results.

Depicting Hierarchical Regression Interaction

When a hierarchical regression analysis suggests moderation, meaning that the addition of the interaction term(s) contributes significantly to the improvement in R^2 and therefore the model F, the best way to interpret the result is using a graphical depiction. A picture is much simpler to understand than a mere report of the regression coefficient for an interaction. Using an extension of the idea for plotting experimental interactions introduced in Chapter 9, we can plot the effect in a graph by calculating the predicted values $\hat{Y}$ at contrasting levels of the independent variable (X) and the moderator (Mod). Suppose the researcher conducted another analysis examining the potential interaction of a moderator, ball price (BP), with an independent variable predicting satisfaction, durability (Dur). After determining that the addition of the interaction significantly improves the model F and R^2, the results suggest the following equation for predicting values of the dependent variable, satisfaction:

$$\hat{Y} = 4.0 + 0.5Dur - 0.5BP + 0.75(Dur \times BP)$$

Both Dur and BP were standardized prior to the analysis. Standardization makes plotting the results simpler and easier to follow. Although lines can be plotted with any contrasting points, a simple way to draw the graph is to compute the predicted values at values of X and Mod of -1 and $+1$. In doing so, the plot depicts results at one standard deviation below and above the mean for both variables. This procedure is easier to see by illustration. When Dur is held constant at its high value ($+1$), the following predicted satisfaction values are found by varying BP from $+1$ to -1:

$$\hat{Y} = 4.0 + (0.5)(1) - 0.5(1) + 0.75(1 \times 1) = 4.75$$
$$\hat{Y} = 4.0 + (0.5)(1) - 0.5(-1) + 0.75(1 \times -1) = 4.25$$

These points can be seen on the right of the plot. When Dur is held constant at its low value (-1), the following predicted values are found by varying BP from $+1$ to -1:

$$\hat{Y} = 4.0 + (0.5)(-1) - 0.5(1) + 0.75(-1 \times 1) = 2.25$$
$$\hat{Y} = 4.0 + (0.5)(-1) - 0.5(-1) + 0.75(-1 \times -1) = 4.75$$

These points can be seen on the left of the plot. From the graph, we see that durability affects satisfaction more strongly in the high-price condition. Notice that the slope of the high-price line is steeper and positively sloping. In contrast, the low-price line (in blue) is sloped less severely and negatively. The term **slopes test** sometimes is used to refer to the comparison of slopes in interpreting an interaction's effect. Here, we see that the combination of high durability and high price is associated with the highest satisfaction. The low durability and high price combination produces the lowest level of satisfaction. The researcher can report back to the golf client that a high-price ball must deliver good durability if the customer is going to be satisfied. Durability seems less important for low-price golf balls.

Slopes test

Comparison of slopes in interpreting an interaction.

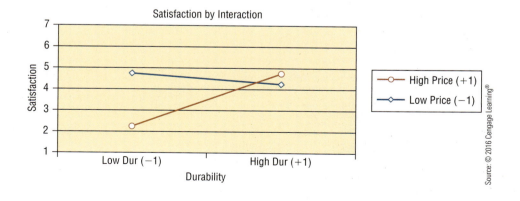

Source: © 2016 Cengage Learning®

EXHIBIT 19.7

Plot of Interaction Effect

TIPS OF THE TRADE

- Hypotheses should be backed with a sound explanatory logic.
  - Hypotheses should not be tautological.
  - Hypotheses should not state a nonevent.
- Mediation tests provide a way to see if some third variable (*M*) goes between the independent and the dependent variable to facilitate the relationship.
  - Mediation tests can be biased if some unaccounted-for variable exists that affects both *M* and *Y*.
  - The bias can be ignored if residuals suggest no substantial underspecification.

- Moderation tests provide a good way to test for context effects.
  - When using continuous variable interactions, standardize the independent variable(s) and moderator(s) prior to analysis.
  - Compute the interaction term from the standardized variables.
  - This facilitates plotting of the effects.

::SUMMARY

1. Test hypotheses with regression. Linear regression provides a useful way to test hypotheses proposing relationships between variables. Well-stated hypotheses invite a confrontation with the data, and are specific, relatively short, questionable, nontrivial, and not tautological. A positive (negative) relationship is supported by a significant positive (negative) regression coefficient.

2. Understand basics of interpreting hypotheses of mediation. A mediator is a variable that intervenes between an independent variable and a dependent variable in a way that facilitates a relationship. One can think of a mediator like a faucet. The relationship flows through the pipes to the extent that the mediator (faucet) is open. Full mediation exists when a relationship between X and Y, demonstrated in a simple regression, becomes insignificant in a multiple regression predicting Y with X and M. Underspecification bias can present a problem in interpreting significance tests of indirect effects in mediation analysis. Macros like PROCESS provide a way of addressing such problems.

3. Know that moderation accounts for context effects. Context effects account for factors unique to time, space, or conditions that may affect some hypothesized relationship. Common context effects include factors like time pressure, culture, or demographic variables. A moderating variable changes the relationship between the independent and dependent variable. A moderator is represented in multiple regression by the interaction term between an independent variable and a moderator. As such, a multiple regression containing the independent variable, moderator, and interaction term could present problems with multicollinearity.

4. Conduct and interpret hierarchical regression. In hierarchical regression, the interpretation shifts away from the individual parameter coefficients more to the change in F and R^2 occurring when a variable or set of variables is added to some base model. The base model typically includes only control variables as predictors of the dependent variable. The second model adds direct effects. The third model adds the continuous variable interactions. If the change in F is statistically significant, evidence of moderation is presented. Standardization of the independent variables representing direct effects facilitates the analysis and the graphical representation of effects.

:: KEY TERMS AND CONCEPTS

bootstrapping, *512*
complete mediation, *510*
context variable, *514*
direct effect, *505*
hierarchical regression, *514*
indirect effect, *509*

mediator variable, *509*
moderation, *513*
partial mediation, *510*
slopes test, *517*
tautology, *504*

:: QUESTIONS FOR REVIEW AND CRITICAL THINKING

1. What are the characteristics of good (well-stated) hypotheses?
2. What does it mean for a hypothesis to be tautological?
3. A researcher proposes the following hypothesis: Brand image is positively related to willingness to pay. After running a regression analysis with data on these variables, how would one know if the researcher's hypothesis is supported?
4. What evidence would a researcher use to prove a negative relationship existed between *X* and *Y*?
5. What does it mean for a variable to mediate the relationship between two other variables?
6. Think about variables that cause one student to perform better in a business class than another student. Propose a hypothesis that captures that relationship. Now, think of a third variable that might mediate that relationship. Propose a hypothesis for that effect. Explain.
7. What is an indirect effect? How is it computed?
8. A research analyst runs the following regression models (see graphic below) used to predict how sales of brand B (the

dependent variable) are influenced by the perceived quality of brand B (PQB) and attitude toward brand B (Brand B). Using the results below,
   a. What is the indirect relationship of PQB on sales of B?
   b. Presuming no issues with underspecification, is evidence of mediation present? Describe the result.
9. What is the difference between partial and full mediation?
10. Define a moderation effect. Give a typical example. How do they account for context?
11. What is hierarchical regression analysis? How does it differ in approach from standard multiple regression?
12. What is a slopes test?

:: RESEARCH ACTIVITY

1. Using the golfer data provided in this chapter (and available as a file in the student resources), conduct an analysis to test these hypotheses:
   a. Durability is positively related to distance of average drive.
   b. Price paid is positively related to distance of average drive.
      i. Control for durability in testing this effect.
   c. Handicap is negatively related to distance of average drive.
      i. Control for durability and price paid in testing this effect.
   d. Suppose the researcher is conducting research for club brand C. Does price mediate the relationship of club brand (C versus others—use a dummy code with 1 = brand C and 0 for other brands)?
   e. Does club brand (using the dummy code) moderate the effect of distance on satisfaction?
2. Using the data from question 8 (available in the student resources), does age moderate the effect of quality (PQB) or brand attitude (Brand B) on sales?
3. Presuming standardized direct effects are included, draw (or use Excel to draw) a graphical representation of moderator effects that would result from the following regression result:
$$\hat{Y} = 5.0 + 0.3X - 0.6Md + 0.8(X \times Md)$$

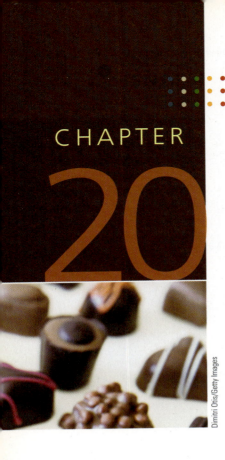

CHAPTER 20

Introducing Multivariate Data Analysis

LEARNING OUTCOMES

After studying this chapter, you should be able to:

1. Understand what multivariate data analysis involves and know the two basic types of multivariate analysis
2. Define dependence techniques
3. Interpret results from multivariate analysis of variance (MANOVA)
4. Know what discriminant analysis can be used to do
5. Interpret a logistic regression output

Introduction

If only business problems were really as simple as most textbook examples. Most coursework involves solving problems that have a definite answer. They are relatively well-defined problems in which the information provided in the problem can be used to produce *one* solution.

Unfortunately, in the real world, most business problems are ill-defined. Not only do they not have a definite answer, but generally information needs to be massaged and generated before any solution can be obtained. Therefore, most business research studies involve many variables that must be organized for meaning. Nowhere is this truer than in the world of big data. Big data analyses require tools that can search sequentially or simultaneously through volumes of information. Thus, today's marketing researchers and marketing analysts know well the multidimensional nature of business. As a consequence, they gain a greater appreciation for multivariate data analysis. This chapter introduces multivariate data analysis and then focuses on techniques particularly useful in prediction.

What Is Multivariate Data Analysis?

Preceding chapters address univariate and bivariate analyses and examine some specific aspects of multiple regression. Although definitions may vary a little from source to source, data analysis that involves three or more variables, or that is concerned with underlying dimensions among multiple variables, will involve **multivariate data analysis**. **Multivariate statistical methods** analyze multiple variables or even multiple sets of variables simultaneously. The marketing analyst applies multivariate statistical methods based on a belief that more intelligence results from looking at combinations of variables rather than any variable or any two variables in isolation.

Many concepts relevant to marketing lend themselves to multivariate analysis. Marketers, for instance, increasingly see nostalgia as a concept with potential to create value for consumers.[1] Nostalgic feelings may make consumers experience heightened emotion, and these emotions could influence customer loyalty. How do we know when someone has experienced nostalgia and whether or not the experience has altered behavior? Nostalgia itself is a latent factor that involves multiple indicators that together represent nostalgia. In addition, a multitude of factors come together to create feelings of nostalgia. Nostalgia, in turn, may be useful in making key distinctions among different consumers.

Many marketing problems benefit from multivariate data analysis, including most psychographic research and most research that seeks to identify viable market segments. In fact, data mining routines search for segments of consumers that share identifiable characteristics. The key characteristic identifying multivariate analysis is the simultaneous consideration of sets of variables rather than variables in isolation.

The "Variate" in Multivariate

Another distinguishing characteristic of multivariate analysis is the **variate**. The variate is a mathematical way of representing the information in a set of variables with one equation. Variates are formed as a linear combination of variables, each contributing to the overall meaning of the variate based upon an empirically derived weight. Mathematically, the variate is a function of the measured variables involved in an analysis:

$$V_k = f(X_1, X_2, \ldots, X_m)$$

V_k is the kth variate. Every analysis could involve multiple sets of variables, each represented by a variate. X_1 to X_m represent the measured variables.

Here is a simple illustration. Recall that constructs are distinguished from variables by the fact that multiple variables are needed to measure a construct. If we measured nostalgia with five variables, a variate of the following form could be created:

$$V_k = L_1 X_1 + L_2 X_2 + L_3 X_3 + L_4 X_4 + L_5 X_5$$

V_k represents the score for nostalgia, X_1 to X_5 represent the observed scores on the five scale items that are expected to indicate nostalgia, and L_1 to L_5 are parameter estimates much like regression weights that suggest how highly related each variable is to the overall nostalgia score.

Don't worry! We do not have to manually calculate these scores anymore. We'll rely on the computer to do the heavy lifting in the vast majority of cases. This type of variate is common to multivariate procedures.

To the Point

"*The essence of mathematics is not to make simple things complicated, but to make complicated things simple.***"**

—S. GUDDER

Multivariate data analysis

Data analysis techniques that analyze three or more variables simultaneously or that are concerned with underlying dimensions among multiple variables.

Multivariate statistical methods

Techniques that analyze multiple variables or multiple sets of variables simultaneously.

Variate

A mathematical way in which a set of variables can be represented with one equation.

As you approach the end of this course, you may be interested in understanding what factors are associated with success in the course. While we may not be able to get at that question specifically, particularly because your grades are not in yet, we can try to understand factors that are associated with studying. Notice that at least two questions deal with how much people study and one in particular deals with how much time students spend studying for marketing research. Take a look at the portion of the questionnaire shown.

Let's examine this research question:

Students' involvement with different social behaviors is related to their study habits.

Use the responses to the items shown in the screenshot or from other portions of the questionnaire as you see fit to explore this research question.

- This could be done by using each item as an individual predictor in a multiple regression model. However, there is a risk of multicollinearity.

Source: www.qualtrics.com

- Q87 assesses whether a respondent is male or female. Is there any evidence that men and women differ in their social involvement as assessed within this set of items?

Multivariate Procedures: Dependence Methods

Two basic groups of multivariate techniques are *dependence methods* and *interdependence methods*. This chapter focuses on dependence techniques. As you will see later, they should be familiar to you because we've already encountered quite a few dependence techniques through the last chapters.

Dependence techniques

Multivariate procedures that predict some observed dependent variable using a combination(s) of predictors that serve as independent variables.

Dependence techniques are those multivariate procedures that predict some observed dependent variable using a combination(s) of predictors that serve as independent variables. With dependence techniques, a clear distinction exists between independent and dependent variables. For instance, when we hypothesize that nostalgia relates positively to purchase intentions, the set of variables indicating nostalgia play the role of an independent variable and variables indicating purchase intentions play the role of a dependent variable.

Predicting dependent variables like purchase intention, sales, web traffic, and so on based on the numerous independent variables is a problem frequently investigated with dependence techniques. *Multiple regression analysis, discriminant analysis, multivariate analysis of variance,* and *logistic regression* are all dependence methods that can help in this task.

Influence of Measurement Scales

Exhibit 20.1 describes some of the most commonly applied multivariate dependence techniques. The exhibit outlines when each technique is appropriate based on the level of measurement and number of dependent variables. For all dependence techniques, the variate predicts

© 2016 Cengage Learning®

EXHIBIT 20.1
An Overview of Multivariate Dependence Techniques

an outcome. When the outcome is less than interval, discriminant analysis or logistic regression are appropriate choices. Discriminant analysis typically involves at least interval independent variables. Logistic regression is used when the outcome is less than interval. The predictors (i.e., independent variable) can be either continuous or dichotomous (coded with a dummy variable). Sometimes, people use the term *nonmetric* to refer to data that is nominal or ordinal and the term *metric* to refer to data that is interval or ratio. Other times, the term *continuous* is used to characterize any data that is at least interval.

Analysis of Dependence

Multivariate dependence techniques are variants of the general linear model (GLM), introduced in Chapter 15. Simply, the GLM is a way of modeling some process based on how different variables cause fluctuations from the average value of a dependent variable. Fluctuations can come in the form of group means that differ from the overall mean as is in ANOVA or in the form of a significant slope coefficient as in regression. The basic idea can be thought of as follows (presented in predictive form):

$$\hat{Y}_i = \mu + \Delta X + \Delta F + \Delta XF + b_c C$$

Here, μ represents a constant, which can be thought of as the overall mean of the dependent variable $\overline{\overline{Y}}$, ΔX and ΔF represent changes due to main effect independent variables (such as experimental variables) and blocking independent variables (such as covariates or grouping variables), respectively, and ΔXF represents the change due to the combination (interaction effect) of those variables. The final term symbolizes the inclusion of covariates (C) that can be included in predicting the dependent variable by estimating a regression or slope coefficient (b_c). While the equation shows only one, any number of covariates might be included. Realize in contrast to Chapter 15, Y_i in this case could represent multiple dependent variables, just as X and F could represent multiple independent variables. Multiple regression analysis, n-way ANOVA, and MANOVA represent common forms that the GLM can take.

Summarizing the Steps in Multivariate Dependent Analyses

An analyst goes about interpreting all multivariate dependence analyses in a sequence of steps that generally corresponds to those provided for interpreting multiple regression analysis in Chapter 15. Once the data are obtained, coded, and any response errors addressed, the steps can be summarized as:

1. Select and run an appropriate multivariate dependence technique.
2. Interpret the overall model results.
3. If the overall model results are statistically significant, proceed to identify the specific variables responsible for the statistical significance of the model by interpreting parameter estimates for individual independent variables.
4. Examine the model for implausible results or other diagnostics that may signal potential statistical problems.
5. Prepare a written description of results.

We now turn to some specific multivariate dependence approaches.

Interpret Results from Multivariate Analysis of Variance (MANOVA)

Multivariate Analysis of Variance (MANOVA)

A multivariate dependence technique in which multiple, related dependent variables are predicted by less than interval independent variables.

Multivariate Analysis of Variance, often abbreviated as **MANOVA**, is a multivariate *dependence* technique involving more than one, related, metric dependent variable predicted by less than interval independent variables. The only difference between MANOVA and *n*-way ANOVA is the inclusion of multiple, related dependent variables as opposed to a single dependent variable. Thus, MANOVA is multivariate on both the predicted and predictor sides of the equation. In the basic GLM equation illustrating multivariate dependence techniques, the only change is that the predicted value now represents a vector (meaning an array of more than one) of dependent variables rather than a single, scalar dependent variable (the predicted value is made bold to signify a vector):

$$\hat{\boldsymbol{Y}}_i = \mu + \Delta X + \Delta F + \Delta XF + b_c C$$

MANCOVA

A variation of MANOVA that can include interval or ratio covariates.

The analyst is not limited to only categorical independent variables. **MANCOVA** is a variation of MANOVA that can include interval or ratio covariates. In the equation above, C accounts for a covariate and in fact, $\boldsymbol{C}$ could also represent a vector meaning multiple covariates are included in the model.

Steps in Interpreting MANOVA

Given that MANOVA is an extension of ANOVA, the analyst follows a similar process in interpreting its results. A key distinction between the two is that MANOVA models produce an additional layer of testing compared to ANOVA. The first layer of testing involves the multivariate F-test. This test examines whether or not an independent variable(s) predicts significant variation among the set of dependent variables within the model. If this test is significant, then the analyst can proceed with interpretation of the F-test results from individual univariate regression models nested within the MANOVA model. The rest of the interpretation results follow from the one-way ANOVA or multiple regression model results given earlier.

EXHIBIT **20.2**
Approach for Interpreting MANOVA

Exhibit 20.2 illustrates a standard process for interpreting MANOVA or MANCOVA results. The process begins by examining the **Multivariate result**, which answers the question of whether or not some hypothesized effect relates significantly to the set of dependent variables. If the multivariate results do not produce a significant F statistic, the analyst concludes that the hypothesized effect does not influence the dependent variables and need not proceed further. Conversely, a significant multivariate F leads the researcher to identify which of the dependent variables are relating to the hypothesized effect. To do so, the analyst examines the individual univariate results. The univariate results are interpreted in the same way as illustrated in Chapter 19.

Multivariate result

Answers the question of whether or not some hypothesized effect relates significantly to the set of dependent variables.

Illustrating MANOVA

The Research Snapshot box on page 537 illustrates how to obtain MANOVA results using SPSS, JMP, or SAS. We illustrate the interpretation of MANOVA using a data set named "GoodBuy," which is available as an EXCEL, SPSS, and JMP file in the student resources for this text. The data contain responses from several hundred consumers intercepted within GoodBuy stores in one of numerous test market areas. The test markets address research questions related to promotion approaches and pricing policies for electronic accessories. Two key experimental variables are manipulated within the test market: EXP1 indicates whether the promotion is delivered via billboards (coded 0) or Internet TV (coded 1). EXP2 indicates whether the products were advertised at a discount price (0 = low, 1 = high). Other items in the data set include whether or not a consumer responded to the promotion by purchasing an accessory (YBUY, 0 = did not buy, 1 = did buy), a host of survey responses including how satisfied the customer is with the purchase (for example, CSD5), and the price the consumer was willing to pay for the accessory (Price). Exhibit 20.3 describes the variables in the data set in more detail. We will use this data set in other illustrations and exercises as well.

In this particular analysis, the researcher examines the research question:

- Do price promotion and media type (TV versus billboard) affect consumers' Willingness to Pay (WTP) and satisfaction with the shopping experience (represented by CSD5)?

EXHIBIT 20.3
GoodBuy Data Set

Variable Name	Variable Description	Variable Type
YBUY	Indicates whether consumer bought the promoted accessory	Dummy coded (0 = did not buy, 1 = did buy)
ATS1	Survey item assessing respondent's impression of other GoodBuy shoppers	5-point scale with high score more favorable
ATS2	Survey item assessing respondent's impression of other GoodBuy shoppers	6-point scale with high score more favorable
ATS3	Survey item assessing respondent's impression of other GoodBuy shoppers	5-point scale with high score more favorable
ATS4	Survey item assessing respondent's impression of other GoodBuy shoppers	5-point scale with high score more favorable
ATM1	Survey item assessing favorableness of GoodBuy atmosphere	0–10 point scale
ATM2	Survey item assessing favorableness of GoodBuy atmosphere	0–10 point scale
ATM3	Survey item assessing favorableness of GoodBuy atmosphere	0–10 point scale
ATM4	Survey item assessing favorableness of GoodBuy atmosphere	7-point Likert scale
EXP	Experience with electronics	Minutes per day browsing electronics-related websites
Hours	Scale item assessing relative amount of time spent using electronic devices	5-point scale ranging from 1 = much less than others to 5 = much more than others
CSD1	Scale item assessing consumer satisfaction with GoodBuy shopping experience	7-point Likert scale (higher score means more satisfaction)
CSD2	Scale item assessing consumer satisfaction with GoodBuy shopping experience	7-point scale assessing how much satisfaction was felt (1 = none to 7 = very much)
CSD3	Scale item assessing consumer satisfaction with GoodBuy shopping experience	6-point scale with high score indicating more satisfaction
CSD4	Scale item assessing consumer satisfaction with GoodBuy shopping experience	5-point satisfaction rating (1 = no satisfaction and 5 = complete satisfaction)
CSD5	Scale item assessing consumer satisfaction with GoodBuy shopping experience	100-point slider item with 100 = complete satisfaction
LOY1	Scale item assessing loyalty toward GoodBuy	0–10 point scale (high score means more loyal)
LOY2	Scale item assessing loyalty toward GoodBuy	0–10 point scale (high score means more loyal)
LOY3	Scale item assessing loyalty toward GoodBuy	0–10 point scale (high score means more loyal)
LOY4	Scale item assessing loyalty toward GoodBuy	0–10 point scale (high score means more loyal)
AGE	Age of research participant	in years
EXP1	Experimental variable representing promotion type	Dummy coded (0 = billboard, 1 = internet TV)
EXP2	Experimental variable representing price displayed in promotion	Dummy coded (0 = low price, 1 = high price)
WTP	Price participant is willing to pay for advertised accessory	in dollars

In the analysis, the researcher wants to statistically control for age by inserting it as a covariate. Exhibit 20.4 displays some of the key results. The analyst reports the following results:

Multivariate Results:

Effect	Wilks Λ	Multivariate F	Num DF	Den DF	p-value
Model	0.73	17.0	8	786	<.001
EXP1	0.98	3.21	2	393	0.04
EXP2	0.79	53.8	2	393	<.001
EXP1*EXP2	0.97	6.85	2	393	0.001
Age	0.98	4.79	2	393	0.009

Univariate Results for Effects on WTP

Effect	F	Num DF	Den DF	p-value
Model	32.2	4	394	<.001
EXP1	3.88	1	394	0.05
EXP2	106.9	1	394	<.001
EXP1*EXP2	8.33	1	394	0.004
Age	3.74	1	394	0.05

Univariate Results for Effects on CSD

Effect	F	Num DF	Den DF	p-value
Model	3.27	4	394	0.01
EXP1	2.98	1	394	0.08
EXP2	0.06	1	394	0.80
EXP1*EXP2	4.51	1	394	0.03
Age	5.21	1	394	0.02

EXHIBIT 20.4
Example MANOVA Results

© 2016 Cengage Learning®

1. The full-factorial MANCOVA tests the effect of the predictors on the dependent variables. Although details are beyond the scope of the text, Multivariate F statistics are computed using one of several alternative statistics provided by most statistical software. Generally, the alternative statistics produce similar results. Among these, **Wilks Lambda (Λ)** is the most commonly applied statistic and the one we'll use in all MANOVA results reported in the text. The user should look for the multivariate F associated with Λ. In this case, Λ is 0.73, which yields the model F of 17.0 ($p < 0.001$). Moreover, the research question posits effects for both the promotion and price experimental variables. Both the price (EXP1) main effect (multivariate $F = 3.21$) and the promotion main effect (multivariate $F = 53.8$) are statistically significant ($p < 0.05$). In addition, the two-way price by promotion interaction also significantly affects the dependent variables (multivariate $F = 6.85$, $p < 0.01$). The covariate, age, also relates to the dependent variables significantly (multivariate $F = 4.79$, $p < 0.01$). Given these significant effects, suggesting that the set of dependent variables is related to predictors, the analyst proceeds to examine the univariate models.

2. The univariate model predicting WTP is significant ($F = 32.2$, $p < 0.001$). Likewise, the univariate model predicting CSD5 also is significant ($F = 3.27$, $p < 0.05$). Given that both models are significant, the analyst proceeds to examine which predictor variables are responsible for these significant results.

3. The analyst now turns to identifying specific independent variables. For WTP, all predictors are significant at $p \leq 0.05$ except for the covariate, age. For CSD5, only the EXP1★EXP2 interaction and the age covariate are significant ($p \leq 0.05$).

4. For each significant effect, the analyst breaks down the nature of the relationship by examining the cell means and/or the parameter coefficients.

Wilks Lambda (Λ)
The most commonly applied statistic for calculating MANOVA model results.

a. Exhibit 20.5 displays the estimated mean plots (LS Means stands for Least Squares Estimated Means) for both dependent variables.

    i.   The results suggest that subjects exposed to the promotional message via TV ($17.71) express a higher WTP than those exposed via billboards ($17.16). Additionally, those exposed to the promotion with a high price express a higher WTP ($18.88) than those in the low price condition ($15.99).

    ii. For CSD5, the means for those in the billboard condition (56.7) are higher than for those exposed via Internet TV (53.2).

    iii. The means for WTP corresponding to the interaction effect suggest that in the low price condition, the mean WTP score is lower in the billboard condition ($15.31) than in the TV condition ($16.67). In contrast, in the high price condition, the means are closer together with a slightly higher mean for those in the billboard condition ($19.01) compared to in the TV condition ($18.75).

    iv. The means for CSD5 corresponding to the interaction effect suggest that in the low price condition subjects report similar levels of satisfaction when exposed to promotion via billboard (54.3) compared to those exposed via TV (55.1). In the high price condition, the mean satisfaction for those exposed via billboards is higher (59.2) than for those exposed via TV (51.3).

b. The parameter estimates for age are **b** = 0.04 ($p > 0.05$) and **b** = 0.33 ($p < 0.05$) for WTP and CSD5, respectively. Thus, age exhibits a positive relationship and significant relationship on CSD5. The older a consumer, the more satisfaction he or she reports.

Based on these MANOVA results, GoodBuy decides to allocate more of its promotion for electronics' accessories toward billboards that advertise relatively higher prices for accessories. The higher prices may signal greater quality. GoodBuy hopes customers, if the MANOVA results hold, will be willing to pay for higher-priced items and experience greater satisfaction with the shopping experience.

EXHIBIT 20.5

Plot of Means by Treatment Combinations

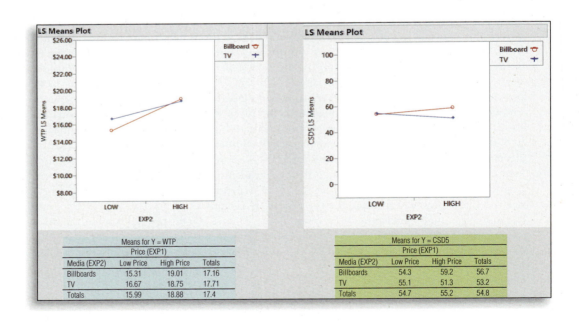

Means for Y = WTP

Media (EXP2)	Low Price	High Price	Totals
Billboards	15.31	19.01	17.16
TV	16.67	18.75	17.71
Totals	15.99	18.88	17.4

Means for Y = CSD5

Media (EXP2)	Low Price	High Price	Totals
Billboards	54.3	59.2	56.7
TV	55.1	51.3	53.2
Totals	54.7	55.2	54.8

Getting MANOVA Results

You can get multivariate GLM results for MANOVA similarly to the way univariate GLM results were obtained. In SPSS, follow this sequence:

1. Follow this sequence of clicks: Analyze → General Linear Model → Multivariate. The box at right will appear.
2. Fill in the relevant Dependent Variables.
3. Place the experimental (or other categorical) variables in the Fixed Factor(s) pane.
4. Place any Covariate(s) in the Covariate(s) pane.
5. Click on "Options" and request estimated means for all predictors, including any interactions. In the "display" section, place a check by parameter estimates. The output will display regression estimates that facilitate interpretation of the covariate.

In JMP, follow the following sequence:
After opening data file, choose "Fit Model."

1. Move the dependent variables into the "Y" pane.
2. Highlight the categorical variables to be used as predictors. Click on "Macros" and then select "full factorial." JMP will populate all main effects and interactions in the Construct Model Effects pane.

3. Enter any covariates in the Construct Model Effects pane.
4. Choose MANOVA from the Personality choices in the upper right-hand corner.
5. Click "Run."
6. In the box that pops up, put a check by "Test Each Column Separately Also" and from the "Choose Response" drop down menu, select "Identity."
7. Then click "Run" to see multivariate and univariate results.

In SAS, the following program will generate MANOVA results (after the data statements):

```
Proc GLM;
Class EXP1 EXP2;
Model WTP CSD5 = EXP1 EXP2 EXP1*EXP2 Age;
Means WTP CSD5;
MANOVA h= _All_;
Run;
```

Steps like these will produce results like those illustrated in this chapter.

Discriminant Analysis

Researchers often need to produce a classification of sampling units. This process may involve using a set of independent variables to decide if a sampling unit belongs in one group or another. A physician might record a person's blood pressure, weight, and blood cholesterol level and then categorize that person as having a high or low probability of a heart attack. A researcher interested in retailing failures might be able to group firms as to whether they eventually failed or did not fail on the basis of independent variables such as location, financial ratios, or management changes. A bank might want to discriminate between potentially successful and unsuccessful sites for electronic fund transfer system machines. A sales manager might want to distinguish between applicants to hire and those not to hire. The challenge is to find the discriminating variables to use in a predictive equation that will produce better than chance assignment of the individuals to the two groups.

What Is Discriminant Analysis?

Discriminant analysis

A multivariate technique that predicts a categorical dependent variable based on a linear combination of independent variables.

Discriminant score

Value determined by the discriminant function as linear regression determines $\hat{Y}$, provides a way of assigning observations to groups.

Cutting score

A number produced by discriminant analysis that serves as a benchmark to which discriminant scores are compared. A discriminant score above the cutting score places observations in one group while a discriminant score below the cutting score places them in another.

Discriminant analysis is a multivariate technique that predicts a categorical dependent variable (rather than a continuous, interval-scaled variable, as in multiple regression) based on a linear combination of independent variables. In each problem above, the researcher determines which variables explain why an observation falls into one of two or more groups. A linear combination of independent variables that explains group memberships is known as a discriminant function. Discriminant analysis is a statistical tool for determining such linear combinations. The researcher's task is to derive the coefficients of the discriminant function (a straight line).

Practically speaking, discriminant analysis shares a lot in common with other multivariate techniques, particularly linear regression and MANOVA. The biggest difference statistically involves prediction of a categorical dependent variable.

From a regression standpoint, the set of independent variables still form a linear combination to predict the dependent variable. Typically though, we use the abbreviation Z_{ij} to represent the predicted values instead of Y_i. Z is known as the **discriminant score**, which is determined by the discriminant function just as linear regression determines $\hat{Y}$, and provides the answer as to which group an observation should belong according to discriminant analysis. Another unique aspect to discriminant analysis involves determination of a benchmark for categorizing observations. Discriminant analysis groups observations by comparing each discriminant score to a **cutting score** produced by discriminant analysis, which serves as this benchmark. A discriminant score above the cutting score places observations in one group while a discriminant score below the cutting score places them in another. For a two-group problem, discriminant analysis produces one cutting score. For a three-group problem, two cutting scores are produced, and so forth.

From a MANOVA perspective, one can think of discriminant analysis as reversing the role of the categorical variable. In MANOVA, the categorical variables help predict continuous dependent variables. Instead, discriminant analysis does the reverse. The categorical variable becomes the dependent variable.

Illustration of Discriminant Analysis

To the Point

"It is not our differences that divide us. It is our inability to recognize, accept, and celebrate those differences."

—AUDRE LORDE

We will consider an example of the two-group discriminant analysis problem where the dependent variable is measured on a nominal scale. Suppose a personnel manager for an electrical wholesaler has been keeping records on successful versus unsuccessful sales employees. The personnel manager believes it is possible to predict whether an applicant will succeed on the basis of age, sales aptitude test scores, and mechanical ability scores. As stated at the outset, the problem is to find a linear function of the independent variables that shows large differences in group means. The first task is to estimate the coefficients of the applicant's discriminant function. To calculate the individuals' discriminant scores, the following linear function is used:

$$Z_i = b_1 X_{1i} + b_2 X_{2i} + \cdots + b_n X_{ni}$$

where

Z_i = ith applicant's discriminant score

b_n = discriminant coefficient for the nth variable

X_{ni} = ith applicant's value on the nth independent variable

Using scores for all the individuals in the sample, a discriminant function is determined based on the criterion that the groups be maximally differentiated on the set of independent variables.

Returning to the example with three independent variables, suppose the personnel manager finds the standardized weights in the equation to be

$$Z = b_1 X_1 + b_2 X_2 + b_3 X_3$$

$$= 0.069 X_1 + 0.013 X_2 + 0.0007 X_3$$

This means that age (X_1) is much more important than sales aptitude test scores (X_2). Mechanical ability (X_3) has relatively minor discriminating power.

In the computation of the linear discriminant function, weights are assigned to the variables to maximize the ratio of the difference between the means of the two groups to the standard deviation within groups. The standardized discriminant coefficients, or weights, provide information about the relative importance of each of these variables in discriminating between the two groups.

A major goal of discriminant analysis is to perform a classification function. The purpose of classification in our example is to predict which applicants will be successful and which will be unsuccessful and to group them accordingly. To determine whether the discriminant analysis can be used as a good predictor of applicant success, information provided in the "confusion matrix" is used. Suppose the personnel manager has 40 successful and 45 unsuccessful employees in the sample. The confusion matrix shows that the number of correctly classified employees (72 out of 85) is much higher than would be expected by chance:

Confusion Matrix			
	Predicted Group		
Actual Group	**Successful**	**Unsuccessful**	
Successful	34	6	40
Unsuccessful	7	38	45

Tests can be performed to determine whether the rate of correct classification is statistically significant. For instance, a chi-square statistic can be applied to the results. A significant chi-square indicates that the discriminant function is classifying observations at a better than chance rate.

For more details on the mathematics and advanced applications of discriminant analysis, we refer the reader to other sources.[2] From a marketing research and marketing analytics standpoint though, discriminant analysis can be very useful. The technique allows data to be searched aggressively for potential information that allows consumers to be sorted into good prospects and poor prospects, those who will stay loyal and those who may switch, among many other questions. Thus, discriminant analysis remains a useful tool in modern marketing analytics.

Interpreting Logistic Regression

Marketing researchers often deal with problems related to the explanation and prediction of why a consumer either responded or did not respond to some marketing effort. The research question that is commonly of interest to business goes as follows:

RQ: What variables determine if a consumer who receives a promotional offer buys the promoted product?

That particular research question can come in slightly different forms to pose questions about whether a consumer clicks through on an e-mail or Web offer, likes a brand or product on Facebook, makes an online recommendation, repeats a purchase, visits a site or store, or any other

Here's how to get basic discriminant analysis results using SPSS:

1. After opening data, click analyze.
2. Choose "classify."
3. Then select "Discriminant."
4. Enter the categorical variable to be predicted as the "grouping variable." Open the dialog box and enter values to "define range." Usually, dummy variables are used so 0 would be the minimum and 1 the maximum. Adjust for other codings or for more groups as needed.
5. Enter the "independent variables" into the respective box.
6. Click on "statistics" and choose Fischer's and other statistics of interest.
7. Click on "classify" and choose "summary table" to get confusion matrix.
8. Click "ok."

To do the same analysis in JMP, follow these steps that reinforce the close connection between MANOVA and discriminant analysis:

1. After opening data, click on "analyze" and choose "Fit Model."
2. Select independent variables and move into the "Y" box (as you see, the software is working in reverse with predictors entered as dependent variables).
3. Select the categorical variable to be predicted and click "add."
4. Select MANOVA as the "personality."
5. Click "Run."
6. Click on the red triangle at the top of the output and choose "Save Discrim." This will add a few variables to your data.

7. Find the predicted categorical variable column just created and in the column information for that variable change it from "continuous" to "nominal" unless it's already nominal (it would show with red mark next to name).
8. Click on "analyze" and "fit Y by X."
   a. Select the observed categorical variable as "Y."
   b. Select the predicted categorical variable as "X."
9. Click "OK."

A simple SAS program to run discriminant analysis looks like this (after the data step is completed which reads Z as a categorical variable and X1, X2, and X3 as independent variables):

```
Proc Candisc;
Class Z;
Var X1 X2 X3;
Run;
```

question that can be phrased as a yes or no response. In fact, these questions can be thought of as trying to distinguish marketing success, yes responses, from lack of success, no responses.

Logistic regression applications are wide-ranging. For instance, research examines whether or not European Union consumers will purchase an item in the informal economy using logistic regression. The informal economy provides a way for consumers to avoid the added expenses and bureaucracy of buying through traditional channels. A consumer in a market may ask if there is a special price for cash. If the merchant accepts payment in cash and does not document the sale, he/she can avoid paying taxes on the transaction and pass some of the savings to the consumer. Research employing a logistic regression, based on a purchase in the informal economy (a success) or no participation in the informal economy (a failure in this case), suggests that the perception of saving money, a conservative political orientation, and living in a multi-person household enhance the probability of participation in the informal economy.[3]

Researchers in other areas also apply logistic regression widely. For example, management researchers build logistic regression models in an effort to understand which employees stay on the job longer. One study showed that CEOs that take on a celebrity status are more likely to remain on the job when the company faces difficulties.[4] Healthcare researchers apply logistic regression widely. In many of these cases, researchers are interested in identifying variables related to someone contracting a specific disease or other health care malady. For instance, one study examined variables associated with a patient contracting either Crohn's Disease or Colitis.[5] One surprising finding in the logistic regression results is that obesity did not increase significantly the likelihood of contracting either disease. This section describes how to conduct a basic logistic regression analysis and how to interpret its results.

What Is Logistic Regression?

Logistic regression is a multivariate technique involving prediction of a categorical, dichotomous dependent variable, usually coded 0 = failure and 1 = success, using metric and/or less than interval independent variables. In many ways, logistic regression functions similarly to linear regression. Consequently, one interprets the results in a similar way as well. In terms of function, logistic regression is applied in the same situation as discriminant analysis. One difference between the two approaches though is that logistic regression only accommodates a dichotomous (meaning two levels) dependent variable. Thus, logistic regression functions to (1) find the independent variables most highly related to the likelihood of an observation being successful (making a purchase rather than not making a purchase) and (2) classifying respondents into success and failure categories.

As such, logistic regression involves prediction of a categorical dependent variable. The analyst prepares for logistic regression by applying a dummy code to the dependent variable. Use 0 to indicate a "failure" or non-instance of the dependent variable and a 1 to indicate "success" or an instance where the behavior of interest actually took place.

Log of the Odds: Logit

Although the precise statistical mechanics of logistic regression are beyond the scope of this book, we provide a grounding in the mechanics by using multiple regression analysis as the basis. The key distinction is exactly what gets predicted by the logistic regression equation. In the end, we want to know the answer to the success or no success question, but to get that logistic regression relies on a continuous number from which success or lack thereof is inferred. In that sense, logistic regression seeks some number to serve the role of the discriminant score described earlier.

The logit value serves as the continuous number predicted by the logistic regression equation:

$$Logit_i = b_o + b_1 X_1 + \cdots + b_k X_k$$

A **logit** of an observation i, is the log of the odds of some occurrence. In logistic regression, a logit is most often the natural log of the **odds of success**. Mathematically, a logit is the ratio of probabilities of an event occurring to not occurring. Put in terms of success or failure (lack of success), a logit is:

$$Logit_i = ln\left(\frac{probability\ of\ success}{probability\ of\ failure}\right) = ln\left(\frac{probability_{success}}{1 - probability_{success}}\right)$$

The right side of the logistic regression equation is the same as in multiple regression. Each b_i represents a parameter estimate that weights the relative predictive power of each independent variable from X_1 to X_k, where k is the total number of independent variables.

Exhibit 20.6 displays some hypothetical values related to the chances of success and the logit values associated with each. Think of each probability as the likelihood of converting a prospect into a customer based on some combination of marketing approaches and demographic variables. In the first row, the company is 90 percent likely to convert a prospective client into a customer. The second row of the column is simple enough because the probability of failure is just 1 minus the probability of success. The third column converts those probabilities into odds of success, which is just the probability of success divided by the probability of failure. We find the logit

EXHIBIT 20.6
Computing Logits from
Probabilities

Probability of Success	Probability of Failure	Odds of Success	Logit
90%	10%	9	2.197
75%	25%	3	1.099
60%	40%	1.5	0.405
50%	50%	1	0.000
40%	60%	0.67	−0.405
25%	75%	0.33	−1.099
10%	90%	0.11	−2.197
1%	99%	0.01	−4.595

To the Point

"Success consists of going from failure to failure without loss of enthusiasm."

—WINSTON CHURCHILL

simply by taking the natural log (ln) of the odds of success. Among these values, the 50 percent row is particularly insightful. Notice that when the chances of success are 50–50, the odds of success are 1.00. The natural log of 1.00 is 0. Thus, when the logistic regression equation predicts a result of greater than 0 (a positive value), the predicted outcome is success. When the equation predicts a result less than 0 (a negative value), the predicted outcome is failure. In this way, 0 for the logit works as a cutting score in discriminant analysis.

Prediction in Logistic Regression

A logistic regression's ability to predict success or failure can be assessed using several statistics. Logistic regression equations are not estimated using OLS because of the statistical distribution created by using logits as dependent variables. Instead, logistic regression relies on maximum likelihood estimation. We will not present the statistical details of maximum likelihood here, but the goal is to create parameters that maximize the likelihood of some event. As a consequence, most logistic regression results will include a likelihood value.

The Likelihood Value

Likelihood value
Provides a way of indicating the overall significance or predictive capabilities of logistic regression because −2 times the log of the likelihood value (abbreviated as −2LL) takes on the value of 0 when every observation is correctly classified as a success or failure.

The **likelihood value** provides a way of indicating the overall significance or predictive capabilities of logistic regression because −2 times the log of the likelihood value (abbreviated as **−2LL**) takes on the value of 0 when every observation is correctly classified as a success or failure. In other words, the resulting cross-classification matrix would look like this (presuming 250 out of 1000 respondents became customers):

Predicted Values	Observed Values	
	Success	**Failure**
Success	250	0
Failure	0	750

−2LL
−2 times the natural log of the likelihood value; serves as an overall indicator of the predictive power of a logistic regression model.

The model predicted each success correctly. Thus, the closer −2LL comes to 0, the better the predictive power of the logistic regression model. Most logistic regression software will produce a cross-classification matrix and chi-square test demonstrating how many observations are correctly classified.

Logistic regression models can be compared with respect to their predictive power by taking the difference of their respective −2LLs. Think of a situation in which an alternative model is compared to a baseline model. The difference in the two −2LL values produces a chi-square statistic for which greater values would represent an improvement in fit for one model over a baseline model. Thus, as this chi-square becomes significant, the alternative model is an improvement to the baseline. Many logistic regression software programs routinely report a chi-square value that compares the proposed model as an alternative to a baseline model that would include no independent variables. That baseline is known as a *null model* result. If this is significant, it provides some evidence of the predictive power of the model. However, the careful market analyst does not rely only on one assessment of predictive capability particularly given the knowledge that large sample sizes tend to show statistically significant model results.

Pseudo R^2

By now, most users will be very comfortable with interpreting multiple regression results. If you are among those, you'll be happy to know that logistic regression can be interpreted in much the same way. In fact, we can even use the concept of the R^2 as another means of assessing the model's predictive ability. In logistic regression, we can employ an **entropy (pseudo) R^2** that we can interpret like the R^2 in multiple regression. Values of 0 mean no predictive power and a value of 1 would mean perfect predictive power. The entropy R^2 is computed as a function of the null $-2LL$ and the observed model $-2LL$:

$$Entropy\ R^2 = \frac{-2LL_{null} - (-2LL_{model})}{-2LL_{null}}$$

Several other R^2 approximations exist for use in logistic regression. We will not go through them all here. But, don't be surprised to find several listed in the output. Typically though, the values do not vary very much and the Entropy R^2 can be computed from the $-2LL$ values provided in the output.

Interpreting Significant Independent Variables

In multiple regression, the statistical significance of independent variables is interpreted using an individual t-test for each predictor. While a t-test is inappropriate in logistic regression, we can interpret the independent variables' strength of relationship to the logit values representing the dependent variable using the **Wald Statistic**. The statistical output should include a list of Wald statistic results for each independent variable. The statistical significance of each can be interpreted just as in multiple regression.

Because the actual parameter estimates express the relationship between an independent variable and logits, they can be perplexing to interpret. In particular, a negative value would indicate a variable that increases the odds of success. Given this problem, logistic regression analysis often includes the **exponential logistic coefficient**, which is nothing more than the antilog of the raw parameter estimate. Also realize that the software may arbitrarily pick one category as "success" and it may not match the user's definition. When this occurs, the signs of coefficients can be reversed. Thus, one way to eliminate doubt about the positive or negative effect of a predictor on the dependent variable is to do an independent samples t-test of the independent variable using the dependent variable as a group variable. Needless to say, the user needs to be cautious before reaching the final conclusion on the direction of effect.

Logistic regression applications are increasing with the advancements in data mining and marketing analytics. In Chapter 13, we illustrated the technique of partitioning as a basic data mining tool. In that chapter, we described partitioning based on chi-square values that require categorization of all variables. Partitioning also takes place using logistic regression. In many partitioning programs, the user will find partitions created based on $-2LL$. Automated logistic regression tools can mine hundreds or even thousands of observations and variables to identify those that create the greatest possibility of success. One advantage to using logistic regression over the chi-square automatic interaction detection approach is that independent variables do not need to be categorical.

When logistic regression is used in an exploratory context, the analyst will routinely apply cross-validation. If the analyst has a relatively large data set, he/she can randomly split it into two and then use one data set to develop the model and the other data set to see how well the results hold up. In other words, do both data sets produce the same results?[6]

Illustration of Logistic Regression

The easiest way to see how to interpret a multivariate technique is to use an example. Here, we'll use the GoodBuy retailer data set to illustrate an application of logistic regression. In this case, the market research team wants the following research question addressed:

RQ: Do consumer perceptions of other shoppers, atmosphere, loyalty and/or type of media exposure help predict whether the consumer buys the promoted product while controlling for age?

Thus, the market analyst sets out to examine a logistic regression model based on the notion of predicting a dichotomous dependent variable (YBUY = 0 or 1, with 1 = buy) and

Entropy (pseudo) R^2
An assessment of logistic regression predictive power that functions like the R^2 in multiple regression.

Wald Statistic
Allows interpretation of the statistical significance of the relationship between each independent variable and the logit values representing the dependent variable.

Exponential logistic coefficient
The antilog of the raw logistic regression parameter estimate.

the independent variables each being continuous with the exception of the dummy variable for EXP1. The analyst operationalizes the logistic regression as follows:

$$Z\ (YBUY) = f(ATS4, ATM4, LOY4, AGE, EXP1)$$

The analyst proceeds to obtain results as follows:

1. Runs the logistic regression analysis using statistical software such as JMP, SPSS, or SAS.
2. Interprets the overall model results shown below:

Model	-LogLikelihood	DF	ChiSquare	Prob>ChiSq
Difference	18.45706	5	36.91411	<.0001*
Full	258.09739			
Reduced	276.55445			

RSquare (U)	0.0667
AICc	528.409
BIC	552.129
Observations (or Sum Wgts)	399

Lack Of Fit

Source	DF	-LogLikelihood	ChiSquare
Lack Of Fit	393	258.09739	516.1948
Saturated	398	0.00000	**Prob>ChiSq**
Fitted	5	258.09739	<.0001*

a. The logistic regression model improves the $-LL$ from 276.6 to 258.1, the difference of 18.5 yields a significant chi-square ($-2LL = 36.9$ with 5 df)) difference. Additionally, the overall model $-2LL$ chi-square of 516.2 with 393 df is likewise significant ($p < 0.0001$). Based on this result, the analyst concludes that the logistic regression model is statistically significant and does help predict the probability of a respondent making the purchase.

b. This conclusion is tempered by the fact the entropy (pseudo) R^2 value is only 6.7 percent. The confusion (cross–classification matrix) that results is as follows:

	Observed Values	
Predicted Values	**Buy**	**No Buy**
Buy	149	109
No Buy	52	89

Thus, 149 of the 201 actual buyers are correctly classified (74 percent) and 89 of the 198 actual nonbuyers are correctly classified (45 percent). Overall, the model predicts 60 percent of the cases correctly. Given that practically 50 percent of the observed sample are buyers ($201/399 - 1$ observation is missing), the model allows a 10 percent improvement in prediction as opposed to assuming everyone will buy.

c. After consulting with the research team, the analyst presumes the model improves prediction enough to proceed with further interpretation.

3. Next, the analyst interprets the specific parameter coefficients that go along with each independent variable. Exhibit 20.7 displays the results. The table displays the parameter estimates, the Wald chi-square and its associated p-value, and the 95 percent confidence interval for each predictor. Two of the five experimental variables are statistically significant using a 0.05 acceptable type I error rate:

a. ATM4, which is the respondent's perception of the GoodBuy shopping atmosphere, yields a p-value of 0.0246. Note that 0 is not in the confidence interval. In addition, LOY4, which is a respondent's perception of how loyal he/she is to GoodBuy, yields a p-value of less than 0.0001, suggesting that it has a stronger influence on the buy decision. Note that one

Term	Estimate (B)	Std Error	Wald X2	p-value	Lower 95%	Upper 95%
Intercept	−2.4286	0.9215	6.9462	0.0084	−4.2691	−0.6474
ATS4	−0.1214	0.1107	1.2028	0.2728	−0.3401	0.0949
ATM4	−0.1984	0.0882	5.0549	0.0246	−0.3759	−0.0287
LOY4	0.3767	0.0760	24.5460	0.0000	0.2367	0.5357
AGE	0.0181	0.0196	0.8494	0.3567	−0.0203	0.0567
EXP1[Billboard]	0.2626	0.1474	3.1753	0.0748	−0.0249	0.5541

EXHIBIT 20.7
Parameter Estimate Results from Logistic Regression

© 2016 Cengage Learning®

significant parameter has a positive parameter estimate and the other a negative. This suggests that they have opposite influences on YBUY. The analyst examines the exponential parameter estimates:

$$ATM4 = 1.22$$
$$LOY4 = 0.69$$

b. The exponential coefficient for ATM4 can be interpreted relative to the 50–50 odds ratio value of 1 by using the formula:

$$100 \times (\text{exponential coefficient} - 1).$$

The 1.22 then can be seen as increasing the odds of purchase by 22 percent:

$$(100 \times (1.22 - 1)) = 22 \text{ percent.}$$

In contrast, the coefficient for LOY4 can be seen as decreasing the odds of purchase by 31 percent:

$$(100 \times (0.69 - 1)) = -31 \text{ percent.}$$

Thus, the results suggest that loyal consumers are less likely to buy the promoted product but that those who like the store atmosphere are more likely to buy the product.

c. To further verify that the direction of relationship is as predicted (given that the software may determine the success category as the reverse of the researcher), an independent samples t-test using YBUY as the group variable and ATM4 and LOY4 as the variables, respectively, confirms that lower LOY4 scores are associated with a buy ($LOY4_{buy} = 8.9$ and $LOY4_{nobuy} = 7.9$). In contrast, the result for ATM4 suggest near similar means for both groups (just under 6.0).

d. Should the analyst realize that the program used an opposite than intended coding, he or she can recode the dependent variable and then redo the analysis, or interpret the reciprocal of the unit odds ratios which are often presented in the statistical output.

4. The analyst examines all results for anomalies. The fact that ATM4 yields a significant parameter estimate despite the small difference in means is noted. Logistic regression is sensitive to multicollinearity. As a consequence, the analyst takes the following steps:

a. Examines the correlations among the predictor variables. Given that a nontrivial amount of correlation exists between ATM4 and LOY4, multicollinearity cannot be ruled out.

b. Thus, the analyst reruns the model without ATM4. The results confirm the predictive power of LOY4 as its parameter estimate is virtually unchanged. However, a model dropping LOY4 but retaining ATM4 suggests that ATM4 is unrelated to YBUY.

5. The analyst and research team conclude that the major finding is that the promotion worked better on nonloyal customers than it did on loyal customers. This is based on the reduced probability of a respondent expressing high loyalty actually making the purchase.

The research snapshot below gives some hints as to how to conduct logistic regression analyses using statistical software. Although we do not cover them here, variations of logistic regression such as multinomial logistic regression and probit analysis can be useful in specific situations. However, the basic logistic regression model for a two-category dependent variable is very widely applied and generally useful.

Here's how to run a logistic regression model to predict a dichotomous dependent variable. In JMP, follow these steps:

1. After loading data, select "fit model."
2. Highlight the categorical dependent variable and move into the "Y" box.
3. Highlight the independent variables and click on "add" to enter them into the model.
4. In the "Personality" window, select nominal logistic.
5. Click "Run."
6. Click on the red triangle at the top of the results that open up. Place a check by "Wald Tests," "Confidence Intervals," and "Odds Ratios."

In SPSS, follow these steps:

1. After loading the data, select "Analyze."
2. Choose "Regression" and then select "Binomial Logistic" from the choices.
3. Click on "Options" and place a check by "Classification Plots."
4. Click on "OK."

In SAS, the following program statements can be executed following the data statement:

```
Proc logistic;
Class Buy;
Model Buy = ATS4 ATM4 LOY4 AGE EXP1;
run;
```

TIPS AND TOOLS OF THE TRADE

- A few basic aspects of the data help determine an appropriate multivariate data analysis dependence technique for analysis.
  - If the dependent variable is less than interval, then choose between:
    - Discriminant Analysis – particularly if more than two categories of the dependent variable exist

- Logistic regression Analysis – particularly for a dichotomous (two group) dependent variable
- If the dependent variable(s) are at least interval, the choose between:
  - Multiple regression – if the independent variables are better than interval
  - MANOVA – if the independent variables are categorical, particularly in the context of executing an experimental design

- The steps in interpreting results from dependence techniques are generally the same.
  - Is the overall model statistically significant?
  - If so, then interpret the meaning of and statistical significance of the individual independent variables.
  - Be alert for data anomalies such as unusual parameter estimates that could signal problems due to multicollinearity or other data issues, just as they might in multiple regression.
- Discriminant analysis and logistic regression are very similar. Logistic regression is particularly useful though when the dependent variable has only two categories as in success versus failure. Success may be purchase and failure no purchase.
- Using maximum likelihood estimation, the log-likelihood value leads to a chi-square value that determines the statistical significance of a logistic regression model. The entropy R^2 can be useful in determining the practical significance of a logistic regression model.
  - For individual parameter estimates for individual independent variables, the Wald statistic and the individual odds ratios are useful in interpretation.
  - Exponential coefficients (i.e., odds ratios) less than 1 indicate a variable associated with a decrease in the chance of success while coefficients greater than 2 indicate a variable associated with an increase in the chance of success.
  - Given that programs may score success the opposite of the intended value, make sure the coefficient is interpreted correctly by taking an independent samples t-test of the independent variable grouped by the dependent variable.

:: SUMMARY

1. **Understand what multivariate data analysis involves and know the two basic types of multivariate analysis.** Multivariate data analysis involves three or more variables or addresses the underlying dimensionality among multiple variables. Multivariate statistical methods analyze multiple variables or even multiple sets of variables simultaneously. The two basic types of multivariate analysis are dependence techniques and interdependence techniques.

2. **Define Dependence Techniques.** Multivariate dependence techniques are those multivariate procedures that predict some observed dependent variable using a combination(s) of predictors that serve as independent variables. Dependence techniques clearly distinguish Y variables from X variables. Multiple regression, MANOVA, discriminant analysis, and logistic regression are common multivariate dependence techniques.

3. **Interpret Results from Multivariate Analysis of Variance (MANOVA).** MANOVA is a multivariate dependence technique involving two or more, related, metric dependent variables predicted by a set (one or more) of less than interval dependent variables. MANOVA can accommodate covariates in the same way as ANCOVA, which turns it into a MANCOVA model. The multivariate F statistic is based on a statistic known as Wilks Lambda (Λ). The test answers the question of whether or not a model or independent variable predicts a significant portion of variance among the set of dependent variables.

4. **Know what discriminant analysis can be used to do.** Discriminant analysis is a multivariate technique that predicts a categorical dependent variable based on a linear combination of independent variables. The results try to explain why an observation falls into one group or another. Discriminant analysis produces a discriminant score that is compared to a cutting score. Group membership is determined by comparing the discriminant score for an observation to the cutting score. The results include a confusion matrix, or cross-classification matrix, which shows how many observations are correctly classified by the discriminant model. Discriminant analysis can be thought of as the reverse of MANOVA.

5. **Interpret a logistic regression model output.** Logistic regression is a multivariate technique involving prediction of a categorical, dichotomous dependent variable (such as success versus failure) using metric and/or less than interval independent variables. The logit value serves as the continuous number predicted by the logistic regression equation. A logit is the log of the odds of some occurrence. The logit is determined from the natural log of the odds of success. A logit of less than 0 is associated with a greater likelihood of failure. A logit of more than 0 is associated with a greater likelihood of success.

∷ KEY TERMS AND CONCEPTS

–2LL, *542*
cutting score, *538*
dependence techniques, *530*
discriminant analysis, *538*
discriminant score, *538*
entropy (pseudo) R², *543*
exponential logistic coefficient, *543*
likelihood value, *542*
logistic regression, *541*
logit, *541*

MANCOVA, *532*
multivariate analysis of variance (MANOVA), *532*
multivariate data analysis, *529*
multivariate result, *533*
multivariate statistical methods, *529*
odds of success, *541*
variate, *529*
Wald statistic, *543*
Wilks lambda (Λ), *535*

∷ QUESTIONS FOR REVIEW AND CRITICAL THINKING

1. Why is multivariate data analysis particularly useful in big data analysis?
2. What is the key characteristic identifying multivariate data analysis?
3. Explain the concept of a variate in multivariate data analysis.
4. Define dependence techniques and give examples of multivariate dependence techniques.
5. What are the steps in interpreting multivariate dependent analysis techniques?
6. What is MANOVA? What distinguishes MANCOVA from MANOVA?
7. What is the additional layer of testing involved in MANOVA compared to ANOVA?
8. Explain the role of Wilks Lambda (Λ) in MANOVA and MANCOVA.

9. How is a cutting score used to determine group membership in discriminant analysis?
10. How are MANOVA and discriminant analysis related?
11. What is a confusion matrix?
12. What is the primary difference in applications between discriminant analysis and logistic regression analysis?
13. What types of research questions can be addressed by logistic regression?
14. Explain what the likelihood value is used for in interpreting logistic regression results.
15. What is an entropy or pseudo R^2?
16. How does an analyst interpret the statistical significance and meaning of individual independent variables used in logistic regression?

∷ RESEARCH ACTIVITIES

1. Use the GoodBuy data set in this analysis. Compute a summated scale for "Loyalty" by summing LOY1, LOY2, LOY3, and LOY4. Then, conduct a MANCOVA analysis using the summed variable and WTP as dependent variables and EXP1, EXP2, CSD5 and Hours as independent variables. Include the interaction of EXP1 and EXP2 to complete a full-factorial analysis. Interpret the results and draw the appropriate conclusions.
2. Using the "Oldskool" data set introduced in Chapter 15, perform a discriminant analysis that examines the following research question:

   a. Do the variables "howplay," "loser," "money," and "winning" predict which "oldskool" group a respondent belongs to?
   b. Interpret the results with a brief report.
3. Using the same data as given earlier, examine the same research question by contrasting the low and high "oldskool" groups. To do this, recode Oldskool into a new variable that includes only those respondents in the low and high group (i.e., discard the middle group). Use logistic regression to obtain the results. Interpret your findings and compare to those obtained from discriminant analysis.

Multivariate Data Analysis: Analytics with Interdependence Techniques

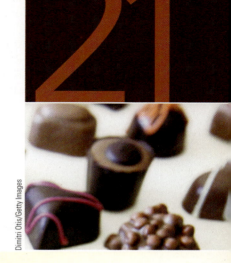

CHAPTER 21

Dimitri Otis/Getty Images

LEARNING OUTCOMES

After studying this chapter, you should be able to:

1. Distinguish interdependence techniques from dependence techniques
2. Conduct exploratory factor analysis
3. Interpret factor analysis results
4. Understand how cluster analysis is a useful big data tool
5. Interpret cluster analysis results

In the previous chapter, we introduced multivariate data analysis. Multivariate data analysis pulls together information from multiple variables to help create meaning and intelligence that no single variable alone could provide. We brought up the concept of nostalgia in the previous chapter as potentially useful to marketing managers. In fact, nostalgia creates a mixture of feelings, but most of the feelings are positive. In addition, nostalgia helps build bonds between people, meaning consumers may feel greater loyalty toward service providers.[1] When someone thinks about a previous vacation destination, the longing to revisit a place associated strongly with pleasant memories creates strong attraction. Nostalgia creates a push factor that motivates consumers to return to a destination.[2] Most of what we know about nostalgia and its role in marketing and consumer behavior comes from multivariate data analysis.

While the previous chapter concentrates on dependence techniques, which the analyst uses to predict some dependent variable, this chapter focuses on interdependence techniques. The focus here will be on ways to simplify the information contained in many, many variables. In a way, these techniques condense information from large amounts of variables and respondents into a more manageable and more understandable form. We begin with an overview of interdependence techniques.

Interdependence Techniques

Multivariate statistical techniques fall into two broad categories: dependence and interdependence techniques. The last chapter described dependence techniques where the main objective is to predict one or more dependent variables. Results from a dependence technique provide us with an idea of how important outcomes like sales, satisfaction, loyalty, or perceived value may respond to changes in other variables like price, quality levels, promotion policies, or even individual difference characteristics.

Interdependence techniques take on a different objective. Rather than predicting some observed outcome, **interdependence techniques** make no distinction between independent and dependent variables and seek to identify the underlying structure of a set of data. That structure could come in the form of identifying dimension or in identifying groups based on similarity. Usually, the analysis of variables into dimensions calls for factor analysis. In contrast, the arrangement of respondents into groups calls for cluster analysis.

Exhibit 21.1 provides a guide as to when to apply specific interference techniques. We provide a working introduction for each in this chapter. Once the analyst realizes that no distinction between independent and dependent variables is necessary to address the research questions, the question becomes whether the research is intended to identify dimensions or groups that will comprise potential segments. **Dimensions** can be thought of as the underlying meanings that help provide structure to common observations. Alternatively, from a mathematical standpoint, dimensions represent the minimum number of coordinates needed to exactly identify some point within a space. Think about any object in a room. Using the distance from the floor, one can determine its height. Using its distance from the two perpendicular walls, one can determine the objects location on the floor. Using all three dimensions, distance from the floor, distance from the entry wall, and distance from the left sidewall, one can exactly identify the object's location. On the other hand, marketing researchers have a strong interest in groups, with each group representing a potential market segment. A **segment** consists of a number of observations, which in marketing research usually means people, who share characteristics that are associated with preference for some firm's value proposition.

The remainder of this chapter focuses on the most common approaches at identifying and studying dimensions and market segments. Both factor analysis and cluster analysis fill these rolls as shown in Exhibit 21.1. Before getting into each technique, the reader should understand that both factor analysis and cluster analysis are not a single technique, but classes of statistical tools that help address issues related to dimensionality and groupings, respectively.

Interdependence techniques are thus different than dependence techniques. The biggest difference in interdependence techniques is the lack of a need to draw a distinction between independent and dependent variables. With interdependence, we focus on how variables and sets of variables simultaneously relate to each other. In other words, the focus is not on how any single variable or small set of variables relate to, or *cause*, any single other variable. Interdependence

Interdependence techniques

Multivariate statistics that make no distinction between independent and dependent variables and seek to identify the underlying structure of a set of data.

Dimensions

Underlying meanings that help provide structure to common observations.

Segment

A number of observations sharing characteristics associated with some outcome of interest.

EXHIBIT **21.1**
Using Interdependence
Techniques

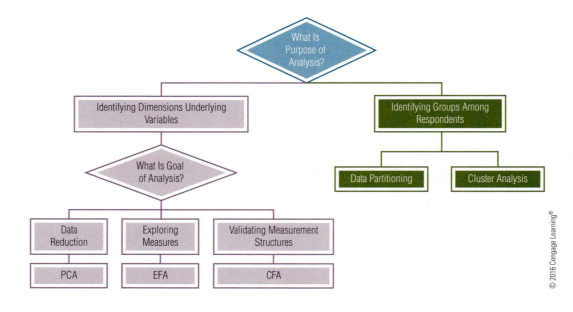

© 2016 Cengage Learning®

techniques sometimes are precursors to dependence techniques as the dimensions that factor anal-ysis uncovers or the segment memberships found in cluster analysis may provide variables useful in regression-based techniques or techniques rooted in ANOVA.

Performing Factor Analysis

Given the lack of a dependent variable, conducting factor analysis is unique in some ways over other techniques covered in this text. We begin with a basic overview of factor analysis.

What Is Factor Analysis?

As described in the previous chapter, all multivariate procedures involve a mathematical variate. We can think of a variate of this form:

$$X_i = L_1F_1 + L_2F_2 + \cdots + L_kF_k$$

X is the observed relationship for the ith variable. L_k is the **factor loading** of a variable on factor k. A factor loading is the correlation between a variable and any factor. Often, we refer to these using only the word *loading*. The greater in absolute value the loading, the stronger the connection between a factor and the individual variable. Each F represents one of k factors. A **factor** is an underlying dimension that helps understand the nature of the variables in a data set.

Mathematically, a data set can produce as many factors as there are variables in a data set. If an analyst is examining 10 variables, it's possible to extract 10 factors. Any observation can be repre-sented without error when the number of factors equals the number of variables. However, most often the analyst does not have interest in that many factors and instead looks for a solution that represents the data with fewer factors than variables. Factor analysis seeks parsimony. **Parsimony** means the researcher seeks a simple solution that still maintains sufficient meaning to represent reality. As a consequence, factor analysis can take on the following form:

$$X_i = L_1F_1 + \cdots + L_fF_f + \varepsilon_i$$

Notice two key differences from the equation above. Now, the number of factors ranges to f instead of k. This is a key distinction because f is less than k. The analyst determines how many fac-tors will be used, often based on the suggestion of or defaults built into factor analysis programs. When factor analysis involves k factors, all of the data about a variable is retained; no information is lost. Each variable is now represented as a linear combination of k factors. When only f factors are retained however, some information about each observation will be lost because the factors beyond the fth factor are not retained. Consequently, this new equation includes ε_i, which repre-sents the error introduced by including less than all possible factors.

Exhibit 21.2 provides a graphical illustration of what factor analysis does. This illustration involves only two variables. Realize that in reality, factor analysis is a tool that deals with many

Factor loading

The correlation between a variable and any factor.

Factor

An underlying dimension that helps understand the nature of the variables in a data set.

Parsimony

Means the researcher seeks a simple solution that still maintains sufficient meaning to represent reality.

EXHIBIT **21.2**
Illustration of Factor Analysis

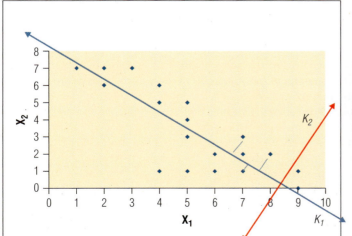

Notice almost all points are uniquely identified on the K_1 axes.

On other axes, several points share the same position and thus cannot be uniquely identified.

© 2016 Cengage Learning®

variables simultaneously. While practically not realistic, the two variable case nonetheless provides a useful illustration. If we use the coordinates for the traditional X_1 and X_2 axes, or dimensions, we can exactly identify each point plotted in the exhibit. What if we wanted to represent these points in a simpler way? If we use only the X_1 dimension, we would introduce considerable error as we can see that several points could not be distinguished from each other. If we traced a line from each point back to X_1, many points would trace back to the same point. Thus, X_1 alone does not do a good job of distinguishing the data. Similarly, if we use the X_2 dimension, we would introduce similar error. Thus, in the X_1-X_2 plane, both dimensions are necessary to represent the data adequately.

However, what if instead we reoriented the data around the alternative dimensions K_1 and K_2? Now, if we use only K_1, we can represent most data points uniquely. If one were to trace a line from each point to the K_1 axis, every point would trace back to a unique spot on the dimension. In contrast, K_2 adds little meaning. Thus, we could use only one dimension, retain most of the information in the data, and introduce a very small amount of error. In contrast to the X_1-X_2 plane, we can simplify the representation by using only K_1 without sacrificing substantial meaning. In essence, this is what factor analysis allows us to do. We reorient the data around alternative dimensions that allow useful and often more clear interpretations by adopting a simpler representation that involves fewer dimensions.

Factor analysis

A prototypical multivariate, interdependence technique. Factor analysis is a technique capable of statistically identifying a reduced number of factors from a larger number of measured variables.

Factor analysis is a prototypical multivariate, interdependence technique. Factor analysis is a technique capable of statistically identifying a reduced number of factors from a larger number of measured variables. The factors themselves are not measured, but instead, they are identified by forming a variate using the measured variables. Factors are usually latent constructs like personality, intelligence, attitude, or perceived value. A **latent construct** is a specific phenomenon that is unobservable directly. We can't accurately tell how intelligent someone is or what their personality is by just looking at a photograph or by knowing their name. Instead, we use multiple observations, or measures, to try to determine what their intelligence and personality are really like.

Latent construct

An unobservable phenomenon that can be inferred from multiple measures.

Factor Analysis Approaches

Analysts apply factor analysis for at least three broad reasons, each requiring a different analytical approach. These three purposes and the corresponding factor analysis approach are:

1. **Data reduction.** Here, the researcher seeks parsimony. Thus, the major objective is to reduce the number of pieces of information needed to interpret the data. Rather than analyzing fifty variables, we will find it simpler to analyze five factors. Furthermore, a data reduction approach helps identify variables that don't relate strongly to the other variables in the data set and as a consequence may not be so useful in understanding the data. Out of the fifty original variables, only forty may be needed to represent five factors. When data reduction is the primary goal, the analyst will likely choose a component-based factor analysis approach. We will describe this later in the chapter.

Exploratory factor analysis (EFA)

Factor analysis that seeks information about how many factors may exist among a set of variables and which variables most represent each factor; used when researcher is uncertain about both questions (number of factors and which variables belong to each).

2. **Exploratory factor analysis (EFA).** EFA is performed when the researcher is uncertain about how many factors may exist among a set of variables or which variables most represent which factors. EFA procedures can overlap with data reduction, but EFA places more emphasis on the creation of **composite factor scores**, which are numbers that represent an individual respondent's score on each individual latent factor; they are determined as a function of the variables in a factor analysis. A summated or averaged scale is one way to represent a factor score on a given factor (see Chapter 10). Another way to compute factor scores is to use a factor analysis program to create scores. The program computes scores like we calculated predicted values in multiple regression. Each variable's contribution to the score is weighted proportionately to its loading. With EFA, the analyst uses these scores in other analyses meaning that EFA is not the end of the analysis.

Composite factor scores

Numbers that represent an individual respondent's score on an each individual latent factor.

3. **Confirmatory factor analysis (CFA).** We will define this in detail in the next chapter. But, the approach is entirely different as the researcher must have strong theoretical expectations about the factor structure before performing the analysis. CFA is the best single tool for assessing construct validity. One big advantage is that CFA provides a test of how well the researcher's "theory" about the factor structure fits the actual observations. CFA requires a rigorous approach to factor analysis that we cover in detail in the next chapter.

To the Point

"Simplicity is the ultimate sophistication."

—LEONARDO DA VINCI

The first two approaches overlap somewhat in that in both cases, the goal is to identify dimensions from variables. A pure data reduction orientation places less of a burden on developing a measure for a latent factor that would represent the dimension. In data reduction, the whole purpose of identifying fewer factors from many variables may be to give some idea of the structure of the data overall. With EFA, the orientation is more toward an exploratory analysis that yields measures of factors represented by the composite factor scores. In this chapter, the illustrations apply well to either the data reduction or EFA approaches.

Illustrations of Factor Analysis

Exhibit 21.3 illustrates factor analysis graphically. Suppose a researcher is asked to examine the effectiveness of creating feelings of nostalgia in a restaurant on customer loyalty. Three hundred fifty customers at themed restaurants around the country are interviewed and asked to respond to the following Likert scales (1 = Strongly Disagree to 7 = Strongly Agree):

X_1—I feel a strong connection to the past when I am in this place.
X_2—This place evokes memories of the past.
X_3—I feel a yearning to relive past experiences when I dine here.
X_4—This place looks like a page out of the past.
X_5—I am willing to pay more to dine in this restaurant.
X_6—I feel very loyal to this establishment.
X_7—I enjoy recommending this place to others.
X_8—I will go out of my way to dine here.

Factor analysis can summarize the information in the eight variables in a smaller number of factors, perhaps two in this case. More than one technique exists for estimating the variates that form the factors. However, the general idea is to mathematically produce variates that explain the most total variance among the set of variables being analyzed. If the factor results suggested two factors, Exhibit 21.3 would represent the results. Thus, EFA provides two important pieces of information:

1. How many factors exist among a set of variables?
2. What variables match up or "load on" which factors?

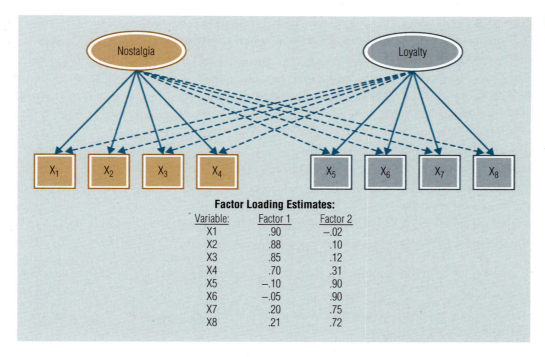

EXHIBIT **21.3**

A Simple Illustration of Factor Analysis

Factor Loading Estimates:

Variable:	Factor 1	Factor 2
X1	.90	−.02
X2	.88	.10
X3	.85	.12
X4	.70	.31
X5	−.10	.90
X6	−.05	.90
X7	.20	.75
X8	.21	.72

Factor Loadings

Each arrow connecting a factor (represented by an oval in Exhibit 21.3) to a variable (represented by a box in the exhibit) is associated with a factor loading. Factor analysis techniques produce loading estimates as regression produces regression coefficient estimates. A factor loading indicates how strongly correlated a factor is with a measured variable. In other words, to what extent does a variable "load" on a factor? EFA depends on the loadings for proper interpretation. The pattern of loadings and the content of the variables provide the means for interpreting each factor's meaning. In this way, the latent factor (construct) represents the variables.

Factor analysis software provides loading estimates. In Exhibit 21.3, the factor loading estimates are shown beneath the factor diagram. The thick arrows indicate high loading estimates and the thin dotted lines correspond to weak loading estimates. We interpret factors by examining any patterns that emerge from the factor results. Here, a clear pattern emerges. The first four variables produce high loadings on factor 1 and the last four variables produce high loadings on factor 2.

When a clear pattern of factor loadings emerges, interpretation is easy. Because the first four variables all have content consistent with nostalgia and the second four variables all have content consistent with customer loyalty, the two factors can easily be labeled. Factor one represents the latent construct nostalgia and factor 2 represents the latent construct customer loyalty.

Data Reduction Technique

Data reduction technique

A statistical technique that allows a researcher to summarize information from many variables into a reduced set of variates.

Factor analysis is considered a **data reduction technique**. Data reduction techniques allow a researcher to summarize information from many variables into a reduced set of variates or composite variables. Data reduction is advantageous for many reasons. In general, the rule of parsimony suggests an explanation involving fewer components is better than one involving many more. Factor analysis accomplishes data reduction by capturing variance from many variables with a single variate. Data reduction is also a way of identifying which variables among a large set might be important in some analysis. Thus, data reduction simplifies decision-making.

In our example, the researcher can now form two composite factors representing the latent constructs nostalgia and customer loyalty. These can be formed using factor equations of this form:

$$F_k = L_1X_1 + L_2X_2 + L_3X_3 + L_4X_4 + L_5X_5 + L_6X_6 + L_7X_7 + L_8X_8$$

where

F_k is the factor score for the kth factor—in this case there are two factors
L represents factor loadings (ith) 1 through 8 for the corresponding factor
X represents the value of the corresponding measured variable

Using this type of equation, factor analysis can compute composite factor scores for factor 1 and factor 2 as a function of the variables X_1–X_8 weighted in proportion to the corresponding loading estimates. If the researcher wants to analyze the relationship among these variables, now all that needs to be done is to analyze the bivariate correlation between factor 1 (nostalgia) and factor 2 (loyalty). This should prove much easier than analyzing an 8×8 correlation matrix.

We can see that because F_1 is associated with high values for L_1 through L_4 (and low values for L_5, L_6, L_7, and L_8) and F_2 is associated with high values for L_5 through L_8 (and low for L_1, L_2, L_3, and L_4), F_1 is determined almost entirely by the nostalgia items and F_2 is determined almost entirely by the customer loyalty items. The factor pattern of high and low loadings can be used to match measured variables to factors in this way.

Creating Composite Scales with Factor Results

When a clear pattern of loadings exists as in this case, the analyst may take a simpler scoring approach. F_1 could be created by summing the four variables with high loadings and creating a summated scale representing nostalgia. F_2 could be created by summing the second four variables (those loading highly on F_2) and creating a second summated variable. This would introduce only a little error given the pattern of loadings. In other words, very low loadings suggest a variable does not contribute much to the factor. The analyst could estimate the reliability of each summated scale by computing a coefficient alpha estimate. Afterwards, the analyst could conduct a simple regression analysis that would test how much nostalgia contributed to loyalty.

Factor analysis is commonly used to reduce the number of variables that need to be included in a regression analysis. For instance, a set of twenty-four variables may be factor analyzed and the results used to create four independent, latent variables (i.e., constructs). The variables could each be represented by a summated or averaged scale for each modeled latent variable.

Communality

A researcher may wish to know how much a single variable has in common with all factors. Communality is a measure of the percentage of a variable's variation that is explained by the factors. A relatively high communality indicates that a variable has much in common with the other variables taken as a group. Communality for any variable is equal to the sum of the squared loadings for that variable across all factors extracted. The communality for X_1 is:

$$0.90^2 - 0.02^2 = 0.8104$$

These values are shown on factor analysis printouts.

Average Variance Explained

Along with the factor loadings and communalities, the percentage of variance explained (or extracted) among the original variables by the factors can be useful. Recall that variance is correlation squared. Factor analysis techniques often present loadings as standardized values that one can interpret in the same way.[3] Thus, if each loading is squared, the result represents how much variance that particular factor and that particular variable have in common. If these summed factor loadings are averaged, we can estimate how much variance a factor has in common with the entire set of variables. This explanation of variance is much the same as R^2 in multiple regression. In this case, though, the variance accounted for among the eight variables by the nostalgia factor is 0.36, and the variance among the eight variables explained by the loyalty factor is 0.35. We can illustrate using the loadings from factor 1:

$$AVE = \frac{(0.90^2 + 0.88^2 + 0.85^2 + 0.70^2 - 0.10^2 - 0.05^2 + 0.20^2 + 0.21^2)}{8} = 0.36$$

Thus, the two factors explain 71 percent of the variance in the eight variables:

$$0.36 + 0.35 = 0.71$$

An extension of this idea is sometimes used to help validate composite factors. Simply put, if only four items are used to create a summated scale, then the average variance explained for each of the four items can be used to indicate convergent validity for a factor. This is one statistic that is sometimes necessary to compute manually. If four items are used to form a composite scale and they have loadings of 0.7, −0.7, 0.8, and 0.9, respectively, the variance explained for the scale is

$$\frac{0.7^2 + (-0.7)^2 + 0.8^2 + 0.9^2}{4} = 0.61$$

In the example shown in Exhibit 21.3, a nostalgia construct made up of $X_1 - X_4$ would produce an average variance explained of:

$$AVE_{Nostalgia} = \frac{(0.90^2 + 0.88^2 + 0.85^2 + 0.70^2)}{4} = 0.70$$

Ideally, the researcher would like scales to explain at least half of the total variation among the measured variables. Thus, the nostalgia measure passes this guideline.

How Many Factors?

Oftentimes, the researcher asks the question, "How many factors will exist among a large number of variables?" While a mathematical discussion is beyond the scope of this text, the question is usually addressed based on the eigenvalues for a factor solution. Eigenvalues are a measure of how much variance is explained by each factor. The most common rule is to base the number of factors on the number of eigenvalues greater than 1.0. This is the default rule for most statistical programs. So, unless some other rule is specified, the number of factors shown in a factor solution is based on this rule.

Factor Rotation

Factor rotation is a mathematical way of further simplifying factor results that involves new reference axes for a set of variables. The most common type of factor rotation is a process called **Varimax**. A Varimax rotation maintains a 90-degree angle between all factors, which means the factors are unrelated to each other ($r = 0$). Not all rotation tools keep this assumption. Some, such as **Promax**, produce factors that represent the degree of correlation among the factors ($r \neq 0$). Rotations that allow correlation are sometimes called oblique because the dimensions do not form right angles; that is they are more or less than 90 degrees.

A further discussion of the technical aspects of the concept of factor rotation is far beyond the scope of this book. However, rotation is critically important because an initial factor solution often proves difficult to interpret. Rotation clears things up by producing more obvious patterns of loadings. Users should experiment with this by looking at unrotated and rotated solutions.

Components or Factors?

Sometimes, the word component is used in place of factor to represent an underlying dimension that is correlated with multiple variables in a data set. Factor analysis shares much in common with **Principal Components Analysis (PCA)**, a multivariate tool that at times can be difficult to distinguish from factor analysis. Many, but not all, statisticians consider PCA a factor analysis tool and software packages often comingle access to the two approaches. PCA employs a different computational approach that involves assumptions about the variance of the variables. Here, we'll only give a basic overview of the differences. The analyst applying factor analysis approaches needs to be aware that a distinction can be made so he or she is not surprised should someone ask a question about why a *common factor analysis* approach is used instead of PCA, or vice versa.

Exhibit 21.4 provides an illustration of the concept of variance, first introduced in Chapter 13. Here, the oval shape represents the combined variance of three variables (X_1, X_2, and X_3). The variance exists in three components that we can think of as having the following sources:

- Common variance—source of variance is common to all variables (communality)
- Specific variance—source of variance is specific to an individual variable
- Error variance—source of variance is external to variables or factors such as faulty measurement or other error sources

PCA identifies components (the term used rather than factors in PCA) based on all three sources of variance.[4] In contrast, common factor analysis approaches ignore variance that could not

Factor rotation

A mathematical way of simplifying factor results that involves a new reference axes for the data; produces more obvious patterns of loadings.

Varimax

Most common type of factor rotation. Maintains a 90-degree angle between all factors, which produces factors that are uncorrelated with each other.

Promax

A rotation technique that produces factors that represent the degree of correlation among factors; i.e., an oblique rotation.

Principal Components Analysis (PCA)

A multivariate tool that at times can be difficult to distinguish from factor analysis and which employs a different computational approach.

EXHIBIT 21.4

Parts of Variance Involved in Data Reduction

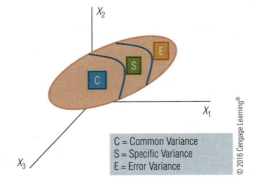

C = Common Variance
S = Specific Variance
E = Error Variance

© 2016 Cengage Learning®

reliably be associated with a factor (i.e., error variance). Because of this difference, PCA has an advantage in identifying variables that just don't seem to belong with the others.

Many articles provide detailed contrasts between the two approaches. However, for most practical purposes the differences are small, particularly when a set of variables has high communality.[5] The steps to conduct the two analyses are virtually indistinguishable in most applications. Thus, we will not dwell further on the distinction. Even though there are technical differences, the reader can consider the terms *component* and *factor* interchangeable in this chapter.

Conducting a Factor Analysis

Exhibit 21.5 provides the steps for conducting a factor analysis. Even before getting to this point, the analyst should have screened the data for as much administrative and respondent error as possible and eliminated outliers. Then, proceed as follows:

1. Select variables for the analysis. The analyst should include variables that are expected to share variance in common either based on some theoretical expectation or based on prior empirical tests suggesting correlation among the set of variables.
2. Identify an initial solution. An initial solution will provide key statistics useful in determining how to proceed through the proceeding steps.
3. From the initial solution, decide on the number of factors to be included in the analysis. The eigenvalues produced by the initial solution provide good empirical evidence to help answer this question.

   a. As described above, the most common decision is to retain the number of factors that display an eigenvalue of at least 1.0.
   b. Alternatively, the analyst may look for a place where the difference in eigenvalues for each component is small relative to other differences. A **scree plot** graphs eigenvalues against the number of factors and provides a visual clue to where the addition of one more factor adds little additional common variance.
   c. Examine item communalities and consider deleting items with low communalities (for instance, below 0.4 could be considered low).
4. Run the analysis again and include rotation of the factors. If the default solution above needed no adjustments, and if the options include factor rotation in the initial solution, this step may not be needed. The analyst also may choose between a common factor analysis approach or a PCA approach.

   a. If PCA is desired or acceptable, then the "initial solution" method should be principal components analysis.
   b. If not, a common factor analysis approach such as maximum likelihood or principle axes factoring, two of the most typical approaches, is selected by instructing the software to do so.

Scree plot

Graphs eigenvalues against the number of factors and provides a visual clue to where the addition of one more factor adds little additional common variance.

	Strongly Disagree	Disagree	Somewhat Disagree	Slightly Disagree	Slightly Agree	Somewhat Agree	Agree	Strongly Agree
I like to have the newest cell phone.	O	O	O	O	O	O	O	O
I don't care what kind of phone I have, as long as it works.	O	O	O	O	O	O	O	O
I prefer to take pictures with a separate camera to the one on a phone	O	O	O	O	O	O	O	O
A smartphone is worth the added expense it costs each month	O	O	O	O	O	O	O	O
Because of my cell phone usage habits, unlimited packages are the best for me.	O	O	O	O	O	O	O	O
I prefer to buy a new computer instead of upgrading my old one.	O	O	O	O	O	O	O	O
I make sure my software always has the latest service updates.	O	O	O	O	O	O	O	O
I want to always have the latest version of my software programs.	O	O	O	O	O	O	O	O
Anti-virus programs are a must on my computer.	O	O	O	O	O	O	O	O
I get confused with all of the choices for computers.	O	O	O	O	O	O	O	O
It is important for me to get the latest HDTV as soon as I can afford it.	O	O	O	O	O	O	O	O
All of the new televisions are too confusing.	O	O	O	O	O	O	O	O

1. Select the variables for analysis
   • Variables believed to share communality
2. Identify an initial solution
   • Factor analysis usually involves multiple runs
3. Decide the number of factors
   • Based on eigenvalues as usual criterion
4. Rotate the solution
   • Varimax most typical rotation
5. Interpret the factors from rotated solution
   • Match variables with factors
   • Delete variables with low communality
   • Repeat process if needed

EXHIBIT 21.5

Steps in Conducting Factor Analysis

5. Interpret the factors from the rotated solution. Examine the pattern of loadings. Match items with relatively high loadings on a single factor to help interpret factors. Many factor procedures, including Varimax rotation, yield standardized loadings that we can interpret like correlation coefficients. A loading of |0.7| or more is considered strong and a loading of at least |0.6| is considered relatively high. The signs of the loadings are irrelevant in determining the strength of relationship between a variable and a factor, but the signs are very relevant in interpreting the meaning of a factor. For instance, the pattern of positive and negative signs could determine whether a factor score meant satisfaction or dissatisfaction. **Simple structure** is a term capturing the type of results that neatly line up variables with only a single factor. **Cross (split)-loadings**, meaning a variable(s) has relatively high loadings on more than one factor, do not exist in a solution with simple structure. In this case, variables with loadings of |0.50| or above on more than one factor create concern about cross-loadings. Cross-loadings make the factor solution difficult if not impossible to interpret.

Simple structure

A term capturing the type of results that neatly line up variables with only a single factor.

Cross (split)-loadings

A variable(s) has relatively high loadings on more than one factor; cross-loadings do not exist in a solution with simple structure.

a. Again, the analyst may examine the solution for items with low communalities or low loadings (communalities are functions of loadings) and consider deleting these items and redoing the analysis. Likewise, items exhibiting cross-loading (i.e., split-loaded) are candidates for deletion.

b. Once the analyst is comfortable with the solution, meaning each factor has an unambiguous interpretation, factor scores for each respondent can be computed if needed.

The research snapshot shows how to obtain factor analysis results using statistical software. Given that factor analysis is not a single technique, but it is a family of techniques, these steps serve as a guide from which the user should experiment to see other variations of the basic factor analysis approach.

Interpreting Factor Analysis

We illustrate factor analysis using variables Q85_1 to Q85_12 from the Qualtrics "Survey This" Feature. An abbreviated data set is included in the resources for this chapter so the user can "click along." The data set includes 309 responses. In this case, maximum likelihood is used as the extraction method. Exhibit 21.6 displays annotated factor analysis results.

The exhibit displays both a chart of eigenvalues and a scree plot. In this case, a four-factor solution would retain 62 percent of the variance in the data. The scree plot suggests nothing that would strongly point to a different conclusion. It does show a slight flattening after the fifth component, but not so much as to move away from the four-factor solution. The analyst chooses maximum likelihood as the extraction method and Varimax as the rotation method. The exhibit shows the loadings estimates that result. A preliminary interpretation can be made by pairing strong loadings with factors.

EXHIBIT 21.6

Interpreting Factor Analysis Output

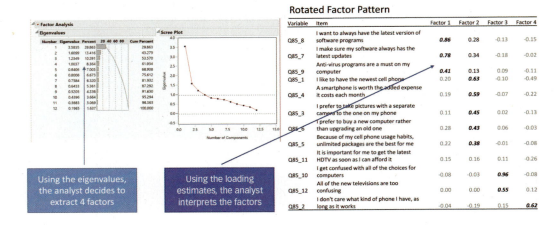

Rotated Factor Pattern

Variable	Item	Factor 1	Factor 2	Factor 3	Factor 4
Q85_8	I want to always have the latest version of software programs	*0.86*	0.28	-0.13	-0.15
Q85_7	I make sure my software always has the latest updates	*0.78*	0.34	-0.18	-0.02
Q85_9	Anti-virus programs are a must on my computer	*0.41*	0.13	0.09	-0.11
Q85_1	I like to have the newest cell phone	0.20	*0.63*	-0.10	-0.49
Q85_4	A smartphone is worth the added expense it costs each month	0.19	*0.59*	-0.07	-0.22
Q85_3	I prefer to take pictures with a separate camera to the one on my phone	0.11	*0.45*	0.02	-0.13
Q85_6	I prefer to buy a new computer rather than upgrading an old one	0.28	*0.43*	0.06	-0.03
Q85_5	Because of my cell phone usage habits, unlimited packages are the best for me	0.22	*0.38*	-0.01	-0.08
Q85_11	It is important for me to get the latest HDTV as soon as I can afford it	0.15	0.16	0.11	-0.26
Q85_10	I get confused with all of the choices for computers	-0.08	-0.03	*0.96*	-0.08
Q85_12	All of the new televisions are too confusing	0.00	0.00	*0.55*	0.12
Q85_2	I don't care what kind of phone I have, as long as it works	-0.04	-0.19	0.15	*0.62*

Using the eigenvalues, the analyst decides to extract 4 factors

Using the loading estimates, the analyst interprets the factors

How to Conduct Factor Analysis

We will begin by illustrating factor analysis in SPSS. Follow these steps:

1. Click on Analyze.
2. Navigate to "Dimension Reduction" and then choose "Factor."
3. Click on "Extraction."
   a. Select "Method" from choices, such as Principal Components," which is the default in SPSS.
   b. Select how many factors will be retained from either "Extract based on eigenvalues greater than 1" or by choosing a number in the "Fixed Number of Factors" choice.
   c. Click Continue.
4. Click on rotation. Choose rotation method, such as Varimax. Click Continue.
5. If the analyst wants the software to automatically compute weighted composite factor scores, click on "Scores" and select "Save as Variables" (use the default regression method of scoring). The scores appear in the data set upon execution. Click Continue.
6. Optional: Click on "Options" and check "Sorted by Size." This only changes the order that SPSS lists variables in the factor pattern output. Click Continue.
7. Click OK.

In JMP, the approach is a little different. Follow these steps:

1. Click on Analyze.
2. Navigate to "Consumer Research" and select "Factor Analysis" from the choices.
3. Select the variables and move them into the Y_i Columns window. Click OK.
4. Initial results will appear. They include:
   a. A list of eigenvalues.
   b. A scree plot.
   c. Using one or both of these, or some other theoretical reason, choose the number of factors and enter it into the "Number of Factors" window.
   d. Select a factoring method: Principal Components Analysis or Maximum Likelihood. If using PCA, select Principal Components for "Prior Communality." Otherwise, select "Common Factor Analysis."
   e. Click "Go."
5. If the analyst wishes for JMP to create weighted composite factor scores, click on the red triangle just above "Final

Communality Estimates" beside "Factor Analysis on Correlations." Choose save "rotated components." Scores for each factor appear in the data set.

In traditional SAS, a program like this will yield factor analysis results:

1. After completing the data step to read the variables, enter the following into the program editor:
   PROC FACTOR ROTATE = VARIMAX METHOD = P SCREE;
   VAR Q85_1 – Q85_12;
   RUN;
2. The "Method = P" means the program will extract factors using the principal components approach. If an initial common factor approach is desired, choose METHOD = PRINIT for principle axes or METHOD = M for maximum likelihood. PROC PRINCOMP also can be used for a PCA approach.
3. The scores option will output weighted factor scores.

EXHIBIT 21.7
2nd Round Factor Analysis

Variable	Item	Factor 1	Factor 2
Q85_8	I want to always have the latest version of software programs	*0.75*	0.30
Q85_7	I make sure my software always has the latest updates	*0.98*	0.18
Q85_1	I like to have the newest cell phone	0.25	*0.84*
Q85_4	A smartphone is worth the added expense it costs each month	0.28	*0.53*
Q85_10	I get confused with all of the choices for computers	−0.24	−0.05
Q85_2	I don't care what kind of phone I have, as long as it works	−0.05	*−0.53*

© 2016 Cengage Learning®

Items related to software and currency load highly on the first factor. Items related to opinions about phones relate to the second factor. For the third factor, the two items related to confusion about electronics load highly. Finally, the fourth factor contains only one item with a high loading, and it has something to do with ambivalence. However, the analyst decides this solution is only preliminary and decides to drop items with low communalities/loadings. In this way, data reduction is accomplished.

Based on low loadings or communalities, six items are dropped (Q85_3, Q85_5, Q85_6, Q85_9, Q85_11, and Q85_12). After dropping these items are rerunning the factor analysis, the results suggest that two factors are appropriate and explain over half of the variation in the data. The factor pattern that result is shown in Exhibit 21.7. Now, as before, the first factor represents concern about the latest software. The second factor, indicated by Q85_1, Q85_4, and Q85_2, represents concern about the latest phone. Notice that Q85_2, which has content expressing an indifference about having the latest phone, loads negatively on the second factor. In contrast, the items expressing concern about having a capable phone load negatively on the second factor. The results suggest that concern for up-to-date software and an up-to-date phone explain the data.

In a big data environment, data reduction is a key goal. From this analysis, we can see how factor analysis plays a big role in data reduction and in understanding the underlying dimensions influencing respondents' survey responses. The ability of factor analysis to explore large numbers of variables and reduce the data to a few underlying dimensions makes factor analysis an important marketing analytics tool.

Cluster Analysis as a Big Data Tool

What Is Cluster Analysis?

Cluster analysis

A multivariate approach for identifying objects or individuals that are similar to one another in some respect. An important tool for identifying market segments.

Cluster analysis is a multivariate approach for identifying objects or individuals that are similar to one another in some respect. Thus, cluster analysis is an important tool for identifying market segments. Cluster analysis classifies individuals or objects into a small number of mutually exclusive and exhaustive groups. Objects or individuals are assigned to groups so that there is great similarity within groups and much less similarity between groups. The cluster should have high internal (within-cluster) homogeneity and external (between-cluster) heterogeneity.

We will illustrate cluster analysis with a hypothetical example relating to the types of vacations taken by 12 individual consumers. We first examine a plot of the consumers' responses in two dimensions: number of vacation days and dollar expenditures on vacations during a given year. Exhibit 21.8 is a scatter diagram that represents the geometric distance between each individual in two-dimensional space. We can find the distance between any two points in two-dimensional space using a distance formula that comes from the Pythagorean Theorem.

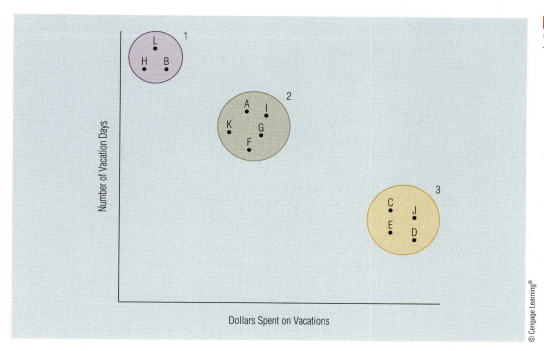

EXHIBIT **21.8**
Clusters of Individuals on
Two Dimensions

© Cengage Learning®

If we think of the distance from A to B on the X-axis as $X_{a\text{-}b}$ and on the Y-axis as $Y_{a\text{-}b}$, then the distance from A to B is:

$$D_{a-b} = \sqrt{X^2_{a-b} + Y^2_{a-b}}$$

Distances can be computed between observations, between a cluster and an observation, and between clusters. Cluster analysis seeks to put observations with low distance scores into the same group while placing observations with a high distance score in a different group.

The diagram in Exhibit 21.8 portrays three clear-cut clusters. The first subgroup, consisting of individuals L, H, and B, suggests a group of individuals who have many vacation days but do not spend much money on their vacations. The second cluster, represented by individuals A, I, K, G, and F, represents intermediate values on both variables—average amounts of vacation days and average dollar expenditures on vacations. The third group, individuals C, J, E, and D, consists of individuals who have relatively few vacation days but spend large amounts on vacations.

In this example, individuals are grouped on the basis of their similarity or proximity to one another. The logic of cluster analysis is to group individuals or objects by their similarity to, or distance from, one another. We will not dwell on the mathematical details for deriving clusters, as our purpose is only to introduce the technique and give an indication of how to interpret cluster results.

Applications of Cluster Analysis

A classic study provides a very pragmatic example of the use of cluster analysis.[6] Marketing managers frequently are interested in finding test-market cities that are very similar so that no extraneous variation will cause differences between the experimental and control markets. In this study the objects to be clustered were cities. The characteristics of the cities, such as population, retail sales, number of retail outlets, and percentage of nonwhites, were used to identify the groups. Cities such as Omaha, Oklahoma City, Dayton, Columbus, and Fort Worth were similar and cities such as Newark, Cleveland, Pittsburgh, Buffalo, and Baltimore were similar, but individual cities within each group were dissimilar to those within other groups or clusters. (See Exhibit 21.9 for additional details.)

This example illustrates the difference between factor analysis and cluster analysis. In factor analysis, the researcher might search for constructs that underlie the variables (population, retail sales, number of retail outlets); in cluster analysis the researcher would seek latent constructs that represent dimensions underlying the objects (cities).

EXHIBIT 21.9   Cluster Analysis of Test-Market Cities

Cluster Number	City	Cluster Number	City	Cluster Number	City
1	Omaha Oklahoma City Dayton Columbus Fort Worth	7	Sacramento San Bernardino San Jose Phoenix Tucson	13	Allentown Providence Jersey City York Louisville
2	Peoria Davenport Binghamton Harrisburg Worcester	8	Gary Nashville Jacksonville San Antonio Knoxville	14	Paterson Milwaukee Cincinnati Miami Seattle
3	Canton Youngstown Toledo Springfield Albany	9	Indianapolis Kansas City Dallas Atlanta Houston	15	San Diego Tacoma Norfolk Charleston Fort Lauderdale
4	Bridgeport Rochester Hartford New Haven Syracuse	10	Mobile Shreveport Birmingham Memphis Chattanooga	16	New Orleans Richmond Tampa Lancaster Minneapolis
5	Wilmington Orlando Tulsa Wichita Grand Rapids	11	Newark Cleveland Pittsburgh Buffalo Baltimore	17	San Francisco Detroit Boston Philadelphia
6	Bakersfield Fresno Flint El Paso Beaumont	12	Albuquerque Salt Lake City Denver Charlotte Portland	18	Washington St. Louis

Note: Points not in a cluster—Honolulu, Wilkes-Barre. Source: Reprinted by permission, Paul E. Green, Ronald E. Frank, and Patrick J. Robinson, "Cluster Analysis in Test-Market Selection," *Management Science*, Vol. 13, P.B393 (Table 2), April 1967. Copyright © 1967, the Institute for Operations Research and the Management Sciences (INFORMS), 7240 Parkway Drive, Suite 310, Hanover, MD 21076 USA

Cluster analysis, discriminant analysis, and logistic regression all represent classification techniques. Cluster analysis differs from multiple discriminant analysis and logistic regression in that the groups are not predefined. It does not involve a measured dependent variable. Cluster analysis searches for useful segment structures within a set of variables. Sometimes, the set of variables is very large. Think of all the variables companies like Facebook, Amazon, and Apple have stored on each consumer. Amazon can mine its Amazon Prime members in an effort to identify market segments that respond to certain types of value propositions, types of products, or types of promotions. Cluster analysis applications are computationally intensive and require a lot of computing power. Given that computers are so powerful and fast today however, cluster analysis proves very useful in exploring large numbers of variables across large numbers of consumers.

Thus, it's no surprise that cluster analysis approaches are increasingly applied as data mining and predictive analytic tools. Cluster analysis routines help identify patterns of similarity in consumers based on all data available about that particular consumer. Beyond marketing, clustering routines may even be useful in identifying groups of consumers who are more or less susceptible to various diseases based on the records that accumulate through each consumer's health care experiences. A consumer's HMO app can help provide data that may make this possible.

Cluster analysis facilitates market segmentation by identifying subjects or individuals who have similar needs, lifestyles, or responses to marketing promotions. Clusters, or subgroups, of recreational vehicle owners may be identified on the basis of their similarity with respect to recreational vehicle usage and the benefits they want from recreational vehicles. The clusters may separate motor home fans from those that prefer campers or tents. Alternatively, cluster analysis helps identify differences among social network users.[7] Some consumers tend to share news from newsfeeds more than anything else, others health-related information, others funny videos, and so forth. These clusters are related to a preference for Twitter, Facebook, Instagram, and so forth. Furthermore, each segment relates to demographic or lifestyle variables that allow us not only to group individuals into clusters to form market segments, but also to reach out to each market segment based on known habits of demographic groups.

Interpreting Cluster Analysis Output

Like factor analysis, cluster analysis actually represents a family of techniques aimed at grouping observations based on similarity of responses. All of these share the principles of grouping similar observations together. Many ways exist to reach that end.[8] Also like factor analysis, cluster analysis takes place in steps.

1. The first step is determining how many clusters to analyze. Ultimately, marketing research dictates this as a practical question. A wide variety of approaches exists to help determine a good number of clusters. The clusters have to be sufficient in size to be useful and yet specific enough to be actionable. Very small groups are not actionable and very large groups are inefficient. Although entire books can be written on the different approaches for determining the number of segments, one way is to use eigenvalues, just as we used in factor analysis. The analyst would use the number of eigenvalues greater than 1 as a guide in exploring the number of groups. This number is only a guide and cluster solutions varying one or two groups in either direction are often also explored.
2. Standardize the data used in the cluster analysis or instruct the software to analyze standardized data.
3. Cluster the observations into the number of groups suggested in the first step. Again, many ways exist to do this. **K-means** is one technique that is among the most widely used tools for assigning observations to groups. K-means requires that the user input the number of groups as part of the analysis. Then, K-means iterates by shifting observations between clusters until some minimal distance criterion is reached (usually determined by software).
4. Analyze the results. Determine the group meaning by looking for relatively high or low scores among the cluster variables on each individual cluster. Do the results make sense and are they actionable? If not, consider solutions with one more or one less group.
5. Assign observations to groups by saving the group membership to the data set.
6. Profile the results on other variables that identify the segment such as key demographics.

Exhibit 21.10 provides a summary of cluster results using the same data as used in the factor analysis example. Typically, we think of factor analysis as forming dimensions represented by variables. In contrast, we think of cluster analysis as forming groups represented by respondents. The results in Exhibit 21.10 suggest that all four groups are of adequate size. The smallest group contains 65 respondents, which represents 21 percent of the data. The largest group contains 103 respondents, or 33 percent of the data. At a minimum, the group membership, as a grouping variable, should significantly predict the variables that used to form the groups. In this case, the ANOVA results confirm that this is the case. Using the means for each group, the analyst interprets the segments. In this case, the following possible interpretations are offered:

1. Group 1 expresses relatively low means with particularly low means on Q85_8. As a result, this segment represents respondents with relative disinterest in electronic technology such as software and smartphones.
2. Group 2 expresses mixed means but is relatively low on Q85_10 and Q85_12. Both of those items indicate confusion about technology. Thus, this segment represents consumers that see themselves as tech savvy.

K-means

Among the most widely used tools for assigning observations to groups in cluster analysis

EXHIBIT 21.10

Example Cluster Results

Number of Cases in each Cluster		
Cluster	1	65.000
	2	103.000
	3	74.000
	4	67.000
Valid		309.000
Missing		.000

	ANOVA					
	Cluster		Error			
	Mean Square	df	Mean Square	df	F	Sig.
Zscore(Q85_1)	38.939	3	.627	305	62.120	.000
Zscore(Q85_2)	17.174	3	.841	305	20.423	.000
Zscore(Q85_3)	16.422	3	.848	305	19.358	.000
Zscore(Q85_4)	34.774	3	.668	305	52.074	.000
Zscore(Q85_5)	15.467	3	.858	305	18.034	.000
Zscore(Q85_6)	27.963	3	.735	305	38.056	.000
Zscore(Q85_7)	43.694	3	.580	305	75.327	.000
Zscore(Q85_8)	49.554	3	.522	305	94.854	.000
Zscore(Q85_9)	18.899	3	.824	305	22.937	.000
Zscore(Q85_10)	49.811	3	.520	305	95.811	.000
Zscore(Q85_11)	16.746	3	.845	305	19.815	.000
Zscore(Q85_12)	43.424	3	.583	305	74.519	.000

	Final Cluster Centers			
	Cluster			
	1	2	3	4
Zscore(Q85_1)	-.78646	.45705	-.56550	.68494
Zscore(Q85_2)	.27156	-.32117	.57953	-.40978
Zscore(Q85_3)	-.39435	.17054	-.42157	.58602
Zscore(Q85_4)	-.78566	.37110	-.46896	.70966
Zscore(Q85_5)	-.51958	.22133	-.30609	.50188
Zscore(Q85_6)	-.92880	.21741	-.01641	.58497
Zscore(Q85_7)	-.96744	.55144	-.45511	.59347
Zscore(Q85_8)	-1.09385	.54520	-.39243	.65648
Zscore(Q85_9)	-.72116	.16634	-.08641	.53935
Zscore(Q85_10)	-.15615	-.86675	.65695	.75836
Zscore(Q85_11)	-.25992	-.18754	-.20299	.76467
Zscore(Q85_12)	-.44968	-.66184	.86503	.49831

Shows number of observations in each group

Individual ANOVAs provide some idea of how well the grouping distinguishes responses. Here, the grouping creates significant differences in all variables

The means by cluster (group) provide a way to interpret each group

3. Group 3 expresses relatively high scores on Q85_2 and low scores on Q85_3. These two items expresses opposing attitudes about smartphones. Q85_2 indicates a desire to have the latest phone and Q85_3 express a desire to use a camera over a phone to take pictures. As a consequence of these results, this segment represents consumers oriented around their smartphone.

4. Group 4 expresses high scores on Q85_1 and Q85_11, both expressing a desire to have innovative products. Thus, this segment represents consumers eager to have the latest electronic technology.

The K-means software contains an option to store the group membership as a variable. After doing this, the analyst can profile the segment on other demographics using tools like cross-classification or *t*-tests. For instance, a cross-classification of this data suggests that segments 1 and 2 are disproportionately female and segments 3 and 4 are disproportionately male.

The ability to find actionable groups of similar respondents provides a primary reason why cluster analysis is such a useful big data tool.

TIPS AND TOOLS OF THE TRADE

- Use interdependence tools to better understand the structure of data.
  - Tools are particularly useful for exploring large amounts of data for meaning.

- Conduct factor analysis in stages.
  - Use eigenvalues to identity the number of factors needed to represent adequately the data.
    - Don't be afraid to explore +/- one factor to find a more interpretable solution.
  - Eliminate variables with low communality (< 0.5) or low loadings or those that load by themselves on a single factor. Do this in early stages. This is acceptable because the analyses are exploratory.
  - Use PCA when the goal is to reduce the number of variables or factors to interpret.

- The distinction between PCA and common factor analysis is not always practically useful because when communalities are high, the two approaches produce very similar results.
  - Simple structure provides easy interpretation and sends a signal that scales formed by the measures are potentially valid.

- Cluster analysis is a useful in identifying groups.
  - A preliminary tool like examination of eigenvalues among a set of variables helps give an idea of how many clusters may provide a useful solution.
  - Explore around that number to look for more useful arrangements of observations into clusters.

:: SUMMARY

1. Distinguish interdependence techniques from dependence techniques. Multivariate statistical approaches fall into two broad categories: dependence and interdependence techniques. Rather than predicting some observed outcome, interdependence techniques make no distinction between independent and dependent variables. Instead, they seek to identify the structure of a data set. The structure could be described either in terms of underlying dimensions or in terms of groups of observations (respondents) based on similarity with each other. In marketing, these groups describe market segments. Interdependence techniques focus on how variables and sets of variables simultaneously relate to each other.

2. Conduct exploratory factor analysis. The variate in factor analysis relates observed variables to an unobserved factor, weighting each observed variable's strength of correlation with the unobserved factor with a loading. The loading is an estimate like a regression coefficient in multiple regression. Factors are usually latent constructs like personality, intelligence, attitude, or perceived value. A latent construct is a specific phenomenon that is unobservable directly. Factor analysis simplifies data by reducing the number of variables needed to portray meaningful information. Exhibit 21.5 provides a sequence of steps to conduct a factor analysis. These steps apply for either data reduction or EFA. The first important question about factors is "how many factors?" Thus, most applications involve a sequence of factor analyses aimed at identifying a simple structure, where each variable loads strongly on only one of the factors. When the analyst is primarily interested in data reduction, reducing the number of variables, PCA makes a good initial extraction tool.

3. Interpret factor analysis results. The initial factor analysis serves to identify the number of factors needed to represent the data. The eigenvalues are useful in this with the most popular rule being to extract as many factors as there are eigenvalues of 1.0 or more. Also, the results are used to delete variables that do not show substantial relationship with other variables based on low communalities and/or loading estimates. In the subsequent factor analysis attempt, the rotated factor pattern suggests the meaning of factors based on how variables load on factors. Cross-loadings interfere with the ability to interpret data.

4. Understand how cluster analysis is a useful big data tool. Cluster analysis is a multivariate approach for identifying objects or individuals that are similar to one another in some respect. Cluster analysis puts distant consumers into separate groups and puts proximal (consumers with little distance from each other) into the same group. Cluster analysis helps identifying useful market segments. Within each segment, consumers are similar, and between each segment, consumers are different. Cluster analysis approaches can search large numbers of variables across large numbers of observations to devise useful segment structures. Given that today's computers are so relatively powerful and quick, cluster applications have become a useful big data tool.

5. Interpret cluster analysis results. Cluster analysis represents a family of techniques rather than a single statistical tool. All of these share the principles of grouping similar observations together. A key question is, how many clusters to analyze? Eigenvalues also can be useful in determining this number. K-means is a very common approach for performing cluster analysis. Once software produces results, determine the group meaning by looking for relatively high or low scores among the cluster variables on each individual cluster. Do the results make sense and are they actionable? If so, save the cluster membership for each observation by adding a group variable to the data. The resulting variable can be profiled on demographic or lifestyle variables as a means of beginning to take action on the cluster results.

:: KEY TERMS AND CONCEPTS

cluster analysis, *560*
composite factor scores, *552*
cross (split)-loadings, *558*
data reduction, *552*
data reduction technique, *554*
dimensions, *550*
exploratory factor analysis, (EFA) *552*
factor, *551*
factor analysis, *552*
factor loading, *551*

factor rotation, *556*
interdependence techniques, *550*
K-means, *563*
latent construct, *552*
parsimony, *551*
principal components analysis, (PCA) *556*
promax, *556*
scree plot, *557*
simple structure, *558*
varimax, *556*

:: QUESTIONS FOR REVIEW AND CRITICAL THINKING

1. Describe the distinction between dependence and interdependence multivariate techniques. Provide examples of each.
2. What is the difference between a dimension and a segment? Describe examples of each.
3. What is a factor loading?
4. How does factor analysis help marketing research obtain greater parsimony?
5. Define the term *latent construct*. How does factor analysis play a role in understanding latent constructs?
6. What are composite factor scores?
7. Explain the concept of communality in factor analysis. How is it related to the concept of factor loadings?
8. Suppose an initial attempt at factor analysis provided the following eigenvalues:
   a. Create a scree plot.
   b. How many factors would you suggest be used in a subsequent factor analysis?

9. What is PCA?
10. What role does rotation play in factor analysis? What does it mean for a rotation to maintain a 90-degree angle?
11. What is simple structure?
12. How does one use a factor loading matrix (factor structure pattern) in interpreting factor analysis output?
13. How is cluster analysis different from factor analysis?
14. What role does "distance" play in cluster analysis?
15. Why has cluster analysis become a more prominent tool in the big data era?
16. If someone conducted one-way ANOVAs predicting the clustering variables using the cluster membership variable that was obtained from a cluster analysis procedure, what should the expectation of the results of those ANOVAs be?
17. Define K-means.

	Eigenvalue	Percent	Cumulative
1	2.81	0.20	0.20
2	2.24	0.16	0.36
3	1.77	0.13	0.49
4	1.37	0.10	0.59
5	1.21	0.09	0.67
6	1.10	0.08	0.75
7	0.96	0.07	0.82
8	0.75	0.05	0.87
	...		

:: RESEARCH ACTIVITIES

1. Interpret the following factor analysis results. The variables represent sample results of self-reported emotions while viewing a film. What two summated scales might be produced based on these results?

Total Variance Explained

Component	Initial Eigenvalues Total	% of Variance	Cumulative %	Extraction Sums of Squared Loadings Total	% of Variance	Cumulative %
1	2.94	36.74	36.74	2.94	36.74	36.74
2	2.51	31.34	68.08	2.51	31.34	68.08
3	0.71	8.84	76.92			
4	0.60	7.53	84.45			
5	0.42	5.20	89.65			
6	0.29	3.67	93.32			
7	0.29	3.64	96.96			
8	0.24	3.04	100.00			

Extraction Method: Principal Component Analysis.

Component Matrix(a)

	Factor 1	Factor 2
Interesting	0.664	−0.327
Anxious	0.444	0.511
Enthusiastic	0.842	−0.332
Worried	0.295	0.828
Exciting	0.812	−0.206
Tired	0.269	0.835
Happy	0.784	−0.383
Guilty	0.398	0.675

Extraction Method: Principal Component Analysis.
2 components extracted.

Rotated Component Matrix(a)

	Component Factor 1	Factor 2
Interesting	0.739	−0.024
Anxious	0.194	0.648
Enthusiastic	0.904	0.044
Worried	−0.073	0.876
Exciting	0.825	0.147
Tired	−0.100	0.872
Happy	0.872	−0.025
Guilty	0.084	0.779

Extraction Method: Principal Component Analysis.
Rotation Method: Varimax with Kaiser Normalization.
Rotation converged in 3 iterations.

2. Use the OLDSKOOL data introduced in Chapter 15 for this exercise. You can download the data from the student resources located at www.cengagebrain.com. The survey captured responses to 9-Point disagree–agree attitudinal scales to the following items:

Label	Item Wording
role_mdl	Athletes should be role models for children.
no_loyal	Today's athletes have no loyalty to their team.
argues	Athletes should not argue with their coaches.
winning	In sports, winning is all that matters.
greedy	Athletes today appear greedy compared to two decades ago
req_rmdl	To represent a team, an athlete should agree to act as a role model at all times.
loyal	The demeanor of an athlete inspires my loyalty to a team
cheating	Winning does not condone cheating.
sec_best	The SEC is the best athletic football conference in college football.
show_off	Today's players are quick to show-off, even for minor accomplishments.
loser	I stick to my team, win or lose.
style	Players should be rewarded for showing style in their play.
obl_rm	Given that they represent their school, college athletes are obligated to be role models.
how_play	It's not whether you win or lose, but how you play the game that counts.
material	Big-time college athletes are only in it for material rewards.
money	There is too much money in college sports.
tm_welfr	Players put themselves before team welfare.

a. Conduct a factor analysis with the goal of reducing the number of variables needed to represent a respondent's opinions about athletes in college sports today.

b. After reducing the number of variables based on initial results, conduct factor analysis to identify the latent constructs that form dimensions among the remaining data. Interpret those constructs' meanings using the resulting factor analysis results. Create a table that shows the factor pattern (including the loadings) that results.

c. Compute the AVE for each factor.

3. Using the OLDSKOOL data, use cluster analysis to identify groups of respondents varying in their opinions on issues related to athletes in college sports today. Use the 17 items above to start.

a. How many clusters would you suggest and why?

b. Perform a K-means cluster analysis using that number of clusters and +/- one cluster. Prepare a summary table showing the results from each analysis.

c. Choose the best of the cluster solutions. Are the groups actionable? Are the groups distinct?

d. Using any available demographic information in the data set, profile the groups by using cross–classification or by comparing means across groups, whatever is most appropriate. Does the profile suggest a pattern in the results?

e. Prepare an executive summary of the results as if it were to be presented to a University Athletic Director.

4. Using the GoodBuy data set from the last chapter, choose 12 variables and conduct an exploratory factor analysis. Describe your results in tables and in a brief summary.

Primer on Structural Equations Modeling

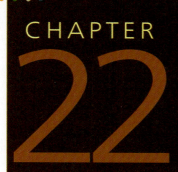

LEARNING OUTCOMES

After studying this chapter, you should be able to:

1. Distinguish SEM as a covariance technique
2. Appreciate SEM as an explanatory tool that tests theory
3. Understand and use the concept of fit
4. Conduct a confirmatory factor analysis
5. Know how to test an elementary structural theory with SEM
6. Be aware of other multivariate statistical techniques

Dimitri Otis/Getty Images

Introduction

By this point in the book, the reader is familiar with important marketing research topics such as prediction, explanation, measurement, multivariate data analysis dependence and interdependence techniques. In this final chapter, we provide a primer on a powerful multivariate technique that involves all of these topics. This particular tool owes its genesis to the fact that researchers often propose theories rather than a hypothesis or even hypotheses. Theories involve process explanations addressing how something may be caused by some sequence of events.

Statistically, testing theories leads us to multiple equation processes. On top of that, in the social sciences and even in some physical science applications, concepts defy direct measurement free from measurement error. Consequently, scientists looked for tools that could simultaneously estimate relationships among such concepts and between the concepts and the items that represent them. In this way, we can begin to understand how things relate to one another with a correction for measurement inadequacies. Although **structural equations modeling (SEM)**, the tool that accomplishes this task, was first introduced in the 1920s by a scientist named Sewall Wright, not until the 1970s with the availability of specialized software did this tool take off. **LISREL**, a program for analyzing Linear Structural Relations, was the first structural equations modeling program to be widely adopted. By the 1980s, marketing researchers started to apply SEM in significant numbers.[1]

SEM is different than other multivariate techniques discussed in the previous chapters. SEM is both an interdependence technique and a dependence technique at the same time. The fact that SEM incorporates a correction for measurement error comes from the fact that SEM combines a confirmatory factor analysis model, an interdependence technique, with structural relationship models that are conceptually similar to multiple regression, a dependence technique. SEM is widely applied in marketing research today. One study estimated that about half of marketing research journal articles apply SEM in one way or another.[2] The purpose of this chapter is to provide a basic primer in SEM.[3] The primer serves as a basic guide and footing from which the interested user can further explore SEM as a powerful analytics tool capable of addressing many types of research questions, particularly those involving latent constructs.

To the Point[4]

"All human actions have one or more of these seven causes: chance, nature, compulsions, habit, reason, passion, desire."

—ARISTOTLE

Structural equations modeling (SEM)

Allows a researcher to build theory and test a theory by assessing its fit with reality; the theory explains how constructs cause other constructs, each theory represented by a series of equations solved simultaneously.

LISREL

The first widely adopted specialized software program for conducting structural equations modeling.

Distinguishing SEM as a Covariance Technique

For many years, SEM was looked at as an extremely rigorous yet difficult technique to apply. Many considered SEM intimidating. That opinion is changing as SEM software has become increasingly user friendly. Computer programming skills were a huge advantage in applying early versions of LISREL. Today, however, LISREL and other software programs such as AMOS allow users to use a graphical interface. If a user can draw a model successfully, he or she can test it. AMOS stands for Analysis of Moment Structures.

AMOS

SEM software that stands for Analysis of Moment Structures.

One reason many found SEM so difficult is that it does involve a somewhat radically different statistical approach. SEM does not analyze raw data as do multiple regression, ANOVA, or most other statistical techniques. Recall from Chapter 18, that all of the information among a set of variables is contained in a covariance matrix (**S**). This is a critical point in understanding SEM. The individual covariances portray the relationships between each pair of variables. The diagonal portrays the variance of each individual variable. The input for SEM does not come from the individual data points but, from the covariance matrix.

Moment

A unique piece of information that serves as input to a SEM model.

SEM uses the term **moment** to represent a unique piece of information that serves as input to the model. One consequence is that the degrees of freedom for analysis are also determined by the covariance matrix. One degree of freedom exists for each unique element of a covariance matrix. Exhibit 22.1 illustrates this point. Positions 1, 3, 6, 10, and 15, are the variances of X1 through X5, respectively. The other positions each represent an individual covariance. Position 2 is where the covariance between X1 and X2 goes. Each position, 1 through 15, represents a unique moment. The positions in the upper diagonal do not add moments because they are not unique. The matrix is symmetric. The upper diagonal repeats only the same values appearing in the lower diagonal. For instance, in the second row, first column, the covariance between X1 and X2 would appear again.

For small covariance matrices, one can easily count up the unique moments. However, an easy computation provides that number:

$$Unique\ Moments = DF\ available = \frac{m(m+1)}{2}$$

DF stands for degrees of freedom and m is the number of measured variables represented in **S**. Not coincidentally, m also equals the number of rows or columns in the covariance matrix. In the Exhibit, one can easily see that $[5(5+1)/2] = 15$.

One disadvantage of using today's easy-to-use software is the fact that SEM is a covariance-based technique may not register as easily. Oftentimes, the software will compute the covariance matrix automatically as part of the analysis. In previous times, the analyst would compute the covariance matrix as a completely separate step, even doing so with software other than that used to conduct SEM. The covariance matrix contains all the information needed to run SEM and through this fact, we sacrifice nothing in terms of information.

We should note at this point that other multiple equation procedures exist that sometimes are referred to as SEM techniques. We will mention some of these later. However, in this chapter, our use of SEM refers specifically to full information, covariance-based structural equations modeling.

EXHIBIT 22.1

Unique Moments in a Covariance Matrix

		X1	X2	X3	X4	X5
S =	X1	1				
	X2	2	3			
	X3	4	5	6		
	X4	7	8	9	10	
	X5	11	12	13	14	15

SEM Is an Explanatory Tool

All of the dependence techniques discussed to this point have the goal of predicting some dependent variable. Multiple regression aims to produce $\hat{Y}$, the predicted value of Y. As these two values differ, the model R^2 gets smaller. Thus, better models are those that *explain* more of the variance in Y. Regression, like ANOVA procedures, is a variance-based approach. Covariances among independent variables are merely a nuisance. Although we use the term *explained* variance, R^2 more accurately describes the extent to which accurate prediction is possible. Even regression models with unreliable parameter estimates can predict well. Statistically and philosophically, prediction does not mean we can explain.

In contrast, analysts apply SEM when explanation is more important than prediction. In contrast to prediction, we can predict to the extent that we can explain. That may seem a little confusing, but we can think of SEM as an explanatory tool from two perspectives.

First, SEM, because it is a covariance technique, requires that models be able to account for every moment in a covariance matrix. That is, the researcher's model must not only tell how independent variables are related to dependent variables, but it must also tell how independent variables are related to one another. To the extent that the model fails in either of these attempts, it is inadequate. SEM uses all information and must account for all information. In contrast, regression seeks only to account for the variances of dependent variables.

Second, SEM is a tool for theory testing. The researcher must be able to offer an explanation of all possible relationships among variables before the technique can even be applied. Before testing a model, theory must tell how measured variables relate to latent constructs and theory must tell how latent constructs relate to one another. Theory provides explanations. Thus, marketing analysts apply SEM when explanation is the primary goal of the research. A good model means the researcher's theory has merit. Prediction becomes a by-product of explanation. SEM is not a good choice for exploring data or for use when prediction is the primary goal.

Fit

SEM models are good models to the extent that they exhibit fit. **Fit** exists to the extent that the SEM model accurately explains the observed covariance matrix. We represent our theory with a model. Like a model in other domains, it is a good model to the extent that it matches the real thing. SEM works by producing equations that represent the processes depicted in a model. Based on that model, the SEM program produces a modeled covariance matrix, which we will represent with the Greek character sigma, Σ.

Fit

Assesses how well a theory fits reality by comparing theoretical covariance matrix with the observed covariance matrix.

Illustrating Fit

Exhibit 22.2 illustrates with a simple example. The top frame shows the observed covariance matrix for four variables representing consumer loyalty. In this case, the variables come from the GoodBuy data described in Chapter 20. The theory put forward is that these four items represent a latent construct, Loyalty. The middle frame shows Σ, the estimated covariance matrix obtained from SEM.[5] The bottom frame shows the residual matrix, which is obtained by subtracting the matching values in Σ from **S**. In cases where the residual element is 0, that particular variance or covariance is perfectly explained by the model.

SEM provides a statistical assessment of fit with a χ^2 test, which is a function of the residual obtained from taking Σ from **S**:

$$\chi^2 = f((N-1)[\mathbf{S} - \Sigma])$$

N is the sample size determined by the number of observations in the data forming the covariance matrix. As the fit gets better, χ^2 gets smaller.[6] Don't get confused by the mathematics involved. A model is a model. It is a replica of the real thing. In the same way, one might look at a replica of the Mona Lisa and judge the extent to which it's a good model by searching for discrepancies

EXHIBIT 22.2
The Concept of Fit in SEM

		LOY1	LOY2	LOY3	LOY4
	LOY1	6.38	2.89	1.97	2.51
S =	LOY2	2.89	4.78	2.14	3.31
	LOY3	1.97	2.14	3.08	2.04
	LOY4	2.51	3.31	2.04	4.22

		LOY1	LOY2	LOY3	LOY4
	LOY1	6.38	2.87	1.76	2.63
Σ =	LOY2	2.87	4.78	2.20	3.29
	LOY3	1.76	2.20	3.08	2.02
	LOY4	2.63	3.29	2.02	4.22

		LOY1	LOY2	LOY3	LOY4
	LOY1	0.00	0.02	0.21	−0.12
S−Σ =	LOY2	0.02	0.00	−0.06	0.02
	LOY3	0.21	−0.06	0.00	0.02
	LOY4	−0.12	0.02	0.02	0.00

© 2016 Cengage Learning®

(i.e., residuals) between the replica and the original Mona Lisa handing in the Louvre Museum in Paris. In this analogy, the replica is Σ and the real Mona Lisa is **S**.

Degrees of Freedom and the χ^2 Result

The χ^2 test is completed by examining the computed value with the critical value of the χ^2 distribution for the appropriate number of degrees of freedom. How are the degrees of freedom obtained? Well, because we started with a 4×4 covariance matrix, we can use the *DF* formula discussed earlier to find that we start with 10 moments. We'll designate the resulting degrees of freedom for a given model with the small letters, *df*.

Thus, the number of degrees of freedom for the estimated model can be found by:

$$df_{model} = \frac{m(m + 1)}{2} - k$$

Where k is the number of parameters estimated. In this case, we have to estimate 8 coefficients to produce a result. How do we know this? Consider Exhibit 22.3. The figure shows a depiction of the proposed factor model. In SEM, ovals represent latent constructs, in this case Loyalty, and boxes represent measured variables (in this case the grey boxes). The blue and orange boxes with numbers inside are added to the output produced by the SEM program. Each one indicates a coefficient that was estimated to test this model. Here, we see that four loadings (*L*) are estimated and take the values shown. In addition, because SEM involves a common factor analysis approach,[7] we have to account for the error variance in each measured variable. Thus, they too must be estimated. Counting up the boxes, we can see that we have used up 8 *df*. That means the χ^2 test has 2 *df* (*DF* − *df* = 10 − 8 = 2).

In this model, the actual χ^2 value (Maximum Likelihood χ^2) comes to 4.6. The critical value with 2 *df* and a 0.05 type I error rate is 6.0. An appendix in the online resources provides the critical values. However, many online sources provide the values or provide the p–value by entering the χ^2 value and *df* (e.g., see http://itl.nist.gov/div898/handbook/eda/section3/eda3674.htm or http://danielsoper.com/statcalc3/calc.aspx?id=11). In this case, the p–value result is 0.10. Thus, we cannot reject the possibility that the χ^2 is 0. What does this mean? It means the model results

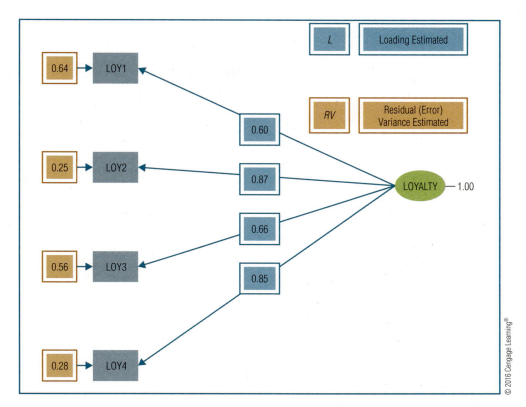

EXHIBIT **22.3**
How Many Coefficients
Estimated?

suggest that Σ and **S** are the same within sampling variance. The insignificant p–value suggests the model provides good fit!

Final Thoughts on Fit

Before leaving the concept of fit, we need to make two points to tie up potential loose ends. First, SEM conventionally uses maximum likelihood estimation. Maximum likelihood produces estimates that are interpreted relative to one another and have no absolute scale. Because of this, SEM software (or the analyst) must **fix** some parameter to an arbitrary nonzero value around which we can interpret the estimated maximum likelihood values for **free** parameters. A free parameter is one that the SEM program estimates. A fixed parameter is one for which the value is specified by the analyst or software. Notice that in the exhibit there is a 1.00 next to the green oval that represents the latent construct, Loyalty. That represents the construct's variance. In this case, that value is fixed to 1.00, allowing the maximum likelihood estimates to be interpreted relative to 1.00. Very often, one of the loadings will be fixed to 1.00 and the variance will be free. Either way works equivalently. In most cases though, we interpret standardized values. They are routinely computed by the software and reported in addition to the raw maximum likelihood estimates (not shown here). But the user needs to be aware that a scale must be set for each construct or maximum likelihood estimation is not possible.

Second, the X^2 test is a function of sample size. Thus, like other statistical tests, as the sample gets larger, the likelihood of finding a "significant" result becomes greater. A good model could get rejected just because the sample provides so much power. As samples get large or models get complex, we do not use the statistical inference test of the X^2 test as the sole indicator of good or bad fit. The X^2 value and the *df* should always be reported, but various other statistics provide guidelines for fit. These other statistics are less affected by power. In nearly every case, they are functions in one way or another of the X^2 residual and *df*. While SEM output provides many of these, we will present two others that are widely used.

■ The **Comparative Fit Index (CFI)** provides an index showing the fit of a model relative to a null model (one that would theorize no relationships among variables). The CFI can range from 0 to 1. Higher values are associated with good fit. While it's impossible to give a single CFI cutoff

Fix

Term used to indicate that the value of a parameter is set to a specific value in estimating an SEM model.

Free

Term used to indicate that the value for a specific parameter will be estimated by the SEM procedures and not fixed to a constant value.

Comparative fit index (CFI)

A goodness of fit index suggesting fit relative to a null model ranging from 0 to 1 where values close to 1 suggest relatively good fit.

that distinguishes good from bad fitting models, a model of moderate complexity ($12 < m < 30$) with a sample size of 200 or more should produce CFI values greater than 0.95 to be a candidate for good fit. As more variables or a very large sample size is involved, the expectation drops slightly (CFI ≥ 0.93). In contrast, with samples below 200 and noncomplex models (12 or fewer variables), CFI values of 0.98 or greater provide evidence of good fit.[8]

Root mean square error of approximation (RMSEA)

Statistic providing an indication of the average squared residual resulting from fitting an SEM model. Values close to 0 suggests good fit.

■ The **Root Mean Square Error of Approximation (RMSEA)** provides an indicator of the average squared residual resulting from fitting the model. While considerable debate exists over the values that are associated with good fit, values below 0.08 suggest reasonable fit for models with small samples (less than 200) and acceptable CFIs, and values below 0.07 suggest reasonable fit for models with large samples and acceptable CFIs.

Thus, we recommend reporting fit by giving the X^2 value, df (and associated p-value), CFI and RMSEA.

SEM tests both the measurement structure (with CFA) and the structural model (explaining the key outcomes) by providing an omnibus assessment of fit. This test of fit is centered around a X^2 goodness-of-fit test. In this case, fit represents how well the researcher's model matches reality as represented by the data. Several software programs are devoted especially to solving structural equations models including LISREL, AMOS (which is currently available with SPSS), and M-Plus, among others.

Conducting Confirmatory Factor Analysis (CFA)

Confirmatory Factor Analysis (CFA)

A type of factor analysis in which the researcher specifies the measured variables that indicate specific constructs based on theory, and then the assessment of validity depends on how well that theory (producing Σ) fits the observed data (**S**).

Exhibit 22.3 provides results of an elementary CFA. In most real-world applications, more than four indicators and more than one construct are involved. We will illustrate the steps for CFA using another simple example. In this case, the analyst tests a measurement theory concerning three constructs from the GoodBuy data, perceived Atmosphere, Customer Satisfaction, and Loyalty.

Exhibit 22.4 shows the proposed measurement theory. The researcher used previously applied scales to represent each construct in the survey. Four variables represent perceived atmosphere and loyalty and five represent consumer satisfaction/dissatisfaction (CS/D). The image makes clear the distinction between CFA and other types of factor analysis. When we depicted the factor analysis results in the previous chapter showing how nostalgia and loyalty are measured (Exhibit 21.3 in previous chapter), each construct was connected to each measured variable. That is not the case here.

EXHIBIT **22.4**
Proposed Measurement Theory for GoodBuy

© 2016 Cengage Learning®

Running a CFA

Programs such as AMOS, which is available as an add-in to SPSS, make running a CFA fairly straightforward. After developing the measurement theory, follow these steps.

1. Open AMOS Graphics.
2. Using the icons on the left and the "page" on the right, draw the measurement theory. Ovals represent latent constructs, boxes represent measured variables, and smaller circles represent error variance terms.
3. Make sure a scale is set for the analysis. AMOS will, by default, specify one factor loading as "fixed" to one for each construct.
   a. Be careful that this is true before running the CFA. Sometimes, when editing a model, the item fixed to one gets deleted.
   b. Fixing the value for a path is easy, just right click on an object, choose object properties, and enter a value (1) in the "regression weight" window.
4. Open the "Select Variables" window by clicking on the appropriate icon (it looks like a ladder).
   a. Drop and drag the corresponding variables into position to represent each respective construct.
   b. The "select variables" window is open in the graphic at the right.
5. Make sure that all relationships (covariances) between constructs are free to be estimated. This can be accomplished by putting two-headed arrows between each set of constructs as shown. In LISREL, these coefficients are called PHI (ϕ) coefficients.
6. Choose the "select files" icon.
   a. A dialog box will open. Click on "File Name."
   b. Navigate to the SPSS file that contains the raw data from which the covariances will be computed to perform the CFA.

7. Choose options for the analysis by opening "Analysis Properties" window. Click on "Output."
   a. Select "Standardized Estimates," "Sample Moments" (the observed covariance matrix, or **S**, will be displayed), "Implied Moments" (Σ will be displayed), "Residual Moments" ($S - \Sigma$), and "Modification Indices."
8. Click on the "Calculate Estimates" icon, which looks like a backgammon board, to conduct the analysis.
9. Results appear on the screen and in the "View Text" pop-up window.

For LISREL, the steps are very similar:

1. Draw the model in a manner similar to that described earlier.
2. Once the model is drawn, click on "Setup."
3. Choose "Build LISREL Syntax."
4. Click on the icon with a person running with an L to run the model.
5. For those with computer programming experience, a LISREL syntax window is available for writing the program code to produce analysis. An appendix to this chapter shows an example of this code.

Estimating a CFA Model

The analyst needs to select software to run the CFA. In addition to LISREL and AMOS, other programs exist such as MPlus, EQS, and SYSLIN in SAS. Each program makes slightly different assumptions about issues such as standardization and missing data. Thus, CFA results may vary slightly from one program to another. In this case, the analyst decides to use LISREL's graphical interface. The steps to conduct a CFA in LISREL graphics and AMOS are essentially the same. The Research Snapshot provides an overview of using SEM software. Using a graphical interface, the analyst reproduces the image shown in Exhibit 22.4, selects the desired options in the analysis, and then runs the program.

Interpreting CFA Results

Exhibit 22.5 displays some of the key results obtained by estimating this CFA model (in this case showing results from LISREL).[9] The overall fit seems good. The $X^2 = 86$ with 62 df. The corresponding p-value is below 0.05, which suggests that we cannot conclude that **S** and Σ are the same within sampling variation. However, the CFI = 0.99 (the maximum value is 1.0) and the RMSEA is 0.031. Both of these values are consistent with a good fit. Given that the sample is rather large, the p-value of 0.03 is likely due to the power of the test. Considering the criterion for valid measures discussed in Chapter 10, this model exhibits fit validity. Fit validity is essential for construct validity.

A CFA result also should provide evidence of construct validity beyond fit. Exhibit 22.5 displays the completely standardized factor loading estimates, the corresponding AVEs and the construct reliability estimate. In CFA, the tradition is to report the Construct Reliability estimate instead of the Cronbach Alpha coefficient. Construct Reliability is considered a more accurate assessment of reliability although the results are usually very consistent. The Construct Reliability estimate for a measure can be computed as follows:

$$Construct\ Reliability \;=\; CR = \frac{(\Sigma_{i=1}^{p} L_i)^2}{(\Sigma_{i=1}^{p} L_i)^2 + (\Sigma_{i=1}^{P} e_i)}$$

Where L_i is the ith item's standardized loading on a factor, p is the total number of items representing a latent construct and e_i is the error variance associated with the ith item loading on the factor.

EXHIBIT 22.5
Key CFA Output

Model Fit Statistics:			
X^2	86		
	62		
df (p-value)	(0.03)		
CFI	0.99		
RMSEA	0.031		
Standardized Loading Estimates, AVEs, and Reliability Estimates			
	CS/D	Loyalty	ATM
CSD1	0.74		
CSD2	0.75		
CSD3	0.68		
CSD4	0.71		
CSD5	0.73		
LOY1		0.59	
LOY2		0.86	
LOY3		0.67	
LOY4		0.84	
ATM1			0.69
ATM2			0.81
ATM3			0.77
ATM4			0.83
Average Variance Extracted	0.52	0.56	0.60
Construct Reliability	0.85	0.83	0.86

© 2016 Cengage Learning®

Validity Component	Evidence
Face Validity	Item content matches construct definition. Determined outside CFA.
Criterion Validity	Do constructs relate to other constructs as expected? Each of the three constructs are positively correlated as expected. Other evidence provided outside this CFA.
Convergent Validity	Do construct indicators converge on a consistent meaning? Factor loadings all above |0.6|, AVEs above 0.50, and Construct Reliability above 0.7 for each construct.
Discriminant Validity	Do measures correlate too strongly with other constructs? Each AVE exceeds the square of the CFA estimated correlation between that construct and other constructs.
Fit Validity	Does the factor structure imposed based on measurement theory produce a good fit? In this case, a good fit is returned upon estimating the model.

EXHIBIT 22.6
Evidence of Construct Validity

© 2016 Cengage Learning®

The fact that all loadings are statistically significant (each loading estimate will produce a *t*-test result and in this case all p–values are less than 0.001; in AMOS, these tests are referred to in the C.R. column for Critical Ratio). More importantly, all AVEs are above 0.50. In addition, each construct reliability estimate exceeds 0.70. In addition, the highest correlation estimate (ϕ) between any two construct is 0.50, between Loyalty and Atmosphere. Squaring that yields 0.25. The lowest AVE is 0.522, which easily exceeds 0.25. Thus, using the criterion set out in Chapter 10, we also have evidence of discriminant validity. Exhibit 22.6 summarizes the assessment of construct validity for this CFA. The analyst reaches the conclusion that the measurement model is supported and thus the measurement theory is valid.

Testing Structural Theory in SEM

Only after establishing adequate measurement validity as shown earlier should the researcher proceed to test the structural theory. Any theory test based on poor measurement is prone to be misleading. At best, results of such an attempt are exploratory. Having established good measurement with a CFA, the analyst proceeds in this case to test a theory that satisfaction (CS/D), acting as an emotion, facilitates the link through which perceptions of the atmosphere cause a consumer to be more loyal. Put in terms discussed earlier, the theory suggests that CS/D mediates the relationship between Atmosphere and Loyalty. Exhibit 22.7 illustrates the proposed structural theory.

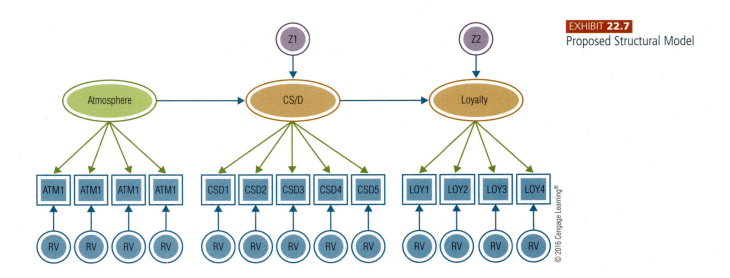

EXHIBIT 22.7
Proposed Structural Model

© 2016 Cengage Learning®

Setting Up the Structural Model

The theory proposes that perceptions of the atmosphere cause satisfaction. A more pleasant atmosphere makes for a more satisfying shopping experience. In turn, the satisfaction driven by atmosphere causes customers to become more loyal. We now must distinguish between independent and dependent latent variables at the structural level. To do that, we adopt a new terminology. **Exogenous constructs** are the latent variable equivalent of independent variables. **Endogenous constructs** are the latent variable equivalent of dependent variables. In addition, we now have **structural coefficients** serving as estimates of the structural relationship between constructs. In other words, they function as regression coefficients in multiple regression.

Taking a look at Exhibit 22.7, we can now see that the endogenous constructs, represented in the dark tan color, now have an error variance term associated with them (Z1, Z2). Endogenous constructs are not expected to be explained fully. Thus, the error variance term accounts for percentage of variance not explained by the model. The value of the error variance can be thought of as $1 - R^2$. While LISREL automatically accounts for this construct level error variance by specifying constructs as endogenous (ETA versus KSI, for endogenous and exogenous constructs, respectively), the analyst must manually insert these in AMOS to create an endogenous construct. In addition, the two-headed arrows are replaced by single-headed arrows to designate causal paths.

Beyond these distinctions, the procedures to execute the models are the same as for CFA.

Exogenous constructs

The latent variable equivalent of independent variables.

Endogenous constructs

The latent variable equivalent of dependent variables.

Structural coefficients

Serving as estimates of the structural relationship between constructs.

Structural Model Results

The structural model results are interpreted in much the same way as the CFA results. The analyst follows these steps:

1. Run the model using software.
2. Carefully consider the model's fit.
   a. Are the *df* for the model correct? A check of this helps spot potential errors in model specification.
   b. Are there any warning messages or indications that the model did not fully execute? Such a message could indicate problems with statistical identification. Models that free more coefficients to be estimated than the number of degrees of freedom (*DF*) available (meaning *df* not positive) are not identified. The statistics can't give back more information than is put in. If the model is not identified, constraints need to be added (parameters fixed) to try to bring it back into an over-identified situation (*df* positive). Oftentimes, factors with less than three indicators, which are themselves statistically underidentified, lead to problems in estimating models.
   c. Barring problems in a or b, is the model fit suggestive of good fit? The same guidelines used for CFA apply here.
      i. Also, the analyst will note the difference between the CFA and the structural model fit.
3. Presuming the model fit is adequate, the analyst proceeds to consider the structural parameter coefficients.
   a. Are the parameter estimates for each path statistically significant? Each is interpreted with respect to the proposed theory.
   b. In addition, the analyst should take a look at the measurement loading estimates. If they have changed more than trivially (more than 0.05, for instance), evidence of interpretational confounding exists and data problems could be evident.
4. Examine residuals. Do the residuals suggest any obvious improvements in fit? If so, the proposed theory is likely deficient.
   a. The standardized residuals are usually easier to interpret. Look for patterns of standardized residuals with relatively high loadings (multiple residuals for a variable above $|2.5|$) or individual high standardized residuals (such as above $|4|$).
5. Draw appropriate conclusions about the theory.

In this case, the analyst uses AMOS to test the proposed structural theory. The overall fit is indicated by a X^2 of 157 with 63 df (p < 0.001).[10] The CFI is 0.96 and the RMSEA is 0.06. Although these results are not clearly indicative of bad fit, falling close to the guidelines for good fit, the difference between this model's fit and the CFA model's fit is considerable. SEM analysts often use X^2 difference test to analyze sequential models. A X^2 difference test is conducted by subtracting the two models' X^2 values and the two df values. Here, the difference between the CFA and the structural model can be computed as:

X^2		df		Δ	
Structural Model	**CFA**	**Structural Model**	**CFA**	**ΔX2**	**Δdf**
157	86	63	62	71	1

The difference of 71 with 1 df is significant (p < 0.001). Thus, the structural model fits significantly worse than did the CFA model. In addition, several relatively high standardized residuals exist (above |5|) between the ATM items and LOY items. These suggest that the relationship between Atmosphere and Loyalty, currently fixed at 0, should be freed. Doing so would produce a fit identical to the CFA, which happens any time all possible structural coefficients are estimated. However, the correlation estimates between constructs would be replaced by regression coefficients. After estimating this model, the analyst finds positive relationships between Atmosphere and Satisfaction (0.24, p < 0.05) and Atmosphere and Loyalty (0.48, p < 0.05). The relationship between Satisfaction and Loyalty is 0.10 producing a t-value of 1.74 (p = 0.07). As a consequence of the weak link between Satisfaction and Loyalty, the researcher's proposed theory of an indirect effect of Atmosphere on Loyalty is not strongly supported. In contrast, the relationship between Atmosphere and Loyalty appears direct.

SEM models are widely applied in marketing research. They are used to test theories related to all manner of marketing-related topics including retail service aesthetics, pricing policies, brand image, cross-cultural issues, market orientation, and much more.[11]

Other Multivariate Techniques

We cannot give attention to all multivariate approaches in this book. Here are a couple of others with which the analyst should be aware. Another interdependence technique is multidimensional scaling. **Multidimensional scaling** provides a means for measuring objects in a multidimensional space based on respondents' judgments of how similar different objects are. Like factor analysis, multidimensional scaling can be useful in identifying the dimensions among which consumers differentiate products. The data typically are collected by having consumers rate how similar product or brand alternatives are to each other. For example, consumers may be asked to rate the similarity of the top auto brands. Here, we may find that Acura and Lexus are very similar but that each is very different from Chrysler and Kia. The researcher may be able to use results to interpret reliability and comfort as key dimensions that distinguish the brands.

Marketing researchers have also sometimes adopted a tool that originated in the physical sciences and is capable of providing statistical results even when only a small amount of data exists or when the measurement quality is not particularly strong. **Partial least squares (PLS)** combines a PCA-based measurement approach with a least-squares based regression approach to simultaneously produce path estimates between factors represented by multiple item measures. The results produce an outer model, the factor analysis model, and an inner model, the regression coefficients between constructs. Unlike SEM described earlier, PLS does not provide a test of fit and it is not a covariance-based technique. Therefore, it has limited ability to validate measures as is done with CFA and it is more capable of exploring individual relationships than testing theory.

Multidimensional scaling

Provides a means for measuring objects in a multidimensional space based on respondents' judgments of how similar different objects are.

Partial least squares (PLS)

Combines a PCA-based factor analytic approach with a least squares based regression approach to produce path estimates between factors represented by multiple item measures.

PLS is particularly useful though when the data are messy, difficult to obtain, and/or the measurement quality is not strong enough for use in SEM. PLS is also very easy to use. PLS programs provide a graphical interface. However, the researcher needs to use caution because although PLS can produce results when other tools may fail, problems such as a lack of generalizability due to a small sample don't go away just because statistical results can be obtained. Also, results based on poor measurement should be considered exploratory. In addition, the analyst has to be especially alert for data anomalies such as implausible results or unstable solutions. Interpretational confounding provides one way of indicating potentially problematic results. SAS, SPSS, and JMP all provide a PLS module. Specialized software also exists such as SmartPLS. Although PLS often is referred to as a SEM technique, analysts are more and more realizing the two approaches vary substantially and should not be considered as interchangeable techniques.[12] The reader is referred to other sources for more information on these more complex techniques.

We give a brief insight into these two multivariate techniques because they are used widely enough so that they are part of the marketing researcher's vocabulary. Surely, the big data era will bring more innovations in multivariate data analysis. At this point, the reader of this book has a good foundation for doing basic multivariate analyses and for diving more deeply into the techniques introduced in this book. We wish you happy data analyses.

TIPS OF THE TRADE

- ■ SEM analyzes covariance structures. This point is critical to accept to understand how SEM works and why it is different from most other techniques.
  - Knowing how *DF* and *df* are determined is very helpful in understanding what SEM does.
- ■ SEM is appropriate for testing theory. The emphasis in testing theory is more on explanation than on prediction.
  - Prediction is not sacrificed however because explanation allows prediction.
  - SEM is not a good exploratory tool.
- ■ Useful hints for CFA.
  - Try to include at least four items as indicators of each construct. This helps in making sure that the model and each individual construct is mathematically identified.
  - We presume constructs are related to one another (with nondirectional correlation/covariance) unless we have a good reason to believe some pair of constructs are independent of each other.
  - Only minor modifications to a factor structure can be made once the CFA stage is reached. Data reduction, such as dropping multiple items that do not perform well, should be accomplished prior to conducting CFA. For instance, if one-fourth items are deleted based on poor performance, more data will be needed to try to confirm the revised measurement model.

∵ SUMMARY

1. Distinguish SEM as a covariance technique. Structural equations modeling (SEM) allows a researcher to build and test a theory explaining how constructs cause other constructs, each represented by a series of equations that are solved simultaneously. Constructs are represented by multiple-item measures. The solution allows correction for measurement error. Unlike most other techniques, SEM is a covariance-based technique. The analysis takes place using the covariance matrix of variables involved in the theory. Because the covariance matrix provides input, no information is lost or sacrificed.

2. Appreciate SEM as an explanatory tool that tests theory. Most other dependence techniques are oriented around prediction. SEM is oriented around explanation. A SEM model ultimately is judged not only based on how much variance in an outcome it predicts, but on how well it accounts for all of the variance and covariance that exists among the relevant set of variables.

3. Understand and use the concept of fit. SEM models are good models to the extent that they exhibit fit. Good fit exists to the extent that the SEM model accurately explains the observed covariance matrix. We represent our theory with a model. SEM estimates the covariance matrix with Σ, which SEM compares to the observed covariance matrix, $\mathbf{S}$, to determine fit. This comparison is accomplished with a χ^2 test ($\chi^2 = f((N-1)[\mathbf{S} - \Sigma])$). If the test turns out statistically significant, then evidence suggests that S and Σ are not the same and that the model does not fit. If the test is statistically insignificant, we reach the opposite conclusion; the model fits. Because of problems with statistical power, we rely on additional statistics such as the CFI and RMSEA in judging fit.

4. Conduct a confirmatory factor analysis. In CFA the researcher specifies which measured variables indicate which specific constructs based on theory, and then the assessment of validity depends on how well that theory (producing Σ) fits the observed data ($\mathbf{S}$). In contrast to EFA approaches, the researcher must know ahead of time the number of factors and the variables that represent each. Thus, like SEM in general, theory drives CFA. With most SEM software, a CFA can be conducted by graphically depicting the arrangement between constructs and the indicator variables that represent them and the relationships among constructs. A CFA provides a thorough assessment of the construct validity of a measurement theory with an emphasis on fit validity, convergent validity, and discriminant validity.

5. Know how to test an elementary structural theory with SEM. The analyst can create a structural model from the CFA by converting constructs into their respective exogenous and endogenous constructs, based on theory. Endogenous constructs include an error variance component. Also, paths with single headed arrows need to be added to represent the causal processes that help form the theoretical explanation. The assessment of fit moves forward in much the same way as the CFA. Analysts often compare models and theories using a χ^2 difference test. The statistical significance of the difference test determines whether one model fits significantly better than the other.

6. Be aware of other multivariate statistical techniques. This book does not describe every multivariate data analysis technique. The chapter concludes with a brief mention of two techniques used frequently enough to be part of the market analyst's vocabulary. Multidimensional scaling is an interdependence technique that uses less than interval data to identify dimensions underlying multiple observations. PLS is a technique useful when data problems exist or measurement is insufficient to allow the use of SEM. PLS combines PCA with least squares regression to estimate relationships between constructs.

:: KEY TERMS AND CONCEPTS

AMOS, *570*

comparative fit index (CFI), *573*

Confirmatory Factor Analysis (CFA), *574*

endogenous constructs, *578*

exogenous constructs, *578*

fit, *571*

fix, *573*

free, *573*

LISREL, *569*

momen, *570*

multidimensional scaling, *579*

partial least squares (PLS), *579*

root mean square error of approximation (RMSEA), *574*

structural coefficients, *578*

structural equations modeling (SEM), *569*

:: REVIEW QUESTIONS

1. Explain why SEM, originally conceptualized in the 1920s, took so long to catch on as a widely applied multivariate data analysis tool.
2. What is a moment in SEM terminology?
3. What do LISREL and AMOS stand for? How do these terms relate to SEM in general?
4. Where do the *DF* originate for a SEM model?
5. Why does the fact that SEM is a covariance technique reinforce its role as an explanatory tool?
6. In a study involving responses of 175 young adult consumers' social networking habits, the marketing researcher proposes that two constructs, credibility of social network posts and central-ity of social networks, are represented by a total of ten measured

variables. How many *DF* are available for use in SEM from this study? After conducting a standard CFA, how many *df* would the resulting χ^2 test be associated with?

7. Describe the relationship between **S** and **Σ** with respect to SEM fit.
8. What is the difference between a fixed and free parameter?
9. Describe how CFA results helps provide evidence of construct validity.
10. Define the terms *exogenous construct* and *endogenous construct*. How does one turn an exogenous construct into an endogenous construct in AMOS?
11. What role does the matrix of standardized residuals produced by SEM play in assessing fit and drawing conclusions?
12. What is PLS and what are its key strengths and weaknesses?

:: RESEARCH ACTIVITIES

1. Using the OLD School data used in the previous chapter, test the following measurement theory: A researcher believes that the items greedy, no_loyal, money, material, and cheating represent a factor called Cynacism, and that the items obl_rm, req_rm, role_mdl, and loyal represent a factor known as Role Model. Use software like AMOS to conduct and interpret a CFA.
   a. Prepare a summary report of the results.
   b. If the model shows a deficiency in validity in any way, can a minor modification be made to produce a better result?

2. Using the GoodBuy data set, add the ATS construct to the model examined in this chapter. Test the theoretical model that both ATS and ATM drive CS/D, which in turn drives Loyalty. Include a direct path from ATM to Loyalty but not from ATS to Loyalty.
   a. Describe the CFA results.
   b. Describe the structural model results.
   c. What are the key conclusions?

Example LISREL Syntax

```
TITLE EMR
DA NO=399 NI=13 NG=1 MA=CM
!
! Lines starting with an exclamation are comments only
! Any TITLE can be added on first line
! The DA line above describes the data
! The LA line indicates that variable labels will follow on next line
!
LA
LOY1 LOY2 LOY3 LOY4 CSD1 CSD2 CSD3 CSD4 CSD5 ATM1 ATM2 ATM3 ATM4
!
!  CM means the Covariance Matrix appears below. SY means it is symmetric.
!
CM SY
6.38
2.89    4.78
1.97    2.14    3.08
2.51    3.31    2.04    4.22
0.21    0.41    0.37    0.44    1.79
0.19    0.27    0.27    0.26    1.02    1.88
0.24    0.38    0.19    0.30    0.91    0.89    1.73
0.19    0.28    0.29    0.25    0.88    0.92    0.86    1.64
4.43    8.47    5.08    7.33    15.07   15.79   12.73   13.47   424.30
0.52    1.01    0.76    1.05    0.16    0.42    0.35    0.27    6.01    3.35
0.94    1.33    1.06    1.26    0.27    0.37    0.26    0.24    4.71    1.78    2.65
0.41    1.02    0.74    0.79    0.18    0.29    0.26    0.19    5.75    1.23    1.33    1.78
0.81    1.01    0.90    0.94    0.17    0.31    0.27    0.22    4.39    1.45    1.47    1.24    1.94
!
! SE stands for select.  Selects the variables included in the analysis
!
SE
CSD1 CSD2 CSD3 CSD4 CSD5 LOY1 LOY2 LOY3 LOY4 ATM1 ATM2 ATM3 ATM4 /
!
! MO stands for Model.  Describes the model that will be tested
!
MO NX=4 NK=1 NY=9 NE=2 PH=SY,FR PS=DI,FR GA=FU,FI BE=FU,FI
!
!VA stand for Value.  Fixes parameters to nonzero value
! FR stands for Free.  Frees coefficients to be estimated
!
VA 1.0 LX 1 1 LY 1 1 LY 6 2
FR LX 2 1 LX 3 1 LX 4 1
FR LY 2 1 LY 3 1 LY 4 1 LY 5 1
FR LY 7 2 LY 8 2 LY 9 2
FR GA 1 1 BE 2 1
!
!  LK stands for Labels for KSI, the name for exogenous constructs
!  LE stands for Labels for Eta, the name for endogenous constructs
!
LK
LOYALTY CSD ATM
!
! PD tells the program to create a path diagram as output
! OU specifies output options
!
pd
OU RS ND=2 SC EF
```

······ **PART SEVEN**

Comprehensive Cases with Computerized Databases

:::::: COMPREHENSIVE CASES

Dimitri Otis/Getty Images

Case 1 Running the Numbers: Does It Pay?

(Download the data sets for this case from www .cengagebrain.com or request them from your instructor.)
Dr. William Ray, a research consultant, has received a government grant of $75,000 to fund research examining how aspects of a student's college experiences relate to his or her job performance. Senator B. G. Shot is being lobbied by his constituents that employers are discriminating against people who do not like math by giving them lower salaries. Senator Shot has obtained $50,000 of the $75,000 grant from these constituents. The Senator was also instrumental in the selection of Dr. Ray as the recipient and hopes the research supported by the grant will help provide a basis to support the proposed legislation making discrimination against those people who do not like math illegal.

The research questions listed in this particular grant proposal include:

RQ1: Does a student's liking of quantitative coursework in college affect his or her future earnings?

RQ2: Do people with an affinity for quantitative courses get promoted more quickly than those who do not?

Dr. Ray has gained the cooperation of a Fortune 500 service firm that employs over 20,000 employees across eight locations. The company allows Dr. Ray to survey employees who have been out of college for three years. Three hundred responses were obtained by sending an e-mail invitation to approximately 1,000 employees

who fit this profile. The invitation explained that the research was about various employee attitudes and indicated that employees would not be required to identify themselves during the survey. Respondents were informed that all responses would be strictly confidential. The e-mail provided a click-through questionnaire which directed respondents to a website where the survey was conducted using an online survey provider. Each invitation was coded so that the actual respondents could be identified by both e-mail address and name. Dr. Ray, however, kept this information confidential so the company could not identify any particular employee's response.

The following table describes the variables that were collected.

Variables Available from Company Records

Variable Name	Variable Type	Coding
PROM	Nominal indicating whether the employee has been promoted	1 = "Promoted" 0 = "Not Promoted"
GPA	Self-Reported GPA in Last Year of College	0 (lowest) to 4 (highest)
Sex	Nominal	1 = "Female" 0 = "Male"
School	Nominal	School Initials
Salary	Ratio	Actual annual salary from last year

Questions from Survey

	Coding	Strongly Disagree (1)	Disagree (2)	Neutral (3)	Agree (4)	Strongly Agree (5)
X_1	The quantitative courses I took in school were the most useful courses.	☐	☐	☐	☐	☐
X_2	Very few topics can be understood if you do not understand the arithmetic.	☐	☐	☐	☐	☐
X_3	I hated going to math classes in college.	☐	☐	☐	☐	☐
X_4	I learned a great deal from the quantitative projects assigned to me in college.	☐	☐	☐	☐	☐
X_5	Students do not need to study quantitative topics in college to succeed in their careers.	☐	☐	☐	☐	☐

586
● ● ●

Please use the following items to describe your undergraduate college experience. For each pair of items, choose the check box closest to the adjective that best describes your experience.

Coding		(–3)	(–2)	(–1)	(0)	(1)	(2)	(3)	
S_1	Dull	☐	☐	☐	☐	☐	☐	☐	Exciting
S_2	Laborious	☐	☐	☐	☐	☐	☐	☐	Playful
S_3	Stressful	☐	☐	☐	☐	☐	☐	☐	Relaxing
S_4	Boring	☐	☐	☐	☐	☐	☐	☐	Fun
S_5	Carefree	☐	☐	☐	☐	☐	☐	☐	Responsible

Questions:

1. Does this grant present Dr. Ray with an ethical dilemma(s) in any way?
2. Derive at least one hypothesis for each research question listed above. Provide a sound rationale or theoretical explanation that leads to the hypothesis.
3. Use the data that corresponds to this case to perform an adequate test of each hypothesis. Interpret the results.
4. Is there evidence supporting the discrimination claim? Explain.
5. List another hypothesis (unrelated to the research questions in the grant) that could be tested with this data.
6. Test that hypothesis.
7. Considering employees' attitudes about their college experience, does the amount of fun that students had in college or the degree to which they thought quantitative classes were a positive experience relate more strongly to salary?
8. Would the "problem" that led to the grant be a better candidate for ethnographic research? Explain.

Case 2 Good Times at GoodBuy?

This case uses the GoodBuy Retail data set introduced in Chapter 20 and referred to several times in the later chapters.[1] The data are available in the online student resources.

GoodBuy is a large big box retailer that has a track record of success offering popular brands of electronics such as Samsung, Sony, LG, and HP. Although the bulk of their sales revenue comes from big-ticket items like computers, big-screen HD televisions, and smartphones (for which they receive supplementary revenue for selling contracts to data suppliers), the margin is higher for small-ticket items (under $100) that include accessories for the other electronics. Many of these accessories are unplanned purchases that customers discover in the store. They sell a disproportionate portion of accessories in-store as opposed to online as customers are able to actually try a lot of them out in the store or have the product demonstrated by a service associate. Management believes one strategy for increasing sales of these items is through more purchases from loyal customers. Thus, the overall decision statement expressed to the research team is:

- In what ways can we allocate resources to consistently encourage our current customers to spend more time in a GoodBuy store and increase purchases of valuable accessories?

In particular, they have approximately $500K allocated per store that can be directed toward enhancing the atmosphere by creating more spacious and luxurious shopping space. This would include leasing out space to Samsung and Apple to operate their own stores within each store. In addition, "living rooms" would allow shoppers to experience all the store's major products in a home-like environment. Alternatively, they could direct this investment toward more multimedia promotion about the low prices at GoodBuy.

After some discussion between the research team and GoodBuy management, the researchers mention that they recently conducted a survey of shoppers (the GoodBuy data from Exhibit 20.3) that

contains relevant data. They translate the decision statement into research questions related to:

- How does the store atmosphere affect customer loyalty?
- Do customers bond with other customers in the store and does this lead to positive reactions among consumers?

In the prospectus for the research, the lead researcher describes the situation background as follows:

The other shoppers are a prominent part of the shopping atmosphere. As shoppers see others who share curiosity about the same sorts of products, they interact and enhance the shopping atmosphere. We know from previous research across other retail types that consumers enjoy shopping with others that they view as similar to themselves. Thus, as a consumer's attitude toward the other shoppers improves, so does their attitude of the shopping atmosphere. Both of these are factors known to increase customer satisfaction, which is a conduit to increased customer loyalty. One of the slides prepared for the presentation summed this theory up as shown in Case Exhibit 2.1.

The lead researcher comes to you and asks you to serve as the analyst for this project. Using the data available, she encourages you to use the scales available to measure the impression of other GoodBuy shoppers (ATS1–ATS4) and the favorableness of the GoodBuy atmosphere (ATM1–ATM4), along with the customer satisfaction (CSD1–CSD5) and loyalty scales (LOY1–LOY4), to test the theory above using multivariate data analysis. Your job is to supply a brief report to her that can be used as a key part of the presentation that will go to GoodBuy management.

Use the following questions to help shape your report:

1. Are the data appropriate for multivariate data analysis? If so, what technique(s) would you suggest as appropriate and why?
2. The researcher suggests that you first use only half of the data to do an initial analysis (split the entire sample randomly into two halves of 200 respondents each). Do you think that is a good idea? Explain.

CASE EXHIBIT **2.1** The Proposed Theory of Customer Loyalty

Impression of others → Favorable atmosphere → CS/D → Loyalty

---

[1]GoodBuy is fictional although elements of the story are based on actual trends in the retail industry.

3. Do the multiple scale items represent distinct latent constructs based on their theoretical expectation (i.e., do the items represent the intended constructs)? Using one of the three approaches to factor analysis (use the most appropriate technique that you are capable with), assess construct validity of the measures (assume the scales have face and criterion validity). Delete any scale items that may be harming construct validity should you find any.

4. Test the theory depicted above using an appropriate statistical technique. Draw a conclusion about the validity of the theory.

5. Do any results suggest a flaw in the theory? Can another model be proposed that provides better fit?

6. Based on your input, and any additional exploration with the data, what would you recommend as a conclusion for the research report?

Case 3 Attiring Situation

(Download the data sets for this case from www .cengagebrain.com or request them from your instructor.)
RESERV is a national level placement firm specializing in putting retailers and service providers together with potential employees who fill positions at all levels of the organization. This includes entry-level positions and senior management positions. One international specialty clothing store chain has approached them with issues involving key characteristics of retail employees. The two key characteristics of primary interest involve the appearance of potential employees and problems with customer integrity.

Over the last five years, store management has adopted a very flexible dress code that allowed employees some flexibility in the way they dressed for work. Casual attire was permitted with the idea that younger customers could better identify with store employees, most of whom are younger than average. However, senior management had just become aware of how some very successful companies tightly control the appearance of their sales force. The Walt Disney Company, for example, has strict grooming policies for all employees, provides uniforms (or costumes) for most *cast members*, and does not permit any employee to work if they have a visible tattoo. Disney executives discuss many positive benefits from this policy and one is that customers are more responsive to the employees. Thus, it just may be that the appearance of employees can influence the behavior of customers. This influence can be from the greater identity that employees display—meaning, they stand out better and may encourage acquiescence through friendliness.

Senior research associate, Michael Neil, decides to conduct an experiment to examine relevant research questions including:

RQ1: How does employee appearance affect customer purchasing behavior?

RQ2: How does employee appearance affect customer ethics?

Mr. Neil decides the problem can best be attacked by conducting a laboratory experiment. In the experiment, two variables are manipulated in a between-subjects design. The experiment includes two experimental variables which are controlled by the researcher and subjects' biological sex which was recorded and included as a blocking variable. The experimental variables (and blocking variable) are:

Name	Description	Values
X_1	A manipulation of the attire of the service-providing employee	0 = Professional Attire (Neatly groomed w/ business attire) 1 = Unprofessional Attire (Unkempt hair w/ jeans and t-shirt)
X_2	The manner with which the service-providing employee tries to gain extra sales—or simply, the close approach	0 = Soft Close 1 = Hard Close
Gender	Subject's biological sex	0 = Male 1 = Female

Four dependent variables are included:

Name	Description	Range
Time	How much time the subject spent with the employee beyond what was necessary to choose the slacks and shirt.	0–10 minutes
Spend	How much of the $25 the subject spent on extra products offered for sale by the retail service provider	$0–$25
Keep	How much of the $25 the subject kept rather than returning to the researcher	$0–$25

Additionally, several variables were collected following the experiment that tried to capture how the subject felt during the exercise. All of these items were gathered using a 7-item semantic differential scale.

Name	Description
SD1	Low Quality–High Quality
SD2	Dislike–Like
SD3	Unfavorable–Favorable
SD4	Negative–Positive
SD5	Easy–Difficult
SD6	Restful–Tiring
SD7	Comfortable–Uncomfortable
SD8	Calm–Tense

The experiment was conducted in a university union. Subjects were recruited from the food court area. RESERV employees approached potential subjects and requested their participation in a study that examined how customers really bought things. Subjects would each receive vouchers that could be exchanged for merchandise in return for their participation. Each potential subject was informed that the participation could take between 20 and 40 minutes to complete. Upon agreeing to participate, subjects were escorted to a waiting area where they were provided with further instructions and mingled with other participants before entering a small room that was set up to resemble an actual retail clothing counter.

Each subject was told to play the role of a customer who had just purchased some dress slacks and a shirt. The employee was to complete the transaction. Once the subject entered the mock retail environment, a research assistant who was playing the role of the retail employee entered the room. As a retail sales associate, one important role was to suggest add-on sales. Several dozen accessory items ranging from socks and handkerchiefs to small jewelry items were displayed at the counter.

As a result of this experimental procedure, each subject was randomly assigned to one of four conditions, each corresponding to a unique combination of the experimental variables described above. In other words, the employee was either:

1. Dressed professionally and used a soft close (i.e., "Perhaps you would like to see some additional accessories") in trying to sell merchandise beyond the slacks and shirt.
2. Dressed unprofessionally and used a soft close.
3. Dressed professionally and used a hard close (i.e., "You really need to match this up with some coordinated accessories which happen to be on sale today only") in trying to sell merchandise beyond the slacks and shirt.
4. Dressed unprofessionally and used a hard close.

Thus, RESERV wishes to use this information to explain how employee appearance encourages shoppers to continue shopping (TIME) and spend money (SPEND). Rather than simply asking purchase intentions, each subject was given $25 (in one-dollar bills) which they were allowed to *spend* on accessories. This allowed each subject to participate in an actual transaction. In addition, the experiment did not provide explicit instructions on what was to be done with the money that was left over. Once the simulated shopping trip was complete, subjects were taken to another small room where they completed a questionnaire containing the semantic differential scales and demographic information alone and at their own pace. Because the instructions did not specifically tell subjects what to do with the money they possessed following the experiment, this allowed the researchers to operationalize a behavioral dependent variable (KEEP) that simulated questionable consumer behavior based on the implied assumption that the money was to be either handed to the research assistant when complete or turned in along with the questionnaire. In other words, subjects who kept money were considered as behaving less ethically than those who left the money behind or turned it in to a member of the research team.

1. Develop at least three hypotheses that correspond to the research questions.
2. Test the hypotheses using an appropriate statistical approach.
3. Suppose the researcher is curious about how the feelings captured with the semantic differentials influence the dependent variables SPEND and KEEP. Conduct an analysis to explore this possibility. Are any problems present in testing this?
4. Is there a role for factor analysis in any of this analysis?
5. Critique the experiment from an internal and external validity viewpoint.
6. What conclusions would be justified by management regarding their employee appearance policy?

Case 4 Values and the Automobile Market

(Download the data sets for this case from www .cengagebrain.com or request them from your instructor.)
In the last decade, the luxury car segment became one of the most competitive in the automobile market. Many American consumers who purchase luxury cars prefer imports from Germany and Japan.

A marketing vice president with General Motors once commented, "Import-committed buyers have been frustrating to us." This type of thinking has led industry analysts to argue that to successfully compete in the luxury car segment, U.S. carmakers need to develop a better understanding of the consumers so that they can better segment the market and better position their products via more effective advertising. Insight into the foreign-domestic luxury car choice may result from examining owners' personal values in addition to their evaluations of car attributes, because luxury cars, like many other conspicuously consumed luxury products, may be purchased mainly for value-expressive reasons.

Industry analysts believe it would be important to assess whether personal values of consumers could be used to explain ownership of American, German, and Japanese luxury cars. Further, they believe they should also assess whether knowledge of owners' personal values provides any additional information useful in explaining ownership of American, German, and Japanese luxury cars beyond that obtained from their evaluations of the cars' attributes.

Personal values are likely to provide insights into reasons for ownership of luxury cars for at least two reasons. First, Americans have always had a very personal relationship with their cars and have used them as symbols of their self-concept. For instance, people who value a *sense of accomplishment* are quite likely to desire a luxury car that they feel is an appropriate symbol of their achievement, whereas people who value *fun, enjoyment, and excitement* are likely to desire a luxury car that they perceive as fun and exciting to drive. An advertiser trying to persuade the former segment to purchase a luxury car should position the car as a status symbol that will help its owners demonstrate their accomplishments to others. Similarly, an advertiser trying to persuade the latter segment to purchase a luxury car should position the car as a fun and exciting car to drive. In other words, effective advertising shows consumers how purchasing a given product will help them achieve their valued state, because brands tied to values will be perceived more favorably than brands that deliver more mundane benefits.

Second, when a market is overcrowded with competing brands offering very similar options—as is the case with the luxury car market—consumers are quite likely to choose between brands on the basis of value-expressive considerations.

METHOD

Data were collected via a mail survey sent to 498 consumers chosen at random from a list obtained from a syndicated research company located in an affluent county in a southern state. The list contained names of people who had purchased either a luxury American car (Cadillac or Lincoln Mercury), a luxury German car (Mercedes or BMW), or a luxury Japanese car (Infiniti or Lexus) within the last year. A cover letter explained that the survey was part of an academic research project. People were asked to return the questionnaires anonymously to a university address (a postage-paid envelope was provided with each survey). Beyond an appeal to help the researchers, respondents were not offered any other incentive to complete the surveys. Of the 498 questionnaires originally sent, 17 were returned by the post office as undeliverable. One hundred fifty-five completed surveys were received, for a response rate of 32.2 percent.

The Survey Instrument

The survey included questions on (1) various issues that people consider when purchasing new cars, (2) importance of car attributes, (3) importance of different values, and (4) demographics (sex, age, education, and family income). Questions relating to the issues that people consider when purchasing new cars were developed through initial interviews with consumers and were measured with a 7-point Likert scale with end anchors of "strongly agree" and "strongly disagree" (See Case Exhibit 4.1). A list of 12 car attributes was developed from the initial interviews with consumers and by consulting *Consumer Reports*. (See Case Exhibit 4.2.) The importance of each attribute was measured with a 7-point numerical scale with end points labeled "very important" and "very unimportant." The List of Values (LOV) scale in Case Exhibit 4.3 was used to measure the importance of values. Respondents were asked to rate each of the eight values (we combined fun, enjoyment, and excitement into one value) on a 7-point numerical scale with end points labeled "very important" and "very unimportant."

CASE EXHIBIT 4.1 Issues That Consumers Consider When Buying Luxury Automobiles

Having a luxury car is a major part of my fun and excitement.[a] (Issue 1)

Owning a luxury car is a part of "being good to myself." (Issue 2)

When I was able to buy my first luxury car, I felt a sense of accomplishment. (Issue 3)

I enjoy giving my friends advice about luxury cars. (Issue 4)

Getting a good deal when I buy a luxury car makes me feel better about myself. (Issue 5)

I seek novelty and I am willing to try new innovations in cars. (Issue 6)

I tend to buy the same brand of the car several times in a row. (Issue 7)

I tend to buy from the same dealer several times in a row. (Issue 8)

I usually use sources of information such as *Consumer Reports* in deciding on a car. (Issue 9)

I usually visit three or more dealerships before I buy a car. (Issue 10)

I would read a brochure or watch a video about defensive driving. (Issue 11)

When buying a new luxury car, my family's opinion is very important to me. (Issue 12)

My family usually accompanies me when I am shopping for a new luxury car. (Issue 13)

I usually rely upon ads and salespersons for information on cars. (Issue 14)

I usually rely upon friends and acquaintances for information on cars. (Issue 15)

When shopping for a car, it is important that the car dealer make me feel at ease. (Issue 16)

Most of my friends drive luxury import cars. (Issue 17)

Most of my friends drive luxury domestic cars. (Issue 18)

I think celebrity endorsers in ads influence people's choices of luxury cars. (Issue 19)

I would not buy a luxury car if I felt that my debt level is higher than usual. (Issue 20)

[a] Note: Subjects' responses were measured with 1 as "strongly agree" and 7 as "strongly disagree."

CASE EXHIBIT 4.2 Car Attributes

Attribute	Code	Attribute	Code
Comfort	Comfort	Low maintenance cost	Lomc
Safety	Safety	Reliability	Rely
Power	Power	Warranty	Warrant
Speed	Speed	Nonpolluting	Nonpol
Styling	Styling	High gas mileage	Gasmle
Durability	Durabil	Speed of repairs	Repairs

CASE EXHIBIT 4.3 List of Values

Value	Code	Value	Code
Fun-Enjoyment-Excitement	Fun	Sense of accomplishment	Accomp
Sense of belonging	Belong	Warm relationship	Warm
Being well respected	Respect	Security	Security
Self-fulfillment	Selfful	Self-respect	Selfres

The Sample

Of the 155 respondents in the sample, 58 (37.4 percent) owned an American luxury car, 38 (24.5 percent) owned a European luxury car, and 59 (38.1 percent) owned a Japanese luxury car. The majority of the sample consisted of older (85 percent were 35 years of age or above), more educated (64 percent were college graduates), and economically well-off (87.2 percent earned $65,000 or more) consumers.

THE CODE BOOK

Case Exhibit 4.4 lists the SPSS variable names and identifies codes for these variables. (Note that this data set is also available in Microsoft Excel.)

CASE EXHIBIT 4.4 List of Variables and Computer Codes

ID—Identification number

AGE (categories are 2 = 35 years and under, 3 = 36–45 yrs, 4 = 46–55 yrs, 5 = 56–65 yrs, 6 = 65 + yrs)

SEX (1 = male, 0 5 female)

EDUC—Education (1 = less than high school, 2 = high school grad, 3 = some college, 4 = college grad, 5 = graduate degree)

INCOME (1 = less than $35,000, 2 = $35,001 − $50,000, 3 = $50,001 - $65,000, 4 = $65,001, or greater)

CAR—Type of luxury car (American car, European car, Japanese car)

ISSUES—The sequence of issues listed in Case Exhibit 4.1. (Strongly agree = 1; strongly disagree = 7)

ATTRIBUTES—The sequence of car attributes listed in Case Exhibit 4.2. (Very important to you = 1; very unimportant to you = 7)

VALUES—The sequence of values listed in Case Exhibit 4.3. (Very important = 1; very unimportant = 7)

ADDITIONAL INFORMATION

Several of the questions will require the use of a computerized database. Your instructor will provide information about obtaining the VALUES data set if the material is part of the case assignment.

Questions

1. Is the sampling method adequate? Is the attitude measuring scale sound? Explain.
2. Using the computerized database with a statistical software package, calculate the means of the three automotive groups for the values variables. Do any of the values variables show significant differences between American, Japanese, and European car owners?
3. Are there any significant differences on importance of attributes?
4. Write a short statement interpreting the results of this research.

Advanced Questions

5. Are any of the value scale items highly correlated?
6. Should multivariate analysis be used to understand the data?

Case materials based on research by Ajay Sukhdial and Goutam Chakraborty, Oklahoma State University.

Case 5   Say It Ain't So! Is This the Real Thing?

INTRODUCTION

David Ortega is the lead researcher for an upscale restaurant group hoping to add another chain that would compete directly with the upscale Smith and Wollensky restaurants (http://www.smithandwollensky .com). Smith and Wollensky is part of the Patina Restaurant Group. The average check for a customer at Smith and Wollensky is approximately $80 to $90.[1] Whenever a new venture of this type is planned, one has to wonder whether there are enough customers willing to pay premium prices given the large number of lesser priced alternatives. In fact, Smith and Wollensky is considering opening a lesser priced "Grill" that would be positioned so that the average customer check would be about half that of the original. What is it that people are willing to pay for and what sacrifices can be made to deliver a satisfying, if not luxurious, experience? How can he create a unique experience at a lower price? These are the questions facing David Ortega.

RESEARCH APPROACH

After considering how to study the issue, David decides a qualitative research approach will be useful. He hopes to develop a deep understanding of how the fine dining experience offers value and perhaps some insights into what intangibles create value for consumers in general. After considering the different options, he decides on a phenomenological approach. The primary tool of investigation is conversational interviewing. David plans to enter into casual conversations with businesspeople in the lounge of the downtown Ritz Carlton. He begins the conversation by commenting on the wine he is sipping—something like, "It isn't bad, but it's hard to believe they get $15 for a glass of this stuff."

[1]MacNealy, Jeremy (2006), "Smith and Wollensky on the Grill," The Motley Fool, http://www.fool.com/News/mft/2006/mft06040425.htm, accessed November 6, 2008.

RESULTS

Two weeks later, David has completed "conversations" with five consumers. He found them very willing and free to talk about the things they indulge in. He develops a field log of notes from the consumers' comments. The notes are recorded verbatim.[2] The following field notes are highlighted:

Respondent	Date/Time	Text
Joe, wm, 55, attorney	12/5/15 – 10:15 PM	Well, wine doesn't have to be expensive to be good. Beyond some basic price point . . . maybe $14 a bottle . . . I find a lot of good wines. But, the wine has to fit the situation. It has to add something. A fake Rolex will tell time; but a real Rolex tells you about you. I don't mind paying for something that's unique—even though it might not be my cup of tea. Chateau Masur is like that. It's from Lebanon! It isn't always elegant or delicious, but it is always real. You always know it comes from some place very unique and is made under the most trying circumstances.
Sally, hf, 45, medical sales	12/7/15 – 5:45 PM	We pay too much for a lot of stuff though. I like things to be genuine. When you ask for crab you get crab—not Krab with a "K." It's made of fish you know!
		. . .
		I love old neighborhood Italian restaurants. They aren't always expensive. But, they have character. I think that it is very easy to spoil. I might not want a checkered red and white table cloth at home, but the Italian restaurant has to have one. I have to smell the garlic from the parking lot. And, that cheap Chianti, the kind with the basket cradle—it had better be from Italy—it tastes sooo good there. You know, you could pay more, but a nice dinner there with a couple of friends is worth a lot.
		You know, the people who make great wine or who have great restaurants kind of luck into it. I don't think they really ever sent out a survey asking what the restaurant or wine should be like. I think they said "I am going to make this the way that I want it to be . . ." and it just happens to be right! They are so committed to the product that it works—no matter the price. But commitment like that costs a little more usually—although they aren't in it for the money.
Hebert, wm, 40, oil executive	12/8/15 – 11:00 PM	How old is it? The older it is, the more it is worth—yeah! I like this French wine that has "depuis 1574," maybe its name is Hugel (trying to recall). Imagine the same family running that company for hundreds of years. I like to think about the family in the vineyards—the old man on a tractor with his sons running around the sides. Their kids are hanging around the barn.
		. . .
		You know, you can buy cheap things and get cheated too. We are free to be cheated at any price point! (laughter) I remember bringing home a bottle of "Louisiana Hot Sauce." Man, that stuff didn't have any heat to it at all. When I looked at the bottle, do you know where it was from? . . . Man, it was from Tennessee . . . can you believe that, Louisiana Hot Sauce from Tennessee!! What a scam.
		. . . .
		When I buy something nice, I want it to be real. Burgundy should be from Burgundy. Bordeaux should be from Bordeaux. Champagne should be from Champagne—not Texas or California! (laughter) Because I know in Champagne, they know how to make Champagne—sparkling wine. They have perfected the methods over hundreds of years. A good glass of Champagne is worth what you pay!
Angela, bf, 60, insurance executive	12/9/15 – 6:45 PM	Look at this hotel . . . when you just look at the price you think "this is crazy!" But, look at the attention to detail. Cleaning the floor is a production. Have you noticed the way they turn down your bed? Taking care of the plants is serious business to these people. I've stayed at a place like this in Florida—I loved it. At first, I couldn't put my finger on it. Then, it hit me. The place smelled like Florida. They have a way of giving everything the smell of sweet grass and citrus. It's terrific. Another one in California smelled of sandalwood and cypress. You have to be willing to pay more for people that care so much about what they do. Maybe that's your wine? Those smells make me think of those special places. When I drink a wine, I think about where it comes from too.
Burt, wm, 35, sales	12/9/15 – 9:30 PM	It's okay for something to be cheap . . . even fake! As long as I know it's fake. I've got three fake Rolexes. This one looks pretty good . . . looks genuine . . . but look at the way the second hand moves . . . it's jumping. A real one wouldn't do that!!
		I ate with this guy the other night who sent back a bottle of wine after ordering it. When the waiter pulled the cork, it didn't have Domaine Mas Blanc written on it—that's the name of the wine. He said, "How do I know it is real?" At first I thought he was crazy but after I looked at my fake Rolex . . . you know, I think he was right. When you spend $100 for a bottle, you want real stuff. But, if you spend $10 for a bottle of wine in a restaurant, who the hell cares? You didn't pay for it to be real . . . one day, when I pony up ten grand for a real Rolex, I'll send back the fakes!

Note: w = white; h = Hispanic, f = female, m = male, etc.

[2]For more comments along this same line, see Beverland, M., "The Real Thing: Branding Authenticity in the Luxury Wine Trade," *Journal of Business Research* 59 (February 2006), 251–258; Beverland, M., "Crafting Brand Authenticity: The Case of Luxury Wines," *Journal of Management Studies* 42 (July 2005), 103–129; and Wolff, C., "Blending High Style and Authenticity," *Lodging Hospitality* 61 (November 1, 2005), 72–76.

RESULTS

David decides to use a word count to try to identify the main themes. Hopefully, these themes can help clarify the business problem. Perhaps if the information can't answer the questions above, it will point him in the right direction. Whatever the case, David feels the project has helped him better understand the total value proposition offered by restaurants, wines, hotels, and other products.

Questions:
1. Comment on the research approach. Do you feel it was an appropriate choice?

2. David did not inform these respondents that he was doing marketing research during these conversations. Why do you think he withheld this information and was it appropriate to do so?
3. Using the Internet, try to identify at least three restaurants that Smith and Wollensky competes with and three with whom the new S&W Grill may compete.
4. Try to interpret the discussions above. You may use one of the approaches discussed in the text. What themes should be coded? What themes occur most frequently? Can the different themes be linked together to form a unit of meaning?
5. What is the result of this research? What should David report back to the restaurant group?

Case 6 TABH, INC., Automotive Consulting

(Download the data sets for this case from www.cengagebrain.com or request them from your instructor.) TABH consulting specializes in research for automobile dealers in the United States, Canada, Mexico, and Europe. Although much of their work is done on a pay-for fee basis with customers such as dealerships and dealership networks selling all major makes of automobiles, they also produce a monthly "white paper" that is sold via their website. This off-the-shelf research is purchased by other research firms and by companies within the auto industry itself. This month, they would like to produce a white paper analyzing the viability of college students attending schools located in small college towns as a potentially underserved market segment.

TABH management assigns a junior analyst named Michel Gonzalez to the project. Lacking time for a more comprehensive study, Michel decides to contact the traffic department at Cal Poly University in Pomona, California, and at Central Missouri State University in Warrensburg, Missouri. Michel wishes to obtain data from the students' automobile parking registration records. Although both schools are willing to provide anonymous data records for a limited number of students, Cal Poly offers Michel a chance to visit during the registration period, which just happens to be next week. As a result, not only can Michel get data from students' registration forms, but a small amount of primary data can be obtained by intercepting students near the registration window. In return, Michel is asked to purchase a booth at the Cal Poly career fair.

As a result, Michel obtains some basic information from students. The information results in a small data set consisting of the follow observations for 100 undergraduate college students in Pomona, California:

Variable	Description
Sex	Student's sex dummy coded with 1 = female and 0 = male
Color	Color of a student's car as listed on his or her registration form
Major	Student's major field of study (Business, Liberal Arts (LA), or Engineering (ENG))
Grade	Student's grade record reported as the mode (A, B, or C)
Finance	Whether the student financed the car he or she is driving or paid for it with cash, coded 0 = cash payment and 1 = financed
Residence	Whether the student lives on campus or commutes to school, coded 0 = commute and 1 = on campus
Animal	Michel asks each student to quickly draw a cartoon about the type of car they would like to purchase. Students are told to depict the car as an animal in the cartoon. Although Michel expects to interpret these cartoons more deeply when time allows, the initial coding specifies what type of animal was drawn by each respondent. When Michel was unsure of what animal was drawn, a second researcher was conferred with to determine what animal was depicted. Some students depicted the car as a dog, some as a cat, and some as a mule.

The purpose of the white paper is to offer car dealers considering new locations a comparison of the profile of a small town university with the primary market segments for their particular automobile. For instance, a company specializing in small pickup trucks appeals to a different market segment than does a company specializing in two-door economy sedans. Many small towns currently do not have dealerships, particularly beyond the "Big 3." Although TABH cannot predict with certainty who may purchase the white paper, it particularly wants to appeal to companies with high sales growth in the United States, such as Kia

(http://www.kia.com), Hyundai (http://www.hyundai-motor.com), and potentially European auto dealerships currently without significant U.S. distribution, such as Smart (http://www.smart.com), among others. TABH also hopes the white paper may eventually lead to a customized project for one of these companies. Thus, the general research question is:

What are the automobile market segment characteristics of students attending U.S. universities in small towns?

This question can be broken down into a series of more specific questions:

- What segments can be identified based on identifiable characteristics of students?
- How do different segments view a car?
- What types of automobiles would be most in demand?

Questions:

1. What types of tests can be performed using the data that may at least indirectly address the primary research question?
2. What do you think the primary conclusions of the white paper will be based on the data provided?

3. Assuming a small college town lacked an auto dealership (beyond Ford, GM, and Chrysler), what two companies should be most interested in this type of location? Use the Internet if necessary to perform some cursory research on different car companies.
4. What are the weaknesses in basing decisions on this type of research?
5. Are there key issues that may diminish the usefulness of this research?
6. What kinds of themes might emerge from the cartoon drawings?
7. Are there any ethical dilemmas presented in this case?

Case 7 Knowing the Way

The Swamp Palace Museum (SPM) is an interactive museum that teaches visitors the ways of life on the swamps of the southern United States. Visitors can visit over 100 exhibits demonstrating the ecology of the swamp and the habits of the animals and insects that call the swamp home. Additionally, the museum includes several fast-food and full-service restaurants and opportunity for swimming and several thrill rides. The park covers over forty acres and includes miles and miles of pathways.

The park was originally supported with one-time government funding but now it has to become self-supporting. After five years of operation, the park has not lacked for visitors but has struggled just to break even. The Swamp Palace has sought help from the Marketivity Group to help them address the long-term viability of the park.

Initially, the Swamp Palace conducts exploratory research employing a participant-observer technique in which trained interviewers pretend to be park guests and engage in dialog with museum patrons. After employing interpretive techniques to the data gathered in these interviews, the Marketivity Group reports the exploratory results to management. The report emphasizes these key findings:

1. Patrons who complain tend to base their complaints over deficiencies in quality. Happy patrons voice nothing indicating a low quality theme.
2. Patrons also express a theme around value. Unhappy patrons believe the value offered by the park is low based in part on what is perceived as a high admission price.
3. Patrons express the difficulty in getting around in the park as a key theme. Even happy patrons joke about how difficult it is to find their way around.
4. As groups get larger, at least one member of the group was unhappy about having to accompany the others to the park.

After further subsequent discussions, Marketivity is hired to undertake a further study aimed at helping in addressing these decision statements:

- In what ways can Swamp Palace use technology to improve a customer's ability to effectively navigate around the museum?
- In what ways can Swamp Palace increase return visits by customers?
- Is participation in online coupon programs an effective way of increasing patronage and value?

Several technologies are considered as ways of enhancing value. One is a mobile phone app that will provide oral and visual navigation aids around the park. For instance, if someone says "take me to the Blind Bayou Bar," the phone will give directions using prominent museum landmarks. Second, Swamp Palace is considering subscribing to an Internet coupon program that would provide patrons with discounts. Marketivity translates these statements into several research questions including the following:

1. Do patrons who use a mobile phone navigation app report higher service quality and have an improved experience relative to those who do not?
2. Do patrons who use the mobile phone app have a greater likelihood of upgrading to a season pass?
3. Do patrons who use a coupon report more positive price perceptions?
4. Do patrons who use the mobile phone app have a greater likelihood of upgrading to a season pass?
5. What factors contribute to improved value perceptions?

Marketivity implements a quasi-experimental design over a one-week period in August. A sample of 200 visitors are randomly intercepted before entering the park. Approximately half are given the opportunity to download a free navigation app for their cell phone. Similarly, about half are invited to go to a kiosk and download a coupon from the Internet. The park provides Marketivity with employees to intercept the patrons and explain the research procedures. Upon exiting the park, the patrons are taken to a desk where they fill out a short questionnaire. The employee then keys the data into the computer. The variables in the data set are described in the table below.

Name	Description*	Values
Wayf	A variable indicating whether the patron was provided the mobile phone app on entering the park	Yes or No
Groupn	A variable indicating whether the patron used a Groupon discount to enter the park	1 = Yes / 2 = No
SQ1	Employees at SPM offer high-quality service	5-point Likert (SD to SA)
SQ2	The attractions at SPM are high in quality	5-point Likert (SD to SA)
SQ3	The food quality at SPM is very good	5-point Likert (SD to SA)
SQ4	The service at SPM is excellent overall	5-point Likert (SD to SA)
SQ5	The quality of SPM is very good	5-point Likert (SD to SA)
VAL1	The time I spent at SPM was truly a joy	5-point Likert (SD to SA)
VAL2	I enjoyed being engaged in exciting activities during my visit to SPM	5-point Likert (SD to SA)
VAL3	While at SPM, I was able to forget my problems	5-point Likert (SD to SA)
VAL4	I think SPM offers guests a lot of value	5-point Likert (SD to SA)
PriceP	The admission price is very fair	5-point Likert (SD to SA)
	Use the terms below to describe your feelings about your overall experience at the museum:	
FEEL1	Favorable —— Unfavorable	7-point Semantic Differential
FEEL2	Exciting —— Boring	7-point Semantic Differential
FEEL3	Happy —— Sad	7-point Semantic Differential
FEEL4	Delighted —— Terrible	7-point Semantic Differential
UPGRADE	Whether respondent agreed to upgrade their ticket to a season pass	1=No / 2=Yes / 3= Undecided
Gender	Sex of respondent	1=Female / 2=Male
Age	Age group	1=less than 18 / 2= 19-24 / 3=25-35 / 4 = 36 - 45 / 5 = 46 or more
Others	How many others were with the patron	0=None / 1=1 / 2=2 / 3=3 / 4= more than 3

*Notes: Missing values in the data set are indicated by either an empty cell (sometimes with a . in the cell) or by the numeral 9. SPM stands for Swamp Place Museum, SD = Strongly Disagree (1) and SA = Strongly Agree (5).

Questions

1. Create frequency tables for Gender, Others, and Age. Are any problems evident with coding? Take any necessary corrective actions.
2. Compute a composite scale for the five SQ items and the four VAL items. Compute a coefficient alpha for each of the resulting service quality and value scales.
3. Perform an appropriate test of each research question RQ1, RQ2, RQ3, RQ4, and RQ5.
4. List an additional research question that can be addressed with a one-way ANOVA. Conduct the test.
5. List an additional research question that can be addressed with a GLM model. Conduct the test.
6. Summarize the implications for the decision statements that arise from the tests above. Make sure you cover whether the park should invest in the navigation system and coupon technologies.

ENDNOTES

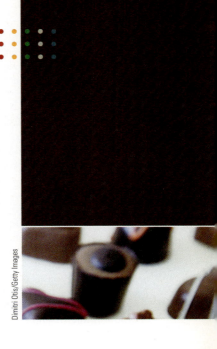

Dimitri Otis/Getty Images

Chapter 1

1 McNeal, M. (2012), "The Secret to Viral Success," *Marketing Research*, (Winter), 10–15.

2 "Coffee: Demographics," in *The 2008 Beverage Market Research Handbook* (Loganville, GA: Richard K. Miller & Associates, 2008), 98–100.

3 Estral, M. and A. Gasparro (2014), "Coming Soon: The Coca-Cola K-Cup," *Wall Street Journal*, (February 6), B1. http://www.marketwatch.com/story/sales-of-single-serve-coffee-have-tripled-since-2011-2013-11-20, accessed March 12, 2014.

4 Garvin, Andrew P., "Evolve Approach to Serve Complex Market," *Marketing News* (September 15, 2005), 22.

5 Burton, S., L. A. Cook, E. Howlett, and C.L. Newman (2014). "Broken Halos and Shattered Horns: Overcoming the Biasing Effects of Prior Expectations through Objective Information Disclosure," *Journal of the Academy of Marketing Science*, 1–17.

6 See, for example, Babin, Barry J., J. C. Chebat, and Richard Michon, "Perceived Appropriateness and Its Effect on Quality, Affect and Behavior," *Journal of Retailing and Consumer Services*, 11 (September 2004), 287–98.

7 Ferrell, O. C., T. L. Gonzalez-Padron, T. Hult, and I. Maignan (2010), "From Market Orientation to Stakeholder Orientation," *Journal of Public Policy and Marketing*, 29 (Spring), 93–96;

Sin, Leo Y. M., Alan C. B. Tse, Oliver H. M. Yau, Raymond P. M. Chow, Jenny S.Y. Lee, and Lorett B.Y. Lau, "Relationship Marketing Orientation: Scale Development and Cross-Cultural Validation," *Journal of Business Research*, 58 (February 2005), 185–94; Nakata, C., and K. Sivakumar, "Instituting the Marketing Concept in a Multinational Setting: The Role of National Culture," *Journal of the Academy of Marketing Science*, 29 (Summer 2001), 255–75; Day, G., "The Capabilities of Market-Driven Organizations," *Journal of Marketing*, 58 (October 1994), 37–52.

8 Gaudoin, T. (2011), "Luggage: An Open and Shut Case," *Wall Street Journal*, (January 28), C12.

9 Manjoo, F. (2013), "The Most Destructive, Unpredictable Force in Tech," *Wall Street Journal*, (October 3), B1.

10 http://wearedevelopment.net/2012/07/11/legos-approach-to-customer-orientation/, accessed March 13, 2014.

11 Arnett, D. and M. Wittmann (2014), "Improving Marketing Success: The Role of Tacit Knowledge Exchange between Sales and Marketing," *Journal of Business Research*, 67 (March), 324–331. Lee, Ruby P., Gillian Naylor, and Qimei Chen (2011), "Linking Customer Resources to Firm Success: The Role of Marketing Program Implementation," *Journal of Business Research*, 64 (April), 394–400; Sin, Leo Y. M., Alan C. B. Tse, Oliver H. M.Yau, Raymond P. M. Chow, Jenny S.Y. Lee, and Lorett B.Y. Lau,

"Relationship Marketing Orientation: Scale Development and Cross-Cultural Validation," *Journal of Business Research*, 58 (February 2005), 185–94.

12 http://opendorse.com/top-100-highest-paid-athlete-endorsers-of-2013/, accessed March 15, 2014.

13 Bojanic, D. C. (2011), "The Impact of Age and Family Life Experiences on Mexican Visitor Shopping Expenditures," *Tourism Management*, 32 (April), 405–14.

14 Wyner, Gordon A. (2005), "Biz Problems Can Get Solved with Research," *Marketing News* (September 15), 33–34.

15 Kesmodel, D., and D. Yadron (2010), "E-Cigarettes Spark New Smoking War," *Wall Street Journal* (August 25), A1–A12.

16 See Allenby, Greg M., Thomas S. Shively, Yang Sha, and Mark J. Garratt (2004), "A Choice Model for Packaged Goods: Dealing with Discrete Quantities and Quantity Discounts," *Marketing Science*, 23 (Winter), 14–21.

17 Mace, S. (2012), "The Impact and Determinants of Nine-Ending Pricing in Grocery Retailing," *Journal of Retailing*, 88 (March), 115–130.

18 http://www.mobilemarketer.com/cms/news/commerce/14694.html, accessed March 16, 2014. http://www.ivycohen.com/MarketingCoach/BrandTransformationDunkinDonuts.html, accessed March 16, 2014.

19 Low, George S. (2000), "Correlates of Integrated Marketing Communications," *Journal of Advertising Research* (May).

20 Li, L.Y. (2011), "Marketing Metrics' Usage: Its Predictors and Implications of Customer Relationship Management," *Industrial Marketing Management*, 40 (January), 139–48.

21 Nielsen Holdings NV (2014), *Continuous Innovation: The Key to Retail Success*. The Nielsen Company: NY, NY.

22 *Express Magazine* (2006), "You Say Tomato, I say Tomahto," (Spring), 19.

Chapter 2

1 Sources: Dwoskin, E. (2014), "What Secrets Your Phone Is Sharing about You," *Wall Street Journal*, (January 13), B1–B7. Walker, J. (2013), "Data Mining to Recruit Sick People," *Wall Street Journal*, (December 16), B1–B2.

2 http://royal.pingdom.com/2008/04/08/the-history-of-computer-data-storage-in-pictures/, accessed March 18, 2014.

3 Belicove, M. (2013), "Discovering Buried Treasure," *Entrepreneur*, 41 (5), 40.

4 Weinberg, B. D., L. Davis, and P. D. Berger (2013), "Perspectives on Big Data," *Journal of Marketing Analytics*, 1 (4), 187–201.

5 Kehrer, D. (2013), "Analysis Shows Jump in Marketing Analytics Jobs," *Forbes*, (8/2), http://www.forbes.com/sites/forbesinsights/2013/08/02/analysis-shows-jump-in-marketing-analytics-jobs/, accessed March 18, 2014.

6 Martinez, M.G. and B. Walton (2014), "The Wisdom of Crowds: The Potential of Online Communities as a Tool for Data Analysis," *Technovation*, 34, 203–214.

7 http://www.fastcodesign.com/1669551/how-companies-like-amazon-use-big-data-to-make-you-love-them, accessed March 18, 2014.

8 Smith, D. G. and D. Strutton (2010), "Has e-Marketing Come of Age? Modeling Historical Influences on Post-Adoption Era Consumer Internet Behaviors," *Journal of Business Research*, 63 (October), 950–956.

9 Evan, A., G. Shankaranarayanan, and P. B. Berger (2010), "Managing the Quality of Marketing Data: Cost/Benefit Tradeoffs and Optimal Configuration," *Journal of Interactive Marketing*, 24 (August), 209–221.

10 Zhou, K. Z. and C. B. Li (2010), "How Strategic Orientations Influence the Building of Dynamic Capability in Emerging Markets," *Journal of Business Research*, 63 (March), 224–231.

11 See Salesforce.com for more about their products and technology.

12 Primack, D. (2014), "Oracle Pays $400 Million for Buekai," *Fortune*, (2/25), 1.

13 Rigby, D. and C. Zook (2002), "Open-Market Innovation," *Harvard Business Review*, (October), 80–89.

14 http://internetworldstats.com, accessed March 20, 2014.

15 Ward, J. and A. Ostrom (2003), "The Internet as Information Minefield: An Analysis of the Source and Content of Brand Information Yielded by Net Searches," *Journal of Business Research*, 56 (Nov), 907–914.

16 Penna, M. D. (2014), "Mobile Marketing: Why Push Technology Notifications Are the Marketer's New Power Tool, New School Marketing Blog, http://www.responsys.com/blogs/nsm/mobile-marketing/push-notifications-marketers-new-power-tool/, accessed March 21, 2014.

17 Fergueson, R. B., "Marines Deploy RFID," *e-Week*, 21 (November 15, 2004), 37. "Benefits of RFID Becoming More Visible" *DSN Retailing Today*, (August 8, 2005), 22.

18 Stevens-Huffman, L. (2013), "Profit from Big Data," *Smart Business Chicago*, (November), 14–17.

19 PR, N. (2014), "Big Data Applications in the Contact Center: Opportunities and Challenges. *PR Newswire US*.

20 Fielding, M. (2010), "C'est Délicieux," *Marketing News*, 44 (September 5), 6.

21 Stevens-Huffman (2013).

22 Hui, S. K., J. Inman, H. Yanliu, & J. Suher (2013). "The Effect of In-Store Travel Distance on Unplanned Spending: Applications to Mobile Promotion Strategies," *Journal of Marketing*, 77(2), 1–16.

23 Strom, R., M. Vendel, and J. Bredican (2014), "Mobile Marketing: A Literature Review on Its Value for Consumers and Retailers, *Journal of Retailing and Consumer Services*, in press, http://dx.doi.org/10.1016/j.jretconser.2013.12.003/; Gao, T., A. J. Rohm, F. Sultan, and M. Pagani (2013), "Consumers Un-tethered: A Three-Market Empirical Study of Consumers' Mobile Marketing Acceptance," *Journal of Business Research*, 66, 2536–2544.

24 Patty Caya, Jakob Nielsen, Kara Pernice, and Amy Schade (2014), "10 Best Intranets of 2014," http://www.nngroup.com/articles/intranet-design/, accessed March 23, 2014.

25 Gabriel, A. R. (2010), "Building Relationships," *Wall Street & Technology*, 28 (December), 16–17. Lamont, J. (2010), "Real-Time Fraud Measures," *KM World*, 19 (Jul/Aug), 12–21.

26 StrongView. (1). StrongView Publishes "A Practical Guide to Modern Marketing Analytics," *Business Wire* (English).

27 Dwoskin, E. (2014), "What Secrets Your Phone Is Sharing about You," *Wall Street Journal* (January 13), B1–B4.

28 Soat, M. (2014), "En Plein Air," *Marketing News*, (February), 29–35.

29 See http://www.turn.com/news/open-data-partnership-announced, accessed March 22, 2014.

30 Hill, K. (2011), "Whac-A-Mole," *Forbes*, 187 (1/17), 36. Vascellaro, J. E. (2010), "Suit to Snuff Out "History Sniffing" Takes Aim at Tracking Web Users," *Wall Street Journal*, (December 6), B1–B2.

Chapter 3

1 Haytko, D. (2008), "Message from the Guest Editor," *Marketing Education Review*, 18 (Spring), 1.

2 *Economist* (2013), "Change Management," 409 (10/12), 80–81.

3 Blumenstyk, G. (2012), "One Business School Is Itself a Case Study in the Economics of Online Education," *Chronicle of Higher Education*, 59 (10/5), B14.

4 Cited in Conant, J. (2008), *The Irregulars*, Simon & Schuster: New York.

5 Sherr, I. (2014), "Zynga Moves to Make Good on Mobile Gaming Pledge," *Wall Street Journal* (Digits), (March 3), blogs.wsj.com/digits/2014/03/03/zynga-moves-to-make-good-on-mobile-gaming-pledge/, accessed April 6, 2014.

6 Zahay, Debra, Abbie Griffin, and Elisa Fredericks (2004), "Sources, Uses, and Forms of Data in the New Product Development Process," *Industrial Marketing Management*, 33 (October), 658–66. Ruiz, D., D. Jain, and K. Grayson (2012), "Subproblem Decomposition: An Exploratory Research Method for Effective Incremental New Product Development," *Journal of Product Innovation Management*, 29, 385–404.

7 Yoon, E., S. Carlotti, and D. Moore (2014), "Make Your Best Customers Even Better," *Harvard Business Review*, 92 (March), 23–25.

8 Research and Markets (2013), "Organic Food & Organic Beverages Market-Global Industry Analysis, Size, Share, Growth, Trends and Forecast 2013–2019, www.researchandmarkets.com /reports/2683746/, accessed April 2, 2014.

9 Jakab, S. (2014), "For Whole Foods, Investors Can Be Finicky," *Wall Street Journal*, (2/12), C1.

10 Hamilton, R., and A. Chernov (2010), "The Impact of Product Line Extensions and Consumer Goals on the Formation of Price Image," *Journal of Marketing Research*, 47 (February), 51–62.

11 Thomas, Jerry W. (2005), "Skipping MR a Major Error," *Marketing News*, (March 4), 50.

12 Kolb, B. (2008), "The Marketing Research Process," *Marketing Research for Nonprofit, Community and Creative Organizations*, 21–41.

13 Einstein, A. and L. Infeld (1942), *The Evolution of Physics* (New York: Simon and Schuster), p. 95.

14 Wunderground (2013), "Coca-Cola Blames Weather for Sales Struggles," (July 16), http://www.wunderground .com/news/coca-cola-blames-weather-sales-struggles-20130716, accessed April 3, 2014.

15 For example, see http://bookstore .gpo.gov/products/sku/703-036-01344-3, accessed April 4, 2014.

16 See Bhardwaj, S., I. Palaparthy, and A. Agrawal (2008), "Exploration of Environmental Dimensions of Servicescapes: A Literature Review," *The ICFAI Journal of Marketing Management*, 7(1), 37–48 for a relevant literature review.

17 Perdue, B. C. and J. O. Summers (1986), "Checking the Success of Manipulations in Marketing Experiments," *Journal of Marketing Research*, 23 (November), 317–26.

18 Babin, B. J., D. M. Hardesty, and T. A. Suter (2003), "Color and Shopping Intentions: The Effect of Price Fairness and Perceived Affect," *Journal of Business Research*, 56 (July), 541–51.

19 Oh, H. and C.H.C. Hsu (2014), "Assessing Equivalence of Hotel Brand Equity Measures in Cross-Cultural Contexts," *International Journal of Hospitality Management*, 36, 156–166.

Chapter 4

1 Sources: Matthes, J., et al. (2013), "Consumers' Green Involvement and the Persuasive Effects of Emotional versus Functional Ads," *Journal of Business Research*, http://dx.doi.org/10.1016/j. jbusres.2013.11.054. Aldhous, P. and P. McKenna (2010), "Hey Green Spender, Spend a Buck on Me," *New Scientist*, 205 (February 20), 6–9. Veal, G. J. and S. Mouzas (2011), "Changes the Rules of the Game: Business Responses to New Regulation," *Industrial Marketing Management*, 40 (February), 290–300.

2 Murphy, L. F. (2013), *GreenBook: Research Industry Trends Report*. AMA Communications Services: New York.

3 Vasishhtha, P. (2010), "Y Worry?" *Advisor Today*, 105 (March), 26–27. https://www .metlife.com/mmi/research/index.html, accessed April 16, 2014.

4 Homomichl, J. (2013), "The 2013 Honomichl Global Top 25 Report," *Marketing News*, (August), 20–55.

5 http://www.jdpower.com/award/2013-initial-quality-study-cadillac-escalade, accessed April 19, 2014.

6 Data taken from Honomichl, J. (2013), "Global Top 25: 2010 Honomichl Report," *Marketing News*, (August 30), 20–55.

7 Reed, B. (2012), "Apple Is Freaking-Out about Top Secret Market Research Being Used in Patent Trial," *BGR*, (August 3), http://bgr.com/2012/08/03/apple-patent-trial-market-research/, accessed April 20, 2014.

8 See Armstrong, J. S. (1989), "Why Do We Know? Predicting the Interests and Opinions of the American Consumer," *Journal of Forecasting*, 5 (September), 464.

9 Terdleman, D. (2014), "Esurance Twitter Contest Goes Viral but Ties Company to Offensive Tweets," *cnet*, (February 3), http://www.cnet.com/news/esurance-twitter-contest-goes-viral-but-ties-company-to-offensive-tweets/, accessed April 20, 2014.

10 Goolsby, J. R., & S. D. Hunt (1992). "Cognitive Moral Development and Marketing," *Journal of Marketing*, 56(1). Cicala, J. E., A.J. Bush, D.L. Sherrell, & G.D. Deitz (2014). "Does Transparency Influence the Ethical Behavior of Salespeople?" *Journal of Business Research*, 67 (September), 1787–1795.

11 Vitell, S., E. Ramos, and C. Nishihara (2010), "The Role of Ethics and Social Responsibility in Organizational Success: A Spanish Perspective," *Journal of Business Ethics*, 91 (February), 467–483. Singhapakdi, A., S. J.Vitell, D. J. Lee, A. M. Nisius, & B.Y. Grace. (2013). "The Influence of Love of Money and Religiosity on Ethical Decision-Making in Marketing." *Journal of Business Ethics*, 114(1), 183–191.

12 Robin, D. P., R. E. Reidenbach, and B. J. Babin (1997), "The Nature, Measurement and Stability of Ethical Judgments in the Workplace," *Psychological Reports*, 80, 563–580.

13 Miller, D. & B. Merrilees (2013). "Rebuilding Community Corporate Brands: A Total Stakeholder Involvement Approach," *Journal of Business Research*, 66(2), 172–179.

14 A firm that conducts surveys and is not involved in selling or telemarketing is generally considered exempt from federal do-not-call legislation. For more on the do-not-call legislation, see www .donotcall.gov.

15 Gillin, Donna L. (2001), "The Evolution of Privacy Legislation: How Privacy Issues Are Changing Research," *Marketing Research*, 13 (Winter), 6–7.

16 MMR Strategy Group (2012), "Should You Worry about Survey Response Rates?" http://mmrstrategy.com/think-tank/should-you-worry-about-survey-response-rates/, accessed April 20, 2014.

17 Ante, S. E. and L. Weber (2013), "Memo to Employees: The Boss Is Watching," *Wall Street Journal*, (October 23), B1–B4. Silverman, R. E. (2013), "Tracking Sensors Invade the Workplace," *Wall Street Journal*, (March 7), B1–B2.

18 Soat, M. (2014), "En Plein Air," *Marketing News*, (February), 29–35.

19 http://www.ftc.gov/news-events/press-releases/2014/02/ftc-approves-kidsafe-safe-harbor-program, accessed April 21, 2014.

20 http://www.kidsafeseal.com /aboutourseals.html, accessed April 21, 2014.

21 Ahuja, R. D., M. Walker, and R. Tadepalli (2001), "Paternalism, Limited Paternalism and the Pontius Pilate Plight When Researching Children," *Journal of Business Ethics*, 32 (July), 81–92; Noguta,V. and C. A. Russell (2014), "Normative Influences on Product Placement Effects: Alcohol Brands in Television Series and the Influence of Presumed Influence," *Journal of Advertising*, 46–62.

22 Spangenberg, E., B. Grohmann, and D. E. Sprott (2005), "It's Beginning to Smell (and Sound) a Lot Like Christmas: The Interactive Effects of Ambient Scent and Music in a Retail Setting," *The Journal of Business Research*, 58 (November), 582–589; Michon, Richard, Jean-Charles

Chebat, and L. W. Turley (2005), "Mall Atmospherics: The Interaction Effects of the Mall Environment on Shopping Behavior," *Journal of Business Research*, 58 (May), 576–583.

23 See, for example, Patterson, M. and J. Schroeder (2010), "Borderlines: Skin, Tattoos and Consumer Culture Theory," *Marketing Theory*, 10 (September), 253–267.

24 Akaah, I. P. and E. A. Riordan (1990), "The Incidence of Unethical Practice in Marketing Research: An Empirical Investigation," *Journal of the Academy of Marketing Sciences*, 90 (Spring), 143–152.

25 Carrigan, M. and M. Kirkup (2001), "The Ethical Responsibilities of Marketers in Retail Observational Research: Protecting Stakeholders through the 'Ethical Research' Covenant," *International Journal of Retail, Distribution and Consumer Research*, 11 (October), 411–435.

26 Sterling, T. (2011), "Committee: Dutch Professor Faked Data for Years," *AP Newswire*, (November 3). Science (2011), "Around the World," 333 (September 16), 1556.

27 Robinson, K. (2009), "Wal-Mart Push Polls Chicago, Claims 74% Support for New Store," *Chicago Sun Times,* (July 29), http://chicagoist.com/2009/07/29/is_wal-mart_push_polling_chicago.php, accessed April 21, 2014.

28 Brennan, M., S. Benson, and Z. Kearns (2005), "The Effect of Introductions on Telephone Survey Participation Rates," *International Journal of Market Research*, 47 (1), 65–74.

29 *Marketing News* (1995), "Marketers Value Honesty in Marketing Researchers," 29 (June 5), 27.

Chapter 5

1 Sources: Russell, M. (2014), "In the Money: VF Corp Outlines 2014 Growth Plans," *Just-Style*, (February 17), http://www.just-style.com/analysis/vf-corp-outlines-2014-growth-plans_id120722.aspx, accessed May 4, 2014. http://www.vfc.com/about/innovation, accessed May 4, 2014.

2 Sayre, Shay (2001); Morse, Janice M. and Lyn Richards (2002), *Readme First for a User's Guide to Qualitative Methods* (Sage: Thousand Oaks, CA).

3 See, for example, Davis, S.F. Golicic, S. F., C. N. Boerstler, S. Choi, and H. Oh (2014), "Does Marketing Research Suffer from Methods Myopia?" *Journal of Business Research*, 66 (September), 1245–1250; Achenbaum, A. A. (2001), "When Good Research Goes Bad," *Marketing Research*, 13 (Winter), 13–15; Wade, K. R. (2002), "We Have Come Upon the Enemy: And They Are Us," *Marketing Research*, 14 (Summer), 39.

4 Harrison III, R. L. (2013). "Using Mixed Methods Designs in the Journal of Business Research," 1990–2010. *Journal of Business Research*, 66 (November), 2153–2162.

5 Babin, Barry J., William R. Darden and Mitch Griffin (1994), "Work and/or Fun: Measuring Hedonic and Utilitarian Shopping Value," *Journal of Consumer Research*, 20 (March), 644–656.

6 Semon, Thomas T. (2002), "You Get What You Pay For: It May Be Bad MR," *Marketing News*, 36 (April 15), 7.

7 New Vision of Beauty. (2013). *Chain Drug Review*, *35*(19), 1–8.

8 Thompson, Craig J. (1997), "Interpreting Consumers: A Hermeneutical Framework for Deriving Marketing Insights from the Tests of Consumers' Consumption Stories," *Journal of Marketing Research*, 34 (November), 438–455 (see pp. 443–444 for quotation).

9 Thompson (1997).

10 While we refer to a hermeneutic unit as being text-based here for simplicity, they can actually also be developed using pictures, videotapes, or artifacts as well. Software such as ATLAS.ti allow files containing pictures, videos, and text to be combined into a hermeneutic unit.

11 Rubinson, J. (2010), "Marketers, Researchers, Lend Me Your Ears," *Brandweek*, 51 (2/15), 34.

12 Winsome, S. J. and P. Johnson (2000), "The Pros and Cons of Data Analysis Software for Qualitative Research," *Journal of Nursing Scholarship*, 32 (4), 393–397.

13 Del Fresno, M. (2011), *Netnografia: Investigacion, Analisis e Intervencion Social Online*. Elsevier: London.

14 See Feldman, Stephen P. (1998), "Playing with the Pieces: Deconstruction and the Loss of Moral Culture," *Journal of Management Studies*, 35 (January), 59–79.

15 www.qualvu.com, accessed May 5, 2014.

16 Reid, D. M. (1999), "Changes in Japan's Post-Bubble Business Environment: Implications for Foreign-Affiliated Companies," *Journal of International Marketing*, 7(3), 38–63.

17 Silber, I., A. Israeli, A. Bustin, and O. B. Zyi (2009), "Recover Strategies for Service Failures: The Case of Restaurants," *Journal of Hospitality Marketing & Management*, 18 (July), 730–741.

18 Strauss, A. L. and J. Corbin (1990), *Basics of Qualitative Research*. Sage Publications: Newbury Park, CA.

19 Geiger, S. and D. Turley (2005), "Personal Selling as a Knowledge-Based Activity: Communities of Practice in the Sales Force," *Irish Journal of Management*, 26, 61–70.

20 Carrington, M. J., B. A. Neville, and G. J. Whitwell (2014), "Lost in Translation: Exploring the Ethical Consumer Intention–Behavior Gap," *Journal of Business Research*, 67, 2759–2767.

21 Gummesson, E. (2014). Commentary on "The Role of Innovation in Driving the Economy: Lessons from the Global Financial Crisis," *Journal of Business Research*, 67 (January), 2743–2750.

22 Beverland, M. (2006), "The Components of Prestige Brands," *Journal of Business Research*, 59 (February), 251–258. Beverland, M. and F. J. Farrelly (2010), "The Quest for Authenticity in Consumption: Consumers' Purposive Choices of Authentic Cues to Shape Experienced Outcomes," *Journal of Consumer Research*, 36 (February), 838–856.

23 2014. "Research and Markets: UK E-Cigarette Market 2014–2018: British American Tobacco Plc, Lorrilard Inc., NIcocigs Ltd & Vivid Vapors Ltd Dominate the New Lucrative Market," *Business Wire*. May 14. Newswires , Ebschost (accessed June 11, 2014). Warren J. R. (2013), "Community-Based Preferences for e-Smoking Cessation," *Qualitative Research Reports in Communication*, 14, 10–18.

24 Woodyard, C. (2010), "Buick Wants to Know How They Really Feel," *USA Today*, (July 20), 3B.

25 Daunt, K. L. and L. C. Harris (2014), "Customers Acting Badly: Evidence from the Hospitality Industry," *Journal of Business Research*, 64, 1034–1042.

26 Babin, Barry J., William R. Darden, and James S. Boles (1995), "Salesperson Stereotypes, Consumer Emotions, and Their Impact on Information Processing," *Journal of the Academy of Marketing Science*, 23 (Spring), 94–105.

27 Murphy, Ian (1996), "Aided by Research, Harley Goes Whole Hog," *Marketing News*, 30 (December 2), 16–17.

28 Boddy, C. (2005), "A Look at the Evidence for the Usefulness, Reliability and Validity of Projective Techniques in Marketing Research," *International Journal of Marketing Research*, 47 (3), 239–254. Carrington, M. J., B. Neville and G. J. Whitwell (2014), "Lost in Translation: Exploring the Ethical Consumer Intention-Behavior Gap," *Journal of Business Research*, 67, 2759–2767.

29 http://www.innovationgames .com/2013/03/fun-with-focus-groups/, accessed Feb. 13, 2015.

30 Arnold, M. (2010), "Sermo Offers On-Demand Physician Focus Groups," *Medical Marketing & Media*, 44 (November), 28.

31 Creamer, Mathew (2005), "Slowly, Marketers Learn How to Let Go and Let Blog," *Advertising Age*, 76 (October 31), 1–35.

32 Fass, Allison (2005), "Collective Opinion," *Forbes*, 176 (November 28), 76–79.

33 Godes, David and Dina Mayzlin (2004), "Using On-Line Conversations to Study Word-of-Mouth Communications," *Marketing Science*, 23, 545–560.

34 Mayo-Smith, D. (2010), "Could You Retweet That Please?" *NZ Business*, 24 (March), 54.

35 Casteleyn et al. (2008).

36 Kozinets, R. (2002), "The Field behind the Screen: Using Netnography for Marketing Research in Online Communities," *Journal of Marketing Research*, 39 (February), 61–72.

37 Smith, A., R. Bolton, and J. Wagner (1999), "A Model of Customer Satisfaction with Service Encounters Involving Failure and Recovery," *Journal of Marketing Research*, 36 (August), 356–372. Bolton, R. and T. M. Bronkhorst (1991), "Quantitative Analysis of Depth Interviews," *Psychology & Marketing*, 8 (Winter), 275–297.

38 http://reviewskeptic.com/, accessed May 12, 2014.

39 Wooliscroft, B., R. D. Tamilia, and S. J. Shapiro (2006), *A Twenty-First Century Guide to Aldersonian Marketing Thought*, Springer: NY.

40 Klahr, S. (2000), "Getting' Buggy with It," *Advertising Age's Creativity*, 8 (May), 9.

41 Nair, G. (2011), "Scientists' Elusive Goal: Reproducing Study Results," *Wall Street Journal*, (December 2), A1–A16.

Chapter 6

1 Sources: http://www.medicare.gov /hospitalcompare/Data/About.html, accessed June 11, 2014. Mathews, M. (2013), "13 Healthstats That Every Healthcare Marketer Should Know in 2013," *Fathom* (January 25), http://www .fathomdelivers.com/blog/healthcare/13-stats-every-healthcare-marketer-should-know-in-2013-and-why/, accessed June 11, 2014. http://www.bmj.com /content/340/bmj.c2016, accessed June 11, 2014.

2 Taves, M. (2014), "If I Could Have More Data…" *Wall Street Journal*, (March 24), R5.

3 Queenan, J. (2013), "Lies, Damn Lies and Revised Numbers," *Wall Street Journal*, (June 9), C11.

4 Vrannica, S. (2014), "A Crisis in Online Ads: One-Third of Traffic Is Bogus," *Wall Street Journal*, (March 24), B1–B5.

5 http://www.npd.com /corpServlet?nextpage=food-beverage-national-eating-trends_s.html, accessed April 2, 2011.

6 Grow, Brian (2005), "Yes, Ma'am, That Part Is in Stock," *Business Week*, (August 1), p. 32 "Servigistics Pricing: Maximizing the Profitability of Your Service Network," Servigistics, http:// www.ptc.com/product/servigistics/, accessed June 21, 2014.

7 Larmer, B. (2013), "Golf in China Is Younger than Tiger Woods, but Growing Up Fast," *New York Times*, (July 14), MM28.

8 Charles, Susan K. (2004), "Custom Content Delivery," *Online*, (March–April), p. 24–29. Fleming, Lee (1997), "Digital Delivery: Pushing Content to the Desktop," *Digital Information Group*, (January 31), p. 7.

9 http://gigaom.com/2013/01/15/from-push-to-pull-why-information-overload-is-changing-our-behavior/, accessed June 17, 2013.

10 https://www.cia.gov/library /publications/the-world-factbook/geos /ez.html, accessed June 17, 2014.

11 This section is based on Levy, Michael and Barton Weitz, *Retail Management* (Homewood, IL: Richard D. Irwin, 1992), pp. 357–358.

12 For illustrations see Mesak, H., A. Bari, B. J. Babin, L. Birou, and A. Jurkus (2011), "Optimum Advertising Policy over Time for Subscriber Service Innovations in the Presence of Service Cost Learning and Customers' Disadoption," *European*

Journal of Operations Research, 211 (June), 642–649. Puneet, M., J. P. Dube', K.Y. Goh, and P. K. Chintagunta (2006), "The Effect of Banner Advertising on Internet Purchasing, *Journal of Marketing Research*, 43 (February), 98–108.

13 See Hanna, R., A. Rohm, and V. Crittenden (2011), "We're All Connected: The Power of Social Media Ecosystem," *Journal of Interactive Marketing*, 1–9.

14 Hayashi, Y.Y., M. H. Hsieh, & R. R. Setiono (2009). "Predicting Consumer Preference for Fast-Food Franchises: A Data Mining Approach." *Journal of the Operational Research Society*, 60(9), 1221–1229.

15 Mehta, N. (2007), "Investigating Consumers' Purchase Incidence and Brand Choice Decisions across Multiple Product Categories: A Theoretical and Empirical Analysis," *Marketing Science*, 26 (Mar/Apr), 457–479.

16 *Wall Street Journal* (2011), "Macy's Catalogs Shoppers' Habits," (March 23), B5.

17 Tirunillai, S., & G. Tellis (2014). "Mining Marketing Meaning from Chatter: Strategic Brand Analysis of Big Data Using Latent Dirichlet Allocation," *Journal of Marketing Research*, 51 (August), 463–479.

18 Ekinci, Y., N. Uray, & F. Ulengin (2014). A Customer Lifetime Value Model for the Banking Industry: A Guide to Marketing Actions. *European Journal of Marketing*, 48(3/4), 17.

19 Totty, Michael (2005), "Making Searches Work at Work," *Wall Street Journal*, (December 19), http://online.wsj.com, accessed February 10, 2006.

20 Shipley, L. (2014), "How Open-Source Software Drives Innovation," *Blue Sky Innovation*, http://bluesky.chicagotribune. com/hub/chi-mit-finding-competitive-advantage-in-open-source-bsi-hub,0,0. htmlstory, accessed June 18, 2014.

21 http://www.jdpower.com/press-releases/2014-north-america-airline-satisfaction-study, accessed June 18, 2014.

22 Weiss, A. M., N. H. Lurie, and D. J. MacInnis (2008), "Listening to Strangers: Whose Responses Are Valuable, How Valuable Are They, and Why?" *Journal of Marketing Research*, 45 (August), 425–436.

23 http://fortune.com/fortune500/wal-mart-stores-inc-1/, accessed June 19, 2014.

24 http://www.retailright.ca/retaillink.htm, accessed June 19, 2014.

25 *Harris Interactive* (2014), "From Talking to Texting, Americans Fess Up to Dangerous Driving Behaviors Despite Recognizing That They're Unsafe," (June 19), http://www.harrisinteractive.com/NewsRoom/HarrisPolls/tabid/447/mid/1508/articleId/1451/ctl/ReadCustom%20Default/Default.aspx, accessed June 19, 2014.

26 Taves, M. (2014), "If I Could Have More Data," *Wall Street Journal*, (March 24), R5.

Chapter 7

1 Swientek, B (2003), "Using Consumer Insights to Guide Package Design: Traditional Research Can Give You Answers. But…" *Brand Packaging* (March 1), accessed at www.interbrand.com, June 30, 2008.

2 Vascellaro, Jessica E. (2005), "Who'll Give Me $50 for This Purse from Nana?" *Wall Street Journal* (December 28), D1–D2.

3 Adams, G. S., F. J. Flynn, and M. I. Norton (2012), "The Gifts We Keep on Giving: Documenting and Destigmatizing the Regifting Taboo," *Psychological Science*, 23, 1145–1150.

4 Brown, M. R., R. K. Bhadury, and N. K. Pope (2010), "The Impact of Comedic Violence on Viral Advertising Effectiveness," *Journal of Advertising*, 39 (Spring), 49–65.

5 Exhibit revised with assistance of Christo Boshoff, Stellenbosh University.

6 Groves, R. and L. Lyberg (2010), "Total Survey Error: Past, Present, and Future," *Public Opinion Quarterly*, 74, 849–879.

7 Cull, William L., Karen G. O'Connor, Sanford Sharp, and Suk-fong S. Tang (2005), "Response Rates and Response Bias for 50 Surveys of Pediatricians," *Health Services Research*, 40 (February), 213.

8 Lee, Eunkyu, Michael Y. Hu, and Rex S. Toh (2004), "Respondent Noncooperation in Surveys and Diaries: An Analysis of Item Non-Response and Panel Attrition," *International Journal of Market Research*, 46 (Autumn 2004), 311.

9 Douglas Aircraft (undated), Consumer Research, p. 13.

10 For an interesting study of extremity bias, see Baumgartner, Hans and Jan-Benedict E. M. Steenkamp (2001), "Response Styles in Marketing Research: A Cross-National Investigation," *Journal of Marketing Research* (May), 143–56.

11 Raven, G. (2008), "Major Holocaust Polls Show Built-In Bias," *Journal of Historical Review*, http://www.vho.org/GB/Journals/JHR/15/1/Raven25.html, accessed February 13, 2015.

12 Network World (2009), "Goodbadugly," 26 (December 21), 5.

13 Wasserman, Todd, Gerry Khermouch, and Jeff Green (2000), "Mining Everyone's Business," *BrandWeek* (February 28), 34.

14 Hof, Robert D. (2005), "The Power of Us," *Businessweek* (June 20), 74–82.

15 Cerrada, C. J., J. Weinberg, K. J. Sherman, & R. B. Saper (2014). "Inter-Method Reliability of Paper Surveys and Computer Assisted Telephone Interviews in a Randomized Controlled Trial of Yoga for Low Back Pain," *BMC Research Notes*, 7(1), 1–10.

16 Kane, J. C., C. Rapaport, A. K. Zalta, D. Canetti, S. E. Hobfoll, & B. J. Hall (2014). "Regular Drinking May Strengthen the Beneficial Influence of Social Support on Depression: findings from a Representative Israeli Sample during a Period of War and Terrorism," *Drug & Alcohol Dependence*, 140, 175–182.

17 Sources for MMS story: Rosen, J. and A. Patel (2014), "Telemarketer Agrees to $3.4 Million FTC Penalty over Unwanted Calls," *Today*, (May 29), http://www.today.com/news/telemarketer-agrees-3-4-million-ftc-penalty-over-unwanted-calls-2D79710375, accessed July 5, 2014. http://simplisafe.com/blog/revolution-will-not-be-robocalled, accessed July 5, 2014.

18 https://gsmaintelligence.com/analysis/2014/02/gauging-the-relationship-between-fixed-and-mobile-penetration/414/, accessed July 4, 2014. http://www.marketingcharts.com/wp/traditional/landline-phone-penetration-dwindles-as-cell-only-households-grow-22577/, accessed July 4, 2014.

19 http://gqrr.com/articles/2013/07/29/the-new-america-a-new-look-at-the-cell-phone-nation/, accessed July 5, 2014.

20 Business Middle East (2010), *Database: Telecommunications* (September), 12.

21 Wang, Y. (2013), "More People Have Cell Phones than Toilets, U.N. Study Shows," TIME.com, http://newsfeed.time.com/2013/03/25/more-people-have-cell-phones-than-toilets-u-n-study-shows/#ixzz2tWBD7ZRW, accessed February 16, 2014.

22 Brick, J. M., P. D. Brick, S. Dipko, S. Presser, C. Tucker, and Y. Yuan (2007), "Cell Phone Survey Feasibility in the U.S.: Sampling and Calling Cell Numbers versus Landline Numbers," *Public Opinion Quarterly*, 71 (Spring), 23–39.

23 Vicente and Reis (2010); Vicente, P. E. Reis and M. Santos (2009), "Using Mobile Phones for Survey Research," *International Journal of Marketing Research*, 51 (5), 613–33.

24 Curtin, Richard, Stanley Presser, and Eleanor Singer (2005), "Changes in Telephone Survey Nonresponse over the Past Quarter Century," *Public Opinion Quarterly* (Spring), 69 (1), 87–95.

25 Cuneo, Alice Z. (2004), "Researchers Flail as Public Cuts the Cord," *Advertising Age* (November 15), 3–52.

26 http://www.people-press.org/2012/05/15/assessing-the-representativeness-of-public-opinion-surveys/, accessed July 6, 2014.

27 Callegaro, M., H. L. McCutheon, and J. Ludwig (2010), "Who's Calling? The Impact of Caller ID on Telephone Survey Response," *Field Methods*, 22 (May 12), 175–91.

28 Hembroff, Larry A., Debra Rusz, Ann Rafferty, Harry McGee, and Nathaniel Ehrlich (2005), "The Cost-Effectiveness of Alternative Advance Mailings in a Telephone Survey," *Public Opinion Quarterly*, 69 (Summer), 232–45.

29 Brennan, Mike, Susan Benson, and Zane Kearns (2005), "The Effect of Introductions on Telephone Survey Participation Rates," *International Journal of Market Research*, 47, (1), 65–74.

30 http://www.marketingresearch.org/calling-cell-phones, accessed July 6, 2014.

31 In a client-based research project using a much higher financial incentive, response rates for courier service reached 55 percent as opposed to 8 percent for snail mail.

32 McLean, S.A., S. J. Paxton, R. Massey, J.M. Mond, B. Rodgers, and P. J. Hay (2014), "Prenotification but not Envelope Teaser Increased Response Rates in a Bulimia Nervosa Mental Health Literacy Survey: A Randomized Controlled Trial," *Journal of Clinical Epidemiology*, 67(August), 870–876.

33 Smith, S. and G. Albuam (2015), "Comparing Panel Respondents to M-Turk Workers in Marketing Research," *Journal of Business Research*, forthcoming.

34 Shih, T.H. and S. Fan (2009), "Comparing Response Rates in E-mail and Paper Surveys: A Meta-Analysis," *Educational Research Review*, 4, 26–40.

35 Fricker, Scott, Mirta Galesic, Roger Tourangeau, and Ting Yan (2005), "An Experimental Comparison of Web and Telephone Surveys," *Public Opinion Quarterly*, 69 (Fall), 370–92.

36 Albaum et al. (2010).

37 Moskowitz, H. R. & B. Martin (2008). "Optimising the Language of E-Mail Survey Invitations," *International Journal of Market Research*, 50(4), 491–510.

38 Porter, P. R. and M. E. Whitcomb (2007), "Mixed-Mode Contacts in Internet Surveys: Paper Is Not Necessarily Better," *Public Opinion Quarterly*, 71 (Winter), 635–48.

39 Gruen, T., T. Osmonbekov, and A. J. Czaplewski (2006), "eWOM: The Impact of Customer-to-Customer Online Know-How Exchange on Customer Value and Loyalty," *Journal of Business Research*, 59 (April), 449–56.

40 Singer, E. and C. Ye (2013), "The Use and Effects of Incentives in Surveys," *Annals of the American Academy of Political and Social Science*," 645 (January), 112–138.

41 Braunsberger, K., H. Wybenga, and R. Gates (2007), "A Comparison of Reliability between Telephone and Web-Based Surveys," *Journal of Business Research*, 60 (July), 758–64.

42 Sinclair, M., J. O'Toole, M. Malawaraarachci, and K. Leder (2012), "Comparison of Response Rates and Cost-Effectiveness for a Community-Based Survey: Postal, Internet and Telephone Modes with Generic or Personalised Recruitment Approaches," *BMC Medical Research Methodology*, 12 (August 31), 132.

Chapter 8

1 Buduson, S. (2014), "Is Your Smartphone Spying on You?" (February 11), http://www.newsnet5.com/news/local-news/investigations/is-your-smartphone-spying-on-you-how-tech-companies-track-your-every-move; Halleck, T. (2014), "Google's New Satellites Can Spy on Apple's Supply Chains, Skybox CEO Says," *International Business Times* (June 17), http://www.ibtimes.com/googles-new-satellites-can-spy-apples-supply-chains-skybox-ceo-says-1603642, accessed July 7, 2014.

2 Dumas, A. (2007), "The Limits of Market Research Methods," *Advertising Age*, 78 (October 18), 27.

3 Naik, G. (2012), "Analytical Trend Troubles Scientists," *Wall Street Journal*, (May 3), A1–A12.

4 Redmond, E. C. and C. J. Griffith (2003), "A Comparison and Evaluation of Research Methods Used in Consumer Food Safety Studies," *International Journal of Consumer Studies*, 27 (January), 17–33.

5 Abrams, Bill, *The Observational Research Handbook* (Chicago: NTC Business Books, 2000), pp. 2, 105.

6 Phillips, A. (2011), "Researchers, Snoppers and Spies—The Legal and Ethical Challenges Facing Observational Research," *International Journal of Marketing Research*, 52 (2), 275–78.

7 Frizell, S. (2014), "There's a Right to Be Forgotten Industry – and It's Booming," *Time* (July 18), http://time.com/3002240/right-to-be-forgotten-2/, accessed July 19, 2014.

8 Phillips (2011).

9 Judah, G., R. Aunger, W.P. Schmidt, S. Michie, S. Granger, and V. Curtis (2011), "Experimental Pretesting of Hand-Washing," *American Journal of Public Health*, 99 (September 2), S405–411.

10 Ivana Mamic, L., & I. Arroyo Almaraz (2013), "How the Larger Corporations Engage with Stakeholders through Twitter," *International Journal of Market Research*, 55(6), 851–872.

11 Parker, J. (2013), "A Typology of Retail Video Advertising," doctoral dissertation, Louisiana Tech University.

12 "Audience Measurement," Nielsen Media Research, http://www.nielsen.com/us/en/solutions/measurement/television.html, accessed July 14, 2014.

13 "Nielsen Releases Radar June 2014 Network Ratings," http://www.nielsen.com/us/en/press-room/2014/nielsen-releases-radar-june-2014-network-ratings.html, accessed July 14, 2014.

14 Barr, A. (2014), "Google Tests a Way to Follow You to the Mall," *Wall Street Journal* (April 14), B1–B4.

15 Lang, B. (2014), "'Gravity' Charts Biggest Social Media Comeback, 'The Heat' Is Twitter's Funniest Movie (Exclusive)," *The Wrap*, (January 27), http://www.thewrap.com/gravity-charts-biggest-social-media-comeback-heat-twitters-funniest-movie-exclusive/, accessed July 15, 2014.

16 Walmsley, A. (2010), "A Lot of Buzz about Nothing," *Marketing* (November 24), 12.

17 Kiley, David (2006), "Google: Searching for an Edge in Ads," *Businessweek* (January 30), 80–82. infotrac.galegroup.com. See also Pieter Sanders and Bram Lebo, "Click Tracking: A Fool's Paradise?" *Brandweek* 46 (June 6, 2005), 46; Klaassen, A., M. Creamer, A. Hampp, and E. Tan (2007), "10 Lessons from the Ad Age Digital Marketing Conference," *Advertising Age* (March 12), 42.

18 Neff, Jack (2005), "Aging Population Brushes Off Coloring," *Advertising Age*, 76 (July 25), 3–49.

19 David M. Hardesty, R.C. Goodstein, D. Grewal, A.D. Miyazaki, and P. Kopalle (2014), "The Accuracy of Scanned Prices," *Journal of Retailing*, 90 (June), 291–300,

20 Barbanel, J. (2014), "Outside Public Housing, Cameras Abound," *Wall Street Journal*, (June 5), http://online.wsj.com/articles/police-identify-suspect-in-prince-joshua-avittos-fatal-stabbing-in-brooklyn-by-matching-dna-on-the-knife-1401906762, accessed September 1, 2014.

21 Horovitz, B. (2007), "Marketers Take a Close Look at Your Daily Routines," *USA Today*, www.usatoday.com/money/advertising/2007-04-29-watching-marketing_N.htm, accessed July 14, 2014.

22 Starr, R. G. and K.V. Fernandez (2007), "The Mindcam Methodology: Perceiving through the Native's Eye," *Qualitative Market Research: An International Journal*, 10, no. 2, 168–82.

23 Hotz, R.L. (2011), "The Really Smart Phone," *Wall Street Journal*, C1.

24 Stringer, Kortney (2005) "Eye-Tracking Technology for Marketers," *Detroit Free Press* (August 1), downloaded from http://www.highbeam.com/doc/1G1-134701284.html, accessed December 18, 2008; Hill, D. (2007), "Face Value," *Marketing Research*, 19 (Fall), 9–14.

25 Lee, N. and A.J. Broderick (2007), "The Past, Present and Future of Observational Research in Marketing," *Qualitative Market Research: An International Journal*, 10, no. 2, 121–29.

26 Yoon, C., R. Gonzalez, and J. R. Bettman (2009), "Using fMRI to Inform Marketing Research: Challenges and Opportunities," *Journal of Marketing Research*, 46, 17–19; Reimann, M., O. Schilke, B. Weber, C. Neuhaus, and J. Zaichkowski (2011), "Functional Magnetic Resonance Imaging in Consumer Research: A Review and Application," *Psychology & Marketing*, 28 (June), 608–37.

27 Krugman's, Herbert B. (1981), statement as quoted in "Live, Simultaneous Study of Stimulus, Response Is Physiological Measurement's Great Virtue," *Marketing News* (May 15), pp. 1, 20.

28 New Media Age (2005), "Mazda Turns to Eye-Tracing to Assist Revamp of European Site," (November 3), 8.

29 Koh, Y. (2014), "Twitter Shakes Up Strategy on Metrics," *Wall Street Journal*, (July 18), B1–B2. http://ssl.marketplace.org/topics/business/twitter-may-change-metrics-reflect-wider-audience, accessed July 19, 2014.

Chapter 9

1 See http://www.law.com and search key terms such as *cigarettes, tobacco, Brown* and *Williamson* for some examples.

2 Doward, J. (2003), "Cigarette Giant to Deny Cancer Link," *The Observer* (October 5), http://www.guardian .co.uk/society/2003/oct/05/smoking .cancercare, accessed Feb. 14, 2015; Seenan, Gerard (2005), "Smoker's Widow Loses Legal Fight," *The Observer* (June 1). http://www.guardian.co.uk /society/2005/jun/01/smoking. publichealth1, accessed Feb. 14, 2015.

3 See, for example, Bolton, L. E., J. B. Cohen, and P. N. Bloom, "Does Marketing Products as Remedies Create 'Get Out of Jail Free Cards'?" *Journal of Consumer Research* 33 (June 2006), 71–84; Smith, K. H. and M. A. Stutts, "The Influence of Individual Factors on the Effectiveness of Message Content in Antismoking Advertisements Aimed at Adolescents," *The Journal of Consumer Affairs* 40 (2006), 261–293; Zhao, G. and C. Pechmann, "The Impact of Regulatory Focus on Adolescents' Response to Antismoking Advertising Campaigns," *Journal of Marketing Research* 44 (November 2007), 671–687.

4 Babin, Barry J., David M. Hardesty, and Tracy A. Suter (2003), "Color and Shopping Intentions: The Intervening Effect of Price Fairness and Perceived Affect," *Journal of Business Research* 56 (July), 541–551.

5 Christie, J., D. Fisher, J. Kozup, S. Smith, S. Burton, and E. Creyer, "The Effects of Bar-Sponsored Alcohol Beverage Promotions across Binge and Nonbinge Drinkers," *Journal of Public Policy and Marketing* 20 (Fall 2001), 240–253.

6 Like Dragnet, the story is true but the brand names are fictitious.

7 Reitter, Robert N. (2003), "Comment: American Media and the Smoking-Related Behaviors of Asian Adolescents," *Journal of Advertising Research* 43 (March), 12–13.

8 HHS (2014), "Trends in Tobacco Use," http://www.hhs.gov/ash/oah /adolescent-health-topics/substance-abuse/tobacco/trends.html#_ftn3, accessed July 30, 2014.

9 Mitchell, Vincent-Wayne, and Sarah Haggett (1997), "Sun-Sign Astrology in Market Segmentation: An Empirical Investigation," *Journal of Consumer Marketing* 14, no. 2, 113–131.

10 Shiv, Baba, Ziv Carmon, and Dan Aneley (2005), "Placebo Effects of Marketing Actions: Consumers May Get What They Pay For," *Journal of Marketing Research* 42 (November), 383–393.

11 Marcus, A.D. (2014), "Researchers Fret as Social Media Lift Veil on Drug Trials," *Wall Street Journal*, (July 30), A1–A10.

12 Albergotti, R. (2014), "Facebook Lab Had Few Limits: Data Science Group Conducted Experiments on Users with Little Oversight," *Wall Street Journal*, (July 3), A1–A2.

13 White, J. B. (2010), "Why Toyota Rolled Over for Its SUVs," *Wall Street Journal*, (April 21), D1–D2.

14 Peterson, R.A. and D.R. Merunka (2014), "Convenience Samples of College Students and Research Reproducibility," *Journal of Business Research*, 67 (May), 1035–1041.

15 Paolacci, G., J. Chandler, and P.G. Iperirotis (2010), "Running Experiments on Mechanical Turk," *Judgment and Decision-Making,* 5 (August), 411–419.

16 Dagger, T. S. and P. J. Danaher (2014), "Comparing the Effect of Store Remodeling on New and Existing Customers," *Journal of Marketing,* 78 (May), 62–80.

17 Riell, H. (2008), "Getting Back to Beer," *Convenience Store Decisions* 19 (February), 14.

18 http://appellationbeer.com/blog/friday-beer-so-this-is-where-all-the-cascade-hops-are-going/, accessed August 1, 2014.

19 Elliot, N. (2014), "Instagram Is the King of Social Media," *Forrester Research,* (April 29), http://blogs.forrester.com/nate_elliott/14-04-29-instagram_is_the_king_of_social_engagement, accessed July 31, 2014.

20 Ramage, Norma, "Testing, Testing 1, 2, 3," *Marketing Magazine* 110 (July 2005), 1196; CNW_Telbec, "Imperial Tobacco Canada Lives Up to Its Corporate Social Responsibility Promise," *Groupe CNW* (2007), http://www.newswire.ca/fr/ releases/archive/September2007/12 /c7976.html, accessed August 1, 2014.

21 Tybout, Alice M. and Gerald Zaltman (1974), "Ethics in Marketing Research: Their Practical Relevance," *Journal of Marketing Research* 21 (November), 357–368.

22 Albergotti (2014).

23 Reprinted with permission from Lee Martin, Geoffrey "Drinkers Get Court Call," *Advertising Age* (May 20, 1991). Copyright © 1991 Crain Communications, Inc.

Chapter 10

1 Reichheld, F. F., "The One Number You Need to Grow," *Harvard Business Review* 81 (2003), 46–54; Keiningham, T. L., B. Cooil, T. W. Andreassen, and L. Aksoy, "A Longitudinal Examination of the Net Promoter and Firm Revenue Growth," *Journal of Marketing* 71 (2007), 39–51; Grisaffe, D. B., "Questions about the Ultimate Question: Conceptual Considerations in Evaluating Reichheld's Net Promoter Score (NPS)," *Journal of Consumer Satisfaction, Dissatisfaction and Complaining Behavior* 20 (2007), 36–53; Kumar, V., I. D. Pozza, and J. Ganesh, "Revisiting the Satisfaction–Loyalty Relationship: Empirical Generalizations and Directions for Future Research," *Journal of Retailing*, 89 (September 2013), 246–262.

2 See Mollen, A., & H. Wilson (2010). "Engagement, Telepresence and Interactivity in Online Consumer Experience: Reconciling Scholastic and Managerial Perspectives," *Journal of Business Research*, 63, 919–925.

3 Periatt, J. A., S. A. LeMay, and S. Chakrabarty, "The Selling Orientation-Customer Orientation (SOCO) Scale: Cross-Validation of the Revised Version," *Journal of Personal Selling and Sales Management*, 24 (Winter 2004), 49–54.

4 Cohen, Jacob, "Things I Have Learned (So Far)," *American Psychologist,* 45 (December 1990), 1304–1312.

5 Theacsi.org, accessed August 14, 2014.

6 In more advanced applications such as those involving structural equations analysis, a distinction can be made between reflective composites and formative indexes. See Hair, J. F., W. C. Black, B. J. Babin, R. Anderson, and R. Tatham, Multivariate Data Analysis, 6th ed. (Upper Saddle River, NJ: Prentice Hall, 2006).

7 Bart, Yakov, Venkatesh Shankar, Fareena Sultan, and Glen L. Urban, "Are the Drivers and Role of Online Trust the Same for All Web Sites and Consumers? A Large-Scale Exploratory Study," *Journal of Marketing*, 69 (October 2005), 133–152.

8 Cronbach, Lee J., "My Current Thoughts on Coefficient Alpha and Successor Procedures," Center for the Study of Evaluation Report, 64, no. 3 (2004), http://epm.sagepub.com/cgi/content/ short/64/3/391, accessed August 14, 2014.

9 Hair et al. (2009).

10 Burke Marketing Research, "Rough Commercial Recall Testing," *Cincinnati*, OH (undated).

11 Cox, Keith K. and Ben M. Enis, *The Marketing Research Process* (Pacific Palisades, CA: Goodyear, 1972); Kerlinger, Fred N., *Foundations of Behavioral Research*, 3rd ed. (Ft. Worth: Holt, Rinehart and Winston, 1986).

12 Patton, L. (2013), "Dunkin Hopes You Stop and Smell the Coffee," *Bloomberg Businessweek*, (June 13), 26–28. Sharf, S. (2014). Starbucks' Earnings Scorch Dunkin's with Same Store Sales Strength. Forbes.com, 22.

13 Hotz, R. L. (2011), "Songs Stick in Teens' Heads," *Wall Street Journal*, (June 13), AA1.

14 Romaniuk, J. (2013). "How Healthy is Your Brand-Health Tracker?: A Five-Point Checklist to Build Returns on a Critical Research Investment," *Journal of Advertising Research*, 53(1), 11–13.

15 Wallace, E., I. Buil, L. de Chematony, & M. Hogan (2014). "Who 'Likes' You... And Why? A Typology of Facebook Fans: From 'fan'-atics and Self-Expressives to Utilitarians and Authentics." *Journal of Advertising Research*, 54(1), 92–109. Bruner, J. (2011). What's a "Like" Worth?. *Forbes*, 188(2), 28–30.

16 Osgood, Charles, George Suci, and Percy Tannenbaum, *The Measurement of Meaning* (Urbana: University of Illinois Press, 1957). Seven-point scales were used in the original work; however, subsequent researchers have modified the scale to have five points, nine points, and so on.

17 Peterson, R. A. and W. Wilson, "Measuring Customer Satisfaction: Fact and Artifact," *Journal of the Academy of Marketing Science* 20 (Spring 1992), 61–71; Dawes, J., "Do Data Characteristics Change According to the Number of Scale Points Used? An Experiment Using 5-Point, 7-Point and 10-Point Scales," *International Journal of Market Research* 50, no. 1 (2008), 61–77.

18 Weigters, B., E. Cabooter, and N. Schillewaert (2010), "The Effect of Rating Scale Format on Response Styles: The Number of Response Categories and Response Category Labels," *International Journal of Research in Marketing*, 27 (September), 236–247.

19 Roster, C. A., R. D. Rogers, and G. Albaum (2007), "A Comparison of Response Characteristics from Web and Telephone Surveys," *International Journal of Marketing Research*, 46 (Fall), 359–373. Albaum, G., C. A. Roster, J.

Wiley, J. Rossiter, and S. M. Smith (2010), "Designing Web Surveys in Marketing Research: Does Use of Forced Answering Affect Completion Rates?" *Journal of Marketing Theory and Practice*, 18 (Summer), 285–293.

20 See Muk, A., "Consumers' Intentions to Opt in to SMS Advertising," *International Journal of Advertising* 26, no. 2 (2007), 177–198; or Summers, T. A., "Predicting Purchase Intention of a Controversial Luxury Apparel Product," *Journal of Fashion Marketing & Management* 10, no. 4 (2006), 405–419, for examples.

Chapter 11

1 Sources: De Jong, M. G., R. Pieters, and J. P. Fox (2010), "Reducing Social Desirability Bias through Item Randomized Response: An Application to Measure Underreported Desires," *Journal of Marketing Research*, 47 (February), 14–27. http://www.huffingtonpost.com/2013/05/03/internet-porn-stats_n_3187682.html, accessed August 18, 2014. http://www.businessinsider.com/decline-of-facebook-user-numbers-2014-4, accessed August 18, 2014.

2 Smith, Robert, David Olah, Bruce Hansen, and Dan Cumbo, "The Effect of Questionnaire Length on Participant Response Rate: A Case Study in the U.S. Cabinet Industry," *Forest Products Journal* 53 (November–December 2003), 31.

3 Giraud, G., C. Tebby, and C. Amblard (2011), "Measurement of Consumers' Wine-Related Knowledge," INRA UMR CESAER Working Paper, Dijon, France.

4 Miller, K. M., R. Hofstetter, H. Krohmer, and Z. J. Zhang (2011), "How Should Consumers' Willingness to Pay Be Measured? An Empirical Comparison of State-of-the-Art Approaches?" *Journal of Marketing Research*, 48 (February), 172–84.

5 Donahue, Amy K. and Joanne M. Miller, "Citizen Preferences and Paying for Police," *Journal of Urban Affairs* 27, no.4 (2005), 419–35.

6 Roll, Charles W., Jr. and Albert H. Cantril, *Polls: Their Use and Misuse in Politics* (New York: Basic Books, 1972), pp. 106–7.

7 Other product attributes are relative advantage, compatibility, complexity, and communicability.

8 Dawson, L., "Will Feminization Change the Image of the Sales Profession?" *Journal of Personal Selling and Sales Management* 12 (Winter 1992), 21–32.

9 Lietz, P. (2010), "Research into Questionnaire Design: A Summary of the Literature," *International Journal of Market Research*, 52 (2), 249–72.

10 Malhotra, Neil (2008), "Completion Time and Response Order Effects in Web Surveys," *Public Opinion Quarterly*, 22 (5), 914–34.

11 Holbrook, A. L. and J. A. Krosnick (2010), "Measuring Voter Turnout by Using Randomized Response Technique: Evidence Calling into Question the Method's Validity," *Public Opinion Quarterly*, 74, 328–43. De Jong, M. G., R. Pieters, and J. P. Fox (2010), "Reducing Social Desirability Bias through Item Randomized Response: An Application to Measure Underreported Desires," *Journal of Marketing Research*, 47 (February), 14–27.

12 See Holbrook and Krosniek (2010) for more details on computation.

13 Malhotra (2008).

14 Smith, S., G. Albaum, and L. Golden (2015), "Comparing Panel Respondents to Crowdsourcing," *Journal of Business Research*, in press.

15 Peychev, A. (2009), "Survey Breakoff," *Public Opinion Quarterly*, 71 (Spring), 74–97.

16 Harzing, Anne-Wil, "Does the Use of English-Language Questionnaires in Cross-National Research Obscure National Differences?" *International Journal of Cross Cultural Management* 5, no. 2 (2005): 213–24.

17 Cateora, Philip R., *International Marketing* (Homewood, IL: Richard D. Irwin, 1990), pp. 387–89.

Chapter 12

1 Brock, Sabra E. "Marketing Research in Asia: Problems, Opportunities, and Lessons," *Marketing Research* (September 1989), p. 47.

2 Rideout, Bruce E., Katherine Hushen, Dawn McGinty, Stephanie Perkins, and Jennifer Tate, "Endorsement of the New Ecological Paradigm in Systematic and E-Mail Samples of College Students," *Journal of Environmental Education* 37 (Winter 2005), 3–11.

3 Krosnick, J., "The Distinguishing Characteristics of Frequent Survey Participants," *Proceedings of Midwestern Political Science Association* 1 (2006).

4 Krosnick, J., D. Rivers, and N. Norman, "Web Survey Methodologies: A Comparison of Survey Accuracy," *Proceedings of the American Association for Public Opinion Research* 1 (2005).

5 Harris Interactive (2011), "Sampling Support and Design," http://www.harrisinteractive.com/vault/HI_SP_Sheet_SamplingSupportandDesign.pdf, accessed August 3, 2011.

6 Hansen, J. M., & S. M. Smith (2012). "The Impact of Two-Stage Highly Interesting Questions on Completion Rates and Data Quality in Online Marketing Research," *International Journal of Market Research*, 54(2), 241–260.

7 Craig, C. S. and S. P. Douglas (2011), "Assessing Cross-Cultural Theory and Research: A Commentary Issue," *Journal of Business Research*, 64 (June), 625–627.

8 Sigenman, Lee, Steven A. Tuch, and Jack K. Martin, "What's in a Name? Preference for 'Black' versus 'African-American' among Americans of African Descent," *Public Opinion Quarterly* 69 (fall 2005), 429–438.

Chapter 13

1 Hayes, B. (2014), "The Hidden Bias in Customer Metrics," Business Broadway, (August 4), http://businessoverbroadway.com/the-hidden-bias-in-customer-metrics, accessed 8/27/2014. "Gaming News," *Marketing News*, 42 (February 1, 2008), 39; Hellebusch, S. J., "Know Sample Quantity for Clearer Results," *Marketing News*, 40 (September 15, 2006), 23–26; Sheth-Voss, P., "How Big Should Your Sample Be?" *Marketing Research*, 20 (Summer 2008), 25–29.

2 Most of the statistical material in this book assumes that the population parameters are unknown, which is the typical situation in most applied research projects.

3 See Jurik, R., M. Moody, and J. Seal, "The Mean vs. the Top Box(es) Scores," *Marketing Research*, 20 (Summer 2008), 41–42.

4 The reasons for this are related to the concept of degrees of freedom, which is explained further in a further discussion of analytics. At this point, just remember that anytime a sample is involved rather than a population, we divide by n-1 as a correction for statistical bias that would occur otherwise.

5 In practice, most survey researchers will not use this exact formula. A modification of the formula, $Z = (X - \mu)/S$, using the sample standard deviation in an adjusted form, is frequently used.

6 Hayes, William L. *Statistics* (New York: Holt, Rinehart and Winston, 1963), p. 193.

7 Wonnacott, Thomas H., and Ronald J. Wonnacott. *Introductory Statistics*, 2nd ed. (New York: Wiley, 1972), p. 125.

8 Note that the derivation of this formula is (1) $E = ZS_X$; (2) $E = ZS/\sqrt{n}$ (3) $\sqrt{n} = ZS/E$; (4) $n = (ZS/E)^2$.

9 Groves, R. M. (2006), "Nonresponse Rates and Nonresponse Bias in Household Surveys," *Public Opinion Quarterly*, 70, 646–675.

Chapter 14

1 Sources: Phau, I. and M. Baird (2008), "Complainers versus Non-Complainers Retaliatory Responses towards Service Dissatisfactions," *Marketing Intelligence & Planning*, 26, 567–604. Ramsey, R. D. (2010), "How to Handle Customer Complaints," *The American Salesman*, 55 (June), 25–30.

2 The Harris Poll (2014), *He Was Both Captain Phillips and Walt Disney and Tom Hanks Is Also America's Favorite Movie Star*. Harris Interactive Inc: New York.

3 Dilmperi, A., T. King, and C. Dennis (2011), "Pirates of the Web: The Curse of Illegal Downloading," *Journal of Retailing and Consumer Services*, 18 (March), 132–140.

4 See Schultz, D. E. and M. P. Block (2011), "How U.S. Consumers View In-Store Promotions," *Journal of Business Research*, 54 (January), 51–54.

5 http://www.wineinstitute.org/resources/statistics, accessed September 4, 2014.

6 See a comprehensive statistics text such as Hair et al. (2010; Multivariate Data Analysis) for a more detailed explanation.

7 http://cherylandsue.blogspot.com/2007/02/shampoo-is-more-than-just-washing-your.html, accessed October 7, 2014.

Chapter 15

1 Sources: De Bock, T. and P. V. Kenhove (2011), "Double Standards: The Role of Techniques of Neutralization," *Journal of Business Ethics*, 99, 283–296. Vermeir, I. and P.V. Kenhove (2008), "Gender Differences in Double Standards," *Journal of Business Ethics*, 81, 281–298.

2 Three nonparametric tests—the Wilcoxon matched-pairs signed ranks test, the Kruskal–Wallis test, and the Mann–Whitney U test—can also be used but are not described here.

3 The formula is not shown here but it can be found in most basic statistics books.

4 See, for example, Armstrong-Stassen, M. (2002), "Designated Redundant but Escaping Lay-Off: A Special Group of Lay-Off Survivors," *Journal of Occupational and Organizational Psychology* 75 (March), 1–13.

Chapter 16

1 Dowling, M., "Mr. Dowling's Rosetta Stone Page," http://www.mrdowling.com/604-rosettastone.html, accessed August 21, 2011. Singh, S. (2011), "The Decipherment of Hieroglyphics," BBC History, http://bbc.co.uk/history/ancient/egyptians/decipherment_01.shtml, accessed August 21, 2011.

2 Yore, L. D., M. K. Florence, T. W. Pearson, and A. J. Weaver (2006), "Written Discourse in Scientific Communities: A Conversation with Two Scientists about Their Views of Science, Use of Language, Role of Writing in Doing Science, and Compatibility between Their Epistemic Views and Language," *International Journal of Science Education* 28 (February), 109–141.

3 Sullivan, E. A. (October 15, 2008), "Twitterpated: Marketers Enamored of Online Communication System," *Marketing News*, 8.

4 An earlier version of this chapter was written by John Bush, Oklahoma State University, and appeared in William G. Zikmund, *Business Research Methods* (Hinsdale, IL: Dryden Press, 1984).

5 "A Speech Tip," *Communication Briefings* 14, no. 2 (1995), p. 3.

6 These guidelines, adapted with permission from Marjorie Brody (President, Brody Communications, 1200 Melrose Ave., Melrose Park, PA 19126), appeared in "How to Gesture When Speaking," *Communication Briefings* 14, no. 11 (1995), p. 4.

7 "Tips of the Month," *Communication Briefings* 24, no. 7 (May 2005), p. 1.

8 Based on Bridis, T. (June 1, 2005), "Study: Shoppers Naïve about Online Pricing," *Information Week*, downloaded from InfoTrac at http://web2.infotrac.galegroup.com; Annenberg Public Policy Center (APPC), "Annenberg Study Shows Americans Vulnerable to Exploitation in the Online and Offline Marketplace," news release (June 1, 2005), http://www.annenbergpublicpolicycenter.org; and Turow, J., L. Feldman, and K. Meltzer (June 2005), "Open to Exploitation: American Shoppers Online and Offline," APPC report, downloaded at http://www.annenbergpublicpolicycenter.org.

Chapter 18

1 Volpe, M. (2013), "The 6 Marketing Metrics Your CEO Actually Cares About," Hubspot: Inbound Marketing, http://blog.hubspot.com/blog /tabid/6307/bid/34054/The-6-Marketing-Metrics-Your-CEO-Actually-Cares-About-Cheat-Sheet.aspx, assessed October 12, 2014.

2 Kedem, B. and K. Fokianos (2003), *Regression Models for Time Series*, Wiley Inc.: New York.

Chapter 19

1 Hunt, S.D. (2010), *Marketing Theory: Foundations, Controversy, Strategy, Resource-Advantage Theory*, ME Sharpe: Armonk, NY.

2 Barring some data anomalies.

3 Yoon, S., S. Oh, S. Song, K. Kim, and Y. Kim (2014), "Higher Quality of Lower Price? How Value-Increasing Promotions Retailer Reputation Via Perceived Value," *Journal of Business Research*, in press.

4 For a thorough discussion of issues related to mediation effects, see Bullock, J.G., D.P. Greene, and S.E. Hu (2010), "Yes, But What Is the Mechanism? (Don't Expect an Easy Answer)", *Journal of Personality and Social Psychology*, 98, 550–558.

5 Preacher, K.J. and A.F. Hayes (2004), "SPSS and SAS Procedures for Estimating Indirect Effects in Simple Mediation Models," *Behavior Research Methods, Instruments, and Computers*, 36 (4), 717–731. Preacher, K.J. and A.F. Hayes (2008), "Asymptotic and Resampling Strategies for Assessing and Comparing Indirect Effects in Multiple Mediator Models," *Behavior Research Methods*, 40 (3), 879–891. 1. Zhao, X., J.G. Lynch, Jr. and Q. Chen (2010), "Reconsidering Baron and Kenny: Myths and Truths about Mediation Analysis," *Journal of Consumer Research*, 37 (August), 197–206.

6 http://www.afhayes.com/, accessed October 29, 2014.

7 http://www.afhayes.com/introduction-to-mediation-moderation-and-conditional-process-analysis.html, accessed October 29, 2014.

8 Sethuraman, R. and K. Gielens (2014), "Determinants of Store Brand Share," *Journal of Retailing*, 90 (June), 141–153.

Chapter 20

1 Merchant. A. and G. M. Rose (2013), "Effects of Advertising-Evoked Vicarious Nostalgia on Brand Heritage," *Journal of Business Research*, 66, 2619–2625. Holak, S. L. and W. Havlena (1998), "Feelings, Fun and Memories: An Examination of the Emotional Components of Nostalgia," *Journal of Business Research*, 42, 217–226.

2 Hair, J. F., W. C. Black, B. J. Babin and R. Anderson (2010), *Multivariate Data Analysis*, 7th edition, Prentice Hall: New Jersey.

3 Williams, C. C. and A. Martinez-Perez (2014), "Why Do Consumers Purchase Goods and Services in the Informal Economy?" *Journal of Business Research*, 67, 802–806.

4 Park, J. H., C. Kim, and Y. D. Song (2014), "Whom to Dismiss? CEO Celebrity and Management Dismissal," *Journal of Business Research*, 67, 2346–2355.

5 Max, J. B., R. Stidham, G. Su, and A. K. Waijee (2013), "Obesity and IBD: Are We Tipping the Scales toward Epidemic? *Gastroenterology*, 145, 478–479.

6 See Hair et al. (2010) for more details on logistic regression analysis.

Chapter 21

1 Wildscut, T., C. Sedikedes, J. Arndt, and C. Routeledge (2008), "Nostalgia: Content, Triggers, Functions," *Journal of Personality and Social Psychology*, 91, 975–997.

2 Leong, A. M. W., S. S. Yeh, Y. C. Hsiao, and T. C. Huan (2015), "Nostalgia as Travel Motivation and Its Impact on Tourists' Loyalty," *Journal of Business Research*, 68, 81–86.

3 The formula for AVE changes with unstandardized loadings. See Hair et al. (2010) for equation.

4 Thus, the primary computational difference being the insertion of a 1.0 in the diagonal of the correlation matrix used for analysis as opposed to the measured variance. For more on PCA, see http://arxiv.org/pdf/1404.1100.pdf, accessed November 29, 2014.

5 Kamtsios, S. and E. Karagiannopoulou (2013), "The Development of a Questionnaire on Academic Hardiness for Late Elementary School Children," *International Journal of Educational Research*, 58, 69-78.

6 Holak, S. L. and W. Havlena (1998), "Feelings, Fun and Memories: An Examination of the Emotional Components of Nostalgia," *Journal of Business Research*, 42, 217-226.

7 Campbell, C., C. Ferraro & S. Sands (2014), "Segmenting Consumer Reactions to Social Network Marketing," *European Journal of Marketing*, 48(3/4), 2-2.

8 For example, do we start by grouping the two most similar observations together (nearest neighbor) or by separating the most distant observations (farthest neighbor)? This is only the tip of the iceberg in terms of the different approaches. Here, we illustrate one commonly applied and simple approach to cluster analysis. For more, see Agresti, A (2014), *Categorical Data Analysis*, John Wiley & Sons.

Chapter 22

1 http://www.ssicentral.com/lisrel /history.html, accessed December 1, 2014. Jöreskog, K. G. and Sörbom, D. (1982). "Recent Developments in Structural Equation Modeling." *Journal of Marketing Research*, 404–416.

2 Babin, B. J., J. F. Hair and J. S. Boles (2008). "Publishing Research in Marketing Journals Using Structural Equation Modeling." *The Journal of Marketing Theory and Practice*, 16(4), 279–286.

3 See http://www.ssicentral.com/lisrel /references.html for a list of sources useful in learning more about SEM. Accessed November 30, 2014.

4 Found at brainyquotes.com, accessed November 30, 2014.

5 LISREL was used to produce these results.

6 The student can get a feel for the actual computations by adding up all the residuals in the lower half of the matrix, taking the average, and multiplying by $N-1$. This won't be exactly the Maximum Likelihood χ^2 residual, but it gives an approximation. The main idea is to see that the χ^2 gets larger as the residuals get larger.

7 As opposed to a PCA approach.

8 See Iacobucci, D. (2010). "Structural Equations Modeling: Fit Indices, Sample Size, and Advanced Topics." *Journal of Consumer Psychology*, 20(1), 90–98 or Hair et al. (2006). *Multivariate Data Analysis*, Prentice Hall, NJ, for more on fit indices and guidelines.

9 The results produced by LISREL. AMOS produces slightly different χ^2 value of 84.7 with 62 df (p = 0.029). The difference in results is negligible.

10 The LISREL results are nearly identical, χ^2 value of 158 with 63 df.

11 Pounders, K. R., B. J. Babin and A. G. Close (2015). "All the Same to Me: Outcomes of Aesthetic Labor Performed by Frontline Service Providers." *Journal of the Academy of Marketing Science*, DOI 10.1007/s11747-014-0407-4, in press; Tobacyk, J. J., B. J. Babin, J. S. Attaway, S. Socha, D. Shows, and K. James (2011). "Materialism through the Eyes of Polish and American Consumers." *Journal of Business Research*, *64*(9), 944–950; Delgado-Ballester, E., M. Hernandez-Espallardo, and A. Rodriguez-Orejuela (2014). "Store Image Influences in Consumers' Perceptions of Store Brands: The Moderating Role of Value Consciousness." *European Journal of Marketing*, *48*(9/10), 1850–1869; Chang, W., G. R. Franke, T. D. Butler, C. F. Musgrove, and A. E. Ellinger (2014). "Differential Mediating Effects of Radical and Incremental Innovation on Market Orientation-Performance Relationship: A Meta-Analysis." *The Journal of Marketing Theory and Practice*, *22*(3), 235–250.

12 Sarstedt, M., C. M. Ringle, J. Henseler, & J. F. Hair (2014). "On the Emancipation of PLS-SEM: A Commentary on Rigdon (2012)." *Long Range Planning*, *47*(3), 154–160.

INDEX